提单及其他付运单证

(修订版)

杨良宜 著

中国政法大学出版社

序

　　本书在出版过程中由于笔者导致的延误，令这本书在2000年9月份写作完毕后，仍拖延了好几个月才得以出版。

　　笔者要感谢的人士有好几位，特别要提及的是给予本书文字编辑的张怡昕先生与打印的陈震英女士。另外，一贯大力协助的张祖跃先生与中国政法大学出版社，在此也再次表达笔者的谢意。

杨良宜
2001年5月

目 录

第一章 简 介

第二章 提单作用之一：物权凭证

§1 物权凭证 ·· (5)
  1.1 定义 ·· (5)
  1.2 转让实质占有权 ·· (5)
    1.2.1 实质占有权,货物/财产主权的区分 ····················· (6)
      1.2.1.1 物权凭证只转让占有权而不转让货物/财产的例子 ······ (7)
      1.2.1.2 转让占有权与货物/财产而不转让主权的例子 ·········· (7)
      1.2.1.3 区分的重要性 ·· (8)
  1.3 侵占货物属侵权下的严格责任 ································ (9)
  1.4 承运人侵占货物也会属运输合约下的严格责任 ·········· (12)
  1.5 承运人作为货物托管人(bailee)的责任 ···················· (13)
    1.5.1 托管的定义 ··· (13)
    1.5.2 托管可以是合约关系 ···································· (14)
      1.5.2.1 分托管的情况 ·· (14)
    1.5.3 托管也可以是侵权关系 ································· (16)
    1.5.4 让与(attornment) ·· (17)
    1.5.5 提单可否提前让与的争议 ······························· (17)
    1.5.6 船东交货单是让与,可构成托管关系 ················ (18)
      1.5.6.1 为何要有船东交货单(ship's delivery order) ········ (18)
      1.5.6.2 对船东交货单的权威定义 ······························ (19)

§2 能成为物权凭证的条件 ·· (20)
  2.1 普通法下完全是根据习惯做法 ································ (20)

2 提单及其他付运单证

　　2.2　什么是习惯? ………………………………………………………（20）
　　　　2.2.1　要求之一：肯定、稳定与悠长历史 ………………………（21）
　　　　2.2.2　要求之二：合理 ……………………………………………（21）
　　　　2.2.3　要求之三：不得与法律规定或合约明示条款有直接矛盾/冲突 …（22）
　　　　2.2.4　要求之四：在有关地区证明习惯被承认和依从 …………（26）
　　2.3　总结有关条件 …………………………………………………………（26）
　　2.4　物权凭证可否光靠单证上的注明/措辞 ……………………………（26）
§3　各种付运单证介绍 …………………………………………………………（27）
　　3.1　装船提单 ………………………………………………………………（27）
　　　　3.1.1　简介 …………………………………………………………（27）
　　　　3.1.2　接受为物权凭证的先例 ……………………………………（28）
　　　　3.1.3　装船提单的优点 ……………………………………………（31）
　　　　3.1.4　装船提单的缺点 ……………………………………………（31）
　　　　3.1.5　提单背书 ……………………………………………………（33）
　　　　　　3.1.5.1　什么是背书 …………………………………………（33）
　　　　　　3.1.5.2　谁有权背书/指示 ……………………………………（33）
　　　　　　3.1.5.3　发货人能否改变背书/指示 …………………………（34）
　　　　　　3.1.5.4　提单什么时候不能再背书/指示 ……………………（36）
　　　　3.1.6　装船提单是流通或只是转让之争 …………………………（37）
　　　　　　3.1.6.1　"转让"历史的简介 ………………………………（38）
　　　　　　3.1.6.2　依权威说法装船提单只是转让 ……………………（38）
　　　　　　3.1.6.3　转让需要约因支持 …………………………………（40）
　　3.2　全程或转运提单（through bill of lading） …………………………（41）
　　3.3　大副收据（mate's receipt） …………………………………………（45）
　　3.4　收货提单（received for shipment 或 alongside bill of lading） ……（46）
　　　　3.4.1　一般不被视为物权凭证的原因 ……………………………（46）
　　　　　　3.4.1.1　原因之一：货物不是义无反顾地付运并锁死在船上 …（46）
　　　　　　3.4.1.2　原因之二：另有最后单证 …………………………（47）
　　　　　　3.4.1.3　原因之三：难有肯定与稳定的习惯 ………………（47）
　　　　　　3.4.1.4　原因之四：以往的先例与立法只针对装船提单 …（47）
　　　　3.4.2　不同看法的案例之一：The "Marlborough Hill" ………（47）
　　　　3.4.3　不同看法的案例之二：The "Lycaon" …………………（48）
　　　　3.4.4　认同不算是物权凭证的案例之一：Diamond Alkali ……（50）
　　　　3.4.5　承认收货提单为物权凭证的好处 …………………………（50）

3.4.6　1992年英国海上运输法已包括在内 ………………………（51）
3.5　海运单(sea waybill) …………………………………………（52）
　　3.5.1　海运单的特征 …………………………………………（53）
　　3.5.2　海运单的格式 …………………………………………（53）
　　3.5.3　海运单的缺点 …………………………………………（54）
　　3.5.4　针对海运单的立法改善 ………………………………（55）
　　3.5.5　海运单的优点与近年兴起的原因 ……………………（56）
3.6　船东交货单(ship's delivery order) …………………………（57）
3.7　多式联运提单/单证(multimodal transport document) ……（58）
3.8　发货通知单(consignment note) ……………………………（60）
3.9　空运单(air waybill) …………………………………………（61）

§4　物权凭证的质押 ………………………………………………（62）
4.1　质押的产生与做法 …………………………………………（62）
4.2　银行对提单货物有特殊货权 ………………………………（65）
4.3　银行的特殊货权受到侵占有诉权 …………………………（65）

§5　无单放货问题的现状与新发展 ………………………………（66）
5.1　怎样才是准确交货/放货 ……………………………………（67）
　　5.1.1　签发了提单就必须坚持收货人退回一份正本提单 …（67）
　　5.1.2　法律坚持对此基本做法保持简单化 …………………（67）
　　5.1.3　真正货方也必须退回提单才能取货 …………………（68）
　　5.1.4　提单一式几份,应退回多少 …………………………（68）
　　5.1.5　提单要全套退回的例外情况 …………………………（70）
　　5.1.6　法院一般不下令船东交货/放货,除非货方出示提单 …（71）
　　5.1.7　提单如果被偷或遗失怎样办 …………………………（71）
　　5.1.8　船东是否应先去卸下货物存仓以减少损失 …………（72）
　　5.1.9　等待提单的船期损失应由谁承担 ……………………（72）
　　5.1.10　易腐货物等不及提单怎样办 ………………………（74）
　　5.1.11　货物卸到岸上仓库是卸港惯常的做法 ……………（75）
　　5.1.12　发货人、承租人等是否有权要求船东无单放货 …（77）
5.2　保函的做法 …………………………………………………（79）
　　5.2.1　船东是否必须接受保函 ………………………………（80）
　　5.2.2　租约规定船东要接受保函 ……………………………（82）
　　5.2.3　对保函的实质要求 ……………………………………（82）
　　　　5.2.3.1　谁出的保函 ……………………………………（82）

4 提单及其他付运单证

  5.2.3.2 保函的措辞/文字 ……………………………………………（84）
 5.3 卸港对货权有争议 …………………………………………………（87）
  5.3.1 船东/船长遇上货权有争议应向法院请求确定权利归属 ………（88）
  5.3.2 船东所花律师费用可获补偿 …………………………………（90）
  5.3.3 向什么法院申请 ………………………………………………（91）
 5.4 船东/船长无辜交货/放货给伪造正本提单的人的情况 …………（92）
  5.4.1 今天航运的现实环境 …………………………………………（92）
  5.4.2 买卖双方互骗是否应由无辜船东承担后果 …………………（93）
  5.4.3 底线是考虑大原则 ……………………………………………（95）
   5.4.3.1 商业机制无法，也不去对付欺诈 …………………（96）
   5.4.3.2 侵占是严格责任 ……………………………………（96）
   5.4.3.3 提单信誉必须维护 …………………………………（97）
   5.4.3.4 总结大原则 …………………………………………（97）
 5.5 船东/承运人责任基础与损失计算 ………………………………（98）
  5.5.1 违约与侵占的不同损失计算 …………………………………（98）
  5.5.2 合约与侵权的并列诉权 ……………………………………（104）
 5.6 对无单放货的抗辩 ………………………………………………（106）
  5.6.1 时效已过 ………………………………………………………（107）
  5.6.2 提单合约内的免责条款 ………………………………………（108）
  5.6.3 海牙规则下的单位赔偿限额 …………………………………（113）
  5.6.4 船舶总的吨位责任限制 ………………………………………（114）
  5.6.5 禁止翻供 ………………………………………………………（115）
  5.6.6 提单不是船东授权签发 ………………………………………（116）
 5.7 船东可否对无单放货协议及时反悔 ……………………………（117）
 5.8 无单放货的损失与保险的关系 …………………………………（119）
 5.9 无单放货的救星：电子提单 ……………………………………（121）
  5.9.1 电子提单必须达致的条件 ……………………………………（121）
   5.9.1.1 条件之一：能去转让货物/财产 …………………（121）
   5.9.1.2 条件之二：能去转让运输合约 …………………（121）
   5.9.1.3 条件之三：能起到文件证明的作用 ……………（122）
   5.9.1.4 条件之四：能提供大家任意使用 ………………（122）
   5.9.1.5 条件之五：防止或减少欺诈 ……………………（123）
   5.9.1.6 条件之六：加快处理单证 ………………………（123）
  5.9.2 1983年的Seadocs（Seaborne Trade Documentation System）经验……（123）

5.9.3　1990年的CMI model ………………………………（124）
5.9.4　1999年的Bolero …………………………………（125）
5.10　有关无单放货的其他问题 …………………………（126）
5.10.1　无单放货的中国判例 ……………………………（126）
5.10.2　班轮提单加上针对无单放货的印就条款 ………（128）
5.10.3　多式联运与无单放货 ……………………………（128）

第三章　提单作用之二：运输合约·谁是其中的合约方

§1　提单的合约方为何混乱 ………………………………（130）
　1.1　谁是承运人或托运人纯是出于自愿 ………………（134）
　1.2　提单比其他合约混乱的原因之一：合约转让 ……（134）
　1.3　提单比其他合约混乱的原因之二：谈判中的证据 …（135）
　1.4　提单比其他合约混乱的原因之三：常有矛盾/隐晦内容，不易解
　　　释 ………………………………………………………（136）
§2　对象要找对的重要性：谁是承运人？ ………………（137）
§3　光船租赁（demise charter） …………………………（140）
　3.1　船长与光船承租人有雇用关系 ……………………（140）
　3.2　光船租赁不必登记，外人不知道 …………………（141）
　3.3　英国法律曾有的漏洞 ………………………………（141）
　3.4　现实中发生的光船租赁 ……………………………（142）
　3.5　期租合约 ……………………………………………（142）
　3.6　识别有否光租的一般做法 …………………………（144）
　　3.6.1　提单上只有船名 ………………………………（144）
　　3.6.2　对人诉讼 ………………………………………（144）
　　3.6.3　对物诉讼 ………………………………………（144）
　　3.6.4　迫船东对有否光租作出披露与保证 …………（145）
　　3.6.5　提单上除船名外印有船公司的名字 …………（145）
§4　班轮提单与租约提单 …………………………………（146）
　4.1　班轮提单如何拟定 …………………………………（147）
　4.2　租约提单合并较早订立的租约 ……………………（147）
　　4.2.1　对租约提单条款不完全符合租约的处理 ……（148）
　　4.2.2　合并的法律 ……………………………………（149）
　　4.2.3　租约提单合并混乱的原因 ……………………（152）

6 提单及其他付运单证

 4.3 总结班轮提单与租约提单的区分 …………………… (154)
  4.3.1 班轮提单针对谁是承运人的条款之一：光船条款(demise clause) ………………………………………………… (155)
   4.3.1.1 内容简介 ……………………………………… (155)
   4.3.1.2 英国法律承认有效 …………………………… (156)
   4.3.1.3 光船条款的历史来由 ………………………… (157)
   4.3.1.4 漠视光租条款会有严重后果 ………………… (158)
   4.3.1.5 美国、加拿大法院有不同看法 ……………… (158)
  4.3.2 班轮提单针对承运人条款之二：承运人身份条款(identity of carrier clause) ……………………………………… (159)
§5 提单由谁签字的重要性 ……………………………………… (160)
 5.1 船长签字约束船东的一般说法 ………………………… (160)
 5.2 期租承租人签字一般也约束船东 ……………………… (161)
 5.3 中国部分人士的不同看法 ……………………………… (164)
§6 如何识别提单承运人 ………………………………………… (166)
 6.1 全凭对提单内明示条款、措辞与签字的全面解释 …… (166)
 6.2 UCP500对承运人说明的要求 ………………………… (167)
§7 近期有关案例简介 …………………………………………… (168)
 7.1 案例之一：The "Venezuela" (1980) 1 Lloyd's Rep. 393 ………… (168)
 7.2 案例之二：The "Rewia" (1991) 2 Lloyd's Rep. 325 …………… (169)
 7.3 案例之三：The "Ines" (1995) 2 Lloyd's Rep. 144 ……………… (170)
 7.4 案例之四：The "Hector" (1998) 2 Lloyd's Rep. 287 …………… (171)
 7.5 案例之五：The "Flecha" (1999) 1 Lloyd's Rep. 612 …………… (172)
 7.6 案例之六：Maritrop Trading Corp. v. Guangzhou Ocean Shipping Co. (1998) CLC 224 …………………………………………… (173)
 7.7 案例之七：The "Starsin" (2000) 1 Lloyd's Rep. 85 …………… (173)
 7.8 总结 ……………………………………………………… (175)
§8 实际承运人(actual carrier) ………………………………… (175)
 8.1 英国法律视为是分包(sub-contract)的做法 ………… (176)
 8.2 实际承运人与货方没有合约关系 ……………………… (177)
  8.2.1 侵权问题之一：海牙/海牙·维斯比规则不包括分包人 …… (177)
  8.2.2 侵权问题之二：以喜玛拉雅条款与分托管去保护分包人 …… (178)
  8.2.3 侵权问题之三：损失时已拥有货物主权才能起诉并获赔偿 …… (185)
  8.2.4 侵权问题之四：不允许以侵权索赔纯经济损失 …… (188)

  8.3 在合约承运人外再加上实际承运人对货方的好处 ………… (189)
  8.4 中国海商法可能对实际承运人过于苛求 …………………… (191)
§9 谁是运输合约的货方 ……………………………………………… (194)
  9.1 总有一方去安排运输 ……………………………………… (194)
    9.1.1 CIF 买卖 ………………………………………………… (194)
    9.1.2 FOB 买卖 ……………………………………………… (196)
    9.1.3 中间商 ………………………………………………… (198)
    9.1.4 全程运输的二程船 …………………………………… (199)
§10 租约、提单这两份运输合约针对同一航次能否一致的探讨 …… (199)
  10.1 无法一致的情况 …………………………………………… (199)
  10.2 运输合约与买卖合约一致与否的探讨 …………………… (202)
§11 订立运输合约的货方才能享有合约权利和承担合约责任 …… (203)
  11.1 合约权利 …………………………………………………… (203)
  11.2 合约责任/义务 …………………………………………… (204)
    11.2.1 例子之一:危险品 ………………………………… (204)
    11.2.2 例子之二:支付运费、亏舱费和滞期费等 ……… (206)
§12 合约相互关系的大原则造成的障碍与解决办法 ……………… (208)
  12.1 背书/交出提单只转让货权,不转让合约 ……………… (208)
  12.2 "合约相互关系"(privity of contract)简介 …………… (209)
    12.2.1 提单的对策之一:Dunlop v. Lambert 先例 …… (211)
    12.2.2 提单的对策之二:转让合约权利(assignment of contractual
        rights) ………………………………………………… (212)
    12.2.3 提单的对策之三:Brandt v. Liverpool 的默示合约 …… (213)
    12.2.4 提单的对策之四:1855 年提单法 ………………… (215)
      12.2.4.1 1855 年提单法的措辞/用字 ………………… (216)
      12.2.4.2 提单法转让合约不是普通法转让(assignment)或一般的
          变更(novation);发货人与收货人负连带责任 …… (216)
      12.2.4.3 1855 年提单法问题之一:只针对装船提单 …… (218)
      12.2.4.4 1855 年提单法问题之二:与为了转让有关货物的目的
          挂钩 ………………………………………………… (219)
    12.2.5 提单的对策之五:1992 年海上运输法 …………… (221)
      12.2.5.1 1992 年立法扩大了对海上运输单证的适用:Section 1 … (221)
      12.2.5.2 1992 年立法针对的运输合约权利可转让与的多种人
          士/对象:Section 2 ……………………………… (222)

12.2.5.3 1992年立法针对运输合约责任的转让:Section 3 ……… (224)
12.2.5.4 1992年立法带来的新问题 ………………………………… (226)
12.2.5.5 总结1992年立法 …………………………………………… (232)
§13 1992年立法没有针对合约相互关系障碍的FOB买卖的情况 ……… (234)
§14 发货人严格的产品责任 …………………………………………………… (236)

第四章 提单作用之二：
运输合约的形式与有关条款的分析/探讨

§1 提单合约形式简介 …………………………………………………………… (237)
§2 租约提单 ……………………………………………………………………… (239)
 2.1 合并条款要寻求双方订约的意愿 ……………………………………… (239)
 2.2 去找出双方订约的意愿是合并哪一份租约 …………………………… (239)
  2.2.1 对船东合并租约进提单的意愿的探讨 ………………………… (240)
  2.2.2 一般准则/说法是合并了船东自己订立的头一份租约 ………… (241)
  2.2.3 头一份是期租租约或多航次程租的情况下合并的是哪一份租约 ……………………………………………………………… (242)
  2.2.4 口头租约能否合并 ………………………………………………… (243)
 2.3 合并的只是租约内有直接关联的内容/条款 ………………………… (244)
 2.4 合并不包括附属性条款 ………………………………………………… (244)
 2.5 合并主要是针对运输与卸港的内容/条款 …………………………… (246)
 2.6 合并的内容/条款必须公平合理和并非不寻常 ……………………… (247)
  2.6.1 针对货物运输/交付责任方面的租约条款 …………………… (249)
  2.6.2 针对滞期费 ………………………………………………………… (250)
   2.6.2.1 装港已经产生的滞期费 …………………………………… (250)
   2.6.2.2 收货人是否要对产生的所有滞期费负责的探讨 ……… (250)
  2.6.3 针对船舱不清洁或不适合的租约条款 ………………………… (252)
  2.6.4 租约仲裁条款 ……………………………………………………… (254)
   2.6.4.1 英美法律不接受一般的合并条款可以包括租约的仲裁条款 ………………………………………………………… (256)
   2.6.4.2 提单可以合并租约仲裁条款的办法之一:仲裁条款既针对租约,也针对提单 ……………………………………… (257)
   2.6.4.3 提单可以合并租约仲裁条款的办法之二:明示合并仲裁条款 ……………………………………………………………… (259)

2.6.4.4　提单成功合并租约仲裁条款的弊端/不利之处 …………… (260)
　　　2.6.4.5　提单合并伦敦仲裁条款对收货人最危险之处：时效已
　　　　　　　逝 ……………………………………………………………… (261)
　　2.6.5　针对无单放货的租约条款 …………………………………………… (265)
§3　班轮提单 …………………………………………………………………………… (266)
　3.1　条款字体太小的影响 ……………………………………………………… (266)
　3.2　Conlinebill 前页的总结条款 ……………………………………………… (267)
　　3.2.1　简介 …………………………………………………………………… (267)
　　3.2.2　邻近条款与其他自由条款的有效性 ……………………………… (268)
　3.3　Conlinebill 前页的承运人条款/空格 ……………………………………… (271)
　3.4　Conlinebill 后页的各条款简介 ……………………………………………… (272)
　　3.4.1　通知人 ………………………………………………………………… (272)
　　3.4.2　首要条款 ……………………………………………………………… (273)
　　3.4.3　适用法律与管辖权 …………………………………………………… (273)
　　　3.4.3.1　普通法地位 …………………………………………………… (274)
　　　3.4.3.2　立法地位 ……………………………………………………… (276)
　　　3.4.3.3　提单合约无效或有争议的明示适用法条款 ……………… (279)
　　　3.4.3.4　对 Conlinebill 适用法与管辖权条款的分析/解释 ……… (281)
　　　3.4.3.5　总结 …………………………………………………………… (282)
　　3.4.4　各自由条款 …………………………………………………………… (283)
　　3.4.5　转船权利/自由 ………………………………………………………… (291)
　　3.4.6　装船前与卸船后的责任 ……………………………………………… (296)
　　3.4.7　装卸货与交货 ………………………………………………………… (296)
　　　3.4.7.1　承运人不另给通知与及时交货或从速提货 ……………… (296)
　　　3.4.7.2　班轮业务下谁有权指定卸货码头/地点 ………………… (296)
　　　3.4.7.3　若收货人不前来提取货物，船长有的权利是什么 ……… (296)
　　　3.4.7.4　若船东/承运人想马上能卸货上岸呢 …………………… (297)
　　　3.4.7.5　承运人私下出售或公开拍卖货物的情况 ………………… (298)
　　　3.4.7.6　分不开货物的处理 …………………………………………… (301)
　　3.4.8　运费与各项有关支出/使费 …………………………………………… (304)
　　3.4.9　留置权 ………………………………………………………………… (307)
　　3.4.10　延误 …………………………………………………………………… (307)
　　3.4.11　共同海损与救助，新杰森与姐妹船条款 …………………………… (308)
　　3.4.12　双方有责碰撞条款 …………………………………………………… (310)

    3.4.13　政府指令、战争、疫症、冰封及罢工等情况下的自由条款 …… (313)
    3.4.14　喜玛拉雅条款 ……………………………………………… (313)
    3.4.15　承运人有权合并货物堆装在集装箱内并装在甲板上 ……… (313)
    3.4.16　额外条款 …………………………………………………… (314)
    3.4.17　总结 ………………………………………………………… (314)

第五章　提单作用之二：运输合约下的货损货差责任

§1　起点是公共承运人有严格责任 ………………………………………… (315)
§2　普通法下合约承诺也是严格责任 ……………………………………… (317)
§3　订约自由受到尊重 ……………………………………………………… (318)
　3.1　公共承运人与私人承运人所享有的订约自由的地位不同 ……… (318)
　3.2　订约自由的技巧：以船舶适航为例 ……………………………… (319)
§4　海上运输责任的立法 …………………………………………………… (321)
　4.1　美国1893年的哈特法 ……………………………………………… (321)
　4.2　1924年的海牙规则 ………………………………………………… (323)
　　4.2.1　历史简介 ………………………………………………… (323)
　　4.2.2　海牙规则下船东与货方各自责任的简介 ……………… (328)
　　4.2.3　海牙规则的适用 ………………………………………… (329)
　　　4.2.3.1　什么航次适用 …………………………………… (329)
　　　4.2.3.2　什么付运单证与运输合约适用 ………………… (338)
　　　4.2.3.3　侵权是否/能否适用 …………………………… (356)
　　　4.2.3.4　什么期间适用 …………………………………… (367)
　　　4.2.3.5　什么货物适用 …………………………………… (373)
　　4.2.4　举证第一步：货方证明货损货差发生在承运人在海牙规则下要
　　　　　　负责的期间 ……………………………………………… (387)
　　　4.2.4.1　清洁提单 ………………………………………… (388)
　　　4.2.4.2　收货人及时通知货损货差的责任 ……………… (388)
　　　4.2.4.3　货损货差书面通知的种类与内容 ……………… (389)
　　　4.2.4.4　及时书面通知是否必要 ………………………… (393)
　　4.2.5　举证第二步：船东/承运人证明造成货损货差的原因 ……… (397)
　　　4.2.5.1　船东/承运人有举证责任才公道和符合实际 …… (397)
　　　4.2.5.2　租约下对举证责任有订约自由 ………………… (398)
　　　4.2.5.3　货损货差原因不明的情况 ……………………… (398)

4.2.5.4 船东/承运人举证责任所要达到的程度 ……………… (402)
4.2.5.5 货损货差原因多于一个的情况 ……………………… (403)
4.2.5.6 原因是否造成货损货差的近因、主因 ……………… (403)
4.2.6 举证第三步:船东/承运人证明船舶适航 ……………………… (404)
  4.2.6.1 适航举证责任在船东/承运人 ……………………… (404)
  4.2.6.2 海牙规则下的不适航须与货损货差有关 …………… (406)
  4.2.6.3 海牙规则要求"克尽职责"令船舶适航是先决条件,不违反
      才能享有免责 ……………………………………… (408)
  4.2.6.4 何谓"克尽职责" ……………………………………… (410)
  4.2.6.5 海牙规则要求"克尽职责"令船舶适航是在开航前与开
      航时 ………………………………………………… (418)
  4.2.6.6 适航的定义 …………………………………………… (421)
4.2.7 举证第四步:船东/承运人证明免责 …………………………… (438)
  4.2.7.1 海牙规则的免责项目 ………………………………… (438)
4.2.8 举证的第五步:货方证明承运人没有妥善与小心装卸,堆放与照
    看货物 ……………………………………………………… (475)
  4.2.8.1 "妥善与小心"的定义 ………………………………… (476)
  4.2.8.2 妥善要求之一:不了解或处理照看不了的货物不应接受
      运载 ………………………………………………… (476)
  4.2.8.3 妥善要求之二:技术水平,良好的制度以及了解货物本
      质/特性的例子 ……………………………………… (477)
  4.2.8.4 装卸货物的定义与要求 ……………………………… (478)
  4.2.8.5 海牙规则不涉及交货 ………………………………… (479)
  4.2.8.6 堆装货物的定义与要求 ……………………………… (479)
  4.2.8.7 运载、保管与照看货物的要求 ……………………… (482)
4.2.9 海牙规则禁止承运人减轻或逃避责任/义务 …………………… (484)
  4.2.9.1 有关例子介绍 ………………………………………… (485)
  4.2.9.2 有关刑事化之说 ……………………………………… (487)
  4.2.9.3 提单条款无效后可否重生 …………………………… (487)
  4.2.9.4 提单条款可否被分割,只判部分无效 ……………… (487)
  4.2.9.5 海牙规则强制适用与纯属合并适用有否分别 ……… (488)
4.2.10 举证的第六步:双方对其他有关方面的争辩 ………………… (488)
  4.2.10.1 非法/不合理绕航 …………………………………… (488)
  4.2.10.2 索赔时效 ……………………………………………… (496)

        4.2.10.3 单位/单件责任限制 ……………………………………(520)
   4.3 海牙·维斯比规则 ……………………………………………(537)
   4.4 汉堡规则 ……………………………………………………(540)
   4.5 三个公约的各签约国名单 …………………………………(545)
   4.6 各国(包括中国)自己的不同立法 …………………………(546)
   4.7 CMI草拟中的运输公约 ……………………………………(548)

第六章:提单作用之三:货物收据

§1 收据内容 ………………………………………………………(549)
   1.1 Congenbill 提单 ………………………………………………(549)
   1.2 海牙规则 ……………………………………………………(550)
   1.3 汉堡规则 ……………………………………………………(550)
§2 发货人提供准确内容的责任 …………………………………(552)
   2.1 发货人的责任是否绝对/严格 ………………………………(553)
   2.2 收货人是否承担发货人的责任 ……………………………(555)
§3 提单的货物内容 ………………………………………………(558)
   3.1 内容之一:货物标号/标记 …………………………………(558)
   3.2 内容之二:货物重量/数量/度量 ……………………………(558)
      3.2.1 岸上货物重量与船舶吃水重量之争 …………………(559)
      3.2.2 岸上油柜度量与油轮油柜空档度量之争 ……………(561)
         3.2.2.1 岸上与船上数字差异主因 ………………………(563)
         3.2.2.2 可依赖船上数字去抗辩货差索赔 ………………(564)
      3.2.3 岸上理货与船舶理货 …………………………………(566)
      3.2.4 岸上与船上货物重量/数量之争的其他实例 …………(568)
      3.2.5 发货人一般以岸上货量为提单货量 …………………(571)
      3.2.6 船东/承运人在海牙规则下拒签岸上货量提单的理由 …(572)
         3.2.6.1 拒签的两个合法理由 ……………………………(572)
         3.2.6.2 集装箱会有合法理由拒签或加否定性批注 ……(573)
      3.2.7 发货人与承运人对货量争议的协调做法 ……………(574)
         3.2.7.1 欺诈性保函无效 …………………………………(575)
         3.2.7.2 实例介绍 …………………………………………(577)
         3.2.7.3 非欺诈性保函有效 ………………………………(579)
   3.3 内容之三:货物表面状况 …………………………………(580)

3.3.1 以什么时候的表面状况为准 …………………………………… (581)
3.3.2 集装箱的表面状况 ……………………………………………… (583)
3.3.3 表面状况只需合理判断 ………………………………………… (585)
3.3.4 货物表面状况的表述是否足够保护买方 ……………………… (587)
3.3.5 对货物表面状况作出批注必须准确且有必要 ………………… (587)
 3.3.5.1 不必要的批注 ………………………………………… (587)
 3.3.5.2 对船东自己不利的批注 ……………………………… (588)
 3.3.5.3 必须准确地批注 ……………………………………… (589)
3.3.6 发货人与承运人对清洁提单争议的折中做法 ………………… (591)
 3.3.6.1 保函 ……………………………………………………… (591)
 3.3.6.2 租约条款 ……………………………………………… (592)
 3.3.6.3 买方/卖方同意某些提单批注 ………………………… (594)

§4 船东/承运人对提单内容不正确的责任 ……………………………… (595)
4.1 普通法下的禁止翻供 …………………………………………………… (595)
 4.1.1 构成的4个要求 ………………………………………………… (595)
 4.1.2 一般情况下很容易证明依赖与损害 …………………………… (596)
 4.1.3 第三者早知真相,没有真正去依赖不正确提单内容的情况 … (596)
 4.1.4 不利提单持有人的 Grant v. Norway 先例 …………………… (598)
4.2 立法下的禁止翻供 ……………………………………………………… (600)
 4.2.1 各立法的措辞/条款 …………………………………………… (601)
 4.2.2 1855年提单法的不当措辞 …………………………………… (601)
 4.2.3 1992年海上运输法的改善 …………………………………… (602)
 4.2.4 海牙·维斯比规则/1971年海上运输法 ……………………… (603)
4.3 合约下的禁止翻供 ……………………………………………………… (603)
4.4 误述侵权(tortuous misrepresentation) ……………………………… (604)

§5 提单内容的否定性批注 ………………………………………………… (605)
5.1 否定性批注如"重量不知"、"据说是有"等的合理性探讨 ……………… (605)
5.2 海牙规则的对策 ………………………………………………………… (606)
5.3 英国法律承认"否定性批注"的有效性 ………………………………… (607)
 5.3.1 先例之一:New Chinese Antimony 1917 ……………………… (608)
 5.3.2 先例之二:Canada and Dominion Sugar 1946 ……………… (608)
 5.3.3 先例之三:Scindia Steamship 1961 ………………………… (608)
 5.3.4 先例之四:The "Herroe" and "Askoe" 1986 ………………… (609)
 5.3.5 先例之五:The "Esmeralda" 1988 …………………………… (610)

5.3.6 先例之六:The "Atlas" 1996 ………………………………… (611)
5.3.7 先例之七:The "River Gurara" 1998 ……………………… (612)
5.3.8 先例之八:The "Mata K" 1998 …………………………… (612)
5.4 对英国法律在这一方面的批评 ……………………………………… (614)
5.4.1 海牙规则的大精神是不准承运人减轻或逃避责任 ………… (614)
5.4.2 以发货人要求签发作为前提并不现实 ……………………… (615)
5.4.3 解决办法 ……………………………………………………… (616)
5.5 美国法律只承认符合事实的否定性批注 …………………………… (616)
5.6 汉堡规则及其他国际公约与美国法律立场一致 …………………… (619)

§6 运费 ……………………………………………………………………… (620)
6.1 表述运费已经预付必须无条件与明确 ……………………………… (621)
6.2 禁止翻供只适用在第三者依赖与信赖这表述的情况 ……………… (621)

§7 提单日期 ………………………………………………………………… (622)
7.1 付运日期在买卖合约中的重要性 …………………………………… (622)
7.2 发货人无法及时装船的困境与对策 ………………………………… (624)
7.3 倒签提单容易被发觉,无可抗辩及后果严重 ……………………… (624)

第七章 总 结

案例索引 …………………………………………………………………… (638)
附 录 ……………………………………………………………………… (666)
 附录一:英国提单法(1855年) …………………………………… (666)
 附录二:英国海上运输法(1992年) ……………………………… (668)
 附录三:美国提单法(1916年) …………………………………… (674)
 附录四:美国哈特法(1893年) …………………………………… (687)
 附录五:海牙规则(1924年) ……………………………………… (690)
 附录六:海牙·维斯比规则(1968年) …………………………… (702)
 附录七:汉堡规则(1978年) ……………………………………… (709)
 附录八:CONGENBILL 1994 租约提单 …………………………… (731)
 附录九:CONLINEBILL 2000 班轮提单 …………………………… (738)
 附录十:英国某著名班轮公司装船或多式联运共用提单 ………… (738)
 附录十一:海运单 …………………………………………………… (754)
 附录十二:CMI 电子提单规则 ……………………………………… (756)
 附录十三:海牙规则、海牙·维斯比规则、汉堡规则的比较 …… (761)

第一章 简　　介

有关提单的法律与实务,是国际贸易与国际航运最为重要的法律与实务。提单这份源于欧洲商人"发明"的单证,通过几百年来的实践、习惯做法与改良,已成为国际贸易与航运的基石。外贸中最普遍的做法:"成本、保险费和运费"(简称 CIF)或"成本加运费"(简称 CFR),常被称为"文件买卖"(不严格是"货物买卖"),而其中的文件主要就是指提单。跟单信用证中的单证,最重要的一份也是提单。对国际航运而言,提单的重要性更是业内人士都耳熟能详的。像绝大部分海员一样,笔者早年作为学徒上船工作后没有几天,刚弄清楚了船首船尾,就听到了提单这份文件/单证。随着时间的推移,笔者也见过好几份不同的提单并开始掌握一些关键之处。例如,发货人有权要求签发提单而船长必须依从;提单内容必须准确,否则后果严重;千万不能在卸港(或其他地方)无单放货,等等。慢慢地,笔者也知道了提单的三个功能:运输合约的证明、物权凭证与货物收据。但这只是表面肤浅的理解。对于一个没有正规学习过并且熟悉合约法、财产法等法律的年轻人,要深入理解也实非是易事。除了要看大量书籍外,也需要时间去磨炼与探讨。

到了近年,提单的各种问题日趋复杂,令业内人士更是迷惑,难以深入理解,如有太多的新资料无法系统与全面吸收。这些问题中有些是一直存在的(例如对 1855 年英国提单法的解释;保护 1 年索赔时效的难处),有些是因为技术的发展或商务做法上的改变所致,或是形势更加恶化(例如集装箱运输:多了短航次与船舶速遣,导致无单放货的情况大增)。

这些问题往往也不只是理论性的,而是会带来实质性严重后果的。这不得不归咎于近一二十年来的人心不古、贪念无穷、皮包公司充斥以及国际商贸整体环境的转坏。近年人们的心态普遍是欠债的能赖就赖;能钻法律空子占便宜的也绝不放过,否则便是傻瓜;还有很多的"讼棍"公司,他们嫌正当生意赚不够,动不动就以起诉来欺压怕事、不懂的人士。但今天投身于国际贸易或航运,如果水平不够,除非他运气一直极好,遇上的都是业内仅有的"好人",否则将会很快消亡。

就货损货差而言,一个看来十分简单、自然明确的案件,在今天的环境下,也不再是只懂二三招[如扣船、海牙规则(或中国海商法)等]的人士(包括律师)能应付得了的。

例如,国际船东互保协会在 19 世纪 80 年代钻 1855 年英国提单法的空子,面对货方索赔货损货差,总会以质疑货方是否有合约的诉权作为抗辩。由于 1855 年英国提单法局限性,确也有不少案件能让国际船东互保协会成功抗辩。这带来了大量的著名先例,如 The "Aliakmon" (1986) 2 Lloyd's Rep. 1; The "Kapetan Markos" (1987) 2 Lloyd's Rep. 321; The "Future Express" (1992) 2 Lloyd's Rep. 79,等等。而随着 1992 年海上运输法(新的提单法)的生效,这方面的问题才告一段落。

近年来,另一大问题是无单放货。由于短航次增多以及今天船舶速遣,产生了对这种做法的需求,但这做法会导致严重的后果,往往仍是归咎于:其一,人心不古、贪念无穷。常见的一种情况是买方无单提取货物后,仍在信用证结汇或托收上为难卖方。结果导致船东被卖方索赔,而船东可能出于"好意"采取无单放货的通融做法,反而变成了傻瓜。其二,业内人士半桶水的特别多。本来知识无限,每人都不会是满桶水,有的只是或多或少的区别。但无可避免的是,在现实世界中,一级吃一级、弱肉强食。所以,经常出现严重事故的往往都是对提单理解不足的船东。他/它们在千变万化的情况中往往无法作出对自己最有利的保障、平衡及决策。

总之,近年此问题多不胜数,光是有报道的案例已够看半天了,诸如 The "Ines" (1995) 2 Lloyd's Rep. 144; Motis Exports v. Dampskibsselskabet AF 1912 (1999) 1 Lloyd's Rep. 837; The "Stone Gemini" (1999) 2 Lloyd's Rep. 255,等等。

做法上(包括实务与法律)的改变也令提单问题日趋复杂而难以掌握。可以说,百年来提单的实务与法律都在不断发展、完善:1855 年英国提单法、1893 年美国哈特法、1916 年美国提单法(Pomerene Act 1916)、1924 年海牙规则、1968 年海牙·维斯比规则、1979 年维斯比规则的特别提款权修改等,再加上数不清的先例/判例。但这些改变/改善都是缓慢出现的。不像近年,改变之多之快,实在令人目不暇接。比如,具有 140 年历史的英国提单法被新的立法(1992 年海上运输法)替代,后者有很不一样的内容和新的创意。这新的立法解决了部分老问题,但又带来了新问题。另外的发展有 1980 年汉堡规则、1993 年中国海商法、制定中的美国新海上运输法以及正在草拟中的国际海事委员会(CMI)新运输法/运输公约。

法律改变往往因实务改变所引起。例如,上百年来,业内人士只知道有一份装船提单的文件/单证,大家把它当做圣旨去膜拜。英国 1855 年的提单法也只是针对装船提单。但近年来各式各样的海上运输单证纷纷出现,令人无所适从。它们各有名称,但很难说它们有多少传统装船提单的特征。他们甚至会自称是提单(例如货运代理签发的"house bill of lading"),但其实不是一般理解上的提单,不具备一项或多项提单必须拥有的特征[比如必须是"可转让/流通"(negotiable),必须有人出面认作是"承运人"(carrier),必须与海运有关以及应有船名等]。多式联运固然带来了很多不同名堂的新单证,其他因素也导致了新单证的出现,如"海运单"(sea waybill)。据知,在欧美一些班轮航线,今天船东签发海运单已经多于传统的提单了。

一涉及国际性业务,往往会遇到"择地行诉"(forum shopping)的问题。简单地说,就是当事人去一个对他/它有利、能取巧的诉讼地点打官司。例如,中美双方订的合资合约,即使有条款说明若发生争议双方要去新加坡法院诉讼,往往也会在后来真正发生争议时,中方去中国法院,美方去美国法院起诉,置合约规定的新加坡法院诉讼于不顾。但这种择地行诉行为相比起提单的择地行诉行为,可算是简单得多了。提单诉讼要考虑的因素之多,是其他业务的同类行为难以比拟的。例如,货方要起诉,首先要明确谁是承运人,"告船"(in rem)"告人"(*in personam*),哪里才能成功起诉(比方"告船"就关系到相关船舶的行走地区),哪是提单的管辖地或有否仲裁明示条款,等等。

法律的急变,更令择地行诉不易。例如海牙规则的一年索赔时效,实在是十分短促,一旦走错了路再回头已是覆水难收:在正确的诉讼地点时效已过。英国法院对此要求十分严格:见 Cia. Colombiana de Seguros v. Pacific Steam Navigation Co (1963) 2 Lloyd's Rep. 479。这给了想择地行诉的货方一个重要的警示。但后来另有案例对此又似有放松:见 The "Kapetan Markos" (1986) 1 Lloyd's Rep. 211 与 The "Nordglimt" (1987) 2 Lloyd's Rep. 470。该两判例是说货方只要及时(交货后 1 年内)在有适当管辖权的法院(它不必是最后真正审理争议的国家法院)提出了告票,也已是足够了。但从近期的 Thyssen v. Calypso (2000) 2 Lloyd's Rep. 243 判例看来,英国法律在这方面又重趋严格。

说到减少与防止择地行诉,一种优越的办法是在相关合约内加一条仲裁条款。因为,在 1958 年的纽约公约下,签约国必须中止自己国家法院的诉讼,把管辖权让给双方在合约中同意了的仲裁机构或仲裁庭(如十分通用的 Congenbill 1994)。但这又带来了新问题,因为收货人手中的提单之所以能成为其与承运人之间的运输合约,纯是因为立法(提单法)所导致,是仅有的一种"合约"而并非是订约双方所同意的产物。加之,在班轮提单长期存在一面倒的情况下,班轮公司就算任意加上一条去南极仲裁的条款也不会有货方反对或有能力去反对。另就个别国家的法院而言,以提单的仲裁条款去剥夺他们的管辖,在感觉上也不是味道,也不符合他们本国的利益。由于国际上使用的标准格式合约若附加仲裁条款,通常会是一条伦敦仲裁条款。而租约的仲裁条款,现实中十之八九去伦敦仲裁。难怪曾听有人说过,在不久的将来,伦敦对租约仲裁的雄霸(甚至是独霸)地位,会同时延伸至提单的仲裁。个别国家对此发展已作出反击,最著名的是美国新的海上运输法,它在修改过的 Section 3 (8)(b)明示外国管辖条款/仲裁条款无效。当然,这新的立法能否通过以及什么时候通过,目前仍是未知数。

中国也受到这一问题的影响,会如何作出反应仍是未知数。或许会是,大家都去承认汉堡规则吧！至少在这一点上，汉堡规则在 Article 22 说明了不论提单怎样写，原告（货方）有权选择多处地点起诉：被告（承运人）所在地、提单签发地点、装卸港（注意：现实中卸港尤其重要）、提单明示地点等。

　　对以上涉及的各方面问题，本书都将会有详论。许多未提到的问题，本书也会去详论。由于提单相关的内容实在太多，笔者自知目前本书只是涉及皮毛，将来肯定还需要出修订本并由业内人士不断去发扬光大，方可写出更精确、更全面的内容。

第二章 提单作用之一:物权凭证

§1 物权凭证

装船提单是一份物权凭证已是众所周知的说法。但何谓物权凭证呢?

1.1 定义

可先去节录权威的 Benjamin's《Sale of Goods》第 5 版,18 - 005 段所说的定义为:"There is no authoritative definition of 'document of title to goods' at common law[1], but it is submitted that it means a document relating to goods the transfer of which operates as a transfer of the constructive possession of the goods[2], and may operate to transfer the property in them[3]."

除了普通法外,英国一项立法("Factors Act"1889)的第 1 条也有对物权凭证下定义并强调了货物占有权和控制权,具体如下:"(4) The expression 'document of title' shall include any bill of lading, dock warrant, warehouse-keeper's certificate, and warrant or order for the delivery of goods, and any other document used in the ordinary course of business as proof of the possession or control of goods, or authorising or purporting to authorise, either by endorsement or by delivery, the possessor of the document to transfer or receive goods thereby represented."

1.2 转让实质占有权

物权凭证一定可去转让货物的实质占有权,否则它也就不是物权凭证了。这

---

〔1〕 在英国普通法/案例法下,对物权凭证没有权威定义。
〔2〕 它应可去转让货物的实质占有权。
〔3〕 它也会可以转让货物/财产。这一点请注意是物权凭证好像提单下,卖方会只去转让占有权但仍保留货权,因为买方仍未付货款,正如著名的先例 The "Aliakmon" (1986) 2 Lloyd's Rep. 1。故此,它只是"会"可以转让货物/财产,但不一定,因为这全凭双方(买卖双方)的意愿,正如 1997 年英国货物销售法之 Article 17(1) 所讲明的。

表示法律需要去默示：

(1)对货物有占有权,想去交出占有权的承运人(或其他人士如货仓经营人),必须把货物交给有物权凭证的持有人。

(2)有物权凭证的持有人,才有权向承运人提出交出货物的要求。

(3)承运人交出货物的占有权之后,即使交给了对货物没有货权或"主权"(title)的一方,承运人也不必承担任何责任。

据以上所讲,表示承运人如果是拒绝交出货物给有物权凭证的持有人,或是把货物交出来给非持有物权凭证的人,都会侵犯后者的权力,实属"侵占"(conversion),承运人会有严重后果。

1.2.1 实质占有权,货物/财产主权的区分

实质占有权(constructive possession)并不代表对占有的货物/财产(property)有主权,这点已在较早段节说清楚。毕竟,在海上运输时,船长/承运人也拥有占有权,但他并不拥有货物主权。

作为主要是在海上运输的物权凭证——装船提单,毫无疑问它可去转让货物的实质占有权,也经常是这样做,卖方/发货人把提单背书与交出给买方/收货人,让买方可去对货物有实质占有权。或是把提单背书与交出给银行作为抵押/质押之用。但在本章 1.1 小段之注〔3〕提及,这样做可以转让货物所有权,但不一定是这样发生。因为把货物/财产所有权转让,如卖方转让给买方,还得去全面地看双方真正意图。而把提单背书或交出只能是"表面证据"(*prima facie transfers* the property in the goods);Lickbarrow v. Mason (1787) 2 T. R. 63;Dracachi v. Anglo—Egyptian Navigation Co. (1868) L. R. 3 C. P. 190。这是因为 1979 年英国货物销售法之 Section 17 清楚说明如下：

Property passes when intended to pass

(1) Where there is a contract for the sale of specific or ascertained goods the property in them is transferred to the buyer at such time as the parties to the contract intend it to be transferred.〔4〕

(2) For the purpose of ascertaining the intention of the parties regard shall be had to the terms of the contract, the conduct of the parties and the circumstances of the case."〔5〕

---

〔4〕 何时转让货物以订约双方意图为准。

〔5〕 从这条款可见,去客观找出双方意图,是要看全面的事实如买卖合约条款(会有一条"保留货权条款"(retention of title clause)等),双方行为与当时环境。

1.2.1.1 物权凭证只转让占有权而不转让货物/财产的例子

这种情况经常会发生,例如把装船提单去背书与交出给银行质押,会是只转让占有权而非是去转让货物。

在卖方与买方之间,也偶尔会发生。例如在本章 1.1 小段提及的 The "Aliakmon" (1986) 2 Lloyd's Rep. 1 先例。

该实例中,涉及韩国卖方卖一批钢材给英国买方。英国买方原是准备马上转售,但安排不成,导致买方无法或不愿意马上支付卖方以交换提单,双方原是以托收方法结算。双方事后同意卖方交出提单而让买方在卸港的 Immingham 向船长提取钢材,但这批钢材的主权保留在卖方手中。换言之,英国买方去占有这批钢材,并设法在 Immingham 岸上转售,以便有钱去支付韩国卖方。这段期间买方只有占有权,钢材(货物)本身是"听卖方指示处理"(held to the order of the sellers)与"让卖方处置"(held at the disposal of the sellers)。

The "Aliakmon" 可说是一个典型例子把货物/财产(或是它的物权凭证)的占有权去转让同时,并不把所有权/主权转让。现实中,同类情况发生很多。

另一好例子是分不开的散货。在 1995 年改法前在英国货物销售法下无法转让货权,不管买卖双方意图(可去参阅《国际货物买卖》一书之第五章 §4 段)。这导致去背书提单只转让占有权,但无法转让货权。

1.2.1.2 转让占有权与货物/财产而不转让主权的例子

再进一步说,去把实质占有权与货物/财产转让,也不一定能转让该财物的主权。比方是,不论是针对一批"真正货物"(real property)或代表它的"物权凭证"(document of title),卖方与买方都同意了去"转让财产"(pass property),买方也付了货价(比方是),完全符合了 1979 年英国货物销售法之 Section 17,但结果仍不一定能把该货物主权转让。怎么会是这样呢?答案是:可能卖方自己也对该批货物没有主权,则何来有主权可去转让买方?这就是著名的 nemo dat 说法,这课题已在笔者的《国际货物买卖》一书的第七章有详述,在此不重复。

1.2.1.2.1 *nemo dat* 说法

最极端也明显的例子是卖方偷或骗或侵占的货物,是没有主权可去合法转让给买方的。

看来,这对无辜的买方很不公平。买了货物,占有了货物,也支付了货款给卖方,却在真正有货物主权的人士出现后再也不能去保留/占有货物。但想到这种互有冲突的说法/看法,在社会科学经常有此情况,往往要去权衡利弊,从大局考虑,然后去定出大政策(法律),也就释然了。nemo dat 说法的考虑,会是:

(ⅰ)去保障财物的真正拥有者不轻易被侵占是更为重要的大政策。

(ⅱ)不鼓励有意无意或/与疏忽去买入贼赃的人士(买方)。否则,会带来社会

1.2.1.2.2 nemo dat 的例外

话说回来，nemo dat 也有很少的例外情况去保障十分无辜的买方买入没有主权的财物，这在笔者的《国际货物买卖》一书之第七章 2.5 小段有详述，不去重复。只说一种例外是称为"买方控制货物"（buyer in possession），书中说（小部分节录）：

> 这种 buyer in possession 的说法，会是主要针对……"保留货权条款"（retention of title clause）。在这情况下，货物是交了给买方，但卖方又私下去保留了货物主权，是无辜的第三者/外人不会知悉的。所以，如果他从买方购进该货物，他应在这说法下获得主权，可以超越/优先原来卖方所保留的主权。公道客观地说，谁叫原来卖方信任买方，虽主权仍是保留，但去让买方占有与控制该货物呢？

1.2.1.3 区分的重要性

区分占有权、主权等十分重要，可以如下段节从各方面去探讨与理解。

1.2.1.3.1 例子之一：没有货权的中间商签发的第二套提单

今天国际贸易商很主要的活动是以 F.O.B. 买入货物，再以 C.I.F. 转售该批货物，从中在货价，运费与保费赚取差价。厉害精明的国际贸易商能发大财，还会在操作中不放过每次能提高利润的机会，例如买卖合约与运输合约条款订得好进而占大便宜。或是，在滞期费计算中取巧。

据知今天涉及中国的出口，会是 80% 左右以 F.O.B. 成交。主因是中国货方"怕麻烦"，不想去碰困难的航运。这一来，代价是中国货方赚不了大钱，也经常受国际贸易商的鱼肉与摆布。

回到正题。国际贸易商派的船舶在中国港口装了货物后，船长签发了一套"装船提单"（shipped bill of lading），并交给中国发货人（也是 F.O.B. 卖方）。但中国发货人会是稍后才结汇（在有信用证的情况下），故为了争取时间，加快资金流通与多赚取利息，该国际贸易商（实是中间商）会在背后多出一套以自己为发货人的第二套提单，并在 C.I.F. 买方开给他的信用证结汇。但注意是在当时，国际贸易商对这批船上货物没有主权，又怎能去转让主权呢？

这一来，如果将来出了争议，例如是国际贸易商突然倒闭，或是他以单证不符为由而在信用证拒绝支付中国发货人，最后会导致中国的 F.O.B. 卖方与在外国卸港的 C.I.F. 买方抢夺这批货物。根据 nemo dat 的说法，货物主权应在中国的 F.O.B. 卖方。

1.2.1.3.2 例子之二：自动交出物权凭证，但保留货物主权

若是拥有货物主权的一方，例如是上一小段的中国 F.O.B. 卖方，自动/自愿去

把第一套真正是物权凭证的装船提单给了国际贸易商而后者又去转售了给一无辜的外国 C.I.F. 买方。

这并不涉及第二套提单,而且有了争议,后果也大不相同,这正是 nemo dat 例外的 buyer in possession。

在本章 1.2.1.1 小段介绍的 The "Aliakmon" (1986) 2 Lloyd's Rep. 1,在同样道理下,Immingham 岸上转售钢材给其他分买方,他们可享有 nemo dat 例外的保护,不受韩国卖方保留货权的影响。

事实上在笔者的《信用证》一书(第 26 页)与《国际货物买卖》一书(第 376 页)提到的"trust receipt",也有同样道理/精神。它的做法是在买方没钱赎单,开证银行交这份单证(主要是物权凭证的提单)给买方,让他转售/处置,之后再付钱给银行。但如果买方不诚实,开证银行针对无辜第三者而言,会失去货物的主权:Lloyd's Bank v. Bank of America (1938) 2 KB 147。

1.3 侵占货物属侵权下的严格责任

侵占货物是民事侵权行为,而且属严格责任,目前也已有立法 [Tort (Interference with Goods) Act, 1977] 对付。这课题也曾在笔者的《国际货物买卖》一书有介绍,不妨节录部分如下:

    4.1 侵占的不同形式

    侵占有很多不同的形式,它会是比"侵犯"(trespasser to goods)广泛得多。例如 A 的货物被 B 偷去,B 是在民事上犯了"侵犯"。但再下去 B 把货物转卖了给 C,C 再转卖了给 D 等,C 与 D 只是犯了"侵占"。当然,B 既是"侵犯",也是"侵占"。所以,侵占会是广泛得多。

    不同的形式有:

    (ⅰ)C 在没有足够合法理由下,拥有主权属于 A 的货物,而在 A 要求归还时拒绝。这正是本章 2.6 小段提及的无辜买方买进赃物后被真正货主要求归还时的困境。当然,也会有其他的各种变化。例如,一个小偷把偷的皮包匆忙中塞进一个不知情过路人士的口袋。这不是侵占,因为过路人的拥有并不知情,"非是自愿"(involuntary)与短暂。但之后真正货主要求归还而过路人拒绝,这变为是侵占了。同样道理也会发生在公众地方拿错了其他人的大衣或雨伞。再举一例是二程船为一程船托运 A 的货物,这不是侵占而是"分托管"。若二程船稍后面对 A 与一程船或其他人对货物主权的争议,正确的做法是请求法院去确定(interplead)。

    (ⅱ)C 把 A 的货物,不论是取自 A 或其他人,去占为己有。

(ⅲ)C 的货物来自(购买或馈赠)B,而 B 对该货物没有"主权"(title)。

(ⅳ)C 把主权属于 A 的货物转送或转卖给第三者如 D、E、F 等,或做同样事情导致 A 对该货物的主权受到损害。船长把货物在卸港无单交货即属这一形式的侵占。

(ⅴ)C 把 A 的货物毁坏。例如,A 把他的车子借给 C,但 C 把车子撞坏。

(ⅵ)作为托管人,C 错误的导致 A 的货物失去或毁坏。这是在本书附录三的 Tort(Interference with Goods) Act,1977 的 Section 2(2)立法所规定的一种侵占。来取代以前的 Detinue。

(ⅶ)C 即使是合法自 A 取得货物,例如是以托管人或承运人身份取得,但事后错误的"保留"(keep)或"使用"(use)该货物。比如是无权去留置货物但却去宣布留置:Finalayson v. Taylor,The Times 14 April 1983。这种形式的侵占常会在航运中发生,即船长/船东非法留置船上货物,有意或无意的当做借口向货方敲一笔钱。

4.2 侵占是严格责任

侵占是一种"严格"(strict)的民事"侵权"(tort)责任:Clerk & Lindsell 的"Torts"第 16 版之§22-67。侵占方自辩说自己无辜,没有疏忽,不知情等并不足够。这也是经常在船东无单(正本提单)交货后面临真正货主(提单持有人)索赔时的一种抗辩,但其实在英国法律下站不住脚。

除非是:侵占方(船东)与真正货主(提单持有人)之间也有合约关系,而合约内有广泛免责条款可去免除侵占方的责任。例如,在笔者的《程租合约》一书的第 126 页至第 128 页所谈及的金康租约第 2 条款。这一来,再根据笔者的《国际商务游戏规则——英国合约法》一书的第 590 页至第 592 页讲法,真正货主会是受合约的约束,而不得以侵权为由的诉因去改变合约与/或取巧。

4.3 侵占赔偿计算的特殊对待

侵占的各种"救济"(remedy)已是在 Tort(Interference with Goods) Act,1977 的立法 Section 3 订明如下:

"(2)The relief is—

(a)an order for delivery of goods, and for payment of any consequential damages, or

(b)an order for delivery of the goods, but giving the defendant the alternative of payment of damages by reference to the value of the goods, together in either alternative with payment of any consequential damages, or

(c)damages."

去详细探讨这三种不同救济之前,也应去看该立法同一 Section 3 的 subsection(3),如下：

"(3) Subject to rules of court—

(a) relief shall be given under only one of the paragraphs(a),(b) and (c) of subsection(2),(b) relief under paragraph (a) of subsection (2) is at the discretion of the court, and the claimant may choose between the others"。

这是说真正货主针对侵占方的法律救济只能是在三种做法中拣一种。而这三种的第一种是取决于法院的裁量权，决定是否给予。但余下两种救济却是完全由真正货主自己决定选用哪种。

4.3.1 三种不同的救济

回头去探讨这三种不同的救济，它们是：

（i）法院下令物归原主，以及侵占方赔偿有关损失（如果有）。但这第一种救济的裁量权既然在法院，表示法院不一定会给予这命令（order for delivery of goods）。而面对这种申请，确是，法院的考虑会与面对"履行指令"（specific performance）的申请一样。这方面是在笔者的《国际商务游戏规则——英国合约法》一书的第584页有详细介绍。例如，法官要考虑双方的"便利与否"（balance of convenience），市场有否代替产品，整个案情的公道，将来金钱上的损失赔偿会否已足够等。

（ii）第二种也是下令物归原主，但侵占方有权去选择赔付所侵占货物的市场价格，而保留货物。另外，再赔偿有关损失（如果有）。这种救济是由真正货主选择决定。而在货物已完全毁坏或失去，侵占方可以说是无法物归原主，也只得是去赔付货物的市场价格了。

（iii）第三种是货物也不想要了，真正货主选择只要侵占方赔偿损失。侵占方不存在有选择权可去说：货物仍在，可以马上物归原主。

要有以上三种不同的救济，也是说得过去。法律是想去尽量帮助真正货主，严厉对待侵占方。所以，要去考虑真正货主的想法。第一种救济权力不在真正货主，所以不必多讲。在第二种与第三种救济之间的选择，会是因为侵占的延误（例如船东非法拒绝交货）导致一个赚钱的分售合约被中止，变了物归原主再也没有作用。或是，侵占的延误导致货物会产生质变，例如是一船的香蕉。自然是，真正货主不想要物归原主，就选择第三种救济了。

相反，如果真正货主仍想要回这票被侵占货物，则他会选择第一种（但法院可能会否定）或第二种救济。可是，侵占方可能无法物归原主。或是这样做太昂贵不便，例如侵占的货物已是安配或混合在其他货物内。所以，第二种救济可去让侵占方有选择权去赔付货物的市场价格，加上有关损失。

显然，承运人拒交或无法交出货物的实际占有权给物权凭证的持有人，即会有民事中侵权的严格责任。

1.4 承运人侵占货物也会属运输合约下的严格责任

民事诉讼除了侵权,就是合约的违约。一般而言,除非物权凭证的持有人就是发货人(卖方),而他原来就是与承运人订有运输合约,则一般是不会与属第三者的物权凭证的持有人(例如是银行或收货人)有任何合约关系。至于立法强制转让合约会后详。

如真有合约关系,而合约有明示或默示的要求:承运人正确交货,不可有误。则承运人做不到也属违约,要面对损失索赔。合约责任也是严格责任,除非另有免责条款可资保护违约方。这一点看来,货物被侵占以侵权或违约起诉应是没有分别,都会是严格责任。但在损失计算上,它们会有分别,这一点在本章5.5.1小段后详。另外,针对合约如果真有免责条款会如何影响特别是侵权的诉讼,也会后详。

无单放货可构成毁约/违约,可去节录 Denning 勋爵在 Sze Hai Tong Bank Ltd. v. Rambler Cycle Company Limited (1959) 2 Lloyd's Rep. 114 有说明如下:"The contract (as embodied by the B/L) is to deliver, on production of the bill of lading, to the person entitled under the bill of lading. In this case it was 'unto Order or his or their assigns', that is to say, to the order of Rambler Cycle Company Limited (seller) if they had not assigned the bill of lading, or to their assigns, if they had. The shipping company (carrier) did not deliver the goods to any such person. They are therefore liable for breach of contract unless there is some term in the bill of lading protecting them."

运输合约有明示条款要求承运人正确交货的例子另可去举 Conlinebill(1978年)提单格式的:"… in the like good order and condition… unto Consignees or their Assigns…"

而即使没有明示条款,也有默示条款,正如 Leggatt 大法官在 The "Houda" (1994) 2 Lloyd's Rep. 541 之第553页所说:"It is necessarily implicit in the power to order the issue of bills of lading which make the goods deliverable 'to order' that the obligation is accepted to deliver to the holder upon production of the bill of lading. It is an incident of the bill of lading contract that delivery is to be effected only against the bill of lading."

当然,明示或默示条款都只是在有合约关系下才有意义。这一来,如果物权凭证的持有人是第三者,本来就没有合约存在,就变得没有意义了。他只能是去依赖民事中侵权的侵占理论。

但在1992年的英国海上运输法(为了去替代1855年的英国提单法),它去把运输合约(不同种类提单等)强制转让给了第三者的提单持有人,以立法将这份运输合约加在后者头上。这可去节录 1992 年立法之 Section 2(1) 所说的:"Subject to the following provisions of this section, a person who becomes:

(a) the lawful holder of a bill of lading;

....

Shall (by virtue of becoming the holder of the bill or, as the case may be, the person to whom delivery is to be made) have transferred to and vested in him all rights of suit under the contract of carriage as if he had been a party to that contract."

第三者的提单持有人——与承运人有了合约关系,则运输合约内的违约(不论是明示或默示条款)就用得上了。

读者会有疑问:既已有了侵权下的侵占责任,何必再去斤斤计较有否合约责任?简单的答案是,侵权下的侵占只针对物权凭证的持有人。但不是所有的提单都会是物权凭证(例如是所谓的记名或非指示提单,实是海运单。或是,提单已是失效),则第三者被侵占了货物就只能靠合约来起诉了,只要与承运人建立了合约关系。

另外的例子会是如 The "Future Express" (1993) 2 Lloyd's Rep. 542 先例,银行虽是提单持有人,但因货物一直不再存在,故不是有效的"质押"(pledge),进而不能以物权凭证持有人的身份以侵权的侵占起诉承运人(船东)而败诉。该先例若在今天发生,有了 1992 年立法的适用,则银行应可胜诉。银行不是以侵权之诉胜诉,而是以违约之诉胜诉。在本章之 3.1.5.4 小段,会较详尽地介绍该案例,目前暂略过。所以总的说来,1992 年海上运输法的生效导致一份付运单证是否属物权凭证的争议的重要性大大降低。而 1992 年英国该立法会在本书第三章详述,届时读者会对此课题更能理解,在此笔者暂时略过。

1.5　承运人作为货物托管人(bailee)的责任

1.5.1　托管的定义

作为承运人(或货仓经营人)也会有托管人的责任。"托管"(bailment)的定义可去节录《Chitty on Contracts》一书之 32 - 001 段,引述了《Possession in the Common Law》一书的定义,为:"any person is to be considered as a bailee who otherwise than as a servant [6] either receives possession of a thing from another [7] or consens to receive

---

[6] 托管关系不适用在主仆之间;仆人照顾主人的货物/财产并非是托管人。
[7] 此人可称为"寄托人"或"委托人"(bailor)。

or hold possession of a thing for another[8] upon an undertaking with the other person[9] either to keep and return or to deliver to him the specific thing[10] or to (convey and) apply the specific thing according to the directions antecedent or future[11] of the other person."

在日常生活中，托管在有意无意之间经常发生。显然，把货物交给承运人托管与运输至卸港，也有了一个托管关系。而承运人就是 bailee，发货人就是 bailor。

最正宗的做法，就是在托管期满把货物交给"寄托人"(bailor)的发货人。但经常要去听从寄托人的指示另作处理，例如把货物交给原是第三者的收货人。托管的法律是会涉及复杂的合约法、侵权法与财产法，这些内容将在以后的段中介绍。

1.5.2 托管可以是合约关系

大部分的托管都会是由合约产生，海上运输也不例外。有了合约关系，则托管也变为 bailment on terms。而有了争议，也会以合约条款为准。例如，内中有免责条款(豁免托管人疏忽责任)。

1.5.2.1 分托管的情况

托管合约内会有条款允许或授权托管人去另找"分托管人"(sub-bailee)。这在航运经常发生，例如，一程船与二程船的"全程提单"(Through bill of lading)。这种提单下，一程船作为承运人签发全程提单，并承诺对发货人作出全程运输。但一程船稍后会把货物转运，交出给二程船，而二程船就是"sub-bailment on terms"了。

关于这一课题，在笔者的《国际商务游戏规则——英国合约法》一书的第四章之5.7小段，有详细介绍，可去节录如下：

> 5.7 有条件的分托管(sub-bailment on terms)
>
> 有条件的托管看来不难明白，但有条件的分托管就较难明白。比如，货方托运，船东的运输就是有条件托管，提单上的条款就是托管条件。到了卸港，船东把卸下货物存放进仓库，而仓库有它的标准合约。这一来，仓库的条款就是分托管的条件(sub-bailment on terms)。肯定是，它们并不是一样的条件：托管是提单，分托管是仓库标准合约。问题是，如果货物在仓库内被偷去，货方以侵权去控告仓库，仓库可否以如下抗辩：

---

[8] 同上。
[9] 同上。
[10] 托管人应在托管期满把货物/财产交还给寄托人。
[11] 或是，根据寄托人以往的指示或将来的指示，在托管期满把货物/财产交出给指示的第三者。

(ⅰ)提单内有的免责等条款?
(ⅱ)它的标准合约内的免责等条款?

在(ⅰ),答案应是提单有否一条喜马拉雅条款,去包括了仓库的独立承包商在内。

在(ⅱ),就关系到这 sub-bailment on terms 的条件能否去约束货主,这问题在贵族院(上议院)的 The "Pioneer Container"(1994)1 Lloyd's Rep. 593 有解答。

该案中,高雄来香港的支线船/二程船"K. H. Enterprise"在途中沉没,时为 1987 年,船上所有集装箱都灭失了。货方在香港把该船台湾船东一条姐妹船"Pioneer Container"扣起来,并起诉,这官司一直上诉到英国贵族院。

在合约的关系是:发货人与一程船船东(韩国的 Hanjin)订约,这提单合约中有一条款是说:"The carrier shall be entitled to sub contract on any terms the whole or any part of the carriage, loading, unloading, storing, warehousing, handling and any and all duties whatsoever undertaken by the carrier in relation to the goods"。

这是一条极广泛的条款去授权一程船,也是提单承运人,去让它另订合约(sub-contract)。

一程船另找了二程船的"K. H. Enterprise",后者也取出了自己的提单,一程船是被当做发货人。所以,合约角度来看是一程船(提单承运人)与二程船(实际承运人)之间的合约,与货方无关。但二程船也是分托管人,而且是有条件的,即二程船提单的条款。其中有一条款是说台湾法院有管辖权。

双方在香港法院争议的是,货方以侵权,托管控告"K. H. Enterprises"船东,二程船船东能否以他的提单条款,作为分托管条件,去加在货方身上? 如果能,这会否包括台湾管辖权条款,而令香港法院要去考虑中止?

贵族院判是:

(a)货方与二程船关系是托管。

(b)如果货方有授权分托管与接受有关条件,货方要受到约束。

(c)这授权可以是写明,如在本案的一程船提单合约。这授权也可以是默示(implied),例如货方以前曾多次这样安排运输:一程船再转二程船。但默示总是比不上明示(写明)的明确。

(d)只有分托管的条件是完全不合理,不正常,才会不能去约束货方,贵族院的 Goff 勋爵是说:"… their Lordships do not perceive a similar need(指租约条款合并进提单不能完全去合并来约束货方) to limit the terms so consented to … where, as here, the consent is very wide in its terms, only terms which are so unusual or so unreasonable that they could not reasonably be understood to fall within such consent are likely to be held to be excluded."

(e)提单不论有否一条喜马拉雅条款可去保护二程船或分托管人,也不影响后者可去依赖分托管的条件。

在本案例,贵族院判是一条管辖权条款(或适用法律等条款)没有不正常不合理之处,所以分托管人的条件可去约束货方,即台湾管辖权有效。

这先例可被视为船东一大胜利,特别是对支线(feeder)业务。以前的二程船或其他的分承包商唯一靠的是一条不能肯定的喜马拉雅条款,今天有一样更稳定肯定的有条件分托管(sub bailment on terms)来保障。

要小心的反倒是一程船:它要肯定它与货方的提单中有一条类似"K. H. Enterprise"一程船的广泛授权,可去另订合约(sub-contract)。否则若没有明示或默示的货方授权去容许它找二程船(如找了"K. H. Enterprise"),答应它的条件,则会在出事后货方控告"K. H. Enterprise"船东时,后者不能依赖分托管条件(因为货方从没有去授权)。这一来,"K. H. Enterprise"船东赔了钱后,可以去回头找一程船(Hanjin)算账,因为它根本没有货方授权去另订合约(sub-contract),是构成严格要负责的"越权行为"(breach of warrant of authority)。

1.5.3 托管也可以是侵权关系

当然,托管也会产生在没有合约关系的情况下,此时双方(托管人与寄托人)只能有侵权关系。毕竟,要构成一个有效合约,是有多样的先决条件。例如,要有对价或约因。另外,双方要有意图去订立有效合约,是要双方"通电"(广东人说法)。"想法一致"(meeting of mind)。这些大道理都在笔者的《国际商务游戏规则——英国合约法》一书之第二章、第三章详述,不必全部节录。

故此,既有"免费托管"(gratuitous bailment),等于没有约因,也就不会有合约了。但这不表示免费为他人的财物作出托管的托管人没有责任,可去疏忽乱来。

托管也会是涉及寄托人是小孩、有神经病或醉酒的情况。他们根本不能订立有效合约。但不表示为他们的财物作出托管的托管人,可去疏忽乱来。

多举一个例子:托管也会发生在无意识的情况下,例如把大衣遗留在餐馆。正如McArthur大法官在Makower, McBeath & Co. Pty. Ltd. v. Dalgety & Co. Pty. Ltd. (1921) VLR 365 之第 373 页所说:"It is not necessary, in order to constitute a bailment that the goods should in the first instance be delivered by the bailor to the bailee; it is quite sufficient, in my opinion, if the bailee, having, in the first instance obtained possession and control of the bailor's goods, without the latter's knowledge or consent, afterwards acknowledges to the bailor that he holds them for him, and thereafter retains possession and control for him with his consent."

1.5.4　让与(attornment)

托管如果涉及寄托人指示托管人把货物/财产交出给第三者,会有"让与"(attornment)的说法,为保护托管人不必对任何不知名的第三者负责。让与的说法可节录《Chitty on Contracts》之 32015 段如下:"If the bailor directs the bailee to hold the chattel in his possession on behalf of a third person(the plaintiff) and the bailee thereupon attorns to the plaintiff by accepting the bailor's direction, or by acknowledging to the plaintiff that the plaintiff now has title to the chattel, the bailee will become the bailee of the plaintiff…"

另可去节录 Lloyd 大法官在 The "Future Express" (1993) 2 Lloyd's Rep. 542 之第 550 页所说的:"There is an attornment when, in simple terms, a bailee of goods acknowledges that he holds the goods on behalf of a person other than the original bailor. The relationship of bailment then springs up between the bailee and that other person, enabling him to sue in conversion for non-delivery."

以上所节录的,可以中文多作一次简介。即寄托人指示托管人交出财物给第三者后,只要托管人一经让与,以后的托管关系变成托管人为第三者负责,而不是向寄托人负责。如果拒交财物或误交财物,控告侵占的原告是第三者,而不是寄托人。

1.5.5　提单可否提前让与的争议

如果承运人一开始签发提单,发货人(寄托人)就已说明收货人是某某第三者,会否构成让与可去容许收货人在承运人交不出货物时以托管人侵占为由而索赔损失?看来,这"提前让与"(attornment in advance)的说法不被法院接受。在 The "Future Express" (1993) 2 Lloyd's Rep. 542 之第 550 页,Lloyd 大法官说:"if the consignee named in the bill of lading could always have sued in bailment for non-delivery, it is very odd indeed that there should have been no record of such a case, as far as I know, in the last 200 years."

而较早时在高院一审,Diamond 大法官说得更明白:"If the 'attornment in advance' theory were to be adopted, at any rate in its broad form, then any consignee or indorsee of the bill could, merely by proving that he was the lawful holder of the bill, make a demand on the carrier for delivery up the goods and, if the demand was not complied with at all or if there was then a short delivery or a delivery of damaged goods, sue the carrier for breach of his duty as bailee to deliver the goods at the port of discharge in the same good order as when shipped. If this were held to be the law then, as was said in The "Captain Gregos" (No. 2) (1990) 2 Lloyd's Rep. 395 at 406… there would have been no need for the 1855 Act."

总结以上所说,光是提单注明了第三者的收货人,或是背书了给他,还不足构成"让与"(attornment),可去令承运人与第三者的收货人有托管关系,进而可令正确的交货方法是交给第三者的收货人,并向后者负责。

1.5.6 船东交货单是让与,可构成托管关系

1.5.6.1 为何要有船东交货单(ship's delivery order)

国际贸易做法上千变万化,现列举一种情况说明:发货人/卖方(A)无法顺利把已装在船上的2万吨糖卖给原买方(B),或因无法结汇,或因(B)拒货,或因(B)倒闭,或因(B)赖皮,等等。这导致(A)要尽快设法转卖这2万吨糖,以免延误船期。如果能找到新买方(C)买下全部的2万吨糖,(A)可很简单地把手中持有的装船提单背书给(C),并交出给(C),一手交单,一手交货价/钱。

但不一定会这么巧,(C)可能只买1万吨糖。可幸运的(A)亦能另找到买家(D)吃下其余的1万吨。但这是货物在海上运输途中的转卖,文件上、操作上怎样办呢? 如何才能相互保障呢?

一种做法是(A)回头去找船东要求交换手中的一套2万吨糖的提单,另签二套各1万吨糖的提单。但这做法会有麻烦与困难,例如船东/承运人不肯合作。而且,运输途中会有不只一次的船上货物转卖,即(A)是中间商而不是真正发货人。

另一种做法是(A)自己签发2份各1万吨糖的交货单(merchant's delivery order),交出给(C)与(D)各一份,并换取货价的支付。但这对(C)与(D)会是保障不足,因为这一份不是物权凭证,也没有船东的任何确认,构成不了托管关系。

再一种做法,也是可行与一般的做法,是船东在(A)的要求下,签发2份各1万吨糖的交货单。注意这是"船东交货单"(ship's delivery order)。这一签发,应是"让与"(attornment),表示今后船东/承运人与(C)/(D)有了托管关系,正确的交货是在卸港把糖交出给(C)与(D),再也不是给(A)了。这一来,船东交货单足以去保障(C)与(D)的利益,让后者可以安心支付货价给予(A),以换取这份单证。

显然,为了防止原来签发2万吨糖的装船提单仍在流通,船东/承运人必须坚持退回这套提单后,才能签发2份各1万吨糖的船东交货单。

以上做法,也可使用在其他贸易情况。例如是(A)顺利以提单把货物转让了给(B),但(B)想在船舶抵卸港前转卖货物。结果找了(C)与(D),各要买1万吨糖,等等。

英国今天已有了 1992 年的海上运输法(本书第三章后详),可以说以上的托管关系、让与等的重要性已减。因为即使是(C)(D)与船东之间没有托管关系,也有了运输合约关系,可去让(C)与(D)对付船东/承运人拒交货或误交货的行为。1992 年立法的 Section 2 (1)(c) 说:"2 (1) Subject to the following provisions of this section, a person who becomes … (c) the person to whom delivery of the goods to which a ship's delivery order relates is to be made in accordance with the undertaking contained in the order, shall (by virtue of becoming the holder of the bill or, as the case may be, the person to whom delivery is to be made) have transferred to and vested in him all rights of suit under the contract of carriage as if he had been a party to that contract."

要强调是,在 1992 年立法前,所适用的 1855 年提单法根本没想到船东交货单,未包括在内。所以,构成"托管关系"(bailment)非常重要,否则收货人持有船东交货单根本是得物无所用,船东/承运人一句话说"我不认识你"就毫无办法。此外,他也不会有其他的侵权或合约诉因/诉权。

1.5.6.2 对船东交货单的权威定义

有了以上解释,笔者估计应很容易去理解英国法律委员会近期对这份单证的权威定义,是在 Law Commission No. 196: Rights of Suit in Respect of Carriage of Goods by Sea (London, 1991), para. 5.26, 所说的:"Ship's delivery orders are either (a) documents issued by or on behalf of shipowners while the goods are in their possession or under their control and which contain some form of undertaking that they will be delivered to the holder or to the order of a named person[12]; or (b) documents addressed to a shipowner requiring him to deliver to the order of a named person[13], the shipowner subsequently attorning to that person[14]. Where the order is issued to the ship and authorities, directs or orders the carrier to deliver to a certain person, it confers no rights against the carrier until the carrier attorns to the person to whom delivery is due[15]. Similarly, where such a delivery order is transferred, there would have to be a fresh attornment to the transferee before he acquired a right of possession against the carrier.[16]"

再强调是,以上报告定义为时早于 1992 年海上运输法。如今的立法已强制了

---

[12] 这第一种单证即是指船东交货单。它显示货物仍在船东/承运人的占有与控制下,并有一定保证把货物交出给船东交货单持有人或他的指定人士。
[13] 这是第二种单证,是指"货方交货单"(merchant's delivery order)。
[14] 货方交货单是要有承运人事后的"让与"(attornment)才能构成托管,才能作准。
[15] 否则,货方交货单的持有人并没有权力去对付船东/承运人,要求交出货物。
[16] 如果货方交货单被转让/转卖,则每一新的持有人都必须另有新的让与才会与船东/承运人有托管关系。

运输合约关系,有否托管关系重要性已不大。

§2 能成为物权凭证的条件

以上§1段谈及物权凭证对有关货物的权力(占有权)以及相关的各种法律后,可去探讨如何才能被定性为物权凭证。

2.1 普通法下完全是根据习惯做法

普通法/案例法会去承认一份单证是一份物权凭证,全是根据习惯做法,与法律可说是无关。而有否这习惯做法,是事实问题,要去靠证据证明。

首先,可去看看什么是习惯。

2.2 什么是习惯?

社会上有不少习惯流传下来而变为法律(立法或普通法),商业活动尤其不少。例如涉及票据、贸易、海事和保险,等等。这些所谓的"商人法则"(law merchant 或拉丁文的 lex mercatoria)不少变为英国法律的一部分。但要去证明一个"认可习惯"(established custom)的存在,应受法律承认,并非易事。这必须是在"事实方面"(matter of fact)证明该种做法已是:

（ⅰ）肯定与稳定;

（ⅱ）悠长历史的做法;

（ⅲ）合理;

（ⅳ）与一般的法律规定或说法(立法或普通法)没有直接矛盾/冲突,习惯只是一种"例外情况"(exception)或"限制条件"(qualification)。同样道理适用在有合约的情况,习惯不能去否定明示条款,不能有直接矛盾/冲突:Kum v. Wah Tat Bank (1971) 1 Lloyd's Rep. 439。习惯充其量只能当做是一种默示的条款,合约下总是先看明示条款,没有明示才去看能否有默示。

（ⅴ）在所有有关地区(可大可小)或/与行业内的人士承认,自动依从这个做法。

对以上说法可节录 2 段权威说法作为支持。一是 Devlin 勋爵在 Kum v. Wah Tat Bank 先例所说的:"Universality, as a requirement of custom, raises not a question of law but a question of fact. There must be proof in the first place that the custom is generally accepted by those who habitually do business in the trade or market concerned. Moreover, the custom must be so generally known that an outsider who makes reason enquiries could not fail to be made aware of it. The size of the market or the extent of the trade affected is neither here not there. It does not matter that the custom alleged in this case applies only to part of the shipping trade within the State of Singapore, so long as the part can be ascertained with certainty …"

二是 Clarke 大法官在 The "Sormovskiy 3068" (1994) 2 Lloyd's Rep. 266 之第 275 页简短的有关习惯说是:"However custom in this context means custom in its strict sense; that is it must be reasonable, certain, consistent with the contract, universally acquiesced in and not contrary to law."

接下去对以上所讲能构成习惯的各种要求稍作更详细的解释。

2.2.1 要求之一:肯定、稳定与悠长历史

再去强调,要成功举证有一个肯定、稳定与悠长历史的习惯做法存在并非易事。光是去证明有"一贯做法"(practice)并不足以构成"习惯"(custom)。但一贯做法与习惯的分水岭是什么也不好掌握。这一点争议在 The "Sormovskiy 3068" (1994) 2 Lloyd's Rep. 266 先例出现。它涉及在俄罗斯港口 Vyborg 的一贯做法,就是船长把货物卸下交给"Commercial Sea Port"(CSP)的港口当局。但该案中发生无单放货(即误交了货物,侵占了货物)。被告的船东/承运人抗辩说货物卸给 CSP 是当地习惯,故可以此"例外情况"(exception)对误交货物免责。但 Clarke 大法官认为船东只能证明 Vyborg 有这样的一个宽松"一贯做法"(practice),不足构成"习惯"令船东免责。

所以,虽然一切付运单证理论上都可去证明有习惯做法视它为物权凭证,但实际并不容易,因为举证难且昂贵。只有"装船提单"(shipped bill of lading),因为有 Lickbarrow v. Mason (1787) 2 T. R. 63 与 Sanders v. MaClean (1883) 11 QBD 327 的先例,加上 1855 年提单法与在本章 1.1 小段提及的 Factors Act, 1889,已被视为一种"不必证明习惯的物权凭证"(documents of title without proof of custom)。而其他付运单证例如是"多式联运提单"(combined transport bill of lading),都要有额外工作去证明习惯才会被法律接受是一份物权凭证。而去证明也会遇上困难,例如某航区尚没有太长历史,说不上有悠长做法。

这说明了很长一段时间,国际贸易只视装船提单为物权凭证,其实并非如此,但这看法有它的原因。

2.2.2 要求之二:合理

合理难下精确定义,要看每一不同案情而定。但要求合理的大精神可以理解为:明示条款可去罔顾合理与否,只要措辞/文字明确。但默示条款就必须是合情合理了。

要作为物权凭证,合理之处之一是:这单证不能是一份暂时的"初步单证"(preliminary document)。即是,稍后另会有付运单证签发,会被用作转让货权,等等。

这方面可举 Nippon Yusen Kaisha v. Ramjiban Serowjee (1938) 60 Lloyd's Rep. 181 的先例。它涉及一宗 F. A. S. 买卖(启运地船边交货),也即是:卖方只要把货物交付到指定的装运港口船边的码头上或驳船里时,就完成了任务。而买方将自负费用与承担风险把货物装船运输。该案中,卖方的 Ramjiban Serowjee 先生只获得了一份"大副收据"(mate's receipt)。因为不是 Serowjee 把货物装船,所以他不是发货人,不存在可要求船东(N. Y. K. 公司)签发装船提单给他,而且根据海牙规则之 Article Ⅲ(3),船东必须要去签发给发货人的。后来,船东也确是签发了一套装船提单,注明发货人是 Serowjee 的卖方,而且在没有要求交换大副收据的情况下把这套装船提单交给了 Serowjee 的卖方。这套提单经过多次背书转让到了最后收货人手中,最终也确以此物权凭证在卸港把货物提走。

再回头说 Serowjee,他持有一份大副收据,并以此向买方索取货款,而买方赖皮,迫 Serowjee 最后只能向船东起诉,指后者违约或侵占了他的货物。

关于违约,这明显不能成立,Serowjee 与船东的 N. Y. K. 不存在有合约关系。而在侵权的侵占货物方面,考虑之处是 Serowjee 手中持有的一份大副收据是否是物权凭证。

贵族院判定大副收据最终不是用来转让货权,或在卸港提货。它只是一份"初步单证"(preliminary document),不是被大家视为"最后单证"(final document),无法被合理当做"物权凭证"(document of title)。

2.2.3 要求之三:不得与法律规定或合约明示条款有直接矛盾/冲突

有关这方面,最好去介绍已多次提及的 Kum v. Wah Tat Bank Ltd. (1971) 1 Lloyd's Rep. 439 先例。它涉及的付运单证是一份"大副收据"(mate's receipt)。已在上一小段详述,这份单证一般不被视为物权凭证。但该案中,原告证明了:

(ⅰ)有一习惯做法,是有关航区/航线把大副收据当做"最后单证"(final document),从来不再签发装船提单以交换大副收据。

(ⅱ)这习惯做法在有关航线的 Sarawak 至新加坡有多达 90% 至 95% 的货物运输是如此办理,从来不签发装船提单。

贵族院接受有此习惯做法的证据,但原告仍败诉,因为要法律去承认习惯,仍有其他要求,而恰恰是该大副收据印有"不可流通/转让"一句。所以,贵族院判定: "The factor that in the end compels them to differ from his conclusion is the presence on the mate's receipt of the words 'NOT NEGOTIABLE'. These words are part of the printed form. Their presence on a mate's receipt which is to be used simply as such may be superfluous, but it is not incongruous. The only meaning, whether it be a popular or a legal meaning, that can be given to this marking is that the document is not to pass title by endorsement and delivery."

Devlin 勋爵说明如下: "The question is whether a Court of law can also ignore them.[17] The Courts are well aware of the tendency of businessmen to retain in the documents they use inapplicable or outmoded expressions[18]; and they endeavour, albeit with reluctance since the retention is inevitably a source of confusion, to give effect to what they take to be the true nature of the document…[19] The rule is plain and clear that inconsistency with the document defeats the custom.[20] If this document had "Negotiable" printed in the right hand corner and "Not negotiable" in the left, the argument could begin.[21] But if the right-hand corner is blank, custom cannot be used to fill it.[22] Whichever way the argument for the respondents is put, it amounts in the end to a submission that the force of custom should expel from the document words that are on it: this is not permissible by law.[23]"

所以，任何付运单证只要去印上"不可流通/转让"字样都一定不会被法律承认为物权凭证。它们会是"海运单"(sea waybill)或是装船提单的副本。正本的装船提单印有"可流通/转让"(Negotiable)字样，往往是一套3份。但副本会取出30/40份，去在各运输环节中任意使用，而副本印有"不可流通/转让"(Non-negotiable)字样。笔者见过商人在提单副本背书，意图转让货权，这显然是乱来，因为提单副本根本变不了为物权凭证。

除了"Non-negotiable"字样外，也可以有其他明示条款/字样去表达同一解释或意义，比如是：

（ⅰ）"不可转让"(non-transferable)。

（ⅱ）在收货人一栏没有"指示"(order)一字，并有条款说明货物在卸港是交出给指明的收货人或他的代表：如马士基公司的"Maersk Line non-negotiable sea way-

---

〔17〕 问题是：法院可否去漠视这"不可流通/转让"字样的存在？
〔18〕 确实有商业人士不去理会他们使用的单证有不适用或已过时的措辞或字样。
〔19〕 而导致对这份单证本质是什么意图的混乱。
〔20〕 但大道理与基本原则是清楚：单证上的矛盾与不同措辞/文字可以去打垮（超越）习惯做法。
〔21〕 如果大副收据的左上角有"不可流通/转让"字样而右上角有"可流通/转让"字样，即一份单证本身的明示条款有自我矛盾/冲突，这还有得争，到底解释起来什么是超越，习惯做法会否有点份量可作补充？
〔22〕 但如果大副收据的左上角有"不可流通/转让"字样而右上角只是空白，像本案例，则不能以习惯来替代或填充，更谈不上是指习惯可去超越明示的字样。
〔23〕 这是法律不允许的。

bill"与 P&O 公司的"non-negotiable waybill for combined transport shipment or port to port, shipment"。

(ⅲ)在收货人一栏注明"不准指示"(not to order):BIMCO 的 COMBICONWAY-BILL 标准格式中字样。

(ⅳ)明示条款说明在卸港货物交出给"承租人指定的一方"(to the party nominated by the Charterers or their authorised agent):BIMCO 的 HEAVYCONRECEIPT 标准格式。

有了以上明示字样/条款,都会难以争辩有习惯做法令此单证成为物权凭证,进而令该单证的持有人(不管他是谁)有权向船东/承运人提出交出货物的要求。

装船提单除了要有"可流通/转让"(negotiable)字样,要注意还要有另一明示字样才会与物权凭证不产生矛盾/冲突。这就是在"收货人"(consignee)一栏有"听指示"(to order)字样。在近期的 The "Chitral"(2000)(Holmes Hardingham Newsletter No. 30)判一份收货人注明是谁而且没有"to order"字样的提单不是一份物权凭证。该案例提到一个 1873 年先例的说法为:"It appears that a bill of lading was made out, which is in the usual form, with this difference, that the words"or order or assigns" are omitted. It has been argued that, notwithstanding the omission of these words, this bill of lading was a negotiable instrument, and there is some authority ... for that proposition: but undoubtedly, the general view of the mercantile world has been for some time that, in order to make bills of lading negotiable, some such words as "or order or assigns" ought to be in them. For the purpose of this case... it may be assumed that this bill of lading is not a negotiable instrument."

另在 The "Delfini"(1990)1 Lloyd's Rep. 252 之 269 页,Mustill 大法官也谈到"听指示"(to order)字样的重要性,如下:"In this regard, The form of the bill of lading is very significant ... if the seller takes from the carrier a bill of lading which makes the goods deliverable to his order, this is strong evidence that the shipment is not an unconditional appropriation, and that the property is intended to be held up in the vendor pending the fulfillment of a condition: almost always, as I have said, pending the payment by the buyer of the price, or the provision of security for it."(有"听指示"字样十分重要,这证明了付运并非是无条件的拨归,而是卖方仍不肯去交出货物,除非能先满足一个条件,就是买方先支付货款或提供担保)。

美国的 1916 年提单法有一种"记名提单"(straight bill of lading),可去节录几段有关立法条款如下:

(ⅰ)Section 2 Straight bill of lading

A bill in which it is stated that the goods are consigned or destined to a specified person is a straight bill(记名提单是去写明货物是交给某人).

(ⅱ)Section 6 Indorsement on straight bill

A straight bill shall have placed plainly upon its face by the carrier issuing it"non-negotiable"or"not-negotiable"(记名提单应在表面上注明"不可流通/转让")…

(ⅲ)Section 8 Duty to deliver goods on demand;refusal

A carrier, in the absence of some lawful excuse, is bound to deliver goods upon a demand made either by the consignee named in the bill for the goods or, if the bill is an order bill,[24] by the holder thereof(记名提单注明的收货人或指示提单[25]的持有人有权要求承运人交货,而承运人没有合法理由下,不得拒绝)…

(ⅳ)Section 9 Delivery;When justified

A carrier is justified, subject to the provisions of sections of sections 90 to 92 of this title, in delivering goods to one who is: (a) A person lawfully entitled to the possession of the goods, or (b) The consignee named in a straight bill for the goods, or (c) A person in possession of an order bill for the goods, by the terms of which the goods are deliverable to his order;or which have been indorsed to him, or in blank by the consignee, on by the mediate or immediate indorsee of the consignee. [船东/承运人可以合法/正确地把货物交给三类人,即(a)合法拥有货物占有权人士,例如是经过法院在多人争夺货权的 interpleader action 中判决谁是胜诉方;(b)或记名提单下注明的收货人;(c)或指示提单的持有人]。

显然,美国有了这立法,自然也不会允许去争辩有习惯做法在某航区把"straight bill of lading"当做物权凭证办事,因为接受这个习惯的默示说法会与美国法律规定有直接矛盾/冲突。

在本小段最后值得一提的是:英国立法没有像美国立法有"straight bill of lading"的说法。当然,滥用名字的付运单证实是不少,许多不能算是提单的都去自称为提单 [例如像货代签发的 "公司提单" (house bill of lading); Gagniere & Co. v. Eastern Co. of Warehouses (1921) 7 Lloyd's Rep. 188; The " Cape Comorin" (1991) 24 N. S. W. L. R. 745 (NSWCA)等情况。在英国,已有权威说法是美国的"straight bill of lading"就是海运单。而且,英国看来鼓励大家称这种付运单证为海运单,省得都叫提单带来混淆。这是在本章 1.5.6.2 小段提过的 Law Commission No. 196, 4.12 段说:"straight bills of lading … resemble waybills in all material respects, and we wish to treat them alike in legislation."

---

[24] 指示提单即是可以流通/转让的提单,这方面后详。
[25] 指示提单即是可以流通/转让的提单,这方面后详。

2.2.4 要求之四：在有关地区证明习惯被承认和依从

这一点在较早各小段已有涉及。例如，Kum v. Wah Tat Bank Ltd. (1971) 1 Lloyd's Rep. 439 一案例（在 2.2.3 小段提到）是证明 Sarawak 至新加坡有多达 90% 至 95% 的货物运输是如此办（不签发提单，只去依赖一份大副收据）。而回头航次，即新加坡至 Sarawak，仍有多达 75% 至 80% 是如此办。看来，这足以成立有此习惯做法。

另可再去强调本章 2.2.1 小段所讲的对习惯做法举证会是不容易与昂贵，所以装船/指示提单一直受欢迎，因为这种付运单证已是"不必证明习惯的物权凭证"（documents of title without proof of custom）。其他所有付运或托管的有关单证，理论上都可成为物权凭证，只要是：

(ⅰ) 去证明有此习惯做法，也是合理做法。
(ⅱ) 没有如海运单的明示条款/措辞矛盾/冲突。

2.3 总结有关条件

简单概括，普通法去承认一份单证为物权凭证的有关条件如下：

(ⅰ) 只有在无法或十分困难去转让"实质占有权"（constructive possession）时，才会需要有一份物权凭证。如果可去把实物（货物）转交，例如卖方交出给买方，进而马上转让实际占有权，就不必要有一份物权凭证了。

(ⅱ) 物权凭证必须可以流通/转让。这转让是包括实质占有权或加上财产权。

(ⅲ) 作为物权凭证，它必须是"最后单证"（final document），不能是"初步单证"（preliminary document）。

(ⅳ) 证明习惯做法（subject to proof of custom）。

2.4 物权凭证可否光靠单证上的注明/措辞

一份单证要被普通法承认为物权凭证，全是根据习惯做法，这一点已在 2.1 小段说清楚。此外，要去立法承认某种单证属物权凭证，这也可以。毕竟是，喜欢怎样立法都可以。在本章之 1.1 小段，就已介绍了 Factors Act, 1889 的立法。

疑问是：可否凭单证本身的措辞/条款去把它提升为物权凭证呢？例如，注明是"可流通"（negotiable）或"可转让"（transferable），而收货人一栏注明"听指示"（to order）。更或是，用更清楚文字在单证上写明是物权凭证？

Diamond 大法官在 The "Future Express" (1992) 2 Lloyd's Rep. 79 之 95 页认为是不

可以，不足够。他说："A bill of lading is not a document of title merely because of its terms.[26] If a document could become a document of title merely by virtue of its terms, it is hard to see why a custom as to the transferability of bills of lading had to be proved in Lickbarrow v. Mason[27] ...A document can only, it seems, achieve the status of a document of title to goods by mercantile custom or by statute.[28] 或许有人问，为何判定是否一份法律接受的物权凭证如此重要？可举一点：在本章1.2小段提到法律会默示一位承运人/托管人以物权凭证交出货物/财产后，即使是交给了实是没有货权或主权的一方，也不必去承担任何侵占的责任。

§3 各种付运单证介绍

3.1 装船提单

3.1.1 简介

装船提单这份付运单证对外贸、航运以及银行都不会陌生。它的重要性可以说是没了它，绝不会有这一二百年来众所周知的以 CIF 进行国际贸易的做法。[29]

其实，它只是发货人把货物装上船舶后，船长签发给发货人的一份收据，一份声明，注明收到什么货物装上船了。与此同时，船长答应把该货物运输去何地交货。笔者可去节录一本很早的书籍（1757年）对提单的定义（Postelthwayt，《The Universal Dictionary of Trade and Commerce》）如下："Bill of Lading, is a memorandum, of acknowledgement, signed by the master of the ship; and given to a merchant, or any other person, containing an account of the goods which the master has received on board from that merchant or other person, with a promise to deliver them at the intended place, for a certain salary."

看来，这两百多年前的定义至今仍是恰当和适用的。

装船提单也确能给所有相关人士信心：它针对货物已经装上船舶，已锁死在船舶的船舱内。船长不会轻易放走，连发货人自己想去取回货物也会面对船长先要

---

[26] 装船提单能成为物权凭证不会只是靠在单证上写明可转让，等等。

[27] 否则，又何需有 Lickbarrow v. Mason (1787) 2 T. R. 63 著名的先例，当事人要花很大的精力去证明习惯，毕竟该提单上亦有同样措辞/字样？

[28] 故此，只有靠商业习惯或是立法才能去令一份单证拥有物权凭证的特性。

[29] 英国最早的一个 CIF 先例应是 Tregelles v. Sewell (1862) 7 H. & N. 574, 158 E. R. 600。FOB 买卖历史早得多，但 FOB 有多种不同的做法。

求退回装船提单。

而对货物能去提供的资料如数量、重量、标记等,装船提单都会有记载。而且,提供与确认这些资料的人是船长。船长是整个国际贸易运输过程中唯一有机会去对货物作出检查的人(卖方自己不算),而且:

（ⅰ）他有水平。

（ⅱ）他应是客观的,不参与买卖双方各自的利益。

（ⅲ）不论是普通法或立法都会否决/禁止船长对这些提单资料的事后否定。在普通法,会依"禁止翻供"(estoppel)的理论;在立法,1855年提单法之 Article Ⅲ 写明提单资料会是"结论性证据"(conclusive evidence)。同样写法也可见英国的1971年海上运输法(海牙·维斯比规则的立法),Section 3 (4) 与1992年海上运输法之 Section 4。故此,船长应十分小心谨慎地在装船提单上作出任何批注、声明与陈述。

此外,海牙规则强制承运人/船长在发货人要求下,必须在装货后签发装船提单,不得推卸责任。而海牙规则已是不少国家的立法,表示船长拒签装船提单会是犯法。这在海牙规则 Article (3) 有规定:"After receiving the goods into his charge the carrier or the master or agent of the carrier shall, on demand of the shipper, issue to the shipper a bill of lading showing among other things…(有关资料)。"

3.1.2 接受为物权凭证的先例

普通法接受装船提单是一份物权凭证的第一个主要先例是 Lickbarrow v. Mason (1787) 2 T. R. 63。显然,在这先例之前,在地中海进行的贸易已有一段长时间了,做法上是船长去签发装船提单给发货人,然后发货人决定货物最终交给谁,而船长在卸港时会把货物交出给第一个装船提单的持有人。没有这习惯做法,并且作出举证,Lickbarrow 也不会是这样判决。

该先例的装船提单收货人写明是"unto order or assigns"(指示或转让一方)。故此,此单证也是一份"指示装船提单"(ordered shipped bill of lading)。Lickbarrow 先例判是:"by the custom of merchants,[30] bills of lading for the delivery of goods to the order of the shipper or his assigns[31] are, after the shipment,[32] and before the voyage performed,[33] negotiable and transferable by the shipper's indorsement[34] and deliver-

---

[30] 根据商人的习惯做法。

[31] 将货物交给发货人指示或转让的一方。

[32] 在货物装船后。

[33] 与在航次终结前。

[34] 以发货人的背书去转让货物占有权/所有权。

y,[35] or transmitting of the same to any other person; and that by such indorsement and delivery or transmission the property in such goods is transferred to such other person[36]."

另一重要先例是 Sanders v. MaClean（1883）11 QBD 327，Bowen 大法官说： "The law as to the endorsement of bills of lading is as clear as in my opinion the practice of all European merchants is thoroughly understood.[37] A cargo at sea while in the hands of the carrier is necessarily incapable of physical delivery.[38] During this period of transit and voyage, the bill of lading by the law merchant is universally recognised as its symbol,[39] and the indor-sement and delivery of the bill of lading operates as a symbolic delivery of the cargo.[40] Property in the goods passes by such indorsement and delivery of the bill of lading, whenever it is the intention of the parties that the property should pass, just as under similar circumstances the property would pass by an actual delivery of the goods.[41] And for the purpose of passing such property in the goods and completing the title of the indorsee to full possession thereof, the bill of lading, until complete delivery of the cargo has been made on the shore to some one rightfully claiming under it, remains in force as a symbol, and carries with it not only the full ownership of the goods, but also all rights created by the contract of carriage between the shipper and the shipowner.[42] It is a key which in the hands of a rightful owner is intended to unlock the door of the ware-

---

〔35〕 另也去交出提单。
〔36〕 这样做可去把船舶上货物转让给第三者。
〔37〕 这又谈到欧洲商人的习惯做法。
〔38〕 货物在船上，船在大海上，发货人/货方很难对货物去作出实物（货物）占有权/所有权的转交：请参阅2.3小段。
〔39〕 只好以提单作为货物标志。
〔40〕 通过背书与交出提单，标志性地把货物交出。
〔41〕 以双方（卖方/买方）意图为准去何时把货权转让，背书与交出提单是表面显示了这意图：Bools 的《The Bill of Lading》一书之第10页所说："the decision［指 Lickbarrow v. Mason（1787）2 T. R. 63］is only authority for the proposition that the transfer of the bill, prima facie, transfers the property in the goods"。

这与在岸上把实物（货物）转交一样，卖方交出给买方。但是否真把货权转让了，仍得全面看买卖双方意图，例如卖方会有"货权保留条款"（retention of title clause）。这情况在岸上的实物转让会发生：Aluminium Industrie Vaassen v. Romalpa（1976）1 Lloyd's Rep. 443，也会发生在海上提单背书与交出：The "Aliakmon"（1986）2 Lloyd's Rep. 1。

〔42〕 这一点涉及"合约相互关系"（privity of contract），是发货人与承运人订的运输合约能否也去转让给收货人（买方）的问题，将在本书第三章详谈。

house,[43] floating or fixed, in which the goods may chance to be."

较近期的权威先例,可去节录 Diplock 大法官在 Barclays Bank Ltd. v. Commissioners of Custom and Excise (1963) 1 Lloyd's Rep. 81 先例所说的话:

"The contract for the carriage of goods by sea, which is evidenced by a bill of lading, is a combined contract of bailment and transportation[44] under which the shipowner undertake to accept possession of the goods from the shipper[45], to carry them to their contractual destination[46] and there to surrender possession of them to the person who, under the terms of the contract, is entitled to obtain possession of them from the shipowners.[47] Such a contract is not discharged by performance until the shipowner has actually surrendered possession (that is, has divested himself of all powers to control any physical dealing in the goods) to the person entitled under the terms of the contract to obtain possession of them.[48]

So long as the contract is not discharged, the bill of lading, in my view, remains a document of title by indorsement and delivery of which the rights of property in the goods can be transferred.[49] It is clear law that where a bill of lading or order is issued in respect of the contract of carriage by sea, the shipowner is not bound to surrender possession of the goods to any person whether named as consignee or not, except on production of the bill of lading[50] [see the "Stettin" (1889) 14 PD 142]. Until the bill of lading is produced to him, unless at any rate its absence can be satisfactorily accounted for,[51] he is

---

[43] 这是耳熟能详的说法,即装船提单好像是去打开船舶这个浮动仓库的钥匙。这对以前通信困难的海上运输与国际贸易是十分恰当的说法。货物装上了一艘船舶,已是"义无反顾"的付运,货物好像是发货人泼了出去的一盆水,收也收不回。船舶在开往卸港中,在大海中没有人能去碰,如同货物锁死在该船舶上。直至到了卸港,船长才凭装船提单交出货物。相比,如果一批货物放置在一处是什么人都可自由进出,都有机会去碰它。这一来,还要钥匙干吗? 这一来,买方不会安心去付出高价(货价)买这无用的钥匙,银行也不会对它有信心,以它作质押而去借出金钱。

[44] 以提单作为证明的海上运输合约既涉及托管协议,也涉及运输。

[45] 在运输合约下,船东/承运人承诺从发货人处接受货物的占有权。

[46] 并把货物运至目的地/卸港。

[47] 然后把货物占有权让出给任何有权去对货物占有的人士。

[48] 直至船东这样履了约,正确地把货物的占有权交出,这运输合约才谈得上已是顺利履行而自动中止。

[49] 这一运输合约一天不中止,即货物的占有权没有正确交出,提单就仍是一份物权凭证。

[50] 法律上如果是指示提单,船东只去交出货物的占有权给退回/呈上正本提单的一方,不论他是否在提单上被注明为收货人。

[51] 除非,船东满意并接受提单为何不存在的理由,例如是毁了或偷了。

entitled to retain possession of the goods[52] and if he does part with possession he does so at his own risk if the person to whom he surrenders possession is not in fact entitled to the goods.[53]"

3.1.3 装船提单的优点

显然,指示装船提单今天已有约一二百年的江湖地位,肯定有它极优越之处。这可去简单总结为:

(ⅰ)它是唯一的"不必证明习惯的物权凭证"(documents of title without proof of custom):本章之2.2.1小段。

(ⅱ)它可去转让船上货物的实质占有权:本章之1.2与1.2.1.1小段。

(ⅲ)它也可去转让货物主权,一般也去这样做:本章之1.2.1.1小段。另,正如3.1.2小段的Lickbarrow v. Mason(1787)2 T. R. 63先例判的"转让提单表面上是转让货物"(the transfer of the bill, prima facie, transfers the property in the goods)。

(ⅳ)不像"衡平法转让"(equitable assignment)或"成文法转让"(statutory assignment),以物权凭证的提单去转让货物的占有权与所有权不必另去通知承运人。这在早期无法与大海上的船长通信的情况下,已表示无法以assignment来处理。关于assignment这一课题,请参阅笔者的《国际商务游戏规则——英国合约法》一书的第四章之§7段。

(ⅴ)装船提单的整个操作过程令人产生信心,加上不断有法律的对此加固。例如,买方以此可知悉卖方已履行了他的承诺,准确地与"义无反顾"地把买卖合约规定的货物装上船舶,并将开航至约定的卸港。特别是在CIF买卖,可以说买方的信心是完全与唯一的建立在此份单证上。而到了约定的卸港,船东/承运人虽然对船上货物的转卖一无所知,货权落在谁的手中完全无法知悉,但也完全有信心只根据收货人退回物权凭证的提单,即使是收货人实非有货权一方,也不必负任何侵占责任:Glyn Mills Currie & Co. v. East and West India Dock Co. (1882) 7 App. Cas. 591.

3.1.4 装船提单的缺点

人为建立起来的制度,也不可能完美。以装船提单为中心的上一二百年的国

---

[52] 否则,船东大可以拒交出货物,继续去占有货物。
[53] 而不这样做,把货物占有权让出给一位根本无权去对货物占有与拥有主权的人士,船东就会有风险。

际贸易与航运，也有不少弊端，而且不断在变化，可去简单介绍如下：

（ⅰ）装船提单不能对货物状况/质量等有太大份量的保证。毕竟它只针对货物的"表面状况"。显然对有些货物，光是靠观察"表面状况"并不足够。近二十多年才发展起来的集装箱运输，只针对集装箱的"表面状况"更只是空话一句。虽然，这只是与岸上进行实物买卖有程度上的差异，岸上买卖也不见得会去或能去全面内外检查，例如将罐头食品全部打开。故此，CIF 或 CFR 买卖下，不表示买方可以只信赖装船提单而完全罔顾卖方的信誉。因为到了收货时发觉"货不对板"，会是无法去怪装船提单的表述，因为它不针对货物质量（这靠表面状况看不见），也不全面针对买卖合约对货物的描述/样本（承运人/船长根本不知道买卖合约内容）。这一来，买方拒货或索赔，仍得去面对卖方。关于这一方面课题，可参阅《国际货物买卖》一书之第四章，不再去重复。

（ⅱ）再举一例说明买方不能把信心全放在一份装船提单而罔顾卖方的信誉，这里涉及假提单的问题。这里说的假提单是卖方伪造一套装船提单去银行结汇，其实根本没有货物的存在，更谈不上货物已装上船。但在 CIF 或 CFR 的买卖，银行与买方也只能去看单证（即装船提单）。故此，卖方的信誉十分重要。卖方如果是著名的国际贸易商，历史悠久，他往往也是不好惹，是厉害角色。但他只会"合法"行骗，这往往已足够发大财了。他不会"非法"去骗，因这会触犯刑法，犯不着。而去无中生有的签发假提单，正是典型的非法欺骗，触犯了刑法。假提单的课题在笔者《信用证》一书的第七章有详论，不再重复。装船提单只是一份单证，一张纸，完全防止不了伪造。所以买方只能靠自己的知识、经验、信息网络与机灵去"带眼识人"，别让骗子冒充一流卖方而有机可乘。

（ⅲ）近年来提单制度出现了一个"死症"（癌症或艾滋病），可说是无治疗良法，就是无单放货的问题。造成的原因是短航次、船舶停港时间短与航速太快、货物部分转卖频繁而每次转卖都要去个别处理（背书提单，结汇，检查单证，递送单证，等等）。整个流程仍是多年来的做法，没有提高效率或利用新科技（电子通信）的改进措施。这样的后果必然是船舶抵达了卸港但装船提单根本毫无踪影，因要经过层层叠叠的处理。的确，现实中常有船舶到了卸港后一个月或甚至是一年后装船提单才姗姗然送抵卸港。

这一来，除非船舶在卸港耽误上一个月或一年，每天无所事事，否则是做不到以物权凭证的装船提单退回船长后才交出货物的。在这"死症"，船东/承运人身处两难局面，漠视严重的、昂贵的与漫无止境的延误船期不是办法；而无单放货，不理会物权凭证，也不是办法。这导致今天在这方面问题与争议极多，例如无单放货后船东/承运人被指控侵占货物。这是在本章稍后之§5段会去详述的。

3.1.5 提单背书

3.1.5.1 什么是背书

一般的说法是装船提单通过背书而转让货物,而背书就显示了这转让货物的意图。在 Dracachi v. Anglo-Egytian Navigation Co. (1868) L. R. 3 C. P. 190 先例有耳熟能详的说法如下:"the transfer of a bill of lading for value is prima facie evidence of intention to pass the property."这一点已在本章之 1.2.1 小段等多处提及。

背书实是有权"指示"(order)把货物交出给谁,即向船长/承运人作出的将货物在卸港应交出给谁的指示。而在远古时代,无法通信的情况下,最安全、最可靠,也是唯一能做的指示方法就是索性写在物权凭证上,所谓"把单证锁死在一起"(lock into the document),而不分开去另作指示。这就是背书在提单上的做法的原由。

背书所代表的指示不必长篇大论,只要够明确并且签个字即可。代表公司的背书则多加一个公司印章已是足够让业内人士知悉。

3.1.5.2 谁有权背书/指示

有权利去作出指示把货物在卸港交出给谁的最初始一方自然是发货人,因为货物原是由发货人交给船长/承运人的。

装船提单若是要成为物权凭证,已在本章多次提到(例如是 2.2.3 小段),提单应该不得有直接矛盾/冲突的明示条款。

故此,装船提单总会印上或写上"可流通/可转让"(negotiable)。另在"收货人"(consignee)的一栏,一定有"指示"(order)字样,即将来货物交出给谁仍得听指示:请看本章之 2.2.3 小段。先写上"听指示"(to order)应已是表示听发货人指示,因为货物来自他。不少提单会写明"听发货人指示"(to shipper's order),这更为明确。这种称为"指示提单"(order bill)或"指示装船提单"(ordered shipped bill)的才是物权凭证,而去转让就是靠背书的指示。例如,代表货物的提单去转让给 ABC 的买方,可背书为"to ABC or his order"或"to the order of ABC"。而发货人(卖方)肯去背书,把这套提单放手给买方,也是在一手交钱(货价),一手交单之时,例如在信用证结汇或托收。

如果 ABC 的买方再去转售这批仍在运输中的货物给 EFG,则转让是由 ABC 去多加一个背书给"EFG or his order"或"to the order of EFG"了。

如果这一批货物多次转售,会令一份提单背页上写满了背书的签字与印章,好像一张大花脸。到了向船长以此物权凭证提货时,船长/承运人应去看是否有"适当的背书"(duly endorsed),也就是适当的指示交出货物给谁。

除了看指示是否够明确,也要看名字(往往是公司)是否正确。另外最重要的是仔细查验背书是否一个跟一个,所谓"Chain of endorsement",始于发货人的背书指示,直至最后一个收货人,没有中断,也没有错漏。如有疑问,即使收货人退回物权凭证的一份装船提单,仍不足让船长/承运人可安心交出货物。之后货方向船东索赔货损货差,也会面对这种质疑。如果提单背书有错漏,不连续,即会面对船东对"诉权"(title to sue)的抗辩。

在 The "Sletter"(1999)(LMLN No.522)一案例,涉及装2万吨化肥从美国运往孟加拉国。在孟加拉国的 Mongla Port 港外,"Sletter"的大船把货物转卸到"Queen of Diamond"(船名)的驳船后,在驳船开往内港时因不适航而沉没。原告向多位被告("Sletter"与"Queen of Diamond"的2个船东,代理等)起诉,而案中首先涉及原告是否有"诉权"。

原告是化肥进口商,他通过他的银行 United Commercial Bank Ltd.开了一份信用证给美国卖方的 Seminole Fertilizer Corp.装船提单显示美国卖方是发货人,进口商的原告是"被通知方"(notifying party),这也是指示提单通常做法/写法。而收货人一栏是写作:"to the order of United Commercial Bank Ltd.,… Dhaka…"

被告(船东)抗辩是没有 United Commercial Bank Ltd.再背书给原告,原告根本没有货权,提单合约与侵权都告不成。该案例中,进口商只有一份注明"不可流通/转让"(non-negotiable)的提单付本有背书给他,作为清关之用。但这显然是乱来,不足够去转让货物给进口商(原告),并去拥有诉权。

这种问题要是有水平能自察,可自己先理顺后再起诉或/与再抖出有关文件证据。否则一经抖出一份没有"适当背书"(duly endorsed)的提单给船东/承运人的被告,让对方找出破绽,就无法逃避事实了。所以,更早一步,货物保险商在赔付货损货差时,因为考虑将来会代位向船东索赔而会面对这种争辩,也应当赔付前先核对提单背书是适当的,没有遗漏的。

如果是一种"空白背书"(endorsement in blank),即不说明是货物交给谁,这将令提单变为一份"持有人提单"(bearer's bill),即谁持有它,谁就有权提取货物,这也是"适当的背书"。好处是转售多次后提单仍是一份简洁的单证,可能只有发货人一个的空白背书。不好之处是有遗失危险,所以现实中不多见。

另可值得一提的是,如果信用证要求装船提单是注明或背书为"有关银行的指示"(to the order of the bank),则注明或背书为"买方的指示"(to the order of the buyer)是一项不符点:Cape Asbestos Co. Ltd. v. Lloyd's Bank Ltd.(1921)W. N. 274。银行要求这样做的原因在稍后3.1.5.4与4.1小段详述。

3.1.5.3 发货人能否改变背书/指示

照说,常识是谁拥有货物谁有权去指示船东/承运人,交出货物给谁。在作出指示后,只要货物仍未曾交出,物权凭证的提单也还在手中,也不必去无故刁难拥有货物一方,禁止他改变主意,改变指示。只要及时,又何必不准人家去修定/更正原来的主意/指示呢?

所以,在 Benjamin's《Sale of Goods》一书第四版之 18-009 段有说:"Even where the bill is made out to the order of a named consignee, the shipper may, nevertheless, be entitled to direct the carrier to deliver the goods to another person, e. g. by endorsing it to such another person. Thus, in The"Lycaon"(1983) 2 Lloyd's Rep. 548, a seller shipped goods under a bill of lading naming the buyer as consignee; and having passed to the buyer to divert the goods from the buyer by endorsing the bill of lading by way of pledge to a bank. The shipper's right to redirect the goods to some one other than the originally named consignee may be compared with the 'right of disposal' (or 'disposal') or the 'right to modify the contract of carriage' give a consignor under the conventions[54] which regulate the international carriage of goods by air, road and rail."(即是在 The"Lycaon"一案例,提单原是写明买方是收货人,是记名提单。但货权仍属卖方,卖方把提单背书给了银行作为质押/抵押。法院判是卖方可以这样做)。

发货人要去改变背书/指示,常会是两种情况。一是真正搞错了对象,正如 The "Aegean Sea"(1998) 2 Lloyd's Rep. 39。二是原来买卖不顺利,例如买方拒绝,导致卖方(发货人)另要去转售给其他买方: The "Stone Gemini"(1999) 2 Lloyd's Rep. 255。改变结果会导致提单背页会有"取消"(cancelled)或"无效"(void)的字样。这不应是问题,而要去注意的是:

(i)错背书一方不必去背书回头。除了对方不合作外,这样做反而与搞错了对象的事实看来有矛盾。因为背书本是空的,本来就不存在任何转让货物的意图给错误对象,故他也没有权去背书回头,也不必要: The"Aegean Sea"。

(ii)如果买方拒绝接受提单,不支付货款,而且最终把这套提单退回给卖方,这表示由始至终提单的合法拥有人是在卖方,而不在可能会短暂持有这套提单的买方。这表示船长不能光看见一份提单就放货,而要去取回并保留一份正本提单才足够。在澳大利亚先例的 The"Stone Gemini",法院说:"The provisions of the UCP recognize that until the documents are accepted and taken up by the issuing bank the bills of lading are to be held for return to the presenter, This position accords with the commercial reality of the present situation where the bills were to provide security to Westpac as negotiating bank until the documents specified in the letter of credit were accepted by BOC. The documents, in my view, were despatched on the basis that until acceptance they were to retain their character as security for the moneys paid out by Westpac. The possession of the bills did not move into a legal hiatus when they were despatched on July

6. They did not pass into the 'possession' of BOC. As it turned out the documents required by the letter of credit were never accepted. In my view, they therefore never left the legal possession of Westpac, notwithstanding that they were not physically in the hands of Westpac at the time when the discharge of cargo was carried out…"

在上述的(ⅱ)会出乱子的情形,可举笔者不止一次见过的同类案件为例。要知道,像中国卖方出口货物,不一定每次都会有信用证的保障,而去叫一家银行代为"托收"(collection)会涉及费用。所以,见过十分"粗糙"的做法是把提单背书后加上一份"汇票'(bill of exchange),快递给海外买方,希望后者"接受"(accept)或/与支付货款。但这十分危险,卖方会完全失控。理论上,提单(与有关的货物)合法拥有人是卖方,不是买方,而买方不接受也应去退回这套提单。这一点实际在 1979 年的货物销售法之 section 19(3) 也有注明如下:"Where the seller of goods draws on the buyer for the price, and transmits the bill of exchange and bill of lading to the buyer together to secure acceptance or payment of the bill of exchange, the buyer is bound to return the bill of lading if he does not honour the bill of exchange, and if he wrongfully retains the bill of lading the property in the goods does not pass to him."

充其量,好像"保留货权条款"(retention of title clause)一样,以上做法只能保障卖方在买方碰巧破产时,可去要回提单与有关的货物。但以上做法完全保障不了卖方,如果是买方不诚实,他把提单转售了给无辜的分买方,而不支付货款给卖方。面对无辜分买方,卖方去争夺对提单与有关货物的主权可不容易了,这正是在本章之 1.2.1.2.2 小段所提及的"buyer in possession"情况。

笔者也见过不诚实买方以暂时持有的提单去刚抵达卸港的船舶提取货物,之后又说服船长退回这张正本提单给他,而船长也这样做了(这是乱来)。买方随后把整套提单退回给托收银行,而对卖方说是货不对板,除非货价打个 5 折等。

3.1.5.4 提单什么时候不能再背书/指示

不论货物是否在卸港卸下,一天没有把货物交出给提单内正确的收货人,该提单仍是一份完全有效的物权凭证:这一点可去看本章 3.1.2 小段所节录 Diplock 大法官在 Barclays Bank Ltd v. Commissioners of Custom and Excise (1963) 1 Lloyd's Rep. 81 所讲的话。较近期,Phillips 大法官在 The"Delfini"(1988) 2 Lloyd's Rep. 599 也曾说:"…the bill of lading, until complete delivery of the cargo has been made on the shore one rightfully claiming under it, remains in force as a symbol, and carries with it not only the full ownership of the goods, but also all rights created by the contract of carriage between the shipper and the shipowner."

从提单是一份运输合约证明的角度来分析,也完全说得过去。一个合约要去中止,"寿终正寝",除了像受阻或合约双方同意等外,也只能以"履约去中止"(discharge by performance）。根据提单去把货物在卸港交出给正确的收货人，正是完成了履约，合约随之而中止，包括了它是物权凭证的特征。

但仍没有直接先例判是货物已经交出了给完全正确的收货人（买方），他是以保函提取货物，但事后不去赎单，而提单是在银行手中，作为质押，以为是一份有效的物权凭证，其实已是失效。这一来，岂非对银行十分不利？因为短航次银行常会面对这情况。一个针对办法会是坚持提单的收货人是银行自己。对这一点，Mustill 大法官在 The "Delfini" (1990) 1 Lloyd's Rep. 252 曾说过："Finally, I should mention the continued status of the bill of lading after the goods have arrived at destination and have been discharged from the ship. It is, I think, quite clear from Meyerstein v. Barber (1870) L. R. 4 H. L. 317, that when the goods have been actually delivered at destination to the person entitled to them, or placed in a position where the person is entitled to immediate possession, the bill of lading is exhausted' and will not operate at all to transfer the goods to any person who has either advanced money or has purchased the bill of lading'. It is equally clear that until the buyer has actually received delivery, the fact that the goods have been discharged at destination subject (say) to a lien for freight, does not entail that the bill is exhausted."

有关这一点，也应去介绍已多次提及（比如在本章之 1.4 小段的）The "Future Express" (1993) 2 Lloyd's Rep. 542 的案情。该案中货物（小麦）是卸下并交给了收货人一年多之后才结汇，注明银行是收货人的提单才被银行接受了。但在当时，货物早已不存在。法院（高院与上诉庭）判这不是一个有效的质押。所以，表面看来银行拥有一套完整的正本装船提单，确实无误是物权凭证，而船东也确是无单放货，银行却不能成功向船东起诉侵占货物。

这一来，不论是指没有有效的质押或是指提单已是失效的物权凭证，都会令银行无法安枕。特别是短航次，每每在结汇时，质押时，背书时，已明知货物早已不存在，已提走或消耗掉。

幸亏是，如在本章之 1.4 小段略及，有了 1992 年的立法，已去把合法持有提单（lawful holder of a bill of lading）的银行与船东/承运人之间强制确立了运输合约的关系。导致像 The "Future Express" 的先例不会再发生，因不必仅是要依赖提单是否是物权凭证这一点才有诉因/诉权了。

3.1.6 装船提单是流通或只是转让之争

经常有人把"流通"（negotiable）与"转让"（transferable）混为一谈。在本小段，去区分它们，是把流通视作一个无辜的受让方在接受了一份物权凭证后，会比转让方原有的权力更大。正如 Bools 的《The Bill of Lading》一书之 10 页所给的定义为:"Negotiability is a term likely to cause confusion. Unless otherwise specified, during this section it is used to mean that quality of a document that enables the transferor of the document to give a transferee a greater right to the goods than he himself has, provided that the transfer is to a bona fide purchaser for value."

显然,一份单证光是去"转让"而不是在严格意义上"流通",受让方的权力就不能超越过转让方。主要情况是:如果转让方没有对单证代表的财物有主权,则在"转让"(transferable)说法下,受让方也无法有主权:请参阅本章1.2.1.2.1 小段有关 nemo dat 说法。但在"流通"(negotiable)说法下,转让方没有主权,无辜受让方也可拥有主权。

3.1.6.1 "转让"历史的简介

英国的普通法一直不愿意承认一个非实物的转让,而实物是指摸得到,看得到,可去真正占有的"thing in possession"。这方面在笔者的《国际商务游戏规则——英国合约法》一书的第四章7.2小段有详述,在此只去节录其中小部分如下:

> 普通法不反对财产(实物)的转让,但对无形的财富,即一个诉权的权利(会要通过法律行动来体现)却无法接受。这权益,可以是由合约也可以不是由合约而产生,称为 chose in action(通过诉讼才能占有的动产权益),因为它要通过"be claimed or enforced by action"来体现,会有很多种类,如债务(debt),股权,流通票据,保单,提单,版权,其他侵权与违反合约的诉权,等等。

普通法的一个忧虑是"揽讼"(maintenance)的危险,这方面的详论不再在此重复。而法律发展下去,有了衡平法与立法去否定普通法忧虑的,就是"衡平转让"(equitable assignment)与 Law of Property Act 1925 的"成文法转让"(statutory assignment)。

但远在衡平法与立法的发展之前,普通法也已承认二种非实物的转让。一种是有关货物,另一种是有关金钱。而它们的转让必须是根据一份"物权凭证"(document of title)的单证,而转让的权力要去"锁死在"(locked up in)单证中,可不必去另通知债务人(或托管人)已可自由流通或转让。这种单证涉及金钱,一般是称为"流通票据"(instruments)。而涉及货物,最著名的自然是"指示装船提单"(ordered shipped bill of lading)。

3.1.6.2 依权威说法装船提单只是转让

提单通常去印上"流通"(negotiable)字样,但看来,它只能是去"转让"(transferable)。显然,流通会严重影响他人(如剥夺他人原有的主权/物权),故必须有法律承认，而不能光是去自说自话。而涉及金钱的票据可去流通，是大政策认为它们在流通/转让时应有更大的信心。以下可节录有关的权威说法。先节录 Benjamin's 《Sale of Goods》一书之18－021段："whether bill of lading negotiable. A bill of lading which satisfies the requirements of a document of title at common law possesses one of the attributes of negotiability, viz. that it is transferable by indorsement (where necessary) and deliver.[55] Statements to the effect that a bill of lading is "negotiable" (or that it has been "negotiated") may be taken to refer to this attribute of transferability alone.[56] Thus it has been said that in Lickbarrow v. Mason (1787) 2 T. R. 63 the word "negotiable" was not used in the sense in which it is used as applicable to a bill of exchange, but as passing the property in goods only.[57] There are, in particular, two legal attributes of bills of exchange as negotiable instruments which are not shared by bills of lading.[58] The first is that the transferee of a bill of lading as a general rule acquires only such interest as the transferor had, and does not take free from defects in the transferor's title.[59] And, secondly, the rules governing the consideration for the transfer of a bill of exchange do not apply to the transfer of a bill of lading.[60] For these reasons the general view is that a bill of lading is not a truly negotiable instrument in the full legal sense.[61] When, in commercial parlance, a bill of lading is described as 'negotiable', what it meant is that it is transferable[62]…"

另可去节录 Wright 勋爵在 Nippon Yusen Kaisha v. Ramjiban Serowgee (1938) 60 Lloyd's Rep. 181 所说的，如下："It is true generally that a bill of lading is not a negotiable instrument in the sense that a bill of exchange is and the transferee of a bill of lading does not get a better title than his transferor. But while that is true of title in law, it can-

---

[55] 提单有一个流通票据共有的特征，就是以背书与交出提单作为转让。
[56] 提单上注明"可流通"，它实际只指"可转让"。
[57] 它只是用作货物的转让/转手。
[58] 最少有二处作为汇票特征的要点是提单欠缺的。
[59] 一是转让人（卖方）如果对货权有不妥之处，也同样影响即使是无辜的受让人（买方）。这 nemo dat 说法，请看本章之 1.2.1.2.1 小段。
[60] 二是转让所需的约因要求不一样，提单转让需要有约因支持才有效。这一方面，会在下一小段详述。
[61] 所以，提单不是严格的流通票据。
[62] 提单指的流通只是转让。

not be asserted of equitable rights."[63]

最后可去节录 Devlin 勋爵在 Kum v. Wah Tat Bank Ltd. (1971) 1 Lloyd's Rep. 439 在 446 页的同样说法如下:"It is well settled that 'negotiable', when used in relation to a bill of lading, means simply transferable. A negotiable bill of lading is not negotiable in the strict sense; it cannot, as can be done by the negotiation of a bill of exchange, give the transferee a better title than the transferor has got, but it can by indorsement and delivery give as good a title."

3.1.6.3 转让需要约因支持

这方面可去节录 Benjamin's《Sale of Goods》一书第 4 版的 18025 段,如下:"The transfer of a bill of lading does not pass property or title,[64] or bar the right of stoppage in transit,[65] unless value is given for the transfer. Thus it has been held that the indorsement of a bill of lading to an agent solely with a view to enable him to collect or store the goods did not pass any property to the agent.[66] one reason for this result was that the agent had not givenany consideration for the transfer;[67] another was that the transfer was not made with the intention of transferring property.[68] There appears to be no support in the authorities for any presumption that value has been given for an indorsement of a bill of lading.[69] There are conflicting decisions on the question whether past consideration a-

---

[63] 该案例是卖方收不到货款去"中止运输"(stoppage in transit)的权利(这课题在笔者的《程租合约》一书 501 至 506 页有详论)会导致提单的转让受影响,因为这权利是衡平法权利,要去看全面的公平合理,不是卖方理所当然的在普通法下拥有。在著名的 Lickbarrow v. Mason (1787) 2 T. R. 63 先例,也是否定了卖方去中止运输的衡平法权利,因装船提单已转让给了无辜的分买方。

[64] 除非是有"价值的约因"(value),典型例子是买方付出货价以交换提单的转让,则不能去以此来转让货物。有关"约因"的课题,在笔者的《国际商务游戏规则——英国合约法》一书之第三章有全面的详论。

[65] 如因为没有约因不能转让货物,自然也不能去阻止卖方去中止运输的权利。这一点在本章 3.1.6.2 小段之有略及。

[66] 故此,曾有先例是把提单背书给一位代理人,可让后者向船长提取货物并代为存入仓库,这并没有把货物转让给后者。要清楚区分是为了避免出了事会说不清。例如,代理人倒闭,这批存在仓库的货物(会以代理人自己名字寄存)算谁? 又或是,提取货物后发觉货损货差,应以谁的名义起诉船东或承运人? 这不能是胡混过关的,因为诉讼中有披露,有反盘问,会赖不掉,"代理人"就只是"代理人",从未付出过"value"来换取提单转让。

[67] 原因之一是代理人不会去为提单转让而作出或给予任何有价值的约因。

[68] 原因之二是双方(货方与代理人)也从未有过前者把货物转让给后者的意图。有关这一点(如 1979 年英国货物销售法之 Section 17)请看本章之 1.2.1 小段。

[69] 并没有先例说背书本身已可去武断是有约因,不必多去额外证明。

mounts to 'value' for the transfer of a bill of lading.[70] Where the transfer is made in consideration of an antecedent debt, the transferee's forbearance to enforce the debt will generally be sufficient 'value' for this purpose. There is no authority on the question whether a transfer of a bill of lading made without consideration can vest the contractual rights under the bill in the transferee,[71] but as such a transfer will not generally pass the property in the goods covered by the bill, it is at any rate clear that the contractual rights will not be transferred by virtue of section of the Bill of Lading Act 1855[72]..."

3.2 全程或转运提单(through bill of lading)

这种提单涉及"转船"(tranship)，有一程船，二程船。原因常会是装港或卸港是小港口，大船不去。故有一程船的"大船"(ocean carrier)先把货物运输至卸港附近，再"分包"(sub-contract)与分托管(sub-bail)给另一小船转运至最后卸港。

分包是给"分包人"(sub-contractor)，而分包的安排在 The "Starsin" (2000) 1 Lloyd's Rep. 85 先例，Colman 大法官有谈及如下："… Where a carrier has chartered a vessel to perform the sea carriage which that carrier has contracted with the shipper to perform, he has in effect employed the shipowners to carry out the substantial part of his own contractual obligations. He has therefore employed the shipowner as an independent contractor just as if he had employed a stevedore to carry out the handling of the goods at the port of loading."

其中一程船的船东/承运人（可能是"大船"船东）去承担全程运输的履约责任，签发一份全程提单。该提单内，有明示条款允许转船，否则在无权下去转船是会导致船东/承运人违约，不合理绕航等。例如，The "Pioneer Container" (1994) 1 Lloyd's Rep. 593 先例中的一程船船东（韩国的 Hanjin），它的全程提单就有一条款说："The carrier shall be entitled to sub-contract on any terms the whole or any part of the carriage, loading, unloading, storing, warehousing, handling and any and all duties whatsoever un-

---

[70] 至于是"已过时约因"(Past consideration)去交换提单的转让是否有效，曾有不同的判决。法律不承认已过时约因，请看《国际商务游戏规则——英国合约法》一书之第三章，5.2 小段。

[71] 没有先例说缺乏约因的提单转让能否把合约权利转让给受让人。

[72] 但在 1855 年提单法，因为立法的措辞/用字是去把提单的合约转让（给买方）与转让货物扯在一起，故此没有约因转让不了货物，也就无法去转让合约权利。另在 1992 年海上运输法，再也没有将提单合约转让与货物转让扯在一起。要产生提单合约的权利转让，只需要是有"善意"(good faith)的"合法持有人"(lawful holder)。1992 年立法的有关措辞是："a person in possession of the bill who is either the consignee or the indorsee to whom the bill has been transferred in good faith."

立法并没有对"善意"多作出解释或给予定义，又好留待将来判例进一步澄清。但会是不去再要求约因。

dertaken by the carrier in relation to the goods."

与货方关系而言,一程船是运输合约,二程船是侵权与分托管。

涉及转船,会发生在散装货的运输。如果是集装箱的货,更是会转船频密,难以避免了。所以,像针对信用证的 UCP500,已说明在没有明示拒绝的情况下(如说明要求直航),全程提单可以接受。这是 Article 23,可节录部分如下:"(b) For the purpose of this Article, transhipment means unloading and reloading from one vessel to another vessel during the course of ocean carriage from the port of loading to the port of discharge stipulated in the Credit. (c) Unless transhipment is prohibited by the terms of the Credit, banks will accept a bill of lading which indicates that the goods will be transhipped, provided that the entire ocean carriage is covered by one and the same bill of lading. (d) Even if the Credit prohibits transhipment, banks will accept a bill of lading which:

(i) Indicates that transhipment will take place as long as the relevant cargo is shipped in Container(s)... as evidenced by the bill of lading, provided that the entire ocean carriage is covered by one and the same bill of lading;

(ii) Incorporates clauses stating that the carrier reserves the right to tranship."

在上述(c)中要求全程提单去包括全程的履行,在笔者的《国际货物买卖》一书有详论,可以节录如下:

7.3.6 提单内容要求之四:要包括全程

这方面大精神是要让 CIF 买方可去盯着提单的承运人(一般会是船东)履约,而在发生违约时,例如有货损货差,买方要起诉也知道他的对象是谁。

7.3.6.1 不包括全程的情况

这提单不包括全程的情况,英文的所谓"no continuous documentary cover",可看先例 Hansson v. Hanel and Horley. Ltd. (1922) 2 A. C. 36。大精神是 Sumner 勋爵所讲的:CIF 卖方必须"cover the buyer by procuring and tendering documents which will be available for his protection from shipment to destination."

在该先例,是 CIF 买卖,目的地是日本,而付运港是挪威的 Braatvag;卖方把货物先运送去汉堡。一程船名叫"Kiev"。在汉堡,货物再装上二程船叫"Atlas Maru"。而卖方把二程船签发的提单去"交单"(tender)给买方,法院判是卖方违约,未做到为买方在单证上提供"continuous documentary cover",因为二程船不会去负责一程船这段的风险,变得买方无法在一程船这一段时间有任何单证上的保障。

7.3.6.2 船东有权转运的情况

不少班轮提单,订明船东有权去"转运"(tranship),而且,他不负责转运后的责任,例如,像 Soproma SpA v. Marine & Animal By-Products Corp. (1966) 1 Lloyd's Rep. 367 先例的有关提单有一条款说得非常清楚如下:

"When, for any cause whatsoever, cargo is transhipped to another vessel… all risks of whatever nature they may be, lie solely and entirely with…receivers of the goods… It is therefore clearly understood and established that the responsibility of the master and owner under the terms of this bill of lading is strictly limited to the time the goods are on board the carrying vessel…"

而这种免责条款能否保障提单承运人(船东)是要看措辞会否足够广泛明确了:Tne"Berkshire"(1974) 1 Lloyd's Rep. 185。

在这情况下,这提单如何影响 CIF 卖方的"交单"(tender)?在英国贵族院,Asquith 勋爵在 Holland Colombo Trading Society, Ltd. v. Alawdeen and Others (1954) 2 Lloyd's Rep. 5 先例有以下看法:"… A bill of lading with a transhipment clause is not necessarily a bad tender under a CIF contract; but it must in some way give 'continuous documentary cover' in respect of the goods over the whole transit; and a bill of lading issued by a shipowner who by the transhipment terms in it disclaims all liability in respect of the goods in the event and as from the time of transhipment, gives no such 'continuous' cover…"

看来,提单允许船东有权去转运,而不影响 CIF 买方的是要该提单的承运人(船东)负责全程。所以 Benjamin's《Sale of Goods》第四版一书的 19-026 段说:"In such cases the buyer would, if the goods were lost or damaged, have a remedy against at least one of the carriers for breach of the contract of carriage. Thus the requirement of continuous documentary cover would be satisfied and the buyer would not be entitled to object to the documents merely on account of the transhipment."看来,这转运问题不好解决。毕竟,CIF 卖方无法去影响班轮公司提单的标准条款。加上其他新发展不知道会如何影响这方面,如汉堡规则与中国海商法都在"提单承运人"(contractual carrier)外多加了一位"实际承运人"(actual carrier)。所以,稳当的做法仍是在买卖合约中订明。例如,CIF 卖方明知有一程船、二程船等,就应在买卖合约订明"允许转运"(transhipment allowed)。

7.3.6.3 习惯性做法的例外

这方面可节录 Benjamin's《Sale of Goods》第四版一书的 19-027 段如下:

"Relaxation of requirement of continuous documentary cover: The requirement of continuous documentary cover may be varied by the terms of the contract of sale, or by the customs or usages of the relevant trade. Thus where it is customary to ship goods by coastal or river steamers to a port for ocean shipment, and to tender the ocean bills of lading only, such a tender is good under a CIF contract. The custom may require the seller expressly to reserve power to tranship in the contract of sale, in which event the buyer will be entitled to reject the documents on account of transhipment if no such reservation was made: Fischel & Co. v. Knowles (1922) 12 Lloyd's Rep. 36."

既有一程船与二程船,自然会签发多于一套的提单。显然,如果一程船签发了全程提单,交给了发货人,发货人也去用来结汇,最后会经过银行而最终落在买方(收货人)手中。至于二程船如果也去签发一套提单,这提单须与第一套的全程提单明示去扯上关系。主要是写明"这提单下的交货是要去退还全程提单"(delivery of goods under the individual bill dependant upon the presentation of the through bill of lading)。

这二程船的提单在发货人一栏会填上一程船的船东/承运人。现实中有的会填上全程提单的发货人,但这并不正确,除合约关系没有理顺外,一程船的代理人安排转运也没有发货人授权去这样做。这也会导致补偿行为时的麻烦,如二程船抗辩一程船不能做原告,订约方应是发货人,他才能去告二程船:The "Xingcheng" (1987) 2 Lloyd's Rep. 210。

至于货物主权在这两套提单下谁属也不难去分析。如果全程提单仍在卖方手中,买方仍未支付货款,表示货权仍在卖方手中,并未转让。而第二套的二程船提单,所谓发货人,签发或转让/背书(如果发生此情况)都肯定是一些没有货权的人士。所以,去持有二程船提单的无辜第三者也就不会有更高更好的货物主权。这一点可去节录 Ralph de Wit 的《Multimodal Transport》一书之 6.22 段,如下:"While at common law, too, the pure through bill may be considered to be a document of title, the outcome of a conflict between pure through bill and individual bill may not always be the same. It should be borne in mind that in the common law system the document of title is merely transferable, not negotiable, and therefore proof to the contrary is possible even as against a third party acting in good faith, at least in principle … the nemo dat rule will apply, and it is obvious that the issuer of the individual bill could not confer any right to the goods upon its holder that he himself did not have."

在 The "Lycaon" (1981) 1 Lloyd's Rep. 92 与 (1983) 2 Lloyd's Rep. 548,虽然案例不是针对全程提单,它判是 1980 年 1 月份签发的一套提单比 2 月份另一套提单优先,就包含有这 nemo dat 说法的原则在其中。

3.3 大副收据(mate's receipt)

主要对散装货,在货物装上船后,船东会马上给发货人一份收据,这就是大副收据。这是因为去备妥一份装船提单仍需要一点时间,它会由发货人去备妥,填上各种有关的资料,再交给船长或有授权的代理人签字。今天往往在签发提单时,船舶业已启航。所以为避免时间上的空隙,需要有一份大副收据充场。

当然,只有一票货物,船东是不应去为同一票货物签发两份收据。所以,在交出提单时应把大副收据收回。

而大副收据上记载的货种、货量、批注等,也必须与提单吻合。提单作为后来签发的"收据",针对的是同一票货物,自然要依照大副收据的内容,否则船长不应去签发这套提单。如果签发了不符的提单,船东将来会面对收货人/货方的索赔,而且难以抗辩。例如在 The "Dona Mari" (1973) 2 Lloyd's Rep. 366,大副收据对木薯的批注是"不太干"(not quite dry),但这批注并没有加在装船提单内。

大副收据不是一份"物权凭证"(document of title),这已在本章之 2.2.2 详述,并有介绍有关的先例 Nippon Yusen Kaisha v. Ramjiban Serowjee (1938) 60 Lloyd's Rep. 181。原因包括没有证明显示有此习惯做法以及大副收据只是一份"初步单证"(preliminary document),不是"最后单证"(final document)。

该案例中,Wright 勋爵说:"The mate's receipt is not a document of title to the goods shipped. Its transfer does not transfer property in the goods, nor is its possession equivalent to possession of the goods. It is not conclusive, and its statements do not bind the shipowner as do the statements in a bill of lading signed with master's authority. It is, however, *prima facie* evidence of the quantity and condition of the goods received, and *prima facie* it is the recipient or possessor who is entitled to have the bill of lading issued to him."

故此,大副收据不是海牙/海牙·维斯比规则与英国 1992 年海上运输法等立法所针对的付运单证。1924 年的海牙规则在 Article(b)注明它所针对的运输合约只是:"'Contract of carriage' applies only to contracts of carriage covered by a bill of lading or any similar document of title…"

1992 年的英国海上运输法也只是针对提单,海运单与在本章 1.5.6 小段谈及的"船东交货单"(ship's delivery order)。换言之,不能以大副收据来转让运输合约,令单证上的收货人可在船东/承运人拒交出货物时起诉其违约。

在罕有的情况下,大副收据可去被证明是习惯做法而被法院接受为物权凭证:请参阅本章之 2.2.3 和 2.2.4 小段之 Kum v. Wah Tat Bank Ltd. (1971) 1 Lloyd's Rep. 439。除了如此,看来大副收据对银行,对买方等人士都不是一份可信赖或应重视的单证。

3.4 收货提单(received for shipment 或 alongside bill of lading)

在散装货运输,一般船东从发货人处收货是在船旁。所以有说法是货方有责任把货物交到船舷(ship's rail),好让船东把货物接过来并装进船舱内:请参阅笔者的《程租合约》一书之第 306~307 页。而对货物的责任与风险分摊,一般也是同样去规定,例如在海牙规则中著名的"吊钩至吊钩原则"(tackle to tackle)或"船栏至船栏原则"(rail to rail)。当然合约可去改变一切:发货人(也会是承租人)如果同意了负责装货/堆货/平舱(free in/stowed/trimmed),则不只是把货物交到船舷,而是应去安排装卸工将货装进船舱了。

至于是油轮,这船旁或船舷就是油管的"歧管"(manifold)了。

散装货运输,一般会涉及大副收据的签发。但涉及班轮,做法有点不一样。即使在多式联运普及之前,也经常会有班轮公司先接收了发货人的托运货物,存放在仓库(会是班轮公司自己拥有),然后在预计的装运船舶抵港后装上船。这样做大家方便,预计装运的船舶也会有改动,例如是船期调动,船舶出事故,或是预计的船舶装不下这票货物。所以,班轮公司在接收了货物会签发一份收据给发货人,它甚至是船名也没写或并不肯定是哪艘船舶运输。这份收据就是通常所称的"收货提单"(received for shipment bill of lading)。

疑问是:这份单证是否属"物权凭证"(document of title)?

3.4.1 一般不被视为物权凭证的原因

比起"装船提单"(shipped bill of lading),收货提单一般不被视为物权凭证,受重视程度也较低,原因会是:

3.4.1.1 原因之一:货物不是义无反顾地付运并锁死在船上

收货提单并非是已"义无反顾"的装上船舶的货物,说不上是锁死在船舱内,要有提单这把"钥匙"才能去打开。所以,把它用在货物买卖或质押等会信心不足。Benjamin's《Sale of Goods》一书之第 18~045 段对这方面说:"There is, moreover, a practical reason for distinguishing, for this purpose, between shipped and received bills. Once goods have been shipped, it is impossible or extremely difficult for the shipper or consignee to deal with them physically and it is that impossibility or extreme difficulty which led to the recognition of shipped bills of lading as documents of title. There is no such impossibility or extreme difficulty in dealing with goods before they have been shipped, and correspondingly less need to regard documents relating to them as documents of title. On the other hand, refusal to recognise received bills as documents of title need not hamper dealings in such goods once they have been shipped, for it is then a simple matter to turn the received into a shipped bill by a notation recording the fact of shipment."

难怪以前在针对信用证的 UCP400,它在 Article 26 (c) (ⅲ) 是写明不接受收货提单作为结汇用的付运单证:"Unless otherwise stipulated in the credit, banks will reject a document which…

(ⅲ) Contains the indication "intended", or similar qualification in relation to:

The vessel and/or the port of loading-unless such document bears an on board notation…and also indicates the actual port of loading."

3.4.1.2 原因之二:另有最后单证

收货提单照说很快会变为一份物权凭证的装船提单。货物一装上船,班轮公司即会在收货提单上加上批注证明已装上船以及是什么船名。而如果没有装上船就去这样批注,班轮公司会是构成"欺诈行为"(fraud):Kallis (Manufacturers) Ltd. v. Success Insurance Ltd. (1985) 2 Lloyd's Rep. 8。

所以,在这短短的时间内,没有必要把收货提单也当做物权凭证。而且,在本章之2.2.2 小段有详述,收货提单应是"初步单证"(preliminary document),装船提单才是"最后单证"(final document)。

3.4.1.3 原因之三:难有肯定与稳定的习惯

要去证明某地某行业有把收货提单视为物权凭证的习惯做法是很不容易的,而再要去证明这习惯既肯定,也稳定(请看本章之2.2.1 小段)则更不容易。这是因为收货提单可以代表多种不同做法,例如"收货"是为了某一艘将抵达的船舶,或是任何船舶都可以,让承运人/班轮公司选择与决定。收货提单也可以是代理人收货而不是承运人/班轮公司收货。所以会是变化无穷。

3.4.1.4 原因之四:以往的先例与立法只针对装船提单

在本章多处(如在3.1.2 小段)提及的主要先例 Lickbarrow v. Mason (1787) 2 T. R. 63,它只针对装船提单。另在1855 年的英国提单法,它也只去针对装船提单。

3.4.2 不同看法的案例之一:The "Marlborough Hill"

但曾有不同看法的案例,主要原因是法官不认为收货提单与装船提单本质上有太大不同,反正都是船东/承运人确认接收了货物托运。

最早的案例是 The "Marlborough Hill" (1921), A. C. 444。先要说明:该案例涉及另一问题,是争议有关是否属海事庭管辖的问题。故此针对收货提单是否物权凭证,只能是法官的"随口说说"(obiter)。该案例的收货提单是写作:"received for shipment by the sailing vessel called the 'Marlborough Hill' or by some other vessel owned or operated by(船公司名字)."

换言之,货物根本未曾装上船舶。但 Phillimore 勋爵不认为本质上有太大不同,说:"It is a matter of commercial notoriety, and their Lordships have been furnished with several instances of it, that shipping instruments which are called bills of lading, and known in the commercial world as such, are sometimes framed in the alternative form 'received for shipment' instead of 'shipped on board', and further with the alternative contract to carry or procure some other vessel…to carry, instead of the original ship.

There can be no difference in principle between the owner, master or agent acknowledging that he has received the goods on his wharf, or allotted portion or quay, or his storehouse awaiting shipment, and his acknowledging that the goods have actually been put over the ship's rail. The two forms of bill of lading may well stand, as their Lordships understand that they stand, together. The older is still in the more appropriate language for whole cargoes delivered and taken onboard in bulk; whereas 'received for shipment' is the proper phrase for the practical business-like way of treating parcels of cargo to be placed on a general ship which will be lying alongside the wharf taking in cargo for several days, and whose proper stowage will require that certain bulkier or heavier parcels shall be placed on board first, while others, though they have arrived earlier, wait for convenient place and time of stowage."

3.4.3 不同看法的案例之二:The "Lycaon"

再接下去是 The "Lycaon"(1981)1 Lloyd's Rep. 92 与(1983)2 Lloyd's Rep. 548,该案例涉及德国卖方把一批杀虫水与电线卖给了非洲买方。货物是分批放在两处不同的仓库,一是德国,一是荷兰。注意是货物根本不在港口,更谈不上是已装上了船舶。该两份仓库收据给了卖方货代后,货代去向船东代理人交换了一份"提单",日期是 1980 年 1 月,装运船舶是写作:"the above mentioned consignment is at the disposal of(船东代理) and that the same is intended to be shipped in one lot with M. S. "Lycaon" from Bremen to Douala."

之后,货物确是装上了"Lycaon"轮而且多去签发了一份"装船提单"(shipped bill of lading),日期是 1980 年 2 月。

本来,船东代理曾有要求先退还第一套提单后才能去使用第二套的装船提单,而卖方货代也同意了。但货代不遵守诺言,去向银行结了汇,导致第二套提单最终到了非洲收货人/买方手中。但第一套"收货"提单,却被德国卖方用来为一笔贷款作为质押/抵押。

这一来,最后就有了谁有权拥有放置在仓库的这批货物的争议?是第一套提单(顶多只算是收货提单)或是第二套提单(这是装船提单)。后一单证毫无疑问是物权凭证:Lickbarrow v. Mason (1787) 2 T. R. 63。但前一的单证呢？它如果也是物权凭证则可去转让货物的实质占有权与物权/主权:请看本章之1.1小段。而且为时较早,这就会比2月份的一套装船提单优先。这 nemo dat 说法的原则已在3.2小段末段略及。该案例中的 Lloyd 大法官受 The"Marlborough Hill"(1921) 1 A. C. 444 影响,判是1月份一套收货提单也是物权凭证,而且优先于2月份一套。他说:"I now come to the third main argument put forward on behalf of Mr. Fuhs. It is said that the January bill of lading is not a document of title. The word 'Shipped' has been deleted;instead there is a typed clause as follows:

'We herewith confirm that the a. m. consignment is at the disposal of Messrs. Karl Geuther & Co. , Bremen, as Agents of the Joint Service (NEPH) and that same is intended to be shipped in 1 Lot with MS "LYCAON" from Bremen to Douala.'

So far from being a shipped bill it is said that this is not even a received for shipment bill as ordinarily understood. All it does is to acknowledge that the goods are at the disposal of the vessel's agents. It is submitted that I ought not to regard such a document as a document to title without proof of custom, such as was found to be proved in the "Marlborough Hill" and Kum v. Wah Tat Bank Ltd. , There has admittedly been no attempt to prove any such custom here. I would not take so narrow a view of the January bill of lading. It is true that it does not use the traditional language 'received for shipment'. But the language which it does use comes to the same thing. Nobody suggests that the goods have to be received by the shipowners themselves. It is enough that they are received by their agents. For myself, I can see no practical or commercial difference between goods being received by agents on behalf of the shipowners and held in their own warehouse and goods being held at the disposal of the agents in the warehouse of another. Nor is there any difference, as was suggested, between 'for shipment' in a received for shipment bill and 'intended to be shipped with' in the present document. The document acknowledges that the goods at the carriers' disposal. It provides for the terms on which the goods are to be carried to their destination, namely, Douala, and there delivered to the consignee or his assigns. It states the name of the ship by which it is intended that the carriage should be performed. In my judgment the legal effect of the bill of lading is precisely the same as in any other received for shipment bill of lading. I would hold that it is covered by the custom as found proved in The "Marlborough Hill". It follows that Mr. Fuhs has failed to satisfy me that the January bill of lading is not a document of title. On the contrary I am satisfied that it is."

但 The"Lycaon"案例备受批评,原因之一是判决时没有去考虑持相反看法的 Diamond Alkali Export Corporation v. Fl. Bourgeois (1921) 3 K. B. 443 案例(在下一小段详述)。原因之二是 1 月份的一套提单连收货提单也谈不上,这可去节录 Benjamin's《Sale of Goods》一书之 18 – 02 段说:"… it merely said that the goods were 'intended to be shipped' on the "Lycaon", without indicating any physical proximity between the goods and the ship; indeed, one of the warehouses in which the goods were stored was not even in the same country as the port of shipment. In these circumstances, it is straining language to say that the goods had been 'received for shipment' on the "Lycaon"; and the view that the January 'bill of lading' was a document of title is, with respect, open to doubt."

3.4.4 认同不算是物权凭证的案例之一:Diamond Alkali

与 The"Marlborough Hill"及 The"Lycaon"唱反调的先例就是 Diamond Alkali Export Corporation v. Fl. Bourgeois (1921) 3 K. B. 443。该案例的提单是写作:"received in apparent good order and condition… to be transported by the S. S. "Anglia"… or failing shipment by said steamer in and upon a following steamer."

McCardie 大法官批评了 The"Marlborough Hill"案例,并说明没有任何"认可习惯"(recognised custom)去把收货提单当做物权凭证。所以,在该先例,判是 CIF 的买方可以拒绝卖方这样一套的付运单证。

McCardie 大法官指收货提单看来只是:"The document seems to me to be (in substance) a mere receipt for goods which at some future time and by some uncertain vessel are to be shipped."但看来主要依据仍是 Lickbarrow v. Mason (1787) 2 T. R. 63 的主要先例以及 1855 年英国提单法都只是去针对装船提单。

3.4.5 承认收货提单为物权凭证的好处

试想,如果去承认收货提单为物权凭证实在也有好处,如:

(ⅰ) The"Marlborough Hill"与 The"Lycaon"的看法有它们的道理,大部分收货提单会在本质上与装船提单没有太大分别。船东/承运人如果在签发中有疏忽或不诚实,都可能会发生在两种之中的任何一种单证。

(ⅱ)本章 3.1.4 小段提到一个提单"死症",就是单证处理太慢导致经常要去无单放货。这一来,如果能去处理(例如结汇)一份收货提单总会比装船提单在时间上能提早一点吧!

(ⅲ)在今天,班轮运输锐变为集装箱运输,也从传统的"港口至港口"(port to port)变为"门口至门口"(house to house 或 door to door),导致承运人(多式联运承运人,他可以是班轮公司,也要以是 NVOC 等人)会一早在内陆(远离港口)已签发了收货提单,并交出给发货人处理/结汇。若是发货人要等待至货物装上船舶才能动,会是劳民伤财。例如在 Customs and Excise Commissioners v. A. p. S. Samex (1983) 1 All E. R. (1043) 1051,收货提单与装船提单相隔是两个月。

这方面也可以节录国际商会(ICC)的"UCP 1974/1983 Revisions Compared and Explained" ICC Publication No. 411 (1984) 在第 51 页所说:"Except in the case of a port to port shipment under a marine bill of lading, the majority of transport documents will indicate that cargo has been accepted for transport from 'a place of final destination'. Also, and especially in the case of combined transport, insistence on an 'on board' document is likely to hold back the document, thereby postponing the time when the beneficiary can present documents in order to secure payment, and delay delivery of the goods at destination (with the possibility of costly demurrage) because the goods arrive before the documents."

所以,针对信用证的 UCP500,Article 26 针对多式联运单证,写法是:

"If a Credit calls for a transport document covering at least two different modes of transport (multimodal transport), banks will, unless otherwise stipulated in the Credit, accept a document, however named, which:…

iii. (a) indicates the place of taking in charge stipulated in the Credit which may be different from the port… or place of loading, and the place of final destination stipulated in the Credit which may be different from the port… or place of discharge, and/or

(b) contains the indication "intended" or similar qualification in relation to the vessel and/or port of loading and/or port of discharge…"

当然,发货人想要去使用收货提单结汇或托收也要其他方面配合,如买卖合约与信用证。如果信用证注明是要求"装船"(on board)提单,像 Robalen Inc v. Generale de Banque SA, 3 September 1999, US District Court (SDNY) LMLN # 525 的美国案例,则以上节录的 UCP500 之 Article 26 就不管用了。

3.4.6 1992 年英国海上运输法已包括在内

总而言之,时至今日,收货提单的问题也业已获得解决。在 1992 年的立法,它并没有去赋予收货提单一个物权凭证的身份,确也没有必要。立法只是不像 1855 年的提单法,去局限在装船提单。相反,立法只说"提单"(bill of lading),而在 Section 4 写明是包括了收货提单如下:

"A bill of lading which—

(a) represents goods to have been shipped on board a vessel or to have been received for shipment on board a vessel…"

该 1992 年立法的 Section 2 (1) 说明了"提单的合法持有人"(the lawful holder of a bill of lading) 会被强制与承运人产生了运输合约的关系。这提单包括了收货提单，而它的持有人也可与船东/承运人产生该单证证明的运输合约关系。如果船东/承运人拒交货或交不出货物，再也不必斤斤计较有否习惯做法，收货提单能否成为物权凭证以便可去以侵权起诉侵占货物。收货提单持有人（例如买方）只要以运输合约起诉好了，内中总有明示或默示条款要求正确交出货物，请看本章 1.4 小段。

3.5 海运单(sea waybill)

首先可去节录笔者的《信用证》一书第 157~158 页对海运单的简介：

> 海运单做法在海上运输只是较近年兴起，只要不涉及运输途中转卖货物或银行要抵押，照说是可以海运单替代提单。而提单的困难，主要是在卸港经常面对无单放货的方面，这带来更多的海运单做法。今天不少立法已把海运单也包括在内，如英国的 1971 年海上运输法（即是海牙·维斯比规则的立法，而海牙与海牙·维斯比规则本身并未去针对海运单，它们只针对提单），1992 年海上运输法（去替代 1855 年提单法）等。
>
> 海运单最主要的分别是它"不能转让"(non-negotiable)，货物只交给海运单注明的"收货人"(consignee)。所以，它不像提单（指的是"不记名提单"），不是货权的证明或凭证。海运单反而是与本书第一章……所讲的"记名提单"(straight bill of lading) 是同一类别的单证。
>
> 当然海运单注明的收货人也可让卖方（他与船东订运输合约）在交货前更改。这等于某人雇用搬运公司指令后者把东西交给谁一样。所以，著名的 OCL 在它的海运单有一条款说：
>
> "Delivery will be made to the consignee named or his authorised agent, on production of proof of identity at the place of delivery. Should the consignee require delivery elsewhere than at the place of delivery as shown below then written instructions must be given by the consignee to the carrier or his agent. Should delivery be required to be made to a party other than named as consignee, authorisation must be given in writing by the shipper to the carrier or his agent."
>
> 除了 OCL 的海运单，笔者还可以节录马士基公司的海运单(Maersk Line's non-negotiable sea waybill)，它对货物应交给谁规定得更清楚："delivery of the goods will be made to the consignee or his authorised representative upon proper proof of identity and

authorisation without the need of producing or surrendering a copy of this waybill."

3.5.1 海运单的特征

简单地总结海运单的特征包括：

（ⅰ）它不是物权凭证，也无意去让它成为物权凭证，所以一般都写明是"不可流通/转让"（non-negotiable）的字样：请看本章之2.2.3小段。

（ⅱ）它与装船提单等物权凭证不一样，在卸港交出货物是"认人不认票"，认的人是发货人说明的收货人。但物权凭证之所以称为物权凭证，表示交出货物是"认票不认人"。

（ⅲ）发货人可去随意指令货物交出给谁，航次半途改变也无妨，这毕竟是他的货物，可自由处理。

3.5.2 海运单的格式

现实中使用的海运单看来与一般提单十分相似。例如货物数量、表面状况与装港卸港等。单证后面是密密麻麻的付运条款。唯一或主要不同之处是海运单不能以其本身去转让货物的占有权或/与所有权。所以，非但不像装船提单注明是"可流通/转让"（negotiable），而且更会明确去显示这一点的不同，一般注明是"不可流通/转让"（non-negotiable）。另在收货人一栏没有"指示"（order）一字或更是印上"不听指示"（not to order），以显示海运单无法以背书方式转让货物。也会有海运单索性没有收货人一栏而只去说明货物在卸港交出给"承租人（或发货人）指定的一方或代理人"（to the party nominated by the Charterers（或 Shippers）or their authorised agent…）。

今天许多班轮公司都备有提单与海运单的标准格式，以供海运的发货人使用。例如是"Maersk Line's non-negotiable sea waybill"，"P&O's non-negotiable waybill for combined transport shipment or port to port shipment"等。著名的国际船东组织BIMCO（Baltic & International Maritime Council），也拟定了海运单的标准格式，一是多式联运海运单的"Combined Transport Sea Waybill"（简称是COMBICONWAYBILL）。其他各有针对的比如是"non-negotiable cargo receipt"（简称是WORLDFOODRECEIPT），等等。

另去重复本章2.2.3小段的后段所讲：straight bill of lading 实际是海运单，这也已有权威说法的支持。海运单另有叫法是像"data freight receipt"，"cargo receipt"或"cargo key receipt"。名字是次要，重要是实质内容。本质上，海运单与空运的"空运单"（air waybill）或是公路/铁路的"发货通知单"（consignment note）实际是一回事。

3.5.3 海运单的缺点

海运单一直少人使用,直至近年才有改观,原因如下:

(i)它不是物权凭证,无法在航次中以单证转售船上货物,导致航次中转售频密的货物像石油产品,部分散装货等根本无法去使用海运单。要以海运单转售货物,可不像装船提单这么容易,只去背书业已足够。如果 A 的卖方是交出了一份海运单(不是装船提单)给买方的 B,收货人注明是 B。则如果 B 想去转卖货物给 C,船东也不会理会,船舶到了卸港仍只会卸货给 B,不是 C。所以,B 要先去要求 A 向船东提出更改收货人为 C 才能成事。但事情一多,时间一拖长,又会有其他疑问。例如是 B 与 C 之间的货价结算以及何时才算把货物主权转让?要知道,他们会有倒闭的危险,更有扯皮的危险。

(ii)买方在不完全相信卖方情况下,去付出货款以换取一份海运单是十分不智与危险的。因为卖方可在后来偷偷去要求船东把货物交出给其他人士,甚至是给他自己。换言之,卖方可去随意更改海运单内的收货人:请看本章 3.5.1 小段。当然,也有办法减低这方面的危险,那就是买方要求海运单内多加一个条款不准卖方去更改收货人,条款称为"non-disposal clause"或简称"NODISP clause"。而措辞/用字例如是:"By acceptance of this waybill the shipper irrevocably renounces any right to vary the identity of the consignee of these goods during transit."

但加了这一条款,对买卖双方保障都不足,例如:(a)如果单证有不符之处而结不了汇或买方拒付货款,卖方仍无法去更改收货人名字,比方把船上货物另转售给他人,或自己去收货。或可以是,条款把不能再更改收货人的时间订在单证被买方(或银行)接受之后。但这要涉及事后如何确认给船东/承运人,而条款的草拟与实际操作也就愈加复杂了。(b)订约方原是发货人与船东/承运人,他们之间可以自己改变运输合约,例如"更改"(vary)甚至"取消"(cancel)。所以,即使海运单有了一条 NODISP clause,也不保障买方,卖方大可征得船东同意先取消这条款再改变谁是收货人。但随着 1992 年的英国海上运输法已在 Section 2(1)[b]加进了海运单,强制去转让这海运单的运输合约到收货人(买方)头上,这就使船东不只是听信卖方就任意去更改或取消海运单内容,进而减少这方面买方的顾虑。

(iii)因为以上(i)与(ii)的原因,国际货物买卖(特别是 CIF/CFR)不会接受与使用海运单。除非买卖合约订明,法律也不会承认卖方只交出一份海运单,就已尽证明付运责任。

(iv)同样是以上(i)与(ii)的原因,银行一般不接受海运单的质押。一定要做也必须有特殊安排,如:(a)海运单内也需要一条"NODISP Clause",防卖方结汇后向船东更改收货人名字。(b)海运单收货人注明是银行,而买方会只是"通知人"

（notify party）。显然，这样做是防止买方不来"赎单"，而船东却在背后把货物交出了给买方，银行全不知情。直至买方"赎了单"，结算了，银行才通知船东把海运单的货物权利"转让"（assign）给买方。但这一来，买方利益又会是有一点牺牲。如果支付了货款后银行不 assign 怎样办？银行在通知船东前突然倒闭怎样办？这都不像背书在物权凭证的装船提单上那样干净利落。

银行的另一做法是在海运单加一条款说明银行对货物有留置权，而船东交出货物给收货人之前必须有银行授权，确认不再留置货物。

（v）因为有合约"相互关系"（privity of contract）的困难，故此有了1855年提单法去把运输合约（包括它的诉权）转让给买方。但这立法并没有包括海运单，导致海运单的收货人无法像装船提单的收货人一样，有货损货差可去直接向船东/承运人索赔，因为海运单下他们之间没有运输合约关系。

（vi）即使是船东/承运人喜欢多使用海运单，决定权也不在他们手中，因为海牙规则（会是多数国家的法律）强制船东/承运人必须签发装船提单，只要是发货人有此要求。这是海牙规则的 Article 3，内中说：…（3）After receiving the goods into his charge the carrier or the master or agent of the carrier shall, on demand of the shipper, issue to the shipper a bill of lading showing among other things…（7）After the goods are loaded the bill of lading to be issued by the carrier, master, or agent of the carrier, to the shipper shall, if the shipper so demands, be a "shipped" bill of lading, provided that if the shipper shall have previously taken up any document of title to such goods, he shall surrender the same as against the issue of the "shipped" bill of lading…

（vii）海牙规则主要针对船东/承运人不得以订约自由去任意豁免责任，此为众所周知。但海牙规则没有包括海运单。它包括的只是"提单或同类物权凭证"（bill of lading or any similar document of title）。这规定于海牙规则的 Article 1（b）："'Contract of carriage' applies only to contracts of carriage covered by a bill of lading or any similar document of title, in so far as such document relates to the carriage of goods by sea…"

这样一来，公约不包括，要去依赖海牙规则也只能靠合约合并海牙规则了，即在海运单加一条"首要条款"（Paramount Clause），如同租约做法一样：The "Saxon Star"（1958）1 Lloyd's Rep. 73。但合并有它的技巧，绝非容易，这方面已在笔者的《期租合约》一书之 45.2 至 45.5 段有详述，另会在本书第五章 4.2.3.2.2.2 至 4.2.3.2.2.6 小段详论，先不去重复。

3.5.4 针对海运单的立法改善

为了鼓励多使用海运单与保障海运单，针对上小段所讲的海运单的部分缺点，

英国有了一些立法上的改良/改善,具体如下:

(ⅰ)英国1971年海上运输法(把海牙·维斯比规则立法)已去包括海运单。它在 Section 1 (6) 说:"Without prejudice to Article X (c) of the Rules, the Rules shall have the force of law in relation to—

(a) any bill of lading if the contract contained in or evidenced by it expressly provides that the Rules shall govern the contract, and.

(b) any receipt which is non-negotiable document marked as such if the contract contained in or evidenced by it is a contract for the carriage of goods by sea which expressly provides that the Rules are to govern the contract as if the receipt were a bill of lading…"

(ⅱ)英国1992年海上运输法(替代1855年提单法)也包括了海运单,让卖方订的运输合约可转让给海运单内的收货人,让后者可与船东/承运人之间有一个合约关系。这是在 Section 2 (1) 如下:"Subject to the following provisions of this section, a person who becomes—

…

(b) the person who (without being an original party to the contract of carriage) is the person to whom delivery of the goods to which a sea waybill relates is to be made by the carrier in accordance with that contract; or… shall (by virtue of becoming the holder of the bill or, as the case may be, the person to whom delivery is to be made) have transferred to and vested in him all fights of suit under the contract of carriage as if he had been a party to that contract."

3.5.5 海运单的优点与近年兴起的原因

海运单的优点只有一点,但这一点却是重要的一点,因为它可去解决在本章3.1.4小段谈及的"死症",就是在卸港无单放货的问题。

因为海运单不是物权凭证,就不像装船提单那样迫使船东/承运人非要去"认票不认人"才敢交出货物。若装船提单不知所踪,船舶又不能遥遥无期等,迫使船东/承运人去接受其他可能是"较次"的保障方法/安排而交出货物(主要是保函),既带来风险,也增加了行政工作与麻烦。

班轮虽然可以通过自己的代理人或分公司拥有自己的仓库/集装箱堆放场,进而可以控制在岸上置放的货物,从而可在不必延误船舶的情况下,仍然无须无单放货。但船东/承运人不一定在每一个卸港都能做到如此,更会遇上收货人(但手中未有装船提单)在当地很有影响力。这一来,会令船东/承运人难以安枕。

一旦使用海运单,这一切的担忧、额外工作与麻烦都会一扫而空。难怪,今天不少班轮公司已在大力鼓吹海运单的使用,特别在欧洲航线。这一点可先节录 Lloyd 大法官的一篇发言(标题是"The Bill of Lading: Do We Really Need it?"刊登在 (1989) LMCLQ49), 所说如下: "I have been told that on the North Atlantic route, for example, perhaps 70 per cent of all liner goods are carried on sea waybills."

另节录 Steyn 大法官在 The "European Enterprise" (1989) 2 Lloyd's Rep. 185 先例所说的: "It is the invariable practice of all English cross channel operators not to issue bills of lading for the cross channel Ro-Ro ferry trade. Instead, they issue commercial non negotiable receipts."

联合国贸发会(United Nations Conference on Trade and Development 或简称 UNCTAD)下属的 International Maritime Committee 在 1985 年 10 月写出过报告认为不少货运其实不必去使用装船提单。当然决定权不在船东/承运人,因为有海牙规则的 Article 3 (3) 与(7)。但海牙规则没有禁止船东/承运人为签发装船提单而多收费用(或加在运费中),相反发货人肯于接受海运单则减收费用(减收运费),以鼓励海运单的使用。

话说回来,也不是所有国际货物买卖与运输都可以使用海运单。像散装货与石油产品因经常要在海上转卖货物,加上有质押等问题,很少听说签发/使用海运单。

而即使在班轮,今天多见海运单而少见装船提单,也是因为国际商业大环境在改变。例如,跨国公司的生产与销售,使得它们母子公司之间或与有着长远合作关系的伙伴之间不会互不信任,因为害怕对方倒闭和扯皮等。这一来,可以不必去依赖装船提单,一份海运单业已足够。而在亚洲班轮业务,据知较少见到海运单。

3.6 船东交货单(ship's delivery order)

这份单证已在本章之 1.5.6.1 与 1.5.6.2 小段详述,不去重复。只需强调一下在 1992 年的英国海上运输法已包括了船东交货单,并给了这份单证一个定义,这是未曾介绍的,故现节录如下(在立法的 Section 1(4)):

"References in this Act to a ship's delivery order are references to any document which is neither a bill of lading nor a sea waybill but contains an undertaking which—

(a) is given under or for the purposes of a contract for the carriage of goods to which the document relates, or to goods which include those goods; and

(b) is an undertaking by the carrier to a person identified in the document to deliver the goods to which the document relates to that person."

另要重复的重要一点是 1855 年提单法只针对装船提单,但 1992 年立法已包括了所有提单(不管装不装上船),海运单与船东交货单。它允许运输合约的转让,绕过"合约相互关系"(Privity of contract)的说法,进而强制船东/承运人与收货人之间也有一个合约关系,可以去互告而不必劳烦原订约方的发货人。(本书第三章会详述这方面内容)。见 Section 2(1)的规定(重复):

"Subject to the following provisions of this section, a person who becomes—
(a)提单的合法持有人;
(b)海运单;
(c) the person to whom delivery of the goods to which a ship's delivery order relates is to be made in accordance with the undertaking contained in the order, shall (by virtue of becoming the holder of the bill or, as the case may be, the person to whom delivery is to be made) have transferred to and vested in him all rights of suit under the contract of carriage as if he had been a party to that contract."

所以,在本章1.5.6.1小段所讲的船东交货单可构成"托管关系"(bailment),因为有"让与"(attornment),已在有了1992年的立法后显得毫不重要。在什么依据都没有的情况下,收货人/买方的货物被侵占或损坏,才会去千方百计找一种关系以便起诉索赔船东/承运人。视当地习惯,有可能船东的交货单并非是物权凭证,所以告不成侵权。又没有运输合约关系,因为1855年提单法不包括。如此一来,合约相互关系的普通法大道理就像一座大山压在头上,动不了。

但今天1992年立法赋予了合约关系,则物权凭证与托管等都显得毫不重要了,起诉的依据只要肯定有一个就已很足够。

3.7 多式联运提单/单证(multimodal transport document)

有关这一课题,笔者会有一本书专门论及,名为《多式联运》。故在此不想多讲或重复。在本章之3.4.5小段,也有谈及多式联运中最重要的集装箱运输。

多式联运的核心内容是由一位承运人(可称为 Multimodal Transport Operator,简称 MTO,或 Combined Transport Operator,简称 CTO),向货方/发货人以运输合约承诺去执行整个运输。这整个运输往往是由门口(发货人门口)至门口(收货人门口),所谓 door to door 或是 house to house。但这可任意作出变化,看需要而定,例如只是码头至门口(pier to house)等。重要的是,这整个运输一定会涉及多于一种的运输方式才能算是多式联运。例如海运加公路运输。一般都会有一程涉及海运,或长或短,特别是有关付运单证能称之为"提单"。

多式联运承运人(MTO 或 CTO)常会是班轮公司,它们提供多式联运,也提供港口至港口的传统运输服务。但也可以是货代,自称为"无船承运人"(Non Vessel Operation Carrier 或简称 NVOC)。既称为"无船",就表示在海上运输这一段,非要"分包"(subcontract)不可。当然,在其他运输方式如公路/铁路,NVOC 也是"分包"

(Sub-contract)而已,非自己拥有。

自然地,多式联运承运人免不了要签发多式联运提单或单证。这些单证名字各不同,所以要去看本质,本质主要是有关的条款/措辞是否反映了多式联运的大精神与基本操作。

例如,多式联运承运人是班轮公司,可举英国著名的 OCL 公司(Overseas Containers Limited)所签发的"OCL Combined Transport Bill of Lading"为例。其中第 6 条是说:"If the Carriage called for by this Bill of Lading is Combined Transport, the Carrier undertakes to perform and/or in his own name to procure performance of the Carriage from the Place of Receipt or the Port of Loading, whichever is applicable, to the Port of Discharge or the Place of Delivery, whichever is applicable, and, save as is otherwise provided in this Bill of Lading, the Carrier shall be liable for loss or damage occurring during the Carriage to the extent set out below…"

又或是,多式联运承运人是货代,可举国际货代组织的 FIATA(全名是 Federation Internationale des Associations de Transitiares et Assimiles)所拥有的标准格式"FIATA Combined Transport Bills of Lading"(最后是 1992 年版本)为例,其中第 2 条是:"By the issuance of this "Combined Transport Bill of Lading", the Freight Forwarder(a) undertakes to perform and/in his own name to procure the performance of the entire transport, from the place at which the goods are taken in charge to the place designated for delivery in this Bill of Lading…"

其实多式联运提单与传统的收货提单(本章之 3.4 小段)或/与装船提单的全程提单(本章之 3.2 小段)本质上区别不大。

多式联运提单是收货提单应是没有争议的,它常会在远离装港的内陆城市已经签发与使用(例如结汇)。多式联运提单也类似于全程提单,区别只是前者分包给不同运输方式,而后者分包给另一船舶(二程船),仍局限在海运。

而由于各种特殊原因,传统的装船提单要涉及一小段的岸上运输,但这并不影响这份单证作为物权凭证的地位。在 Marshall, Knott & Baker Ltd. v. Arcos Ltd. (1933) 44 Lloyd's Rep. 384 先例,涉及一个 CIF 买卖,卖方租用的船舶("Orland")太大,进不了买卖合约与装船提单上注明的目的地(一个码头)。卖方同意以火车等把货物转运至买方地点。该案例是针对买方是否可以拒绝这份提单。现在看来,仍不能说明该装船提单因此而失去了物权凭证的功能。但针对多式联运提单是否为一份物权凭证有过不少质疑,如同装船提单一样。多式联运提单可分为两种:一种注明是"不可流通/转让"(non-negotiable);另一种是"可流通/转让"(negotiable)及有相关字样如"听指标"(to order)等。但在本章之 2.4 小段提到,光靠自说自话并不足够。

当然,任何单证都可以成为法律承认的物权凭证,只要能证明有此"习惯做法"

(proof of custom)即可。见本章之 2.1 小段。但这会是劳民伤财,也可能会失败。即使有此习惯,也会因存在时间较短,没有悠长历史而不成立。而且,一天没有定论,就总会有怀疑。

但 1992 年英国海上运输法一生效,可以说已解决了该问题。已经详论过,这项立法适用于收货提单,也适用于海运单。故应可视 negotiable 的多式联运提单为收货提单,而 non-negotiable 的多式联运提单可视为海运单。在该立法下,都会强制有一个运输合约在这些单证内的收货人与船东/承运人之间存在,可去互告,例如因为拒交货物或货损货差。有了这种合约关系,是否为物权凭证的担忧就会减少或者不必要了。

3.8 发货通知单(consignment note)

这不是海运的付运单证,但也可略为提及。

公路(或/与铁路)的承运人在收货后,通常会出具一份发货通知书,而它的作用可节录"公路运输公约"(CMR Convention)之 Articles 8 - 59(另有其他有关条款)如下:"Article 8 (1) On taking over the goods, the carrier shall check:

(a) the accuracy of the statements in the consignment note as to the number of packages and their marks and numbers, and

(b) the apparent condition of the goods and their packaging

…

Article 9 (1) The consignment note shall be prima facie evidence of the making of the contract of carriage, the conditions of the contract and the receipt of the goods by carrier…"

显而易见,它的职能及其做法与提单相同。内中有不少资料是发货人才能填上的(请看 CMR Convention 之 Article 6)。而由承运人或它的雇员(公路运输就会是卡车/货柜车司机)签发,这实际是收据的作用与做法。

此外,像提单一样,发货通知单的一个职能是运输合约的证明。它只能是一个证明,因为在签发时,双方已部分履约(装货上车或上船)。在这之前双方一定有合约存在。而在货代的粗糙做法上较多会是在饭桌上的口头协议,或纯粹是以行动构成一个合约:货方一言不发,把货物交给以前有过交往的货代或只是叫货代来取货。

装船提单具有的三个职能中唯一剩下的,也是发货通知单所欠缺的就是物权凭证。众所周知,要有习惯做法才会有法律承认的物权凭证的地位。而发货通知单没有这个习惯是因为商人不这样做,也没有必要这样做。原因是公路运输时间不会太长,不像航运般旷日持久。也不需要去创造一个代表货物的标志,以便去马上处理/运用。加之货物不会像装上船那样被"锁死"在卡车内,令大家有信心。所以,不像提单,没有人去以一把"钥匙"来形容一份发货通知单,好像没有这钥匙的人就无法碰这批货物。而只涉及公路运输的货物,一般是实物买卖,无须以发货通知单在运输中进行买卖。

3.9 空运单(air waybill)

空运单是华沙公约的说法,英国的立法(Carriage by Air Acts)称它为"空运发货通知单"(air consignment note)。

与3.8小段的发货通知单一样,它也有货物收据与证明运输合约的职能及其做法。这可以节录华沙公约的 Aritcle 11 如下:

"(1) The air waybill shall be prima facie evidence of the conclusion of the contract, of the receipt of the goods and of the conditions of transportation.

(2) The statements in the air waybill relating to the weight, dimensions, and packing of the goods, as well as those relating to the number of packages, shall be prima facie evidence of the facts stated; those relating to the quantity, volume, and condition of the goods shall not constitute evidence against the carrier except so far as they both have been, and are stated in the air waybill to have been, checked by him in the presence of the consignor, or relate to the apparent condition of the goods."

但空运单亦是欠缺了装船提单的另一个职能:不是一份"物权凭证"(document of title)。所以,承运人在空运单下只是把货物交给空运单上写明的收货人,这在华沙公约的 Article 13 有说明如下:

"(1) Except in the circumstances set out in the preceding article, the consignee shall be entitled, on arrival of the goods at the place of destination, to require the carrier to hand over to him the air waybill and to deliver the goods to him, on payment of the charges due and on complying with the conditions of transportation set out in the air waybill."

显然从以上的措辞/文字可见,它根本不是类同装船提单的做法,在卸港一手交单(提单),一手交货。提单也不会跟船,而是会另外处理,或银行结汇,或海上进行 CIF 买卖(单证买卖),但空运单却跟货物走在一起,到了目的地承运人要去作出通知并同时去交给记名的收货人。

当然,如果收货人写得不明确肯定,例如是"care of Mr. X",这会带来争议。这方面笔者可去节录 R. H. Mankiewicz 的 The Liability Regime of The International Air Carrier 一书之 116 段所说的:"The consignee is the person designated as consignee on the air waybill, and not the final recipient of the goods; Court of Appeals, Paris, 11 July 1975; 1976 RFDA 127, recently: U. S. Court, Southern District of New York, Swiss Bank Corp. v. First National City Bank er al. ,11 May 1979: 15 Avi 17.631… It follows that if the goods are addressed 'cares of Mr. X' the latter is not the consignee; Court of Appeals, Bremen, Germany (Fed. R.), 24 November 1966: 1968 ETL 1254;... Conversely if, instead of the bank which was to pay the carrier, the final recipient has been designated as the consignee in the air waybill, the carrier was entitled to delivet the cargo to him without requesting payment from him; Austrian Supreme Court, 23 June 1977: 1979 Transport Recht, No. 3 P. 75."

显然,并没有习惯把空运单当做是物权凭证。理由同样是:空运太快,不必在运输途中另去有"标志"(symbol)代表飞机上的货物,否则只是自我麻烦。例如,本来货物一到目的地即可去交给写明是谁的收货人。有了一份会在流通/转让的物权凭证,会令承运人不敢交出货物,而物权凭证会"飞"得比货物更快到达目的地吗?这岂不是每次付运都会造成交货的延误。

§4 物权凭证的质押

"质押"(pledge)在笔者的《国际货物买卖》一书之365/366页有简单提及,可先去节录如下:

> ……即"质押人"(pledgor)把货物作为抵押品质押给"承押人"(pledgee),例如是"当铺"(pawn shop)的做法。另一例子是今天常会发生的把股票质押给银行,以求借贷。质押虽是把抵押品交给承押人控制,但一般所有权仍属质押人。只是在质押人偿还欠债日期届满时未能偿还,才会是承押人对抵押品的所有权"加强"(strengthen),而质押人(也是原来所有权拥有人)对抵押品的所有权"减弱",导致承押人可去合法把抵押品出售,把所有权转让给第三者的买方……"抵押"(mortgage)与"质押"(pledge)有重要不同之处。以上可见,mortgage是不必把抵押品交给贷款的银行……

在 Sale Continuation Ltd. v. Austin Taylor & Co. Ltd. (1967) 2 Lloyd's Rep. 403, Paull 大法官曾说:"Now the essence of a pledge is that it is security against either an immediate advance or against a present Liability to make a future payment."

显然,把装船提单或其他相同的物权凭证放在银行去作为抵押品就是一个"质押"(pledge)。

4.1 质押的产生与做法

最常会发生的是在信用证的操作,银行往往会先去支付货款给卖方,这是在信用证结汇之时。但该银行只会稍后才能向开证人（买方）或开证银行要回这笔钱（加上它的费用）。所以，质押就成了这笔"先垫付了的钱"（advance）的"担保"（security），而银行也因此而变为了"有担保债权人"（secured creditor）。质押的安排会是，申请人（一般是买方）一开始去填写一份申请开信用证的表格时，该表格内已有一条款，措辞/文字如下："I/We hereby authorise you to hold the documents called for by the terms of this credit and the merchandise to which they relate and the relative insurances as security for all liabilities incurred by you or your correspondents or agents in connection with this credit including expenses and charges of whatever nature incurred in relation to the said merchandise or the obtaining of possession or the disposal thereof (which expenses and charges I/we hereby authorise you to incur and undertake to repay to you) and you may sell the said merchandise either before or after arrival at your discretion and without notice to me/us. I/we further agree to give you any additional security that you may from time to time require to cover my/our liabilities to you hereunder and in the event of your selling the merchandise to pay on demand the amount of any deficiency."

在 The "Future Express"（1993）2 Lloyd's Rep. 542，另有不同措辞/文字在该案例的申请开信用证表格中，如下：

"We undertake to receive the documents relating to this credit from you on receipt of your first invoice, against payment of remaining balance notwithstanding non-arrival of respective goods.

In case of being failure in settlement, we hereby authorise the Yemen Bank for Reconstruction and Development to debit our account with the remaining value of the documents, if our account is sufficient to cover the same, and if there is insufficient fund in our account you are authorised to put hand on the goods[73] or to clear through the customs... and sell same in order to obtain full settlement."

至于保兑银行有否质押？如果有，是从何处来，因为不是向它申请开信用证的啊？而它也谈不上是开证银行的代理人。保兑银行也需要质押的保障，因为开证银行也可能会倒闭。在这一点，Lloyd 大法官在 The "Future Express（第 547 页）说道："the bank's security depends, not on the contract between the buyer and his bank, but on the ability of the seller to pledge the documents of title on his behalf, or with his consent. Otherwise the confirming bank would be unsecured in the perhaps unlikely event of the issuing bank becoming insolvent."

保兑银行的质押来自卖方/发货人作为信用证受益人去交出这套物权凭证的

---

[73] 这几个字"to put hand on the goods"与接下去授权银行出售货物抵债即是同意一个质押。

提单给保兑银行。在本章之3.1.5.4小段提及,银行也要求提单背书给它。这一点在多个先例谈及,如 Kum v. Wah Tat Bank Ltd（1971）1 Lloyd's Rep. 439 的第442页,Devlin 大法官说:"At common law a pledge of goods is not complete without delivery. Delivery is likewise necessary to give the bank the possessory right without which they cannot sustain an action for conversion."

Diamond 大法官在 The"Future Express"（1992）2 Lloyd's Rep. 79 之第93页也持同一看法说:"At common law a pledge cannot be created without delivery or constructive delivery of the thing pledged and delivery is necessary to give the bank the possessory right without which it cannot sustain an action for conversion."（交出了抵押品才能去产生一个质押,这才给了银行对抵押品的一个占有权并可在抵押品在被他人侵占时起诉）。

信用证的做法常会涉及"中介银行"（intermediary bank）,它们也会要先去垫付了钱,而只得一套物权凭证的提单在手中,其地位又是如何呢? 应是,它们有一个"默示的质押"（implied pledge）,可以说是与一般的明示质押地位一样。这一点可去节录 Gutteridge & Megrah 的《The Law of Banker's Commercial Credits》1984年一书,在第210页说:"As regards the issuing bank such right (of resort to the documents of title for reimbursement of sums of moneys paid against them) is usually given by the agreement between it and its customer identified in the application for the credit. The intermediary bank has an implied pledge when it pays or negotiates documents tendered by it by the seller."（即开证银行与申请开证方会有明示协议,一般是印在申请表格中允许银行把物权凭证所代表的财产/货物用来清偿所欠的钱。而中介银行则有一个默示的质押……）。这说法应也可适用在保兑银行。

质押不一定涉及银行,只有少见的例子如已提及过的 The"Lycaon"（1981）1 Lloyd's Rep. 92 与（1983）2 Lloyd's Rep. 548 案例,1980年1月签发的第一份提单（只是一份收货提单）是用来向原告的 Ishag 先生作质押,因为 Ishag 先生借出150万美元给被告。而计划如何去偿还这笔钱与提单所代表的货物（如果是物权凭证的话）无关,质押纯是用作担保。偿还计划是发货人（欠债方）将进口的一批价值不少于800万美元的"未曾切割钻石"（uncut diamonds）,将来转售后,利润由发货人（欠债方）与 Ishag 先生（债权人）共同分享。但其后,发货人不诚实地把第二份的装船提单背书和转让给了非洲的买方/收货人。同时,这批钻石根本交不出。这导致 Ishag 先生想去提取这批提单所代表的货物（存放在德国的仓库内,待法院下令）,而与买方/收货人发生了谁才拥有所有权的争执。

4.2 银行对提单货物有特殊货权

银行作为承押人,自然对提单所代表的货物有"担保利益"(security interest)。但货物所有权仍在货方,说法是银行(或其他承押人)只是有一个"特殊货权"(special property)。因为直至质押人(货方)赖债,银行不得去碰这批货物,例如看见货价急升去转售/转让这份物权凭证。

这可以节录几个相同的权威说法。先是 Selbourne 勋爵在 Sewell v. Burdick (1844) 10 App. Cas. 74 说:"… that the endorsee by way of security, though not having 'the property' passed to him absolutely and for all purposes by the mere endorsement and delivery of the bill of lading while the goods are at sea, has a title by means of which he is enabled to take the position of full proprietor upon himself with its corresponding burdens, if he thinks fit; and that he actually does so between himself and the shipowner, if and when he claims and takes delivery of the goods by virtue of that title."

另可节录 Delvin 勋爵在 Kum v. Wah Tat Bank Ltd. (1971) 1 Lloyd's Rep. 439 在第 447 页的说法如下:"A pledgee is said to have a special property in the goods. (被告/船东大律师) referring to The"Odessa"(1916) 1 A. C. 145, has rightly pointed out that this is not property in the ordinary sense; the pledgee has not even temporarily the use and enjoyment of the goods but simply the right to retain them until the pledge is honoured and if it is not, to sell them and reimburse himself out of the proceeds."

4.3 银行的特殊货权受到侵占有诉权

如果提单项下的货物被侵占,主要/常见的就是无单放货,则银行作为承押人可以有诉权向侵占方索赔损失(货价)。这一点可去节录 The "Stone Gemini" (1999) 2 Lloyd's Rep. 255 在第 262 页的说法如下:"Westpac(结汇银行) says that as a consequence of being furnished with the shipping documents upon negotiating the letter of credit and making payment on the drafts, it acquired a 'special property' as pledgee in the cargo sufficient to entitle it to sue in conversion."

这种案例并不少见,The"Stone Gemini"本身就是一个典型的例子。它涉及山东冶金公司从澳大利亚进口约 6 万吨价值 170 多万美元的矿砂,冶金向 Jindalee 买(实际上是通过它),Jindalee 再向发货人(Mount Newman Joint Venture)买。Jindalee 并去以金康租约程租了"Stone Gemini"的船舶把矿砂自 Port Hedley 运送至青岛。但在青岛,矿砂以 Jindalee 出的保函(冶金也多加了一份保函)无单放了货。至于信用证的情况是:冶金向交通银行申请开证,受益方一是 Jindalee,二是 Mount Newman。Jindalee 把信用证转了给 Westpac 的银行去结汇并支付了 Mount Newman 货款,换取得装船提单与其他单证/文件。但 Westpac 再向开证银行的交通银行要求偿还,却因两个不符点而被拒绝。

再接下去是 Westpac 直接与冶金交涉,而冶金也分两期支付了部分货款,但仍欠下约 100 万美元。于是 Westpac 扣船/诉船,指无单放货的侵占行为导致它作为承押人或提单持有人(该提单是空白背书,是持有人提单)损失,结果胜诉。

§5 无单放货问题的现状与新发展

提单总是物权凭证,故此一旦签发提单,[74] 船东/船长马上应警惕到会有法律千方百计去保障的无辜/善意的买方会依赖该提单付出货价/代价(value)。另外也会有银行的承押人去依赖/信赖它,这也是法律要保障的。这在本章之 1.2 小段早已说明,持有物权凭证的人有权向船东/承运人提出交出货物的要求。船东如果拒交或无法交出,会构成侵占货物的侵权。再加上,船东/船长在提单下既是去"运输"(carriage),也是去"托管"(bailment)货物,会有运输合约的明示/默示条款约束;见本章之 1.4 小段。而作为托管人,理所当然要把货物交还给正确的货主或它的授权/指示人士。而船长去无单放货,实在是漠视正确货主的利益,乱交货给无权提取的人士。这既是船东的违约行为(提单合约),也是"侵占"(conversion)行为。这方面的严重后果,在笔者的几本书都已详述,如《国际货物买卖》第七章的§4 段;《国际商务游戏规则——英国合约法》第七章之 4.4 小段;《程租合约》第一章的 3.2.3.2 小段等。请恕笔者又在此再提及这老生常谈的问题,因为它仍是出事的热点,有不少近期的判例(有被报道,也有未被报道的),一般都是船东败诉,损失极其惨重,甚至是致命的。因为它不同于一般货损货差,互保协会是不保的。船东/船长可千万不能轻视这足以致命的问题,应完全掌握整个概念才可去轻重恰当地在每一次遇事时作出对策。

---

[74] 这提单主要是指装船提单(本章 3.1 小段),但也包括任何可能会是物权凭证的提单,例如是注明"可去流通/转让"(negotiable)的多式联运提单。多式联运一样会涉及无单放货。例如在 Westwood Shipping Lines Inc v. Ceo International Inc. (1998) 150 FIR 125,涉及有多个集装箱的皮鞋从上海运去加拿大的多伦多,货从温哥华卸下然后再陆路联运给收货方的 GEO。提单是"听指示"(to order),而 GEO 只是"通知方"(notified party)。GEO 手中没有提单,但说服了多式联运承运人(班轮公司)无单放货。但事后,GEO 不去支付中国卖方货款,导致中国卖方/发货人在上海海事法院起诉班轮公司无单放货。而班轮公司也赶紧在加拿大法院采取行动对付 GEO,如申请 Mareva 禁令防止皮鞋(货物)流失。另一例子是在"Fairplay"杂志 2000 年 8 月 24 日一期的第 27 页报道的新加坡法院判货代坐牢 4 年至 5 年,因为他无单放货后再去对货方谎称货物仍在他手中,这构成欺诈与合谋盗窃罪。该货代的谎言很可能只是为了拖时间,不敢面对现实。

5.1 怎样才是准确交货/放货

5.1.1 签发了提单就必须坚持收货人退回一份正本提单

只要船长在装货后签发了(或授权签发了)提单,就应意识到这是去创造了一份物权凭证。再想到整个外贸、信用证等的做法,就应坚持收货人必须退回一份正本提单才去交货/放货。这是 Neill 大法官在 The "Houda"(1994) 2 Lloyd's Rep. 541 之第 550 页所说的: "The case for the owners is based on the general principle that once a bill of lading has been issued only a holder of the bill can demand delivery of the goods at the port of discharge.[75] It is because of the existence of this principle that a bill of lading can be used as a document of title[76] so that the transfer of the document transfers also the right to demand the cargo from the ship at discharge[77]."

Neill 大法官还说: "It is necessarily implicit in the power to order the issue of bills of lading which make the goods deliverable 'to order' that the obligation is accepted to deliver to the holder upon production of the bill of lading[78]."

5.1.2 法律坚持对此基本做法保持简单化

不少英美法官也曾说过要对此沿用了几百年的基本做法予以"简单"(simple)化。因为一旦复杂化,在有些案例,若允许例外情况可以无单放货,就会导致船东"无所适从",或存在侥幸心理,每次事件都会要打官司,而且多少总会降低大家对提单作为物权凭证的信心。但保持简单做法,就是一句话说:"船东/船长无单放货就要负全责",又会带来僵化或不公平的感觉,因为在个别案件中船长确实是无能为力,根本没有疏忽犯错,但仍要对无单放货负责: Motis Exports v. Dampskibsselskabet AF 1912(1999) 1 Lloyd's Rep. 837。

这项大原则可节录 Clarke 大法官在 The "Sormovskiy 3068"(1994) 2 Lloyd's Rep. 266 在第 274 页的一段话: "It makes commercial sense to have a simple rule[79] that in the absence of an express term of the contract[80] the master must only deliver the

---

[75] 若签发了提单,卸港交货只能是给提单持有人。
[76] 这是因为有一份物权凭证的存在。
[77] 它会去转让而且转让到谁的手中,谁就有权在卸港向船舶提取货物。
[78] 只要曾经去签发了'指示'提单,就默示船长有责任只去交货给退还该份提单的持有人。
[79] 坚持一个简单做法符合商业利益。
[80] 除非是提单合约另有写明(例如是注明"不准转让")。

cargo to the holder of the bill of lading who presents it to him[81]."

确实在绝大部分案例,这大原则也得到贯彻。即:船东总逃脱不了要对无单放货负全责,没有例外,也没有同情,只是简简单单的一句话:不准无单放货。所以,船东/船长对无单放货千万不可心存侥幸。

5.1.3 真正货方也必须退回提单才能取货

真正货方(卸货当时或在事后证明)也必须退回提单才能向船东/船长提取货物。道理是,他/它可去转让/转售这套是物权凭证的提单。看来,"记名提单"(named bill of lading)若可去流通/转让,仍须在提取货物时先退回正本提单也是同样的道理。

这一点可去节录 Legatt 大法官在 The "Houda" (1994) 2 Lloyd's Rep. 541 至 553 页所说:"Delivery without production of the bill of lading constitutes a breach of contract even when made to the person entitled to possession…"

也可再节录 Rix 大法官在 Motis Exports v. Dampskibsselskabet AF 1912 (1999) 1 Lloyd's Rep. 837 所说:"In my judgment a true owner cannot in the absence of some special arrangement oblige a shipowner to deliver his goods to him without presenting his bill of lading.[82]"

5.1.4 提单一式几份,应退回多少

提单正本(不是指副本)会去出几份,或 3 份,或 5 份。在 The "Nai Matkeini" (1988) 1 Lloyd's Rep. 452 先例中,出了 4 份正本提单。一式几份一定要写明在提单上。这有长远历史做法的原因,不妨重复一下:以前的纸张质量差,邮政不可靠,所以怕损坏或遗失,而在通信困难时代是无法请航行中的船长再补一份的。所以,提取货物时船东/船长仍要收货人退回一套完整的提单就不合逻辑了,因为可能有一份损坏了或遗失了。而要去退回一套的话又何必一式几份,倒不如只签发一份更干净利落,不怕失散。

其实何止是提取货物,其他方面的行动(例如交出单证与结汇),法律也不要求是全套完整的提单。这可去节录笔者在《国际货物买卖》一书的第二章 7.3.13 小段如下:

7.3.13 提单内容要求之十一:完整一套包括所有的正本提单

---

[81] 船长只能去交货给出示这份正本提单的提单持有人。
[82] 真正货方也不能不退还提单而"逼"船东/船长交货。

提单是货权凭证,凭一份正本提单,也足够向船长提取货物了。照说,只签发一份正本提单已是可以,也有这样做,但较普遍的做法仍是一式三份正本提单。这古老做法纯是为了保险,怕把一份正本提单以较快的客轮邮寄去卸港时遗失,则另有其他两份顶上。而每次签发多少份正本提单,提单表面会显示,例如在 Congenbill 的船长签字旁边有一栏可供填上。

既然每一份正本提单都会是针对同一票货物的货权凭证,CIF 买方自然想卖方交单时全部交出。但看来,买卖合约不去订明会有不肯定。在 Sanders v. Ma Clean (1883) 11 Q. B. D. 327,CIF 卖方自己保留了一份,只交出两份正本提单。英国上诉庭说可以,只要卖方不是去把另一份正本提单背书给了第三者。但这怎会是买方在单证买卖时能去查明的事呢?Bowen 大法官说:

"The bill of lading... may be regarded as a key of the warehouse where the goods are. Can a person who has contracted to pay on delivery of the keys of the warehouse refuse to accept the keys tendered to him on the ground that there is still a third key in the hands of the vendor which, if fraudulently used, might defeat the vendee's power of taking possession? I think business could not be and is not carried on upon any such principle."

看来,买方要保障自己,应在买卖合约与信用证(如果有涉及)去订明"交单"(tender)是要"完整一套"(a full set of bills of lading)才成:Donald H. Scott & Co. Ltd. v. Barclays Bank Ltd. (1923) 2 K. B. 1.

显然,只去以一份正本提单交货/放货仍会有危险交错货。比如稍后有另一人持有同样一份正本提单(是一式几份的另一份)要求船东/船长交货。造成这种情况会是不小心或不太懂的承押人(银行)或买方只要了一份正本提单(以为足够去提取货物),而不是坚持要一整套正本提单,给了不安好心的卖方有机可乘。在著名的先例 Glyn Mills & Co. v. East and West India Dock Co. (1882) 7 App. Cas. 591,就是类似这个情况。该案例中,货方以一式三份的其中一份质押,而手中的另外两份的其中一份,货方用来私下提取货物,并且不去清还债务。

该先例判船东/船长只要是善意的,无法知道另有不同的提单持有人,是不必对后来才提出要求交货的另一份正本提单持有人(也是正确的收货人)负责。至今,该先例仍是对船东/承运人这样的做法(只凭一套几份中的一份正本交出货物,但结果交错了人),提供了主要的保障。只要是,表面一切正常,没有特殊情况。

除了 Glyn Mills 的保障,船东/承运人在运输合约(提单)以及一个名为"*volenti*"的说法下也有额外保障。这是在提单格式(一般在一式几份之处)加上一句说:"the one of which bills being accomplished the others to stand void"(其中一份正本提单要是

"完成任务",即凭其提取了货物,其他的正本提单就此失效/无效)。这正是警告买方,承押人或其他所有有关人士光是持有一份正本提单不会有足够保障,因为它会变"无效"(void)。提单一写明,就合约法精神而言,就表示船东/承运人去这样做,就有了依据而不会构成违约。而"volenti"的说法,是单证持有人光去看单证,已可知道另有几份正本的存在,因都是物权凭证,可据以去把货物提走,因而应有所警惕。

最后要一提的是船长一定要保留退回的提单,千万别交了货后又还给收货人。这样乱来的话,根本也是无单放货。

5.1.5 提单要全套退回的例外情况

一般,在卸港交货/放货只要退回一份正本提单,但也有情况是船东/船长要保障自己,与买方在买卖合约以及银行在信用证规定的做法一样,要求货方退回"完整一套提单"(a full set of bills of lading)。至于是什么情况,在理解了整个外贸/航运的运作后应可去判断。

例如,在本章 3.4.3 小段提及的 The "Lycaon" (1981) 1 Lloyd's Rep. 92 与 (1983) 2 Lloyd's Rep. 548 案例,可去联想到出两套提单的危险。

但船东今天仍要去面对签发两套提单的现实,这会是在租约中订明。如果订约前船东拒绝会导致拒租,如果后来才拒绝则会是违约。要去出两套提单的原因会是:

(ⅰ)第二套提单去改掉任何有关第三者(往往指货物供应方/原卖方)的资料。第一套提单在装港出,涉及原卖方与中间商(第一买方)的买卖合约,而提单发货人自然填上原卖方。但这"显示第三者的文件"(third party document)不一定适用在中间商转售给第二买方的买卖合约。中间商也不愿意让第二买方知悉货物来源。故此,要去与船东换一套第二套提单,发货人是中间商的名字。

(ⅱ)在以往三角贸易盛行之际,常有自欺欺人的做法,就是中国大陆去台湾地区的货物运输,中国装港出的第一套提单装港是上海,而卸港会是香港或是日本的 Ishigaki。但货物根本没在香港(或 Ishigaki)卸,顶多是船舶象征性地到一到。而第一套提单就被"换上"(switch)第二套提单,把装港写作香港(或 Ishigaki),卸港写上真正的卸港例如是高雄。

(ⅲ)在装港装货后船长签发了第一套提单给发货人,发货人慢吞吞地去结汇。但中间商(也是承租人)等不及了,他/它想尽早在第二买方开出的信用证中结汇。但没有最最重要的代表物权凭证与可去转让货权的提单,中间商是束手无策的。于是,他/它会去说服船东(或早在租约订明)去先出另一套:第二套提单。在发货人/原卖方结汇后中间商获得第一套提单,才退还给船东作为取消之用。

总之,在以上种种情况,船东即使这样去做,冒一定的险,也要要求完整一套提单(例如,去交换另一套),而不光是像卸港的正常交货,只收回一套中的一份正本已足够。

船东应坚持货方退回"完整一套"(a full set)提单的另一种情况是改卸港,只要回一份正本恐怕是不够,因为仍有两份(或更多,看实际是签发了一式几份)在外面流通/转让。Glyn Mills & Co. v. East and West India Dock Co. (1882) 7 App. Cas. 591虽保障船东在"正常情况"下以一份正本提单交货/放货,但不去依照原提单注明的卸港卸货并非是正常情况,这样更改卸港会令其他提单持有人蒙在鼓里。

5.1.6 法院一般不下令船东交货/放货,除非货方出示提单

在Trucks and Spares Ltd. v. Maritime Agencies (Southampton) Ltd. (1951) 2 Lloyd's Rep. 345,收货人因提单迟到,去向法院申请下令船东交货,法院拒绝下令。

这种情况会发生在如船舶半途出事或船东倒闭,收货人只好在半途出事港口自己去安排转运货物到目的地。但如果船长不合作,甚至要敲一笔钱才肯交货。那么收货人要去合法地强制船长交货/放货,就只能通过当地律师向出事港口的法院出示全套正本提单,证明货方所有权人的身份,并申请下命令交货。

5.1.7 提单如果被偷或遗失怎样办

提单如果被偷或遗失,常常不会只是其中一份这么简单和无伤大雅。往往会是,一整套的被偷或遗失或损坏。这一来,去等待正本提单(即使只要一份)也会是白等。

看来,正确做法是收货人向法院证明自己的货权后,充分去解释与证明提单消灭的原因/过程,进而要求下令交货/放货。除非是,收货人能与船东达成协议,例如以保函交货。

在Carlberg v. Wemyss (1915) S. C. 616, Johnson勋爵在第624页略为提到:"… and in the event of total loss of the bill of lading might have to be resorted to, if necessary at the sight of the court."

另Leggatt大法官在The "Houda" (1994) 2 Lloyd's Rep. 541至第553页说:"… Where a bill of lading is lost, the remedy, in default of agreement, is to obtain an order of the Court that on tendering a sufficient indemnity the loss of the bill of lading is not to be set up as a defence."

The "Houda"正是一个整套提单不知所踪的案例。该船装港是科威特的Mina Al Almandi,也在该港签发了装船提单,时为1990年。该年8月2日,伊拉克入侵导致这套提单自此不知所踪。

该先例除了已节录的 Leggatt 大法官所言,也可去节录 Millett 大法官所言如下:
"… for unless the bills of lading are produced he(指船长)cannot know for certain that the person to whom he has been ordered to deliver the cargo is entitled to it. One solution, no doubt, is that, since the master's duty is not one of instant obedience(指听从期租承租人命令)but only of reasonable conduct, he can delay complying with the order for as long as is reasonably necessary to satisfy himself that the order is lawful, possibly by obtaining the directions of the court in the exercise of its equitable jurisdiction to grant relief in the case of lost bills."(最后一句是船长最好向法院寻求指引,这方面在本章 5.3.1 小段详论)。

5.1.8 船东是否应先去卸下货物存仓以减少损失

也许有人会说,船东应先去把货物卸下,寄存在仓库等待正本提单的交换。这样做可去减少比如是昂贵的船期损失。当然,岸上仓库寄存也会是昂贵,而散货/油货则更会难以安排,这要看实际情况。

确实,部分船东也会这样做。例如,班轮常会这样做。不少卸港也会有一些习惯做法,例如给多少天免费的"free time"。但重要的仍是要肯定即使货物寄存在岸上,船东仍能去充分控制。这一来,表示如果岸上不是船东自己的仓库,或是,卸港在法纪不明,贪污盛行与乱糟糟的国家,船东最好是不先去卸下货。一去卸下,会失控,这是绝对要避免的,例如在 Carlberg v. Wemyss (1915) S. C. 616,就涉及船长拒绝把货物先卸下岸,Johnson 勋爵同意地说:"The master must therefore, prior to presentation of the bills of lading, do nothing with the cargo which will place it beyond the owner's and his own control, that is, which will amount to delivery."

在本章之 2.4 小段详述的 The "Lycaon" (1981) 1 Lloyd's Rep. 92 与 (1983) 2 Lloyd's Rep. 548,船东/船长不敢在非洲卸港把货物先卸下,但船舶(班轮)又不能去久候,结果是把货物原封不动地运回德国装港,再卸下去仓库寄存,等待英国法院判决货物谁属。

在第五章 4.2.8.7.4 小段介绍的 The "Iran Bohonar" (1983) 2 Lloyd's Rep. 620 也有类同情况,该先例也稍后在 5.1.11 小段有所涉及。

5.1.9 等待提单的船期损失应由谁承担

提单迟延抵达卸港导致船期损失收货人不一定有错,例如,航程太短,令处理单证怎样也赶不上。没有说法是船舶一抵达卸港而提单仍未抵达,收货人已是违约。正确答案是在"合理期间"内抵达即可,除非是合约另有写明,但这情况较少,通常不会有条款去针对。这一来,要靠默示,就是以合理为准,即收货人在合理时间内要以提单交换提货。这一通用大原则,可见 Hick v. Raymond & Reid (1893) A. C. 22 所说的(在第 32~33 页): "When the language of a contract does not expressly, or by implication, fix any time for the performance of a contractual obligation, the law implies that it shall be performed within a reasonable time. The rule is of general application, and is not confined to contracts for the carriage of goods by sea... so long as such delay is attributable to causes beyond his control, and he has neither acted negligently or unreasonably."

但何谓合理伸缩性可就大了,这稍后会在本小段详述。

像 The "Houda" (1994) 2 Lloyd's Rep. 541,伊拉克入侵导致提单丢失也说不上货方或收货人有责,有疏忽或不合理之处。

至于船期损失,班轮不大会发生,原因已有略及。但油轮(虽然石油运输经常是无单卸货)或散装货轮会损失船期,因不敢先卸货上岸(怕失控)或无法卸货上岸(没有办法安排或太昂贵)。那么它应否等待,要等待多久?

该问题可以节录《Voyage Charters》一书的第 150 页所说。虽然它实际主要是针对船东对货物的留置权,不是无单放货。但两者都涉及船东不要对货物失控、流失,后者的问题固然是严重得多,也严格多了,但道理仍是相同。它说:"Failure of the consignee to take delivery."

It is the duty of the consignee to take delivery of his goods when duly tendered to him by the shipowner, and to perform any obligations to be performed by him which are a precondition of the shipowner's duty to deliver, such as surrendering the bill of lading and paying any freight and other charges for which the shipowner has a lien.[83] If the consignee fails to present the bill of lading and take delivery the shipowner has the following remedies:[84]

(1) In the absence of agreement, or custom, to the contrary the shipowner must wait for a reasonable time to allow the consignee to claim the goods, since the consignee who is ready to receive the goods within a reasonable time is entitled to delivery direct from the ship[85]: see Erichsen v. Barkworth (1858) 3 H & N 601, 616; Proctor, Garratt, Mar-

---

[83] 收货人有责任去退回提单,提取货物。
[84] 否则船东有以下的措施。
[85] 一般是,收货人在一个"合理时间"内提取货物,这不是未尽责任,可以说是法律默示允许的。什么算是合理时间要看个别案件的事实,可以有十分大的幅度。而在收货人没有错的情况下,提单迟延抵达卸港,也避免不了,难去证明这时间是不合理。总之,应是收货人犯有本可避免的错,才能去指控它/他没有在合理时间内提取货物,要负责船期损失。例如是利用船舶作为临时仓库之用,或对轻微货损有过敏反应,提出不合理要求,否则不卸货。

ston v. Oakwin SS Co. (1926) 1 K. B. 244; Turner, Nott v. Bristol Corporation (1928) 31 Lloyd's Rep. 359.

(2) However, many charterparties and bills of lading contain express provisions which entitle the shipowner to land the goods immediately.[86] Also, the Merchant Shipping Act 1894, sections 492 – 501, where it applies, entitles the shipowner to land the goods after the expiry of 72 hours from the report of the ship,[87] or after such other period as may be expressed in the charterparty or bill of lading. The shipowner's rights under the Act are in addition to any conferred by the contract of carriage.

……"

所幸的是在散装货轮，多数情况是不必理会什么是"合理时间"、"不合理时间"，什么原因造成等待提单，等等。因为：

（ⅰ）在程租下如果一抵达卸港就能开始起算卸货时间（一般都有这样的租约条款），则"卸货时间"（discharge laytime）或"滞期"（demurrage）不会中止计算，船东没有船期损失；Erichsen v. Barkworth (1858) 3 H & N 601。

（ⅱ）在期租下承租人不能去停租：The "Houda" (1994) 2 Lloyd's Rep. 541。

这一来，表示船东仍要去追究什么是"合理时间"等只会发生在程租租约中卸港订的是 C. Q. D. . (customary quick despatch) 条件或卸货时间无法始算时。或是，船期损失外，船东会另遭受损失，如因延误错过销约期而失去下一个高利润的租约。

5.1.10 易腐货物等不及提单怎样办

接上一小段所谈的内容，可联想到易腐货物怎么办？这"易腐"也不仅指生果食品，可包括像中国进口的大量鱼粉，因为怕自燃/发热，必须尽快从船上卸下，但收货人却没有正本提单。看来，除非船东能很快与收货人达成其他协议（例如以保函交货），船东应考虑向法院（或提单有仲裁条款则会是仲裁庭）申请下令马上拍卖。这是在英国的高院规则（Rules of Supreme Court）的 Order 29 rule 4，航运人士熟悉的法院提前拍卖被扣船舶也是同样精神，可去节录如下："The Court may, on the application of any party to a cause or matter, make an order for the sale by such person, in such manner and on such terms (if any) as may be specified in the order of any property (other than land) which is the subject-matter of the cause or matter or as to which any

---

[86] 一般班轮提单总会有明示条款允许船一到卸港马上卸货，不必等待"合理时间"，以免延误船期，请看第四章之 3.4.7.4 小段。

[87] 另外，英国商船法另有 72 小时（除非提单另有写明）的期限，过了后船东可去把货物卸下。

question arises therein and which is of a perishable nature or likely to deteriorate if kept or which for any other good reason it is desirable to sell forthwith."

早卸下这种货物可避免日后处理麻烦/昂贵。也会有这种情况,就是船东仍未被付清运费,所以应趁货物仍有剩余价值而早日行动。

5.1.11　货物卸到岸上仓库是卸港惯常的做法

这种情况并不少见:卸港有惯常做法,甚至要求船舶把货物卸下寄存在(通常会是)当地政府管理的港口或仓库。那么,船东可否安心去无单卸下货物,寄存在岸上,等将来收货人退回提单才交货/放货呢? 说到是否安心,货物一卸下会否失控,全是看情况/事实而定,例如:

(ⅰ)在 5.1.8 小段所讲,卸港是否法纪不明、贪污盛行与乱糟糟?

(ⅱ)收货人是否在当地极有势力?

(ⅲ)船东有否自己的代理人,在卸港有势力/影响,本身也是大公司,有信誉,曾保证可为船东控制寄存在岸上仓库的货物。

总之,如果货物卸了上岸而被代理人或仓库/港口当局无单放货,可怜的船东看来仍是难辞其咎。首先可去介绍一些美国案例;在《Voyage Charters》一书的第151 页说:"Discharge to governmental authorities charged with receiving it and distributing it to the consignee under the law and custom of the port is "proper delivery" under the general maritime law and the Harter Act[88]…In such a case, however, the carrier remains absolutely liable for misdelivery[89] unless the shipper induces him to make the mistake[90] or the contract of carriage provides otherwise.[91] Allied Chemical v. Companhia

---

[88]　根据卸港法律与习惯做法把货物卸到岸上,让政府部门负责交付给收货人,在一般海事法与哈特法应已足够去构成承运人或船东做到"适当的交货"。

[89]　但船东/承运人仍绝对要对交错货物/无单放货负责。这看来矛盾的说法能去说得通的是"适当的交货"应属合理、正确的做法。但无单放货的情况会是另一个层次,因为侵占是严格责任(在 5.1.15.3.2 小段后详),不光是"合理"、"适当"已足够抗辩。

[90]　除非是,原告的发货人自己引诱船东/承运人无单放货,则不得事后去怪责后者犯错。这涉及禁止翻供的争议,稍后会在 5.1.16.5 小段谈到。

[91]　或是,运输合约写明可这样做。但这种条款是否一定能保障船东也难说,像在美国的 Hoffman-Laroche Inc v. TFL Jefferson 1990 AMC 1388;731 F. Supp. 109 (SDNY 1990),提单有条款说:"If a carrier was obliged to hand over the goods to customs or other port authority, such handover shall constitute due delivery."

但判是该条款违反了美国的哈特法而无效,因哈特法不像海牙规则(美国是 1936 年海上运输法)只管辖货物在船舶上的一段,它对岸上的一段也管。至于英国法律的有关论述,请见 5.1.16.2 小段。

de Navegacao Lloyd Brasileiro,775F. 2d 476,483（2d Cir. 1985）（carrier liable when he,without compulsion, gave consignee documentation which allowed consignee to obtain the goods from Brazilian officials without production of the bill of lading）;Nebco International v. M/V'National Integrity',752 F. Supp. 1207. 1221 – 1222（SDNY 1990）（shipper who induced the carrier to release the goods to the consignee improperly is estopped from recovering on claim against carrier for misdelivery）.[92]"

另外再介绍 The"TFL Jefferson"先例,它涉及货物在苏丹港卸上岸交给政府当局管理的港方,但后者事后无单放货给当地势力更大的"苏丹农业部"。而未获得支付货款的卖方自然去扣船诉船,指船东无单放货。船东抗辩说这样做是卸港的"习惯"（custom or usage）,但这并未被法院接受。

对此美国法很严格,英国法也松不了。在 The"Sormovskiy 3068"（1994）2 Lloyd's Rep. 266 的 275 页,Clarke 大法官说:"It would not however in my judgment be good performance of the defendant's（shipowner）obligations under the contract if it were merely the practice for vessels to deliver goods without presentation of a bill of lading[93] in circumstances where neither the law nor custom（in its strict sense）[94] required it."

该先例涉及俄罗斯的 Vyborg 港,惯常做法是把船上货物卸下给港口当局的 Commercial Sea Port（CSP）。但 CSP 事后没有取回正本提单就交出了货物,这导致后来船东被起诉无单放货。船东抗辩指卸货交出给 CSP 已是准确交货,因为这是 Vyborg 的习惯做法。但 Clarke 大法官既不同意这做法是当地法律规定,也不是"习惯做法"（custom）,而只是一个当地的"宽松惯常做法"（loose practice）,不足以保障船东无单放货。

卸港有明示的法律不准船东把货物控制在船上,一定要无单的马上卸上岸,不管你船东对货失控不失控,恐怕不多见,这会令该卸港国家看似是"强盗国度"。

至于卸港有这习惯要船舶卸下货物,寄存在岸上,恐怕这习惯也不容易确立与证明。何谓"习惯"（custom）在本章之2.2小段已谈及。像习惯被认可所要求的因素如"合理"、"与一般的合约或/与法律规定或说法没有直接矛盾/冲突"等,就不易满足了。

更深一层地考虑这问题,如果卸港真有法律或做法确实是迫船舶抵港后马上卸货上岸,而货物肯定会失控而最后导致无单放货,则船东在海牙规则下会有小心与妥善照顾货物的责任不进卸港,直到这问题获得理顺或转去其他附近卸港卸下。

---

[92] 一般做法是无单卸货上岸不保障船东。
[93] 同样,一般做法是无单卸货上岸不保障船东。
[94] 必须是卸港法律或严格的习惯才可保障船东。

这方面可参阅笔者《禁令》一书的第二章之 3.1.8 小段所说的 The "Iran Bohonar" (1983) 2 Lloyd's Rep. 620 先例,在本书第五章之 4.2.8.7.4 小段有节录。

5.1.12 发货人、承租人等是否有权要求船东无单放货

显然,除了法院,应该不会有人有权利去要求船东无单放货。发货人无权,这已在 Carlberg v. Wemyss (1915) S.C. 616 先例明确,它涉及发货人与收货人联合要求船长卸货上岸等待提单抵达,但被船长所拒绝。确是,提单作为物权凭证,不会光是在发货人与收货人手中。其他持有人如承押人的银行,第二、三、四的买方等,它/他们的权益(货权)也不能去罔顾。

至于承租人,程租更不用说,连一般有更大权力在营运方面下令指挥船长的期租承租人,也已在好几个著名先例中被明确了他不能去下令船长无单放货,而即使下了令船长也可去漠视而不会面对停租或索赔。

在 Strathlorne Steamship v. Andrew Weir (1934) 50 Lloyd's Rep. 185,上诉庭同意期租承租人下令无单放货是"错误行为"(wrongful act)。

而在 The "Sagona" (1984) 1 Lloyd's Rep. 194,Staughton 大法官总结说:"I would summarise the effect of these authorities as follow: (1) Under a bill of lading contract or a voyage charter a shipowner is only obliged to deliver cargo against presentation of a bill of lading (2) Under a time charter the charterer cannot lawfully order the shipowner or the master to deliver the cargo to a receiver who is not entitled to possession of the cargo."

另在 The "Houda" (1994) 2 Lloyd's Rep. 541,Leggatt 大法官说:"It is an incident of the bill of lading contract that delivery is to be effected only against the bill of lading.[95] It is nothing to the point that if there were no bill of lading contract the time charterer could give a lawful order to deliver with which the master would be obliged to comply.[96] In my judgment delivery to a time charterer entitled to possession without production of the bill of lading is a breach of the bill of lading contract[97]."

以上所说的是租约没有明示条款的情况。随着今天越来越多的情况需要无单放货,(否则会带来延误,例如是短航次),变得今天航运市场财大气粗的承租人常会迫使船东接受一条无单放货条款,否则不租人该船。在油轮,这更是一般做法,多数油轮租约都会印上这一条款。

---

[95] 期租承租人要船长出了代表物权凭证与运输合约的提单,就不得迫船长/船东在有了提单合约下去无单放货。

[96] 所以,承租人不能说在从未有过签发提单的情况下,它在租约下有权去下令船长交货给谁,而船长必须遵令,因为命令涉及营运。这两种不同情况不能去相比。

[97] 再要船长无单放货就是逼船长/船东在提单合约下毁约/违约了。

这方面的做法可去节录笔者的《程租合约》一书第一章之2.2.3.2小段如下：

"3.2.3.2　无单交货

今天更重要的事情是卸货无正本提单。众所周知，一直以来的做法是收货人没有正本提单，船长不会把货物卸给他，交给他。即使卸上岸，船长也要有充分的控制，确保不会失控导致误交货才可：Barclays Bank Ltd. v. Commissioners of Customs and Exercise (1963) 1 Lloyd's Rep. 81；The "Sormovskiy 3068" (1994) 2 Lloyd's Rep. 266.

但今天船跑得太快，结汇与邮递等又太慢，加上短航次太多，经常导致船到了卸港，但正本提单根本未到，往往更会是仍在发货人手中。听说，这情况发生的概率达百分之五十之多。

一般解决的办法有两种：一是收货人以一流银行的保函来替代提单，实际是去保障船东在如果误交货的情况下，可靠的银行会赔给船东一切损失与费用。二是让船舶等待直至正本提单到了卸港，在等待中当然要去敦促发货人与银行，试图减少延误。

但这两种办法都是昂贵的办法，而且花的是不必要浪费的钱。以银行保函来说，银行除了手续费以外，会要收保额的百分之一的费用作为"担保收费"(bail fee)。所以货价是450万美元，船东要的保额最少是500万美元，"担保收费"即会是5万美元，去加上手续费等，往往是买方/收货人在这笔买卖中的利润也没这么多。此外，安排银行保函需要时间，所以对卸货来说延误两三天仍会是不可避免。

要是让船等提单到才卸货，就会延误8至10天。给收货人造成不便与损失不算，还会在提单终于到手可去卸货前被船东突然告知要留置货物，除非收货人支付这8至10天延误的滞期费或滞期损失，每天1.5万美元。这一来，收货人又会是损失难逃。

但要是收货人掌握航运，即以FOB买货，并负责去租船，他或许可以轻而易举地解决这问题。他可以坚持租约内放进一条款规定船东必须在卸港无单放货，文字上会是：

"In case original bills of lading cannot be made available at the discharge port, then vessel to release the cargo against Charterer's letter of indemnity in accordance to Owner's P&I Club wording."

如果担心这条款有时会涉及非法无效(主要情况是货物所有权明确在发货人手中，船东会以他不应去"明知故犯，即使犯的是民法中的侵权"(intentional civil wrong)为由去拒绝无单放货)，收货人，也是承租人也可用一条更好的条款说明等提单才卸货的时间损失不算滞期损失或滞期费。这不是去要求船东无单放货,所以在任何情况下都不会有非法味道。用字上可以是如下:

"Should the original bills of lading not arrive at discharge port in time, it is at the discretion of the Owners to release the cargo against the charterer's letter of indemnity in accordance with Owner's P&I Club's wording without any bank endorsement. In case Owner elects to wait for the presentation of original bills of lading before discharging the cargo, time lost thereby shall not count as laytime and/or as demurrage."

反过头来,如果收货人不控制航运,如以 CIF 或 CFR 买货,此时卖方也是承租人,他是不会去理会这问题的。正常情况下,货款已有银行信用证的保证,他对这宗买卖再没风险也没兴趣。在卸港的延误,船东一般会通过货物的留置直接向收货人追讨,不必去麻烦卖方的承租人。所以,卖方怎么会自找麻烦地在租船谈判时坚持放进一条款去保障买方可去无单提货而且是要卖方作为承租人为此出担保(letter of indemnity)?确实我也听过有这种事发生,买卖合约有一条款说:"如果船抵卸港没有提单,卖方协助买方去尽快取货。"船到了卸港,给买方以此条款一逼,CFR 卖方便稀里糊涂地取出了保函给船东无单卸货。结果卖方虽能结汇,但买方不去银行"赎单"。结果银行扣船指控其无单放货,而船东以卖方出的保函要求补偿,最后损失仍在卖方。这真是傻事,卖方要是肯去为无单放货负责,他要信用证保证付款干吗?根据简单的合约法原则去解释买卖合约的条款,卖方也不必这样去做。卖方去"协助"买方尽快取货,如果由我作为仲裁员来判,来解释,卖方去请求船东接受买方(不是卖方)的银行保函也已是足够合理的"协助"了,因为船东不一定要接受。卖方一点合约法概念没有,心中无底,所以被买方一逼,即去过分地"协助",从而自招损失。

5.2 保函的做法

用保函解决这问题可说是一贯的做法。无数案例、文章也有所提及。随便举一些例子,在 The "Sormovskiy 3068"(1994)2 Lloyd's Rep. 266, Clarke 大法官说:"In trades where it is difficult or impossible for the bills of lading to arrive at the discharge port in time the problem is met by including a contractual term requiring the master to deliver the cargo against a letter of indemnity or bank guarantee."(在一些提单无法及时抵达卸港的航次,例如是短航次,解决无单放货这问题是去在租约中加一条款要求船长以接受保函或银行担保换取卸货/交货。)

在 The "Houda"(1994) 2 Lloyd's Rep. 541，Leggatt 大法官说："In practice, if the bill of lading is not available, delivery is effected against an indemnity."

确实，像短航次，例如，在青岛装货去神户，船在星期五下午才装完货开航，船长授权外代签发提单，外代等青岛发货人备妥一套提单并与大副收据核对无误后代船长签字。可以说，船舶在星期一抵达神户，很可能因为周末，这套提单根本仍未备妥与签发，更谈不上会及时送抵神户准备向船长退回以交换提取货物。所以，可以肯定地说，船抵时提单一定不在神户。这变得不去把货物卸下岸（这是本章 5.1.8 小段与 5.1.11 小段所详述的），只能是损失船期的等待提单的到来（请看本章 5.1.9 小段）。但这可能是漫长的等待，因为签发了提单仍有其他单证/文件的要求才能结汇。也会有其他中间商/中间银行。反正是，如广东的俗话所说："多一个香炉，多一个鬼"，每多一个人/公司去沾手，或多或少都会增加延误。虽然船东可继续赚取滞期费（程租）或租金（期租），但会有其他损失，例如下一租约的销约期赶不上，已同意了下一位承运人一个"估计可装货日期"（expected ready to load）而带来严重后果（请看《程租合约》一书之第 154 页至第 160 页），等等。所以常会是：货方/承租人/收货人与船东都不想看见这种船期损失发生。

5.2.1　船东是否必须接受保函

在租约没有明示条款要求这样做，法律会否默示船东/船长必须接受保函（来自收货人或承租人）换取无单放货？有一些案例曾涉及，但说法也不一致。例如在 Carlberg v. Wemyss (1915) S. C. 616, Johnson 勋爵曾说："Neither the owner, his agent, nor the master can, I think, be called upon to accept a banker's or any other guarantee or an indemnity, though such a thing is not unknown…"

但 Lord President（该案例是苏格兰法院判）说："I am of the opinion… that the shipowner is bound, if it be reasonably practical at once to load the cargo into wagons or onto the quay, as the case may be, reserving his lien. If that be not reasonably practical, then I hold the shipowner is bound to discharge into the waggons of the consignee upon receiving a suitable indemnity from him against any loss which may emerge."

撇开太老的案例，近期的说法应是没有这个默示要求。在 The "Houda"(1994) 2 Lloyd's Rep. 541 至 551 页，Neill 大法官说："It is by no means uncommon in the oil cargo trade for the cargo to be discharged before the bill of lading is received. This practice was noticed by Mr. Justice Staughton in The "Sagona" (1984) 1 Lloyd's Rep. 194 at P. 201. As Mr Justice Staughton explained, there may be a number of reasons for this practice, but it does not seem to me that the existence of the practice or the right to a letter of indemnity can impose on the owners a contractual obligation which does not otherwise exist."

笔者也相信没有这个法律的默示要求,换言之,船东可不去理会接受保函的请求。原因是在现实中无法行得通。这不是"保函"一句话,而是实质细节与内容无法去规范。正如笔者的《海事法》一书99页提及的澳洲案例(The "MSC Samia"(1991) LMLN NO. 482)就很好地说明了这一点。该案例是这样说:

"... the objections raised in the present case were concerned with the terms of the undertaking and the acceptability of the entity giving it. It was not easy for the Court to make a properly informed determination as to whether the refusal by the plaintiffs for the security was oppressive. In cases where the dispute turned purely on quantum, the Court could more easily make a reasonable estimate as to an appropriate figure. Where, however, conditions proffered in the undertaking were in contest, and where there was a dispute as to whether the entity providing the undertaking was satisfactory, it was generally inappropriate for the Court to interfere with the negotiations of the parties or to impose terms on them, It would often be more appropriate for the Court to leave that question to commercial negotiation between the parties. If they could not agree, the procedures relating to the provision of a bail bond or payment into Court could be pursued. The Court should not be placed in a position of arbitrating or mediating in respect of ongoing negotiations between the parties as to what were the terms of an acceptable security. If there was to be any involvement of the Court it should occur where it was established that there had been an abuse of the negotiating process in a way which amounted to clearly oppressive conduct or an abuse of the Court's process…

… Where it was clearly evident that sufficient security had been provided on appropriate terms, by a person or entity with ample assets and means to make good the undertaking, it might be that "just terms" could be formulated. However, the Court could not impose an obligation on a party to provide or accept a satisfactory undertaking. If a stance adopted by a party was manifestly unreasonable as to terms, quantum, or the form of undertaking, there might be an abuse of process in insisting on such unreasonable security. Otherwise, the parties should avail themselves of the payment into Court or bail bond options."

还记得亚洲金融风暴后,约1998年底,曾知悉一欧洲船东坚持若是亚洲银行出保函,只接受汇丰银行。其他亚洲银行包括一些最大的日本银行,一概不接受。该票可能要无单放货的货物,价值高达1000万美元。你可以说该欧洲船东胆小,太谨慎。但能说他不合理或违约吗?毕竟,谁敢保证呢?所以,如果法律来一个默示要求以保函放货,船东会说,那好,我要比尔·盖茨(Bill Gates)的私人担保。但承租人/收货人根本不认识 Bill Gates,那么这默示条件/要求还不是空话一句。

5.2.2 租约规定船东要接受保函

法律既没有默示,有些航次(如短航次,或发货人不马上交出提单等)又必须这样做不可,那就只能在租约上明示了,即加一条明确条款。去明示了,再不存在公平/合理与否,纯是去解释该明示条款的措辞/文字。

这些条款的草拟在较早的 5.1.12 小段的节录部分(节录《程租合约》一书)已有详述,故不再重复。在此只举一个不当措辞/不足用字的例子去让承租人警惕。在 The"Honda"(1994) 2 Lloyd's Rep. 541,它的主要有关条款第 50 条说:"Charterers hereby indemnify Owners against all consequences or liabilities that may arise from…(… delivery of cargo without presentation of Bills of Lading…)…Letter of Indemnity to Owners' P&I Club wording to be incorporated in this CharterParty."

以上措辞/文字显然不足,它只说承租人去补偿船东,并说保函是什么格式而已。它并没有说船东必须去这样做,必须去听令行事。

所以 Neill 大法官判该条款不足以约束船东去接受保函以交换无单放货,他说:"Clause 13 and 50 do not in my view impose any express obligation on the"Charterers"(注:这应是"Owners"才正确,法律报告应是印错了)to discharge a cargo in the absence of the bill of lading. They merely provide for a letter of indemnity if such discharge takes place. But I do not construe the clauses as imposing a contractual duty on the owners."

但类似规定在 The"Delfini"(1990) 1 Lloyd's Rep. 252 却是强制得多了,有关条款是:"Should Bill of lading not arrived at discharge port in time then Owners agree to release the entire cargo without presentation of the original Bills of Lading against delivery by Charterers of letter of indemnity issued in accordance with Ownels P & I Club wording."

5.2.3 对保函的实质要求

已经说过,这不是"保函交换无单放货"一句话而已。最重要的是什么样的"保函"? 是谁出的保函? 保函是什么措辞/文字才恰当? 这等等涉及实质内容或细节的方面。

5.2.3.1 谁出的保函

谁是保人显然最为关键。正如 5.1.13.1 小段说笑话提到的 Bill Gates 出的保函就与一个乞丐出的保函有天渊之别。但也会有变数,因此轻重掌握要恰当,毕竟世界上也不只 Bill Gates 有钱。另外,对于值 1000 万美元的货物笔者确没能力去出一个足以令船东安心接受的保函,但若只是取出一个几千美元的保函也被拒,笔者就会感到被羞辱了。

归纳地说,对出保函的一方(保人)的实质要求是:

(ⅰ)拥有作出担保金额的资产/财力。故此自然人不能是讨饭的,公司(包括银行在内)不能是巴拿马的皮包公司。担保金额愈大,对保人的资产/财产要求就愈高。

(ⅱ)保函的保障要延续一段时间,因此,这保人的资产/财力估计在中、短期不会改变/逆转。

(ⅲ)资产/财力位处可去执行的地点,这表示只有在一些法纪不明,贪污盛行与乱糟糟国家才拥有资产的自然人或公司,他/它的保函不一定可去安心接受。这显然是指部分"名誉扫地"的发展中国家,会是理论上在本国有资产/财力,但无法去当地法院以法律执行。例如,收货人是"苏丹农业部",是政府部门,它取出保函换取无单放货,就难以令船东安心接受:请看在 5.1.11 小段介绍的 Hoffman-Laroche Inc v. TFL Jefferson 1990 AMC 1388; 731 F. Supp. 109（SDNY 1990）。

(ⅳ)最好是不涉及利益的第三方,例如是银行做保人。因为既不涉及利益,又为了自己的信誉,变得银行出了保函会应付则付,不会去扯皮。

许多出事的保函,就是因为这个问题。或是接受来历不明承租人的保函去无单放货;或是接受收货人自己出的保函,而他/它也不是可靠与有财力的公司;或是接受一个名誉很差的发展中国家(发展中国家也有名誉好的)的当地小银行出的保函。

近日遇到的一个典型案件是:中国船东将船出租给马来西亚承租人,以他的保函无单放货。他也是买方,提取了货物就"不安好心",在开给卖方的信用证中挑出少少毛病就以不符点拒付。这一定是"不安好心",因为已提取了货物,没有什么不满意,还有什么需要去在单证上挑毛病,不去支付货价呢？结果,澳洲的卖方/发货人,仍持有一套正本提单,就扣船诉船,中国船东败诉,损失惨重(数以几百万美元的赔偿),但以保函去找马来西亚的承租人,后者已不知所踪。用 Mareva 禁令去冻结承租人的银行账号也是一无所获,只是劳民伤财。

难怪一位有水平的油轮船东曾在闲谈中对笔者说:他对承租人的财务/背景最关心。这不光是怕收不到运费、租金或滞期费,这些相对是小问题。最大问题是油轮租约都有条款要求船东去接受承租人(不是银行或其他第三者)的保函以换取无单放货,这可不是开玩笑的。

说真的,今天的世界涉及外贸人士"不安好心"的可多的是。所以这不是去分好人坏人,笔者也无暇、无法去细分。但只要出保函的收货人财雄势大,或更是涉及银行担保,变得他/它"不安好心"之余也会去想想:我能否逃得掉？如果只是枉做小人,最终赖不掉,该收货人也就会乖乖地去支付货款给卖方/发货人以取得这套正本提单,或是向开证银行赎单,然后再以正本提单向船东交换较早出的保函/银行担保。换言之,就是船东或任何人别做傻事或错事,不要给他人起歹心,起贪念的机会。

可见,船东只要在这方面多加注意就会趋吉避凶了。

5.2.3.2 保函的措辞/文字

保函只是一个合约,在订约自由的大原则下,它写什么就解释为什么。这表示船东想在保函获得"天衣无缝"的保障,也必须在措辞/文字上做到"天衣无缝"。

国际船东互保协会的标准措辞/文字十分完整,常为船东所采用。所以像 The "Houda" (1994) 2 Lloyd's Rep. 541 的租约条款会规定保函要依照"Owners' P & I Club wording."

当然,这只是要求以船东互保协会的标准措辞/文字出保函,没有明确要否银行去加签,充当保人,而在这标准措辞/文字中是有这一栏的。

这一来,船东就想取巧了。事情经过是:船东起先不答应无单放货的条款,承租人于是不肯承租他的船舶。后来船东被迫答应了却心有不安,因为承租人虽不是光棍的巴拿马公司,但也好不了多少。于是船东就想找合法借口逃避这条款。当时,承租人再不能说不继续租,因这会是毁约。船东的技巧不外乎是:

(i) 在条款的措辞/文字里挑毛病,好像 The "Houda" (1994) 2 Lloyd's Rep. 541 先例。

(ii) 遇上适当机会,主要是发货人明确表示货权仍在他手中,不属买方/收货人(也会是 FOB 下的承租人)的情况下,船东可以借口不得故意协助侵权,这样是以非法为由拒绝照租约条款行事:这一点可去看《国际商务游戏规则——英国合约》一书的第七章4.4小段,不再重复。

(iii) 指船东互保协会标准措辞/文字内既然有银行加签一栏,双方在租约同意以此措辞/文字为准也就表示了应有银行加签。显然,光棍承租人多了一个银行去共同作为保人,对船东的保障自然是大大提高了。但在 The "Nemea" (1980) LMLN 280,法院不同意船东的争辩,不让船东取巧。虽是如此,仍有小心的承租人对此点专门有说明,例如在 The "Aegean Sea" (1998) 2 Lloyd's Rep. 39,有关条款是"… Wording of Letter of Indemnity to be in accordance with Owners P & I Club, excluding Bank Guarantee."相反,如果船东坚持承租人当做保人不足保障,要银行加签,则相关文字应是:"including Bank Guarantee"或"to be additionally endorsed by first-class bank",等等。

以下不妨去节录国际船东互保协会的标准措辞/文字或格式(这格式刚在修改/更新,但不影响本段讲的道理/原则),并在一些地方对其背后原因加以解释:

"STANDARD FORM LETTER OF INDEMNITY TO BE GIVEN IN RETURN FOR DELIVERING CARGO WITHOUT PRODUCTION OF THE ORIGINAL BILL OF LADING.

To:[insert name of owners]

the owners of[insert name of ship]

Dear Sirs,

Ship:[insert name of ship]

Voyage:[insert load/discharge port, as stated in bill of lading]Cargo:[insert description of cargo]Bill(s) of lading:[insert identification number, date, place of issue]

The above cargo was shipped on the above vessel by[insert name of shipper] and consigned to[insert name of consignee or to whose order the Bill of Lading is made out, as appropriate]for delivery at the port of[insert name of discharge port stated in the Bill of Lading]but the Bills of Lading have not arrived and we,[insert name of party requesting delivery], hereby request you to give delivery of the said cargo to[insert name of party to whom delivery is to be made]without production of the original Bill(s) of Lading.[98]

In consideration of you complying with our above request, we hereby agree as follows:

1. To indemnify you, your servants and agents and to hold all of you harmless in respect of any liability, loss, damage or expenses of whatsoever nature which you may sustain by reason of delivering the cargo in accordance with our request.[99]

2. In the event of any proceedings being commenced against you or any of your servants or agents in connection with the delivery of the cargo as aforesaid to provide you or them on demand with sufficient funds to defend the same.[100]

3. If, in connection with the delivery of the cargo aforesaid, the ship or any other ship or property belonging to you should be arrested or detained or if the arrest or deten-

---

[98] 以上是去写明/注明有关的细节/资料,如船东、船名、装卸港、有关货物、提单日期、签发地、编号、发货人与收货人名字,等等。接下去是说因提单不能及时到达,货方/承租人(注明是谁提出要求)要求船东无单放货,并答应下列条件。

[99] 条件一是补偿船东因无单放货的所有损失与费用。注意它的用字十分广,如"of whatsoever nature…"。也请注意保函的保障也延展到去保护"雇员"(servants)与"代理人"(agents)。因为无单放货是严格的侵权行为,会祸及从旁协助的雇员或代理人,故也须去保障。

[100] 条件二是同意在有人(自称提单持有人)起诉船东等无单放货时,预付船东足够的金钱去抗辩。这主要是律师费用的支付,律师会要求预付费用或中间收费,绝少会同意打完了整个官司或解决了所有问题才收费。有了这条件二,船东不必自己先掏荷包支付律师费用,而事后才能向保人要求补偿。

tion thereof should be threatened to provide on demand such bail or other security as may be required to prevent such arrest or detention or to secure the release of such ship or property[101] and to indemnify you in respect of any liability, loss, damage or expenses caused by such arrest or detention or threatened arrest or detention[102] whether or not such arrest or detention or threatened arrest or detention may be justified.[103]

4. As soon as all original Bills of Lading for the above cargo shall have come into our possession to deliver the same to you, whereupon our liability hereunder shall cease.[104]

5. The liability of each and every person under this indemnity shall be joint and several and shall not be conditional upon your proceeding first against any person, whether or not such person is party to or liable under this indemnity.[105]

6. The liability of each and every person under this indemnity shall in no circumstances exceed 200% of the CIF value of the above cargo.[106]

7. This indemnity shall be governed by and construed in accordance with English law and

---

[101] 条件三是涉及船舶被扣,保函中的保人同意去代提供担保放船。关于这方面请去参阅笔者的《海事法》一书第一章。扣船是为了诉前保全,对案件本身的"是非曲直"(merits)尚未有定论。所以,光是有保人的"补偿"(indemnify)仍不足够,保人会说你船东并未败诉,补偿你什么？故要迫使保人代垫付诉前保全的担保,就必须明示。要知道,这会是好几百万美元的事。

[102] 情况会是,扣了船即使是马上安排诉前保全,也已造成损失,如延误、额外港口使费、承租人(后来新的租约)索赔/停租等。这一切也是要保函的保人去补偿。要去明示这些已造成,已产生的损失/费用的补偿是独立出来,即使最后在"是非曲直"上船东胜诉,判是不必负无单放货的责任,也不影响这些损失/费用的补偿。

[103] 这扣船行动可能也会是乱来/过火的,但船东被扣船舶的损失去向扣船东反索赔可不容易,英国法律是要去证明扣船东"恶意"(male fides),现实中一般做不到,这可去参阅《海事法》一书的第一章7.6小段。而即使像中国有反担保这回事,也可能会金额不足赔偿损失。这一来,在这条件三去向保函的保人要求补偿这损失/费用,因是有关无单放货导致扣船所引起,保人会抗辩说这是扣船东乱来/过火,而这行为足以打断"因果关系"(causation)。为此,这"天衣无缝"的措辞/文字说明是"不管该扣船是否乱来",保函的保人也要作出补偿给船东。

[104] 条件四是当保人要把全部正本提单退回给船东,才可中断或取消这保函下保人的责任。注意退回的提单是"所有正本"(all original)而不光是一式多份中的其中一份。

[105] 条件五是指保人(有两位,注[4]的要求方与注[5]的银行)要共同的与各自的对船东负责。这表示船东向银行要钱,要垫付诉前保全,银行不能说:"你为何不先找要求你无单放货的承租人,而要先麻烦我？"答案是船东先找谁或一起找(如去诉讼就把它们列为第一、第二被告)都可以。

[106] 特别是银行加签保函,总会要一个限额。这限额光是货款(加运费,保金)并不足够。这是因为无单放货之时或之后,若市场货价急升,则提单持有人(也是真正拥有货权一方)会是损失惨重(或严格说,本来可赚取更高利润但因无单放货而坐失良机了,或要在急涨市场另去买入替代货物)。但总要有一个限额,所以这船东互保协会的格式印明是 CIF 价格的双倍。现实中见过双方讨价还价,结果把保函最高金额改为120% 或 150% 的 CIF 价格。

each and every person liable under this indemnity shall at your request submit to the jurisdiction of the High Court of Justice of England.[107]

>   Yours faithfully
>   For and on behalf of   For and on behalf of
>   [insert name of requestor][108]   [insert name of bank][109]
>   Signature·······················   Signature······························ "

把保函写得如此清楚,不厌其烦,其重要性可去比较近期的 Rank Enterprises v. Gerard (1999) 2 Lloyd's Rep. 666 先例。该案例的保函倒也不是针对无单放货,故不去节录与详论。但大道理一样,措辞/文字不足就会被挑骨头。其中有趣的一点是担保人被起诉要求补偿,担保人说受保人应先去抗辩第三者的起诉,如果抗辩成功,就不存在有任何补偿。没理由在第三者无理取闹,受保人明明可去成功抗辩的情况下,也要保人补偿。但这一来,受保人会要打几年官司才可知道抗辩成功或失败,麻烦多多不说,还要不断地花律师费用,要自己先掏腰包。更会加上变数,如保人目前财力尚好,但几年后难说。所以受保人争辩说如果要是这样,那么它去向第三者投降赔钱,以利早日向保人取回补偿岂非更好。保人回驳说:"这可不成,这是没去"减少损失"(mitigation)"。长话短说,该案例在这一点是保人的争辩被高院法官接纳,可见保函措辞/文字不足之危险。

5.3 卸港对货权有争议

在本章之 5.1.4 小段谈到一般正常情况下,一式几份中的一份正本提单交换提取货物业已足够保障船东。那不正常的情况呢?例如有两位人士各持有一份正本提单要求提取货物?或是,发觉出了两套提单落在不同人手中。又或是,有一方(甚至会是发货人)指它有货权,但没有提单,因为被另一方不合法扣起了。这一来,看来 5.1.4 小段的 Glyn Mills & Co. v. East and West India Dock Co. (1882) 7 App. Cas. 591 并不足以保障船东。正如 Motis Exports v. Dampskibsselskabet AF 1912 (1999) 1 Lloyd's Rep. 837 先例中 Rix 大法官在第 840 页清楚地提到:"One must start with the nature of a bill of lading contract, irrespective of any special clauses like…It is

---

[107] 这是适用法律与管辖权条款,是国际性合约应该有的,为了肯定/稳定。也免不了是注明适用英国法与英国高院管辖。说真的,去同意一条仲裁条款也无不可了!
[108] 要求无单放货的一方签字作为保人,它会是承租人,也会是收货人。
[109] 银行加签。

of essence of such a contract that a shipowner is both entitled and bound to deliver the goods against production of an original bill of lading, provided he has no notice of any other claim or better title to the goods..."

5.3.1 船东/船长遇上货权有争议应向法院请求确定权利归属

"请求法院去确定权利谁属"(interplead)的做法,可在此多加介绍。其做法在英国"高院规则"(Rules of Supreme Court)有详细注明,而在跟从英国做法的国家/地区也有同样的法院规则。在香港高院,Order 17 就全部是针对 interpleader 的做法,在此部分节录以说明一些主要之处,具体如下:

首先在 Order 17, rule 1, 它说:

"Entitlement to relief by way of interpleader1 (1) Where—

(a) a person is under a liability in respect of a debt[110] or in respect of any money, goods[111] or chattels and he is, or expects to be, sued for or in respect of that debt or money or those goods or chattels by two or more persons[112] making adverse claims thereto, or

(b)...

the person under liability as mentioned in sub-paragraph (a)... may apply to the Court for relief by way of interpleader.[113]"

向法院申请,是以传票方式,并要送达给所有争议有权利收取或提取的人士。这是在 Order 17, rule 3 (1) 与(2), 说:

"3 (1) An application for relief under this Order must be made by originating summons unless made in a pending action, in which case it must be made by summons in the action.

(2)... the summons must be served on any person who made a claim under that rule to or in respect of that money or those goods or chattels, and that person may attend the hearing of the application."

去作出申请的人必须是(1)本人对争议的金钱或货物财产没有利益,除了是一些仍要收的费用如运费。他(申请人)如果因为被欠下费用/运费而要留置货物并

---

[110] 或是它/他手上有一批货物要交付。
[111] 如果一方有责任去付一笔债或手上有一笔钱要交付,或是运费,或是佣金等。
[112] 但有两个或以上的人提出各自不同的收取/提取权利,并可能会以此向拒绝交付的一方采取行动(即不是讲笑的)。例如,船东与二船东一齐向货方/收货人索要欠下的运费。或是,船东面对多方对货权有争议。
[113] 该方为了小心(也无法去百分之一百肯定交付给谁才是正确),可向法院申请,让法院去审理决定。

不影响 interplead 的权利,这是两码事:De Rothschild Freres v. Morrison, Kekewich & Co. (1890) 24 QBD 750 (C. A.)。显然,如果他本人也有利益,即抗拒他人前来索取,不肯交出金钱或货物,则不管这个人不只有一位,也只属正常诉讼的控辩做法,不是 interpleader 的做法。(2)不得与主张权利提出索取的其中一位同谋。(3)愿意照法院的命令交出金钱、货物或财产给法院或以其他办法保管。确实,法院也常下令把金钱交给法院或货物由争夺货权几方的律师共同去保管。这可以早日让申请人作出交付,之后再没有责任,可以松一口气,省一点律师费用和不用再理会该诉讼。正常情况下,这正是他的愿望。这方面是在 Order 17, rule 3(4)所说:

"(4)... a summon under this rule must be supported by evidence that the applicant—

(a) claims no interest in the subject-matter in dispute other than for charges or costs.

(b) does not collude with any of the claimants to that subject-matter, and

(c) is willing to pay or transfer that subject-matter into Court or to dispose of it as the Court may direct."

至于法院的做法,可以节录 Order 17, rule 5 所说的:

"5(1) Where on the hearing of a summons under this Order all [114] the persons by whom adverse claims to the subject-matter in dispute (hereafter in this Order referred to as "the claimants"[115] appear, the Court may order—

(a) that any claimant be made a defendant in any action pending with respect to the subject-matter in dispute in substitution for or in addition to the applicant for relief under this Order, [116] or

(b) that an issue between the claimants be stated and tried and may direct which of the claimants is to be plaintiff and which defendant.[117] (2) Where—

…

(c) all the claimants consent or any of them so requests, or

---

[114] 法院开庭审理,要传唤所有曾经诉称它/他有收取/提取权利的人士出庭。

[115] 这些人可以称为"索取方"(claimants)。

[116] 法院可以在这 interpleader 的做法中理顺各方所戴的帽子。例如,申请人在另一诉讼中是被告,该诉讼的原告与另一位第三者都对一笔金钱或一批货物提出索取。法院为去让已交出金钱/货物的申请人脱身,会下令第三者代替申请人做该另一诉讼中的被告。如果仍需申请人参与,则第三者可一齐去并列为第一、第二被告等。如果有仲裁条款/协议,法院也可下令去让仲裁庭审理:Phoenix Timber Co. Ltd's Application (1958) 2 QB 1;(1958) 1 All ER 815。

[117] 或法院可下令索取方之间的争议事项另行安排审理[如由"聆案官"(master)审理]以及决定谁做原告、被告。

(d) the question at issue between the claimants is a question of law and the facts are not in dispute, the Court may summarily determine [118] the question at issue between the claimants and make an order accordingly on such terms as may be just.

(3) Where a claimant, having been duly served with a summons for relief under this Order, does not appear on the hearing of the summons or, having appeared, fails or refuses to comply with an order made in the proceedings, the Court may make an order declaring the claimant, and all persons claiming under him, for ever barred from prosecuting his claim against the applicant for such relief and all persons claiming under him, [119] but such an order shall not affect the rights of the claimants as between themselves."

5.3.2 船东所花律师费用可获补偿

所以船东/船长遇上有怀疑,有多人争夺船上货物的货权时,最妥善/安全的做法就是向法院申请所谓的 interplead。尤其是这些费用(主要是律师费用,但也可包括像货物存放仓库的费用等)都会获得补偿。这补偿要在争议的金钱(存放在法院)中扣除后才发还给真正有权利的一方,或是争议的货物如果拍卖掉也会有一笔金钱可从中扣除补偿。总的大原则仍是:谁败诉谁要承担所有的费用,包括了申请人(船东)的费用。所以,去申请之前,船东也可先警告争夺货权的双方,例如说:"我给你们两天时间去和解谈妥货物谁属,以免延误船期。否则我马上请律师向法院 interplead。这一来不可避免要多花很多的律师费用,最后总是你们一方或双方去承担。"

现实中可能在第二天,争夺货权的双方就会回来向船东确认/同意如何做,以防止船东花钱去向法院 interplead。

船东无法去获得费用补偿情况是他自己犯错而导致有 interplead 的必要。例如,已在本章之 3.4.3 小段详述的 The "Lycaon" (1981) 1 Lloyd's Rep. 92 与 (1983) 2 Lloyd's Rep. 548,法院就拒绝判给补偿,指是因为船东自找麻烦出了两套提单,才导致要去 interplead。

---

[118] 法院有些情况下可以马上判决金钱/货物/财产权利谁属。这情况是前述的如(b)索取方要求;(c)争议只涉及法律不涉及事实,因为事实会要去取证,光是靠 interpleader 行动中的宣誓书/宣誓证明不足够。

[119] 如果任何一位索取方不出庭,不理会这 interpleader,法院会下令该方以及以其名义主张的有关人士今后再不能主张权利,甚至下禁令不准对申请人采取任何其他行动(例如去外国法院起诉侵占)。

5.3.3 向什么法院申请

一涉及国际的问题,就会马上面临这个考虑。船东要去申请的法院,一定要对案件有"管辖权"(competent jurisdiction),也最好是"恰当的诉讼地"(appropriate forum)。这一来 interpleader 对大家方便外,将来判决受外国承认或尊重的机会也大,船东不会在其他国家被再次干扰。这些问题已在笔者的《禁令》一书之第六章有详述,不再重复。

一般船东去考虑的会是在卸港的法院,毕竟事情发生在该处,也最有可能对争夺货权的"索取方"(claimants)有地域主权。加上,还会有其他理由赋予其管辖权,例如是汉堡规则适用。但卸港不一定有法院或可信赖的法院。在本章之 5.1.8 小段提到"法纪不明,贪污盛行与乱糟糟"的卸港,船东根本不敢把货物先卸下岸,以免失控导致无单放货。这一来,当地法院会好得了多少呢?如果法院乱来,它所做出的判决也不会受其他国家承认或尊重,而且判错的可能性大,这会导致遭受损失的其中一个索取方(他才真正拥有货权)再去其他国家的港口干扰船东,去诉船/扣船,指船东无单放货,而卸港法院乱来的判决并不能保障船东。这方面类同于《海事法》一书之第一章§12 段"法院出售的船舶有清洁所有权",但这要获得外国承认方可,该小段中说道:

> 离不开的说法是扣船出售地的法院应是"有能力"(competent),"诚实"(honest),"合法"(lawful)的根据当地立法,有权去管辖(jurisdiction),等等。

加上船东也应寄望有相对正确的判决,货物是给了真正有货权的一方。这不光是为了公道,也可去避免将来有麻烦。这一来,卸港法院即使廉洁,但依其水平不足以了解这复杂的商业做法,也会令判错机会相应提高,导致有不服气的败诉方,留下后患,这也不是好事。

这一来,除了卸港法院外(即使有),船东还会动脑筋向其他法院申请。例如,英国法院常会是一个优先选择,而管辖权会来自提单内,或提单所合并的租约内(The "Delfini" (1988) 2 Lloyd's Rep. 599)有一条伦敦仲裁条款,或写明适用英国法,甚至是写明英国法院有管辖权。总之在英国法院"无远弗届"的管辖权(这一点请参阅《禁令》一书的第六章)之下,要找一个理由去管辖并不会难。

这类问题可去看 The "Irini A" (1999) 1 Lloyd's Rep. 189,它涉及一批大米从越南运去东加的 Lome。案件也涉及出了第二套提单,而在 Lome 的法院,判决是第二套提单有效。在英国法院,Tuckey 大法官说英国法院会判法不同,但结论不同再也无关。只要是东加法院好好地针对争议的"是非曲直"(on the merits)来判,而非是程序上有问题,则构成"一事不再理"(issue estoppel),不再翻案。换言之,英国法院承认或尊重该东加判决,但很难说其他同类案件也会是同样结果。

5.4 船东/船长无辜交货/放货给伪造正本提单的人的情况

这是近期十分热门的话题,因为有 Motis Exports v. Dampskibsselskabet AF 1912 (1999) 1 Lloyd's Rep. 837 的先例。该案例最近(1999年12月,尚未报道)被上诉庭驳回,仍是要无辜船东承担后果,结果带来很大反响。严格来讲它不是无单放货,只是正本提单是伪造的。

5.4.1 今天航运的现实环境

要深入了解这方面的困境,可先去列举介绍一下今天航运的现实环境与其他事实:

(ⅰ)今天极少是船长自己签发提单,为了不延误开航,总会授权代理签发。

(ⅱ)今天期租很多,一般都非要去全权授权承租人代签发提单不可(请参阅笔者的《期租合约》一书之§25段)。随着多次分租,这授权会一路延展下去。而今天乱来的承租人或分承租人充斥市场,在背后乱出提单或多套提单去约束船东/船长的情况,船东可说是无从防范也无能为力:The "Antaios" (1984) 2 Lloyd's Rep. 235。

(ⅲ)笔者一直说靠单证/文件防不了欺诈,美钞难伪造得多了,一样经常听到有假的。早在1982年出版的《提单》一书第17页就已提及名画"蒙娜丽莎"(又称"永远的微笑")都被伪造,挂在巴黎卢浮宫几年后才被发觉。如果装船提单是船长自己签发,那么自己去细看自己的签字是否伪造会比较容易。但今天航运不是这个现实,变得船长在卸港看到一份提单,是正本的,好像是承租人签字或装港代理签字,也就交货/放货了。

(ⅳ)不诚实的收货人怎么能去伪造呢?毕竟它/他需要掌握真的一份提单内的资料,例如是实际货量。否则乱去填写资料马上会被船长揭穿。答案是由于卖方自己的行为,如先去把一份或多份副本提单给买方/收货人作为报关等之用:例如是在3.1.5.2小段提到 The "Sletter" (1999) LMLN # 522 一案中的做法。这一份副本落入不诚实收货人/买方手中,即给了它/他机会去照版伪造一份。这种事情笔者十多年前已听说过,但当时仍很局限,只是在去尼日利亚的船/货才面临这种危险。看来,今天这不法伎俩是有更多骗子掌握了。船东可真不能掉以轻心。

当然,买方以假提单欺骗卖方远远比不上卖方欺骗买方容易。卖方以假提单骗买方的手法,在笔者的《信用证》一书有详述,不再在此重复。而买方要去欺骗,则要看机缘巧合了。例如,一般卖方会坚持以信用证支付货款。这一来,买方已无法去以假提单进行欺骗了。即使是结汇发生问题或托收发生问题,卖方也会马上通知船东/承运人在卸港不能乱交出货物,因为整套提单仍在卖方/发货人手中。故此,不存在买方可去偷偷伪造一份正本提单去向船长提取货物。因此能以此手法进行欺骗,纯是看机遇。

5.4.2 买卖双方互骗是否应由无辜船东承担后果

国际外贸/航运是虎狼当道,不诚实的卖方骗买方或是转过来买方骗卖方的种种事件与不同手法是不断听说。如果船东参与或协助一方去骗另一方,可说是自己活该,理应承担后果。例如是损坏的货物装上船却去签发清洁提单(Brown Jenkinson v. Percy Dalton (1957) 2 Lloyd's Rep. 1)或是倒签提单(SCB v. PNSC (1995) 2 Lloyd' Rep. 365),这显然是去协助卖方欺骗买方。已有无数的案例明确是要船东承担可能是极严重的后果。

但如果船东是无辜的呢?这仍要船东承担后果看来有点"欺人太甚",但这正是目前的趋势。

在较早的 The "Nea Tyhi" (1982) 1 Lloyd's Rep. 606,涉及三合板被装在船舶舱面,但期租承租人与他的代理人却在背后越权(船长无授权)去签发"舱内提单"(underdeck bills)。结果三合板装在舱面受海水损坏严重,本来这种货物不应该装在甲板/舱面,纯是承租人乱来。但英国法院仍要船东负责赔偿收货人/提单持有人,虽然这明显是承租人(也会是 CIF 卖方或他委托去租船运输的人)在欺骗,船东并不知情,也很难知情。Sheen 大法官说:"As to Mr. Colman's(船东大律师)submission that one of two 'innocent' parties must suffer,[120] if I had to choose whether the shipowner or the endorsee of a bill of lading should be the loser I would have no hesitation in saying[121] that there is more reason that he who contracts with the charterer and puts trust and confidence in him to the extent of authorizing the charterers' agents to issue and sign bills of lading[122] should be a loser, than a stranger."

以上看来,船东仍有可怪责之处,即"所托非人"。但去细究,也看个别案子,则收货人/提单持有人又何尝不会犯同样的错误?它/他作为买方对不诚实的卖方不去了解就订约,也是没带眼认人。如果是有水平、诚实的卖方/发货人,它/他会把货物乱放在甲板/舱面,然后出一套虚假的"舱内提单"吗?

要是说提单会背书转让,持有人不是原买卖合约的买方,那就不能这样去怪责了。但船东一样可以是小心谨慎地找对了承租人,但毛病却出在分租约或分分租

---

[120] 船东的大律师说是两位无辜的人(收货人与船东)中的一位肯定要遭受损失了。
[121] 在这两位无辜的人中选择一位去承担后果,我(Sheen 大法官)毫不犹豫会选船东。
[122] 谁叫他去信任一位不值得信任的承租人,甚至授权他去代签发提单呢?

约,是其他人士"所托非人",这又怎能怪责船东,要他承担后果呢?

或者说,船东承担后果后可向"正直"的承租人要求补偿,一步步地告下去直至由"所托非人"的承租人或分承租人去承担后果为止。但这说法又何尝不能适用在买卖合约:被骗的收货人向它/他的上一手卖方索赔,一步步告下去直至不诚实的卖方/发货人或值得怪责的卖方(明知提单虚假不能去背书转让)为止。

这只是理论,现实中补偿并非易事,劳民伤财外,变数也太多,失败的可能性颇高。所以,归根结底,仍是要看应否由无辜的船东承担买卖双方互骗的后果,作为代罪羔羊?要知道"Nea Tyhi"涉及的是虚假的舱内提单,但按同样原则,承租人背后偷偷去签发倒签提单、清洁提单等,也是要船东承担后果。

或者说,船东作为代罪羔羊是为了维护国际商贸的一套机制,令大家对提单作为"物权凭证"(document of title)不会有任何缺乏信心的理由。特别是,这也能配合国际公约的说法。这国际公约是指海牙·维斯比规则的 Article 3(4)说:"However, proof to the contrary shall not be admissible when the Bill of Lading has been transferred to a third party acting in good faith."(提单在善意的第三者手中,船东不得去反证提单内容不正确)。

汉堡规则的 Article 16(4)也有同样说法,是:"However, proof to the contrary by the carrier is not admissible when the bill of lading has been transferred to a third party, including a consignee, who in good faith has acted in reliance on the absence in the bill of lading of any such indication."

所以,船东是不准去推翻提单所载的内容,如声称货物数量写错了,没有装这么多:Grant v. Norway(1851) 10 CB 665。如此类推,船东也不准去反证说提单写错了,货物不装在舱内,是装在甲板上。

但要船东作为代罪羔羊的趋势,到了 Motis Exports v. Dampskibsselskabet AF 1912(1999)1 Lloyd's Rep. 837,又"升华"到另一境界。它不涉及承租人背后做手脚,或是船长任由提单上有不正确内容,可去怪责船东,或指这是国际公约所分摊给船东的责任。

该案例是罕见的不诚实买方去欺骗卖方(一般总是卖方去骗蒙在鼓里的买方,特别在 CIF/CFR 买卖),另去伪造一套提单提取货物,而在信用证上则挑不符点去拒付(托收则拒绝接受单证)。这一来,要去怪责船东船长会是只能怪他为何不是字迹专家。说真的,真是专家也没有用,因为根本没有"真迹"在手可供比较。而"真迹"就是在船长背后由装港代理、承租人或分承租人等所代船长签发的提单。

或者会说,船长/船东可以在卸港交货放货前先去查核收货人前来提取货物而退回的一份正本提单是否"真迹"。但这谈何容易,会严重延误船期,无法开卸不说,这也不是今天的惯常做法。经常是开始卸货后船长才上岸去代理公司要一份

正本提单。今天卸货很快,再也很难先去查核提单是否真迹了,因这会花上好几天。而且即使如此,仍有如下重大困难:

（i）若涉及期租,承租人或其中的分承租人会不合作,不肯让船东直接去接触分租下去的当事方。相反,承租人会施加压力要船长马上卸货,不得延误,否则停租索偿,等等。

（ii）即使真能接触到手上有"真迹"（原正本提单）的发货人/卖方,它/他也可能会不合作,不作声,希望船东犯错去无单放货。因为它/他若遇上没法在信用证结汇或买方拒绝单证的情况,会面对极大困难去处置船上这票"浮动货物"（floating cargo）。可能不得不廉价转售或甚至是要去求船东回航装港才能处置这票"无人要"的货物。这一来,不安好心的卖方会希望船东最好无单放货,而不小心但又贪心的收货人/买方也去提取了货物后,他就大可理直气壮地向船东索赔整票货物的价值,说是损失,而不必去扣减完全只能是靠猜测的卖方若是要处置货物可能会带来的损失。卖方这种手段在笔者的《信用证》一书第四章之5.5.2小段有提及:

> （货物市场不涨的情况）也吃不准买方会不会要这批货物,加上卖方另去转卖给其他买方也不容易,对策是应不去惊动船东与买方,只是去静观其变。或会是到了卸港,特别是在 FOB,买方随便与无意识地去无单交货,一无单交货后,卖方才出现向船东与买方施压,要求支付货款……

只要这不安好心的卖方不乱讲话、乱行动,也不会造成"禁止翻供（estoppel）,让船东将来以此去抗辩无单放货的指控,这一点在5.1.16.5小段后详。

换一角度去看 Motis Exports 判例:看来相比较仍是大同小异的,在本章之5.1.4小段详述的 Glyn Mills & Co. v. East and West India Dock Co.（1882）7 App. Cas. 591,也是买方不诚实,一式三份的正本提单一份去质押,另一份去向船长提货。众所周知,船东可以不必负责。

两个先例比较,唯一不同的重要事实是 Glyn Mills 的提单是真的一份,Motis Exports 的提单是伪造的一份。其余重要事实都是一致的;船东船长无辜,善意;收货人欺诈,不诚实。这一来,这不同的唯一一点事实是否能公道与足够地去作出有天壤之别的责任区分呢:Motis Exports 要船东负全责,Glyn Mills 船东不必负责任？

5.4.3　底线是考虑大原则

看来,船东是有错或是无辜,是否是买卖双方互骗后果的代罪羔羊,都不是重要的考虑因素。重要的仍是一些大原则,大精神,具体如下:

5.4.3.1 商业机制无法,也不去对付欺诈

这大原则、大精神在《信用证》一书第七章之§1段"世界上没有制度可防止欺诈"有谈及,可去节录如下:

> 首先要清楚的是不会有制度可以完全防止欺诈,因为总会有"道高一尺,魔高一丈"的情况。非但如此,信用证的做法本身也从未想过去对付欺诈。信用证所起的作用在本书第一章§6段已有介绍,是在双方有"信用"的大前提下给予保障;对卖方是会获支付货款,对买方是货物已付运。而且,如第一章3.2小段之(ⅰ)所说,信用证的保障尤其体现在卖方倒闭清盘(insolvency)的情况。

Lloyd 大法官在 The "Future Express" (1993) 2 Lloyd's Rep. 542 的第 546 页说: "If… Dalali(骗子) had been insolvent, instead of fraudulent, the plaintiffs would have been fully secured. No system, however carefully devised, is proof against fraud… if there is a lesson to be learned, it is not that banks should eschew their traditional function of financing commerce by way of letters of credit, but rather that they should be more carefully in selecting their customers."

而早在 Sanders v. Maclean (1883) 11 Q. B. D. 327, Bowen 大法官曾说: "The object of mercantile usage is to prevent the risk of insolvency, not of fraud; and anyone who attempts to follow and understand the law merchant will soon find himself lost if he begins by assuming that merchants conduct their business on the basis of attempting to insure themselves against fraudulent dealing. The contrary is the case. Credit, not distrust, is the basis of commercial dealings; mercantile genuis consists principally in knowing whom to trust and with whom to deal, and commercial intercourse and communication is no more based on the supposition of fraud than it is on supposition of forgery."(任何人去做生意,若以为他可以对免被欺诈遭受损失投保,会是感到失落与不现实。任何生意的起点是双方有"信用",可信任而不会欺诈,而非是不信任。做生意精明的人士最关键是知道信任谁,信任到什么程度,应在某情况下跟谁打交道)。

国际贸易制度无法去防止欺诈,实在是与法律不能去,也无法去保障不懂的傻瓜一样的道理。

这样说来,应是被骗的卖方买方自理损失,在这种商业机制下不应将损失嫁祸到无辜船东头上。但涉及提单下的无单放货,仍有接下来的更大的原则与精神要加以考虑。

5.4.3.2 侵占是严格责任

这大原则、大精神在《国际货物买卖》一书第七章之4.2小段"侵占是严格责

任"有说道：

> 侵占是一种"严格"(strict)的民事"侵权(tort)责任"：Clerk v. Linsell 的《Torts》16 版之 §22~67。侵占方自辩说自己无辜，没有疏忽，不知情等并不足够。这也是经常在船东无单(正本提单)交货后面临真正货主(提单持有人)索赔时的一种抗辩，但其实在英国法律下站不住脚。

另可去节录 Diplock 大法官在 Marfani & Co. Ltd. v. Midland Bank Ltd. (1968) 1 WLR 956 清楚明了的说法如下："Such, however, is the common law of England, and one of the consequences of the historic origin of the tort of conversion and its application to negotiable instruments as "goods" is that the tort at common law is one of strict liability in which the moral concept of fault in the sense of either knowledge by the doer of an act that it is likely to cause injury, loss or damage to another, or lack of reasonable care to avoid causing injury, loss or damage to another, plays no part."

5.4.3.3 提单信誉必须维护

这大原则、大精神在《信用证》一书的第一章有详述：为何英美法律要尽力去维护大家对提单(与信用证)的信心与尊重，由于内容较多，在此不去重复或节录。但不妨另去节录 Rix 大法官在 Motis Exports v. Dampskibsselskabet AF 1912 (1999) 1 Lloyd's Rep. 837 所作的老生常谈之言如下："If one of two innocent people must suffer for the fraud of a third, it is better that the loss falls on the shipowner, who responsibility it is both to look to the integrity of his bills and to care for the cargo in his possession and to deliver it alright, rather than on the true good's owner, who holds a valid bill and expects to receive his goods in return for it.

In my judgment, therefore, it is no defence to a shipowner or to the defendants in this case, innocently to be deceived by production of a forged bill of lading into release of cargo. When the proper bill of lading is produced, he has no defence."

5.4.3.4 总结大原则

一去总结以上所谈的大原则、大精神，就不难理解为何英国高院与上诉庭在 Motis Exports v. Dampskibsselskabet AF 1912(1999) 1 Lloyd's Rep. 837 的判决。会是发货人/卖方自己不小心与不诚实的收货人/买方打交道，但恶果反而落在无辜的船东头上。

这样看，较早的对船东严格的案例，如在 5.1.11 小段提及的 Hoffman-Laroche Inc v. TFL Jefferson 1990 AMC 1388；731 F. Supp. 109 (SDNY 1990) 与 The "Sormovskiy 3068" (1994) 2 Lloyd's Rep. 266 等，亦不难去理解了。

四十多年前,Denning 勋爵在 Sze Hai Tong Bank Ltd. v. Rambler Cycle Co. Ltd. (1959) 2 Lloyd's Rep. 114 曾说过以下的至理名言,用它来警示今天的船东仍是完全适宜:"It is perfectly clear law that a shipowner who delivers without production of the bill of lading does so at his peril. The contract is to deliver, on production of the bill of lading, to the person entitled under the bill of lading. In this case it was "unto order or his or their assigns", that is to say, to the order of the Rambler Cycle Company,[123] if they had not assigned the bill of lading, or their assigns if they had. The shipping company did not deliver the goods to any such person. They are therefore liable for breach of contract unless there is some term in the bill of lading protecting them. And they delivered the goods, without production of the bill of lading to a person who has not entitled to receive them. They are therefore liable in conversion unless likewise so protected."

而在 5.1.4 小段详述的 Glyn Mills v. East and West India Dock Co. (1882) 7 App. Cas. 591 让船东不必对交错货物(不严格是无单放货)负责,也会是出于调整及使这方面的商业机制合理化(即一式几份正本提单只要退回一份即可去交货),令该船东有所适从,而多于是法院同情无辜的船东才这样判决。

5.5 船东/承运人责任基础与损失计算

船东/承运人如果要对无单放货负责,其责任基础已详谈过。一是侵权下的"侵占"(conversion):本章之 1.3 小段。二是运输合约下的错误交货:本章之 1.4 小段。三是"托管关系"(bailment):本章之 1.5 小段。情况会是,三种责任基础都可成立。特别是在今天生效的 1992 年英国海上运输法下,有运输合约关系,也可以此合约关系向船东/承运人起诉无单放货的违约/毁约,因此机会是大大增加了。例如银行,它是提单合法持有人,也可去起诉了。这一来,托管关系不再重要,因为它本是以合约条款为准的 bailment on terms:请看本章之 1.5.2 小段。

剩下来的责任基础也就是侵权(侵占)与合约。照说,在无单放货下,它们都是严格责任,应不必太去计较,设法区分。但实际并非如此,在订约自由的大原则下,总有合约会出现古怪的条款要去解释,而这是纯侵权不必面对的。另外,损失计算也会有不同。

5.5.1 违约与侵占的不同损失计算

如果以违约计算损失,大原则大精神是"复原"(restitutio in integrum),这方面已在笔者的《国际商务游戏规则——英国合约法》一书第十四章有详论,无须在此

---

[123] 它是发货人/卖方,而交货给谁提单是注明"听指示",听他的指示。

重复。只简单提一下,船东/承运人交不出货物的损失计算,Esher 勋爵在 Rodocanachi v. Milburn(1886) 18 QBD 67 先例曾有过以下的指引:"I think that the rule as to measure of damages in a case of this kind must be this: the measure is the difference between the position of (buyer) if the goods had been safely delivered and his position if the goods are lost. What, then, is that difference? If the goods are delivered he obtained them, but in order to obtain them he must pay the freight in respect of which there is a lien on them. If there were no lien, he would be entitled to the goods without paying anything. Upon getting the goods he could sell them. He therefore would get the value of the goods upon their arrival at the port of discharge less what he would have to pay in order to get them. But what is to be the rule in getting at the value of the goods? If there is no market for such goods, the result must be arrived at by estimate, by taking the cost of the goods to the shipper and adding to that the estimated profit he would make at the port of destination. If there is a market there is no occasion to have recourse to such a mode of estimating the value when the goods ought to have arrived. But the value is to be taken independently of any circumstances peculiar to the (buyer)."

以上大意是:

(ⅰ)损失以卸港的货物市场价格为准,但要减去货方应付给船东/承运人才能提取货物(因为船东对货物有留置权)的有关费用。Esher 勋爵只提到提单仍欠下的运费。但照说,已产生了的滞期费,也可以有留置权,也应包括。毕竟,大原则大精神是复原。

(ⅱ)卸港若没有该货物的市场,损失只好去推算估计了:货价原是多少,利润应是多少等。

有关市场价格的课题,在笔者的《国际货物买卖》一书之第八章 4.1 小段有详述,不去重复。只说一点:市场价格会有卖方与买方价格,虽然一般相差不远:The "Texaco Melbourne"(1994) 1 Lloyd's Rep. 473。看来,《McGregor on Damages》等权威书籍倾向是以买方价格为准,因为买方失去了货物的话(被拒交、误交),这会是他要去市场买入替代品的代价。

这损失的计算也不是一成不变。在另一颇著名的无单放货案例 The "Ines" (1995) 2 Lloyd's Rep. 144,涉及电话的货物,判损失是买方本来会支付原告(被无单放货的提单持有人)的货款,这才是真正的"复原"。以上讲的是以违约为准的损失计算,而若是基于侵权的"侵占"(conversion),又会有何不同呢? 本来,公道与客观地看也应只是市场价格。受害的原告拥有的财物被侵占了,赔足够的钱给他让他在市场另买入替代品不是很好吗? 的确在 Hall v. Barclay(1937) 3 All ER 620 的先例曾判是:"Where you are dealing with goods which can be readily bought in the market, a man whose rights have been interfered with is never entitled to more than what he would have to pay to buy a similar article in the market."

但之后大政策有了改变,法律也改为要特殊对待侵占的损失赔偿计算,用意是要严厉对付侵占方(无单放货的情况下就会是船东/承运人了)。这方面可去节录《国际货物买卖》一书之第七章 4.3 小段如下:

4.3 侵占赔偿计算的特殊对待

侵占的各种"救济"(remedy)已在 Tort (Interference with Goods) Act, 1977 的立法 Section 3 订明如下:

"(2) The relief is—

(a) an order for delivery of goods, and for payment of any consequential damages, or (b) an order for delivery of the goods, but giving the defendant the alternative of payment damages by reference to the value of the goods, together in either alternative with payment of any consequential damages, or (c) damages."

去详细探讨这三种不同救济之前,也应去看该立法同一 Section 3 subsection(3),如下:

"(3) Subject to rules of court—

(a) relief shall be given under only one of the paragraphs (a), (b) and (c) of subsection (2), (b) relief under paragraph (a) of subsection (2) is at the discretion of the court, and the claimant may choose between the others."

这是说真正货主针对侵占方的法律救济只能是在三种做法中拣一种。而这三种的第一种法院有裁量权,决定是否给予。但余下两种救济却完全是由真正货主自己决定选用哪种。

4.3.1 三种不同的救济

回头去探讨这三种不同的救济,它们是:

(ⅰ)法院下令物归原主,以及侵占方赔偿有关损失(如果有)。但这第一种救济的裁量权既然在法院,表示法院不一定会给予这命令(order of delivery of goods)。而面对这种申请,确是,法院的考虑会与面对"履行指令"(specific performance)的申请一样。这方面是在笔者的《国际商务游戏规则——英国合约法》一书的第 584 页有详细介绍。例如,法官要考虑双方的"便利与否"(balance of convenience),市场有否代替产品,整个案情的公道,将来金钱上的损失赔偿会否已足够等。

(ⅱ)第二种也是下令物归原主,但侵占方有权去选择赔付所侵占货物的市场价格,而保留货物。另外,再赔偿有关损失(如果有)。这种救济是由真正货主选择决定。而在货物已完全毁坏或失去,侵占方可以说是无法物归原主,也只得是去赔付货物的市场价格了。

(ⅲ)第三种是货物也不想要了,真正货主选择只要侵占方赔偿损失。侵占方不存在有选择权可去说:货物仍在,可以马上物归原主。

要有以上三种不同的救济,也是说得过去。法律是想去尽量帮助真正货主,严厉对待侵占方。所以,要去考虑真正货主的想法。第一种救济权力不在真正货主,所以不必多讲。在第二种与第三种救济之间的选择,会是因为侵占的延误(例如船东非法拒绝交货)导致一个赚钱的分售合约被中止,变了物归原主再也没有作用。或是,侵占的延误导致货物会产生质变,例如是一船的香蕉。自然是,真正货主不想要物归原主,就选择第三种救济了。

相反,如果真正货主仍想要回这票被侵占货物,则他会选择第一种(但法院可能会否定)或第二种救济。可是,侵占方可能会无法物归原主。或是这样做太昂贵不便,例如侵占的货物已是安配或混合在其他货物内。所以,第二种救济可去让侵占方有选择权去赔付货物的市场价格,加上有关损失。

4.3.2 侵占赔偿的"市场价格规定"

侵占赔偿的起点是去看被侵占货物的市场价格,这道理在一个较早期案例的 Hall v. Barclay (1937) 3 All ER 620 已有说明如下:

"Where you are dealing with goods which can be readily bought in the market, a man whose rights have been interfered with is never entitled to more than what he would have to pay to buy a similar article in the market."

这"市场价格规定"(market value rule)也在1977年立法的 Section 3(2)(b)再次订明:请看本章4.3 小段。

确定市场价格的"市场"会有各方面争议,这在本书第八章的4.1 小段会有详论。

而市场上下波动,变得是哪一天的市场价格为准呢? 答案是在货物被侵占的一天,原因是自该天起,侵占方的行为令真正货主无法及时去转售/处理这票货物,例如估计有关市场将会大幅度下挫:Soloway v. McLaughlin (1938) AC 247。

这答案在 BBMB Finance (Hong Kong) v. Eda Holdings (1991) 2 All ER 129 先例被 Templeman 大法官再次强调:

"The general rule is that a plaintiff(真正货主) whose property is irreversibly converted has vested in him a right to damages for conversion measured by the value of the property at the date of conversion…The inexplicable failure by the defendant to collect the sale price cannot mitigate or reduce the damages recoverable by the plaintiffs and cannot alter the measure of damages."

这一来,表示货物被侵占后市场下跌,那么即使原来真正的货主不会有眼光或机会在市场下跌前转售,但有了侵占赔偿的规定,他仍然可去索赔市场价格,进而把以后市场下跌的风险与损失转嫁给侵占方。要知道,侵占方不一定有过错或疏忽,只是侵占属严格责任而已。所以,这看来会造成不公平,如 Andrew Tettenborn Cambridge Law Journal,52(1), March 1993 发表的一文"Damages in Conversion-The Exception or the Anomaly?"所举的例子如下:

"In other cases the present conversion rule simply over-compensates P(真正货主,以原告 Plaintiff 的 P 为号). Assume, for example, a cargo belonging to P is mistakenly collected from a third party's warehouse by D(侵占方的被告以 Defendant 的 D 为号);a week later, when D notices the mistake and returns it, its market value has fallen. P can claim this drop in value (i.e. the value of the cargo when taken, less its reduced value when returned)[124]; but unless it is clear that P would have realised the cargo in the meantime, awarding P anything at all simply gives him a windfall. Or take another example: suppose D takes P's property in error, but when he later offers it back P refuses to accept it[125]. The logic of conversion dictates that P is entitled to do this, and so effectively force D to 'buy him out' by paying what the property was worth at the time he took it. There seems little to be said for this. The sensible solution is for P to be bound to mitigate his loss like any other tort plaintiff; even if his property has gone down in value, no injustice would be caused by making him accept it back and then recover from D any actual loss he could show."

至于在货物侵占后,市场价格不是下挫而是上升,岂非不会对侵占方不利,而且还会令他可去赚?因为他可以去选择第二种救济,去赔付侵占一天的市场价格,而不去归还市场价格业已大涨的货物。答案是侵占方别去妄想,因英国法律对他十分严厉与不利。在 Sachs v. Miklos (1948) 2 KB 23,上诉庭说:

"The value of the goods converted, at the time of their conversion, is one thing ... but it does not follow that that sum is the measure of the plaintiff's(真正货主) loss. The question is what is the plaintiff's loss, what damage be has suffered, by the wrongful act of the defendants(侵占方)."

在该先例,上诉庭判是货物侵占后市场价格上涨的差价(与侵占一天的市

---

[124] 第二种救济,市场价格下跌的部分视为"有关损失"(consequential damages)。
[125] 第三种救济。

场价格比较)是"有关损失"(consequential damages),侵占方也要对此作出赔偿。

在The"Playa Larga"(1983) 2 Lloyd's Rep. 171,上诉庭认为侵占货物后市场价格上涨,不表示真正货主可去拣市场价格最高的一天作为比较,其差别算是"有关损失"。真正货主去证明他会在市场价最高时出售货物图利也只是去讲故事,事后诸葛亮,侵占方无法去反证/反驳。

在这方面最后可回头去介绍已经提及的 Solloway v. McLaughlin 先例。该案例中,股票经纪把寄存在他手中的股票侵占出售。往后在市场以便宜得多的价格再去购进,及时归还给股票主人。这一来,股票经纪赚了一大笔,但股票主人也谈不上有损失。股票主人发觉这件事后以侵占损失向股票经纪索赔,并且成功。判是侵权一方不能在"侵权"(tort)中图利;如果有,这好处要归还受害方。这方面看来与"合约"(contract)有点不同,违约方可去图利,只要对方没有损失:请看《国际商务游戏规则——英国合约法》一书的604页介绍的 Surrey County Council v. Bredero Homes Ltd. (1993) 1 W. R. 1361。但连这判法也已有了疑问:Attorney General v. Blake (1998) 1 All ER 833。

4.3.3 如何取巧?

有了4.3.1与4.3.2小段的介绍,现在可去看真正货主如何取巧,选择最佳的救济:

(ⅰ)首先看侵占方是否皮包公司/小公司。如果是,表示索赔损失将困难重重,甚至无望。所以应从速去要求物归原主。

(ⅱ)如果侵占方是大公司,有实力,而货物市场价格在侵占后下跌,或难以处理,则应选择第三种救济,拒绝侵占方物归原主,向他索赔侵占一天的货物市场价格。

(ⅲ)如果货物市场价格在侵占后上涨,则对侵占一事诈作不知(有些情况下可做得到)。市场到了高位时再当做想把货物出售而发觉被侵占,造成巨大损失。也不要去接受侵占方将货物物归原主。

4.3.4 无单交货的救济/赔偿

上一小段的取巧做法,可去套用在经常发生的无单交货,而真正货主(正本提单持有人)仍是收不到货款的卖方。

卖方可去以侵占向船东/船长起诉,而船东一般无法去将货物归原主,因为已是给买方无单提货的取走。所以只能去赔偿货物在侵占一天的卸港市场价格,加上"有关损失"(如果有,例如市场之后涨了)。卖方也可去以侵占向买方起诉,这一点在笔者的《信用证》一书的94页有提到说:

(ⅲ)买方没有货权而占有了卖方的货物,是与船东无单交货一样,构成了

"侵占他人货物"(conversion of cargo)的侵权行为。若是货物市场上涨,卖方以这理由向买方索赔甚至可不必去局限在买卖合约的货价,而是更高的市价。

这样说太简短,其实去向买方(侵占方)起诉,所有在 4.3.3 小段提及的取巧考虑都用得上,可从中选择对卖方最佳的救济。

5.5.2　合约与侵权的并列诉权

无单放货既可在 1992 年的海上运输法下让提单合法持有人以合约起诉船东/承运人(有没有托管关系不再重要),加上持有物权凭证的提单也可以侵权的侵占起诉船东/承运人,这就有了"并列诉权"(concurrent action 或 parallel action)的存在。问题是:原告可否取巧。例如选一个对他有利的诉权起诉,往往是以侵权起诉而去漠视合约,进而逃避一些对他不利的合约条款或时效已过等问题。

在无单放货,这样做显然也有好处,例如上一小段显示了以侵占起诉可去索赔更大的"损失",因为立法有特殊对待。

在英国普通法下,Goff 勋爵在 Henderson v. Merrett Syndicates (1994) 2 Lloyd's Rep. 468 先例去比较其他国家有关法律后,说:"My own belief is that, in the present context, the common law is not antipathetic to concurrent liability,[126] and that there is no sound basis for a rule which automatically restricts the claimant to either a tortious or a contractual remedy.[127] The results may be untidy; but given that the tortious duty is imposed by the general law, and the contractual duty is attributable to the will of the parties,[128] I do not find it objectionable that the claimant may be entitled to take advantage of the remedy which is most advantageous to him,[129] subject only to ascertaining whether the tortious duty is so inconsistent with the applicable contract that, in accordance with ordinary principle, the parties must be taken to have agreed that the tortious remedy is to be limited or excluded.[130]"

这样看来,无单放货下大可以侵占与违约的并列诉权起诉船东/承运人,而且可去任意取巧,例如损失计算是以侵占为准。而就这一点而言,侵占与违约也不像有什么太大的"矛盾"(inconsistent),或许后者已有明确针对的条款。但目前不少无单放货的案例中,仍未见过有这方面(并列诉权)的争议与判决。最后,不妨去节录

---

[126]　普通法不反对并列诉因/诉权。
[127]　也没有太大理由去剥夺原告的权力,迫他只准以侵权或合约一种诉权起诉。
[128]　但考虑到"侵权"是一般法律所强加的而"合约"代表双方自愿。
[129]　我(Goff 勋爵)认为任由原告在 2 种诉权间取巧之余。
[130]　应去看侵权是否与相关合约的责任相差太远,互有矛盾。如果是,就应以合约为准了。

《国际商务游戏规则——英国合约法》一书第十四章对这一课题的内容如下：

3.2 告违约？告侵权？

有不少情况会是受害方同时面对违约或侵权。例如1924年的海牙规则适用在提单合约，规则内容有一年时效与件装责任限制等。但货方以侵权（如果有关，例如不小心照顾货物）起诉船东，则可避过一年时效与责任限制，例如有长至 Limitation Act 的六年时效。

为此在1971年的海牙·维斯比规则，对海牙规则的 Article 4 多加了如下一句："The defences and limits of liability provided for in this Convention shall apply in any action against the carrier in respect of loss or damage to goods covered by a contract of carriage whether the action be founded in contract or in tort."

可见，大精神是尽量减少受害方选择违约或侵权来取巧的可能，以免带来混乱。而最主要的先例是在 Tai Hing v. Liu Chong Hing Bank (1985) 2 Lloyd's Rep. 313，它是关于银行与客户之间的既有合约，但亦有侵权关系。Scarman 勋爵在321页说：

"Their Lordship do not believe that there is anything to the advantage of the law's development in searching for a liability in tort where the parties are in a contractual relationship. This is particularly so in a commercial relationship. Though it is possible as a matter of legal semantics to conduct an analysis of the rights and duties inherent in some contractual relationships including that of banker and customer either as a matter of contract law when the question will be what, if any, terms are to be implied or as a matter of tort law when the task will be to identify a duty arising from the proximity and character of the relationship between the parties, their Lordships believe it to be correct in principle and necessary for the avoidance of confusion in the law to adhere to the contractual analysis: on principle because it is a relationship in which the parties have, subject to a few exceptions, the right to determine their obligations to each other, and for the avoidance of confusion because different consequences do follow according to whether liability arises from contract or tort, e. g. in the limitation of action."

Scarman 勋爵接着说，合约的规定应是主导，不得以侵权之诉来改变：

"Their Lordship do not, however, accept that the parties'/mutual obligations in tort can be any greater than those to be found expressly or by necessary implication in their contract…the respondent banks cannot rely on the law of tort to provide them with greater protection than that for which they have contracted."

以上判词在之后不少的案子中被接受,跟从的有:Banque Keyser Ullmann SA v. Skandia (U. K.) Co Insurance Ltd. (1990) 1 QB 665,(1991) 2 A. C. 249; National Bank of Greece S. A. v. Pinios Shipping (No. 1) (1990) 1 A. C. 637; Bank of New Zealand v. Cinivan (1991) 1 N. Z. L. R. 178(新西兰案例)等。

在 Banque Keyser Ullmann SA 一案中,Slade 大法官说 Scarman 勋爵的判词是一个宝贵的警告,即不应让侵权去侵害合约关系:"a valuable warning as to the law of tort to fill in contractual gaps."在 Bell v. Peter Browne & Co. (1990) 2 QB 495,Mustill 大法官也说这(指 Scarman 勋爵的判决)应是英国法律对一部分案子所持的观点,并对并列诉权这种做法引起的混乱表示可惜:"a pity that English law has elected to recognise concurrent rights of action in contract and tort."

3.3 告违约同时可告侵权的例外

其实即使有了上小段的解释,英国法律在这方面的观点,即可同时告违约与侵权,仍是不明确,正如 Mustill 大法官在 The Eras Eil Actions (1992) 1 Lloyd's Rep. 570 在 598 页所说:"it has to be said that this area of the law is in a state of disarray."

这不明确之处是仍有一些例外情况可去同时告违约与侵权,我在这里举其中两个例外:

(ⅰ)专业服务的合约带来的责任(professional liability),受害方(客户)可去选择告违约与侵权:Caparo Industries v. Dickman (1990) 2 AC. 605 的核算师;Punjab National Park v. de Boinville (1992) 3 All ER. 104 的保险经纪人。

(ⅱ)在合约产生以前的责任(pre-contractual liability),这包括了如非法威迫订立合约等行为。但最主要应是误述(misrepresentation)导致合约的产生,尤其这误述是欺诈性的(fraudulent misrepresentation)。普通法下,受害方有权中止因此而带来的合约,并且以"欺诈侵权"(tort for deceit)索赔损失:Derry v. Peek (1889) 14 App. Cas. 337。这也进一步解释了前面 3.1 小段所提的倒签提单日期的例子。相对于合约已在履行中,如提单或租约,它所会有的违约或侵权行为,好像是没有小心照顾货物,这应是以 Scarman 勋爵在 Liu Chong Hing Bank 先例的说法为准。

5.6 对无单放货的抗辩

船东能提出的抗辩可真不多,而成功的会是更少,以下不妨介绍一下船东常在无望中用来"聊胜于无"的一些抗辩理由:

5.6.1 时效已过

英国法律对合约或侵权规定的 6 年时效实在太长,一般不会涉及,难以想象提单持有人会过了 6 年才起诉船东/承运人无单放货。但真正有关的时效应是 1971 年的英国海上运输法,它的一年时效可就短多了。这方面可去节录笔者的《国际货物买卖》一书的第 325 页所说:

> ……是 1971 年的"海上运输法"(Carriage of Goods by Sea Act 1971),即对海牙·维斯比规则的立法,说明在交货后(或应交货后)一年的时效。有关的措辞/文字十分决断、广泛,说是"… the carrier and the ship shall in any event be discharged from all liability[131] whatsoever in respect of the goods, unless suit is brought within one year of their delivery or of the date when they should have been delivered"。这样的措辞/文字,应是货损货差外,连无单放货这类的索赔,也应包括在内:可参阅 The "Antares"(1987) 1 Lloyd's Rep. 424;The "Captain Gregos"(1989) 2 Lloyd's Rep. 63 与 The "Ines"(1995) 2 Lloyd's Rep. 144…

在 The "Antares",Steyn 大法官指基本违约或非基本违约,或绕航不绕航,一年时效都一概适用。而海牙·维斯比规则也说明,不论以"合约"或"侵权"起诉船东/承运人,一律相同对待:这加在海牙规则的 Article Ⅳ。

这一年时效的抗辩在个别案件可能无关。例如 The "Future Express"(1992) 2 Lloyd's Rep. 79,结汇已是无单交货后一年多。该先例中的发货人/卖方(著名粮商的 Tradax)十分精明,同意延迟结汇以助"代理"(实有中间商的味道)在金钱上周转,但为了防止将来结汇(信用证当然要不断延期)时因不符点遭拒绝付款,而货物(小麦)早已吃光了,所以要求它的保兑银行"瑞士联合银行"(UBS)先接受这份单证/文件,再收回暂不结汇。估计 UBS 也是老关系,也这样做了。如果早发觉有不符点,也会趁对货物仍有控制,未曾卸下,可去干预无单放货而迫使买方马上修改信用证。只要是完全妥当,不怕 UBS 将来在保兑信用证之下会拒付,Tradax 才让船舶无单放货。之后 Tradax 从 UBS 获得支付,UBS 亦从开证银行的账号中扣除同样一笔货款。但没人前来赎单,开证银行只好出面诉船指控无单放货。不会太离题:时隔这么久才结汇,发觉出了事(不赎单)才去起诉肯定一年时效已过。该先例也面对这争议,只是根据案情不必再去针对时效,所以 Diamond 大法官不肯对此点作出判断。该先例要是在 1992 年新提单法下,搬到今天再去审理的话,开证银行作为

---

[131] 措辞是针对"所有责任",没有去局限在只是规则所针对的"吊钩至吊钩"运输中的责任。

"合法提单持有人"（lawful holder of bills）应不再有诉权的问题，Diamond 大法官就非要对一年时效已过的抗辩作出判决了，但估计开证银行仍会凶多吉少。

再比如澳大利亚上诉庭在中远的 The"Zhi Jiang Kou"（1991）1 Lloyd's Rep. 493 一案中的判决，该判决称涉及无单交货（该单证是一份多式联运单证，算是一份物权凭证，收货人是"To Order"）可以时效已过作为抗辩。

5.6.2　提单合约内的免责条款

提单合约内的免责条款（如果有）与此很有关，因为无单放货导致真正提单持有人损失。它要求船东交货不果，提出侵占的起诉，这都是 1992 年新提单法下行使的在 Section 3（1）的权利；该法实际上令它变为"合约的一方"（as if he had been a party to that contract）。所以，在订约自由下，提单合约怎样写，就会怎样解释，也会去约束提出索赔的提单持有人，即使是涉及无单放货。因为原告即使以侵权的侵占为诉因/诉权起诉也难以否认侵权外另有合约存在，故此属"并列诉权"（concurrent action）；请看本章之 5.5.2 小段。而在合约有相关明确与广泛的条款针对下，原告不能以侵权作出回避。

虽然海牙规则/海牙·维斯比规则也有一些方面去禁止订约自由，但因为针对不同，应该不会有影响。海牙规则针对海上运输中的货损货差责任，责任期限是所谓的"吊钩至吊钩原则"（tackle to tackle）或"船栏至船栏原则"（rail to rail）。但无单交货一般是发生在岸上，即货从船上卸下之后，尤其是班轮业务。此外，海牙规则强加责任要船东小心与妥善处理货物只是说"卸货"（discharge）没有"交货"（delivery）：Article 3（2）。而不准以订约自由豁免船东责任的 Article 3（8）也只是涉及该章所针对的责任。

更进一步，去参考海牙规则的 Article 7，应是对以上所谈更为明了，现节录如下："Nothing herein contained shall prevent a carrier or a shipper from entering into any agreement, stipulation, condition, reservation or exemption as to the responsibility and liability of the carrier or the ship for the loss or damage to, or in connection with, the custody and care and handling of goods prior to the loading on and subsequent to the discharge from, he ship on which the goods are carried by sea."

班轮提单一般都会有这种免责条款，反正船东喜欢怎样拟定，发货人在现实中都不会或无能力去反对。但能否在无单放货方面去保障船东，曾有过不少先例都显示了法院极大的敌意，总是千方百计去在条款的解释中挑毛病令船东无法免责。其中也有过颇难去区分的矛盾先例。首先可以列举一古老先例，是颇为罕见的保障船东错放货的上议院（贵族院）先例：Chartered Bank v. British Steam Navigation（1909）A. C. 369。该提单有一条款说："…in all cases and under all circumstances the liability of the company shall absolutely cease when the goods are free of the ship's tackle, and thereupon the goods shall be at the risk for all purposes and in every respect of the shipper or consignee."(货物从船上吊钩卸下脱钩后,船东所有责任绝对中止,货物风险全在发货人或收货人头上)。

船东把货物卸下驳船,交给卸港"作业代理人"(landing agents)照顾,但因为他不诚实,与骗子串通,导致无单放货。但上议院判是船东受到免责条款保障,Macnaghten 勋爵说:"it may be admitted that the bills of lading cannot be said to be spent or exhausted until the goods covered by them are placed under the absolute dominion and control of the consignees. But their Lordships cannot think that there is any ambiguity in the clause providing for cesser of liability. It seems to be perfectly clear. There is no reason why it should not be held operative and effectual in the present case."

该案例虽常被无单放货的船东援用来抗辩,但常被后来的案例所加以区别(distinguish),虽然没有明言去推翻它(级别低的法院也无法去这样做)。

在 Compania Importadora de Arroges Collette y. Kamp S. A. v. P & O Steam Navigation Co. (1927) 28 Lloyd's Rep. 63, Wright 大法官说 Chartered Bank 先例的不诚实 landing agents 不严格是船东代理人,实际只是"中间人"(intermediaries),意即船东不必为他去承担责任有合理/说得通之处。Wright 大法官也说:"such a clause has never been extended to a simple case of misdelivery."

在 Sze Hai Tong Bank Ltd. v. Rambler Cycle Co. Ltd. (1959) 2 Lloyd's Rep. 114, Denning 勋爵简单地去加以区分,说:"... on the simple ground that the action of the fraudulent servant there could in no wise be imputed to the shipping company. His act was not its act."

而在 Motis Exports v. Dampskibsselskabet AF 1912 (1999) 1 Lloyd's Rep. 837, Rix 大法官说:"It has to be said, however, that Chartered Bank(先例)has not appeared to have been influential."

但更多的先例是判船东不得去依赖免责条款,部分例子如下:

(ⅰ)在著名的 Sze Hai Tong Bank Ltd.,提单有第2条款说:"During the period before the goods are loaded on or after they are discharged from the ship on which they are carried by sea, the following terms and conditions shall apply to the exclusion of any other provisions in this bill of lading that may be inconsistent therewith, viz... (c) In all other cases the responsibility of the carrier whether as carrier or as custodian or bailee of the goods shall be deemed to commence only when the goods are loaded on the ship and *to cease absolutely after they are discharged therefrom.*"

以 Denning 勋爵为首的上诉庭主要是以与"基本毁约"(fundamental breach)类

似的"相悖理论"(doctrine of repugnancy)为由去漠视该条款。这方面干脆可以节录《国际商务游戏规则——英国合约法》一书的第十章5.1.1小段部分内容如下：

案中卖方售一批自行车给新加坡买方，海运提单属(凭发货人)指示提单(to order B/L)。因此承运人有义务按发货人(卖方)的指示(或提单背书)，凭提单放货。可提单第2条又规定："承运人的责任自货物卸离船后绝对终止(cease absolutely)。"结果货物在新加坡卸船后，承运人的代理未经指示就将货物放给买方，是无单放货，而事实上买方当时根本就未支付货款。放货当时，买方向承运人提供了一份银行担保。事后，当承运人根据此份保函就卖方提出的索赔向担保银行追偿时，银行却提出：根据提单第2条，"货物一旦卸船，承运人责任即告终止。"根本不存在承运人要承担之后的责任的问题，既然如此，出具保函的银行亦无须负责。该案最后在贵族院判下来，丹宁勋爵(Lord Denning)在判词中指出：本案提单中的这条免责条款，从字面上看似乎是再清楚不过的了，同时被告(银行)也辩称这条规定足以令原告(承运人)免除其诉称的对发货人的责任，即放货给无权收货的他人的责任。可是如果真这样去解释，那么根据同样理由，似乎承运人将货物随便交付给一个过路人甚至干脆把它们扔到海里也不用负责任了。这显然是讲不通的。如果事前订约时去问提单双方当事人，上述情况承运人能否免责，他们肯定会回答当然不能。因此，对这样一条极度广泛的免责条款，实际上存在一种默示的限制(implied limitation)。另外，从解释合约的角度讲，若给予该条免责条款如此广泛的适用，也将违背(run counter)合约的主要目标和宗旨。根据判案法官们的观点，"依(发货人的)指示凭提单适当交货"是本案合约(提单)的主旨之一，若承运人可随意将货交于他人而无须承担责任，无疑将彻底破坏这一主旨。因此，上述免责条款只能在符合合约宗旨的范围内适用，否则无效。这个判例的确为"相悖理论"作出了很好的注释。

在某种程度上，上述"相悖理论"与后来发展起来的"基本违约"(fundamental breach)理论似乎有类同之处，后者以前在合约解释上曾一度被英国法院所采用，就是说，如果一方的行为已触及到合约的根基(a breach which went to the "very root" of the contract)，违反了整个合约的根本目标(main purpose)，那么所有免责或限制责任的条款对违约方无效，不予适用，等于违约方由此丧失了所有合约规定的免责、限责权利与保障。比如甲卖一样货品给乙，结果货是烂的，可买卖合约中有一条免责条款，使卖方得以连这种违约下的责任都免掉，又或者有一限责条款称出现任何货物质量问题，包括货全部烂掉，卖方只需赔一毛钱。那么这种条款以前法院往往就用"基本违约"的理论去予以否定,不过自 Photo Production Ltd. v. Securicor Transport Ltd. (1980) 1 Lloyd's Rep. 545,贵族院就合约条款的有效问题革命性地确立了"以合理性为检验标准"(test of reasonableness)的原则后,基本违约的理论就不再适用了……

在这以后,"基本违约"作为解释合约的理论等于是不复存在了,对于合约的条款(主要是免责限责条款),法官单凭违约的性质(构成所谓基本违约)去全盘否定掉已行不通了。正如丹宁勋爵在 Mitchell v. Finney Lock Seeds (1983) 2 Lloyd's Rep. 272 中所讲的,现在法律上的观点已相当清楚,不论违约的性质如何,免责(包括限责)条款都不因此而自动终止、失效。各条条款都必须经过解释,以确定合约方是否意欲将这些条款适用于案中违约的情况,而这种解释、确定合约方意愿的标准,就是综合考虑整个案件后得出的对条款公平、合理性(fairness and reasonableness)的判定。

虽然"基本违约"的理论已不复存在,但前面讲述的"相悖理论"作为解释合约的一种机制是仍然存在的。毕竟两者是有区别的,按照前者的概念,一旦一方的违约行为构成所谓的"基本违约",他就等于走出了合约的框架(step outside the four corners of the contract),合约中的一切免责、限责等权利性条款包括船东可收取多少运费再不适用,也不必再追究这些条款本身的内容、性质如何。而相对起来,"相悖理论"则仍是基于对合约条款本身的解释,只有在条款的适用与合约的宗旨完全相悖的情况下,才会否定其效力。至于违约的性质,并不是唯一的考虑因素。可见,两种理论的角度和出发点都有不同。另外还要指出,在解释合约中运用"相悖理论"否定合约条款的情况毕竟不多,法官也不会轻易援用。往往只有在通过其他方法均不能获得对条款的满意解释之后,法官(或仲裁员)才会引用这一解释机制。从这个意义上讲,"相悖理论"可以算是法院解释合约条款(尤其对免责、限责条款)的最后武器。

(ⅱ)在较近期的 The "Ines" (1995) 2 Lloyd's Rep. 144,提单合约中的第3条(另有其他条款)说:"PERIOD OF RESPONSIBILITY: Goods in the custody of the Carrier or his Agents or servants before loading and after discharge whether being forwarded to or from the ocean vessel or whether awaiting shipment landed or stored or put into hulk or craft belonging to the carrier or not or pending transhipment at any stage of the whole transport are in such custody at the sole risk of the owners of the goods and thus the carrier has no responsibility whatsoever for the goods prior to the loading on and subsequent to the discharge from the ocean vessel."

Clarke 大法官在分析有关先例后否定这免责条款可在无单放货方面保障船东,说:

"One of the key provisions of the bill of lading, so far as the shipper is concerned, is the promise not to deliver the cargo other than in return for an original bill of lading.[132] That principle protects the shipper from fraud.[133] It also protects the shipowner. The parties would not in my judgment be likely to have contracted out of it.[134] Thus clear words would be required for them to be held to have done so.[135] The clause should be construed so as to enable effect to be given to one of the main objects and intents of the contracts,[136] namely that the goods would only be delivered to the holder of an original bill of lading. The question is thus whether the words in any of the clauses relied upon are sufficient to excuse misdelivery of the goods after discharge. In my judgment they are not."[137]

Clause 3... That clause seems to me to be concerned with loss of or damage to the goods and may well include the case where the goods are stolen,[138] but it is not concerned with misdelivery..."

(ⅲ)在 Motis Exports v. Dampskibsselskabet AF 1912 (1999) 1 Lloyd's Rep. 837，提单也有一条"5.3b"的免责条款说："Where the carriage called for commences at the port of loading and/or finishes at the port of discharge, the Carrier shall have no liability whatsoever for any loss or damage to the goods while in its actual or constructive possession before loading or after discharge over ship's rail, or if applicable, on the ship's ramp, however caused."

Rix 大法官也不接受该条款可去保障船东"有单放货"但提单是伪造的。他说："... I do not see why natural reading of this language should regard it as including the misdelivery of the goods by the defendants out of their possession, whether such misdeliv-

---

[132] 对发货人而言，提单最主要的承诺之一是不把它的货物乱交给他人。
[133] 这才可以保障它免受骗也。
[134] 双方即使有订约自由也不像会把这么主要的承诺去加以改变/豁免。
[135] 所以，要真去这样做，就非要有十分明确清楚的措辞/文字不可。比方，说明船东可在卸港把货物任意交给它高兴给的第三者，收货人一栏也去写上"To order of shipowner"，以免提单内有矛盾解释起来又会对船东有敌意。
[136] 这有 Sze Hai Tong Bank Ltd. 先例的"相悖理论"(doctrine of repugnancy)讲法的味道。
[137] 判是我(Clarke 大法官)不认为本提单内有任何条款可足够明确去对无单放货免责。
[138] 这里的免责条款大可以对货物被偷(如寄存在岸上)免责,但对无单放货不能免责。虽然,它们的后果会是一样:货物全部失去。这导致在 5.1.15 小段的 Motis Exports,船东争辩说伪造提单前来提取货物形同偷取货物。但 Rix 大法官不同意,说两者不同:"In my judgment, however, Mr. Justice Clarke was thinking of the case where goods are physically taken by theft from the custody of the shipowner, rather than the delivery of the goods against a void and worthless, albeit deceptive, bill.

ery lie in the absence of any bill of lading or in the absence of an original or genuine bill of lading.[139] If that alternative were a possible reading,[140] it is not one which should lightly be adopted against the background of the fundamental importance of the shipowner's promise to deliver up only against an original bill of lading.[141] If that was what the defendants had intended to provide, they could so easily have done so."

以上的例子多是班轮提单。在多式联运提单也会加上这种免责条款。这些运输,合约条款的拟定权在船东/承运人,而面对的千万货方/发货人往往知识与实力均不足够与之抗衡,所以可以加入这种广泛免责条款。但显然,这在无单放货方面仍是不足以保障船东/承运人。而进一步去扩大改善这免责条款,不是说不可以(这可从刚节录的 Rix 大法官所说的最后一句话中理解)。但个别货方/发货人(发货人公会)会对抗,当局会干预(如美国的 FMC)。毕竟无单放货,主动权在船东/承运人,可不是开玩笑,不比其他外来的风险。而且也不一定管用,在法院解释起来,照目前的敌意与相悖理论等,船东/承运人不易免责。但有关这一点,请稍后看 5.10.1 小段。

至于租约提单,有关条款的拟定或去合并什么,决定权一般不在船东/船长,所以不大会有这种免责条款。即使合并的租约就是船东自己订的租约,今天的环境下也不可能迫承租人在租约中接受一条这类的免责条款。加上,散装货物去理会卸下后作业的也不多。

5.6.3 海牙规则下的单位赔偿限额

船东即使要对无单放货负责,能否少赔一点,例如享有海牙规则下的单位赔偿限额? 毕竟时至今天,仍有案例在争议一个集装箱是否算一个单位,只赔海牙规则下的 100 英镑:The "River Gurara" (1998) 1 Lloyd's Rep. 225。所以,这一点在高价货的无单放货肯定会对船东有帮助。

但看来,船东的运气不会好。首先是上一小段已谈到海牙·维斯比规则除了一年时效外,不会适用在无单放货。而即使提单有类似的条款(也属一种免责条款,可去局限赔偿),也会遭受法院的敌意解释或"相悖理论"(doctrine of repugnancy)的引用。

这可节录在《国际商务游戏规则——英国合约法》一书的 5.1.1 小段最后一句

---

[139] 免责条款 5.3b 的措辞/文字,从文义上看不能去包括无单放货,或是因没有一份正本的或一份真确的提单而交错了货物的责任。
[140] 即使该 5.3b 条款可以有这样的内容,去作出这解释。
[141] 也不会轻易去支持,因为不能无单放货实在是船东太重要的承诺了。

所说:

> 另一'相悖理论'案例是 The "Chanda" (1989) 2 Lloyd's Rep. 494,判是海牙规则的单位赔偿限额不适用在船东违约把货物装在甲板(如此类推也包括船员偷货,无单交货等性质的违约)。

这一方面在本书第五章之 4.2.3.5.3.7 小段再详论,在此只去挑一个权威的说法,是 Hirst 大法官在 The "Chanda" 案例中所说: "…clauses which were intended to protect the shipowner provided he honoured his obligation to stow goods under deck did not apply if he was in breach of that obligation; the package limitation fell within this category since it could hardly have been intended to protect the shipowner who as a result of the breach exposed the cargo in question to such risk of damage; the package limitation clause being repugnant to and inconsistent with the obligation to stow below deck, was inapplicable."

Hirst 的说法显然是相悖理论的说法,如果不适用在 The "Chanda" 的违约,怎会适用在具有同样性质但严重性有过之而无不及的无单放货呢？

至于海牙·维斯比规则去加强了一年时效的适用性,欲去局限了单位赔偿限额的适用性(不适用在有意/故意的违约)原因何在,这在本书第五章 4.2.10.3.7 小段有详述。

5.6.4 船舶总的吨位责任限制

船东还有另一个责任限制的权利,在笔者的《海事法》一书第二章有详述,因内容太多,无法在此重复。它涉及国际公约,例如新加坡是签约国的 1957 年责任限制公约与英国、香港地区等签署承认的 1976 年责任限制公约。它们允许在出了大事时,可让船东以船舶吨位计算出一个最高赔偿金额,而不是陷入无底深渊地赔下去。能去受到保护的损失类别,1976 年公约是在 Article 2 (1) (a) 说明如下: "Claims in respect of loss of life or personal injury or loss of or damage to property (including damage to harbour walls, basins and waterways and aids to navigation) occurring on board *or in direct connexion with the operation of the ship or* with salvage operations and consequential loss resulting therefrom."

以上斜体字显示该公约应可适用在货损货差,而不像海牙·维斯比规则的"局限"措辞/文字并不适用在无单放货。

当然,也要去看是什么样的无单放货。在 Motis Exports v. Dampskibsselskabet AF 1912 (1999) 1 Lloyd's Rep. 837,船东被作为第三者欺诈的代罪羔羊,船东可去享

受总的责任限制应不是问题。但如果船东自己鲁莽,恶意地去无单放货,则会被拒绝责任限制。因为1957年责任限制公约的大前提是船东不得"有错或知情"(actual fault and privity)。而1976年责任限制公约也有适用的大前提,就是船东不得"意图去造成损失"(committed with the intent to cause such loss)与"轻率并知道这损失很可能会产生"(recklessly and with knowledge that such loss would probably result)。这立场与海牙·维斯比规则的单位赔偿限责相近。

但话说回来,这笔以船舶吨位计算的最高赔偿金额会是一笔大数,对无单放货的船东作用不大。除非是十分昂贵的货物例如值好几百或上千万美元,这一课题会是无关。

5.6.5　禁止翻供

关于这衡平法的救济,笔者在《国际商务游戏规则——英国合约法》一书第十一章有详论,内容太多,无法去节录或重复。

它会适用在无单放货,也常会有这种抗辩。例如,在The "Stone Gemini" (1999) 2 Lloyd's Rep. 255,船东抗辩原告的提单持有人(承押人/银行的Westpac)知道并同意无单放货,构成禁止翻供。但法院根据证据认定的事实不认为如此,法官说: "on the facts and the evidence Westpac were not aware of the letter of indemnity until much later in 1995; and any question of the bank's prior assent, waiver or estoppel to the use of the letter of indemnity to obtain discharge of the cargo did not arise."

涉及发货人/卖方是提单持有人而后成为原告向船东索赔无单放货的损失,如果放货当时他知道,并同意或是行动上配合船东去这样做,只是后来信用证结汇发生困难才又倒过头来想把船东作为代罪羔羊,那他就会面对船东禁止翻供的抗辩。例如在5.6.1小段等详述的The "Future Express" (1992) 2 Lloyd's Rep. 79,假如卖方Tradax不是精明小心,而是允许并协助无单放货,那么他自己事后因文件有不符点结不了汇,就会面对船东的这种争辩。但Tradax精明小心,先向保兑银行确定了单证/文件可获支付/接受。在本章5.4.2小段后部分的(ⅱ)提到不安好心的卖方对无法处理的浮动货物会巴不得船东去无单放货,然后再向船东索赔损失。但这里又会涉及禁止翻供的考虑。很可能,它(卖方/发货人)应该事前知道无单放货,例如涉及短航次,几乎大家都是这样在做/在操作。或者有关租约有条款涉及无单放货。但卖方/发货人光是知道但保持沉默,一般不足以构成禁止翻供。保持沉默只能属"中性"(neutral),难去说死他若是开口会讲什么话,是同意或是反对无单放货。毕竟,衡平法讲公道。在《国际商务游戏规则——英国合约法》一书之第十一章之5.3小段有说:

……但是,如果一方什么也没有做,什么话也没讲,一般是很难说他弃权和禁止翻供的,除非是一种沉默构成禁止翻供(estoppel by silence)的情况,即一方应为而不为,应说而不说的情况。从严格的法律意义讲,这种被动的不作为(inaction)也算是一种行为,如果实际上是诱导了对方,也可能构成弃权或禁止翻供……

可随便去挑一个先例的说法,在 The "Zhi Jiang Kou" (1991) 1 Lloyd's Rep. 493, Kirby 大法官在 511 页提到一种情况,是一方明知对方不知道某种情况而故意不去讲明,让对方踏进陷阱,而整个过程造成不公道,也是禁止翻供。他说:"…that it would not be pleaded or otherwise relied upon and refrained from correcting that assumption when it was a duty and conscience to do so, and estoppel would arise. It is also clear that an estoppel may arise from silence, if the circumstances otherwise sustain the conclusion of unconscionability."

在以上精神下,把 Motis Exports v. Dampskibsselskabet AF 1912 (1999) 1 Lloyd's Rep. 837 的伪造提单(5.4 小段)事件稍为改动一下,即会涉及禁止翻供的抗辩。比如,船长告知承租人,也是发货人,船舶正准备开卸,一份正本提单已退回。但承租人会知道这份是伪造的正本提单,因为正确的一套仍完整在他手中,因不符点而结不了汇,或无法托收成功。可是,承租人不去提醒船长,让他/船东踏入陷阱,这即会是禁止翻供。

衡平法重视公道、公平,而适用不适用的个别案件事实总会不同。能去下准确判断,自己必须先了解这套游戏规则,这套机制反映出英美高层次人士(例如大法官)的想法。毕竟,去跟不懂的人士或部分来自发展中国家人士讲英美高层次人士眼中的何谓公道、公平,会有天南地北的差距。

5.6.6 提单不是船东授权签发

这是船东在面对货损货差时很喜欢提出的抗辩,就是提单不是他或他的雇员(船长)授权签发,对他没有约束。换言之,在散装货常有的期租安排下,提单实际是承租人提单,而不是船东提单:这方面在第三章 5.2 小段等会详论。

事实上,若去否定这套提单作为物权凭证的存在与有效性,只因为没有授权,是行不通。因为期租下船东早已实际授权承租人签发提单:请参阅笔者的《期租合约》一书第 25 页。

稍为想想也知道船东这种争议会站不住脚。货物毕竟是装了上船,若船东可以否定提单作为物权凭证(与运输合约),岂非不去无单放货也可以把货物占为己有?

即使在租约中没有实际授权承租人签发提单（租约毕竟只是私人合约，双方怎样同意都可以），涉及签发提单，还有一个表面授权的问题。对一位发货人或无辜提单持有人来说，他们只看到/知悉某某船舶在装港装载了他的货物，接下去某某承租人或代理人为船东签发提单，而船东并没出面否认或阻止这个做法。好像一家有限公司去任命了一位董事，放他在这位子，就很难去否定他在任内所做的事对公司的约束力，不论内部有否实际授权。

实际授权与表面授权的课题在笔者的《国际商务游戏规则——英国合约法》一书第四章之§6段有详述，内容太长，无法节录。在此只说说近期的 The "Starsin"（2000）1 Lloyd's Rep. 85 先例，它有十分详细的内容针对这方面争议。很明显，该先例判是没有实际授权，也有表面授权。Colman 大法官说："… It is against that background that the position of the time charterer and the loading port agent respectively authorized to issue bills of lading by the terms of the time charter and the master's letters of authority falls to be analyzed.[142] Once such a time charter has been entered into or letter issued, the shipowners have placed the time charterer or local agent in the position of their representative in respect of the issue of bill of lading contracts relating to the cargo to be loaded[143] and have hereby indirectly represented to the shippers and to indorsees of the bills that they, the shipowners, have authorized the time charterers or agents to bind them to contracts of that kind[144]. Consequently, the shippers and indorsees are entitled to assume that the owners are content to be bound by the terms of the bill even if, unknown to them, there was no actual authority to issue the bill in precisely the terms in which the bill was issued.[145]

5.7　船东可否对无单放货协议及时反悔

这情况会发生在本章 5.2 小段谈到的保函做法上，即船东同意以保函交换无单放货。这同意会早早订明在原先的租约，也会在卸港才与收货人谈妥，而构成一个合约。但在卸货前，或卸了一半货，或刚卸完，会有情况船东反悔，不肯继续无单放货或要求收货人退回不属于他的货物。改变主意的原因会有多种，举例如下：

（ⅰ）突然对保函的可靠性有怀疑，例如保人的银行出事。

（ⅱ）突然接获发货人警告全套提单仍在他手上，而且买方在向他扯皮，不支付

---

[142] 期租下的承租人与船长授权签发提单的装港代理人地位一样。
[143] 一去订立期租或一去授权代理，他们就有权为将装上船舶的货物去签发提单。
[144] 并且以行动间接向发货人与提单背书受让人表述了他们有权签发提单。
[145] 所以，发货人与提单背书受让人有权认为船东愿意授权给他们，即使背后真相是没有实际授权。

货款。

（iii）船东刚看了一篇关于无单放货巨大危险的文章。

这一来，就出现船东要去反悔，推翻原先的合约的情况。这一般会有各种借口，看情况而定。一是收货人去说服船东同意无单放货时，曾有过"误述"（misrepresentation）。另会是以非法为由，这可节录《国际商务游戏规则——英国合约法》一书第七章之4.4小段的"故意去侵权"如下：

> 这会令一个合约变为非法，设法去法院执行，这在《Chitty on Contracts》27版的16-016段有清楚说明如下：'If a contract has as its object the deliberate commission of a tort, it would seem that the contract is illegal, even though no criminality or fraud is involved. Thus a printer cannot recover the cost of printing matter which he knew to be libellous and the purchaser cannot recover a sum of money deposited with the printer on account of the cost to be incurred in printing it.' 这个类别会构成非法合约对国际航运与外贸在有一方面影响非常大，就是交货没有提单的问题。众所周知，今天因航次短，船速快，带来估计50%的情况是卸货时正本提单仍未到达卸港。今天一般的做法是收货人提供银行担保（保函），金额最少要是货物价格，来换取船东无提单卸货。这保函没有去欺骗任何人，不是非法。它只是针对一个情况：收货人说货物属他，也没有理由不相信，只是代表主权的正本提单仍未在手，因结汇延误或其他延误。而没有主权的证明，船东有权不交货，收货人于是用银行保函来保障船东，交换卸货。但银行提供保函价值不菲[一般是金额的1%年费作为保费（bail fee），再加手续费]，所以，收货人不会甘心，正常情况下这本来是他的货，为何要他赔上可能是他所能赚取的利润去换取本来是他的货？所以，今天愈来愈多船东面对承租人（比如他也是FOB的买方）强迫在租约加一条条款去同意没有提单卸货，而且只能有承租人的保函，不能索取银行保函。要是船东拒绝，承租人会不去租进，令今天是承租人市场下出租船东往往被迫去让步。但如果承租人是皮包公司，这保函又得物无所用，这不是非法的问题，而是保人的信用不值保函的金额。这变得如果船东想赖掉，会可去利用这类别的非法制定令有关租约条款变为非法。这是，如果发货人通知船东，或船东咨询发货人，得知已结汇，提单正在转往收货人途中。这情况下，根本不必太担心。但如果发货人告诉船东提单仍在他手中，甚至指信用证无法结汇，因已过期或有不符点。这一来，表示货物主权仍属发货人。如果在知道的情况下，仍去把货物交给没有货物主权的收货人，是故意去做出侵权行为（deliberately commit a tort of conversion）。所以，这时船东会可去指这租约条款要船东必须无单放货是非法，是迫船东故意去侵权，因为明

知货权是在发货人手中。这样的判法已有一个伦敦裁决：The "Etalofos" (1995)。所以，对承租人/收货人来讲，如何能保证船东同意无单放货仍是一个昂贵的大问题。在我看来，除非电子提单全面去替代，这问题无法真正解决。但去全面替代到今天已有上百年采用的以上做法谈何容易。

对收货人而言，去抗拒船东的反悔，特别是要求退回货物，会在无法依赖曾有合约之余，依赖像"承诺性禁止翻供"（promissory estoppel）。即指船东同意了，即使合约不成立，也构成禁止翻供。这一点在本章§5段的（注）所提及的加拿大先例 Westwood Shipping Lines Inc. v. Ceo International Inc (1998) 150 FTR 125 有涉及，是在船东获得一个 Mareva 禁令防止皮鞋（货物）流失，并要求收货人退回后，收货人所提出的抗辩。加拿大法院判要成功依赖禁示翻供，必须有以下条件：

（ⅰ）an unambiguous promise intended to affect legal relationship between the promisor and promisee；

（ⅱ）intention that promisee should rely on the promise；

（ⅲ）a change in promisee's position because of reliance on the promise.

以上三个条件应是理所当然，毕竟禁止翻供是衡平法，追求公道/公平。首先，船东无单放货的承诺难以满足（ⅰ）的条件，因为船东是根据 Geo 的误述而作出承诺。再说（ⅲ）的条件，被承诺方的 Geo 能说它的地位因此承诺而改变，故允许反悔对它不公道吗？要知道，无单交货后 Geo 若去支付货款，不扯皮，因为货物也已到手，又何来卖方起诉船东，船东被迫要求退货？故 Geo 的地位有了改变，也是因它自己扯皮而起，它才是罪魁祸首，怎么可去依赖衡平法呢？显然，Geo 在该案例中败诉。换言之，船东可以及时去反悔，要求收货人退还货物或/与拒绝再卸货/交货。

5.8 无单放货的损失与保险的关系

这要分两方面来谈，先是船东，他/它的责任险一般是在互保协会投保。而针对无单交货，互保协会的立场十分明确，写明是不在承保范围以内，贵客（船东）自理。

另是提单持有人，他拥有的货物被无单放货，被他人侵占。这一来，他可去对付侵占方，例如是收货人或是船东，各种救济办法也在本章之 5.5.1 小段有谈及。但各种行动都有它的风险与麻烦。例如收货人是皮包公司或身处法律不明确/稳定国家。至于对付船东，采取扣船以取得适当管辖地点/法院与诉前保全，好是好，也是惯常做法，但也会有以下问题：

（ⅰ）5.6.1 小段的时效已过。

（ⅱ）5.6.4 小段的责任限制。

（ⅲ）最危险与可能的是船东赔不起，因此而倒闭，而货物索赔的赔偿顺序要后于银行抵押。

这一来,提单持有人,也是真正货主,会动脑筋去向货物保险人索赔。据说中国的法院(一宗在上海海事法院)已判过两次是要保"一切险"(all risks)的保险公司赔付。

无疑,如果整批货物被"盗窃"(theft)而在运输途中消失,这在一切险应是承保范围。即使犯法之人是船员或船东自己,也不例外。这一来,无单放货导致的消失,又有何实质分别呢? 当然,去把盗窃与无单放货区别开来并作不同处理,在本章之 5.6.2 小段提的 Motis Exports v. Dampskibsselskabet AF 1912 (1999) 1 Lloyd's Rep. 837 先例,Rix 大法官也有这样做。但毕竟感觉有一点牵强,只是非要去一刀切找出一条分水线罢了。

但在一切险的保险,英国是 A 条款(Institute Cargo Clause A),拒赔的举证责任是在保险公司头上。当然,如果提单持有人不隐瞒事实(也不容易做到),货物损失是因无单放货而非盗窃而导致的事实会是明确。否则,光是去调查并举证不是盗窃而是无单放货就会不易了。但事实明确了,仍有该不该赔的疑问。不妨先去看不属一切险的 B 与 C 条款,也会对这种风险去加保一种称为"Institute theft, pilferage and non delivery clause"的风险条款。

从这加保的用字,"non delivery"好像是包括了无单放货所导致的货物损失,属承保的风险。但已有先例否定,认为"non delivery"不是新的风险,而是与盗窃的风险同类。在 Forestal Land, Timber and Railways Co. Ltd. v. Rickards (1940) 4 All ER 96, Hillery 大法官在第 110 页说:"Where such words occur in such a context, the insured need not prove loss by theft or pilferage. It is enough if he proves non delivery and gives prima facie proof that the goods were not lost in any way other than by theft or pilferage."

但是否 A 条款的一切险仍会有不同解释,与 B 或 C 条款另去加保在本质上不同? 即使如此,因无单放货遭受损失,而在一切险下索赔仍会困难重重,争议多多,如:

(ⅰ)一切险保的是运输风险,无单放货一般是涉及买卖合约的争议,常是买方赖债扯皮,与运输无关。

(ⅱ)因果关系成疑,因为损失难说是因无单放货引起,而会是来自后来的变化导致卖方(提单持有人)收不到货款,如结不到汇。变了同一事实下,原来不是承保的,也不属"损失",却因后来非有关任何运输风险的"新事实"(intervening fact)而变为"损失"。

(ⅲ)短航次,石油运输,租约内有无单放货条款等事实都涉及无单放货,应在投保时尽"告知"(disclosure)责任。

(ⅳ)无单放货在一些运输已属正常做法:短航次,石油运输等。而"风险"是指"不该发生而发生了"。所以,会否不属风险,而"一切险"(all risks)毕竟仍需是风险才承保?

(ⅴ)其他方面例如被保险人(提单持有人)有否去尽义务减少/避免损失等:请参阅笔者与汪鹏南教授合著的《英国海上保险条款详论》一书之第 324 至 326 页。

5.9 无单放货的救星:电子提单

"电子提单"(electronic bill of lading)近年讲得很多,看来也确实只有它才能去根本解决这个无单放货的"死症",因为它:

(ⅰ)可去大大加快整个操作所需的时间。

(ⅱ)可让船东/承运人在交出货物前很容易查获谁是真正有权的收货人。

在技术上,这不应是个问题。困难是如何去建立一套可行,完善与能为广泛接受的国际游戏规则与做法,去替代一二百年的现有的一套纸面提单做法。

5.9.1 电子提单必须达致的条件

电子提单想去替代"纸面提单"(paper bill of lading),有一些条件必须达致;如:

5.9.1.1 条件之一:能去转让货物/财产

能够去转让货物的占有权与所有权,靠的是传统提单的物权凭证地位:请看本章之 1.1 小段和 2.3 小段等。而能有物权凭证的地位,靠的是习惯做法:请看本章之 2.2 小段。

这一来,电子提单若想享有同样的物权凭证地位,会是不易,因为:

(ⅰ)目前仍未起步,难有此习惯做法,更谈不上是有悠久历史了。

(ⅱ)法院会难以接受一份根本不是有形存在的电子提单(只是电子记录的一些资料)可以成为物权凭证。

(ⅲ)电子提单也难去背书、签字。照说,"电子识别"(electronic authentication)应比人手签字更可靠、更难冒充。

以上看来,只能是靠立法才能把电子提单提升至物权凭证的地位。

5.9.1.2 条件之二:能去转让运输合约

在本章之 3.5.4 小段,提到海运单已包括在 1992 年英国海上运输法,可让卖方把运输合约转让给海运单的收货人。

在本章之 3.7 小段,也同样提到多式联运提单/单证。但电子提单的地位又如何呢?只能说因时机仍未成熟,所以 1992 年英国海上运输法只去埋了一个伏线,留待将来英国政府在时机成熟时去订规则而不必另去立法,这可节录 1992 年立法之 Section 1(5)如下:

"The Secretary of State may by regulations make provision for the application of this Act to cases where a telecommunication system or any other information technology is used for effecting transactions corresponding to—

(a) the issue of a document to which this Act applies;

(b) the indorsement, delivery or other transfer of such a document; or

(c) the doing of anything else in relation to such a document."

5.9.1.3 条件之三:能起到文件证明的作用

众所周知一有了争议,而且是有关"事实"(matter of fact)的,判断/裁决就要靠证据了。而证据的类别中,近年看法是"文件证据"(documentary evidence)会优越于"口头证据"(oral evidence),也比较稳定。这方面在笔者的《国际商务仲裁》一书第十一章有详述,不去重复。

这一来,一涉及电子提单与相关文件,就存在如何去作为证据的做法以及证据的份量如何的问题了。在做法上,像涉及文件披露,都会存在一定困难。而更重要是电子提单可去随意删改而外人(除非是专家)无法知悉。

在国际商会文件的 452 号(1988 年)第 8 页提到这问题,说:

"Because of its physical characteristics, the traditional paper document is accepted as evidence. It is durable, and changes or additions will normally be clearly visible. The electronic document is quite different. It takes the form of a magnetic medium whose data content can be changed at any time. Changes or additions will not appear as such.

Computer records are subject to accidental corruption, a phenomenon almost unknown to paper based records, and are intrinsically more subject to deliberate alteration than are paper based records."

当然,这方面法律也在改变。例如香港在 2000 年 1 月 7 日立法的 Electronic Transactions Ordinance,内中就涉及电子记录/文件可作为证据,但仅局限于可靠的电脑等先决条件,这方面在笔者不日出版的《英美证据法》一书中有详论。

国际商会的"1987 年远距传送贸易数据交换行为统一规则"(The Uniform Rules of Conduct for Interchange of Trade Data by Teletransmission 或简称 U. N. C. I. D.)的第 10 条有一个"日志"(Trade Data Log)的做法,即是为去记录所有对电子文件的改动。但笔者不知实情如何,也是外行人,只断断续续地听闻反正是有不少地方在改变/改善。

5.9.1.4 条件之四:能提供大家任意使用

因为国际外贸与航运领域是什么人都可以进入,自由竞争的。所以,电子提单建立起来的一套做法与规则也必须是能广泛让有关人士适用。这一来会有一定矛盾,例如 1990 年的"国际海事委员会电子提单规则"(CMI Rules for Electronic Bills of Lading)就是完全公开的一套,任何人不必加入任何组织,只要有电话/电报通信,加上电脑与"解调器"(modem),大家联成网络,就已可操作。

但完全公开,问题会是像难以规范的地方,欺诈的机会也大大增加。

如果不是公开的一套,例如像 Bolero,则存在要有管理机构的费用,进而涉及要收集会员,会员给予会费,才能进行。但除非法律规定或是现实中非这样做不可,一般国际外贸与航运人士都不会有如此远见,肯去先掏钱参加 Bolero。这方面会在稍后之 5.9.4 小段再详述。

5.9.1.5 条件之五:防止或减少欺诈

固然,今天以纸面提单为中心的一套国际外贸与航运做法也面对大量欺诈。但去另建立一套做法与规则,至少在理论上应是可以防止或减少欺诈的,才值得支持。

比方在"国际海事委员会"(CMI)公开的一套做法,规则的第 8 条有一个"密匙"(private key)的做法,以识别电子提单持有人。但在公开的通信往来,容易被外人知悉。身为外人的骗子可假装是电子提单持有人将提单转售或质押给无辜第三方。除非,密钥能去"加密"(encryption)而有关人士又能去"解密"(decryption)。这便又有了它们在操作上的考虑。

5.9.1.6 条件之六:加快处理单证

电子提单当然应该是能加快处理与检查单证才有吸引力。但如果有关单证太多太乱(如 Bankers Trust Co v. State Bank of India(1991) 2 Lloyd's Rep. 443 的结汇涉及 967 张文件),则以电子或人手处理分别也不大。为了能去加快,单证的格式,内容等方面就要在一定程度上规范化。

5.9.2 1983 年的 Seadocs(Seaborne Trade Documentation System)经验

在 1983 年,美国大通银行(Chase Manhatten Bank)与国际独立油轮船东会(Intertanko)推出了一个 Seadocs 的计划。它主要是想对付油轮的无单放货问题,而做法上是既有纸面提单,又利用电子去加快整个转让过程。要提一提的是石油产品经常在海上运输途中买卖,几十次或上百次也有。其中的纸面提单将存放在 Seadocs 的伦敦中心,之后的货权转让以电子通信去处理。这可以大大节省时间,而任何有关人士仍可去安排检查正本的纸面提单。在交出货物时,船东/承运人一去问 Seadocs,也应该不会弄错。

但 Seadocs 还未起步就已胎死腹中。部分原因会是:

(i)由商业机构带头弄一套"不公开的机制/做法"(closed system),总免不了受其他人士/公司的猜疑。例如,其他银行(大通银行的竞争者)会怕商业机密外泄。

(ⅱ)时机,法律等未成熟。Seadocs做法在没有"实质去签字背书与交出提单"(physical indorsement and transfer)以及"处于静态的提单"(static bill)方面难被法院接受为物权凭证。当时实行的1855年提单法也不会适用,而这一来,就不存在运输合约与诉权转让给最后的买方,而Seadocs也没有针对这方面的解决办法。

(ⅲ)Seadocs的计划既有纸面提单的签发与存在,就免不了会有关方想去检查这份提单与相关单证。但安排上却并不方便甚至困难,正如Kathy Love女士在她的书《Seadocs: the Lessons Learned》所说:"A more serious problem, from the point of view of the banks, was that without physical presentation of the bill a bank would not be able to scrutinise the bill (and the documents associated with it, which could also be lodged in the Registry) for conformity with a letter of credit. In order to meet this objection the Registry, somewhat grudgingly, undertook to examine a bill, if requested to do so, to see whether it complied with particular requirements stated by the requesting party. It was hoped that this facility would also go some way towards satisfying the concerns of cargo buyers who, particularly in view of the frequency of fraudulent bills, often had careful inhouse programmes for scrutinising documents."

5.9.3 1990年的CMI model

在1990年,国际海事委员会(Committee of Maritime International或简称CMI)推出了电子提单规则(CMI Rules for Electronic Bills of Lading),规则在本书《附录十二》。它的主要做法是在第4条,即货物装了上船,船东/承运人根据发货人的指示,向约定的"电子地址"(electronic address)发出一份电子提单,内中有所有纸面提单的内容。这可说是好像传统的签发一式三份纸面提单的做法。除此外,船东/承运人另去给发货人一个"密匙"(private key),而这也只有他们两位知道。发货人以此密匙可去控制货物以及将来转让给第三者。做法上是规则的第7(b)条款,如下:
"A transfer of the Right of Control and Transfer shall be effected [146]: (ⅰ) by notification of the current Holder to the Carrier of its intention to transfer its Right of Control and Transfer to a proposed new Holder,[147] and (ⅱ) confirmation by the Carrier of such notification message,[148] where upon (ⅲ) the Carrier shall transmit the information as re-

---

[146] 去转让货权(货物控制权)的做法是。
[147] 先由当时的"电子提单持有人"(Holder),也就是拥有货权(密匙)的一方(最先的一位应就是发货人)通知船东/承运人他意图转让给谁。
[148] 船东/承运人确认知悉通知。

ferred to in article 4 (except for the Private Key) to the proposed new Holder[149], where after (ⅳ) the proposed new Holder shall advise the Carrier of its acceptance of the Right of Control and Transfer[150], whereupon (ⅴ) the Carrier shall cancel the current private Key and issue a new Private Key to the new Holder.[151]"

从以上简介粗略看来,整个规则及其操作并不困难,也十分"大众化",只要有关方均有办法去通信与在网上互联。但这套"公开的体系/机制(open system)使用的人并不多,也有很大缺点,部分也已提及,如:

(ⅰ)在5.9.1.4小段提到的难以规范,例如,每一位船东/承运人会去签发什么样的电子提单?不合作怎样办?等等。

(ⅱ)整个体系放了太多责任在船东/承运人头上。后者其实根本不必去理会货物每一次的转售,他/它只要在卸港交出货物时,知道谁是有货权,能去控制货物的一方即可。

(ⅲ)在5.9.1.5小段提到欺诈的危险以及公开的机制难去保密。

(ⅳ)以纸面提单能去做到一手交单,一手交钱,对买卖双方(也包括银行)均有保障,而在这CMI规则下会有不明确,因为涉及通知船东/承运人与处理(例如给予新的密钥)的时间。

(ⅴ)在5.9.2小段提到的时机,法律等仍未成熟。例如一些港口当局海关仍坚持要纸面提单或付本;世界上有的地区太落后,电脑并不配套;等等数不尽的问题。

5.9.4 1999年的Bolero

由SWIFT(环球银行财务电信)与TT Club(多式联运互保协会)等合资组成的Bolero国际有限公司,在1999年9月27号推出了Bolero的一套规则与做法。它与CMI规则不同之处是它并不公开,属"不公开的一套系统/机制"(closed system)。去参与的人士/公司,都必须加入为Bolero Association的会员,并缴纳会费。成了会

---

[149] 并直接告知意图转让与的人士(新的受让人)所有在第4条有关的电子提单的内容(货物,数量,标记,装卸港,等等)。除了当时拥有货权一方的密钥不能去披露,毕竟转让仍未成事,披露了会被冒名欺诈。

[150] 如果新的受让人接受转让/转售,他应直接通知船东/承运人。在CMI规则之第4(c)条款,也说明新的受让人可去拒绝(这应是理所当然)或如果过了合理时间仍无消息/确认接受,船东/承运人均去当做什么也没有发生,货权仍在当时拥有密匙一方,可作另一次的转让/转售。

[151] 但要是新的受让人接受了,转让/转售成功,则船东/承运人会去取消原有的密匙,另去给受让人一个新的密匙,而受让人也可以此有了货权(控制货物),变为"电子提单新持有人"(new Holder),并有权另去转让/转售或提取货物(在EMI规则第7(a)条款)。估计如涉及银行与信用证,也是以同样做法令银行成为"new Holder"。

员,会发给一本会员手册(rule book),也就是 Bolero 的规则与做法。据知,近日中远与台湾的长荣都先后加入成了会员。

据知 Bolero 通过一套称为"Core Messaging Platform"的机制,会是能去提供通信高度可靠的保安保密。通过电子签字与加密等做法,外人进不来。

它的电子提单称为"Bolero 提单",而 Bolero 提供了一个"注册中心"(registry)去记录每次的转让/买卖或/与质押。这记录会作为证据保存若干年,以防将来有任何争议。重要的是:船东/承运人不必去理会船上货物每次的转让,只要在卸港交货前,向 Bolero 一查就能马上知道交货给谁或只去听谁的指示就是准确交货了。

人为的制度总会有疏忽错漏的危险。故此,Bolero 也去投保了责任保险并规定每次事故(如失去或延误电子通信)赔 10 万美元。

Bolero 面对的困难是:

(ⅰ)如何去扩展业务,吸收会员。毕竟不是太多人愿意去支付一笔会员费。而在外贸与航运的整个过程,只要有一位不参与,操作即有困难。

(ⅱ)国际上的法律仍未跟上,主要是对电子提单的承认。毕竟,连英国的 1992 年海上运输法也只是去埋了伏线:请看 5.9.1.2 小段。

(ⅲ)Bolero 不享有任何法律地位,没有专利/专营权,将来难保有各种竞争。

(ⅳ)如何去耐心地改变这几百年来的习惯做法呢? 毕竟,要去改变一个成年人的想法(在任何方面)都会是最困难的事。

5.10 有关无单放货的其他问题

这方面要去探讨仍有课题可讲下去,笔者在结束本章前,只去挑两个不同课题探讨,是以下段节:

5.10.1 无单放货的中国判例

无单放货的争议在各国均不少,据知中国法院也判了不少这方面的案件。听说近期一宗是以卖方(正本提单仍在他手中)与买方接触为由,判这行为构成"追认"或"弃权/禁示翻供"从而令卖方失去了就无单放货向船东/承运人索赔的权力。笔者不知道中国法律对这些说法的权威定义与准则,但在英美法,它们是十分清楚的。首先是"追认"(ratification),这方面在《国际商务游戏规则——英国合约法》一书第四章之 6.4 小段有详述。这是涉及有否授权的课题,与无单放货的违约是两码事。故就英美法而言,"追认"说法在无单放货的争议是套不上的。

至于"弃权/禁止翻供"的说法也在《国际商务游戏规则——英国合约法》一书第十一章有详论。它有好几个准则/条件,符合了才能成立。例如它是衡平法,故必须公平合理。它必须要对违约方有"诱导"(inducement)的行为,令对方(违约方)

"误以为"他(原告)放弃或不再坚持合约权利,可放胆去违约。此外,违约方要有"损害性依赖"(detrimental reliance)。

这一切表示"弃权/禁止翻供"行为必须发生在违约前,否则根本说不通。例如,违约方放胆违约是因为他"预期"受害方将来会有"诱导行为"? 故此,在无单放货前若发货人去协助/参与无单放货,则事后翻脸不认人去控告船东,这是典型的"弃权/禁止翻供"。但发货人在无单放货后的所作所为就很难被认为是"弃权/禁止翻供"。

或许有人会说,这"弃权/禁止翻供"不是针对无单放货,而是针对仍未开始或推进的向船东/承运人索赔的无单放货的损失。即是,放弃索赔权利。但这一来讲不通的地方同样十分多,而且是根本的,具体如下:

(i) 原告的发货人是与买方接触,非是与船东/承运人接触,对后者何来"诱导"行为或言论?

(ii) 船东/承运人即使能说明/证明发货人曾有过"诱导"言行,具体是什么,也难去进一步证明有何"损害性依赖"。这会是,若非发货人的诱导言行,船东根本不会这样做,或这样去违约。难道是,船东/承运人本已备妥一笔钱赔偿无单放货的损失,但因发货人的"诱导"言行而去把这笔钱花光了,再也没有钱可赔? 但要知道,这话也不是空口说说,而是要去证明。所以,笔者难以想象对船东/承运人有任何"损害性依赖"。

(iii) "弃权/禁止翻供"是衡平法理论,一切以公平合理为最高原则。故此像这种案情,卖方先去接触买方,寄望后者提取了货物(无单放货),也应去支付货款,支付后一切问题就解决了,万事皆休,这完全可以理解,也是值得支持的做法。笔者想不通为何要以法律去对付/禁止这完全公平合理、符合商业习惯的做法,指发货人这样做是在"背后"诱导了船东/承运人,令他/它遭受"损害性依赖",所以构成"弃权/禁止翻供",再也不能向船东/承运人索赔。这是迫发货人今后休想以和平的商业做法去解决问题,而非要动不动马上告船抓船不可,免得一与买方接触(或任何其他人一接触),即被船东/承运人指是"背后"弃了权或禁止翻供。

(iv) 从另一角度看公平合理以适用衡平法理论,会是:船东/承运人违了约,无单放货,后果严重。有什么天大的"公平合理"的理由要让他/它去以"弃权/禁止翻供"脱罪? 为何发货人一去接触买方,让船东脱罪就会变得是"公平合理"了,好像中了彩票头奖?

(v) 无单放货只是违约中的一种,而法律原则上应一视同仁地运用/适用,否则会令人无所适从,也令法律失去肯定性。所以,是否所有其他违约如货损货差,倒签提单等,也是同样对待。即是,发货人接触了买方就构成对船东"弃权/禁止翻供",而接触了船东就对买方构成"弃权/禁止翻供"? 若这是正确解释,不单说这与英美法和国际上的理解很不一样。而且，疑问仍不断有，如，发货人同时与买方及船东接触/谈判呢？或是，与买方接触但同时电传了船东说明保留索赔无单放货损失的权利？又或是，发货人先接触了船东但没有结果（例如船舶突然沉没），再去找买方，买方也以同样道理去抗拒？虽然，是买方提走了货物但不付钱，难道中国法律要对此行为支持吗？

要知道，"弃权/禁止翻供"理论今天在不少国际公约也有体现，据笔者所知解释上是与英美法一致。所以中国的法律若去下新定义，新解释，会令下一代的中国年轻人在国际上格格不入，与外国人无法沟通。要去这样做在没有重大的理由下，应该避免。

总之，这中国案例的判决在笔者看来与国际做法不一样，无助于提高/保护提单的信誉与可信性，并且也有违对船东/承运人无单放货行为绝不鼓励的精神。

另笔者在一份律师所报道中看到新加坡也有一案例 The "Timur Gueen"（2000），是判收货人迟迟不来提取货物，货物也将被拍卖，则承运人身份变了是"不情愿托管人"（involuntary bailee），责任可以降低，包括在无单放货方面。

5.10.2　班轮提单加上针对无单放货的印就条款

较早之 5.6.2 小段举了不少订得不错的免责条款，但"道高一尺，魔高一丈"，笔者已知有班轮公司在他们的班轮提单中多加一条条款去明示针对无单放货，例如是在 Motis Exports v. Dampskibsselskabet AF 1912（1999）1 Lloyd's Rep. 837 先例吃了大亏的马斯基公司。已在 5.6.2 小段略及，海牙规则不针对"交货"（delivery），所以班轮公司有完全的订约自由。唯一重要局限的是"相悖理论"，因为提单合约的主要目标和主旨之一是去准确交货，所以合约整体解释起来，不可能双方再去同意一条条款让船东/承运人可去随意乱交货而无须承担责任，进而彻底破坏提单合约的主旨。

为此，该条款会要明示针对"误交货"（misdelivery）与/或"不交货"（non-delivery），以免将来法院指不够明确。另外，会讲明除非证明是船东/承运人的"故意不良行为"（wilful misconduct），否则不必对其他原因导致的误交货/不交货负责，以显示合理性与并非全盘否定合约的主旨。要是这种条款能在法院过关，将会令班轮公司对无单放货的责任大减，因为货方要证明"故意不良行为"可不容易，这方面在笔者的《海事法》一书第二章之 4.4.2/4.4.3 小段有谈及。

5.10.3　多式联运与无单放货

这方面已在本章之 §5 段一开始的注脚中介绍了有关案例，如 Westwood Shipping Lines Inc. v. Geo International Inc.（1998）150 FTR 125。可见，无单放货也经常

发生在多式联运的运输中。此处再举一例,最近在香港法院判的 The"Brij"一案(见 2.2001 Johnson Stokes & Master 刊物"Focus"的报道)。它涉及货方告船东无单放货,但该票货物原与一位货代(NVOC)订约,货代作为承运人在收取货物后也签发了一份多式联运提单,并且注明"to order",为不记名提单。仅此措辞能否令其成为"物权凭证"(document of title)呢?本章之 2.4 小段有探讨,不再重复。该单证亦非"装船提单"(shipped bills of lading),很难肯定是一份物权凭证(见本章之 3.4.1.4 小段)。但香港已成立了类似英国 1992 年的"海上运输法"(Carriage of Goods by Sea Act, 1992),这可让立法扩大包括多式联运提单,而且立法将该运输合约在较大程度上扩大了转让的对象/人士(见本书第三章之 12.2.5 小段)。其后果在许多情况下令双方(收货人与多式联运承运人)有赖不掉的合约关系,而合约有明示或默示的责任要求准确交货,否则属违约,须作出赔偿。而多式联运提单注明"to order",就是一条明示条款。有了这样的肯定的运输合约关系,就不必再斤斤计较有否"物权凭证"了。还回到香港的先例:作为承运人的货代事后找到"Brij"一船付运。照说,这是本章 3.7 小段中所讲是"分包"(sub-contract)那一种情况。但"Brij"船东也签发了一份"to order"的海运提单。"估计"(详情不知,因报道很短)提单发货人应是货代(NVOC),提单收货人也应是货代的代理人。可以说若在正常的操作下,货代(NVOC)应在卸货港从"Brij"提取货物后再运送至目的地交给收货人(持有正本多式联运提单与 to order 的一方),但该案例报道说货物没有交给收货人(不知为何原因是否货代倒闭了?)。然而收货人不起诉作为合约一方的货代(NVOC),却起诉船东("Brij"的船东)无单放货。从短短的报道中,笔者没有看明白收货人依据什么起诉的船东。该运输合约关系是收货人与货代通过信用证结汇的多式联运提单;而海运提单被货代放置一旁好几个月,不应在收货人手中,与收货人也没有关系。至于侵权,"Brij"的船东在装港从货代手中收取货物后,又在卸港交还给货代,也是再正常不过的"分包"。"Brij"的船东与/或货代所做错的,就是不应签发一份不记名(to order)的海运提单,导致混乱,好像同一票货物出了两套提单一样(请看本章 3.4.3 小段的 The"Lycaon"(1983) 2 Lloyd's Rep. 548)。何不出一份海运单(sea waybill)呢?最终,香港法院判是收货人告船东无单放货败诉。从表面看,这应是正确的。

第三章　提单作用之二：
运输合约·谁是其中的合约方

§1　提单的合约方为何混乱

任何合约,照说谁是订约方都不应有任何混淆。任何头脑清醒的人都不会在还未清楚对方是谁的情况下贸然同意与他/它订立一个可能是昂贵的合约。毕竟,这不是盲婚哑嫁的年代。

但现实中也经常发生有关合约订约方到底是谁的争议,特别是涉及中国贸易。毛病常出在订约方自己乱来,或不知道如何去区分,或不知道后果的严重。例如,笔者近日知悉一宗事件,涉及中国一家照说很有经验的公司。它原是经纪人,但订约时中方当事人有异议,该公司竟以自己名义顶上为当事人。外国公司也不在乎,因为它更有财力,将来索赔损失更为容易,后来也确是如此。但整个合约(是租约)就很可笑,很矛盾,租约在当事人一栏订明是该公司,另在经纪人一栏与赚取佣金又是该公司。

这方面问题,任何的合约都会发生,已在笔者的《国际商务游戏规则——英国合约法》一书之第四章 6.5.1 小段至 6.5.4 小段有详及,可节录如下:

6.5.1　如何解释合约去确定身份:代理人或是订约方?

如果,代理人在一个租约下一贯的自称是承租人,签字也是以承租人的称谓去签(这只是一种表现,因为签字只是例行手续),那么这代理人就要负起承租人的责任去履约。即使对方船东会知悉背后另有人,但解释起来仍只是看双方同意的合约,而不是非正式的以往意向。况且,船东虽然知道仍可能不愿意与背后的人士订约。

在这方面,Halsbury's Laws of England,第 4 版 Vol. 1,854 段是抄了 Brandon 大法官在 The "Swan" (1968) 1 Lloyd's Rep. 5 的话,作为如何去解释一个合约以找出正确身份的指引,具体如下:

"*Prima facie* a party is personally liable on a contract if he puts his unqualified signature to it. In order, therefore, to exonerate the agent from liability, the contract must show, when construed as a whole, that he contracted as agent only, and did not undertake any personal liability. It is not sufficient that he should have described himself in the contract as an agent for the contract if the surrounding circumstances may indicate that he is liable. If he states in the contract, or indicates by an addition to his signature, that he is contracting as agent only on behalf of a principal, he is not liable, unless the rest of the contract clearly involves his personal liability, or unless he is shown to be the real principal."

这既是公道,也是大原则,解释合约本来就应整体去看,客观找出订约方的意向。举一个简单的例子,A 在租约内签字一栏是写为承租人代理(as agent),但在许多其他条款都说他要负责,如装货后 3 天 A 要付运费给船东,船长每 3 天要向 A 报告船舶位置,滞期费在卸货后 30 天船东与 A 结账。而且租约说明没有经纪参与,不必付佣金。这一来,你说总的印象会是 A 只是代理人或是承租人?看来应是后者更像。而且租约可以有一个以上承租人,所以稍有疑问,大可以说 A 与租约写明是承租人的另一家公司是共同承租人。

6.5.2 合约说明是代理人仍被判作为订约方的先例

去举两个相似的先例,都是租船业务,而且都涉及一著名粮商 Tradax,可更好表达这方面的精神。它们是 The "Virgo" (1976) 2 Lloyd's Rep. 135 与 The "Sun Happiness" (1984) 1 Lloyd's Rep. 381。在这两个先例,都是船东向 Tradax (承租人)索赔大笔滞期费时,Tradax 以自己只是代理人来抗辩,称承租人实是埃及的公司,船东应向埃及公司追偿。但两次 Tradax 都败诉要负责赔偿滞期费。

在两个租约,都有条款说明:

—— The "Virgo" 有 31 条款为:"This vessel was chartered on behalf and for account of General Organization for Supply Goods Cairo."

—— The "Sun Happiness" 有 36 条款为:"This Charter Party contract is signed for and on behalf of the receivers, General Authority for Supply Commodities Cairo."

但法院很重视其他租约条款,也拿来一起解释,如在 The "Virgo" 有:

(i)在租约一开头是说:"It is this day mutually agreed, between (船东名字) Owners of the Panamanian S. S. "Virgo"…and Tradax Export, S. A., Charterers, that…"

(ii)签字是:"Greenwich Marine, Incorporated, as Agents for: Tradax Export S. A."

(iii)有附件说:"It is mutually agreed that Charterers are to be ultimately responsible for demurrage payments. Very truly yours, Greenwich Marine Incorporated."

(iv) 其他方面。

可以看到,租约有一处是写明 Tradax 是承租人(Charterers), Tradax 是完全知道的,他如何能自圆其说去免掉合约责任呢?

再多举一先例是 The "Scaplake" (1978) 2 Lloyd's Rep. 380,它是一个运载木材的租约,使用的是金康程租格式,在第4栏(box 4)的承租人写明是一家 CDM 的塞浦路斯公司,是一家皮包公司。船东也不是傻瓜,所以租约内有一条29条款如下:"Freight and demurrage will be guaranteed by actual Charterers Messrs. Dritsa & Kaglis Bros. Ltd... or personally by their director"。要注意的是这条款指 Dirtsa & Kaglis 是"真正承租人"(actual Charterers),而不光是付运费及滞期费的担保人(guarantor)。它是一家比 CDM 有经济实力的公司。另外,要注意这条款只局限在担保运费及滞期费,而非是所有方面的履约责任(performance guarantee)。在这租约,承租人签字的是 CDM,但租约(金康格式)反面及附页第四面,与附件(addendum)第2页,Dritsa & Kaglis 也有加签。

船在卸港搁浅受损,修理费超越20万美元。船东向 CDM 追讨没有意义,转向 Dritsa & Kaglis,并开始向它仲裁。后者争辩它不是承租人,CDM 才是,它也没有对这种损坏责任作出担保,但法院判根据这租约的写法与签字,它与 CDM 同属共同承租人。

6.5.3 委托人被命名或未命名(named or unnamed principal)

合约如有命名谁是委托人,谁就是订约方,这应是最明确的。只要合约其他条款也是一致没有任何矛盾的,则代理人的地位不容置疑。但如果合约内不去命名,而其他条款上、签字上,又明确表达了双方是了解有一个未命名的委托人存在,签约或订约的一方仅被接受为代理人而已,这会是未命名委托人(unnamed principal)的情况。要注意的是:这不是6.5.1小段的对方知道代理人背后会有人,这里的情况是合约的用字表达出其中的订约一方只是代理人,只是未命名谁是委托人而已。这一来,代理人仍可以代理人身份不必去负责履约或承担责任。这在2.12小段提到的 The "Santa Carina" (1977) 1 Lloyd's Rep. 478,是同一精神。

二手船舶买卖也常见这种情况,一家大船公司说明他只是代理来订约买船,另有一未命名委托人存在,而且其他条款也与他这地位没有矛盾。租约也会有,我见过两次是租约由头至尾都说明"马士基作为代理"。租约另一方以为与马士基订约,其实不是。这种情况一般会有危险,因为你等于跟不知名的一方订约。将来出事或市场逆转,突然钻出来一家巴拿马皮包公司说他才是未命名的委托人,你就惨了。

6.5.4 从未透露委托人(undisclosed principal)

这种情况是双方订约时合约文字上显示不知道另有委托人存在,或会是,像6.5.1小段所述那样代理人以自己名义订约。这一来,这代理人要对合约负责:Sims v. Bond (1833) 5 B & Ad. 389,393。但在这种情况下,英国法律仍允许有一些例外。这是:

(ⅰ)在3.10小段谈到的合约"相互关系"的例外之一,即允许代理人去为第三者(未透露的委托人)向对方订约方追偿实际损失。

(ⅱ)未透露的委托人可以出面以自己名义起诉对方订约方,或被对方控告。道理在什么地方看来有点争议。说这是因为合约实际是他与对方所订,则与代理人也要对合约负责的原则有矛盾。看来,还是像Treitel的《Law of Contract》在第8版631页所说:"未透露的委托人的权力是一个合约'相互关系'概念的例外,是一个独立权力,因为商业方便而设立"(His right is an independent right which constitutes an exception to the doctrine of privity, established in the interests of commercial convenience)。它也举了如The"Havprins" (1983) 2 Lloyd's Rep. 356的案例。

在(ⅱ)的例外会对合约的另一方不公平,因为他一直以为是与代理人打交道,订约。他也会面对未透露的委托人以及他的代理人分别的起诉。所以,法律会限制未透露的委托人的情况,尤其是在另一订约方能证明仅仅想与代理人打交道的所谓有个人考虑(personal consideration)的情况,等等。

但有些情况下仍须去允许这(ⅱ)的例外,如委托人本是要求代理人与第三者订约时命名出委托人,但代理人没有这样做,甚至不安好心,想把第三者要付的一笔钱吃掉。这令委托人要以未透露的委托人身份插手进来,以自己的名义起诉作为第三者的合约另一方以取得这笔钱。例如,原船东出租船舶,委托经纪人。但经纪人看见有差价可赚,不以原船东名义与承租人订约,而用上自己名义,但他实际只是代理人。

提单合约本来应是千万种商业合约中的一种,一方是"承运人"(carrier),另一方是"托运人"也通常是"发货人"(shipper)。既然是合约,则合约的基本要求也必须符合。在笔者的《国际商务游戏规则——英国合约法》一书第二章之1.2小段,也列明了有三个基本要求。一是对价或约因(consideration),二是双方同意每一条他们想同意的条款/条件(agreement on all terms),三是双方意图去订立有效合约(intention to create contract)。

特别在第三个基本要求下,可以看到合约关系完全出于自愿,合约当事一方在自己不情愿下被迫订了合约也往往可去以胁迫(duress)、误述(misrepresentation)等违反公共政策的理由去推翻该合约。

1.1 谁是承运人或托运人纯是出于自愿

故此,在提单合约下,谁是承运人就完全出于自愿了。这正是1924年海牙规则的界定,"与托运人订有运输合约的船东或承租人"。这也是英美及许多海运大国的立法与看法。这一来,不能去简单地说提单的承运人一定是原船东。可能会是,一著名班轮公司只是承租了一艘船舶(即它不是船东),然后投入自己名下营运。而托运人完全是在你情我愿的情况下,去与班轮公司订下运输合约,托运人根本无意去与船东订约。而班轮公司亦与该托运人有多年交往,一直以来运输的船舶是班轮公司自己拥有的(只是这一航次碰巧使用承租船舶),情愿自己做承运人。这一来,怎能去说原船东是承运人,是提单合约的一方呢?

在多式联运有一种"NVOC 提单",由"无船承运人"(Non-Vessel Operation Carrier 简称 NVOC)签发,也是一样道理。既然是"无船",表示承运人不是船东,他/它一般是由货代(Freight forwarder)的身份转过来。但反正是他/它愿意充当承运人,而托运人愿意让他/它运输,进而订立运输合约,以"NVOC 提单"为证,这又有什么不妥呢?

不幸的是:现实中提单的合约方经常有混乱。特别是,搞不清谁是承运人。

造成这种现象,可以是与其他合约出现这种问题一样。即订约方自己乱来,或不知道如何区分,或不警觉,或漠不关心。就好像结了婚仍不知道爱人的名字,或与媒人混淆。在多式联运经常发生的争议是:去向货代索赔时他/它以自己只是代理人来抗辩。实际会是在订约时,托运人根本未去问清楚货代是以代理人身份还是承运人身份来订运输合约? 反正是,双方草草商量了就开始运输。事后有了争议,才被迫要去把身份弄清楚。

但提单合约还会有其他的因素导致混乱,这是其他合约不会有的,具体如下:

1.2 提单比其他合约混乱的原因之一:合约转让

通过提单法(以前的1855年提单法与当今的1992年英国海上运输法),提单合约可以转让给收货人(买方),并强制地把收货人与承运人扯上一个合约关系。这方面在本章之§12段详及。

总之,像这种立法的情况十分罕有,因为普通法下合约的基本要求之一就是订约方自愿。而现实中的争议,又往往发生在收货人(买方,提单持有人)与承运人之间。特别是,收货人面对货损货差要向承运人索赔。这一来,他会面对更大的困扰与无法知情。因为原来的订约方(托运人)不是他,这正是 CIF 买卖一贯的做法。若他真是原订约方,总会了解得多一点,即使有混乱也较易去对付。

1.3 提单比其他合约混乱的原因之二:谈判中的证据

其他合约一涉及这方面的争议,经常会有一种称为"谈判中的证据"(parol evidence)的问题。这种证据一般在解释合约条款的争议中是不准加以考虑,不被接受的。这可去节录《国际商务游戏规则——英国合约法》一书第十章之 2.2 小段所说:

一般合约是不必双方签字的,口头的协议也是完全有效的,只是证明困难而已。但一个合约一经双方签字,在解释它的条款时后果就会相当不同。一份合约一经成立,除非出现法律规定的某些可能导致合约或其条款被废止或修正的情况,一般是涉及公共政策的诸如胁迫(duress)、误述(misrepresentation)及错误(mistake)等,合约的条款、文字对订约双方往往就是终局的。在解释合约时与已订条款、文字不符合的东西法院均不予采纳,即使是合约谈判过程中的有关文件、证据甚至合约草案,若与已签订完的合约不符,亦不能作为有效证据影响合约的解释。法官、仲裁员还是只能依照合约所订的文字本身去寻找订约双方的意愿。而不会考虑双方在谈判过程中是怎么讲的,来往文件是怎样写的,这在法律上叫"parol evidence rule"(谈判中证据的准则)。

该书接下去在 2.3 小段说:

"不过,作为 parol evidence,也有好几种例外的情况可以被法院采纳,一是经纪人或代理人所代表的委托人未经披露(undisclosed principal)或任何对谁才是真正订约方,委托人有纠纷的情况:Fung Ping Shan v. Tong Shun (1918) A. C. 403。"

换言之,在提单合约如果有这种争议,例如被告的承运人自辩不是承运人,并去提出谈判中的证据,例如订舱时已向发货人/托运人说明并获接受,这将令原告的收货人十分被动,无法去反证,因为实际上他根本没有参与订约的谈判。代表货方的是发货人(卖方)而不是收货人(买方),而去向外国卖方请求协助举证常会是不可能的事。

有一点要明确的是运输合约的谈判是早在订舱(booking)时: The "Uhenbels" (1986) 2 Lloyd's Rep. 294; The "Jalamohan" (1988) 1 Lloyd's Rep. 443,等先例。但立法把运输合约转让给收货人的不是订舱合约(booking contract)而只是提单合约。故此,订舱时的谈判,对收货人无关。正如 Leggatt 大法官在 The "Rewia" (1991) 2 Lloyd's Rep. 325 之第 333 页说:"As Mr. Gaisman(船东大律师)forcefully points out, the original plaintiffs in this action were consignees of the goods who could only have title as assignees of the bills of lading, and not by way of an assignment of an oral booking contract. What are sued on are the contracts contained in or evidenced by the bills of lading… the Court would therefore derive no assistance from a factual inquiry into the circumstances in which the booking contract was made."

这方面难处 Rix 大法官在 The "Hector" (1998) 2 Lloyd's Rep. 287 也谈到:"It is uncertain to me on the authorities whether the question of whether a bill of lading is an owner's or a charterer's bill is a pure question of construction, or depends on all the circumstances of the case… It is further complicated, it seems to me, where the question is concerned with a negotiable document like a bill of lading. Such documents are replied on by third parties, far removed from the original circumstances of the bill's creation. That should mean that the rule should either be a matter of construction in its purest form, to be decided on the face (the two faces) of the bill itself, or that the position may well be different depending on whether the issue is joined between immediate parties to the creation of the bill or after negotiation to a third party."

综上所述,现实中针对提单合约这种争议,英国法院一般只能去客观解释提单合约的措辞/内容,而不另去接受其他证据。这在一定程度看来,可令争议稍为简化。正如 Colman 大法官在 The "Starsin" (2000) 1 Lloyd's Rep. 85 所说:"As a matter of basic principle the resolution of the issue of the identity of the party undertaking the obligations of carriage is one of construction of the words on the bill of lading."

1.4 提单比其他合约混乱的原因之三:常有矛盾/隐晦内容,不易解释

可惜的是,提单措辞/内容常有矛盾、遗漏、隐蔽之处,造成不易解释。其原因可以班轮提单为例,会是:

(ⅰ)历史原因,例如是"光船条款"(demise clause),这方面后详。

(ⅱ)班轮公司能一面倒的去订立条款,不存在发货人有真正机会就运输合约的内容进行谈判。若真能不这样做,多少总会有改进,会澄清。目前则是任由班轮公司有意无意的去订立与加减条款,故弄玄虚。随便去拣一个例子,在 The "Venezuela" (1980) 1 Lloyd's Rep. 393,由班轮公司自己一手拟定的提单条款十分混乱,被 Sheen 大法官批评说:"The question is whether, as between the shipper and CAVN, the contract of carriage made CAVN or the shipowner liable as the carrier. To answer this question I must look at all the terms of the bill of lading and construe the document as a whole. It was printed in Japan and appears to have been drafted by someone whose command of the English language is faulty."

而该提单的抬头印上两家公司,一是 CAVN(Compania Anonima Venezolana de

Navegacion），另一是 FMG（Flota Mercante Grancolombiana S. A.），这两家南美国家船公司合作行走一班轮航线，是日本去南美。该提单并没有像光船条款的条款，但却有一条"承运人定义"（definition of carrier），措辞是："Carrier is either the Compania Anonima Venezolana de Navegacion or the Flota Mercante Grancolombiana S. A. depending on whichever of the two is operating the vessel carrying the goods covered by this Bill of Lading."

而该出事的航次，真正承运的船舶"Samjohn Govenor"是期租进来，它的船东是一家巴拿马单船公司。但这一来，提单上就含糊不清地有了三个潜在的承运人：CAVN，FMG 与巴拿马船东。

（iii）航运本身有多元化的做法，导致常会有多于一家公司是承运人。例如，班轮公司是通过皮包公司拥有船舶，然后去光租回来以供营运。去光租而不去期租可避免另要成立管理公司去处理期租中分摊给名义船东的部分工作。或是，船舶是向外人光租或期租进来的。

这一来，任由班轮公司决定提单条款，例如加上一条光船条款，再在每一航次任意派不同背景的船舶，难免"承运人"会一会儿是班轮公司自己，一会儿是皮包公司的船东，再一会儿是从外面租进来船的船东。对航运没有足够了解的托运人，也无法从一个船名可去追查谁是船东，身处何地。而一直作为对手的班轮公司，最终只会是代理人，不是承运人。可以说，托运人也会感到无所适从，更不用说只持有一份提单的收货人。这变化多端的做法早在 Paterson Zochonis & Co. v. Elder Dempster & Co. (1922) 12 Lloyd's Rep. 69 案例，Rowlatt 大法官有提到说："...This is a case where a well-known line of ships found it necessary to supplement its fleet by getting in another upon a time charter; and people in the commercial world who use the line know nothing at all about that. They think they are shipping by this line; and unless it is clear to the contrary the contract should be regarded as being made with the line. In this case the mate's receipt – as the bill of lading itself which goes just as far – it is the more material document – proclaims to the people who took the bill of lading that those who are going to carry the goods are the African Steamship Co…"

§2 对象要找对的重要性：谁是承运人？

这是很简单的道理：合约出了事，双方就要找谁负责了，找的也就是合约的对方当事人。涉及提单合约，意味着有了货损货差，收货人也要找谁是承运人了。

在笔者的《国际货物买卖》一书，第六章之 6.3.1 小段详述找对对象的重要性如下：

6.3.1 对象要找对的重要性

这方面的重要性在于:

(i)不浪费律师费用——今天律师费用高昂,如果处理不当,找错对象索赔,会是严重劳民伤财。

(ii)诉前保全——今天去取得诉前保全会十分关键。船舶会是一船公司,卖方会是皮包或经济不稳定的公司。这涉及要尽快去扣船或申请禁令,以求取得诉前保全。有了它,可安心打官司外,不必怕胜诉也是空高兴,还会迫对方不会在诉讼途中使用拖延手法,也大大增加了庭外和解的可能性。

(iii)保险要求——货物保险(包括一切险)的保单中一般有条款要求买方及时采取适当行动保护保险公司的代位求偿权,否则遭受损失可向买方反索赔。这在笔者的《英国海上保险条款详论》一书 324 至 327 页提及,不去重复。所以正确索赔对象如果是船舶,也表示买方应采取适当行动向船东起诉,取得诉前保全等。

(iv)其他相关行动——对象找对了,可能要马上采取一些紧急的措施,例如去保留证据。对象是船舶,买方会要考虑在它开航前向当地法院申请上船检查,以确定它是否适航/适货。这会比将来诉讼只去靠凭空争论、臆猜、船东单方面递交的证据(会是一面倒对己方有利)等,优越得多了。一经上船检查,明确了舱盖多处漏水腐蚀,有了录像或照片,而货损又是因为海水所造成的,那么在这种情况下,船东马上就会投降赔钱,官司根本不必继续下去。

其他保留证据的行动会是如:申请上船把航海日志复印一套,例如若涉及倒签提单,即可显示装货日期与提单日期不符。

其他相关行动也包括了在法院/法律以外的多方面,例如货损货差装船前已存在,则正确索赔对象应是卖方而不是船东。这一来,会涉及买方要否去"拒绝接受"(rejection)货物。这方面问题在本书第四章有详论,不再去重复。

而如果正确索赔对象是船东,不是卖方,则在卸货时发觉货损货差就拒绝接受货物会是十分错误的决定。这是因为在货物买卖,会有几项在 1979 货物销售法规定的默示条件,例如是货物符合描述,要求是"商售质量"或"满意质量",等等。而卖方违反了这些条件,买方可去中断合约,拒绝接受货物。但货物销售法并不适用在提单或租约,而适用在提单的立法如海牙规则或中国海商法并没有同样的默示条件去让买方在货不对板时把货物"退回"给船东(即拒绝接受),而货物及风险自此归船东。提单或租约也不见得会有明示的条件可去达致这种讲不通的后果,因为即使是船舶不适航导致货损货差,不适航也只是"中间条款",并非是可去允许中断合约的"条件条款": The "Hong Kong Fir" (1961) 2 Lloyd's Rep. 478。所以,买方碰到货损货差就不分皂白地拒绝接受,会是小事变大事,导致货物全损。这种错误行为的例子已在本章6.1小段有所介绍。

（Ⅴ）时效——这又是重要的环节,因为针对不同的索赔对象,面对的时效会不同。在笔者的《国际商务仲裁》一书282至286页提到时效的四大种类。一是来自英国法律的6年时效针对一般合约如买卖合约;二是来自其他国家适用法的法律;三是合约内规定一个时效必须开始仲裁或起诉;四是合约内规定一个时效必须做一些事。

笔者不会去重复详论这些不同的时效,只去增加一些与本章/本书有关的内容。

在第一种类,涉及货物买卖,英国还有一立法针对"内在缺陷"(latent defect)。内在缺陷会在很后期才表露出来,所以买方享有不同时效去向卖方提出索赔,即另再有3年时间。这方面对国际货物买卖关系不大,因为国际上的"商品"(commodity)买卖固然是无关,而且国际上认为本来的6年时效已经太长,经常会以明示条款去缩短这6年时效。英国也另有一立法,是1971年的"海上运输法"(Carriage of Goods by Sea Act 1971),即对海牙·维斯比规则的立法,说明在交货后(或应交货后)1年的时效。有关的措辞/文字十分决断、广泛,说是:"…the carrier and the ship shall in any event be discharged from all liability whatsoever in respect of the goods, unless suit is brought within one year of their delivery or of the date when they should have been delivered"。这样的措辞/文字,应是除货损货差外,连无单放货这类的索赔,也应包括在内;可参阅 The "Antares" (1987) 1 Lloyd's Rep. 424; The "Captain Gregos" (1989) 2 Lloyd's Rep. 63 与 The "Ines" (1995) 2 Lloyd's Rep. 144。这一来,如果买卖合约与提单/租约都没有明示的时效条款,表示买方向卖方索赔,他不必心急,英国法律下时效有6年之久。但如果索赔的正确对象是船东,则在提单下往往只有1年,这一年时效很短,加上船舶的流动性很强,"择地行诉"(forum shopping)需要时间,导致买方一不小心就会错过时效。

第二种类的时效是在货物买卖合约如果适用外国法律(即在英国法律的眼中)时,则外国法律的相关时效就会适用。合约会去适用外国法律,要么是有明示条款(这情况不多见,但不是没有,例如笔者刚在一个外地仲裁被指定为仲裁员,合约说明适用中国法律),要么是靠默示(如法律冲突下寻找最密切关系的法律)。记得曾有一个外地仲裁,涉及香港法律(与英国法律一致)还是德国法律(德国与合约有密切关系)是该钢材买卖的适用法律。如果是香港法律,明显有6年时效之久。但德国法律,它的 German Commercial Law,377 条款明确要求买方要在货物交付后马上进行检查,如有货不对板,必须马上通知卖方,否则买方会失去索赔权力。

这是否算是一条时效条款不无争议之处,因为措辞/文字不够明确,这可参考英国高院的 The "Ocean Dynamic" (1982) 1 Lloyd's Rep. 88 先例。但该仲裁判是香港法律适用,是 proper law of contract,否则还要听德国法律专家对这 377 条款的解释作证才好下定论说这条款所定是否够明确作为时效。

第三种类时效在租约或货物买卖合约经常遇到,也是挺危险的,因为变化太多,防不胜防。说句公道话,英国立法的 6 年时效也是长了一点,在今天动得快、变得快的商业环境下,当事方想以明示条款去缩短 6 年时效完全可以理解。但一去缩短时效至不合理不实际的程度,如买方必须在一星期或半个月内向遥远的外国卖方起诉,否则时效已逝,这又变得是去为难买方。所以,在订约时买方要抗拒这种太短的时效条款,因为将来要去起诉对方多数会是买方而不是卖方。

提单以明示条款去缩短时效并不多见,毕竟海牙规则的一年时效已是够短了。而且,再去缩短这一年时效在海牙规则下也是无效。

最后的第四种类时效,《国际商务仲裁》一书已有详述,笔者不多讲了。这种类时效也会与国际货物买卖合约有关,如著名的贵族院先例 Ok Petroleum v. Vitol (1995) 2 Lloyd's Rep. 160,即是一个 CIF 买卖。该案例的详细介绍请参阅《国际商务游戏规则——英国合约法》一书的第 335~336 页。

§3 光船租赁(demise charter)

3.1 船长与光船承租人有雇用关系

去进一步根据提单措辞/内容找出谁是承运人,有必要对一些航运做法有所了解。首先是对光船租赁的简介。它其实是财产租赁的一种,与期租程租很不一样。其中重要的区别是承租人可去完全占有控制船舶,而做法上是通过他/它派上船舶的船长与船员。所以,光船租赁下船长船员根本与原船东本人没有主仆关系。这一来,船长签发的提单只能去约束光租承租人,不能去约束实是陌生人的原船东: Baumwoll v. Gilchrest (1892) 1 Q. B. 253, (1893) A. C. 8。顺理成章的是船长与船员犯错,如疏忽航行/管船,不适航,缺乏合理维修保养船舶,未曾小心谨慎照顾货物或误交货物等,要去对"诉人"(in personam)负责的是有主仆关系的光船承租人而不是陌生人的原船东。换言之,光船承租人才是船长签发提单的承运人,而不是原船东。

3.2 光船租赁不必登记,外人不知道

对收货人的困难是:光船租赁无须登记,故此有了货损货差应向谁起诉呢?要求对光船租赁进行登记也不是没有人谈及,但在国际上去对私人协议作出全面的管制与登记会是劳民伤财,难以操作(像如何去公开任人查阅)与强制执行,比较起来可能会利弊不成比例。

所以,收货人应警觉会有此私人协议的安排,导致寻找提单合约的承运人时搞错目标,承运人实际不是原船东,而是光船承租人。

3.3 英国法律曾有的漏洞

对收货人曾经有的另一困难是英国法律一度无法对物诉讼/扣船。这方面在笔者的《海事法》一书之第一章6.4小段有详及,说:

> 但光船承租人是否是受惠船东呢?照说,他/它虽有利益,对船舶安全占有控制,可是与船东应扯不上关系:不论是"合法"(legal)或"衡平"(equitable)的,但这方面有不同的先例。
>
> 在 The "Andrea Ursula" (1971) 1 Lloyd's Rep. 145,原告的修理厂为被告光租的"Andrea Ursula"轮修理,被告欠钱,原告向船舶对物诉讼。判是光船承租人也是属"受惠船东"(beneficial owner)。但这看法不被稍后的 The "I Congreso del Partido" (1977) 1 Lloyd's Rep. 536 认同。
>
> 这一来,船东岂非可去以光船出租的安排来取巧?例如,班轮公司的船舶是以光船经营,变得有了货损货差也永远不必害怕货方对物诉讼/扣船?……要知道,英国法律下这些类别的索赔都不是船舶优先权,只是"诉物"(in rem)行为而已……
>
> 这漏洞已在 Supreme Court Act, 1981 被补救。在 Section 21 (4) (i),已明确加上"光租承租人"(the charterer of it(指诉物的船舶) under a charter by demise)。说明是光租承租人,就不包括期租,程租了……

Supreme Court Act, 1981 的条款是:"If the person who would be liable on the claim *in personam* was the charterer when the cause of action arose, an action *in rem* may brought against the ship concerned if the person against whom the action *in personam* would lie is the charterers under a charter by demise."(如果诉因发生时面对对人诉讼请求会要负责任的人是承租人,而且这承租人是光船租承租人,那么就可以同时对有关船舶实施对物诉讼)。

3.4 现实中发生的光船租赁

光租租赁会在许多情况下发生,甚至会是与融资有关或是内部安排为了去挂光租承租人的国旗。较正常的情况是让承租人全面占有控制的经营该船舶,而真正船东则可以撒手不理,纯变为是投资人一个,按时收取租金。也可能会是,名义上的船东与光船承租人实际上关系密切,甚至是同一利益集团。例如,班轮公司去以单船公司的名义拥有船舶。以单船公司(经常是方便旗国家如巴拿马、利比里亚等,但可以是任何国家注册的有限公司)拥有个别船舶会有机会在出大事情时将责任局限在出事的船舶而不会延展至祸及整个船队。单船公司也可在经营时令外人(如债权人)对付起来难度增大,例如对手无法以姐妹船扣船以寻求有利的管辖地。

故此,一家班轮公司需要全面占有与控制多艘船舶方能顺利经营一条或多条航线,这就需要去光租一批船舶。船东可能就是自己集团的单船公司,而光租租约也纯是内部安排。当然船舶也会来自外人的船东,光租租约每一条款与租金都要艰苦谈判后才订得下来。

班轮公司是如此,散货运输一样会是这种安排。例如,一个"营运人"(operator)为他手中的长期运货合约(contract of affreightment 或简称 COA)要去履行而希望能控制一些船舶,但又无意或无能力去自己成为原船东。

3.5 期租合约

当然,要使用、经营船舶的承租人,若不计较太全面的占有与控制,加上租期可能不长,也可去考虑期租。像著名的期租标准格式合约的纽约土产(NYPE 46)著名的第 8 条款,称为"受雇及赔偿条款"(employment and indemnity clause),即说明在船舶的营运方面,承租人有决定权。这广泛决定权包括事实使用什么提单格式船长必须签发,纽约土产不像少数租约会局限承租人只能签发某一种提单格式:The "Paros" (1987) 2 Lloyd's Rep. 269。而船长虽然是船东聘请的,但根据这条款,船长必须依从承租人的命令与指示,形同受雇于承租人及作为承租人的代理人一样。

但与光租相比,这里船长的"受雇"并不完全听命承租人。期租下船东与承租人有了利益冲突,就难免船长会听命于船东而与承租人对抗。这种情况无处不在,例如第 8 条款的受雇范围究竟有多大,这在笔者的《期租合约》一书有详及,不去重复。

在签发提单方面,船长一般是约束原船东而不是期租承租人,这与光船租赁很不一样:The "Berkshire" (1974) 1 Lloyd's Rep. 185 与《期租合约》之 25 段。

期租下,船长与船东才有主仆关系。船长签发的提单,船东也很难去否定船长没有实质授权或表面授权(这方面请参阅本书第二章之 5.6.6 小段)。

正如 Leggatt 大法官在 The "Reiwa"（1991）2 Lloyd's Rep. 325 之第 333 页所说："That formulation has never been doubted. The cases are all of a pattern. In my judgment they support the conclusion that a bill of lading signed for the master cannot be a charterer's bill unless the contract was made with the charterers alone, and the person signing has authority to sign, and does sign, on behalf of the charterers and not the owners."

今天会让船长亲自签发提单的情况不多，因为这会延误船期，而承租人也会怕节外生枝。所以，期租租约（如 NYPE 46 的第 8 条款）会授权承租人或代理人去代船长签发提单：The "Berkshire"（1974）1 Lloyd's Rep. 185。再进一步说就是期租承租人这样做，签发了的提单也就约束船长与船东了。正如 Rix 大法官在 The "Hector"（1998）2 Lloyd's Rep. 287 先例说："For these purposes, I would regard an owner as giving his time charterer ostensible authority to bind him (in signing bills of lading on the master's behalf) by reason of putting his vessel under his time charterer's orders and directions regarding employment. That is not simply a matter of private contract; it is reflected in the reality of what happens when a time chartered vessel enters port in order to load cargo. An owner in such circumstances holds out his time charterer as a disponent owner with powers over the employment of his vessel, and thus as having power to bind him by signing a bill of lading."（船东去让期租承租人营运，进装港装货，让货方看是二船东的承租人在全权经营，即表示有表面授权给承租人去签发提单并可去约束船东）。

在另一更早的先例 Tillmans v. Knutsford（1908）1 K. B. 185 之 191 页，Channell 大法官更清楚的说明如下："…the time charterers, instead of directing, as they were entitled to do, the captain to sign, signed it themselves. I am of opinion that the effect of their so signing is exactly the same as if they had directed the captain to put his name to the bill of lading and he had accordingly signed it. If they had struck out the words 'for the captain and owners', and then signed it, I think they would, on the face of it, have been purporting to make it their own contract; but they did not purport to make it their own contract. They purported to sign it for the captain and owners; and, therefore, to make it the contract of the captain and owners, and they had absolute power to do that by the terms of the charter-party."（期租承租人若把提单上"为船长/船东"签字一栏涂掉后才签字，还可以说他这样做是把他作为提单中的承运人/合约方的行为。但仅代船长/船东签字，而且在租约中也完全有权这样做，那承租人根本就不是把自己当做承运人/合约方）。

若是早已答应了 NYPE 46 的第 8 条款，事后船东又去干预承租人签发"运费已经预付"的提单，这是违约行为，可以带来严重后果：The "Nanfri"（1979）1 Lloyd's

Rep. 201。

3.6 识别有否光租的一般做法

现在进一步分析，如果收货人向承运人索赔货损货差，又不知背后是否有一个光租租赁，应如何去做。

3.6.1 提单上只有船名

这情况可能会是，收货人手上是一份背书给他的散货装船提单，像著名的Congenbill提单（可去看本书之附录八）。这种标准格式是供大众使用，不会印上个别船公司的名字。所以，要去识别承运人只能先从船名追查。另外，该提单有船长或船长授权的签字。但这并不代表什么：船长可为船东或光船承租人签字，收货人一开始无法知悉。而收货人去询问，也会不知向谁问，反正也不会有人好心去披露。

因而，从查船名的这第一步，可凭像"Lloyd's Maritime Directory"一书甚至像国际互保协会参加的船舶名单中找出真正船东的名字与所在地。譬如说，真正船东是中远公司或是英国一家老牌的船公司。当然，也可能会是一家名不见经传的巴拿马公司如名为"ABC Navegacion S. A."至此，收货人凭提单上的船名，已可去采取两种行动。一是对物诉讼（*in rem*）的钉住该船舶，在适当港口行动，起诉并扣船要求诉前保全。二是对人（船东）诉讼（*in personam*），起诉地点会是被告所在地。

3.6.2 对人诉讼

对人诉讼的行动一般不多，原因会是：

（ⅰ）难以获得诉前保全。

（ⅱ）可能是一场空，对象找错，因为背后有光租。固然，船东在抗辩请求书中会指出这个事实，但已足以令原告的收货人白干一场，劳民伤财，甚至令一个应起诉光租承租人的货损货差索赔错失时效。或者会是，一开始收货人已可询问船东有否光租的安排，而在会被起诉的威胁下，船东也许会坦白。

（ⅲ）最大原因仍应是，今天大量的巴拿马、利比里亚单船船东不值得去对它对人诉讼，也无从下手（哪里是适当法院）。

3.6.3 对物诉讼

这一来，惯常的行动仍是对物诉讼，只要及时，即船舶仍未沉没，或是出告票前船舶未转卖等，成功索赔的机会会大得多。原因会是：

（ⅰ）可在有利与适当的港口（管辖地点）行动。例如是，新加坡。因为货损货差责任有互保协会的保赔，加上船舶在国际上营运与出租，有些主要港口如新加坡是避无可避的。所以,迟早等得到目标船舶的到临,以采取行动送达对物诉讼告票并进行扣船。当然,目前的做法与法律变化很多,且愈加复杂,故最后的审理管辖权仍可能无法保留在采取行动的有利港口法院。例如,提单合约有一条有效仲裁条款。这方面在本书第四章之 2.6.4 小段与第五章之 4.2.10.2.5.2 小段等后详。

(ii)不论怎样,保不住管辖权也保得住诉前保全。

(iii)这一来,不管背后的船东是如何隐蔽,也会被迫曝光去面对这个索赔:或应诉,或庭外和解,否则会被缺席判决了。

3.6.4 迫船东对有否光租作出披露与保证

而对物诉讼如何针对背后有光船租赁的可能呢?在做法上应有三点要注意:

(i)对物诉讼告票需要把船东或/与光租承租人的名称都列为被告。当然,准确是谁尚不知道。但去提了他/它的身份已可避免有遗漏并带来其他像一年时效已届等的争议。要知道,告票会因送达不到而要延期。

(ii)到了真正送达告票与扣船时,就可真正迫船东披露有否光租的事实。届时收货人应要船东保证在产生货损货差时,船舶并未光租出去。省得在事后诉讼(诉物往往变为诉人),船东自辩无辜,被告应是光船承租人(首次披露光船租赁),那收货人可就告错对象了。

(iii)以船东的披露与保证为准,诉前保全(一般会是互保协会的担保函)的措辞/文字要配合。如针对的是船东的责任或是光船承租人的责任。一天不弄清楚,就不同意放船。

3.6.5 提单上除船名外印有船公司的名字

在班轮运输或部分的散货运输,经营的船公司可能会不想放过机会做广告或是为自己闯出名堂,故在签发的提单上印有他/它的名字。但没有法律规定班轮运输的提单必须在船名外印有船公司名字。像 BIMCO 拥有的标准班轮提单格式 Conlinebill(本书的附录九),供大众使用,亦是不会印上个别班轮公司的名字。话说回来,今天印刷便宜方便,一家班轮公司连自己的单证/文件也没有,在客户眼中看来会是太短视,不肯投入和太儿戏了。这一来,有了船名再去多印一家船公司名字,成了班轮公司普遍做法,这又如何去分析呢?

会是,第一步仍是从船名去找出真正原船东的名字与地址。之后,再与提单上印的船公司比较。如果完全一致,例如都是中远,这表示应没有期租或光租涉及在内,诉人或诉物(船)都应是明确不过。

但若是真正原船东与提单上印的船公司不一致,则初步显示了它们之间很可能有期租或光租的联系/关系。这要搞清楚才能开始诉人。但考虑到收货人仍会去

"对物诉讼"(in rem),因为有本章之 3.6.3 小段所讲的优点,则可去迫船东讲出有否光租的事实,这可参阅 3.6.4 小段所讲的做法。

§4 班轮提单与租约提单

对这方面的航运做法也应略去介绍,虽然对于班轮与不定期船的不同做法已是众所皆知,不必去细谈。不定期船主要是在散装货与石油运输,一般涉及租约。

先可给予一个权威介绍,是 Mustill 大法官在 The "Anwar Al Sabar" (1980) 2 Lloyd's Rep. 261 先例所说的如下不同做法:"In the liner trade it is the practice for the owner to use his own form of bill of lading[152]; this is done for convenience[153], and the practice tells one nothing about the right of the owner to insist on his own form where the vessel is under charter[154]. In the liner trade there is almost invariably an antecedent contract between shipper and carrier in the terms of the booking note[155] which incorporates the carrier's standard form of bill of lading[156]. If the shipper does not wish his goods to be carried under such a bill of lading he simply does not ship the goods by that carrier's line[157]. There is no other way he can get them carried by that carrier otherwise than to agree to his standard form[158]. If the booking note does not expressly incorporate the standard form, it will usually be implied into the contract of carriage by course of dealing[159]. When one turns to goods carried pursuant to a charter – party the practice is, in my experience, completely different[160]. So far from it being usual for the owner to employ his own form of bill of lading, to prepare it spontaneously, as it were, sign it and tender it to the charterer, I should have thought that this was a very rare occurrence indeed[161]. By far the most usual course is for the charterer to prepare the bill of lading[162], and present it for

---

[152] 班轮业务总是船东有自己的提单格式。
[153] 这是为了方便。
[154] 若船舶是程租,船东能否有权坚持使用他/它的提单格式则是另外课题[注:期租一般措辞是提单格式的决定权在承租人:The "Berkshire" (1974) 1 Lloyd's Rep. 185]。
[155] 班轮业务一早已另有一份运输合约,就是订舱单。
[156] 订舱单合并了班轮提单格式。
[157] 若是发货人对该提单格式(条款)不满意,他/它就不要该班轮承运好了(即不订约)。
[158] 一般是要该班轮去承运,发货人只好答应提单格式/条款。
[159] 订舱单不是明示也会是默示去合并班轮提单格式。
[160] 但租船业务做法上很不一样。
[161] 很少会是船东以他的提单格式去签发了,然后交给承租人。
[162] 一般是承租人去备妥提单(包括决定格式)。

signature to the master or ship's agent [163], who, after verifying that it is in conformity with the requirements of the charter – party [164] will sign it without further ado [165]."

4.1 班轮提单如何拟定

对提单的内容,班轮公司会去拟定一份完整全面的运输合约,条款尽量不去对该航次应该针对的事项有所遗留或不明确。好的合约应是对将来履行中会出现的所有问题,不明朗与会有争议处都去事前约定/针对,并各自争取对自己有利的条款。毕竟,对发货人而言,该提单会是运输合约最佳的证明。它只是最佳证明的原因在本章之1.3 小段已略及,更早的订舱(booking)才是原始的运输合约。而订舱单(booking note)常合并班轮提单内容,如 The " Jalamohan" (1988) 1 Lloyd's Rep. 443 先例中的订舱单印有"other terms as per carrier's bill of lading"。所以,发货人很难去对后来签发的提单的印就内容提出异议。但也会有在订舱谈判时双方曾另有额外协议的情况,例如在 The "Al Battani" (1993) 2 Lloyd's Rep. 219 先例的承运人口头答应直航,但发货人在后来签发提单时才发觉不是这回事,因而可去以承运人违约/毁约来对付,包括来得及去卸下货物,中断运输合约,并且索赔损失。

而对收货人而言,通过 1992 年英国海上运输法的强制转让运输合约到他/它头上,提单更是无可争议的唯一合约。

正如所有大公司面对成千上万消费者的订约方时所采用的一贯做法,班轮公司拟定与印好提单后,就不愿意再去与个别订约方谈判条款并作出每次不同的增减修改。这会带来不稳定、大量增加班轮公司的工作等不良后果。所以,不论航运市场的当事方强弱如何,一般班轮公司都不肯去碰拟定的提单条款。

这对订约方另一方的发货人而言,倒也无所谓。反正提单内容(印就条款)一般不影响信用证结汇,而运输的风险或提单下的争议,往往也与发货人无关。

有关班轮提单常见的条款,会在本书之第四章详及。而在附录九与附录十也有班轮提单样本。

4.2 租约提单合并较早订立的租约

至于租约提单的内容,却因为事前有一份租约的存在,变得与班轮提单很不相同。

首先,已有了一份经过谈判同意的租约(例如是程租合约)存在,作为运输,就

---

[163] 然后交给船长或船东代理人,要求他签字。
[164] 船长或船东代理人在查核提单内容正确与符合租约要求后。
[165] 即照签无误。

不应后来另有一份不同的运输合约去替代或修改。要知道,任何合约的修改/更改都需要约因或对价,双方有此意图,等等。难怪,有说法是提单在承租人手中,因为双方已有租约存在,所以提单不会是运输合约或是它的证明(这只是班轮提单的说法),它只能是一份收据:Rodocanachi v. Milburn (1886) 18 QBD 67;The "Dunelmia" (1969) 2 Lloyd's Rep. 476. Denning 勋爵在 The "Dunelmia" 说:

"…The charterparty is not merely a contract for the hire of the use of a ship. It is a contract by which the shipowners agree to carry goods and to deliver them. If the shipowners fail to carry the goods safely, that is a breach of the contract contained in the charterparty; and the charterers can claim for the breach accordingly, unless that contract has been modified or varied by some subsequent agreement between the parties. The signature by the master of a bill of lading is not a modification or variation of it. The master has no authority to modify or vary it. His authority is only to sign bills of lading "without prejudice to the terms of the charterparty…"

In this case, therefore, the bill of lading did not modify or vary the charter. And there is nothing else. So the charter governs…

Even though the charterer is not the shipper and takes as indorsee of a bill of lading, nevertheless their relations are governed by the charter at any rate when the master is only authorized to sign bills of lading without prejudice to the charter."

话说回来,在租约下装了货物上船,发货人仍需要承运人/船东签发提单。毕竟,这是海牙规则的 Article 3(3) 与 (7) 条款赋予的法定权力。加上,船长收取了货物总要签发收据而发货人也要有物权凭证的提单去在信用证结汇。所以,有了租约一样免不了有提单。唯一分别是,发货人在 CIF/CFR 买卖,很可能也是承租人。则提单根本与运输合约(双方已有租约)扯不上关系。

4.2.1 对租约提单条款不完全符合租约的处理

但租约提单仍会通过背书去转让货物所有权,而随之而来的"剧变"是运输合约会强加到收货人头上:根据是业已过时的 1855 年提单法或当今的 1992 年英国海上运输法。可以说,这给了租约提单一个合约的新生命。此时也有了一个三角关系,互相以合约联系在一起:船东与承租人(发货人)是租约,船东与收货人(提单持有人)是租约提单。

故此,遇上合约有争议,仍需独立处理,虽然最后它们之间互有关系。例如货损货差,收货人以租约提单的合约关系向船东索赔。船东不得以租约条款下他/它不必负责为由抗辩,因为租约只是另一个合约,不约束收货人。固然,赔付了货损货差后,如果租约条款原不必船东对此货损货差负责,或是因提单加大了责任(会有可能,因为提单会强制适用海牙/海牙·维斯比规则,而租约在自由订约下会有比海牙/海牙·维斯比规则轻松得多的责任,例如,著名的"金康租约"(Gencon charter party),或因承租人负责的有关工作有了失误(例如堆放货物),船东大可以租约有关条款去向承租人追偿,要求"补偿"(indemnity)。

再举一例是租约提单注明了"运费已预付"(freight prepaid)或承租人签发了班轮提单(liner bill)而导致条款下要求船东支付卸货费用,在面对收货人的提单持有人时,船东也是无法抵赖。或是会因"禁止翻供"(estoppel)的理由不准船东去否定提单的批注与/或内容,以免影响无辜收货人。甚或是干脆以一个合约内的条款必须严格执行为由而不准船东去否定。或许有人说,这提单合约是 1992 年立法强加在双方头上的。但这都不必细究,反正有合约就需严格执行,不存在一个合约的不同形成(只要合法)会导致履行上的不同。至于之后船东另根据租约可否成功向承租人追回欠下的运费或已支付的卸货费(租约条款是"free out"——免费卸货,没有理由要船东支付卸货费用),是不关收货人的事了,也完全符合不同合约各自独立处理的原则。

就船东而言,既然有了一份经谈判双方你情我愿订立的租约,而且针对的是同一航次,自然希望后来签发的提单也有与租约一样的条款。这省得行走同一航次会面对两个有不同履约责任或/与权利的运输合约。一般的做法也确有这个考虑。故此,租约提单通常没有预先印好的条款,完全不像班轮提单。它只去说明合并了某租约所有有关条款。由于租约常在每一点上都要进行谈判,而谈判结果的变数也多,致令往往不到最后一分钟都无法去预测会谈出什么样的条款。因此也就无法像班轮提单那样去事前印就好条款。

4.2.2 合并的法律

以合并作为合约内容的一部分经常发生,这方面也在笔者的《国际商务游戏规则——英国合约法》一书第十章之 4.3 小段有详及如下:

4.3 并入条款(Incorporation Clause)

在一些存在并入条款(Incorporation Clause)的合约中,也存在着并入条款所含内容与合约主文条款相冲突的情况。这时,合约解释上的原则就是合约主文(the main contract)内的明示条款、条款超越并入条款的内容。实务中,并入条款所指向引入合约的条款在形式上是多种多样的。它可以是某项或几项具体的条款,也可以是另一份完整的合约,更可以是一套完整的法规。海上货运中最常见的并入(条款)有如租船提单(C/P B/L)之对租船合约的并入;租船合约中(往往通过首要条款——Paramount Clause 的形式)对海牙规则的并入,如著名的期租标准合约 NYPE 格式第24条并入1936年美国海上货物运输法(类同于海牙规则);货物买卖合约(FOB,CIF 买卖)则常见有在装、卸港装卸时间、延滞费计算方面适用承运船舶租约规定的并入(as per C/P)。应注意法律上不存在并入的内容,要去附上一份才有效的要求,否则租约去合并海牙规则、哈特法、约克·安特卫普规则、油污公约等就会变成一本厚书了,加上更会有去并入尚未存在的文件,如买卖合约并入将来租约。这些并入条款所指向的条款、合约或法规如何引入,适用到合约中,除上述合约主文明示条款优先的原则外,在合约解释上还受到一套"与标的事项直接关联"(direct germane to subject-matter)或"附属性条款"(ancillary clauses/terms)理论的限制。这方面以下两个英国法院的判例有很好的说明。

在 The "Annefield" (1971) 1 Lloyd's Rep. 1 中,提单中订有并入条款称租船合约并入本提单,而租船合约中有一条仲裁条款。原被告双方就该条仲裁条款是否适用进提单产生争议,结果官司打到上诉院,丹宁勋爵(Lord Denning)在判词中称:租约中与提单的标的事项直接关联(即与货物的装船、运输以及交付直接关联)的条款可以也应该引入到提单合约中适用,即使需要在措辞上作出一定的改动以贴切适用于提单。但如果租约中的条款并非与提单直接关联,那么除非在提单中或租约中有明确文字表明其适用于提单,该条款不能引入提单。租约中的仲裁条款与提单中货物的装船、运输以及交付并无直接关系,因此仅用普通的用语(general words)不能将其引入提单。这一案例表明"并入条款"所指向的内容必须与合约的标的事项直接关联,方能以一般的并入用语引入合约适用。具体地说,该案也确立了租约中仲裁条款不能简单地以提单中的"租约条件、条款并入提单"的并入条款并入提单的先例。鉴此,当事人要将租约中的仲裁条款并入提单,最稳妥的做法就是在提单的并入条款上写明"租约的条款"条件包括仲裁条款引入本提单。这一来,因有明确并入租约中仲裁条款的字眼,该仲裁条款自然可适用在提单。不过,"Annefield"轮案对租约中仲裁条款能否引入提单的判例也有一种例外,那就是当租约中的仲裁条款写有"所有由租约或于租约下签发的提单所引起的争议须提交仲裁……"的字眼时,提单中一条一般性的并入条款(如"租约条款、条件并入提单")已是足够将租约内此类仲裁条款并入提单中适用:The "Merak" (1964) 2 Lloyd's Rep. 283。

另一个很新的案例,OK Petroleum v. Vitol (1995) 2 Lloyd's Rep. 160。也反映了上述并入条款在合约中如何适用的理论。该案中,原告 CIF 价售卖汽油予被告,买卖合约规定(卸港)延滞费依租约(租用承运船的航次租约)的规定。买卖合约订立之后,卖方租船将油付运,结果在卸港发生了延滞(注:买方负责卸货)。该租约有关延滞费的条款中,有一项索赔时效(Time Bar)的规定,称除非自卸除油管后90天内收到有关索赔通知,承租人对租约下产生的延滞费及其他费用不予负责。在高等法院,原告依买卖合约向被告索赔卸港产生的延滞费,而被告则以合约中有关"延滞费按租约"(Demurrage as per Charterparty)的并入条款辩称,租约中有关延滞费的条款规定了卸货后90天的索赔时效,而原告并未在此90天内提出索赔,通知被告,因此索赔时效已中止,被告无须赔付。该案争议的焦点显然就在于租约延滞费条款中的索赔时效规定能否也一齐并入买卖合约中。结果法院判有关索赔时效的规定不能并入买卖合约,原告仍可索赔延滞费。法官在判词中称:a) 有关并入的一般性用语(General words of incorporation)通常不能解释为足够广泛可以将从外引入的合约的所有规定并入进本合约,除非这些规定构成引入合约的标的事项的一部分(part of subject-matter),例如所有有关如何计算卸货/滞期时间与滞期费的条款,或是租约内的航行疏忽免责条款可在挂靠卸货码头碰坏岸上设备时用以抗辩收货人/提单持有人的索赔:The "Ikaraiada" (1999) 2 Lloyd's Rep. 365,而非诸如仲裁、管辖权和时效条款等,仅属附属性质(ancillary)。附属性的规定通常被视为与本合约下当事人的权利、义务无关;b) 本案中索赔时效的规定,虽然在租约下专门适用于延滞费的索赔,但本质上仍是附属于租约有关延滞费的主体或标的事项的。这种附属性表现为该规定的功能仅限于对已产生合约权利的执行,是专门针对已产生延滞费的收取的;c) 在买卖合约中的并入(incorporation)一词,作为一般性用语,并无明显表达双方欲将租约中那些并不属延滞费标的事项本身一部分,而仅属附属性质的规定并入买卖合约之意。而本案也无特殊的情况显示对"并入"的一般性用语的通常解释应予背离。因此,被告提出的索赔时效并入买卖合约的辩称不会被采纳。原告的索赔不会因时效而中止。这一判例进一步说明,并入条款引入的条款、合约中并不构成标的事项本身部分的附属性条款、条款(ancillary terms/clauses)不能以普通的并入用语并入进本合约中适用,要想并入则要去明示了。

即使能并入,根据开始已提到的原则,即并入不能超越合约主文中的明示条款,很多纠纷也能够解释。譬如,常见的运费已付(freight prepaid)提单并入的租约,往往会有不同的规定。如80%运费先预付,20%以后付;或是,在出运费已付提单7天之后才付,而现实中并没有付;更可能是,租约说明虽然出运费已付提单,但运费实际是要到卸完货租方才付。这种千变万化的租约条款都不能去超越在提单中对受货人而言的明示条款,即"运费已付"。再举一例,提单中注明目的地/卸港是古巴,船东就不能对提单下的收货人说并入的租约条款是不允许去古巴的,因为即使是事实,也被提单上明示的卸港所超越。

合约的有效性、合理性要求订约双方应该了解与自愿受合约条款的约束。所以，应该清楚知道合并了什么内容，不应让其中一订约方抵赖。或许有人会问，可否不合并，而把合并租约的有关条款全数搬过来，在租约提单中重复一次？这样做会徒然增加工作量，而实际作用极少。首先如果租约有不利收货人的条款，例如是十分优待船东的卸货时间的计算（例如是船舶一抵达长江口就起算），或是高昂的卸港滞期费，会要货方去承担，则去搬到租约提单中无论是以合并方法或把条款重复一次，都不会丝毫改变结果。至于说收货人难以知悉租约内容，不知道合并了什么，可回应说只要收货人警觉一点，在买卖合约说明要卖方限时呈交有关租约，没有理由是收货人（买方）想看也看不到的。如买卖合约合并了国际商会的"国际贸易术语解释通则"（Incoterms），针对 CIF 与 CFR 也有要求卖方给予一份租约副本。故此只要买卖合约合并了 Incoterms，买方是不会无法见到一份有关租约，进而知悉它的内容的。另在 Thyssen v. Calypso（2000）2 Lloyd's Rep. 243，Steel 大法官也不接受买方真想去获取一份有关租约会有实质困难。当然，知悉了内容也不会在实质上有何改变，提单一结汇，已是成为一个合约强加到收货人头上，改也改不了了。

4.2.3　租约提单合并混乱的原因

但一份一般的租约提单，通常不会自动去附有一份合并的租约，因为：

（ⅰ）签发提单时租约根本仍未备妥，特别是订约后不久马上去装货（好像短航次）。租约虽已有，但内容/条款只是记录在电传来往，例如主要条款是一份传真的"recap fixture"。

（ⅱ）签发提单时即使已备妥了一份租约，双方（承租人与船东）也签了字，但若要把租约附在提单，会存在提单签发多于一套，而租约只有一份。固然，纯为了让提单持有人马上知道合并了什么内容/条款，可只去附上一份副本的租约，正本则自用。

（ⅲ）但除非是合约（买卖合约或信用证）明示规定，法律大原则是不要求一个合约去合并的同时必须附有一份合并的文件。例如，信用证合并了 UCP500 就必须去附有一份 UCP500。要真是有此法律要求，会带来无谓的工作并且劳民伤财。好像一份租约，经常会合并大量其他的文件：针对货差货损责任合并海牙/海牙·维斯比规则；针对油污责任合并 Civil Liability Convention，美国油污法；针对共同海损理算合并 York-Antwerp Rules 或北京理算规则，等等。都要去附上相关文件会令一份租约变为一本厚厚的书。再说，即使这样去做，也只能在合约订立之后，这是费时失事的"例行文书工作"（formality paper work）。但有效与约束的合约早在传真谈拢时已经产生。这一来，法律怎能去要求有此善后文书工作呢？时间上根本无法配合。

(ⅳ)现实中,不论是谁去签发提单(船长,承租人或代理人)或/与发货人备妥提单,大家在做法上都是得过且过,十分粗略。别说不会去查问有否一份租约业已备妥签妥,例如向经纪人查问,他/它们根本连想都不会去想,所以经常导致租约提单合并了哪一份租约都不明确/不肯定。如果该航次只有一份程租租约,还可去默示合并的就只能是此租约。怕就怕有太多份租约,又有程租,又有期租。英国法律本来遇上太不明确太不肯定的合并,显示订约双方根本不知道所协议的为何物,会以双方没有"一致看法"(meeting of minds)而判合并无效。

但在租约提单的情况下,合约(该有关航次)已经履行。当时提单在无辜收货人手中想去为货差货损索赔。而根据1992年立法(之前是1855年提单法),在提单持有人/收货人与船东之间被强制有了一个提单的运输合约。以上种种因素加起来,可见法院是不能去随口说合并太不明确太不肯定,所以这是一份没有任何内容/条款的提单合约,干脆判没有合约的存在。相反,遇上这种情况,英国法院想尽办法也会去判默示的合并到底是哪一份租约。

例如,第一份船东与承租人的程租合约下卸港滞期费是1万美元一天,而第二份承租人(二船东)与分承租人的分租约下卸港滞期费是1.5万美元一天。这一来,没有明示说明哪一份被合并,就会有争议了,因为这关系到提单持有人/收货人若在卸港延误,为避免货物被留置而支付的滞期费是1万或1.5万美元的分别。而根据 The "San Nicholas" (1976) 1 Lloyd's Rep. 8,默示去合并的是第一份1万美元的租约。因为提单是船长授权签发的,约束船东。对船东而言,它/他对分租约不会了解太多,也不受约束。相反,它/他会很合理地希望在同一航次,尽量只有一个标准、划一的履约责任或/与权利在租约与提单中同时出现。众所周知,默示的条件之一就是要合理。

但现实中,船东不一定如愿以偿,因为:

(a)租约(特别是期租)通常去全面授权承租人签发提单:请参阅《期租合约》一书之25段与《程租合约》一书之第十三章。所以,最终租约提单去合并哪一份租约的决定权不在船东。

(b)说真的,承租人去代船东签发比租约的责任重大得多的提单,例如是班轮提单(船东在提单下要去承担卸货费用等),通常也是允许的。唯一局限的说法是承租人不能去签发"欺诈性"(fraudulent)或/与"租约绝对相异/矛盾"(manifestly inconsistent with charter party)或/与"完全不正常条款"(extra-ordinary terms)的提单。例如,提单的卸港是租约禁止的地区。但即使是如此,在面对提单持有人/收货人时,船东仍难以抗辩,因为承租人会有表面授权(虽没有实质授权):请参阅本书第二章之5.6.6小段提及的 The "Starsin" (2000) 1 Lloyd's Rep. 85。船东唯一能做的仍只是在事后向承租人要求补偿额外的支出或/与损失。

154 提单及其他付运单证

(c) 正如 Brandon 大法官在 The "Berkshire" (1974) 1 Lloyd's Rep. 185 的权威说法,可去节录如下:"The effect of such a clause (指该先例中纽约土产格式的租约第 8 条) in a charter party is wellsettled. In the first place, the clause entitles the charterers to present to the master for signature by him on behalf of the shipowners bill of lading which contain or evidence contracts between the shippers of goods and the shipowners, provided always that such bills of lading do not contain extraordinary terms or terms manifestly inconsistent with the C/P, and the master is obliged, on presentation to him of such bills of lading, to sign them on the shipowner's behalf. In the second place, the charterers may, instead of presenting such bills of lading to the master for signature by him on behalf of the shipowners, sign them themselves on the same behalf. In either case, whether the master signs on the directions of the charterers, or the charterers short-circuit the matter and sign themselves, the signature binds the shipowners as principals to the contract contained in or evidenced by the bills of lading."

4.3 总结班轮提单与租约提单的区分

综合以上所讲,可去简单总结班轮提单与租约提单的区分如下:

(i) 班轮提单有固定的印就格式,条款不会因不同航次或/与面对不同发货人而轻易改变。

(ii) 班轮提单多数印有班轮公司的名称/抬头(或部分的长期散货运输:本章 3.6.5 小段),以收广告/建立商誉之效。租约提单没有这考虑。它的签发与使用怎样格式的决定权在承租人(在 CIF 买卖亦是发货人):The "Berkshire" (1974) 1 Lloyd's Rep. 185。除非该发货人除了进行国际货物买卖外也经营航运,他/它是不会有兴趣为他自己或船东在提单格式上做广告。所以,租约提单经常只有船名(因为是货物装船提单),不会印有任何船公司的名称。当然也会有例外的情况,例如"营运人"(operator)租船去履行一个长期的 COA。

(iii) 班轮提单的拟定往往是单方面决定,谈不上与发货人有谈判。精明的船公司一有不利形势出现,例如是一个案例刚判下来(如在本书第二章之 5.10.1 小段的介绍),会马上去更改与重印他/它的班轮提单合约格式,务求去抵消这不利新形势的影响。但租约提单做不到这点,它只能去合并较早的租约条款。该些条款在今天租船市场上不会任由船东自说自话。

(iv) 所以班轮提单背后条款密密麻麻,包罗万象。但租约提单只凭合并租约,看来十分简洁。

(v) 虽然两种提单拥有不少雷同条款,但亦有不少条款会各自有不同的针对,导致条款上的相异或有/无。例如是针对装卸货时间与滞期费的条款,对租约船东事关重大。但对班轮而言,因为船舶极少会为了一批货物而遭受延滞,一切装卸作业与靠泊码头亦是班轮自己一手安排,故班轮提单即使有一条滞期费条款也只是为了以防万一(如危险品发生了危险而延误船期,因卸不下来)。

另一例子是针对谁是承运人的光船条款与承运人身份条款,也是班轮提单才有。租约提单讲过,通常只有船名,不印有船公司名称/抬头,不存在去界定谁是承运人的必要。

现对这两条条款略作介绍如下:

4.3.1　班轮提单针对谁是承运人的条款之一:光船条款(demise clause)

班轮提单因为印有班轮公司的抬头(如中远或马士基等公司),而实际使用的船舶却不一定是名下拥有,导致一份提单看来会有两个不同船公司,都可能被指认是承运人。一是提单抬头的公司,另一是真正的原船东。当然,如果某班轮公司使用在营运的都是自己名下的船舶,承运人在提单内找来找去也只有一家船公司,只可能他/它是承运人。但如果该班轮公司营运的船舶是租进来(或期租,或光租),就会导致有两个可能的承运人。这船舶即使是属班轮公司集团的单船公司所拥有,但不同公司仍是不同法人,仍需要有合约(租约)关系才会讲得通是单船公司的真正船东让班轮公司去控制并使用船舶。

还有,班轮公司即使使用自己名下的船舶,也会存在周期性的航线中货量一多或自己船舶进坞修理保养或出了意外,被迫临时租入外人拥有的船舶以免营运中断/受扰的可能。

在一个合约(如提单合约),完全可以有多于两位的订约方。所以,班轮公司与真正的原船东如果是不同法人,但同时出现在提单内,并且愿意同时承担承运人的责任,所谓的"jointly and severally responsible",完全可以。但一切合约构成的基本要求(本章§1段),都必须符合。这就不容易了,很少情况下会是班轮公司(也是承租人)与船东同时愿意去充当提单合约下的承运人,负共同责任,而这纯是去便利收货人/提单持有人而已。

4.3.1.1　内容简介

相反,历来的做法是班轮公司针对期租进来的船舶,会在提单说明承运人只是真正的原船东,而不是它的班轮公司。这说明的条款就叫"光船条款"(demise clause)。已有上百年历史,班轮提单内通常有此条款,可去节录的措辞一般会是:
"If the ship is not owned by or chartered by demise[166] to the company or line by whom

---

[166] 如果该提单下的船舶并非是[167]的公司或班轮公司所拥有或光租进来(换言之,若是船舶碰上是自己拥有或光租的,本条款不适用。如此措辞是因为班轮提单只印就一个式样,供所有航次使用,不再去区分会有个别航次期租了船舶,以专供其使用)。

this bill of lading is issued [167] (as may be the case notwithstanding anything that appears to the contrary) this bill of lading shall take effect only as a contract with the owner or demise charterer as the case may be as principal [168] made through the agency of the said company or line who acts as agent only [169] and shall be under no personal liability whatsoever [170] in respect thereof."

4.3.1.2 英国法律承认有效

有此条款,若发货人作为另一订约方同意(一般也是如此,从未听说发货人在订舱位时或付运时对班轮公司提出对此光船条款有异议),即是接受了真正船东或光船承租人(在有期租情况下)为订约方、承运人。同时,亦接受一直在打交道的班轮公司,也是提单的抬头人,只是一个代理人而已。

而船东或光船承租人看来"无端"成为班轮提单的订约方、承运人,也难抵赖,例如说没有授权期租承租人的班轮公司代它/他去订约。这方面可回头参阅本章之4.2.3小段后段的(a)至(c)。

或许会感觉这与事实不符,太虚假。但真正一手操纵谈判的当事人在合约名义上的订约方方面另去推出一家公司"充数"的情况经常发生,例如在船舶买卖。只要双方订约方你情我愿,合约也就是这个关系,即真正当事人会只是代理人或经纪,而不是合约一方。

笔者把这些基本合约法概念说清楚,是为了说明英国法院在这样分析下,是认为光船条款完全有效的:The "Berkshire" (1974) 1 Lloyd's Rep. 185; The "Vikfrost" (1980) 1 Lloyd's Rep. 560。在 The "Berkshire",提单抬头印了一家船公司的名字为"Ocean Wide",但有关船舶是期租进来的,即真正船东不是 Ocean Wide。Brandon 大法官判说:"I see no reason not to give effect to the demise clause in accordance with its terms. The company or line by whom the bill of lading was issued, within the meaning of that clause, is clearly in this case Ocean Wide. It is not in dispute that the ship was not owned or chartered by demise to that company, but was on the contrary owned by the shipowners, it follows that the bill of lading is, by its express terms, intended to take effect as a contract between the shippers and the shipowners made on behalf of the shipowners by Ocean Wide as agents only…"… therefore, I hold that the contract contained in or evidenced by the bill of lading purports to be a contract between the shippers and the shipo-

---

[167] 指签发提单给发货人的公司或班轮公司,亦即是提单抬头印上它的名字。
[168] 本提单只是一个真正船东或光船承租人作为订约方的合约,而[167]的公司或班轮公司只是一个代理人。
[169] 提单抬头印有的班轮公司只是一个代理人。
[170] 不就提单负任何个人的责任。

wners, and not one between the shippers and the charterers."

4.3.1.3 光船条款的历史来由

这条款的历史来由是在英国商船法(Merchant Shipping Act 1894)的Section 503,英国立法允许船东在遇上一个重大事故时可以一次申请责任限制,或以此来抗辩过高的索赔金额。有关责任限制的课题,在笔者的《海事法》一书第二章有详及,不去重复。在该立法,遇上重大事故对财产损失负有责任,船东或光船承租人可去限制责任,每船舶吨位以8英镑为准。要知道,一百年前有限公司的做法尚未流行,故此遇上大事故大责任,船东可以是倾家荡产地赔光每一毛钱。故此,责任限制是十分重要的保障。而对货差货损负上的责任会可大可小:不适航会导致船舶沉没,船货全损,也可能只是海水浸湿一件的货物。后者即使扯上责任限制也只会是海牙/海牙·维斯比规则的每一单位的责任限制。但前者则很有可能扯上以船舶吨位计算的责任限制。全损的货价会是上千万美元,如果责任无法抵赖,可去限制赔偿金额在二三百万美元的责任限度内仍是事关重大:The "Penelope II" (1980) 2 Lloyd's Rep. 17。

但1894年的商船法没有把期租承租人(或程租承租人)包括在内,这带来一个危险是如果班轮公司期租一艘船舶来营运,再自己去作为承运人,那么遇上船货全损而面对索赔时,就会无法去限制责任,而要赔上千万美元: Paterson, Zochonis v. Elder Dempster (1922) 2 Lloyd's Rep. 69。

看来对班轮公司不公道之处是:若该沉没的船舶不是期租进来,而是自己拥有或光租进来,则面对同样索赔反而可去享有责任限制。

所以,班轮提单去增加一条光租条款,实际是为了在期租(或程租)时万一出了大事故,可让班轮公司以代理人身份躲在背后,先推真正船东或光船承租人到前台面对提单持有人/收货人的索赔。即使最后要赔偿,而且船东可向班轮公司获得"补偿"(indemnity),班轮公司也可间接享有责任限制。

到了1958年的商船法(Merchant Shipping (Liability of Shipowners and others) Act 1958),已把期租承租人也放入可享受责任限制的行列。这一来,照说光租条款已完成它的历史任务,可从此在班轮提单内删除。但事实上目前仍保留了这条款,这会是班轮公司认为该条款仍有其他好处。例如,提单持有人/收货人索赔只能针对船东(或光租承租人),他/它才是提单合约的承运人。真有诉讼,抗辩起来在举证方面船东(或光租承租人)会比班轮公司优胜方便得多。虽然在操作上,班轮公司或会去处理货损货差的索赔,但会以代理人自居。

这有关光船条款的历史,Colman大法官在The "Starsin" (2000) 1 Lloyd's Rep. 85 之第89页也略有提及:"That such issue arise is almost always the consequence of bills being issued on time charterers' forms, as here, and bearing words in the signature box which, it is argued, supersede the effect of the identity of carrier clause (cl. 33 in this case) and the demise clause (cl. 35 in this case). The latter has survived from the era when a time charterer who was party to a bill of lading contract as carrier was not entitled to limit his liability under the Merchant Shipping Act. It was therefore necessary, particularly for liner companies who issued bills, to avoid being held liable as carriers. Since the enactment into English law of art. 1.2 of the Convention on Limitation of Liability for Maritime Claims, 1976 by s. 186 of the Merchant Shipping Act, 1995 such precautions have become unnecessary."

4.3.1.4 漠视光租条款会有严重后果

这一点可去介绍 The "Antares" (1987) 1 Lloyd's Rep. 424 先例，它涉及烧焊机 (flash butt welding plant) 的货物错误装在船舶甲板上导致损坏。照说，这在责任方面是再清楚不过，提单承运人难辞其咎。但谁才是承运人呢？

该提单格式印有一家名为 "Mediterranean Shipping Co" 船公司的抬头，收货人/提单持有人 (Kenya Railways) 与它的律师没有去细究 Mediterranean 是否是承运人就向它起诉。若有去细究与进一步调查，会发觉 "Antares" 的船东并非是 Mediterranean，这显示 "Antares" 会是光租或是期租给 Mediterranean。而要进一步地澄清，则是靠本章 3.6.4 小段所讲的做法。换言之，正确的处理方法应是去对物诉讼并在届时迫船东披露有否光租。如果有，诉人对象改为 Mediterranean，但诉前保全仍然在手。如果没有，诉人对象继续是真正船东，而不是 Mediterranean。更何况，该提单有一条光租条款，说明了这安排。

在 1984 年 11 月，该提单持有人 (Kenya Railways) 在英国法院向 Mediterranean 起诉。而在卸货后 1 年零 2 天，Mediterranean 告诉 Kenya Railways 的律师一是提单有光租条款，二是 "Antares" 只是期租进来，故它只是代理人。当时，海牙·维斯比规则（英国 1971 年海上运输法）措辞十分明确严厉的一年时效已届，Kenya Railways 再也来不及调转矛头去起诉 "Antares" 的船东了，结果，一个责任十分明确，索赔金额达 75 万英镑的案件就因为对象找错而以失败告终。

4.3.1.5 美国、加拿大法院有不同看法

美国法院一向倾向货方利益，对光租条款这种会令货方无法充分理解而导致上当的条款自然是抱有敌意。在 Pendleton v. Benner Line (1918) 246 U.S. 353，判是 Benner Line 的班轮公司公开以"公众承运人"(common carrier) 身份去揽货，之后接受货物再去租船，安排小工装货上船，订下并收取运费后才自己签发提单。这一来，Benner Line 不能靠在提单内自说自话，自称为代理人，只代原船东签提单，就妄想去合法脱身。

但是，笔者想如果不是等到签发提单时，而是在一早订运输合约时，就已获发

货人同意班轮提单的内容包括光船条款,再加上已期租了船舶,就很难去指责船公司/班轮公司是事后自说自话,改变身份了。

也有其他美国案例像 Epstein v. United States(1949)86 F. Supp. 740(SDNY);The "Anthony Ⅱ"(1966)2Lloyd's Rep. 437 判光租条款实质是减轻承运人责任,违反1936年的美国海上运输法(海牙规则)。但这看法与英国法院不同,后者认为海牙规则讲明船东或承租人都可以是承运人,只要他/它其中一位肯出面与托运人/发货人订立运输合约:见本章1.1小段。故此,光船条款去说明谁是承运人有何不妥,有何违反海牙规则之处呢?

另在加拿大也有类同美国的判法:The "Mica"(1973) 2 Lloyd's Rep. 478 与双方同意的上诉在(1975) 2 Lloyd's Rep. 371。

4.3.2 班轮提单针对承运人条款之二:承运人身份条款(identity of carrier clause)

有部分的班轮提单,除了光租条款外,另会有一条近似内容的承运人身份条款。实际上,光租条款亦只是承运人身份条款的一种。可去节录在 The "Starsin"(2000)1 Lloyd's Rep. 85 先例的提单33条(35条是光租条款)如下:"IDENTITY OF CARRIER The contract evidence by this Bill of Lading is between the merchant and the owner of the vessel named here in or substitute and it is therefore agreed that said ship owner only shall be liable for any damage or loss billed(SIC)to any breach or non performance of any obligation arising out of the contract of carriage whether or not relating to the vessel seaworthiness. If despite the foregoing, it is adjudged that any other is the carrier and/or bailee of the goods ship here under, or limitation of, and exoneration from liabilities provided for by law or by this Bill of Lading shall be available to such other. It is further understood and agreed that as a line, company or agent who has executed this Bill of Lading for and on behalf of the master is not a principal in the transaction and the said line, Company or agent shall not be under any liabilities arising out of the contract of carriage, nor as carrier nor bailee of the goods."

以上条款在措辞/用字上不尽如人意,例如漏了针对光船租赁的可能,但明显是意图去说明船舶的真正原船东才是承运人,不是班轮公司。但在订约自由下,加上草拟的班轮公司水平也不一样,所以也有过承运人身份条款是说承运人是该班轮公司,而不是可能期租进来船舶的真正原船东的。这种条款的例子可去看本章1.4小段节录的 The "Venezuela"(1980)1 Lloyd's Rep. 393。在此只提一点,如果有像 The "Venezuela"的承运人身份或定义条款,而在同一份提单又去印上一条意思/措辞完全相反的光船条款,那么可以说合约整体解释起来,会是只能完全罔顾这两条正面冲突的条款的存在。这种情况笔者见过,可见这世界上不知所谓的订约与履约的人士并不少。

§5 提单由谁签字的重要性

提单是一份货物装上船舶的收据,正常情况下都会是船长或代船长(通常是船东代理人)签字。而船长与船东有主仆关系,除非是光船租赁:本章之 3.1 段。而涉及期租,也通常会是承租人或他的代理人代船长签字,这权力来自租约:本章之 3.5 小段。但会有混乱情况,例如船长或代理人注明提单是代承租人的某班轮公司作为承运人而签发。

提单谁签字/代谁签字的重要性在于该签字是后来用手写,加在提单格式上的前页的,因此合约解释起来有矛盾时该签字的内容自然要超越印就在背页的光船条款或承运人身份条款。加上,它会被视为是一种"表述"(represent),表述谁愿意作为承运人。正如 Colman 大法官在 The "Starsin" (2000) 1 Lloyd's Rep. 85 之第 90 页所说:"…if a party signs a charter-party or any other commercial contract, just as he may do so in a way which indicates that he does not accept personal liability, so conversely he may do so in a way which represents that he does accept personal liability. Having regard to the fact that the printed form of the bill of lading clearly indicates by the words of attestation and by cll. 33 and 35(承运人身份与光船条款)that the shipowner is the carrier and is as such bound by the contract of affreightment, that conclusion can be displaced only if by the additional writing it is clearly represented that some other party is to assume the obligations of carriage under that contract. In approaching this problem of construction, just as 'preponderant importance' is to be attached to a qualification to a signature indicating that the signatory is only an agent…so in ascertaining whether the signatory has accepted personal liability under the contract it is necessary to give preponderant importance to the words used in conjunction with the signature and other relevant words written on to the printed form."

5.1 船长签字约束船东的一般说法

有一个"一般说法"(rule)是因为船长受雇于船东(没有光租情况下),所以他的签字总是去约束船东。在外人来看,他有船东实质或名义的授权。所以,权威的说法一直是如果光是以提单签字为准来认定谁是提单合约的承运人,则船长签字就是船东的提单:Turner v. Haji Goolam (1904) A. C. 826;Wehner v. Dene (1905) 2 KB 92;Limerick v. Coker (1916) 33 T. L. R. 103;The "Hector" (1998) 2 Lloyd's Rep. 287 等。

在《Scrutton on Charterparties》一书 20 版之第 80 页有提到 Wehner v. Dene 先例

中 Channell 大法官的说法如下:"If the charter is not a demise, a bill of lading signed by the master or by the charterer as authorized agent of the master is usually a contract with the shipowner. In ordinary cases, where the charterparty does not amount to a demise of the ship, and where possession of ship is not given up to the charterer, the rule is that the contract contained in the bill of lading is made, not with the charterer, but with the owner."

另在参阅了所有有关先例后,Leggatt 大法官也在 The"Rewia"(1991)2 Lloyd's Rep. 325 总结了这说法,他的话已在本章之 3.5 小段有节录,不再重复。

5.2 期租承租人签字一般也约束船东

有关这一点,也有在较早的 3.5 小段详及,不去重复。只提提节录在该小段的 Tillmans v. Knutsford(1908)1 KB 185,Channell 大法官提到期租承租人把提单上的"为船长与船东"(for the captain and owners)涂掉再签上自己名字,情况就不一样了。可以说,这会把一份所谓的"船东提单"(owner's bill)变为一份"承租人提单"(charterer's bill)。这种情况不多见,但也曾经有,会是签发提单的承租人或他的代理人不小心/不理解所导致。

在 Harrison v. Huddersfield SS Co(1903)19 T. L. R. 386,船长签字并批注"作为期租承租人代理"(as agent for time charterers),而原有的"as master"印在提单上却被涂掉,即是这样的情况/例子。Walton 大法官说:"… if the Master had signed as master he would have been making a contract for the shipowners. But he did not do so. Under the whole circumstances of the case, the contract by the bill of lading was not made for the shipowners, nor did the master propose to act for the shipowners,[171] nor had he apparent authority."

另在 Samuel v. West Hartlepool Co. (1906) 11 Com. Cas. 111,提单是印上期租承租人的抬头,而签字的船长没有加上任何批注(即代谁签发),判是一份承租人提单。但在《Voyage Charter》一书之 382 页,作者认为该案例今天再审理判法应会不一样。期租下船长是船东雇用,不加批注的签字约束谁应是很明确。

在 Paterson, Zochonis & Co. v. Elder Dempster(1922)12 Lloyd's Rep. 69 先例(已在本章 1.4 小段提及),涉及一家十分著名的班轮公司(African Steamship Co.,),它也很少租用外轮,一般以自己拥有的船舶营运。这导致持有该班轮公司提单的货方,都会以为是与它订立运输合约。Rowlett 大法官因此判不加批注的船长签字仍改变不了提单是承租人提单的性质,他说:"…it seems to me that there is a contract

---

[171] 该案例中船长出庭证明船东指示他不能去代船东签发提单,只能代承租人。

with the African Shipping Co. on this bill of lading. This is a case where a well-known line of ships…proclaims to the people who took the bill of lading that those who are going to carry the goods are the African Steamship Co; and there is the signature at the bottom which may be the signature of the master without qualification. Therefore, I think, in these circumstances it is a bill of lading with the African Shipping Co."

但在后来的 The"Rewia"(1991)2 Lloyd's Rep. 325,事实大致相同(除了一点),上诉庭的判法却不同。该船舶分租给了一家集装箱班轮公司,并以它的抬头签发提单,而签字是"代船长"(for the master)。货物装在集装箱,但集装箱航次途中被冲下海。货方向船东与分承租人的班轮公司起诉。上诉庭判该案提单是"船东提单",说(已节录在本章 3.5 小段):"a bill of lading signed for the master cannot be a charterer's bill"。

至于与 Paterson, Zochonis & Co. 的先例矛盾,判法相反,Leggatt 大法官区分的理由是有一点事实不相同:Paterson, Zochonis & Co. 的班轮公司极少期租船舶,基本上使用自己拥有的船舶营运;但 The"Rewia"的集装箱班轮公司营运全靠租人的船舶。Leggatt 大法官在第 331 页说:"But no impetus is to be derived from that case for present purposes, because although the bills were liner bills all the tonnage used by the first defendants(班轮公司) appears to have been chartered in."

对笔者而言,以班轮公司自拥或期租船舶的多寡作为区分有不妥之处。毕竟,这事实不会反映在一份提单上,收货人/持有人也无法知道事实。这一来,无助于他们去寻找谁是提单承运人,向他及时起诉索赔货差货损。

总结起来,承租人提单的情况不多(看个别提单的措辞/用字而定,特别是签字代表谁)。而对期租承租人而言,也有实质或/与表面授权去代船长/船东签发"船东提单"(owner's bill):请参阅第二章之 5.6.6 小段。即使没有实质授权(这情况很罕见,也不是一般期租租约标准格式像 NYPE 46 的第 8 条款的说法,但考虑到订约自由,难保不会有情况是期租加上一条附加条款说明承租人无权签发约束船东的提单,应由船东代理人或船长签发才有效),对货方而言,特别是收货人/提单持有人,承租人仍有表面授权,因为他们不会知道租约的私下安排。正如 Colman 大法官在 The"Starsin"(2000)1 Lloyd's Rep. 85 先例说道(第 92 页):"At the primary stage of construction, the issue is what was represented, not what was authorized to be represented. In answering this question facts, such as the existence of actual authority of the signatory to bind the owners, which would not normally be within the shippers' knowledge, cannot be part of the context or commercial setting."

对船长(与期租承租人)是否有表面授权去签发"船东提单"(owner's bill)并约束船东曾有过质疑并予否定的唯一先例是著名的 Grant v. Norway(1851)10 C. B.

(N. S.)665。它涉及船长为未曾装上船舶的货物签发了提单,而法院判船长没有实质(这是肯定)或表面授权去这样做并约束船东。

但这判法十分有争议,因为若有表面授权说法的话,就不应再去区分是否有疏忽或不诚实。正如一位雇员有他所属公司的表面授权处理某些事项,对无辜与无法知情的外人看来,这位雇员在他工作分内有疏忽或不诚实或干得不好,所属公司也要负责,是表面授权的一部分,无法去区分。去想想,既然没有实质授权,而要去依赖表面授权,就已表示不必有受约束的一方认同。

所以 Colman 大法官在 The "Starsin" (2000) 1 Lloyd's Rep. 85 之第 97 页说"At p. 611, col. 1 of his judgement [The "Nea Tyhi" (1982) 1 Lloyd's Rep. 606] Mr. Justice Sheen drew attention to that passage in the judgement of Lord Justice Mackinnon in Uxbridge Permanent Benefit Building Society v. Pickard, (1939) 2 K. B. 248 in which he had attempted to rationalize the distinction between Grant v. Norway and Lloyd v. Grace Smith (1912) A. C. 716. Mr. Justice Sheen commented that he did not understand how the conclusion (that there was no ostensible authority) followed from the premise (that anyone dealing with the captain of a ship must be taken to know that he could only have authority to sign a bill of lading for goods which have been in fact shipped). In my judgment, this explanation is not consistent with the true conceptual basis of ostensible authority to which I have referred. The application of that basis would not lead to any distinction between the contractual rights acquired by the innocent shipper or consignee under a bill of lading issued by a time charterer or other agent clothed by the shipowner with authority to issue bills of lading generally, where the bill was issued negligently or fraudulently in respect of goods not shipped (and therefore without actual authority) and the contractual rights of a third party in respect of a contract signed by an agent who had been placed by his principal in a position to conclude contracts of the kind in question. In this connection the words of Lord Robertson in George Whitechurch Ltd. v. Cavanagh, (1902) A. C. 117 at p. 137 are directly in points:

'It seems to me extremely doubtful whether Grant v. Norway can be held, or has ever been held, to represent the general law, or to do more than determine the law about ship-masters and bills of lading, and whether, assuming it to have the wider bearing, it is reconcilable with the doctrine of Lord Selbourne in Houldsworth v. City of Glasgow Bank. *I found it extremely difficult on principle to hold that the scope of an agent's employment can be limited to the right performance of his duties, or to say that an agent within whose province it is truly to record a fact is outside the scope of his duties when he falsely records it, when the question of liability to be decided is whether a loss is to be borne by the princi-*

pal who placed him there, or by an innocent third party who had no voice in selecting him'."

接下去，Colman 大法官基本上否定了 Grant v. Norway 的先例，说："Accordingly, as the law has now developed, Grant v. Norway should be treated as conceptually aberrant and should not be used as a basis for the extension of the protection of shipowners against being bound by bills of lading issued by time charterers, or other agents on behalf of the owners, which by reason of some inaccuracy on their face, have been issued without actual authority. Not only does this conclusion give effect to the conceptual basis of ostensible authority but it also reflects a further important policy consideration. That is that if an innocent shipper, indorsee or consignee could not rely on statements on the face of a bill of lading as to such matters as the date of shipment and the absence of clausing and was obliged to verify the accuracy of the date and the apparent good order and condition of the goods each time he took a bill of lading, that would represent a most serious impediment to international trade which depends so heavily on the accuracy of bills of lading as negotiable instruments."

再近期的是 Alimport v. Soubert Shipping Co. Ltd. (2000) 2 Lloyd's Rep. 447，判是"无辜"的船东要对承租人代理签发的倒签提单负责。该先例的 Timothy Walker 大法官认同 The "Nea Nyhi"，The "Saudi Crown" (1986) 1 Lloyd's Rep. 261，The "Hector" (1998) 2Lloyd's Rep. 287 与 The "Starsin"，并说："…the agents had ostensible authority to issue bills of lading, and the shipowners are bound by the bill of lading as issued."（承租人代理有表面授权签发提单，该提单约束船东）。

该先例也说 Grant v. Norway 已完全被 1992 年海上运输法的立法所废除了（finally given its "guietus" by sec. 4 of COGSA 1992）。

5.3　中国部分人士的不同看法

笔者据闻大陆有部分人士认为期租承租人才是提单的"承运人"，因为他/它可以"胡作非为"，船东经常失控。加上许多工作是由承租人承担，如装卸货物。所以，有了期租则船东不再是提单的"承运人"，这不公平。

笔者不清楚的是：在此说法下，凡涉及期租，提单"承运人"是否一定是承租人，而不论提单表面的写法；或是"承运人"尚须看看提单的写法如何？

若是后者，则该说法与英国的说法并无不同之处，如上小段所讲，提单表面的签字（是认定"承运人"的重要依据）若"为船长"，而船长又是船东雇用，其是"船东提单"，船东是"承运人"，但若签字是为了承租人，则会是"承租人提单"了。

若是前者，则该说法会与国际社会很不一样了。而且，它会否定了"订约自由"

原则，因为提单上注明了签字"为船长或/及船东"也不算数，"承运人"仍硬性算是承租人。如果仅仅是以不公平就可以否定合约的内容，将会导致合约的约束力在中国法律下大减。其原因是要想在合约条款中挑出不公平之处实在不难，即使在订约当初是公平的，后来也会变得不公平的，例如货价在市场大起大落。在英国，能够否定合约内容的只是违反公共政策，而不仅仅是不公平，因此英国法的地位可令大家对合约有信心。

再者，把期租承租人当做提单的"承运人"有其他方面的严重缺陷，如：

（ⅰ）与其他航运习惯做法难于接轨，例如期租标准格式一般有授权承租人代船东签发提单的条款，见"纽约土产（NYPE）第8条"（请阅《期租合约》一书之§25段）；在本书第五章之4.2.3.2.2.7小段曾提到另一期租标准格式的 Gentime 1999，第17条写得更明确如下："… If requested, the Owners may authorise the Charterers and/or their agents in writing to sign bills of lading, waybills, through bills of lading or multimodal bills of lading (hereafter collectively referred to as Contracts of Carriage) on the Owners' and/or Master's behalf…"

试想，若提单的"承运人"一定（或作为起点）是承租人，为什么还有要求船东授权的普遍条款？承租人签发自己作为"承运人"的运输合约，何需他人（船东变成分包人）授权才能作为呢？

（ⅱ）提单是货物的收据（请看本书第六章）。从发货人手中接收货物的是船长，不是承租人，因此正常情况下不应是承租人签发收据。

（ⅲ）今天一般的反映与做法是：若船东/船长在装港知悉承租人在背后签发了不准确提单，会跳起来，并与互保协会一起设法去阻止该提单的流通。如向法院申请禁令［请见本书第六章之3.2.4 小段详论的 The "Phassa"（1990）SMA No. 2640 案例］，通知收货人与开证/保兑银行等。著名的 The "Antaios"（1984）2 Lloyd's Rep. 235 也是同类事件。再可举另一著名的 The "Nanfri"（1979）1 Lloyd's Rep. 201 案例。若是提单的"承运人"根本不是船东，何苦紧张？

（ⅳ）本质上，期租与程租接近，但与光租不接近。主要不同之处是船长的雇用。鉴于通过船长可以有效控制船舶，而船长的雇用关系到其权利的来源，授权必须有根有据。故光租下船长的所作所为约束光租承租人，签发的提单也是光租承租人提单，此点相信大家没有异议：请看本章§3段。若期租下船长不是承租人雇用，但签发（或代其签发）的提单却是承租人提单，岂非程租也应如此解释？除了期租程租下船长都由船东雇用外，今天 TCT（time charter trip）的普遍做法更是现实中令期租与程租难以区分。这样说来，难道只要有租船的安排，所签发的提单都是承租人提单？或是期租/TCT 是承租人提单，程租才是船东提单？而在前者说法下，岂非所有租约提单无论写法如何/签字如何均为"承租人提单"？而"船东提单"只会在班轮中出现了？而说法是去增加复杂性？例如，收货人难以凭手中的一份提单就知悉原船东是 TCT 或是程租，他/它应去起诉承租人或是船东呢？谁是承租人呢？

（v）这部分人士的说法并没有充分考虑中国货方的利益。已经在上段列举了一种情况，再多举一种情况：承租人若是提单的承运人、运输合约的对象，当他/它们是隐蔽（租约提单上不写明）的，或是皮包公司，或是外国（甚至是方便旗国家）公司，中国货方要想起诉他们绝非容易（请看 3.6.2 小段）。中国法律不承认"对物诉讼"（请看 3.6.3 小段），只有当船东是"承运人"（暂且不讲"实际承运人"这一与国际不一致的说法）时，才可通过扣船取得"诉前保全"，这才是中国货方的利益所在。

（vi）这一说法也没有考虑到后果的严重性。例如船东/船长十分容易去做手脚，毕竟货物由船长照管的。他可以做了手脚而不负责，因为提单的承运人是承租人。而以"实际承运人"的说法去约束船东/船长不一定管用，这不是合约关系，况且除事实不容易查明外，诉讼也不一定在中国大陆法院。

（vii）笔者另一重大忧虑是中国法律在这方面（航运与外贸），最好不要与国际做法/说法太脱节，这会误导一大批中国的年轻人，且会令他/它们与国际上格格不入。除非涉及中国重大利益、且非如此作为不可时。不过，即使如此，也要先想出一套完整的方案，避免前后矛盾和难以自圆其说，最后才考虑决定是否去做。

（viii）其实中国部分人士何必愁不公平。船东作为提单"承运人"或是承租人作为提单"承运人"先承担起提单责任后再去追偿，这是船东与船东互保协会惯常的做法，最终责任属谁怎会摆不平？

§6 如何识别提单承运人

6.1 全凭对提单内明示条款、措辞与签字的全面解释

综合以上段节所讲，可以说识别提单承运人的整个做法与中心思想并不复杂。第一是只去解释提单上的措辞/用字，如 1.2 小段节录 The "Starsin" (2000) 1 Lloyd's Rep. 85 所讲的："As a matter of basic principle the resolution of the issue of the identity of the party undertaking the obligations of carriage is one of construction of the words on the bill of lading". 第二是解释一份商业合约，应全面去解释所有有关条款/文字。正如 1.4 小段节录 The "Venezuela" (1980) 1 Lloyd's Rep. 393 所讲的："To answer this question（谁是承运人？）I must look at all the terms of the bill of lading and construe the document as a whole."

笔者的《国际商务游戏规则——英国合约法》一书第十章详细讲述了有关"合约的解释"，不少内容完全适用在提单的解释，但无法在此全部节录。

因为其中有千奇百怪的写法，也会导致有不同的判决。有时看来小小的一点不同就会带来完全不同的判决，毕竟这涉及个别法官在看了整份提单合约后总的感觉可以很灵活，但也不稳定。例如，提单上用了一个极大的红字印章，甚至加有"重要"一字，说"本提单承运人不是任何其他人，而是某班轮公司"。可能是，这加上的印章解释上会带来极大的比重，会去超越内容矛盾/不同的其他条款或船长签字：The"Hector"(1998) 2 Lloyd's Rep. 287。另在 The "Starsin"，笔者原认为 Colman 大法官判得十分好，有说服力，但这给上诉庭推翻了，因为解释同一份提单有不同结论：请看本章 7.6 小段。

另要去提的一点是谁签发或代谁签发提单的重要性：本章 §5 段。强调这点是考虑到今天所见的提单（租约或班轮提单）都会是代船长签发，更有在 5.1 小段的"一般说法"(rule)去约束船东，视提单为"船东提单"(owner's bill)，而且这一般说法在近年也明显愈来愈被法院所接受。尽管提单明示条款重要还是签字重要（如果有了矛盾）仍会有不同看法：请看 7.7 小段的 The "Starsin" 一审与上诉。另去重提的是本章 1.3 小段讲到的发货人与承运人之间订约谈判中的证据在提单这一特殊的合约下一般是不被接纳的，只能看提单并作出解释。

6.2　UCP500 对承运人说明的要求

现实中令这方面疑问/混乱以及判决不稳定而造成货方很不公平的后果会能较大程度减少的另一个发展是 UCP500 的修改，它明确要求海运提单的正面/前页上要去写明谁是承运人。这是在 Article 23(a)(ⅰ) 所说的：

"Marine/Ocean Bill of Lading

a) If a Credit calls for a bill of lading covering a port-to-port shipment, banks will, unless otherwise stipulated in the Credit, accept a document, however named, which:

(ⅰ) appears on its face to indicate the name of the carrier and to have been signed or otherwise authenticated by:

— the carrier or a named agent for or on behalf of the carrier, or

— the master or a named agent for or on behalf of the master.

Any signature or authentication of the carrier or master must be identified as carrier or master, as the case may be. An agent signing or authenticating for the carrier or master must also indicate the name and the capacity of the party, i.e. carrier or master, on whose behalf that agent is acting …"

故此，在本书附录九的"Conlinebill 2000"提单标准格式，为符合 UCP500，BIMCO 文件委员会马上作了修改并在正面提单的左下角加上一大格专门填上承运人名字与地址。这一来，今后收货人/提单持有人光看提单也不再会难以捉摸谁才是承运人了。而只要去填上,将来真有争议要去作出解释,这一大格的注明的谁是承运人恐怕是有极大的分量了。

若是提单没有填上承运人,会被视为有不符点而遭受银行拒绝结汇。在笔者的《信用证》一书第六章1.3小段曾讲到:

> 在UCP500的新规定下,有一些班轮提单会是不符合。它一般会有抬头的一家船公司,例如马士基的班轮提单抬头自然是马士基。但马士基不一定是承运人:如果船是租回来再加上一条光租条款的话。要去符合UCP500,照说提单应有一处或一条款清楚说明谁是承运人,反正总有一方要出来顶上。
>
> 香港最近有一案例名为Southland Rubber Co Ltd v. Bank of China(1997) 3 HKC 569,提单是有抬头公司的,名为"P. T. Kemah Nusasemesta",并称是"船东、进出口商等"(Shipowner's Export-Import, General Contractor),但就是没有讲谁是"承运人"(carrier)。签字应是代理,说是由船长授权代船东签。法院严格解释UCP500,说这提单有不符点。

话说回来,UCP500虽可减少这方面的疑问与不稳定,但也不会完全消除之,因为:

(ⅰ)不是所有提单都与UCP500有关,国际货物买卖不一定都以信用证支付。

(ⅱ)提单即使填上承运人一栏/一格,还会有其他批注/增加条款导致要整体解释,也会把承运人填错填漏,承运人是谁仍会有争议。

(ⅲ)UCP500的Article 25针对租约提单,规定不对此(注明谁是承运人)作同样要求。固然,大部分租约提单并没有抬头的船公司名字,而且往往代船长签发,毫无疑问是"船东提单"(owner's bill)。但这也无法说死:会有租约提单有船公司抬头而它不是真正船东或光船承租人,也会有签字是代期租承租人而非代船长的。

§7 近期有关案例简介

7.1 案例之一:The"Venezuela"(1980)1 Lloyd's Rep. 393

它涉及一批2000吨的菱镁矿(magnesite UBE 95)从日本运去委内瑞拉途中遭受海水损坏,故收货人要找出谁是提单承运人,向他索赔。

揽货承运的是一班轮公司,由两家南美国家船公司CAVN与FMG经营。它也签发了它们公司抬头的提单,并有一条说明承运人是CAVN或FMG的"承运人定义"(definition of carrier)条款,这一切都在本章之1.4小段有提及。

出事的船舶属一家单船的巴拿马公司拥有，它期租了给一中国公司，再分租/期租给 CAVN，因为 CAVN 不够船舶使用。

签发提单的是 CAVN 在日本的代理人：日本著名的 NYK。签字是说明代船长签发："Nippon Yusen Kaisha general agents and as agents for the Master."

照说，根据"一般说法"（rule），这代船长签字的提单应逃不了是"船东提单"（owner's bill）。但 Sheen 大法官认为这说法不是一成不变的，并引述 Roche 大法官在 Wilston Steamship Company Ltd. V. Andrew Weir & Co. (1925) 22 Lloyd's Rep. 521 的说法："But that is not an invariable rule and it always falls to be decided on the facts and documents of the particular case."

而且，Sheen 大法官认为"承运人定义"条款说明 CAVN 是承运人比船长授权签字更重要，虽然前者只是印就条款。Sheen 大法官说："If those goods had been carried in a ship owned by CAVN, the shipment would have been made in precisely the same manner as in this case. NYK would have issued a bill of lading identical in every material respect. Only the names of the Master and the ship would have been different. It seems to me that if CAVN did not wish to contract as 'the carrier', then the bill of lading issued by CAVN should at least have made it clear with which company the shipper was entering into the contract of carriage. Until the shipper or holder of the bill of lading was told that 'Samjohn Governor'（承运船舶）was on time charter for the voyage in question there was nothing on either side of the bill of lading which indicated that anyone other than CAVN was contracting as carrier."

对原告而言，判 CAVN 是承运人的好处是它经济实力较强，本身也拥有船队可供对物诉讼。若是单船的巴拿马公司（真正船东）是承运人，则除非能成功去对物诉讼并取得诉前保全，否则根本无从下手去向它索赔。

7.2 案例之二：The "Rewia" (1991) 2 Lloyd's Rep. 325

它也是涉及货物损坏，集装箱被冲下大海。该案例的船舶"Rewia"以 NYPE 标准格式期租了给一班轮公司。签发的提单印有班轮公司与它"经理人"（manager）的抬头。但提单上另有两处显示船东才是承运人的内容如下：

（ⅰ）在提单正面，有一条常见的条款，是所谓的 attestation clause，在本书第二章之 5.1.4 小段已提过这种条款的作用，措辞是："In Witness whereof the Master of the said Vessel has signed the number of original Bills of Lading stated below, all of this tenor and date, one of which being accomplished, the others to stand void."

（ⅱ）提单签字一栏印有"代船长"（for the Master）。

上诉庭判是"船东提单"（owner's bill），船东才是承运人。该案由 Leggatt 大法官作主要的判词,而 Dillon 大法官则总结说:"Lord Justice Leggatt has summarized the relevant English authorities in his judgment. The key words in the bills are the words 'for master' against which the stamp and signature of St. John Agencies have been placed. Unless the words 'for master' can be rejected as surplusage or repugnant to the references to the sub-charterers in the heading of the bills, these bills must, on the English authorities analysed by Lord Justice Leggatt be held to be owners' bills signed for the master so as to bind his employers, the owners. But I can, for my part, see no basis of construction which would entitle the Court to reject the words 'for master' and the preceding words 'In Witness whereof the Master… has signed the… Bills' in this way. Therefore, in my judgment, the bills are, by English law, owners' bills…"

在此先例,可见上诉庭重申船长或代船长签字约束船东的"一般说法"(rule)。这令笔者想到在 7.1 小段谈及的 The"Venezuela"(1980)1 Lloyd's Rep. 393 先例,如果考虑了 The"Rewia"的说法再判,结果会否有所不同?

7.3　案例之三:The"Ines"(1995)2 Lloyd's Rep. 144

它是一个著名的无单放货案例,已在本书第二章如 5.6.2 小段略为提及。显然,要以提单合约去向承运人提出无单放货的违约索赔,又要涉及谁是承运人之争了。

该案例的班轮公司名为 Maras Linja,它向"Ines"的德国船东期租了该船 3 个月来营运,并在装港指定了 EIMSKIP 为代理人。

在装港签发的提单,签字是代理人,并有含糊不清的批注。首先,提单格式印有代"Maras Linja"签发(signed for the carrier Maras Linja)。但又以打字加上了两处:"pp EIMSKIP-Rotterdam"与"as agents only."

这一来,Maras Linja 说它的解释是:EIMSKIP 代它签而它又是承运人(指船东)的代理人;即:"signed by or on behalf of Eimskip as agents of Maras Linja who were in their turn agents for the carrier."

"Ines"的船东反驳说这签字应很明确,是为 Maras Linja 作为承运人签署(signed as agents for the carrier Maras Linja)。这也是 Clarke 大法官所倾向接受的。

但该提单却仍有两条条款是指或显示船长/船东才是承运人:

(ⅰ)在提单正面,有一条常见的条款,在本书第二章之 5.1.4 小段已提过这种证明(attestation)条款的作用,措辞是:"IN WITNESS whereof the Master or the Agent of the said vessel has signed the number of original Bills of Lading stated below all of this tenor and date, one of which being accomplished the others to be void."

(ⅱ)在提单背面,有一条类似"光船条款"(demise clause)的条款说:

"19. RESPONSIBILITY WHEN JOINT SERVICE. The Contract evidenced by this Bill of Lading is between the Shipper and the Owner of the ocean vessel named therein (or substitute) and it is therefore agreed that the said shipowner only shall be liable for any loss, damage or delay arising or resulting…"

在衡量了所有相互矛盾的条款/措辞后,Clarke 大法官判船东才是承运人,说: "Although the signature box itself is ambiguous, a consideration of the other clauses and the document as a whole leads in my judgment to the conclusion that the parties intended that the contract should be between the shippers and the shipowners. It follows that I have reached the conclusion that the parties to the contract of carriage contained in or evidenced by the bills of lading were the plaintiffs on the one hand and the owners on the other. I have reached that conclusion as a matter of construction of the bill of lading itself. A consideration of the surrounding circumstances does not seem to me to lead to any other result."

由此案例可见,签字一栏与它的批注虽然重要,但若有严重矛盾而要去超越像光船条款等条款,它必须足够肯定与明确,否则谈不上在整体解释中能去超越。或者是,"一般说法"(rule)针对的是船长/代船长签字,并不适用在约束承租人方面。

7.4 案例之四:The "Hector"(1998)2 Lloyd's Rep. 287

此案例涉及分承租人(也是 FOB 买方)已根据程租约把所有运费支付给了二船东,但二船东(也是期租承租人)失踪,不再支付租金给原船东。这一来,船东不肯自掏腰包去完成航次,除非分承租人再付一次运费。分承租人当然不肯,因为他手中有一份注明"运费已预付"(freight prepaid)的提单。但问题是:该提单是否约束船东? 它是"承租人提单"(charterer's bill),也即二船东的提单,还是"船东提单"(owner's bill)?

有关的提单格式是 BIMCO 印发的 Conline Bill(本书之附录九),故没有船公司抬头。但它在提单正面/前页加上一图章说:"CARRIER: U. S. EXPRESS LINES (USEL)"。USEL 就是承租人/二船东。

除此之外,提单其他多处条款却都显示承运人应是船东,如:

(i) 签字是"代船长"(FOR AND ON BEHALF OF THE MASTER-MR V. ILNITSKY WITHERFIELD LIMITED AS AGENTS)。

(ii)提单背面有一条第 17 条款是"承运人身份"条款,措辞/文字如本章之 4.3.2 小段所节录,说明船舶的真正船东才是承运人。

但最终 Rix 大法官受加上的图章所影响,判 USEL 才是承运人,而船东不受约束。判词说:"As a matter of construction, then, I have found the issue an intriguing one, largely I think because of the pressure created by the general rule that a bill of lading signed by the master is an owner's bill. There is also of course the powerful pointer of cl. 17. However, I have not been able to satisfy myself that the stipulation that the carrier is USEL is to be shrugged off as ambiguous. What does it mean, and why was it been inserted, unless it is intended to have effect as the definition of the carrier? The term 'carrier' is a critical terms. It is not like an expression which might merely indicate that USEL was the operator of the vessel or the owner of the line. 'Carrier' is the expression in which the party with the obligations to carry out the bill of lading contract is clothed… The bill of lading therefore stipulates that the carrier under the bill of lading is USEL. Although the master may be the servant of the owners, and cl. 17 say that the owners are the carriers, the only party which is identified expressly by name in the bill of lading as the carrier is USEL…"

7.5　案例之五:The"Flecha"(1999) 1 Lloyd's Rep. 612

本案例也是涉及货损索赔,有关船舶"Flecha"期租给了一家名为 Continental Pacific Shipping Ltd. 的船公司/营运人(operator),装载木材产品从远东港口运去欧洲,签发的提单全是装港代理人"代作为承运人的承租人签发"(as agents for the carrier Continental Pacific Shipping)。

但提单另有相互矛盾之处如下:

(ⅰ)提单正面有一 attestation clause 说:"In witness whereof the Master of the said vessel has signed the number of original Bills of lading stated below all of this tenor and date, one of which being accomplished, the others to stand void."

(ⅱ) 提单背面33 条款的"承运人身份"说:"The contract evidenced by this bill of lading is between the merchant and the owner of the vessel…and… the said shipowner only shall be liable for any damage or loss due to any breach or non-performance of any obligations arising out of the contract of carriage…"

(ⅲ)提单背面第35 条的"光船条款"。

Moore-Bick 大法官对所有有关条款作整体解释后判是"船东提单"(owner's bill),说:"If it were the intention of the shipping line to undertake personal liability for the carriage of the goods in contradiction to what was stated in the bills of lading terms something far clearer would be required in order to bring that about; the form of signature while they raised questions of describing Continental Pacific as carriers did not go far enough to make it clear contracting in place of the owners contrary to all the terms of the bills of lading."

看来，这判法与 7.3 小段的 The "Ines"（1995）2 Lloyd's Rep. 144 一致：请参阅该小段的最后一段/一句，本案例同样适用。唯一不同之处是：The "Ines" 提单签字的批注含糊不清，但 The "Flecha" 的提单应是清楚明确，但判决却结果一样。

7.6 案例之六：**Maritrop Trading Corp. v. Guangzhou Ocean Shipping Co.**（1998）**CLC** 224

此涉及广远的先例中，提单签字是"代船长"（Arete… as agents for and on behalf of Capt. Deng Zuo Tai, Master of M/V "Hung Jiang"）。以此为依据，货方向广远起诉。广远实际是把该船期租给了一家名 Pacific Asia Line Inc 的公司，它签发的提单抬头也有印上它的公司名字。

但该提单格式另印有一条矛盾的"承运人身份条款"（Identity of Carrier clause）：本章的 4.3.2 小段。它是说"承运人……只是……"（carrier…shall only refer to Project Asia Steamship Ltd），条款并印上 Pacific Asia 的地址、电话与传真号码。

总之，判是该提单承运人不是广远。

7.7 案例之七：The "Starsin"（2000）1 **Lloyd's Rep.** 85

本案例与 7.5 小段的 The "Flecha"（1999）1 Lloyd's Rep. 612 十分相似，而且有关的船公司也正是 Continental Pacific Shipping Ltd. 它向 "Starsin" 的船东期租了 "Starsin" 这艘船。提单的签字也有批注是 "as agents for the carrier Continental Pacific Shipping."

而提单另有矛盾之处亦是一样：正面前页有一 attestation clause，背面后页有第 33 条款的"承运人身份"与第 35 条款的"光船条款"。此外提单背面有第一条款的"定义"（definition）说明承运人就是"提单代签发的一方"（the party on whose behalf this Bill of Lading has been signed）。

照说，如果受先例约束，则有了 The "Flecha" 的判决也就应有了定论，不必再审理一次，劳民伤财。但 The "Flecha" 只是英国高院的判决，不是上诉庭或贵族院的判决，所以判 The "Starsin" 的 Colman 大法官不必受此约束，而只需以此作参考。

而代表船东的大律师 Steven Berry 先生为了胜诉，不让提单去约束船东，也只好去攻击 The "Flecha" 案例实在是判错。这记录在判词中说："Mr Steven Berry, on behalf of the defendants, has attacked the correctness of the decision of Mr Justice Moore-Bick in The 'Flecha'.[172] He submits there the Judge started with the small print and

---

[172] 船东大律师攻击 The "Flecha" 判决不正确。

then asked himself the question whether there was anything to contradict it, [173] instead of beginning with the writing in the signature box which he should have treated as the dominant factor [174] ... Mr. Berry submits that, whereas the signature in The 'Ines (1995) 2 Lloyd's Rep. 144 was of ambiguous effect [175], that in The 'Flecha' was totally unambiguous in its description of Continental as the carrier [176], which is exactly this case."

在判决时,Colman 大法官却作出了与 Moore-Bick 大法官完全相反的"解释"(construction),判提单是"承租人(Continental)提单",而不是"船东提单"(owner's bill)。

Colman 大法官说,提单签字的一栏是清楚明确的批注说"as agents for the carrier Continental Pacific Shipping",这不可能会导致货方去认为这是代船长/船东签字,即使提单背后再另有条款说什么不同的反话:"Above all, no shipper reading the contents of the signature box would assume either that the bill had been signed by the master, as stated in the attestation box, or that the agents had signed on behalf of Continental acting in turn on behalf of the carrier. By the words used the agents had represented that Continental was content that it could be treated as the carrier whenever that word appeared in the reverse-side terms."

所以,Colman 大法官的结论是:"... I am not able to accept the argument, based on The "Flecha", that the use of that word is too vague and uncertain to displace the printed provisions, cll. 33 and 35, and the attestation wording. By analogy with the reasoning of Mr. Justice Rix in The "Hector(1998) 2 Lloyd's Rep. 287, with which I entirely agree. I therefore conclude that as a matter of construction these where charterers' bills and not contracts binding the shipowners."

但 Colman 大法官的原判前不久被上诉庭以 2:1 的多数推翻[The "Starsin" (2001)1 Lloyd's Rep. 437]。看来,上诉庭(多数)很受第35条的"光船条款"影响。Chadwick 大法官说:"...Whether the description of Coninental Pacific as 'carrier' in the signature box must yield to the opening words of Cl. 33 was answered by construing the bill of lading as a whole; when that was done it was clear that parties had provided the answer to that question by incorporating Cl. 35 as a term of the contract; the shipowner

---

[173] Moore-Bick 大法官在整体解释提单合约时不应先从小字体的印就条款开始,之后才问有否其他的批注去否定它们(小字体的印就条款)。

[174] 正确的步骤应是先从关键的签字一栏开始,之后才去看其他像小字体的印就条款。这一来,整体的感觉与印象就会不一样。

[175] The "Ines"的提单签字一栏并不明确。

[176] 但 The "Flecha"的提单签字却十分明确,是代"承运人 Continental Pacific Shipping"签发。

was liable in contract under the bills of lading".

笔者对上诉庭的"解释"(construction)有一定保留,也不觉得提单格式印上"光船条款"应给予太大重量。但不管怎样,原判是"承运人提单"却被改成"船东提单",对原告的货方可说是事关重大,也可见这方面的不稳定与不肯定。

7.8 总结

从以上的近期案例简介可见,这方面问题仍是不容易解决,仍存在不肯定/不稳定的因素。在本章6.2小段曾提到UCP500的要求,并说该要求应可去减少这方面的争议。这话虽然正确,但提单正面/前页有了新加的承运人一栏/一格,还是难保在提单的其他地方不会有相互严重矛盾/冲突的条款/批注,以供争辩。银行也无法在结汇时去作出整体解释,而即使作出,也不一定会与将来的法院判决一致,毕竟法官与法官之间也会不一致。

而另一危险是:提单的拟定、签发以及另加上条款/批注等全是由班轮公司或船公司一手包办。托运人/发货人通常无从质疑,更不用说是后来的提单持有人了。这一来,船公司故意把承运人是谁搞得混乱或是写明承运人是一家光棍的皮包公司,都会令货方利益受损,而且这又是海牙规则/海牙·维斯比规则没有想到去对付的。

而就货方向承运人索赔而言,这"承运人"是谁也不好确定,陷阱处处。通常他会是船东,这样的好处是可以去对物诉讼:见本章之3.6.3小段。若是光租,承运人是光船承租人也一样。

但若有期租加插在内,而且期租承租人签发的是有自己名字/抬头的提单,就常会导致究竟船东还是承租人才是提单承运人的争议了。而又要强调的是:提单条款/批注等的拟定/签发却全是由承租人(通常是班轮公司或营运人)一手包办。

此外,能去对物诉讼,货方还要借此机会去澄清背后有否光船租赁的安排:请参阅本章之3.6.4小段。而这是另一层次的问题了,但也必须去顾及。

若针对船东而提单看来承运人是谁会有争议之处,也别忘了加上合约外的侵权/托管诉因,因为一旦船东判不是合约承运人,即提单是"承租人提单"(charterer's bill),则要向船东告下去而不必投降,原告的货方就要依赖侵权/托管了。而届时,作为分包人,船东也会依赖像喜玛拉雅条款或分托管条件(本章之8.2.2小段将详论)以寻求保障。

§8 实际承运人(actual carrier)

在英美法等大部分国家的立法,以及海牙/海牙·维斯比规则的国际公约中,只有合约承运人而没有实际承运人的概念。但 1978 年的"汉堡规则"(Hamburg Rules)首次引入了这个概念,这可去节录第一条款的定义如下:

"Article 1. Definitions

In this Convention:

1. "Carrier" means any person by whom or in whose name a contract of carriage of goods by sea has been concluded with a shipper.

2. "Actual carrier" means any person to whom the performance of the carriage of the goods, or of part of the carriage, had been entrusted by the carrier, and includes any other person to whom such performance has been entrusted."

这概念也引入到中国海商法,有关规定如下:

第 42 条:(二)"实际承运人"是指接受承运人委托,从事货物运输或者部分运输的人,包括接受转委托从事此项运输的其他人。

第 61 条:本章对承运人责任的规定,适用于实际承运人。

8.1 英国法律视为是分包(sub-contract)的做法

英国法律对于合约的承运人自己不去部分或全部履行合约责任,而将其分包给"分包人"(sub-contractor)去代他履行的做法,完全没有异议。而有了合约承运人外再有实际承运人,则后者正是一位"分包人"。

常有此情况发生,如本书第二章 3.2 小段的"全程提单"(through Bill of lading)。而在多式联运提单下,合约承运人(常会是无船承运人的 NVOC)更常会把所有运输的合约责任分包给不同的公路、海路等实际承运人。

在本章 7.6 小段的 The "Starsin"(2000) 1 Lloyd's Rep. 85 案例,既然判了承租人 Continental Pacific Shipping 是提单合约承运人,则真正去进行货物运载的"Starsin"船东也就成了"实际承运人"(actual carrier)了。

分包人也被称为"独立承包商"(independent contractor),他与代理人不同之处是他可去独立行事,不像代理人每每要听命于"委托人"(principal)。提单合约下除了分包运输给实际承运人外,另一种常见的分包是将本属合约承运人分内的装卸货物的提单责任分包给装卸公司。在 The "Starsin",Colman 大法官也谈及这种关系与做法如下:"Ordinarily understood the word "independent contractor" in the context of a head contract means a third party with whom a party to a contract enters into a contract under which the third party contracts to perform some or all of the obligations which that party had undertaken to perform under the head contract, in other words, a sub-contractor. Where a carrier has chartered a vessel to perform the sea carriage which that carrier has contracted with the shipper to perform, he has in effect employed the shipowners to carry out the substantial part of his own contractual obligations. He has therefore employed the shipowner as an independent contractor just as if he had employed a stevedore to carry out the handling of the goods at the port of loading. Accordingly… the defendants (实际承运人的船东) are independent contractors in this case."

8.2 实际承运人与货方没有合约关系

在英国法律下,货方(托运人或收货人/提单持有人)只是与合约承运人有合约关系,而与后来的分包人(实际承运人或装卸工)没有合约关系。这是因为合约关系不是天上掉下来的,而是要符合各种基本要求[本章一开始提到了三个基本要求,如"对价/约因"(consideration)等]。而这一般不会发生在货方与分包人之间。正如 Goff 勋爵在 The "K. H. Enterprise"(1994)1 Lloyd's Rep. 593 之第 597 页说:"However, so far as English law and the law of Hong Kong are concerned, a technical problem faces shipowners who carry goods, for example under the feeder bills of lading in the present case, where there is no contractual relationship between the shipowners(指实际承运人) and certain cargo-owners. This is because English law still maintains, though subject to increasing criticism, a strict principle of privity of contract, under which as a matter of general principle only a person who is a party to a contract may sue upon it. The force of this principle is supported and enhanced by the doctrine of consideration, under which as a general rule only a promise supported by consideration will be enforceable at common law… The present case is concerned with the question whether the law of bailment can here be invoked by the shipowners to circumvent this difficulty."

这一来,若是货方要向没有合约关系的实际承运人起诉索赔,民事诉讼也只能是依赖"侵权"(tort)了。但这会带来多方面的问题,具体如下:

8.2.1 侵权问题之一:海牙/海牙·维斯比规则不包括分包人

海牙·维斯比规则针对已有提单合约关系的承运人,并不鼓励货方再以侵权去取巧,故它否定一种既有合约,也有侵权的"并列诉权"(concurrent action 或 parallel action)。这方面课题已在本书第二章 5.5.2 小段详及,不再重复。

而海牙/海牙·维斯比规则本质上也只去针对提单承运人(他可以是船东或承租人)与持有人(货方)在运输中对货物责任的公平分配。公约本来是为去约束班轮公司/船东以订约自由去鱼肉货方,原意根本与侵权无关。至于分包人(独立包商)像装卸工等,根本不在规则考虑之列。他们与货方也不存在有并列诉权,因为双方从未有过合约关系。

这一点可去节录海牙·维斯比规则的 Article Ⅲ,说:

"Between Articles 4 and 5 of the Convention[177] shall be inserted the following Article 4 bis:

"1. The defences and limits of liability provided for in this Convention shall apply in any action against the carrier in respect of loss or damage to goods covered by a contract of carriage whether the action be founded in contract or in tort[178].

2. If such an action is brought against a servant or agent of the carrier (such servant or agent not being an independent contractor[179], such servant or agent shall be entitled to avail himself of the defences and limits of liability which the carrier is entitled to invoke under this Convention."

8.2.2 侵权问题之二:以喜玛拉雅条款与分托管去保护分包人

为去保护分包人/独立承包商,班轮提单一般会加印一条喜玛拉雅条款。有关这课题,不妨去节录《国际商务游戏规则——英国合约法》(修订版)一书第四章§5段如下:

§5　困难的可能解决方法之三:喜玛拉雅条款与分托管去保护分包人

5.1　喜玛拉雅条款的作用

已经谈了不少第三者去要求合约权利的情况,对此已添加了新一段的 4.3.5 小段加以介绍。现在转个话题谈谈第三者应有的责任。当然,在绪言已谈到,基本精神是不能在第三者没有同意的情况下,去强加"合约"责任到他身上。但如果这是"侵权"或"托管"(bailment)的责任,不需要合约为前提,这责任就不一样了,会可去加在第三者身上。侵权的责任主要是疏忽,等于第三者(比如船员、装卸工)的疏忽,会带来合约一方(如货主)侵权的起诉。这种情况

---

[177] 这是指海牙规则,海牙·维斯比规则并不是一个完整的新国际公约,它只是去修改/补充海牙规则的部分内容。

[178] 这是去针对并列诉权,侵权也同样适用海牙/海牙·维斯比规则,货方不得取巧,例如指承运人在提单合约的一年时效虽已届,但另有普通法的 6 年侵权时效仍可供慢慢去起诉,分别只是不以合约而是以侵权为由起诉。

[179] 规则也保护承运人的雇员(如船长/船员)与代理人,但明确表示不包括分包人/独立承包商。后者不像前者,承运人无法去控制或监管分包人的一举一动。这一来,会导致货方为回避时效已届或责任限制金额太低,索性放弃向承运人起诉而转而以侵权起诉像装卸工等的分包人:Midland Silicones v. Scruttons(1961)2 Lloyd's Rep. 365。

已在 1.2 小段的 Midland Silicones v. Scruttons 及 2.8 小段的 Adler v. Dickson 介绍过。问题是，第三者不是合约一方，他如何去依赖合约内会有的保障条款（免责条款，时效，责任限制等）呢？

若任由货主去以侵权成功向船员、装卸工或代理等索赔，最后仍会是会要船东来承担，这一来船东就失去了合约原有的保障，等于给货主从后门攻了进来。

船员与船东的密切关系自不必言，很难想象货主控告船员，船东不是在船员背后顶住。即使是装卸货的装卸工，主要在班轮运输，往往也会与船东有密切关系，或是有长期服务合约，而合约内会包括一条条款去补偿装卸工在为船东服务中带来责任而要赔的钱。

这一来，要防止后门被攻进来，船东常在提单合约或其他合约中放进一条名叫喜玛拉雅的条款，作用是以代理或信托人身份去把本是第三者的装卸工、船员等人也扯进来作为合约一方。它所以名为喜玛拉雅条款是因为 Adler v. Dickson 的先例是发生在一艘名为"喜玛拉雅"(Himalaya)的客轮上。

5.2 喜玛拉雅条款的用字

这类型的条款，用字上不尽相同，因为有订约自由，而一个好的版本可以 The "Eurymedon" (1974) 1 Lloyd's Rep. 524 的条款为例：

"It is hereby expressly agreed that no servant or agent of the Carrier (including every independent contractor from time to time employed by the Carrier) shall in any circumstances whatsoever be under any liability whatsoever to the Shipper, Consignee or Owner of the goods or to any holder of this Bill of Lading for any loss, damage or delay of whatsoever kind arising directly or indirectly from any act, neglect or default on his part while acting in the course or in connection with his employment and, without prejudice to the generality of the foregoing provisions in this Clause, every exemption, limitation, condition and liberty herein contained and every right, exemption from liability, defence and immunity of whatsoever nature applicable to the Carrier or to which the Carrier is entitled hereunder shall also be available and shall extend to protect every such servant or agent of the Carrier acting as aforesaid and for the purpose of all the foregoing provisions of this Clause the Carrier is or shall be deemed to be acting as agents or trustee on behalf of and for the benefit of all persons who are or might be his servants or agents from time to time (including independent contractors as aforesaid) and all such persons shall to this extent be or be deemed to be parties to the contract in or evidenced by this Bill of Lading."

这一来，如果装卸工或船员被货主以侵权起诉，他们可以出示一份有此条款的提单,并以合约一方向法院抗辩这索赔已过了提单内的一年时效,或可享受免责、责任限制,等等。

这种做法也不光是在航运,它可伸延到其他行业,只要是作为合约一方的雇主想去保障为他服务履约的雇员或独立承包商(independent contractor),免他们被侵权(或托管)索赔。

喜玛拉雅条款更可伸延去说明对方万一成功控告第三者(如装卸工、船员),也要用回这笔钱去补偿船东,即要吐出来。文字上会是如下:

"The Merchant undertakes that no claim… shall be made against any servant or agent or sub-contractor of the Carrier which imposes or attempts to impose upon any of them… any liability whatsoever in connection with the goods and, if any such claim… shall nevertheless be made, to indemnify the Carrier against all consequences thereof…"

这一来,因为法院要去禁止这种"兜圈子补偿"(circle of indemnity),因为是"无用的诉讼"(useless litigation),会在船东去插手(intervene)并提出证明后,不允许原告的货方对装卸工或船员控告下去:The "Elbe Maru"(1978)1 Lloyd's Rep. 206。

5.3 喜玛拉雅条款的有效性

这条款在多个国家打过官司,大原则是承认有效。但肯定是,法院会严格来解释,所以在草拟上一定要全面、清楚:见美国的 The "Skulptor Vuchetich"(地方法院,Southern District of Texas,在 UK Club 1981 年 Legal Decisions 报道)。美国早在 Carle and Montanari Inc. v. American Export Isbrandtsen Lines Inc. and others(1968)1 Lloyd's Rep. 260 已承认这种喜玛拉雅条款。但 Burlingham 的 1997 年 12 月报道指出一个不知名的上诉(巡回)庭刚有案子说这条款因违反公共政策而不能去保障船舶经理人因海牙规则下的航行疏忽造成的货损去免责。

在加拿大上诉庭这条款不被接受,但不是在原则上,而是该案中装卸工犯的不是一般疏忽,而是"极度疏忽"(gross negligence),而加拿大法律是不允许用合约去豁免极度疏忽的责任的:Eisen und Metall A. G. v. Ceres Stevedoring Co. Ltd.(在 UK Club 1977 年 legal Decisions 报道)。

在英国,也已有很多案例,这条款的有效性不容置疑:比如在 The "Eurymedon"(1974)1 Lloyd's Rep. 534;The "Elbe Maru"(1978)1 Lloyd's Rep. 206;The "New York Star"(1980)2 Lloyd's Rep. 317;Raymond Burke Motors Ltd. v. The Mersey Docks and Harbour Co. (1986)1 Lloyd's Rep. 155,等等。

这种条款要有效,令雇员或独立承包商成为合约一方,要符合 Reid 勋爵在 Midland Silicones v. Scruttons(1961)2 Lloyd's Rep. 365 所列下的如下四点要求:

(ⅰ)提单应清楚写明装卸工等人可去受提单条款保障,这一般不成问题。

(ⅱ)提单应清楚写明船东是以代理身份替装卸工等人订约,去把提单免责等条款延展给他们,这一般也不成问题,只要写清楚。

(ⅲ)船东作为代理,是有装卸工等人的授权去订这提单合约。如果发出提单时仍没有授权,例如卸港装卸工仍未找好,何来授权?但应仍可去事后追认(ratification)。有时仍会看到在不同的事实情况下,会有争论,例如,装卸工是由港口在当时才指定[Metalimport v. S. S. Italia, 1976AMC 2347 (S. D. N. Y. 1976)],而在这一点上也的确常有争辩。

(ⅳ)装卸工等人要有约因给货方才会有有效合约,这一点已在 The "Eurymedon"的先例被解释了。本来在订约(出提单)时,卸港装卸工是谈不上有何约因对价给货方的。但贵族院说,提单订约时只是单方面合约(unilateral contract),但它在卸港装卸工提供服务时(这是约因)就变为双方(装卸工与货主)的全面合约(full contract)了。

回头总结一下,Reid 勋爵的四点要求是如此说明:

"I can see a possibility of success of the agency argument if (first) the bill of lading makes it clear that the stevedore is intended to be protected by the provisions in it which limit liability, (secondly) the bill of lading makes it clear that the carrier, in addition to contracting for these provisions on his own behalf, is also contracting as agent for the stevedore that these provisions should apply to the stevedore, (thirdly) the carrier has authority from the stevedore to do that, or perhaps later ratification by the stevedore would suffice, and (fourthly) that any difficulties about consideration moving from the stevedore were overcome."

5.4 喜玛拉雅条款用字不广泛的危险

这危险可用两个案例说明:一是加拿大的 The "Suleyman Stalskiy"(1976) 2 Lloyd's Rep. 609。装卸工在卸清了船中的钢材后,没有依照收货方的要求将货存进有盖仓库,而放在露天地上。这令钢材受到水湿并生锈。法院判是提单的喜玛拉雅条款只针对船东/承运人的履行责任,而钢材在船舶卸下后,船东责任已完,所以装卸工以后的疏忽不在提单的喜玛拉雅条款范围。

话说回来,The "Suleyman Stalskiy"的条款用字并不广泛,只是说:"装卸工等人 used or employed by the carrier for the purposes of or in connection with the performance of any of the carrier's obligations under this bill of lading."

比起 The "Eurymedon"(在5.2小段),可见是有局限。The "Eurymedon"有去说明"directly or indirectly",而且是针对"雇用期间有关的疏忽"(...neglect or default... in connection with his employment)而非只是针对"履行承运人提单责

任有关的疏忽",后者在时间上受到了局限。

另一先例是上一小段所提的 Raymond Burke Motors 一案。这是在货物尚未开始装时,已被装卸工损坏,法院判是不能去依赖提单中的喜玛拉雅条款。

5.5 海牙·维斯比规则的情况

1968 年的海牙·维斯比规则,在 Article Ⅲ,其实已明确规定"雇员与代理"(servant or agent)是受到保障的,这是海牙规则所缺乏的(因此带来像 1961 年 Midland Silicones v. Scruttons 的先例)。但即使如此,提单或海运单等仍是需要有一条好的喜玛拉雅条款,因为:

(ⅰ) Article Ⅲ (2) 说明"such servant or agent not being an independent contractor"。像船员的身份会很明确,但装卸工会是船东的直接雇员或代理,也会是独立承包商,身份会不明确。而其他方如二程船等,更明显只是独立承包商。

(ⅱ) 可能有的航次只是适用 1924 年的海牙规则,而不是海牙·维斯比规则;

(ⅲ) 提单内会有其他保障,是超出海牙·维斯比规则所给予的,例如货物在岸上的免责、时效等。

5.6 托管与分托管(bailment and sub-bailment)

看来,喜玛拉雅条款的保障也不是十全十美。但今天要去保护装卸工与独立承包商的重要性已是更大,因为今天二程船运输(在 2.10 小段所提到)与多式联运已相当盛行。危险会是,货物在二程船上因碰船后沉没,货方直接以侵权(因碰船一般总有船员疏忽)控告二程船的船东。

二程船船东因为明显是独立承包商(independent contractor),所以应不受海牙·维斯比规则保障,更不用说是 1924 年的海牙规则了。

这一来,在货主以侵权行为控告下,二程船船东会无法以著名的海牙规则的"航行疏忽"免责。在以往的做法,为了保障二程船及所有多式联运的独立承包商,一直是靠一条详尽的喜玛拉雅条款。但已见到,这保障并非十全十美与肯定。

在 2.10 小段提到的 The "Pioneer Container" (1994) 1 Lloyd's Rep. 593,是在这方面一个非常重要的案例。

在谈论"分托管"(sub-bailment)之前,先去很简单的谈谈"托管"(bailment)。在 N. E. Palmer 教授的《Bailment》一书,他指出最重要的是对一样东西的占有,就可构成托管:"The essence of bailment is possession"。现在托管也不必另有一个合约或是物主的明确同意,而托管人的责任就是在他托管期间"合理小心"照顾(reasonable or due care)托管物。托管往往会是有收费的,所谓 bailment for reward;但也会是免费的,所谓 a gratuitous bailment。分别会是前者要有较高的"小心"(care)标准去照顾托管的东西。

托管的情况比比皆是,我可随意去举一案例,是 Moukataff v. B. O. A. C. (1967) 1 Lloyd's Rep. 396。其他岸上林林总总的托管,比如东西寄放在大饭店的衣帽间,贵重东西放在银行保险箱等,都是托管。在航运,明显的例子是货物在船上,船舶也是"占有"了货物,所以船东也是托管人。在货方向船东起诉货损货差时,告票中总是把侵权,合约与托管都放进去,以免遗漏。因为有可能双方并没有提单合约存在(可看4.1~4.3小段),则侵权与托管就用得上了。而托管会是要船东(托管人)证明货物虽在他手中损坏,但他已有"合理小心"照顾,这一点比以侵权控告强,因为举证不一样。

但如果双方有提单合约关系,这托管只是"Bailment upons terms",而条件(terms)也就是提单合约的条件,包括海牙规则,所以以合约或托管来起诉船东其实是一样。

5.7 有条件的分托管(sub-bailment on terms)

有条件的托管看来不难明白,但有条件的分托管就较难明白。比如,货方托运,船东的运输就是有条件托管,提单上的条款就是托管条件。到了卸港,船东把货物卸下存放进仓库,而仓库有它的标准合约。这一来,仓库的条款就是分托管的条件(sub-bailment on terms)。肯定是,它们并不是一样的条件:托管是提单,分托管是仓库标准合约。问题是,如果货物在仓库内被偷去,货方以侵权去控告仓库,仓库可否以如下抗辩:

(ⅰ)提单内有的免责等条款?

(ⅱ)它的标准合约内的免责等条款?

在(ⅰ),答案应是提单有否一条喜玛拉雅条款,去包括了仓库的独立承包商在内。

在(ⅱ),就关系到这 sub-bailment on terms 的条件能否去约束货主,这问题在贵族院(上议院)的 The "Pioneer Container" (1994) 1 Lloyd's Rep. 593 有解答。

该案中,高雄来香港的支线船/二程船"K. H. Enterprise"在途中沉没,时为1987年,船上所有集装箱都灭失了。货方在香港把该船的台湾船东另拥有的一艘姐妹船"Pioneer Container"扣起来,并起诉,这官司一直上诉到英国贵族院。

在合约的关系是:发货人与一程船船东(韩国的 Hanjin)订约,这提单合约中有一条款说:

"The carrier shall be entitled to sub-contract on any terms the whole or any part of the carriage, loading, unloading, storing, warehousing, handling and any and all duties whatsoever undertaken by the carrier in relation to the goods."

这是一条极广泛的条款去授权一程船,也是提单承运人,让它另订合约分包(sub-contract)。

一程船另找了二程船的"K. H. Enterprise",后者也取出了自己的提单,一程船被当做是发货人。所以,从合约角度来看该提单是一程船(提单承运人)与二程船(实际承运人)之间的合约,与货方无关。但二程船也是分托管人,而且是有条件的,即二程船提单的条款。其中有一条款是说台湾地区法院有管辖权。

双方在香港法院争议的是,货方以侵权、托管控告"K. H. Enterprises"船东,二程船船东能否以他的提单条款,作为分托管条件,去加在货方身上?如果能,这会否包括台湾地区管辖权条款,进而令香港法院要去考虑中止?

贵族院判是:

(a)货方与二程船的关系是托管。

(b)如果货方有授权分托管与接受有关条件,货方要受到约束。

(c)这授权可以是写明,如在本案的一程船提单合约。这授权也可以是默示(implied),例如货方以前曾多次这样安排运输,一程船,二程船等。但默示总是比不上明示(写明)的明确。

(d)只有分托管的条件是完全不合理、不正常的,才不能去约束货方,贵族院的 Coff 勋爵说:"…their Lordships do not perceive a similar need(指租约条款合并提单不能完全合并去约束货方)to limit the terms so consented to… where, as here, the consent is very wide in its terms, only ters which are so unusual or so unreasonable that they could not reasonably be understood to fall within such consent are likely to be held to be excluded."

(e)提单不论有否一条喜玛拉雅条款去保护二程船或分托管人,也不影响后者可去依赖分托管的条件。

在本案例,贵族院判是一条管辖权条款(或适用法律等条款)没有不正常不合理之处,所以分托管人的条件可去约束货方,即台湾地区管辖权有效。

这先例可被视为是船东一大胜利,特别是对支线(feeder)业务。以前的二程船或其他的分承包商唯一靠的是一条不能肯定的喜玛拉雅条款,而今天就有了一样更稳定肯定的有条件分托管(sub-bailment on terms)来保障。

要小心的反倒是一程船:它要肯定它与货方的提单中有一条类似"K. H. Enterprise"一程船的广泛授权,可去另订合约(sub-contract)。否则若没有明示或默示的货方授权容许它去找二程船(如找了"K. H. Enterprise"),答应它的条件,则会在出事后货方控告"K. H. Enterprise"船东时,后者不能依赖分托管条件(因为货方从没有去授权)。这一来,"K. H. Enterprise"船东赔了钱后,可以回头去找一程船(Hanjin)算账,因为它根本没有货方授权去另订合约(sub-contract),是构成严格要负责的"越权行为"(breach of warrant of authority)。"

8.2.3 侵权问题之三:损失时已拥有货物主权才能起诉并获赔偿

这方面的课题在笔者多本书已有详细论及,对此可去节录像《国际货物买卖》一书第五章的1.2小段如下:

> 1.2 拥有货物才能以侵权起诉
>
> 英国法出于政策上的理由,怕一打开"大水门"(floodgate)会带来太多的侵权起诉,所以一向坚持只准拥有真正货物或托管的人士才能以侵权起诉。其他不拥有货物,但有各种合法利益的人士受同一侵权而损失,也是投诉无门。正如在 The "Aliakmon"(1986) 2 Lloyd's Rep. 1 的先例,Brandon 勋爵说:
>
> "…there is a long line of authority for a principle of law that, in order to enable a person to claim in negligence for loss caused to him by reason of loss of or damage to property, he must have had either the legal ownership of or a possessory title to the property concerned at the time when the loss or damage occurred, and it is not enough for him to have only had contractual rights in relation to such property which have been adversely affected by the loss of or damage to it."
>
> 有"possessory title"(占有权)的托管人以侵权起诉很少见到,变得主要仍是合法拥有"真正货物"(legal ownership)的人才能以侵权起诉。
>
> 所以,承租人在船舶碰撞后是不能就对方疏忽而导致的船舶有关损失以侵权起诉的,只有"legal ownership"(合法所有权)的受损船东,才能向对方船舶以侵权起诉: Chargeurs Reunis Compagnie Francaise de Navigation a Vapeur v. English & American Shipping Co. (1921) 9 Lloyd's Rep. 464; The "World Harmony"(1965) 1 Lloyd's Rep. 244; The "Mineral Transporter"(1985) 2 Lloyd's Rep. 303。
>
> 这一局限,也对国际货物买卖带来极大影响,这方面在 The "Aliakmon"(1986) 2 Lloyd's Rep. 1 有最好反映。它涉及钢材买卖,英国买方付不出货款,运输途中买卖双方另达成协议是钢材货物仍属卖方,先由买方以提单[是空白背书的"持有人提单"(bearer bill)]向船东提取钢材去安排转售后才支付卖方,而付清货款后钢材才归买方。换言之,这类似"保留货权条款"的做法。
>
> 在卸货时,钢材有损坏。事后买方向船东索赔,但在侵权方面,判是买方在钢材受损时,并非真正拥有货物,有的只是一份说明买方将会取得货物的买卖

合约而已。所以，买方不准以侵权起诉船东。

The"Aliakmon"只是在20世纪80年代中无数同类案件中的其中一宗，问题出在1855年英国提单法的文字/措辞十分局限。它只在以提单托付或背书纯是为了去转让货物的情况下，才承认提单合约的转让，以方便买方直接根据提单起诉船东。但很多情况的"托付"（consignment）或"背书"（endorsement）非是如此，导致买方（提单持有人）无法以合约（提单）起诉船东。但改以侵权起诉船东，又会面对是否拥有货物的质疑。

这方面的问题，在笔者的"外贸及海运诈骗"一书的第134页开始与《国际商务游戏规则——英国合约法》一书的第81~84页有详谈，不去重复。

而在英国通过了1992年的"海上运输法"替代1855年的提单法，大大扩充了买方（合法提单持有人）的提单合约诉权后，应是很大程度减少了这方面问题。但仍会有例子是买方（提单持有人）无法以合约（提单）向船东起诉，只能是以侵权与/或"托管"（bailment）起诉疏忽造成损失的被告。光是以"托管"起诉，也要怕"有条件的分托管"（sub-bailment on terms）会有不知详情的"条件"。这方面请看笔者的《国际商务游戏规则——英国合约法》一书的93~94页。要是以侵权起诉，则又要面对有否真正拥有货物的质疑。例子是：

（ⅰ）买方持有的提单只是一程船东所签发，但货物在二程船随船沉没；

（ⅱ）买方持有的提单明确是承租人才是唯一承运人，不是船东，船东不是提单合约一方。但货物是在船上受损，承租人又是皮包公司：The "Venezuela"（1980）1 Lloyd's Rep. 393; The "Ines"（1995）2 Lloyd's Rep. 144; The "Hector"（1998）2 Lloyd's Rep. 287。

（ⅲ）买方持有多式联运单，但签发该单证的"承运人"（carrier），实是一家皮包公司的货代，不值得去向他起诉。而货物是在某处仓库受损。

以上情况（加上其他情况），买方去向无直接合约关系的二程船、船东、仓库等以侵权起诉，都要去注意自己在造成损失之时是否拥有货物。

例如，货物在8月1日装上一程船，并签发全程提单。在8月5日装上二程船，而二程船在8月7日沉没。当时，卖方尚未在信用证下结汇，更未曾在不记名提单背书，去把货物转让。当然，稍后（例如是8月9日）卖方如此做了。但事实上，在货物损失之时，买方并没有真正拥有货物。当然，买方可以提单合约去起诉一程船，让一程船另去向二程船追讨补偿。但只要买方想以侵权起诉二程船，例如一程船东不知所踪，那么看来安全的方法还是去加上卖方的名义（如果卖方肯借出名义），作为共同原告方。

这种问题也出现在7.6小段的The"Starsin"（2000）1 Lloyd's Rep. 85先例。已

经说过 Colman 大法官判该案提单是"承租人提单"(charterer's bill),不是"船东提单"(owner's bill),这一来,原告(收货人/提单持有人)向被告(船东,实际承运人)起诉就改为是以侵权了,正如 88 页所讲的诉因是:"The claims are advanced in each case primarily on the basis of the defendants' breach of the bills of lading contract and alternatively in tort on the basis that the defendants were bailees and/or carriers for reward and negligently permitted the cargo to be damaged in the course of the bailment."

但该案例同时带来一个新的争端,对此也未曾有过判例,就是有关疏忽行为发生在原告有货物主权之前,然后由于时间上的消逝,造成无可避免的"递增损失"(progressive damage),而部分的递增损失发生在原告后来获得货物主权后。

该案事实是:木材货物堆放不妥,造成无可避免的递增损失,而原告正是在后来航次中通过提单背书与交出而获取货物主权的。但在疏忽发生时(堆放不妥),原告实际并未有货物主权。这一来,代表船东 Mr. Berry 争辩:"It is submitted by Mr Berry, on behalf of the defendant shipowner, that, in as much as the shipowners' duty to the owners of the cargo arises only out of his being a bailee, he owes no duty to exercise due care of the cargo to anyone who, at the time when care ought to be exercised, is not owner of the cargo[180]. In the usual case of cargo damage, the want of proper care and the occurrence of damage happens more or less at the same time, as, for example, where a hatch cover is not properly secured and not checked during the voyage with the result that the cargo is wetted due to continuing negligence[181]. It is therefore unsurprising that the authorities, such as The 'Wear Breeze' (1967) 2 Lloyd's Rep. 315; The "Aliakmon" (1986) 2 Lloyd's Rep. 1, have been concerned to emphasize the principle that a plaintiff cannot only recover in respect of damage suffered by the cargo while he had title[182]. Whereas that principle also arises from the fact that the tort is not complete until damage has been caused[183], it is fundamentally the case that there can be no right of action unless there has also been a breach of duty owed to the plaintiff after title has passed to him[184]. In the present case, once the cargo has been badly stowed and the voyage had commenced, there was, on the evidence, nothing that could have been done to prevent

---

[180] 船东说如果他的责任只是源于他是一位没有合约关系的托管人,那么他对任何不是货物主人的人士没有"谨慎从事"(duty of care)的法定责任。

[181] 一般货差货损的案件,疏忽行事或不谨慎从事往往与产生货损货差同时发生,例如是舱盖不固导致海水进入损坏货物。

[182] 故著名先例都只去强调当其时,原告的货方必须拥有货物主权才能以侵权索赔损失。

[183] 也会是侵权早已开始,且一直持续至真正产生损失,而当时原告刚拥有货物主权,道理也是一样。

[184] 反正,基本原则是在货物主权转让与获得后,曾有不谨慎从事才会给该货方(原告)有诉权。

the progressive damage to the cargo during the whole of the voyage[185]. Since title did not passto any of the claimants until after the commencement of the voyage, the shipowners could not at the time of the bad stowage, have been in breach of any duty owed by them as bailee to any of the claimants and, since there was no negligence on the shipowners' part at any time after title passed to the claimants there was no breach of duty on which the claimants could find any cause of action in tort[186]."

但 Colman 大法官拒绝了船东以上的争辩，并在参考了房子建筑与产品责任的案例/精神后，判是原告的货方只要在货损产生时已拥有主权业已足够。Colman 大法官说："For these reasons I have no doubt that the shipowners submission is misconceived:what determines whether cargo-owner,who has no contract with the shipowner can sue in negligence for cargo damage caused by negligent acts of the shipowner before title passed to the cargo-owner is solely and simply whether by the time when the cargo was lost or damaged the title in the cargo had passed to the claimant."

话说回来，这要求仍会对依赖侵权起诉的货方造成困扰。在 The "Starsin"，也要去区分和估算原告获得货物主权前后的损失，而产生在前的损失船东也是不必负责。

8.2.4 侵权问题之四：不允许以侵权索赔纯经济损失

除了货物真正的损坏灭失外，对货方也会造成损失的是一种"纯经济损失"（pure economic loss）。这主要会是船舶延误（造成违约的原因，例如是不适航或不合理绕航），导致货物迟到卸港，对收货人/提单持有人造成市场下跌或转售时机已失等纯经济损失。如果以提单合约的关系起诉，这种损失也可以成功索赔：The "Heron Ⅱ"(1967) 2 Lloyd's Rep. 457。但若是没有合约关系，例如是实际承运人（分包人）的延误，货方想以侵权向他索赔纯经济损失会难以成功。这是因为英国法律的大政策，顾虑有太多诉讼而不允许在侵权诉讼中去索赔纯经济损失。这方面在笔者的《海事法》一书之第七章§9 段有略及，可节录如下：

§9 船舶碰撞常会带来对无辜第三者的损失。例如，承租人（期租或程租）会失去分租的利润，或是已备好货物但因碰撞而无法履约。其他受害的第三者会是碰撞船之一的下一港口装卸工、代理等，因为事故而令船舶取消此

---

[185] 本案特殊之处是货物在装港堆放不妥，无可避免导致递增损失。
[186] 在不谨慎从事的堆放不妥时，原告（货方）尚未获得货物主权。而且，在货方获得主权的转让后，船东反而并未做过任何不谨慎的事。

行。反正是,会有千变万化的情况出现。

问题是:对方船舶被判有责任,这批受害第三者能否以侵权索赔损失?答案是不能,因为英国法律至今不允许以侵权去索赔"纯"经济损失。

这法律有悠久历史: Cattle v. Stockton Waterworks Co. (1875) L. R. 10 QB 453; Simpson & Co. v. Thomson (1877) 3 App. Cas. 279; Societe Anonyme de Remorquage a Helice v. Bennetts (1911) 1 KB 243; Elliott Steam Tug Co. Ltd. v. Shipping Controller (1922) 1 KB 127; The "Aliakmon" (1986) 2 Lloyd's Rep. 1,等等。

这方面的原则主要是为了防止有太多诉讼,因为有"纯"经济损失的无辜第三者会有很多。而且,这会带来侵权责任方近乎无限的赔偿责任。例如,疏忽驾驶车辆要去赔偿被碰伤的行人是理所当然。但如果还要去赔偿受伤的行人所工作的公司、亲友、生意伙伴等的"纯"经济损失,这会是近乎无限、无止境的赔偿责任。而且别忘了,船舶可以限制责任,若太多人可去索赔这笔钱自然会分薄了传统承认的损失索赔。

所以,承租人以侵权向对方船舶索赔"纯"经济损失,虽有过多次尝试,但都不成功: Chargeurs Reumis Compagnie Francaise the Navigation a Vapeur v. English & American Shipping Co. (1921) 9 Lloyd's Rep. 464; The "World Harmony" (1965) 1 Lloyd's Rep. 244 美国案例的 Federal Commerce & Navigation v. Marathonian (175) AMC 738; The "Mineral Transporter" (1985) 2 Lloyd's Rep. 303。

至于承租人能否向租船给自己的船东索赔"纯"经济损失,这全要看双方合约的措辞/用字了。他们之间一定会有合约:期租合约,程租合约。一般说来,租约下的船东在航行方面的责任总不会超过海牙规则所定。所以,航行的疏忽/过失导致承租人损失,一般船东也是免责。期租的 NYPE 标准合约是如此,程租的金康标准合约更是如此。当然也会有变数,因为大原则仍是订约自由。大家可去参阅笔者的《期租合约》一书第 331~332 页提及的 The "Emmanuel C" (1983) 1 Lloyd's Rep. 310 与 The "Satya Kailash" (1984) 1 Lloyd's Rep. 588 等对船东十分危险的先例。

8.3 在合约承运人外再加上实际承运人对货方的好处

汉堡规则(与中国海商法)增加了"实际承运人"的概念,这显然是为货方利益着想。虽然在现实中,很大部分的提单都会是船东提单,因为是船长或代船长签字:请看本章之 5.1 小段。这一来,合约承运人与实际承运人是同一人:船东本人,无从区分。但只要看看近期案例，就会发觉仍有一定数量的提单还是有上述区分，如：

（ⅰ）The "Hector"（1998）2 Lloyd's Rep. 287 的合约承运人是 U. S. EXPRESS LINES（承租人），实际承运人是船东。

（ⅱ）The "Starsin"（2000）1 Lloyd's Rep. 85 的合约承运人是 Continental Pacific Shipping Ltd.）（承租人），实际承运人是船东（注意：上诉庭刚推翻了原判）。

加上，还有全程运输的像 The "K. H. Enterprise"（1994）1 Lloyd's Rep. 593 的先例，一程船（韩国的 Hanjin 船公司）是合约承运人，二程船的 "K. H. Enterprise" 台湾船东是出事（船沉）时的实际承运人。

如果照英国法律视实际承运人为分包/独立承包商，只有侵权关系，会导致货方原告面对种种困难，如 8.2.1 小段至 8.2.4 小段所讲。像 The "Aliakmon"（1986）2 Lloyd's Rep. 1 就是著名例子，收货人因卖方保留货权（因此收货人自己没有货权）而无法以侵权成功向船东索赔货损货差。

但汉堡规则加上了实际承运人的概念，并在 Article 10（2）说："All the provisions of this Convention governing the responsibility of the carrier also apply to the responsibility of the actual carrier for the carriage performed by him…"

而在 Article 11 对"全程运输"（Through Carriage），也有（2）小段说："The actual carrier is responsible in accordance with the provisions of para. 2 of Art. 10 for loss, damage or delay in delivery caused by an occurrence which takes place while the goods are in his charge."

总而言之，汉堡规则以立法手段（在承认的国家）去强加了规则的责任、义务与权利到实际承运人头上。这可说是"法定责任"（statutory liability），而非是合约或侵权责任之争。例如，也要对 Article 5 内的船舶延误负责，而这是纯经济损失：8.2.4 小段。

汉堡规则没有去理会在本章 8.2.3 小段谈及的有关损失时货方要有货物的真正"主权"（legal title）或"占有权"（possessory title）才能获得赔偿的问题。这会被视为是本国法，例如，英国法律适用于侵权，但不适用在合约。后者只要去证明船东能预见有此类损失（提单会在海运途中的任何时间被转让，运输风险去了收货人头上，导致整个航次造成的损失都要收货人承担），损失有因果关系等，即可获赔偿。

但考虑到汉堡规则是把实际承运人的地位放在与合约承运人一样，估计本章 8.2.3 小段的困难/问题不应对货方产生。当然，英国不承认汉堡规则，所以也不会面对这问题。

另要注意的是，汉堡规则只是要实际承运人对他履行部分的任务负责。这当然是完全公平合理与可行。例如，卸货装卸工不会去为装货装卸工的疏忽负责。

8.4 中国海商法可能对实际承运人过于苛求

中国海商法有关实际承运人的章节已在8段略为提及,其中较重要的是第61条。该条的英文翻译是:"The provisions with respect to the responsibility of the carrier contained in this Chapter shall be applicable to the actual carrier."

要注意的是相比于汉堡规则,它少了几个重要的字:

(ⅰ) Article 10(2)的"for the carriage performed by him."

(ⅱ) Article 11(2)的"caused by an occurrence which takes place while the goods are in his charge."

而且,中国海商法在第63条接下去说:"承运人与实际承运人都负有赔偿责任的,应当在此项责任范围内负连带责任"(Where both the carrier and the actual carrier are liable for compensation, they shall jointly and severally be liable within the scope of such liability)。

这一来,在笔者看来,恐怕会有实际承运人要去为不是他分内履行的任务负责:或会是过去的行为如合约承运人(但已倒闭,所以不值得去对付)装货时堆放疏忽,本来与二程船的实际承运人无关;又或会是将来的行为,如合约承运人(已倒闭)不去安排卸货或转运等。

相比而言;笔者反倒觉得,中国海商法对合约承运人反而比较务实与宽松。在第60条第2款说:"虽有前款规定,在海上运输合同中明确约定合同所包括的特定的部分运输由承运人以外的指定的实际承运人履行的,合同可以同时约定,货物在指定的实际承运人掌管期间发生的灭失,损坏或者迟延交付,承运人不负赔偿责任。"

故此,比如按中国海商法之第49条说:"承运人应当按照约定的或者习惯的或者地理上的航线将货物运往卸货港"。

会否是:承运人不履约,实际承运人也要代履约去将货物运往卸货港?本来该第49条的原意是针对不合理绕航,但却又似在强制承运人在提单合约下将货物运往卸货港。毕竟,提单合约会有"邻近条款"(这方面请去参阅本书第四章之3.2.2小段),或"中止运输的法律权利"(stoppage in transit)(请参阅本书第四章之3.2.2小段),这些都会导致承运人不必将货物运往卸货港。所以,主要是针对货损货差责任的海牙/海牙·维斯比规则对此没有立法要求,而汉堡规则更不是针对不合理绕航(虽然它有实际承运人的说法),更不用说是有"要运到卸货港"的义务/责任了。

这种争议出现在一近期案例,涉及单船公司 Tonbo Maritime Inc(船东)所拥有的"益盛"轮在1998年10月9日以期租(NYPE 标准格式)3至5个月给名为 Ceasar

Marine S. A. 的光棍巴拿马公司的承租人,该租约第 5 条规定在拖欠租金的情况下,船东可以撤船。

在该年 10 月份中,"益盛"根据承租人指示在蓬莱装了 1.6 万吨水泥,原是去尼日利亚拉格斯卸。在蓬莱,中国外代获授权代承租人的 Ceasar Marine S. A. Inc. 签发了"运费已预付"(freight prepaid)提单。提单签字处清楚注明是:"as agent for the carrier Ceasar Marine S. A. Inc."

而且,为符合 UCP500 对海运提单的要求,提单正面在显眼之处注明:"The Carrier:Ceasar Marine S. A. Inc."

另外,该提单并没有"光船条款"(本章之 4.3.1 小段)以及任何类似"承运人身份条款"(本章之 4.3.2 小段)的条款。

换言之,根据英美法律或国际上的一套做法(包括像挪威等国),这是百分百明确不过的"承租人提单"(charterer's bill),合约承运人是承租人的船公司,不是船东。去比较 7.4 小段的 The "Hector"(1998)2 Lloyd's Rep. 287,"益盛"轮的提单对谁是合约承运人在重要的两点上更明确:

(ⅰ)The "Hector" 签字是"代船长"。

(ⅱ)The "Hector" 提单有一条矛盾/冲突的"承运人身份条款"(第 17 条)。

但不论怎样,The "Hector" 一案也是判不是"船东提单"(owner's bill),而是"承租人提单",所以船东不受约束,没有必要去履行提单合约责任。所以估计在 The "Hector" 一案判决后,船东可以理直气壮的:

(a)去向分承租人(也是 FOB 买方)要求再付一笔运费,甚至敲一笔更高的运费,因为分承租人无力讨价还价,而双方实际是在谈判一个新的运输合约,无法去质疑船东漫天开价。

(b)把货物卸下不理,只要做法合理和尽量给货方通知前来提货。这是"不情愿的托管人"(involuntary bailee)的地位与权力。这在岸上也经常会发生,如访客遗留了东西,导致主人变为不情愿的托管人。不情愿归不情愿,托管人仍有责任"合理小心"(reasonable or due care)去照看,而不能占为己有或故意/疏忽毁坏。但看管照顾他人的东西是要花费成本的,甚至是所费不菲且不值得(看是什么东西)。幸好天下间离不开一个"理"字,所有事情必以合理为度,好的法律亦是如此。因此,超过合理时间而仍不去提回东西的,特别是在不情愿的托管人已给了合理通知的情况下,则该托管人有权去以合理的办法自行处理这些东西。而在 The "Hector" 即是作为不情愿托管人的船东可去合理处理船上货物。

回头再去谈"益盛"轮,该提单既然是 100% 明确的承租人提单,船东也应是一位"不情愿的托管人"(involuntary bailee)了。

介绍了提单,可去谈谈该案其他的事实。由于承租人欠付租金及燃油费,船东依约在 1998 年 10 月底撤船,但当时船上("益盛"轮)有 1.6 万吨在蓬莱装的水泥。

船东既然不受提单的约束,就不必去履行、去无偿(因提单注明"运费已预付")把货物运至拉格斯。

撤船后,船东通知了各方货方(托管人、通知人与收货人)尽快提取船上货物或/与它商讨新的运输合约以代取与它无关的承租人提单,以便顺利完成航次至拉格斯。但货方无意再支付任何运费而导致接下去的 1 个月均无法达成任何协议。众所周知,水泥只是廉价货物,而且"生命周期"有限,即时间一长就会报废。所以,船东必须早日处理这批货物。

船东在听取尼日利亚律师的意见,并比较过各个就近港口的费用后,决定选择去海口把水泥卸下以便"解放"船舶。在卸下前,船东向海口海事法院取得批准,也通知了货方,要求尽速前往海口提取水泥。但结果在无人前往办理提货的情况下,法院下令拍卖该批水泥,而卖得的货款留存在法院等候定夺。

水泥被拍卖后,该批货物尼日利亚的收货人向船东提出起诉。诉因是:
(1)船东是实际承运人。
(2)它在中国海商法第 49 条有法定责任将货物运往卸货港(拉格斯)。
(3)船东未尽此法定责任。

可说,若是货方胜诉,中国海商法强加在实际承运人头上的责任应是在国际上独一无二的,是汉堡规则引入实际承运人这概念时也未曾去想到的,毕竟汉堡规则也主要是针对货损货差责任而已,而不是在其他方面如何履约。

据知,原告货方也在香港等地法院出了告票对付原船东(对付提单合约承运人 Ceasar Marine S. A. Inc. 毫无实际意义,因它是皮包公司),但不敢下手,因明知败诉,于是去了中国法院企图利用海商法取巧。

最后中华人民共和国海口海事法院(1999)海事初字第 01 号判船东胜诉,正确之余(笔者看来),但判决理由没有去针对这方面主要的争议。故此,这仍可被视为是中国海商法的一处疑点:至少在笔者看来。

再多举一例是笔者近日查询的有关一船上千万美元的铜精矿从欧洲运往中国,在途经新加坡加油时被扣而导致船东倒闭,船舶被法院拍卖。新船东购入该船舶,改了新船名,也有了"清洁主权"(clean title),照说是不对中国收货人有任何运输合约责任的。中国收货人的一份提单合约是由倒闭了船东的船长签字,倒闭船东才是承运人。新的船东只是"不情愿的托管人",因船上仍有这票铜精矿。因不好处理,在新加坡难以卸掉,加上德国卖方游说新船东,总算令新船东愿意"免费"把货物运至中国目的地卸货。但中国收货人因延误遭受损失,所以想找人索赔。去告德国卖方应不会成功,因为运输风险在收货人头上,去告新船东就英美法而言也不会成功,因他/它没有疏忽/过错外,也不欠收货人一个合约责任去及时交货,而非合约关系也不存在纯经济损失的索赔（本章之8.2.4小段）。但中国收货人却提出一个"实际承运人"的说法，指新船东是"实际承运人"，并想在中国卸港去扣船。对这说法笔者无法分析，因不懂中国海商法。会是，该案件的事实是新船东从未受倒闭的老船东（承运人）委托，所以并非是"实际承运人"，但这说得通吗？只想说这说法与国际上的做法/说法很不一样，而且长远对中国收货人也不一定有利。今后新船东再面对此情况，是无论如何也不会再"做好人"把货物运至中国卸港了。他/它会将货在新加坡卸下，只要有预先通知中国收货人前去提货。若新加坡卸不下，也只会去其他港口如曼谷、日本等港口卸下。总之不要去中国，省得从"不情愿的托管人"无端变成"实际承运人"。笔者只是随口说说，对中国海商法，例如在这一方面，读者请去参阅司玉琢老师的权威说法。

§9 谁是运输合约的货方

9.1 总有一方去安排运输

"货方"是指发货人（卖方），中间商或/与收货人（买方），他/它们之间都有可能去安排运输订约。而既然是国际买卖，总免不了有运输（尤其是海上一段运输），也免不了要有一方货方去负责安排，至于有关费用应是最终由买方直接或间接承担。如在 CIF 或 CFR 买卖，卖方安排海上运输，有关费用（运费）已是加在货价内，买方最终间接承担这笔运费，毕竟是他/它买的货物。而在 FOB 买卖，若由买方安排海上运输的话，运费是由买方直接支付给船东。

有关 CIF 或 FOB 买卖，在笔者的《国际货物买卖》一书已有详述，不在此重复。在此只讨论谁是运输合约中与承运人发生关系的货方。

9.1.1 CIF 买卖

在 CIF，很明确是卖方与承运人去订立运输合约。这也是像国际商会 Incoterms 1990年的规定（如果买卖合约有去合并）所说："卖方责任：……（a）运输合同——按惯例，自费签订运输合同，用通常用以运输该类合同货物的那种远洋船（或内河船），经由通常的航线，将货物装运至商定的目的地港口。"

作为卖方对手的"承运人"（carrier）是谁已在本章较早段节详述。他/它可以是船东，也可以是光船承租人，也可以是二船东/三船东（期租承租人），也可以是"无船承运人"（NVOC），等等。反正是，谁愿意做承运人而卖方也相信他，即可订立完全是他们之间的私人协议：一个运输合约。可能二船东/三船东或无船承运人订了运输合约之后才去租船/找船。

第三章　提单作用之二：运输合约·谁是其中的合约方　195

　　卖方订立的运输合约可以千变万化，这本是订约自由的大原则。它会是口头的：卖方与无船承运人草草地口头协议后随即付运。也会是寥寥数句写在一张白纸上，然后双方签字。好像 The "Sevonia Team" (1983) 2 Lloyd's Rep. 640 案例，涉及一份运输合约称为"transportation agreement"，内容只有 5 段。

　　而正规一点的做法，如果涉及大宗货物，卖方是要去租船。通过经纪人或其他渠道，卖方会联系上心目中船舶的真正船东或二船东进而谈妥一份有完整内容的租约，也就是运输合约。而后来装完货再签发给卖方（也是承租人）的提单，不管内容如何，也不可能改变租约的内容，因提单只是收据一份：请参阅本章 4.2 小段。

　　如果涉及小量货物，适合班轮运输，卖方则会去订舱位，签订"订舱单"（booking note），内中通常会合并了该班轮公司的提单条款（有关如何拟定请看 4.1 小段），这就是运输合约了，此点也已在本章之 1.3 与 4.1 小段有详述。至于后来装完货签发的给卖方（也是托运人）的提单，只能是较早时订立的运输合约的证明：The "Ardennes" (1950) 84 Lloyd's Rep. 340。另外 Devlin 大法官在 Pyrene v. Scindia Navigation Co (1954) 1 Lloyd's Rep. 321 也曾说："In my judgment, whenever a contract of carriage is concluded, and it is contemplated that a bill of lading will, in due course, be issued in respect of it, that contract is from its creation 'covered' by a bill of lading."

　　另《Scrutton on Charter-Parties》一书之 Article 30 也说："The bill of lading is not the contract[187], for that has been made before the bill of lading was signed and delivered[188], but it is excellent evidence of the terms of the contract[189]… But it is open to the shipper to adduce oral evidence to show that the true terms of the contract are not those contained in the bill of lading[190], but are to be gathered from the mate's receipt, shipping cards, placards, handbills announcing the sailing of the ship, advice-notes, freight-notes, or undertakings or warranties by the broker, or other agent of the carrier[191]."

　　一般来讲，对提单内的标准印就条款，发货人（卖方）不会异议。且不说这些条款在较早订约时确已合并，就算在心态上发货人也不会关心，因为一般不影响结汇：见本章之 4.1 小段。但在其他某些内容上会有异议，例如订约时班轮公司或揽货代理曾保证直航，但后来签发提单却并非如此。或是有关船期或船上设备，与订约时的保证/讲法不一致。这一来，若是来得及，发货人甚至可以对方"毁约"（repudiation）去对待，例如中断合约（接受毁约），要求把货物卸下退回，并事后向班轮公

---

[187]　提单不是运输合约。
[188]　运输合约较早时已存在。
[189]　但提单会是运输合约极佳的证明。
[190]　如提单不反映较早时所订的运输合约，发货人可去提出反证。
[191]　这些文件或事实都可以去支持发货人对提单不符的异议。

司索赔。这方面较早时已在 4.1 小段略为谈及。

9.1.2 FOB 买卖

FOB 对谁安排海上运输有不同与多种的灵活做法，这与 CIF 不一样，在《国际货物买卖》一书第三章也有详述。像 Devlin 大法官在 Pyrene Company Ltd. v. Scindia Steam Navigation Company Ltd. (1954) 1 Lloyd's Rep. 321 提到的就有三种以上的不同做法。这说法在 The "El Amria" (1982) 2 Lloyd's Rep. 28 被 Donaldson 大法官重复如下：

"In Pyrene Co Ltd v. Scindia Navigation Co Ltd., Devlin J. instanced three types of FOB contract…

In the first, or classic type, the buyer nominated the ship and the seller put the goods on board for the account of the buyer, procuring a bill of lading[192]. The seller was a party to the contract of carriage and if he had taken the bill of lading to his order[193], the only contract of carriage to which the buyer could become party was that contained in or evidenced by the bill of lading which was endorsed to him by the seller[194].

The second is a variant of the first, in that the seller arranges for the ship to come on the berth[195], but the legal incidents are the same.

The third is where the seller puts the goods on board, takes a mate's receipt and gives this to the buyer or his agent who then takes a bill of lading[196]. The buyer was a party to the contract *ab initio*[197]."

---

[192] 第一种做法是买方指定是什么船舶(与班轮公司)，卖方把货装上该船舶，并获签发一套提单(这是发货人在海牙规则 Article Ⅲ(3) 与 (7) 的法定权力，在本书第二章之 3.5.3 小段中有详述)。

[193] 若提单是指示提单(一般也是)，则提单合约中的货方是卖方。否则，没有合约关系承运人干吗要听卖方的指示呢？

[194] 而买方要成为这运输合约的一分子就必须根据提单法的立法将合约强制转让，这是在提单稍后背书给他/它之时。

[195] 第二种做法与第一种大致一样，除了买方连指定什么船舶也省掉，全部运输安排都交托给卖方处理。看来，这二种做法与 CIF 买卖无大分别，除了在 FOB，运费会是分开结算，而在 CIF 则运费已加在货价里。这第二种 FOB 做法请看稍后详述的 The "El Amira" 先例。

[196] 第三种做法是卖方把货物装上船并取得一份大副收据(请看本书第二章之 3.3 小段)，把这大副收据给买方或买方装港代理，以便他/它去向船东/承运人换取一套提单。这会是买方自己在装港指定了一位"货运代理"(forwarding agent)，订了舱位预付了运费，到时通知 FOB 卖方把货物装上船舶，取得一份大副收据后再没有他的事。这第三种 FOB 做法请看 Pyrene Company Ltd v. Scindia Steam Navigation Company Ltd. (1954) 1 Lloyd's Rep. 321 的例子。

[197] 这一来，买方从一开始就是以提单为证明的运输合约的一方。提单上的发货人是买方名字。提单也会订明是听他/它的指示交货。

以上主要是讲班轮运输做法，在散装货往往涉及整艘船舶，其在 FOB 做法上一般是由买方租入船舶后将船派往装港。正如在 Miserocchi v. Agricultores（1982）1 Lloyd's Rep. 202 先例中 Staughton 大法官说："… under an FOB contract it was the buyer's obligation to provide a ship at the place of shipment on the day when shipment was to take place; the seller had then to bring his goods to the ship's rail for loading."

这也是国际商会 Incoterms 1990 的说法，即"FOB 卖方对运输没责任，而是由 FOB 买方去签订自指定港口装船时起的运输合同，费用自理。"

以上可见 FOB 不像 CIF 明确，与承运人订立运输合约的可能是卖方，也可能是卖方代理买方，或是买方自己。

举个例子，在 The "El Amira" 先例，它涉及每年大批的洋葱从埃及运去欧洲各国。这些洋葱都以 FOB 埃及港口的价格出售。但为了促销，并且让埃及卖方可向欧洲买方保证 FOB 之外的运价是多少以及一定有船可供付运，有关商会（名为"Supreme Onion Shipping Committee"）与个别船东/承运人谈判并订立了运输合约，可称为"Continental Contract"。在合约中，商会自称代表发货人与收货人："Supreme Onion Shipping Committee on behalf of the Receivers and their Shippers only."

而 Continental Contract 有多达 30 条条款去针对各个方面，如在 1977 年度总货量是 1.3 万吨洋葱，运费是多少，要签发班轮提单，适用海牙规则，卸港的地理顺序，船东负责积载，验查船舱权力、仲裁条款，等等。可说，它根本就像一份系列航次租船合约的包运合同（Contract of Affreightment，简称 COA）。唯一的大问题是：这商会在订约当时不可能有"所有"的洋葱买方的授权，将来的买方会是谁也是天知道。

在 The "El Amria"，就涉及其中一次付运并发生货损，收货人（提单持有人）向船东起诉。而首先面临的争议就是双方间的合约到底是哪一份运输合约？是班轮提单呢，还是 Continental Contract？如果商会真能代表 FOB 买方去订立这份实际是租约的 Continental Contract，则后来签发的班轮提单只能是一份收据，不会去改变双方已受约束的 Continental Contract。相反，若是商会不能代表 FOB 买方（也是本案原告的收货人），Continental Contract 不能约束 FOB 买方，则 FOB 买方与船东的运输合约也就是班轮提单了。正如 Donaldson 大法官说："In deciding whether the receivers were parties to a contract of carriage on the terms contained in the bills of lading, which contained the exclusive jurisdiction clause, or on the relevant terms of the Continental Contract, which did not, the law to be applied is that of Egypt. However, it was not suggested that the law differed in any material respect from that of England. Accordingly, the position is that if the receivers were the charterers of the vessel on the terms of the Continental Contract, the bills of lading would be bare receipts and not contracts of carriage in their hands（see The "Dunelmia"（1969）2 Lloyd's Rep. 476）. It is true that in that case the charter-party required the master to sign bills of lading "without prejudice to this charterparty" and there is no equivalent clause in the Continental Contract, but part of the ratio of the decision was that a master normally has no authority to vary the terms of a charter-party and that to issue a contractual bill of lading to a charterer would have this effect. So the issues come to this: (a) was the Continental Contract a contract of carriage or a tonnage contract? And (b) if it was a contract of carriage, were the receivers parties to it?"

以上节录也可见,两份运输合约内容不一样,例如在管辖权条款(只有 Continental Contract 有仲裁条款)与适用法条款方面。

Donaldson 大法官(与上诉庭)判该案是第二种 FOB 做法,提单才是约束收货人与船东的合约,他说:"accordingly, all we know is that the sellers arranged for the ship to become available, that the sellers shipped the onions, that the sellers took an order bill of lading and that the sellers endorsed that bill of lading in favour of the receivers and delivered it to the receivers on payment of the price. Using Mr. Justice Devlin's classification, this is a type 2 FOB contract, and the buyer's only rights are under the bill of lading."

9.1.3 中间商

国际贸易商,也是"营运人"(operator),常有的一种做法是以 FOB 买入货物再以 CIF/CFR 卖出给第三者,从中赚取货价差价,保费或/与运费差价(会包括像滞期费差价等)。航运十分复杂,陷阱处处,不少发展中国家的货方不敢去碰,也只好让中间商去赚了。像中国的外贸,据说因进出口公司怕麻烦,有 80% 的进口是 CIF/CFR,而出口则是 FOB,反正不去碰航运。所以在这环境下,能去掌握航运的中间商(国际贸易商)就可以大展拳脚了。

至于运输合约的关系,针对大宗货物,首先会是中间商去市场租船,并订立一个租约。之后,派船去装港装载 FOB 买入的货物。装完货物,在发货人(FOB 卖方)要求下,船长/承运人要签发提单,这是海牙规则之 Article Ⅲ (3) 与(7)下发货人的法定权利,船东无法去抗拒,这一点在本书第二章之 3.5.3 小段有详述。

这提单一般会是指示提单,所以是发货人与承运人(多数是船东)之间的运输合约,而且海牙规则之 Article Ⅰ(b) 也说明:"'Contract of carriage' applies only to contracts of carriage covered by a bill of lading… including any bill of lading… issued under or pursuant to a charter party from the moment at which such bill of lading… regulates between a carrier and a holder of same."

可见,船东至此已受两个运输合约约束:与中间商是租约,与发货人是提单。这两个运输合约都是针对同一航次,所以不能有太大矛盾,令船东(承运人)无所适从。例如,去两个不同的卸港,一南一北。所以,租约授权承租人(中间商)签发的提单,即使是最宽松的一种授权用字以"呈上"(as presented)来表达,法律上也是局限在后来"呈上"的提单不能与租约有绝对相异/矛盾之处:The"Berkshire"(1974)1 Lloyd's Rep. 185。例如,签发提单的卸港不能是租约不准去的地区:Halcyon Steamship v. Continental Grain (1943)75 Lloyd's Rep. 80。这方面在笔者的《期租合约》一书 25.3 段与《程租合约》一书第十三章都有详述,不去重复或节录。

9.1.4 全程运输的二程船

当一程船船东是承运人(全程提单请参阅本书第二章之 3.2 小段)而将运输再给分包二程船时,二程船提单的发货人严格上应是填上一程船的承运人。这是少有的发货人不是真正的货方的情况。见过不少二程船提单在发货人一栏由安排转运的一程船代理人填上"代原发货人",这不一定正确,因为该代理人没有货方(发货人)的授权。在本书第二章之 3.2 小段亦说到在诉讼时会带来谁是当事人的混乱:The "Xingcheng"(1987)2 Lloyd's Rep. 210。

§10 租约、提单这两份运输合约针对同一航次能否一致的探讨

除了不要无所适从外,船东更希望两个运输合约在每一条款都能"背靠背",完全一致。毕竟,去履行的是同一航次,是去干同一件事。所以,一般简单与肯定的做法是在提单合并租约所有条款("All the terms, conditions, clauses and exceptions contained in the said charterparty apply to this bill of lading and are deemed to be incorporated therein":在 Akt. Ocean v. Harding(1928)30 Lloyd's Rep. 249 先例的提单合并条款)。

10.1 无法一致的情况

但即使如此,仍会无法做到完全一致,例如在以下情况:

(ⅰ)一些与提单合约没有直接关联的条款不能泛泛去合并,除非特别写明。例如是租约内的仲裁条款:The"Annefield"(1971)1 Lloyd's Rep. 1,或是 FOB 买卖的租约内的"中止责任条款"(cesser clause):Gullischen v. Stewart(1884)13 QBD 317。

(ⅱ)合并的内容(租约条款)不得与提单明示的条款/批注冲突,如果有,后者解释起来要超越前者。例如,提单注明"运费已预付",但租约条款却规定有 30% 运费要留待卸完货 1 个月后才结算。

(ⅲ)在货损货差方面,提单往往受海牙/海牙·维斯比规则(甚至汉堡规则,中

国海商法等）定下的承运人法定最低责任所约束，并不准以订约自由为名去减轻责任或加大权利：见海牙规则 Article Ⅲ(8)。当然，承运人以订约自由去加大自己的责任，减少权利/免责，这是可以：见海牙规则 Article V。此外，同一 Article V 也说明海牙规则不适用在租约。所以，租约条款有完全的订约自由，双方可去同意对承运人（船东）比海牙规则更苛刻或另一极端是宽松得多的条款。这一来，会一个极端是租约有一条款说明船东要让船舶绝对适航，绝对负责货物安全，而这租约合并到之后签发的提单，会是提单下船东承担了"加大的责任"（increases responsibilities），而这在海牙/海牙·维斯比规则下仍然有效。但另一个极端是租约有一条款说明船东不必对货损货差负任何责任，或另有条款去减轻船东责任至比海牙规则低多了（这情况毫不奇怪，著名的"金康租约"第二条款即是如此，请参阅《程租合约》一书第四章）。这租约合并到之后签发的提单，会是租约内容中有违反海牙/海牙·维斯比规则的部分无效。这一来，显然会造成租约与提单无法一致，出了事会增加船东的麻烦。典型的是多了诉讼：如货方/提单持有人根据提单向船东索赔货损货差，船东败诉或和解后再根据租约（责任较轻）向承租人寻求"补偿"（indemnity）。

（ⅳ）如果租约是程租租约，它的内容与后来的提单应是为了针对同一航次，所以合并起来可能会十分配合。例如，装卸港口/码头，装卸作业，装卸时间与滞期费，留置条款，等等。但如果租约是期租租约，而且是唯一的一份租约，或者明示是合并了这份期租约入提单，又是怎样办呢？毕竟，这2份合约内容不同，难以合并：The "San Nicholas"（1976）1 Lloyd's Rep. 8；The "SLS Everest"（1981）2 Lloyd's Rep. 389。

情况会是，若明示去合并一份期租约，则期租约内大部分的内容会被漠视。毕竟大原则是只有是"直接关联"（direct germane to subject matter）的内容才能去合并：请看（ⅰ）段。另外，有部分是直接关联的内容/条款，但用字不当，因为是期租，这就有可能要对其加以"篡改"（manuplate）以便配套。这一切有关如何去合理解释并入条款的问题，在笔者的《国际商务游戏规则——英国合约法》一书的第十章有详述，不去重复。稍后本书第四章也会在§2段详述这一方面。

至于只有一份期租约，根本没有程租存在，"并无可并"，而提单也没有任何明示去合并该期租约的话，也可以光看提单本身十分简陋的内容（这可不是班轮提单）去作出解释。有必要也可以默示一些条款（可能会有许多方面要默示）。毕竟，内容十分简陋的合约在现实中不是少见。

以上可举 Mallozzi v. Carapelli（1976）1 Lloyd's Rep. 407 为例说明，读者因此会更清楚。该案例首先涉及一个 CIF 买卖（散粮的货物），买卖合约中有一条款针对卸货率（每工作天3000吨）以及买方负责支付租约下的滞期费。而卖方较早时已期租了一艘名为"Italmotor"的船舶。在卸港以卸货率计算，共产生了14天多的滞期费，但什么是滞期费呢，因为只有一份期租约，没有程租？结果卖方硬是去算出一

个"滞期损失"(damage for detention)的金额,但这被上诉庭否定。Megaw 大法官说:

"The first sentence of the clause[198] sets out an 'average rate of discharge'. But the second sentence[199] provides:

…Demurrage/half dispatch on unloading at the rates indicated in the Charterparty for buyer's account.

The relevant charter-party contains no provision for demurrage on unloading and no rates for demurrage. So the buyers' case was really perfectly simple: Never mind how long the time was that was occupied and whether or not that involved not complying with the 'average rate of discharge'…having regard to the fact that the sellers had chosen-no doubt for their own purposes-to enter into a contract with shipowners, namely the time charter -party[200], which did not involve any provision for demurrage nor indicate any rates for demurrage, there was nothing to be paid. In my judgment it is as simple as that; and that contention is right…

…

The clause[201] would have worked perfectly sensibly in accordance with its literal and natural meaning if the sellers had… made a charter-party which involved an obligation of, and rates for, demurrage[202]."

以上案例可见,只有一份期租约或明示合并的只是期租约,船东/承运人就无法去说提单合约有任何明示/默示的卸货率与滞期费率可强加到提单持有人/货方头上。可是,现实中今天愈来愈多的是只有一份期租约:CIF/CFR 卖方以"time-charter-trip"(TCT)期租船舶来跑这航次。若是之后签发的提单去合并这 TCT 租约,哪来卸货率/滞期费?

(ⅴ)如果 CIF 卖方在买卖合约,同意了一些条款是后来在租船时无法说服船东接受的(或无法改以灵活性较大的期租来取代程租),那就无可避免地会存在矛盾而导致后来签发的提单无法在买卖合约(或/与信用证)下被接受。例如,买卖合约是"免费卸货"(liner discharge),或是 CQD(customary quick dispatch)。但在谈租约时,船东坚持是不负责卸货(free out),或是要有卸货率/滞期费。那么订了这样的租约(虽是程租),要合并到后来签发的提单就会产生困难;Seng v. Glencore Grain (1996)1 Lloyd's Rep. 398。一种办法是在提单正面/前页去明示 liner discharge 或/

---

[198] 这是指买卖合约的条款。
[199] 这是指买卖合约的条款。
[200] 卖方自己去订立一份期租约。
[201] 这是指买卖合约的条款。
[202] 卖方如果是订立了一份有滞期费/卸率的程租租约就好办了,完全配套了。

与CQD,进而去超越合并的条款。但这就造成两个运输合约(程租租约与提单)不是内容"背靠背"了。

其他有关租约提单的合并条款,在本书第四章会再详论。

10.2 运输合约与买卖合约一致与否的探讨

上一段略为提到了买卖合约与运输合约是否一致,有否矛盾的问题,这又是须探讨另一方面了。对船东/承运人而言,如果订立的程租租约顺利合并进了提单,而且两份运输合约确能做到"背靠背",那应是没有问题了。但换了对买卖合约而言,可能两份内容一致的运输合约(比方说,都订明是 free out)都与买卖合约有矛盾,不一致(比方说,订明是 liner discharge):Seng v. Glencore Grain (1996) 1 Lloyd's Rep. 398。这一来,又怎样办呢?

首先,如果买方"能把好关",会是能在买卖合约或/与信用证以不符点拒绝接受这份不足保障的提单合约。这一来,会迫 CIF/CFR 卖方去修改提单,令它与买卖合约内容一致。而这样的话,二份运输合约却又无法一致了,但买方对此不必理睬,反正船东(承运人)与发货人(承租人)会去想办法,或对于加大的提单责任事后再为补偿而诉讼,或私下谈判,等等。

但如果不能把好关,就会导致买方最后要自己先掏腰包卸货(提单是 free out),或先要支付船东一笔滞期费(而买卖合约原是 CQD),事后再去向卖方要求"补偿"(indemnity)了。但别高兴:补偿不一定会成功,因为有太多变数了,如:买卖合约有一条乌干达仲裁条款;卖方是皮包公司,法官/仲裁员判错;自己不懂又乱来导致好事变坏事,等等。

在此介绍一著名先例,可反映各合约之间的"网络"或"环节"。在 The"Spiliada"(1987)1 Lloyd's Rep. 1,涉及船舱被硫磺的货物腐蚀。货物是由温哥华运去印度,合约"网络"与当事人是:

(ⅰ)印度买方 MMTC 以 FOB 向加拿大卖方 Cansulex 购入 2 万吨硫磺。

(ⅱ)MMTC 程租租进了 The"Spiliada"轮,船东是希腊船东。

(ⅲ)在温哥华装了 2 万吨硫磺。

(ⅳ)船长签发了指示提单,写明 Cansulex 是发货人。

(ⅴ)该提单背面有印就的条款,与租约不一致,其中第 21 条注明适用英国法(这一来就能给英国法院以管辖的理由/借口)。

(ⅵ)船东与 MMTC(承租人)的租约内有一条伦敦仲裁条款。当然,也可以是印度仲裁条款,这是订约自由嘛。

(ⅶ)MMTC 与 Cansulex 之间的买卖合约也有一条伦敦仲裁条款。同样,它可以是加拿大或新加坡仲裁条款。

第三章　提单作用之二：运输合约·谁是其中的合约方　203

在该"Spiliada"轮被严重腐蚀/损坏后，船东采取了两个行动：

其一，对承租人 MMTC 开始仲裁，这是根据程租租约。至于对危险品的责任，在稍后 11.2.1 小段详论。其二，对发货人 Cansulex，在英国法院起诉，这是根据它们之间的运输合约：一份提单，内中注明适用英国法。

当然，如果最后 MMTC 真要赔钱，而买卖合约下错在 Cansulex，更会有另一个的仲裁（依据买卖合约的仲裁条款行事），就是 MMTC 要求 Cansulex "补偿"（indemnity）。这一切的合约"网络"，Coff 勋爵是如此介绍的："The owners have advanced their claim against Cansulex as shippers under the contract of carriage contained in or evidenced by the bills of lading to which I have already referred, basing their claim on art. 4, r. 6, of the Hague Rules incorporated into the bills, and on a warranty implied by English law that dangerous cargo will not be shipped without warning. Arbitration proceedings have also been commenced by the shipowners against MMTC in London under the arbitration clause in the voyage charter. It is open to MMTC to bring arbitration proceedings in London against Cansulex under the sale contract between them, by virtue of the London arbitration clause in that contract. Leave was obtained by the owners to issue and serve a writ upon Cansulex outside the jurisdiction on a ground contained in the then RSC., O.11, r.1 (1)(f)(ⅲ)[203], viz., that the action was brought to recover damages in respect of breach of a contract which was by its terms governed by English law."

§11　订立运输合约的货方才能享有合约权利和承担合约责任

在本章 §9 段已详论了谁是订立运输合约的原始货方。可以说，就提单这份运输合约而言，不论其形式或条款（班轮提单或租约提单）如何，只要是指示提单，都会导致发货人是该合约的一方，受约束。若提单只是一份货物收据，这表示发货人与船东（承运人）早已有了一份租约，是提单所无法替代的。现实中，后者的情况不多。故可从总体上说，除了本章 9.1.2 小段所讲的第三种 FOB 做法，发货人作为合约一方在提单合约中既有权利，也有责任和义务。

11.1　合约权利

货方的权利包括对船东（承运人）有诉权，这针对的是承运人违反提单合约的明示、默示或法定条款/责任，例如是无单放货，就是明确的违反了提单的明示或默

---

[203] 有关这方面的英国法院管辖权以及送达告票往外国被告，请参阅笔者与杨大明先生合著的《禁令》一书第六章。

示条款:请参阅本书第二章5.5小段等多处。当然承运人也可以提单合约内的免责条款去抗辩,只是很难成功而已:请参阅本书第二章之5.6.2小段。

又例如是不适航导致货损货差,即是明确的违反了海牙规则的法定责任,诉权又是在发货人,因他才是提单这份运输合约的一方。固然,海牙规则内的免责,限制赔偿责任,时效等权利/好处,如果适用,承运人/船东作为提单合约的另一方也尽可引用来提出抗辩。

11.2 合约责任/义务

合约责任/义务会有多种,所以发货人作为提单合约一方(货方)也不是闹着玩的。可在接下来的段节举几种典型的例子。

11.2.1 例子之一:危险品

今天危险品的运载十分多,它可能会带来的严重后果/灾难性意外,绝不可轻视。提单合约会有明示条款禁止发货人(合约另外一方)去偷偷的运危险品,例如在 Ministry of Food v. Lamport & Holt Line, Ltd. (1952) 2 Lloyd's Rep. 371 的班轮提单第11条款说:"the shippers shall be liable for any loss or damage to ship or cargo caused by…dangerous goods, shipped without full disclosure of their nature."

而即使没有明示的提单条款,英国法律也会去默示,这一点十分明确,在《Scrutton on Charter-parties》一书之 Article 51 说:"By the common law of England the shipper of goods impliedly undertakes to ship no goods of such a dangerous character or so dangerously packed that the shipowner or his agent could not by reasonable knowledge and diligence be aware of their dangerous character, unless notice be given to the shipowner of his agent of such dangerous character…"

如果提单只是收据,因发货人较早已订立有一份租约,则地位一样:没有明示条款也有默示条款去在租约作出同样的禁止危险品的规定。著名的先例如 The "Atlantic Duchess" (1957) 2 Lloyd's Rep. 55 与 The "Athanasia Comninos" (1990) 1 Lloyd's Rep. 277 都是这种例子:承租人同时是发货人。

当然,就算承租人不是发货人(如本章之9.1.3小段的情况),也一样在租约下有此默示的法律责任。有关何谓危险品,笔者可去节录《程租合约》一书第八章3.3小段如下:

3.3 危险品

我在《期租合约》一书的第101页,给危险品下的定义是:"会对船舶、船员、其他货物造成危险的货品就是危险品"。该书已有这方面详论,不再重复。

程租不像期租,货物品种在租约中已有订明。所以,若租约订明是去装鱼粉,则船长不可以它有自燃危险而去拒绝。既然出租,船东应接受这类货物品种一般性危险的预防与风险。

但如果这批货物有船长一般不应知道的特殊类别(different kind)的风险,承租人或发货人有责任在装船之前通知船长,让他去熟悉防备:The "Atlantic Duchess" (1957) 2 Lloyd's Rep. 55 (货是 butanised crude oil):The "Athanasia Comninos" (1990) 1 Lloyd's Rep. 277 (货是发出爆炸气体的煤炭):The "Fiona" (1993) 1 Lloyd's Rep. 257 (货是 Residual fuel oil)。如果不去事先通知,承租人等于是违反了这方面的法律默示责任。而如果租约有去合并首要条款,海牙规则下的 Article IV, Rule 6 也适用。

如果船长收到通知后,发觉货物根本不能安全运抵目的地,他可否拒装呢?毕竟,这是租约订明的货物。例如租约订明是铜精矿,但装之前被通知水分很高,航程中移动会产生危险:The "Agios Nicolas" (1968) 1 Lloyd's Rep. 57。这方面法律并不太明确,可去看 Voyage Charters 一书的第 112 页说:

"Where the cargo has been described specifically in the clarterparty, but presents unusual risks which are different in kind from those usually associated with a cargo of the charterparty description, it is unclear whether the carrier is entitled to refuse the goods on the grounds that they fall outside the charterparty description or whether, having received the appropriate notice, he is obliged to carry them. The former view was taken by Evans J. in The "Amphion" (1991) 2 Lloyd's Rep. 101, purporting to follow The "Athanasia Comninos" at page 283 The latter view seems more in accord with The "Atlantic Duchess" (1957) 2 Lloyd's Rep. 55, 95 and The "Fiona" …It is also the view taken in Scrutton, page 103, subject to the qualification that if it is impossible to carry the goods safely, the carrier is justified in refusing them."

看来,关键是危险程度的确定,如果通知了船长后他是可以预防的,或多花点钱加设备,就可以解决问题,那么船东仍要履约,去装这租约订明的货物品种,即使它有一点特殊类别的危险。

但要是危险太大,避免防备不了,则总不能让船长船员去跑这个航次送死吧,这变成是"不可能"(impossible)去履约了。

随着在海上运输中危险品的种类愈来愈多,各国法律强加的责任也不断加重,而一出事也往往是天文数字的损失灾难,出口商可要小心了。随便拣近期几宗事故作为例子如下:

(ⅰ)Navigas v. Enron(1997) 2 Lloyd's Rep. 759 与 The "Berge Sisar" (1998)2 Lloyd's Rep. 475 都涉及沙特阿拉伯装的"丙烷"(propane)腐蚀性太高,这会损坏船舱。

(ⅱ)这种货物腐蚀船舶的案件老早已有,如 Brass v. Maitland (1856) 6E. & B. 470 的漂白粉(有高腐蚀的 chloride lime)。

(ⅲ)硫磺严重腐蚀船舱的 The "Spiliada" (1987)1 Lloyd's Rep. 1。

(ⅳ)近几年有一种叫 Calcium hypochlorite 的漂白粉(中国出口不少)会带来在海上运输途中严重火灾,甚至最后船舶遭受全损:例如,The "Kapitan Sakharov" (2000)2 Lloyd's Rep. 255。问题严重至国际互保协会集团(The International Group of P & I Clubs)出资成立工作小组去研究解决或减少危险的办法。这工作小组在1999年底出了报告与建议,建议有:只装在甲板上,但要远离船员房间及避免太阳直晒,要用铁桶而不是麻包袋包装;使用的集装箱不要大于 20 尺的 teu;如果预计航次中会遇上高于35℃的温度,应设计保证集装箱内的堆放货物能够有通风,如不要装超过 14 吨的重量,或干脆集装箱配有机动冷却通风,等等。

(ⅴ)在 The "Kapitan Sakharov" (2000)2 Lloyd's Rep. 255,涉及一种名为 calcium hypochlorite 与 isopentane 的货物发生爆炸,导致船舶全损/沉没,损失严重。船东指 calcium hypochlorite 的发货人偷偷把危险品装在集装箱内,不去宣告。

由于发货人总是逃不了责任,笔者建议中国的国营出口商要十分小心。毕竟,不像私人公司,前者出了灾难性事故会是要中国老百姓世世代代的去赔偿外国人。鉴此,可否避免自己出面作发货人而转由私人公司甚至是皮包公司去出面安排运输呢? 例如,在 The "Aegean Sea" (1998)2 Lloyd's Rep. 39 案例,就反映了西班牙国家石油公司的进出口全部是通过一家它背后控制但表面上完全独立的 ROIL 公司进行的。该公司甚至故意不在西班牙注册,而是一家 Liechtenstein 的公司。

至于无辜收货人/提单合法持有人会否也有这方面的责任,请参阅第六章之2.2 小段。

11.2.2 例子之二:支付运费、亏舱费和滞期费等

发货人要支付运费,而运费是多少应去看提单合约。班轮提单下会是早已(订舱位时)同意运费费率与回扣。租约提单下会是合并租约所同意了的运费。

发货人要支付运费的合约责任,可去节录《Scrutton on Charter-Parties》一书的 Article 171 如下:

"Freight is *prima facie* payable according to the terms of the contract of affreightment, and by the person with whom such contract is made…

From shipment of goods upon a vessel for a certain voyage a contract by the shipper to pay freight for such goods is implied…

…The shipper does not free themselves from such liability by indorsing the bill of lading so as to pass the property…"

至于滞期费道理也是一样,但不像运费,发货人(也是 CIF/CFR 卖方)可以很快在信用证获支付包含了运费的货价,而且提单往往也要求注明是"运费已预付",所以发货人很愿意负责支付运费给船东(或二船东的承运人)。可是发货人并不想付滞期费,特别是对在卸港会发生的滞期费负责。但发货人是运输合约的一方,仍是无法逃避。

首先在班轮提单,这问题应不必太去关心,毕竟班轮绝少会产生滞期。

至于租约提单,由于较早会已有一个程租租约的存在,甚至是发货人与船东双方订立的也不一定,则发货人去逃避对滞期费负责的一般做法是在程租租约内加一条"中止责任与留置条款"(Cesser and Lien Clause)。这方面问题在《程租合约》一书第十二章有详论,内容较多,无法去重复或节录。

在此只简单说明该条款是明确去说船东要在卸港通过留置货物直接向收货人(买方)结算/收取卸港滞期费,而别来找承租人(也是发货人)。只有在毫无留置办法情况下才准船东去找承租人支付。这清楚不过的措辞/用字,可见于"金康租约"1976 年版的第 8 条款如下:"Owners shall have a lien on the cargo for… demurrage[204]…Charterers shall remain responsible for… demurrage… incurred at port of loading[205]. Charterers shall also remain responsible for… demurrage (including damage for detention) incurred at port of discharge[206], but only to such extent as the Owners have been unable to obtain payment thereof by exercising the lien on the cargo[207]."

这明示条款完全有效:见 Hansen v. Harrold Bros. (1984) 1 QB 612;The "Zitella" (1938) 61 Lloyd's Rep. 97;The "Sinoe" (1972) 1 Lloyd's Rep. 201;The "Kavo Peirtis" (1977) 2 Lloyd's Rep. 113;The "Boral Gas" (1988) 1 Lloyd's Rep. 342;The "Miramar" (1984) 2 Lloyd's Rep. 129;The "Aegis Britannic" (1987) 1 Lloyd's Rep. 119;等许多先例。

曾有过案例判中止条款不合并进提单:Gullischen v. Stewart (1884) 13 QBD 317。但该古老案例涉及的承租人也就是收货人,变了留置货物仍是针对承租人,故

---

[204] 允许船东有权为滞期费留置货物。这一条款将被合并进提单,变得提单下船东也有合约权利去为滞期费留置货物。
[205] 对装港产生的滞期费,承租人(发货人)要无条件负责。
[206] 但对卸港产生的滞期费承租人若要负责,先决条件是……
[207] 船东要通过留置货物向收货人索取,只有在无法做到或只能取回部分滞期费的情况下才能回头找承租人。

何必要中止责任去迫船东为滞期费先留置货物呢？

若承租人是发货人，或是像9.1.3小段的中间商，反正不是收货人，如果签发的提单顺利合并了程租租约的中止条款，那么船东/承运人不去留置货物是不能成功向承租人（根据租约）或发货人（根据提单）索取滞期费的。这方面请阅《程租合约》一书第十二章之§4段。

§12 合约相互关系的大原则造成的障碍与解决办法

在§9段可见，就提单合约而言，99%都会是发货人（卖方）与承运人（船东）之间的运输合约。这一方面是因为CIF/CFR买卖盛行，故是由卖方安排运输。另一方面是因为即使是FOB买卖，是买方租船，发货人仍是有权在海牙/海牙·维斯比规则下要求签发装船指示提单的"运输合约"（contract of carriage）。这便形成了租约这份运输合约是买方（承租人）与承运人/船东的，但提单这份运输合约仍是卖方（发货人）与承运人/船东的这样一种三角合约关系。

12.1 背书/交出提单只转让货权，不转让合约

在本书第二章多处已详谈了提单是"物权凭证"（document of title），可去通过背书与交出而转让货物的占有权与所有权：请重点看3.1.2小段所提的主要先例Lickbarrow v. Mason (1787) 2 T. R. 63。但疑问是：转让货物的同时能否去转让提单这份运输合约？若是不能，这会严重影响提单作为物权凭证的地位，因为提单持有人/收货人不能因转让而与船东产生合约关系。他/它们之间只有侵权的关系。可能双方最终会有"托管"（bailment）的关系，因为船东在卸港交出货物给收货人会构成"让与"（attornment）（请看本书第二章之1.5.4小段），但这仍是侵权关系而非是合法关系（请看第二章之1.5.3小段）。

这一来，遇上货损货差，收货人只能以侵权起诉船东。但这十分不利，如：

（ⅰ）本章8.2.1小段谈到的海牙/海牙·维斯比规则不适用。

（ⅱ）本章8.2.3小段谈到的损失当时收货人尚未拥有货物主权。

（ⅲ）本章8.2.4小段谈到的无法/无权索赔纯经济损失。

当然，收货人也会有有利之处。例如卸港产生的大量滞期费，船东只能根据提单合约向发货人索赔。侵权没有滞期费这种责任与索赔，它实际是纯经济损失，合约关系下可去索赔，但在侵权不行。

对于本章11.2.1小段讲到的危险品造成损失，船东也是只能去向发货人追究，跟没有提单运输合约关系的收货人无关（除非收货人碰巧是FOB买卖的承租人，但这是以租约为根据，不是以提单）。

在 Thompson v. Dominy(1845)14 M & W 403;153 E. R. 532,这疑问有了答案,但这并不是一个好的答案。Parke B 大法官判是提单背书与交出只转让货权,但不转让运输合约,说:"I have never heard it argued that a contract was transferable, except the law merchant, and there is nothing to show that a bill of lading is transferable under any custom of merchants. It transfers no more than the property in the goods, it does not transfer the contract."

有此判决其实不奇怪,这要去先了解"合约相互关系"(privity of contract)的大原则。

12.2 "合约相互关系"(privity of contract)简介

这个大原则、大精神在笔者的《国际商务游戏规则——英国合约法》一书已有第四章整章详论。内容实在太多,无法在此重复。只强调在这大原则下,普通法坚持一个合约只是属订约双方之间的事,与第三者无关。有如下两点可以明确:

(i)除了订约方,第三者不能去要求合约的权利(to acquireright under a contract)。

(ii)除了订约方,不能去强加合约的责任给第三者。

这大原则涉及提单方面,首先在上一小段提到的 Thompson v. Dominy(1845)14 M & W 403;153 E. R. 532,显然已造成障碍。

但还有其他一连串重要先例确立了这一大原则。在著名的 Tweddle v. Atkinson(1861)1 B & S 393 先例,它涉及男女双方的娶嫁,事前女方父亲与男方父亲同意了前者给新郎一笔钱。事后女方父亲食言,新郎起诉,法院判合约即使是为了把好处给新郎,但由于他不是合约方,因而就不能去依赖合约起诉。显然,这种事情也不会与侵权扯得上任何关系,这等于是新郎只能是不了了之。

另去节录 Haldane 勋爵在 Dunlop Pneumatic Tyre Co Ltd v. Selfridge & Co Ltd. (1915) A. C. 847 的名言如下:"In the law of England certain principles are fundamental. One is that only a person who is a party to a contract can sue on it. Our law knows nothing of a jus quaesitum tertio arising by way of contract(指只有订约方才有合约的诉权,这是英国法律的基本原则)。"

到了 Midland Silicones v. Scruttons(1961)2 Lloyd's Rep. 365,这大原则已有了多个先例确认,可以说已是"根深蒂固",再也动不了。所以 Viscount Simonds 在判词中说:"If the principle of jus quaesitum tertio(拉丁文,指第三者有权加入一个合约要求他应有的利益)is to be introduced into our law, it must be done by Parliament after a due consideration of its merits and demerits."

这表示法院本身已是无能为力,不能靠案例法再在个别的案例事实下,东改西改,这既不全面,也机遇难逢。所以必须依赖议会去立法更改,在立法前要清楚考虑优劣,去怎样改与改多少。而早在说这话之前,在提单合约方面早已是这样做了,这就是稍后要详论的 1855 年提单法的立法。

相互关系的大原则在不应强加"合约责任"(contractual obligations)到非自愿的第三者身上这一点是没有太大异议。确实,如果法律允许这样做岂非人人自危,无端天上便掉下来一份合约责任要他/她去履行。而有异议的是:如果合约想去把一个或多个好处给第三者,这第三者为何不能去起诉/执行呢? 正如 Steyn 勋爵在 Linden Gardens Trust v. Lenesta Sludge Disposals (1994) 1 AC 85 先例所说的:"The case for recognizing a contract for the benefit of a third party is simple and straightforward[208]. The autonomy of the will of the parties should be respected[209]. The law of contract should give effect to the reasonable expectations of contractual parties[210]. Principle certainly requires that a burden should not be imposed on a third party without his consent[211]. But there is no doctrinal, logical or policy reason why the law should deny third party where that is the expressed intention of the parties[212]. Moreover, often the parties, and particularly third parties, organize their affairs on the faith of the contract[213]. They rely on the contract. It is therefore unjust to deny effectiveness to such a contract[214]."

读者或许会问:为何不去让订约方/合约方起诉,而要斤斤计较第三者能否有诉权以自己名义去起诉并执行他/她的"合约"好处/利益呢? 例如,在 Tweddle v. Atkinson 先例中不是由新郎起诉,而是他父亲起诉,因他是订约方,被告的女方父亲应是无话可说了。但这问题在《国际商务游戏规则——英国合约法》一书已有详述,可简单介绍的不可行之处是:

(i) 原订约方(例如 Tweddle v. Atkinson 的新郎父亲)可能死亡。在另一著名的同类先例,Beswick v. Beswick (1968) AC 58 正是这情况。人寿保险也常有这情况,保险好处/利益去给了第三者(投保人的妻子、儿子、朋友、情人等),投保人死亡,承保人(保险公司)不肯支付,谁去起诉执行呢?

(ii) 原订约方可能不愿意麻烦,不想打官司,好处/利益反正是他/它的。或

---

[208] 去承认合约中给于第三者的好处/利益十分简单。
[209] 这是合约双方订约时的意愿,应以尊重。
[210] 合约法本来就是去尽量尊重/承认合约双方的合理期望。
[211] 当然,这不能是去将这合约的责任或承担强加到一位非自愿的第三者头上。
[212] 但没有什么逻辑上或政策上的理由不让法律去承认第三者在这合约所有的好处或利益。
[213] 现实常会是:第三者知道了他有这合约的好处或利益,会依赖它去作出计划,例如在 Tweddle v. Atkinson 案例的新郎,考虑到女方的父亲将会付他一笔钱,就可能会去买房子,先付订金,等等。
[214] 法律不去承认会造成极大的不公道。

是，要去敲第三者一笔竹杠才肯帮忙，例如好处/利益能要回来须平均分摊，等等。

（ⅲ）更大的问题是：原订约方没有真正损失。他/它能起诉对方违约/毁约，并在责任方面会胜诉只是一方面，另一方面是他/它无法证明有损失，因为损失的是没有诉权的第三者。正如在《国际商务游戏规则——英国合约法》一书所说明的，这困境是"the third party suffering losses but cannot sue, and the promisee may sue, but has suffered little or no losses from the promisor's breach."

12.2.1 提单的对策之一：Dunlop v. Lambert 先例

提单是最早在合约相互关系的大原则下面对困难并能找出可行与说得通对策的一环。众所周知，提单这份运输合约的原订约方一般是船东作为承运人与发货人（卖方）作为托运人，特别是随着 CIF 买卖的兴起，尤为如此。而收货人的买方只是第三者，可以说由于海上转卖频繁，会有新买方在运输合约订立时根本仍未存在，故其怎会不是第三者呢？

提单在背书转让的过程中，因为习惯与法律（Lickbarrow v. Mason（1787）2 T. R. 63）承认它是物权凭证，所以货物主权是转让给了买方。但提单的另一个职能：运输合约，并未能因此而转让。从未有说法是背书可去转让合约权利与责任：请看本章 12.1 小段介绍的 Thompson v. Dominy（1845）14 M & W 403；153 ER. 532。相反，合约相互关系这大原则可不容易去跨越。这一点可去节录 Scrutton 大法官在 Brandt v. Liverpool（1924）1 KB 575 的说法："Before the Bills of Lading Act. 1855, was passed, by the custom of merchants the indorsement of the bill of lading passed the property in the goods contained therein, but it did not assign the contract contained therein, and therefore the person who by indorsement became the owner of the goods did not by the same indorsement acquire a right to sue the shipowner upon his contract which was evidenced in the bill of lading."

这一来，就会带来严重不妥。卖方（发货人）在转让了货权，同时收到货款后，他/它对这宗买卖再也不会关心，因为运输风险不在卖方头上（请参阅《国际货物买卖》一书的第六章），所以卖方是想最好别去烦他/它。但可能当时只是在海上运输的初期，离卸港尚远，要这提单合约履行下去，要去关心、依赖或尽责的，实在都是买方（收货人）这一方。提单合约固然有不少责任（支付运费、滞期费等），但也有不少好处/利益。而且是明示或默示给于第三者的买方的（例如船东根据提单要把货物运送至写明的目的地/卸港，并免费卸货与交货给收货人等）。但问题是，这第三者的买方不是订约方，他/它没有诉权去向船东起诉索赔或强制履约。例如，船东违约不开往卸港，买方去向船东提出提单合约内的要求甚至会被嘲弄，如被质问："我跟你有什么关系？"

另外，货损货差经常会发生，造成真正受害的买方无法去依据提单合约向船东起诉，例如指称船东没有"克尽职责"（due diligence）令船舶适航。而如果真能起诉，又存在船东无法以提单合约内的免责条款抗辩。原因很简单，就是双方没有合约关系。

若买方只是依赖与船东的侵权/托管关系，这已在本章多处详述（如12.1小段），会十分不完整而且缺陷重重。毕竟，提单内容也不光是针对货损货差，像在买方/收货人与船东之间谁应去负责卸货这方面就与侵权完全扯不上关系，必须去以提单合约关系才能找出答案，毕竟提单内会对这点有明示或默示条款。

另一做法是买方/收货人请卖方/发货人（他/它是提单合约的一方）出面代为向船东/承运人以提单合约起诉/索赔或要求执行/履约。但会面对真正受损的是买方，不是卖方，变得船东/承运人即使有责任也只需赔名义上的损失。这正是Dunlop v. Lambert (1839) 6 CI & F 600先例所面对的船东抗辩。而法院为此作出的一个新理论就是发货人与船东在订约时都知道/默认合约是为了以后这票货物的买方利益所订立的，因为国际外贸几乎一定是这种情况，提单与货物在航次中转让给买方，所以发货人可以代买方（合约利益方，在订约时双方已知道）去索赔全部损失："is entitled to recover by way of damages for breach of contract the actual loss sustained by those for whose benefit the contract is entered into"。

这方面在《国际商务游戏规则——英国合约法》一书的第四章3.11小段有详论，不再重复。

显然，这解决了"合约相互关系"（privity of contract）的一小部分困难，但不是全部困难。例如，买方怎样才可获得卖方协助去向承运人/船东起诉，并让卖方在胜诉后诚实地退回索赔金额呢？在国际买卖中，货物多次转售，最后买方/收货人（也是真正的受害方，例如在货损货差或船东其他违约方面）更是无法找回原订约方的发货人协助/帮忙诉讼。

12.2.2 提单的对策之二：转让合约权利（assignment of contractual rights）

转让合约利益这一复杂的课题在笔者的《国际商务游戏规则——英国合约法》一书的第四章§7段有详论，无意在此重复或大量节录。只去提一提的是，"衡平法转让"（equitable assignment）早已有案例涉及与允许：Crouch v. Martin (1707) 2 Vern. 595; Row v. Dowson (1749) 1 Vern. Sen. 331; Ryall v. Rowles (175) 1 Ves. Sen. 348; Wright v. Wright (1750) Ves. Sen. 409 等。

但疑问是，卖方可否把提单的合约转让给买方呢？例如是因遭受货损货差而产生的诉权？毕竟，这种情况确有发生，也曾获法院承认/允许：The "Kelo" (1985) 2 Lloyd's Rep. 85。但这对策的严重缺点是：

（ⅰ）转让只局限在合约利益，不能去包括合约责任。故此，在买方向船东（或承运人）索赔的同时，船东却不能反过来向买方反索赔运费或滞期费，他仍要另外去向发货人起诉。这对整个制度的公平与简化来说，非是好事。

（ⅱ）转让必须一环扣一环，不能有中断。但后来的提单持有人是无法知悉较早的环节的，这就会产生大问题。例如，曾有过5次转卖，其中第三次转卖并没转让合约利益（对船东的诉权）。这就会导致最后的买方（收货人，提单持有人）即使有了他/它自己一环的卖方转让也是毫无用处。

（ⅲ）买方无法去独立行事，他/它向船东起诉仍要将原来的订约方（发货人）等牵扯进来，作为"共同原告"（Co-plaintiff）。若是发货人不合作，则要去把他/它当做"共同被告"（Co-defendant），另一被告自然是提单的船东或承运人了：The "Aiolos"（1983）2 Lloyd's Rep. 25，去这样要求，在国际通信并不发达的当年，实在是苛求。另外也会碰到像发货人倒闭的困境。

12.2.3 提单的对策之三：Brandt v. Liverpool 的默示合约

关于怎样才能构成默示合约或/与合约条款的问题，笔者的《国际商务游戏规则——英国合约法》一书的第十章§7段有详论，请参阅，无法在此重复，但大原则/大道理是完全相通的。

在著名的 Brandt v. Liverpool（1924）1 K. B. 575 先例，涉及"锌粉"（zinc ashes）的货物，它装上船舶时已看得见潮湿，这表示它会在海运途中发热，但船长仍去签发了清洁提单。而且，还把它与棉花（容易火烧）的货物装在同一船舱。这货物半途果然出事，导致要转运去目的地/卸港。

航次中，提单被发货人质押，并背书给了原告的银行。银行为了提取这批货物，被迫在抗议下支付了748英镑的运费与其他费用。之后，银行向船东起诉，索赔的项目一是这笔748英镑的款项，另一是因货物延误抵达而货价大跌导致的损失。

当时，已有针对提单的立法（1855年的提单法），但它不适用在银行以承押人身份去持有这份提单的情况。换言之，提单是物权凭证，故此银行可以它去提取货物。但提单合约关系就不会去转让给银行了。

这对银行不一定是坏事，因为有了合约关系也可带来重大的合约责任：请看本章之 11.2.1 与 12.2.4.1 小段。当然在本案的 Brandt v. Liverpool，是银行想以提单合约的关系向船东起诉，因为若以侵权起诉，银行有如下好几个严重的困难：

（ⅰ）这748英镑不属与侵权有关的损失。

（ⅱ）货物延误的损失会是纯经济损失，无法以侵权去索赔：这一点请参阅本章之 8.2.4 小段。

（ⅲ）该先例还涉及船长乱签清洁提单，虽然货物实在有不妥。故此只有靠合约上的说法,即船长/船东是"禁止翻供"(estopped)去对无辜提单持有人否定提单上的资料的。但以侵权的说法,这就说不通是凭什么了。

上诉庭在 Brandt v. Liverpool 先例判是双方在交货时另有一个默示合约,这不光是银行去提取货物而船长放货的双方行为(这只是提单的物权凭证职能),而是因为银行支付了这 748 英镑,本身就是约因。换言之在该先例,原告银行可以提单合约起诉。可能是法院对船东不满意,而该案例的事实又可让法院去作出这种说法,即使有点牵强。

这默示合约的说法在以后好几个案例也有涉及,如:The "Dona Mari"(1973)2 Lloyd's Rep. 366;The "Elli 2"(1985)1 Lloyd's Rep. 107;The "Aramis"(1989)1 Lloyd's Rep. 213 等。

但看来,这说法/论点并不稳定,也颇牵强,正如英国 Law Commission No. 196 报告之 2. 12 小段说的"often involved an element of fiction, even detective work"。例如,运费已预付的提单,不必再付运费,已不容易去默示一个合约,也说不出再有什么约因。又如,提单仍未到手,是以保函放货,也难去说船东/收货人有一个默示合约,后者可能根本不会知道提单的内容。当然,收货人也可在提取货物时与船东另去同意任何方面的问题,但这就不再光是默示合约了。

所以,May 大法官在 The "Elli 2" 曾说:"… I agree that the boundaries of the doctrine are not clear[215]. I would not expect them to be so. As the question whether or not any such contract is to be implied is one of fact, its answer must depend on the circumstances of each particular case[216]——and the different sets of facts which arise for consideration in these cases are legion.[217] However, I also agree that no such contract should be implied on the facts of any given case unless it is necessary to do so[218]: necessary, that is to say, in order to give business reality to a transaction and to create enforceable obligations between parties who are dealing with one another in circumstances in which one would expect that business reality and those enforceable obligations to exist[219] …"

在 The "Aramis",法官对 Brandt v. Liverpool 的说法作出了颇局限的解释,判是必须要在案件的事实中能"推定"(infer)双方有意图订约,有发盘与接受,否则构成不了默示合约。Bingham 大法官说:"… it would in my view be contrary to principle to countenance the implication of a contract from conduct if the conduct relied upon is no

---

[215] 我(May 大法官)同意这说法/论点的范围并不明确,也无法去明确。
[216] 这要去看每一个案件的不同事实/各自的行为。
[217] 而要考虑的事实/双方的行为会是多不胜数。
[218] 我同意如没有必要不应去默示有一个合约。
[219] "必要"是指有商业上的需要/效用,不光是合理不合理的问题。

more consistent with an intention to contract than with an intention not to contract. It must, surely, be necessary to identify conduct referable to the contract contended for or at the very least conduct inconsistent with there being no contract made between the parties to the effect contended for. Put another way, I think it must be fatal to the implication of a contract if the parties would or might have acted exactly as they did in the absence of a contract"(Bingham 大法官认为双方如果没有过什么特别的言论或行为与没有提单合约的做法不同,则不应去默示一个有合约,例如,作为收货人〔包括银行〕去向船长提货,这是有提单合约或没有提单合约做法上都一致的,因为提单持有人有物权凭证,可去提取货物。故不应以这一行为/做法去默示双方在提货与交货时另订立了一个提单合约。而收货人支付运费也不一定代表什么。例如当时的事实是:"船东/船长向收货人(银行)说:货物你可以提取,因为你退还了正本提单。但根据提单合约,这批货尚欠下运费与一些费用。那些费用我无法向你追讨,因为我们之间没有合约关系,我也不会去"无中生有",但运费我根据普通法是可以留置货物索取的,所以你想提取货物只好先付清,这与合约无关"。这一来,即使要支付运费才能提取货物,又怎可以此去默示有一个合约呢?)

看来 Brandt v. Liverpool 先例解决不了多少问题,仍须另去立法,在全面考虑后作出针对性的规定,以令绝大部分的情况都能成功去绕过"合约相互关系"(privity of contract)的羁绊,能把提单这运输合约的所有权利与责任从原订约方(发货人)转让给买方(收货人),让收货人与船东他们双方之间互有合约诉权。而争议中的索赔与抗辩(反索赔)也以提单条款为准,货损货差方面的责任与赔偿也去适用海牙/海牙·维斯比规则(只要是法律强制或/与提单合约内有像"首要条款"(paramount clause)那样的条款去明示合并该规则)。与此同时,漫无约束的侵权诉讼则可去尽量减少/收缩。

12.2.4 提单的对策之四:1855 年提单法

在 12.1 小段提及的 Thompson v. Dominy(1845)14 M & W 403;153 E. R. 532 先例后,英国马上开始研究如何经全面考虑后用立法去针对这一会严重影响外贸的难题,看怎样才能最好地去绕过或跨越这合约相互关系的障碍。之后,这带来了著名的英国提单法,它节录在本书的附录一。

这个关系,可去看 Scrutton 大法官在 Brandt v. Liverpool (1924) 1 KB 575 先例中十分清楚的说明如下:"Before the Bills of Lading Act, 1855, was passed, by the custom of merchants the indorsement of the bill of lading passed the property in the goods contained therein, but it did not assign the contract contained therein, and therefore the person who by indorsement became the owner of the goods did not by the same indorsement acquire a right to sue the shipowner upon his contract, which was evidenced in the bill of lading."

12.2.4.1　1855 年提单法的措辞/用字

这立法很短(相比今天的立法),而针对合约相互关系的更只有第一段(section 1),可以顺便节录如下:"Every consignee of goods named in a bill of lading, and every endorsee of a bill of lading to whom the property in the goods therein mentioned shall pass, upon or by reason of such consignment or endorsement,[220] shall have transferred to and vested in him all rights of suit, and be subject to the same liabilities in respect of such goods as if the contract contained in a bill of lading had been made with himself."

以上备注可多加说明。据闻当时立法者的一种忧虑是怕会影响银行,怕硬去把银行拖进来成为提单合约一方,要是有了灾难性索赔(请看本章之 11.2.1 小段),银行可就再也不敢去干这业务了,那这立法岂非弄巧成拙。确实,这也是后来的贵族院判决,很受银行欢迎:Sewell v. Burdick(1884)10 App. Cas. 74。

故此,立法局限在仅是为了转让有关货物的情形,表示受让人绝大多数只会是买方。如果提单是托运/托付或背书给卖方在卸港的代理人,以提取货物,内中不涉及买方,这并不适用 1855 年提单法,故不会转让提单合约,有争议仍只是承运人与发货人之间的合约纠纷。

将提单背书给银行或空白背书作为"质押"(pledge)之用也不适用 1855 年提单法,不会转让提单合约给银行,因为在背书时从未想过要转让有关货物给银行,这转让只在真正的货物买卖关系下才会有。因此,银行不必怕因持有这份提单,身为"承押人"(pledgee),而被船东(承运人)索赔欠下的运费、滞期费或其他损失。毕竟,提单所代表的货物可能是低价或已严重损坏而"资不抵债"。但没有运输合约关系,银行持的一套提单仍有物权凭证的功能。故此,银行可进退自如,只要小心不去订立一个默示合约(本章 12.2.3 小段)给自己带来合约责任就行。而在船东无单放货的情况下,银行一样可去控告船东"侵占"(conversion):The "Stone Gemini" (1999)2 Lloyd's Rep. 255。而且,银行也可以侵权/托管向船东索赔货损货差,双方只是没有提单合约关系罢了。

12.2.4.2　提单法转让合约不是普通法转让(assignment)或一般的变更(novation);发货人与收货人负连带责任

1855 年提单法 Section 1 最后一句是要收货人/受让人承担提单合约"所有的责任"(same liabilities),好像他/它就是原来订立提单合约的一方(这应是发货人)。

---

[220] 请注意立法是局限在提单的托运/托付或背书必须是为了去转让有关的货物给收货人/受让人,否则立法不适用,即提单合约不转让。

故此,这实在不是普通法或立法下的"转让"(assignment),因为后者只转让合约利益,不能转让合约责任。有说法是1855年提单法是一种"法定转让"(statutory assignment),这其实并不准确。

比较接近的反而是合约变更,所以也有说法称它是一种"法定变更"(statutory novation)。但仍不完全准确,因为变更是去把原来合约中断掉,由另一个与第三者的合约来替代,由第三者去把合约的履行接过来:请参阅《国际商务游戏规则——英国合约法》一书之第四章7.1小段。

但根据1855年提单法,原来合约并未中断,发货人的合约责任仍在(如违约装危险品,付运费,滞期费等)。而提单合约去转让给了买方,只是多加一个人,多一个货方的合约方。有了责任,可以说发货人与收货人对船东/承运人是负上了"连带责任"(jointly and severally liable)。只有是再去转卖/转让这份提单,即A(发货人)背书给了B(中间商),B再背书给了C(收货人),在B与C之间才会是"变更"(novation),因为可让B在合约关系中脱身。这一来,余下来对船东/承运人负上"连带责任"的就是A与C两位。去扯上发货人,不容其脱身,是怕对船东/承运人不公平。因为他/它往往是冲着发货人财雄势大、名誉好才肯订立这份运输合约。如果发货人凭一个背书即可脱身,而船东/承运人则要找不明来历的收货人去负责这样那样,那就不公平了。

这法律地位在 The "Berge Sisar"(1998)2 Lloyd's Rep. 475 先例有详论,如 Millet 大法官所说:"The section(1855年提单法的第1段)has been considered in a number of cases, most recently by the House of Lords in Effort Shipping Co Ltd v. Linden Management S. A.(1998) 1 Lloyd's Rep. 337. Lord Lloyd pointed out that Section 1 dealt with the rights and the liabilities under the contract of carriage differently[221]. Whereas the rights were transferred with the property in the goods, the liabilities were not[222]. They were vested directly in the endorsee by force of the section[223], not by assignment. The consignor remained liable[224], and the holder of the bill of lading came under the same liability as the consignor[225]. His liability was by way of addition, not substitution …[226] The liability of an endorsee was by way of addition to that of the consignor but by

---

[221] Lloyd 勋爵指出,第1段措辞中故意分开两句去将权利与责任区分来讲。
[222] 提单合约下的权利是转让了给收货人/受让人,发货人确也不能另去申张权利,如要求船东交货或赔付。
[223] 但责任只是说要收货人/受让人也承担。
[224] 发货人仍要继续负责。
[225] 提单持有人加入后就有了同样的责任。
[226] 这是去加入责任方而不是去替代原来的责任方。

way of substitution for that of a previous endorsee[227]."

12.2.4.3　1855年提单法问题之一:只针对装船提单

1855年提单法立法当时,国际外贸的付运单证也只有装船提单:请参阅第二章之3.1小段。因而该立法只针对装船提单也就理所当然了,这在该立法的 Section 3 有说明是"装上船舶的货物":

但近年随着付运单证的多元化,光去针对装船提单已是追不上时代。在今天的国际买卖,付运单证经常会是"船东交货单"(ship's delivery order):见本书第二章之1.5.6与3.6小段;或"海运单"(sea waybill):见本书第二章之3.5小段;或"多式联运单证"(multimodal transport document):见本书第二章之3.7小段。它们也一样会面对"合约相互关系"(privity of contract)的困扰。特别是若也想去鼓励像海运单等的使用,法律更应去配套。

目前商业人士解决的办法是在海运单上硬加上发货人代表收货人去同时作为"货方",这使得收货人将来可自己以合约方的身份去直接向船东/承运人起诉(或被诉)。例如在"General Council of British Shipping non-negotiable sea waybill"的标准格式说:"The shipper accepts the said Standard Conditions on his own behalf and on behalf of the Consignee and the owner of the goods and warrants that he has authority to do so[228]. The Consignee by presenting this Waybill and/or requesting delivery of the goods further undertakes all liabilities of the Shipper hereunder, such undertaking being additional and without prejudice to the Shippers own liability[229]. The benefits of the contract, evidenced by this Waybill shall thereby be transferred to the Consignee or other persons presenting this Waybill[230]."

另举一例是 CMI(Comite Maritime Internationale)拟定的"1990 Uniform Rules for Sea Waybills",其中的 Article 3 说:"The shipper enters into the contract of carriage not only on his own behalf but also as agent for and on behalf of the consignee(and warrants to the carrier that he has authority to do so)."

多式联运单证也是采纳相同的技巧,举例是 P&O 船公司的提单,其中对"商人"(Merchant)的定义说:"…holder, Consignee, Receiver of the Goods, and Person owning or entitling to the possession of the goods or of this Bill of Lading, any Person having a present or future interest in the goods and anyone acting on behalf of such person."

---

[227]　只有纯是中间商的背书人,他/它的责任才会被收货人(买方)所替代。
[228]　说明发货人有授权代表收货人去加入作为合约方。
[229]　这说法与上一小段(12.2.4.2小段)讲法一样,即收货人去加入作为海运单的责任方,但发货人仍不能脱身。
[230]　这海运单的权利转让给了收货人。

许多其他的标准格式均可见有类似措辞,如 BIMCO 拟定的"COMBICONBILL"(第 2 条款)或"COMBIDOC"(1995 年改为"MULTIDOC"),等等。

但这能否顺利跨越合约相互关系的大原则仍难以估计,这就好像"喜马拉雅条款"(Himalaya Clause)被 Reid 勋爵在 Midland Silicones v. Scruttons(1961)2 Lloyd's Rep. 365 加上 4 个先决条件一样,不一定每次都能符合。

例如,卖方/发货人是否真有收货人授权? 虽然,海运单因为"不可流通/转让"(non-negotiable),确定收货人是谁以及事先安排授权应不困难。加上,订约时没有授权仍可事后去"追认"(ratification)。但总是多一层手续/麻烦。

也可能会追究收货人如果真是合约方,它/他们与承运人之间有否约因/对价。

所以总的说来,最好仍是去立法,把这些付运单证在类似提单法下的装船提单之外都增加进来。当然,这立法也不能再称为提单法了,因为针对对象不止是装船提单一项。

12.2.4.4　1855 年提单法问题之二:与为了转让有关货物的目的挂钩

为何有此挂钩的估计原因在本章 12.2.4.1 小段业已略述。立法的措辞/文字本身也带来一定的疑点。如严格去解释,立法可以是要求作背书这一行动就转让有关的货物,两者必须同步,但这在现实中问题可就大了。读者或许会觉得这说法难以理解,不是在本书第二章之 3.1.5.1 小段说过背书提单就显示了转让这货物的意图吗? 问题是,意图归意图,但这不是结论性的证据,证明这票货物以此行动转让。例如,买卖双方在买卖合约已另同意货物主权在背书提单前的较早时间,如货物装上船舶时,即已转让给买方。也会是,双方同意卖方保留货权(retention of title),好像著名的"The "Aliakmon"(1986)2 Lloyd's Rep. 1(此先例的案情请看本章之 8.2.3 小段的节录部分)。

或是,意图归意图,卖方实际无法以背书提单去转让货物给买方,例如有以下情况:

(i)背书当时货物装在船舶上仍分不开,这是一船货(如 2 万吨糖)卖给多位不同买方时常见的情况。在 1995 年前的英国法律,1979 年的货物销售法 Section 16 说明尚未分开的货物不能转让货权("The title to goods which form part of a larger bulk cannot pass until those goods are ascertained")。

这课题在《国际货物买卖》一书之第五章§4 段有详谈,不去重复。

通常,能去分得开一船货给多位的买方,要等待至卸港卸货,这表示航次途中背书提单实在是无法以此去转让货物。

(ii)货物早已卸下,之后才背书提单(例如结汇),像 The "Future Express"(1993)1 Lloyd's Rep. 542 先例是卸货与背书相隔一年以上,这一来,就有了这"过时提单"(stale bill)作为物权凭证是否已失效之争。如果已失效,显然不可能再以背书转移货物主权。这方面问题在本书第二章之3.1.5.4小段有详论。以上所谈的困境,部分是新问题(如stale bill与短航次导致货物一早卸下已是近年愈来愈多的情况),也有不少应是一直存在。或许有人会问,这疑点与困难为何到20世纪80年代才大量冒出来,1855年提单法不是已上百年,一直执行没有问题吗?答案会是:人心不古,一旦有承运人/船东能第一次成功找出这个法律空子,则今后每位被告都会去钻这空子。每当船东/承运人被诉,他就会通过文件披露去寻找有否可能在背书提单时,事实上无法,不能或无意去转让货物主权。如果是,即表示1855年提单法不适用,合约相互关系的大原则没有跨越,提单合约的诉权只在卖方,不在买方/收货人,后者根本没有"诉权"(title to sue),与船东/承运人也没有合约关系。

估计20世纪80年代前,人心没有这样"无情",会承保船东这方面责任的国际互保协会即使想到可能有此法律漏洞也不会去钻营。如果对货损货差有责任(以海牙规则为准),船东应该赔则互保协会也就赔了。

总之,20世纪80年代有不少这种案例,也有不少是船东/承运人成功以"title to sue"抗辩成功的例子,即使是责任明确得不能再明确,例如是不适航(The "Kapetan Markos NL"),或是错签发提单(The Aliakmon"),或是无单放货(The "Future Express")。

比方是: The "San Nicholas" (1976) 1 Lloyd's Rep. 8; The "Albazero" (1976) 2 Lloyd's Rep. 467; The "Elafi" (1981) 2 Lloyd's Rep. 679; The "Sevonia Team" (1983) 2 Lloyd's Rep. 640; The "Elli 2" (1985) 1 Lloyd's Rep. 107; The "Kelo" (1985) 2 Lloyd's Rep. 85; The "Kapetan Markos" (1987) 2 Lloyd's Rep. 321; The "Aliakmon" (1986) 2 Lloyd's Rep. 1; The "Aramis" (1989) 1 Lloyd's Rep. 213; The "Delfini" (1990) 1 Lloyd's Rep. 252; The "Filiatra Legacy" (1991) 2 Lloyd's Rep. 337; The "Future Express" (1992) 2 Lloyd's Rep. 79 等。

这对原告的收货人非常不公平,他/它明明有一个"很站得住脚的索赔"(cast-iron claim),怎知道原来在同一船舱另混有其他买方的货物,所以货权无法转让?倒不如根本没有1855年提单法,明知有合约相互关系的障碍,买方可一早去:

(A)在买卖合约迫卖方转让诉权,订下条款说:"should the buyer so request, seller hereby agrees to irrevocably and unconditionally assign all rights of suit against third parties causing loss or damage to goods onboard..."

(B)以卖方/发货人名义起诉,反正可代收货人取回全部损失;请参阅本章之12.2.1小段谈到的 Dunlop v. Lambert (1839) 6 Cl & F 600。

当然,如果提单转让/转售多次,以上安排也不易。但至少收货人一早明知有合约相互关系的障碍,也就不会乱花律师费去起诉船东/承运人了。

即使不去严格解释1855年提单法对转让货物与背书的挂钩,像Mustill大法官在 The"Delfini"的中间说法,以上困难仍在所难免。唯一的办法是去把货物转让的局限与挂钩完全去掉,不再与提单背书同步,甚至不再是重要因素。Mustill 大法官在 The"Delfini"的讲话是:"Section 1 (of the Bills of lading Act, 1855) presents two alternative situations in which the contract is transferred to the endorsee. The first is where the property passes "upon" the endorsement (and delivery of the document). This means that the passing of property is simultaneous with the endorsement and that the endorsement is the act which brings it about… The second is where the property passes 'by reason of' the endorsement. This must signify something different since the expression is 'upon or by reason of' not 'upon and by reason of'. In my judgment it means that although the endorsement of the bill is not the immediate occasion of the passing of the property nevertheless it plays an essential causal part in it."

读者对以上所讲的也不必去细究了,因为英国的 1992 年海上运输法(后详)已替代了 1855 年提单法,前者正是将提单合约的转让完全与货物主权的转让脱了钩。像在香港,立法也已追随英国作了更改:见 1996 年的"提单及相类似装运单据条例"。但据知悉仍有像加拿大的提单法(参照英国 1855 年提单法)尚未更改,目前仍在考虑。这一来,以上所讲的困难(如 The "Aliakmon")仍会影响加拿大等国家的有关案件。

12.2.5　提单的对策之五:1992 年海上运输法

有关这新的"提单法",较早(如在第二章)已有多处略为谈及。可以说,它已全面地针对了 1855 年提单法的漏洞或不足。而且,它带来了一套新做法、新概念。

12.2.5.1　1992 年立法扩大了对海上运输单证的适用:Section 1

立法已扩大适用在其他海上运输单证,如海运单(请参阅第二章 3.5.4 小段),等等。难怪,1992 年立法不再称为"提单法",虽然它是为了替代 1855 年提单法。Section 1 说:

"1(1)This Act applies to the following documents, that is to say-(a) any bill of lading[231]; (b) any sea waybill[232]; and

(c) any ship's delivery order[233]. (2) References in this Act to a bill of lading—

(a) do not include references to a document which is incapable of transfer either by in-

---

[231]　请注意立法再也不讲是"装船提单",它只是"提单"二字。
[232]　刚已提到,海运单已是包括在内。美国法律的 straight bill of lading,实际也是英国法律的海运单。
[233]　这种海运付运证请参阅第二章之 1.5.6 与 3.6 小段。

dorsement, or, as a bearer bill, by delivery without indorsement[234] but; (b) subject to that, do include references to a received for shipment bill of lading[235]."

12.2.5.2　1992 年立法针对的运输合约权利可转让与的多种人士/对象：Section 2

立法接下去在 Section 2 以十分细致的文字与简单的英语说明可以把提单合约下的权利(包括诉权)转让给收货人/买方。要注意的是立法的措辞再也不将运输合约转让与转让货物挂钩。虽然 1992 年立法已在本书之附录二，但为了方便阅读，在此仍去节录 Section 2(1) 如下：

2 (1) Subject to the following provisions of this section, a person who becomes—

(a) the lawful holder of a bill of lading[236];

(b) the person who (without being an original party to the contract of carriage)[237] is the person to whom delivery of the goods to which a sea waybill relates is to be made by the carrier in accordance with that contract[238]; or

(c) the person to whom delivery of the goods to which a ship's delivery order relates

---

[234] 不包括一些不能以背书或/与交出来转让货权的"提单"，即不是物权凭证的"提单"。本来能称之为"提单"的，它应有能去"流通或转让"(negotiable)的功能，正如立法专员 Diana Faber 女士在 Lloyd's Maritime and Commercial Law Quarterly, Part4, 1996 之第 512 页所说：

"The characteristics of a bill of lading suggested in the above cases are as follows: it must be signed and negotiable; it may have to evidence acceptable by the carrier of legal responsibility for the entire transportation; it certainly has to evidence the terms of the contract of carriage and it may be that these should include terms relevant to maritime transport and the name of the intended vessel."

但现实中常有乱套的情况，例如 straight bill of lading 或 non-negotiable/non order bill of lading 的叫法。

故此，在这小段说明它们都不属提单：虽然它们仍会是本立法包括的单证，如实属海运单。

[235] 立法也包括"收货提单"这种付运单证：请参阅第二章之 3.4.6 小段。立法没有讲明包括"多式联运单证/提单"(multimodal transport document/combined transport bill)，但估计也应包括在内，这一点也在第二章之 3.7 小段略有谈及。

[236] 可获转让提单合约的一种人首先是提单的"合法持有人"(lawful holder)。1992 年立法没有说明什么才是"合法持有人"，只在 Section 5(2) 要求是"善意"(good faith)的。估计除了是非法持有(例如骗来，偷来一份提单)，都应包括。收货人/买方固然包括，另外也应包括中间商(曾一度合法持有提单)，承押人(银行)等。

[237] 海运单中原来与船东/承运人订约的一方立法并不包括，因他/它们一直有运输合约关系，何必再立法转让？海运单不像提单，海牙规则并不适用，所以原订约方不一定是发货人。

[238] 海运单下被转让这运输合约权利的人士是单证内的收货人。故此，以 CIF/CFR 买卖为例，今天买方可以不再采用装船提单而转用海运单，因为就独立自主的诉权而言(有了货损货差直接向船东/承运人索赔)，已因有了这立法而有了保障。

is to be made in accordance with the undertaking contained in the order[239],

shall (by virtue of becoming the holder of the bill or, as the case may be, the person to whom delivery is to be made)[240] have transferred to and vested in him all rights of suit under the contract of carriage[241] as if he had been a party to that contract[242]."

Section 2 接下去的各小段(由(2)至(5))是针对其他各种情况,可简介如下:

—Section 2(2)[243]之(a)段针对并讲明包括了"过时提单"(stale bill)(这方面在本章之12.2.4.4小段的(ii)有略述)。只要是有买卖合约或质押安排在交出货物前业已存在。有这项要求是因为立法不想鼓励的一种情况是货物占有权早已不存在(货物已交出),但仍去把提单事后协议转手/转卖,纯是去转卖诉权。这虽可让买的人成为提单合法持有人,但他买的光是诉权,而不是早已不存在的货物。

—Section 2(2)(b)段针对的是买方拒绝货物,导致他/它的卖方(多次转售下他/它不一定是发货人)变得最终拥有货物,则这卖方也变了有该运输合约的权利(包括诉权)。例如,发觉有货损货差,船东有责任。要知道,拒货会发生在买方从船舶收货后的岸上。至于因"货不对板"而导致买方(收货人)拒货的课题,请参阅《国际货物买卖》一书之第四章。有关这一小段,可转而节录本立法的Section 5(4)说明同样的立场/地位:

"Without prejudice to sections 2(2)... above, nothing in this Act shall preclude its operation in relation to a case where the goods to which a document relates—

(a) cease to exist after the issue of the document[244]; or

(b) cannot be identified (whether because they are mixed with other goods or for any other reason)[245]..."

—Section 2(3)针对船东交货单,应不必多解说,措辞/文字十分明了。

—Section 2(4)是针对万一真正损失的人(遭受货损货差)不是有权索赔的人,则船东/承运人不准以代为索赔的人士只有名义上损失,没有真正损失为抗辩。换言之,本章12.2.1小段提到的 Dunlop v. Lambert(1839) 6 Cl & F 600 先例所持的立场仍是保留不变。可举一个会发生这种情况的例子:在一个"CIF out-turn"(同样情

---

[239] 船东交货单的收货人:这种付运单证请参阅第二章之1.5.6与3.6小段。
[240] 以上各种人士会因他/它们持有提单或是被指定为收货人,而……
[241] 可获转让与给予所有的运输合约权利(包括诉权)。
[242] 好像他/它们就是原订约方一样(提单就会是发货人了)。这一来,他/它们也要去承担合约责任了,而不光是享有权利。而责任方面在立法的 section 3 有分别针对,后详。
[243] 不再节录立法的有关段节,请读者看附录二。
[244] 货物已不存在不受影响(只要是有关买卖合约事前已订明)。
[245] 货物与其他货物混合分不开的情况也不受影响。这请参阅本章之12.2.4.4小段中的)(i)。

况会发生在"ex-ship")买卖,会是海上运输风险在卖方头上。虽然风险在卖方,但提单合法持有人的买方(没有风险)才是 1992 年立法下拥有合约诉权的人士。那么情况会是,如有货损货差,买卖双方结算是要卖方去承受这货损货差的损失,但他/它却无法去以提单合约起诉船东/承运人索赔,因为合约已转让给买方(这在 Section 2(5)有讲明)。除非卖方与船东/承运人另有租约关系,因为 1992 年立法对运输合约的定义[在 Section 5(1)]并不包括租约,则卖方才可根据租约内容索赔。但双方不一定有租约,这一来,卖方只好请买方借出名义去起诉船东/承运人了。但买方会面对他/它没有实质损失的抗辩,所以要加上这 Section 2(4)的规定不让船东/承运人去取巧。

—Section 2(5)刚才已提到,是去消灭运输合约原订约方的权利(包括诉权)。这可避免船东/承运人会面对合约上的"双重责任"(double liability),如被提单合法持有人(买方)刚索赔成功,提单发货人(卖方)又为同一事故起诉。

12.2.5.3　1992 年立法针对运输合约责任的转让:Section 3

立法在运输合约的权利方面是扩大了转让的对象/人士,因为不再与货物转让挂钩,而且包括了多种付运单证。但合约的责任是否同时转让呢?对一般的收货人/买方而言,看来既有权利,也有责任应是理所当然。如果收货人向船东索赔货损,船东也可以在同一诉讼中反索赔运费,滞期费或货物对船舶造成的损失。这一点已在本章 12.2.4.1 与 12.2.4.2 小段详论。而在 1992 立法,亦是有同样想法。这清楚反映在该立法出台前的报告(report by Law Commissions):

"We see, in general no unfairness in making the person who either claims delivery or who takes delivery of the goods, from being subject to the terms of the contract of carriage, since in both cases the person is enforcing or at least attempting to enforce rights under the contract of carriage (3.18 段).

Furthermore, it is unfair that the carrier should be denied redress against the indorsee of the bill of lading who seeks to take the benefit of the contract of carriage without the corresponding burdens(3.22 段)."

但立法有一重大政策考虑,就是在目前的措辞/文字下,银行、承押人、中间商等都会变为提单合法持有人或被指定为收货人。如果因为这样就要他/它们去承担来自船东可能是天文数字的合约责任索赔(这方面仍有不明朗之处,请参阅第六章之 2.2 小段的详论),显然会严重打击银行意欲资助国际外贸或贸易商参与国际买卖的兴趣。例如,船上一票石油产品会以提单转卖多次(据知在一个航次内会有上百次的买卖),岂非出了大事每一个中间商(曾一度短暂的合法持有提单),都会人人自危?这方面也在本章 12.2.4.1 小段有略述。而要中间商负责也不是英国法律过往的立场:Smurthwaite v. Wilkins (1862) 11 C. B. (N. S.) 842;The "Giannis NK"

(1998)1 Lloyd's Rep. 337 之 344 页。

1992 年立法所想出来的对策是去把合约权利放在 Section2,而合约责任另分开放在 Section 3。而且,Section 3 尽量收缩了要负责的对象/人士。这 Section 3 较短,为了方便阅读,不妨节录如下:

"3(1) Where subsection (1) of section 2 of this Act operates in relation to any document to which this Act applies and the person in whom rights are vested by virtue of that subsection – (a) takes or demands delivery from the carrier of any of the goods to which the document relates[246];

(b) makes a claim under the contract of carriage against the carrier in respect of any of those goods[247]; or

(c) is a person who, at a time before those rights were vested in him, took or demanded delivery from the carrier of any of those goods[248],

that person shall (by virtue of taking or demanding delivery or making the claim, or in a case falling within paragraph (c) above, of having the rights vested in him) become subject to the same liabilities under that contract as if he had been a party to that contract.

(2) Where the goods to which a ship's delivery order relates form a part only of the goods to which the contract of carriage relates, the liabilities to which any person is subject by virtue of the operation of this section in relation to that order shall exclude liabilities in respect of any goods to which the order does not relate[249].

(3) This section, so far as it imposes liabilities under any contract on any person, shall be without prejudice to the liabilities under the contract of any person as an original

---

[246] 1992 年立法收缩责任对象的做法是去列举三行动,而 Section 2 下有运输合约权利人士,只有做了这三项行动的其中一项,才会负上运输合约责任。而这(a)段就是第 1 项行动:去向船东/承运人要求交货或去提取货物。故此,如果银行是提单合法持有人,它可享有立法 Section 2 的权利,加上提单本是物权凭证(这一特点与 1992 年立法无关),银行可安心以提单为质押。而银行一天不真正去提取货物,也就不必怕运输合约的责任会是"祸从天降"。真要去提货,银行大可先去衡量得失,看清楚有何权利与责任后才行动。

[247] 三项行动中的第二项是向船东/承运人提出运输合约(不是侵权)下的索赔。例如,船舶沉没,不再存在交货,提单持有人或海运单收货人指船舶不适航导致船货全损,要求赔偿。这一来,原告也负上了责任,船东可抗辩外还可去反索赔。

[248] 三项行动之三(最后一项行动)是针对诸如收货人较早时已凭保函提货(无单放货),后来才去持有提单等的情况。

[249] 针对船东交货单,收货人只对他那部分的货物负责。这是因为船东交货单会写上船上所有货量。

party to the contract[250]."

12.2.5.4　1992年立法带来的新问题

社会科学总不会是百分之百地完善。一个草拟得十分好的立法或合约,也难免有想不到或欠周详考虑之处。只要这漏洞/空子是同级世界一流高手/专才也无法预见,草拟时挑不出来的,那就是了不起了。事后诸葛亮般的批评毕竟谁也会讲。

以下去介绍2个有关1992年立法的重大案例。

12.2.5.4.1　错误背书下的"lawful holder"

案例一:The "Aegean Sea"(1998)2 Lloyd's Rep. 39

该案例涉及"Aegean Sea"轮在La Coruna搁浅后,造成重大损失(船舶断开)以及油污等,是当时著名的海难事件。当时船舶是出租给ROIL.,该公司的母公司是西班牙国家石油公司的Repsol。显然,Repsol才会有资产,ROIL只是皮包公司,任何人想索赔,且金额也大的话,自然想拖Repsol下水,这正是船东的意图。

能去拖Repsol下水是因为船上为整船原油开出了两套提单,而其中的一套本是背书给ROIL的,但在文书上搞错了,结果背书给了Repsol。这错误事后也被发觉因而在该背书上加印了一个"无效"(void)的章,另去更正为背书给ROIL。

这里不妨再详细介绍一下,该套提单所代表的其中一票原油的原卖方/发货人是Sun Oil,Sun Oil的FOB买卖合约是与Louis Dreyfus订的。而Louis Dreyfus再以FOB转售给ROIL。ROIL长期以来出面为Repsol去进口原油供应给各炼油厂使用,从中赚取15%~20%的利润。该票原油也不例外,以ex-ship La Coruna的条件转售给了Repsol。在这安排下,显然应是ROIL去租船,因为向Louis Dreyfus买入是FOB,向Repsol卖出是ex-ship La Coruna。ROIL也确实这样做了,以程租(ASTANKVOY标准格式)向"Aegean Sea"船东租入该油轮。程租合约中免不了有一条条款要求无单放货:"13. Should Bills of Lading not arrive at discharge port in time then Owners to release the entire cargo without representation of the original Bills of Lading. Charterers hereby indemnify Owners against all consequences of discharging cargo without presentation of original Bills of lading. Wording of Letter of Indemnity to be in accordance with Owners P & I Club, excluding Bank Guarantee."

而装船提单签发后,首先是Sun Oil将提单背书给了Louis Dreyfus(to,or to order of,Louis Dreyfus),并在纽约把这一套正本提单"转交"(deliver)。根据Louis Dreyfus与ROIL的买卖合约条款规定,应把所有单证/文件送去ROIL的Liechtenstein地址结算,并把一份不可转让的提单付本寄给Repsol,可让Repsol知道情况。

---

[250]　这方面已在本章之12.2.4.2小段详述,即原订约方(如提单的发货人)与提单合法持有人或收货人负有"连带责任"(jointly and severally liable),法律地位一样,只在1992年立法表明得更清楚。

第三章　提单作用之二：运输合约・谁是其中的合约方

因为"Aegean Sea"出了大事，ROIL 就请 Louis Dreyfus 尽快把单证/文件送给它，以便向保险公司索赔。结果匆忙中，Louis Dreyfus 将提单不是背书给了买方的 ROIL，而是背书给 Repsol。之后 ROIL 便把这套提单转给了 Repsol 处理，再过了两个星期（因为圣诞节），这错误背书才被 Repsol 一位负责人看到。于是他电告 Louis Dreyfus，后者也承认背书有错误，不符合买卖合约，并要求退回以便更改。之后，Louis Dreyfus 去加印了一个"无效"（void）的章在给 Repsol 的背书上，而另再去将提单背书给 ROIL。不像电子提单，这改动是明显可见在这份传统纸张的提单上的。

但这却给了"Aegean Sea"船东一个借口去把 Repsol 拖下水，指 Repsol 是提单的"合法持有人"（lawful holder），并曾要求提取货物，所以要在提单上负全责。而提单上卸港是写作"西班牙港口"，船东指货方在提单下指定 La Coruna 这个不安全港口是违反了默示责任。看来，这有点像"列名港口"或"不列名港口"是否安全的责任应由谁负的争议，对此请看笔者的《程租合约》一书第 187 页至第 192 页。

船东根据提单合约，以 Repsol 在 1992 年新提单法下是"lawful holder"（提单合法持有人），向 Repsol 索赔数以千万美元计的损失（光是船价已是 1200 万美元，还有其他许多项目诸如庞大的油污责任、救助、燃油运费，等等）。

这显然是新问题，在 1855 年提单法下不会出现，因为 Louis Dreyfus 背书提单给 Repsol，不论是否错误，总之当时不是为去转让货物（肯定不是，因买卖合约是与 ROIL 订立的），凭这背书并不能同时转让提单合约给 Repsol，也就是这背书不包括在 1855 年立法所定的转让提单合约的情形内。但 1992 年新提单法并不再理会是否有意图转让货物，而是扩大了提单合约的转让范围，这反而带来了这新问题，等于是强加了合约的责任到第三者（Repsol）身上。

所幸的是依该案例的事实经过，Thomas 大法官判是 Repsol 从来未拥有提单，也不需要这套提单，判词说："Moreover the bill of lading was never delivered to Repsol by Louis Dreyfus: Louis Dreyfus sent the bill to ROIL, under cover of a letter addressed to ROIL, It was sent to ROIL, as principals; it was not delivered by Louis Dreyfus to ROIL, to receive as Repsol's agents as it was intended for ROIL, and the covering letter was addressed to them. There was therefore no delivery by Louis Dreyfus to Repsol, only a delivery to ROIL… In my view Repsol therefore never obtained possession of the bill of lading as the result of completion by delivery of the bill by endorsement… Even if Repsol had obtained possession of the bill of lading from Louis Dreyfus, they never accepted delivery of it as the endorsee or transferee. As soon as they saw the endorsement to them, they sent it back to be endorsed to the rightful endorsee and transferee."

针对 Louis Drefus 事后把错误背书加上印章说"无效"，而不是由 Repsol 再回头背书将提单转回给 Louis Dreyfus 的事实，Thomas 大法官认为这加强了他的看法，即

Repsol 从未拥有提单,所以不存在要插手进去背书提单。判词在这一点上说:"The owners(船东)contended that if Repsol had become the lawful holders, then as there was no endorsement back to Louis Dreyfus, Louis Dreyfus could not re-indorse the bill of lading to ROIL[251], It is clear that there was no endorsement back by Repsol to Louis Dreyfus, but that was no doubt because Repsol never regarded themselves as entitled to endorse the bill as it had been endorsed to them in error[252]. In my view, this submission made by owners reinforces the conclusion that Repsol never became the lawful holders[253]. It cannot have been intended by the draftsman of the Act that a person to whom a bill of lading is endorsed and sent in error has then to act as if he was a person entitled to endorse the bill of lading[254] as a precondition[255] of the person who made the mistake being enabled to rectify his error by re-indorsing and delivering it to the correct party[256]; the person to whom it was sent was not the lawful holder and not therefore entitled to endorse it."

12.2.5.4.2 曾经一度的提单持有人在 1992 年立法下要否负提单责任之争

案例二:The "Berge Sisar"(1998)2 Lloyd's Rep. 475

该案例涉及的问题与"案例一"有关联,也是船东出了事后(指"丙烷"(propane)的货物腐蚀弄坏船舶,这种问题看来常有发生,如 Navigas v. Enron(1997) 2 Lloyd's Rep. 759)想拖第三者下水,指它在 1992 年新提单法之下属"合法持有人" (lawful holder),有权利也有提单合约的责任。

当然,这也并非是新概念,1855 年的提单法已是如此。在本章 12.2.4.1 小段节录的 Section 1 讲明转让的不光是权利(have transferred to and vested in him all rights of suit),同时也有提单的责任(subject to the same liabilities…)。但 1992 年新提单法的危险是它扩大了提单合约可以转让给的"人士的类别"(class of people),并不计较背书当时是否是为了转让货权,只要是提单背书受让人,都可变为"lawful holder"(提单合法持有人),在提单下既有权利,也有责任。

---

[251] 船东争辩说 Repsol 不去将提单回头背书给 Louis Dreyfus,因而后者根本无从去再背书给 ROIL。
[252] 事实确实如此,但因提单是错误背书给 Repsol 的,所以 Repsol 从未认为自己有权在该份提单作出任何背书。
[253] 船东的争辩反而加强了 Repsol 从来不是提单合法持有人的看法。
[254] 1992 年新提单法的立法者不可能有意图凭错误背书的提单,要求可能是无端卷入的"受让人"去假扮作有货权而去将提单回头背书。
[255] 以此作为一个先决条件。
[256] 去让弄错的原背书人有机会去改正,重新背书给正确的受让人。要真是如此去要求,试想想,如果被错误背书的受让人不肯合作去回头背书怎样办? 或是,要敲一笔钱才协助又如何?

The "Berge Sisar"案也涉及在一连串的背书过程中,有一中间商曾短时间作为"lawful holder"。但很快地,船舶仍在航程中,提单再被背书转让给了其他买方。这曾经一度是提单合法持有人的中间商,会否有提单责任,例如船东向收货人、承租人等索赔都碰壁,最后可找到他头上呢?

在 1992 年新提单法以前,已有过这种案例。在 Smurthwaite v. Wilkins(1862) 11 C. B. (N. S.)842,法院不接受"一度的提单持有人"(an intermediate holder of a bill),在早已将提单背书给了其他人(买方)而与货物无关后,仍要对欠下运费负责。在这方面还可以参阅 Lloyd 勋爵在 The "Giannis NK"(1998) 1 Lloyd's Rep. 337 和 344 页的讲话。这也很对,否则海上转卖频繁的货物好像石油产品,转让会多至上百次,一出事岂非船东就可去控告全世界的石油公司。

但这"一度的提单持有人"不是指发货人,只是指中间商。对原订约方的发货人英国法律一直是不让他脱身的,不论提单背书了多少次,提单货物转让了多少次。在 Fox v. Nott(1861) 6 Hurl & Nov. 630,Pollock 大法官说:"The statute creates a new liability, but it does not exonerate the person(i. e. the original shipper) who has entered into all express contract."

1992 年新提单法(海上运输法)也是同一原则,Section 3(3)讲明:"This section, so far as it imposes liabilities under any contract on any person, shall be without prejudice to the liabilities under the contract of any person as an original party to the contract."

这一切已在本章之 12. 2. 4. 2 与 12. 2. 5. 3 小段有详论。

回头去介绍"Berge Sisar"先例的事实/案情。Borealis 是瑞典买方,以 CFR 条件向 Jersey 的一家名为 Stargas 的公司买入 4 万多吨的丙烷。Stargas 则是向 Saudi Arabian Oil Co. (简称 SA)以 FOB 买入这批货物(直接或间接,即可能另有中间商,因该批 4 万多吨的丙烷共签发了 5 套提单)。而 Stargas 因负责航运也是以程租向船东 (Bergesen)租入"Berge Sisar"轮。

在丙烷运抵瑞典的 Stenungsund 后,Borealis 去船上取了样本后发觉货物不合规格,腐蚀度太高。几天后,Borealis 把这批货物以"CIF Terneuzen"转卖给了 Dow Europe。"Berge Stsar"最后是把船上的丙烷卸下在 Ostend 的 Dow 私人码头。之后,为了有关损失,各方摆下战线/战阵如下:

(a) Borealis 在英国法院出告票向 Stargas 起诉,指货物不符合买卖合约的规定与要求。在 Stargas 作出抗辩请求后(估计是把责任推到船东身上,而货物运输的风险不是由卖方承担),Borealis 把船东 Bergesen 也追加为第二被告,指控它违反租约的一些条款,如 1936 年美国海上运输法(海牙规则)。这正是笔者的《国际货物买卖》一书第六章 6.3 小段之"买方面对货损货差应去向谁索赔"命题所详述的困境,不去重复。

(b)被告的船东 Bergesen 作出抗辩(应是去否认船舶不适航,有疏忽或不妥善照顾货物等的指控),并提出船舶受货物腐蚀的反索赔。

(c)Bergesen 也去把发货人的 SA 拖了进来,令这反索赔针对 Stargas 是依据租约,而同样的反索赔针对 Borealis 是因为它是提单的"合法持有人"(lawful holder),而最后针对的 SA 是因为它是提单的发货人:1992 年提单法之 Section 3(3)。

(d)SA 与 Bergesen 之间的争议,因为提单有仲裁条款,SA 不肯放弃,所以在 1958 年的纽约公约下英国法院非要去承认仲裁并且中止在英国的诉讼不可。但 Borealis 则放弃了仲裁,变得它与 Bergesen 的争议是由英国法院管辖。

(e)Borealis 之后再出一招,向英国法院申请去追加 SA,并列为原告或被告。理由是如果这丙烷的货物真是不妥,腐蚀性太高,会对 Bergesen 承担的赔偿责任就可以以同一诉讼在 Borealis 与 SA 之间分摊清楚。策略上,把 SA 拖进来可以取得证据,因为这票丙烷是妥还是不妥的资料 SA 才会有,Borealis 不会有。

(f)SA 拒绝被卷进英国的诉讼,申请英国法院自己去中止诉讼。这种做法在笔者的《禁令》一书的第七章有详论,不去重复。

不在这些各方的战略/战术上多谈,以免离题太远,只说说这些争辩涉及的其中一点,即 Borealis 会否是 1992 年新提单法下的一位"lawful holder",导致它既有权利(可提取货物或在提单下拥有诉权),但也有责任(货物对"Berge Sisar"造成腐蚀的责任)。

这案例有它特殊的事实,就是较早提到的"Berge Sisar"先抵达的卸港是瑞典的 Stenungsund,而且 Borealis 也曾向船长/船东要求提取货物(丙烷)。这一来 Borealis 看来已是符合了 1992 年新提单法的 Section 3(1)(a),变得既有提单合约的权利,也负有提单责任。

但其中的变化是,Borealis 在取了丙烷样本发觉不合规格后,无法自用,于是拒绝卸货。之后又将货物转售给了 Dow Europe,而船上货物(丙烷)最后也是卸给了 Dow Europe。提单后来到了 Borealis 手中,不到 24 小时就背书转交给了 Dow Europe。

问题是:Borealis 是否有提单责任,在 1992 年立法下是否是"lawful holder"呢?或者,它只是"一度的提单持有人"(an intermediate holder of a bill),在 Smurthwaite v. Wilkins 的先例或是 1992 年新提单法都没有强加提单责任到它头上?

在上诉庭,占少数的 Neill 大法官认为 Borealis 既然在 1992 年新提单法下有了提单责任,就看不出它有什么理由可去转让掉或消灭掉,他说:"But, though Borealis was the holder of the bills for only a short period, I do not see any escape from the conclusion that by seeking to enforce prospective rights under the bills and then becoming the holder of them it became subject to their liabilities. Once these liabilities attached, as it is conceded they did, it seems to me that it would require clear words in the statute to effect a transfer or extinction of them."

Neill 大法官继续说 1992 年新提单法的 Section 3(3) 不准原订约方的发货人脱身免责,既然这样去对发货人明确规定,但又不提"一度是提单持有人"而且曾要求过提取货物的人士的地位如何,会是立法者没曾想到有本案例的特别情况。但总之,这并不足以说明 1992 年立法下可转让掉或消灭掉 Borealis 责任。Neill 大法官的话是:"The facts of the present case are unusual and it does not seem that they were within the contemplation of those who drafted COGSA, 1992… It may be said that the special provision in s. 3(3) relating to the original shipper indicates sub silentio that an intermediate holder is no longer liable after indorsement of the bill, but I do not find this argument a sufficient ground for construing s. 3(1) so as to bring about a statutory transfer or extinction of accrued liabilities."

Neill 大法官的总结认为若"纯"是一位"一度的提单持有人"的确没有提单合约的责任,但它/他一去行使提单合约权利,陷入 1992 年新提单法的 Section 3(1),就再无法脱身,即使再把提单与货物转让/转售也改变不了。他说:"In my judgment the decision in Smurthwaite v. Wilkins is not affected by s. 3(1). The intermediate holder who does not seek to enforce the contract of carriage does not come within any of the paragraphs in s. 3(1) which act as triggers for the attachment of liability. The report[257] makes it clear that only a restricted class of holders will be 'subjected to the same liabilities under (the contract of carriage) as if he had been a party to that contract.'"

"But that class includes those who seek to enforce the contract."

上诉庭持相反意见的(占多数)有 Schiemann 与 Millett 大法官。他们认为 Borealis 没有提单责任。而 1992 年新提单法所针对的"一度的提单持有人"(只要不是发货人)与 1855 年提单法并没有任何不同之处。即使是该"一度的提单持有人"曾做过 Section 3(1) 所讲的一些行动如"要求交货"(demands delivery),只要它不是最后真正去提取货物的人,这情况并非不可逆转。它仍可去背书转让提单给第三者/新买方(本案例是 Dow Europe),而自己(Borealis)的提单责任则告中断/消灭。Millett 大法官说:"a lawful holder of a bill of lading who had taken one of the steps specified in s. 3(1) in relation to any goods and afterwards endorsed the bill of lading and transferred the goods to a third party was thereby discharged from liability under the contract of carriage; intermediate holders of a bill of lading remained potentially liable under the contract of carriage and became actually liable if they took actual delivery of the goods their position was not ir-

---

[257] 指对 1992 年新提单法委员会所出的报告。

reversible... if the holder endorsed the bill in favour of a third party[258] who became liable the previous holder was exonerated..."

12.2.5.5　总结1992年立法

以上两小段所介绍的两个重要的近期案例，希望能带给读者几个讯息。一是1992年新提单法（海上运输法）解决了1855年旧提单法的缺点，主要是将提单背书转让与货物的所有权转让脱钩，进而扩大提单合约能予转让的人士的类别，使之都可以成为"合法持有人"（lawful holder）。这一来，可以同步减少以侵权起诉承运人/船东的各种弊端。但立法者思前想后，以为拟定得天衣无缝，这立法还是在新案例意想不到的事实下出现了漏洞以及难以解释之处。由此可见，在相对更紧迫的情况和时间下拟定一个复杂合约，想要天衣无缝更是谈何容易。

也觉得有点滑稽：1855年提单法是措辞/文字太局限，使得收货人想变为运输合约一方并享有诉权（Title to sue）不易：请看本章之12.2.4.3与12.2.4.4小段。但该法被1992年海上运输法替代后，却又嫌太多人会陷入运输合约的"罗网"而负上各种责任。

另一讯息是在提单合约下既有权利（提取货物方面主要只靠物权凭证的功能，而其他所有权利是诸如以提单合约向船东起诉等），但同时也有责任。而且，这责任会是十分庞大。例如，像The "Aegean Sea" 案涉及的不安全港口问题，或The "Berge Sisar" 案涉及的危险品严重损坏船舶等。的确，笔者听过、见过，也处理过不少同类的案件，如危险品出事导致人命伤亡，船舶全损，等等。往往是很容易出毛病：记得一次只是工人没有把盖子扭紧以致半途危险品漏出，导致人命伤亡，船舶被迫回航装港去清除危险品，损失上百万美元。其他像精矿（水分过高）、硫磺、鱼粉等的货物出事更是频繁。出这种事，发货人难辞其咎：见Fox v. Nott (1861) 6 Hurl & Nov. 630 先例与1992年新提单法 Section 3(3)。看来，中国的大出口公司若涉及危险品运输，也应小心这种庞大的责任，或去投保，或去组织一下公司的结构，以便去与船东/承运人订立运输合约的一方（发货人）不用由母公司出面，做法就像The "Aegean Sea"案例中的ROIL与Repsol。

但"lawful holder"（提单合法持有人）看来有点无辜，提单责任应该不关他的事。而且，1992年新提单法的"lawful holder"还包括作为承押人的银行，可不能乱去强加庞大的提单合约责任到他们头上。所以，有关这1992年立法的委员会报告中的2.31段说明光是去持有提单，如银行、中间商等，并不自动与船东产生合约关系。报告2.31段说："...in accordance with the recommendation that there should not be an automatic linking of contractual rights and liabilities, pledges and others holding the bill

---

[258] 看来本案例的Dow Europe有危险，是真正有提单责任的lawful holder，可被Bergesen/船东索赔。

merely as security would not be liable for such matters as freight and demurrage unless they sought to enforce their security."

但持有提单的人士(不论是收货人或银行)一去行使权利,即在 12.2.5.3 小段节录的 1992 年立法 Section 3(1)去向船东提取货物或要求交货(船东也愿意,构成了所谓的 attornment),或以提单合约起诉索赔,就有提单合约责任了。这在立法者认为完全公道:既有权利也就应有责任。

这一来,总结下来就是:

(ⅰ)1855 年提单法下因为提单的背书与货物的转让同步与挂钩,所以银行绝不会面对提单合约责任(本章之 4.6.4 小段),除非银行贸然地以行为构成一个默示合约(Brandt v. Liverpool(1924)1 KB 575):见本章之 4.6.5 小段。但在 1992 年新提单法下,银行或其他人士(如 The "Aegean Sea"(1998)1 Lloyd's Rep. 39 的 Repsol)都会被卷进去/拖下水,只要提单是背书给他/它,由他/它持有并去行使权利。(ⅱ)提单责任可以是非常庞大的,特别是常见的危险货物的发货人处理不当,或是不宣告/宣载[The "Kapitan Sakharov"(2000)2 Lloyd's Rep. 255)]船长又无法知悉,例如盛装容器的盖子没有扭紧,包装处理不符合 IMO 的要求,对鱼粉没有进行过延缓自燃的处理(The "Amphion"(1991)2 Lloyd's Rep. 101),等等。航次中若危险品造成意外带来损失,责任在发货人身上应是顺理成章,毕竟过错在他/它。这在海牙规则有明确规定,Article 4 (6) 说:"Goods of an inflammable, explosive or dangerous nature to the shipment whereof the carrier, master or agent of the carrier has not consented with knowledge of their nature and character, may at any time before discharge be landed at any place, or destroyed or rendered innocuous by the carrier without compensation and the shipper of such goods shall be liable for all damages and expenses directly or indirectly arising out of or resulting from such shipment…"

(ⅲ)发货人对提单的责任固然难以脱身,但正如(ⅰ)所讲,行使权利的提单"合法持有人"(lawful holder)也会被扯进去并要承担与发货人一样的提单合约责任。这在 1992 年新提单法的 Section 3(1)说得明白,已节录过,但可再去强调该段的最后一句,它说:"…that person(行使权利的提单合法持有人)…become subject to the same liabilities under that contract as if he had been a party to that contract."

这方面仍有疑问,本书第六章之 2.2 小段还会再予针对性较强的详论。(ⅳ)这表示发货人/收货人/银行都要十分小心,例如:

(a)大企业,如国家公司、大炼钢厂等,利用资产少的贸易公司进行进口/出口,如 The "Aegean Sea"(1998)2 Lloyd's Rep. 39 的 Repsol 与 ROIL。

(b)买卖已装在船舶上的"浮动货物"(floating cargo),一定程度上已显示会有麻烦,买方在确定买卖合约之前,应独自向船东询问是否有任何提单合约责任,有否欠下运费、欠下装港滞期费与其他各种的责任。

(c) 估计或害怕有麻烦的货物到了卸港,例如听说船上鱼粉曾发生自燃,收货人/买方可去另订一个新的买卖合约,然后把提单背书转让给这新买方(实际是原收货人控制或有关系的皮包公司),让它去提取货物。如有提单责任也只会算到它头上,而不可能去把真正有资产的原收货人拖下水。原收货人这样做,船东也无从知道,就算知道也无从反对。但不这样去做,提单背书就只到他/它为止,若去向船长提取货物并退回一份正本提单,这之后才发觉船东索赔比货价更高的提单合约责任就会后悔都来不及了。

(d) 银行作为承押人如要去提取货物,也应考虑(c)的技巧,去隔一层关系。

(iv) 另外也会有其他的空子可钻,例如订立海运单的卖方责任难逃,但在知悉或估计要出大事后,就去把海运单内的收货人(可能是一家财雄势大贸易公司,可能是一家银行)名字及时更改,以协助后者从运输合约的责任中脱身,这做法请看第二章之3.5.3小段。

(v) 中国/亚洲的货方或许会问:英国立法与我何干?这可以有多个答案。第一是在今天的航运/外贸英国法律可以说就是国际上的一套游戏规则,中国国际贸易商/进出口公司以及从事国际营运的船东总不能只顾中国海商法,这在现实中根本行不通。第二是中国海商法也会要去改进,例如去针对愈来愈普遍使用的海运单。第三是在中国港口卸货的收货人,也愈来愈多要面临去伦敦仲裁,受英国法管辖,因为提单有一条伦敦仲裁条款(这一点会在本书第四章之2.6.4小段详论)。

§13 1992年立法没有针对合约相互关系障碍的FOB买卖的情况

在本章结束前可去探讨一下1992年立法没有针对的一种情况。这影响倒也没有,因为已有普通法(先例)给了答案/解决方法。这是一种FOB买卖的情况。一般FOB买卖,由买方派船,卖方装货上船,然后要求船东签发指示提单,卖方是发货人,这不成问题,卖方(发货人)是提单运输合约的一方,与船东/承运人有合约关系。

唯一的问题是,提单是装完货后当天或多天后才会签发。而如果在装货过程中发生争议,发货人/卖方与船东/承运人有否运输合约关系呢?船东可否说:"我不认识你,我只是与买方订有运输合约,如一份订舱单或租约?"答案应是既然大家预计会签发一份装船提单,也会强制适用海牙规则,所以装货过程中的争议仍受未签发的提单与海牙规则管制/约束。在 Pyrene Company Ltd. v. Scindia Steam Navigation Company Ltd. (1954) 1 Lloyd's Rep. 321, Devlin 大法官说:"In my judgment, whenever a contract of carriage is concluded and it is contemplated that a bill of lading will in due course be issued in respect of it, that contract is from its creation 'covered'[259] by a bill of lading and is therefore from its inception a contract of carriage within the meaning of the Rules[260] and to which the Rules apply."

在 Pyrene Company 先例,还涉及另一问题,因为卖方将不会是提单(将来签发)的发货人,该案例是本章之 9.1.2 小段所提及的第三种 FOB 买卖做法。这一来,卖方凭什么会是提单合约的一方?

该先例涉及以 FOB 买卖 5 辆昂贵的救火车从伦敦运去印度。FOB 买方安排了运输(班轮运输)而卖方准时交货装上船。但在装港把救火车吊上船时,因船东装卸工的疏忽而掉到码头上被摔坏了。卖方后来花了 966 英镑才修理好,但以当时的海牙规则,船东的单件责任限制只有 200 英镑。当然,海牙规则只有在卖方与船东有运输合约关系时才适用。而双方要有了合约关系,就再不能以侵权去取巧,例如卖方企图以侵权来索赔 966 英镑:请参阅本书第二章 5.5.2 小段有关"并列诉权"(concurrent action 或 parallel action)的介绍。

显然,在 Pyrene Company,卖方坚持没有合约关系,与船东只有托管/侵权关系,所以海牙规则(只针对有提单等的运输合约)不适用,他可完全索赔回这 966 英镑。

Devlin 大法官判是卖方受提单运输合约的约束,理由是 2 个或其中之一,具体如下:

(i)根据是本章 12.2.1 小段 Dunlop v. Lambert(1839)6 Cl & F600 的说法,就是发货人与船东/承运人订约时已知道/默认合约是为了以后这票货物的买方利益所订(contract for the benefit of the buyer)。当然在 Pyrene Company 先例,关系倒了过来,因为是 FOB 买卖,是买方"contract for the benefit of the seller"。

Devlin 大法官说:"In this type of case the seller as shipper makes the contract for the benefit of the buyer. The converse may be equally true. There is no difficulty in principle about the concept of an FOB buyer making a contract of affreightment for the benefit of the seller as well as for himself … In brief, I think the inference irresistible that it was the intention of all three parties that the seller should participate in the contract of affreightment so far as it affected him…"

(ii)或根据在本章 12.2.3 小段所讲的"默示合约"(implied contract)。Devlin 大法官说:"If this conclusion(指刚提及的(i))is wrong, there is an alternative way by which, on the facts of this case, the same result would be achieved. By delivering the

---

[259] 这是海牙规则在 Article 1(b)对运输合约的定义所用的措辞/文字:"applies only to contract of carriage covered by a bill of lading…"。

[260] 这指海牙规则。

goods alongside the seller impliedly invited the shipowner to load them, and the shipowner by lifting the goods impliedly accepted that invitation. The implied contract so created must incorporate the shipowner's usual terms; none other could have contemplated; the shipowner would not contract for the loading of the goods on terms different from those which he offered for the voyage as a whole."

§14 发货人严格的产品责任

还有,发货人/卖方另有一个危险的责任,就是严格的产品责任。产品责任在西方国家已普遍是严格责任,即不管有否疏忽亦要负全责。而且,受害的用家或消费者不必要有任何合约关系即可去控告发货人/卖方等人士。在美国,这种索赔可高达上千万上亿美元,会毁掉一家大型/中型的公司,这可不是开玩笑。

一般是需要四个要素才能构成严格的产品责任。一是产品/商品有缺点,有不妥之处;二是这缺点/不妥令产品/商品有危险;三是这缺点/不妥造成/导致损失或伤亡;四是这问题的产品/商品出售与出事故时情况一样(例如没有被改装过),而且是合理与可预见的使用下出事故的(例如商品有说明某情况下使用会有火灾危险或应如何使用)。

不管发货人/卖方是不是生产商,他/它都会要负责,在美国的 Pan-Alaska Fisheries v. Marine Const. & Design Co. 56S F. 2d 1129,1978 AMC 2315(9 Cir. 1977)先例,说是所有生产商、"贸易商"(dealers)与"分销商"(retailers)都要负上责任,因为他/它们都是"整体的去生产与行销这最终造成伤害的缺陷商品"(an integral part of the overall producing and marketing enterprise that should bear the cost of injuries resulting from defective products)。

至于中国出口商(特别明知出口产品/商品有危险性)如何去减低这个产品责任的风险呢?读者或可去参阅笔者的《禁令》一书第六章有关 Adam v. Cape Industries(1990) Ch 433 的先例。

第四章　提单作用之二：
运输合约的形式与有关条款的分析/探讨

§1　提单合约形式简介

众所周知，船舶以班轮和不定期船（出租）的形式经营在做法上很不相同，这也反映在提单这份重要的运输合约上。在本书第三章之§4段，已对班轮提单与租约提单有详论，故不在此重复。本章是分析/探讨这些提单常见的一些条款，毕竟，它们绝大部分最后会约束船东/承运人与收货人/提单合法持有人之间的合约关系，赖也赖不掉；而收货人作为合约一方以他并不完全知道合约内容为由去抗辩也不会成功。

在预早拟定条款的班轮提单或是临时合并租约条款的租约提单，都会有内容雷同的条款。毕竟，大家都有需要以条款去针对各种在履约时会出现的问题。例如，针对共同海损以 York-Antwerp Rule（约克、安特卫普规则）来理算，针对美国法律独有之处的"新杰森条款"（New Jason Clause）与"双方有责碰撞条款"（Both to Blame Collision Clause），针对去合并海牙规则的"首要条款"（Clause Paramount）等。

也会有另一极端是只有一种提单才需要这些条款，例如，"光船条款"（Demise Clause）或/与"承运人身份条款"（Identity of Carrier Clause）这些条款在本书第三章之 4.3.1.3 与 4.3.2 小段已详论。班轮提单才需要这些条款是因为班轮公司的名字通常印在提单格式的抬头，而真正承运的船舶实际是班轮公司期租进来的，班轮公司无意在这种情况下仍被当做是运输合约承运人，但又怕被误会而被诉，所以要以此光船条款或/与承运人身份条款去说清楚。这种做法在通常没有抬头的租约提单是不必理会的，以致光船条款与/或承运人身份条款一般不会出现在租约提单。原因是租约提单一般不会有期租承租人名字的抬头，只会填上船舶名字，大家通常都使用某类航次、货种的标准提单格式，而没有自己公司的格式。而一般通用的标准租约格式，都会另有一份相配套的标准提单格式，例如，金康租约有"Congenbill"（见本书之附录八），Austwheat 1990 有"Austwheat Bill"，Norgrain 1973 有"North American Grain Bill of Lading Form"等。

与光船条款相反，有另一种条款是租约提单才需要，班轮提单不必理会的，这是针对滞期费的条款。这方面也已在本书第三章之4.3小段与11.2.2小段有谈及。该两小段讲到班轮绝少会产生船舶滞期，特别是今天的班轮都变为集装箱运输，船舶一抵达港口，马上就靠泊私人集装箱码头进行卸装，不要几个小时已可以开航，绝少听过有船期延误、产生滞期的。除非遇上意外，比方是集装箱内的危险品外泄，导致港口当局干预，进而延误船舶，例如，像 The "Orjula" (1995) 2 Lloyd's Rep. 395 先例中的集装箱外泄 hydrochloric acid 与 sodium hypochlorite 的危险品。况且，把一个固定的金额印在班轮提单格式，而同样的格式使用在多艘不同成本的班轮/船舶，会被视为是并非依"真正的损失预测"(genuine pre estimate of damages)所得出的对某艘船舶造成"滞期损失"(detention loss)而要支付给船东的"议定赔偿金"(liquidated damage)，导致很容易被当做是"罚款"(penalty)而判无效。这方面课题在《国际商务游戏规则－英国合约法》一书第十四章之§15段有详论，不去重复。只是总结一下，由于以上原因，班轮提单很少印有滞期费条款。但这滞期费条款对租约提单却绝对重要。原因一是不像班轮，散货运输中船东/承运人难以控制船舶在港内的速遣，往往要依赖货方，例如，靠泊的是收货人的私人码头，由收货人负责卸货的"Free out"等。原因二是散货运输经常会遇上严重压港或其他原因，导致船舶被延误，产生大量滞期，而若是班轮，即使去同一港口也不会面对这问题。难怪曾听过出租船做短航次运输（但两头港口有压港/拥挤的情况）的船东说：不收取运费都无所谓（短航次运费也多不了），但滞期费可不能定得低，这会是一笔比运费高得多的钱。

以上所讲，基本的大精神仍是去订好一个合约，这就要懂业务，把将来履约时可能会发生的各种事情都全面与完整去针对了，明确了，责任后果都去分摊了。这可带来合约双方履约时的肯定，使每事都已预计到，减少或避免争议。由于班轮业务与租船业务并不完全相同，其中作为与收货人/货方的相关运输合约提单的内容也自然不会完全相同。甚至同是班轮提单，也会因行走的航线不同而出现不同的条款。例如，在集装箱搜出毒品时有所闻，这在美国十分严厉的1986年"反毒品法"(U. S. Anti Drug Abuse Act 1986)下会带来重罚。故此，提单要有条款去针对这严重问题，如说明货方对集装箱或包装内可能藏有毒品的预防与举证责任，要严格承担后果等。

行走美国航线还有其他独特的事情要针对是班轮行走其他航线所不必面对的。例如，《期租合约》一书之53.1段提到了所有进口美国的货物的提单/海运单都要有统一编号(Carrier or Bill of Lading Issuer Standard Character Alpha Carrier Code 或简称 SCAC Code)。

§2　租约提单

租约提单的内容/条款是去合并较早订立的租约,这一方面已在本书第三章之 4.2 至 4.3 小段有详论。经常出现在租约提单的一条普通的合并条款是:"All the terms, conditions, clauses and exceptions contained in the charter-party dated… apply to this bill of lading and deemed to be incorporated"。至于合并的一些大原则,也已在第三章之§10 段有探讨/详论。在此,笔者想先再去谈谈这些大原则。

2.1　合并条款要寻求双方订约的意愿

像所有合约的明示条款一样,合并条款也一定要寻求双方订约的意愿。而如果条款本身写得不够明确,有了争议仍是要客观地找出双方的订约意愿应是什么,到底双方想合并的是什么。而难以找出或难以解释并不表示法官或仲裁员可轻易去否定/漠视合并条款,这毕竟不是正确与妥善的做法:请参阅《国际商务游戏规则——英国合约法》一书第十章之§5 段。除非在没可能解释的情况下,例如,合并条款中想去合并的文件根本就不存在,也不会有,也不是仅对某文件稍作"篡改"(manipulate)即可去套用,才会迫不得已去否定/漠视该合并条款。

双方想去合并的文件尚不存在,但将会存在,只要双方意愿明确而且行内人士都按同样做法,这合并仍是无妨。例如,CIF/CFR 买卖中针对将来所租的船舶会有支付其卸港滞期费之责,卖方(租船东)为避免支付船东后,自己夹在当中,无法向买方要求补偿(注意卸港延误是买方之责,卖方难以控制),所以会一早在订立买卖合约时已合并进将来租约的有关卸货时间与滞期费条款,所用措辞/文字通常是简短的"as per charter-party"。卖方无法说得更清楚,因为租约会是买卖合约订立几个月后去找船付运时才订立,时隔太久,根本无法预测租约最后会是什么条款,例如,滞期费会是高是低。这一方面在笔者的《国际货物买卖》一书第九章 3.1 小段有详论,并提到有关先例如 Suzuki & Co. v. Companhia Mercantile Internacional (1921) 9 Lloyd's Rep. 171; Gill & Duffus v. Rionda (1994) 2 Lloyd's Rep. 670。在 Gill & Duffus 先例, Clarke 大法官说:"the expression' as per charter-party' referred to the charter-party pursuant to which this cargo was being carried… Provided that the charter concerned was a genuine commercial arrangement it did not matter that the charter had not been drawn up at the time when the contract of sale was made…"

2.2　去找出双方订约的意愿是合并哪一份租约

这一点已在本书第三章之§10 段略述,在此再多加详论。

若是相关的航次只有一份程租约,再加上租约提单明确了是合并该租约(通常以填上该租约日期作为识别),那么在这明示合并条款下双方的意愿应是明确得不能再明确,解释起来也无从去扭曲。但现实中今天的船舶经常转租,二船东、三船东,甚至多达十船东也曾听闻。这一来,涉及相关的一个航次,只有一套的货物装船提单,但租约会有3份、5份,这就会有疑问这只有一套的租约提单合并的到底是哪一份租约?或许有人说,去看看提单所注明合并的租约日期不就可以识别与明确了吗?但现实中这也会面对两个问题。一是在这多份租约中会有相同的日期,二是在第三章之4.2.3小段与本章之2.6.4.2小段提到的承运人与发货人在备妥与签发提单时往往十分粗略,得过且过,不常去查问有关租约,反正不去填上合并租约的日期通常也不影响发货人结汇,所以不予理会。

2.2.1 对船东合并租约进提单的意愿的探讨

这一来,这份租约提单合并了什么就会有争议了。毕竟,不同的租约常有重大不同的条款,合并哪一份会有天壤之别。或会有人说,可否借此去否定/漠视这条"含糊不清"的合并条款?答案是应避免这样做,这会是懒惰,不肯用脑的法官或/与仲裁员推卸责任的判法。客观地想想,双方订约当时的意愿会是期望或不期望合并租约呢?例如,船东/承运人签发一份提单运输合约,若不希望合并原先艰苦谈判所得的租约,会导致在卸港面对以下困境:

(ⅰ)提单格式本身(如 Congenbill)没有卸货时间与滞期费条款,若不去合并租约相关条款,在这提单合约就根本不会有这些条款。但若在卸港遇上延误,岂非会是在本书第三章§10段所讲的 Mallozzi v. Carapelli(1976)1 Lloyd's Rep. 407 先例一样的结果?

(ⅱ)留置货物的权利对船东十分重要,它允许船东以此手段合法地去扣押属收货人所拥有的货物,迫收货人/货方去支付欠下的债务。若能成功,船东可避免在国际上追债常会带来的昂贵、漫长与结果不稳定的法院诉讼或/与仲裁。但正如《程租合约》一书第十二章之§3段所讲,英国普通法只对欠下的运费(主要这项)给予默示的留置权,即运输合约不去明示也有这权利。而像欠下滞期费等债务,船东想去享有留置权必须依赖明示条款。就英国合约法而言,若订约双方有订约自由,则除非是违反公共政策,合约明示了什么条款,就应看该条款的措辞/用字,以各种"解释合约的准则"(rules of construction)去协助解释/分析。现实中绝大多数程租租约标准格式均赋予船东可就欠下的滞期费留置货物的权利,只有把该租约再合并进租约提单,船东才谈得上提单合约有条款给予其权利可为欠下的滞期费留置货物。所以,船东怎会不期望提单去合并原先的租约呢?

(ⅲ)今天的程租租约通常是同意装卸货费用不必船东/承运人承担的"free in

and out"(或简称 FIO),船东一般都会拒绝承担和安排他/它不熟悉港口的货物装卸,这种做法、心态与班轮完全相反。但在没有明示条款下,英国法律默示的地位是船东/承运人要在装港把货物装上船舱并在卸港将货物从船舱卸下。所以在一般的租约提单标准格式,因本身没有这方面的明示条款,若不去合并租约的 FIO 条款,会导致船东/承租人在提单合约下面对收货人,要负责与安排卸货。顶多将来去向承租人要求补偿这笔额外的费用(因为租约本是同意为 FIO),但已是够麻烦了。

所以综上所述,客观、合理与现实的判断应是船东/承运人与发货人订约时(签发提单时)已有意愿/期望去合并租约,而不会不希望去合并租约。而作为另一订约方的发货人,也不见得会反对或有任何理由去反对,反正能顺利在信用证结汇就万事大吉了。最后可以节录 Denning 勋爵在 The "SLS Everest" (1981) 2 Lloyd's Rep. 389 所讲的如下一段话作为总结:"…Unless the charter-party was incorporated, all sorts of terms and arrangements would have to be implied-or discovered in some other way-in order to make the whole thing workable[261]. But it works simply and completely by incorporating the terms of the charter[262] – this is, the terms of the voyage charter[263]."

2.2.2 一般准则/说法是合并了船东自己订立的头一份租约

笔者尚未谈到正题:就是有意愿,有期望去合并租约,但多个租约下应去合并哪一个呢?根据以上所讲的推理,船东应是想去合并他/它自己艰苦谈判所得的租约,而不是不知内容/细节的分租约。这也是英国法律的地位,正如 Gatehouse 大法官在 The "Nai Matteini" (1988) 1 Lloyd's Rep. 452 先例所讲的:"That, of course, is not to say that the purported incorporation of an unidentified charter-party by the bill of lading had no effect[264]. The question is which of the two charter-parties is referred to[265]. According to Scrutton[266], art. 35, at p. 65, the normal rule in a case such as the present is that the presumed intention of the parties to the bill of lading contract is to incorporate the head charter[267] (See the 'San Nicholas' (1976) 1 Lloyd's Rep. 8 at p. 11, approving

---

[261] 若是不合并租约,一份租约提单会难以去解释,许多条款与安排都需要去默示才能让这份运输合约履行下去。
[262] 但若能去合并租约,则解释起来会十分简易与完美。
[263] 当然,这租约是一份程组合约才能相配套地去合并。
[264] 在提单合约合并一份没有识别的租约并非无效。
[265] 问题是哪一份租约才是被合并的呢?
[266] 指权威的《Scrutton on Charter-Parties》一书。
[267] 一般准则/说法是合并的应是船东自己订立的"头一份租约"(head charter),而不是"分租约"(sub-charter)。另要注意"估计的双方意愿"(presumed intention)的措辞/文字,表示合约法的大原则仍是要以客观地寻找的订约方意愿为准。

this passage in Scrutton and The 'Sevonia Team' (1983) 2 Lloyd's Rep. 640 at p. 644)."

2.2.3 头一份是期租租约或多航次程租的情况下合并的是哪一份租约

若头一份是期租租约,说这份租约被合并进提单才是"估计的双方意愿"(presumed intention)有说不通之处,具体如下:

(ⅰ)租约提单标准格式内的合并条款一般都会说明运费多少/如何支付是依照某日期(识别之用)的租约,进而带出合并这回事。原因会是运费的重要性,非要明确不可。例如,著名的 Congenbill 1994 只是简单的一句:"Freight payable as per CHARTERPARTY dated(日期,也经常不去填上)"。

也会有多写几个字、更为明确的合并条款,如:(a)在 The "San Nicholas" (1976) 1 Lloyd's Rep. 8,提单上印就的合并条款是:"This shipment is carried under and pursuant to the terms of the Charter dated(日期空白) at(地点空白) between(订约方空白) as Charterer, and all the terms whatsoever of the said Charter except for the rate and payment of freight specified therein apply to and govern the rights of the parties concerned in this shipment"。(b)在 The "SLS Everest" (1981) 2 Lloyd's Rep. 389,提单上印就的合并条款是:"Freight and other conditions as per(租约与日期) including the exoneration clause"。(c)在 The "Nai Matheini" (1988) 1 Lloyd's Rep. 452,提单上印就的合并条款是:"…he or they paying Freight for the same as per Charter Party between(订约方名字) dated(日期) all the terms, conditions and exceptions (including but not limited to Due Diligence, Negligence, Force Majeure, War Liberties and Arbitration clauses) contained in which Charter Party are herewith incorporated and form part hereof."

笔者在此要提出的一点只是:期租租约哪来运费?至于15天一期的租金,它与运费根本是两码事,计算基础也很不一样,这是即使去努力"篡改"(manuplate)仍毫无办法配套的。

(ⅱ)若头一份是期租租约,说真的,在船东签发提单合约时,很难说他/它当时是意愿与期望去合并该份期租租约。在本章之 2.2.1 小段的情况并不会发生。船东也不会关心提单没有滞期费条款,不可去为欠下的滞期费留置货物等。说真的,去合并是期租的"头一份租约"(head charter),也不会令提单有滞期费条款,留置权条款等。对船东而言,他/它只关心租金的准时支付,这要去盯紧承租人而不是提单下的收货人。

(ⅲ)船东也知道,合并的大原则是只有与提单事项"直接关联"(direct germane to subject matter)的内容才能去合并。所以去合并一份期租怎样说也是作用不大或甚至是没有作用;请参阅本书第三章之 10.1 小段。

(iv)在期租租约下的一般条款如纽约土产(N. Y. P. E)标准格式,通常是承租人而不是船东有权去选择提单的形式或/与内容,而船长一般不得拒绝签发:The "Berkshire" (1974) 1 Lloyd's Rev. 185;The "Nanfri" (1979) 1 Lloyd's Rep. 201。这方面笔者《期租合约》一书之25段有详论,不再重复。这样一来,客观地寻找订约方的意愿到底是想合并哪一份租约,推论到的对象也应是期租承租人(二船东)而不是原船东。若二船东订下的分租约是一份程租租约,内容有运费、滞期费等条款,那么这份提单合约订约方的意愿与期望看来应是合并这程租合约。以此类推,若是二船东的分租约也是期租约,则要去看三船东、四船东等的"分分租约",直至找到一份可以与提单配套的程租约为止。在 The "SLS Everest" (1981)先例,正是这样的判法。

最后另去一提的头一份租约是"多航次程租租约"(head consecutive voyage charter)的情况。在这情况下,相比一份单一航次的程租约的合并仍会增加了配套的困难,例如,有不同金额的运费与滞期费。但看来仍是与期租租约有不同的对待,可以被视为是订约双方所意愿/期望所合并的一份租约。在 The "Nai Matteini" (1988) 1 Lloyd's Rep. 452, Gatehouse 大法官说:"Of course, the head charter was a consecutive voyage charter, and (货方大律师) … referred to the inappositeness of certain provisions of the head charter if one were to incorporate them into the bill of lading. There are arguments the other way, but I am not persuaded that the normal rule should not be followed in this case."

2.2.4 口头租约能否合并

口头的租约或部分租约内容能否包括在合并条款内呢?若能包括,这会对收货人/提单合法持有人不利,因为谈判租约时他们并不在场。这方面在近期的 The "Al Battani" (1993) 2 Lloyd's Rep. 219 与 The "Heidberg" (1994) 2 Lloyd's Rep. 287 先例有涉及。在 The "Heidberg",Diamond 大法官说:"it would be commercially unsound to hold that on the proper construction of the bill of lading, it was capable of incorporating the terms of an oral contract; what was transferred to the consignee or indorsee consisted only of the terms which appeared on the face and reverse of the bill of lading; collateral oral terms were not transferred and the same principles applied where the bill of lading incorporated a charter-party; and as a matter of construction of the bill of lading it did not incorporate the terms of a charter which at the date of the bill of lading was issued had not been reduced to writing…"

2.3 合并的只是租约内有直接关联的内容/条款

合并的大原则是除非特别去写明(这是另外的明示条款,订约自由下写什么都可以),否则一般只有"有直接关联"(directly germane)的内容/条款才可以被合并。说真的,也只有这些内容/条款才有必要去合并,而其他不必要的都应去摒弃。毕竟合并是一种隐晦、粗糙并容易令合约一方或双方不警觉或/与看漏的订约做法,所以解释起来应去局限而不是扩大。

而与提单这份运输合约有直接关联的程租租约的内容/条款,也只能是与运输、装卸和交付这同一票货物有关的才能算得上。针对这一点的权威说法是Denning勋爵在 The "Annefield"(1971)1 Lloyd's Rep. 1 的讲话如下:"I would say that a clause which is directly germane to the subject matter of the bill of lading, (that is to the shipment, carriage and delivery of goods) can and should be incorporated into the bill of lading contract[268], even though it may involve a degree of manipulation of the words in order to fit exactly the bill of lading[269]. But if the clause is one which is not thus directly germane, it should not be incorporated into the bill of lading contract unless it is done explicitly in clear words either in the bill of lading or in the charter-party[270]."

另再节录 Brandon 大法官在 The "Rena K"(1978)1 Lloyd's Rep. 545 先例中相同的说法如下:"In the authorities mentioned above a distinction had been drawn between clauses in the relevant charter-party which are directly germane to the shipment, carriage and delivery of the goods covered by the bill of lading and other clauses which are not directly germane to such matters…"。

2.4 合并不包括附属性条款

这方面与上一小段所讲的是同一道理,只是把"直接关联"与"不直接关联"再去区分为"构成合约标的事项的部分"(part of subject-matter)与"附属性条款"(an-

---

[268] 与货物付运、运输和交货有直接关联的内容/条款才能被合并。

[269] 这些内容/条款或许要稍作修改才能在提单合约内完全配套,但这也无妨。例如,租约是写承租人延误船期一天要付多少运费,为能合并在提单则或许要把"承租人"更改"货方(发货人与/或收货人)"了。这认可的做法在笔者《期租合约》一书之 45 段有详论,它是关于把海牙规则合并进租约的惯常做法。在贵族院的 The "Saxon Star"(1958)1 Lloyd's Rep. 73,该合并被判有效,虽然这样做要大量地删改海牙规则,因为海牙规则写明只适用在提单,不适用在租约。

[270] 租约中不是直接关联的内容/条款,除非另以明示条款表明并入提单内,是不能,也不必包括在一般的合并条款内的。例如,租约有一条款说承租人有权多跑一个航次。或是,要求船东在卸完货后 30 天把一些航次的文件交给承租人。当然,最著名也是打官司最多的一条"不是直接关联"(not directly germane)条款就是仲裁条款,这方面在稍后的 2.6.4 小段再详论。

cillary terms/clauses),前者可以一般的合并条款包括在内,而后者却不能。后者的"附属性条款"被视为是与合约双方执行权利义务无关,不论有没有它合约都可获得执行。这可以节录笔者的《国际商务游戏规则——英国合约法》一书第十章之4.3小段的有关内容如下:

> 另一个很新的案例,OK Petroleum v. Vitol(1995)2 Lloyd's Rep. 160. 也反映了上述并入条款在合约中如何运用的理论。该案中,原告以 CIF 价售卖汽油予被告,买卖合约规定(卸港)延滞费依租约(租用承运船的航次租约)的规定。买卖合约订立之后,卖方租船将油付运,结果在卸港发生了延滞(注:买方负责卸货)。该租约有关延滞费的条款中,有一项索赔时效(Time Bar)的规定,称除非自卸除油管后90天内收到有关索赔通知,承租人对租约下产生的延滞费及其他费用不予负责。在高等法院,原告依买卖合约向被告索赔卸港产生的延滞费,而被告则以合约中有关"延滞费按租约"(Demurrage as per Charterparty)的并入条款辩称,租约中有关延滞费的条款规定了卸货90天的索赔时效,而原告并未在此90天内提出索赔,通知被告,因此索赔时效已中止,被告无须赔付。该案争议的焦点显然就在于租约延滞费条款中的索赔时效规定能否也一齐并入买卖合约中。结果法院判有关索赔时效的规定不能并入买卖合约,原告仍可索赔延滞费。法官在判词中称:a)有关并入的一般性用语(General word of incorporation)通常不能被解释为足够广泛可以将引入合约的所有规定并入进本合约,除非这些规定构成引入合约的标的事项的一部分(part of subject matter),而非诸如仲裁条款,管辖权条款等,仅属附属性质(ancillary)。附属性的规定通常被视为与本合约下当事人的权利、义务无关;b)本案中索赔时效的规定,虽然在租约下专门适用于延滞费的索赔,但本质上仍是附属于租约有关延滞费的主体或标的事项的。这种附属性表现为该规定的功能仅限于已生合约权利的执行,是专门针对已产生延滞费的收取的;c)在买卖合约中的并入(incorporation)一词,作为一般性用语,并无明显表达双方欲将租约中那些并不属延滞费标的事项本身一部分,而仅属附属性质的规定并入买卖合约之意。而本案也无特殊的情况显示对"并入"的一般性用语的通常解释应予背离。因此,被告提出的索赔时效并入买卖合约的辩称不会被采纳。原告的索赔不会因时效而中止。这一判例进一步说明,并入条款引入的条款、合约中并不构成标的事项本身部分的附属条款、条款(ancillary terms/clause)不能以普通的并入用语并入进本合约中适用,要想并入则要去明示了。

从以上节录看来,程租租约内的仲裁条款,管辖权条款,时效条款等,均属"附属性条款",不会成为提单合约中涉及运输、装卸与交付货物的主体或标的事项,非要让它们有效的合并进来提单合约才能顺利执行。

2.5 合并主要是针对运输与卸港的内容/条款

照说,一份程租租约为去针对某一航次,某一特定货物的运输,绝大部分的内容/条款都应与后来签发的提单合约有直接关联,可以包括在合并条款。有这方面的争议(即提单有否合并),只会发生在装货后签发提单之时或更后的履约。在这之前发生在装港的装货,提单尚未存在,不会有此种争议。例如,租约的销约期条款,装货作业的责任属谁等。

这方面的争议在发货人与船东之间也少有产生(也会有少见的例子,比方 The "Garbis"(1982) 2 Lloyd's Rep. 283 先例,后详),因为通常发货人获得提单后不久就会去在信用证结汇。在成功取得货款后,对该航次/买卖再也不会关心。而之后要去关心的是提单合约强加到他/它头上的收货人。收货人(买方)要去承担该航次的风险,唯一的保障一是一份保单,另一是一份提单。保单只保障部分海上风险,提单则提供了更大的履约保障,可让收货人盯着船东/承运人把货物运抵卸港交付,并获得与买卖合约相同的"合约权益与保障"(continuous documentary protection)。故此有 Seng v. Glencore Grain(1996) 1 Lloyd's Rep. 398 的判法。该案中,CIF 买卖合约是约定卖方负责卸货,即所谓的"班轮条款"(linerterms)。但卖方去租进一艘船舶时却在程租租约中答应了"免予(船东)卸货"的"Free out"条款。而后来签发的提单也合并了这份"Free out"的租约。这一来,可见买方/收货人无法从该份提单获得与买卖合约相同的"合约权益与保障"。收货人在买卖合约下原本不必负责卸货,但在提单合约下面对船东却要去负责卸货,因为提单合并了租约的"Free out"条款而非买卖合约。这一来,卸港出了争议,收货人只好回去找卖方,要求承担卸货费用。但如果届时卖方倒闭了,或赖皮,买方/收货人可就夹在当中了。所以该先例判是这份不能给买方提供相同"合约权益与保障"的提单,买方可在托收时拒单,拒绝支付货款。Mance 大法官说:"The documents will identify the agreed cost, freight and destination, and will give the buyers the contractual right as against the carriers to delivery for such freight and at such destination. 'Linerterms' refers to responsibility for… discharge, a matter directly involving the carrier. When the sale contract price clause refers to 'Linerterms', the natural conclusion is in my view that it refers to a right which buyers are to be given as against the carriers. So viewed, the contract remains, from shipment, an essentially documentary transaction, under which the buyers part with payment in return for continuous documentary protection against the carrier."

总之,不论收货人是否从提单合约获得了与买卖合约相同的"合约权益与保

第四章 提单作用之二：运输合约的形式与有关条款的分析/探讨 247

障"，或是并没有获得（原因会有多种，如收货人不懂，或是自己弃权等），他/它与船东/承运人之间今后的关系就是这份运输合约。正如 Goff 大法官在 The "Garbis"（1982）2 Lloyd's Rep. 283 说："If a receiver of goods accepts a bill of lading in this form without/ascertaining the terms of the charter-party, he must accept that his contract with the shipowner for the carriage of goods, contained in or evidenced by the bill of lading, is subject to the charter – party terms relevant to the loading, carriage and discharge of the goods…"

在海上航次中发生了共同海损，租约订明以什么规则理算也合并在提单内，双方（收货人与船东/承运人）都不能有异议。租约若有像"邻近条款"（near clause）、罢工条款、战争条款等可允许船东在某些情况下避免去卸港的条款，也会被合并进提单内，而关于这些条款的详论，在《程租合约》一书第七章可见到，不在此重复。

航次完毕到了卸港（租约与提单都是同样的卸港），收货人与船东/承运人有更多的关系会发生了。例如，若要先减载谁去负责？或是，谁负责卸货（"Free out"或是 Linerterms 之争）？又或是，允许的卸货时间有多久及如何计算？而有了延误，每天滞期费是多少？船东若被欠钱，他/它对货物有否留置权利等。这一切的重要事项都涉及双方的合约权利与义务，都应在程租租约有约定，而去合并进了提单，表示提单也有了相同的内容/条款去针对这些事项，并且约束双方（收货人与船东/承运人）。而去局限与"控制"（control）能予合并的租约内容/条款，不让其无限度的扩大，也有保护提单持有人/收货人的考虑，以免令他/它受意料之外、不合理、不寻常的合并所约束。

最后还要一提的是如果 FOB 买卖下收货人租船，那么提单在他手中就只是收据一份，毫无运输合约之作用：Rodocanachi v. Milburn（1886）18 QBD 67；The "Dunelmia"（1969）2 Lloyd's Rep. 476。这一来，提单合并什么或不合并什么也就无关重要，反正不是运输合约或它的证明，所以根本不会有合并的到底是哪一些条款这样的争议。

2.6 合并的内容/条款必须公平合理和并非不寻常

法律在解释合并条款时处处要求公平合理，例如，在 2.4 小段就有很强的这种意识。要知道，订约自由下会有很短的时效（即使针对货损货差的海牙规则的一年时效其实也很短，转眼间即届满），或会有去世界上某稀奇古怪的地方仲裁的条款，附属性条款如果可以借合并这种隐晦的手法带进另一份合约，很容易令不警觉的对方上当。在另一角度看，订约自由下只要不违反公共政策，什么不合理不公平的内容/条款都可以有效，但它必须以清楚、明确无误的措辞/文字说明，这是解释合约基本的准则。这一来，一条一般的、通用的合并条款就难以说做到了这一点，足可以把另一份合约或文件内不公平合理的内容/条款包括在合并之内。

若另一份被合并的合约内有"不寻常"的(extraordinary 或 unusual)条款,道理也是一样,会被视为不包括在合并内,要合并必须另去清楚明确无误的明示。

就这大精神可以介绍贵族院的 The "K. H. Enterprise" (1994) 1 Lloyd's Rep. 593 先例,它是关于"有条件的分托管"(sub-bailment on terms)的。这课题,在《国际商务游戏规则——英国合约法》一书第四章5.7小段与本书第二章1.5.2.1小段有详论。该先例也涉及合并问题,但这是另一种"合并",是发货人与一程船船东订约时(一程船提单),广泛地授权后者去另订分包合约(sub-con-tract)。这一来,将来与二程船或仓库订立的分包合约,其内容/条款能有多少是可以约束发货人?是发货人一早的广泛授权条款能包括进去,已被合并的呢?

贵族院认为这种"预期的合并"与租约提单合并程租租约的"合并"并不相同,前者不必去严格局限/控制,但后者需要。前者只要是在订约双方"商业/行内的预期"(commercial expectation)之内,例如,明知仓库的分包合约条款一面倒偏向仓库是行业的习惯做法,则已可包括在合并内。而在 The "K. H. Enterprise" 先例,涉及二程船东提单内的一条台湾管辖权条款能否包括在一程船的授权分包/预期合并条款内,进而可去约束发货人/货方。要知道,行业内(班轮运输)的班轮提单都会印有一条管辖权条款。因此,这是在订约双方(一程船提单合约)的"商业预期"(commercial expectation)之内,可以合并。

由此可见,"有条件的分托管"形式的合并并不受2.4小段所讲的附属性条款的局限,而且解释起来较为宽松,主要是看双方订约的"商业/行内预期"是些什么。看来,英国法律的一些大原则在实践中运用起来可以十分灵活,而这样做也是为了追求公平合理,符合实际客观地寻求订约双方真正的订约意愿等"更大"的原则。这可去节录 Goff 勋爵的部分判词(多次强调公平合理)如下:"Here, however, the question is whether consent given by the owner of goods to his bailee to bail the goods to a sub-bailee on any terms is wide enough to embrace an exclusive jurisdiction clause in the contract governing the sub-bailment…

In such a case… the element of control must be derived from the scope of the owner's consent[271]; and where, as here, the consent is very wide in its terms, only terms which are so unusual[272] or so unreasonable that they could not reasonably[273] be understood to

---

[271] 在这种预期合并,局限/控制(即合并包括些什么内容/条款)要去看货方订约时预期会在分包合约包括些什么样的内容/条款,并对此同意/接受。

[272] 局限只是针对分包合约内有很不寻常的条款,是原来订约时发货人/货方不大可能同意/接受的,这些条款不能被包括。

[273] 也不包括不合理的条款,这是原先不能去合理预期的。

第四章　提单作用之二：运输合约的形式与有关条款的分析/探讨　249

fall within such consent are likely to be held to be excluded.

　　Bearing this in mind, their Lordships perceive a number of consideration which militate in favour of the incorporation of the exclusive jurisdiction clause in the present case. First... second, a provision in this form is by no means uncommon in shipowners' standard forms of bill of lading; indeed such a provision must, their Lordships imagine, be very common in the case of shipowners engaged in the container trade[274]. Third, their Lordships do not consider that it can possibly be said that the incorporation of such a clause in a bill of lading is per se unreasonable[275]...

　　...they(指贵族院) consider that the incorporation of the relevant clause in the sub-bailment would be in accordance with the reasonable commercial expectations[276] of those who engage in this type of trade, and that such incorporation will generally lead to a conclusion which is eminently sensible in the context of the carriage of goods by sea, especially in a container ship, in so far as it is productive of an ordered and sensible resolution of disputes in a single jurisdiction, so avoiding wasted expenditure in legal costs and an undesirable disharmony of differing consequences where claims are resolved in different jurisdictions."

　　现在再回头去讨论程租租约合并进提单合约的课题。总地说来，就是对合并的解释要有公平、合理的考虑，排除不寻常条款的考虑以及要保障无法警觉的无辜收货人权益的考虑等。所以，英国法律对这种合并的局限与"控制"(control)也就相应"合理"地严格。话说回来，知道了一些要考虑的精神/原则，但去运用在不同实例中仍是很不容易，毕竟何谓"合理"可以从不同角度去看，得出很不同的结论，也会因事、因人而异。以下段节会介绍几个方面的实例来加以探讨。

2.6.1　针对货物运输/交付责任方面的租约条款

　　程租租约享有订约自由，故此什么古怪的条款都会有。也会有减轻或豁免船东对货物运输/交付责任的条款，例如，著名的金康租约的第二条，也会有像 Jones v. Hough(1880)1819 5 Ex. D. 115 的一条"船东对7月1日前不能抵达卸港而要增收税金的后果不负责"(The vessel was not liable for duties on cargo by non-arrival before July 1st)。

　　这些条款/内容若去合并，甚至是明示在提单内，都会受到海牙规则 Article 3

---

[274] 班轮船东的标准提单格式普遍有一条管辖权条款，特别是从事集装箱运输的班轮船东。
[275] 去合并这管辖权条款也没有什么不合理之处。
[276] 这分包/分托管合约内的管辖权条款完全在双方的"商业/行内的预期"之内。

(8)的约束而被局限禁止,导致无效:这一点请参阅本书第五章之4.2.9小段。这可以说是以立法手段去局限/控制一些不合理的合并,以保障/强化提单在国际贸易中的可信性、认受性。

2.6.2 针对滞期费

2.6.2.1 装港已经产生的滞期费

在英国法律下,滞期费(demurrage)一词包括了装港与卸港产生的滞期费:见 Kish v. Cory(1875)LR 10 QB 553。毕竟,订约双方可以对该词加以局限,但没有这样做,在解释上就不应去"扭曲的"指它只是针对卸港的滞期费。此外,有不少租约(像油轮租约)只约定了一段时间给予货方进行装卸作业,超出了支付滞期费,并不再去区分装货占多少时间,卸货占多少时间。所以,在这种约定下根本没有装港(或卸港)滞期费的说法,而只有一个总的滞期费是多少,既包括装港,也包括卸港。这一切在《程租合约》一书第十二章§6段已有详论。

而程租租约若条款允许对货物进行留置以索取欠下的滞期费,一般的措辞/用字也不去区分(若是能去区分)只是针对卸港而不是装港的滞期费。

这程租租约的留置权条款,可以一条一般措辞的合并条款合并、引入提单合约内;见 The "Anwar Al Sabar"(1980)2 Lloyd's Rep. 261; The "Miramar"(1983)2 Lloyd's Rep. 319。换言之,船东在提单合约下也有权利为欠下的滞期费而去留置货物,而且不用区分是装港还是卸港产生的滞期费。

但这英国法律的立场与少数国家的法律有冲突,例如,The "Anwar Al Sabar"提及的埃及法律与《程租合约》一书提及的中国海商法(第78条款),对装港产生的滞期费要求在提单中明确注明,否则不准以留置货物手段索取。这一来,会令船东夹在当中;根据租约适用的英国法,他/它无权,也不必在租约提单中另加明示条款(即写明装港滞期费多少),只需依赖一般措辞的合并条款已有足够保障。但现实中,去了像埃及或中国的卸港,合并条款却被视为不是把装港欠下多少滞期费合并进来。而现实是卸港的法律立场才是重要的,因为留置货物一般要在卸港执行。

2.6.2.2 收货人是否要对产生的所有滞期费负责的探讨

照说,程租租约内的装卸时间与滞期费条款应在广泛的一般措辞的,提单合并条款下被包括在内。这种条款与货物付运、运输、交货与装卸有"直接关联"(directly germane)。但这是否意味着承租人欠下的滞期费(不论金额多高),收货人都要负上个人责任,因为提单合并了租约的滞期费条款呢?

在 The "Miramar"(1984)2 Lloyd's Rep. 129 先例,涉及的就是这一疑问。该先例涉及一大笔的滞期费(约25万美元),而且程租租约的第8条写明是:"承租人要支付滞期费每天多少…"(Charterer shall pay demurrage per running hour and pro-rate

…)。该租约也有第 21 条允许船东针对欠下的滞期费留置货物。

该先例的承租人倒闭,显然是不会支付船东任何滞期费了。于是船东在卸货后期留置货物(1 万多吨的柴油),并向收货人索取这笔欠下的滞期费。最后双方暂时和解,以收货人提供 15 万美元为担保,换取继续卸货/交货。

事后,双方去英国法院寻求对各项争议的判定。高院一审,Mustill 大法官判是:

(i)该租约提单的合并条款可以包括装卸时间与滞期费条款。

(ii)但租约的滞期费条款只写明是承租人要支付,而合并并不表示一定要去更改每一条款,把"承租人"自动改变为"收货人"或"提单持有人"。

(iii)而没有必要更改,或是不合理的更改,应予避免。

(iv)租约留置权条款也可包括在租约提单的合并条款内。

总结以上,Mustill 大法官拒绝去更改滞期费条款,将"承租人"改变为"收货人",即收货人并不负个人责任要代承租人支付滞期费(以租约所订的计算办法)。但是,船东有权为欠下的滞期费留置货物,不管最后是谁前来付清欠款以换取不再留置货物。Mustill 大法官说:"…I am of the opinion that cl. 21(留置权条款)can be incorporated into the bill of lading contract without any strain. If this is so, the incorporating words have produced a really useful practical result. The rights which the shipowner most wishes to preserve are those relating to his freight, dead-freight and demurrage. In theory, a power to sue the consignee directly in respect of the indebtedness will be of value. In practice, however, the shipowner is not really interested in litigating for his freight and demurrage. For practical purposes, what he needs is the capacity to enforce his claim on the spot, and for this purpose the lien is what matters…"

这段话的意思是船东并不关心能否向收货人起诉追讨运费与/或滞期费,他/它一向只关心能否通过留置货物去马上迫出这笔欠款,不论最后是承租人还是收货人或承押人(银行)愿意去支付。所以,不必再去更改滞期费条款令收货人负上一项"个人责任"(personal liability)。

故此 Mustill 大法官判船东可获担保的 15 万美元,但尚欠下的滞期费余数,船东不能向收货人追索,要求后者负责。

Mustill 大法官的判决为上诉庭与贵族院所支持。贵族院的 Diplock 勋爵也指出去任意更改条款令收货人要代承租人支付滞期费在某些情况下会带来不公平/不合理及说不清的问题。特别是一船货签发了几份租约提单给多位不同的收货人,合并的都是同一份程租租约。这一来,如何计算个别收货人负担的滞期费?几票货物早卸晚卸会否影响不同收货人应支付滞期费的多少(或早卸的根本不必支付)?会否船东可向每位收货人索取承租人应在租约支付的滞期费,以致加起来发大财?或是,船东可去挑一个收货人索取承租人欠下的滞期费,然后让该收货人向其他收货人要求分摊/补偿？所以，贵族院判是没有硬性"规定"（rule）是合并条款能包括的租约内容/条款，就可以自动去更改，以收货人替代承租人。每当这样做时仍要看看是否必要，是否合理公平。

这 The "Miramar"先例也不必太令船东/承运人担忧，实践中，有了对货物的留置权往往业已足够有保障。值得去向收货人个人索赔的情况是有，但不经常。若是卸港法纪不明，难以执行留置，英国法律倒也接受船舶去邻近港口留置。怕的是很不幸货价太低，留置权作用不大，而承租人是光棍，但收货人碰上大公司，船东/承运人才会动脑筋去拖收货人下水，指他要对欠款负上个人责任。但这看来不成，除非租约有滞期费条款（合并条款可将其包括在内）根本不必更改已完全在提单适用，例如，相关条款是"中止责任条款"（cesser clause），另再说明船东在卸港的滞期费直接与收货人结算，承租人不负责任。或是，租约条款已说明"承租人/收货人要支付滞期费"。而 The "Miramar"先例也印证了本章 2.6 小段所讲的解释合并条款要考虑必要性、合理性、公平性，同时也可以十分灵活。

2.6.3　针对船舱不清洁或不适合的租约条款

在 The "Garbis"（1982）2 Lloyd's Rep. 283，涉及一票石油（Naptha）从 Bahrain 装运去菲律宾。它的租约中同意了一条"不寻常"（unusual）条款（M6 条款）如下："Charterers agree that some colour drop in the clean Naptha parcel is acceptable and Charterers also agree that the clean Naptha parcel will be loaded into the two tar epoxy painted holds."

承租人（CIF/CFR 买卖的卖方）租入了一艘可能污染清洁货物的船舶，这会有多种原因。会是，收货人也知道此事，也无所谓，因货物受到小程度污染也可以接受。也会是，发货人/卖方匆忙中找不到清洁与适合的船舶，所以随便去租进一艘曾装过不清洁货物，不适当的船舶作为"权宜之计"。但这一来，船舶在卸港会面对收货人提出货物受污染的可能性很高，而责任也清楚，是船舶不适航、不适货。所以，即使承租人对船舱不清洁无所谓，在租约明示同意与接受，船东仍会担心提单又如何？是否也已合并有关条款，可去约束收货人同意与接受？

在 The "Garbis"，它的提单有一条十分广泛的合并条款如下："This shipment is carried under and pursuant to the terms of the Charter dated（租约日期）between（船东）and（承租人）as Charterers and all the terms whatsoever of the said Charter except the rate and payment of freight specified therein apply to and govern the rights of the parties concerned in this shipment."

争议是：租约的一条"不寻常"条款（M6 条款）可否以合并条款包括，而不必另在租约提单中明示？在仲裁庭，判是该条款"不寻常"（unusual），要在提单明示。当然,这样做会带来其他后果,例如,在信用证结汇中银行会对这份提单提出质疑。但该案上诉到高院,Goff 大法官推翻了裁决,并且判:

（ⅰ）同意该租约条款是不寻常。

（ⅱ）提单的合并条款是十分广泛的措辞/用字。

（ⅲ）要考虑的不应只限于寻常不寻常,也要去（或更重要的是去）考虑合并条款的措辞/用字是否广泛。

Goff 大法官的判词说:

"… The arbitrators concluded that it was not[277], because it was an unusual clause which a bill of lading holder would not have anticipated[278], and in the nature of an exclusion clause. On this point, I have formed a view different to that formed by the arbitrators[279]…

In my judgment, in applying these principles to a particular case, it is not enough simply to categorize the relevant terms as "unusual"[280] or as an "exclusion clause". The question to be asked is whether the words of incorporation in the bills of lading were wide enough to incorporate this particular condition[281], which is (as the arbitrators have held) an unusual condition…

…If a receiver of goods accepts a bill of lading in this form without ascertaining the terms of the charter – party[282], he must accept that his contract with the shipowner for the carriage of the goods, contained in or evidenced by the bill of lading, is subject to the charter – party terms relevant to the loading, carriage and discharge of the goods, even though they may be unusual terms[283] … Whether he has any recourse against, for example, the seller of the goods who endorsed the bill of lading over to him, must depend upon the terms of the relevant sale contract[284]."

但对 The "Garbis"先例,笔者仍有不少疑问,如:

---

[277] 仲裁庭认为这 M6 的不寻常条款没有被合并,不包括在合并条款内。
[278] 这不寻常条款不是提单合法持有人可以预期/估计得到的。
[279] 我（Goff 大法官）与仲裁庭看法不一样。
[280] 我认为光去分类何谓寻常或不寻常条款并不足够。要注意 Goff 大法官只是说"不足够"（not enough）,不是说完全无关或完全不重要。
[281] 主要仍是看提单的合并条款是否有足够广泛的措辞/用字。
[282] 收货人如果接受了一份有此广泛合并条款的租约提单而不先去了解其中的内容/条款。
[283] 他将来要受约束,只要租约的内容/条款是涉及装卸与运输同一票货物,这也包括了不寻常条款。
[284] 至于他将来可否去向卖方追偿,这是另一回事,要去看买卖合约。但针对船东而言,他（收货人）若受不寻常条款约束,表示再不能向船东采取索赔行动,例如,指证货物受到污染,除非该不寻常条款因违反海牙规则而无效。

（ⅰ）Goff 大法官所讲的如收货人在接受租约提单前可以、应该去了解合并的内容/条款与现实的做法不符。即使能先去了解并且不满意合并,也不是可以拒绝托收或/与结汇的理由。这一点稍后在 2.6.4.1 小段再详论。

（ⅱ）收货人若不能抗拒不寻常条款的合并,只能将来根据买卖合约向卖方追究,这就不能为收货人/买方提供本章 2.5 小段详述的与买卖合约相同的"合约权益与保障"（continuous documentary protection）,而在国际外贸这套制度的运行中,主要依赖文件/单证是相当重要的。

（ⅲ）提单通常印就的合并条款措辞/用字都十分广泛,现实中并不能令收货人/买方因此提高警觉而意识到包括了不寻常条款。

（ⅳ）Goff 大法官没有说明条款寻常或不寻常是否仍是考虑因素,只说是"不足够"。而后 Goff 大法官升任为勋爵。在后来的 The "K. H. Enterprise"（1994）1 Lloyd's Rep. 593 先例,针对的是另一种更加宽松、不去局限/控制的"合并",但 Goff 勋爵仍去把货方不大可能同意/接受的不寻常条款排除在"合并"外:这方面请看本章之 2.6 小段。

2.6.4　租约仲裁条款

这方面的问题,在进一步详论前,不妨先去节录笔者的《国际商务仲裁》一书第三章 14.1 与 14.2 小段如下:

　　这方面争论不少,其实是个简单的问题,纯是针对合并另一个合约的条款能包括些什么,范围去到哪里？班轮提单不会合并（incorporate）任何其他合约的条款,它去印上一条仲裁条款,在英美法下即有一条有效的仲裁条款,这毫无疑问。但在租约提单（charter - party bill of lading）,一般做法是靠合并租约的有关条款,写法会是:

　　"All terms and conditions of the charter - party dated（XX）to be in - corporated in this bill of lading."

　　然而,英美合约法对合并条款一直是限制在只有"与标的事项直接关联"（direct germane to subject matter）的才可以不必特别注明也能合并进去。其他"附属性条款"（ancilliary clauses/terms）,想要去合并就必须明示,而不能泛泛地靠一条一般的合并条款。这要求也完全合理,可令另一方当事人警惕。这要求也不只针对租约的仲裁条款（只是附属性条款）,还包括其他条款如索赔时效等:OK Petroleum v. Vitol（1995）2 Lloyd's Rep. 160。

　　所以,可以很简单地说明这问题:租约提单若没有明确表示租约的仲裁条款也一起合并进来,则提单并无仲裁协议在内。但如果说明合并包括了租约仲裁条款,则英美法完全接受提单也会有一有效的仲裁协议:The "Annefield"(1971)1 Lloyd's Rep. 1(英国):The "Sky Reefer"(1995)63 USLW 4617;AMC 1817(美国最高法院)。

租约提单越来越多地明示租约的仲裁条款已被合并进来,其中最重要的是 BIMCO 在 1994 年对 Congenbill 这一最常见,最多使用的租约提单格式的修正。该 1994 年版合并条款为:

"(1)All terms and conditions, liberties and exceptions of the Charter – party, dated as overleaf, including the Law and Arbitration Clause, are herewith incorporated."

考虑到今天的租约多数是伦敦仲裁条款,即表示今天很大部分的租约提单实际上已有一条有效的伦敦仲裁条款。收货人有货损货差的索赔,要保护一年的时效等,都会去伦敦仲裁。而有关法院,即使是接受了起诉,也会在被告马上申请中止(stay)之下根据 1958 年纽约公约非要中止诉讼不可。

这会对中国带来很大的冲击,因为中国进口的不少是散装货,买卖与结汇中常会使用 Congenbill 1994,变得非要去面对这多数是伦敦仲裁的事实。近年来,一有外轮在中国港口卸货发觉有货损货差,中国收货人与他的保险公司(如人保)往往就会在船离港前很快起诉并取得担保。之后,会在中国海事法院继续诉讼直至判决或庭外和解。这样的做法,往往对国内收货人很有利,因能掌握主动。

但今天面临 Congenbill 1994 的普及使用,外轮可马上申请法院中止诉讼,要求去伦敦仲裁。而因为涉及国际层面,估计海事法院一般也不会拒绝申请(笔者听闻是各有不同对待)。这一来,后果会是在不久的将来,中国海事法院、中国海事律师等有关人士将无事可干。至于中国收货人与他的货物保险公司,将会面对伦敦的昂贵与不方便诉讼,变得至少在较少金额的货损货差案,中方索性放弃。

去解决这个问题,我认为并不困难,因为美国已在考虑立例去否定提单中的外国仲裁条款,这是在 The "Sky Reefer"的判决后。基于的是同样的原因,即要去保护美国收货人与保险公司。所以,中国只要作出同样的一步就好了。而除了美国,澳大利亚亦有相似的立例,虽然它并非为了针对外国的仲裁条款而订:请看3.4.3.4 小段。

至于这样做会否违反了 1958 年纽约公约,我想美国肯定有强而有力的理由,而这也会适用于中国作出同样的立例。很随便地想想,已可估计到至少有两个以上的理由可作为借口:一是 1958 年纽约公约与另一国际公约(海牙规则)在这一点上有冲突,即提单中不能有减轻承运人责任的条款(这一直是美

256 提单及其他付运单证

国针对外国管辖权条款的说法）。二是这在中国发生的货损货差是不能仲裁的争议（arbitrability），这在本书本章节的§16段有详论，所以判提单的仲裁条款无效（null & void）。

不论怎样，我希望中国尽快去找出面对这不利局面的对策，以保护自己的巨大利益。"

此外笔者另一本书《禁令》第六章的最后一段，在节录了以上相同内容后，接下来写道：

综上所述，笔者这一年已碰过不少这种案件，中国货方/律师十分被动。有好几个案件是咨询，来自上海、北京等地。有一宗涉及广州，代表外轮的英国互保协会要聘请笔者出一份书面意见，请求广州海事法院中止审理，迫中国货方去伦敦仲裁，笔者因为不再接案而拒绝了。另一宗案件涉及80万美元的索赔，进口货是鱼粉，大概是青岛海事法院以提单合并了租约的伦敦仲裁条款为由而中止审理，反正详情笔者不清楚，只是笔者被中国货方任命为仲裁员。笔者也欣然接受，今天笔者也接受为数不多的伦敦仲裁的仲裁员任命。但后来在细看了该案租约的伦敦仲裁条款后，发觉有一句说："仲裁员必须居住在伦敦"（The arbitrator (s) shall be resident (s) in London）。换言之，笔者会不符合对仲裁员的资格要求，所以马上辞退，让货方另去任命另一位伦敦仲裁员，因为一年的时效已很紧迫。

总而言之，这重大困难在处处严重影响中国货方，代位的保险公司、海事法院与律师。希望有权利改变此状况的人士尽快行动，不要多花时间在收集一百个、二百个不同意见去慢慢分析上，反正社会科学的事情总有话说。只要看一点，美国也这样做了，去用立法抢回对提单的管辖权，这还会错吗？美国又不是发展中国家，它会不知轻重，不明事理就去做出不保障自己利益的事吗？

2.6.4.1　英美法律不接受一般的合并条款可以包括租约的仲裁条款

这一方面的英国先例可真不少，随意可去挑出如 Hamilton & Co. v. Mackie & Sons (1889) 5 T. L. R. 677；T. W. Thomas & Co. Ltd. v. Portsea S. S. Co. Ltd. (1912) A. C. 1；The "Njegos" (1935) 53 Lloyd's Rep. 286；The "Merak" (1964) 2 Lloyd's Rep. 527；The "Phonizien" (1966) 1 Lloyd's Rep. 150；The "Annefield" (1971) 1 Lloyd's Rep. 1；The "Rena K" (1978) 1 Lloyd's Rep. 545；The "SLS Everest" (1981) 2 Lloyd's Rep. 389；The "Varenna" (1983) 2 Lloyd's Rep. 592；The "Nai Matteini" (1988) 1 Lloyd's Rep. 452；The "Nerano" (1994) 2 Lloyd's Rep. 50；The "Heidberg" (1994) 2 Lloyd's Rep. 287 等。

而英国法律在这一方面的立场，可去节录 Brandon 大法官在 The "Rena K" 先例所说的如下:"A long series of authorities has established that, where a charter-party contains an arbitration clause providing for arbitration of disputes arising under it, general words in a bill of lading incorporating into it all the terms and conditions, or all the terms, conditions and clauses, of such charter-party, are not sufficient to bring such arbitration clause into the bill of lading so as to make its provisions applicable to disputes arising under that document…"(有一连串的先例已明确了在提单以一条一般性措辞的合并条款是不足以将租约内的仲裁条款包括在内的)。

2.6.4.2　提单可以合并租约仲裁条款的办法之一:仲裁条款既针对租约,也针对提单

这种说法是来自 The"Merak"(1964) 2 Lloyd's Rep. 527 先例。一般租约的仲裁条款措辞上只是针对租约下的争议要去哪里或/与如何仲裁(仲裁庭人数,适用规则,等等)。该条款会在一开始说:"All disputes arising out of this charter-party…",或是说:"Any disputes relating to or in connection with this charter-party…"。但在 The "Merak",租约仲裁条款一开始说:"Any dispute arising out of this charter or any bill of lading issued hereunder…(接下去是说仲裁的细节)"。

即是条款写明既针对租约,也针对提单的争议。这一来,上诉庭判是租约提单一般措辞的合并已可去包括这种措辞/文字的租约仲裁条款。有人质疑这判决,因为无辜的提单持有人仍是没有被警觉。他只看到手中的一份租约提单有一条一般措辞的合并条款(如"All the terms, conditions, clauses and exceptions contained in the said charter-party apply to this bill of lading and are deemed to be incorporated herein"),他怎会知道租约仲裁条款是怎样的写法? 而租约的一种写法会影响到提单同样的合并条款可以包括仲裁条款,换了另一种写法却不包括似有不合理之处,毕竟提单是另一份合约。

话虽是说(如 2.6.3 小段的 The"Garbis"(1982) 2 Lloyd's Rep. 283 先例)收货人可先去了解租约的内容/条款才接受提单,但现实中做不到,或不是这样操作。这在笔者的《信用证》一书第六章 1.4 小段有略述。首先,针对信用证的 UCP 500,Article 25 (b)说:

即使信用证要求提交与租船合同提单有关的租船合同,银行对该租船合同不予审核,但银行将予以照转而不承担责任。

《信用证》一书接下去说:

Article 25 (b)是值得多去探讨的另一处主要不同,即银行不去检查租约条

款,即使一套单证文件中包括了一份租约。毕竟,租约不容易看得明白。但现实中信用证明确要求附一份租约的情况不多,因为即使是注明"允许租约提单结汇",也不存在合并的租约也要一齐递交的要求:S. I. A. T. di dal Ferro v. Tradax Overseas S. A. (1978) 2 Lloyd's Rep. 470; (1980) 1 Lloyd's Rep. 53。

这毕竟做起来不容易:在 1.2.2.3 小段谈到特别在短航次,租约成立只是通过电传与传真。而其中双方同意了的条款会是要去仔细比较,整理双方在谈判中的来往通信,这需要时间去备妥一份租约,再由各散东西的船东承租人签字。但届时船舶可能早已去了装港装货,所以根本来不及送一份签好字的租约给卖方让其与租约提单一起拿去结汇。的确,因为整理、备妥以及让双方签署一份租约既需时间又很麻烦,不少短航次根本不去理会这一步的例行手续。反正航次完毕,双方履了约,没有什么纠纷,也就结束档案了。

另一个困难是,签字的租约只有一份,但同一航次的租约提单会多于一份。这一来,有几点要注意:

(a) CIF 或 CFR 的买方如果想有一份租约,了解租约提单到底合并了什么,他应在信用证上提出要求。或是,在买卖合约加一条款说装货后一个星期(不等),卖方要提供一份有关的租约。如果买卖合约合并了 Incoterms 1990,它也有要求卖方提供一份副本(不是正本)租约……

因此总结起来,现实做法中收货人/租约提单持有人经常看不到合并的一份租约,可去让他了解其中内容如仲裁条款是如何写法[但 Steel 大法官 Thyssen v. Calypso (2000) 2 Lloyd's Rep. 243 一案中认为,收货人设法取得一份合并的租约并不存在任何不现实的情况: the claimants had failed to show that it was not reasonably practicable to obtain a copy of the charter party]。这或许是由于没出事他就不予理会,或没有权马上去要求卖方提供一份租约(只要买卖合约没有合并 Incoterms),或是根本不存在有备案/签字的一份租约(fixture 只是一份传真确认双方同意的主要条款的文件,加上多份传真对租约细节谈判与最后同意版本的记录)的缘故。而法律的地位也支持没必要在一份租约后随附上其提单。所以,一般措辞的提单合并条款如果可以合并/包括租约的仲裁条款,只因该仲裁条款明示适用在提单争议,很容易令收货人上当,例如,在某国家法院起诉,索赔货损货差,但提单若有仲裁条款他去起诉应是根据仲裁条款来做。结果错误的做法除了劳民伤财外,还会令海牙规则的一年时效逝去。而这在今天的英国法律下是不予同情的:The "K. H. Enterprise" (1994) 1 Lloyd's Rep. 593。而且 1996 年的英国仲裁法 Section 12 下延长仲裁时效(即使能去这样做,因海牙规则也是以合约的形式适用)也极不容易,因对延长的尺度已大大收紧。

第四章　提单作用之二：运输合约的形式与有关条款的分析/探讨　259

但不论对 The"Merak"先例是满意还是质疑，看来这已是英国法律的立场，且也被后来的判例所认同，例如，在 The"Annefield"（1970）2 Lloyd's Rep. 252, Brandon 大法官说："First, in order to decide whether a clause under a bill of lading incorporates an arbitration clause in a charter-party...Fourthly, where the arbitration clause by its terms applies both to disputes under the charter-party and to disputes under the bill of lading, general words of incorporation will bring the clause into the bill of lading so as to make it applicable to disputes under that document."

显然，Brandon 大法官以上的讲话是针对 The"Merak"先例的。

2.6.4.3　提单可以合并租约仲裁条款的办法之二：明示合并仲裁条款

租约提单若是明示去合并程租租约的仲裁条款，这在"解释"（construction）上所得的结果会很不一样，再也不是本章2.3小段所指的该仲裁条款"不是直接关联"（not directly germane），或是2.4小段所指的该仲裁条款只是"附属性条款"（ancillary terms/clauses）而可去否定它了。

在 The"Rena K"（1971）1 Lloyd's Rep. 545 先例，租约提单的合并条款的措辞/文字是："All terms, clauses, conditions and exceptions including the Arbitration Clause, the Negligence Clause and the Cesser Clause of the Charter-party dated London 13 April 1977 are hereby incorporated."

Brandon 大法官判如此去明示，可成功地在提单中合并相关租约的仲裁条款。他说："...the further specific words 'including the Arbitration Clause', The additions of these words must, as it seems to me, mean that the parties to the bills of lading intended the provisions of the arbitration clause in the charter-party to apply in principle to disputes arising under the bills of lading; and if it is necessary, as it obviously is, to manipulate or adapt[285] part of the wording of that clause in order to give effect to that intention, then I am clearly of the opinion that this should be done."

这样解释确有道理，也符合合约法精神和公平合理的要求。首先，不管它合并不合并，光是有"仲裁"一字出现在一份合约（不论是提单或是任何其他合约），在今天支持商业仲裁的大环境之下已会被视为是一份有效的仲裁协议。这方面可去参阅笔者的《国际商务仲裁》一书第三章之11.2小段谈到的简漏的仲裁协议也是有效的论述，如在 Hobbs Padgett & Co. Ltd. v. FC Kirkland Ltd. and Kirdland (1969) 2 Lloyd's Rep. 547 之第549页；The"Petr Shmidt"（1995）1 Lloyd's Rep. 202。而公平合理的是租约提单既有此明示，收货人/提单持有人在起诉时应向卖方或/与承运人

---

[285]　这租约仲裁条款合并进提单显然要去更改一些文字，如"All disputes arising out of this charter-parties..."改为"All disputes arising out of this bill of lading..."。

查查合并的仲裁条款到底是怎样一回事，有此明示应足够给予他警示去小心，去多加了解后才行动。

而今天的租约提单，已越来越多是这样的做法。像被最普遍使用的标准租约提单格式 Congenbill 199（附录八），它印就的合并条款就是："All terms and conditions, liberties and exceptions of the Charter Party, datedas overleaf, including the law and Arbitration Clause[286], are herewith incorporated."

2.6.4.4 提单成功合并租约仲裁条款的弊端/不利之处

这方面在一开始的 2.6.4 小段所节录的内容中已有详论。在此仍可作一总结如下：

（ⅰ）租约提单毕竟仍是颇受船东影响，例如，船长或代理人在签发提单时要求加上仲裁条款。一般发货人只要不影响结汇也就不加理会，他也可能是所懂的业务知识不足与船东抗衡。总之，后果是在租约提单要求明示加上合并租约的仲裁条款并不难。去使用 Congenbill 1994 标准格式已是这种情况，可达致这样的结果。

而假若合并的仲裁条款是去南极仲裁，或去莫名其妙的国家仲裁，那岂非就是船东赖掉对货损货差责任的一种上佳办法？这正是美国最高法院在 The "Sky Reefer"（1995）63 USLW 4617；AMC 1817 所表示的担忧之处。照说这也是英国法院的相同立场：请参阅本书第五章之 4.2.3.1.5 小段介绍的 The "Morviken"（1983）1 Lloyd's Rep. 1 先例与 Diplock 勋爵的讲话，它说明船东/承运人以提单的适用法条款（或管辖权条款）取巧去减轻或逃避对货物的责任，在海牙规则下一样会被视为无效。

（ⅱ）今天租约的仲裁条款，十之七八去伦敦仲裁。以往租约提单下的争议（主要是货损货差，但也会是其他方面），管辖权是在各国各地的法院，如中国的海事法院，因为提单通常没有仲裁条款。今天以及将来，若租约提单普遍去明示合并租约的伦敦仲裁条款，会导致伦敦仲裁生意额倍增，而其他国家（包括像美国、中国）的法院会大受影响，管辖权被剥夺，由伦敦仲裁所取代。这些国家的律师、收货人、保险人等也会受到严重的不利影响。

（ⅲ）说是说 1958 年的纽约公约的签约国（英国与中国都是）必须尊重一条有效的仲裁条款，但这国际公约没有想到提单这份合约是罕有的并非依订约双方意愿而成立的合约。这提单合约的合约关系（收货人与船东/承运人之间）是立法（提单法）强加到他们的头上。

（ⅳ）难怪，美国为保障本国利益已立法去针对提单内的外国仲裁条款。这立法就是新的美国海上运输法。另外，汉堡规则在这方面有对货方十分有利的条款，

---

[286] 明示把租约的仲裁条款合并在提单内。

见 Article 22。例如,一艘丹麦船从东京运货去悉尼,提单有一条伦敦仲裁条款。收货人受仲裁约束,但汉堡规则允许其去丹麦、东京、悉尼或伦敦仲裁。

(v)据知中国海事法院对此问题仍是有不同的做法/判法。但照说,严格或光靠"解释"(construction)租约提单,如使用 Congenbill 1994 标准格式,是很难去否定/漠视确有这明示的"仲裁条款"(Arbitration Clause)清楚写在提单的合并条款的。这一来,该条款(Arbitration Clause)代表什么呢?法官不是订约方,不由他任意去删除明示的措辞与/或条款。在笔者看来,正规与全面的做法仍会要像美国一样,去立例/立法改变这不利的情况。

2.6.4.5 提单合并伦敦仲裁条款对收货人最危险之处:时效已逝

直至中国能去立例/立法改变这不利的局面,或另想出其他国际上认可的解决办法前,中国收货人/货方与代位的保险公司务必要去了解这方面对他/它们的危险。而其中最危险的是针对索赔货损货差海牙/海牙·维斯比规则所规定的一年时效。

众所周知,收货人要保护一年时效,是要去法院起诉(在英国法院就是去出告票)或去开始仲裁(若提单内有仲裁条款)的。英国法律的地位一向是,去保护时效就要在正确的诉讼地点采取行动,一点都错不得。故在 Compagnia Colombiana de Seguros v. Pacific Steam Navigation Co. (1963) 2 Lloyd's Rep. 479,提单有英国管辖权条款。美国收货人为货损而去索赔,却在美国起诉,出了"告船告票"(in rem writ)。后来因种种原因没有在美国行动下去(原因会是诸如船舶不往来美国等),于是收货人转而去英国法院起诉,但当时一年时效已届。收货人争辩在这一年内,它已在美国法院出了告票,应已中断了一年的时效。但英国法院支持船东,判是要以最后与正确无误的诉讼地点为准,要保护一年时效也要在该地保护,而在其他国家法院出的告票不能去代为保护。

这导致收货人每每要去出大量保护时效的告票在船舶可能会出没的港口,这常是劳民伤财之举。而且,有部分国家没有这种做法,或是出告票十分昂贵(如法院收费是根据索赔金额的百分比)。

而能成功在某港口送达告票并以扣船取得诉前保全,并不表示保得住管辖权。船东/承运人会成功申请"中止"(stay),因为说服了法院有更适合的外国法院或提单合约的外国法院管辖权条款应被尊重。最后决定中止或不中止,英国法律是以法官的裁量权为准。这一切的详论可参阅笔者的《禁令》一书第六章。

以往,若是外国法院更适合,有更密切与真实的关系,或该外国是提单合约的明示管辖权地点,但一年时效已逝。而如果英国法院不中止让官司继续下去,原告的收货人则不会面对时效已逝的困境。这样一来,就会影响法官去中止的裁量权,因为一中止也就等于判了原告的索赔"死刑"。所以,船东/承运人为了博取法官同情,常在申请中止的同时向法院承诺不会在更适合的外国法院以时效已逝为抗辩:The "Blue Wave" (1982) 1 Lloyd's Rep. 151; The "Adhigunda Meranti" (1981) HKLR 904。

但在 The "Spiliada" (1987) 1 Lloyd's Rep. 1, Goff 勋爵看来已把这一点仅当做是中立/中性的因素来考虑。Goff 勋爵说:"Suppose that the plaintiff allowed the limitation period to elapse in the appropriate jurisdiction, and came here simply because he wanted to take advantage of a more generous time bar applicable in this country; or suppose that it was obvious that the plaintiff should have commenced proceedings in the appropriate jurisdiction, and yet he did not trouble to issue a protective writ there; in cases such as these, I cannot see that the court should hesitate to stay the proceedings in this country, even though the effect would be that the plaintiff's claim would inevitably be defeated by a plea of the time bar in the appropriate jurisdiction."

这一来,原告的收货人可能就要多做不少工夫。例如像 The "K. H. Enterprise" (1994) 1 Lloyd's Rep. 593,有关的提单有一条台湾管辖条款。但收货人不一定想在台湾起诉,或该处扣不了船去索取诉前保全。根据出事船舶的营运,可能去的港口(而且适合对物诉讼与扣船)是香港、新加坡与英国港口。这就表示收货人出于小心,要在台湾、香港、新加坡与英国都去采取行动保护时效。否则在香港成功诉船/扣船,却被船东成功申请中止,而且香港法院不理睬在台湾法院(是明示管辖地,也被视为更适合)一年时效已逝的事实,收货人可就惨了。

估计出于同情无所适从的收货人在这方面的困境,曾有案例如 The "Kapetan Markos" (1986) 1 Lloyd's Rep. 211 与 The "Nordglimt" (1987) 2 Lloyd's Rep. 470 判是收货人/货方只要在一个有适当管辖权的法院(不需要是最后进行诉讼的法院)在一年时效内出了保护告票,就可以保护海牙/海牙·维斯比规则的时效。在 The "Nordglimt",货物是 1984 年 1 月份在吉大港卸下,结果发现有货损。在刚好一年内的 1985 年 1 月 8 日,收货人在比利时(装港)法院向承运人起诉(诉人)。但因为没有诉前担保,收货人 1987 年 4 月 16 日又在英国另去开始诉船/对物诉讼。但显然,当时一年时效已逝,而承运人也以此点作为在英国法院的抗辩。但 Hobhouse 大法官不接受这说法,判定:"the proceedings in personam Belgium, having been started in Belgium within time and it being accepted that both parties and the Court were competent, the defendants' liability had not been discharged under art. III, r. 6 [287]; the liability which was the subject matter of the English action continued to exist upon the true construction

---

[287] 被告(船东/承运人)的责任并不因海牙规则的IV⑥条款下的一年时效已逝可以免除,因为在比利时法院的诉人行动已在一年内开始了。

of the bill of lading and the legislation to which it was subject[288]; the defendants could not assert that the suit had not been brought within the relevant period[289] and their case that the plaintiffs had no subsisting cause of action upon which to sue failed[290]."但这些案例又带来讲不通的新问题,导致英国法律在这一课题上又在向收货人/货方的原告收紧要求。这有一连串的案例如 The "Amazona"(1989)2 Lloyd's Rep. 130;The "Havhelt"(1993)1 Lloyd's Rep. 523 和 The"Finnrose"(1994)1 Lloyd's Rep. 559 等。

在 The"Finnrose",Rix 大法官提到讲不通的地方是:

(ⅰ)原告收货人可否在英国法院[应算是"恰当与可靠的"(proper and competent)法院]一年时效内出一张告票而不送达,所以船东/承运人根本不知道有其事。然后,收货人任由该告票失效。但会否是,从此收货人可在 6 年内任意去任何国家的法院(该国家也有 6 年时效)起诉,因为较早时已保护了海牙/海牙·维斯比规则的一年时效?

(ⅱ)若原告的收货人在一年时效内出了告票,也去送达,诉船并扣船。但后来因原告自己推进诉讼延误/怠慢,导致索赔被法院"撤销"(strike out for want of prosecution)。这一来,收货人可否另去英国法院或外国法院起诉,指一年时效已被早先一个及时行动的诉讼所保护了?

所以,在 Thyssen v. Calypso(2000)2 Lloyd's Rep. 243,涉及一票钢材货物运去美国费城,但发生货损。租约提单是 Congenbill 标准格式(请参阅 2.6.4.3 小段),也合并了租约的仲裁条款。收货人在美国法院及时出了告票,但这诉讼最终被船东成功向美国法院申请中止。这应是类同于 The "Sky Reefer"(1995)63 USLW 4617;AMC 1817 的 Supreme Court 的判决,因为直至美国改了立法(新的海上运输法),美国法律仍是受制于 1958 年的纽约公约;这方面在 2.6.4.4 小段已有谈及。

但该美国收货人去伦敦仲裁,发觉一年时效已逝,而船东也以此点来抗辩。因此,收货人被迫向英国高院申请:

(ⅰ)宣告一年时效已被美国法院较早的诉讼(虽最后被中止)所保护。

(ⅱ)若一年时效确实已过,要求法院以 1996 年仲裁法之 Section 12 去延长时效。

但以上申请均被拒绝,等于索赔"死亡"。

在(ⅰ),Steel 大法官认为,若说收货人去任何可以诉船(in rem)的法院出一张告票就从此可保护了海牙/海牙·维斯比规则的一年时效是不可接受、不可思议

---

[288] 英国的诉船/诉物行动只是同一诉讼的延续。
[289] 被告(船东/承运人)不能以时效已逝为由抗辩。
[290] 被告对原告(收货人)再没有诉因的指称。

的。他也考虑了 The "Finnrose" 先例。估计 Steel 大法官也受到仲裁条款的影响,因为有 1958 年纽约公约,表示更难去回避仲裁。而收货人不去采取保护仲裁时效的行动,更是难辞其咎。Steel 大法官说:"It is not enough for the correct claimant[291] to commence proceedings before a competent court[292] against the correct defendant[293]. The proceedings must remain valid and effective at the time when the carrier seeks to rely on rule 6[294] in the second set of proceedings[295]. Thus where the first action has been dismissed for want of prosecution[296] or stayed by reason of the invocation of an arbitration clause[297], suit has not been brought[298]."

在(ⅱ),Steel 大法官鉴于 1996 年仲裁已大大收紧了时效的延长,而收货人错过时效又谈不上是"无法预见"(outside the reasonable contemplation)或是船东有"不公平"(unjust)行为,因此收货人的申请无法达到立法可允许延长时效的先决条件。

总结以上,中国收货人/货方与代位的保险公司应可看到这方面的危险。或许,货方也不要把解决这方面问题的责任全都推给中国海事法院与立法者,毕竟中国是 1958 年纽约公约的签约国,有一定难处。不妨这样,今后中国买方买货,干脆就在买卖合约与信用证上明示要求一套提单正面写上"没有仲裁条款在本提单"(no arbitration clause in this bill of lading)的字样。若是班轮运输,发货人/卖方会难以办到,因为改不了班轮提单条款。但换了是租约提单,照说发货人/卖方这样做只是举手之劳,而这已可以免除收货人的"百日之忧"了。

而按目前做法,即使能在中国海事法院成功扣船,但由于外国船东会去申请中止,因此中国收货人要有两手准备,例如,在一年时效将届满前在伦敦提起仲裁,以保护时效,给被告船东的一份传真可以说:"纯是为了万一要保护时效,无损我目前抗拒中止的行动而且我坚决认为提单没有有效仲裁条款,我已指定了杨良宜为仲裁员……"(Solely for the purpose of protecting time bar if it shall becomes relevant, and entirely without prejudice to our present action in resisting a stay before the Chinese Maritime Court which we deem the bill of lading does not have a valid arbitration clause, we

---

[291]　"准确"的原告是指本书第三章 §9 段谈及的有提单合约诉权的货方/收货人。
[292]　原告去一个恰当的法院起诉。
[293]　向"准确"的被告(本书第三章 §2 段谈及的提单合约内的承运人)及时起诉并不足够。
[294]　这 rule 6 是海牙规则的一年时效。
[295]　必须是在进行第二个诉讼时,第一个诉讼(有保护 1 年的时效)仍然有效。
[296]　若第一个诉讼已因怠慢而被法院撤销。
[297]　或是因为违反有效的仲裁条款而被法院中止。
[298]　等于从未在海牙规则的一年时效内起诉。

have appointed Mr Philip Yang as our arbitrator[299]...）

但一开始仲裁,会给船东机会去推进以造成"既成事实"。中国收货人可以请求仲裁庭暂缓推进,先等待中国海事法院决定是否中止,但仲裁庭不一定听从。这最后会导致的结果仍是由伦敦仲裁审理,把案子从中国海事法院抢过去。这表示做法上可能要更加取巧,例如指定一位很忙碌的仲裁员,甚至是中国的仲裁员,估计在其如此繁忙下不会很快推进仲裁。这一课题在本书第五章之4.2.10.2.5小段还会论及到其他方面。

2.6.5 针对无单放货的租约条款

在本书第二章之5.1.12与5.2.2小段,谈到程租租约在这方面的明示条款。会有疑问是:这针对货物交付的租约条款可否以一般措辞/文字的合并条款包括入租约提单内? 若是可以,对船东会有极大影响,因为无单放货事关重大。而本来租约下是承租人有权要求无单放货,并由承租人提供担保,一旦成功合并,经过修改,在提单下就变了是收货人有权要求无单放货,并由收货人提供担保:"The vessel to release the cargo without original bill of lading against Consignee's letter of indemnity in accordance with Owner's P&I Club wording."

但很可能船东肯去接受租约这种条款就是基于承租人财雄势大,例如是大石油公司。若是换了其他人/其他公司,例如可能是光棍或身在难以对付国家的收货人,船东肯定会坚持要有国际一流银行的保函才肯无单放货了。

可是船东能以什么理由去抗拒租约提单内的一条一般措辞的合并条款将租约内的无单放货的条款包括入内呢? 说是2.3小段的"不是直接关联"（not directly germane）有不通之处;说是2.4小段的"附属性条款"（ancillary terms/clauses）又不像。看来,还是要以2.6小段的说法,即该无单放货条款是"不寻常"（unusaul）,也不公平合理的,所以一般措辞的提单合并条款并不足以将其包括。或是,即使可以包括,也不能把承租人更改为收货人,让后者去提供担保以换取无单放货。若以此说法为据,读者应去参阅前文有关的段节如在2.6.3小段介绍的 The "Garbis"（1982）2 Lloyd's Rep. 283（判不寻常条款不影响合并）与2.6.2.2小段介绍的 The "Miramar"（1984）2 Lloyd's Rep. 129（判有必要,公平合理才去更改租约条款,以利适用在提单内）。笔者迄今仍未见到这一方面的案例,但估计会是接近 The "Miramar"先例的判法,毕竟 The "Miramar"是贵族院的判例,在时间上也较后。

---

[299] 如何指定仲裁员要看仲裁条款的准确措辞/用字。

§3 班轮提单

班轮提单的内容/条款是由班轮公司一早单方面拟定,并印妥班轮提单合约格式以供将来普及与大量使用的。它不像租约提单去合并另一份程租租约,也不会有这份程租租约的存在,因为业务上的做法不同。这一切已在第三章之4.1小段有详论。在此,笔者只去详论和分析这种提单内一般常见的内容与条款。而提单格式是以本书附录八的 Conlinebill 2000(仍在草拟阶段)为准,虽然各班轮公司会有不同的条款/内容。

3.1 条款字体太小的影响

班轮提单背面的明示条款密密麻麻,字体很小(否则在一页纸内写不下),这早已为人所批评。例如,Scrutton 大法官在很早的 Paterson, Zochonis & Co. v. Elder, Dempster & Co. (1922) 13 Lloyd's Rep. 513 先例的 517 页说:"Like many other Judges, I desire to protest against the extremely illegible condition of this bill of lading. Shipowners have had a good deal of warning from the courts; and some day they will find themselves deprived of the protection of their exceptions on the ground that they have not given reasonable notice of them as terms of the contract."

说真的,实际上不论字大字小,都不影响发货人。发货人根本不会去看它(班轮提单背面的内容/条款)。他们既看不懂,也漠不关心(运输风险不在他们头上),而且就算不满意也无能为力。但做戏仍要做得好看,故此班轮公司仍是不遗余力地花时间花金钱(例如请著名的大律师/专家来拟定一条密不透风的条款)去不断完善它的班轮提单。这才能在将来出了事故时,班轮公司可以凭背面的某一条款说:"不关我的事,没有我的责任,我对无单放货(误交货)没有严格责任等,而这是双方'意愿'的运输合约条款规定的。"

而争议去了法院或仲裁庭,也会将条款当做是双方的"意愿"来解释。其实这是做戏,已经说过,不论发货人还是收货人都谈不上对此班轮提单条款有意愿。虽然收货人有海牙规则立法去强制的保障,但看来范围太窄,因它连准确与妥善交货的问题都不针对(这方面可去看本书第二章之5.6.2小段),看来或许需要更广泛的国际公约/立法,有类同于英国保护消费者立法的1977年"不公平合约法"(Unfair Contract Terms Act)或是更广泛的针对,才能真正在各重要方面去保护收货人,保证一份提单作为物权凭证能真正赢得买方或/与其他人士的信心,信任与肯定。

不把话题扯得太远,再回头去讨论提单背面条款字体太小的问题。在解释一份文件或合约(不光是提单,它只是千万种合约中的一种)时,若在一个极端的例子,合约文件简直看不出有文字,好像武侠小说中的一份"无字天书",或是只有一些难辨的符号,另一订约方难以去理解,很难说内中有什么是双方订约时意愿的明示条款。而换一个稍为不那么极端的例子,要解释一份文件与/或合约的条款/内容,但其内的字迹很潦草(用手写的文件/合约),也很小(用放大镜才看得见),甚至在语言/文字上是俄文。这一来,是否也可以同样的理由指称订约时不会有另一合约方(非拟定合约的一方)的意愿,因为他/它无法理解呢?

合理的分水线应是,难看(字体小,外文等)不表示可以不看,不去解释。否则今后就难有合约与合约条款了,因很容易就会被推翻/否定。但若到了一个程度是不光难看,而且无法合理地去看得到内容/条款,无从去理解,那就可以去推翻/否定了。以此为大原则/大精神,它也应适用在提单以及其他千千万万不同种类的合约中。若是提单合约可以作为例外,将来定会有其他合约也试图作为例外对待,那么法律就会变得不肯定与混乱。

因此,英国法院虽然对班轮公司的做法有一定敌意,倒也不会轻易以班轮提单的字体太小实在"难看",难理解为由去否定它的条款。在 Wilson v. Cie des Messageries Maritimes (1954) 1 Lloyd's Rep. 229 的澳大利亚先例,就有这种反映。但在 The "Iran Vojdan" (1984) 2 Lloyd's Rep. 380, Bingham 大法官曾判提单中一条适用法条款因看不清楚而无效。他说:"on the basis that the proper law was German, applying that law it appeared that the clause would be treated as invalid because the conditions were not decipherable."

除英国法院外,其他国家的法院对班轮公司会有更大的敌意。在荷兰法院,The "Bundesgerichtshof" May 30, 1983 (1984) ETL217 判是要用放大镜才看得见的提单内容/条款不被视为是合约的一部分,因而无效。而在美国法院,更有不少先例去否定字体过小的提单条款,如所谓的"fine print": Allstate chs. Co. v. Int'1 Shipping Corp. 1985 AMC 760 (11 Cir. 1983); Nemeth v. General S. S. Corp. 1983 AMC 885 (9 Cir. 1982); Calmaquip Eng. West Hemisphere v. West Coast Carriers 1984 AMC 839 (5 Cir. 1981); The "Hong Kong Producer" (1969) 2 Lloyd's Rep. 536. 德国法院亦有类似先例,是 Allianz v. Indian Steamship Co. 11 Z. R., 135/82, 30.5.1983。

3.2 Conlinebill 前页的总结条款

3.2.1 简介

在本书附录八的 Conlinebill 2000,前页有许多空白格子以供填上各项资料/内容,但另有一条款总结性地针对了多方面,可以节录如下:

"SHIPPED onboard [300] in apparent good order and condition, weight, measure, marks, numbers, quality, contents and value unknown,[301] for carriage to the Port of discharge[302] or so near thereunto as the vessel may safely get[303] and lie always afloat, to be delivered in the like good order and condition at the Port of discharge unto the Consignee or its assignees,[304] on payment of freight as indicated to the right plus other charges incurred in accordance with the provisions contained in this Bill of Lading.[305] In accepting this Bill of Lading the Merchant expressly accepts and agrees to all its stipulations on both Page 1 and Page 2,[306] whether written, printed, stamped or otherwise incorporated, as fully as if they were all signed by the Merchant.

When consigned to order one original Bill of lading must be surrendered duly endorsed in exchange for the cargo delivery order.[307] IN WITNESS whereof the Carrier, Master or their Agent has signed the number of original Bills of Lading stated below, all of this tenor and date, one of which being accomplished, the others to be void[308]."

3.2.2 邻近条款与其他自由条款的有效性

上一小段注[309]谈到提单前页有一条"邻近条款"(near clause),这一条款通常也出现在程租租约,这已在笔者的《程租合约》一书有详论。不妨先去节录该书第七章§4段如下:

> 在本章 3.6.5 小段已重申过,港口一经列名或指定,船东一定要去履约,除非是受阻。该段也提到,不论有任何延误,时间上的损失也是由船东自己承担。

---

[300] 这是装船提单。
[301] 这一条"否定性批注"(disclaimer)的有效性及其他有关方面在本书第六章之§5段有详论,请参阅。
[302] 承运人承诺把货物运往提单前页填上的卸港。
[303] 这一条称为"邻近条款"(near clause),作用在于减轻承运人要去列名卸港的严格责任。这条款有进一步详述的必要,将在注脚之后再去谈论。
[304] 承运人承诺在卸港把货物如同装上船时般完整无误地交给收货人或他/它的受让人。
[305] 交出货物的同时承运人有权收取/获得支付运费和其他在提单欠下的金钱,注意措辞/文字并不只提滞期费,因为这不一定与班轮有关:这一点已在本书多处谈及,如本章之§1段。
[306] 明示货方接受本套提单也就同时接受前页与后页的条款/内容,受到约束。注意它不是去合并租约,故没有合并条款。
[307] 若是指示提单,交货时收货人必须退回一份正本提单以换取船东的交货单。这一点请参阅本书第二章之 1.5.6.1 小段与 5.1.4 小段。
[308] 有关这一条款,在本书第二章之 5.1.4 小段有详论。
[309] 303

这"邻近条款"也在本章 3.3 小段提到过,它是金康租约的第 1 条。有了这条款,文字上去看船东所答应的装港应是(例):"上海或邻近的船可安全前往的地方"(Shanghai or so near thereto as she may safely get)。船东并未说死他承诺一定去上海。

在 The "Varing" (1931) P.79 的先例,这"邻近条款"下是由船东去选择,去受益,去免除他必须去所同意的装卸港的绝对责任(除非是租约受阻)。

也是因为它有免责的味道,所以有一个说法是若订租约时船东已明知自己虽然答应了,但实际上不会去上海,而只会去邻近的宁波,这不会被允许。要知道,这样开承租人的玩笑会要他的命。如是装港,待装的货物在上海,船东去了宁波,你说承租人该怎么办?把货物转运去宁波港?这方面的费用及时间浪费可不得了。但别忘了,船东没有违约,他在租约下只应允去上海或邻近地区。所以,若船东订约前就单方面知道自己会去依赖免责条款,而不会去履行合约主旨的话,那么去援引这"邻近条款"是不允许的:The "Angelia" (1972) 2 Lloyd's Rep. 154 等。

但在订约后,不论是列名或承租人后来指定港口,如果发生任何会带来船舶延误或额外使费的事情,船东可在合理情况下去邻近港口装或卸。这包括 3.6.5 小段所讲的暂时不安全的情况。

所以,在 The "Alhambra" (1881) 6P. D. 68,租约的卸港写作:"safe port… as ordered or so near thereto as she may safely get…"。判是若一个港口必须花钱轻载才能进去,则船东可不必去,他可去邻近港口卸货。当然,这应是租约没有特别条款针对轻载,如一条说:"Lightening, if any, for Owners' account"。

在另一著名的案例 The "Athamas" (1963) 1 Lloyd's Rep. 287,租约订明船是去柬埔寨的金边卸水泥,也有一条"邻近条款"。因船速太慢,船要等待 5 个月后湄公河流水较弱时才能开进去,船东于是在相隔 250 海里的西贡(今天的胡志明市)把货物卸下,算是交差,并索要运费。要知道,这样一来收货人可就惨了,把货物再转运到金边去的费用很高。但上诉庭判船东在这邻近条款下可这样做。至于相隔 250 海里是否太远,会否船东取巧一装完货就马上在附近卸下,说是邻近港口,从而可以交差并要求运费? Sellers 大法官说是要以合理为准,要船货利益都考虑到。看来,"合理"仍应是尽量接近卸港的其他安全港口。Sellers 大法官说:

"… so in considering whether a substitute discharging place is within the phrase 'so near thereto as she may safely get' the Court or tribunal should apply the conception of reasonableness in relation to distance. The distance might be so great in relation to the contemplated length, duration and nature of the adventure that notwithstanding that it was the nearest safe port or place the substituted place of discharge could not be assumed to be within the contemplation of the parties as fair and reasonable men."

相隔的距离要以合理为准,船东要等待多久才能去其他邻近港口也是要以合理公平为准。船东肯定不能一需要等一两天潮水,便马上要去邻近港口装卸,甚至以此为借口来刁难承租人或收货人。

考虑到免责条款会严格针对船东去解释,小心的船东会在何谓"合理"的时间上尽量克制自己,不要太早作出反应。反正是"合理"要看每一不同案情才能作出判定,所以无法说死。我只去举一个案例,它不是严格涉及"邻近条款",但原则是一样。在 Knutsford S. S. Co. Ltd. v. Tillmanns & Co. (1908) A. C. 406,提单卸港是海参崴,如果因冰封进不了海参崴是有条款容许船东去邻近港口。船东在海参崴等了三天后自己改去日本长崎卸货。贵族院说这三天时间太短。

再强调,这也不是三天或三星期的分别,完全看合理与否。例如,有准确消息说航道出了事故,要封闭两三个月,船东可以一天也不等待就改去邻近港口。有这邻近条款的分别是没有它,船东只好干等,直至航道重新通航,两三个月时间不见得会是受阻延误(frustrating delay)。

最后可去提醒收货人的是,金康提单(Congenbill)已在格式上针对卸港订明了这"邻近条款"。这一来,买卖合约及信用证若指明是用金康提单,买方或收货人会无话可说。否则,有先例说有"邻近条款"的提单在 CIF 或 C&F 买卖下可被拒绝接受:The "Orland" (1933) 44 Lloyd's Rep. 384. 在 Benjamin's Sale of Goods,14 版,19-029 说:"The bill of lading must provide for the carriage…A bill of lading may fail to satisfy this requirement even though it is expressed to be for the delivery of the goods at the c. i. f. destination if it does not in fact oblige the carrier to deliver is qualified by the words 'of so near as the ship can safely get' and she cannot safely get to the particular wharf named as the destination in the contract of sale."

显然,船东/承运人也需要这方面的保障与灵活性(即不必严格要去列名卸港),不论是在程租租约或提单合约。但提单涉及海牙规则的强制适用。这一来,会有疑问是这条"邻近条款"的有效性如何?有否违反海牙规则去减轻船东/承运人责任?这会否是不合理绕航?要知道不合理绕航会是大事:请参阅本书第五章之 4.2.10.1 小段。

答案是:英国法律下应是有效,它不是针对绕航(合理与否),而是说明"履约"下的航次应是什么。这在《Scrutton on CharterParties》一书第 9 版之第 452 页有说:

"The Rule(海牙规则) has no effect upon the right of the carrier under a liberty clause in a bill of lading in certain stated circumstances to discharge the goods at a substituted port; the exercise of such a right, if valid on common law principles, is no deviation, but is a performance of the contractual voyage."

Scrutton 一书提到了贵族院的 The"Caspiana"(1956) 2 Lloyd's Rep. 379 先例作为对这个说法的支持。该先例涉及提单适用 1939 年加拿大海上运输法(海牙规则),但同时有一条明示的"自由条款"(liberty clause)允许船舶在某些情况下[如卸港发生罢工,劳资纠纷,其他"妨碍"(obstruction),疫症,冰封等],不必为进列名的卸港干等,而可以去邻近的"安全与方便"(safe and convenient)港口卸下货物。因为列名卸港(英国伦敦等)发生罢工,班轮进去了货也卸不下,而且会延误班轮船期,所以船东转去汉堡把货物卸下。收货人事后要自己去安排转运回英国。结果,收货人向船东索赔损失,指该自由条款违反海牙规则,而且也违反了提单的主旨是为了去伦敦等卸港卸货(这看来是与本书第二章之 5.10.1 小段谈及的"相悖理论"(doctrine of repugnancy)相似)。但贵族院判该自由条款不是针对绕航,而是针对出了某些事故后的履约替代做法。贵族院说(Viscount Kilmuir):"that clause should not be regarded as giving liberty to deviate but rather as providing, in circumstances particularly envisaged, an agreed substituted method of performance of the contract of carriage; that in proceeding to Hamburg, which was a convenient port, the ship was acting in accordance with the contract of carriage; and that what she did was to be regarded as performance of the contract of carriage."

Morton 勋爵也说:"No conflict arises when an obligation in a contract, unqualified in its terms as it is first stated,[310] is subsequently qualified by a proviso modifying or altering the obligation if certain events happen which are outside the control of either party.[311] Original obligation and the qualification of it form part of the intention of the parties and neither part is repugnant to the other[312]."

这样看来,提单的"邻近条款"(near clause)应是有效。

3.3 Conlinebill 前页的承运人条款/空格

在本书附录九的 Conlinebill 2000,前页左下角有一条款,实际是许多空格,以供

---

[310] 这是指提单合约先是毫不保留的写明去某某卸港。
[311] 但之后另有保留说某些情况下(如罢工、冰封等),双方无法控制,则原先的去某某卸港的义务/责任将有更改。
[312] 这两条条款之间没有冲突/矛盾,应合起来考虑作为双方同意履约的替代做法。

填上承运人的资料。它包括了承运人的名字（会是船东，也不一定是他/它）、地址、签字（可以由船长或代理人代签）。

Conlinebill 要如此编排显然是为了去符合 UCP500 的新规定，要求提单说明谁是承运人。这一点在本书第三章之 6.2 小段有详论，不再重复。这也是好事，可去减少在第三章谈到的提单承运人到底是谁的通常争议。

3.4 Conlinebill 后页的各条款简介

在本书附录九的 Conlinebill 2000，后页共有 18 条条款，另外还有选择性的两条。当然在订约自由的大原则下，使用 Conlinebill 格式提单的班轮公司/船公司可去随意增减这些条款。以下就对这些条款作一简介。

第 1 条：定义这里对"货方"（merchant）作出了定义，他们包括了发货人、收货人、受让人、提单持有人以及拥有货物主权的人士等。有了此定义，在提单所有其他条款提到"货方"要负责什么事情等，就可去包括发货人，又包括收货人。不必再理会货物会航次半途被转让，若提单光是写发货人显然有不足之处。至于定义不去提及"承运人"（carrier），是因为提单前页已有条款/空格明确了。

3.4.1 通知人

第 2 条：通知在提单（不论是班轮或租约提单）的前页左上角，"收货人"（Consignee）一栏的上面或下面，通常另有一栏是"通知人"（notify party），以供填上名字与地址。但要注意若提单是物权凭证的"指示提单"（order bill），则并不表示可去无单放货给"通知人"。这一切的课题已在本书第二章之 3.1.5 小段（与其他小段）有详论，不再重复。

这一来，要有通知人的资料干什么呢？答案是船东/承运人会需要知道如何与收货人（或他的代理人）接触。例如是半途发生救助（会需要货方前来提供救助担保），或是货物在邻近港口而不是列名卸港已经卸下（请看本章之 3.2.2 小段）等。

但班轮公司也怕被解释为它有合约责任去在卸港（船舶抵达前后）统一通知"收货人"（或"通知人"）前来提取货物，即使在正常情况下。要知道，班轮一船会有上千票货物，这通知起来可是大量的工作，何不要收货人自己看报纸，查海关/港口当局，自己留心船舶的抵达/船期？故此，Conlinebill 在此条款说明承运人不必给通知，如下："Any mention in this Bill of Lading of parties to be notified of the arrival of the cargo is solely for information of the Carrier and failure to give such notification shall not involve the Carrier in any liability nor relieve the Merchant of any obligation hereunder."

3.4.2 首要条款

第3条:首要条款 Conlinebill 2000 这一条款是为去合并海牙或/与海牙·维斯比规则。有关这方面,本书第五章之4.2.3.2.2.1 至 4.2.3.2.2.6 小段有详论,先不去重复。只提提本条款最后一段/一句说明承运人不负责装船前或卸货后,或转船时在二程船发生的任何货损货差。同时,对甲板货与动物也不负责。这完全符合海牙/海牙·维斯比规则,在本书第五章会有详论,例如,在该章之4.2.3.4 小段谈及规则只是强制适用在"船至船"的期间。在该章之4.2.3.5.2 小段谈及规则不适用在动物。另在该章之4.2.3.5.3 小段说到规则也不适用在甲板货。

一不适用或不受制于海牙或/与海牙·维斯比规则,就表示双方可享有订约自由,而一般的做法是班轮公司会利用自己比发货人优越的订约地位去减轻或/与豁免责任。这种做法与技巧在第五章之4.2.3.5.3.4 小段有详论,先不去重复。在此只说说在 Conlinebill 条款中所用的措辞/文字,看来不够广泛去保障承运人,例如,在船长/船员等疏忽导致的对动物或甲板货造成的货损货差方面;这方面请参阅本书第五章之4.2.3.5.3.4 小段。

3.4.3 适用法律与管辖权

第4条:在一个国际性合约,会涉及多于一个国家,适用法律显然十分重要。这法律是指"实体法"(substantive law),它将解释该合约的一切争议如"构成"(formation),"效力"(validity),"条款解释"(interpretation/construction)与"如何去履约"(right performance)等。困难是,国与国之间的法律会有重大差异。随手便可举出这种例子,如在 The "Grangefield" (1972) 1 Lloyd's Rep. 53 先例,提到租约的免责条款,在英国法律有效,但在荷兰法律却无效。这会在相关案件带来天渊之别的后果。

而即使在同一国际公约,虽然按理解释起来各国法院应尽量接近,甚至是一致,但现实中并非如此。例如在 The "Blue Wave" (1982) 1 Lloyd's Rep. 151 与 The "Komninos S" (1991) 1 Lloyd's Rep. 371,就反映了希腊法律的 Civil Code, Article 75,禁止双方协议去延长时效,如海牙规则的一年时效。但在英美法(与世界上大部分国家的法律)下,这却是完全有效。在商业现实中双方也经常是这样做,如双方在谈判或仍在调查案情,而不会动不动因时效将届而去起诉。

像中国法律也与世界其他国家的法律(包括英美法)有不少巨大的差异。例如在新的合同法生效之前,据知是有法律不承认双方没有签字的合约的。这导致中国实体法如适用的话,会有许多外国或/与国际上承认完全有效的合约/协议,变了在中国法律下无效。

3.4.3.1 普通法地位

以上讲了适用法律的重要性,接下去可谈谈合约若没有明示规定(明示条款),则要去找出默示的适用法的问题,这是英文所谓的"find the proper law of the contract"。在英国法院,这方面原则上的做法可去引述 Denning 勋爵在 The "Grangefield" (1972) 1 Lloyd's Rep. 53 案针对海上运输合约的著名讲话如下:"In order to determine the proper law of the contract, the Courts at one time used to have a number of presumptions to help them.[313] Now we have to ask ourselves: What is the system of law with which the transaction has the closest and most real connection? [314] This is not dependent on the intentions of the parties. They never thought about it. They had no intention upon it. We have to study every circumstance connected with the contract and come to a conclusion.[315] This new test is all very well. It is often easy to apply.[316] But, there are sometimes one country only.[317] They point equally to two countries, or even to three.[318] What then is a legal advisor to do? What is an arbitrator or a Judge to do? Is he to toss up a coin and see which was it comes down? [319] Surely not. The law ought to give some help.[320] It ought to provide a pointer to a solution, if only as a last resort. One such point is that, in a contract of charter-party, other things being equal, the law of the ship should govern[321] …"

在普通法下,特别是针对各种不同的合约,还有其他许多因素要考虑,例如:

(i)若双方订约是以一份英文的标准格式合约为准,为基础,这尚不足以说明默示适用英国法。但像 The "Al Wahab" (1983) 2 Lloyd's Rep. 365 先例,双方订约使用

---

[313] 法院会考虑多项因素/事实以找出适用法。

[314] 总之会问:什么国家的法律才是与整个合约/交易有最密切与最真实的联系呢?

[315] 法官要去考虑合约的每一个环节以求找出结论,例如,提单/租约的货物是哪里出口,哪里装船?提单在哪里签发(Megaw 大法官在同一案例中认为这一点极其重要)?当事人的身份与所在地在哪里?运费的支付(如货币)与如何支付(如地点)?争议的证人/证据/船员在哪里,等等。但注意英国目前已有立法针对这方面[Contracts (Applicable Laws) Act 1990],该立法有条款[Article 4(4)条款]专门针对货物运输合约,故此不再是刚提到的普通法下的众多考虑因素。

[316] 有时候得出结论十分容易,因为众多考虑因素都指向一个国家。

[317] 但有时候难以取舍。

[318] 众多考虑因素会指向二个或三个国家[例如 The "Iran Vojdan" (1984) 2 Lloyd's Rep. 380 即涉及伊朗、德国与英国]。

[319] 法院当然不能简单以"掷硬币"而定,这样做纯是赌博,不存在有任何考虑,而且对维护法院的尊严地位也不利。

[320] 法律应给一些指引,以指点迷津。

[321] 其中包括,如果一个租约有众多考虑因素难以取舍,作为最后的考虑,适用法就应是船舶的船旗国法律(但这一说法随后因方便旗的流行已失去意义。但碰上不是方便旗,而是像德国旗,仍会有一方当事人去大力争辩,坚持这仍是有关适用法最重要的考虑因素:The "Iran Vojdan")。

的是英国的 SG 保单加协会条款,英国贵族院大部分法官认为非要适用英国法,否则就难以解释了。

(ii)英国贵族院另在 James Miller & Partners Ltd. v. Whitworth Street Estates (Mancester) Ltd. (1970) AC 583 一案也受到一份英国通用的标准格式合约的困扰。订约双方一方是英国公司,一方是苏格兰公司,合约的目的是去改造在苏格兰的建筑物,而订约是以英国的 RIBA(建筑师学会)标准格式合约为准(虽然苏格兰亦有自己类似的标准格式合约)。后来有了争议,双方首先要找的答案是到底适用英国法还是苏格兰法。贵族院意见有分歧:Hodson 勋爵与 Viscount Dilhorne 认为订约方选择了一份英国的标准格式合约这一因素十分重要,说:"determined by the use of the English form, the selection of which shows the intention of the parties to be bound by English law."但 Guest, Reid 与 Wilberforce 勋爵认为苏格兰法律有更密切与真正的联系。

(iii)如果合约有一条仲裁条款(arbitration clause),例如是伦敦仲裁,这会被视为是一个十分重要的考虑因素:在 Cie. Tunisienne de Nav. v. Cie. 'Armement Maritime (1970) 2 Lloyd's Rep. 99。Diplock 勋爵说:"an arbitration clause is generally intended by the parties to operate as a choice of the proper law of the contract… Unless there are compelling indications to the contrary in the other terms of the contract of the surrounding circumstances of the transaction…"

他还说即使另有更密切联系国家的法律也取代不了这个十分重要的考虑因素:"the mere fact that there are systems of law which the transaction has a closer connection is not sufficient to rebut the implication."

在租约提单,通过合并租约的伦敦仲裁条款(本章之 2.6.4 小段),也会带来默示英国法律适用的后果:见 The "Agia Skepi"(1992)2 Lloyd's Rep. 467。

(iv)如果不是一条仲裁条款,而是一条某国家法院的管辖权条款(jurisdiction clause)呢?好像在 The "Komninos S"(1991)1 Lloyd's Rep. 371,涉及一批从希腊运去意大利的钢材,英文的提单内有一条款说有争议去英国法院,具体如下:"All Dispute(s) to be referred to British courts."

双方(货方与船方/承运人)争议的提单适用法有希腊、意大利与英国法(因为有英国法院的管辖权条款)。在高院,Leggatt 大法官判希腊法律是适用法,因为关系最密切,他说:"Thus the contract was made in Greece between Greek shippers and Greek managers on behalf of the Cypriot owners of a Panamanian vessel to carry Greek steel from Greece to Italy for freight payable in Greece in Greek Currency pursuant to Greek exchange control regulations. In my judgment, these factors do predominate over the equivocal reference to British Courts, and other English references, some of which many have been influenced by the use of English as the language of commerce..."

但去了上诉庭,判决被推翻,判是双方订约意向是英国法律才是适用法。

(ⅴ)其他像 The "Grangefield"(1972)1 Lloyd's Rep. 53 与 The "Komninos S"(1991)1 Lloyd's Rep. 370 等先例,涉及的一个考虑因素是有关免责条款(或其他条款)在英国法律有效,但在另有密切联系的国家法律下无效。考虑到解释合约是要尽量令它的条款有效而不是无效,故应选择英国法律才是适用法。

总结以上所讲,可以说,普通法去默示并且找出订约双方的意图,是既不科学也不稳定的做法。正如在 Cheshire & North 的《Private International Law》11 版(1987年)的第461页所说:"Surely the only situation where it is clear what the parties' actual intentions are is where they have expressly provided for the governing law by a choice of law clause. The whole notion of inferring an actual intent is based, at best, upon making assumptions which may or may not be correct, and, at worst, upon a form of dishonesty. It would be better to apply a purely objective test in all cases where there is no express choice of law clause."

3.4.3.2 立法地位

首先,笔者要节录《信用证》一书有关这方面的第九章之3.1小段如下:

目前英国这方面的法律,可以简单地看这1990年的立法。该立法的根据是"罗马公约"(Rome Convention)。该公约虽然是欧共体法律,但不局限在欧共体国家。所有去英国法院的案件,即使涉及非欧共体国家,全都要适用这立法。该立法是针对合约内不同国家的法律选择与适用的。

首先由双方订明会是最简单明确了,这在1990年立法完全被尊重。这在 Article 3(1)有说明如下:

"A contract shall be governed by the law chosen by the parties. The choice must be express or demonstrated with reasonable certainty by the terms of the contract or the circumstances of the case. By their choice the parties can select the law applicable to the whole or a part only of the contract."

但如果双方没有同意,没有订明,就好像信用证那样呢?这另在 Article 4(1)有说明如下:

"To the extent that the law applicable to the contract has not been chosen in accordance with Article 3, the contract shall be governed by the law of the country with which it is most closely connected (即适用最密切联系国家的法律)…"

说实在的,去找出最密切联系国家的法律的做法也是英国普通法遇上法律冲突时的一贯做法,这1990年立法也没有改变什么。但在 Article 4(2),它

去包括了一个"可去反证的推定"(rebuttable presumption)来协助找出最密切联系国家的法律。它是说:

"Subject to the provisions of paragraph 5 of this Article, it shall be presumed that the contract is most closely connected with the country where the party who is to effect the performance which is characteristic of the contract has, at the time of conclusion of the contract, his habitual residence, or, in the case of a body corporate or uncorporate, its central administration. However, if the contract is entered into in the course of that party's trade or profession, that country shall be the country in which the principal place of business is situated or, where under the terms of the contract the performance is to be effected through a place of business other than the principal of business, the country in which that other place of business is situated."

换言之,每一个合约"本质上"(characteristic)会是由其中订约的一方去履约,他可被称为"本质上的履约方"(charateristic performer)。去把他/它找出来后(如果有),他的住所地(自然人)或公司的行政/管理中心或商业上的主要业务所在地国家的法律可被推定为有最密切联系,从而作为适用法。

例如在一个 CIF 的买卖,从中国运货至印度,卖方公司是在香港,看来"本质上的履约方"应是卖方,这变得最密切联系的法律是香港法律了,而不是中国(装港)或印度(卸港)法,等等。

当然也会有不少情况是无法找出谁是"本质上的履约方的",这一来,1990 年立法的 Article 4(5)是这样说:

"Paragraph 2 shall not apply if the characteristic performance cannot be determined, and the presumption in paragraph 2 shall be disregarded if it appears from the circumstances as whole that the contract is more closely connected with another country.(如果整体看来合约另有更密切联系的国家,则不必理会"本质上履约"的问题了)。

涉及提单合约,还想去节录也在该立法(Contracts(Applicable Law) Act 1990)附件的罗马公约的有关条款:

该公约第一条说明公约是为了针对在合约中选择适用不同国家法律的问题,并列出了一连串的合约种类(不包括提单合约)不适用此公约。显然,这些除外的合约有了争议仍要以英国普通法去解释。该条款说:

Article 1. Scope of the Convention

1. The rules of this Convention shall apply to contractual obligations in any situation involving a choice between the laws of different countries.

2. They shall not apply to:

(a) Questions involving the status or legal capacity of natural persons, without prejudice to Article 11;

(b) Contractual obligations relating to:

——wills and succession,

——rights in property arising out of a matrimonial relationship,

——rights and duties arising out of a family relationship, parentage, marriage or affinity, including maintenance obligations in respect of children who are not legitimate;

(c) obligations arising under bills of exchange, cheques and promissory notes and other negotiable instruments to the extent that the obligations under such other negotiable instruments arise out of their negotiable character;

(d) arbitration agreements and agreements on the choice of court;

(e) questions governed by the law of companies and other bodies corporate or unincorporate such as the creation, by registration or otherwise, legal capacity, internal organisation or winding up of companies and other bodies corporate or unincorporate and the personal liability of officers and members as such for the obligations of the company or body;

(f) the question whether an agent is able to bind a principal, or an organ to bind a company or body corporate or unincorporate, to third party;

(g) the constitution of trusts and the relationship between settlors, trustees and beneficiaries;

(h) evidence and procedure, without prejudice to Article 14…

3. The rules of this Convention do not apply to contracts of insurance which cover risks situated in the territories of the Member States of the European Economic Community. In order to determine whether a risk is situated in these territories the court shall apply its internal law.

4. The preceding paragraph does not apply to contracts of re-insurance.

而针对提单合约等的货物运输合约,罗马公约有一明示条款[Article 4(4)]说:

"Article 4 Applicable law in the absence of choice…

4. A contract for the carriage of goods… In such a contract if the country in which, at the time the contract is concluded, the carrier has his principal place of business is also the country in which the place of loading or the place of discharge or the principal place of business of the consignor is situated, it shall be presumed that the contract is most closely

connected with that country. In applying this paragraph single voyage charter-parties and other contracts the main purpose of which is the carriage of goods shall be treated as contracts for the carriage of goods."

可见,立法规定了四个考虑因素:承运人主要营业地/国家、装港、卸港与发货人主要营业地/国家。

若承运人是在 A 国,装卸货是在 B 国与 C 国,发货人是在 D 国,这一来,主导思想是以 Article 4(1) 的最密切联系国家的法律为适用法 (the contract shall be governed by the law of the country with which it is most closely connected)。而针对合约明显是适用某国法律的情况,Article 4 (5) 更给予了伸缩性,指可去不顾前述规定的四个考虑因素,它说:"disregarded if it appears from the circumstances as a whole that the contract is more closely connected with another country."

虽然立法不能彻底解决普通法的不稳定/不科学,但已有所改良,毕竟列下了四项考虑因素。这会令多数的争议有了明确答案,如 The "Assunzione" (1954) P. 150,涉及意大利船东的船舶从法国运货去意大利,显然是适用意大利法律。立法以承运人主要营业地/国家为起点,再去联系其他考虑因素即会有答案。虽然答案仍不一定科学,但至少会变得较稳定/可预测。

3.4.3.3 提单合约无效或有争议的明示适用法条款

看来,有明示的适用法条款仍是最佳的解决办法,省得有了争议会多一项争议课题。涉及提单合约的适用法条款,首先要提醒的是在 The "Morviken" (1983) 1 Lloyd's Rep. 1 先例中 Diplock 勋爵所说的(海牙规则下承运人去减轻或豁免责任的条款属无效的规定应予广泛包括)以下一段话:"…for that matter, a country whose law recognized and unfettered right in a shipowner by the terms of the bill of lading to relieve himself from all liability for loss or damage to the goods caused by his own negligence, fault or breach of contract."

这方面在本书第五章之 4.2.3.1.5 小段有详论。

另外,一条无法解释/无法肯定或实施的"浮动条款"(floating law clause),也会被判无效:见 The "Iran Vojdan" (1984) 2 Lloyd's Rep. 380。该先例提单内有关适用法的条款是:"2. (a) The contract of carriage, the bill of lading and all disputes arising hereunder or in connection therewith… shall… in the option of the carrier to be declared by him on the merchant's request be governed (i) either by Iranian law, in particular by the Hague Rules… as enacted in the Iranian Maritime Code… with exclusive jurisdiction of the Courts in Teheran Iran; (ii) or by German law, in particular by the Hague Rules as enacted in German Commercial Code… with exclusive jurisdiction of the Courts in Hamburg… (iii) or by English law, in particular by the Hague Rules as enacted in the

Carriage of Goods by Sea Act, 1924... with exclusive jurisdiction of the Courts in London ... (b) In case the law of the country in which a suit is filed does not recognize this agreement on the exclusive jurisdiction of the Courts of Teheran, Hamburg or London... and/or this agreement on the exclusive application of Iranian, German or English law... then the Hague Rules as enacted in that country shall apply."

Bingham 大法官谈到一条任由一方去选择适用法的"浮动条款"无效的原因是:"The proper law is something so fundamental to questions relating to the formation, validity, interpretation and performance of a contract that it must, in my judgment, be built into the fabric of the contract from the start and cannot float in an indeterminate way until finally determined at the option of one party. As I say, it is, as I understand, common ground that as a matter of English law effect cannot be given to that part of this clause. That is, however, the limit of the common ground."

再去多举一个例子是合约有一条明示的适用法条款但难以解释的情况。在已提及的 Cie. Tunisienne de Nav. v. Cie. D'Armement Maritime (1970) 2 Lloyd's Rep. 99, 程租约(是有多个航次的租约)的承租人是突尼西亚公司,船东是法国公司,航次是来往阿尔及尼亚港口之间。租约的第 13 条是说:"(适用法是) the laws of the Flag of the Vessel carrying the goods."

法国船东虽拥有四五艘挂法国旗的船舶,但在起初的 6 个航次,共用了 5 条不同船旗国的船舶履约。在第六航次后,中东爆发战争,运费市场与风险大大变动,结果法国船东中止履约。若是履约下去,实际仍有至少 6 个航次以上。承租人为此提出损失索赔,但马上就面临适用法的争议。而根据较宽松的法国法,租约确会是因"受阻"而合法中止。

在贵族院,少数法官认为第 13 条没有意义,是无效的,说是"as having failed in its purpose to determine the proper law of the contract"。

但多数法官认为既然有明示条款,即使难以解释也应尽量给予支持。而订约双方明知船东是法国公司,履约的主要会是法国船,所以租约的第 13 条应是法国法适用。Diplock 勋爵说:[I] commerce business men frequently find it convenient to use printed forms of contract with which they are familiar to record their agreements about transactions for which the printed clauses are not literally apt, as they were drafted for use as contracts about transactions which have somewhat different characteristics. If the law is to give effect to their intentions... the court must construe the words of the printed form not exclusively literally but, if necessary, analogistically... By clause 13 when used for a single voyage charter the parties clearly intended to choose the system of law with which the contract had its connection through the nationality of the carrying vessel. Had the parties contemplated that the contract would be performed exclusively by vessels owned or controlled by the French company there could be no question but that the parties intended to choose French law as the proper law of the contract. Is the court to treat the clause as meaningless simply because, notwithstanding that they did contemplate that vessels owned by the French company would be used primarily to perform the contract, they also contemplated that there might be exceptional occasion son which chartered vessels might be used? It does not seem to me that from the business point of view this could make any significant difference so far as choice of proper law was concerned.

3.4.3.4 对 Conlinebill 适用法与管辖权条款的分析/解释

现在,不妨去看看 Conlinebill 2000 的明示条款。大精神看来是条款难解释仍要尽量去给予支持,判为有效。

这份标准格式合约是英文的措辞/文字,照说也可以准确无误地去明示适用英国法。但这样做在国际性机构(即使是对英国法十分友善的 BIMCO)不容易得到各国代表的支持。加上就各班轮公司而言,它们都希望适用自己最熟悉/理解的本国法律。所以在这现实下,Conlinebill 写的是以"承运人的主要业务所在地"(Carrier has his principal place of business)的法律与管辖权为准。

这一来,对收货人要起诉承运人索赔货损货差而言,又增加了困难、疑问,且是外行人难以充分了解的。

首先,收货人/货方律师要去找出谁是"承运人"。这一困难课题在本书第三章之§2 段有详论。"承运人"会是班轮公司,例如马斯基公司,则它的主要业务所在地应是丹麦的哥本哈根。但承运船也可能是马斯基期租的船舶,由船长授权签发提单,加上提单有"光船条款"(demise clause)等。这一来根据第三章之4.3.1.2 小段(还有前后其他小段)所述,表示提单"承运人"会是该船原船东,而马斯基公司只是代理人。若该船是挂巴拿马旗,由挪威船东拥有,香港船公司(如华林公司)管理。这一来,什么才是适用法与管辖地呢?

这方面可去介绍两个先例。第一个是 The "Blue Wave" (1982), Lloyd's Rep. 151,涉及一航次自南美去欧洲,发生了几票货损。货方在英国法院起诉,而船东要求中止,理由是提单的管辖地点是希腊法院。

该提单的管辖权条款与 Conlinebill 一样,是"承运人的主要业务所在地"。而船东被认定为是提单合约的"承运人"。船东是利比里亚公司(方便旗船舶),但由一家希腊船公司在处理日常业务。Sheen 大法官判希腊是管辖地,他说:"Undoubtedly the defendants(船东) have a place of business in Piraeus (希腊比雷埃夫斯). They have no office or staff in Liberia. "Blue Wave" is not operated from Liberia. There can be no doubt that the defendants have their principal place of business in Greece."

第二个先例是 The"Rewia"（1991）2 Lloyd's Rep. 325，提单也有一样的条款说明管辖地是"承运人的主要业务所在地"。船东又是利比里亚公司，但背后股东是德国银行，另外船舶是交给香港公司管理。在高院，判香港是提单合约承运人的主要业务所在地。但去了上诉庭，改为是德国。Leggatt 大法官说："the principal place of business was not necessarily the place where most of the business was carried out; there was nothing uncommercial or inapposite about the conclusion that the principal place of business was in Hamburg of a company registered in Liberia owning a ship, the earning of which would ultimately be remitted to Germany, and about which most important decisions would be taken in Germany; although in practice Turbata（香港管理公司）had a free hand in the day to day management of the vessel from Hong Kong all that they did was subject to the control of the directors in Hamburg; that was the centre from which instructions were given when necessary and ultimate control exercised; the reference to 'principal place' did not require identification of a particular building…"

从以上简介可见，Conlinebill 2000 明示但隐晦的法律与管辖权条款实在是给原告的收货人/货方出了难题。首先，原告先要找对谁是"承运人"（Carrier），这已十分不易，以上介绍的两个先例尚未涉及有另一变数的光船租约。之后还要去摸底，搞清楚承运人的业务操作才谈得上能去知道哪里是"主要业务所在地"。再之后，才说得出什么是提单合约的适用法以及哪里的法院有权管辖。

难怪，收货人对"诉人"（action in personam）的诉讼不会感兴趣：请看本书第三章之3.6.2小段。收货人仍会尽可能去"对物诉讼"（action in rem），这其中的好处已在本书第三章之3.6.3小段谈及。考虑到提单的承运人多数会是船东（请看本书第三章之5.1.5.2小段等），对物诉讼通常应是错不了。但危险是，若像 Conlinebill 的提单有一条明示的管辖权条款，而船东也能说明哪里才是他/它的"主要业务所在地"，那表示船东可去成功申请诉船地法院"中止"（stay）审理的机会会大增，因为提单合约已有一条外国法院管辖权条款是英国法院会考虑的重要因素：见 The "Eleftheria"（1969）1 Lloyd's Rep. 237。

这一来，收货人诉船/扣船成功后仍可能保不住管辖权（只会保得住诉前保全的担保如互保协会出的保函等），但可以先弄清楚提单合约的管辖地点到底在哪里。可是弄清楚后，是否又会面临 2.6.4.5 小段所讲的一年时效已逝的问题，除非收货人早有两手准备？

3.4.3.5　总结

看来，还是美国法律考虑得周到，简简单单的便保护了自己人（货方）的利益。虽然表面看来海牙规则并未特别针对管辖权的课题，但美国的 Indussa Corporation v. The Ranborg（1967）2 Lloyd's Rep. 101 判是提单中的外国管辖权条款无效，因它们违反海牙规则去减轻了承运人的责任。

另外澳大利亚也考虑得周到,它的海上运输法(是海牙规则的立法)多加了一句是其他国家引入海牙规则为国内立法时没有做的,它讲明不准在提单内豁免澳大利亚法院的管辖权。该条款是:"All parties to any bill of lading document relating to the carriage of goods from any place in Australia to any place outside Australia shall be deemed to have intended to contract according to the laws in force at the place of shipment, and any stipulation or agreement to the contrary, or purporting to oust or lessen the jurisdiction of the courts of the commonwealth or of a state in respect of the bill of lading or document, shall be illegal, null and void, and of no effect."

近年来曾令美国尴尬的是提单合约内的一条仲裁条款,因为 Supreme Court 已在 The "Sky Reefer" (1995) 63 USLW 4617 先例判该种条款有效,因为 1958 年纽约公约比 1924 年海牙规则(美国是 1936 年立法)为时更晚,也对仲裁更有针对性,所以有了冲突效力就更高。而且,The "Sky Reefer" 对 Indussa 先例的说法(只针对外国的法院的管辖权,不是仲裁)也有了质疑,这导致以后一连串的案例,大多背弃了 Indussa 的判法,如 Union Steel America Co. v. M/V Sanko Spruce, 14F. Supp. 2d 682 (DNJ July 21, 1998)(针对韩国法院管辖); Nippon Fire & Marine Ins. Co. v. M/V Coral Halo, 2000 U. S. Dist. LEXIS 1548 (ED. La. Feb. 11, 2000)(针对日本东京法院管辖); Reed & Barton Corp. v. M/V Tokio Express, 1999 U. S. Dist. LEXIS 1807, 1999 AMC 1088 (SDNY Feb. 22, 1999)(针对德国汉堡法院管辖)等。故此,美国只能去改立法(海上运输法)以求改变这种不利地位了。

3.4.4 各自由条款

第 5 条:航次所包括的做法;

第 6 条:另用替代船舶履约的权利/自由;

Conlinebill 2000 的这两条条款可一并去谈,它们具体的措辞/文字可以看本书的附录九。条款的用意是去给予承运人各种营运的自由、伸缩性与方便。例如,第 5 条允许船舶在航次半途加添燃油,装卸其他货物(毕竟这是班轮业务)。而第 6 条则涉及另用替代船舶履约,例如,用支线船/二程船把货物运抵卸港。但若不在合约说明,这样去做会是严重的违约/毁约。

在 3.2.2 小段提到过,英国法律并不禁止提单合约内说明要"履约"的航次应是什么:见 The "Caspiana" (1956) 2 Lloyd's Rep. 379。自由条款(另称为"Caspiana Clause")起的作用就是去说明这履约的航次,例如,不是直航。至于如何去合理解释这些自由条款,由于提单合约与程租合约的类似条款原意是一样的,所以可干脆去节录笔者《程租合约》一书第五章的 §2 段如下:

在这一段先谈谈何谓绕航,程租下到底什么航次适用哪种绕航是法律所允许的。

2.1 何谓正常及习惯航线?

谈到绕航,首先要确定何谓正常及习惯航线(usual and customary route),这也是英国海上保险法在 Section 46(2)(6)所用的词语。

一般而言,这是指装卸港之间地理上最直接的航线(direct geographical route):The "Indian City" (1939) 64 Lloyd's Rep. 229; Achile Lauro v. Total (1968) 2 Lloyd's Rep. 247。

当然,这也会有变化。例如习惯上去某卸港时先要去另一港清关或让领航员上船。或者,可取道好望角或通过苏伊士运河。又或者,无法在一个漫长航次前装足燃料,需要在中途港加燃料或油水,尤其在早期船舶要以大量煤炭作燃料。

这样一来,要证明虽不是地理上最直接的航线,但仍是正常与习惯的航线,就要看每一案子的具体证据了。例如,几乎所有其他同类的船舶跑这航次也都会是这样。

在这方面,Porter 勋爵在 The "Indian City" (1939) 64 Lloyd's Rep. 229 的有如下说法:

"It is the duty of a ship, at any rate when sailing upon an ocean voyage from one port to another, to take the usual route between these two ports. If no evidence be given, that route is presumed to be the direct geographical route, but it may be modified in many cases for navigational or other reasons, and evidence may always be given to show what the usual route is, unless a specific route be prescribed by the charter party or bill of lading…

"In some cases there may be more than one usual route. It would be difficult to say that a ship sailing from New Zealand to this country (英国) had deviated from her course whether she sailed by the Suez Canal, the Panama Canal, round the Cape of Good Hope or through the Straits of Maggelan. Each might, I think, be a usual route. Similarly the exigencies of bunkering may require the vessel to depart from the direct route or at any rate compel her to touch at ports at which, if she were proceeding under sail, it would be unnecessary for her to call."

对班轮的所谓正常及习惯航线,会更不好判断。班轮不像散货船,它从装港直航至卸港的机会不多,一般它会挂靠多个港口。在 Leduc v. Ward (1888) 20 Q. B. D. 475,判是发货人知悉班轮不是直航并不能约束收货人。只要提单上明示会从装港直航去卸港,收货人即可指控船东绕航。

但问题是,一般只有发货人才会知道班轮的行程、航线,以便去订舱位。幸亏在之后的先例,Evans v. Cunard (1902) 18 T. L. R. 374 以及贵族院的 Frenkel v. MacAndrews (1929) A. c. 545,均认同船东可去证明该轮正常及习惯的航线,只要提单没写明是直航去卸港(proceed directly to the port of delivery)。而在 Evans. v. Cunard 提单是写"bound for Liverpool";而在 Frenkel v. MacAndrews 提单则是写"with destination Liverpool";这并不影响船东去举证班轮的一向正常及习惯的航线。

2.2 程租下什么航次适用?

在一个程租,载货的航次肯定是适用这不能绕航的默示或明示条款(如果有)。而对空放去装港的航次,这也适用,即不得绕航。毕竟,空放航次也是程租的一部分:The"Noel Bay" (1989) 1 Lloyd's Rep. 361。

2.3 哪种绕航为法律所允许?

即使是偏离了正常或习惯的航线,仍有被法律所允许的情况。这已在上一章的4.2.2小段指出,主要是英国海上保险法的Section 49所作的说明,例如是为了船货安全(避风或浮冰等),以下会更详细地讨论各种情况:

2.3.1 航行所需要

这方面在 The"Indian City" (1939) 64 Lloyd's Rep. 229 也曾提到 Phillimore 大法官在 Morrison v. Shaw Savill (1916) 2 K. B. 783 先例所说的:

"This call is one of the incidents of the voyage and is no departure. There are many similar instances, such as calling at weather stations to inquire about ice, or going to some station for a Government pass through territorial waters, or to pick up a pilot, of calling at a preliminary port to lighten the ship in order that she may finish the voyage with a less draught. These are not, in my view, departures from the usual and customary course of the voyage."

2.3.2 因不适航导致半途需要绕航

这方面会是如船舶主机不妥的不适航,导致半途被迫要绕航中途港修理。或是在装港积载不当,半途货物移动,船必须去中途港重新积载才能继续航行。这种绕航也是法律所允许的,这是贵族院在 Kish v. Taylor (1912) A. C. 604 所作的判决,再早以前也有另一同样判法的 The "Europa" (1908) P. 84。

照说,不适航也是一项违约,何必再与绕航相区分呢?答案是,两者后果的严重程度差远了。不适航只会对它所引起的损失负责,但绕航的后果就严重了,这会在后文详述。

这样也很有道理,因为一切要以船货安全考虑为重。否则岂不是船舶在半途一有不适航引起的不妥,船长便会对是否应去绕航或继续冒险感到很矛盾,毕竟不适航比起绕航,后者要可怕得多。

2.3.3 船会被扣押或遇上其他风险

船如果按预定航次跑下去,会遇上扣押(往往发生在战时,而和平年代也可能发生在极不稳定的地区),也可被允许绕航,即使是船上货物属于中立,或危险程度不一样,也不影响绕航的合法性:见 The "Teutonia" (1872) L. R. 4 P. C. 171。毕竟,这是基于对船货安全考虑的大精神。在该先例,Mellish 大法官说:

"It seems obvious that, if a master receives credible information that, if he continues in the direct course of his voyage, his ship will be exposed to some imminent peril, as, for instance, that there are pirates in his course, or icebergs, or other dangers of navigation, he must be justified in pausing and deviating from the direct course, and taking any step which a prudent man would take for the purpose of avoiding the danger."

2.3.4 为了救助人命

人命无价,所以为了救助人命去绕航不被允许是说不过去的。但救助财产,如仅是施救其他船舶,这是法律所不允许的:Scaramanga v. Stamp (1880) 5 C. P. D. 295。2.3.5 海牙规则下的合理绕航:

海牙规则也是法律,只不过它属于成文法而不是普通法。海牙规则多会适用在提单,而在租约则要看是否有一条"首要条款"了。而把因救助财产而绕航也算是法律所允许的,可在本章第§1段见到。该段提到海牙规则将合法绕航扩大至包括救助财产,但这在现今不大会发生。另外,海牙规则也增加了一种叫"合理绕航"(reasonable deviation)的情况。何谓合理绕航在不少著名先例都曾针对过:如 The "Ixia" (1931) 41 Lloyd's Rep. 165;The "Macedon" (1955) 1 Lloyd's Rep. 459;The "Daffodil B" (1983) 1 Lloyd's Rep. 498;The "Al Taha" (1990) 2 Lloyd's Rep. 117 等。

每件事故要看合理与否,都要具体地去看该事故的事实,它们各有不同。所以很难用一句话说死何谓合理绕航。但明确的是:要合理,就要船长在作出绕航决定时,把所有因素考虑在内,如必要性,运输合约的性质及条款(装载的是否为易腐烂货物,有否允许绕航条款等)以及所有各方(货方、船东等)的利益。这是 Atkin 勋爵在 The "Ixia" 所说的如下:

"The true test seems to be what departure from the contract voyage might a prudent person controlling the voyage at the time make and maintain, having in mind all the relevant circumstances existing at the time, including the terms of the contract and the interests of all parties concerned, but without obligation to consider the interests of any one as conclusive."

很明显,在判定是否合理绕航时并不会对船东太优待。这在 The"Ixia"一案可见:它是自 Swansea 装煤去 Istnbul。在装港,船东派了两个工程师去检查新装的传热器。本想他们完工后可与装港领航员一齐离船,但因有所延误,结果是开航后,沿英国海岸走了一段,才绕航约 5 海里去 St. Ives 放下这两个工程师。之后,船仍是沿英国海岸走,但由于距岸太近,结果搁浅而船货全损。贵族院判这不是合理绕航,因为去 St. Ives 只是考虑船东的方便与利益。但从判词看来,它是强调了绕航后,船没有回到原来较安全的航线,仍是沿英国多礁石的沿岸跑。看来,这一点也影响了对合理与否的判断。

2.4 合约条款所允许的绕航

考虑到法律上对这方面要求严格,船东在运输合约内放进允许绕航的条款具有重大意义。首先,即使在海牙规则看来,有一条足够广泛的允许绕航条款也会成为考虑绕航是否合理的一个因素:The"Ixia"。

而在海牙规则不适用的情况下,如在一份程租,则会有更大的订约自由。例如,去允许船东半途加燃油。

2.4.1 允许绕航加燃油条款

首先要说明这不是 2.1 小段的情况,即早期船舶必须沿途加燃油或燃料(煤炭)才能完成一个漫长的航次。今天船舶续航能力强,往往没有必要去半途加油。这一来,在装港开出而没有足够燃油去完成航次会是不适当。而在明知后果、有预谋的情况下,不是半途被迫而去加油也仍会构成非法绕航。这在美国一先例有说明:Hurlbut v. Turnure,81 F. 208(2d Cir. 1897)。

但船东常会想半途去加油,或贪其便宜,或可因此而多装货。这一来,就要依赖适当的合约条款了。在 The"Macedon"(1955) 1 Lloyd's Rep. 459 的澳大利亚案例,它有一条看似广泛的条款去允许半途加燃料,如下:

"The ship to have liberty either before or after proceeding towards the port of discharge to deviate from any advertised or other route in any manner and for any purpose whatever (although in a contrary direction to or out of or beyond the ordinary or usual route to the said port of discharge) once or oftener in any order backwards or forwards, to touch and stay at ports… Take in coal or supplies… and all such ports, places and sailings shall be deemed included within the intended voyage, and the company shall not be responsible for any delay occasioned by the matter aforesaid, or for any loss or damage caused by or arising from such delay…"

船装了煤炭货物后,偏离了直接航线约 4 海里去澳洲的 Newcastle 添加燃料,因为当地便宜。注意的是,该船本来有足够燃料去卸港,去添加只是为下一航次备用。在 Newcastle 港内,不幸遇上麻烦,带来重大延误。时间一久,船上煤炭发生自燃,最后整个航次放弃。

在解释以上的条款能否保障船东,以及能否算是海牙规则下的合理绕航时,Kindella 大法官认为加的燃料与该航次无关,则该条款不会有允许此种绕航的意思。他说

"In my view, a deviation which is not in any way connected with the contract voyage or its purposes cannot be said to be a deviation within the terms of the contract."

这一来,有一些租约条款就订得更详尽了。例如在 Austwheat 1996,它的 29 条是:

"Before loading the Vessel shall have the right of proceeding to and bunkering at any usual bunkering port in Australia and/or bunkering at the loading port. After loading the Vessel shall have liberty as part of the contract voyage to bunker at the loading port and/or to proceed to any port or ports at which bunker oil is available for the purpose of bunkering at any stage of the voyage whatsoever and whether such ports are on or off the direct and/or customary route or routes between any of the ports of loading or discharge named in the Charterparty and may there take oil bunkers in any quantity of the discretion of Owners even to the full capacity of fuel tanks and any other compartment in which oil can be carried whether such amount is or is not required for the chartered voyage."

看来,著名的 P&I Bunker Deviation Clause 也是近似,如下:

"The vessel in addition to all other liberties shall have liberty as part of the contract voyage and at any stage thereof to proceed to any port or ports whatsoever whether such ports are on or off the direct and/or customary route or routes to the ports of loading or discharge named in this Charter and there take oil bunkers in any quantity in the discretion of Owners even to the fill capacity of fuel tanks, deep tanks, and any other compartment in which oil can be carried whether such amount is or is not required for the chartered voyage."

写得如此清楚明白,看来在程租的订约自由下,难以针对船东去挑毛病,但这还要看下一段的"相悖理论"。当然在海牙规则下,合理与否仍有其他较多的因素要看,要加以考虑。例如,加油港是否严重偏离航线?是否严重损害货方的利益?是否有较大危险,等等。

2.4.2 针对极广泛的允许绕航条款的"相悖理论"

第四章 提单作用之二：运输合约的形式与有关条款的分析/探讨

允许绕航条款是一种免责条款：去免除船东对绕航本应承担的严重后果。所以在第四章谈到的针对免责条款的有关精神完全适用。例如，5.2 小段提到的要考虑整个合约，5.3 小段讲到的法官对其有一定敌意等。这一来，也带来 5.7 小段论及的"相悖理论"。这就是，无论绕航条款在措辞上如何广泛，若是与合约主旨（main object or purpose）有冲突，则解释起来会被相应地局限或超越。

这合约主旨的说法首先就是来自绕航的先例。在 Glynn v. Margetson (1893) A.C. 351，船是装载橘子去英国利物浦。运输合约中有一条广泛的绕航条款，允许船去很多列名地区，不论是为何原因（for any other purpose whatsoever）。结果船绕航，偏离了航线 350 海里，这严重延误带来了橘子的腐烂。贵族院判是这允许绕航条款所指的港口，只能是沿航线的港口，不能严重偏离，否则就违反了合约的"主旨"，这也是首次提出了"相悖理论"。Herschell 勋爵说：

"…the main object and intent, as I have said, of this charterparty is the carriage of oranges from Malaga to Liverpool. That is the matter with which the shipper is concerned; and it seems to me that it would be to defeat what is the manifest object and intention of such a contract to hold that it was entered into with power to shipowner to proceed anywhere that he pleased, to trade in any manner that he pleased, and to arrive at the port at which the oranges were to be delivered when he pleased."

在 2.4.1 小段所谈到的 The "Macedon" 一案，Kinsella 大法官也有类似说法如下：

"I think that expedition was of the essence of such a contract and I find it impossible consistently with this to read it to mean that the parties intended that the defendants（船东）should have a right within the contract, to call not only at Newcastle but at every port on the coast or off it, on the contract route or off it, for any purpose whatever, whether connected with the journey or not. To do so would stultify the object of the contract. If the whole contract is read, as it must be, as a commercial document, I think that（允许绕航条款）, while they cannot be treated as expunged, must be treated as subordinate to the dominant purpose of the contract to carry the cargo with all reasonable expedition to its destination."

美国法院在 General Elec. Co. Int'l Sales Div. V. The Nancy Lykes, 706 F. 2d 80 (2d Cir. 1983) 也说明了为何允许绕航条款说清楚了仍不一定能得到充分的文字上的解释：

"Even before COGSA was enacted in 1936, it was well settled that liberties clauses, though broad in language, were limited in scope... Because liberties clauses refer to the voyage contemplated by the parties, and not to different voyage which the shipper is concerned; and it seems to me that it would be to defeat what is the manifest object and intention of such a contract to hold that it was entered into with power to shipowner to proceed anywhere that he pleased, to trade in any manner that he pleased, and to arrive at the port at which the oranges were to be delivered when he pleased."

在 2.4.1 小段所谈到的 The "Macedon" 一案, Kinsella 大法官也有类似说法如下:

"I think that expedition was of the essence of such a contract and I find it impossible consistently with this to read it to mean that the parties intended that the defendants (船东) should have a right within the contract, to call not only at Newcastle but at every port on the coast or off it. on the contract route or off it, for any purpose whatever, whether connected with the journey or not. To do so would stultify the object of the contract. If the whole contract is read, as it must be, as a commercial document, I think that (允许绕航条款), while they cannot be treated as expunged, must be treated as subordinate to the dominant purpose of the contract to carry the cargo with all reasonable expedition to its destination."

美国法院在 General Elec. Co. Int' Sales Div. V. The Nancy Lykes, 706F. 2d 80 (2d determined unilaterally by the carrier, these clauses have long been interpreted to give the carrier only a limited right to deviate when such a deviation is reasonable under all the circumstances."

2.4.3 允许绕航条款所起的作用

撇开 2.4.2 小段的"相悖理论",允许绕航条款对船东仍是极为重要的,如本段一开始所讲,这是考虑绕航合理与否的一个因素。而且,在一些不与合约主旨或主要义务有冲突的情况下,主要是那些轻微的绕航,仍会是看条款如何说就如何解释。这一来,一条广泛且有针对性的允许绕航条款就会显得重要。

这可以去举两个先例来说明,一是 The "Ragnvald Jarl" (1934) 49 Lloyd's Rep. 183。在一个 Palermo 去伦敦的 22 天航次,船是装了柠檬。它半途绕航去英国的 Hull,延误了 3 天。表面看来,本案与上一小段讲的 Glynn v. Margetson 的橘子案例事实相近,除了绕航及延误的严重性不同外。但 Branson 大法官判是船东可去依赖一条广泛的允许绕航的条款,并说:

"In so far as the liberty which has been reserved can be used without frustrating the contract, then there is no reason for disregarding it in construing the contract. It can stand with that limitation, and why it should be necessary to disregard it altogether I do not see... nor do I find any authority for the proposition that one should disregard it altogether(除非允许绕航条款会令整个合约变为无意义,看不出有什么理由在解释整个合约时,可不考虑它的存在)."

另一个例子是美国的 The "San Giuseppe" 122F. 2d 579, 582 (4th Cir. 1941)。它也涉及一条广泛的允许绕航条款,也说明准去加油。一个不严重的绕航[航次是新奥尔良去伦敦,船绕航去诺福克(Norfork)加油],被判为不算违约的绕航。

2.4.4 金康租约下的允许绕航条款

经过以上各段的分析,回头去看本章§1段的金康租约第3条,会发觉它的措辞看似广泛,其实不然,但也绝非没有任何保障船东的作用。

首先,它说船可去挂靠任何次序的港口(to call at any port or ports in any order)。这在2.4.2小段的 Glynn v. Margetson 一先例可见,它只会允许沿航线的港口,不能严重偏离,次序也不应是太颠倒。

接着,它说是绕航可为了任何事情(for any purpose),这应是指船东可去为了修理、加油、换船员、装卸其他货物等这些仅与船东有关的其他事情而绕航。但在2.4.1小段的 The "Macedon" 一案可见,所有这些事情必须与该航次有关。所以,装了货半途去作年度修理,实与航次无关,这仍不被允许。加油也是一样,船东想去为下一航次加油恐怕要在金康租约内多加一条如2.4.1小段所提的 P&I Bunker Deviation Clause 才能获得更好的保障。

该条款最后也提到可绕航去救助财产,这已很清楚,就不多谈了。

3.4.5 转船权利/自由

第7条:转船的自由

Conlinebill 2000 的第7条款很简短,为了方便看,不妨节录如下:"Transhipment:The Carrier shall be at liberty to tranship, land and store the cargo either on shore or afloat and reship and forward the same to the Port of Discharge."

"转船"这课题带来几个有趣与实际的问题。例如,普通法下船东/承运人有默示的权利去转船吗?如果有,是什么情况下可以这样做?另外,既然有了默示权利可去转船,为何船东/承运人要去另加明示条款允许转船?这样有何额外的好处?适当措辞/文字应是怎样?

先去节录《Scrutton on Charter-Parties》一书第19版之 Article 129 如下:

"Where a vessel in which goods are shipped is hindered by an excepted peril from completing the contract voyage, (1) the shipowner must, if the obstacle can be overcome by reasonable expenditure or delay, do his best to overcome it. (2) It is only where an excepted peril renders the completion of the voyage physically impossible, (3) or so clearly unreasonable as to be impossible from the business point of view, (4) that the shipowner is justified in throwing up the voyage without the consent of the charterer or shipper. (5) The test of whether completion of the voyage is impossible from a business point of view may depend on the possibility of effecting repairs or the cost of repairs. (6) In either case the question to be considered is the repair necessary to enable the ship to complete the voyage with the particular cargo carried. (7)

Where the shipowner is prevent from completing the contract voyage by a peril which cannot be overcome in a reasonable time, or by damage which cannot be repaired at a reasonable expense, he is not bound either to repair or tranship; (8) though, if he elects to do neither, he must hand over his cargo to the cargo-owner freight free, (9) or, if the cargo-owner is not present to receive it, and cannot be communicated with, the master must act for the best as the cargo-owner's agent. (10) He has, however, the right to earn his freight either by repairing his own ship and proceeding to the port of destination, or by transhipping the goods into another vessel to be forwarded thither, (11) and he may delay the transit a reasonable time for either of these purposes. (12) If he spends an unreasonable time in making up his mind which course to adopt, and the cargo is damaged during the delay, the shipowner will be liable to the cargo-owner for the damage. (13)

In case of justifiable transhipment by the master as agent for the shipowner, the cargo-owner will be bound to pay the full freight originally contracted for, though the transhipment was effected by the shipowner at a smaller freight. (14)

Semble, the master cannot, without express authority, bind the cargoowner to more unfavourable terms in the contract of transhipment, as by wider exceptions, or to pay a larger freight than that originally contracted for, unless communication with the cargo-owner is impossible, and forwarding the cargo on such terms would appear to a reasonable man to be the most beneficial course of the interests of the cargo. (15)

If the hindrance of the ship's voyage is not caused by an excepted peril, the shipowner is not entitled as of right to tranship on his own account on terms more onerous to the shipper than the original contract (though he may be bound to do so on account of the cargo-owner); but he is liable for delay or failure to deliver. (16)

Note: In many bills of lading (especially through bills of lading and bills issued by regular steamship lines) there is an express provision that the shipowner shall have liberty to tranship and forward the goods "by any other line", or "by any other steamer or steamers". The terms of such clauses vary considerably, but there is not usually much doubt as to their meaning. (17)

Where in such a clause there was liberty to tranship and forward "at ship's expense but at shipper's risk", it was held that the phrase "at shipper's risk" applied only to the process of transhipment, and did not supersede the general provisions of the bill of lading as to the transit after transhipment to the destination. (18)"

在以下小段,将对以上节录的内容加以详论,并引用同样的序号以便阅读:

(1)如果船舶在航次半途遇上事故(由于免责原因造成的)导致有障碍无法完成航次。

(2)船东/承运人如果花合理的费用或/与时间就可克服此障碍(通常的一种情况是修理船舶),则他/它必须这样做。毕竟,履约责任(把货物运至卸港)是严格的。

(3)除非航次完全无法再履行,例如是船或货业已因免责风险而遭受了全损。

(4)或是商业上不值得去做;这主要是船舶发生了"推定全损"(constructive total loss)。

(5)这一来,提单合约可说是已受阻,船东/承运人不必经货方同意(他/它怎会同意呢!)就可以放弃航次。

(6)可否修理或修理是否太昂贵这两点都会成为是否构成"推定全损"与航次受阻的考虑因素。

(7)总之要考虑有关船舶的修理(可否修理或太昂贵)是否可行。但会有一种情况是出了事故,船舶显然是不可修理或修理太昂贵,但仍可花一笔钱去"勉强修补",只为让船/货去卸港后才把船放弃与作废(推定全损)。这会带来争议指这笔钱不多,所以航次不应受阻。至于如何算"勉强修补",这会是一个"很"暂时的修理或/与加上拖带去卸港。疑问会是,若推定全损能成立而足以构成受阻,船东对这票船上货物再也没有合约责任,那么他顶多只是一位"不情愿的托管人":如在 The "Medina Princess" (1965) 1 Lloyd's Rep. 361 之 522 页。这一来,怎会有责任去"勉强修补"去把货物运到卸港呢?如果说只要"勉强修补"就能继续去卸港就不是受阻,而不论船舶本身是否推定全损,那么就不应又去针对很暂时的修理,只为完成航次着想。这会变成是不修理,船已完全作废,但仍要船东安排拖带或其他办法把货物运去卸港。这看来对船东/承运人有苛求之嫌。

这一点在 Kulukundis v. Norwich Union Fire Ins. Society (1936) 55 Lloyd's Rep. 55 先例, Greene 大法官曾谈论到,他说:"…I may point out in passing that if this view is correct the case would be one where, although the vessel would be a total loss for the purposes of a policy on hull, there would be no loss of freight under a policy on freight, since the sea damage would not in fact have been sufficient to excuse performance of the contract of affreightment."

而 Greene 大法官举的例子是船舶在卸港外搁浅,从当中截断,但船东/承运人很容易就可以安排把货物卸下驳船转运去卸港,费用也不高,从这角度看则提单合约会是并未受阻。但 Greene 大法官的话受到 Goff 大法官的质疑,后者在 The"Pythia"(1982) 2 Lloyd's Rep. 160 之 166 页说:

"…Lord Greene contemplated that the shipowner might be bound to unload the cargo into lighters and bring them into port first the remark was obiter, second that it was prefaced by the words 'it may well be', and third that Counsel did not apparently advance any argument to the contrary. Furthermore in the same case, Lord Justice Scott described transhipment as 'a privilege or liberty of the shipowner and not a duty'.

There must be considerable doubt whether, in this respect, this tentative dictum of Lord Justice Greene is one which should be followed, example which he was considering, the contract was prima facie frustrated when the back of the ship was broken. In any event, removal of the cargo from the ship by the shipowner might, depending on the circumstances, constitute a general average act giving rise to a right to contribution from cargo. Indeed, if it were practicable to communicate with the bill of lading holders or their agents at the port of discharge, it is difficult to see why they should not, though the contract was frustrated, be given the opportunity to come and collect their cargo in lighters."

[Greene 大法官所讲的只是"附带意见"(obiter),他并没有把话说死,这一点也没有大律师的陈词/反驳。更重要的是,这说法与"船东为赚取运费去转船是特权而不是责任"的提法有矛盾/冲突。既然提单合约因船舶截断而受阻,但又可以很容易卸下驳船转运去卸港,何不让船东只去通知收货人而让后者自己安排驳船来提取货物呢?]

(8) 若船东无法在合理时间内克服障碍或/无法以合理费用修复船舶去完成航次,他/它就再没有责任去进行修理或去转船,把货物运至卸港。

(9) 这等于是受阻而船东也应去交出货物(虽在半途但交出货物仍要收货人退回整套正本提单:请看本书第二章之 5.1.5 小段)。若运费尚未支付(运费到付情况),船东也不得要求运费(部分或全部),因为普通法是要求船东/承运人完成服务,到了卸港,才赚取运费的。这方面在笔者的《程租合约》一书第九章 1.2 小段有详论。

(10) 如果无法联系收货人,船长就是收货人的代理人/托管人了,包括会以"紧急代理人"(agent of necessity)的身份去处理货物。

(11)但船东有赚取运费的权利,即如果划算,船东/承运人可把货物转船。当然,是否去转船纯是船东/承运人的选择权[请看(8)]。而去这样做,往往会是:

(ⅰ)运费到付(freight collect)。如果运费已经预付,去转船对船东/承运人不会有好处,他/它不会去干。提单合约受阻了就算了。

(ⅱ)可赚取的运费比转船使费高,最后总账仍有得赚。

(12)去安排转船无疑会带来延误,但只要合理,船东/承运人不必对此货物延误向货方负责[当然,整件事故的起因应就属免责事项,这请看(1)]。

(13)但船东不得去不合理地延误转船,例如因保险或其他原因而迟迟不行动,否则要对收货人延迟收货的损失负责。

(14)只要是这种合法的转船把货物运抵卸港,收货人就不得借此提单合约早已受阻而拒付运费,也不得去托词转船运费较低,因为若非如此,船东/承运人根本不会主动去转船。

(15)若不是以上自己为赚取运费的转船,而是在提单合约受阻后代收货人转船,则船长在没有明确授权下,不得去代收货人订立更苛刻的转船条件或/与更昂贵的运费。除非是"紧急代理人"身份,因联系不到收货人,但又认为非这样做不可(代收货人转船,接受苛刻条件/昂贵运费),全是为了货方/收货人利益着想。

(16)如果整件事故的起因不是免责[这一点请看(1)],例如是船舶开航时严重不适航,则怎样说船东/承运人对收货人遭受的损失(包括因转船的延误)都要负责了。

(17)许多提单(特别是班轮提单)都印有一条自由转船条款,措辞/用字明确。

(18)若条款说明转船的风险是在发货人,它只是指转船的行为。提单合约其他方面的承诺仍要执行,而且"风险"并不表示船东/承运人的疏忽被包括在内,可以免责:见 The "Oroya" (1926) 25 Lloyd's Rep. 573。

作一总结,有关船东/承运人转船的权利/自由是:

(1)提单合约即使没有写明,船东/承运人在普通法下也有默示权利/自由(但没有责任)在免责事故导致受阻时把货物转运至卸港以赚取运费。收货人若去干预,例如在 The "Bahia" (1864) 2 Asp. M. C. (O. S.) 174 向半途避难港法院申请强制卸货/交货,这是违反默示条款的行为。

(2)提单合约若有明示条款允许转船,会带来额外权利/自由,例如去合理地在港外把货物卸下驳船,让驳船完成航次:(Marcelino Gonzalez v. Nourse (1935) 53 Lloyd's Rep. 151。

(3)根据该明示条款的实际措辞/文字,会更广泛去允许船东/承运人在不同情况下为自己的利益转船,而且对转船后的风险不负责。

3.4.6 装船前与卸船后的责任

第 8 条:装船前/卸船后的责任这段期间再不受海牙/海牙·维斯比规则约束,所以承运人不会承担责任,安排接驳运输也只是以货方代理人的身份作出。当然 Conlinebill 这条款的措辞/文字也并非过分偏袒船东/承运人,他/它有疏忽仍是免不了责任。读者不妨比较这 Conlinebill 的条款与有类似意图的其他班轮公司提单格式的条款:见本书第二章之 5.6.2 小段。

3.4.7 装卸货与交货

第 10 条:装卸货与交货 Conlinebill 2000 这一条款分(a)至(g)小段,各有针对,而且措辞/文字一目了然。(a)是承运人一般负责装卸与交货,这是班轮做法,与租约的 FIO 相反。(b)是装卸上/下船舶与仓库等费用由货方负责。另可一提的是第 9 条说明承运人负责装卸港的"过驳船"费(lighterage),而将货物卸下过驳船的权利/自由应是来自第 7 条。

3.4.7.1 承运人不另给通知与及时交货或从速提货

(c)小段是说明承运人不另给货方关于装卸的通知,这方面可参阅本章之 3.4.1 小段。

(d)小段要求货方及时/准时交货以便装船。而(e)小段针对卸货,要求货方(收货人)去配合从速提取货物。在承运人要求下,甚至要超时工作去配合。提单合约若不去说明,应默示以当地港口习惯做法为准,例如一般不超时工作。但提单合约若说明,就应以明示条款为准了。

(f)小段说明货方不前来提取货物,则承运人有权/有自由去把货物卸下码头/岸上,而且这样做就算是已完成了提单的履约。若有必要(如易腐烂货物),承运人更可合理地去把货物以私下出售或公开拍卖掉。

这一小段带来的好几处问题可在如下段节加以详述:

3.4.7.2 班轮业务下谁有权指定卸货码头/地点

在班轮业务下,一般是由船东/承运人指定卸货码头/地点。这也完全合理与符合现实,否则上千个不同收货人,各有主意,各有主张,能去听谁呢? 这与租约的情况完全不一样,租约一般会规定承租人指定安全港口/码头/泊位,变得权利不在船东。而即使没有明确规定,英国法律默示的地位也是权属承租人(若持有正本提单),或提单合法持有人(收货人),或多数的收货人(若不只有一位):请参阅《Scrutton on Charter-Parties》一书,第 19 版之 Article 147。

3.4.7.3 若收货人不前来提取货物,船长有的权利是什么

针对收货人不前来提取货物的困境,由于班轮/集装箱船不能延误,船东/承运

人有何办法？这方面在本书第二章之5.1.8小段有详论，另在5.1.9小段也谈到收货人有"合理"时间前来向船长提取货物。

但会是班轮承运人等过了合理时间收货人仍无影无踪，则他/它应如何办呢？笔者可先去节录《Scrutton on Charter-Parties》一书第19版之Article 151，它说：

"If the consignee or holder of the bill of lading does not claim delivery within a reasonable time,[322] the master may land and warehouse the cargo in a statutable warehouse[323] at the expense of its owners, still preserving his lien on it,[324] and it is his duty to act reasonably in doing so rather than render the charterers, if they are not the defaulting consignees, liable for demurrage.

In such a case the warehouseman holds the goods as the common agent of the shipowner and of the consignee or indorsee of the bill of lading; agent of the shipowner to retain the goods and his lien for freight; agent of the consignee or indorsee to hold or deliver the goods for him on his producing the bill of lading and paying the freight.[325]

…if there are no statutable warehouses, delivery into which preserves his lien, he can still retain it by hiring a warehouse for the purposes.[326]

If, in unloading by the master owing to the delay or absence of the consignee, difficulties arise from the inaccurate description of goods in the bill of lading, the consignee must bear the resulting loss.[327]

If the master is forbidden to land the goods by the port authorities, or cannot obtain warehouse accommodation, he may, and must, at their owner's expense, deal with them in the matter both most reasonable to preserve his lien and must convenient in his judgment for their owner[328]."

3.4.7.4 若船东/承运人想马上能卸货上岸呢

若船期紧迫，连"合理"时间也不想等待呢？这情况不少，但这一来就违反了普通法的地位。所以，很早已有班轮提单明示规定要求收货人"船抵达后马上"（immediately after arrival）提取货物：Major v. Grant（1902）7 Com. Cas. 231。

---

[322] 若过了合理时间收货人仍不见影。
[323] 船长可把货物卸下并存放在一个"立法许可"的仓库；立法是指英国商船法（Merchant Shipping Act 1894, Section 494）。
[324] 仓库费用由货方承担，并可同时保留对货物的留置权（如有必要，如针对欠下的运费）。
[325] 仓库主是承运人的代理人（要去保护留置权），也是收货人的代理人（将来把货物交给他）。
[326] 若卸货港没有"立法许可"的仓库，船东/承运人也可以自己安排岸上仓库。
[327] 这一点是货物标号/标记的问题，在本书第六章之3.1小段中有谈及。
[328] 但一切以合理为准，包括要考虑到收货人的地位/利益。

而 Conlinebill 2000 第 10 条(f)小段的第一句,通称为"London Clause",也是为了同样目的。它让船东/承运人可以自由把货物卸到岸上,而且明示不必为岸上货物负责,以防有当地习惯或港口规定是这货物在岸上仍要船东/承运人负责,除非收货人或他的代理人已去提取并把责任接收过来。

这一点可去节录《Carver Carriage by Sea》一书第 12 版之 1017 段,它说:

"Where the bill of lading contained the clause known as the London clause, entitling the shipowner 'to land these goods on the quays of the dock where the steamer discharges immediately on her arrival',[329] it was held to override a custom of the port which would have entitled the consignee to have delivery overside into lighters.[330]

A clause enabling the shipowner to discharge in the consignee's absence, and in his risk and expense, is for the shipowner's protection.[331] He is not bound to exercise the power…"

说到这里,仍须明确的是虽有"伦敦条款"(London Clause),也不表示船东/承运人可以乱来,不必合理与妥善/小心地照看货物。这在两点可见:

(i)接下去一句针对承运人可以在有合理需要时把货物以私下出售或公开拍卖处理掉。这有"紧急代理人"(agent of necessity)的味道,稍后详论。

(ii)仍有本书第二章详述的必须退还正本提单才能交出货物的要求。

3.4.7.5 承运人私下出售或公开拍卖货物的情况

这是 Conlinebill 2000 第 10 条(f)小段的第二句,写明(重复英文的措辞):

"should the cargo not be applied for within a reasonable time, the Carrier may sell the same privately or by auction."

承运人作为货物的托管人,即使货卸到了岸上,也会有"合理小心照看"(reasonable or due care)的责任。例如,不去眼看着易腐货物烂掉,或是昂贵的仓库费用将很快把剩余货价冲抵掉。这方面的托管人责任,可去节录《国际商务游戏规则——英国合约法》一书第四章之 6.3 小段有关"紧急代理人"(agent of necessity)的论述,如下:

6.3 没有授权的紧急代理人(agent of necessity)

在特殊情况下,会是没有任何授权也可以以紧急代理人的身份去为委托

---

[329] 若提单有一条 London Clause(措辞/文字类同 Conlinebill 2000 之第 10 条(f)小段)。
[330] 则它可去超越卸港习惯的做法,例如原先收货人有权要求货物在船旁另一边卸下驳船而不是卸在岸上,也计划这样去作业。但根据 London Clause,承运人在船舶一抵达后马上就可把货物卸到岸上。没去理会(与通知)收货人,判可以这样做而不构成违约。
[331] 这条款是保障船东/承运人可在收货人不出现时自由卸下货物,并对其不再负责,而费用与风险则由收货人承担。

人订一个合约,做一些事情,而委托人要受约束,比如不能去赖掉紧急代理人用他名义与第三者订的合约。

对航运来说,这种情况最典型的例子是海上救助。船长与救援人员签订的救助合约,船长对船东而言,身份是被默示授权的代理人:见 The "Unique Mariner" (1978) 1 Lloyd's Rep. 438。但船长对货方而言,身份则是紧急代理人。同样的,救助合约对船东货方都有约束力。

6.3.1 紧急代理人的构成条件

总的来说,法院不大愿意去承认紧急代理人,因为这会剥夺了委托人(比如是货方)的自主权。这情况一般会发生在托管(bailment)的情况,托管人要为货物采取一些紧急行动。但其他情况下也可以,只要是符合如下要求:

(ⅰ)无法与委托人(如货方)取得联系,或即使取得联系,也无法取得明确指示如何办:见 The "Winson" (1982) 1 Lloyd's Rep. 117。在这一点上,随着通信日益发达,法院看来有收紧船长以紧急代理人身份订下救助合约去约束货方之可能,如美国的 The "Belle Ville" (1970) AMC 663, 284, F. Supp. 1002 与英国的 The "Choko Star" (1990) 1 Lloyd's Rep. 516。如果货方可去以船长越权赖掉这救助合约,则他不会受救助合约内的伦敦仲裁条款约束,或是要去付定额救助奖金。而即使救助成功,货方也只需负责一般性无合约救助(pure salvage)的奖金。但船长则会是因越权要对救助方负上责任了。考虑到即使今天通信容易,但船上会有上百上千个集装箱,各有不同货主,所以要求船长去向每一位货方取得授权也不现实。看来,在救助的情况下,法院仍应尽量支持紧急代理人这一理论。

(ⅱ)紧急代理人必须是为了保障或改进情况(preservation and improvement)。所以,除了救助,也包括其他情况,如船长花钱去半途处理、修理损坏的货物,免损坏进一步扩大。

(ⅲ)紧急代理人所做的是合理且必须要做的,例如他可去把货物存放(然后让货方自己决定如何处置),则不应匆忙去拍卖掉。

(ⅳ)紧急代理人所做的必须是合理、善意而且是为了货方(或委托人)好的。

6.3.2 紧急代理人享有的权利

这权利会有如下三方面:

(ⅰ)这样做了,可完成紧急代理人本来会有的责任,比如船长在海牙规则下有合理与妥善照看货物的责任,托管人(bailee)对存放货物有"合理小心照看"(reasonable or due care)的责任等。

(ⅱ)与第三者订了合约(如救助合约、修理合约、买卖合约等),紧急代理人只是代理人身份,可以退出,不必负责履行或不履行。

(iii)紧急代理人所花的费用,可向委托人(货方)要回来。这种使费本来没有授权,会被视作是"自愿花费"(volunteer)。在有关约因的第三章5.4小段提过,自愿者因为没有约因或对价,是一方自愿作出贡献,所以法律一般不予协助去寻求补偿(indemnity)。但紧急代理人实质是被当做有授权了,所以可去要求补偿使费。

6.3.3 紧急代理人的实例

这方面也提过,如船长订立救助合约,货物半途有损船长认为无法完整运至卸港而在半途拍卖,或是安排作出修理以免进一步损坏,等等。

船长是这身份,同样理论也可去适用在岸上仓库的负责人,等等。

我也遇过装运牛羊的船舶,半途因天气坏而延误,结果要去花钱多加粮草,否则牛羊活不到卸港,这也是典型的紧急代理人所为。

最后再举一种最常见的例子是:国际买卖中在卸港交货,买方发觉质量不妥而去拒绝接受(rejection)货物。但卖方一般也不理睬,况且去安排收回在卸港的货也谈何容易。这一来,货物弃置在卸港会进一步扩大损失费用,这时谨慎的买方会可以以紧急代理人身份(给了卖方通知但没有明确指示)去把这票货转卖掉:见 Graanhadel T. Vink B. W. v. European Grain & Shipping Co. (1989) 2 Lloyd's Rep. 531; Treitel on Law of Contract,第8版,第622页。

买方这样做会对他有利,因为减少损失总是对的。而且买方往往已付了钱给卖方(通过信用证),虽然去拒绝货物,但将来能否成功追偿回这笔货款仍是天知道。"

读者或许会问,既然普通法有此"紧急代理人"的说法,Conlinebill 2000 又何必再多加一句去说明承运人可以私下或公开出售货物呢?答案是:

(i)有明示条款去授权承运人这样做比普通法安全与稳定。从节录中可见,"紧急代理人"的说法毕竟不容易成立。

(ii)例如,Conlinebill 2000 明示条款说合理时间一过收货人不前来提取货物,承运人已可去这样办。但普通法的地位却颇重视与货方能否取得联系:见 The "Winson", The "Choko Star"等先例。而收货人不前来并不表示承运人无法去联系他,通知他,不知道他是谁。只是承运人不想与不肯去背上通知收货人的责任而已:请参阅本章之3.4.1小段。但这一来,表示去把货物出售/拍卖,承运人就不一定能成为"紧急代理人",从而变成是越权了。

(iii)所以,还是有必要以此明示条款去预先授权。

3.4.7.6 分不开货物的处理

这是 Conlinebill 2000 第 10 条款之(g)小段,很短一句,不妨节录如下:

"The Merchant shall accept his reasonable proportion of unidentified loose cargo."

这里涉及一个相当复杂的分不开货物/货物混在一起的问题。特别是在航次半途发生事故而导致几票分不开货物如何分摊短少/货差等问题。

首先,可去节录《国际货物买卖》一书之第五章,笔者已有多处提到这方面的问题,虽然主要是涉及货物主权若分不开便难以从卖方转让给买方的方面。该书在第五章之 4.1 小段说:

如果船舶载重量是 2.5 万吨,装的是 2 万吨食糖,分属三份不同买卖合约。食糖都混在一起,说不出哪部分是归某买卖合约的,反正是船舶到了卸港,买方前来提货,才慢慢去分。但这一来,却令"不记名提单"的背书也在 1979 年货物销售法的 Section 16 下无法去转让货物,因为在船上的食糖"意外"的分不开而尚未可去确定。

1979 年立法也不是在这方面故意为难,本小段已介绍过 10 个买方去卖方仓库"提取"(实际是形同抢掠)单车的困境,不妨再举这 2 万吨混合在一起的食糖为例。该例中船舶半途遇险,海水进到舱内令 1 万吨食糖变为"糖水"流失。到了卸港,有三位买方,各买了 1 万吨、5000 吨及 5000 吨,上船提货。他们知悉遇险,都说变"糖水"流失的货物不属他的一票。这一来,船长怎样办呢? 先到先得? 但他们都一齐到呢? 看谁给船长的红包大? 这合法吗?

而船长如果去向三位买方质问:你们说变"糖水"流失的货物(装在 1、2 号舱)不属于你们的,可否证明较早时,货物已转让给你们(提单背书时)并已确定是装在 3 或 4 或 5 船舱。可以说,三位买方都会无法回答。

可见,分不开的货物要到了卸港,真正去分得开,才能分别转让给个别买方。但这对买方不便也不利,因为他支付货款后(例如以信用证支付),仍无法拥有货物。如果卖方倒闭怎样办,因为债权人会来索取这票仍属卖方的货物? 而发生货损,买方如果要以侵权起诉船东,也会因没拥有货物而寸步难行。"

针对上述,该书第五章之 4.4 小段接着讲到了英国立法的改变,就是对分不开货物引进了"共同拥有者"(tenancy in common)的概念,并考虑到了如何在几票货物中分摊短少/货差,具体如下:

4.4 英国在 1995 年立法的修改

在英国法律下,这"共同拥有者"的概念并不稀奇。在岸上的土地/房子,常会有这概念。如大厦一单位由几位业主照比例的拥有,各占一份,所谓"tenancy in common"。同样做法,一早已在对商船的拥有上实行,根据"商船法

(Merchant Shipping Act),可以有多达64人共同拥有一船。货物买卖也没有理由不能这样处理。所以在 Sale of Goods（Amendment）act 1995，它在1979年货物销售法的规定上增加了 Section 20（A）与20（B）。这可在本书的附录一找到，由于内容稍多，故不在此节录。

另外，在 Section 16，原条款仍被保留，表示大原则不变，只是去加了几个字说"Subiect to Section 20A below"，以表示新增加的 Section 20A 只是唯一例外的情况，大原则仍是货物要能去"确定"（ascertained）才能转让给买方。

这一来，英国法律在这问题上已与美国法律看齐。英国法律也针对了一些细则，例如是：

（i）一大批货有了短缺的情况如何分摊这是在 Section 20（A）（4），说明要"共同拥有者"照比例分摊。如在较早讲到的2万吨食糖有1万吨变了糖水，余下的1万吨只好照比例分：1万吨的买方只有5000吨；其余各5000吨的2位买方只能各有2500吨。要知道，这1万吨变了糖水的损失起因，船东在海牙规则或中国海商法下不一定有责任。所以遇上不幸要由共同的买方分摊承担。

这实际是与中远提单上的一条款一样，只是做法上以前要靠提单条款的明示，今天则可以靠立法给予的默示。这中远提单条款是说：

"Where bulk cargo or goods without marks or cargo with the same marks are shipped to more than one consignee, the consignees or owners of goods shall jointly and severally bear any expense or loss in dividing the goods or parcels into pro rate quantities and any deficiency shall decide"。

（ii）无法避免先到先得的情况——这是在 Section 20（B）（2），它针对了另一种情况，是无可避免的先到先得，例如上例的2万吨食糖分不同港口卸，加上流失不多，船长也不知道有短缺。这一来，最后一位买方（提单持有人）会发觉少了1000吨，而这总共1000吨的损失全要由他来承受，看来很不公道。要知道，这1000吨损失的起因可能是船东不必负责的。这一来，这位不幸的买方可否去起诉船长，指他分摊损失不当呢？但是，船长又要怎样做才是恰当的呢？或者是，去起诉比他先一步提货的买方，要求他们将照比例多提取了的食糖归还给他？

英国法律为了避免过多的诉讼，复杂的理算/分摊以及不现实/昂贵的做法，决定不追求绝对的公道。立法在这一条款下是谁倒霉则谁自负损失。

当然，英国法律并不禁止订约自由，当事方可另去协议：见 The"Ypatianna"（1987）2 Lloyd's Rep. 286；Re Stapyton Fletcher（1994）1 WLR 1181"。另请看第十章6.1小段所介绍分析的 CAFTA 100 详尽的第26条。

第四章　提单作用之二：运输合约的形式与有关条款的分析/探讨　303

有关航次中发生事故导致分不开的货物整体的短少/货差，笔者想再多讲一讲。它会涉及海上事故是承运人可以免责或不能免责的，船东/船长的平均分摊短少货物的权利等问题。而较先的节录比较多地针对货物的主权转让，即不是遇上事故，一大批货物装上船舶时已属多位买方，混在一起，一直至卸货时才分得开，也会有无法转让货权的问题，而并没遇上事故，也不应有货物短少发生。而涉及半途遇上事故这一方面的问题，则可以节录《Scrutton on Charter-Parties》一书第19版之 Article 150 部分如下加以论述："Where goods of one description, shipped under different bills of lading, become unidentifiable in the course of the voyage:[332]

(A) If this result has happened by reason of excepted perils (so that the shipowner has a defence against the claim of any bill of lading holder for damages for his failure to deliver the actual goods shipped under that bill of lading),[333] the owners of the goods so mixed become tenants in common of the whole of the mixed goods in the proportion in which they have severally contributed to that whole.[334] It will therefore be the duty of the shipowner to deliver the indistinguishable goods,[335] or their proceeds,[336] to the various holders in proportion to the extent to which full delivery on each bill of lading remains unsatisfied by the delivery under it of its proper identifiable goods.

(B) The shipowner may be relieved of this duty of apportioning the goods among the bill of lading holders by the provisions of the various bill of lading, or by the custom of the port as to discharge.[337]

(C) This principle has no application where various shipments become mixed and unidentifiable in the course of the voyage, but the shipowner on the terms of his contracts

---

[332] 如果货物是同一种类的商品，分别有几份不同的提单，几个不同的收货人，半途遇上事故而出了分不开的问题。

[333] 如果造成事故的是船东可免责的原因（有关提单合约的一般免责事项，也就是海牙规则的各项免责，可参阅本书第五章之4.2.7.1小段）。

[334] 这一来，这一大批分不开但又有了短缺的货物属所有收货人"共同拥有"(tenants in common)，各自有权去平均或按比例分配他们应有的一份货物。

[335] 而船东/承运人也有责任去这样公平/合理分配并交出货物。他/它不能去"厚待"其中一位收货人，导致其余收货人被"分薄"了应得的货量。或是，纯为自己方便去随意交货给先到先得的收货人。否则就算他/它原本可以在海牙规则下免责（对事故而然），也会因后来对货物处理不妥或违反这方面默示的法定责任而要对这部分货差负责。

[336] 也可能货物被私下出售或公开拍卖（请看3.4.6.5小段），这时船东/承运人仍应去公平/合理分配卖货所得的金钱/货价。

[337] 如何分配若在提单合约另有明示规定或卸港另有习惯做法，则去照做亦可免除船东/承运人在这方面的责任。

has no defence to a claim by any particular bill of lading holder that he has failed to deliver the specific goods shipped under the particular bill of lading.[338]"

3.4.8 运费与各项有关支出/使费

第 11 条：运费与使费 Conlinebill 2000 这一条款分为(a)至(e)小段，针对运费与各项有关使费（如关税、熏舱费用、货物整理与额外处理费用、货物修补/包装费用、量重费用，等等）与罚款（如违反海关或进出口国家法律/条例等）。最后的(e)小段，是针对班轮业务常见的情况，发货人出于各货物品种运价不同，为了省钱，故意瞒骗或/与误述货物的本质/品种，例如本是危险品却不作声明。在散货运输中较难去瞒骗，但在班轮业务，货物有包装甚至是铅封了的集装箱，船东/承运人不易觉察。发货人也会在宣告货物重量、计算或货价时做手脚或无意中出错。这一切如果后来承运人发觉可疑，可在这明示条款下[第 11 条(e)小段]开箱检查或验看发票等，并在查明真相后去收取双倍的运费。在此只提一提这条款有可能会被指为是"惩罚条款"(penalty clause)而无效：这一点请去看笔者的《国际商务游戏—英国合约法》一书第十四章之§15 段。当然，班轮公司也会去争辩这样订只是因为额外带来的行政工作/麻烦，难以证明具体的金额损失，所以要去估计一个"议定的赔偿"(liquidated damage)。

讲到运费这一课题，笔者的《程租合约》一书第九章有详论，内容太多，无法节录或重复，就此略过。

至于各项使费的争议，该书多处也有详论，如第十五章之§2 段，因为内容少得多，故去节录如下（它针对航次租约，但在提单合约也是一样道理，一样的争议）：

> 这一条款常见于金康合同 1976 年格式的附加条款，所以在 1994 年格式，索性增加为第 13 条。它的内容是讲只有船舶的税金与使费(all dues, charges and taxes)才由船东负责支付。其他的对货物及运费征收的税金与使费则由承租人负责支付。
>
> 关于运费的税金以及有关争议，已在本书第九章之§8 有详细介绍，不再重复。
>
> 至于何谓"船舶"、何谓"货物"的税金与使费，这有时会分不清楚，因为在计算的方法上可能会混在一起。例如明明是港口的泊位费或使费，但却与所

---

[338] 如果事故不是可以免责的事由，则分配归分配，但并不存在船东/承运人可去免除责任。事实上，他/它要对所有收货人遭受的货差损失负上责任，作出赔偿。

装货物的品种与数量挂上钩。而 1994 年金康租约对此已写明不理会计算或核算方法,而主要是看它的本质。

这方面的争议,实际与第十章的 2.11 小段一样。例如,其中举到一案例的争议是德国港口一种叫"Kajegebubr"的使费是否算港口使费,虽然它的计算是根据货量。

因为这种争议颇多,也不好决定,即使每次都去仔细看使费的本质或是看有关条款的写法,也常会有矛盾的裁决,所以我想多举几个这方面的纽约仲裁的例子,具体如下:

(i)在 The "Sun Pollux" SMA No. 1468(1980),它的金康租约有一条附加条款写作:

"25. Normal port dues including customary agency fee to be for Owners' accont. Owners to put ship's agents both ends in funds for disbursements prior to vessel's arrival. Any dues and/or taxes on cargo and/or freight or calculated onsame as per custom of the port to be for Charterers' account. Any dues and/or taxes on vessel to be for Owners' account."

在南美厄瓜多尔的卸港有一笔港口使费是以卸货量来计算,每吨 3 美元,针对该使费,港口的规定是:

"Taxes Levied Against the Vessel;

5.1 The present tariff comprises the utilization of the piers and dock facilities; the use of buoys… and it will be applicable in the quantity and under the conditions outlined later on all ships which use the mentioned facilities…

5.5 Taxes Per Ton Discharged…

5.5.2 General cargo, homogenous, US $ 3.00…."

仲裁庭判是根据这特定的第 25 条附加条款,只因为它写得不好,说是以"货物"计算的费用由承租人支付,那么这笔钱自然也不必看其本质,由承租人承担是明确不过的了。

(ii)在 The "Vassilios Bacolitsas" SMA No. 2259(1986),是一笔 7000 多美元的在 Rostock 卸港的部分港口使费。该港的港口使费计算办法是分别根据船舶的毛吨位(GRT)与卸货量。租约有一条简单的附加条款说:

"22. Any dues and/or taxes on cargo and/or freight at discharge to be for Receivers' account. Any dues and/or taxes on vessel to be for Owners' account."

两位仲裁员判承租人要负责这 7000 多美元的根据卸货量计算的港口使费。但另一位仲裁员 Michale A. van Gelder 先生不同意,他不认为这第 22 条附加条款清楚明确地改变了在程租合约下船东要负责港口使费的基本责任与安排。他也说港口使费拆开两部分计算的办法并不表示本质上有何改变。他说："The fact that the Port Tariff breaks up the total cost is not any reason to decide that port charges are to be interpreted as '… dues and/or taxes' within the meaning of Clause 22."

　　在这里，大家可回头看 1994 年金康租约第 13 条已讲明的不理会计算或核算的办法，只看收费或税金本质的规定。所以，这案例的争议应不会在 1994 年的金康租约发生。

　　(ⅲ) 在 The "Koeaeli" SMA No. 2417 (1987)，是关于葡萄牙所有港口都征收的一项使费，称为 Maritime Commercial Tax (以前叫 Gold Dues)。它的计算也是根据卸货量。但仲裁员在该仲裁中判船东要负责，而原因倒不是去分析这使费的本质，而是指该租约为列名港口，船东早应知道会有这笔使费由港口当局向船东征收。所以如果他不想承担，他应事先在租约讲明以转嫁给承租人。

　　(ⅳ) 在 The "Ermis" SMA No. 2960 (1993)，涉及船在中国天津新港装货，但被指超出了安全吃水 9 米，所以每超出一公分的吃水要加收 1500 元人民币，共达 1.6 万美元。外代指这笔钱是"赶装费用"(arrange rush loading charge and sailing by hightide)，这带来争议，到底它是否是港口使费？仲裁员判它的本质应如"清理航道费用"(dredging dues) 一般，在程租下一向由船东承担，是正常港口使费的一部分，所以由船东负责。

　　(ⅴ) 在 The "Punica" SMA No. 3023 (1993)，是关于何谓"码头费"(wharfage)，何谓"停泊费"(dockage)。这两笔使费在国际海商词典 (International Maritime Dictionary) 的定义是：

　　—码头费：The exact meaning of this term varies in different port. It can be defined in a general way as a charge assessed against all cargo conveyed on, over, or through a wharf, quay or pier. Sometimes called transfer charge tolls, port toll.

　　—停泊费：A charge or due levied against a vessel in cases where, in addition to harborage, the vessel makes use of the dock accommodation of a port for the purpose of taking in or discharging cargo.

　　这一来，看它们的本质，一般应是：码头费的本质在于针对货物，应由承租人负责；而停泊费的本质在于针对船舶，应由船东负责。至于它们会如何计算或核算，各港口做法也不同，这不必去理会。这也是 1994 年金康租约第 13 条的写法。

　　但在 The "Punica" 一案，它的有关条款是：

　　"27. Any taxes/dues/wharfage on cargo to be for Charterers' account. Any taxes/dues/wharfage/dockage on vessel and/or freight to be for Owners' account."

在马来西亚的 Port Kelang，有一笔 2 万 5 千元的"码头费"，它以卸货量计算，有了争议。两位仲裁员判在第 27 条下，应由承租人负责。但另一位仲裁员，Jack Berg 先生不同意，认为这笔钱应细看港口规则，它的本质是"停泊费"而非"码头费"，所以应由船东自己负责。

3.4.9 留置权

第 12 条：留置权 Conlinebill 2000 这一条款很短，为方便读者，不妨节录如下："The Carrier shall have a lien on all cargo for any amount due under this contract and the costs of recovering the same and shall be entitled to sell the cargo privately or by auction to satisfy any such claims."

这又是一个重要课题，在《程租合约》一书第十三章有详论，内容太多，无法节录或重复，请读者自己去参阅，所讲内容的道理与先例在提单合约也一样适用。

例如，英国法律只默示有针对欠运费的留置权，所以船东/承运人想要就其他代货物垫付了的使费（如在第十一条所列举的）保留留置权，就要靠明示条款了，否则不一定有合法权利去留置。在租约业务是先要在租约订有此广泛的留置权条款，之后再合并进租约提单。在班轮提单就要印妥在一份标准格式内，再供以后使用。

书中也提到留置货物所花的费用不一定能要回：The "Olib"（1991）2 Lloyd's Rep. 108。所以，Conlinebill 的第十三条款有这样 "the costs of recovering the same" 的用字/措辞。

3.4.10 延误

第 13 条：延误船东/承运人从装港去卸港的航次法律默示的地位是应采取"恰当"（proper），"习惯性"（usual）与"合理"（reasonable）的航线，不应去"不合理绕航"或"不合理延误"（unreasonable delay）。有关不合理绕航，留待本书第五章之 4.2.10.1 小段（有关海牙规则）再详论。Conlinebill 2000 的第 13 条也只提及延误，所以，在此只谈这方面问题。由于第 13 条不长，也先作节录如下："If the carrier is held liable in respect of delay, (1) consequential loss or damages, other than loss of or damage to the cargo, (2) the liability of the carrier shall be limited to the freight for the carriage covered by this Bill of Lading, (3) or to the limitation amount as determined in Clause 3 (4) and Clause 4, (5) whichever is the lesser."

以下小段，将详论以上第 13 条的内容，并引用同一序号以便阅读：

(1) 延误会严重至构成不合理绕航。这可去节录 MacKinnon 大法官在 The

"Storviken"(1927) 27 Lloyd's Rep. 227 先例所说的:"Deviation, it is logically obvious, means a departure from the agreed via by which the ship is to carry out the charter voyage. It has been extended to include not merely its proper meaning but to extend to delay in the carrying out of the voyage beyond the agreed period of time-usually the shortest reasonable time in which the voyage can be carried out… In both of these cases, having regard to the deviation or delay, the deviation or delay is of course a breach of that which is expressed or implied in the contract as the route or the period of time by which or during which the voyage is to be accomplished."

故此,如果船舶在航次中延误且并不合理,例如停留中途港口过久,被扣船而不去尽早提供诉前保存,出了事故应修理但迟迟不作出决定(即使是因为保险公司的延误)等,都会构成违约。

至于延误会带来货物实质损坏,在本书第五章之4.2.6.6.6.1小段会有详论。例如易腐货物烂掉、煤炭/鱼粉等自燃、水泥变质及大豆发霉,等等。

但同样危险或更危险的是纯经济损失,如失去了市场/季节(The"Heron Ⅱ"(1967) 2 Lloyd's Rep. 457),或要在分销合约赔钱,等等。

(2)+(3)故此,Conlinebill 这条款把对经济损失的赔偿责任只局限在所收取的运费上。这运费不会有多少钱,一个集装箱会是只有几千美元或更少。

(4)但这会违反海牙规则令条款无效——如果在有关航次/出口国家该规则刚好是强制适用。这一来,就要以海牙规则的单位责任限制为准。

(5)也会是当地其他法律会强制适用在某航次,如汉堡规则或中国海商法,则也要以这些法律的立场为准,而不是只赔偿运费。要知道,班轮提单印妥后去用在所有不同航次,各有不同的立法/规定针对,故条款要用广泛与多包容的措辞/文字。

3.4.11 共同海损与救助,新杰森与姊妹船条款

第14条:共同海损与救助——Conlinebill 2000 这一条款不算长,可去节录如下:"General Average shall be adjusted, stated and settled in London according to the York-Antwerp Rules 1994, (1) or any modification thereof, in respect of all cargo, whether carried on or under deck. In the event of accident, danger, damage or disaster before or after commencement of the voyage resulting from any cause whatsoever, whether due to negligence or not, for which or for the consequence of which the Carrier is not responsible by statute, contract or otherwise, (2) the Merchant shall contribute with the Carrier in General Average to the payment of any sacrifice, losses or expenses of a General Average nature that may be made or incurred, and shall pay salvage or special charges incurred in respect of the cargo. If a salving vessel is owned or operated by the Carrier, salvage shall be paid for as fully as/if the salving vessel or vessels belonged to strangers. (3)"

有关共同海损与救助这两个关系密切的不同课题,请读者自己去参阅笔者的《海事法》一书第五章与第六章。内容实在太多,无法在此复述,就此略过,在此只对以上条款中加注码处作一说明如下:

(1)共同海损若不讲明,一般国家的法律规定/默示是以卸港法律为理算基础。现实也是到了卸港才执行共同海损。但各国有不同的法律,相异之处会很多很大。而且班轮上的货物会涉及多个不同卸港。这一来,撇开某些国家的法律好/坏,可否被接受,明确与否等问题,光是要去顾及多个不同卸港与不同国家的法律已可令共同海损理算严重增加麻烦。故此,班轮提单以明示条款规定理算一律依照York-Antwerp Rules 1994 作为基础/准则,不论事故时船上货物各去不同卸港。有关 York-Antwerp Rules 的内容,请参阅《海事法》一书第六章之3.3.3.1小段。

(2)这一部分是"新杰森"(New Jason)条款,在笔者《期租合约》一书§39段有详论,可节录如下:

39.1 新杰森条款的产生

新杰森条款是针对美国法律的独特之处而订的,条款源于一宗很古老的案例叫 The"Irrawaddy"(1898)171 U.S. 187,该案判是船东虽在1893年哈特法(相当于海牙规则)下可对航行疏忽免责,但仅此而已,它的作用像块盾牌(shield),而不能作为一把宝剑(sword),可以进一步向货方追讨共同海损的分摊。

这判法明显与英国不一样[The"Carron Park"(1890)15 P.D. 203],英国法院认为既然是免责,即没有错,因此不应妨碍船东去追讨共同海损的分摊。大家知道,一方的错引起共同海损是要负全责的。

这新杰森条款加在提单与租约内,就是去说明船舶有错但若是免责(这主要是航行疏忽),则共同海损货方不得拒绝分摊。这条款已被美国法院确认为有效(The"Jason"(1910)225 U.S. 32),并未因哈特法而无效。而本来的杰森条款因为1936年美国海上运输法的生效而作出相应修改从而变为"新"杰森条款。

39.2 订入新杰森条款的必要性

船东船长一定要记得在租约与提单内订下这一条款,虽然,需要这个保障也只限于共同海损的理算是在美国,以及货物运输是与美国有关而可能要在美国执行及收取共同海损分摊。当然,船舶在国际海上运输特别是期租下到处都会去,船东跟美国打交道的机会仍多得很。

如果忘了放进一条新杰森条款,导致在美国法律下无法向货方收取共同海损的分摊,一般船东互保协会章程都说明是不赔偿给船东的。

另外,如果提单漏了去放进一条新杰森条款,由于租约内一般都规定提单要有此条款,船长也往往有权不签租方呈交的提单。

现实中,因为一般所见的标准格式,不论租约或是提单,都早已印上这条款,所以漏掉的机会绝微,船长与船东都不怕。

(3)这一部分是"姊妹船"(sistership)条款,在笔者《期租合约》一书§40段有详论,可节录如下:

"此条款在现今已很少被应用,原因是:一船公司(one-ship company)的策略已大行其道,再也不容易找到有姊妹船互救的情况。连最有名望、水平与崇高地位的船公司,如马士基、包玉刚的环球等,亦是这样的公司结构。这样一来,即使是马士基船互救,也非是姊妹船互救。一船公司的好处很明显。这样做可以在发生大灾难时,把责任局限在一条船上。即使不能完全这样做,如在美国1990年油污法(OPA 1990)下的油污责任,也可以增加和解谈判的余地。一船公司也可避免给其他债权人(如租方、货主)去取巧施压抓其姊妹船,这也配合了现代营运,如向银行借贷等,银行会有此要求。但对像中国拥有这样大的商船队而不采用一船公司政策的特异情形来说,这姊妹条款就显得很重要,一定要在提单与租约中加入。

尽管这是一生之中也未必会碰到的巧事情,船东仍应明确在提单订有此条款(在期租情形下,应坚持承租人所签发的提单应订有此条款)。由于法律上是不承认自己(公司)可以控告自己要求赔偿或付钱的,法院对此也不会受理,因此即使是姊妹船相互救助成功也是不能获得救助费用的。所以根据此条款,船东虽然法律上没有权去收取救助费用,但在合约上却有这权利。船东只需交由仲裁员判定救助费用,然后向承租人/货主及被救助船舶的保险公司收取此费用的分摊部分"。

3.4.12 双方有责碰撞条款

第15条:双方有责碰撞条款

Conlinebill 2000 这一条款,也可去节录如下:"If the Vessel comes into collision with another vessel as a result of the negligence of the other vessel and any act, negligence or default of the Master, Mariner, Pilot or the servants of the Carrier in the navigation or in the management of the Vessel, the Merchant will indemnify the Carrier against all loss or liability to the other or non-carrying vessel or her Owner in so far as such loss or liability represents loss of or damage to or any claim whatsoever of the owner of the cargo paid or payable by the other or non-carrying vessel or her Owner to the owner of the cargo and set-off, recouped or recovered by the other or non-carrying vessel or her Owner as part of his claim against the carrying vessel or Carrier. The foregoing provisions shall also apply where the Owner, operator or those in charge of any vessel or vessels or objects other than, or in addition to, the colliding vessels or objects are at fault in respect of a collision or contact."

这方面在笔者的《期租合约》一书§43段有详论,可节录如下:

46.1 租约中订立双方有责碰撞条款的原因

双方有责碰撞条款是海上货物运输合同(提单或租约)中的一条标准条款。不少标准格式都印上了这条款,如出名的 Congenbill 提单。这一来,可防止遗漏。船东的互保协会要求船东在有关合约中必须放进本条款,而货物保险的 A 条款,在第三条也有这条款。至于原因何在,笔者在"英国海上保险条款详论"一书的 273 和 276 页曾谈到。

简言之,本条款源自美国碰撞法不同于 1910 年布鲁塞尔碰撞公约的特殊的"货物无辜规则"(innocent cargo rule)。根据公约,也是英国以前的判例法[The"Milan"(1861) Lush. 388;31 L. t. Ad. 105;5 L. T. 590],船货被视为是一家,船有错,即货也有错。会这样判估计是由于从前的做法是船货一家人,所以保险也保在一起,使用的是已存在了 200 年的 SG(ship & goods)保单格式。

可以举个例子,甲乙船相撞,判各有一半错(反正双方有错,至于比例并不重要)。则甲船上的货亦被视为有一半错,向乙船(non-carrying ship)索赔将只能得回一半赔偿。如果讲数字,甲的货物损失达 2000 万美元,它向乙船只能以侵权之诉索回 1000 万美元。至于余下的 1000 万,只好是自己(往往是货物保险公司)承担了。去告甲船(即自己的承运人或 carrying ship)是没有用的,因为海牙规则会对航行疏忽给予免责,而碰船正是典型的免责例子。

但美国的看法却不一样,它认为货方是无辜的一方,所以美国也不去签 1910 年的公约。在美国,"无辜"的货方是可以向对方船(只要有错)100% 索赔回损失的[The"Atlas"93 U. S. 302,315(1816)]。以上举的例子,即甲船货方损失的 2000 万美元全可向乙船要回来(除了乙船会申请责任限制外)。乙船不能抗辩说我只有一半错,甚至是只有 10% 的错,因为乙船面对的是无辜的货方,不存在货方也有部分比例的错,所以要分摊损失。但乙船赔了 2000 万美元后,可去向甲船(船东)要回一半[The"Chattahoochee"173 U. S. 540(1898)],因为双方各错一半。这一来,岂非通过后门或兜了个圈,甲船最终还是赔付了给自己船上的货方1000万,而照理在海牙规则或有关立法下,它是根本不必负责的,因为是航行疏忽。

有鉴于此,甲船船东索性去兜更大一个圈子:在与其船上货物一方所订的运输合同,不论是提单或租约,都去加上一条"双方有责碰撞条款"。这条款为求完整,加上又是律师草拟,所以不容易看得明白,除非是全面了解了背景。

这条款的作用是:有了它,甲船在被迫付了1000万美元给乙船后,可依照提单或租约(要看那一个才是承运合约)向货物装在甲船的货方讨回这一笔钱;依据便是本条款是这样讲明的,是订约自由下经双方同意加进合约的。

成功的话,则甲船的货方早前从乙船追到手的2000万美元,又要再吐出1000万来给甲船。结果是大家兜了个大圈,又返回原地,而得益只是律师。

有了这"双方有责碰撞条款",互保协会才会保障船东。比如,会代垫付给乙船1000万并根据提单或租约再向甲船货方要回这1000万。

46.2 双方有责碰撞条款的效力

美国曾判决"公共承运人"(public carrier)的运输合约,受哈特法或美国海上运输法(1936)的管制,因而加上这一条款是无效的:(United States v. Atlantic Mut. Ins. Co 343 U.S. 236, 1952 AMC 659(1952);The "Frances Hammer"(1975)1 Lloyd's Rep. 305)这一来,照说班轮提单就没必要再加这一条"双方有责碰撞条款"了。但仍是每一提单都去加,管它有效无效。一方面是船东互保协会要求这样做,另一方面是如果案子不在美国法院审,不适用美国法,或是美国法院中止审理而去承认在班轮提单上的外国仲裁条款[The "Sky Reefer"(1995)63 USLW 4617],则在外国(如英国)不论是法院判或是仲裁判都会承认这"双方有责碰撞条款"是有效的。如其他合约条款一样。

这条款如果是在非公共承运人的合约,明显就是指租约。连美国法院也接受它的有效性:American Union Transport Inc. v. United States, 1976 AMC 1480;Alamo Chemical Transp. Co. v. The Overseas Valdes, 1979 AMC 2033。

即使租约合并了美国海上运输法(1936),如 NYPE'46 的第24条,这条款也应是有效:Allseas Maritime v. The Mimosa, 574 F. Supp. 844(S. D. Text. 1993)。这方面的条款在外国,如英国是更不用说了,明显是有效,所以船东千万不要漏了加一条"双方有责碰撞条款"在租约(与所出的提单)内。特别是碰船,即使甲乙两船在亚洲范围的公海上碰,甲船的货方也可去美国扣乙船,把损失的2000万美元全索赔回来。这种"择地行诉"(forum shopping)的做法很常见,因此,不是船走美国,在美国碰船,甲船才需要一条"双方有责碰撞条款"来保障的。

看来,因为汉堡规则没有对航行疏忽给予免责,所以,如果全球性的接受该规则,就不应再存在有"双方有责碰撞条款"的必要了。但众所周知,这一天的来临遥遥无期,连中国《海商法》也是继续沿用此航行疏忽的免责。

3.4.13 政府指令、战争、疫症、冰封及罢工等情况下的自由条款

第16条:政府指令、战争及疫症等这一连串的自由条款,大原则/大精神与3.2.2小段的"邻近条款"(near clause)相同,因此不再多讲。Conlinebill 2000的该条款也较长,所以不去节录,请读者自己参阅附录九。

因为合约中的承诺是严格责任,所以船东/承运人同意了去某列名港口,可以说除非有像"受阻"(frustration)等罕见情况,他是绝不能半途去拒绝履约,拒去卸港的,这方面的大原则/大精神在本章之3.4.5页也可看到。

好像"邻近条款"一样的作用,为减轻或避免绝对要去列名卸港的责任,针对各种不同的突发事故如政府指令和战争等,船东/承运人会拟定一些自由条款,以避免"受阻"不易证明或/与成立,但为了履约到卸港要等待下去却又太昂贵或太遥遥无期的困境。

这些自由条款如针对战争的"战争条款",针对冰封的"冰封条款",以及针对罢工的"罢工条款",在笔者《程租合约》一书第七章之§5、§6和§7小段有详论,不在此重复。

3.4.14 喜玛拉雅条款

第17条:喜玛拉雅条款 Conlinebill 2000的这一条款太长,不去节录,请读者自己去看附录九。而内容方面,也已在本书第三章之8.2.2小段详述,故就此略过。

3.4.15 承运人有权合并货物堆装在集装箱内并装在甲板上

第18条:有权堆装,单位化 Conlinebill 2000这一条款分(a)与(b),条款不长,可去节录如下:

(a) Cargo may be stowed by the Carrier as received, or, at the Carrier's option, by means of containers, or similar articles of transport used to consolidate cargo.

(b) Containers, trailers and transportable tanks, whether stowed by the Carrier or received by him in a stowed condition from the Merchant, may be carried on or under deck without notice to the Merchant.

特别在二十多年前传统班轮转型走向集装箱船,发货人的货物若不是已堆装在集装箱(发货人自己堆装/铅封或交由货代/NVOC代劳),会对船东/承运人造成困难。所以,有这(a)条款可让船东/承运人有权/有自由去合并货物(与其他人的货)在一个集装箱内,以便装上专门的集装箱船运输。

而(b)涉及去把集装箱堆放在甲板上,这课题在本书第五章之4.2.3.5.3小段有详论,不先去重复。它详尽的内容包括了探讨把集装箱堆放在甲板上是否习惯做法(在4.2.3.5.3.9.2小段),要事先取得发货人同意货装甲板(在4.2.3.5.3.5小段)等,读者看了自然会对这条款(b)小段有完全的了解。

3.4.16　额外条款

Conlinebill 2000 标准格式(本书附录九)另有(A)与(B)的额外条款,任由船东/承运人选择适用与否。

(A)针对滞期费。正如本章一开始之§1段已讲到,由于班轮极少会因一票货物产生延误/滞期,加上不容易去预计延误船期的"真正"损失,进而将有关滞期费印在标准格式内,年年岁岁去适用,所以一般班轮提单都没有滞期费条款。

(B)针对美国航线的如下两个问题:

(ⅰ)美国有1893年哈特法,适用装船前与卸下船舶后的一段时间。换言之,船东/承运人在美国并不能将责任局限在海牙规则或/与1936年美国海上运输法的"船栏至船栏"(rail to rail)期间。这方面在本书第五章之4.1小段有详论。

(ⅱ)在美国,有先例说船东/承运人若不给发货人一个合理/公平的机会去宣告货价,就不能依赖海牙规则或1936年美国海上运输法下货物每件/每单位500美元的责任限制:见 The "Lady Sophie" (1979) 2 Lloyd's Rep. 173 等。要知道,一宣告了货价,将来赔偿也就不能限责了。但这一来,班轮公司也不客气,一开始会收取更高的运费(称为 ad valorem 运费)。现实中,多付运费会影响发货人,而将来能多赔只是保险公司或收货人受益。因此,发货人不愿宣告货价,也导致现实中很少有这种 ad valorem 货价的提单。但少归少,工夫仍要做足,以防将来美国法院不准限责。所以,便有了这一条款在 Conlinebill 2000,即(B)(ⅱ)条款。它属选择性使用是因为船舶行走美国航线才需要。

3.4.17　总结

还有其他一些条款/条款没有包括在 Conlinebill 2000 标准格式的班轮提单,例如在本书第二章5.10.1小段讲到的针对无单放货的免责条款。

至于本书第三章4.3.1小段的"光船条款"(demise clause)或4.3.2小段的"承运人身份条款"(identity of carrier clause),因 Conlinebill 2000 已在前页要求填上谁是承运人及其详尽资料(在本章3.3小段谈及),故不再需要。重要的只是别忘了填或乱填。

讲到这里,希望已把班轮提单的一般内容/条款作了一个全面介绍,可以让读者理解一般做法及背后的原因。

第五章　提单作用之二：
运输合约下的货损货差责任

海上运输中，对船上货物造成损坏的风险难免会有，本章正是要探讨有关这些风险应由谁承担及如何承担的问题。这在历史上曾涉及各方利益的拉锯战，至今仍在延续。

§1　起点是公共承运人有严格责任

英美普通法有所谓"公共承运人"（common carrier）与"私人承运人"（private carrier）的区分，这是大陆法国家所没有的。公共承运人的定义是："公共承运人出面招揽，为获取报酬（运费）而代大众运输货物，并且不保留拒运的权利，除非是无法代劳，如货装不下或不适合这运输"（common carriers are those who hold out as being prepared to carry goods for reward for all and sundry without reserving the right to refuse the goods tendered）"。

这正是班轮运输的做法，至于私人承运人，是"只为个别人士运输货物"（private carriers are those who undertake to carry goods for certain persons）。这正是租船的做法。

传统以来，法律一直对公共承运人盯得很紧，因为与公众利益有关。加上班轮的运输合约涉及同时也是物权凭证的提单，而这份提单是会通过背书转让给无辜的买方或承押人的银行（本书之第二章在这方面已有详论），它的可靠性关系到整个国际贸易的制度与信心，故此法律会抗拒作为公共承运人的班轮公司去逃避承担货物在海上运输中遭受损坏的风险。

因此，英美法律在这方面的起点是，"公共承运人"（public carrier）对货物负有一个严格或绝对的责任。这可节录 Carver《Carriage by Sea》一书之§2段："The common law, with regard to the liability of a public carrier of goods, is strict[339]. Apart

---

[339] 公共承运人有严格责任。

from express contract[340] he is, with certain exceptions[341], absolutely responsible for the safety of the goods while they remain in his hands as carrier[342]..."

之所以这样对待公共承运人，Bcat 大法官在 Rilcey v. Horne（1825）5 Bing. 217 的判例中说明如下："When goods are delivered to a carrier, they are usually no longer under the eye of the owner[343]: he seldom follows or send any servant with them to the place of their destination[344]. If they should be lost or injured by the grossest negligence of the carrier or his servants[345], or stolen by them[346] or by thieves in collusion with them[347], the owner would be unable to prove either of these causes of loss[348]; his witnesses must be the carrier's servants, and they, knowing that they could not be contradicted[349], would excuse their masters or themselves[350]. To give due security to property[351], the law has added to that responsibility of a carrier, which immediately rises out of his contract to carry for a reward, namely, that of taking all reasonable care of it[352], the responsibility of an insurer[353]."

另可节录 Brett 法官在 Liver Alkali Co v. Johnson（1874）L. R. 7 Ex. 267 案中所言："I think that by a recognized custom of England, a custom adopted and recognized by the courts in precisely the same manner as the custom of England with regard to common carriers has been adopted and recognized by them, every shipowner who carries goods for hire in his ship, whether by inland navigation, or coastways, or abroad[354], undertakes to carry them at his own absolute risk[355], the act of God or the Queen's enemies alone

---

[340]　除非运输合约另去订明（即承认订约自由）。
[341]　或法律默示的几个免责原因（即：天灾/天意、公敌与货物内在缺陷）。
[342]　公共承运人要绝对负责货物在它/他手中时的安全。
[343]　货物一旦交托了给承运人，货方再也看不见，管不着了。
[344]　货物/发货人一般不会派人随船或卡车看管货物至目的地。
[345]　如果是因承运人极度疏忽的原因导致货损货差。
[346]　或是承运人或它/他的雇员自己偷了货。
[347]　或是承运人或它/他的雇员串通的盗贼偷了货。
[348]　货方都无法去证明什么。
[349]　货方能有的证人只能是承运人的雇员，而这些雇员知道就算瞒天过海其谎言也无法被拆穿。
[350]　肯定会为自己说好话。
[351]　为了保障货物。
[352]　法律除要求承运人采取一切合理行动照顾货物外。
[353]　还给承运人加上了作为货物保险人的责任，即对货物有严格责任。
[354]　不论是内河、沿海或国外的海上运输。
[355]　承运人都有绝对责任。

excepted[356], unless by agreement between himself and a particular freighter, on a particular voyage, or on particular voyages, he limits his liability by further exceptions[357]."

§2 普通法下合约承诺也是严格责任

私人承运人(像程租)的责任起点其实也是大同小异,因为普通法下合约的承诺(如承运人承诺把货物从甲地运至乙地)也是严格责任,承诺方必须严格去执行。这方面在笔者的《国际商务游戏规则——英国合约法》一书已有多处谈及。例如在第十二章"合约受阻"之§1段说到:

……必须先明白英国法律下合约承诺方的严格或绝对责任。这方面最主要的先例早自 Paradine v. Jane (1647) Aleyn 26 一案,法院说:

'When the party by his own contract creates a duty or charge upon himself, he is bound to make it good, if he may, notwithstanding any accident by inevitable necessity…Because he might have provided against it by his contract.'

……

换言之,一经合约承诺,天塌下来也要履行。如果无法履行,便要面对违约索赔。其中根本没有合理不合理(即使是客观上看来合理,而非是常见的一方主观认为合理)的讲法"。

另在该书的第二章之1.1小段,也提到普通法下严格履约的责任,除了两三种默示的免责/除外责任。现节录如下:

……要知道,英国法律下,一个合约一经订立,是必须绝对或严格履行的。所谓"严格",就是除非合约中另有明确规定,只有普通法默示的除外情况出现才可免履行之责。而普通法默示的,即不必写明也可享受的除外情况,只有极少的两三种,如天灾、公敌等。对一方无法履行已经订立的合约,这普通法的免责或除外会起到保护作用的,可以说是万中无一。

故此,Carver 在《Carriage by Sea》一书的第 90 段说道,公共承运人的法律责任实际与租约没有大分别:"We have already considered, in Chapter I, the liability at

---

[356] 除了天意(天灾)或公敌外。
[357] 除非是运输合约另有规定,即订约自由仍受尊重。

common law of carriers by sea. Apart from any special terms in the contract of affreightment. Whether the contract appear in a bill of lading or charter party or otherwise, their liability is, generally speaking the same as that of a common carrier …"

难怪像海牙规则、海牙·维斯比规则以及汉堡规则等，根本没去区分公共承运人与私人承运人。

§3 订约自由受到尊重

公共承运人与私人承运人另有一重要的相同之处，就是二者均享有订约自由。公共承运人的订约自由，在§1段所节录的Carver《Carriage by Sea》一书之注[2]有提及。一有订约自由，在合约双方的争议，法官或仲裁员的职责也只能是合理客观去解释合约条款（明示或默示）。毕竟，订约自由本就是英美法律的基本大原则。

公共承运人与私人承运人的不同之处倒在于，二者在订立运输合约时所处的地位。

3.1 公共承运人与私人承运人所享有的订约自由的地位不同

首先说说私人承运人所处的订约地位，了解租船市场如何操作的人士都会认同其地位不会优于是承租人的货方。应该说，近一二十年来，承租人一直处于优越的、更具实力的谈判地位。而订约所必须拥有的法律与专业知识，承租人也不比船东逊色。所以，在租船市场，若要立法去保障弱者，对象应是承运人而不是承租人。而总体来说，大家均接受这样的看法，即对于双方谈判合约的实力与知识，租船市场有相对的平衡。所以，最好少去干预，让市场的力量自动去调节会更好。

但对于公共承运人所处的订约地位，情况却大不一样。这种承运人面对的是大量的"小货主"，他们像一般的小市民，小消费者，也不靠航运为生。所以就知识与实力而言，货方完全无法平起平坐地去与公共承运人（班轮公司）订立一个公平合理的运输合约。

班轮公司也老实不客气，上百年来都不断地对班轮提单的运输合约加以改善以增加对自己利益的保障。这种状况直至今天仍未改变，班轮公司总是任意去拟定或修改它的提单条款，而货方则是闭了眼睛去接受订约。

班轮公司的"心狠手辣"，占尽好处，可从本书第二章之5.6.2小段所介绍的提单合约内的免责条款看到。所介绍的这些提单都是班轮提单，内中的免责条款完全是一面倒的保障班轮公司，如 Chartered Bank v. British Steam Navigation (1909) A. C. 369 判例的："…in all cases and under all circumstances the liability of the company shall absolutely cease…and thereupon the goods shall be at the risk for all purposes and in every respect of the shipper or consignee."

或是较近斯的 The "Ines" (1995) 2 Lloyd's Rep. 144 判例,内有的提单条款第 3 条是:"Goods in the custody of the Carrier or his Agents or servants before loading and after discharge…at the sole risk of the owners of the goods and thus the carrier has no responsibility whatsoever for the goods…"

3.2　订约自由的技巧:以船舶适航为例

以船舶适航这重要一项为例,普通法的地位(也就是法律默示的地位)是船舶必须严格适航,正如 Blackburn 勋爵在 Steel v. Stateline (1877) 3 App. Cas. 72 所说:"where there is a contract to carry goods in a ship, whether that contract is in the shape of a bill of lading or any other form, there is a duty on the part of the person who furnishes or supplies that ship, or that the ship room, unless something be stipulated which should prevent it,[358] that the ship shall be fit for its purpose. That is generally expressed by saying that it shall be seaworthy; and I think, also, in marine contracts, contracts for sea carriage, that is what is properly called a warranty, not merely that they should do that best to make the ship fit,[359] but that the ship should really be fit[360]."

就私人承运人的租约而言,早在 1531 年已有判例涉及明示条款要求严格或绝对适航。明示条款是说:"and the said owner shall warrant the said ship strong and stanche well and sufficiently vitualled and apparelled etc."

看来,这明示条款与普通法的默示地位基本相同。该明示条款延续至今变为是:"tight, staunch and strong and in every way fitted for the voyage"它可在不少租约格式内看见,例如在 Americanized Welsh Coal Charter (Amwelsh form) 的条款第一条;Baltimore Form C 的条款第一条,C(Ore)7 的条款第 2 条,等等。

而就订约自由而言,长期来讲船货双方确也做到"势均力敌",即有时候船东/承运人要承担严格的适航责任,否则承租人不租。另有时候船东/承运人可很大程度去豁免适航的责任,例如作为明示条款的金康租约的条款第 2 条(有关偏袒船东的金康租约这一条款请参阅笔者的《程租合约》一书第四章)。

但就公共承运人的班轮运输而言,订约自由实际是一面倒,即倒向船东的自由,这时根本谈不上可通过谈判最后达成一份你情我愿的运输合约。

---

[358] 又再次表明了可以订约自由去作出改变。
[359] 令船舶适航的责任不单是承运人已经做到最好、毫无过错就已够。
[360] 而是要求船舶的确百分之百在各方面都是严格的适航。既然百分之百适航,也表示航次中不会出事,那就根本也不必再探讨了。

针对普通法严格的适航要求,班轮于是就开始在运输合约(班轮提单)中订下各种免责条款/条款。

这种条款或会因措辞不当,用字不清,加上法院的敌意,对船东起不了保护作用。但无所谓,输了一次官司败仗,有了一次教训,班轮公司就在它的免责条款更改或增加内容,慢慢令提单变得在措辞/文字上密不透风,让法院找不到任何漏洞。

在这种拉锯战中,整体上最后总是班轮胜利,只会在个别先例看到船东曾经在"小战役"中失败。这可以节录 Carver 的《Carriage by Sea》一书第 122 段开始部分的内容如下:

"Ineffective words 'negligence,' Thus an exception of negligence does not relieve the shipowner where the loss was caused by unseaworthiness, or unfitness, although it was due to negligence of master or crew, unless there is an express exception relieving him from unseaworthiness or want of fitness…

"Damage capable of insurance". A clause relieving the shipowner from liability for "damage capable of insurance" will not generally relieve him from liability for unseaworthiness, In Nelson Line v. Nelson (No. 2) (1908) A. C. 16, Lord Lorebum L. C. said that in his opinion the words "The owners not being liable for any damage or detriment to the goods which is capable of insurance…" seem, if considered by themselves, to excuse the shipowners "form any imaginable liability, except such as by law cannot be underwritten". But as he then proceeded to deal with the contract as a whole and decided that the shipowners were not protected from liability for a loss due to unseaworthiness…

或许会说,既然班轮公司可去一面倒拟定提单条款,何不干脆清楚地说明不必对适航负责?其实这种例子不是没有,像 Weiner & Co. v. Wilsons & Furness-Leyland Line (1910) 15 Com. Cas. 294 先例中的提单,就有条款去对此豁免:"unseaworthiness or unfitness of the vessel at commencement of or before or at any time during the voyage."

但想要推卸责任(或赖皮)的人,也会想表面上做得好看,说得冠冕堂皇。班轮公司若公然在提单上白纸黑字写明对适航绝不负责,总是有点那个。更何况,措辞/文字隐蔽一点,也一样可达到卸除责任的结果,这又何乐而不为呢?加上,不同人有不同想法、不同水平,所以有了千变万化的不同条款/条款,但拟定这些条款的班轮公司的目标都是一致,就是去免责、限责,诸如:

(ⅰ)"defects, latent or otherwise, in hull… (whether or not existing at the time of the goods being loaded or at the commencement of the voyage" 可免责:见 Bond, Connolly v. Federal S. N. Co. (1905) 21 T. L. R. 438。

(ⅱ)"Neither the steamer, nor her owners, nor her charterers, shall be accountable for the condition of goods shipped under this bill of lading, nor for any loss or damage thereto, whether arising from failure or breakdown of machinery, insulation, or other appliances, refrigerating or otherwise, or from any other cause whatsoever, whether arising from a defect existing at the commencement of the voyage or at the time of shipment of the goods or not."见 Elderslie SS Co. V. Borthwick (1905) AC 93。

(ⅲ)"It is agreed that the maintenance by the shipowners of the vessel's class... shall be considered a fulfilment of every duty, warranty or obligation and whether before or after the commencement of the voyage."见 Ingram &. Royle v. Services Maritimes (1914) 1 K. B. 541。

§4 海上运输责任的立法

4.1 美国1893年的哈特法

随着国际贸易的急剧发展(如 CIF/CFR 买卖单证),若承运人到底应负什么责任(或不负责任)的问题不能解决,或完全不稳定(比方要看个别班轮公司的良心或拟约的水平),那将严重动摇提单的信用地位。在国际上,代表货方利益的美国力主立法统一提单规定,而另一方面代表船东利益的英国却坚持保留订约自由,双方各不相让。而当时美国进出口的货物,大量是由英国班轮公司/船舶来运输。后来美国感到要订立国际法必定很困难,干脆就在国内单独采取行动来管制,它自恃国力强大,强制推行对提单的统一管制。于是在1893年制定和通过了哈特法(Harter Act 1893),订立了一套船东应尽义务和可获免责极限的标准。现就其主要内容简介如下:

1. 哈特法规定:在美国国内或美国与外国港口之间从事水上货物运输的承运人,在提单上加注条款借以使他(们)免除对装船(Load)、积载(Stow)、保管(Keep)、照料(Care)、运输(Carry)和卸货/交货(Discharge/delivery)的疏忽所负的责任,均属非法,所订条款亦属无效。

2. 同样,在提单上加注条款使船东克尽职责使船舶适航(Exercise due diligence to make the ship seaworthy)等责任得以有任何减少、减轻或避免者,均属非法,所订条款无效。

3. 哈特法之 Section 2 说明适航责任包括了:"船东要克尽职责去妥善地装备船舶,配备船员,供应所需物品,令船舶适航可面对计划中的航次,令船长等小心处理、积载与照顾货物以及适当交付货物的责任不得以减轻(...the obligations of the owner or owners of said vessel to exercise due diligence properly equip, man, provision, and outfit said vessel, and to make said vessel seaworthy and capable of performing her in-

tended voyage, or whereby the obligations of the master, officers, agents or servants to carefully handle and stow her cargo and to care for and properly deliver same, shall in any wise be lessened, weakened, or avoided)…"

4. 船东只要克尽职责,使船舶适航,对"驾驶或管理船舶的过失、天灾、公敌行为、货物固有缺点、包装不固、依法扣押、海上救助等方面所造成的损失"(faults or errors in navigation or in the management of the vessel … dangers of the sea or other navigable waters, acts of God, or public enemies, or the inherent defect, quality, or vice of the thing carried, or from insufficiency of package, or seizure under legal process, or for loss resulting from any act or omission of the shipper or owner of the goods, his agent or representative, or from saving or attempting to save life or property at sea, or from any deviation in rendering such service)船东无须负责。但这是免责的极限,就此再也没有更多的订约自由。

5. 船东有责任签发提单,注明货物的标志、件数或容积、重量及外表状况,该提单并应作为收到上述货物的表面证据(Prima facie evidence of the receipt)。拒绝签发会被科以2000美元的罚金,并可为此带来对船舶的留置权。

哈特法被认为是有史以来最好与最重要的海事法例之一,在以后的实践中亦证明了此点。由于它的成功,亦导致了国际性的海牙规则的出现,而该规则亦是以哈特法为蓝本的。

哈特法免除船东对驾驶过失(error & negligence in navigation)等所负的责任,是法律方面的一大突破,此前的法律从来不会明文规定任何人可以对所犯的错误无须负责,因为这一来岂非要无错的对方去负责承受损失,但哈特法却是破天荒第一回作了这样的规定。由于航运毕竟是较具危险性的事业,因此应当对从事这一事业的人有一定的保障和鼓励,这样才不至于使人们对此事业裹足不前。另一方面,事实上船舶在海上航行,尤其在以前通信差的时代,船东不能像陆上事业一样事事可直接管到,因此船东只要克尽职责使船舶适航,之后发生的在法定范围内的过失和事故责任给予船东免责,在当时的历史条件下是很合理和实际的。也由此可见这立法(与后来的海牙规则)实际是一种"妥协"(compromise),是平衡了船货双方各自的利益与所持观点后所作出的决定。

再要强调是,船东必须先尽了适航的责任,才能去享有各种免责。适航是先决条件,是船东应尽的本分、义务。这在哈特法之 Section 3 说得清楚具体,如下:"If the owner of any vessel transporting merchandise or property to or from any port in the United States of America shall exercise due diligence to make the said vessel in all respects seaworthy and properly manned, equipped, and supplied, neither the vessel, her owner or owners, agent, or charterers, shall become or held responsible for damage or loss resulting from."(接下去是一连串的免责)。

最后再提两点:一是哈特法适用在装货前与卸货后直至交付货物的一段时间,比海牙规则所谓的船舶责任期间只是"船栏至船栏"(rail to rail)或"吊钩至吊钩"(tackle to tackle)稍长。故此来往美国港口的国际航次,虽适用 1936 年美国海牙规则的立法:海上货物运输法(Carriage of Goods by Sea Act,1936,简称 COGSA 1936),但像货物卸到岸上仍待交付这段期间,则 COGSA 1936 不再适用,而要由哈特法顶上。二是海牙规则虽以哈特法为蓝本,两者之间仍有不少重要差别,毕竟是由不同的两批人去草拟立法,时间与客观环境上也不一样,这差异是正常的,比如:

(ⅰ)海牙规则针对的适航责任是在船舶开航前和开航当时。哈特法对此则没有局限在任何时间。

(ⅱ)哈特法也没有把出事的事故与不适航联系在一起。这会十分危险(对船东),因为整艘巨大复杂的船舶总会挑得出毛病:见 The "Isis" 290 U. 8. 333 (1933).

(ⅲ)在免责方面,两个立法大致相同,除了哈特法没有特别针对"火灾"(fire),也没有一条海牙规则 Article Ⅳ (2) (q)的"一揽子免责"(catch-all exception)条款。

(ⅳ)海牙规则不去针对货物的"交付"(delivery)。

4.2 1924 年的海牙规则

4.2.1 历史简介

哈特法开了头,其他货方利益比船东利益大的国家也跟随着立法。当时没有第三世界或发展中国家,这些国家是澳大利亚、新西兰与加拿大。它们制定了类似哈特法的立法:1904 的 Australian Carriage of Goods by Sea Act;1908 的 New Zealand Shipping and Seaman Act;与 1910 的 Canadian Water Carriage Act。它们都是英联邦国家,这迫使宗主国的英国也非要去采取一些动作不可。在 1920 年,这个问题被提交到帝国海运委员会研究。委员会在 1921 年 2 月作出报告,赞成在英国范围内根据加拿大法案统一立法。

但当时英国国内有部分人士提出了折中的做法,就是制定了的规则(类同于哈特法)不以立法手段强制执行,而是仿效 1890 年对共同海损计算的"约克·安特卫普规则"(York-Antwerp Rules,1890),让业内人士在订约时自觉自律去采用,以合约法去约束双方。这个折中做法的精神其实体现在原先 1924 年的海牙规则,即想以提单加入一条"首要条款"(Clause Paramount)才令海牙规则适用。像 The "Hurry On"(1939) 63 Lloyd's Rep. 21,该著名先例(另名为: Vita Foods Products, Inc v. Unus Shipping Co. Ltd.)的有关立法(Newfoundland Carriage by Sea Act, 1932)的 Section (3)有此说明如下:"Every bill of lading, or similar document of title, issued in this Domininon which contains or is evidence of any contract to which the Rules apply shall contain an express statement that it is to have effect subject to the provisions of the said Rules as applied by this Act."

该先例的提单没有一条首要条款,但有条款讲明适用英国法。英国贵族院判有关立法(海牙规则)不是"强制性"的(mandatory),只是指导性/自愿性的(directory),它的适用要依赖合约确有加入一条首要条款。这判决并不受欢迎,因为它提供了逃避适用海牙规则的机会,所以海牙·维斯比规则已改为强制性执行,不论提单有否加入首要条款。本章之4.2.3.1小段会再详述此先例。

不偏离话题,英国自己立法将有关义务/责任强加到英国船东头上,无疑会导致它/他们对外国船东(主要是欧洲国家如荷兰、挪威、法国、希腊等)的竞争力下降。所以为了不让外国船东享有"无法无天"的"订约自由"优势,而自己却自绑手脚,英国决定通过"国际海事委员会"(Comite Maritime Internationale 或简称 CMI)去推动国际性的立法。

在1921年9月在海牙举行的国际性协会会议上,由各有关方组成的代表团草拟并通过了规则的主体,即1921年海牙规则,并建议各国采纳。当时的海牙规则对立法强制执行是有所保留的,但在后来的谈判和讨论中,主张立法的呼声甚高,促使1922年10月在比利时布鲁塞尔(Brussels)举行的讨论海事法律的外交会议的代表们作出决定,建议其本国政府对海牙规则稍作更改即采纳作为国内立法的基础。会议的目的是各参加国都应促使一切出口提单均有采用该规则的义务。

在英国,帝国经济会议在1923年11月已建议英帝国各成员国政府和议会(当时的大英帝国)采用修正后的规则。因此有了"1924年英国海上货物运输法"(Carriage of Goods by Sea Act. 1924),并在1924年8月1日经英王批准。而国际方面亦于1924年8月25日在布鲁塞尔签订了"统一提单的若干法律规定的国际公约"(International Convention for the Unification of Certain Rules Relating to Bills of Lading),亦即众所周知的"1924年海牙规则"(The Hague Rules 1924)。

总结以上(与较早段节)所讲,笔者不妨节录较权威的、在近期澳大利亚上诉庭的一个案例所提到的有关这段历史。该案例是 The "Bunga Seroja"(1999)1 Lloyd's Rep. 512,上诉庭说:"History of the Hague Rules…

10. By the early 19th century, shipowners had come to be regarded as common carriers by both English and American law[361] Accordingly. The carrier was strictly liable for damage to or loss of cargo that was damage or loss occurring in the course of carriage un-

---

[361] 主要是针对班轮,不是租船,先例有:Laveroni v. Drury (1852) 8 Ex. 166 at 170; Liver Alkali Co. v. Johnson(1874) L. R. 9 Ex. 338 at pp. 340~341。

第五章　提单作用之二：运输合约下的货损货差责任　325

less the carrier could prove not only that its negligence had not contributed to the damage or loss, but also that one of four excepted causes (act of God, act of public enemies, shipper's fault or inherent vice of the goods) was responsible for the loss.[362]

11. To avoid this liability (sometimes spoken of as tantamount to that of an insurer[363]) carriers began to include more and wider exculpatory clauses in their bills of lading.[364] In England, it was held that carriers and shippers could agree to terms by which the carrier assumed virtually no liability, even for its own negligence[365]. In Australasian United Steam Navigation Co. Ltd. v. Hiskens, Mr. Justice Isaacs said[366]:

Common law relations based on reasonableness and fairness were in practice destroyed at the will of the shipowners, and as fast as Courts pointed out loopholes in their conditions, so fast did they fill them up[367], until at last the position of owners of goods became intolerable.

In the United States, however, the Federal Courts held that contractual clauses which purported to exonerate carriers from the consequences of their own negligence were void as against public policy[368] and strictly interpreted clauses which attempted to exonerate carriers for the failure to provide a seaworthy ship[369]. This did not help United States Cargo interests when much of their trade was carried on British ships pursuant to bills of lading containing choice of forum Clauses nominating England as the place in

---

[362] 先例有：Laveroni v. Drury；Nugent v. Smith (1876) 45 L. J. (C. L.) 697 at p. 701；Propeller Niagara v. Cordes 62 U. S. 7 at pp. 22~23 (1859)。

[363] Mansfield 勋爵在 Forward v. Pittard (1785) 1 T. R. 27 at p. 23 所讲的。

[364] 船东/承运人开始在提单合约内大量加入广泛的免责条款。注意这只是班轮公司，租约的船东可没有这能耐。

[365] 先例是：In re Missouri Steamship Company (1889) 42 Ch. D. 321。

[366] 这先例是：Australasian United Steam Navigation Co. Ltd. v. Hiskens (1914) 18 C. L. R. 646。

[367] Isaacs 大法官说普通法想去实现的公平合理的大精神全被船东单方面的订约自由毁了。法院一挑出提单条款的漏洞，船东就马上填补，直至提单对他/它而言密不透风。

[368] 美国(但不是英国)曾以违反公共政策为由否定对船东疏忽免责的条款，先例有：Railroad Co. v '. Lockwood, 84 U. S. 357 at p. 384 (1873)；Phoenix Insurance Co. v. Erie and Western Transportation Co. 117 U. S. 312 at p. 322 (1886)；Liverpool and Great Western Steam Co. v. Phoenix Insurance Co. 129 U. S. 397 at p. 441~442 (1889)；Compania de Navigacion la Flecha v. Brauer. 168 U. S. 104 at p. 117 (1897)等。在英美法下，违反公共政策是普通法唯一去否定订约自由下明示条款的理由。但是英国法院显然不认为班轮公司以明示条款豁免疏忽是什么了不起的事，层次不应高至违反公共政策。

[369] 美国有关先例有：The "Caledonia", 157 U. S. 124 at p. 137 (1895)；The "Carib Prince", 170 U. S. 655 at p. 659 (1898)。

which suit must be brought.[370]

12. These problems led, in the United States, to the Harter Act, 1903 of 1893 ('the Harter Act')[371]. This Act was a compromise between the conflicting interests of carriers and shippers.[372] A carder could not contract out of its obligation to exercise due diligence to furnish a seaworthy vessel[373] or to relieve it from 'liability for loss or damage arising from negligence, fault, or failure in proper loading, stowage, custody, care or proper delivery of any and all lawful merchandise or property committed to its or their charge'.[374]

13. New Zealand, Australia and Canada each passed legislation modelled on the Halter Act: the Shipping and Seamen Act (N.Z.), the Sea-Carriage of Goods Act, 1904 and the Water Carriage of Goods Act, 1910 (Can.). All of these Acts, although modelled on the Hatter Act, made some changes to the model. Thus the 1904 Australian Act was, in some respects, more generous to cargo interests than the Harter Act.

14. Pressure grew for uniform rules. In February, 1921, the British Imperial Shipping Committee recommended uniform legislation throughout the British Empire based on the Canadian Act[375]. Draft rules were prepared, considered and amended. By 1922 the Comite Maritime International had adopted a draft. The Diplomatic Conference on Maritime Law then took up the matter and in August 1924, the International Convention for the Unification of Certain Rules of Law Relating to Bills of Lading was concluded and opened for signature[376]. Australia enacted the Sea-Carriage of Goods Act (Cth) as soon as the final diplomatic steps had been taken.

15. The new rules quickly gained international acceptance, although United States legislation was not passed until 1936. By the start of World War II 'the overwhelming

---

[370] 但美国法院的严厉对待并不解决问题,因为英国班轮公司/船舶的提单合约格式都订明管辖权地点是英国,英国法院。

[371] 美国被迫推出哈特法加以对付。推出当时,估计在国际上(英国为主)受到不少压力。即使今天美国强大多了,在推出油污方面的 Oil Pollution Act (1980)时也遭受国际上不少威吓,压力,误导,游说等。例如恐吓说"如果立法通过,今后世界油轮都不跑美国了"。美国政府是谈判高手,知己知彼,最终胜利,这实在不是仅具一般知识/谈判水平与国力较次的国家所能做到的。

[372] 哈特法是一个船东与货方的妥协。

[373] 这在 4.1 小段已略述。

[374] 也在 4.1 小段已略述。

[375] 这部分历史在多本书有记载,如 Sturley 的《The Legislative History of the Carriage of Goods by Sea Act》或海牙规则的工作报告(1990),第 2 册之第 138 页。

[376] 可参阅《Benedict on Admiralty》一书,第 7 版,Vol. 2A, § 15 之 2~14 段。

majority of the world's shipping was committed to the Hague Rules'[377].

16. The Hague Rules represent a compromise about the allocation of risk of damage to cargo (a compromise which was different from what had been represented in domestic statutes). Thus, to take only one example, shipping interests gained the advantage in Australia and the United States of elimination of the rule established in McGregor v. Huddart Parker Ltd.[378] and The Isis[379]. In those cases, the High Court of Australia and the Supreme Court of the United States held that a carrier could claim exemption from liability on the bases set out in the 1904 Australian Act and the Hatter Act if (and only if) the carrier had complied with its obligation relating to the seaworthiness of the vessel, regardless of whether the cargo's loss or damage was caused by lack of seaworthiness, Under the Hague Rules, however, some causal connection must be shown between the loss and the matter in respect of which due diligence was not demonstrated[380].

17. The complexity of the history which we have touched on is such that, as Mr. Justice Dixon said in. William Holyman & Sons Pty. Ltd. v. Foy & Gibson pty. Ltd.[381] 'the case law, English, Australian and American, dealing with other legislation thought to be in pari materia cannot be applied to the Hague Rules, except with great care and discrimination'.

18. Similarly, it may be that similar care and discrimination must be shown in applying decisions about marine insurance to the Hague Rules. Many of the issues which arose under the exempting provisions of bills of lading issued before the Hague Rules find parallels with issues arising under policies of marine insurance. Whether, however, principles developed in connection with one area should be applied in the other was open to argument for many years and may still be so. In Arbib & Houlberg v. Second Russian Insur-

---

[377] 见 Sturley 的《The Legislative History of the Carriage of Goods by Sea Act》一书。

[378] McGregor v. Huddart Parker Ltd. (1919) 26 C. L. R. 336 的澳大利亚先例在海牙规则产生前曾判对于不适航的船舶，即使不适航与损失无关，船东/承运人仍不能享有免责。这对船东/承运人十分严厉的判例是针对 1904 年的立法所作出的。

[379] 在 The "Isis", 290 U. S. 333 (1933), 美国最高法院也作出相同的判决, 虽然针对的是大同小异的哈特法。

[380] 但在海牙规则的 Aticle 4 (1), 船东/承运人在适航责任方面的地位改善了, 现在立法的措辞/文字是不适航需要与损失有实质因果关系。

[381] 在 William Holyman & Sons Pty. Ltd. v. Foy & Gibson Pty. Ltd. (1945) 73 C. L. R. 622 的澳大利亚先例中, Dixon 大法官说海牙规则背景复杂, 加上是一个国际上的妥协, 所以处理被视为具相同性质的本国其他立法(比如是"海上保险法")的判例法并不适用于海牙规则, 除了应小心区别外。

ance Co.[382], the Court of Appeals for the Second Circuit identified as follows the distinction drawn in the United States between the two areas:

The phrase 'perils of the seas' occurs in bills of lading, where it is used as a ground of the carrier's exemption from liability, and it is also employed in policies of insurance in stating the ground of the insurance company's liability. In the interpretation of the phrase when used in bills of lading, the courts have adopted great strictness, as the carrier is seeking exemption of liability; but in the interpretation of the phrase when used in insurance policies, the courts in many cases have given to it great elasticity of meaning[383]."

4.2.2 海牙规则下船东与货方各自责任的简介

海牙规则以美国哈特法为蓝本,在讨价还价地平衡船东与货方利益及各自所持的立场后,订下了一连串各自要承担的先后责任。显然,作为主要的履约方,船东身上的责任肯定是较多与较重的。当然,船东也不是毫无所得,例如船舶适航责任方面,再不是普通法的严格或绝对适航而是"克尽职责"令船舶适航。可对航行与管船东面的船长/船员疏忽或/与过失免责,这一项十分重要,海难如碰船搁浅造成严重货损货差都会与这项免责有关。船东另可以享有单位赔偿限额与较短索赔时效等好处。这一切的课题会在后详述,在此简要介绍各自的先后责任,可以各自举证责任的先后排列及要举证的内容加以说明,这样会更好理解。

这方面可以节录 William Tetley 教授的《Marine Cargo Claims》一书第 3 版的第 373 页,它说:

"My order proof is as follows:

1) Cargo claimant proves his loss and damage in the hands of the carri-er[384].

---

[382] 这是美国上诉庭的先例: Arbib & Houlberg v. Second Russian Insurance Co. 294 F 811 at p. 816 (2 Cir. 1923)。

[383] 美国先例举例说同是"海难"一词,出现在提单是免责事项,应严格去解释。但出现在保单,是承保风险,应宽松去解释。

[384] 第一步是货方证明货损货差发生在承运人手中。而货在承运人手中并要负上海牙规则的责任,是指 Article 1 (e) 的货物装上船舶直至卸下的一段时间,即所谓"吊钩至吊钩"或"船栏至船栏"。而一般证明的方法十分简易:装上船舶的货物表面看良好无损是依赖于一份清洁的装船提单;卸下船舶的货物表面看是否良好(或短缺)是看"卸货理货单"(discharge tally sheet),"货物收据"(cargo receipt)与/或"检验报告"(survey report)等。几份装卸文件一比较对照,马上可看出是否曾经有过货损货差发生在承运人手中,而且是在要负责的一段时间。

有时会是表面看货损不明显,要稍后才会发觉,这也无妨,只是货方举证难度会增加,例如在 The "Ocean Dynamic" (1982) 2 Lloyd's Rep. 88。

2) The carrier must prove the cause of loss[385].

3) The carrier must prove due diligence to make the ship seaworthy before and at the beginning of the voyage in respect to the loss[386].

4) The carrier must prove one of the exculpatory exceptions[387].

5) The cargo claimant then attempts to prove lack of care of cargo[388], or attempts to disprove the above evidence of the carrier including lack of seaworthiness and lack of due diligence[389].

6) Both parties then have various arguments available to them[390].

4.2.3 海牙规则的适用

海牙规则的适用有几个方面要探讨,如什么航次(进口/出口/进出口/转运)适用?什么运输合约适用?什么期间适用?什么货物适用等等。

4.2.3.1 什么航次适用

原来海牙规则只要求其适用在签发提单的地点/国家。例如,澳大利亚签发的一份提单,之后对物诉讼/扣船发生在香港。因澳大利亚与香港都承认海牙规则,故香港法院会尊重海牙规则并将其适用在该诉讼。

但各国以海牙规则制定的国内立法,对其适用航次的规定却并不相同。其中

---

[385] 举证责任接下去转了过来,是承运人/船东一定要证明是什么原因导致货损货差。这也公道,可参阅本章§1段的 Riley v. Horne (1825) 5 Bing. 217 先例,道理一样。有此举证责任,也表示若不知是什么原因导致货差货损,则承运人仍要负上赔偿责任。

[386] 承运人/船东接下去要证明它/他在开航前已克尽职责令船舶适航(与货损货差有因果关系的适航方面)。

[387] 承运人/船东接下去要证明货损货差的原因是海牙规则 Article 4 列出的各项免责的其中一项或多项,因而可对事故免责。

[388] 下一步是货方要去主动一些,证明货损货差发生在承运人手中是因为它/他不妥善或不小心照顾货物所导致的。海牙规则只对船长/船员的"部分"疏忽行为与过失免责,这"部分"是管船与航行方面。但针对船长/船员管货方面(照顾货物),海牙规则非但不准对疏忽与过失免责,反而明示强加了适航之外的另一个义务/责任,这就是在 Article 3 (2) 要求承运人小心与妥善去照顾货物。

但不像开航前履行适航的义务/责任是一个可去享有免责的先决条件,这妥善小心照顾货物的义务/责任与各项免责并不存在优先先后,纯是以事实的认定去看货损货差主要是什么所导致的。例如,水湿的货物虽是海难所引起,但如果船长/船员马上把涌进的海水泵走,是不至于导致这严重与扩大了的货损的。而这方面的举证责任是在货方,不像开航前的适航可去留待承运人/船东自己证明已尽了义务/责任。

[389] 货方也可反证承运人/船东自辩自证的已尽适航义务/责任。货方会在承运人/船东提供或"披露"(discovery)的文件中挑出漏洞/毛病。

[390] 之后双方会就所有其他有关方面进行争辩,例如不合理绕航、时效,承运人如果有责任也可享有赔偿限制,等等。

美国的 1936 年海上运输法跟随哈特法,讲明其适用在美国进出口外贸的航次。在该立法(1936 COGSA),一开始便说:"Every bill of lading or similar document of title which is evidence of a contract for the carriage of goods by sea to or from ports of the United States, in foreign trade, shall have effect subject to the provisions of this chapter…"

4.2.3.1.1 英国立法只适用在出口航次

但在英国,立法规定只适用在出口的航次,不论目的地是外国或英国本地港口。这是在 1924 年英国海上运输法(1924 COGSA)中规定的:"Subject to the provisions of this Act, the Rules shall have effect in relation to and in connection with the carriage of goods by sea in ships carrying goods from any port in Great Britain or Northern Ireland to any other port whether in or outside Great Britain or Northern Ireland."

考虑到签发提单一般(但不一定是)在装港或出口国家,英国 1924 COGSA 实际与海牙规则本意一样。

另在 1924 COGSA,有 Section 3 针对提单要去明示合并该立法,即海牙规则,内容如下:"Every bill of lading, or similar document of title, issued in Great Britain or Northern Ireland which contains or is evidence of any contract to which the Rules apply shall contain an express statement that it is to have effect subject to the provisions of the said Rules as applied by this Act."

这要求一般不成问题,现实中提单格式都会印上这种明示条款,名为"首要条款"(Clause Paramount)。例如在附录八的 Congenbill,背面印有:

"General Paramount Clause.

(a) The Hague Roles contained in the International Convention for the Unification of certain rules relating to Bills of Lading, dated Brussels the 25th August 1924 as enacted in the country of shipment, shall apply to this Bill of Lading. When no such enactment is in force in the country of shipment, the corresponding legislation of the country of destination shall apply, but in respect of shipments to which no such enactments are compulsorily applicable, the terms of the said Convention shall apply…"

以上所讲,在一份提单是针对英国出口,而且印上首要条款时,则适用 1924 COGSA 应是毫无疑问。若是提单没有明示的首要条款呢?这一来,如果发生争议而且是由出口国的法院审理(即英国法院),也应是没有疑问,因为 1924 COGSA 是强制的立法,适用在出口的航次。怕是怕一个航次,装卸港都是适用海牙规则的国家的港口,立法是适用在出口航次。而在提单内,明示或默示的适用法却是卸港国家法律。加上,在卸港发现货损货差而导致在该处起诉。这一来,若是提单没有一条明示首要条款,又不是诉讼国家立法强制适用的航次(该航次是进口,不是出口),适用或不适用可就有得争了。

在英国上诉庭的 The "Torni"（1932）p. 78，就遇上这疑问，上诉庭一致判海牙规则适用。Scrutton 大法官担心船东可任意地首先在提单内不去加一条"首要条款"，另再去说明卸港的法律适用（注：海牙规则没有禁止这样做），从而逃避海牙规则。这一来，Scrutton 大法官怕"搅乱了"（upset the apple cart）。

4.2.3.1.2　出现的漏洞：Vita Food（案例）

但六年后，由有了另一个具争议的案例：The "Hurry on"（1939）63 Lloyd's Rep. 21 去了英国的上议院（也即是贵族院）。该先例的提单没有加一条"首要条款"，反而有条款说明适用英国法。有关航次是 Newfoundland 到纽约，而 Newfoundland 的 1932 年立法，在出口航次强制适用海牙规则。所以，争议若在 Newfoundland 法院审理，海牙规则适用，正如 Wright 勋爵所说："A Court in Newfoundland would be bound to apply the law enacted by its own Legislature…"

但若是不在 Newfoundland 法院而在英国法院审理，提单又适用英国法，则上议院认为是例外了，缺乏强制适用海牙规则的依据。正如 William Tetley 教授在《Marine Cargo Claims》第 3 版之第 6 页所说，该案带出的原则是："The principles are roughly to the effect that the Hague Rules will apply in almost every case, the main exception being where a bill of lading was issued in a contracting state, which bill of lading invoked English law and did not contain a paramount clause, and the case was tried in England."

Tetley 教授认为上议院在 The "Hurry on" 是错判。但仍是去总结海牙规则只适用在：

（ⅰ）在出口国法院审理/诉讼，则海牙规则强制适用。

（ⅱ）如果审理/诉讼不在出口国法院，希望是提单有明示"首要条款"。若没有，则需要提单的适用法就是出口国家的法律，否则海牙规则不适用。

显然，这给船东逃避海牙规则提供了一个漏洞。而且这是十分奇怪的结论：运输合约的条款（是否适用海牙规则）是要看受理法院是否出口国家的法院。

另一个漏洞是海牙规则没有说明提单若未加上"首要条款"会有什么后果/惩罚。这一点探讨得也不多，仅在美国 Gilmore 教授的《The law of Admiralty》186（2d ed. 1975）一书中谈到，其后果应是："it may not seem too drastic to hold the carrier estopped from claiming the benefit of the statute, or of the exceptions in his illegal bill, while permitting the cargo to claim whatever benefit the statute gives…（应不算极端去剥夺承运人在海牙规则下可享有的好处与免责）"

但这一观点是否会被英国（较同情船东）认同尚有疑问。

4.2.3.1.3　海牙·维斯比规则扩大了适用航次

在之后的国际会议（1959 年至 1963 年），有与会方提议将规则扩大适用至签约国的进出口航次,指出:"The provisions of this Convention shall apply to every Bill of Lading for carriage of goods from one state to another, under which Bill of Lading, the port of loading, of discharge or one of the optional ports of discharge is situated in a contracting state whatever may be the law governing such Bill of Lading and whatever may be the nationality of the ship, the carrier, the shipper, the consignee or any other interested person."

但在1967年的第12次外交会议中,有国家反对海牙规则强制适用在进口航次,认为这是干预签约国的主权。这导致在1969达成一个谅解协议,加在"维斯比修定稿"(Visby Protocol)中。该谅解协议是否适用在进口航次/货物随签约国的意愿。另出口航次强制适用则不改变。这带来海牙·维斯比规则的 Article X,它显示了这谅解/妥协如下:

"The provisions of these Rules shall apply to every bill of lading relating to the carriage of goods between ports in two different states if;

(a) the bill of lading is issued in a contracting state, or

(b) the carriage is from a port in a contracting state, or

(c) the contract contained in or evidenced the bill of lading provided that these Rules or legislation of any state giving effect to them are to govern the contract, whatever may be the nationality of the ship, the carrier, the shipper, the consignee, or any other interested person."

众所周知,海牙·维斯比规则在英国已立法为《1971年海上运输法(1971 COGSA)》。除了 Article X 外,1971 COGSA 另在两处针对/增加了规则适用的航次如下:

(ⅰ) Section 1 (3):

Without prejudice to subsection (2) above, the said provisions shall have effect (and have the force of law) in relation to and in connection with the carriage of goods by sea in ships where the port of shipment is a port in the United Kingdom, whether or not the carriage is between port in two different states within the meaning of Article X of the Rules.

(ⅱ) Section 1 (6):

Without prejudice to Article X (c) of the Rules, the Rules shall have the force of law in relation to—

(a) any bill of lading if the contract contained in or evidenced by it expressly provides that the Rules shall govern the contract, and

(b) any receipt which is non-negotiable document marked as such if the contract contained in or evidenced by it is a contract for the carriage of goods by sea which ex-

第五章　提单作用之二：运输合约下的货损货差责任　333

pressly provides that the Rules are to govern the contract as if the receipt were a bill of lading.

but subject, where paragraph (b) applies, to any necessary modifications and in particular with the omission in Article Ⅲ of the Rules of the second sentence of paragraph 4 and of paragraph 7.

4.2.3.1.4　对英国 1971 COGSA 适用航次的总结

总结下来，1971 COGSA 适用的 6 种航次如下：

(1) 英国港口的出口航次，不管目的地是外国或英国本土。注意这立法不再像 1924 COGSA 的 Section 3 那样要求明示合并 1971 COGSA 在提单内：1971 COGSA 之 Section 1(3)。

(2) 任何从签约国港口去另一外国（不必是签约国）港口的航次：1971 COGSA 之 Article X(b)。

(3) 任何航次在两个国家港口之间（都不必是签约国），而签发提单是在另一签约国：1971 COGSA 之 Article X(a)。

(4) 任何航次在两个国家港口之间（都不必是签约国），而提单内有"首要条款"(clause paramount)：1971 COGSA 之 Article X(c)。

(5) 任何航次在两个港口之间，不论是否属两个不同国家（不必是签约国），而提单内有"首要条款"(clause paramount)：1971 COGSA 之 Section 1(6)(a)。[注意 (5) 与 (4) 不同之处是 (4) 来自海牙·维斯比的国际公约，适用在国与国之间。但 (5) 是针对英国立法去增加的 Section 1(6)(a)，不必是国与国之间的关系]。

(6) 任何航次在两个港口之间，不论是否属两个不同国家（不必是签约国），代替提单签发了"不可转让"的单证（如海运单），且内有"首要条款"(clause paramount)：1971 COGSA 之 Section 1(6)(b)：McCarren v. Humber International Transport (1982) Lloyd's Rep. 301。

读者会问：可否举一些例子是海牙·维斯比规则或 1971 COGSA 并不适用的航次？这当然有，例如澳门（回归前）来香港的航次。香港有类似 1971 COGSA 的立法，即适用海牙·维斯比规则；澳门回归前属葡萄牙的殖民地，不是海牙·维斯比规则签约国。而该航次签发的提单或付运单证并没有一条"首要条款"。我们不妨再看看 The "Komninos S" (1991) 1 Lloyd's Rep. 371，该案是从希腊装钢材运往意大利。希腊不是海牙·维斯比国家，而提单的适用法则判希腊，提单也没有一条"首要条款"，仅第 24 条列明英国法院有管辖权，上述庭认为这一事实不足以适用海牙·维斯比规则。

4.2.3.1.5　以提单适用法逃避 1971 COGSA 适用的 The "Morviken" 先例

1971 COGSA 所带来的分别，可见于 The "Morviken" (1983) 1 Lloyd's Rep. 1 的贵

族院先例。它涉及一个航次从英国(苏格兰)的 Leith 装一台机器(铺柏油路机)经 Amsterdam(荷兰)去 Bonaire (Netherlands Antilles)卸。承运人是一程船的船东(名"Haico Holwerde"),而二程船是他/它租来的"Morviken"。在 Bonaire 卸货时,机器被摔坏了。看来,在海牙规则或海牙·维斯比规则下,承运人都难逃责任。分别只是在单位赔偿限额的 Article 4(5)(后详),在海牙规则只是 250 英镑,但在海牙·维斯比规则已提高至约 1.1 万英镑。

该航次开始时英国的 1971 COGSA 刚生效了 9 个月,照说该航次适用该立法是明显不过的,依据是 Article X(a)(因为提单也在 Leith 签发)与 Article X(b)(航次出口港是英国的 Leith)。但提单上有一条款讲明适用荷兰法律(荷兰只承认海牙规则)以及 Amsterdam 法院有管辖权,说:

"Law of application and jurisdiction: The law of the Netherlands in which the Hague Rules, as adopted by the Brussels Convention of 25th August 1924 are incorporated-with the exception of article 9 – shall apply to this contract…

…All actions under the present contract of carriage shall be brought before the Court of Amsterdam and no other Court shall have jurisdiction with regard to any such action unless the Carrier appeals to another jurisdiction or voluntarily submits himself thereto."

这一来,承运人就向英国法院申请"中止"(stay),把管辖让给提单合约上所同意的 Amsterdam 法院。有关这种中止申请与英国法院的各种考虑因素,在笔者的《禁令》一书第六章有详论,内容太多,无法去节录。

承运人所持的理据是:

(ⅰ)海牙/海牙·维斯比规则确在 Article 3(8)不准承运人以订约自由等手段去减轻或逃避责任,但选择什么法律适用并非与责任有关。

(ⅱ)若果该条款不是说 Amsterdam 法院有权管辖,而是一条仲裁条款,如荷兰仲裁,则英国法院也必须中止,以符合 1958 年的纽约公约(当时英国已立法为 1975 年仲裁法)。

可以想象,英国法院肯定会对此中止申请有所抗拒,因为明知去了荷兰法院,它就会以海牙规则的赔偿限额来判。所以承运人在上诉庭与贵族院都败诉。而针对承运人的理据,Diplock 勋爵说:

(ⅰ)海牙/海牙·维斯比规则之 Article 3(8)有关减轻或逃避责任的条款"无效"(null, void and of no effect)并不应局限地解释为仅针对规则所列明的责任(如适航,小心/妥善装卸货物等),而应扩大至其他可达到同样后果的像适用法条款或管辖权条款等。只要它们会导致减轻或逃避责任,即应被视为"无效"。Diplock 勋爵在这一点的英文判词是:"… I have no hesitation in rejecting this narrow construction of article Ⅲ, r. 8, which looks solely to the form of the clause in the contract of carriage and wholly ignores its substance. The only sensible meaning to be given to the description of provisions in contracts of carriage which are rendered 'null and void and of no effect' by this role is one which would embrace every provision in a contract of carriage which, if it were applied, would have the effect of lessening the carrier's hability otherwise than as provided in the rules, to ascribe to it the narrow meaning...would leave it open to any shipowner to evade the provisions of art. Ⅲ, r.8 by the simple device of inserting in his bills of lading issued in, or for carriage from a port in, any contracting state a clause in standard form providing as the exclusive forum for resolution of disputes what might aptly be described as a Court of convenience[391], viz. one situated in a country which did not apply the Hague-Visby Rules or, for that matter, a country whose law recognized an unfettered right in a shipowner by the terms of the bill of lading to relieve himself from all liability for loss or damage to the goods caused by his own negligence, fault or breach of contract."

（ⅱ）不接受外国仲裁条款在提单内会带来同样矛盾，因为仲裁庭可去裁定合约适用法。而以明示条款去适用另一国家法律已是被视为"无效"（请回头看（ⅰ）段），仲裁庭不见得会有不同看法。Diplock 勋爵在这一点的英文判词是："... I do not accept the analogy... An arbitration clause providing for the submission of future disputes to arbitration is to be distinguished from a clause making a choice of the substantive law by which the agreement containing the arbitration clause is to be governed. What the arbitration clause does is to leave it to the arbitrator to determine what is the 'proper law' of the contract in accordance with accepted principles of conflict of laws and then to apply that 'proper law' to the interpretation, and the validity of the contract and the mode of performance and the consequences of breaches of contract. One, but by no means the only, matter to be taken into consideration in deciding what is the 'proper law' is a particular choice of substantive law by which the contract is to be governed, made by an express clause in the contract itself. But if the particular choice of substantive law made by the express clause is such as to make the clause null and void under the law of the place where the contract was made, or under what, in the absence of such express clause, would be the proper law of the contract,[392] I am very far from accepting that it would be

---

[391] Diplock 勋爵接下去只说这种法院不去适用海牙·维斯比规则或有不同的适用法律。但估计他更怕的会是乱来或/与不懂的外国法院，只是出于外交上的礼貌所以说不出口。

[392] 确实，合约的适用法明示条款为去逃避原来视为无效/非法的适用法，实是违反公共政策而无效。例如，中国禁止赌博，但双方订约方在中国订约，一切涉及中国，所以无可置疑默示适用中国法，但合约中去加上一条明示适用法条款，说是拉斯韦加斯的 Nevada 州法律适用，肯定不禁止赌博，即属无效，因为违反中国公共政策。

open to the arbitrator to treat the clause as being otherwise than null and void, or to give any effect to it."

笔者对以上的(ii),仍有无法完全明白之处。因为若说外国仲裁庭可去裁定合约适用法而不一定接受一条原来默示法律下是无效的明示适用法条款,则外国法院亦可去这样考虑与判决。世界上不少法院(包括英国)只是对自己的程序法不会改变,没有弹性,但对采用外国的实体法会是十分开明,也经常有。

但总结说来,The"Morviken"判决是符合海牙·维斯比规则的立法意图的,应是正确。当然,这也解决不了所有问题,例如是其中国家法院之间的管辖权。试想,一个航次从荷兰出口,而提单在伦敦签发,提单内没有一条"首要条款",但有一条适用法/管辖权条款是葡萄牙。这一来,就要看案件在哪里审理,后果会分别如下:

——英国法院审理/诉讼:适用海牙·维斯比规则,根据1971 COGSA之Article X(a)。

——荷兰法院审理/诉讼:出口航次,适用海牙规则。

——葡萄牙法院审理/诉讼:因不是它的出口航次,提单内又没有"首要条款",所以海牙与海牙·维斯比规则都不适用。

看来,遇到上述例子,择地行诉仍十分重要。会将一年时效已过的案子挽救回来。

4.2.3.1.6 转运的情况

货物在中途港转运会发生几种情况,例如:

(i)它本是一份"全程提单"(through bill of lading)下的航次:有关全程提单请参阅本书第二章之3.2小段。

(ii)提单有一条款允许承运人为了方便或其他原因去安排转运,称为"自由条款"(Liberty Clause),好像 OCL 船公司的提单就有第21条说:"The Carrier may at any time and without notice to the merchant;…transfer the Goods from one conveyance to another including transhipping or carrying the same on another vessel than the vessel named overleaf… The liberties set out in sub-clause 1 may be invoked by the carrier for any purpose whatsoever… and anything done… or any delay arising therefrom shall be deemed to be within the contractual carriage and shall not be a deviation."

(iii)遇上意外/海难无法完成航次或共同海损下的替代费用(转运货物比在避难港储藏货物划算),等等。

如果出口港的国家适用海牙·维斯比规则但中途转运港的国家适用海牙规则,而货损货差发生在二程船,则会有疑问是什么规则适用了。照说规则是针对出口进口国家,但有得争。

首个有关先例是加拿大法院的 Captain v. Far Eastern Steamship Co. (1979) 1 Lloyd's Rep. 595。判是在一个从印度马德里经新加坡转运去温哥华的航次,虽提单明示适用海牙规则,但海牙规则并不适用在当货物放置在新加坡岸上待转运时。加拿大法院判:"the Hague Rules did not apply to the part of the contract under which the goods were on the dock at Singapore since that part of the contract which related to holding the goods on the dock at Singapore awaiting loading upon the second vessel, was not within the rules because it did not relate to the 'carriage of goods by water'."

这导致承运人无法享有单位赔偿限制的 500 加元,而要全部赔上 3 万多加元。

但在英国的 Mayhew Foods v. O. C. L. (1984) 1 Lloyd's Rep. 317, Bingham 大法官有不同判法。该案例涉及一个冷藏集装箱内装有冻肉,本应保持温度在 -18℃,但到了卸港是 2℃,冻肉变坏,最后改作牺畜食用处理掉。有关的航次是从英国的 Shoreham 港出口,卸港是沙特阿拉伯的 Jeddah。承运人 OCL 根据它提单内的"自由条款",先把货物从 Shoreham 用一程船"Voline"运去法国的 Le Havre,再从 Le Havre 上二程船的大船(名为"Benalder")运去 Jeddah。

OCL 承认了责任,但在赔偿限额上又有争议。承运人/被告 OCL 认为海牙・维斯比规则只适用在集装箱装上"Benalder"的二程船之后,而 OCL 一早已违约,没有去保持低温,所以当时冻肉已是毁坏。因此适用的赔偿限额是提单第 7 条款的以 2 美元 1 公斤计算。而 1971 COGSA 是以 2UOA(联合国的"特别提款权"或另称为 SDR/Special Drawing Rights) 1 公斤计算,比美元稍高。

但 Bingham 大法官判是 1971 COGSA 一开始就适用,因为出口航次是从英国港口出口,而且这强制立法一直适用至卸货,因此中途转运也一样适用。判词部分说:"the rights and liabilities under the rules attached to a contract; they did not apply to carriage or storage before the port of shipment or after the port of discharge [393] but between those two ports the contract was for carriage by sea [394] and if during that carriage OCL chose to avail themselves of their contractual right [395] to discharge, store and tranship, those were operations in relation to and in connection with the carriage of goods by sea; [396] the rules having applied on shipment at Shoreham remained continuously in force until discharge at Jeddah."

介绍的第三个案例是香港法院的 Ryoden Machinery v. Anders Maersk (Sup. Ct. of Hong Kong 1986); (1986) 1 Lloyd's Rep. 483。它涉及两个昂贵的锅炉从美国的 Baltimore 出口,经香港转运去上海(据知是用于和平饭店)。在香港去上海的二程船"Lin-

---

[393] 1971 COGSA 不像美国哈特法,前者只适用在"船栏至船栏",装港装上船前与卸港卸下船后再不适用 1971 COGSA,即承运人可享有订约自由。
[394] 但在装卸港之间,就是海上运输。
[395] 这是指提单内的"自由条款"。
[396] 中途转运也是海上运输的一部分,适用 1971 COGSA。

jiang"（应是香港明华公司的船），两个锅炉掉落海中。货方向承运人马斯基（Maersk）索赔，并为了援用较高的赔偿限额，称美国的1936 COGSA不适用（只赔500美元），而应适用香港已立法的海牙·维斯比规则。笔者估计是美国至中国香港的一程船不是甲板货，所以1936 COGSA适用，但二程船变了甲板货，所以会掉下海。

货方律师争辩说香港立法适用在"出口航次"（shipment），而"shipment"根据字典解释也包括"transhipment"。看来货方律师并不充分理解像 The "Morviken"（1983）1 Lloyd's Rep. 1 与 Mayhew Foods v. O. C. L. 的判例，故只在文字上挑毛病而漠视了海牙·威斯比规则的精神/本意。结果货方败诉，索赔回来的1000美元肯定是远远不够支付律师费了。据船东律师说，该案例一判下来，马上派人送给对方这1000美元，也有点嘲笑的意思。该案例的 Mayo 大法官说："I entirely reject（货方大律师）argument that 'shipment' includes 'transhipment'. All the references to shipment in the Rules are consistent with shipment being confined to the initial shipment referred to in the bill of lading. The result of this is that the plaintiffs cannot establish that the Hague-Visby Rules are applicable to the shipment of these boilers. The COGSA provisions incorporated in the bill of lading are applicable to the contract with the consequence that the limitation I have referred to is operative. The plaintiffs will only entitled to the very small amount under the limitation."

笔者对该案件并不完全了解，但从案例报告分析，笔者更多地想到货方（和平饭店？）会否有更好的战略？毕竟适用海牙·维斯比规则仍是要受制于单位赔偿限制，好处有限。会否货方更好是去：

（ⅰ）以侵权向二程船（明华公司有好几条姊妹船）起诉，若成功可索回全部损失。但会有第二章之1.5.2.1小段的"有条件的分托管"的危险。即使如此，也不应只赔付1000美元。

（ⅱ）去美国向马斯基（Maersk）索赔，估计1936 COGSA虽然适用，但在美国会有很多理由（包括不应中途去把货物装在甲板，这方面请看本章之4.2.3.5.2.7小段）去否定承运人可以限制责任：The "Hong Kong Producer"（1969）2 Lloyd's Rep. 536；Calmaquip v. West Coast Carriers Ltd. 650 F. 2d 633, 1984 AMC 839（5 Cir. 1981），等等。

4.2.3.2　什么付运单证与运输合约适用

海牙规则所适用的运输合约及付运单证在 Article 1（b）说得很清楚，具体如下：
"'Contract of carriage' applies only to contracts of carriage[397] covered by a bill of lading

---

[397] 海牙规则（与海牙·维斯比规则）只适用于海上运输合约关系。换言之，非合约的关系比如是货方与二程船，装卸工人等，不适用海牙规则。

or any similar document of title,[398] in so far as such document relates to the carriage of goods by sea, including any pursuant to a charterparty[399] from the moment at which such bill of lading or similar document of title regulates the relations between a carrier and a holder of the same[400]."

像美国的 1936 COGSA, 也在一开始说明:"Every bill of lading or similar document of title[401] which is evidence of a contract for the carriage of goods by sea[402] to or from ports of the United States, in foreign trade, shall have effect subject to the provisions of this chapter."

从以上节录可见:提单是被明确包括的。立法也没有去局限在装船提单,所以像本书第二章的 3.2 小段详述的"全程提单"与 3.7 小段的多式联运提单,海牙规则都适用。

4.2.3.2.1 海运单

但对于第二章 3.5 小段的海运单呢,毕竟它在班轮运输是愈来愈普及,比提单使用得更多,这在 1924 年是没有想到的。要知道,海运单注明"不能转让"(non-negotiable),也不是物权凭证,所以不属海牙规则定义中的"相关/类似物权凭证"(Similar document of title)。

在海牙规则的 Article 4,实际有去针对"不能转让"的付运单证,它没有说明是海运单,但明确说允许它不必适用海牙规则,可享有完全的订约自由。但为了防止船东/承运人采取不鼓励签发提单的做法(虽然按照海牙规则,发货人有权要求,承运人不得拒绝,但承运人可以使用其他手段,如加收运费等令发货人放弃此要求),进而逃避海牙规则的适用,所以 Article 6 说明即使付运单证是"不能转让",也不能用于一般的商品运输,一般的外贸,而是只能用于像军火/军备运输等的特殊情况。对该 Article 6 只节录部分(全文请看本书附录五)如下:

"…provided that in this case no bill of lading has been or shall be issued and that the terms agreed shall be embodied in a receipt which shall be non-negotiable document and shall be marked as such.

…

---

[398] 有关的付运单证是提单(也是运输合约的证明)或相关/类似的物权凭证。
[399] 不适用在租约,正如本章之 3.1 小段所说,租船业务下会是船东而不是货方需要保护。
[400] 但租约下签发的提单一旦转让到了无辜第三者手中,也适用海牙规则:这在稍后的 4.2.3.1.3 小段有详论。
[401] 有关的付运单证是提单(也是运输合约的证明)或相关/类似的物权凭证。
[402] 海牙规则(与海牙·维斯比规则)只适用于海上运输合约关系。换言之,非合约的关系比如是货方与二程船,装卸工人等,不适用海牙规则。

provided that this article shall not apply to ordinary commercial shipments made in the ordinary course trade, but only to shipments where the character or condition of the property to be carried or the circumstances, terms and conditions under which the carriage is to be performed are such as reasonably to justify a special agreement."这一来,海运单又是不上不下了,因为它涉及的都会是一般的商品运输,一般的外贸。

这不明朗之处,以 William Tetley 教授的看法,是海运单也强制适用,他在《Marine Cargo Claims》一书第3版第11页说:

"The Rules are ambiguous and themselves state that they apply by art. 1(b) and art. 2 to bills of lading or similar documents of title. But art. 3(8) declares that the Rules to be of public order, while art. 6 stipulates that the Rules may only be avoided by the issue of non-negotiable receipts under certain specific conditions. From art. 1(b), art. 2, art. 3(8) and art. 6, taken together, one must conclude that, most rational interpretation (and the best solution to the ambiguity) is that the Hague or Hague-Visby Rules apply to all contracts of carriage of goods by sea, except for carriage under non-negotiable receipts which comply with art. 6…

The Hague or Hague-Visby Rules thus apply to non negotiable receipts (waybills), unless the shipment is an extraordinary shipment in a non commercial trade…"

在英国的 1971 COGSA,更是明示增加了立法在海运单上的强制适用,这是在 1971 COGSA 之 Section 1(6)(b),已在本章之 4.2.3.1.3 小段详述。

4.2.3.2.2 租约

海牙/海牙·维斯比规则不适用在租约,它可享有完全的订约自由(除非是违反公共政策),其中道理也已在本章之 3.1 小段解释过。

立法虽然不强制适用,但租约完全可以去合并海牙/海牙·维斯比规则,进而令该立法适用,这毕竟也是订约自由。

4.2.3.2.2.1 租约合并海牙/海牙·维斯比规则的做法

但合并的技巧可要多加注意,因为这完全是合约法,写什么算什么,合并的是海牙规则就是海牙规则,合并的是海牙·维斯比规则就是海牙·维斯比规则。这方面的困难,早在笔者《期租合约》一书的 45.1 至 45.2 段已有详论,可节录如下:

45.1 在租约中订立此条款的初衷和结果

很明显,这条款是想把美国的有关法律(海上货物运输法,即相关的海牙规则)合并到租约内。这做法其实不只是期租,往往在程租也有,而一般是在租约内加一条条款,如"航次租约的首要条款"。估计是租方船东都想在责任与免责方面能与提单配合,因为提单往往会强制适用海牙规则。这一来,通过合并双方就都有了肯定,知道不论在租约下或提单下,什么该做什么不该做。这也同时可以减少事后补偿(indemnity)的起诉与仲裁。比如,船东或租方在面对提单的索偿后,因租约条款、责任的不同而去事后要求租约另一方补偿。

但是,这做法所带来的困难可真是不少。比如,租约内所有的活动是远远不止货物的装卸运载的,所以,海牙规则的适用应去到哪里?对这问题,本书已在34章节的"免责条款"有详论,现在不再重复。

更大的困难是,海牙规则,特别是美国海上货物运输法,充满了与租约格格不入的条款。海牙规则本身就在 Article 5 说明只用在提单而不用在租约。所以,要合并进租约可不好解释。

45.2 对海牙规则合并入租约的解释

在一个著名的案例[403]可见到这方面的困难与矛盾,即是(a)要把海牙规则下的"提单"变为"租约";(b)海牙规则只是针对货物,所以,租约下的空放航次又如何?要是载货的航次是要船东"克尽职责"令船舶适航,而空放航次却不必(因海牙规则不适用),这会否令整个租约履行起来矛盾重重?(c)在美国海上货物运输法,S.13(第13条)是说明:"This Act shall apply to all contracts for carriage of goods by sea to or from ports of the United States in foreign trade …"。这一来,是否只有期租内(使用 NYPE46 格式)去跑美国的航次才适用这第24条,其他航次则不受制于美国的有关法律?

"Saxon Star"这一案例一直打到上议院,多位著名的大法官意见明显相异。在高院[404],Delvin 大法官判是:

a)"提单"与"租约"应可被视为相通。

b)有关法律(海牙规则)的适用,包括免责条款,不受地理的局限。即是,不跑美国的航次也可以适用。

c)对没有装货,即空放的航次,并不适用。

这案例上诉至上诉庭[405],整条的所谓"首要条款"被完全否定,说是这条款毫无意义(insensible),没法给予任何意思。

最后,案子上诉到了上议院,上诉庭的判决再次被推翻。所有五位大法官都认为"租约"既然合并了海牙规则(或是美国法),该法应是适用。至于其适用应否只局限在行走美国的航次,则只是以3对2的多数通过适用于租约内所有的航次,不管与美国有否接触。而对没有装货的空放航次,也是以多数压倒

---

[403] The "Saxon Star" (1958) 1 Lloyd's Rep. 73(上议院)。
[404] The "Saxon Star" (1957) 1 Lloyd's Rep. 79(高院一审)。
[405] The "Saxon Star" (1957) 1 Lloyd's Rep. 271(上诉庭)。

少数判决要适用。

所以在"Saxon Star"之后,可以说NYPE46第24条(或附加的"首要条款")的法律地位是:

a) 租约内所有的活动都适用海牙规则(或相关的美国法)的规定。

b) 所以,不只是在载货航次(laden voyage),就是在空放航次(ballast voyage),船东也有海牙规则要求的开航前克尽职责令船舶适航的义务。

c) 海牙规则或相关法律不受地理局限,例如要行走美国。事实上,在往后的"Satya Kailash"[406],这一点更是再度得到确认。该租约下的船舶仅是在印度港外空载时,也完全适用美国海上货物运输法(NYPE46的第24条)。

The "Saxon Star"是英国先例,但美国法院也是类同的判法,其先例有:Sun Company, Inc. v. s. s. Overseas Arctic, 27 F. 3d 1104 (5th Cir. 1994); Shell Oil Co. v. M. T. Gilda, 790 F2d 1209 (5th Cir. 1986); United States v. Wessel, Duval & Co., 115F. Supp. 678 (S. D. N. Y. 1953)。

4.2.3.2.2.2　合并条款的技巧之一:合并海牙规则还是海牙·维斯比规则

这种合并条款称为"首要条款"(Clause Paramount),现实中既有很短也有很长很详尽的条款。有把有关规则全部照录的,也有只将规则豁免部分内容合并的。它们会有不同的后果。首先去举的例子是租约中常有的简单一句话:"'首要条款'适用/合并在此租约"。这一来,合并的是什么规则呢?在The "Agios Lazaros" (1976) 2 Lloyd's Rep. 47,Denning勋爵判是海牙规则,不是海牙·维斯比规则,他说:

"What does 'paramount clause' or 'clause paramount' mean to shipping men? Primarily it applies to bill of lading. In that context, its meaning is, I think, clear beyond question, It means a clause by which the Hague Rules are incorporated into the contract evidenced by the bill of lading and which overrides any express exemption or condition that is inconsistent with it…[407]

Such being the clear meaning of 'clause paramount' in a bill of lading, we have to see what its meaning is in this charterparty.[408]

It seems to me that when the 'paramount clause' is incorporated, without any words of qualification, is means that all the Hague Rules are incorporated.[409] If the parties in-

---

[406] The "Satya Kailash" (1984) 1 Lloyd's Rep. 588.
[407] "首要条款"主要加在提单上,用以说明海牙规则适用与超越提单所有其他有冲突或矛盾的条款。
[408] "首要条款"加在租约又如何呢?
[409] 也应是适用海牙规则。

tend only to incorporate part of the rules (for example Art. IV),[410] or only so far as compulsorily applicable, they should say so. In the absence of any such qualification it seems to me that a 'clause paramount' is a clause which incorporates all the Hague Rules.[411] I mean of course, the accepted Hague Rules, not the Hague-Visby Rules,[412] which are of later date."

以上判例受到质疑,虽然当时海牙·维斯比规则的 1971 COGSA 仍未生效:1971 COGSA 是在 1977 年 6 月 23 日生效。所以像《Time Charter》一书第 561 页提到 The "Agios Lazaros"时说:"However, if a paramount clause is incorporated into a Baltime[413] charter-party governed by English law it is likely, following the coming into force in 1977 of the Carriage of Goods by Sea Act 1971, the Hague-Visby Rules would be regarded as incorporated."

到了近期的 The "Bukhta Russkaya" (1997) 2 Lloyd's Rep. 744,这一问题有了澄清的机会。该租约(也是 Baltime 格式)适用英国法,规定伦敦仲裁,并有一"首要条款"说:"… in trades involving neither US or Canadian ports, the general paramount clause to apply in lieu of the USA clause paramount."

航次是从非洲的毛里塔尼亚去日本东京,货物是高价的海产。这两国之间,海牙规则与海牙·维斯比规则都不强制适用。

航次中发生货损,承租人作为承运人先要面对收货人索赔,最后赔付了 22.6 万美元。承租人之后马上向船东要求"补偿"(indemnity),但当时海牙规则的一年时效已届。有关海牙规则并入租约引起的时效问题,在笔者《期租合约》一书的 45.3 段有详论,因内容较多不去节录。只提已有先例判船东是租约中的"承运人",所以承租人去向船东起诉,也只有一年时效:The "Khian Zephyr" (1982) 1 Lloyd's Rep. 73;The "Strathnewton" (1983) 1 Lloyd's Rep. 219。这方面将在后面 4.2.10.2 小段详述。

但如果租约适用的是海牙·维斯比规则,承租人可就有救了,因为它在 Article 3(6) 多加了一段,专门针对补偿行动,这是海牙规则原先所没有的。内容是:"An action for indemnity against a third person may be brought even after the expiration of the year provided for…"

---

[410] 若只想适用海牙规则的一部分,例如,Article 4 的免责部分,应写清楚。在本章 4.2.3.2.2.3 小段介绍的 The "Mariasmi" (1970) 1 Lloyd's Rep. 247 先例中的"首要条款",即是这种措辞。
[411] 否则海牙规则全部适用。
[412] 但不适用海牙·维斯比规则。
[413] 其他租约格式也是一样道理。

所以，到底"首要条款"是指海牙规则还是海牙·维斯比规则实在是事关重大[414]。

在参考了当时已通用的 BIMCO 1994 的"首要条款"后，Thomas 大法官判是解释如下："…'the general paramount clause' has the following essential terms: (1) if the Hague Rules are enacted in the country of shipment, then they apply as enacted; (2) if the Hague Rules are not enacted in the country of shipment, the corresponding legislation of the country of destination applies or, if there is no such legislation, the terms of the Convention containing the Hague Rules apply; (3) if the Hague-Visby Rules are compulsorily applicable to the trade in question, then the legislation enacting those rules applies."

看来，适用海牙规则还是海牙·维斯比规则是要看租约的航次而决定了。而在 The "Bukhta Russkaya" 先例，因为装卸港的两国都不强制适用海牙或海牙·维斯比规则，表示以上(2)的情况适用，即适用海牙规则。这表示承租人向船东要求补偿这 226 000 美元已是过了时效。

4.2.3.2.2.3　合并条款的技巧之二：首要条款与其他租约条款的冲突

因为租约的"首要条款"纯是以合约法去解释，所以必须要注意一个合约应如何去整体"解释"(construction)。例如在笔者的《国际商务游戏规则——英国合约法》一书第十章的 4.2 小段提到说：

> 在鉴于此，不少当事人在订约时就相当谨慎了。比如期租要用 NYPE 格式，其中有一首要条款(U.S.A. Clause Paramount)在第 24 条，讲适用美国 1936 年的海上货物运输法(实际是援用海牙规则)，那么很多船东或租家在订约时就把第 24 条涂掉，然后在越后面越好的附加条款加一条普遍的首要条款(General Clause Paramount，实际就是海牙规则)，将海牙规则引入本租约。这看起来似乎是多余，为什么把本来已订明用海牙规则的第 24 条涂掉而又在后面重新加一条说要用海牙规则呢？这里面实际上有讲究，因为既然要让适用海牙规则这一条超越所有有关货损货差的条款，那么把它放在第 24 条并不稳妥，因后面附加条款中若又有一条诸如"船不适航船东无须负责"的规定。那么一旦出了事，就会有争论了，到底哪一条超越哪一条？毕竟后者是附加条款。所以干脆就把第 24 条涂掉，然后再在附加条款重新写一条首要条款适用海牙规则，那么它便能超越其他条款与之不一致的规定了。这的确不失为一种非常谨慎的订约方法。在这方面，Denning 勋爵在 The "Agios Lazaros" (1976) 2 Lloyd's Rep. 47 说道：It (首要条款) brings the

---

[414] 另有许多情况下这问题也是事关重大，如 4.2.3.5.3.8 小段有关把货物装在甲板上的违约。

Hague Rules into the charter party so as to render the voyage or voyages subject to the Hague Rules, so far as applicable thereto; and it makes those Rules prevail over any of the exceptions in the charter party."

至于这"首要条款"与租约其他条款发生冲突带来谁优谁劣之争,更是经常见到。在以下段节介绍的两个案例,会令读者更好地理解这个问题。

首先是 The "Mariasmi"(1970)1 Lloyd's Rep. 247 先例,涉及一程租租约(金康租约格式),内中有两条有冲突的附加条款。一是第 29 条的"首要条款"。但措辞/用字上纯是为船东着想,即只在海牙规则中抽出针对免责的 Article 4 合并进租约,并明示不承担普通法的严格或绝对适航责任。该"首要条款"英文版本是:"Voyage Charter Party Clause Paramount(Carrier's Rights and Immunities) : Notwithstanding anything herein contained no absolute warranty of sea-worthiness is given or shall be implied in this charter party, and it is expressly agreed that the owners shall have the benefit of the 'Rights and Immunities' in favour of the carrier or ship contained in the Enactment in the country of shipment giving effect to the Hague Rules as set out in the International Convention for the Unification of Certain Rules relating to Bills of Lading. If no such Enactment is in force in the country of shipment the terms of Article 4 of the said Rules shall apply…"

但该租约同时有第 21 条说明船舶如果在给了抵达装港的通知后(另有条款针对如何给通知)发生延误,船东就要承担所有额外的装港费用,如货物运至码头但无法装上船而要多占用火车卡或驳船的费用。

在去第二个装港途中(Antwerp),该船因航行疏忽与他船碰撞,导致延误了十多天才开始装货。承租人以租约第 21 条提出索赔有关额外的装港费用,船东则以船员的航行疏忽属海牙规则的免责事项辩称不必去负责与作出任何赔偿。

Mocatta 大法官在整体解释租约时说,第 29 条的所谓"首要条款",其实是很有限度的"首要",并没有去针对太多方面。他说:"that it was wrong to place too much weight on the word 'Paramount' in the rubric to clause 29; that clause 29 contained a limited provision of paramountcy; and that, therefore, clause 29 did not necessarily prevail over clause 21."

相反,Mocatta 大法官觉得第 21 条更有针对性,专门针对晚抵达装港的情况,所以应超越第 29 条的"首要条款",因后者针对更广泛的各种情况。Mocatta 大法官说:"that on the facts in the case, clause 21(being tailor-made for purpose of contract) prevailed over clause 29…"

第二个例子是 Sabah Flour v. Comfez (1988) 2 Lloyd's Rep. 18 先例,它是程租,

租约内有第 23 条"首要条款"（合并的是澳大利亚海上运输法，也即是海牙规则）。众所周知，内中 Article 3(6)规定的是一年的索赔时效。

但该租约另有第 34 条的仲裁条款，内有规定 6 个月的时效，英文措辞是："…any claim must be in writing and claimant's arbitrator appointed within six months of the vessel's arrival at final port of discharge, otherwise all claims shall be deemed to be waived."

承租人向船东提出一个货损货差索赔，他/它在一年时效内，但已过了 6 个月，才开始任命仲裁员仲裁。这一来，时效是 6 个月（第 34 条）还是一年（第 23 条）？上诉庭判是第 34 条（仲裁条款）针对的是所有争议，而海牙规则/首要条款的第 23 条只针对货损货差，所以表面看来冲突的两条条款实际可去协调，即第 23 条的一年时效只去适用在租约的货损货差索赔。

美国也有不少类同的先例与仲裁。如 The Granville 1961 A. M. C. 2229，判是"首要条款不能剥夺 Baltime 1939 租约格式内对船东很优待的免责条款"（第 9 条与第 13 条）。

当然能以"首要条款"超越租约（或提单）其他矛盾条款的先例与仲裁也很多，如：

（i）美国的 Standard Oil Co. of California v. United States, 59 F. Supp, 100 (S. D. Calif. 1945), aff'd, 156 F. 2d 312 (9th Cir. 1946)判租约的另一条款说明船东不必对多装不同种类货物的后果负责无效。

（ii）澳大利亚的 The "Penrith Castle" (1954) 2 Lloyd's Rep. 544 判提单另有法国法院的管辖权条款无效。

（iii）英国的 W. R. Varnis & Co. Ltd. V. Khoti (1949) 82 Lloyd's Rep. 525，案情请参阅本章之 4.2.9.5 小段。

（iv）英国的 The "Amazonia" (1990) 1 Lloyd's Rep. 236 判是租约合并了澳大利亚的海上运输法（内有条款保障澳大利亚法院的管辖权）可以超越另一伦敦仲裁条款。

以上例子仅涉及有关的大原则，而个别案例的判决是否正确还涉及其他许多因素，例如双方争议是否全面。然而毕竟对合约内相互矛盾的条款的解释并不容易/固定，很多时候是取决于法官或仲裁员的印象/感觉了。正如 Shaw 大法官在 The "Agois Lazaros" (1976) 2 Lloyd's Rep. 47 之第 59 页所说："The interplay between COGSA (or the Hague Rules) and the provisions of the Charter to which it is appended, is not so easily resolved; The courts have not found it easy to make sense of the Hague Rules in the context of a charter-party since clearly those rules were not designed to be incorporated in such a contract."

4.2.3.2.2.4　合并条款的技巧之三：写明首要条款不在租约适用，只在提单适用

这方面可举的例子是 The "C. Joyce"（1986）2 Lloyd's Rep. 285，它的租约是使用金康租约。该租约格式的第 2 条对船东十分优待，责任比海牙规则轻多了，例如写明并不要求"克尽职责"（due diligence）使船舶适航，当然也不会要求更高的普通法的严格或"绝对适航"（absolute seaworthy）了。

该租约另有附加条款要求船长签发提单，并有一句（看来像"首要条款"）简单地说："… all bills of lading signed under this charter party to include … Clause Paramount."

航次中因船舱进海水而造成货损，面对海牙规则适用的提单的持有人/收货人，船东作出了赔偿。之后船东/互保协会认为船东虽在海牙规则下有责任，但在金康租约下可不必负责，于是向承租人提出"补偿"（indemnity）要求。

Bingham 大法官判船东败诉，因为细看条款的措辞/文字，实际是约定了船长必须去签发内有"首要条款"的提单。本案例正是这样去做了：提单有"首要条款"，适用海牙规则，而不是其他有更高责任的规定如汉堡规则等。Bingham 大法官说此举既然没有带来比租约已约定的更高的责任，何来补偿？Bingham 大法官认为完全可以在租约同意一套责任，但提单是另一套更高的责任，这本是订约自由嘛！

这要是灵活运用到现实中，就会带来先机/成功。笔者记得在 The "C. Joyce"先例报道后不久曾遇上一宗货物（散粮）去中国的案子。中方收货人以 FOB 进口，委托了香港一家中资公司代租船。其实他们之间的合约关系也是租约，虽然这个航次的程租只有口头几句，内容或/与条款十分粗糙。

很巧，香港中资船公司租入外轮的租约正是与 The "C. Joyce"案例相似：也是采用金康租约，也有条款要求船长签发内有"首要条款"的提单。

该航次发生了严重货损，中国收货人没有直接向外轮索赔，虽然，他/它们之间有提单合约关系，也适用海牙规则，因提单有明示的"首要条款"。相反，中国收货人（可说是分租方的身份）是去迫香港中资船公司向外轮追索。但这一来，他/它们之间是租约关系，而在金康租约下，条款对船东（外轮）十分保护，中方的货损索赔不会成功。

香港中资船公司在尚未行动之前（向船东开始伦敦仲裁）向笔者咨询，我想起 The "C. Joyce"的案例，马上加以劝阻。笔者认为以租约索赔货损只能是死路一条，相反，以提单起诉才大有机会。更妙的是，外轮赔付后是不能向香港中资公司要求补偿的，这正是 The "C. Joyce"的判决。但这劝阻并不容易，也不知是这些合约关系太复杂难明，或是笔者自己表达水平差，或更会是部分中国人怕面对外国人麻烦而只敢欺负自己人（香港中资船公司），总之要说服中国收货人仍是困难重重。

4.2.3.2.2.5 合并条款的技巧之四:赔偿限额的币值方面

这方面问题可先去节录笔者《期租合约》一书的45.4段如下:

45.4 海牙规则并入租约引起的赔偿责任限制的问题

海牙规则或有关法律合并到租约内还有其他的疑问,比如在金额限制方面。在海牙规则中,这方面条款是在Article IV的(5),全文为:

"Neither the carrier nor the ship shall in any event be or become liable for any loss or damage to or in connection with goods in an amount exceeding £ 100.00 per package or unit, or the equivalent of that sum in other currency…"

对这£ 100.00,海牙规则在Article IX再有解释:

"The monetary units mentioned in these Rules are to be taken to be gold value." 当然,海牙规则变为某国法律,这金额已被改为当地货币,如美国海上运输法是500美元。这一来,在金额的限制上就要看租约合并进去的是哪一个立法。要是美国法,应是500美元。要是英国法,应是100英镑。当然,如合并的是英国1971年的《海上运输法》,会是"海牙·维斯比规则"适用,那么这金额与计算方法又会不同。

但如果纯是合并1924年海牙规则,因有本段所提的Article IX,故已有多个不同国家的案例有不同的判法,即是,1924年100英镑的黄金价格在今天应相当于接近7000英镑的币值。多数的判例,包括英国[415],均认同这个看法。这在"Rosa S"一案有详细分析。

所以,若双方有意愿将海牙规则并入,用首要条款的方式加在租约中,用字便要小心了。当然,NYPE46的第24条是合并美国法,金额限制是500美元,这方面没有问题。但要是涂掉该条再以附加条款合并1924年海牙规则,则会面临"Rosa S"一案的危险,船东可要小心。

这金额限制的另一问题是针对哪一种的索赔船东可享用此限制?是否只是针对货物的损失(loss or damage to goods),或是更广泛?毕竟,Article IV(5)的用字"in connection with goods"是广泛的。比如像"Satya Kailash"一案[416]轻载时发生的碰撞损失,判下来是NYPE46第24条下的免责船东可享受。但是,在金额限制方面又如何呢?如果船东可以享受,这金额限制又如何计算:照该航次装的(或意图装的)货为准?每件500美元?或是散装货用重量计算(如果租约合并了海牙·维斯比规则)?

---

[415] The "Rosa S" (1988) 2 Lloyd's Rep. 574.
[416] The "Satya Kailash" (1984) 1 Lloyd's Rep. 588.

第五章　提单作用之二：运输合约下的货损货差责任　349

看来,对于海牙规则或有关法律合并在租约的普遍做法(在 NYPE93 是第 31 条),仍会有官司可打。

从以上节录可见,有几点要注意:

(ⅰ)若货物价值不高(一般散装货),这一点不必太关心。

(ⅱ)如果货物品种价值会有关,"首要条款"合并某国法律较佳。例如 NYPE'46 租约格式的"首要条款"是合并美国的 1936COGSA；Austwheat 租约格式的"首要条款"是合并澳大利亚的 1924COGSA；等等。但这并不保险,因为订约方可另去附加"首要条款"并不合并某国法律,而只合并全部的海牙规则,这包括了 The "Rosa S"案例的 100 英镑的黄金价格。

(ⅲ)"首要条款"合并海牙·维斯比规则也没有 The "Rosa S"的问题,因为它的赔偿限额已不再是黄金价格,而是改为联合国国际货币基金组织的"特别提款权"(Unit of Account 或简称 UOA,亦称为 Special Drawing Rights 或简称 SDR)了。

(ⅳ)"首要条款"只合并海牙规则的部分内容,例子是 4.2.3.1.2.3 小段的 The "Mariasmi"(1970) 1 Lloyd's Rep. 247 先例的"首要条款",对船东/承运人会是安全的做法。

4.2.3.2.2.6　期租使用的"首要条款"版本的介绍

看来,去拟定一条好的"首要条款"以便把海牙/海牙·维斯比规则合并进租约并非易事。当然,这"好"的拟定还要相对公平,不要一面倒,保障船东,像 The "Mariasmi"(1970) 1 Lloyd's Rep. 247 案例中的有关条款那样。

特别是涉及期租,NYPE'46 租约格式的"首要条款"在合并美国的 1936 COGSA 方面,已打了不少官司,澄清了许多疑点,但问题/困难仍不少,其中包括一年时效方面,因为海牙规则与 1936 COGSA 没有针对补偿行动的时效。在 4.2.3.1.2.2 小段提及的 The "Bukhta Russkaya"(1997) 2 Lloyd's Rep. 744 先例,正是有这问题。另一重要疑点是"首要条款"的适用范围包括了什么纠纷,或只是针对货损货差的纠纷？笔者的《期租合约》一书 45.3 段针对这一方面有详细论述,内容稍长,不去节录。只提一提,"首要条款"若只针对货损货差,则货物若属承租人,就只涉及向船东索赔。若货物属第三者,就会涉及承租人与船东相互之间的"补偿"(indemnity)行动。但 NYPE 是期租,它不同于程租,双方关系复杂且涉及面不光是一个特定航次,特定货物。所以 NYPE 粗略地以"首要条款"合并海牙规则,便带来了这样的疑惑,即其他所有的租约纠纷,如航速耗油索赔,迟放发提单,船泵有问题,洗舱不清洁等,是否包括在海牙规则的适用范围内,例如受否一年时效约束？这疑惑带来多个先例,但看来疑点仍在,分水线并不明显,如：The "Standard Ardour"(1988) 2 Lloyd's Rep. 159,The "Stena Pacifica"(1990) 2 Lloyd's Rep. 234,The "OT Sonja"(1993) 2

Lloyd's Rep. 435,The"Marinor"(1996) 1 Lloyd's Rep. 301 等。

所以近期推出市场的 Centime 1999 标准期租合约格式,为求与 NYPE'46、'93 标准格式分享市场使用率,在这方面采取了截然不同的措辞/写法,这会在下一小段详述。在此可先介绍 BIMCO 近期的"首要条款"版本,它是准备去供 Gentime 1999 选择性使用的,措辞/文字上是去合并海牙·维斯比规则,内容如下:

CLAUSE PARAMOUNT

The International Convention for the Unification of Certain Rules of Law relating to Bills of Lading signed at Brussels on 24 August 1924 ("the Hague Rules") as amended by the Protocol signed at Brussels on 23 February 1968 ("the Hague-Visby Rules") and as enacted in the country of shipment shall apply to this Contract When the Hague-Visby Rules are not enacted in the country of destination shall apply, irrespective of whether such legislation may only regulate outbound shipments.

When there is no enactment of the Hague-Visby Rules in either the country of shipment or in the country of destination, the Hague-Visby Rules shall apply to this Contract, save where the Hague Rules as enacted in the country of shipment or if no such enactment is in place the Hague Rules as enacted in the country of destination apply compulsorily to this Contract.

The Protocol signed at Brussels on 21 December 1979 ("the SDR Protocol 1979") shall apply where the Hague-Visby Rules apply whether mandatorily or by this Contract.

The Carrier shall in no case be responsible for loss of or damage to cargo arising prior to loading, after discharging, or while the cargo is in the charge of another carrier, or with respect to deck cargo and live animals.

4.2.3.2.2.7 Gentime 1999 期租约格式的替代"首要条款"做法

上一小段谈到了 BIMCO 最近推出了这一份标准期租合约格式,以供市场使用。今日租船市场以期租为主,程租相对为辅。而期租中估计 95% 以上使用 NYPE'46 (或 '93)的标准格式,它的第 24 条是一条"首要条款"。或会是,Gentime 1999 并不容易改变由 NYPE 长期雄霸/独霸的局面。对市场大部分用家而言,人性是一样的,即不喜欢改变,怕改变。大家也不会去细究 Gentime 是否比 NYPE 好,好多少,值不值得去改用另一标准格式,等等。但笔者在此纯是以理论的角度去介绍 Gentime 的第 18 条,它替代了 NYPE 的"首要条款"以及因不够明确而带来的 Inter-Club Agreement(请看本章之 4.2.10.2.8.4 小段,对此有略述),而采取了截然不同且是全新概念的措辞/写法。可先去节录该条款如下:

18. Responsibilities

(a) *Cargo Claims*

(ⅰ) Definition[417]——For the purpose of this Clause 18 (a), Cargo Claim means a claim for loss, damage, shortage, (including slackage, ullage or pilferage), overcarriage of or delay to cargo including customs fines or fines in respect of such loss, damage, shortage, overcarriage or delay and includes:

(1) any legal costs or interest claimed by the original claimant making such a claim;

(2) all legal, Club correspondents' and experts costs reasonably incurred in the defence of or in the settlement of the claim made by the original claimant, but shall not include any costs of whatsoever nature incurred in making a claim or in seeking an indemnity under this Charter Party.

(ⅱ) *Claim Settlement*——It is a condition precedent to the right of recovery by either party under this Clause 18 (a) that the party seeking indemnity shall have first properly settled or compromised and paid the claim.[418]

(ⅲ) *Owners' Liability*[419]——*The Owners shall be liable for any Cargo* Claim arising or resulting from:

(1) failure of the Owners or their servants to exercise due diligence before or at the beginning of each voyage to make the Vessel seaworthy;

(2) failure of the Owners or their servants properly and carefully to carry, keep and

---

[417] 从定义可见，本条款只针对货损货差与有关费用。这可避免了上一小段介绍的 NYPE 以"首要条款"合并海牙规则所带来的不明确，即不知其适用于租约纠纷的范围包括到哪里。

[418] 这一句说明了原提单索赔可以庭外和解，只要合理（如有法律依据、和解前通知了补偿方或有称职律师的建议），也不影响补偿。固然，这也是普通法的地位：The "Krspan J" (1999) 1 Lloyd's Rep. 688。这一句也要求必须支付了原索赔才能提出与寻求补偿。这也应是普通法的地位，否则哪有真正损失？但遇上对补偿责任有争议，经常会先去起诉（或开始仲裁），以获得一个只针对责任的"宣告"的判决或裁决，从而明确应否补偿：请看本章之 4.2.10.2.8.2 小段。

[419] 这一条款明确列出船东对货损货差应负之责，计有四种情况。一是每一相关航次开航前没有"克尽职责"令船舶适航（本章之 4.2.6 小段）。二是没有妥善与小心装卸，堆放与照顾货物（本章之 4.2.8 小段）。三是不合理绕航，除非是承租人下令或批准的绕航，如乱绕航去加燃油或揽货（本章之 4.2.10.1 小段）。四是针对航行/管船过错，这表面看来难以理解，因为海牙/海牙·维斯比规则对此是免责（本章之 4.2.7.1.1 小段），何必要让船东在 Gentime 期租租约下对承租人负责？但读者若细看这一句，便可发觉这其实是与汉堡规则有关。在本章之 4.4 小段会提到，汉堡规则对航行/管船过错或/与疏忽并没有免责。这一来，若遇上航次是强制适用汉堡规则（例如去埃及卸货），航次中发生了这类事故提单下不准免责，导致原索赔是船东要去赔偿收货人。若根据 NYPE 标准格式，船东会向承租人要求补偿，因为"首要条款"下船东对航行/管船过错或/与疏忽照样免责。或是，换一种情况，承租人是提单下的承运人，因强制适用汉堡规则而要赔偿因航行/管船不当导致的货损货差，他事后亦是无法在 NYPE 标准格式下向船东要求补偿。但承租人管不了航行与船舶管理，所以在期租下这样分摊责任看来并不公平。所以在 Gentime 标准期租租约，把这赔偿责任（但只在汉堡规则下才有责任）明示地分摊到船东头上。

care for the cargo while on beard;

(3) unreasonable deviation from the voyage described in the Contract of Carriage unless such deviation is ordered or approved by the Charterers;

(4) errors in navigation or the management of the Vessel solely where the Contract of Carriage is subject to mandatory application of legislation giving effect to the Hamburg Rules.

(ⅳ) *Charterers' Liability*[420]——*The Charterers shall be liable for any* Cargo Claim arising or resulting from:

(1) the stevedoring operations enumerated under Clause 13 (d) unless the Charterers prove that such Cargo Claim was caused by the unseaworthiness of the Vessel, in which case the Owners shall be liable;

(2) any transhipment in connection with through-transport or multimodal transport, save where the Charterers can prove that the circumstances giving rise to the Cargo Claim occurred after commencement of the loading of the cargo onto the Vessel and prior to its discharge;

(3) the carriage of cargo on deck unless such cargo is stowed in fully closed containers, placed on board the Vessel in areas designed for the carriage of containers with class-approved Vessel's lashing gear or material.

(ⅴ) *Shared Liability*[421]——*All Cargo Claims arising from other causes than those enumerated under sub-clauses* (ⅲ) *and* (ⅳ), *shall be shared equally between the Owners and the Charterers unless there is clear and irrefutable evidence that the claim arose out of pilferage or the act or neglect of one or the other party or their servants or sub-contractors, in which* case that party shall bear the full claim.

---

[420] 这一条款明确列出承租人对货损货差应负之责,计有三种情况。一是装卸工所造成的,因为Gentime 期租租约的第13 条把装卸工所有的作业(装卸,堆装,堆装集装箱,理货,捆绑货物等)的风险与责任均加在承租人头上。除非是,装卸工的不妥作业(如堆装货物)提升至船舶不适航的程度(如不妥堆装影响船舶稳性)。这一来若承租人能予以证明则货损货差责任仍是归船东。这一方面请看本章之4.2.6.6.5 小段。二是全程提单或多式联运下的转运。情况会是承租人(他/它会是一个货代或多式联运承运人)去签发了全程提单,提单承运人会是承租人自己或是船东(因为代船长签)。但显然一涉及转运,船东不会管也管不到。所以这方面责任是在承租人头上,如转运中发生货损货差。三是甲板货,除了是专门去装载集装箱:这一方面请看本章之4.2.3.5.3 小段。

[421] 其他情况的货损货差(例如无法解释原因:本章之4.2.7.1.16.2 小段),承租人与船东各分摊一半赔偿(赔提单持有人/收货人),除非一方能证明损失是对方(或他/它的雇员/分包人)所造成,才可避免分摊此赔偿,例如承租人证明是船员偷窃货物或反过来船东证明是装卸工偷窃货物。照说在提单下,收货人不必去理会偷窃货物的是船员还是装卸工,反正他们都是提单承运人的雇用人员,要负责的话都一样赖不掉(本章之4.2.7.1.16.4 小段)。但在此之后的期租下的补偿,则有去区分的必要了。

(ⅵ) *Charterers' Own Cargo*[422]——*If the cargo is the property of the Charterers, the Owners shall have the same responsibilities and benefits as they would have had under this Clause had the cargo been the property of* a third party and carried under a Bill of Lading incorporating the Hague-Visby Rules.

(b) *Fines, etc.*——The Charterers shall also be liable to the Owners for any losses, damages, expenses, fines, penalties, or claims which the Owners may incur or suffer by reason of the cargo or the documentation relating thereto failing to comply with any relevant laws, regulations, directions or notices of port authorities or other authorities, or by reason of any infestation, contamination or condemnation of the cargo or of infestation, damage or contamination of the Vessel by the cargo.[423]

(c) *Deck cargo*——The Charterers shall be liable to the Owners for any loss, damage, expense or delay to the Vessel howsoever caused and resuiting from the carriage of cargo on deck save where the Charterers can prove that such loss, damage, expense or delay was the result of negligence on the part of the Owners and/or their servants.[424]

(d) *Death or Personal Injury*——Claims for death or personal injury having a direct connection with the operation of the Vessel shall be borne by the Owners unless such claims are caused by defect of the cargo or by the act, neglect or default of the Charterers, their servants, agents or sub-contractors.[425]

---

[422] 期租一样可能会运载承租人自己的货物,即承租人是收货人,并非是"经营人"(operator),或是"多式联运承运人"等。这一来,遇上货损货差,承租人索赔的责任分摊完全一样。提单在他手中,只是当做货物收据,双方合约关系纯是期租租约:The "Dunelmia"(1969) 1 Lloyd's Rep. 32。本条也说明船东与承租人之间的索赔以海牙·维斯比规则为准,省得将来有争议时租方说汉堡规则才适用,所以航行/管船不当导致的货损货差,船东照样应赔偿承租人损失。

[423] 这一条针对承租人在期租下营运其所作所为带来的后果,若对船东造成损失,全归承租人负责。如因为船上货物或相关文件的问题而遭港口当局罚款、干预等;或是货物生虫、污染等。这一条并没改变什么,NYPE 标准格式的"雇用及赔偿条款"(employment and indemnity clause)也有同样作用。

[424] 这一条说明承租人要对甲板货负责;有关甲板货,请看本章之 4.2.3.5.3 小段。在期租,是承租人把货物装上船舶。将货物装在甲板上也是他/它的用意/安排,也有权这样做(期租包括使用甲板,如 NYPE'46 之第 7 条)。

[425] 这类问题常在美国港口发生,装卸工动不动就会指控因船舶不安全(如灯光不够,甲板湿滑,告示不足,等)或作业不安全,导致他受伤。这常是事实,但也有少了一根头发,然后索赔天文数字的赔偿。诉讼途中,也往往会去庭外和解。这之后就是船东与承租人之间的补偿行为了。这一条款就是针对这一方面。故若然事实上是船舶不安全,疏忽等原因导致人员伤亡意外,这是船东自己负责。但若是承租人或他的雇员/分包人等的行为/疏忽或货物的缺陷引起伤亡(如装卸作业中疏忽伤及其中一装卸工人),承租人要负责,并补偿船东。

(e) *Agency*——The Owners authorise and empower the Charterers to act as the Owners' agents solely to ensure that, as against third parties, the Owners will have the benefit of any immunities, exemptions or liberties regarding the cargo or its carriage. Subject to the provisions of Clause 17 the Charterers shall have no authority to make any contracts imposing any obligations whatsoever upon the Owners in respect of the cargo or its carriage.[426]

(f) *Indemnity and Limitation*——The Owners and the Charterers hereby agree to indemnify each other against all loss, damage or expenses arising or resulting from any obligation to pay claims, fines or penalties for which the other party is liable in accordance with this Charter Party. Both the Owners and the Charterers shall retain their right to limit their liability against the other party in respect of any claim brought by way of indemnity, notwithstanding that the other party has been denied the right to limit against any third party or has failed in whatever manner to exercise its rights of limitation.[427]

(g) *Time Bar*——In respect of any Cargo Claims as between the Owners and the Charterers, brought under sub-clause 18 (a), unless extensions of time have been sought or obtained from one party by the other or notice of arbitration has been given by either party, such claim(s) shall be deemed to be waived and absolutely time barred upon the expiry of two years reckoned from the date when the cargo was or should have been delivered. When the Hamburg Rules apply compulsorily the above time bar shall be extended to three years.[428]

---

[426] 这一条款提到第 17 条,该条即授权承租人去签发提单与海运单。所以,承租人签发的提单一般约束船东,令船东成为承运人:请看本书第三章之 3.5 小段。但本条款说明承租人无权以船东的名义去订立其他的运输合约,例如是全程运输/提单或多式联运的转运。

[427] 这一条针对的情况如承租人没有充分利用船舶吨位责任限制(请看本章之 4.2.10.3.9 小段),就去赔付巨额货损货差赔偿,并不影响在要求补偿的行动中,船东可以提出或再提出这船舶吨位责任限制,以图少去补偿。承租人未充分利用赔偿会有多种原因,如不懂、忘了,被有关法院草草否定等。

[428] 这一条针对补偿行为(为主)的仲裁时效,订明是交货或应交货后的 2 年。换言之,它比海牙·维斯比规则的 6 年(而且是从补偿诉因浮现时始算)要短多了:请看本章之 4.2.10.2.8.5 小段。但一般情况下仍应足够,因为原提单索赔只有一年时效。所以到了 2 年,总会知道有否原索赔的存在,会否要补偿。届时,即使原索赔仍未结案或/与和解(这到很可能),要求补偿的一方也可在对方不明确同意补偿的情况下开始仲裁以保护时效,甚至推进仲裁以取得一个确定补偿责任的"宣告裁决"(declaratory award)。另要注意的是,本条最后一句说明若汉堡规则强制适用在提单,因为有了 2 年索赔时效,所以租约的补偿时效也从 2 年延长为 3 年。读者或会问:货损货差的责任在这 Gentime1999 标准期租格式的第 18 条会是足够详尽明确了,但其他的期租纠纷呢?船东有否免责呢?这方面的答案是在第 19 条详述。

19. Exceptions As between the Charterers and the Owners, responsibility for any loss, damage, delay or failure of performance under this Charter Party not dealt with in Clause 28 (a), shall be subject to the following mutual exceptions;

Act of God, act of war, civil commotions, strikes, lockouts, restraint of princes and rulers, and quarantine restrictions.

In addition, any responsibility of the Owners not dealt with in Clause 18 (a) shall be subject to the following exceptions;

Any act, neglect or default by the Master, pilots or other servants of the Owners in the navigation or management of the Vessel, fire or explosion not due to the personal fault of the Owners of their Manager, collision or stranding, unforeseeable breakdown of or any latent defect in the Vessel's hull, equipment or machinery.

The above provisions shall in no way affect the provisions as to offhire in this Charter Party.

4.2.3.2.3　租约下的提单

本书第三章之 4.2 小段已说过租约下签发的提单若是在承租人手中，提单只起货物收据的作用，而承租人（也是货方）与船东的合约关系纯是早已约定的一份租约：The "Dunelmia" (1969) 1 Lloyd's Rep. 32。

租约下签发的提单也是物权凭证，一样可以通过背书转让货物的占有权/所有权给第三者的买方。这一切在本书第二章的多处（如 3.1.5 小段）已论及，不再重复。

而一去背书转让，与船东/承运人以提单为准的一个运输合约关系也同时转让给了第三者的买方/提单受让人。这正是英国 1855 年提单法 Section 1 以及今天替代提单法的 1992 年海上运输法的立法意图与作用，这已在本书第三章之 12.2.4/12.2.5 小段论及。

上述立法并没有去区分班轮或租约下的提单，1855 年提单法只是针对（货物）"已装船的提单"（shipped bill of lading），但这也不影响租约下的提单，因它们都会是"装船提单"。

从以上所讲可以想象到一种情况，即：租约有完全的订约自由，结果某一租约同意使用金康租约，没有大改动，导致租约中对船东有利，责任十分轻微。在装了货物后签发提单，该提单合并了租约条款，意味着提单下也对船东有利，责任十分轻微。该套提单在承租人手中无所谓。一是他/它与船东承运人之间已有租约，合约关系以租约为准；二是即使提单有任何的合约的作用（其实没有），与租约一致也是公平合理。但如果再往后该套提单被背书转让，去了无辜的买方手中，该买方再因立法而与船东/承运人有了以提单为准的合约关系，则如果合约条款仍是稳定不变,一致地以合并了的金康租约条款为准,那就会对无辜的买方十分不利。所以海牙规则也一定要去对付这一个环节,禁止订约自由(这自由源自租约订立时),强加给船东/承运人最起码的一套责任如"克尽职责"使船舶适航等,否则会出现诸如以下一些不妥的现象:

(ⅰ)同是提单,同是 CIF/CFR 买卖,卖方以班轮运输,不存在租约,则班轮提单受立了法的海牙规则强制约束。但卖方若以租约运输便有了订约自由,进而令其后签发的租约提单可以不受海牙规则适用。这完全不同的结果实在令人无法接受。

(ⅱ)租约提单现实中转卖/转让频繁,比班轮提单转让的次数/机会多得多了,所以它代表的价值、信心等,在国际外贸中的重要性更大,因此怎能任由船东以订约自由去逃避海上运输的各种责任呢?

所以海牙规则的 Article l(b)说明租约提单一旦到了无辜第三者的提单持有人(包括买方、承押人等)的手中,规则也强制适用。即不存在订约自由,合并进来的金康租约部分如果让船东减轻或逃避责任,将被视作"无效"(null, void and of no effect)。

4.2.3.3 侵权是否/能否适用

这问题简单的答案当然是"不适用"。确实是,海牙/海牙·维斯比规则的主旨是为了压制船东(特别是班轮公司,请回头看本章之 3.1/3.2 小段)的订约自由,而侵权与订约自由无关。但侵权会在两种主要的情况下与海牙规则发生关系并产生矛盾。

4.2.3.3.1 矛盾之一:承运人既违约,又侵权

4.2.3.3.1.1 英国法律承认并列责任/并列诉讼

如果合约一方(比方是承运人)既违了约又构成侵权,侵权主要是以"疏忽"(negligence),责任方未尽"谨慎从事"(duty of care)的法定责任为由,另一合约方在英国法律下可去"并列诉讼"(concurrent action),即可以违约,同时又可以侵权为诉因起诉:就这方面本书其他地方已有涉及,如第二章之 5.5.2 小段。船东/承运人会惹上"并列责任"(concurrent liability)的典型例子是装卸或照顾货物有疏忽导致货物损坏;这既违反提单合约(适用海牙规则),也是侵权行为。

有关这方面的法律,本书第二章之 5.5.2 小段已节录了笔者《国际商务游戏规则——英国合约法》一书的第十四章 3.2 小段与 3.3 小段,不再在此重复,请读者自己参阅。

4.2.3.3.1.2 为何要以侵权起诉

要知道,违约与侵权的起点很不一样。合约是严格责任,但有宽松的订约自由。而侵权一般是以疏忽为起点,也不存在订约自由与谈判合约的过程。这一来,最后合约下的责任与免责,通常与侵权不一样。例如合约会对某种疏忽免责(像海牙规

则有著名的 Article 4(2)(a)针对航行或管船中的疏忽或过失免责),但侵权恰恰就要对这疏忽负责。又例如,合约会约定半年,1 年、2 年不等的索赔时效(像海牙规则有 1 年),但侵权是法定的 6 年(Limitation Act 1980),侵权也不会有谈判,事先约定另一时效。

的确,海牙规则(适用在提单合约)的一套责任实在与侵权太不一样了,正如 Donaldson 大法官在 The "Aliakmon"(1985) 1 Lloyd's Rep. 199 所说:"I have, of course, considered whether any duty of care in tort to the buyer could in some way be equated to the contractual duty of care owed to the shipper, but I do not see how this could be done. The commonest form of carriage by sea is one on the terms of the Hague Rules. But this is an intricate blend of responsibilities and liabilities (Article Ⅲ), rights and immunities (Article Ⅵ), limitations to the amount of damages recoverable (Article Ⅳ, r. 5), time bars (Article Ⅲ, r. 6), evidential provisions (Article Ⅲ, rr. 4 and 6), indemnities (Article Ⅲ, r. 5 and Article Ⅳ, r. 6) and liberties (Article Ⅳ, rr. 4 and 6). I am quite unable to see how these can be synthesized into a standard of care."

这一来,收货人/提单持有人在某件有关的事故就会想取巧了。例如海牙规则一年时效刚过,或是,海牙规则的单位赔偿限额太低了:请看 4.2.3.1.6 小段提及的 Ryoden Machinery v. Anders Maersk(Sup. Ct. of Hong Kong 1986)(1986) 1 Lloyd's Rep. 483。想以侵权起诉便是其中一种的取巧。

4.2.3.3.1.3　海牙·维斯比规则把侵权之诉的大门关上

在英国,如 4.2.3.3.1.1 小段的节录可见,法律是不鼓励当事方在已有合约关系的情况下再把侵权扯进来去取巧的。英国法律认为一切应以合约为准,这是双方一开始愿意发生关系时所达至的平衡,必须去尊重。所以,合约方被另一方以侵权起诉,仍然可以提出相关合约条款来抗辩,而且最后的判决/裁决是以合约所规定为准。

但世界各国对这并列责任的看法并不相同(或没有看法),所以海牙·维斯比规则在 Article 3 同意在原来海牙规则的 Article 4 多加几段来明确针对这问题,在此可节录部分如下:

"1. The defences and limits of liability provided for in this convention shall apply in any action against the carrier in respect of loss or damage to goods covered by a contract of carriage[429] whether the action be founded in contract or in tort.[430]

---

[429] 在已有一个运输合约(注意,海牙规则在 Article 1 (b)对它的定义是"提单与相关/类似物权凭证")的大前提下。

[430] 诉讼不论以合约还是以侵权为诉因,此公约(海牙·维斯比规则)均强制适用。

2. If such an action is brought against a servant or agent of the carrier[431] (such servant or agent not being an independent contractor)[432], such servant or agent shall be entitled to avail himself of the defences and limits of liability which the carrier is entitled to invoke under this convention[433]?

3. The aggregate of the amounts recoverable from the carrier, and such servants and agents, shall in no case exceed the limit provided for in this Convention.[434]

…"

4.2.3.3.2 矛盾之二:独立承包人的侵权

以上讲到海牙·维斯比规则明示去保护曾在作业中犯了疏忽的承运人的雇员与代理人不受侵权干预。这也没有什么大不了,本来这就是英国普通法地位。在 Elder, Dempster v. Paterson, Iochonis (1924) 18 Lloyd's Rep. 319, Scrutton 大法官说:"…where there is a contract which contains an exemption clause, the servants or agents who act under that contract have the benefit of the exemption clause. They cannot be sued in tort as independent people, but they can claim the protection of the contract made with their employers on whose behalf they are acting."

4.2.3.3.2.1 代理人与独立承包人的区分

但这不包括独立承包人,虽然他/它与代理人有何大分别也不一定是太明显。

原则上代理人是受委托人授权而代其办事,代理人只能是处处对委托人负责(accountable for principal),扮演一个局限的角色。而独立承包人则是去依约办妥"分包"(sub-contract)的工作。履约中不必事事都去取得对方订约方的授权,对方一般也管不到独立承包人如何履约。固然,在订约自由下,分包合约也可让分包方更多去插手承包方的内部事务。但一般不会这样做,甚至做不到。比方是像修船厂或船级社的独立承包人。

至于"独立承包人"的定义,也已在本书第三章之8.1小段提到的 The "Starsin"(2000) 1 Lloyd's Rep. 85 先例略有提及。

不保护独立承包人的理据在 Midlands Silicones v. Scruttons (1961) 2 Lloyd's Rep. 365 的著名先例稍有提及。Reid 勋爵在第377页说独立承包人的分包合约与受害方无关,如果他/它因侵权造成受害方受损,本质上与疏忽侵权造成任何第三者受损一样,为何在前一种情况下因受害方与分包的雇主另有一个合约,就可让独

---

[431] 如果向承运人的雇员(像船长,船员)或代理人起诉,本公约同样适用。

[432] 除非是针对独立的分包人,本公约才不适用。这表示货方仍可以侵权起诉有疏忽的独立分包人(像装卸工、二程船等)。这方面的各种问题在接下去的小段会详论。

[433] 如果向承运人的雇员(像船长,船员)或代理人起诉,本公约同样适用。

[434] 从承运人及其雇员与代理人处所索赔获得的金额,不得超出本公约的限额。

立承包人插进来取巧或少赔一点呢？这既没有法律依据，也没有任何政策上的需要去分出两种不同后果的侵权。

但雇员及代理人的本质就不一样，他/它们只是雇主或委托人的"手脚"，做什么事情都不是独立而为，而是要听从"大脑"的指挥。而这"大脑"就是雇主或委托人。

4.2.3.3.2.2　货方取巧成功的先例：Midlands Silicones

Midlands Silicones v. Scruttons 先例涉及一批桶装化学品从美国运往伦敦，而提单（当然不止一桶）明示的"首要条款"合并了美国的 1936 COGSA。在伦敦卸货时，装卸工疏忽摔坏了一桶。如果收货人以提单合约向承运人起诉，只能获赔 1936 COGSA 的单位赔偿限额的 500 美元，但每桶化学品远不止是此价格（高出 4 至 5 倍）。因此，收货人以侵权起诉疏忽的装卸工，并成功获得全部赔偿。

在贵族院，判是装卸工不属 1936 COGSA 的"承运人"，运输合约（提单）也不关他的事。船东与发货人订约时并没有把装卸工包括在内，他完全是第三者，所以不能去享有船东在提单合约下的免责或限责。

Midlands Silicones 先例对海牙规则是一个冲击，肯定会"造成混乱"。货方利益、船东利益以及他/它们背后的保险公司/互保协会已在海牙规则达到风险分摊上的平衡，货方也乐于接受即使承运人有责任，仍会在高价货赔不足，即承运人可以限制责任。但现在从后门攻进去，货方仍可迫使船东全数赔偿，因为装卸工肯定要在服务合约中（stevedoring contract）要求船东/承运人（也是订约方）对他作出保障/补偿。

4.2.3.3.2.3　贵族院大政策摇摆不定的先例：The "Nicholas H"

对货方这种从后门进攻，而把海牙规则建立的利益平衡"搅乱"的做法，贵族院的大政策看来也有摇摆/不一致。在 Midlands v. Silicones 先例是允许货方从后门突击船东成功（虽然贵族院中的 Denning 勋爵大力反对）。但三十年后的 The "Nicholas H" (1995) 2 Lloyd's Rep. 299 先例，又大力维护海牙规则所达到的平衡，不惜给予船级社免受侵权诉讼的豁免权。

该先例涉及"Nicholas H"轮在秘鲁 Callao 港与智利 Antofagasta 港满载了铅和锌精矿，准备开航去意大利等卸港。航次途中因发觉船身破裂而绕航去了波多黎各的 San Juan 港避难。在避难港，日本船级社上船检查，并建议完全修理好才重新开航。但估计这样做昂贵且不方便（因船上有货物），可能是在船东的压力和交涉下，日本船级社最后让步改为只要求临时修理，永久修理留待将来卸了货再算。显然，临时修理便宜与粗糙多了，只会是在裂缝两头钻两个洞以防止/减轻裂缝继续扩大，另再以烧焊加一块铁板暂时把裂口封住。

"Nicholas H"在重新开航去意大利途中，海浪一大，临时修理马上失败，结果海水涌入导致船舶沉没。

货方向"Nicholas H"船东索赔且成功,但海牙规则下只赔得50万美元。于是,货方就尚差的货价余额约550万美元以侵权向日本船级社起诉。日本船级社要赔钱之外,疏忽也很明显,毕竟允许临时修理是不当的决定。

但在贵族院,判是日本船级社可享有豁免权,它对货方没有"谨慎从事"(duty of care)的责任。而考虑因素主要仍是怕货方从后门突击船东从而导致海牙规则的风险平衡被打破,正如Steyn勋爵所说:"the recognition of a duty would be unfair, unjust and unreasonable as against the shipowners who would ultimately have to bear the cost of holding classification societies liable, such consequence being at variance with the bargain between shipowners and cargo-owners based on an internationally agreed contractual structure; it would also be unfair, unjust and unreasonable towards classification societies, notably because they acted for the collective welfare and unlike shipowners they would not have the benefit of any limitation provisions; the existing system provided the cargo-owners with the protection of the Hague Rules or Hague-Visby Rules although that protection was limited under such rules and by tonnage limitation provisions; under the existing system any shortfall was readily insurable and the lesser injustice was done by not recognizing a duty of care."

所以,有说法是船级社不要太高兴,因为The "Nicholas H"先例给予的豁免权主要是因为有上述考虑。故一旦不涉及货损货差,没有海牙规则要加以考虑,船级社的豁免权可能就没了。

4.2.3.3.2.4 喜玛拉雅条款

回到正题,Midlands Silicones v. Scruttons (1961) 2 Lloyd's Rep. 365 先例中提到船东/承运人可享有合约内的免责(像一年时效)限责。之后班轮提单也就纷纷这样去做,把装卸工包括进来的办法是去加一条称为"喜玛拉雅条款"(Himalaya Clause)的条款,有关这条款,可以节录笔者《国际商务游戏规则——英国合约法》一书之第四章5.1~5.5小段如下:

5.1 喜玛拉雅条款的作用

已经谈了不少第三者要求合约权利的情况,也添加了新一段的4.3.5小段,现在转个话题是第三者应有的责任。当然,在绪言已谈到,基本精神是不能在第三者没有同意下,强加"合约"责任到他身上。但如果这是"侵权"或"托管"(bailment)的责任,不需要合约为前提,这责任就不一样了,会是可以加在第三者身上,侵权的责任主要是疏忽,等于第三者(比如船员、装卸工)的疏忽,会带来合约一方(如是货主)基于侵权的起诉。这种情况已在1.2小段的Midland Silicones v. Scruttons 及 2.8 小段的 Adler v. Dickson 介绍过。问题是，第三者不是合约一方，如何去依赖合约内会有的保障条款（免责条款、时效、责任限制等）呢？

若任由货主以侵权成功向船员、装卸工或代理等索赔，最后仍会是船东要承担，这一来船东就失去了合约原有的保障，等于给货主从后门攻了进来。

船员与船东的密切关系自不必言，很难想象货主控告船员，船东不是在船员背后顶住的。即使是装卸工，主要在班轮运输，往往也会与船东有密切关系，或是有长期服务合约，而合约内会包括一条款去补偿装卸工在为船东服务中带来责任而要去赔钱的。

这一来，要防止从后门被攻进来，船东常在提单合约或其他合约中放进一条名叫喜玛拉雅的条款，作用是以代理或信托人身份把本是第三者的装卸工、船员等人也拖进来作为合约一方。它名喜玛拉雅条款是因为 Adler v. Dickson 的先例是发生在一艘名为"喜玛拉雅"（Himalaya）的客轮上。

5.2 喜玛拉雅条款的用字

这类型的条款，用字上不尽相同，因为有订约自由，而一个好的版本可以 The "Eurymedon"（1974）1 Lloyd's Rep. 524 的条款为例："It is hereby expressly agreed that no servant or agent of the Carrier (including every independent contractor from time to time employed by the Carrier) shall in any circumstances whatsoever be under any liability whatsoever to the Shipper, Consignee or Owner of the goods or to any holder of this Bill of Lading for any loss, damage or delay of whatsoever kind arising directly or indirectly from any act, neglect or default on his part while acting in the course of or in connection with his employment and, without prejudice to the generality of the foregoing provisions in this Clause, every exemption, limitation, condition and liberty herein contained and every right, exemption from liability, defence and immunity of whatsoever nature applicable to the Carrier or to which the Carrier is entitled hereunder shall also be available and shall extend to protect every such servant or agent of the Carrier acting as aforesaid and for the purpose of all the foregoing provisions of this Clause the Cartier is or shall be deemed to be acting <u>as agents or trustee</u> on behalf of and for the benefit of all persons who are or might be his servants or agents from time to time (including independent contractors as aforesaid) and all such persons shall to this extent be or be deemed to be <u>parties to the contract</u> in or evidenced by this Bill of Lading."

这一来，如果装卸工或船员被货主以侵权起诉，他们可以出示一份有此条款的提单，并以合约一方向法院抗辩这一索赔已过了提单内的一年时效，或可享受免责、责任限制，等等。

这种做法也不光是在航运，它可伸延到其他行业，只要是作为合约一方的雇主想去保障为他服务履约的雇员或独立承包商（independent contractor），使他们免于侵权（或托管）索赔。

喜玛拉雅条款更可伸延至说明对方万一成功控告第三者（如装卸工、船员），也要用回这笔钱去补偿船东，即还要吐出来。文字上会是如下：

"The Merchant undertakes that no claim… shall be made against any servant or agent or sub-contractor of the Carrier which imposes or attempts to impose upon any of them… any liability whatsoever in connection with the goods and, if any such claim… shall nevertheless be made, to indemnify the Carrier against all consequences thereof…"

这一来，因为法院要去禁止这种"兜圈子补偿"（circle of indemnity），因它是"无用的诉讼"（useless litigation），法院会在船东插手（intervene）并提出证明后，不允许原告的货方对装卸工或船员控告下去：The "Elbe Maru"（1978）1 Lloyd's Rep. 206。

5.3 喜玛拉雅条款的有效性

该条款已在多个国家得以，其大原则被承认有效。但有一点可以肯定，法院对它的解释都会非常严格，所以在草拟时一定要全面、清楚，比如：美国的The "Skulptor Vuchetich"（地方法院，Southern District of Texas，在 UK Club 1981 年 Legal Decisions 报道）。美国早在 Carle and Montanari Inc. v. American Export Isbrandtsen Lines Inc. and others（1968）1 Lloyd's Rep. 260 就已承认这种喜玛拉雅条款。但 Burlingham 1997 年 12 月的报道曾指出一个不知名（巡回）法庭刚有案子说这条款因违反公共政策而不能保障船舶经理人对海牙规则下的航行疏忽造成的货损免责。

在加拿大上诉庭，这条款不被接受，但不是在原则上，而是该案中装卸工犯的不是一般疏忽，而是"极度疏忽"（gross negligence），而加拿大法律是不允许去用合约豁免极度疏忽责任的：Eisen und Metall A. G. v. Ceres Stevedoring Co. Ltd.（在 UK Club 1977 年 Legal Decisions 报道）。

在英国，也已有很多案例对该条款的有效性不容置疑：比如在 The "Eurymedon"（1974）1 Lloyd's Rep. 534；The "Elbe Maru"（1978）1 Lloyd's Rep. 206；The "New York Star"（1980）2 Lloyd's Rep. 317；Raymond Burke Motors Ltd. v. The Mersey Docks and Harbour Co. (1986) 1 Lloyd's Rep. 155；等等。

若使这种条款有效，可令雇员或独立承包商成为合约一方，且必须符合 Reid 勋爵在 Midland Silicones v. Scruttons（1961）2 Lloyd's Rep. 365 所列出的

如下四点要求:

(ⅰ)提单应清楚写明装卸工等人是可以受提单条款保障。这一般不成问题。

(ⅱ)提单应清楚写明船东是以代理身份替装卸工等人订约,从而把提单免责等条款延展给他们。这一般也不成问题,只要写清楚。

(ⅲ)船东作为代理,是有装卸工等人的授权去订这提单合约的。如果发出提单时仍没有授权,例如卸港装卸工仍未确定,何来授权? 但仍可事后去追认(ratification)。有时仍会看到在不同的事实情况下会有争论,例如,装卸工是由港口当时才指定的,而在这一点上也的确常有争辩。

(ⅳ)装卸工等人要有约因给货方才会有有效合约,这一点已在 The "Eurymedon"先例被解释了。本来在订约(出提单)时,卸港装卸工是谈不上有何约因或对价给货方的。但贵族院说,提单订约时只是单方面合约(unilateral contract),它在卸港装卸工提供服务时(这是约因)变为双方(装卸工与货主)的全面合约(full contract)。

回头总结一下,Reid 勋爵的四点要求是这样说明的:

"I can see a possibility of success of the agency argument if (first) the bill of lading makes it clear that the stevedore is intended to be protected by the provisions in it which limit liability, (secondly) the bill of lading makes it clear that the carrier, in addition to contracting for these provisions on his own behalf, is also contracting as agent for the stevedore that these provisions should apply to the stevedore, (thirdly) the carrier has authority from the stevedore to do that, or perhaps later ratification by the stevedore would suffice, and (fourthly) that any difficulties about consideration moving from the stevedore were overcome."

5.4 喜玛拉雅条款用字不广泛的危险

这危险可以用两个案例说明。一是加拿大的 The "Suleyman Stalskiv" (1976) 2 Lloyd's Rep. 609。装卸工在卸清了船上的钢材后,没有依照收货方的要求存进有盖仓库,而是放在露天。这令钢材受到水湿并生锈。法院判决提单的喜玛拉雅条款只针对船东/承运人的履约责任,而钢材在船舶卸下后,船东责任已告完结,所以装卸工以后的疏忽不在提单的喜玛拉雅条款范围。

话说回来,The "Suleyman Stalskiy"案中的条款用字并不广泛,只是说:"装卸工等人 used or employed by the carrier for the proposes of or in connection with the performance of any of the carrier's obligations under this bill of lading."

比起 The "Eurymedon"(在 5.2 小段),的确是有局限。The "Eurymedon"有去说明"directly or indirectly",而且是针对"雇用期间有关的疏忽"(…neglect or default… in connection with his employment)而非只是针对"履行承运人提单责任有关的疏忽",后者在时间上受到了局限。

另一先例是上一小段所提的 Raymond Burke Motors 一案。它是在货物尚未开始装时,已被装卸工损坏,法院判不能依赖提单中的喜玛拉雅条款。

5.5 海牙·维斯比规则的情况

1968 年的海牙·维斯比规则,在 Article Ⅲ 当中其实已明确规定"雇员与代理"(servant or agent)是受到保障的,这是海牙规则所缺乏的(因此带来像 1961 年 Midland Silicones v. Scruttons 的先例)。但即使如此,提单或海运单等仍是需要有一条好的喜玛拉雅条款,因为:

(ⅰ)Article Ⅲ (2) 说明"such servant or agent not being an independent contractor"。像船员的身份会很明确,但装卸工可能是船东的直接雇员或代理,也可能是独立承包商,身份会不明确。而其他人如二程船等,更明显只是独立承包商。

(ⅱ)可能有的航次只适用 1924 年的海牙规则,而不是海牙·维斯比规则。

(ⅲ)提单内会有其他保障,是超出海牙·维斯比规则所给予的,例如货物在岸上的免责,时效等。

4.2.3.3.2.5 有条件的分托管(sub-bailment on terms)

另一种保护独立承包人的办法是称之为"有条件的分托管"的做法,就此也可节录《国际商务游戏规则——英国合约法》一书之第四章5.6~5.7小段的详论如下:

5.6 托管与分托管(bailment and sub-bailment)看来,喜玛拉雅条款的保障也不是十全十美。但今天要去保护装卸工与独立承包商的重要性已是更大,因为今天盛行的二程船运输(在 2.10 小段所提到)与多式联运已相当盛行。危险会是,货物在二程船上因碰船后沉没,货方直接以侵权(因碰船一般总有船员疏忽)控告二程船的船东。

二程船船东因为明显是独立承包商(independent contractor),所以应不受海牙·维斯比规则保障,更不用说是 1924 年的海牙规则了。

这一来,在货主以侵权之诉控告下,二程船船东会无法以著名的海牙规则的"航行疏忽"免责为抗辩。在以往的做法,为了保障二程船及所有多式联运的独立承包商,一直是靠一条详尽的喜玛拉雅条款。但已看到,这保障并非十全十美与肯定。

在 2.10 小段提到的 The "Pioneer Container" (1994) 1 Lloyd's Rep. 593，会是这方面一个非常重要的案例。

在谈论"分托管"(sub-bailment)之前，先去很简单的谈谈"托管"(bailment)。在 N. E. Palmer 教授的《Bailment》一书，他指出最重要的是对一样东西的占有，就可构成托管："The essence of bailment is possession"。现在的托管也不必另有一个合约或是物主的明确同意，而托管人的责任就是在他托管期间"合理小心"的照顾(reasonable or due care)。托管往往会是有收费的，即所谓 bailment for reward；但也会是免费的，即所谓 a gratuitous bailment。分别会是前者要有较高的"小心"(care)标准去照顾托管的东西。

托管的情况比比皆是，我可随意举一案例如 Moukataff v. B. O. A. C. (1967) 1 Lloyd's Rep. 396。其他岸上林林总总的托管，比如是东西寄放在大饭店的衣帽间，贵重东西放在银行保险箱等，都是托管。在航运，明显的例子是货物在船上，船舶对其也是"占有"，所以船东也是托管人。在货方向船东起诉货损货差时，告票中总是把侵权、合约与托管都放进去，以免遗漏。因为有可能双方并没有提单合约存在，则侵权与托管就用得上了。而托管会是要船东（托管人）证明货物虽在他手中损坏，但他已有"合理小心"照顾，这一点比以侵权控告强，因为举证不一样。

但如果双方有提单合约关系，这托管只是"Bailment upous terms"，而条件(terms)也就是提单合约的条件，包括海牙规则，所以以合约或托管来起诉船东其实是一样。

可以再举一个近期的案例：在香港终审法院(the Court of Final Appeal)审理的 Bewise v. Hoi Kong 5th Nov. 1998，涉及 4 辆名贵汽车交给货代运输，货代（以分包合约）交给一个货场(depot)去负责堆装汽车进集装箱，装妥后准备转到另一有较佳保安设施的货场，然后待运。但由于疏忽忘了做，汽车在当天晚上被窃。货方要向谁起诉或如何起诉就涉及原来与货代的运输合约了。如果是多式联运(Multimodal Transport)，对象应是货代。但货代往往会在运输合约（多式联运单证）内订有对货方不利的条款（如责任限制、短时效等），或货代只是皮包公司。但同时，该合约允许货代"分包"(sub contract)与"分托管"(sub-bail)（这一点十分重要）。这一来，货方要以侵权/托管直接起诉"独立承包人"或"分包合约方"(sub-contractor)，他将面对的困难是赖不掉分包合约方与货代（多式联运承运人）双方同意了的合约条款，这就是所谓的"有条件的分托管"(sub-bailment on terms)。

至于若是全程运输(Through Transport)，更明显是货方与"分包合约方"实际就有直接的合约关系。换言之，货代（作为代理人）所同意的"分包合约方"的合约条款,都对货方有约束。除非是根本没有授权货代去分包/分托管,则货方可不受此约束。

在 Bewise v. Hoi Kong 案例,"分包合约方"是疏忽导致汽车失窃的货场(depot)。但它的标准合约条款有一条写明:"shall not be liable for any loss or damage due to theft unless the theft was carried out by employees of the depot, its agents, servants or subcontractors."(对失窃不负责,除非进行盗窃的是货场的雇员、代理人或分包人)。

该案例没有证据证明盗窃涉及"内贼",所以香港终审法院判汽车的货方败诉。

以上香港的先例是货物尚未装船;而事实上从船上卸下来的货物交给码头装卸工托管,稍后再交付给收货人,这也是"分托管"(sub-bail)的一种。码头装卸工可以是有条件的分托管(这样做对他有利,当然还要看什么条件了),也可以是纯自愿的去接受分托管,什么条件也没有。这一来,他就有普通法的"谨慎从事"的责任了。在 The "Regenstein"(1970)2 Lloyd's Rep.1,两箱德国的闹钟从船上卸下交给悉尼港码头装卸工,让他们堆放在仓库并保管。但后来一箱被偷,而收货人只起诉码头装卸工。贵族院判被告的码头装卸工要负责全部损失,判词说道:"that the defendants were independent contractors and there was a sub-bailment to them by the shipowners; and although there was no contractual relationship between the plaintiffs and the defendants, the defendants, by voluntarily taking possession of the plaintiff's goods in the circumstances, assumed an obligation to take due care of them and were liable to the plaintiff for their failure."

4.2.3.3.2.6 英国立法的 Contracts (Rights of Third Parties) Act 1999

英国这个近期的重要立法在《国际商务游戏规则——英国合约法》(修定本)一书之 4.3 小段有详述。该立法的目的是让合约外的第三者可以自己的名义起诉,去要求合约下的权利,虽然他并非合约一方当事人。该立法中的 Section 1 (6) 说:"Where a term of a contract excludes or limits liability in relation to any matter references in this Act to the third party enforcing the term shall be construed as references to his availing himself of the exclusion or limitation."

这段措辞/文字等于第三者(包括独立承包人)可在该立法下享有合约内免责/限责的保护。这保护会比喜玛拉雅条款肯定、安全及完善得多,因为立法没有订下像针对喜玛拉雅条款那样的四点要求(先决条件),或要看条款的用字是否足够/广泛。

难怪有说法认为有了这立法的适用,提单合约再不需要喜玛拉雅条款了。

4.2.3.3.2.7 对保护独立承包人林林总总方法的总结

这方面又可以节录《国际商务游戏规则——英国合约法》一书之第四章 4.3.5.7 小段如下:

海上货物运输常会涉及"转包承包方"（subcontractors），即承运方把部分的任务交由转包承包方履行。只要有了多式联运，则会有更多的转包承包方了。例如，装卸工，码头仓库主，驳船船东，二程船船东，其他运输方式承运人，等等。

英国传统法律有关"合约相互关系"的理论，曾带来十分不公平，不稳定与复杂的后果。这就是：货方不以合约起诉承运人又或是"多式联运承运人"（Combined Transport Operator），而以侵权直接起诉出事的转包承包方。这可能会是现实需要，例如承运人倒闭。但更多机会是货方想取巧去避开运输合约一定会有的时效，最高赔偿金额及免责等条款。有许多著名先例都是这种情况，如 Midland Silicones v. Scruttons (1961) 2 Lloyd's 是承运人与所有的"转包承包方"（subcontractors）的合约都明确给予货方/提单持有人一个好处/利益（to confer a benefit）。而将来货方直接以侵权起诉转包承包方，有了这立法（指在 4.2.3.3.2.6 小段的 1999 年立法）就构成了既有侵权，也有合约的"并列责任"（concurrent liability）。加上提到的 1971 年 COGSA（即海牙·维斯比规则）的 Article 4 规定以侵权或合约起诉被告，它/他都可以享有相关的免责，这意味着货方将无法像以往那样去取巧了。

……

另外说明一下，租约提单很少去理会这些技巧，主要是因为租约业务中很少涉及独立承包人。例如，租约多数会是船东不负责货物装卸（free in and out），所以不需要分包给装卸工。租约业务不像班轮，不会预先收货和卸船后慢慢交货，也不会与岸上的仓库、驳船等发生关系。一般也不会去安排转运，签发全程提单。租约业务一般只会关心船员等雇员不受侵权攻击，而这已在海牙·维斯比规则中包括了：请看本章之 4.2.3.3.1.3 小段。

但租约业务也不见得完全不涉及独立承包人，The "Nicholas H" (1995) 2 Lloyd's Rep. 299 正是一个例子。另外的例子会是船舶管理人（ship-manager），货方对于因他/它的疏忽导致船舶不适航而出事的，以侵权向他/它起诉。所以，船舶管理人为了有保障，对于一般船东的互保协会保险，会要求加上他/它作为"共同受保人"（co-assured）之一，虽然这样做也有坏处，因为即使是他/它，也要为支付保费负责（如果船东倒闭/赖皮）。

4.2.3.4 什么期间适用

海牙/海牙·维斯比规则只适用于货物在船舶上的一段期间，即所谓的"船栏至船栏"。这在 Article 1(1) 对货物运输的定义中有说明如下："'Carriage of goods' covers the period from the time when the goods are loaded on to the time they are discharged from the ship."

而且，为了避免不够明确，规则更在 Article 7 说明船东/承运人若在货物装上船舶之前或卸下船舶之后已占有/受托管了这票货物（这典型是班轮公司的做法），这之前、之后的期间可享有完全的订约自由，不受海牙规则的强制约束。对此，Article 7 规定："Nothing herein contained shall prevent a carrier or a shipper from entering into any agreement, stipulation, condition, reservation or exemption as to the responsibility and liability of the carrier or the ship for the loss or damage to, or in connection with, the custody and care and handling of goods prior to the loading on, and subsequent to, the discharge from the ship on which the goods are carried by sea."

有了这订约自由，班轮公司也实在不客气。面对发货人，它们仍享有完全一边倒的订约自由。照理说，班轮公司可在它的提单格式中加入一条"首要条款"，令海牙规则或海牙·维斯比规则基于合约法而适用。但班轮公司不会这样"笨"，所以不少班轮提单会印上像本书第二章之 5.6.2 小段所述的一边倒地保护船东/承运人的免责条款。

在英国法律下，这种做法完全有效：Anselme Dewavrim v. Wilsons & North-Eastern (1931) 39 Lloyd's Rep. 289; K. Chellaram & Sons Ltd v. Nissho Shipping Co Ltd (1967) 2 Lloyd's Rep. 578; The "Arawa" (1980) 2 Lloyd's Rep. 135, 等等。在 K. Chellaram 先例，Buttrose 大法官说（第 586 页）："…as the discharge on to the quayside by ship's tackle is not repugnant to or inconsistent with the Hague Rules the carrier is afforded complete protection."

4.2.3.4.1　海牙规则只针对船栏至船栏期间的原因

船东/承运人抗拒船栏至船栏以外的法定责任，是可以理解的。毕竟海牙规则只是一个平衡船货双方利益的妥协。

在散装货（干的或湿的）的租船业务下船东的立场，完全站得住脚。因为货物未装上船前或卸下船后，船东很少可能有权去"控制"（control）。这一来，要船东去承担法定责任是毫无道理的，也没有一点好处。要船东对他/它控制不了、也与他/它无关的事负责的话，无非是要找"代罪羔羊"，根本无助于促使船东小心处理货物，以图减轻/避免赔偿责任的长远的大局利益。另外，若船东控制不了但仍要负责，会产生其他的许多不便及不公平，如取证困难等。

至于在班轮情况下，船东/承运人的确会在未装上船前或卸下船后（但仍未交付货物给收货人）控制、占有及托管货物。但班轮公司在这期间也不一定事事管得到，通常他也只能去依赖独立的承包人。班轮公司在装港时还好一点（但仍有像 4.2.3.3.2.5 小段所讲的 Bewise v. Hoi Kong 5. Nov. 1988 的香港先例的情况），若到了卸港就更容易失控了。毕竟，有的卸港会在法纪不明的国家！本书第二章之 5.1.8 小段对此有提及。而即使在发达国家，也会出事频频，班轮公司经常也管不到。像在 William Tetley 教授的《Marine Cargo Claims》一书中,随便就可挑出几个有此类情形的美国案例,如:

(ⅰ)货物卸下后在岸上存放时被水湿:Standard Brands Inc. v. N. Y. Kaisha, 42F. Supp43,1942 AMC 477(D. Mass. 1941)。

(ⅱ)货物卸在纽约某个码头,码头倒塌,货物全失:Stein Hall & Co. v. Sealand Dock and Terminal Co. 1956 AMC 253 at p. 942(N. Y. Supr. Ct. 1956)。

(ⅲ)货物卸在码头遭受火灾:Kinderman & Sons v. Nippon Yusen Kaisha Lines, 322F. Supp. 939 at p. 942,1971 AMC 743 at pp. 746-747(E. D. Pa. 1971)。

(ⅳ)至于货物在卸下后被盗窃或原因不明地丢失的案件,更是数不胜数。

4.2.3.4.2 英国普通法下船东对交货的责任

笔者在此不再重复本书第二章§5段已详论的"无单放货",那也涉及普通法下船东对交货的责任。在此介绍的是船东对交货的其他责任,这有二方面可谈。

4.2.3.4.2.1 不能马上卸船了事,要给收货人合理的时间提货

就这一方面,可以节录《Scrutton on Charter Parties》一书第 19 版的 Article 149 的有关内容如下:"In the absence of statutory provisions, customs of the port of discharge, or express stipulations in the charter or bill of lading, the master on the arrival of the ship at destination must allow the consignee a reasonable time to receive the goods, and cannot discharge his liability by landing them immediately on the ship's arrival."

另外也可以节录 Denman 大法官在 Gatliffe v. Bourne(1838)4 Bing. N. C. 314 所讲:"The defendants(指船东)were bound to keep the goods on board (or at the wharf at their own risk) for a reasonable time, and they continued liable until such reasonable time had elapsed."

这一普通法的要求对租船业务不构成问题,一般收货人迟来提货会产生滞期费,这对他自己不利,所以一般不会拖延,而船东/承运人对此也无所谓,反正延迟有滞期费可收。但对班轮公司而言,这要求却带来很大的不便,因为船舶为赶船期必须准时开航,而班轮一般也不会有滞期费。所以尽快把货物卸下,交由岸上保管,之后再交付给收货人是班轮公司的一般做法。在不少港口,会有立法或习惯做法给予收货人 3、5、6 天或更长时间免费在岸上仓库贮存货物,即所谓的"free time",也会规定该段时间内货物的风险与责任仍在班轮公司身上:The "Emilian Marie"(1875)44 L. J. Adm. 9。

4.2.3.4.2.2 承运人要亲自把货物交给收货人

普通法的这一要求对租船业务也不是问题,一般收货人前来卸货也是交货之时。在此之前货物一般仍在船上,因为船东/承运人要自己去找一个码头卸下并贮存几万吨小麦或化肥并非易事。但班轮业务不一样,船舶要准时开航,收货人成百

上千,各人有不同的"合理"或"不合理"时间前来提取货物,所以去"亲自交货"(personal delivery)实在不易安排。

这方面可以节录 The "Regenstein"(1970) 2 Lloyd's Rep. 1 案例报道中的第 6 页,它提到《Halsbury》一书所讲的英国法律是:"Under the general law the obligation of the ship is to deliver the cargo, the subject of the bill of lading, on the production of the bill of lading by the holder thereof and *prima facie* the contract of affreightment remains unperformed[435] until such a delivery has been effected and, accordingly, a delivery to a wharfinger is not a compliance with the obligation.[436] But it is always open for the ship, by special terms in the bill of lading, to provide that personal delivery to the holder of the bill of lading is not required[437] and that the ship's obligation to deliver the goods can be satisfied by delivery in some other specified manner."

同样说法,也在 Carver 的《Carriage by Sea》一书第 12 版的 1018 段提到,具体如下:"The undertaking of the shipowner by his contract is, that he will deliver the goods to certain indicated persons.[438] We have to consider whether he can, under any circumstances,[439] discharge that obligation in any way short of finding out those persons, and delivering the goods to them. *Prima facie*, no delivery can suffice except a personal delivery to the agreed consignee, or his agents; until that has been made the contract remains unperformed."

这样的亲自交货也不光适用在岸上仓库。如果是全程运输,要把货运分包给二程船运至目的地交货,则普通法下提单的承运人(一程船船东)应对货物在二程船的期间也负全责,直至亲自交货。在 Carver 的《Carriage by Sea》一书之 1021 段是这样说的:"Where the contract is that the shipowner will deliver to another carrier that the goods may be forwarded to a further destination, his responsibility in the matter will not generally be terminated when the goods leave the ship."

显然货物在二程船期间,一程船船东实际对货物也已失控,出了事故连举证都不易,这正是较早时在 4.2.3.4.1 小段所讲的船东的困境。

另要提到的是如果岸上仓库或某贮存地点是收货人所指定的,卸货至此应算是已亲自交货了,如果货物在该仓库出事,应与班轮公司无关。这也公平合理。有关案例可见美国 Commercial Trading v. Coordinated Caribbean 178 So. 2d 890, 1865

---

[435] 未亲自交货,则运输合约尚未完全履行。
[436] 船东把货物交托给了码头并不足够,风险/责任仍在船东。
[437] 但船东有订约自由可在提单合约内豁免其亲自交货的责任,而另外说明其他替代做法。
[438] 提单合约会明示或默示货物交付给谁。
[439] 表示船东不一定在每次不同的情况下都能做到。

AMC 2539 (Fla. Ct. of Appl. 1965)。该案例是收货人要求把货物冻肉交付一冷冻库贮存,但之后该冷冻库误交货物,法院判船东无须负责。

但现实中多数是班轮公司自己安排岸上仓库或贮存地点,或是当地港口对卸下货物有专门规定(请看本书第二章之 5.1.1.1 小段提及的案例,其中 The "Pormovskiy 3068" (1994) 2 Lloyd's Rep. 266 先例涉及俄罗斯的 Vyborg 港有惯常做法是把货物从船上卸下给港口当局的 CSP),这样就很难去怪收货人了,这时班轮公司即使对货物失控也仍要负责。

4.2.3.4.2.3 以班轮提单豁免/改变普通法下的交货责任

以上各小段所讲的种种对班轮公司不利的普通法下的亲自交货的要求,船东/承运人只能以订约自由去豁免或改变。而针对自船上卸下直至真正交货的期间,海牙规则也允许这样做。所以,Carver 的《Carriage by Sea》一书的 1020 段有如下说明:"Any personal delivery to the shipper or consignee may be excused by the special terms of the contract."

这种提单条款的措辞/文字五花八门,可以 The "Regenstein" (1970) 2 Lloyd's Rep. 1 为例,它涉及的班轮提单有第 1 与第 4 条款说:"1. The carrier shall not be liable in any capacity…for any…loss…occurring…after the goods leave ship's tackle to be discharged, transhipped or forwarded…4…. The carrier or the master is not required to give notice of discharge of the goods or the forwarding thereof. When the goods are discharged from the vessel, they shall be at their own risk and expense; such discharge shall constitute complete delivery and performance under this contract and the carrier shall be freed from any further responsibility…"

细读以上提单条款,可看到它在各方面对普通法原来加在班轮公司身上的有关交付货物的各种责任均有针对。

4.2.3.4.2.4 美国哈特法针对妥善交货

美国在哈特法下(适用于美国进出口货物)的地位与英国只适用海牙/海牙·维斯比规则的地位不一样。哈特法也有针对货物在卸港的"妥善交货"(proper delivery),而且禁止订约自由。所以像 4.2.3.4.1 小段提到的 Standard Brands Inc. v. N. Y. Kaisha,42F. Supp. 43,1942 AMC 477 (D. Mass. 1941)先例,虽然提单合约实际有明示条款豁免班轮公司对货物自船上卸下后的责任,但美国法院判该条款无效:

"…where the consignee is not present to accept immediate delivery of the goods, regardless of the form of the contract of carriage the carrier cannot exempt itself from its negligence in exposing goods to loss or damage after discharge from its ship.

Of course, where the loss would not have occurred except for the negligence of the consignee in failing to remove his goods promptly he cannot then be heard to charge the carrier for their loss."

4.2.3.4.2.5 何谓"船栏至船栏"或"吊钩至吊钩"

海牙规则下的船栏至船栏的确切分水线有时也会难以确定。例如用岸吊装货,有说法是分水线在船栏。但使用船吊呢?如果货物已被船吊钩起,但因船吊操纵不当导致货物摔落,难道摔在码头与摔在船舶甲板上会有区别吗?这分水线十分重要,因为若海牙规则适用,意味着船东责任难逃(海牙规则 Article 3(2)要求妥善/小心装卸货物),但可享有单位赔偿责任限制、一年索赔时效等。但若是海牙规则不适用,则意味着提单合约会有条款完全豁免责任(请看4.2.3.4.2.3 小段),而不这样做或因措辞/用字不善导致班轮公司有责任,则单位赔偿责任限制或一年索赔时效等也无法去享有,除非提单合约另有条款说明。

在 Pyrene Company Ltd v. Scindia Steam Navigation Company Ltd. (1954) 1 Lloyd's Rep. 321 一案,涉及船吊吊起的一架消防车掉下码头摔坏,结果带来海牙规则是否适用的争议。Delvin 大法官拒绝去想象一条虚线,画在船栏/船舷上当做分水线。他认为海牙规则要整体来解释,因为 Article 3(2)要求妥善与小心装卸,表示应包括整个装卸作业过程。此重要先例会在本书第六章之3.3.1 小段再作详论。

另有情况会是货物在驳船上待装上船时受损,例如风浪造成驳船沉没,这是否算是装货作业的一部分?《Marine Cargo Claims》一书在第530页提到两个美国案例,判决结果相异。判承运人要负责的是 The "Yoro" 197 F. 2d 241,1952 AMC 1094 (5 Cir. 1952),但判承运人不必负责的是 E. T. Barwick Mills v. Hellenic Lines,331 F. Supp. 161,1972 AMC 1802 (S. D. Ga. 1971)。

至于在卸港作业的驳船,若货物已经自船吊脱钩,堆放于驳船之后遭受损坏(如被后来的货物压坏),已有英美先例一致判决这种情况包括在海牙规则要求船东要妥善与小心地卸货作业过程中,海牙规则完全适用。在英国的 Goodwin, Ferreira & Co. v. Lamport & Holt (1929) 34 Lloyd's Rep. 192 先例,Roche 大法官说:"In my judgment, the discharge of these goods was not finished when they were put into a lighter when other goods were being discharged into the same lighter to make up the lighter load which was to start for the shore. When it is contemplated that these goods are to form the lighter load with other goods, the discharge of the goods themselves within the meaning of the Act of Parliament is, in my judgment, going on so long as other goods are being raised into the lighter and stowed into the lighter alongside or on top of them."

以上所讲,表示驳船装满了货安全离开大船后,海牙规则的卸货作业才告一段落。

至于美国的有关案例是 Hoegh v. Green Truck Sales Inc. ,298 F. 2d 240 at p. 242,

1962 AMC 431 at p. 434 (9 Cir. 1962)。

最后还要提到,在装港船栏至船栏的风险分水线也完全适用于国际货物买卖(不论是 FOB 或 CIF)中风险由卖方转移给买方的做法。一过船栏,货物运输风险开始,风险归买方,他/它应去投保(在 FOB 或 CFR 买卖下):The "Galatia" (1980) 1 Lloyd's Rep. 453。若出了意外,买方不应找卖方而应找保险人(根据保单)或/与承运人(根据提单)。买方与承运人的关系是依据海牙规则,若是承运人要负责或可免责或限责,这差别只会涉及保险人,买方/货方只要有足够的投保,并不受任何影响。而在该赔的情况下,保险人应先赔付买方,之后再代位去追索船东。整个国际外贸的运作经过这些年来的发展与健全可以说已相对天衣无缝了。

4.2.3.5 什么货物适用

海牙/海牙·维斯比规则强制适用在所有货物/商品,只除了以下三种情况:

4.2.3.5.1 非一般的外贸/商业货物

这方面在本章之 4.2.3.2.1 小段已有谈及,它是海牙规则之 Article 6,允许在不签发提单的情况下,可以不适用海牙规则,换言之可享有订约自由。但估计这种运输例如军火、救援物资等,货方强大、内行,船东不见得能像班轮公司那样一边倒地享有自说白话的订约自由。

4.2.3.5.2 动物

动物是指活生生的动物(live animal),海牙规则在 Article 1(c)讲明不包括动物在内(也表示班轮公司或租船业务下的船东/承运人可享有订约自由)。至于不包括的原因,据说是除了风险较大外,还因为动物若受伤或有潜在疾病遭至损失,往往无法保留至卸港,导致损失原因不明,承运人难以成功举证从而可享有免责。

4.2.3.5.3 甲板货

海牙规则在 Article 1(c)也讲明不包括甲板货(或称"舱面货"),只要在提单有此注明。原因也是风险太大,不适宜强制规定船东/承运人的责任。

何谓甲板货或非甲板货,应很容易区分:非甲板货就是被船体遮蔽保护在内,不是暴露在外受天气因素影响的货物。例如,装在船舱或"深水舱"(deeptank)。在此意义下,只要符合上述概念,即使货物装在不该装载货物之处,例如船上医院,也不存在甲板货的问题:Lossiebank (Massce & Co. Inc. v. Bank Line),1938 AMC 1033 (Sup. Ct. of Cal. 1938)。

4.2.3.5.3.1 不特别批注的清洁提单下的货物视为舱内货

这一点在 William Tetley 教授《Marine Cargo Claims》一书第 3 版之第 651 页至第 652 页有说明如下:"It is a basic principle that a clean bill of lading, both before and since the Hague and the Hague-Visby Rules has always meant that the cargo is to be carried below deck. In other words, where the carrier contracts to carry goods without describing the actual place of stowage, it is understood that the goods are carried under deck. This principle must be recognized in any consideration of deck cargo and the Rules."

故此,承运人签发了清洁提单却把货物装在甲板上,那就不是海牙规则 Articlel(c)所指的甲板货了,也意味着海牙规则要强制适用了。一旦强制适用,船东会有以下不妥之处:

(i)除非这种货物是习惯性的、可安全装在甲板上,否则明显会是船东/承运人违反了海牙规则的"妥善与小心堆装……货物"。另外出了事故(如水湿或掉下大海)也难以寻求适合免责的事由。

(ii)运输合约内订有的对甲板货完全免责条款(会在 4.2.3.5.3.4 小段详述)在海牙规则下因属减轻/逃避承运人的责任而变得无效。例如,若涉及租约,其内有条款说明若装甲板货船东"在任何情况下概不负责"(not in any circumstances whatsoever be responsible)。这是十分强烈、明确和广泛的措辞/文字,可对船东的疏忽也予以免责:Gillespie Bros. Ltd. v. Bowles Transport Ltd. (1973) 1 Lloyd's Rep. 10。该租约条款被合并进租约提单,提单就包括了该条款。提单若批注是甲板货,海牙规则不强制适用,有订约自由,这合并的租约条款也就有效。但若提单不批注(或是无效的批注)而货物又装在甲板上,则海牙规则仍强制适用,该合并的租约条款也就无效了。

(iii)美国法律视其为"非法绕航"的一种,借此剥夺船东/承运人在海牙规则享有的一年时效与单位赔偿责任制:The "Hong Kong Producer" (1969) 2 Lloyd's Rep. 536 等。

(iv)英国法律也会因此剥夺船东/承运人享有的单位赔偿责任限制:The "Chanda" (1989) 2 Lloyd's Rep. 494。

4.2.3.5.3.2 习惯装于甲板上的货物要否批注

在海牙规则之前,曾有说法是习惯装在甲板上的货物可不必在提单上加批注:Schooner St. Johns N. F. 263 U. S. 119 at p. 124, 1923 AMC 1131 at pp. 1132 – 1133 (1923)。但海牙规则的 Article 1(c)并没有区分有否习惯的做法(这也不容易成立),只是说凡甲板货均要在运输合约中注明:"…cargo which by the contract of carriage is stated as being carried on deck and is so carried."

对此,仍有法院不予认同或态度不明确,如美国法院在 The "Hong Kong Producer" (1969) 2 Lloyd's Rep. 536 一案,就曾追究集装箱从美国运往日本装在甲板上是否习惯做法。William Tetley 教授在《Marine Cargo Claims》一书之第 652 页指出这是错误的:"Some courts and authors erroneously take the position that the principle of custom in respect to deck cargo still exists although the Rules stipulate just the opposite…"

4.2.3.5.3.3 怎样批注才有效

批注只是针对事实,因此有什么货物部分或全部装在甲板上,只要在提单/运输合约上写明"on deck"就可以了,十分简单。

不少班轮提单经常印有一条"船东/承运人有选择权装货在甲板上"的条款,如在 Svenska Traktor Aktiebolaget v. Maritime Agencies (Southampton) Ltd. (1953) 2 Lloyd's Rep. 124 先例的条款是:"Steamer has liberty to carry goods on deck and shipowners will not be responsible for any loss, damage, or claim arising therefrom."

另在 The "Hong Kong Producer" (1969) 2 Lloyd's Rep. 536 的判例,条款是:"The shipper represents that the goods covered by this bill of lading need not be stowed under deck and it is agreed that it is proper to and they may be stowed on deck unless the shipper informs the carrier in writing before delivery of the goods to the carrier that under deck stowage is required.

With respect to goods carried on deck, all risk of loss or damage by peril inherent in or incidental to such carriage shall be borne by the shipper…"

以上这类的条款,都在相关的英美法院被判无效,因为它不足以说明货物事实上的确装在甲板上。这类条款只是说船东"有选择权"(option),但有权可以不用,而且条款是印在提单背面,总不能份份提单都属甲板货提单吧!再者,要求批注是为了让买方或提单持有人/受让人对该事实能有警觉,而在提单背后密密麻麻的条款中"偷偷"地多加一条,现实上是起不到警示作用的。

班轮为何要加印这样的一个条款呢?估计是:

(i)发货人对甲板货提单抗拒,因这会令他在信用证结汇等方面遇到麻烦。

(ii)但货物装船时可能临时决定要放在甲板上。这情况会在集装箱运输中发生;或因船舶重心,或因货物堆装,或因箱内货物是危险品等各种原因,导致班轮公司临时决定将货装放在甲板上。

(iii)也可能涉及转运后变为甲板货,如本章之 4.2.3.1.6 小段谈到的 Ryoden Machinery v. Anders Maersk (Sup. Ct. of Hong Kong 1986) (1986) 1 Lloyd's Rep. 483。

4.2.3.5.3.4 船东如何以订约自由对甲板货免责

对甲板货运输享有的订约自由,船东要好好利用了。班轮提单下班轮公司固然可以独断专行地去订约,租约(将来会合并进租约提单)下大概承租人也自知甲板货的风险大,因此一般也不太抗拒船东订下广泛的甲板货免责条款。要知道,海牙规则虽不适用,普通法仍适用,而责任的起点对船东仍是十分严格的(§2 段)。所以,船东需要免责条款的保障。

一种常见的免责条款的措辞/文字是说"甲板货属发货人(或承租人)的风险"(Deck cargo at shipper's risk)。这措辞/文字算不上太保障船东,因为没有豁免疏忽。疏忽可以是航次中应照顾好甲板货(例如不断检查/加固绑扎)但未做到,或应避开风浪/或减速而没有做等。

在 The "Fantasy" (1992) 1 Lloyd's Rep. 235,涉及一个从巴西去西非的航次,但是以期租方式向船东租人"Fantasy"轮承运。租约格式是著名的纽约土产(NYPE 格式),另有一附加条款的第 63 条说:"Deck cargo:Charterers entitled to load deck cargo provided regulation permit. Deck cargo, if any, to be checked and protected by crew up to twice a day during sea passages, if required by charterers and/or circumstances deem it appropriate. Same to be tightened up or replaced or additional lashing to be added appropriate to circumstances:such cargo to be carried at charterers' risk."

船舶自 Santos 装上多个集装箱堆放在甲板上。开航后遇上坏天气,导致集装箱移位,其中 1 个掉下大海,另外 14 个与船舶本身均有受损,迫使船舶紧急绕航去避难港的 Rio de Janeiro。

在高院,Evans 大法官认为 "at charterers' risk"(风险在承租人)并不能豁免船东与他的船员/雇员的疏忽,但可能豁免第三者的疏忽,例如是装卸工"疏忽堆装"(negligent stowage)。Evans 大法官说:"The words 'at charterers' risk' were not of themselves sufficient to confer an exemption from liability for negligence but the meaning and effect of the words depended on the context in which they were found and the words might have the effect of relieving a party from liability for the risks of damage caused by not his own or his servant's negligence but caused by third parties who carried out operations entrusted to them."

从以上判法看来,1994 年的金康租约第 1 条的措辞:"if shipment of deck cargo agreed same to be at the charterers' risk and responsibility",在船东或其雇员船员/雇员)有疏忽导致货损货差时,仍不足以保护船东。这也正常合理,想要对疏忽免责就必须明确说明,含糊其词并不足够,例如只说对"航海错误"(error of navigation)免责而不是对"航海疏忽或过错"(neglect or default... in the navigation)免责,并不足以保护船东:The "Emmanuel C" (1983) 1 Lloyd's Rep. 310。

但针对甲板货,若在提单有批注会导致海牙规则不适用,从而令海牙规则下著名的免责—管船或/与航海疏忽/过错免责的好处也失去,更不用说是照顾甲板货过程中有疏忽了。这改变了船东要享有有关免责,务必要利用订约自由去订下有关免责的条款,令自己的责任或/与好处不会劣于海牙规则的地位。

这样看来,船东以订约自由把船长/船员等疏忽豁免掉仍很有必要。其中一种有效的措辞在笔者《程租合约》一书第八章的 4.2 小段有提及,是将上段所讲的金康条款多加一句变为:"if shipment of deck cargo agreed same to be at the Charterers' risk and responsibility, Owners not responsible for loss or damages whatsoever and/or howsoever caused."

明确判定"whatsoever"一词含义极其广泛,可包括疏忽的,是在 Gillespie Bros. Ltd. v. Bowles Transport Ltd. (1973) 1 Lloyd's Rep. 10 一案,该先例在《国际商务游戏规则——英国合约法》一书第十章的 6.3.1 小段有详论,因为内容较多,不再节录。

这一点也可从近期的 The "Imvros" (1999) 1 Lloyd's Rep. 848 先例得到确认,该先例涉及的租约有一条款针对甲板货:"Charterers are permitted to load cargo on the vessel's deck…provided always that the permissible loads are not exceeded…The vessel is not to be held respensible for any loss of or damage to the cargo carded on deck whatsoever and howsoever caused."

承租人争论说船舶适航是船东最重要的责任,而货物损失是因不适航引起的(因为甲板货捆绑不足够,而仲裁员判这是不适航的一种),因此它超越了以上针对甲板货的免责条款。但 Langley 大法官不同意承租人的讲法,他说:"the submissions by the owners were correct; for cargo carried on deck the owners had no responsibility for loss or damage however caused; the exclusion covered any cause and there was no justification for excluding unseaworthiness as a cause; the bills of lading incorporated the Hague Rules and in respect of cargo carried on deck the parties were free to exclude the carriers' liability under the Rules; the words were clear and could not be qualified by in effect adding 'but not if the loss is caused by unseaworthiness of the vessel'…"

4.2.3.5.3.5 货装甲板要否取得发货人的同意

船东若在订约时(班轮运输会是在订舱位时)没有取得发货人对货物装在甲板上的同意,更或是,同意的是货要装在船舱内,则事后船东/承运人把货物装在甲板上就是严重的违约行为。这与提单是否批注甲板货无关,无论批注不批注,这都是对发货人的违约。若来得及,发货人可接受毁约而中断合约,并把船上的货物卸下。若来不及这样做,船东也会有很多麻烦。首先,船东/承运人去签发没有批注的清洁提单,光是海牙规则就强制适用了。在 4.2.3.5.3.1 小段已谈到,这是违反海牙规则的,责任难逃。而若是船东/承运人签发有批注甲板货的提单,则马上会遭到发货人的拒绝并采取索赔损失等行动,因后者会面对诸如信用证结汇等方面的困难。

就以上所讲可以举一先例说明,它是美国的 Sheerwood et al. v. The Lake Eyre et al (1970) Ex. C. R. 672。在该先例中,发货人在订约时要求并坚持要将货物(他个人的东西,估计是搬家)装在船舱内,而不能装在甲板上。船东代理没有答应,只是说会想办法。结果货物装在甲板上,也签发了甲板货提单。事后发货人暴跳如雷,要求船东/承运人马上改把货物装到船舱内或在途经加拿大 Montreal 往澳大利亚(目的地)前,把货物卸下。但最终船东没有这样做,而货物在前往澳大利亚的航次中遭受坏天气而损坏。

发货人于是向船东/承运人索赔损失,美国法院判发货人胜诉。判决认为,既然双方没有达成货是否装在甲板上的协议,双方并未谈拢船东/承运人就去履约,表示普通法的地位适用,而在普通法下,船东是应把货物堆装在船舱内的。

4.2.3.5.3.6　发货人/承租人同意或要求货装甲板但货物实不适宜的情况

发货人/承租人若同意或要求货物装在甲板上,在班轮运输,一般不会有疑问,往往是确有需要。但在散装货的租约业务下,船东/船长对此就要有所警觉。

曾有不少次是发货人/承租人(也会是 CIF/CFR 卖方)因租错船舶(如舱容太少、船舱太短,等等)而无法把预计的货量装进船舱内。或是,船舶没有租错,但因"堆装"(stowage)失误、装卸工疏忽等原因导致部分货物装不进船舱内。这一来,发货人/承租人可能会把心一横,索性同意或要求船长把余货装在甲板上。在租约下,装货通常由承租人负责,即货物装在甲板上包括加固绑扎都由承租人来安排,只要船长不加阻止即可。

这种情况不会在班轮发生,因为每位发货人的货物数量有限,配载与装货不关发货人的事。表面看来,只要是发货人/承租人自己要求货装甲板上甚至是他主动地去这样做,货物是他的,他愿意冒额外风险,又与船东何关,船东便大可不必理会。只要将来签发的提单有批注说明是甲板货以及有合并租约,而租约内又有针对甲板货的广泛免责条款可供合并即可。但仔细琢磨就会看出毛病了,因为除非货物的确可装在甲板上,也是习惯装在甲板上的,买卖合约与信用证不大可能会允许甲板货提单。这就意味着可能发货人/承租人在犯了错(如租错船舶)、闯了祸之后,为了"很短视"地作出补救,不惜采用不诚实的手段以求暂时过关,于是背着船东/船长私下签发了一套清洁提单先去结了汇。但这至少在两个方面是严重违反了买卖合约:一是货物应装在船舱内,正如《国际货物买卖》一书的第二章7.3.9 小段所述如下:

7.3.9　提单内容要求之七:货物要装在船舱内

除非买卖合约允许货物可以装在甲板上,买方可以拒绝一份显示货物装在甲板上的提单。货物装在甲板上会带来多方面的不良后果:货损货差风险大大增加,保险不赔,船东在提单下一般没有任何责任,海牙/海牙·维斯比规则也不予管制与适用,等等。

所以,Benjamin's Sale of Goods 第四版一书的 18—121 段说:"...Indeed The position seems to be that the buyer is entitled to reject goods which are carried on deck unless the contract of sale expressly permits such carriage. The 'general proposition that the deck is not the place upon which to put cargo except by some special arrangement' appears to apply as much to contracts of sale as to contracts of carriage."

另一方面是提单内容必须真实,如《国际货物买卖》一书的第二章 7.3.11 小段所述如下:7.3.11 提单内容要求之九:所有内容必须真实。

在本章 7.3.2 小段已提到普通法有这"真实"(genuine)的要求,即表示提单内容必须真实,否则构成违约/毁约,包括如:(ⅰ)没有货物存在的假提单;(ⅱ)倒签提单;(ⅲ)冒船长签字;(ⅳ)其他各方面。

现实中,买方在"交单"(tender)时往往不会知道内容不真实。但在支付货款后才发觉,买方仍应可以"事实搅错"(a mistake of fact)为据去向卖方追讨回已付的钱。这在 Benjamin's Sale of Goods 第四版一书的 19—034 段说道:"Where a bill of lading is not 'genuine', the buyer is entified to reject it. But the further question arises whether, if he pays against such a bill, the buyer has a quasi-contractual right for the recovery of that payment. In Kwei Tek Chao v. British Traders and Shippers Ltd. (1954) 2 Lloyd's Rep. 114, a buyer paid against a bill of lading which stated that goods had been shipped in October, when in fact they had been shipped on November 3 (outside the shipment period specified in the contract of sale). It was held that the buyer could not recover back the payment as having been made on a consideration which had totally failed; for the bill of lading, though not genuine, was not an utter nullity. This decision may be contrasted with that in The 'Raffaella' (1984) 1 Lloyd's Rep. 102; (1985) 2 Lloyd's Rep. 36 where a bill of lading was alleged to represent cement shipped on the 'Rafaella' in May 1979 at Constanza for Port Said. In fact the cement had been shipped elsewhere a year earlier...and was, by the time of tender, much deteriorated. Leggatt J. described the bill of lading as 'a sham piece of paper', and held that money paid against the bill could be recovered back by the buyer as having been paid under a mistake of fact..."

当然,在使用假提单的情况下,骗子卖方会早已不知所踪,这样的追讨不会有结果。但也可能是,假提单的卖方只是中间商,而且他有实力。这一来,买方在支付货款后才发觉提单有假,仍可以向卖方(中间商)追讨回已付的钱或提出索赔。这情况就曾发生在 Hindley & Co. v. East Indian Produce (1973) 2 Lloyd's Rep. 515 的先例,Kerr 大法官说:"...it was an implied term in a C&F contract that the bill of lading should not only appear to be true and accurate in the material statements which it contained, but that such statements should in fact be true and accurate, and in the present case the bill of lading which was tendered was not a proper one, and therefore the sellers were in breach on thatground also..."

所以，前面所说的卖方以不诚实的手段去补救其实是"很短视"的，因为：

（ⅰ）这货物很可能受损坏，表面看似乎风险已转给买方，而且信用证也已结汇，但其实风险仍在卖方。

（ⅱ）因为买方可以拒货并向卖方追讨回已付的钱，而卖方则难以抗辩/抗拒。

（ⅲ）这甲板货没有保险，卖方最终要自己承受损失，而这损失往往也会是全损。

（ⅳ）严重影响商誉。

但对船东/船长而言，仍要警觉的是：

发货人/承租人（也是卖方）若是皮包公司/小公司，也谈不上有商誉，它/他们会不在乎是否"短视"。本来就不能也没法把眼光放远。水平不够，犯了严重错误（也是经常犯）后，也只能以不诚实的手段去拖一天算一天了。

遇上这种卖方，买方会无法成功地向他/它追讨回已结汇支付了的货款，这导致买方会把矛头转向船东，因为提单一般都会约束船东（请参阅本书第三章之 5 小段的例外情况）。船东也难以推搪说承租人签发的清洁提单没有他/它的实质、默示或表面授权（请参阅本书第二章之 5.6.6 小段的详论）。而矛头一转向船东，第一步往往就会是对物诉讼与扣船，要求诉前担保。这种情况下船东互保协会不会代出保函。而去找承租人协助/补偿（因这是他的所作所为导致的），结果会与买方无法成功向卖方追讨一样，都是一场空。这一来，船东可就惨了。

所以，对一切不该装在甲板上的货物，明知这样会受损，例如是钢材、机器（The "Antares"（1987）1 Lloyd's Rep. 424；The "Chanda"（1989）2 Lloyd's Rep. 494 等）、棉花（Royal Exchange Shipping Co. Ltd. v. Dixon (1886) 12 App. Cas. 11）等，船长应予以警觉并应干涉这种并不妥善的堆装，同时应迫使发货人/承租人交代清楚这是在买卖合约/信用证允许的做法。发货人/承租人若是心虚，会很快被迫讲出真相。

对以上所讲，可引述 The "Nea Tyhi"（1982）1 Lloyd's Rep. 606 的先例来加以总结并让船东加强认识。该案中船舶期租给哥本哈根一间名为 Pership Aps 的公司，租约（NYPE 格式）授权承租人签发提单，有关条款是："8. …the charterers are to load, stow, …the cargo at their expense under the supervision and responsibility of the Captain, who is to sign bills of lading for cargo as presented in conformity with mate's or tally clerk's receipts. 39. The charterers hereby agree to indemnify the owners against all consequences of liabilities that may arise from the charterers or their agents…signing bills of lading…inconsistent with the mate's or tally clerk's receipts."

该船被承租人调派去马来西亚的 Port Kelang 装货前往美国的 Newport。在装港，部分三夹板（plywood）被堆装在甲板上，但承租人签发的提单却是注明货装舱内的清洁提单。航行中，三夹板受海水损坏。收货人/提单持有人因此向船东起诉，而船东去找承租人 Pership Aps 时,后者却已倒闭。

船东以承租人没有被授权去签发不符事实的提单,所以船东不应受约束为由去抗辩收货人的索赔。但 Sheen 大法官认为承租人仍有"表面授权",他说:"In my judgment the charterers' agents had ostensible authority to sign the bills of lading on behalf of the master. Accordingly that signature binds the shipowners as principals to the contract contained in or evidenced by the bills of lading. It follows that the defendants(船东) are liable in damages to the plaintiffs(收货人/买方) for breach of the contract."

这一判决完全正确,也符合近期一贯的判法,如 The "Starsin"(2000) 1 Lloyd's Rep. 85(请参看第二章之 5.6.6 小段)。

另外 Sheen 大法官也强调了维护提单信誉的重要性,即使这样会牺牲船东的利益,谁叫船东不小心乱将船出租给皮包甚至是骗子的承租人呢。Sheen 大法官说:"As to(船东代表律师) submission that one of two 'innocent' parties must stiffer, if I had to choose whether the shipowner or the endorsee of a bill of lading should be the loser I would have no hesitation in saying that there is more reason that he who contracts with the charterer and puts trust and confidence in him to the extent of authorizing the charterers agent to issue and sign bills of lading should be a loser, than a stranger."

4.2.3.5.3.7 船东如果违约装货于甲板能否享有单位赔偿责任限制

在海牙规则的 Article 4(5) 有条款允许船东/承运人即使有责任,也可享有单位赔偿责任限制。这方面已在较早的 4.2.3.2.2.5 小段略有提及,稍后还会再加详论。

今天作为英国法律的 1971 年海上运输法(1971 COGSA),已把海牙·维斯比规则立法,同时也把提单下的 100 英镑的单位赔偿责任限制大大提高了。但美国的 1936 COGSA 仍是以海牙规则为版本,单位赔偿责任限额仍定在 500 美元。

本小段题述问题的关键在于:船东即使有责任(对发货人或是收货人),不应把货物装在甲板上,他/它是否也只需赔 500 美元。显然,英美法院肯定会对此种违约下给予船东责任限制存有敌意。

在美国,这违约装货于甲板上的行为会被视为"准绕航"(quasi-deviation)从而令船东/承运人被剥夺在海牙规则下享有的所有免责/责任限制。在 The "Hong Kong Producer"(1969) 2 Lloyd's Rep. 536,上诉庭(2nd Circuit)也同样持此看法,不准船东限制责任。这方面还有许多其他先例,如:Jones v. Flying Clipper, 116F Supp. 386, 1954 AMC 259(SDNY 1953);Sealane (Searoad Shipping CO. v. E. I. Du Pont de Nemours), 361 F. 2d 833 at p. 838, 1966 AMC 1405 at p. 1412 (5 Cir. 1966);State Motors Inc. v. SS Espa, 1967 AMC 1447 (S. D. Ga. 1966),等等。

但在美国也有少数矛盾的判例,这在 William Tefley 教授的《Marine Cargo

Claims》一书第 3 版之第 657 页有提及。其中有名的是 The "Mormacvega"（1974）1 Lloyd's Rep. 296。但该先例的大前提是集装箱堆装在特别设计的船舶甲板上没有不合理之处，不构成"准绕航"，所以船东即使有责任仍可享有 1936 COGSA 的单位赔偿责任限制。该先例的概述提到："Where goods are shipped under a clean bill of lading on the deck of a container ship built for the purpose of carrying deck cargo, such shipment does not constitute an 'unreasonable deviation' from the contract of carriage and the shipowner is not prevented thereby from limiting his liability under the United States Carriage of Goods by Sea Act in the event of goods being lost."

这看来并不适用在船东根本不应该将货堆装在甲板上的违约情况。因此，船东在完全不合理的情况下，装货于甲板上在美国法律下仍会被视为"准绕航"而被剥夺单位赔偿责任限制。这也与英国近期的判例相符。

在 The "Chanda"（1989）2 Lloyd's Rep. 494，涉及一整套设备（是一个沥青厂）从德国运往沙特阿拉伯。但其中的控制室部分（内有精密电子零件，为整套设备中最昂贵的部分，占价值的 90%）被堆装在甲板上。航次途中遇上风浪，结果设备遭至全损。在责任明确的情况下，主要的争议是在于船东能否享有单位赔偿责任限制。若能享有，根据适用的德国法律（照海牙规则）船东只需赔 1250 马克，这与真正损失会有天壤之别。

要知道，英国当时已放弃了"基本违约"的说法：Photo Production Ltd. v. Securicor Transpoa Ltd.（1980）1 Lloyd's Rep. 545。但纯是去解释合约的措辞/文字与条款，仍有"相悖理论"（doctrine of repugnancy）。这一方面在笔者的《国际商务游戏规则——英国合约法》一书第十章之 5.1.1 小段有详论，因内容较长，不便在此节录。在"相悖理论"下，与合约的宗旨原意有违背的免责条款均要靠边站，否则岂非是去否定了整个合约？

正如 Roskill 大法官在 Evans v. Merzario（1976）2 Lloyd's Rep. 165 所说："…the defendants（承运人）promise that the container would not be shipped on deck would be wholly illusory.[440] This is not a case of fundamental breach.[441] It is a question of construction.[442] Interpreting the contract as I find it to have been, I feel driven to the conclusion that none of these exemption clauses can be applied,[443] because one has to treat the promise that no container would be shipped on deck as overriding any question of ex-

---

[440] 承运人对货装在船舱内的承诺会变得完全空泛（若可以违反而同时又可免责）。
[441] 这不是基本违约的说法。
[442] 纯是解释合约。
[443] 整个合约去解释，免责条款并不适用。

第五章 提单作用之二：运输合约下的货损货差责任 383

emption condition.[444] Otherwise, as I have already said, the promise would be illusory[445]."

但曾有过表面看有矛盾的 The "Antares"（1987）1 Lloyd's Rep. 424 一案例，判海牙·维斯比规则的一年时效适用，虽然也是同样的情况违约，即船东把应在船舱内的货物（机器）去装在甲板上。这表面看有矛盾，其实没有，因为海牙·维斯比规则相比海牙规则1924年已明确的肯定了一年时效在任何情况下适用。有关这一点在下一小段再详述。

在考虑了各先例后，在 The "Chanda" 一案，Hirst 大法官判是单位赔偿限责不适用，道理是 "相悖理论"。Hirst 大法官说："I am quite satisfied that neither the Dixon[446] nor the Evans[447] case rested on the discredited fundamental breach rule,[448] but rather on a principle of construction,[449] which in my judgment is to be derived from both these two cases, that clauses which are clearly intended to protect the shipowner provided he honours his contractual obligation to stow goods under deck do not apply if he is in breach of that obligation…[450]

I am satisfied that the package limitation clause falls fairly and squarely within this category,[451] since it can hardly have been intended to protect the shipowner who, as a result of the breach, exposed the cargo in question to such palpable risk of damage.[452] Otherwise the main purpose of the shipowners obligation to stow below deck would be seriously undermined…[453]

In my judgment there is nothing in the Antares case which conflicts with this view.[454] The exception at issue them…was also not of a nature which in any way under-

---

[444] 集装箱（货物）不装在甲板上的承诺是合约主旨，超越免责条款。
[445] 否则这承诺变成是空气了，是空话一句。
[446] 这是一个古老的先例，名为 Royal Exchange Shipping Co. Ltd. v. Dixon (1886) 12 App. Cas. 11，涉及棉花被违约堆装在甲板上受损，贵族院判船东不能去享受免责条款。
[447] 这是 Evans v. Merzafio (1976) 2 Lloyd's Rep. 165 先例，已详述过。
[448] 指基本违约的说法已过时，但以上2个先例也并非依据这说法而作出。
[449] 而纯粹是根据对合约的整体解释。
[450] 合约的免责条款只在船东遵守货物堆装在船舱内这一合约主旨时才能保障船东。
[451] 单位赔偿责任限制就是这类免责条款，即要遵守合约主旨才能去享有。不遵守合约主旨，如偷了货然后要限制赔偿责任，实在是说不通。
[452] 运输合约从未想过船东会把货物堆装在甲板上，让其面对无可避免的损坏风险。
[453] 若船东可限制责任，他以后大可乱来，如估计赔偿有限，不妨乱去收货堆装在甲板上冒一冒险。
[454] The "Antares" 虽是判一年时效有效，也并无矛盾。

mined the purpose of the shipowners obligation to stow below deck.[455]

As a result I hold that the package limitation clause, being repugnant to and inconsistent with the obligation to stow below deck, as inapplicable."

4.2.3.5.3.8　船东如果违约装货于甲板能否享有时效

上一小段提到美国视这种违约为"准绕航"（quasi-deviation）而会剥夺船东/承运人在海牙规则下享有的所有免责/限责。故针对时效，这立场也是一致，即（船东）不再享有或适用。在 Aetna Insurance v. Carl Matusek Shipping Co. 1956 AMC 400 (S. D. Fla. 1955)，原告的货方是在14个月后才起诉，虽然一年时效已过，但美国法院判不受影响。

但在英国法律下，这方面的地位有所不同。在 The "Antares" (1987) 1 Lloyd's Rep. 424 先例，涉及班轮公司把货物（机器）堆装在甲板上，导致机器严重受损。收货人（肯尼亚铁路公司）向班轮公司索赔，但其实对象弄错了，因为班轮公司只是期租了"Antares"轮，而提单内订有"光船条款"（demise clause）。换言之，正如本书第三章4.3.1小段所详论的，这提单合约的承运人实际是船东而不是承租人的班轮公司。这发展中国家可怜的收货人（与他的律师）却不太熟悉这些技巧/专业知识，到了把合约关系弄清楚再向真正船东起诉时，一年时效已过。

英国上诉院判这一年时效适用，因为1971 COGSA（海牙·维斯比规则的立法）适用，它在Article 3⑥针对一年时效的措辞/用字十分广泛，也未区分严重与不严重违约之间会有不同的对待。正如 Steyn 大法官所说："article Ⅲ, r.6 made no distinction between fundamental and non-fundamental breaches[456] of contract nor did it make any distinction between breaches which did and breaches which did not amount to deviation;[457] the board purpose underlying art. Ⅲ. r.6 was that the time limit was of general applicability which would promote certainty and predictability in judicial decisions and the one year time limit was apphcable.[458]"

就同一观点，可另再节录 Bingham 大法官在 The "Captain Gregos" (1990) 1 Lloyd's Rep. 310 所说的如下："…I would hold that' all liability whatsoever in respect of the goods' means exactly what it says. The inference that the one year time bar was intended to apply to all claims arising out of the carriage (or mis-carriage) of goods by sea under bills subject to the Hague-Visby Rules is in my judgment strengthened by the con-

---

[455]　这免责并不会导致船东乱来，因为他/它在违约时怎会知道货方会迟于1年后才起诉索赔？所以这时效条款是另一种性质的免责条款。

[456]　没有区分是否属基本违约。

[457]　没有区分是否属绕航的违约。

[458]　总之这措辞/文字显然是为了令判决肯定与可预见，因此这一年时效都应适用。

sideration that art. Ⅲ, r. 6 is, like any time bar, intended to achieve finality and, in this case, enable the shipowner to clear his books."

有关这方面,也请读者看看本书第二章的 5.6.1 小段,其中谈到无提单放货的违约在海牙·维斯比规则下也适用一年时效,道理与推理也是一样的。

看来,英美法在这点上有所不同也说得过去,因为美国的 1936 COGSA 只是对海牙规则的立法而已。若是说得过去,也意味着本章 4.2.3.2.2.2 小段谈及的"首要条款"(Clause paramount)到底是指海牙规则还是海牙·维斯比规则会是事关重大了,除非"首要条款"的版本已十分明确地讲明合并什么。

另外也请读者看看上一小段提及的 The "Chanda"(1989) 2 Lloyd's Rep. 494 先例中 Hirst 大法官的有关讲话。

4.2.3.5.3.9 集装箱装于甲板上的争议

今天的班轮运输/业务基本上是以集装箱为主。众所周知,集装箱船会把 1/3 以上的集装箱装在甲板上。这一来也带来了许多疑问,例如是风险如何?这可否算是"习惯做法"?船东/承运人应否先获得发货人同意才将集装箱装于甲板上?如果办不到又如何?提单不批注"甲板货"(一般不批注)会有何后果?海牙/海牙·维斯比规则适用否?等等。

4.2.3.5.3.9.1 风险有否增加

在 William Tetley 教授的《Marine Cargo Claims》一书第 3 版的第 653 页,明确是说"风险肯定增加",内容如下:"Certain container ships are especially equipped to carry containers both under deck and on deck. Yet containers on deck are at greater risk than those under deck or at least it would seem that those containers which are swept or slide overboard have always been those carried on deck[459]."

另外该书在同一页的注脚中提到风险增加的原因有如下:"Especially equipped or especially built containers ships do not necessarily mean safety for the deck cargo or even stability or seaworthiness of the vessel. Problems arising from containers are due to the large cubic space they occupy as compared with their weight and the weight of their contents. A conminer ship has in consequence a high centre of gravity so that it is not unusual for containers on top to slide overboard. Besides, it is the containers on deck which are usually stove in by storms or their contents are otherwise damaged or wetted. Large high automobile ships incidentally are the answer for the carriage of automobiles, because of the same problem."

以上提到船舶"重心"(centre of gravity)太高,会导致集装箱掉下大海。重心高

---

[459] 显然,能被海浪冲下大海的集装箱,只会是堆装在甲板上的。

会是因集装箱堆装得太高;而导致集装箱掉下大海,直接的原因会是遇上坏天气横摇太厉害。影响船舶横摇程度的主要因素之一是船舶的"稳性高度"(metacentric height)。一般船舶的"稳心"(metacenter)应在"重心"(centre of gravity)之上,这被称为"positive GM"(正稳性高度)。这样船舶在横摇时才能有自我纠正的力量去重新"摆正"(upright)。但如果这"positive GM"太大,即稳心与重心相隔太远,会令船舶"太硬"(too stiff),有偏摆便迫不及待去纠正、摆正,从而导致急促与剧烈的横摇,容易造成甲板上集装箱松脱加固并掉下大海。但若到了另一极端,即稳心与重心在一起或相隔太近(如果重心在稳心之上,会令船舶横摇时翻侧),又会令船舶"太软"(too tender),坏处是船舶更容易横摇倾斜,且程度上更严重,但摇摆频率会较慢。在这种情况下船若横摇超过25度,甲板部分会被海水冲到。情况总的说来也是危险的,所以"国际海事组织"(简称IMO)的"载重线公约"(Loadline Convention)对船舶有要求最低、最起码的"positive GM"。

集装箱船今天装卸极快,在港时间短,所以必须提早就计算/计划好各不同重量的集装箱的堆装。今天这些都是由岸上/集装箱码头所谓的"planner"(计划员)去做的工作,在电脑的协助下,计算可以很快。而船长预先告知他所要求的GM(稳性高度)是多少,将是重要的考虑因素。船长的要求会涉及面对的航次长短?天气如何?耗油多少(会影响重心)?个人的判断喜恶,等等。之后对装船的快速作业,船长也难以再插手。

在The"Bunga Seroja"(1994) 1 Lloyd's Rep. 455,船长要求的GM是0.8米~0.9米。但最后开航时GM却是1.31米,船舶可说是"相对硬"了(relative stiff)。在航次中船舶遇上坏天气导致货损(与船损),船东随即面对索赔,被指船舶不适航。船长被质疑的是:如果GM只是0.8米~0.9米,损失会否减少?或是,船长应否坚持船要达到他所要求的GM才开航,等等。

4.2.3.5.3.9.2 货装甲板上是否习惯做法

要构成"习惯做法"必须满足的条件,本书第二章之2.1小段已有详论,不再重复。在The "Hong Kong Producer" (1969) 2 Lloyd's Rep. 536 的美国判例,上诉庭否定了有此习惯做法,判词说:"The record in this case discloses that the carrier did not prove the existence of such a custom in the port of New York. It produced two witnesses who testified on this point. The First, one Rand who was a representative of the Grace Line, stated that his company would stow any container on deck even if the shipper desired under deck stowage. Such testimony is certainly insufficient to show a custom of the port. A party cannot claim to have proved a valid custom merely by showing that it is the habit of some carriers to stow goods on deck contrary to the wishes or knowledge of shippers. The mere habit of a carrier to stow cargoes anywhere it chooses, even if it is in breach of its contract, cannot be said to establish a custom."

但要警觉这"Hong Kong Producer"不是一艘专门建造的集装箱船,而且该案例为时较早,故有此判法并不奇怪。

而不久后在另一不同组合(除了 Hays 大法官)的美国上诉庭,看法已经不一样:The "Mormacvega" (1974) 1 Lloyd's Rep. 296。该集装箱船是正式改装的,可以在甲板上安全堆装集装箱,正如一审法院所说的:"containers on the deck of the 'Mormacvega' were not necessarily subject to greater risks than those stowed under deck; that deck stowage was required by the realities and exigencies of Mormac's cargo terminal and ship loading procedures; that the vessel was specially reconstructed to permit safe carriage of cargo on deck; and that the stowage lashing and checking of the cargo was approved shortly before departure by a surveyor from the National Cargo Bureau."

今天,载运集装箱的船舶也极少不是专门为集装箱运输建造/设计的,因此估计集装箱装于甲板已构成习惯做法。此外,提单格式内也常有一条甲板货"选择权"条款允许船东可选择装货于甲板上:见 4.2.3.5.3.3 小段。这提单格式是发货人订约时所同意的,等于集装箱堆装在甲板上有发货人的允许。唯一要注意的是,集装箱船签发的提单通常不会有甲板货的批注,这仍是清洁提单。

一个集装箱会否堆装在甲板上在一定程度上会是碰巧。例如,要看港口的次序以方便将来卸下;是否有较重的集装箱以及数量多少?有否危险性货物?有否对天气敏感应装在船舱内的货物?有提前或迟了送至码头的集装箱,等等。

4.2.3.5.3.9.3 提单不批注有何后果

上一小段已谈到集装箱堆装在甲板上,提单一般不予批注,这仍是清洁提单。时至今日,这习惯做法应已成立,所以难以指责船东/承运人违约。除非双方(发货人与承运人)曾明确同意过货装船舱内,但这情况很少。这一来,唯一的影响是这甲板上的集装箱仍适用海牙/海牙·维斯比规则,班轮公司也就不能享有订约自由,仍必须做到"克尽职责"令船舶适航,妥善小心管货与堆装货物等,即责任与一般舱内货物看齐。但如 4.2.3.5.3.1 小段所讲,可按习惯性或/与安全性这样做,不能说是违反了"妥善与小心堆装货物"。

这里规则适用的原因是,货物(集装箱)不在提单注明是甲板货,则不符合海牙规则 Article 1(c)对甲板货的定义,因此不能豁免海牙规则的强制适用。

4.2.4 举证第一步:货方证明货损货差发生在承运人在海牙规则下要负责的期间

对于货损货差的索赔诉讼,本章的 4.2.2 小段曾提到其中举证责任的先后排列顺序,也就是船、货双方各自一步步进行举证的做法。这里第一步便是货方(一般是收货人/提单合法持有人)的举证。这举证一般是出示一份清洁提单以及一份不清洁的"货物收据"(cargo receipt),前者在装港签发,作为货物装船收据;后者在卸港签发,作为货物卸船交付收据。两份一比较若有差异,就表示货物在船东/承运人手中及负责期间曾出过事,从而导致有此差异。

有说法是,这样一去证明并作出比较,表面上已显示或可推断出船东/承运人曾违约(an inference of a breach of the obligation):Pearson 勋爵在 The "Albacora" (1966) 2 Lloyd's Rep. 53 的 63 页所说。

4.2.4.1 清洁提单

有关清洁提单,本书在第六章 3.3 小段曾有详论,先不去重复。货物装完船一般都会签发清洁提单,确认货物装上船舶时表面状况良好,否则发货人(卖方)难以通过信用证结汇或向买方托收这一关。

假若货物并非表面状况良好但船东/承运人却违背事实去签发清洁提单,那么在普通法或/与海牙・维斯比规则[460]下,他/它在面对收货人(买方)时也会被禁止再去否定提单的内容,试图指证提单记载不代表事实,亦即所谓的"禁止翻供"。这方面本书第六章均有详论。

4.2.4.2 收货人及时通知货损货差的责任

在卸港,收货人如果在货物交付时发觉货损货差,他应马上给予船东/承运人通知。这要求既合理,也是常识。若在交付货物时明显可见有货损(表面状况不妥),收货人怎能违背事实(也有违自己的利益)去签发清洁收据呢?若这样做了,将来再说反话指货物交付时已有货损,索赔恐怕难于登天。没有人(法官或仲裁员)会相信收货人所讲的是一个方面,另一方面船东/承运人也会反驳说交付时货物表面状况就是良好,否则收货人怎会肯签发清洁收据呢?再者,这也是海牙/海牙・维斯比规则立法的要求。这立法要求也有其他合理考虑之处,例如,有了货损货差通知,船东/承运人才会有所警觉去调查原因及其他有关方面(例如是否在有关的适航方面尽了责任),因为之后一连串的举证责任都在他/它身上。

在海牙/海牙・维斯比规则,这通知的要求是规定在 Adicle 3(6),可节录如下:

"Unless notice of loss or damage and the general nature[461] of such loss or damage

---

[460] 海牙・维斯比规则之 Article 3(4) 最后一句说:"However, proof to the contrary shall not be admissible when the bill of lading has been transferred to a third party acting in good faith."

[461] 货损货差通知还必须包括损差的性质,例如是破包、水湿、短少多少、受污染,等等。这才能让船东/承运人真正知道发生了什么事故以便作出一连串的对应措施,如通知互保协会、调查、取证,等等。

be given in writing[462] to the carrier or his agent at the port of discharge before or at the time of the removal of the goods[463] into the custody of the person entitled to delivery thereof under the contract of carriage[464] or, if the loss or damage be not apparent, within three days,[465] such removal shall be *prima facie* evidence of the delivery by the carrier of the goods as described in the bill of lading.[466]

The notice in writing need not be given if the state of the goods has, at the time of their receipt, been the subject of joint survey or inspection.[467]

……

In the case of any actual or apprehended loss or damage the carrier and the receiver shall give all reasonable facilities to each other for inspecting and tallying the goods[468] …"

4.2.4.3 货损货差书面通知的种类与内容

已经提到这书面通知的重要性:不去通知,会被视为货物已按照提单表述完整无缺地被船东/承运人交付,构成"表面"(*prima facie*)证据。除非有很合理且很具说服力的解释与证据,要推翻这表面证据绝非易事。

没有这通知,收货人(买方)不光是面对船东/承运人时有困难,在其他方面也会有麻烦,例如向保险公司进行货损货差的索赔。在一般的保单条款,如英国的A.B.C学会货物条款之第16条(称为"被保险人的义务条款"),都明确订明"被保险人"(收货人)有责任去保留索赔权力,而在此过程中花了费用(如进行共同检验),保险人也会额外补偿。保险人之所以关心这方面(货损货差书面通知)是因为他/它将来会代位向船东/承运人索偿。若是收货人漏了给通知,进而影响损害了保险人的索偿权益,会导致保险人拒赔。固然,争辩下去会有情况是船东/承运人根本不应负责,或可限制责任,那么保险人怎样也应赔付一部分,因为漏了给书面通知导致的"损害"(prejudice)算得出来。但仍然可见,漏了书面通知会有诸多麻烦。

---

[462] 要以书面通知,普通法下,通知可以口头,也可以是书面的,只是前者证明起来较困难,不稳定,所以立法要求是书面。

[463] 通知的时间是针对收货人把货物提走之前或当时,而不是刚从船上卸下来的船栏至船栏之时(本章之4.2.3.4.1小段)。也不是提走后才通知,令船东/承运人无法或极不方便去提出异议。

[464] 收货人是指运输合约(提单)下有权提取货物的人士,而不是像码头当局等人士。

[465] 不明显的货损货差,不能马上看出来,可以3天内通知。

[466] 若以上要求做不到,收货人把货物提走就是证明这货物已按照提单的表述从船东/承运人手中交付的表面证据(不是结论性证据)。

[467] 若对货损货差有一个共同检验,则书面通知便不必要了,因这纯粹是多此一举。

[468] 双方(承运人与收货人)都应相互合作,提供给对方检查与点算货物的机会。有关的货物(如受损部分)会是在岸上或是船上。

这书面通知只是针对有了货损货差这样的事实,而不是为了去争议责任。在事实尚未清楚、调查仍未完成的情况下,去争辩责任实在也不成熟。所以,收货人不必去抗议什么,承运人也不必去抗辩什么。这些都应留待将来去谈判,若最后和解不成功,就去诉讼。

这都是合情合理的推理与思维,可同样运用在所有其他大小事情,甚至国家大事。例如,两国之间出了事故或意外,客观看真相(即使是表面真相)显然需要取证、调查等工作才能获得。如若仅根据自己一方人士在事故或意外之后所言,就马上作出定论,仍为操之过急。因为这不是较全面和确切的资料/证据的来源,也容易有偏差,例如某些人士为了避免受到惩罚而将责任推卸给对方。

一般来讲,有水平的国家(或公司,或人士)不会马上下定论,断言为谁的责任(当然会指责对方),把话说得过于绝对而不给自己留有余地。因为他知道这样说了也无法取信于有水平的公民(或/与其他人士)。然而有个别国家(或公司,或人士)会马上断言责任,把话讲死(例如讲:"百分之百是对方的责任","全是对方的错"等)。遇上思维能力不高的公民,听后即深信不疑。

显然,这种心态并不健康,也无助于找出事故或意外的真相来,只能促使两国关系恶化、互不信任、难有共同语言。

在刚节录的海牙规则 Article 3(6),有提到货损货差书面通知的三个种类,可在以下段节略加介绍。

4.2.4.3.1　书面通知种类之一:不清洁的货物收据

这书面的"不清洁货物收据"(bad cargo receipt 或 bad order receipt)没有什么形式/格式上的要求,手写打字都可以。但应是:

(ⅰ)说明货损货差的性质,应尽量写得详尽。会有情况是卡车/拖车去提取货物,司机没有能力或/与时间去作出通知。则司机应先作口头通知,其后收货人尽快以书面追加通知。

(ⅱ)通知要给船东/承运人或他/它的代理人,别给错了对象如海关,装卸工,港口当局等人士。

(ⅲ)只是在卸港才需要给这通知。若在中途港进行卸货,收货人鞭长莫及,没有这通知责任。

(ⅳ)在收货人把货物提走之前或当时要作出通知。海牙规则不基于船东/承运人的责任只是船栏至船栏而把这通知时间定在更早的货物从船舶卸下时,是因为在班轮业务中,不少港口会有特别规定或做法令到货物卸下来不是直接交付给收货人。货物或许会先卸下给海关或码头当局等(这一方面请看本书第二章5.1.11 小段所介绍的多个案例,如 The "Sormovskiy 3068"(1994) 2 Lloyd's Rep. 266),但当时收货人不一定知道,更谈不上已见到他的这票货物,又怎能凭空去作出货损货差的书面通知呢？但之后，货物一从（比如）海关交付到收货人手上，后者即有了书面通知的责任：Rechtbank van Koophandel te Antwerpen, September 4, 1979, (1980) ETL 291。

（ⅴ）至于货物从船舶卸下到海关或港口当局将其交付给收货人这一段期间内已发现货损货差，这又如何处理呢？苛求收货人在此期间作出通知仍是不现实或做不到。所以有说法是对货物从船舶卸下给海关/港口等时是"清洁"的证明仍是船东/承运人的举证责任。William Tetley 教授在其《Marine Cargo Claims》一书第 3 版之第 294 页说："In France it is generally held that in such circumstances the burden of proof is on the carrier to show the condition of the goods at discharge into the hands of the port authority."

（ⅵ）收货人也不应在提走货物后才作出书面通知。因为这会剥夺了船东/承运人检查货损货差是否属实或安排共同检验的机会。

换一个角度去分析，如果漏了给书面通知，是否有其他文件可替代，可补救？答案应是"可以"，只要其他文件能起到同样的作用，如记录了货损货差的事实，通知了船东/承运人让他/它警觉，等等。从另一角度也可说是其他文件可以推翻原来因漏了作出通知而构成的卸下货物符合提单表述的"表面"（*prima facie*）证据。故William Tetley 教授在其《Marine Cargo Claims》一书第 3 版之第 868 页，举了两个例子去说明其他文件证明是可以替代书面通知的，具体如下："when written reserves are not made upon delivery the presumption that the goods were delivered in the same good order and condition as described in the bill of lading can be overcome by a number of means. For example, reservations made by the port company when the goods were put into their warehouse immediately after discharge can be sufficient to upset the presumption of delivery in proper form.[469] similarly, a bill of lading holder may rely on reservations appearing on tally slips prepared by the stevedore or the ship's agent[470]."

当然，也不是每一种文件都可以替代书面通知，如果它无法起到同样的作用。例如，在《Marine Cargo Claims》一书之同一页（第 868 页），就举了两个例子，如下："On the other hand, not everything is equivalent to a written receipt. Thus a Lloyd's survey report made by a Lloyd's agent in favour of the underwriter of the cargo[471] was held to be

---

[469] 第一个例子是货物从船舶卸下交付给港口寄存时，港口当局的收据或记录内有货损货差的批注。

[470] 第二个例子是装卸工或船东代理编制的理货单，加有货损的批注（如多少是破包、水湿），或记录货物有短少（The "Juno" (1986) 1 Lloyd's Rep. 190）。有关理货是否可靠/准确的问题，请参阅本书第六章之 3.2.3 小段。

[471] 保险人的检验报告。即使它记录了货损货差的事实，也没有及时通知船东/承运人，让他/它警觉，作出调查、取证，等等。

of little value…Nor do receipts belatedly produced on the occasion of inland transport,[472] constitute a reservation sufficient to establish the reality and amount of an alleged shortage of goods at delivery from the ocean carrier."

4.2.4.3.2　书面通知种类之二：不明显的货损货差应在3天内通知

这类书面通知的要求，与上一类的"不清洁货物收据"大致一样；也没有什么格式或形式上的要求；内容上只要求说明货损货差的性质；通知要给船东/承运人或他/它的代理人，等等。唯一的分别是，由于货损货差不明显，所以有三天多的宽限期去作出通知。

或许有人会问：清洁提单只是针对货物的表面状况，故不明显的货损货差会与船东/承运人有关吗？这里就要看不明显的短缺实质是什么性质了。

若"不明显"的短缺实际是来自装船前已经存在的问题，如货物质量或生产技术有问题，那便与船东/承运人无关，而是买卖双方之间的事。但若"不明显"的短损"显示"是海上运输中出的问题，那就与船东/承运人有关了，反倒是不关卖方的事，因一般CIF/FOB买卖下，货物装船后风险已转让给了买方。例如，包装了的货物表面看不出，但内部已受水湿，或部分在运输中被盗。这在今天集装箱运输经常发生，但其他货物品种也常有，如石油产品卸上岸后才发觉污染短少，等等。

读者也许会问，这通知过了3天后才作出又会否有什么影响或损害呢？这一点稍后会详述。

4.2.4.3.3　书面通知种类之三：共同检验

海牙规则没有硬性规定双方（承运人与收货人）要进行一个"共同检验"（joint survey），但这不失为一个好的安排，对双方应该都有利。小心的船东/承运人在知悉有货损货差后，往往会马上安排一个检验，并邀请收货人参与并给予合作。它的好处会是：

（ⅰ）能详尽、清楚、准确、客观及专业地记录事实，这比4.2.4.3.1小段的一份货物收据强多了。

（ⅱ）可对损失程度与补救办法等作出判断。例如，货物若是机器，水湿后仍可修复，这就构成不了全损。若失去这共同检验的机会，在确定损失方面船东/承运人就会被动了，变了将来会是收货人的一面之词（当然也要有一定证据支持）。

若是一方拒绝参加这共同检验，这在将来会对他很不利，届时他将无法提出反证去质疑这份检验报告，因为他根本不在场。另外，他也失去了若参加共同检验，可以当场提出异议、多了解情况等好处。

参加共同检验并不会影响责任的确定。有时船东/承运人（或收货人）事先说

---

[472] 迟来的一份岸上运输收据。

明参加检验并不代表承认责任(without prejudice to liability)。但不去说明也无妨,正如4.2.4.3小段所说,当时去争论货损货差的责任为时尚早。

4.2.4.4 及时书面通知是否必要

及时书面通知是否必要或重要是有争议的,因为海牙/海牙·维斯比规则的措辞/文字没有对不及时通知作出任何惩罚规定。这与针对一年时效的规定大不相同,后者在措辞/文字上清楚写明时效—过船东/承运人再没有任何责任。

通知及时与否的分别只会是:有及时书面通知,就有了表面证据证明曾有货损货差发生在船东/承运人负责期间,而要推翻这表面上的"事实",会是承运人的责任,而且也不会容易。相反,没有及时通知,收货人要证明这货损货差发生在船东/承运人负责的期间,举证上就多了许多责任。而且,船东/承运人肯定会有诸多挑剔,这又会增加收货人的举证责任。例如,一个简单的货物水湿事件,如果表面看货损十分明显却不及时通知,就已经很难解释了。再者,收货人不去及时通知,即使有可以令人接受的解释,他也会要举证货物自船舶卸下至岸上存放期间,没有可能接触过任何的水源。这包括没有下雨记录,货物寄存的地点与情况(有否遮盖?如何堆放?记录如何?),水湿的是什么水等等,借此希望能说服法官/仲裁员。这一点可节录 William Tetley 教授在其《Marine Cargo Claims》一书第3版之第872页所说的如下:"It has been said that the notice is of little value or legal effect because the consignee has the burden of proof in any event. It is true that the consignee has the burden of proving that damage took place in the hands of the carrier, but if notice of loss has been given, the consignee has the advantage of having made *prima facie* proof of the condition of the goods at discharge."

4.2.4.4.1 没有及时书面通知而又成功证明货损发生在船上的先例

收货人没有在提走货物时,也没有在提货后3天内及时作出通知,他如何去举证货损货差发生在船东/承运人负责期间呢?这可以先举一个英国的先例:The "Ocean Dynamic"(1982)2 Lloyd's Rep. 88。

该先例涉及50吨的美国樱桃经海路运往英国,用作制造馅饼。货物包装是用箱子,不完全密封,每箱装有30磅的樱桃。货物装上一艘名为"Ocean Dynamic"的冷藏船,被堆装在第二货舱的底层。该船自美国开航后,先去了法国的 Le Havre 卸货,再去英国的 Harwich 卸货,其中包括把樱桃卸下。这批樱桃在1976年9月12日卸下,寄存在码头的冷藏库。几天后,部分的樱桃开始用冷藏货车运给收货人分销的买方的冷藏库,时为9月17日。9月20日,分销的买方开始生产。9月22日,在生产线上首次发现碎玻璃。这可不是小事,因为这樱桃馅饼是用来食用的。之后,发现碎玻璃愈来愈多,而且有很大片的,印有"Johnnie Walker"威士忌的招牌纸,显示碎玻璃来自碎酒瓶。这导致生产被迫停止,所有货物被销毁,生产线要重新清理后才能恢复生产。这一来，损失自然惨重。

　　船东否认这会是发生在船舶的运输过程中，指卸货时如有玻璃片应可从表面看见。而在船上时第二货舱并没有其他货物，谈不上会有威士忌酒堆装在一起。在装卸时也很难想象会有人故意将威士忌空酒瓶掉进第二货舱，蓄意捣蛋，若真如此也总该会有人看见。

　　这一来，收货人就要对整个运输储存与作业过程作出调查与举证了，看看有否任何可能在其中某个环节中发生了事故。

　　首先是在装港，船东也承认不可能在装船前已发生这种事故，只是未被发觉才签发了清洁提单。

　　而从卸下船至交到生产的工厂，有几个环节：船上卸下，寄存在码头的冷藏库（名为 Anglia Cold Store），冷藏货车运去分销买方的工厂（名为 Samor's factory）。

　　在考虑了所有的举证后，Coff 大法官认为事故"不大可能"（balance of probability）在这些环节中发生。他的分析仿如福尔摩斯（Sherlock Holmes）侦探小说般抽丝剥茧："The probability is, therefore, that the whisky bottle must have been smashed in the vicinity of a number of the cartons, and that the broken glass must have entered some of the cartons because their lids were missing. Moreover, the smashing of the bottle is likely, on the evidence, to have been the result of a considerable impact; for example, through dropping the bottle from a considerable height. Is this likely to have happened on the quay at Harwich? Plainly not. The cartons, being refrigerated cargo, were loaded without delay straight from the pallets on which they were discharged into the refrigerated lorries. It was suggested that some may have been put in warehouses nearby by the stevedores during a lunch break, but on the evidence I consider this to be unlikely. In these circumstances, it is most improbable that any whisky bottle could have been shattered in the vicinity of the cartons at that stage at all, still less without being observed.

　　Once the cartons had been loaded inside the refrigerated lorries, the door of each refrigerated container was sealed. The seal remained unbroken until the lorry was backed up to the bay at the Anglia Cold Store for discharging of its contents into the store. At the cold store there were, for obvious reasons, stringent precautions to prevent any bottles or glass coming into the cold store or its immediate vicinity. It is difficult to imagine that at the stage of discharge at the cold store, when the checker and handlers were always present, any whisky bottle could have been shattered in the vicinity of the cartons. It is inconceivable that this could have happened inside the cold store, particularly bearing in mind the manner in which the cartons were stacked. The same comments, of course, apply at the stage of discharge from the cold store and of carriage in sealed refrigerated containers to Samor's factory at Didcot. Similar stringent precautions were in force at Samor's factory. Indeed, one fact alone excludes the possibility of the glass having got into the cartons at Didcot; that is, that one fragment of glass was found between two cartons on the same pallet at Didcot and must, therefore, have got into that position before the cartons arrived at Didcot."

而且，十分幸运的是调查发现了其中一块碎片附有 Johnnie Walker 威士忌的招牌纸，这提供了重要线索，经追查，这是来自一批 1974 年卖给汉堡船舶供应商的威士忌。换言之，酒瓶来自船上。此外，收货人也派人去过"Ocean Dynamic"轮的姊妹船观察它的卸货情况，发觉装卸工在船上喝酒，边喝边干活，对此也有证人出庭作证。

这一切综合起来，Goff 大法官判"重大可能"（balance of probability，民事诉讼的举证准则，也称为"盖然性的权衡"）的事实是船员向装卸工提供/出售廉价的免税威士忌，装卸工在卸货时喝酒（因为带不走），之后把空酒瓶到处乱丢而导致此次事故。

结果船东要负责，因为收货人举证证明了（只是根据可能性而已）货物自船舶卸下时已发生货损。显然，在这一事实认定下，船东是违反了海牙规则，如没有妥善与小心卸货，为此船东也没有免责可以去依赖。

4.2.4.4.2 集装箱的情况

"门至门"的集装箱运输下经常是运到收货人的仓库、工厂或地点再打开，这时才会发觉有否货损货差。这一来，在码头"提走"（removal）货物时或提货后 3 天内作出书面通知，在现实中都是无法做到的。通常，收货人凭推理及其他客观环境或/与科学方法去证明货物损坏发生在船东/承运人的承运中，从而说明货物交付时并非状况良好。显然，这也包括了货方在拆箱时，发觉货物有损坏短缺，马上通知承运人。若可以的话，由双方共同对货物进行检查。如果不是收货人拆箱，比方是货代或多式联运人的"groupage operator"拆箱，再把集装箱内多批货物分别交给不同的收货人，则拆箱的货代等人在发觉货损短缺后应马上通知收货人，以免将来怪在它/他头上。在拆箱时如有海关人员在场，应作批注说明货物的表面状况，省得说不清。例如，是海水导致损坏：The "Fedtrade"，1983 AMC 774（S. D. Tex. 1981）。

像 The "Alex"（1974）1 Lloyd's Rep. 106 的加拿大先例，涉及集装箱顶部有一小洞，导致雨水渗入。承运人的其中一项抗辩是收货人没有及时作出通知，这一来，又要涉及诸如水分的来源，所含盐分，当时的下雨量等的证明，之后法官才判是雨水渗入大部分是发生在承运人看管期间。

在另一荷兰的案例（The "Isnis" s'Gravenhage, 4 October 1988, S & S, 1989, no. 77; aff'd by H. R., 5 October 1990, S & S, 1991, no. 98），涉及 55500 Litres 的 Port

酒从葡萄牙运去荷兰。货物装在 3 个集装箱(运载液体货物的"Liquitainer"),后来在装货作业中发觉其中一个集装箱的 Port 酒受到一种化学品的污染。该化学品可加进 port 酒作为"加强口味"(taste enhancer)之用。故此,承运人极力争议这污染发生在岸上交货给他之前。但法院衡量后仍认为如果污染发生在岸上(如岸上存放的"storage tank"),则所有 3 个集装箱的 Port 酒都会受污染,而不应仅 1 个。故更大的可能仍是该一个集装箱本身不清洁、不适货。

其他案子也应是同样道理,根据已证明的事实推断出货物损坏发生在船东/承运人的承运期间的判决,可简要举例如下:

(ⅰ)金属货物刚产生的氧化(生锈)应在航次中发生:M. Paquet & Co. v. Dart Cantainerline,1973 AMC 926(N. Y. Civ Ct. 1973)。

(ⅱ)集装箱顶部有洞导致雨水渗入,而承运人签发的提单没有对此作出批注:比利时判例的 The "Transontario", Antwerp, 15 June 1977, J. P. A. 1977—1978, 40, aff'g Comm. Antwerp, 19 March 1976, J. P. A. 1975—1976, 187。

(ⅲ)酒被"冻坏"(frost damage)不可能发生在意大利装货/交货前,Insurance Company of North America v. Italica, 567 F. Supp 59, 1984 AMC 136 (S. D. N. Y. 1983)。

(ⅳ)检验报告受潮损坏是由于通风不足够导致出汗与冷凝:All American Trading Corp. v. New York Maru, 1988 AMC 2208 (SDNY. 1987)。

(ⅴ)有关环境的证据证明水湿很大可能不会在装港发生已足以推断其更有可能在承运人负责期间发生:Arkwright Mutual Insurance Co. v. Oriental Fortune, 745 F. Supp. 920, 1991 AMC (2237) 2240 – 2241, ref. Cited (SDNY 1990)。

当然,要这样去证明货损货差发生在船东/承运人承运期间总归会不容易也不肯定,无法与 4.2.4.3.1 小段所提的做法相比,即在货物从船上卸下时已可作出一份不清洁的货物收据,并同时对尚在码头(或船上)的受损货物安排一个共同检验,从而能清清楚楚说明损坏发生在船上的事实。但在集装箱业务下,这也是别无他法。这样证明的不容易不肯定可以举一例来说明。在美国上诉庭的 The "Zim America" (1994) LMLN # 390,涉及集装箱内的名牌 Bally 皮具从意大利运往纽约。在纽约,船舶挂靠承运人 Zim 自己的码头,并由 Zim 自己雇用的装卸工把集装箱从船上卸下。当天下午,Bally(收货人)安排了货车/拖车(属 Maypo Trucking Corp 公司)来提走货物,但载了货的货车/拖车当晚先停在"港口保护区"(Port Security),到第二天才开走,而到了 Bally 的仓库,却发觉集装箱内的部分皮具被偷。

上诉庭判 Bally 无法证明货物是在船上,而不是在 Maypo 手中,把集装箱放置在港口保护区的那天晚上被偷。Bally 提出了有关该保护区保安设施的证明,但上诉庭认为并不足够,判词说道:"Accordingly, there was insufficient evidence to support a finding that the 65 cartons of leather goods were missing at outturn. Even if there was any doubt on that point, there certainly was insufficient evidence to overcome the presumption of good delivery created by section 3(6) of COGSA. Accordingly, Bally had failed to prove… its *prima facie* case under COGSA."

4.2.5 举证第二步:船东/承运人证明造成货损货差的原因

本章之4.2.2小段提到这是第二步的举证责任,且举证责任是从货方转移到了船东/承运人身上。要知道,若不立法规定,在订约自由的大前提下,船东/承运人可以提单条款把这方面的举证责任加在收货人身上。这显然会带来很大的不公平,也不符合实际,因为相关的证据常会是船东/承运人才拥有或能去取证。例如,向船长/船员取证(口头证据),查看航海日志,等等。

4.2.5.1 船东/承运人有举证责任才公道和符合实际

的确,若举证责任是在货方身上而他/它对海上运输中发生了什么事情又一无所知,事后调查也不会容易(比如试想一下,船长/船员会否对货方坦白? 或自动交出航海日志)。这只会令事故的真相无法大白。

这纯粹是常识与简单推理,也有不少权威的说法予以支持。例如美国最高院曾在 Commercial Molasses Corp. v. New York Tank Barge Corp. 314 U.S. 104 (1941), 1941 AMC 1697 先例说:"… the law takes into account the relative opportunity of the parties to know the fact in issue[473]…Since the bailee in general is in a better position than the bailor to know the cause of the loss[474] and to show that it was one not involving the bailee's liability,[475] the law lays on him the duty to come forward with the information available to him[476]…If the bailee fails it leaves the trier of fact free to draw an inference unfavourable to him[477] upon the bailor's establishing the unexplained failure to deliver the goods safely… whether we label this permissible inference with the equivocal term

---

[473] 法律(也是合理客观的地位)应考虑到双方对事件/事实了解的相对机会/能力。
[474] 总地说,受损货物出事时是在托管人手中,作为托管人的船东/承运人总应比寄托人的货方了解更多的事实。
[475] 托管人也能去证实不是他的责任造成货损货差(如果属实)。
[476] 所以,法律要求托管人前来提供资料,说明事实真相。
[477] 若托管人做不到这一点,对事实作出判断的法官(或仲裁员)就会自由地作出对其不利的推断。一个常会有的不利推断是:船东/承运人是否因有关资料/证据对其不利,故此有所隐瞒,这毕竟是人性自私的一面? 另一不利的推断是:船东/承运人对这么明显,严重的事故竟然说一无所知,即使是真话,也显示了他/它的管理水平极差。

'presumption'[478] or consider merely that it is a rational inference[479] from the facts proven, it does no more than require the bailee, if he would avoid the inference,[480] to go forward with evidence sufficient to persuade that the non-existence of the fact, which would otherwise be inferred, is as probable as its existence[481]…"

4.2.5.2　租约下对举证责任有订约自由

租约虽不适用海牙规则，但在没有明示条款的情况下，普通法仍是默示（接受托运的）船东/承运人有这方面的举证责任。

美国的 Glenn Bauer 律师在"Responsibilities of owners and charterer to Third Parties-consequences under Time and Voyage Charters" 49 Tul. L. Rev. 995,1009(1975) 曾写道："As a general rule, as between a time charterer and a vessel owner, the responsibility for cargo loss falls on the one who agreed to perform the duty involved."

但在较早的 4.2.5 小段已提到，合约方可以订约自由把有关的举证责任改变。但现实中在租约很少见到这种做法，或许是，承租人都懂业务，谈判力又强，不会轻易接受船东/承运人去改变他/它应尽的举证责任。

4.2.5.3　货损货差原因不明的情况

在海牙规则适用的情况下，船东/承运人一开始要证明/说明货损货差的原因也确实有必要，否则他/它下几步的举证都走不下去了，即去证明已"克尽职责"令船舶适航（适航是指与相关货损货差有因果关系的方面），接着再要证明是某免责事项导致该货损货差的。若不先去说明货损货差的原因，上述的举证根本无从说起。

4.2.5.3.1　无法说明/证明原因船东就要负责

现实中，确会有货损货差其原因是无法知悉的。这一来，船东/承运人仍要承担责任，理由是他/它"未尽举证责任"（failed to discharge the burden of proof）。这方面可举 The "Destro" (1927) 29 Lloyd's Rep. 133 先例中，Mackinnon 大法官在第 136 页的讲话如下："That being so, under Art. IV, r. 2(q) the burden is on the defendants to show that these goods were lost and taken out of the case without（船东）any fault or privity on the part of the carrier or neglect by his servants or agents. Have they discharged that burden? If I accept all their evidence, in a sense they have. But in another sense they have not, because that which they seek to prove is wholly irreconcilable with the evi-

---

[478]　法律允许这样的推断。
[479]　或只是合情合理的推断。
[480]　若作为托管人的船东/承运人想避免这不利的推断，就必须去提供资料/证明。
[481]　这要求只是为了确定"可能性"的程度（balance of probability），例如损失可能被推断是托管人疏忽造成，则托管人须提供资料/证据说明损失非其疏忽造成同样有可能，而且更有可能。

dence for the plaintiffs. There is in truth a mystery about the loss. If I accept the evidence given for the defendants the loss of the goods is quite inexplicable. In those circumstances one side or the other must win. I cannot give victory to both. I think the only logical result is that defeat must be on the side on which rests by this statue the burden of explaining that which would be otherwise inexplicable. Having regard to the wholly inexplicable conflict of evidence on both sides I think I must hold that the defendants have not discharged the burden which is put upon them by Art. IV, Rule 2(q) of the Act."

这方面近期的一些案例也不少，随便挑一个，可以举在 4.2.4.3.1 小段详述的 The "Ocean Dynamic"(1982) 2 Lloyd's Rep. 88 先例，法官在事实的判断上认为碎玻璃自船舶卸下前已经存在，已发生货损事故（虽只是"可能性"较大的判断而已）。之后举证责任便到了船东身上。船东若同意或再证明确是 Goff 大法官的估计（即装卸工在卸货时边喝船员出售的威士忌酒边干活），并无好处，在海牙规则下要承担责任。因为这样船东除没有免责可适用外，还违反了妥善与小心卸货的义务。但不去同意这估计/判断，船东确实又调查不出什么原因。而说不出及无法证明货损的原因，船东仍要负责，正如 Goff 大法官说："…on the balance of probabilities, the glass did indeed get into the cartoons while on board the ship. It follows that I decide this issue in favour of the plaintiffs（收货人）Furthermore, it must follow that the defendants（船东）are in these circumstances unable to involve the exceptions in s.4(2)(q) of the United States Act（美国的 1936 COGSA）; because since they cannot show, on the balance of probabilities, how the whisky bottle came to be broken, they cannot discharge the burden of proof which rests on them to show that neither the actual fault or privity of the carrier, nor the fault or neglect of the agents or servants of the carrier, contributed to the loss or damage…"

以上两个判决笔者认为十分合理公平。正如 Mackinnon 大法官所说，民事诉讼总要有一方败诉而另一方胜诉，不可能"双方都胜诉"（I cannot give victory to both）。所以，若船东/承运人无法说明与证明货损货差的原因反而可以胜诉，岂非会是：

（i）败诉方变了是原告的收货人/提单持有人？

（ii）无法说明/证明原因反而可免责，可胜诉，船东/承运人以后还会去说明与证明原因吗？肯定不会，特别是明知货损货差原因披露出来反而自己要负责的情况。

（iii）这岂不是不鼓励判明真相，无法令该负责的一方负责，长远上也不利于迫使负责一方不断改善以减少货损货差的良性循环。

4.2.5.3.2　船舶保险方面同样如此判决的著名先例 The "Popi M"

船舶保险虽与海牙规则下的货损货差是两码事，但也有雷同之处。这就是船东作为被保险人有责任举证说明与证明损失是列名的承保风险所引起的。

在 The "Popi M"(1985) 2 Lloyd's Rep. 1 先例,涉及船舶在风平浪静的情况下沉没。什么原因造成只有天知道,而由于沉没地点太深,根本无法派人潜水下去弄清真相。

一般在这种情况下沉没,总会带来对船东不利的猜疑。简单的就是怀疑船舶(特别是老船,像"Popi M"已二十多年)沉没是由于"正常磨损"(fair wear and tear)造成,不属承保风险。严重的(例如被保险人是名誉不好的船东)更会怀疑是船东故意凿沉去骗取保险费。在高院对 The "Popi M" 的一审中,Bingham 大法官不接受保险人以专家意见说是由于正常磨损造成事故,因船东的专家更有说服力,他以沉船的经过说明沉没不大可能是因正常磨损造成。由于船员全获救,特别是最早的目击证人(三管轮)看见机舱船底破裂而海水大量涌入,船东的专家可了解沉没的经过。

船东也就船底破裂提出了几种可能。一是碰上海底礁石。二是碰上海上浮动物(如大木)。三是被一艘不明潜水艇碰上。但 Bingham 大法官不接受会存在第一种"可能",因为出事地点水很深,是惯常航道,不可能有未知的海底礁石。第二种"可能"也不会存在,因为以"Popi M"轮当时 11/12 节的船速,船首的浪应会把所有海上浮动物推开,不可能碰上机舱船底。这剩下了第三种可能,就是与不明潜水艇碰上。当然,要是说与其他船舶碰上,不可能没有人看见相碰船的船名或是什么类型的船舶。且其他船舶也会有损坏,不会事后不知所踪。再说,这样又怎会碰上"Popi M"的机舱船底?只有是碰上某国潜水艇才会这样,而且后来查不出,因为涉及高度军事机密。

Bingham 大法官认为这第三种可能有点天方夜谭,但在"无可选择"之下,也只好选了它去作为"Popi M"轮沉没的原因。Bingham 大法官还提到了大侦探福尔摩斯的名言,就是在筛选出的几个"可能"的原因中一个一个去抽丝剥茧,在逐个排除了"不可能"(impossible)的原因后,剩下的看起来"不大可能"(improbable)的原因也就是真正的原因(该名言的英文是"when you have eliminated the impossible, whatever remains, however improbable, must be the truth")。

但案件到了贵族院,Bingham 大法官的判决被推翻,其考虑问题的方法也被质疑,Brandon 勋爵指出了以下几点:

(i)这是最重要一点,即法官不必非要去"硬找"一个原因。法官(或仲裁员)总是倾向于要说出一个原因或一个可能的事实,好像这样才算尽了责去判决/裁决。法官(或仲裁员)往往都不想去推说原因不明,因为应举证的一方没能举证,这有卸责的味道。但在证据实在不完整,疑点太多时,这恰恰是法官(或仲裁员)应有的思维方法。即船东有法律加于其身上的举证责任,他/它所说明/证明的东西疑点太多,说不清原因,也就是举证失败了。船舶保险是如此,海牙规则下的货损货差也应是如此。在这一点上,Brandon 勋爵是说:"…I have already sought to emphasize as being if great importance, namely, that the Judge is not bound always to make a finding one way or the other with regard to facts averred by the parties. He has open to him the third alternative of saying that the party on whom the burden of proof lies in relation to any averment made by him has failed to discharge that burden. No Judge likes to decide cases on burden of proof if he can legitimately avoid having to do so. There are cases, however, in which, owing to the unsatisfactory state of the evidence or otherwise, deciding on the burden of proof is the only just course for him to take."

(ⅱ)大侦探福尔摩斯的名言,只能适用在所有相关事实都知道,之后才去抽线剥茧排除"不可能"而剩下唯一的"不大可能"。但在"Popi M",未知的事实太多(如船沉之处太深无法探摸,出事地点有否活跃的潜艇在活动等),因此这名言用不上。

(ⅲ)任何根据"可能性"(balance of probability)去推断事实的做法,总离不开要合情合理,要符合所谓的"一般常识"(common sense)。法官(或仲裁员)应想到这事实发生会比不发生的可能性为高。否则什么天方夜谭的说法与臆测都会有人提出来了,如"Popi M"轮沉没是因为火星人入侵地球,或是这世上有鬼,等等。

归结一下,Brandon 勋爵判是:"In my opinion Mr. Justice Bingham adopted an erroneous approach to this case by regarding himself as compelled to choose between two theories, both of which he regarded as extremely improbable, or one of which he regarded as virtually impossible. He should have borne in mind, and considered carefully in his judgment, the third alternative which was open to him, namely, that the evidence left him in doubt as to the cause of the aperture in the ship's hull, and that, in these circumstances, the shipowners had failed to discharge the burden of proof which was on them."

以上思维方式,在海牙规则下的货损货差举证责任方面完全适用。

4.2.5.3.3 原因不明会对船东作不利的推断

这一点已在本章之 4.2.5.1 小段谈到,即法官(或仲裁员)可合法地作出对船东"不利的推断"(adverse inference),注脚还列举了二个不利推断的例子。涉及海牙规则下的货损货差,更曾有著名判例指出针对某些情况应作出船舶不适航的不利判断。在 Ralston Purina Co. v. U.S.A. 1952 AMC 1496 at pp. 1498—1499 (E.D. La 1952),判词说道:"When the cause of damage by seawater to an ocean shipment is unexplained, the rule has always been that the damage must be presumed to have been caused by unseaworthiness of the vessel on account of failure of the carrier to exercise due diligence to make the vessel seaworthy."

另有美国先例曾判正常天气下(不是在10级台风中心),出事船在一般船舶应能承受的海况下却沉没,而且原因不明(好像 The "Popi M" (1985) 2 Lloyd's Rep. 1),应可以推断船东没有"克尽职责"去令船舶适航。但要注意的是,这说法不一定能套用在船舶保险的 The "Popi M"案,因船舶保险的适航责任并非要"克尽职责"那样的严格。该美国的先例是 The "Southern Sword", 190 F. 2d 394 at p. 397, 1951 AMC 1518 at p. 1521 (3 Cir. 1951),判词是说:"…the logical inference of unseaworthiness which follows from the unexplained sinking of a vessel in weather she should be able to withstand suffices to discharge that burden unless and until the carrier shall affirmatively show exculpatory circumstances."

在英国也有相同的判例:The "Torenia" (1983) 2 Lloyd's Rep. 210。

4.2.5.4　船东/承运人举证责任所要达到的程度

法律并不要求举证要证明"绝对"(absolute)是什么原因造成货损货差,这也不是民事诉讼所要求的举证责任的程度。举证在程度上只要求这说明/证明的"事实"(肇事原因)发生的可能性比没有发生的可能性稍高(有另一叫法是"盖然性的权衡")。这一点 Brandon 勋爵在 The "Popi M" (1985) 2 Lloyd's Rep. 1 也略有谈及。

另外也不必去详尽说明/证明每一细节,仿如船东/承运人自己有参与,在现场一样。在 The "City of Baroda" (1926) 25 Lloyd's Rep. 437,涉及货物被窃。既然货物是被偷偷地盗窃,船东/承运人不可能说明太多细节,他只能举证船上做了什么以防盗窃,晚上有人看管,有何制度保证看管好,等等。Roche 大法官同意这是举证所要达到的程度,而海牙规则下的举证与岸上其他托管的举证是一样的,他说:"…speaking for myself, I do not adopt the view that that involves in a matter of this sort the proof of the whole of the circumstances that may attend or explain a very obscure cause, or involves the obligation of explaining such a matter to show how and why that care was used with regard to them. The law I take to be that which is laid down with regard to a bailee in general…

In many cases it would be sufficient I think to prove general care that was exercised with regard to the management of a ship and cargo, but in this case(盗窃)it has become, on my view of the facts, material for the defendants(船东)also to say that, besides general care in arranging for watching, the watching was vigilantly and properly carried out."

这种因盗窃引致货差的情况并不少,而海牙规则的 Article 4(2)(q)对此是规定船东/船员/雇员没有任何疏忽与过错则可以免责。所以遇到这种情况很多时候船东/承运人只能举证没有疏忽与过错,这也可被接纳,正如 The "Clan Macdougall" (1943) 76 Lloyd's Rep. 58 先例(涉及冷藏兔肉卸货时发觉部分解冻受损)的判词说道:"It is not necessary for the defendants(船东)to establish exactly why and how the damage occurred, provided they can disprove negligence; but of course it is not easy to do that unless they can establish some reasonably possible alternative explanation. If the damage is entirely unexplained, it is difficult to see how the onus can be discharged."

4.2.5.5 货损货差原因多于一个的情况

船东/承运人说明/证明的货损货差原因如果多于一个(这情况也不少),则若是两个或更多的原因都可以免责,也不存在不适航,那船东/承运人固然可以安枕无忧。但若是一个免责而另一个要负责,则船东/承运人还须去举证如何区分。即哪部分货损货差属免责,要是分不开,则船东/承运人要全部负责。例如,海难(免责)造成部分货损,但涌入的海水却因船舱"舱壁"(bulkhead)腐蚀穿洞(不能免责的不适航)渗进隔舱从而扩大了货损。总之货损如能明确区分出来,则船东/承运人仍可对免责部分免责,否则要全部负责,正如 Hobhouse 大法官在 The "Torenia" (1983) 2 Lloyd's Rep. 210 之第 218 页说道:"Where the facts disclose that the loss was caused by the concurrent causative effects of an excepted and a non-excepted peril, the carrier remains liable. He only escapes liability to the extent that he can prove that the loss or damage was caused by the excepted peril alone."

针对这一点实在有不少先例同样判过,这也不单单局限在货损货差索赔的争议。例如,保险如果涉及一个是承保风险但另一个不是,而两个风险同时导致损失,且损失也分不开,则保险人可以不赔。在涉及船舶保险的 Leyland Shipping Co. v. Norwich Union Fire Insurance Co. (1918) AC 350,Wright 大法官说:"…where there are two perils both of which are proximate causes of the loss and are in an open policy the shipowner could have recovered on either, then, if one of those perils is excepted by the warranty the underwriters are not liable."

另 Denning 勋爵在 Wayne Tank & Pump v. Employers' Liability (1973) 2 Lloyd's Rep. 237 也有以下讲话:"…and that there was not one dominant cause, but two causes which were equal or nearly equal in their efficiency in bringing about the damage. One of them is within the general words and would render the insurers liable. The other is within the exception and would exempt them from liability. In such a case it would seem that the insurers can rely on the exception clause."

4.2.5.6 原因是否造成货损货差的近因、主因

有关"近因"(proximate cause)或/与"主因"(dominant cause)这一重要课题,笔者的《国际商务游戏规则——英国合约法》一书第十四章§10 段的"因果关系"有详论,内容太多,无法节录。在此只简单提一下,如果造成货损货差看似有多个原因,但仔细分析一下,这些原因会部分实属关系不大,影响微不足道,但另有一二个原因却重要得多,与货损货差的发生在时间上也接近得多。虽然单是时间上接近并不代表太多,但若同时也是重要原因,则表示即使更早时另有重要原因,其"因果

链"(chain of causation)也可能被该较近发生的重要原因所打断。这一来,看货损货差的原因是否属海牙规则下的免责事项就要看它是否是"近因","主因"。这方面典型的先例是加拿大的 Eisenerz GmbH v. Federal Commerce & Navigation Co. Ltd. (1974) SCR 1225,它涉及船舶搁浅受损后去干坞修理,为了修船底,要把货物从船上卸下待船修复后重装,在此过程中船东疏忽导致货损货差。加拿大最高法院判造成货损货差的原因(近因/主因)不是搁浅(这是海牙规则的免责事项)而是船东疏忽照看货物(违反海牙规则的 Article 3(2)条款),因此船东/承运人要负责。

同样案情也发生在著名的英国先例 Gosse, Millerd v. Canadian Government Merchant Marine (1928)32 Lloyd's Rep. 91,它涉及"锡块"(tin plate)的货物遭受淡水损坏。原因是航次中船舶曾因碰撞码头(这可以免责)而要去修理,但修理中没有好好盖严船舱货物,导致货物遭受雨水损坏。法院判货损的主因/近因是船东/承运人违反了海牙规则,没有小心照看货物。而较早时船舶碰撞码头受损导致修理,只能是"远因"。除非是碰码头的一刹那造成部分货物当即受损,那这部分货损的近因/主因才算是船碰码头,船东/承运人对此可以免责。

4.2.6 举证第三步:船东/承运人证明船舶适航

在本章之4.2.2小段,提到了这是第三步的举证责任,这举证责任仍是在船东/承运人身上。海牙/海牙·维斯比规则之 Article 3(1)规定:"承运人在航次开始前和开始当时应克尽职责,使船舶处于适航状态(exercise due diligence to make the ship seaworthy);适当地配备船员,装备船舶和配备供应品,使货舱、冷藏舱、冷气舱和该船其他载货处所能适宜和安全地接受,运送和保管货物。"

这著名的条款有好几方面需要详论,例如:
(ⅰ)适航举证责任谁属与举证要达到的程度?
(ⅱ)适航是否与货损货差有关?
(ⅲ)是否先决条件,不违反才能去享有免责?
(ⅳ)何谓"克尽职责"?
(ⅴ)什么时候必须尽此责?
(ⅵ)何谓适航?
(ⅶ)其他

以上各重要方面/课题将在接下来的段节详论。

4.2.6.1 适航举证责任在船东/承运人

4.2.6.1.1 原因何在

这一点在较早段节已明确:举证责任是在船东/承运人身上。这在 William Tetley 教授的《Marine Cargo Claims》一书有多处提到,例如在第372页。这举证是要针对所有方面,例如有否与货损货差相关的不适航?如果有,船东/承运人是否已"克尽职责",等等。这举证责任在船东/承运人身上实在很公平合理,因为是否适航纯粹是对事实的认定,全要靠证据支持,而这些证据全部掌握在船东/承运人手中,货方一无所知。不去要求船东/承运人举证只会令事故真相无法查明,而这一来,就更谈不上今后以此为训去作出改善以预防同类事故发生了。此外,本章 4.2.5 小段已详论过,船东/承运人对造成货损货差的原因是有举证责任的。经常会是,调查取证起来,它们(事故原因与是否涉及不适航)根本是同一回事。

就"以上所述,随便任意引用一个权威的说法加以支持,可节录 Hobhouse 大法官在 The "Yamatogawa"(1990)2 Lloyd's Rep. 39 先例所说如下:"The breakdown... were caused by the unseaworthiness of the vessel at the commencement of the voyage; accordingly the burden of proof is upon the defendants(船东)to prove either that in all respects they exercised due diligence to make the vessel seaworthy or that in so far as they failed to discharge that duty it did not cause or contribute to the casualty(船东要不证明已"克尽职责",要不证明不适航与事故无关)。"

4.2.6.1.2 货方申请检查船舶的做法

收货人虽没有举证责任,但一般也不会坐着干等船东/承运人来举证,特别是遇上较大的货损货差事故。做法上往往是,货方若怀疑船有不适航,例如货物遭海水损坏,怀疑舱盖漏水或其他地方漏水,会设法上船检查。当然,船东/船长不会轻易合作,特别是心中有鬼时。对船东而言,即使心中没鬼也不要随便答应货方上船检查,别以为那样是坦白,实际很容易会给对方挑出毛病。这一来,收货人就要考虑强制手段了,这强制手段就是向法院申请下令船东允许检查船舶,英国与香港法院的高院程序法都有这方面的规定(香港的 Rules of Supreme Court, Order 29)。这做法在笔者《禁令》一书第五章之 9.3/9.4 小段有详论,内容较长,不在此节录。

检查船舶最好是一出事故就尽快进行,这常会是就在卸港进行。若错过时机,例如过了几个月等保险人赔付、代位后,找了懂行律师向船东追索时才想到这个做法,虽然可以,但会有一定的危险与麻烦,例如是船舶已出售或沉没或不适航之处已修理妥,而即使不适航的情况仍在,船东也可去狡辩说这是新问题,几个月前出事时并不存在,没有漏水。

在《禁令》一书中,详述了 The "Mare del Nord"(1990)1 Lloyd's Rep. 40 先例,在此可以再略作介绍,毕竟该案十分典型。该先例涉及汽油货物的短卸,原因不明。内行人对这种货差可能原因的一个估计是船上偷油。当然这样去估计要在整体上合情合理,例如船东不是中远,马斯基等大公司,因这些大公司不可能会自毁商誉于这种偷鸡摸狗的不法事情。若是船上偷油,一般做法是加装管道去连接船舱与燃油柜,否则它们之间并不相连。所以一旦能上船检查,会马上真相大白,人赃并获。

而如果收货人坐着干等船东将来举证(且手中什么证据都没有,仍肯冒险花钱去起诉),若真是船上偷了油,你想船东会"坦白从宽"吗?船东肯定会另找理由推搪,例如船东说没有过错是意外造成的货差,并以不多及空泛的证据(如船长讲"故事"的口头证据)作支持。天知道,在收货人无法反证之下,船东会蒙混过关,成功抗辩。

再回去讲 The "Mare del Nord" 先例,收货人的代表律师在威胁船东律师后仍无法取得船东合作允许上船检查,只好向法院申请强制下令了。

总结上述,收货人虽不必举证货损货差的原因及相关的适航,通常仍不会坐着干等,他会主动去调查。这其中的原因或好处是:

(i)别太天真,以为留待船东/承运人去举证即可来一个真相大白。精明但不诚实的外国(中国)船东多的是,去振振有词地挑一个理由还不容易?有水平的船东更能天衣无缝地杜撰一个故事,这全是看表达与做戏的"水平"(skill),尤其在明知对方收货人无从反驳,全是他/它一面之词的情况下。打官司虽有诸如文件披露、反盘问等手段可能令船东/承运人不能蒙混过关,但现实中仍是斗智的游戏,并不保证真相大白。

(ii)又何必将官司打到底才令真相大白呢?这毕竟是十分劳民伤财的事。若能较早迫出真相(上船检查后),马上就可公平地、知己知彼地进行庭外和解了。

4.2.6.2　海牙规则下的不适航须与货损货差有关

在本章之4.1与4.2.1小段,提到美国《哈特法》下的不适航不必与货损货差或要分摊共同海损的事故有关:The "Isis",290 U.S. 333(1933)。这对船东十分危险、苛刻,因为任何船舶都有可能挑得出不适航之处,但该不适航却与事故毫无因果关系。例如第五货舱失火引致货损,但挑出的一个不适航毛病是第一货舱漏水。

《哈特法》导致法院有此解释(The "Isis")纯粹是因为立法所用的措辞/文字,当然这会是立法的本意,但也不一定,正如合约一样,常会有词不达意或想得不够周密的情况出现,顶多在层次上比一般合约的草拟水平要高不少就是了。但后来有了海牙规则,美国也将其立法为1936 COGSA,则这方面的问题就明确了,即如不适航,它必须与货损货差事故有因果关系。这也是英国法律(1971 COGSA)的立场。这方面权威的说法可先节录 Heinz Horn-Marie Horn, 1968 AMC 2548 at p.2558 (5 Cir. 1968)(1970) 1 Lloyd's Rep. 191 所说的如下:"Under the Harter Act…the owner whose diligence in providing a seaworthy vessel is found deficient is liable for damage to cargo without causal relation between the defect and the disaster…COGSA, however calls for such casual relation as a prerequisite to a finding of liability. Although sect. 1303(1)(a)…has been construed as requiring that the loss be casually related to the want of due diligence before liability can be imposed on the carrier."

另也可节录《Marine Cargo Claims》一书的第374页所说:"Some American cases

on due diligence and the burden of proof seem confused and contradictory…But the confusion seems to arise from the difference between the Harter Act and COGSA, under the Hatter Act due diligence to make the vessel seaworthy had to be proved in every respect, while under COGSA, which is the American version of the Hague Rules, due diligence need only be proved in respect of the loss."

至于何谓有关或无关（没有因果关系），除了前面提到的第五货舱失火与第一货舱漏水无关是最明显不过的例子外，还可多举如下一些例子：

（ⅰ）在美国先例 Captayannis "S", 1969 AMC 2484（D. Ore. 1969），船确是因为船员（除了船长）不合资格而不适航，但偏偏后来的事故是船长航行疏忽所致。这一来，不适航与事故就扯不上因果关系了。

（ⅱ）在美国先例 Dir. Gen. of India Supp. Miss. v. S. S. Maru, 1972 AMC 1694（2 Cir 1972），涉及船舶超载，超吃水达13吋之多，这显然是不适航。之后船舶搁浅，但船东却证明/说明了多此13吋或少此13吋，搁浅仍是避免不了，所以不适航与事故（搁浅）无关。

（ⅲ）英国也曾有类似的超载案件，后来船因坏天气沉没。但因航程中已消耗了部分油水，船沉时已没有超载。结果法院判不适航与沉没事故无关：Walker v. Dover Navigation Co. (1950) 83 Lloyd's Rep. 84。

（ⅳ）在英国先例 The "Yamatogawa" (1990) 2 Lloyd's Rep. 39, 涉及一船原油从青岛运往新加坡，提单（与租约）合并了海牙规则。途中，船舶因为主机的"减速齿轮"断裂而失去动力，船货被迫接受救助并拖带至新加坡。这带来救助费用与共同海损费用的承担与分摊问题。货方在承担了货物部分的救助费用后，为了向船东/承运人追偿（同时也为了拒绝分摊余下部分的共同海损费用），就要好像一般的货损货差索赔那样，去指控船东违反了海牙规则，如船不适航，等等。在经过专家证人的取证及十分复杂的技术分析后，Hobhouse 大法官认为该"减速齿轮"（reduction gear）的构造根本无法打开去检查，而且即使检查也无法看到这断裂之处。虽然不适航是事实（否则怎会出事故？）船东也承认没有"克尽职责"（但照理说他/它也不必去承认，因为无法看到和查到这毛病，应不能说是没有"克尽职责"）但 Hobhouse 大法官仍判这些与事故无关，他说道："In my judgment, on the evidence that I have heard and read, the correct assessment of what good engineering practice involved in relation to this reduction gear on Yamatogawa was that it should not be dismantled, whether on the guarantee inspection or on the CMS first survey, and that the input shaft should not be withdrawn nor the sun wheel removed. It follows that the defendants'（船东）failure fully to exercise due diligence had no relevant causative effect on this casualty. The casualty would have occurred even if due diligence had been exercised."

4.2.6.3 海牙规则要求"克尽职责"令船舶适航是先决条件,不违反才能享有免责

这方面最著名的说法是 Somervell 勋爵在 Maxine Footwear v. Canada Government Merchant Marine(1959) 2 Lloyd's Rep. 105 先例所作的讲话。他针对海牙规则的 Article 3(2) 开头一句话("Subject to The provisions of Article 4")和 Article 4 说:"Article III, rule 1, is an overriding obligation. If it is not fulfilled and the non-fulfillment causes the damage the immunities of articles IV cannot be relied on. This is the natural construction apart from the opening words of article III, rule 2. The fact that that rule is made subject to the provisions of article IV and rule 1 is not so conditioned makes the point clear beyond argument."

该先例本身很能说明这一点:它涉及一艘名为"Maurienne"的船舶在加拿大的 Halifax 港装货。装货途中,因发觉船的排污水管因天冷而被冰封(当时是 2 月份),船长于是雇用了岸上工人去"解冻"。工人在安装了"板架"(stage)后,用"喷灯"(torch)烧污水管。但这导致污水管的软木部分被烧着而酿成火灾,最后严重至要把船舶在港内凿沉才能成功灭火。这一来,已装上船的货物全损是无可避免了。

照理说,海牙规则有一项对船东/承运人十分宽待的火灾免责,这是在 Article 4(2)(b),它规定"火灾,除非是承运人自己引起的"(Fire, unless caused by the actual fault or privity of the carrier),均可免责。这一来,船员、装卸工等随处吸烟、疏忽行事等导致火灾都不影响船东/承运人可享有火灾的免责。而在 Maxine Footwear 先例,岸上工人乱去使用喷灯也看似应该不影响船东/承运人可享有火灾的免责。

但海牙规则有一步步的法定举证责任,其中包括对适航举证的先决条件,所以不能简单地只跳去针对免责项目。

要对适航举证,就可分析出 Maxine Footwear 先例中的"Maurienne"轮有如下不妥:

(a)是否不适航?——显然是,一艘火光熊熊的船舶怎会是适航、适货?所以判是:"From the time when the ship caught fire she was unseaworthy. This unseaworthiness caused the damage to and loss of the goods"。

(b)有否"克尽职责"?——应该没有,因为火灾是船长雇用的工人疏忽所致。有关"克尽职责"的问题会在稍后的 4.2.6.4 小段详论,只说说,如果这场火灾是一个完全陌生的第三者引起,例如恐怖分子冲到船上放火,则谈不上船东/承运人没有"克尽职责"了。

(c)是否开航前发生(因开航后再没有这适航责任了)?——显然也是,因为事故发生时,"Maurienne"轮仍在装货,尚未开航。有关开航前才有适航责任的问题,会在稍后的 4.2.6.5 小段详论。在此只说说,若该事故发生在开航后(或在卸港),

例如船员在航行中疏忽用喷灯去"解冻"而引致一模一样的事故,船东/承运人仍可以享有火灾免责。因为已与适航无关(要求的时间已过),而火灾免责又十分广泛,不因船员/雇员的疏忽/过错而受影响。像 Maxine Footwear 的贵族院判法,已为国际上多数国家的人士接受和认同。例如《Marine Cargo Claims》一书的作者也持同样观点。但在不同事实的案例中,这一点仍不易区分,如下面谈到的近期另一案例。

近期另一同类的案例是 The "Apastolis"(1999)2 Lloyd's Rep. 292,在第一审(The "Apastolis"(1996)1 Lloyd's Rep. 475),Tuckey 法官就是根据 Maxine Footwear 先例判船舶一失火即构成不适航。该船在希腊的 Salonika 港装棉花,发生火灾。起因是第五货舱有火花掉落引致棉花着火,而这火花可能来自两个原因,一是装卸工乱掉香烟头,二是甲板上/舱盖烧焊所引起。但这就带来一点重要的区别:若只是香烟头乱掉在棉花上引发事故,这怎会与船舶适航/适货有关? 可以说,在发生火灾损坏货物前,船舶毫无不适航/不适货之处。只有是船员烧焊不小心,才会与适货有点关系,因为它导致第五货舱无法安全堆装易燃的棉花。要注意的是,Maxine Footwear 先例的案情是喷灯烧着了用于绝缘的污水管软木部分,是船舶先着火,其后才烧至货物。所以 Tuckey 大法官在认定了是船员疏忽烧焊引致火灾的事实后说:"I have not found this point easy to resolve.[482] I do not think that the short judgment in Maxine Footwear is decisive.[483] I accept of course that if it is simply fire in the cargo itself which makes the vessel unseaworthy, as might be the case with a fire caused by a discarded cigarette, then there can be no breach of art. Ⅲ, r. 1.[484] But here the threat to the cargo posed by the spark is associated with welding carried out to the ship.[485] Which side of the line does this case fall? …If one were to ask rhetorically whether the carrier had made the hold of his ship fit and safe for the preservation of an inflammable cargo when he was carrying out welding work above the hold which resulted in sparks raining into it, there could I think be only one answer: No;[486] his holds was not fit and safe for the cargo; his ship was unseaworthy.[487]"

在上诉庭(The "Apostolis"(1997)2 Lloyd's Rep. 241),案子改判为火灾是因装卸工乱掉香烟头引起的。但仅在这一点上看来,说法仍是一样。Leggatt 大法官说:

---

[482] 这方面不易区分。
[483] Maxine Footwear 短短的判词并没有作出全面的解释。
[484] 我(Tuckey 大法官)同意如果火灾是因乱掉香烟头直接引起,这并不涉及船舶的不适航/不适货。
[485] 但若火灾是烧焊所引起就难说了。
[486] 若是客观地问,一个货舱不断有烧焊火花从上像降雨般落下,它是否"适货"去装载易燃货物呢? 答案肯定是"不"。
[487] 所以,"APostolis"并不适航,也不适货。

"(In Maxine Footwear) It was fire in the fabric of the vessel, namely the cork lining of the hold, which rendered her unseaworthy. Here the ship only became so on account of the fire in the cargo. It cannot even be said that the welding was taking place in order to render the ship unseaworthy. The fire might as well have been caused by a discarded cigarette, which, as the Judge accepted, could not be a breach of art. Ⅲ, r. 1."

综上所述,笔者有以下看法:

(ⅰ)这方面不必去斤斤计较公道不公道,这纯粹是按海牙规则的条款的措辞/用字去解释。正如本章4.2.2小段所节录的《Marine Cargo Claims》一书所提的一步一步的举证次序。

(ⅱ)海牙规则只是一个妥协的产物,它是历经船货双方及各有关国家出于各自的利益/理由长期争论后取得的平衡。国际上应尽量尊重并一致地解释。

(ⅲ)而且,像 Maxine Footwear 先例那样判船舶一失火就是不适航,不适货又有什么不公道呢?毕竟,船长/岸上工人为何不在解冻冰封的污水管方面做得更好,却随便就乱使用喷灯呢?要知道,船舶当时在装港,船东/承运人能够控制得到。

(ⅳ)笔者不是中国海商法专家,但据知中国海商法不是这样规定(或没有这样规定)。然即使针对海牙规则(如合约合并了"首要条款"),听说中国海事法院也有个别案件不是按国际上一般的解释。若真是如此,笔者总觉得不妥,除非有很合理的原因。如果有,外国法院也会依法判决。

4.2.6.4 何谓"克尽职责"

在本章之3.2小段,曾介绍过普通法的地位是要求船东/承运人做到令船舶严格或绝对地适航。但因有订约自由,所以提单会完全或大部分地豁免船东/承运人对适航的责任。而豁免的程度完全是看有关条款的措辞/用字,这并没有太大的奥妙。这其中的一个程度就是定位在"除非是船东本人或其经理人本人的行为或错误引起,以及没有尽到'本人应尽的克尽职责'(personal want of due diligence)使船舶适航",船东/承运人不必对船员/雇员的过错或疏忽所导致的不适航、不适货负责:The "Dominator" (1959) 1 Lloyd's Rep. 125; The "Bmbant" (1965) 2 Lloyd's Rep. 546 等。这一适航要求的程度并不高,对船东优待而对货方不利。它虽然来自合约而并非任何国际公约或立法,双方想改就改,但因为著名的金康租约格式第2条(虽然合约方仍是要改就去改好了)就是这样的措辞/文字,所以这一程度的适航要求也就变得出名和常见了。这方面在笔者的《程租合约》一书第四章§6段有详论,内容太多,不再重复。

在这适航要求的高程度(普通法)与低程度(合约的惯常措辞/文字)之间,看来海牙规则是想作出折中,其要求是船东要做到"合理"的程度。这一点尤其在海牙规则的法文版本有所显示,而这是"正式版本"(official version),对适航要求是"diligence reasonable"（合理尽责）。但英文版对适航要求的措辞/文字是用了"due diligence"（克尽职责），而这也是美国 1983 年《哈特法》中所使用的措辞。

4.2.6.4.1 解释"克尽职责"一词的先例

有关这"克尽职责"一词，英国实际早有判例作出解释。这是在 C. E. Dobell & Co. v. Steamship Rossmore Company Ltd. (1895) 2 Q. B. 408 先例，涉及美国哈特法以合约方式合并进提单内，而英国上诉庭要对《哈特法》（不当做是立法，纯粹是以合约条款来看待）的"克尽职责"作出解释。该案例中因船上木匠（船员）疏忽导致不适航，船东争辩他不必为他的船员/雇员或代理人的疏忽负责。但上诉庭不同意，Esher 勋爵说："It is obvious to my mind…that the words of the 3rd section[488] which limit the owner's liability if he shall exercise due diligence to make the ship in all respects seaworthy, must mean that this is to be done by the owner by himself or the agents whom he employs to see to the seaworthiness of the ship before she starts out of that port…"

另外，Kay 大法官也说："…It seems to me to be plain on the face of this contract that what was intended was that the owner should, if not with his own eyes, at any rate by tile eyes of proper competent agents, ensure that the ship was in a seaworthy condition before she left pert, and that it is not enough to say that he appointed a proper and competent agent（注意最后一句说船东光是找了一个妥当与可靠的代理人去代劳令船舶适航仍不足够，也就是，该代理人要确实做妥，不犯错，不疏忽才足够）…"

对船东/承运人同样严厉/苛刻的判法也发生在美国法院，毕竟哈特法是美国的立法：The "Colima" (1897) 82 Fed. 665。

英国以 1924 COGSA 把海牙规则立法后，早期仍有判例如此解释"克尽职责"，如 The "Newbrough" (1939) 64 Lloyd's Rep. 33（不够煤炭/燃料的不适航），Wright 勋爵说："…The obligation to make a ship seaworthy is personal to the owners, whether or not they entrust to the performance of that obligation to experts, servants, or agents…."（这是船东个人的责任，不能推给专家，雇员或代理人）。

也早有先例警告说船东/承运人在海牙规则所获得的适航"好处"（相比普通法的地位）其实是虚无缥缈，不实在的。这是在 The "Lilburn" (1939) 64 Lloyd's Rep. 87，Mackinnon 大法官所说的："The limitation and qualification of the implied warranty of seaworthiness, by cutting it down to use 'due diligence on the part of the shipowner to make the ship seaworthy', is a limitation or qualification more apparent than real,[489] because the exercise of due diligence involves not merely that the shipowner per-

---

[488] 指哈特法第 3 条，内中要求"克尽职责"使船舶适航。《哈特法》在附录四。
[489] "克尽职责"看来虚无缥缈，没有实质好处。

sonally shall exercise due diligence, but that all his servants and agents shall exercise due diligence,[490] as is pointed out in a note in Scrutton of Charter-parties which says that this variation will not be of much practical value[491] in face of the dilemma that must constantly arise on the facts. In most cases if the vessel is unseaworthy due diligence cannot have been used by the owner, his servants, or agents;[492] if due diligence has been used the vessel in fact will be seaworthy.[493] The circumstances in which the dilemma does not arise[494] (e.g., a defect causing unseaworthiness but of so latent a nature that due diligence could not have discovered it) are not likely to occur often.[495]"

4.2.6.4.2 The "Muncaster Castle" 先例

到了著名的 The Muncaster Castle (1961) 1 Lloyd's Rep. 57 先例，它的案情反映出这严厉/苛刻的适航要求对船东/承运人确有不合理之处，于是这一问题开始受到广泛注意，有观点认为这并非是海牙规则谈判中船货双方为各自利益所取得的平衡与妥协。

该先例涉及一个从悉尼运牛舌罐头（当然还有其他货物装在此班轮）至伦敦的航次，航次中第五货舱进海水浸坏了 100 多只罐头。海水渗入的原因可追朔至船舶在这航次前曾入坞进行"特检"（special survey）及"载重线年检"（Annual Load Line Inspection）的事实。检验时曾将船底旁的所有 31 个"防浪阀"（storm valve）全部打开让"劳合社"检验师（Lloyd's surveyor）进行检验，在验毕及满意后，由船坞的钳工把防浪阀重新盖好。但由于一个很有经验的钳工没有把其中 2 个防浪阀的螺丝钉以均力旋紧，导致后来出事。

该"Muncaster"轮出坞后往澳洲装货前往英国。其间当然不会发现有防浪阀未盖好旋紧。后在去英国的航次中遇上恶劣天气，令船舶颠簸，结果未盖好的防浪阀进一步松脱导致海水涌入第五货舱。船舶抵达伦敦卸港时，发觉舱中积水达 15 吋，并已浸坏牛舌货物。

经对上述事实的调查，认定造成货损的主因/近因是船坞的钳工疏忽没有盖好旋紧防浪阀而让海水涌入这一点是明确的。若是以绝对适航的程度要求来看待，船东也应是违反了适航义务，因为不适航的事实摆在眼前。但从整件事故看，船东

---

[490] 因为它要求不光是船东本人"克尽职责"，而是所有雇员/代理人都要"克尽职责"。
[491] 这带来一个严重的困境导致对船东没有实质好处。
[492] 这困境是：一有不适航，也往往没有"克尽职责"。
[493] 而一有去"克尽职责"也往往不会再有不适航，不会出事故了。
[494] 这困境不会出现唯一情况是潜在的不适航（一般是指船体，机器等潜在的缺陷），因为这是所有人去"克尽职责"仍无法事前发觉的。
[495] 但以上的情况现实中发生不多。

似乎又十分冤枉,因为他/它对此毫无预防办法。船东是英国一家著名的班轮/船公司,船舶的检验是由英国著名的劳合社进行,而船舶进的船坞也是著名及有悠久历史的。再者,该船坞也是雇用了有经验的钳工去干这工作,但偏偏就是在这钳工的环节出了问题。而且,这个疏忽表面上还看不出来,即使劳合社检验师或/与船东盯着钳工去旋紧螺丝钉(一般不会这样,去盯着每件小事),也没有作用。

该案到了贵族院,判是"Muncaster Castle"轮的船东违反了"克尽职责"使船舶适航的先决条件,所以什么免责都免谈了,船东要对货损负责。

贵族院拒绝不依照先例而仅针对海牙规则下的"克尽职责"重新作出不同解释或定义。同时,也拒绝区分船员、雇员或代理人的过错疏忽与其他"独立承包人"(independent contractor)的过错/疏忽,以作出不同对待。要求去区分疏忽属后者的独立承分包人的作用在于:如果船东对该独立承包人的任命/委托并没有不妥之处,该过错/疏忽不算在船东身上。其原因有:

(i)曾有这种先例:Searle v. Laverick (1874) L. R. Q. B. 122; Green v. Fibreglass, Ltd. (1958) 2 Q. B. 245 等。

(ii)船东/承运人无法控制/管不到。

(iii)也会有情况是船东/承运人根本没有资格与技术去管,例如独立承包人是劳合社、专家等。

但贵族院拒绝区分,因为分水线不容易找。例如船舶要修理会让船员进行或另找修理厂。找了修理厂也会是船员仍然对部分修理自己去做;反正会有变化多端的做法。在讨论该案带出的问题时,英国代表曾提出所谓的"'Muncaster Castle'修定"(The "Muncaster Castle" Amendment),意图在海牙·维斯比规则加上一条款——说明只要船东/承运人雇用了一个优良可靠的独立承包人(independent contractor),就不必再对独立承包人本身过错/疏忽所造成的损失负责。

但其他国家代表并不支持,认为这 The "Muncaster Castle"先例只是英国自己的问题,不必以国际公约来对付。这一来,这修定也就无疾而终了。

4.2.6.4.3 判是已"克尽职责"的先例

可以想象得到,绝大部分的不适航如果确是事实而且与货损货差有关,船东/承运人往往也没有去"克尽职责"。能成功举证已"克尽职责"的案例,寥寥可数。在此不妨举几个为数不多的先例如下:

最著名的可以先举 The "Amstelslot"(1963)2 Lloyd's Rep. 223 的贵族院判例。该案中船舶从美国波特兰装小麦去印度孟买,到达离檀香山约 90 海里的位置时,由于主机的减速齿轮断裂,失去动力,最后要由救助的拖轮拖去日本神户港。在该港把小麦转运去孟买。收货人提出索赔损失并同时拒绝分摊共同海损的 7536 英镑。

收货人指减速齿轮的断裂是由于"鼓轮上的螺旋轮箍安装不合适或该轮箍使

用过久已有裂缝所造成的",而这缺陷在波特兰开航时已存在,即船舶不适航。收货人的诉状对不适航是说:"certain screwed dowels which had been fitted to the after helix try of the main gear drum had been fitted improperly in that they were too tight and so forced the try, away from the drum. By reason of the foregoing repeated flexing of the try occurred during operation resulting in ultimate fatigue and fracture of the metal of the try."

船东/承运人承认船舶是不适航(出了事故是事实,无从抵赖),但他已是"克尽职责"。该"金属疲劳裂缝"(fatigue crack)是从内部逐步扩大的,属潜在缺陷,检验无法发现。事实上,该船这一部分(减速齿轮)曾被劳合社检验师检查过,但裂缝没被发现。收货人指检验师如果以仔细的方法检查,而不光是"表面看看"(superficial inspection),应可以看到这小裂缝。这方法包括把上盖移走就可更接近地检查减速齿轮,把齿轮上的牛油擦去然后检查每个螺丝,每一螺旋(helix)逐一检查等。

在贵族院,判是船东/承运人已做到"克尽职责"。如果有几个正常的检验方法,在没有特别需要注意的情况下,检验无须自动提升至最高要求的一种办法。即这方面仍是以惯常的,合理的做法为准。

Eventide 勋爵说:"It is clear on the evidence that the examination made in fact of the 'Amstelslot' was in all respects in accordance with the standard generally applied to ships of the same kind on a continuing survey and was founded on the skill and experience of Lloyd's Register of shipping.[496] If, therefore, there was no lack of care in so examining the ship[497]…, it would appear to follow that the appellants(船东)satisfy the burden of proving that due diligence was taken by them,[498] unless it can be shown that upon the facts and in the circumstances of the case the duty of diligence required the appellants to apply some higher standard[499]…?

除了 The "Amstelslot"先例,还可以从《Marine Cargo Claims》一书挑出其他一些船东成功举证"克尽职责"的英美案例如下:

(ⅰ)在英国的 The "Cathay"(1927)28 Lloyd's Rep. 202,据知是有关海牙规则的第一宗先例,判是建造船舶时的监督员已"克尽职责"。

(ⅱ)在英国的 The "Anglo Colombian"(1937)58 Lloyd's Rep. 188,第一货船舱进水损坏了小麦货物。进水之处是某个松动了的螺铆钉。法院判这是"内在/潜在

---

[496] 证据显示该检验的做法符合劳氏船级社对这类船舶适用的一般标准。

[497] 所以没有不小心或疏忽之处。

[498] 船东已"克尽职责"。

[499] 除非当时有特别需要注意的情况,如"Amstelslot"轮的减速齿轮经常出毛病或表面看已应有怀疑,要去更深入检验,则船东才有采用更高检验办法/标准的责任。

缺陷",而且船东/承运人也不必每次开航前去敲一敲每个螺铆钉看是否松了("I cannot myself believe that in every case if is obligatory...to go and tap every rivet to find if it has a defect or not")。

(ⅲ)在英国的 The "Highland Monarch"（1939）64 Lloyd's Rep. 188,冷藏系统在航程中坏了,漏出盐水(Brine)把货物(羊肉)损坏,漏水的"联轴节"(coupling)已曾二次(其中一次在装港开航前)被劳氏船级社检查过。

(ⅳ)在英国的 The "Australia Star"（1940）67 Lloyd's Rep. 110,涉及燃油柜的铆钉/对接铆松脱,无法发现,导致航次中漏油。该案例另外也提到"克尽职责"要以造船年代当时的技术水平为准,不能过分去要求。

(ⅴ)在美国的 Iarembo,136 F. 2d 320,1943 AMC 954（2 Cir 1943）,判是虽然有船旁钢板已 75% 腐蚀,但较早曾有表面检查与"锤击试验"(hammer test),只是没有发现而已。

(ⅵ)在英国的 The "Hellenic Dolphin"（1978）2 Lloyd's Rep. 336,船舶投入班轮服务,从希腊的 Piraeus 开航,去地中海各港口装货后,开往东南非各港口,在 Mombasa 卸清欧洲装的货物后,开始回航,同时去各港口装货回欧洲。其中在 Lourenco Marques 港装了 5000 多包石棉,堆装在第四下层货舱。到了卸港威尼斯,发觉其中 3000 多包遭海水浸坏。经后来调查,发觉海水是从船旁钢板的一条裂缝渗入。该裂缝与 16 粒松脱铆钉是由船旁钢板出现了一个约半寸至 1 寸深,4 尺长的"凹陷"(indent)造成。这样的凹陷,专家认为是由重击造成,而重击之时,船长/船员也不会感觉不到。但偏偏船上没有任何记录显示有过类似意外,例如被拖轮碰撞、与码头碰撞等。这一来,自然也无法去举证说明何时发生这导致不适航的事故,是否在 Lourenco Marques 开航前或开航后,因为海牙规则只针对开航前才要求承运人"克尽职责"令船舶适航。

另在有否"克尽职责"方面,船东自辩称他在管理上有一套良好的检查船旁与船舱的制度。一是每航次在船东的所在地港口 Piraeus,都会派主管的监督轮机长(chief superintending engineer)去上船作检查,包括从表面上察看船旁/船舱有否看得见的毛病。这检查不像船级社的特检(Special Survey),例如要去测量钢板厚度,正如该主管作为证人说道:"if the ship does not have something obviously wrong and we do not see anything wrong, there is no need to proceed centimetre by centimetre because then we will never finish."二是船长与大副在航次中的例行检查,也没有发觉该凹陷。

收货人的专家指这些检查并不足够,应在回航港口 Mombasa 也进行检查,当时船已卸空,船旁大部分露出水面。另船东应指示船长每次装货前从内到外检查船舱,并把检查报告公司/船东,如发现有新的凹陷等（A prudent shipowner issues instructions to the Master to inspect the ship internally and externally prior to loading, and to submit a record of this inspection to head office)。但在此事故,什么书面文件都没有。

但 Lloyd 大法官接受船东的主管与船长这两位证人的证言(相信他们),判船东已"克尽职责",不再苛求他在检查船舶上做更多。Lloyd 大法官说:"although some additional precautions were desirable at the turn-round port over and above the ordinary routine inspection which the master said he carried out, a detailed examination was not such an obvious precaution that the failure to carry it out showed a want of due diligence …if the defect existed before loading at Lourenco Marques then it was a true latent defect not discoverable by due diligence and the defendants(船东) had not only discharged the burden which rested on them under art. IV, r. 1 of the Hague Rules but they were also entitled to rely on the exception and latent defects contained in art. IV, r. 2(p)."

(vii)在英国先例的 The "Admiral Zmajevic"(1983) 2 Lloyd's Rep. 86,因为主机"曲柄箱"(crankcase)的润滑油受酸(acid)而污染,导致主机受损,在航次中发生故障。这带来拖带救助与共同海损。收货人不肯分摊,指船舶不适航。船东承认船不适航,因装港开航时润滑油已受污染。但他/它辩称已做到"克尽职责",因为对此污染他/它的确无法发现,一般船东都是把使用中的润滑油样本定时交给石油公司(该案例是 Shell 公司)作出化验,看看水分,酸的指标等,而以前的报告都没有不妥,不正常之处。结果法院判船东已"克尽职责",毕竟,也没有说法是 Shell 的化验出错了。

(viii)在英国的 The "Tilia Gorthon"(1985) 1 Lloyd's Rep. 552,涉及木材(timber)装运在船甲板上。这并没有什么问题,"Tilia Gorthon"轮本身就是一艘木材船,有设备去装甲板货。发货人也同意这是习惯做法。加拿大装港有专门"法典规则"(code)针对装于船甲板的木材,如堆装多高、堆装要紧密、不得有空隙等。海牙规则本不适用于甲板货,但提单以合法方式合并引入了海牙规则也适用在甲板货,故此出了事就要一步步照该规则去举证了,如船东要证明"克尽职责"使船舶适航/适货。

船舶在航次中遇上大风浪,其中一个捆绑甲板木材的"张力器"(tensioner)断裂,导致甲板上的许多木材冲下大海。

Sheen 大法官判是捆绑的铁链与"张力器"均有证书说明力量符合加拿大的法典规则,而即使张力器断裂,从证据上看来也应属无法发觉的潜在缺陷,所以船东并没有违反"克尽职责"的适航义务。Sheen 大法官说:"…the chains and tensioners used on board "Tilia Gorthon" were certified to be substantially stronger than the criteria specified by the Canadian Code… the strength of the chain was greater than the strength of the tensioner… even if the tensioner had less than its designed strength the evidence supported the view that any defect was latent; it could not have been discovered by any reasonable inspection of the tensioner and it would be unreasonable to expect any shipowner or his crew to do more than that; in those circumstances the loss did not result from any failure to exercise due diligence to make the ship seaworthy."

(ix)已在 4.2.6.2 小段详述过的英国先例 The "Yamatogawa"(1990) 2 Lloyd's Rep. 39,不再重复。

4.2.6.4.4 总结"克尽职责"的适航要求

总结以上各段节,笔者对"克尽职责"有以下看法:

(i)"克尽职责"的适航要求对船东/承运人十分严格/苛刻,法官(或仲裁员)会有"事后诸葛亮"倾向的危险。多数货损货差与船舶相关方面有不适航会扯得上关系。海水渗入,正常天气下船舶沉没,主机故障等,更常常是明显不过,可凭此去推断不适航,除非船东/承运人能够成功举证以改变这不利的推断:见本章之 4.2.5.3.3 小段。而即使普通一点的事故像碰船搁浅等导致货损货差,船东/承运人也难以安枕无忧。这方面也会有像船员不足,水平/训练/指引不够,海图过时等相关的问题经调查后被挑出来。而一有了不适航的事实存在,船东/承运人再进一步去举证已"克尽职责"在现实中往往会陷入像 4.2.6.4 小段提及的 The "Lilburn"(1939) 64 Lloyd's Rep. 87 先例中所讲的"严重困境"。难怪一有涉及不适航,船东/承运人十有八九(或是更高比例)会对货损货差难逃责任。船东互保协会也往往只能天南地北地去争辩一轮(总会有话可讲),实质上人仍是为了寻求庭外和解。由于适航的争议会涉及十分复杂的技术问题,所以打起官司来十分昂贵。这是代表船东或货方的律师应理解的,所以能在真相大致清楚后早日去合理和解实在对双方都是好事。

(ii)"克尽职责"相比于普通法对适航的要求唯一较宽松之处是船东/承运人可以对潜在缺陷或无法合理看见的不适航免责。"潜在缺陷"(latent defect)本身也是海牙规则 Article 4(2)(p)的一项免责,这里并没有矛盾。故船东/承运人一旦成功举证了他/它已"克尽职责",即可自动去举证他/它所依赖的免责项目(这是下一步的举证责任)。

(iii)何谓"潜在"或"看不见/查不到"应以合理为标准,不应苛求,除非事实表明需要这样做,例如有所怀疑(如对老龄船或经常出的某类故障/毛病)。所以"锈蚀"(corrosion)或"正常损耗"(wear and tear)很少会被视作是"潜在缺陷",例如一条完全隐蔽的管道因锈蚀而漏水漏油。原因是老船应多去检查,有这锈蚀除非是比正常的加速,否则正常使用年期一到,船东/承运人应自动去更换或多加注意。正如 William Tetley 教授在《Marine Cargo Claims》一书第 3 版之第 509 页说道:"Nevertheless, corrosion is unlikely to be a latent defect because corrosion takes so long to develop that it is a defect that should have been discovered before and at the beginning of the voyage and many previous voyages, Even when the corrosion is the result of a defective manufacturing process, because the corrosion took place over a long period and could have been discovered by due diligence, it is not a latent defect…"

（iv）"克尽职责"是船东/承运人的"个人责任"（personal liability），任何其他人代劳去修理、供应、检验以及进行其他各方面的安排的过程中有过失/疏忽，仍要算在船东/承运人身上。这"其他人"即使是世界最一流最可靠的，像船级社、专家、船厂等，也都一视同仁，反正是代劳中不能犯错。

（v）由于船东/承运人有举证责任，因此装货前，开航前要多去保留证据。在此过程中如果发现不妥，也可作出补救/修理，万事总是预防胜于治疗。例如在上一小段的 The "Hellenic Dolphin"（1978）2 Lloyd's Rep. 336 货方的专家曾提到："A prudent shipowner issues instructions to the Master to inspect the ship internally and externally prior to loading, and to submit a record of this inspection to head office."

（vi）冷藏货是另一例子，这种货物十分危险，冷藏设备在航程中一旦出现故障，即使十分短暂，也会造成重大货损甚至全损。而有了故障，也很可能是开航前缺陷/毛病已存在了，也即是不适航了。船东要再进一步去证明已"克尽职责"，会是更困难了，除非一早已作出准备。这正是船东互保协会对船东所作的要求，即在每一装港开航前要安排由船级社作出检验确保冷藏设备是妥善、没有毛病与操作正常的，否则将来出了事故将不予赔偿/补偿。互保协会的规则会是以下措辞/文字：
"Except where the Association shall have previously agreed in writing, there shall be no recovery in respect of perishable cargo carried in insulated or refrigerating chambers unless:(a) the space, apparatus and the means used for the carriage and safe custody of the perishable cargo have been certified and approved before the commencement of each voyage, by a surveyor of the entered ship's Classification Society, and…"

4.2.6.5　海牙规则要求"克尽职责"令船舶适航是在开航前与开航时

在英国普通法下，对绝对或严格适航的要求是存在于每一阶段。当然，所要求的也只是不同阶段所需要的，如装货、内河航行、远洋航行等。但总之，适航要求是不光只针对在装港开航前或当时。例如，一个航次如果分几个阶段进行，半途要补充燃料（以前烧煤经常这样操作），则每一阶段，每次从半途港开航，都要做到绝对或严格适航：The "Vortigern"（1899）p. 140。班轮业务中半途有其他的装卸港，地位也应如此。

但海牙规则的措辞/文字对适航时间上的要求是在"开航前与开航时"（before and at the beginning of the voyage），这代表什么呢？要知道，海牙规则是国际公约，是船货双方利益的平衡/妥协，因此解释起来不应去受英国普通法"阶段理论"（doctrine of stages)的影响。

开航是指船舶起锚或再没有缆绳系在码头,并意图离港始航:可参考船舶保险的先例如 The "Neptunus"（1914）4 Camp. 84; Baines v. Helland（1855）10. Exch, 802。故此船舶在拖船带动下离开码头时,碰撞了混凝土码头,以致船壳出现裂缝。但当时船舶仍有两根缆绳系在码头。碰撞后,船长未检验就继续开航。途中,海水从裂缝进入,货物被损坏,这应是船东/承运人在海牙规则下负有责任。

4.2.6.5.1 开航仅指提单内的装港

The "Makedonia"（1962）1 Lloyd's Rep. 316 一案,判海牙规则的航次仅指提单的航次,也就是适航要求只在该受损或短缺货物的装港而已,不再受以后中途港开航时的不适航所影响。Hewson 大法官在 The "Makedonia"中指出:"'Voyage' in this context means what it has always meant: the contractual voyage from the port of loading to the port of discharge as declared in the appropriate bill of lading. The rule says 'voyage' without any qualification such as 'any declared stage thereof'. In my view, the obligation on the shipowner was to exercise due diligence before and at the beginning of sailing of sailing from the loading port to have the vessel adequately bunkered for the first stage to San Pedro and to arrange for adequate bunkers of a proper kind at San Pedro and other selected intermediate ports on the voyage so that the contractual voyage might be performed…"

4.2.6.5.2 如何影响多个装港的货损货差

在班轮业务,船舶常会挂靠多个装港。这影响会是:船舶去 A、B 两港装货;在 A 港开航时适航但在 B 港开航时不适航(而且没有"克尽职责"),导致 A、B 两港装的货物均受损。在责任方面,会是船东/承运人可对 A 港的货物免责(注意尚有下一步的举证要说明依赖什么免责项目),但对 B 港装的货物就难逃责任了,因为在 4.2.6.3 小段讲过,适航是先决条件。

怎会有这种情况出现呢? 在 The "Makedonia"（1962）1 Lloyd's Rep. 316 先例船舶在中途港加的燃油受污染就是一个典型例子。再多举一个例子是 The "Chyebassa"（1966）2 Lloyd's Rep. 193 先例,涉及在 Calcutta 装的货物航次中被海水损坏,而海水渗入是因为在 Calcutta 之后的下一装港,苏丹的 Port Sudan 装货时,防浪阀的铜盖被装卸工拆掉偷去。这常会发生在赤贫的发展中国家港口,当地人为了以烂铜烂铁卖上一点小钱,往往上船拆东西,偷东西。船从 Port Sudan 开航后,遇上大风浪,海水从没有盖的防浪阀渗入,损坏货物。可以说,船舶从 Calcutta 开航时适航,不适航是在 Port Sudan 开航时后。如果在 Port Sudan 开航时无法合理发觉防浪阀盖子被窃(这举证并不容易),加上偷窃的人不是装卸工而是陌生人,则船东仍有机会成功抗辩已"克尽职责"。但在 The "Makedonia",偷窃却是装卸工所为,而装卸工又是船东所雇用的,船东怎谈得上"克尽职责"呢? 所以他/它仍是难逃责任。

根据以上所讲,可以设想出以下更多的变化:

（ⅰ）Port Sudan 装的货物受损,船东责任难逃,不论后来遇上的天气有多坏。若天气坏至某一程度是没有这不适航货物也会遭受同一程度、同一样的损坏的,则会像 4.2.6.2 小段所讲的那样,不适航会是"无关"的了,即与货损没有因果关系。

（ⅱ）Calcutta 装的货物受损,与不适航无关,因该不适航只是后来在 Port Sudan 发生的,海牙规则对此没有要求。船东/承运人下一步只需对免责项目作出举证。

（ⅲ）免责项目中,船东/承运人其实没有太多项目可去依赖。遇到大风浪人们会想到"海难"或"海上危险"(perils of the sea)这一项免责。但在 The "Chyebass",判是海难若是由于船东/承运人或其雇员/代理人等的过错或疏忽所导致,船东/承运人不能享有海难免责。这一点在笔者的《国际商务游戏规则——英国合约法》一书之第十章 6.3 小段已有详论。这纯粹是基于"针对规则"(contra proferentem rule)等理由,即免责中不明确说明对过错/疏忽免责,一般不能包括。这一来,装卸工（偷了防浪阀盖子）的过错是否可算在船东/承运人头上,令后者不能享受海难的免责呢? 第一审的高院确是这样判。但案子到了上诉庭这一审判决被推翻,上诉庭判是雇员在受雇范围内的过错/疏忽,雇主是要负责。但装卸工的偷窃不在这受雇范围,只是上船装货提供了一个机会给他去偷东西,而这与他受雇去装货无关,因此这偷窃不能算在船东/承运人头上。Salmon 大法官说:"The fact that his employment on board present him（装卸工）with the opportunity to steal does not, in my judgment, suffice to make the defendants（船东）liable."

这一课题在本章后面的 4.2.7.1.16.4 小段将就重要部分再度进行探讨。

（ⅳ）必须区分以下:在讨论船东有否"克尽职责"的命题下,装卸工偷防浪阀盖子令船舶不适航,船东/承运人要负责。但不涉及"克尽职责"的问题,光是讨论免责,则装卸工偷防浪阀盖子引起的责任不再算在船东/承运人头上。

4.2.6.5.3 何谓开航

海牙规则只针对货物运输,所以开航时刻应是指船舶装完货物,开始离开码头之时。正如《Marine Cargo Claims》一书之第 377 页所说:"The exact moment of the beginning of the voyage is difficult to determine. one gathers it is when all hatches are battened down, visitors are ashore and orders from the bridge are given so that the ship actually moves under its own power or by tugs or both. Thus it is submitted that the controversial decision in S. S. "Del Sud", 1959 AMC 2143 (5 Cir. 1959) is correct. There the vessel, while leaving a dock with the assistance of a tug, was swung around and stuck the dock. It was held that the voyage had commenced."

要区分得如此仔细可以刚提到的"Del Sud"轮为例,美国法院判该轮碰上码头当时,实际已经开航,船东再也没有适航责任,故可进一步去举证并依赖航行疏忽等免责项目。相反,若船舶未算开航就发生了这事故(例如在装货码头之间移船,尚未开航),造成船舶受损进而导致货损(如海水渗入),那就会是像4.2.6.3小段详述的 Maxine Footwear v. Canada Government Merchant Marine (1959) 2 Lloyd's Rep. 105 著名先例那样的后果了。

另要提的是,有些适航工作是准备在开航后才做,也能做得到,而且没有不合理之处,这并不影响船舶开航时的适航。毕竟,对海牙规则的解释若能合理配合现实的做法,就应该如此解释。这些适航工作会是:开航后在船舶尚行驶于河道/航道中的几个小时内把船舱盖好,甲板货捆绑好,等等。或是,继续去打压舱水:Orient Ins. Co. v. United S. S. Co. 1961 AMC 1228 (SDNY 1961)。

4.2.6.5.4 适航责任何时开始

较前面的段节只提到适航责任何时终结,即装港开航前与开航当时。那么责任又是何时开始呢?应该在"开航前"(before the voyage)的多久呢?答案应是:在开始装货时直至开航:Maxine Footwear v. Canada Government Merchant Marine (1959) 2 Lloyd's Rep. 105。毕竟,适航包括适货,所以开始装货前,船东已有责任令船舶的货舱,冷藏设备等都妥善、安全及没有缺陷/毛病。

另外要提一下,开始装货即适用海牙规则的准确时间在本章4.2.3.4.2小段的 Pyrene Company Ltd. v. Scindia Steam Navigation Company Ltd. (1954) 1 Lloyd's Rep. 321 先例有介绍。

4.2.6.6 适航的定义

这适航的定义大致是指船舶在各方面都能满足在本航次适当并安全地装运预定货物的可合理预见的要求。其英文定义可以节录《Marine Cargo Claims》一书第3版第370页的说法如下:"Seaworthiness may be defined as the state of a vessel in such a condition, with such equipment, and manned by such a master and crew, that normally the cargo will be loaded, carried, caxed for and discharged properly and safely on the contemplated voyage."

不难想象,船舶有缺陷/毛病即会构成不适航,例如是救生衣不足,救生艇漏水等。但海牙规则只针对货物运输,因此与货运不会有任何关系(因果关系)的不适航可以不必理会。但即使如此,这适航的针对面已是够广泛了。常会涉及的会有:

（ⅰ）水密并能抵挡风浪的船身、舱盖等。

（ⅱ）船舶主机、发电机、抽水机、冷藏设备等状况良好,操作正常,不会在预定航次中出任何故障/毛病。

（ⅲ）所有航行设备状况良好,操作正常。

（ⅳ）所有机器设备有适当标签,有说明书,有指示图表等,可让船员可以很快理解并掌握如何操作。

（ⅴ）船长/船员要有足够水平，曾受过各方面训练（救火、应急等），有适当和足够的指示，人员数目足够。

（ⅵ）有质好量足能满足这预定货物及航次/航线合理所需的供应，如燃油、润滑油、海图、"船员通告"（Notice to Mariners）、舱盖布，等等。

（ⅶ）货舱清洁，适合预定货物的堆装与运输。根据货物的类型与需求，配有安全/妥善的通风设备，救火（二氧化碳设备），惰性气体设备，没有病疫细菌，没有过多铁锈或脱漆会污染货物等。

（ⅷ）船舶开航时与航次中的稳性，这包括货物堆装是否良好安全，压舱水的存量、分布方面等，这都会影响稳性。

（ⅸ）其他。

以上针对的各方面或各类适航要求也只是实例中的沧海一粟。反正收货人在面对货损货差（或要分摊共同海损）时，主导的想法便是这类事故会否是船上的毛病或缺陷所引起？如果是海水渗入会否是不水密所致？船舶半途要求救助拖带是否是主机的问题，或是燃油不够/质量差？雾中搁浅是否与船上海图过时，或船员水平问题，或雷达失灵有关，等等。

这些船上的缺陷/毛病若是属实，且又与所出的事故扯得上因果关系，即是不适航了。至于如何去查明真相，本章之 4.2.6.1.1 与 4.2.6.1.2 小段已有详论，不再重复。若真相查明的确是不适航，船东/承运人若想脱身下一步要做的便是举证自己"克尽职责"。

最后举一个近例以显示这方面的变化多端。The "Kapitan Sakharov"［(2000) 2 Lloyd's Rep. 255］装了一个集装箱，内有危险品（calcium hypochlorite）。对此，船东/船长是不知情的。该集装箱被堆装在第三货舱甲板上，航行中发生爆炸并引起火灾。火灾蔓延至货舱下，那里堆装了 8 个集装箱，内有高度易燃的 Isopentane。虽经船员奋力扑灭（2 名船员死亡），仍未成功。大火令邻近油柜内的船用柴油遇热后爆炸，结果使船舶沉没，所有货物（含其他集装箱内的货物）全损。在该案例中，Clarke 大法官与上诉庭判是：

（a）由于 calcium hypochlorite 集装箱装上船令船舶不适航，但因船东/船长无法知道，所以算"克尽职责"。

（b）船长应知道第三货舱没有通风设备，8 个集装箱的 Isopentane 根本不应堆装在该货舱内，导致泄出易燃气体无法排除。这样的堆装构成不适航，而且是未"克尽职责"。它是导致船/货全损的另一有效/相关的原因，故船东负有责任。

4.2.6.6.1　必须结合预定的货物与航次来考虑

已经提到，适航只是针对预定的货物与航次。这可以按几种不同讲法来表达，例如说适航要求只是"相对"的（relative）。也可以说适航要求不应吹毛求疵，不应过分,而应完全根据具体的实际情况来考虑。

在笔者1982年出版的《提单》一书,第42页对此曾作了比喻,笔者至今仍十分满意,不妨介绍如下:

> 以一个日常生活的例子说明:有人请教你道:"请问出门旅行应带备些什么衣物呢?"你会怎样回答呢？难吗？一个头脑清醒的人在回答这个问题之前必先要对方说得具体一点。例如:目的地是什么地方？途中经过些什么地方？……否则他无法回答。你是准备到非洲猎大象呢,还是到瑞士阿尔卑斯山滑雪呢？是到地中海享受阳光呢,还是要攀登喜马拉雅山呢？是到澳门两日游呢,还是坐豪华邮船作环球旅行呢？根据每一个不同的具体情况都可能得出不同的答复,这是一个日常生活的例子,但用于适航的要求亦同此理。对不同的航线有着不同的具体要求,我们不能要求一艘渡轮要具备行走四大洲五大洋的能力才算适航。同样并不能以此航线的标准来要求彼航线的船舶,而只能具体地以该轮预定行走的航线作为制订适航标准的准绳。以一个较具体的例子来说:一艘远洋货轮在越洋航程途中,由于无法盖好舱盖,被大浪打上甲板,而这些浪是可预见的,使海水涌入货舱,浸湿了货物,这艘船当然是不适航。但在另一种情况下,若它在行走内河时没盖好舱盖,在绝大多数情况之下是不可能有河水涌入的,但突然间,河中掀起一股莫名的大浪——像这样的大浪在该河道上是少见的,河水打入舱内浸湿货物,该轮是否同样由于没有盖好舱盖而不适航呢？我看这种情况跟上一例子不一样,法庭很有可能接受这一股莫名大浪是属于天灾(Act of God)或海难(Perils of the navigable waters),由于该航道从来都是风平浪静,船舶没有必要经常保持舱盖的密封,亦算是适航,属于天灾或海难所造成的损失船东当然无须负责。若真是因舱盖应盖好没有做到而不适航,等于先决条件没有达到,那就谈不上下一步去以天灾或海难免责了。
>
> 以上是讲航次的相对适航要求,在货物的适货方面,可举一例是针对矿砂、煤炭等货物货舱生锈脱漆无关重要。但针对清洁要求十分高的像散粮、化肥、陶土(China clay)等,同样的货舱会是不适货了。

4.2.6.6.2 不适航类型之一:船员

今天船员素质水平下降已是共知的事实,遇上涉及船员疏忽/过错的事故要打官司,笔者经常不敢想象部分见过的船员如何胜任地应付一个被对方精明的大律师和专家"刨根问底",每一细节或矛盾之处都不放过,绝不容胡混过关的反盘问。这绝不是懂不懂英文的问题,反盘问可以中文通过翻译进行。

现实中，出事故的原因也主要是由于船员疏忽/过错，但要知道，海牙规则下的平衡/妥协是船舶在装港开航前，船东/承运人能管得到，故此他/它应尽一切能力（克尽职责）去做好各方面的适航。满足了这一大前提（先决条件），才能在之后发生的称职船员一时犯错时得到免责。

不妨先列举部分有关先例：

(ⅰ)在 The "Roberta" (1938) 60 Lloyd's Rep. 84，是涉及一位不称职的轮机员错误打开了旋塞，让水渗入货舱损坏了货物。法院判是轮机员没有证书，完全不称职，船东要负责。

(ⅱ)在 The "Makedonia" (1962) 1 Lloyd's Rep. 316，判定大管轮与二管轮不称职，而船东没有在雇用前采取适当步骤去了解他们的水平与经验。

(ⅲ)在 The "Brabant" (1965) 2 Lloyd's Rep. 546，是船员清洁货舱有疏忽而引致货损。

(ⅳ)在美国先例的 Heinrich Horn-Marie Horn, 1968 AMC 2548；(1970) 1 Lloyd's Rep. 191，涉及没有足够的称职人员熟悉如何操作冷藏设备。

(ⅴ)在美国先例的 Liberty Shipping Linm. Procs., 1973 AMC 2241 (W. D. Wash 1973)，涉及船员没有接受防火/灭火的训练。这看来与英国的 The "Star Sea" (1997) 1 Lloyd's Rep. 360 先例有雷同之处。在 The "Star Sea" 先例中，船东没有培训船长/船员了解、掌握对二氧化碳灭火装置的使用，以致他们一无所知，也没去加强救火演习，等等。这导致船长犯上严重错误，灭火时应释放全部二氧化碳却只释放了一半，结果功效大减，无法灭火。

(ⅵ)在美国先例的 Ta Chi Lim Proc. (Eurybates) 513 F. Supp. 148, 1981 AMC 2350 (E. D. La. 1981)，船长犯严重航行错误导致船碰撞后沉没，船货两失。这方面也与英国判例大同小异。英国著名的先例 The "Lady Gwendolen" (1965) 1 Lloyd's Rep. 335，即涉及船长习惯性地在雾中超速，船东的总管犯错没有去警觉并作出纠正。事故是雾中超速发生碰船，从"克尽职责"令船舶适航的要求看，船东显然未做到。另在 The "Eurysthenes" (1976) 2 Lloyd's Rep. 171，船舶搁浅导致货损，对船东的其中一项指控是驾驶员不足。

(ⅶ)在 The "Ert Stefanie" (1989) 1 Lloyd's Rep. 349，船舶装的是一种极其危险的硅铁(ferro silicon)，遇水即挥发出毒气。半途中，货舱进水，导致船员死亡、船舶绕航及最终放弃了航次。判是船舶不适航，其中的一项不适航就是船长对这种危险品一无所知，而船东也没有去指导他。

(ⅷ)在 The "Safe Carrier" (1994) 1 Lloyd's Rep. 589，涉及大管轮根本没有时间去熟悉、了解机器/主机船就开航了。今天船舶停港时间短，更换船员时常会有此危险。

从以上各先例可见，船员方面的问题也不光是持有一张合格证书就足以"打遍天下"的，而是有关船员本人实质上要有专业水平，素质高，受过所有方面的培训（包括法律方面），有足够的指示，等等。

4.2.6.6.3 不适航类型之二：适货

4.2.6.6.3.1 船舶设计与设备方面

适航包括了适货，而光是适货针对面已是很广。会涉及技术性很高的争议，当然也有不少只凭常识已可判断。适货固然是包括该船舶、船型、货舱与设备适合装运这预定的货物。任意挑几个案例或例子作为介绍如下：

（i）在 The "Gudermes"（1993）1 Lloyd's Rep. 311 先例，涉及船上油温太低，而货舱没有加温设备，导致在意大利卸港（Ravenna）无法卸下货油。该卸港靠长 13 公里的海底管道卸油上岸，管道也没有加热设备，所以过于低温的燃油（货物）一卸下，会马上塞死管道。结果该案中解决办法是把"Gudermes"轮的低温燃油转去另一有加温设备的船舶（"Sea Oath"），然后加热再卸上 Ravenna。

这也令笔者想到近期一案件所涉及的像糖酱或棕油等的货物，运载的船舶也必须要有很清洁并配有良好加温设备的货舱，否则在寒冷的冬天去预定卸港，会因无法维持温度（40℃/105℃）而带来同样的困难。

（ii）在 4.2.6.3 小段已详论过的 The "Apastolis"（1996）1 Lloyd's Rep. 475 一案的一审判决也有涉及货舱无二氧化碳灭火装置的"老龄"船舶去装运易燃的棉花是否属不适航的问题。

（iii）笔者记得曾遇到过这样的争议，即没有冷冻设备但通风良好的船舶是否适航去装运香蕉，行走一预定的短航次。

4.2.6.6.3.2 不污染预定货物/清洁方面

4.2.6.6.3.2.1 干散货

这方面的问题，随着做法的改良或技术的进步，也常在变化。例如散粮，笔者很久以前常听说诸如货被堆装在深水舱受到污染等的事故。随着专门为装散粮设计的散货船出现，另在美加，澳大利亚等主要装港都有十分严格的装货前验（货）舱程序，这方面的事故（散粮受污染）现在已很少听见。有关美国港口对散粮装船前的严格检查，由美国农业部（U.S.D.A.）负责的部分细节，笔者的《期租合约》一书 8.2 段有详述。

但其他品种的货物，并没有一套良好的预防/预先检查方法，或者也不易检查，因此仍常会出毛病，导致船舶不适货。

在 The "Good Friend"（1984）2 Lloyd's Rep. 586 先例，船装了木材与 6000 吨袋装的"豆渣"（soya bean meal）从加拿大去古巴的哈瓦那。在卸港，发觉豆渣受两种害虫（各为 Trogoderma variable 与 Latheticus oryzae）污染，当局禁止卸货，结果船要另

去其他港口把货物处理掉/毁掉。

在听取了所有证据后,包括像"Cood Friend"轮以前走的航次及其所装运的货物,熏舱情况等,法院判害虫应是由货舱内以前余下的货物所滋生,而不是由本航次货物(不论是木材或豆渣)带上船的。Staughton 大法官说:"…on the evidence as a whole, it was distinctly more probable that there was infestation on board the vessel before loading began;[500] the owner had accordingly failed to establish a defence of inherent vice[501] and the cause of the prohibition on discharge[502] was the condition of the vessel before loading….

there were substantial residues from previous cargoes in the thinking in No. 2 tween-deck and on the balance of probabilities those residues were infested before loading with Trogoderma variable,[503] and were the major cause of the trouble which the vessel encountered…the undertaking of seaworthiness…included under cargoworthiness an undertaking that the vessel should be reasonably fit to receive and carry the cargo and deliver it at the specified destination;[504] if the vessel's condition was such that she was not reasonably fit for those tasks, the undertaking was broken…"

另再举一些近年的例子,如发生在化肥的货物,就有一些农业国家(主要像澳大利亚,也包括中国大陆)一发现船上货舱有以前剩余的散粮,当局就拒卸整批货物,生怕散粮滋生的 Kernel bug 害虫混进化肥内,而将该批化肥用在该国的农业耕种会带来大灾难。笔者记得一二年前中国为此曾拒绝了好几条船,迫使部分货物被转卖去不怕这问题的国家如马来西亚或印尼等。这同类的事故近月仍听闻了一宗,是在澳大利亚被拒卸的。

4.2.6.6.3.2.2 湿散货

讲了干的散货,再去谈谈湿的散货,这主要是石油产品,但也可括其他的液体货物如"甲醇"(methanol),"苛性钠"(caustic soda),"棕油"(palm oil),等等。它们的受污染的案件也不少,原因往往是货舱,管道,船上抽油机/泵等没有清洁妥,以前的货物尚未清洗。例如,近期的 The "Liepaya"(1999)1 Lloyd's Rep. 649 先例,即涉及 1 万吨的 caustic soda 被以往航次装运过的 palm oil 所污染。

但照理说,今天特别是涉及石油产品,总会在装货前先由发货人安排检查货舱

---

[500] 从证据看来开装前船上已出现生虫。

[501] 虫害不像是豆渣货物本身带上船的(而如果那是事实,这会是货物本身的内在缺陷造成事故,船东可去免责)。

[502] 在古巴被禁卸货的主因在于船上不适货。

[503] 害虫应是由以前余下的货物所滋生。

[504] 适航包括适货,适货包括可以妥善接受货物并安全运至目的地卸货及交货,做不到就是不适货。

(船上油柜),满意后才开始装,这是油码头的一贯做法。这一来,如果整套做法完善,会像散粮船经 U. S. D. A. 或 N. C. B. (National Cargo Bureau)严格检验后,确认货舱清洁及货物不受污染后才准许开始装货,从而就会大幅度减少这种事故。但笔者感觉两者仍不能相比,原因会是:

(ⅰ)货舱(船上油柜)可以看见,但船上管道、抽油机/泵等隐蔽之处无法看见。

(ⅱ)即使看得见之处,也会是十分粗糙地凭肉眼看看就算。

(ⅲ)个别货物运量不多以及世界装港太多,没有政府当局去制定一套检验方式/程序,由富经验的检验师执行。

当然也会有更保险的做法/检查办法逐步发展起来,如针对一些不能受丝毫污染的货物,会在买卖合约就约定所有货舱(油柜)装了1尺后要先停装,然后所有货舱取一个综合样本化验看看货物有否受污染(同时卖方看看是否有"货不对板"),如没有才继续装,这一来,如果船上油管等隐蔽处导致污染,会被马上发觉,并可在装港就地解决问题,如换上另一批清洁货物。例如在 The "Athenian Harmony"(1998) 2 Lloyd's Rep. 410,涉及飞机油(jet kerosene)运输,就有类似要求如下:"After one foot loaded in all tanks. loading to be stopped for analysis on key tests (colour, gum, wism, flash, S9) and loading to be continued if no sign of contamination."

做得这样保险小心,坏处是会浪费不少时间(化验样本等)。另外对发货人也不大有利,因为像信用证等的结汇都有时限。所以发货人最怕货舱不清洁,化验不合格(off spec)等问题导致无法如期装妥货物,签发提单。

现实中上一航次的剩余货物未被清洗而污染了下一票货物的情况时有所闻。当然,以前装运清洁石油产品而这次装运秽油/重油(dirty oil),就不会有受污染的危险。但以前装运重油之后却改装清洁石油产品,那么即使是多次洗舱,仍会有污染危险,这就像 The "Gippsland"(1994) 1 Lloyd's Rep. 335 先例。

这方面可以举一些近期的著名先例如下:

(ⅰ)The "Fiona"(1994) 2 Lloyd's Rep. 506,涉及燃油货物被上一航次剩余下的"凝结油"(condensate cargo)污染而引起爆炸。有关事故的主因/近因,Diamond 大法官说:"Having thus identified the various causes of the explosion I turn to consider, in case it be relevant, which of these causes had the greatest efficacy in bringing about the explosion.[505] Of the various causes I have identified, viz the condensate contamination, the leaking heating coils, the use of the unearthed thermometer, the shipment of the fuel oil cargo, I have no hesitation in concluding that the dominant or most efficient cause of the explosion was the contamination of the fuel oil in tank 1 by residues of the previous

---

[505] 要找出爆炸的主因/近因。

condensate cargo[506]... The failure to remove condensate residues from the vessel, and in particular the failure to carry out a proper line and duct wash at Rotterdam before loading commenced,[507] constituted a breach by the owners of their duty under art. Ⅲ, r. 1 to exercise due diligence to make the ship seaworthy and to make the holds and all other parts of the ship in which goods are carried fit and safe for their reception carriage and preservation.[508] It follows that the dominant cause of the explosion was a breach by the owners of art. Ⅲ, r. 1[509]."

（ⅱ）已提及的 The "Athenian Harmony"（1998）2 Lloyd's Rep. 410 先例，涉及飞机油（jet kerosene）被上一航次装运的燃油所污染。开装前，大副对检验师所讲的每一货舱（油柜）已用"溶剂"（solvent）清洗再加热水冲洗了 1.5 小时，并不属实。

（ⅲ）在笔者的《国际商务仲裁》一书第十一章之 7.5 小段曾举了一个有趣的仲裁案例，不妨节录如下：

> 当事人的专家证人一般不会说谎，只是各为其主，意见的侧重点有所不同。但如果有开庭审理，有水平（competent）的对方大律师的反盘问往往可以让仲裁员看到一位专家证人避重就轻之处，进而分得出意见的强弱。在反盘问时，一方大律师往往有己方的专家在旁提点应去问什么专业的问题。
>
> 特别是在对一些仲裁员本人也不懂的专业，一位专家的真正水平，对他作证的事情是否真正了解，以及能否对尖锐的反盘问作出合理回答，会对仲裁员的决定起非常重要的作用。

在这里可举两个例子。第一个是关于一条油船的货物——煤油（kerosene），在卸货时发现颜色转变（discoloration），这自然带来货物污染（contamination）的索赔。双方争辩的变色原因是：

（ⅰ）承租人（货主）自然是指船的油柜（tank）不清洁，是不适航，不适货（uncargoworthy），船东在海牙规则下（合并进租约）要负责。

（ⅱ）船东称是煤油本身不稳定（unstable）引致变色，所以是货物的内在缺陷（inherent vice）所引致。

一般来说，这种案子对船东都不利，货物明明是出了清洁提单，但卸下时颜色

---

[506] 有好几个可能的原因：货物（燃油）本身有问题，加热管道破漏，计温器没有接地/接船壳，等等。判是受上一航次的凝结油污染，进而引起爆炸，才是主因/近因。

[507] 应是在装港开装前没有把管道清洗。

[508] 这是不适航的不适货。

[509] 不适货导致爆炸，是主因/近因。

大变,这就要船东来好好解释了。

在该案,双方都有专家。而船东的专家合情合理地解释了该船在上三航次装运的货物都是"汽油"(gasoil),所以技术上不可能仍会有未洗净的油柜、油管,令这次装运煤油受到任何污染。而承租人的专家却无法去反驳,去举证说明如何在刚装运过三次汽油后,仍会有可能及什么可能令煤油污染。

另外,对引起变色的可能,船东专家也能合情合理,引经据典地证明在20世纪30年代炼油技术不完善时常有煤油本身不稳定而自动变色的情况。这种情况虽在近代不经常发生,但从这批货物化验的高硫醇(high mercaptar)、高酸值(high acid number)与高焦炭(high char)数据,可证明货物本身有问题,提炼不好,因而引致自动变色。对这些争论,承租人的专家也是无法反驳或充分解释。裁决的结果应可想而知。

4.2.6.6.3.2.3　发货人或承租人的检验师验定货舱适货的后果

既然许多货物(干湿散货)开装前都会涉及先要让检验师检查满意,那么之后若仍有货物受污染,这会对船东/承运人在海牙规则下"克尽职责"令船舶适航的义务有何影响呢?

首先,若检验师是由船东/承运人雇用,那么他的疏忽/过失一样属于船东/承运人没有"克尽职责":请看本章4.2.6.4小段之The "Muncaster Castle" (1961) 1 Lloyd's Rep. 57先例。

而换一种情况,若检验师是发货人或承租人指派的(如装运石油产品),情况可否有所改变?在The "Giamla M" (1937) 57 Lloyd's Rep. 247,涉及租约有一条款允许承租人先去检查满意。事实上,在开装"汽油"(benzine)前,检验师也的确对货舱情况满意,但汽油仍受到污染。上诉庭判定适航及适货责任是基本与重大的,不是一句话让承租人先去检查满意就可以超越的,合约应整体作解释,所以适航适货责任仍然存在。承租人只是在条款中多了一项检查的权利,希望以此预防事故,这并不等于要替代船东的责任。

这是以租船合约的情况,而不少油轮租约也常有类似条款,如著名的 ASBATANKVOY 租约格式的第18条说:"Cleaning: The Owner shall clean the tanks, pipes and pumps of the vessel to the satisfaction of the charterer's Inspector."

换了是提单合约,这种事情不大会发生在班轮业务,因它在今天多数是集装箱运输。这种事情总是发生在租船业务,尤其是油轮租约。这一来,提单合约总有机会去合并租约,导致租约像 ASBATANKVOY 的第18条也并入了租约提单。但这并不影响船东"克尽职责"使船舶适航/适货的先决条件,这应是很明确的,原因在于:

(ⅰ)这本是整体解释合约得出的结果:见 The "Gianna M"先例的判决。

(ⅱ)海牙规则不强制适用在租约,但强制适用在提单。而海牙规则是不允许船东/承运人减轻其责任/义务的。因此,如果说这合并的第 18 条可以豁免与取代了船东/承运人"克尽职责"令船舶适航适货的义务,在海牙规则强制适用下是说不通的。

但船东/承运人或许仍会感到不服气,毕竟确实是发货人或/与承租人的检验师检查满意后才开装的,出了事故却只去怪船东似乎并不公道。一讲到不公道,自然会想到弃权与禁止翻供的说法。有关这一课题,笔者的《国际商务游戏规则——英国合约法》一书第十一章有详论,内容太多,无法节录。但这说法难以套用在提单合约,因为它是衡平法,处处要顾及公道。而如此套用会造成不公道导致弃权/禁止翻供难以成立的理由是:(a)套用此说法去针对的对象一般是收货人(索赔货损的原告),他常会被称为无辜的第三者。不如对象是发货人时,船东/承运人会可以反驳说发货人的检验师已检查并满意,怎能什么责任也不负,只去怪责船东呢?面对收货人时,以同样的话去反驳可就说不通了。加上考虑到要保护提单制度的可靠性,可信性,怎能以发货人在装港所做的事(检查货舱)去责怪收货人,说他已弃权/禁止翻供呢?(b)再说,即使针对检查本身,大家也是明知会无法看见船舶管道及船泵内部的清洁状况,而发生污染却常来自这方面,所以怎能出了事故就赖在一个无法完全肯定的检查上面呢?

4.2.6.6.3.2.4 仲裁实例介绍

作为对以上所有段节的总结,可以介绍笔者经历的一次仲裁。该仲裁涉及一份租约提单,货物是称为"MIDW Bottoms"的基础油,经加工成滑油再出售。它是美孚石油公司的产品,中国大陆是其主要市场。案中涉及一批 MIDW Bottoms 从新加坡装运至南京,卖方租了一艘一向装运重油(dirty oil)的油轮去履约。该船上一航次装的是"碳黑原料油"(carbon black feedstock),它有很强的粘着力,不易清洗。船东专家声称用热海水洗 1 个小时即可将其洗净,但货方专家认为不用溶剂无法彻底清洗。显然,证据显示(船东自己也承认)货舱只用热海水洗了 1 个小时就去装 MIDW Bottoms 了。

在新加坡开装前,发货人的独立检验人 SGS 检查货舱(油柜)后表示满意,但在证书上说明"管道与船泵已清洗只是据大副所说"(pumps and lines are said to be clean and dry by the chief officer)。

船舶到了南京,卸货前取了样本,拿去与装港样本一比较,马上发现颜色大变,一黑一白。化验结果是货物受到上一航次的碳黑原料油污染。收货人于是提出索赔并扣船,这最终带来仲裁。

在笔者看来,这种案子不难处理,提单有首要条款,双方也同意是以海牙规则为准。而且,表面看来案情对船东不利,都会是要船东举证。

船东不否认污染是在船上造成,但提出了许多争议点诸如:

（ⅰ）MIDW Bottoms 属秽油/重油，不是清洁油，所以不应怪船东只以重油标准洗舱。

（ⅱ）若 MIDW Bottoms 是清洁油，承租人实在不应去租用该轮，因明知它是重油船。

（ⅲ）船东的洗舱已被 SGS 检查认可，船东已是"克尽职责"。

对笔者而言，以上争议只是在枝节上挑毛病，或意图去转移视线。笔者粗略的观点是：(a)提单合并租约并非是所有租约条款都会合并进来，所以有关租错船舶之争（其实租约中也没有有关条款），根本不能并到提单合约中，怎可以此来抗辩收货人/提单持有人的索赔呢？（b）MIDW Bottoms 属重油或清洁油毫无关系，MIDW Bottoms 已清楚写明在提单及租约内是预定的货物，反正适航适货都要针对它。船东不了解这种货物的实际要求就应去了解清楚，毕竟一无所知也是不适航的一种。(c)SGS 的检查满意不能简单化地算作是船东已"克尽职责"，况且 SGS 也说明最可能造成污染的管道与船泵的有关状况只是听大副所说。

但以上各点在仲裁庭内也有不同意见，讨论了很久才能最后定调。所以现实中，一个看来简单的货损案件也会变得复杂混乱。

4.2.6.6.4 不适航类型之三：货舱舱盖水密

舱盖漏水导致货损经常发生，据知这方面的索赔占船东互保协会所有货损货差索赔 15% 多。笔者曾在伦敦一个会议上听说，世界上有高达 40% 多的船舶舱盖因保养不善而漏水或不够水密。

老式舱盖是以一条条钢铁拱梁为框架，然后在上面铺上一块块木板，再在上面铺上 2 层至 3 层油布，最后在四周用木楔（wooden wedge）把油布稳住。这种做法也颇为可靠，通常能保持水密。但缺点是太慢，太耗费人力，往往装完货后要 10 多个船员一起花上大量时间才能做妥，而且工作危险，特别是在横梁上走动去铺上木板。所以今天几乎已完全淘汰。

现今替代的做法是船舶都装置了全钢材与机动的舱盖，它以油压或电力来开关舱盖，十分快捷安全，完全替代了人力的操作。生产这种"钢舱盖"（steel hatch-cover）最出名的厂家是美国的 MacGregor 公司，所以钢舱盖现已被统称为"MacGregor 舱盖"了。钢舱盖也有不同的设计和型号，这可以 The "Sabine Howaldt"（1971）2 Lloyd's Rep. 78 先例中的钢舱盖为例，它谈道："MacGregor hatch covers are composed of joined steel sections of the 'single-pull' type. They are made up of a number of steel panels chained together, each about 5 ft. in length and extending across the width of the hatch.[510] The panels are equipped with rollers so that they may be rolled open and closed

---

[510] 它是由多块钢板组成，每块长约 5 尺，拱跨舱的宽度，各块之间由铁链串起来。

on tracks by means of wire attached to the ship's winches.[511] When the covers are in the closed position, they are lowered from the rollers and presumably made watertight by a rubber gasket or packing fitted around each panel which is compressed tightly between the panel and a knift edge on the hatch coaming or adjoining panel by means of side wedges or clamps and cross-join wedges[512]."

但钢舱盖保养不易,老船更是经常有生锈腐蚀,橡胶衬垫老化/硬化失去弹力而无法再保持水密等问题。而且,装卸作业是粗重工作,过程中常会损坏舱盖。

曾有说法是如果明知预定航次会遇上坏天气,加上货物对海水敏感,应多盖上1层至2层油布更为安全,但这在 The "Sabine Howaldt" 的美国先例被批评是幼稚的做法,因保养得好的钢舱盖根本不需要如此做。

倒是有另一做法笔者曾多次遇过,就是在钢舱盖的接缝处加上一条"绝缘胶布带"(adhesive tape)。

船员常会在每一航次装货前检查舱盖是否水密。检查方法会是以肉眼看有否损坏之处,有否弯曲、水渍,等等。针对水密还会有一种称为"白垩检验"(chalk test)的方法,它是把白垩铺在接缝处然后把舱盖关上再重开,从白垩的双面痕迹可看到接缝处的橡胶衬垫是否仍有弹力和"压缩压力"(compression)。

更仔细的方法会是以高压水喉向舱盖接缝处射水,然后开舱看看有否漏水。

但这些检查水密的方法都无法设计出这样一种境况,就是船舶若真遇上大风浪引致严重拱摇(rolling)或/与前后摇(pitching),造成船体产生扭力(torsion),钢舱盖因此变型而导致海水渗入的情况。

这正如在 The "Sabine Howaldt" 先例所提到的:"MacGregor hatch covers, if properly maintained, will not, under almost all foreseeable circumstances, raise and lower above the coaming. They should prevent the entrance of sea water under almost all foreseeable sea and wind conditions. However, no suitable means have yet been found to completely seal a hatch so as to provide absolute insurance against the entry of sea water under every possibte combination of circumstances. Conceivably, an extremely severe storm of prolonged duration could so affect a vessel having the architectural characteristics of the vessel as to place so severe a strain upon properly maintained MacGregor hatch covers that the jerking, shaking and vibration pounding by and submersion in green seas, could over-

---

[511] 钢板下有滚轮,开关舱盖时只要把一端的钢索接上船舶的绞车/起货机再用力一拉,所有钢板就会滚动至开或关的位置。

[512] 关舱时,钢板拉到所在位置即会放下,它本身的重量加上周围的橡胶衬垫压在"舱口围板"(hatch coaming)上,再用上楔子(wedge),夹子(clamps)等,应可保证水密。

come such hatch covers to the point of leakage."

The "Sabine Howaldt"先例就是少见的几个少数案例之一,判是舱盖渗水但船舶并没有在开航时不适航(这一来再不必再追问船东有否"克尽职责"了),因此船东可以海难免责。该案例的事实是:

（ⅰ）船舶在冬季横越大西洋,从欧洲去美国遇上12级风浪。

（ⅱ）船舶只有约3500吨载重量,但是7年的"新"船,保养良好,船东是德国船东(可能会有印象上的分别),船出事故不久前才刚被著名的德国船级社检验(包括舱盖)并通过。

（ⅲ）事故(遇上大风浪)同时导致船舶甲板多处受损,这会是说明风浪确实巨大的事实证据。

（ⅳ）船长／大副对钢舱盖不断有检查钢舱盖并在航海日志对此作了书面记录。例如开航前检查舱盖无恙后在航海日志写上:"Seaworthy, closed and wedged"。但即使是如此的"事实",船东也在第一审败诉,只是后来在上诉中才变为是胜诉。一审败诉是由于法官认为德国船长曾故意夸大坏天气,实际当时应没有12级风。原因之一是航海日志中的记录比船长口供所讲的风级较低,有矛盾。另是大副被反盘问时曾说过一句"这是阵风,不是飓风"(winds were gusts and not hurricanes)。

4.2.6.6.5 不适航类型之四:船舶稳性,货物堆装,绑扎方面

货物堆装不妥会影响适航,也会只影响货物本身。这一点很早以前在 The "Grelwen (1924) 18 Lloyd's Rep. 319 先例曾被贵族院提到,Sumner 勋爵也为此说了以下名言:"Bad stowage, which endangers the safety of the ship, may amount to unseaworthiness, of course, but bad stowage which affects nothing but the cargo damaged by it is bad stowage and nothing more, and still leaves the ship seaworthy for the adventure, even though the adventure be the carrying of that cargo."

想一想这也是常识。若是把有异味的杂货堆装在食物旁边(这种事故在今天的集装箱运输已不会再发生),这"堆装不妥"(bad stowing)不会与适航有关。去举一个实在的例子,在加拿大法院的 C. E. Crippen v. Vancouver Tug Boat Co. Ltd. (1971) 2 Lloyd's Rep. 207,涉及只应堆装3层高的"货盘"(pallet)却堆装了4层高,这导致倒塌与货损,这也明显与船舶适航无关。但在本章之4.2.6.6小段的 The "Kapitan Sakharov" (2000) 2 Lloyd's Rep. 255,该集装箱堆装不妥却是与不适航完全有关。

会与适航有关的另一个典型例子是"堆装不妥"(bad stowing)影响船舶稳性。这种情况会发生在集装箱运输,对此已在本章4.2.3.5.3.9.1小段详论并提到了 The "Bunga Seroja" (1994) 1 Lloyd's Rep. 455 先例,它的上诉曾在(1999) 1 Lloyd's Rep. 512 被报道。

至于非集装箱的例子,可以举 The "Friso" (1980) 1 Lloyd's Rep. 469 先例为例。"Friso"轮是一艘小船,在葡萄牙的 Leixoes 港装木材及酒去英国,木材是堆装在甲板上。半途经过 Biscay 湾,遇上大风浪,船舶突然倾侧至 40 度~50 度,结果船长弃船。但最终该"无人驾驶"的船舶仍被救并被拖至法国的 Brest,拖带前甲板上的木材被抛下大海,以减少倾侧。这造成了不小的货损货差事故,也产生了大笔与救助费用,结果收货人向船东索赔。

船东以"海难"(perils of the sea)为抗辩,指冲上船的海水令甲板上左边木材增加重量(因倾侧是向左边)并与移动导致船倾。船东的专家证人出庭作证说若左边木材吸收了 40% 水分而右边木材只吸收了 3% 水分,加上木材向左边移动了 20 厘米,综合起来已会造成船舶左倾 29 度。

但 Sheen 大法官不接受这个讲法,原因之一是证据显示海水是从各个方向冲上甲板而不光是在左边。原因之二是倾侧不是慢慢形成的,故不像是左边水分重量慢慢积聚。原因之三是甲板上的木材再去吸收水分只能是微量的。

这一来,Sheen 大法官判船东无法成功举证开航前已"克尽职责"令船舶适航。而且船东陷入的困境就是这严重倾侧的主因是甲板上的木材因绑扎不固而严重移动(不是 20 厘米),导致左倾,这已构成不适航(绑扎不固导致的不适航)。若不是此原因,这突然的严重左倾估计便是由于船舶稳性不足,这也是不适航。至于船舶遇上的坏天气,法官判是完全可预见得到,所以不属海难的免责。

另在本章之 4.2.6.4.3 小段,也举了涉及类似事故的 The "Tilia Gorthon" (1985) 1 Lloyd's Rep. 55 先例,不再重复。至于美国类似的先例有"Anthony Ⅱ"(1966) 2 Lloyd's Rep. 437。

在 William Tetley 教授的《Marine Cargo Claims》一书第 3 版之第 386 页还提到另一种"微妙"的情况,就是船舶先后在 A、B 两港装货。在 A 港开航时,船舶只有半载,也没有不适航之处。到了 B 港加载货物后,却令船舶失去稳性。这一来,自 B 港开航后发生事故,对 B 港装的货物船东难逃责任,因为适航这一先决条件没有达到,但 A 港装的货物并不受 B 港发生的不适航影响。而 B 港的不适航涉及船舶稳性(虽是堆装不妥或绑扎不固导致),这正是船长、船员管船疏忽的免责,船东可以此成功抗辩。

4.2.6.6.6 不适航类型之五:燃油数量与质量

显然,开航前燃油数量(加上安全系数以防航次延长)足够与燃油质量良好是适航的要求之一。但早期的燃料是煤炭,若要足够供应一漫长的航次,会是没有办法(主要是载重方面)再去装足够的货物。所以,一向做法是"分段加油"(bunkering by stages),即一步步分阶段在航次的中途港补充燃料(煤炭)。这也是英国普通法所承认的、接受的; Mc Iver & Co. Ltd. v. Tate Steamers Ltd. (1903) 1 K.B. 362; The

第五章　提单作用之二：运输合约下的货损货差责任　435

"Newbrough"(1939) 64 Lloyd's Rep. 33。当然，在每一中途港开航，普通法也要求船舶要绝对或严格地适航，这在本章之4.2.6.5小段已详述。

今天船舶的燃料不再是煤炭而换了是燃油，但仍有不少情况是船舶要去中途港补充燃油。这或许是因为装港没有足够燃油供应，或是价钱太贵，或是航次很长若多装了燃油就少装了货物，等等。

好的法律应配合实际，所以一向的说法是只要有妥善与良好的燃油补充计划去完成整个航次，这样分段加油并不影响适航。不要求船舶在装港开航时已存有整个航次的燃油在船上。普通法的地位固然如此，海牙规则也是这样。在The "Makedonia"(1962) 1 Lloyd's Rep. 316 先例，针对海牙规则（加拿大海上运输法1936），Hewson 大法官说道："…the obligation on shipowners was to exercise due diligence before and at beginning of sailing from loading port to have vessel adequately bunkered for first stage and to arrange for adequate bunkers at intermediate ports so that voyage could be performed; that that obligation as to bunkering included provision of feed water…"

4.2.6.6.6.1　燃油数量、质量方面的不适航会引起怎样的货损货差

不妨先去解释一下这方面的问题，因为读者或许会问：怀疑燃油不足或质量不妥会带来怎样的货损货差？答案会是：

（i）燃油问题会带来船在半途中失去动力，导致要拖轮救助及产生共同海损费用，要收货人去分摊，这就类同于货损货差的损失了，为此收货人可向船东追索或拒付（后者的情况是船东先垫付了费用再向收货人追付分摊部分）：The "Evje"(No. 2)(1978) 1 Lloyd's Rep. 351。

（ii）失去动力，带来延误，有些品种的货物会损坏，例如水果肉食。在The "Fjord Wind"(1999) 1 Lloyd's Rep. 307，涉及2万多吨的散装"大豆"(soya bean)，本是一个月的航次拖长至5个月，导致大豆严重发霉，这也是典型的货损货差。

（iii）失去动力，带来延误，会令某些品种的货物失去了市场/季节，这在英国法律下亦算是货损货差：The "Heron II"(1967) 2 Lloyd's Rep. 457。

4.2.6.6.6.2　燃油质量差：在装港与在中途港对适航影响的分别

燃油质量差是今天普遍的问题，主因是炼油技术提高以及炼油商追求最大的利润。今天一桶原油已能被更多地提炼为更高价的产品油，令剩余下来可提炼的燃油比例降低，进而使这较少量的燃油内含一桶原油中更多的杂质。这一来，可以想象同是一吨的燃油在今天内含的杂质比一二十年前的多得多了。这些杂质会导致机器损坏进而令船舶失去动力或造成事故，也可能导致原来以为数量足够的燃油变得不足够，因为供应的燃油内含太高水分或"热值"(calorific value)不足。

若在装港供应燃油而其质量不妥导致后来出事故造成货损货差，这会是不适

航,而且船东/承运人责任难逃。即使他/它本身没有犯错,也极难控制其雇员、代理及合同方等,而"克尽职责"要延伸至这所有有关的人都"尽了责",如化验燃油的船级社/实验室,燃油供应商等:请看本章之4.2.6.4.1小段等。

但去了中途港补充燃油,若其质量不妥导致开航后出了事故,因海牙规则的适航责任只是针对提单装港而已,故不再适用。这与普通法的地位不同,即此时船舶不算不适航。这方面与前面4.2.6.5.1.小段所讲的情况是同一精神/原则。而根据不同的事实,船东/承运人这时可以成功依赖像"内在缺陷"或海牙规则Article 4 (2)(q)项等去免责。

4.2.6.6.6.3 有关先例介绍

前文已提到过的The "Newbrough"(1938)64 Lloyd's Rep. 33先例(4.2.6.4与4.2.6.6.6小段)与The "Makedonia"(1962)1 Lloyd's Rep. 316先例(4.2.6.5.2与4.2.6.6.小段),都涉及燃油方面。在此只对著名的The "Evje"(No. 2)(1978)1 Lloyd's Rep. 351先例作一详细介绍,反正这类事故的事实往往都是大同小异。

"Evje"轮在美国波特兰装了一船小麦开出,计划中途在日本横滨补充燃油后再往印度的卸港。但在正常天气下,船舶在尚有2天才抵达横滨时已耗尽所有燃油,失去动力,被迫请求救助并被拖带去横滨。收货人拒绝分摊共同海损,指船舶在美国装港开航时已不适航。不适航处有几方面:(1)把不适合不相配的燃油混合在一起;(2)船上有一个燃油管道阀/开关坏了;(3)船舶超载导致多耗油;(4)燃油质量不适合主机以及数量不足。Donaldson大法官判(1)至(3)项的不适航指控不成立。(1)项即使是事实,船东也已"克尽职责",因为这混合是无法知悉的。(2)项即使是事实,也不会引致多耗油。(3)项下船确有少许超载,虽是不适航,但不会造成耗油过多,故没有因果关系。这些都可以精密计算出来,且有专家作证,不能蒙混过关。只是(4)项,Donaldson大法官和上诉庭均同意是事实,且船东也没有去"克尽职责"令船舶适航。如在计算燃油的足够数量方面,船东、船长显然有错误。

波特兰与横滨之间的距离是4400海里(大圆航线)或4600海里。船长第一个错误是以4400海里计算燃油需求,但船舶真正航行的却是恒向航线。

第二个错误是以船速13节计算,而事实上因为逆流,船速只能达到12.5节。

另外还有像错误估计船上存油量等,导致开航时已是燃油不足构成不适航,而船长的错误自然算是船东没有"克尽职责"了。

4.2.6.6.7 不适航类型之六:船上供应

上一段详论的燃油,实际是船上供应的主要一项。但船东对船上的供应远不止这一项。当然,上百上千种供应中,也不是每一项都与是否适航扯得上关系。例如,供应洋酒香烟给船员。但仍有不少项目的供应不妥会构成不适航,且会导致事故带来货损货差。例如,在The "Agios Vlasios"(1965)2 Lloyd's Rep. 204,就涉及船东没有供应盖舱的油布，导致在卸港下雨时来不及关舱而让雨水损坏了大米的货物。

一项经常会与不适航扯上关系的供应是海图、航海通告及其他有关航行安全的刊物。使用过时的海图十分危险，会导致船舶搁浅，碰撞，下锚损坏海底油管/电缆等严重的事故。有关这方面的先例也不少，如《Marine Cargo Claims》一书之第 383 页就举了不少美国的先例，如：Calif. and Hawaiian S. Corp. v. Columbia SS CO. 1973 AMC 676；American Smelting v. Irish Spruce 1977 AMC 780（2 Cir. 1977）；Consolidated Mining v. Straits Towing Ltd（1972）F. C. 804；Temple Bar 1942 AMC 1125（D. Md. 1942）；Heddernheim 1941 AMC 730（SDNY 1941）；Aakre 1941 AMC 1263（2 Cir. 1941）；Iristo 1943 AMC 1043（2 Cir. 1943），等等。

英国这方面案例也不少，随便挑几个著名的有：搁浅触礁的 The "Norman"（1960）1 Lloyd's Rep. 1；The "Eurysthenes"（1976）2 Lloyd's Rep. 171；损坏海底电缆/油管的 The "Marion"（1984）2 Lloyd's Rep. 1 等。

4.2.6.6.8　不适航类型之七：船舶历史

船舶的历史导致它可能在航次中被扣押也会变为对船舶不适航的指控，这在《Marine Cargo Claims》一书第 3 版之第 388 页有提到说："A ship is not seaworthy if, when it sails, it is susceptible of being arrested and there is no system in place of quickly providing a bond such as is normally provided by a protection and indemnity club（P & I Club）."

为支持以上观点，该书作者 William Tetley 教授举了美国先例的 Morrisey v. S. S. A. & J. Faith, 252 F. Supp 54, 1966 AMC 71。

也有英国判例认同这一说法：在 The "Maestro Giorgis"（1983）1 Lloyd's Rep. 66，船舶被扣押也被说成是与船舶本身的历史有关。Lloyd 大法官判事故的原因是："directly attributable to the history, if not the condition of this particular vessel"。在这说法下，船舶很容易被迫究为不适航。而今天在营运的船舶，谁敢说绝对不会有人去扣押？这一来，岂非每艘船舶的历史都会令其变为不适航？当然，这不适航不一定会造成损害后果，如船东互保协会能很快提供保函放船。但这也难说，因为不少扣押与互保协会无关。这一来，被扣时间一长而船舶仍在中途港（如在卸港被扣应不会影响卸货），就会导致航次延误，进而带来像本章 4.2.6.6.6.1 小段介绍的货损货差类型。

说到船舶的历史，也令笔者想到一宗仲裁案件——The "Nan Fung" 1988（伦敦仲裁），它涉及在美国装上化肥的一条船舶被拒绝进高雄港卸货，因为该船舶曾经直航大陆港口，所以进了黑名单。这导致要另外安排把货物转港/转船，损失重大。

4.2.6.6.9 不适航类型的总结

经常会发生的不适航主要是在船舶主机,辅助机器(发电机泵、锅炉等)及设备等方面。对此笔者不准备多作介绍。这方面不少的案例涉及冗长且复杂的技术方面的争议,没有专家协助外行人难下判断。若真要为此去详述几个有关的著名先例,恐怕也够出版另一本书了。所以笔者在此只好略过,只强调一点是虽有船东举证"克尽职责"成功的例子[如 4.2.6.4.3 小段介绍的 The "Amstelslot"(1963)2 Lloyd's Rep. 223 先例],但很大部分仍是失败的例子。

所以有一定数量的案例是船东/承运人承认不适航及未尽"克尽职责"之责,但又以"纯技术性"(purely technical)的理由来抗辩货损货差的索赔。这种"纯技术性"的理由一度主要是质疑原告收货人的"诉权"(title to sue),如 The "Kapetan Markos"(1987)2 Lloyd's Rep. 321。有关"诉权"的问题,本书第三章之 1.2.2.4.4 小段曾有详论,而随着第三章之 12.2.5 小段详述的 1992 年海上运输法(1992 COGSA)在英国立法生效,也少了这种纯技术性争议的借口,导致船舶不适航下船东对货损货差负责的机会大增。

4.2.7 举证第四步:船东/承运人证明免责

在本章之 4.2.2 小段,提到这是第四步的举证责任,这责任也仍在船东/承运人身上。读者或许会想:作为先决条件的"克尽职责"令船舶适航这一关船东都这么难通过,再考虑下一步很可能是无关的免责有必要,有意义吗?答案是:

(ⅰ)仍有不少案件与装港开航时船舶适航与否无关。

(ⅱ)即使有关,一有了争议要去诉讼,船东/承运人要抗辩一开始就要面对全部举证,不存在"分段"去抗辩,先对第一、第二步举证,成功证明了他/它在开航前或当时已"克尽职责"令适航后,才在另一次开庭审理时确定哪一项免责可适用。所以船东一去抗辩就要全面考虑到,缺一不可。这一来变得船东/承运人即使对证明适航有把握,但若估计到要依赖任何一项免责并无把握,则这场战事(官司)对他/它来说仍不值得打,故此应争取庭外和解。

4.2.7.1 海牙规则的免责项目

海牙规则在 Article 4(2)列举了从(a)至(q)共 17 项的免责,这各项免责实质内容的具体分析会在接下去的段节详论。

该条款明显属免责条款,因为它一开始就开门见山地说"承运人"(这是针对诉人的 in personam)与船舶(针对诉物的 in rem)不必对如下原因引起或造成的"灭失"(loss)或"损坏"(damage)负责。

如果真有货损货差的实质损失,这当然是"loss or damage"了。但英国法律对"loss or damage"有宽松的解释,即也包括了非实质性的、纯属经济上的损失。例如,在章 4.2.6.6.6.1 小段提及的 The "Heron Ⅱ" (1967) 2 Lloyd's Rep. 457 先例中市场下跌带来的损失。有关这纯经济损失的问题也可以参阅 The "Saxon Star" (1958) 1 Lloyd's Rep. 73。

即使是因为不适航引起的债务,也包括在"loss or damage"这一措辞/文字的含义中:Marifortuna Naviera S. A. v. Government of Ceylon (1970) 1 Lloyd's Rep. 247。

在开始讨论每一项免责前,读者应对解释和分析免责条款的一般原则/精神有所掌握。这些原则/精神在《国际商务游戏规则——英国合约法》一书第十章之 6.3 小段有详论,如"针对规则","同类规则"等。

4.2.7.1.1 免责项目之(a):航行/管船疏忽与过错

这是在海牙规则的 Article 4(2)(a),为方便读者查看,不妨先把这项免责的措辞节录如下:"Act, neglect, or default of the master, mariner, pilot, or the servants of the carrier in the navigation or in the management of the ship."

这带来好几方面的问题需要探讨,例如:

(ⅰ)什么人的行为(act),疏忽(neglect)或过错(default)才是这免责所包括的?

(ⅱ)何谓航行?

(ⅲ)何谓管船?

在详细分析前,先要说明这一项免责在现实中十分重要,因为严重的货损货差经常是来自海上事故如碰撞、搁浅等,而这些事故又往往与航行疏忽/过错有关。

4.2.7.1.1.1 何谓疏忽/过错

这项免责中的"行为"一词应是指不当行为/犯错行为,因为只有如此才会有责任,才需要免责。因此这里的"行为"一词本身并没有增加什么新的内容(不同于本书第六章 2.1. 小段对同样措辞/文字所作出的解释),可以仅针对疏忽/过错的措辞稍作解释。

对构成侵权的疏忽,笔者的《海事法》一书第三章之 2.1 小段有介绍如下:

一般而言,构成疏忽要有如下三个成立要素:

(ⅰ)责任方有一谨慎从事的法定义务(A duty in law to take care)

(ⅱ)责任方违反了这一法定义务(A breach of that duty)

(ⅲ)这导致可预见的损失/损害(Consequential foreseeable damages resulting therefrom)。

另在《Shorter Oxford Dictionary》这本字典中,对疏忽的定义是:"Something incorrectly done through ignorance or inadvertence; a mistake"。(错误与/或不正确地行事,或因无知,或因疏忽/不留心引起)

也有定义指是"错误行为或懈怠(该做而不做)行为"(wrongful act or omission)。

4.2.7.1.1.2 谁的疏忽/过错可去免责

该免责说明只针对船长、船员、引水员以及承运人的雇员,因此要严格去解释,没有列名的人士不能包括在内。甚至是疏忽/过错由列名与不列名的人士共同造成,船东也不能免责。这大原则/大精神类同于本章 4.2.5.5 小段提到的一宗事故可以免责,另一事故则要负责,两宗事故共同造成的损失无法区分时则船东就要全部负责的道理。故在 Minister of Food v. Reardon Smith Line (1951) 1 Lloyd's Rep. 265, McNair 大法官说:"…if the damage was caused partly by the chief officer's negligence and partly by the negligence of the repairers' men, that would not give the shipowners the protection they seek…a finding of joint negligence by two persons, one being within the exception and the other without, would disentitle the shipowner to rely upon the exception…"

船东/承运人本人的疏忽/过错即使不是发生在开航前的适航方面而是发生在航行中,也不包括在免责内,除非他本人恰巧就是船长/船员: Westport Coal Co. V. McPhail (1899) 2 Q. B. 130。这方面可以举的一个例子是,船东/承运人通过电信或在中途港参与船舶的航行事务,与船长共同作出了一个有关航行的疏忽或错误的决定,导致海难,例如雾中超速航行导致碰撞。

4.2.7.1.1.3 何谓航行

"航行"(navigation)是指载货船舶从开航至抵达并挂靠好码头在海上航行的一段时间。但有关航行的行为与决定也会在开航前(或抵达后)作出,这种疏忽又会是怎样的地位呢? 在 SS Lord (owners) v. Newsum Son & Co. (1920) 1 K. B. 846 先例,Bailhache 大法官认为"航行疏忽"只适用在船舶"有这动力"(in motion)的时候。但这先例受到批评,因为像船长在海图上选择航线有错误,要区别这是在开航前还是开航后犯的有必要和合理性吗? 要是有,岂非会令船长能押后到开航后才决定就都一律这样做,以便有错误时可以免责。这方面的争议在近期的 The "Hill Harmony" (1999) 2 Lloyd's Rep. 209 又再出现,它涉及船长选择大圆航线(路程较短)与恒向航线,这方面在 4.2.6.6.6.3 小段提到的 The "Evje" (No. 2) (1928) 1 Lloyd's Rep. 351 先例也有介绍。本案亦涉及船长过错,他选错了航线。在高等法院与上诉庭,法官推翻了仲裁庭的裁决,判是免责适用,无须区分船长错误的决定是在开航前还是开航后作出。

上诉庭的 Potter 大法官说:"Finally,…I consider that the Judge(指高院的一审法官) was correct in rejecting the reasoning of Mr. Justice Bailhache in the Lord case as a reason for finding in this case that the master's decision not to follow the charterers' directions, but to sail a rhumb line course(恒向航线) was not a decision as to navigation simply because, when taken, the vessel was still in port prior to commencement of the voyage. Whether or not the word 'navigation' is *prima facie* limited to acts done or measures taken on the voyage itself, I have no doubt, like the Judge, that a decision as to navigation, reached as part and parcel of the owners' responsibility for navigation... may be made either before or after the vessel has left port."

该案(The "Hill Harmony")后上诉至贵族院,刚刚(2000 年 12 月 7 日)判下来船东败诉。按该判决,选择航线的权力不再属于船长,因此这方面有错不再算是"航行疏忽过错"了。在这方面去争论照理说是不必要的,因为有些情况下无法作出区分,以判定是否一定是在开航前已犯错/疏忽。例如,在 William Tetley 教授的《Marine Cargo Claims》一书第 3 版之第 403 页提到了一荷兰先例,名为 Gerechtshef te's-Gravenhage, January 12, 1966, (1968) ETL 345,它判是船长决定在极坏的天气下开航/离港属"航行疏忽或过错"。

4.2.7.1.1.4 何谓管船

对"管船"(management of the ship)的解释比对"航行"的解释困难多了。从字面看,它的范围十分广泛,因为凡是涉及船舶,每一个决定或行为,都可以算是"管船"。在 The "Rodney"(1900) P. 112, Gorell Bames 大法官对"管船过错"给予的定义是:"The words 'fault or errors in the management of the vessel' include improper handling of the ship, as a ship, which affects the safety of the cargo."

要在"航行疏忽/过错"免责之外再追加"管船疏忽/过错"免责也是没有办法,因为船长/船员在航次中犯错,而航次是空放的,不存在有照看货物的考虑,也不是所有犯错都可以归咎为"航行疏忽/过错",例如对水泵或发电机的操作错误。由于"航行"(navigation)实在太局限、太片面,所以要再加上"管船"一词。

但总体去解释,仍有许多局限。首先是免责条款本身的局限,在解释上它会被严格针对。其次是这方面的"疏忽或过错"(neglect or default)仅于 4.2.7.1.1.2 小段提到的列名人士,像船东等非列名人士在"管船"上犯错并不包括在免责内。第三是海牙规则的 Article 3 明确要求承运人要妥善并小心地运载与照看货物,这自然是船长与船员要负的责任,因为承运人/船东本身不在船舶上,非要依赖其船员/雇员才能尽此明示责任。

就这第三个局限而言,总体地解释海牙规则,也必须区分出何谓运载与照看货物,这方面的责任是必须严格的妥善/小心,犯了疏忽/过错也不能免责。与运载及照看货物无关的方面,才能算是"管船",才能在犯了疏忽/过错时免责。而且,要区分属管船而非管货疏忽/过错的举证责任也在承运人身上,因为是他/它要享受该免责。这方面权威的说法可以节录 Hourani v. T. & J. Harrison (1927) 32 Com. Cas. 305 先例的如下讲法:"'Management' means management of the ship and not the general carrying on of the business of transporting goods by sea; it does not include management of the cargo. In order to bring any particular matter within the exception, it must therefore be something which can definitely be said to be in the management of the ship; if all the carrier can prove is an act in relation to the goods, the goods alone, and has no relation to the ship herself, that act is not within the exception."

在另一著名先例 Gosse Millerd v. Canadian Government Merchant Marine (1928) 32 Lloyd's Rep. 91(该先例案情已在本章之 4.2.5.6 小段有略及),贵族院同意上诉庭 Greer 大法官所说的:"If the cause of damage is solely, or even primarily, a neglect to take reasonable care of the cargo, the ship is liable,[513] but if the cause of the damage is a neglect to take reasonable care of the ship, or some of it, as distinct from the cargo, the ship is relieved from liability;[514] but if the negligence is not negligence towards the ship, but only a negligent failure to use the apparatus of the ship for the protection of cargo,[515] the ship is not relieved."

在 Gosse Millerd 先例,判是船舶在修理时没有盖好货舱货物,导致货物遭受雨水损坏属管货的疏忽,不属管船,所以船东不得免责。这行为若发生在装卸货时,也是同样判法。但虽有了 Gosse Millerd 等先例的解释,现实中适用起来仍是困难重重。固然,有些情况明显不会是管船的疏忽/过错(例如是装卸工/船员偷货: Hourani v. T. & J. Harrison 先例;船员检查货舱货物后忘了把水密门关紧等),但仍有太多情况是"边沿"(borderline)案子。船长/船员的一个疏忽/过错行为可能是既为船舶,也为货物,轻重难以区分。接下去的段节会对这方面略作介绍。

4.2.7.1.1.4.1 船员疏忽使用船上设备/机器要看该使用本质是否为了货物

船员经常会在航行中错误/疏忽使用(或不使用)船上各种设备/机器,因而导致事故。区分这种使用的目的,大原则看来是:如果这船上设备/机器的使用是为了船舶本身运行/航行,如主机、雷达的使用等,这错误应属管船方面的;但若使用是以照看货物为主,如通风设备、冷藏设备的使用等,这错误应属管货方面的。

这方面较近期的判例有 The "Iron Gippland" (1994) 1 Lloyd's Rep. 335,法院判油轮上的"惰性气体设备"(inert gas system)虽是为了船舶安全,本质上仍是为了管理货物。所以对其疏忽操作不属"管船疏忽"的免责。

但每个案件中不同的事实都会导致有不同的考虑,不同的法官也可去自由发挥,只要不偏离大的原则。在 Rowson v. Atlantic Transport Co. (1903) 2 K. B. 666,疏

---

[513] 如果疏忽主要是在合理照看货物方面,船舶要对货损负责。
[514] 如果疏忽主要是在合理照看船舶,而非货物方面,则船舶可对这间接带来的货损免责。
[515] 如果疏忽是在于不使用船上保护货物的设施,则船舶也不能免责。

忽/过错是在冷藏设备的使用,但该船的冷藏设备是同时为船员伙食及货物共设的,这因此就影响了英国上诉庭的判决,判是属"管船"的疏忽。到了 Foreman and Ellams v. Federal Steam Navigation Co. (1928) 30 Lloyd's Rep. 52 先例,涉及大管轮判断错误,太晚才启冷藏设备,导致牛肉的货物损坏,Wright 大法官判这不属管船过错,船东不能免责。对于船上的各种不同设备/机器的区分,Wright 大法官说:"…A modern steamship is not only a complicated steel structure of frames, girders and plates, but contains complicated machinery such as propelling engines and boilers which have steering gear, ballast tanks, and pumps and elaborate piping. Negligence in handling these directly affects the ship in its essential functions of floating, being water-tight, being steered and of being navigated safely and correctly. If a ship is stranded or sunk, if the sea connections are improperly opened, and so on, there is a fault in navigation and management which directly affects the ship, but there is also, in so far as the cargo is thereby damaged by such negligence, a breach of the obligation to care for the cargo, and it is to such negligence in my opinion that exception of Article IV (2) (a) applies.

On the other hand, many modern steamships… have holds which are insulated and which can be cooled by elaborate refrigerating machinery and apparatus. All this constitutes parts of the ship and of its equipment, but these are solely provided for the care of the special cargo. The ship can, as a seagoing vessel, be safely and efficiently navigated and managed even though the refrigerating equipment is in disorder and the cargo perishing. This equipment is not in use at all on voyages where no refrigerated cargo is being carried. The same is true of the elaborate system of tanks, pipes and pumps necessary for the carriage of fuel oil. I take these illustrations as sufficient to indicate the distinction between "navigation and management of the ship" on the one hand and "management of the cargo" on the other.

There are also some parts of the ship which for this purpose may be regarded as ancipitis usus; for instance, the hatches may in one aspect be regarded as part of the outer skin of the vessel as when decks are actually or potentially swept by seas, so that the proper battening down of the hatches with tarpaulins and cleats is as much a part of the management of the ship as the closing of portholes. Under other circumstances, as in dock or in calm waters, the hatches belong to the management of the cargo, either because they have to be removed for ventilation or keep tight to keep wet from perishable cargo. Similarly, ship's derricks and winches may be used for ship's purposes so as to appertain to the management of the ship."

以上三段讲话的第一段是说,船上有一些设备/机器纯粹是为了船舶航行、安全等方面的,如主机、舵机、压舱水以及有关管道/水泵等。第二段是指纯粹为了照看货物的设备/机器,如冷藏设备,它坏了会导致货物损坏,但这并不影响船舶航行与安全。可以说,没有这种货物在船上,船舶在航行中根本不必动用这些设备/机器。

第三段是指一些船上设备/机器在不同环境下会有不同的侧重/针对。例如,舱盖,它在大海航行中起到水密的作用。不论是货舱内是否有货物,船员在航次中疏忽使用/处理舱盖都会影响船舶的安全,这应属"管船的疏忽与过错"的免责项目。所以,在 The "Hector" (1955) 2 Lloyd's Rep. 218, 涉及船员没有及时加上铁条(locking bars)加固舱盖,导致大风浪中舱盖油布被吹破,海水涌入,损坏货物。McNair 大法官判这是管船疏忽/过错的免责。显然,有看法认为这判决对承运人太宽松了,认为它解释这项免责的"极限"(highpoint):请看《Voyage Charters》一书之第 757 页。

若换了一个环境,比如船在港内装卸,那么,船员疏忽使用/处理舱盖(如下雨忘了去关舱盖),就会与船舶安全无关,因下雨不会导致船沉。在这一环境下,同样的船员疏忽/过错便是属于管货过失,而不属管船过失,船东不得免责。

这正是 Gosse Millerd v. Canadian Government Merchant Marine(1928) 32 Lloyd's Rep. 91 先例的案情。Wright 大法官说道:"What did the damage was misuse of the tarpaulins. Now the tarpaulins were used to protect the cargo. They were put over the hatch as they always are to keep water out of the cargo holds'. They should have been so arranged, when the hatch boards were taken off, to prevent water from getting to the cargo…the particular use of the tarpaulin, which was neglected, was a precaution solely in the interest of the cargo. While the ship's work was going on these special precautions were required as cargo operations…"

4.2.7.1.1.4.2 大风浪与/或坏天气下起航或/与继续航行

船长若在这方面有疏忽或过错,表面看似乎是偏重于航行/管船,但有关先例及权威的说法对此有很不一样的观点。

首先,在荷兰法院的 Gerechtshef te's-Gravenhage, January 12, 1966, (1968) ETL 345 案,曾判是在很坏天气下起航属航行/管船疏忽/过错,与适航无关。

但在 The "Washington" (1976) 2 Lloyd's Rep. 453 的加拿大先例,却判船长不顾坏天气而继续航行是对货物照料上的疏忽,法官说:"the master's negligence…in maintaining his course and speed on November 18 and 19 in view of the weather reports he was receiving was an error constituting a negligent failure to use the apparatus of the ship for the protection of the cargo and affected the cargo alone."

另外在权威的 *Marine Cargo Claims* 一书,William Tetley 教授在第 402 页(第 3 版)说道:"On occasion a master will force his ship through a storm, instead of heading at slow speed into the wind, with the result that the cargo is damaged. This is really an error in the management of the cargo, because the master has disregarded possible damage to cargo in favour of arriving in port a day or two early."

在加拿大另一先例 The "Mormacsaga" (1969) 1 Lloyd's Rep. 519 案中,曾判是若船长明知港口(美国的 Jacksonville)罢工,却罔顾船上货物(橙)性质上不能承受延误而仍然让船进港,这属疏于照看货物,不属管船疏忽/过错,或是罢工的免责。有说法是这种"明知山有虎,偏向虎山行"的错误做法实质是与大风浪或坏天气下继续航行一样。正如 Marine Cargo Claims 一书在第 403 页所说: "Entering a strike- bound port, like entering an ice- bound port, is equivalent to maintaining a course through a storm and the carrier cannot exculpate himself."

虽然有了以上解释,但仍有说不清的地方。比如在前面 4.2.7.1.1.3 小段提到的像 The "Hill Harmony" (1999) 2 Lloyd's Rep. 209 先例船长选错航线的情况,那本应是航行疏忽/过错的免责。但选了大圆航线而不选恒向航线,在冬季肯定会遇上更坏天气,从而导致船货遭受损坏可能性也大增。这一来,它在本质上与船长在坏天气下错误决定继续航行又有何不同呢?所以这到底是船东/承运人可以免责还是仅属"明知山有虎,偏向虎山行"的疏于照看船上货物的行为呢?在 The "Hill Harmony",贵族院判是期租承租人而不是船长可以选择航线。但承租人通常都不大理会船上的货物,他更关心的是船能早点抵达卸港,省时间,省燃油。这正是 William Tetley 教授批评类似该判决的情况。The "Hill Harmony" 一判下来,船长/船东作为承运人便被夹在了中间:提单合约下他会因罔顾坏天气而要对货损负责;期租合约下他又必须让船行走最短航线,不存在选择,以避开坏天气。

最后略提一下技术方面的问题。有时也会是事实上船长已充分考虑到货物的安全,但由于货物会因延误而变坏,或卸港快要冰封,或收货人催促等事实导致船长决定在大风浪或/与坏天气下继续航行,这种情况下判决也会有不同的结果。船舶遇上大风浪或/与坏天气,可以绕航避风或改变航速或/与航向等,严格来讲并不是选择航线,不会受 The "Hill Harmony" 先例的影响。若船舶硬去闯坏天气,则很可能会造成船货损坏,例如即使是一艘适航的好船也会被海水渗入,或是甲板货被一扫而空;或是货舱内货物无法通风,等等。

4.2.7.1.1.4.3 加压舱水

加压舱水表面看来是为了船舶稳性、安全,应是典型的"管船行为"。这行为也经常会出现疏忽与过错,例如是管道漏,开错开关阀等。笔者记得早年在船上工作时,曾发生过好几次木匠不小心没看紧压舱水是否已快满溢,结果导致"深舱" (deep tank) 的压舱水从打开的"人孔" (manhole) 溢出从而损坏已堆装在同一货舱内货物的事故。这一来,它可否算是"管船疏忽/过错"的免责?

在《Marine Cargo Claims》一书,William Tetley 教授在第 404 页(第 3 版)提到一般而言,加压舱水疏忽可以当做是管船疏忽而免责,但有以下例外:

(ⅰ)若开航前已发生这事故,这会是不适航,不适货。这方面请参阅本章 4.2.6.3. 小段提及的 Maxine Footwear v. Canada Government Merchant Marine (1959) 2 Lloyd's Rep. 105 先例,其中也有类似情况,它涉及的是"火灾",而压舱水满溢流出则是"水灾"。另外,两种"灾祸"都是船长/船员疏忽所引起,而不是恐怖分子上船放火放水,所以可归咎为船东没有"克尽职责"。

(ⅱ)即使事故发生在开航后,但与不适航仍扯得上关系,比如像 The "Farrandoe" (1961) 2 Lloyd's Rep. 276 的船员水平不足,对船舶的了解受到质疑。另外像开关,指示器等开航前已坏,也涉及不适航之争。

(ⅲ)若船长/船员加压舱水时应该想到货物而要作出一定保护措施,例如货物在邻近的同一货舱内,他一定要这样去做了,之后再发生疏忽/过错,这才是"管船"的免责。正如 Marine Cargo Claims 一书在第 405 页所说的:"In other words to flood a ballast tank continually without thought to the cargo is an error in the management of the cargo. The carrier should check cargo holds periodically when ballasting, to see that the cargo is not being wetted. Otherwise, the error is in respect to the care of cargo."

4.2.7.1.2 免责项目之(b):火灾

这是在海牙规则的 Article 4(2)(b),为了方便读者阅读,不妨在分析前先把这项免责的英文措辞节录如下:"Fire, unless caused by the actual fault or privity of the carrier."

4.2.7.1.2.1 什么是"火灾"

"火"或"火灾"(fire)应包括燃烧带来的爆炸。但光是爆炸(如机器受压),没有火光,这不包括在火灾的免责内:The "Inchmaree" (1881) 12 App. Cas. 484。

看来,火灾应是指"看得见的热与光"(visible heat or light)或"火焰"(a flame or a glow)。光是有烟,例如装了鱼粉货物的货舱冒烟,并不足以构成火灾:The "Sante Malta" (1967) 2 Lloyd's Rep. 391 的第 394 页。

若是有看不见的发热,例如货舱内的电灯发热(heat)损坏了附近的散粮货物,这并非是火灾:Buckeye State,39F. Supp. 344,1941 AMC 1238 (WDNY 1941)。

但有判例说:

(ⅰ)灭火时导致部分货物遭受水/烟损坏,可包括在火灾的免责:The "Diamond" (1906) 10 Asp. M. L. C 286。

(ⅱ)不少货物会发生自燃,但在真有火光/火焰产生前,总会有一个发热过程。若是这要想免责的船东/承运人去区分损失,否则要全部负责(这一点请参阅本章之 4.2.5.5 小段),往往无法办到,顶多只是一些专家的臆测。所以,干脆不要求区分,货物自燃导致火灾船东均可免责,不再分是发热或燃烧:Amer. Tobacco Co. V. S. S. Katingo Hadjipatera,81F. Supp. 438 at p. 446,1949 AMC 49 at p. 58(SDNY 1948)。

4.2.7.1.2.2 是火灾但无法免责的情况之一:开航前发生导致不适航、不适货

这情况已在本章之4.2.6.3小段详论,并介绍了Maxine Footwear v. Canada Government Merc9倒是有另一做法笔者曾多次遇过,就是在钢舱盖的接缝处加上一条"绝缘胶布带"(adh 的相关先例,不再在此重复。只提一点,火灾发生在开航前并导致船舶不适航、不适货,这是违反海牙规则的(免责)先决条件,船东/承运人难辞其咎之下将无法以火灾来免责。

4.2.7.1.2.3 是火灾但无法免责的情况之二:火灾是船东/承运人错误或知情所导致

关于"实际错误或知情"(actual fault or privity)的解释,笔者的《程租合约》一书之第四章6.2.1小段与《海事法》一书之第二章3.2小段都有详论。因内容太多,不再重复与节录。只是说,这"实际错误或知情"一词也出现在1957年的船东"责任限制公约"(Limitation Convention)。原意是在船东本人有错时才去否定他/它的责任限制权利,这从"实际"(actual)一词加在"错误与知情"一词之前可见。但曾有过一连串的案例就何谓"实际错误或知情"对船东作出了极严厉的解释,如 The "Lady Gwendolen"(1965) 1 Lloyd's Rep. 335,The "Marion"(1984) 2 Lloyd's Rep. 1 等,会是十分容易就扯上船东/承运人有"实际错误或知情"。

但在海牙规则下这会造成很大影响倒也不见得,因为海牙规则有"克尽职责"适航的先决条件,这十分严格,而船东/承运人能被挑出有"实际错误或知情"的毛病,恐怕多数情况下是开航前已存在,反正这已构成未"克尽职责"令船舶适航。例如 The "Lady Gwendolen"先例,船东雇用船员不当,并"视而不见",既是"实际错误或知情",也是开航前未"克尽职责"令船舶适航。后者的适航先决条件只在海牙规则出现,并不在责任限制公约提及。至于与适航与否无关的,例如船员抽烟不小心导致航次中发生大火,也难以想象这类事故会涉及船东/承运人的"实际错误/知情"。

倒是在举证责任方面可以提提。因为在海牙规则的谈判中,美国代表坚持以他们美国的"火灾法"(Fire Statute)为准加上这"承运人的实际错误或知情"这一措辞,而美国法院判火灾法对此指控的举证责任在原告的货方:Westinghouse v. Leslie Lykes,734 F. 2d 199 at p. 206 - 207,1985 AMC 247 at p. 256 (5 Cir. 1984)。所以,有说法是海牙规则下要货方去举证船东/承运人有"实际错误或知情",而在1957年责任限制公约下是要船东去举证没有"实际错误或知情"。而进一步去分析,则船东要免责比限责更容易,这可有点可笑了。当然,今天1957年责任限制公约已逐步

为1976年责任限制公约所取代(这课题可参阅《海事法》一书之第二章),后者已加强了对船东限责权利的限制,而不再只是泛泛的"船东实际错误或知情"了。

4.2.7.1.2.4　英美火灾法

英、美等国家(加拿大没有火灾法)早已有"火灾法"(Fire Statute)。美国的立法是在1851年,远远早于海牙规则。具体如下:"No owner of any vessel shall be liable to answer for or make good to any person any loss or damage, which may happen to any merchandise whatsoever, which shall be shipped, taken in, or put on board any such vessel, by reason or by means of any fire happening to or onboard the vessel, unless such fire is caused by the design or neglect of such owner."[516]

现今英国的"火灾法"是在商船法(Merchant Shipping Act,1979)之Section 18。笔者对此不去多谈,除了只强调一点,就是在Section 18(3)已没有"实际错误或知情"导致火灾不可免责的讲法,而代替的是货方的原告(尤其是如果有举证责任)更难证明的"意图去造成损失或明知可能会造成损失而轻率地作为或不作为"(with intent to cause such loss, or recklessly and with knowledge that such loss would probably result)。这也与1976年的责任限制公约(Limitation Convention)取代了1957年的责任公约是同步的:这方面请看《海事法》一书之第二章。

至于为何一早就有立法光是针对火灾这风险,笔者找不到权威的依据,但推断或估计是当时火灾危险颇大,也常发生。而且不像岸上,船上无法自救之余,也不能获得其他人(如救火员)的救援。再说,航运投资是当时英美两国大力鼓励的行业。

这一来,今天船舶若发生火灾,造成严重货损,英美法下船东/承运人(英国火灾法也允许期租承租人享有免责)会有两个立法的免责。一是火灾法,另一是海牙规则(英美的海上运输法)。

4.2.7.1.2.5　火灾法与海牙规则之火灾免责的重叠与差异之处

要知道,海牙规则只在Article 3(8)禁止承运人/船东为豁免或减少对货物的责任而享有订约自由。但海牙规则并没有否定其他立法的有效性,而且在Article 8也说明了另一责任限制公约/立法的有效性(即使它会造成对海牙规则下单位赔偿最低金额的影响,导致赔偿更不足)。故此,就有必要比较一下海牙规则与两个针对火灾的立法了,这会有以下几项:

(ⅰ)沿用海牙规则的海上运输法适用在所有船舶,不像英国火灾法仅适用在英国船,美国火灾法仅适用在美国船。

(ⅱ)沿用海牙规则的海上运输法下的火灾免责保护船东及承租人,英国火灾法的免责对象也包括了承租人、经理人与"营运人"(operator)。但美国火灾法只包

---

[516]　"design or neglect"被视为与上一小段详论的"实际错误或知情"同义。

括船东与光船承租人。

（iii）在海牙规则下，船东要想享受免责，必须先满足"克尽职责"令船舶适航的先决条件：见本章之4.2.6.3小段。但火灾法没有这种条件。故此，在本章4.2.6.3小段详论的 Maxine Footwear v. Canada Government Merchant Marine (1959) 2 Lloyd's Rep. 105 先例，有说法是如果加拿大也有火灾法的立法，船东可以火灾法去免责。

（iv）可能船东/承运人会是对火灾有"实际错误或知情"，但达不到"意图去造成损失或明知可能会造成损失而轻率地作为或不作为"这一更高的程度：请参阅4.2.7.1.2.4小段。

4.2.7.1.2.6　火灾举证次序

最后，可以火灾为例介绍火灾引起的货损货差索赔在海牙规则下的举证次序，具体如下：

（i）首先货方的原告要证明他的损失：拥有货物主权，损失金额计算，等等。

（ii）轮到船东/承运人要证明损失（货损货差）的原因：请参阅本章之4.2.5小段。例如，火灾如何发生，如何真正造成货物损失，等等。

（iii）接下去，船东/承运人要证明已在开航前"克尽职责"令船舶在有关防火方面适航、适货。例如，船舶不是在开航前发生火灾导致不适货（Maxine Footwear v. Canada Government Merchant Marine (1959) 2 Lloyd's Rep. 105）；船员对灭火训练有素；船上有足够及设计合理的消防设备，比方船首有独立灭火泵，可在机房发生火灾时使用：The "Marquette" 480 F.2d 669 at p.672, 1973 AMC 1683 at p.1666 (2 Cir. 1973)等。

（iv）又轮到由货方的原告证明船东/承运人对火灾有"实际错误或知情"。

（v）船东/承运人对这指控提出反驳。

（vi）货方的原告另去举证像船东/承运人不妥善或/与疏忽照看货物才是导致部分或全部货损货差的主因/近因，而非因火灾。例如，已经在驾驶台的显示器上发觉了船舱有烟火，但仍等了4天才施放灭火气体，结果延误了灭火行动：American Mail Line v. Tokyo M. & F. Ins. Co., 270 F.2d 499 at p.501, 1959 AMC 2220 at p.2222-3 (9 Cir. 1959)。

有关这方面也请参阅本章4.2.2小段，内有清楚的介绍。

虽有以上所讲的举证次序，但这并不代表当事方可在准备开庭前不去全面考虑整个案情并在所有方面对有关争议及证据作好准备，因为这不是分段去审理，这一点在本章之4.2.7小段已有略及。

4.2.7.1.3　免责项目之(c)：海难/海上风险

这是在海牙规则的 Article 4(2)(c)，为了方便读者阅读，不妨把这项免责的英文措辞节录如下："Perils, dangers and accidents of the sea or other navigable waters."

4.2.7.1.3.1 定义

"海难"一词用在不同的范畴都应有相同的定义,如在海上保险也是一样定义。但因举证责任以及适航责任会有不同,也不能一概而论。在海牙规则下,笔者可以节录一个经常被人引述及接受的定义,它是:"a fortuitous action[517] of the elements at sea[518], of such force as to overcome the strength of a well-found ship[519] or the usual precautions of good seamanship[520]."

4.2.7.1.3.2 必须是不可预见的

从海牙规则的用字看,"perils"与"accidents"(意外)都含有不可或难以预见/预防的性质。这可以节录多个英国相关先例的说法如下:

(ⅰ)在 The "Xantho"(1881) 12 App. Cas. 503,Herschell 勋爵说:"There must be some casualty, something which could not be foreseen as one of the necessary incidents of the adventure."

(ⅱ)在 The "Friso"(1980) 1 Lloyd's Rep. 469, Sheen 大法官说:"Those particulars(指答辩状中的事实说明) do not include an allegation that the weather conditions were exceptional or such as could not reasonably have been anticipated…If the matter had stopped there I would have held that the facts pleaded do not amount to 'perils of the sea'."

(ⅲ)在 The "Tilia Gorthon"(1985) 1 Lloyd's Rep. 552, Sheen 大法官说:"The evidence as to the weather has not satisfied me that the conditions encountered were such as could not and should not have been contemplated by the shipowners."

(ⅳ)在 The "Coral"(1992) 2 Lloyd's Rep. 158, Sheen 大法官说:"The unsuitability of the ship does not provide the defendants(船东) with a defence. The weather encountered by 'Coral' was such as ought to have been contemplated."

美国也有类同的不少先例,试举两例如下:

(ⅰ)在 The "Demosthenes" 189 F. 2d 488 at p. 491 (4 Cir. 1951),法官说:"The excepted 'perils of the sea' does not come into play merely upon proof that the vessel en-

---

[517] 一定要是意外的,偶然的。

[518] 是海上才有的因素,事故。

[519] 海上因素力量超越了一艘良好/坚固的船舶,若是船舶不良好/坚固,这会是不适航而不是海难了,更不说适航是先决条件。

[520] 这海上因素也是一般船长/船员的良好船艺可去超越。若是船长/船员船艺不成,水平不够,这又会是不适航的一种。而若是船艺成,水平够但疏忽/过错,这主因会是违反海牙规则 Article 3 的妥善与小心照看货物而不是海难或管船疏忽的免责:请看 4.2.7.1.1.4 小段。例如,在 4.2.7.1.1.4.2 小段提及的大风浪/坏天气推进航行,不避风,绕航或减速。

countered heavy seas and high winds, if the weather encountered might reasonably have been anticipated and could have been withstood by a seaworthy vessel."

(ⅱ)在 RT Jones Lumber Co. V. Roen Steamship Co., 270 F. 2d 456 at p. 458 (2 Cir. 1959)的上诉庭先例曾提到以下说法:"Perils of the seas are understood to mean those perils which are peculiar to the sea, and which are of an extraordinary nature or arise from irresistible force or overwhelming power, and which cannot be guarded against by the ordinary exertions of human skill and prudence."

加拿大法院与美国法院对海难的判法看来很接近,也十分强调海难的"不可预见"(unforeseen)与"不可预防"(could not be guarded)性。在 Charles Goodfellow Lumber Sales v. Verreault, Hovingfon and Verreault Navigation Inc. (1971) 1 Lloyd's Rep. 185,加拿大最高院曾说(该先例是针对提单货损)海难免责只针对的风险是:"Which could not have been foreseen or guarded against as one of the probable incidents of the voyage."

4.2.7.1.3.3 海难免责难以成立

也是以上"不可预见"性的要求(在美加法院看来特别严格),导致海难这项免责很难成立。试想想,现实中能有多少坏天气、大风浪是不可预见、前所未有,而且无法预防的呢? 特别是在今天天气预报越来越准,且预测期也越来越长的情况下。

例如在冬季横渡大西洋,已有几个先例判是10级风或11级风也不能算是"不可预见",所以无法以"海难"为由对货损免责。

在美国先例的 Thyssen Inc. V. S/S Eurounity 21 F. 3d 533(2d Cir. 1994),上诉庭判:"…The Vessel's bridge log book,… recorded Beaufort Scale winds that did not exceed a level of 10 – 11 on January 4. Expert testimony at trial indicated that there were significant wave heights of between 10 and 11.5 meters. We find nothing of an extraordinary nature, nor do we find irresistible force or overwhelming power in these conditions. Indeed, the testimony of the meteorological expert witnesses for both sides revealed that, for the most part, the weather conditions experienced by the vessel were not unusual in the North Atlantic in the winter-time. Dr. Austin Dooley, the defendants' expert, testified that force 11 winds and significant wave heights of 10 to 11.5 meters were foreseeable …both experts indicated that cross-seas generally could have been expected…Given that severe storms occur on a regular basis in the North Atlantic and that the winds, waves and cross-seas experienced by the vessel were to be expected, we conclude that the vessel has not proven that it is entitled to exonerated based of a peril of the sea."

另在早期的 Edmond Weil v. American West African Line 147 F. 2d. 363 (2 Cir. 1945),著名的 Learned Hand 大法官说在大西洋10级风不是无法预见的,不算

是海难。他还说："gales-indeed even 'whole gales' – are to be expected in such water at such a season."在加拿大先例的 The "Grumant"（1913）2 Lloyd's Rep. 531，也提到冬天在大西洋12级风也可预见。

另在美国先例的 Nichimen Co. v. M/V Farland 1972 AMC 1573（2 Cir. 1972），曾判冬天横渡太平洋遇上11级风也是可以预见的。

读者要稍为留心的是，这种争议全是要看"事实"（facts），而事实认定要靠证据。所以，判决结果会有法官对证据不满意或怀疑的因素在内，例如对航海日志的天气记录抱有怀疑，估计会夸大，或是一方的气象专家说服力差，讲错话被对方专家挑出毛病来等，但判词中不一定会明确说出来。

4.2.7.1.3.4　是否一定要不可预见之争

这方面的争议可见于近期澳大利亚上诉庭的先例 The "Bunga Seroja"（1999）1 Lloyd's Rep. 512 之第 529 页，有关内容可节录如下："Under the Anglo-Australian approach, the critical question is not whether the peril can be foreseen or guarded against but whether the harm causing event was of the sea and fortuitous, accidental or unexpected[521]. If it was, a further question arises as to whether that event was the effective cause of the loss. This approach restricts the immunity of the carrier's negligence rather than by reference to the foreseeability or severity of the peril.

The reasoning of the majority of this Court in The 'Gamlen'（1980）147 C.L.R. 142 correctly indicates that the foreseeability of the peril does not preclude the carrier from relying on the perils of the sea immunity[522]…Many perils of the sea may be reasonably foreseen[523]. The sinking of a ship after hitting an iceberg while crossing the North Atlantic in mid winter is a clear example[524]. And hitting an iceberg does not cease to be a peril of the sea because it could have been avoided by lessening speed or keeping a proper lookout[525]…The "Titanic" was sunk by one of the perils of the sea even though the presence of icebergs in the relevant latitude was reasonably foreseeable and the colli-

---

[521]　英国（有说法是较美国法院宽松）与澳大利亚法院并非视海难"可否预见"或"可否预防"为最关键，而是要看海上事故是否具"偶然性"（fortuitous），"意外性"（accidental）或是"估计不到"（unexpected）。而"不可预见"（unforeseen）与"估计不到"（unexpected）在程度上会有不同。

[522]　在澳大利亚一个较早的判例"Gamlen"，曾被认为海难属"可以预见"并不一定会令承运人无法成功依赖海难的免责。即"不可预见"不是唯一或最主要的考虑因素。

[523]　有许多海上风险实际上可以合理预见、预报。

[524]　例如冬天在大西洋碰上浮冰。

[525]　这是海上风险（海难），不因它"可以预防"（如通过减速或加强瞭望）而性质有所改变。

sion could have been avoided by reducing the speed of the ship[526]."

4.2.7.1.3.5　其他考虑的因素

这在 The "Bunga Seroja" (1999) 1 Lloyd's Rep. 512 先例也有详论。即是否构成海难免责并不是考虑其是否"不可预见",而是要考虑其他多方面的因素,具体如下:

(ⅰ)船舶结构良好,设备良好,保养良好,等等。

(ⅱ)船舶大小。

(ⅲ)这海上风险是否很偶然?

(ⅳ)针对这海上风险承运人是否已谨慎及恰当行事,但仍无法避免事故?

而其他权威的说法(如 William Tetley 教授的 *Marine Cargo Claims* 一书)也提到了其他考虑的因素,如:

(ⅴ)船舶本身有否受到损坏?

(ⅵ)地理环境。

(ⅶ)坏天气/大风浪持续多久?

4.2.7.1.3.5.1　考虑因素之一:船舶构造、设备、保养、大小等方面

这些方面如果不妥当,存有不适航之嫌,导致不得不去享受海难的免责。例如,在加拿大最高院的 C. N. R. v. E. & S. Barbour Ltd. (1963) S. C. R. 323,判一艘船舶估计会遇上浮冰,但没有相关设施是不适航的(也没有"克尽职责"),不能以海难免责。如此看来,船舶若太小,即使本身一切良好,但驶往不常去的大风浪海域,一旦出事如海水渗入船舱,其结果是不适航而不是海难。

4.2.7.1.3.5.2　考虑因素之二:偶然的风险

船舶会在完全正常、可预见的天气中,突然遇上巨浪的袭击。这英文所谓的"freak waves"或"queer seas"或"one big waves",可导致一艘完全适航的船舶遭受严重损坏,进而导致船上货物损坏。例如是南非海域的鬼浪。

在 Hiram Walker & Sons, Ltd. V. Dover Navigation Co. Ltd. (1949) 83 Lloyd's Rep. 84 先例,第 90 页曾提到船出事当时有"一条水柱从天而降,重击在舱盖上"(a conical head of water which came down heavily upon the hatch covers),这判是海难。

另在 Nichimen Co. V. M/V Farland 1972 AMC 1573 (2 Cir. 1972),船上证供说遇上 60 尺巨浪袭击不为美国法院接受与信任,因为航海日志没有批注,而事故后马上发给船公司的电报中也没有提及。

---

[526] 例如像"铁达尼"号客轮的著名"海难",浮冰可以预见,也可以预防,只要"铁达尼"当时有去减速。这一来,事故的主因/近因会变得不再是海上风险(海难),而是在 4.2.7.1.1.4.2 小段详述及的情况。

4.2.7.1.3.5.3　考虑因素之三:船舶损坏

如果一艘适航和坚固的船舶在坏天气,大风浪中遭受损坏,这会强烈显示出它很可能遇到了不寻常和估计不到的海难。例如在 The "Bunga Seroja"(1999) 1 Lloyd's Rep. 512 先例,风浪过后,发觉船首锚机坏了,左锚掉了,当然还造成货损。看来,这种船舶损坏会是导致澳大利亚法院接受海难免责的主要因素之一。

同样判法的其他判例还有 The "Ulvern"(1928) 32 Lloyd's Rep. 7,另在 The "Grumant"(1973) 2 Lloyd's Rep. 531 之第 533 页与 The "Washington"(1976) 2 Lloyd's Rep. 453 之第 459 页也涉及这方面。

4.2.7.1.3.6　除了大风浪以外其他情况的海上风险/海难

一讲到坏天气/大风浪,大家往往就会想到海难的免责。的确它经常会是造成货损货差事故的原因,如海水渗入,甲板上的集装箱被冲下海,甚至船货沉没。也会是船舱通风因天气太坏无法打开,导致因通风不足造成货损:The "Segundo"(1941) A. C. 55 的大米。

这方面的例子还包括船在风平浪静下碰上水底物或礁石,或是被其他疏忽航行的船舶碰撞:The "Xantho"(1887) 12 APP. Cas. 503 之第 509 页。

另在 The "Stranna"(1938) 60 Lloyd's Rep. 51,涉及装货时船舶突然倾侧,导致甲板上部分木材掉下水丧失。上诉庭判是船舶突然(原因也无法解释)的"短暂不稳"(temporary instability)属海难/海上风险。在 *Voyage Charter* 一书之第 760 页,指此案例属"下不为例"(does not represent the general rule)。这估计是基于承运人/船东有举证责任,而若事故原因不明会对他/它作出不利的推断:请看本章之 4.2.5.3.3 小段。此外,在装货时出这种事故会有船舶不适航,适货之嫌:请看本章 4.2.6.3 小段之 Maxine Footwear v. Canada Government Merchant Marine (1959) 2 Lloyd's Rep. 105 先例。海水进入通常被视为是"海上风险",因为若不在海上而在岸上就不会有此危险。所以在船舶保险方面的著名先例 The "Inchmaree"(1881) 12 App. Cas. 484,判是船员疏忽导致机器受损并非是海难/海上风险(承保风险),因为这在岸上也同样可能发生。而若是船舶机器/设备损坏导致海水进入而损坏货物,则虽然前者不是海难/海上风险,但后者造成货损则正是这项免责。这一点在 *Voyage Charter* 一书之第 759 页有提到:"…Also, if damage to the ship's equipment leads to cargo damage through, for example, the incursion of seawater, the latter damage would be characteristic of sea transit and would be within the definition of a peril of the seas,…"

另在 Hamilton Fraser & Co. V. Pandorf & Co. (1881) 12 App. Cas. 518 先例,涉及航次中老鼠咬破海水管导致海水进入货舱损坏大米的货物,贵族院判船东可以海上风险免责。贵族院说本质上,这与一条剑鱼(swordfish)把船旁弄穿一个洞一样。当然,这种案例是发生在以前的船舶,在今天这已失去现实意义。而且,还要更全面去看待这种争议,例如,船上有鼠患则会有不适航、不适货之嫌。

至于若是由于不合理的或/与恶意的人为因素致令海水进入,这不会被认为主因/近因是海上风险/海难。例如是船员的反叛行为(barratry):The "Chasca" (1875) 1. R. 4A. BE. 446,或是船东弄沉船舶的行为(scuttling):P. Samuel v. Dumas (1924) 18 Lloyd's Rep. 211。

4.2.7.1.4　免责项目之(d):天意

这一项免责早在英国普通法已是被默示的,但海牙规则是国际公约,不只是英美两国的法律,所以对这项免责作出明示也是理所当然。比方它与大陆法的"不可抗力"(force majeure)就不相同。有关"不可抗力"的解释,笔者的《国际商务游戏规则——英国合约法》一书第十二章§8段有详论,不再重复。

在英国法律下,天意必须有三个要素。一是"外界因素"(exteriority),二是"不可预见"(unforeseeable),三是"无法预防"(irresistible):Nugent v. Smith (1876) 1 C. P. D. 421 之第 435~436 页。

"外界因素"是指没有任何人为的因素包含在内。若含有人为的因素,因"人"非"上帝",故也不存在天意了。所以,大雾中航行出事不是天意:Liver Alkali Co. V. Johnson (1875) L. R. 9 Ex. 338,但闪电雷击造成火灾是天意:Forward v. Pittard (1785) 1 T. R. 2。

至于"不可预见"与"无法预防",在 4.2.7.1.3 小段的海难/海上风险免责项下已有略及。读者或许会问,既然构成要素/要求一致,为何再要区分海难和天意?答案是:像闪电雷击,海上岸上均会发生,故若援用海难/海上风险免责并不能保障承运人/船东。

4.2.7.1.5　免责项目之(e):战争行为

有关这项免责,可以 The "Wise" (1989) 1 Lloyd's Rep. 96 为例说明,该案中船舶在往澳大利亚卸港途中不幸被伊拉克火箭摧毁,船货尽失。另也可以 The "Safeer" (1994) 1 Lloyd's Rep. 637 为例,该案涉及一船白米运往科威特,但伊拉克突然入侵,船长被迫把货卸给伊拉克当局而不是科威特的收货人,货物因此丧失。

至于有关战争行为的简单定义,在笔者与汪鹏南教授的《英国海上保险条款详论》一书第 205 页说道:"战争可表达为主权国家或事实上具有主权国家特征的政治实体之间动用武力,或进攻,或抵抗"。该书随后有更详尽的内容谈及战争或/与类似风险/事故,但内容较长,不再全部节录/重复。

4.2.7.1.6　免责项目之(f):公敌行为

"公敌"(public enemies)一词从字面看来,应包括与本国对敌、作战的其他国家,例如对英国而言,"二战"时的公敌就是德国。在没有战事、和平的日子,公敌是很少甚至没有的：Spence v. Chadwick（1847）10 QB 517。能想得到的公敌或许只有"海盗"（pirates），而这项风险今天仍大量存在。它会造成货损货差的情况是诸如海盗把船上货物抢走（1990 年 9 月 30 日，印尼海盗上船把二千多吨汽油泵抢走），或因把船员捆绑令船舶失控而出事故，等等。

古代在海上纵横的海盗造成的祸害，曾被法院判定属"海难"（peril of the sea）：Pickering v. Barclay（1648）Styles l32。但今天的海盗到底来自海上还是岸上也难以区分，也许更多是来自岸上，因此已谈不上是"海难"（这一点请看本章之 4.2.7.1.3.6 小段），故此"公敌行为"才是恰当的免责项目。

4.2.7.1.7 免责项目之（g）：君主、统治者或人民的扣留或禁制，或法律程序的扣押

这项免责分两部分。第一部分简称"君主的禁制"（restraint of princes）的免责项目，这已有很长历史，常在租约、提单等合约内被作为明示的免责。随着历史的进步，越来越多的国家再也不是"君主"一言堂，甚至再也没有"君主"这回事。所以，免责的措辞／文字要将范围扩大，就加上了"统治者"（rulers）和"人民"（people）的概念。但这些文字都是专指政府或"准政府"（quasigovernment），它们均有一定的法定权力。故在 Nesbitt v. Lushington（1792）4 T. R. 783，判定"人民"（people）不包括一群"暴民"（tumultuous mob）。

至于"禁制"（restraints）一词，是指"强行干预"（forcible interference），而政府或准政府一般都会有力量／权力去这样做，例如强制把船上货物没收。正如 Martin B 大法官在 Finlay v. Liverpool and Great Western Steamship Co.（1870）23 L. T. 251 先例说："The 'acts and restraints of princes and rulers'...have reference to the forcible interference of a state or of the government of a country taking possession of the goods manu forti…"

一般只要政府或准政府下了命令，就被视为有"力量"（force）去执行，免责不必再要求它"赤裸裸"地显示力量，例如出动公安、军队，刀刀枪枪都要抖出来。贵族院在 British and Foreign Marine Insurance Co. v. Samuel Sanday & Co.（1916）1 A. C. 650 先例说："I am not impressed by the circumstance that force was neither exerted nor present, for force is in reserve behind every State command…"

当然，是否真有"禁制"要讨论清楚。例如，各国都会有海关港口等条例禁止没有清关的船／货离开，这种"正常的法律实施"（ordinary operation of law）不属"禁制"。其他正常的各国港口当局的操作／规定，例如禁止晚上航行也不属"禁制"。实际上，这一行为或命令是"协助"航行而不是干预／禁止航行。还有涉及纯商业的，例如欠代理人钱或其他合约纠纷而遭受扣押，这也谈不上是政府或准政府的禁制／扣留。

有关这一点,在 The "Wondrous"(1991) 1 Lloyd's Rep. 400 先例有详论。它涉及船东出租船给一个伊朗的光棍承租人去装糖浆,从伊朗的 Bandar Abbas 运往欧洲。但在装港,货只装了一半,而且货物也不对劲(不是蔗糖浆而是甜菜糖浆),承租人就失踪了。而船舶也就滞留在 Bandar Abbas 达一年之久,船舶因失修而在一年后才能开航。船舶动不了,船东自然损失惨重。法院判这滞留并非政府扣押或禁制,主因/近因实际是在商业上(commercial)遇上光棍承租人。而伊朗当局在货物没有支付税金,没有清关的情况下,也不准开航,但这纯属正常海关法律/规定的实施。

那么,有什么是君主扣留/禁制的例子呢?这方面案例应有不少,在此只挑几个来介绍,反正万变不离其宗:

(ⅰ)在 The "Denbigshire"(1896) 2 QB 326,船经香港再去日本卸余下货物。抵达香港那一天,中日宣战。船长担心继续该航次会有危险,因附近都是中国军舰,所以"合理"(这一点是法院认定的事实)地在香港把货物卸下。后来日本收货人向船东索赔损失,英国法院判船东可以依赖提单内明示的"君主禁制"免责。

(ⅱ)在本章之 4.2.7.1.5 小段提到 The "Safeer"(1994) 1 Lloyd's Rep. 637 先例,看来,本项"君主禁制"的免责也完全适用,可在海牙规则下保护承运人/船东。

(ⅲ)在本章之 4.2.6.6.8 小段提到 The "Nan Fung" 1988(伦敦仲裁),是涉及船舶被列入黑名单,被高雄港当局拒绝进港卸货,这也应是"君主禁制"的免责。但问题是海牙规则有克尽职责令船舶适航的先决条件,满足了才能去享受免责。此外,也有说法是若订约时应已可合理知道这"君主禁制"的事项将会在履约时"无可避免地发生"(inevitably doomed),则船东不准享受免责:Ciampa v. British India Steam Navigation Co. (1915) 2 K.B. 774;The "Angelia"(1972) 2 Lloyd's Rep. 154。

(ⅳ)两伊战争曾带来 70 多艘船舶被封锁在 Shatt-el-Arab 河,这导致一连串的案例,如 The "Bamburi"(1982) 1 Lloyd's Rep. 312(船舶保险),以及 The "Evia"(1982) 2 Lloyd's Rep. 307,The "Wenjiang"(1983) 1 Lloyd's Rep. 400,The "Chrysalis"(1983) 1 Lloyd's Rep. 503,The "Lucille"(1984) 1 Lloyd's Rep. 244,等等(租约方面)。在 The "Bamburi",判损失属"君主禁制"造成,虽然伊拉克无意将船舶据为己有,占有或使用该船舶,以免引起国际事端。

(ⅴ)在 1982 年的英阿福克兰群岛之战,英国征用了 P&O 船公司的"Strathewe"轮作为运兵之用。P&O 安排将船上货物在马尔他转运去美国,再把空船交给英国政府。在马尔他,因为货物标记与舱单不符,导致遗失,货物也失去价值。美国法院判 P&O 要负责。因为"君主禁制"(英国政府征用)不是近因,货损货差是事后在转运时不妥善/小心处理与照看货物所造成的:The "Strathewe"(1986) LMLN 180。请注意此案例判法与 4.2.5.6 和 4.2.7.1.1.4 小段介绍的 Gosse Millerd v. Canadian

Government Merchant Marine（1928）32 Lloyd's Rep. 91 先例有类同之处。

有关"君主禁制"最后再谈谈它会带来什么样的货损货差。答案应是各种各样的都会有。例如在 The "Denbighshire" 是把货物从香港转运至日本的额外费用；在 The "Safeer" 是全船货物丧失；在 The "Nan Fung" 以及其他被封锁在 Shatt-el-Arab 河的船舶，严重的延误也会导致全船货物损坏。别说是易腐货物了，就是像水泥也会因质变而全损。再说，延误也会带来延误交货的损失，如市场下跌：The "Heron II"（1967）2 Lloyd's Rep. 457 或损坏扩大：The "Panaghia Tinnou"（1986）2 Lloyd's Rep. 586。

接下来谈谈这免责项目的第二部分："法律程序的扣押"（seizure under legal process）。这种例子不多，较早提到的 Finlay v. Liverpool and Great Western Steamship Co. 算是一个例子，它涉及原告起诉索取货物的占有权，在纽约法院申请获得法院下令把货物扣押。该先例判是光有"君主禁制"的免责不足以保障船东。但海牙规则加了这第二部分的免责，应可在同样情况下起到作用。

4.2.7.1.8　免责项目之(h)：检疫

"检疫"（Quarantine restrictions）可导致延误交货或/与货物全损，例如怀疑肉类货物曾受污染或来自瘟疫国家而遭没收/销毁，即会适用这项免责。当然，没有这项明示免责也可以，因为上一项的"君主禁制"免责一样适用。正如《Voyage Charter》一书第 767 页说道："…it is difficult to think of any cases where a 'quarantine restriction' will protect a shipowner where a 'restraint of princes' would not."

或许是，拟订海牙规则的前辈们特别小心，宁可多说，总比漏说好。

4.2.7.1.9　免责项目之，(i)：货方自己的行为或错漏

4.2.7.1.9.1　简介及例子

这一项免责所指的"货方自己的行为或错漏"（Act or omission of the shipper or owner of the goods, his agent or representative）看来与稍后提到的另三项免责有相同之处，它们是：

(i)(m)项的货物固有缺陷。

(ii)(n)项的包装不足。

(iii)(o)项的标记不足。

但货方（主要是发货人）会犯错或作出不当行为导致货损货差的情况远远不止这三项。例如，因发货人申明的货物（一台机器）重量有误，以致在装货或卸货中被吊机吊起时，因过重而掉落损坏。显然，本项免责对此应可适用。另再多举一例子是 *Voyage Charter* 一书第 767 页讲到的，对冷藏货发货人要求的在航次中保持的温度不对，导致货损，这一来承运人又应该可以享受这一项免责。但要再提醒和强调的是承运人/船东在海牙规则 Article 3 下的妥善与小心照看货物责任，常会与免责

项目纠缠不清,这在 4.2.7.1.1.4 小段之"管船"与 4.2.7.1.3.1 小段之"海难"都有涉及。故此,若是船长应可合理发现发货人所申明的错漏而防止事故,这会令因果关系中断,或者说,出事故的近因实际归咎为船长疏于照看货物。

4.2.7.1.9.2　危险品

这一项免责常会涉及另一种常见的事故。危险品的事故可以十分严重,既会有货损货差,也会有船舶损坏/全损、人命伤亡、共同海损、救助,等等。而且,事故的起因也会涉及发货人自己的行为或错漏。例如,发货人为了省运费故意不向班轮公司申报集装箱内的危险品:The "Kapitan Sakharov" (2000) 2 Lloyd's Rep. 255。或是,申报不足或/与申报错误。例如,在 The "Atlantic Duchess" (1957) 2 Lloyd's Rep. 55 一案的货物,向承运人/船东申报的是"原油"(crude oil),但其实是加了"丁烷"(butane)的原油,应称为"butanized crude oil",导致有船长不知的其他危险。就这方面的问题(即申报不足/错误),Donaldson 大法官在 Micada Compania Naviera S. A. v. Texim (1968) 2 Lloyd's Rep. 57 先例曾说道:"The danger consisted in the fact that the cargo was not what it seemed to be. The master, on the findings of fact, had proffered to him what one might describe as a non-shifting board cargo and it was offered, as it were, labelled as a non-shifting board cargo. In fact we now know what it was, at least as to part, a shifting board cargo and as to part it may not have been loadable at all. In a word, what he was being offered was a wet wolf in a dry sheep's clothing and there was nothing to put him on notice that the cargo was something radically and fundamentally different from that which it appeared to be. In those circumstances it seems to me that the cargo was dangerous beyond all argument."

有关危险品的课题,在本书第三章之 11.2.1 小段已有详论,但侧重不同,那段是讲中国出口商对危险品运输会带来灾难性意外和庞大金额索赔的危险务必要有所警惕。在此则着重是谈海牙规则给予承运人/船东享有的免责项目之(i):货方自己的行为或错漏。这会发生在发货人没有事前通知船长,让后者去熟悉、防范该批货物会有的特殊风险的情况下。

事实上,海牙规则还另有一条条款特别针对这一情况,那是 Article 4 (6),可节录如下:"Goods of an inflammable, explosive or dangerous nature to the shipment where of the carrier, master or agent of the carrier has not consented with knowledge of their nature and character, may at any time before discharge be landed at any place, or destroyed or rendered innocuous by the carrier without compensation and the shipper of such goods shall be liable for all damages and expenses directly or indirectly arising out of or resulting from such shipment. If any such goods shipped with such knowledge and consent shall become a danger to the ship or cargo, they may in like manner be landed at any place, or destroyed or rendered innocuous by the carrier without liability on the part of the carrier except to general average, if any."

以上条款可分两部分去分析。第一部分是针对发货人不申报(或申报不足/错误)货物是危险品,也没有获得承运人同意就装上船,那么一经发觉,承运人可随时随地半途卸下,或销毁,或令它变为无害而不必负上任何责任,甚至所花费用以及所受损失(如船期延误)也要发货人去承担(若能成功追索)。"随时随地"表示不必是出了事故,或有了货损货差,承运人才可以这样做。所以,光是靠海牙规则 Article 4(2)(i)的一项免责(货方自己的行为或错漏)并不足以保障承运人:它只是针对发生了货损货差(loss or damage to goods)的免责。说真的,条款的这一部分有惩罚发货人的味道。所以它还说明了发货人要承担"所有"后果/费用。发货人唯一可以对这一方面抗辩是承运人仅凭货物描述已可合理知道它有一般性的危险:Ente Nazionale v. Baliwag Nav. 1986 AMC 1184(4 Cir. 1985)。这一来,可以说是承运人同意了运载这货物,同时也接受了(并应了解到)它一般性/合理可知道的危险。

以上条款的第二部分是针对承运人知道并同意去装运这票危险品,这时他/它再不可以任意和随时去将货物处理掉,例如开出装港就把该货物抛下大海。承运人只能在真正出了事故,危险品真正对人命、财产(船舶等)构成危险时,才可以卸下、销毁或处置它。承运人这样做了,也不必对货方(拥有危险品)的损失负责,作出任何赔偿。除非是要分担共同海损,这主要会是把危险品销毁(抛下大海)恰好也属共同海损牺牲,那是要所有受益方(包括船东)去分摊的。

4.2.7.1.10 免责项目之(m):货物固有缺陷

这一项免责类同于前面 4.2.7.1.9 小段的"货方自己的行为或错漏",所以在此提前先谈。为了方便阅读,不妨先将海牙规则的这(m)项免责节录如下:"Wastage in bulk or weight or other loss or damage arising from inherent defect, quality or vice of the goods."

先要说清楚:这一项的"固有缺陷"(inherent defect)与海牙规则另一项(p)的"潜在缺陷"(latent defect)的分别是:前者针对货物,后者针对船舶。

这一项免责下首先会介绍货物的自然流失/短重可免责,接着再谈谈其他的货物"固有缺陷"所造成的损失,这可包括许多情况,稍后详论。

4.2.7.1.10.1 定义

"固有缺陷"的定义可节录美国"统一商业法典"(Uniform Commercial Code)所说的如下:"any existing defects, diseases, decay or the inherent nature of the commodity which will cause it to deteriorate with a lapse of time."(因时间一久会导致货物变坏/变质的任何货物存在的缺陷、毛病、腐烂或潜在本质)。

William Tetley 教授的 *Marine Cargo Claim* 一书第 3 版第 479 页对此所给予的定

义是:"An inherent vice is one which is an innate or natural or normal quality of the goods. For example, it is an inherent vice of flour that it shrinks and loses weight with the passage of time."(固有缺陷是货物固有的、自然及正常的本质。例如,面粉会随着时间的过去而发生收缩和失去重量)。

最后还可节录 Diplock 勋爵在 Soya Gmbh v. White(1983)1 Lloyd's Rep. 122 先例所说的如下:"If(固有缺陷)means the risk of deterioration of the goods shipped as a result of their natural behavior in the ordinary course of the contemplated voyage without the intervention of any fortuitous external event or casualty…"(付运货物在预计航次中变质/变坏的风险,来自货物本身自然的反应,并没有任何外来事故去导致)。

从以上一段可见,"预计航次"(contemplated voyage)如何也很有关系,这会导致同一样货物[例如是 I. W. L(Institute Warranty Limit)中的印度煤炭]在一个短航次,冷天气下可以抵受,不存在"固有缺陷"。但若在一个长航次,途经高温地区等,则无可避免要变质/变坏,不能抵受,这显然是"固有缺陷"了。这方面问题在 The "Maltasian"(1966)2 Lloyd's Rep. 53 先例有详论,而 Reid 勋爵也说道:"…that whether there was inherent vice depended on transit required by contract."

4.2.7.10.2 自然流失/短重

上一小段已提到面粉会有短重,曾有法国先例判"袋装面粉"(bagged flour)减少 0.5%~1% 的重量属可接受的范围:Cour d'appel de Douai, Nov. 22,1956, DMF 1957, 100。当然,这百分比的多少不好说死,它会受许多因素影响。例如,其中一个重要因素便是航次的长短。其他品种的货物还会受不同因素的影响,如原油/石油产品会有蒸发,其速度快慢会与航次中所遇温度有关。农产品也有水分蒸发,影响因素之一是该产品/货物的含水量。

酒是另一种免不了会减少重量的货物。法国曾有案例判短重 0.25% 属可以接受/免责:Cour d'Appel de Montpellier, January 7,1958, DMF 1958, 220。另也有判例指短重 0.45% 可以接受/免责:Cour d'Appel de Montpellier, January 10, 1974, DMF 1974,341。

已经提过,农产品常有水分蒸发,"收缩"(shrinkage)等导致自然流失/短重。例如在美国先例的 Shui Fa Oil Mill Co., Ltd. V. M/S Norma, 1976 AMC 936(SDNY 1976),判是散装大豆可接受 1.55% 的短少。

一些较不明显的货物品种一样会有这问题。例如曾有案例判袋装水泥可以有 4% 短重:Cour d'Appel de Rouen, December 14, 1956, DMF 1957, 536,或是散装化肥可有 1.5% 至 2% 的短重:United States v. Central Gulf Lines, 699 F.2d 243(5 Cir. 1983)。

至于原油/石油产品,更是有 0.5% 的所谓"习惯性短重"的说法,这在本书第六章之 3.2.2.2 小段有涉及,不再多谈。有关先例是 The "Ypatianna" (1981) 2 Lloyd's Rep. 286。最后略提一下涉及这一问题的其他有关方面,如下:

(ⅰ)这争议的举证常会以专家的意见作为支持。同一品种货物在以往相同航次曾经历过的自然流失/短重比率会是重要依据。

(ⅱ)海上货物保险不保/不赔这种短重/短少。

(ⅲ)若有货物短重/短少超出了可接受/免责的百分比,承运人便要负责,不过法院仍会扣除可接受/免责的部分,余下部分才要承运人赔偿。

4.2.7.1.10.3 其他形式的固有缺陷

这方面的例子会是多种多样,有些货物品种的固有缺陷已是众所周知的,如鱼粉、煤炭会发生自燃,水果、肉食会腐烂,农作物与皮革等货物会生虫,等等。

在本书第三章 11.2.1 小段提到的危险品在航次中发生危险,常会与货物可能存在的固有缺陷有关。在本章之 4.2.6.6.6.1 小段提到的 The "Fjord Wind" (1999) 1 Lloyd's Rep. 307,涉及大豆因延误而发霉,这也会是货物的固有缺陷所引致。另外还有许多不同的例子,如:

(ⅰ)The "Hobsons Bay" (1933) 46 Lloyd's Rep. 189 的苹果。

(ⅱ)Wm. Fergus Harris & Son Ltd. V. China Mutual S. N. Co. (1959) 2 Lloyd's Rep. 500 的木材因未"经干燥"(seasoned),交货时出现损坏,而装船时看不出未经干燥。

(ⅲ)The "Maltasian" (1966) 2 Lloyd's Rep. 53 的咸鱼变坏/"变红"(reddening)。(ⅳ) The "Ahmadu Bello" (1967) 1 Lloyd's Rep. 293 的"coco yams"发生腐烂。(ⅴ)The "Hoyanger" (1979) 2 Lloyd's Rep. 79 的过熟苹果装船,经过 45 天的航程后交货时已腐烂。

4.2.7.1.10.4 与船东/承运人尽责的关系

这方面有好几点要提提。首先是货物有固有缺陷并不影响签发清洁提单,因为这缺陷不是装船时可从表面看到的。自然,签发了清洁提单也不影响船东/承运人以固有缺陷去作为抗辩。

第二点是不少货物都会需要特别照看,而船东在海牙规则的 Article 3(2) 下也有妥善与小心照看货物之责。如提单合约有明示或默示要求而船东却疏于特别照料导致货损,近因/主因就并非是货物固有缺陷。例如,芝士需要通风却缺乏通风:S. M. Sartori Inc. v. Kastav, 412 F. Supp. 1181,1977 AMC 126 (SDNY 1976)。或是,货物需要冷藏却没做到,正如 Lord Reid 在 The "Mattasian" (1966) 2 Lloyd's Rep. 53 所讲的:"It follows that whether there is an inherent defect or vice must depend on the kind of transit required by the contract. If this contract had required refrigeration there would have been no inherent vice. But as it did not there was inherent vice because the goods could not stand the treatment which the contract authorized or required."

第三点是船东/承运人对所运载的货物应有所认识才能妥善与小心地照看,这认识/了解的程度只是一般性的,不要求船东/承运人是专家。若货物真有特别之处需要照看,但不为一般人所知,发货人有责任通知船东/承运人。这方面在 William Tetley 教授的《Mafine Cargo Claim》一书第 3 版第 485 页是说:"The degree of knowledge of the cargo expected of the carrier is not, however, of the highest expertise; such knowledge is the domain of the shipper who provides the cargo. Thus a carrier was not expected to know that a cargo of volatile fertilizer had been improperly treated to avoid caking. The carrier in consequence was not held to be negligent in failing to reduce the height of the stow."

4.2.7.1.10.5　与船东/承运人违约的关系

这种关系上的争议经常有:货物发生损坏/变质,船东/承运人会指这是货物本身的固有缺陷所造成,而货方则常会指是承运人违约,如疏忽堆放货物(堆得太高或太接近机房等),航次中疏于通风,等等。而在海牙规则之 Article 3(2),是要求船东/承运人要妥善与小心堆放、照看货物,有疏忽自然是违约:请看本章之 4.2.8 小段。而要区分或找出货物变质/损坏的主因/近因是什么,是货物本身的固有缺陷还是船东/承运人本身的疏忽/违约,实际是一个事实问题,而认定事实就要靠证据了。

例如在 The "Maltasian" (1966) 2 Lloyd's Rep. 53,涉及咸鱼变坏,承运人抗辩称是由于货物的固有缺陷,而货方(提单持有人/受让人)却指是由于承运人疏忽堆放与通风。

另在 The "Ahmadu Bello" (1967) 1 Lloyd's Rep. 293,涉及一新品种的货物(食物),是袋装的"coco yams",在卸港被发现发生腐烂。其中对承运人的一个主要指控是货物堆放得太高,达 16 层之高,结果是全凭专家的意见去判定,正如上诉庭的 Sellers 大法官讲道:"This was not a very confident reliance by the surveyor on high stacking and weight. The problem was raised quite properly with scientists. Little was know of the peculiarities and propensities of coco yams and laboratory experiments were made. In the laboratory, tests under pressure were make but the results were inconclusive as far as the issues raised in this case are concerned. A pressure of over about 5 lb. to the square inch it was found would cause bruising of an average coco yam of the type of these parcels and would lead to a mould forming over an area of the surface in a temperature of 80 deg. F. humid heat. This in itself was not shown to have caused a rupture in the cell walls which would be a state of decomposition. One of the consultants spoke of distortion of the cells at a pressure over 5 lb. rather than rupture. The judgment finds and accepts, in accordance with the evidence of both Dr. Williams and Dr. Milton, both of whom were consultants who had no prior knowledge of coco yams, that there must be cell ruptures to enable the anaerobic micro-organisms to work and cause decomposition."

由于每袋 coco yam 是 12 寸至 15 寸高,而船舶二层舱高只有 9 尺,所以法院推算堆放顶多是 8 层高,不会是货方所讲的 16 层高。而这只会造成底层有 4 磅压力而不是足以造成破裂的 5 磅压力。故 Lyell 大法官说:"…that bags could not have been stowed more than nine bags high, and probable height was eight; that pressure at bottom of cargo was 4 1b. per sq. in. and cell rupture would require pressure of more than 5 lb. per sq. in. ; and that lowest bags were not damaged;…that damage to yams did not arise from faulty stowage…but from defect inherent in goods before shipment which was not apparent…"

最后要举的例子是 The "Hoyanger" (1979) 2 Lloyd's Rep. 79,涉及货物(苹果)在阿根廷装船时,曾有承运人的保险人雇用的水果专家(名为 Agrotec)检验了苹果,认为没有问题,于是船东签发了清洁提单。后来在加拿大卸港(温哥华)发现苹果已坏掉。收货人为此起诉承运人,指控他/它没有安排"冷风的通风"(circulation of cool air)及将一箱箱苹果堆放得太近,以致之间无法透风。但加拿大法院认为承运人成功证明了货物堆放与照看并没有不妥善或/与不小心之处。毛病实际是出自航次太长(45 天之久)、苹果过熟以及专家错用阿根廷标准验货(标准较低,而阿根廷苹果过往的航次不超过 15 天等)。而专家犯错并不代表什么,因为承运人签不签清洁提单本来没有必要去找专家协助:这方面可参阅本书第六章之 3.3.3 小段。只要苹果过熟是承运人不能合理看出的(这也不是对苹果没有专门知识的一般人士可从外表看得出的),就不能怪承运人签发了清洁提单。该先例中 Addy 大法官判道:"…the poor condition of the apples discovered on discharge was caused by their overripeness previous to loading which rendered them unfit to withstand the rigours of a 45 day voyage and that such overripeness would not have been evident to the ordinary observer without particular expertise in the physiological condition of the fruit; this constituted an inherent defect, quality or vice…It was obvious that neither the defendants, who issued clean bills of lading, nor Agrotec who had been engaged to carry out the inspections actually knew or suspected that the cargo was unfit because Agrotec erroneously applied the Argentine standards; the carriers had not contented themselves with an ordinary inspection and it would be both improper and without legal justification to fix liability on a carrier based on lack of knowledge or expertise of an expert which the carrier was not by law nor by duty to the consignee bound to engage.

The carrier is responsible for the proper stowage, carriage and care of the cargo but it was the shipper and consignee who were presumed to know the hidden weaknesses and defects of the cargo…[527]"

除了与海牙规则之 Article 3(2)难以区分而导致争议外,货物的"固有缺陷"与船东/承运人的另一种违约之间,也常会引起争议,那便是航次的延误。若延误属不正常,但可免责,例如是搁浅/碰撞,属航行/管船疏忽与过错(本章之 4.2.7.1.1 小段),则货物损坏/变坏不论近因/主因是"固有缺陷"还是"航行疏忽与过错",反正都属免责项目,船东/承运人均不必负责。

但若延误是由于船东/承运人不能免责的违约造成,而这延误导致货物损坏/变质,那么船东/承运人就要负责了。这种违约会是不适航或未克尽职责(海牙规则之 Article 3(1))或不合理绕航(海牙规则之 Article 4(4))。这更不用说海牙规则本来就把适航要求当做先决条件了:请看本章之 4.2.6.3 小段。即使在英国普通法,也早有 Pickford 大法官在 The "Cid"(1909) 2 K.B. 360 先例说道:"…although a common carrier is not responsible for damage arising from the nature of the article itself, so long as he performs the voyage properly, he is responsible if he aggravates that damage by any breach of contract on his part."

4.2.7.1.10.6 举证责任在谁

在 4.2.7 小段一开始的标题,已说明是由"船东/承运人证明免责"。但有关货物"固有缺陷"的争议,看来举证责任在谁有点不稳定,也并非一成不变是在想去免责的船东/承运人身上。对此,可先去节录 William Tetley 教授的《Marine Cargo Claims》一书第 3 版第 481、482 页的所说如下:"The rule that the party which has access to certain facts is expected ultimately to prove those facts is especially pertinent in respect to inherent vice and hidden defect because on these matters the shipper is better informed than the carrier.

In consequence, in case of inherent vice and hidden defect the burden of proving good order soon shifts to the claimant despite the fact that the carrier normally has the burden of proof in all exculpatory exceptions."(因为对货物有否"固有缺陷",发货人拥有更多的资料,例如付运前如何处理等,所以有准则/规则是把举证责任转到发货人的身上。这导致承运人虽然对免责通常有举证责任,但针对"固有缺陷"而言,承运人一旦提出货物有"固有缺陷",通常再加上专家或验货师的质疑作为支持,举证责任会很快转到发货人的身上)。

---

[527] 承运人没有法律责任要聘请专家(不过聘请了也不是坏事),不应去惩罚承运人或调高他/它签发准确提单的责任。所以若专家和船长都可合理地察觉出不应签发清洁提单,而都犯了错误,则承运人负有责任;但若专家应察觉而犯了错误,船长根本无法察觉,则承运人免责,因签发提单是以船长为准。

对这一点，美国先例有明确的说法，那是在 Salzman Tobacco Co. v. S. S. Mormacwind 1967 AMC 277 (2 Cir. 1967) 所说的: "…when cargo damage may have resulted from a hidden defect present at the time of shipment, the shipper has the burden of proving that the cargo was in good condition when delivered to the carrier, because the shipper has access to the facts concerning the cargo's then condition…However this burden does not mean that the shipper must always introduce direct evidence that the cargo was in good condition when shipped. The shipper may also meet his burden by showing, from the condition of the cargo as delivered or otherwise, that the damage was caused by the carrier's negligence and not by any inherent vice of the cargo."（当货损可能是由付运时货物固有或潜在的缺陷造成时，发货人要举证这货物交给承运人托运时，实属良好，因为发货人才会有相关的资料。发货人倒也并非总是要提供这货物装船时实属良好的直接证据，他/它也可以凭货物交付时损坏/变坏的情况去指证货损是由承运人自己的疏忽造成，而非由货物固有缺陷引致）。

在英国，有关的先例是 The "Flowergate" (1967) 1 Lloyd's Rep. 1, 说法有点不同, Roskill 大法官说: "that burden of proving inherent vice was on defendants, but, there was no obligation on defendants to prove inherent vice and to negative negligence, although in proving that damage was caused by inherent vice they might have to exclude negligence（货物固有缺陷的举证责任在被告/承运人。但承运人不必同时去证明固有缺陷以及自己清白没有疏忽。指证承运人疏忽照看货物才是货损主因/近因实属货方下一步的责任，这可参阅本章 4.2.2 小段提及的举证责任先后顺序之(4)与(5)，以及 4.2.8 小段。但被告/承运人在证明货物固有缺陷的同时，往往已要去排除自己有任何疏忽，等于仍是免不了有举证之责）"。

所以，William Tetley 教授在其 *Marine Cargo Claims* 一书第 483 页提到安全的做法仍是承运人与原告的货方都应努力寻找证据以证明、支持对自己有利的事实，去节录如下: "From the foregoing one can conclude that the carrier and claimant are advised to do everything possible to prove the facts available to them in a case of hidden defect and inherent vice."

4.2.7.1.11 免责项目之(n): 包装不足

这一项免责也是类同于 4.2.7.1.9 小段的"货方自己的行为或错漏"，为了方便阅读，先节录如下: "Insufficiency of packing."

4.2.7.1.11.1 何谓足够包装？

这方面要求的是要有合理和习惯性的包装。过分的包装要求会是既不实际又昂贵。这里习惯十分重要，因为如果一直是这样的做法，也未曾出过事，即显示货物没有包装不足。正如 William Tetley 教授在 *Marine Cargo Claims* 一书第 3 版之第 492

页说道:"where cargo in customary packing is damaged, although ordinarily cargo so packed does not suffer damage, it can be concluded that the packing was sufficient and that the carrier was at fault for failing to exercise proper care."

同样的说法也出现在 The "Lucky Wave" (1985) 1 Lloyd's Rep. 80, Sheen 大法官说:"when a cargo had been carried frequently over a number of years without suffering from the stresses and strains necessarily encountered during a sea voyage, that suggested that the packing of the cargo was sufficient; if similar cargo packed in a similar way was discharged in a damaged condition that suggested that it had been roughly handled…"

所以有了这方面争议,货方会去举证说服法官过去 23 年都是以同样做法包装货物,却从未出过事故: Hunt Foods v. Matson Navigation Co., 1966 AMC 50 (E. D. La. 1966)。

4.2.7.1.11.2　表面可见包装不足就不应签发清洁提单

包装不足与上一小段的货物固有缺陷的不同之处是前者会在装货上船时已可觉察、看见。这一来,会有船东/承运人本来就不应去签发清洁提单之争:The "Aeneas" (1929) 35 Lloyd's Rep. 49。有关清洁提单的课题,请参阅本书第六章之 3.3 小段。

当然,也会有包装不足是表面无法合理觉察或看见的。这一来,就不能责怪船东/承运人签发清洁提单了,这种情况下他/它自然也可以包装不足(如果是货损的近因/主因)作为抗辩。

4.2.7.1.11.3　与船东/承运人违约的关系

这方面的大精神与 4.2.7.1.10.5 小段所讲的大致一样,反正举证责任一般是在承运人身上。如果包装不足与违约都是造成货损的原因,则去区分出损失比例具体归因于哪项也是承运人的责任。若做不到,承运人就要负赔偿全责。这可以节录 William Tetley 教授的《Marine Cargo Claims》一书第 3 版第 495 页所说的如下: "Where there is insufficient packing and any other cause of loss, the burden is, of course, on the carrier to show what percentage was due to the insufficient packing and what was due to the other cause. The carrier will be responsible for the whole loss if he is unable to separate the damage arising from the two causes."

Tetley 教授还就此举了一些案例,如法国的 Cour d'Appel d'Aix, October ll, 1960, DMF 1962, 276 先例的香蕉损坏,属"不妥善堆装"(improper stowage)引起,但包装不足也令损坏加大。结果判承运人要赔偿一半损失。

举证之责虽在船东/承运人,但考虑到包装足或不足的证据是在货方手中,如过往航次是如何包装或是否有过同样货损等。因此,船东/承运人应可要求货方披露有关资料,而法官/仲裁员也应合理地下令货方去披露。William Tetley 教授在该书同一页也有说到这点:"Because the burden of proof is on the carrier, he has been held entitled in discovery proceedings to range in his questions over the broad field of the shipper's experience in shipping similar cargoes."

4.2.7.1.11.4 包装不足之货损其他货物可否免责

货物本身不妥亦会影响其他装在同一艘船舱的货物,不论是固有缺陷还是包装不足。例如固有缺陷,像 The "Amphion"(1991) 2 Lloyd's Rep. 101 先例中,会自燃的鱼粉没有去处理过(antioxidant)就装了上船,后来果真发生自燃,这免不了会波及其他货物。

包装不足也是一样,像 The "Biela"(1929) 34 Lloyd's Rep. 192 先例,涉及包装不足的机器掉下驳船,撞穿了洞,结果海水涌入损坏了已卸下驳船的棉花。争议是:包装不足这项抗辩可否适用在其他受波及货物的损坏? 即不光是针对受损机器,还包括受损棉花?

应明确的是,"固有缺陷"的免责只适用在有关的货物,不包括受波及的其他货物。这是因为海牙规则在这一项免责后面说明是"of the goods"。但"包装不足"并没有相同字句,看来规则并不想局限这项免责的适用。所以在 The "Biela"先例,Roche 大法官说:"It has been argued…that as regards [海牙规则之 Article 4(2)(n)], insufficiency of packing' has reference to the packing of the particular goods in respect of which loss or damage arises. I have no doubt that (n) is intended chiefly and maindy to apply to such a case, but I am not satisfied and I do not decide that insufficiency of packing of another parcel which is to be shipped with the damaged cargo cannot be prayed in aid or used under(n)…"

话说回来,对受到固有缺陷或包装不足货物波及而受损的其他货物而言,若是船东/承运人没有犯错/疏忽,他/它可以依赖最后一项"总揽"(catch-all)的免责(q):G. E. Crippen and Another v. Vancouver Tug Boat Co. Ltd. (1971) 2 Lloyd's Rep. 207:请参阅本章之 4.2.7.1.16 小段。

4.2.7.1.12 免责项目之(o):标记不足

有关货物标记不足会导致的损失/麻烦,本书第六章之 3.1 小段有谈及。其他大原则与前述的数项免责类同,笔者不再重复。

4.2.7.1.13 免责项目之(j):罢工/停工

笔者现在返回讲这(j)项的免责,前文跳过这项而先讲(m),(n)与(o)项的免责,是因为这 3 项免责本质上类同于(i)项。为方便读者,不妨先将这一项(j)的免责节录如下:"Strikes, lock-outs or stoppage or restraint of labour from whatever cause, whether partial or general."

4.2.7.1.13.1 定义

"罢工"(strike)是指雇员由于劳资纠纷暂时拒绝上班。罢工工人的要求(如增加工资)得不到及时满足时,可能诱发暴力行为而损坏货物。而光是罢工造成的延误,也会造成易腐货物的变质/变坏:The "Arawa"(1980) 2 Lloyd's Rep. 135。

对罢工所下的权威定义,可节录一处说法,一是在 Williams Bros.(Hull) v. N. V. W. H. Berghuys Kolenhandel (1915) 21 Com. Cas. 253 之 257 页所说的: "a general concerted refusal of men to work in consequence of an alleged grievance."

另外在 The "New Horizon"(1975) 2 Lloyd's Rep. 314 先例,Denning 勋爵说:"a concerted stoppage of work by men done with a view to improving their wages or conditions or giving vent to a grievance or making a protest about something or other, or supporting or sympathizing with other workmen in such endeavor[528]. It is distinct from a stoppage which is brought about by an external event such as a bomb scare or by apprehension of danger."[529]

"被迫停工"(lock-outs)是指资方关闭工作场所或阻止复工而令工人无法继续上班。而"任何原因导致的停工或阻碍工人劳动"(stoppage or restraint of labour from whatever cause)这一措辞/文字十分广泛,已在较早时提及,其后加上"whether partial or general"一句,表示工人人数不足,来不及重新雇用已辞退的工人,也可包括在此免责 Re Richardsons & Samuel (1898) 1 Q. B. 261。

而海牙规则在开始列出所有各项免责前已广泛地说明免责是针对所列事项"导致或引致"(arising or resulting from)的损失。故此,罢工/停工后的后遗症如港口拥挤等,这些延误一样包括在此项(j)的免责。

4.2.7.1.13.2 什么人的罢工

海牙规则这一项免责并没有局限罢工或停工须是何人所为。因此免责可包括诸如船员、装卸工人、驳船船员、拖船船员、海关或检疫人员,等等。甚至岸上如铁路工人的罢工/停工也会包括在这一项广泛的免责之内,正如 *Voyage Charters* 一书第 768 页说道:"Indeed, on this basis, the exception might even cover the situation where a vessel operating on a liner trade is delayed by a strike of workers inland delaying the bringing forward of cargo, which delay then causes damage to cargo already loaded; see

---

[528] 一个协调一致的停工,工人是为了加工资,或改善工作条件,或发泄个人不满,或对某事提出抗议,或支持或同情其他罢工工人,等等。

[529] 但外来因素导致停工,不存在工人的自发性,例如恐防有炸弹或危险导致停工,这不算罢工。但要注意的是海牙规则这一(j)项的免责措辞十分广泛,并非只包括"罢工"(strike),还包括了"任何原因导致的停工"(stoppage...from whatever cause),故它应包括外来因素导致的停工如"炸弹警告"(bomb scare),疫症恐慌等:Stephens v. Harris (1887) 17 L. T. 618。

Smith & Service v. The Rosario Nitrate Co. (1893) 2 Q. B. 323, affirmed at (1894) 1 Q. B. 174."

4.2.7.1.14　免责项目之(k)：暴动与内乱

可先节录这短短一项的海牙规则 Article 4(2)(k) 如下："Riots and civil commotions."

"暴动"(riots)与"内乱"(civil commotions)的区别在于：前者并非以颠覆现政权为目标，可能仅仅是"无心的暴徒"(mindless mob)所为。参与后者的虽不是无心的暴徒，但也不一定是要去推翻颠覆现政权，只要参与的人员有一些共同的意愿或/与企图，其行动也造成了大规模的混乱与暴力，即构成"内乱"。看来，中国历史上的梁山伯好汉造反应属"内乱"。正如 Mustill 大法官在 Spinney's (1948) v. Royal Insurance Co. (1980) 1 Lloyd's Rep. 406 所说的："I find nothing in the authorities compelling the Court to hold that a civil commotion must involve a revolt against the Government, although the disturbances must have sufficient cohesion to prevent them from being the work of a mindless mob...There must be some unanimity of purpose among those participating...It must involve a really substantial proportion of the populace...and that there should be tumult and violence on a large scale..."

至于权威性的定义，"暴动"一词在英国刑法有明确的定义，海牙规则这一项免责也应同样适用。这一点可以节录 Voyage Charters 一书第 769 页所说的如下："'Riot has a specific meaning in criminal law, namely that at least three persons[530], with a common purpose[531] and an intention to give mutual assistance, by force if necessary, against opposing them in the execution of that common purpose[532], should use force or violence in and about the accomplishment of that purpose in such a manner as to alarm at least one person of reasonable firmness and courage[533]. Field v. Metropolitan Police Receiver (1907) 2 K. B. 853. Mere malicious injury, even by three or more persons, does not constitute a riot[534]. This meaning has been held to apply to provisions in a policy of insurance: London and Lancashire Fire Insurance Co. v. Bolands (1924) A. C. 836. There is therefore good reason for thinking that the same definition would apply to the present exception."

而"内乱"的权威定义可节录 Mansfield 勋爵在 Langdale v. Mason (1780) 2 Park

---

[530]　暴动要有 3 人以上。
[531]　他们有一个共同意愿/目标。
[532]　若遇上阻力，他们会不惜使用暴力，相互合作去对付。
[533]　这使用暴力的企图可令一个有合理决心与勇气的人士也警觉得到。
[534]　但光是 3 人或 3 人以上纯为恶意伤害他人（如流氓打架伤人），这不算暴动。

on Insurance 965 所说的:"…an insurrection of the people for general purposes, though it may not amount to a rebellion, where there is usurped power."

显然,船舶遇上暴动或/与内乱,会造成货损货差,或是延误交货,这些都需要该项免责来保护船东/承运人。

4.2.7.1.15 免责项目之(l):海上救助或试图救助人命或财产

这一项免责的英文措辞如下:"Saving or attempting to save life or property at sea."

这一项免责与海牙规则 Article 4(4)涉及的不准船舶不合理绕航有密切的关系,这方面稍后会详论:4.2.10.1 小段。

它们之所以有关是因为救助人命或财产总免不了要绕航,并延误航次。在海上救助人命是不容置疑的,但英国普通法并不允许为财产而进行救助:Scaramanga v. Stamp(1880)5 C.D. 295。

毕竟,进行救助会大大增加船货本身的风险,比如去拖曳搁浅中的船舶可能会令自己反倒出事,导致船货全损:Stuart v. British & African Nav. Co.(1875)321 L. T. 257。或是,拖曳其他船引致船速大减:Potter v. Burrell(1897)1 Q. B. 97。这一来,遇上装载的是易腐货物就麻烦了。而即使不是,也免不了延误交货。

海牙规则虽在这一项免责中增加了救助财产,但在今天通信发达,到处有专业救捞公司随时待命,且现今救助专业化,技术装备要求高的大环境下,海上救助财产再不是简单的拖拖拉拉,所以,普通路过的商船去进行救助并不多见。

4.2.7.1.16 免责项目之(p):克尽职责无法发觉的潜在缺陷

可先节录这项免责的英文如下:"Latent defects not discoverable by due diligence."

这一项与 4.2.7.1.10 小段的固有缺陷的分别是:这一项是针对船舶与它的供应(例如本章之 4.2.6.6.6.2 小段提到的质量差的燃油),不是针对货物。但照理说,这方面的问题在对船舶适航的要求上已有涉及,且有极大关联:请看本章之 4.2.6.4.4 小段等。所以,多加这一项免责有否必要呢?

答案应是肯定,因为:

(i)装卸可能是用岸吊/吊车,它有潜在缺陷而导致货损,例如令货物从高处掉下,《Scrutton on Charter Parties》一书第 19 版第 450 页是认为可包括在本项免责内,虽然岸吊根本不是船舶的一部分。

(ii)在 The "Highland Monarch"(1938)64 Lloyd's Rep. 188,Branson 大法官在192 页讲到了这项免责的额外好处/保障,例如船东/承运人无法对开船前已克尽职责成功举证,但该潜在缺陷却实际存在。

(iii)在 The "Kapitan Sakharov"(2000)2 Lloyd's Rep. 255,把潜在缺陷延伸到

没有申报危险品的集装箱发生爆炸/火灾。Auld 大法官质疑说:"Those responsible for the…stuffing and shipping of containers are plainly not carrying out any part of the carrier's function for which he should be held responsible. I can find nothing in the Hague Rules or at common law to make a carrier responsible for the unseaworthiness of its vessel resulting from a shipper's misconduct of which it, the carrier, has not been put on notice …It is not liable for latent defects in a vessel before it acquired it…So why, as a matter of unseaworthiness, should it be liable for latent defects in cargo shipped in it?"

4.2.7.1.17　免责项目之(q):总揽条款

这一项总结性的条款,也是海牙规则的最后一项免责,在现实中也颇为重要,可先去节录它的英文措辞/文字如下:"Any other cause arising without the actual fault or privity of the carrier, or without the fault or neglect of the agents or servants of the carrier, but the burden of proof shall be on the person claiming the benefit of this exception to show that neither the actual fault or privity of the carrier nor the fault or neglect of the agents or servants of the carrier contributed to the loss or damage."(任何其他非因承运人或他/它的代理人/雇员的实际过错或私谋所造成的货损货差,但对此的举证责任在承运人)。

4.2.7.1.17.1　给予广泛解释

对这种"总揽"(catch-all)条款,解释起来要受"同类规则"(ejusdem generis rule)的局限。这同类规则在笔者《国际商务游戏规则——英国合约法》一书第十章之6.3.2小段有详论。在此只节录其中的一小部分如下:"……其含义是:当合约条款先列举了一些特定的事项,其后再用概括性用词(general word)附加上一般事项时,后者的解释只能局限于与前面列明同类性质的事项(things of like nature)……"

但海牙规则所列的各种免责,各有完全不同的针对,很难说什么才属同类性质,所以有说法是这项(q)的免责不受"同类规则"的局限,仍可广泛解释,只要能证明承运人与他/它的代理/雇员没有过错或私谋即可免责:请看 Scrutton on Charter-Parties 一书第19版之第450页。在 William Tetley 教授的 Marine Cargo Claims 一书第3版之第516页,也说道:"Most authorities have also taken the view that the (q) exception is to be construed broadly."

4.2.7.1.17.2　无法解释原因的货损货差的举证责任

海牙规则只在这一项免责明确说明举证责任是在船东/承运人身上,可见在举证这一点上,责任应很明确。这也十分公道,因为货物在船东掌管下发生意外,能去说清楚(举证)的也只有他/它自己,不要求他/它去举证只会令事故真相无法查明,大家也不会从中吸收教训,等等。

本章之4.2.5小段已详细论述了船东/承运人须证明造成货损货差原因的理

由,加上本项免责又明确把举证责任加在他/它的身上,这表明对无法合理解释的货损货差,船东/承运人要承担责任。这在 Pendle & Rivett Ltd. v. Ellerman Lines, Ltd. (1927) 29 Lloyd's Rep. 133 先例也有清楚的说明如下:"That being so, under article Ⅳ, role 2 (q), the burden is on the defendants (被告的承运人) to show that these goods were lost…without any fault or privity on the part of the carrier or neglect by his servants or agents. Have they discharged that burden? If I accept all their evidence, in a sense they have. But in another sense they have not, because that which they seek to prove is wholly irreconcilable with the evidence for the plaintiffs (原告的货方). There is in truth a mystery about the loss[535]. If I accept the evidence given for the defendants the loss of the goods is quite inexplicable.

In these circumstances one side or the other must win[536]. I cannot give victory to both. I think the only logical result is that defeat must be on the side on which rests by this statute the burden of explaining that which would be otherwise inexplicable[537]. Having regard to the wholly inexplicable conflict of evidence on both sides I think I must hold that the defendants have not discharged the burden which is put upon them by Art. Ⅳ, Rule 2 (q) of the Act."

对无法解释的货损货差,船东/承运人不得以此项(q)的免责来逃避责任也在另一著名先例有提及。在 Phillips & Co. v. Clan Line Steamers Ltd. (1943) 26 Lloyd's Rep. 58, Atkinson 大法官说:"It is not necessary for the defendants (被告的承运人) to establish exactly why and how the damage occurred, provided they can disprove negligence[538]; but, of course, it is not easy to do that unless they can establish some reasonably possible alternative explanation[539]. If the damage is entirely unexplained, it is difficult to see how the onus can be discharged[540]."

4.2.7.1.17.3 适用(q)免责的情况

这种情况很多,也常会与其他免责项目并列作为抗辩,例如以"天意"(4.2.7.1.4 小段)作抗辩同时也结合本项免责。的确,既然是"天意",本项免责也

---

[535] 这是一宗神秘的事故,难以解释/说明事故原因,双方提供了对立/矛盾的证据。

[536] 但打官司总有一方胜一方败,无法判双方都胜诉。

[537] 所以只好让有举证责任的一方败诉了。顺便提一下,这判法与本章 4.2.5.3.2 小段详述的 The "Popi M" (1985) 2 Lloyd's Rep. 1 先例可以说是有不谋而合的一致说法。

[538] 承运人不必去证明货损确实是如何发生,只要能排除他/它有任何的疏忽,即可享有本项免责。

[539] 但要这样做,总得要合理解释/说明可能发生了什么事故造成这货损货差,而不能天马行空,"含糊不清"(vague)与/或"令人难以置信"(questionable, doubtful)地随意去发挥。

[540] 所以对完全无法解释原因的货损货差,船东/承运人仍难以满足本项免责对其举证责任的要求。

肯定适用了。

在本章较前的段节,也曾涉及本项免责的适用,例如在 4.2.7.1.11.4 小段提到的其他货物被无辜波及受损,因为同一货舱装有船东/承运人也无法得知的存在"固有缺陷"(inherent vice)或"包装不足"(insufficient packing)的货物。

还有大量其他不同的情况会适用这(q)项的免责,笔者不妨又再多举如下两种情况:

(ⅰ)船舶完全无辜地被其他船舶碰撞,导致货损或延误: M. Golodetz Export Corp. v. Lake Anja, 1985 AMC 891 (2 Cir. 1985)。这碰撞会发生在锚泊、靠泊等非航行情况下。所以其他免责不一定完全适用,如(a)项的"航行疏忽与过错"。而即使有可适用的免责,如(c)项的"海上风险",承运人把(q)项的免责结合起来抗辩也是安全与通常的做法。

(ⅱ)装卸工也算是承运人的代理人/雇员,因此要他们对事故也没有过错或私谋,承运人才能享有这项(q)的免责。但曾有美国先例判是承运人可对因卸货工人疏忽造成的货损以这项(q)去免责: Metalimport v. S. S. Italia, 1976 AMC 2347 (S. D. N. Y. 1976)。该先例的案情是,卸港为罗马尼亚的 Constanza,班轮运费是以"不负责卸货"(free out)为基础,再加上该港装卸工的指定与控制权全在港口当局手中,班轮公司/船长根本插不上手。

4.2.7.1.17.4 适用(q)免责的情况之一:偷窃货物

偷窃货物既会来自岸上也会来自船员/装卸工等"自己人"。若来自岸上,而船东/承运人也能证明他/它已尽了一切努力防盗,做到了妥善与小心照看货物,且该失窃也不应有"内鬼"所为(如通风报信,告知什么集装箱内有贵重货物),那么他/它应可依赖这(q)的免责。

若是船员或装卸工偷窃,看来船东/承运人是难辞其咎了,因此也不能享受这(q)项免责。的确,英国先例就这样判的: Heyn v. Ocean S. S. Co. (1927) 27 Lloyd's Rep. 334。美国先例也是同样判法,并判班轮提单中对货物失窃予以免责的条款实际是违反了海牙规则,因而无效: Remington Rand v. U. S. A., 1951 AMC 1364 (S. D. N. Y. 1951)。但英国法律目前对这一方面的看法仍有不稳定之处,这反映在本章 4.2.6.5.2 小段曾详述过的 The "Chyebassa" (1966) 2 Lloyd's Rep. 193 先例。在第一审的高院,判是装卸工偷窃导致的货损,船东/承运人要负责,这判法与 Heyn v. Ocean S. S. Co. 先例一致。但到了上诉庭这一判决被推翻,理由是偷货(装卸工的过错)"不在受雇范围以内"(outside the scope of his employment)。但这一来就有点混乱了。首先,船东自己若没有参与,永远不会授权或容忍船员/装卸工偷货。那么,可否说船员/装卸工偷货永远是在受雇范围外,船东/承运人在任何严重/恶意的货物失窃情况下都可去免责?若这太过分,不可以这样去放纵船员/装卸工并厚待船东/承运人，会否还要去区分装卸工是在上班时偷货还是下班后偷货呢？

所以，英国上诉庭这一判决受到了批评，如 William Tetley 教授在 *Marine Cargo Claims* 一书第 3 版之第 523 页说道："The Court of Appeal failed to consider the Hague Rules as a statute which specifically calls on carriers to carefully and properly care for cargo at article 3 (2) and only exculpates carriers if they prove that they and their servants or agents did not contribute to the loss under article 4 (2) (q).

It is submitted that the opinions of McNair J. in first instance in Leesh River Tea Co.[541] and MacKinnon J. in Heyn v. Ocean S. S. Co. are a better interpretation of the law than that of the Court of Appeal in Leesh River Tea Co.."

4.2.7.1.17.5　适用(q)免责的情况之二：船员的背叛

上一小段的探讨，也会影响其他情况的货损货差。例如被解雇的船员离船前放火泄愤，或是在笔者《提单》一书第 79 页提及的绰号为 Gun Gun 的一位船员，在航次中精神失常，把船上其他人杀死后，自己乘救生艇逃走，船舶在无人操纵的情下，导致货物受损。

试想，船员背叛总不会是船东雇用范围内的行为。岂非是船东/承运人对此也可享有这(q)项的免责？

这在美国已有先例判是船员背叛并非属海牙规则的免责（请看本章 4.2.7.1.3.6 小段的末段），也不属这(q)项的免责，船员背叛仍属他受雇范围内所犯的行为/过错：Mimi Limitation Procs（Matter of Intercontinental Properties Management）1979 AMC 1680 (4 Cir. 1979)。该案例也是涉及船员杀死其他同事并把船舶弄沉。

4.2.8　举证的第五步：货方证明承运人没有妥善与小心装卸，堆放与照看货物

海牙规则的 Article 3(2) 加了一项责任或义务在承运人身上，可节录其内容如下："Subject to the provisions of Article 4, the carrier shall properly and carefully load, handle, stow, carry, keep, care for, and discharge the goods carried."

在本章 4.2.2 小段曾提到这是下一步，第五步的举证，货方要以此来对抗船东/承运人试图援用各项免责去避免责任。货方是希望通过举证与分析（证据可能来自共同检验，强制上船检查，文件披露等方法），去说服法官或仲裁员接受货损货差的近因/主因是船东/承运人违反了这一项责任/义务，而不是各项免责事由。或是，

---

[541] 这即是 The "Chyebassa" 先例，只是称谓上一种是以船名为标记，另一种是以其中一方当事人的名字为标记。

即使免责适用,但货损至少部分是由于这一项违约造成的。若真是这种情况,船东/承运人就要去区分出到底哪一部分的货损货差是由免责造成,这样才可就这一部分免责。若是区分不开,则船东/承运人要负全责作出赔偿。有关这一原则可以节录 William Tetley 教授在 *Marine Cargo Claims* 一书第 3 版之第 520 页所说的如下:

"The rule that the carrier must not contribute in any degree to the loss is thus, in effect, the same as the rule that the carrier is responsible for the whole loss when the loss results from two causes, one for which the carrier may exculpate himself and one for which he may not, and the carrier cannot show which cause did what damage."

4.2.8.1 "妥善与小心"的定义

"小心"一词应该不难理解,它的反义词应是"不小心"或疏忽。但海牙规则还加上了"妥善"(properly)一词,它的含义是:

(ⅰ)承运人要有技术水平,能去照看与处理这种货物,并且有一套良好的制度。正如在 The "Maltasian" (1966) 2 Lloyd's Rep. 53 先例,Pearson 勋爵所说的:"The word 'properly' adds something to 'carefully', if 'carefully' has a narrow meaning of merely taking care. The element of skill or sound system is required in addition to taking care."

(ⅱ)能做到既有技术水平又有良好的制度,也意味着承运人必须了解这种货物的本质/特性,正如 Reid 勋爵所说:"…the obligation is to adopt a system which is sound in light of all the knowledge which the carrier has or ought to have about the nature of the goods."

(ⅲ)这一来,加了"妥善"一词,可以说是令海牙规则的另一项责任变得对承运人十分苛刻/严格。这不光是一般对托管人的要求,即只要合理小心照看受托管的货物即可。正如 William Tetley 教授在 *Marine Cargo Claims* 一书第 3 版之第 554 页所说:"The addition of the word 'properly' to the word 'carefully' makes the degree of care very close to the common carrier's obligation of insurer as opposed to the bailee's obligation of reasonable care and ordinary diligence."

4.2.8.2 妥善要求之一:不了解或处理照看不了的货物不应接受运载

这方面可以参阅美国的先例 The "Ensley City", 1947 AMC 568 (D. Md. 1947)。在此先节录有关船东/承运人要先了解有关货物的本质/特性的部分判决如下:"The law imposes upon shipowners the duty to use all reasonable means to ascertain the nature and characteristics of goods tendered for shipment, and to exercise due care in their handling and stowage, including such methods as their nature requires."

判决接着也提到船东/承运人应拒绝接受自己处理照看不了的货物,千万别不自量力,其内容如下:"There is no absolute obligation on a vessel to accept a cargo. Indeed, it should not be accepted unless it can be given the type of stowage that its character requires, and the placing of conditions in a bill of lading does not relieve the vessel of the obligation to take appropriate care of the cargo."

此外也可节录另一美国先例的同样说法：Armour & Co. v. Compania Argentina de Navegacion（1958）2 Lloyd's Rep. 49 之第 52 页是说："where cargo is offered for transportation and the carrier cannot give it the type of stowage or ventilation its nature requires, the accepted practice is for the carrier to refuse it, or in the alternative to notify the shipper of its inability to provide proper ventilation and to obtain its authorization to carry the cargo under the available stowage and ventilation."

4.2.8.3 妥善要求之二：技术水平，良好的制度以及了解货物本质/特性的例子

这方面有许多例子，毕竟货物有许多不同的种类，各有不同的本质/特性，是笔者也不懂或只懂皮毛。而这些不同的货物中，自然有难以处理和照看、储运技术水平要求很高的货种，例如像冷冻肉食或水果等。也有简单易运的货物如水泥、矿沙等。在此，笔者只选一种货物（卷筒纸/新闻纸（newsprint）为例略加介绍，以说明何谓"妥善"的要求。首先节录《提单》一书第53页所说的如下：

妥善一词是指对7个列明的工作环节有一个良好的系统，它的本质是技术性的。例如，某欧洲班轮公司经常自北欧严寒的地方装运卷筒纸往远东。在北欧装货的时候是冰天雪地的，卷筒纸的温度亦很低，装船时简直像冰块一般。但在运往远东途中经过炎热的地区，温度相差很大，若没有良好的温度及通风控制，任由货物的温度自由变化，就会使暖空气种的湿气遇冷凝聚为水珠，这对其他的货物影响都不大，但对纸张来说就很不利了，由于纸张的吸水性强，若吸收了湿气就会起皱纹从而影响印刷质量。而这家班轮公司由于有丰富的经验，经研究制定了一整套的温、湿度通风控制程序：严格控制运输中舱内的温度及湿度，作出预定的图表规定何时通风及何时关闭通风，甚至途中按不同地区的水温而将舱壁的压舱水（ballast）更换六次，以期使舱内气温随之逐渐改变。他们以这样的一个系统做法使纸张运抵日本仍保持平滑洁白为荣。这是一个说明如何妥善运输的很好例子……总的来说，要做到妥善就需要有一定的业务水平，它与"小心"是不同的，如前例，若无这样一整套操作系统，尽管全船船员不分日夜守护在卷筒纸的旁边，亦于事无补，纸张仍会吸入湿空气起皱纹，这样承运人大可以说自己已是极小心，但这并没用，因为未能做到妥善。

有关对卷筒纸/新闻纸的妥善处理与照看，特别在运输中的通风方面，The

"Evrgrafov"（1987）2 Lloyd's Re. 634 先例有大量资料，技术性颇高，无法在此一一节录。在此只选取其中第 638 页的一小段，以补充较早前节录的内容，具体如下："Similarly in a publication dated 1980…It says at p. 216: Condensation occurs when reels are stored and loaded in a cold climate and then transported to countries of warm and humid climate. If during the voyage holds are ventilated with air of higher dew point than the temperature of the cargo, the vapour in the air condenses in drops in the reels. Condensation continues until the surface of the reels reaches the same temperature as is the dew point of the air. The same phenomena occur in case reels are still cold and discharged in a warm humid climate…Condensation water can damage a paper reel in two ways. It weaken the wrapper, which then easily tears and exposes the paper to damage. A reel on end is liable to damage as the water runs down on the wrapper and through the end shields. This may result in rejection of the entire reel.

The risks are obvious. Whenever the cargo is loaded in a cold climate and being carried through or to a warmer climate it is axiomatic that ventilation must not take place during the voyage, or, at any rate, not until the cargo has warmed up to a temperature at least as high as that of the ambient air."

4.2.8.4　装卸货物的定义与要求

何谓装卸货作业，何时算开始或结束，卸下驳船的情况等，都已在本章之 4.2.3.4.2 小段略有谈及。而海牙规则要求妥善与小心地装卸，也表示装卸工不得疏忽外，还必须有一套良好的制度或系统去进行装卸。尤其是有的货物品种会需要特别的装卸做法、技术或/与设备。这要求也意味着承运人应去任命称职的装卸工：The "Saudi Prince"（1986）1 Lloyd's Rep. 347。

所以，像装卸工疏忽导致一架灭火车从船吊掉下来，若海牙规则适用，船东/承运人会难辞其咎，要负上赔偿责任：Pyrene Company Ltd. v. Scindia Steam Navigation Company Ltd.（1954）1 Lloyd's Rep. 321。或是下雨中装货，也是一样：The "Anna H"（1994）1 Lloyd's Rep. 287。涉及卸货方面的责任，也不单单局限在装卸工的作业，针对班轮的承运人还有其他的要求，这可以节录 Tan Hi v. U. S. A.，1951 AMC 127（N. D. Cai. 1950）先例所说的如下："The duty imposed by the common law upon water carriers was merely to transport from port to port, or from wharf to wharf. The carrier was not bound to deliver at the warehouse of the consignee; it was the duty of the consignee to receive the goods at the wharf. But the carrier was duty bound to notify the consignee of the vessel's arrival and time of discharge. The carrier was also obliged to discharge its cargo at a fit wharf, to separate each consignment so as to afford the consignee ready access for inspection and removal, and to protect the cargo until the consignee had a reasonable opportunity to remove it from the wharf. If the consignee failed to remove his goods within a reasonable time, the carrier could relieve itself from further responsibility only by depositing the goods in a warehouse for the account of the consignee."

4.2.8.5　海牙规则不涉及交货

讲到卸货,也可提提"交货"(delivery)的问题,按理它也要妥善与小心。交货是指承运人把货物实际交出给收货人或他指定的人士(如卡车司机)。海牙/海牙·维斯比规则没有针对"交货",但这显然不是无意之失,而应是故意不去针对。因为在规则 Article 3(6)的有关一年时效的规定,就曾提到过"交货",所以不会是不知道有此重要的一步行为/工作环节。

在英国法律下,若船舶卸下货物后船东仍占有货物(一般在班轮运输就是这种情况,但很少发生在不定期船的大宗货物运输),船东/承运人仍有托管的责任。由于与收货人有提单合约关系,也表示这是合约的托管,托管的责任和义务最终要去看合约的条款。而班轮公司也不客气,往往会以一面倒保护船东/承运人的免责条款明示在它的提单标准格式中,以豁免托管的责任。这种例子在本书第二章之5.6.2 小段有略及。

无单放货也只涉及不妥善和小心地"交货",海牙规则管不到,这导致班轮公司去拟定对无单放货免责的条款,将其明示在它的提单标准格式内,也是有效。这方面的例子在本书第二章之5.10 小段有略及。

有关卸货后的其他各种分包人(如装卸工、仓库主等)应有的责任,如托管/分托管责任等,在 York Products Pty v. Gilchrist Watt & Sanderson Pty (1970) 2 Lloyd's Rep. 1 的贵族院先例有论及。在美国,因为有哈特法强制适用在货物从船上卸下直至交货这一段期间,所以美国法律在这方面的地位与英国法律很不一样,它不允许订约自由,尤其是不允许订下对船东/承运人免责的条款。因此,不少情况是行走美国航线的班轮公司的提单干脆把这一段时间也订明以海牙规则(美国1936年的海上运输法)为准。这种做法实际是通过合约来适用海牙规则。有关这一方面的课题,请参阅本章之4.2.3.4.2.4 小段。

4.2.8.6　堆装货物的定义与要求

对"堆装"(stowage)的定义可以节录在 The "Visurgis" (1999) 1 Lloyd's Rep. 21g 的近期先例中, Gatehouse 大法官所说的如下:"The first problem is to decide what is meant by the word "stowage" in this contract. When the word is used alone…It must necessarily embrace all the sequential operations required to put the cargo safely onboard ready for safe sea transport, craning the goods onto the ship, positioning them, subject of course to the overriding discretion of the master to ensure seaworthiness of his vessel, and then securing them in position by lashing, dunnaging and any other steps required. These might, I suppose, include shoring up if this is not included in dunnaging, or perhaps, for example, adjusting position in the hold so that individual items are packed tightly against each other and the bulkhead so that they cannot move."

"堆装"货物一向是一项十分复杂/精密的作业,特别是涉及多个货物品种以及多个港口的班轮运输。这里有多方面需要顾及,如货物的本质、包装、特性、运输要求,等等。还要顾及船舶的稳性/重心(如重货不要过多堆装在甲板或上层舱),船舶前后吃水,卸港次序,等等。

随着班轮运输走向集装箱以及散货运输日益使用专门的散装船,对船长/船员在这方面的船艺要求也相应降低。虽然货物在集装箱内的妥善与小心堆装仍很重要,但这不一定是船舶的工作。常会是发货人自己先堆装并铅封好集装箱后再把它交付给船东/承运人。这一来,堆装不妥导致货损,船东/承运人也有多项海牙/海牙·维斯比规则的免责可去享受,如货方自己的行为或错漏(4.2.7.1.9 小段),"固有缺陷"(4.2.7.1.10 小段),"包装不足"(4.2.7.1.11 小段),总揽条款(4.2.7.1.16 小段)等。

4.2.8.6.1 海牙规则对堆装的要求

海牙/海牙·维斯比规则在两处给船东/承运人强加了堆装货物的责任/义务。一是 Article 3(1)的开航前要求船东/承运人"克尽职责"令船舶适航,而不妥堆装货物若影响到船舶的适航(典型的如令船舶失去稳性/重心),就违反了这项先决的要求。这在本章之 4.2.6.6 小段也有略及。二是 Article 3(2)要求的"妥善与小心"堆装货物。这两处的责任/义务的分别是:

(ⅰ)一是要求"克尽职责",另一是要求"妥善与小心"。对船东/承运人两者的要求都十分高。实质分别会是不大。

(ⅱ)适航要求是在开航前,但另一要求却是贯穿于整个航次。有时堆装或重新堆装可能会发生在航次途中,比如是发生海难、意外后。

(ⅲ)不是每次堆装不妥都涉及不适航。有时堆装不妥只会影响货物本身。

(ⅳ)适航要求是先决条件,不违反才能享受免责:请看本章之 4.2.6.3 小段。但"妥善与小心"堆装的要求即使违反了,它也不是先决条件,承运人/船东仍可去区分货损哪一部分是由某项免责造成的,哪一部分才是由不妥堆装所导致,请看本章之 4.2.8 小段。

(ⅴ)会有情况是发货人自己负责在船舱堆装货物,这在租约提单下常会发生,根据的是租约的所谓 FIOS (free in and out, stow)。若堆装不妥损坏发货人自己的货物(但不影响适航),而船长又无法察觉到,谈不上有疏忽/过错。这一来,道理与较早前谈及的发货人自己堆装集装箱一样,船东/承运人不必负责。正如 William Tetley 教授在《Marine Cargo Claims》一书第 3 版之第 545 页说道:"The carrier is protected, however, if the shipper improperly stows its own goods and damage results to them under art. 4 (2) which reads:《Neither the carrier nor the ship shall be responsible for loss or damage arising or resulting from: (i) Act or omission of the shipper or owner of the goods, his agent or representative》."

但仍要区别的是,若这堆装不妥导致不适航或对其他货物不适货,船东/承运人仍是难辞其咎。原因之一是海牙规则的"克尽职责"是船东/承运人"个人的责任"(personal liability),不得由他人代劳:请看本章之 4.2.6.4.4 小段。原因之二是发货人本身难以知道船舶是适航还是不适航,例如影响船舶稳性。

故此,针对堆装货物影响到什么,要有一分为二的做法,例如在 Heinrich Horn-Marie Horn (1970) 1 Lloyd's Rep. 191 之第 198 页是说:"The Captain occupies a dual role with regard to such decisions. He acts for the shipowner where his stowage decisions are made with regard to the seaworthiness and safety of the vessel; he acts for the cargo owner where his decisions do not affect the seaworthiness or safety of the vessel, but affect the safety of the cargo only."

4.2.8.6.2 海牙规则不准承运人减轻或豁免对堆装的责任

众所周知,海牙/海牙·维斯比规则的 Article 3(8) 禁止承运人/船东减轻或豁免规则强加给他/它的责任/义务。所以提单条款(班轮提单是明示印在标准格式,租约提单则是合并租约条款)若是说船东/承运人不对货物堆装负责,那实际是无效的。即使货物在船上堆装是由发货人进行,去减轻或豁免船东/承运人对此的责任/义务仍被禁止,因为船东/承运人有最终的责任/发言权,正如 William Tetley 教授在《Marine Cargo Claims》一书第 3 版之第 545 页说道:"The final responsibility for proper stowage remains in all circumstances with the carrier. In consequence a clause in the bill of lading stating that the carrier is not responsible for stowage carried out by shipper is invalid under art. 3(8) of the Hague or Hague-Visby Rules. Questions of stowage are under the absolute control of the master of the vessel and as such he has the final say as how stowage is to be effected. This is not only because of the carrier's responsibility for the stability of the ship and the safety of the ship and crew, but also because of the carrier's obligation to care for other cargo…"

对某些货物的堆装,例如一座大型的机器,船东/承运人会雇用有经验的专家或验货师协助,他们之后也可能就此签发证明。若提单条款说这是"最终及结论性"的证据证明承运人已做好货物堆装,这条款在海牙/海牙·维斯比规则下又会是无效的。正如 William Tetley 教授在《Marine Cargo Claims》一书第 3 版之第 544 页说道:"Surveyors' certificates alone are insufficient to overcome the burden of proving good stowage. In the 'Anthony II' (1966) 2 Lloyd's Rep. 437 (S. D. N. Y. 1966) 之

445 页, it was held that: Mere certificates and surveys are not sufficient to discharge a carrier's obligation for proper stowage since it cannot delegate the duty to others. See Leerdam, (1927) AMC 509, 510, where the court stated:' Due diligence to make to vessel seaworthy must in fact have been exercised. It is not sufficient for a shipowner to show that he had employed competent men to do the work, but he is held responsible for the failure of the men he employed."

4.2.8.7 运载、保管与照看货物的要求

"运载、保管与照看"(carry, keep and care for)定义应很明确,这在前文谈到的不少方面也已提及,如4.2.8.2 小段提到的承运人对不了解或照看不了货物不应接受运载,或在4.2.8.3 小段提到的卷筒纸在运输途中的温度及通风控制。在此再选几方面去谈谈,它们是其他几种要求船东要"妥善与小心"的作业,具体如下面几小段所列。

4.2.8.7.1 船长作为紧急代理人出售货物以挽救其剩余价值

若货物在途中变坏(例如因免责风险引起的延误),明显无法保存至卸港,加上联络不上货方,那么船长应有责任及时出售该批货物。这样做的授权来自船东作为紧急代理人身份,这方面课题可参阅笔者的《国际商务游戏规则——英国合约法》一书第四章之6.3 小段。若船东/承运人不去这样做,会构成对妥善与小心运载,保管与照看货物的违反。在美国的 Lakas & Drivas v. Basil Goulandris, 1962 AMC 2366 先例是说:"…Circumstances may arise when the master of a ship has not merely the authority[542] but, under sect. 3(2) of COGSA[543], the duty to sell cargo that is at risk of further deterioration, communicating with the owner if that is feasible, but still having both the authority and duty if it is not."

该美国先例涉及芝士的货物因"君主的禁制"(这属免责项目,在本章之4.2.7.1.7 小段已详论)延误航次而变坏。货方指承运人对货物的照看不妥,后者本应半途安排冷冻或出售货物。但美国上诉庭判货方未能成功举证证明承运人有此违约(请看4.2.8 小段的标题)。若真能成功,才会轮到承运人要去举证并区分哪部分损失(芝士的变坏)属"君主禁制"所致,哪部分损失属照看不妥所致。

4.2.8.7.2 船长为照看货物而花费特殊费用

这方面可举例的一种情况是笔者很早前已提及的一船牛羊(提单合约合并了海牙规则,如在 The "Tilia Gorthon" (1985) 1 Lloyd's Rep. 552,故此海牙规则适用),半途因风浪延误引致饲料不足维持至卸港,船长基于妥善与小心照看货物(牛羊)

---

[542] 这授权来自紧急代理人的身份。
[543] 这是海牙规则要求承运人必须妥善与小心运载,保管与照看货物的 Sect. 3(2)条款。

的要求即有责任/义务绕航去中途港加添饲料。而他合理花费的一切"特殊费用"（special charges），承运人可在卸货前通过留置货物向收货人索取。这留置的权力来自普通法的默示，不必以明示条款加以允许，这在笔者《程租合约》一书第十二章之3.1小段有详论。

4.2.8.7.3　船长不应进入明知有罢工的卸港

若船长明知卸港罢工，船舶进去了也无法卸下货物，再加上货物若是易腐品种，延误不起，那么仍然进港也会构成船东对妥善与小心运载，保管与照看货物责任的违反。正如William Tetley教授在 *Marine Cargo Claims* 一书第3版之第743页所说道："It is reasonable to deviate away from a strikebound port; by the same token, it is unreasonable to enter a strikebound port"（The "Mormacsaga"（1969）1 Lloyd's Rep. 515）."

4.2.8.7.4　船长不应进入会丧失货物的卸港

这方面在笔者的《禁令》一书曾提及一个相关的先例，那是在第二章之3.1.8小段，可以节录如下：

> 这可以介绍The "Iran Bohonar"（1983）2 Lloyd's Rep. 620 先例，它涉及美国公司Conti Grain将价值250万美元的6000吨"豆油"（soya bean oil）卖给Interice，再由Interice转卖给伊朗买方。买卖是以FOB方式进行，即伊朗买方派船，它派了一艘伊朗国家船公司I. R. I. S. L拥有的"Iran Bohonar"。
>
> 但在货运途中，Interic经济出现问题，没钱支付Conti Grain。这一来，Conti Grain可就担心了，因为货物到了伊朗卸港很可能控制不了。虽然提单仍在Conti Grain手中，但估计伊朗买方可不会被难倒，肯定会去无单提货。而船东的IRISL，不会听命于Conti Grain，它们之间根本没有租约关系。唯一的关系是Conti Grain是提单持有人，而IRISL既是承运人，也是"托管人"（bailee）。另还要提两点：一是当时美伊关系很差；二是IRISL在伦敦有一分公司专门负责租船，这一来，变了英国法院对IRISL能管辖得到。
>
> 面对这困境，估计Conti Grain会有两种对策：
>
> （ⅰ）向IRISL施压，警告其无单放货的严重后果，毕竟IRISL有好几艘姐妹船在世界各地营运，去扣一艘并不难。这一来，压力会转到伊朗买方身上，导致令其直接与Conti Grain磋商，跳过Interice，付出货价以换取提单。当然，这样会需要一点时间去谈判，也可能被伊朗买方压价，毕竟会有可能伊朗买方虽未有提单在手，但已支付了部分钱给Interice。
>
> （ⅱ）至于另一办法，也是Conti Grain真正采用的，就是向英国法院申请一个禁令，迫使IRISL把"Iran Bohonar"轮转开去其他港口（巴基斯坦的Karachi），

而不去伊朗。IRISL 对此当然抗拒,指提单与租约(与伊朗买方是租约)都不是去 Karachi,怎会这样?

但英国上诉庭还是给予了禁令,迫船舶开往 Karachi,因为 IRISL 与 Conti Grain 之间的承运/托管关系是根据海牙规则,海牙规则有要求船东小心/妥善地运输与照看货物。而货物明显会因为不绕航去 Karachi 而丧失,则船东仍坚持船往伊朗看来是会违反海牙规则里的"默示禁止性协议"(请看本章 3.1.7.1 小段,虽然案例报告并不明显显示在这一点上有争辩)。在此不妨节录 Ackner 大法官所说的如下:

"there was an obligation under Art. III, r. 2 of the Hague Rules properly and carefully to carry and care for the goods, the subject matter of the bill of lading, and there was in the circumstances a serious question to be tried whether the fact that the delivery of the oil to Iran was going to result in its loss to the plaintiffs(原告)obliged(船东)in pursuance of their duty of care to take the goods to the place which was acceptable to be the reasonable alternative if there was to be a deviation."

4.2.9　海牙规则禁止承运人减轻或逃避责任/义务

众所周知,英国一向崇尚订约自由,合约的明示条款,只要明确清楚写什么,就算什么。法官/仲裁员的权限只是去解释合约,他们并非订约方,因此不能自作主张地修改合约。唯一的例外是明示条款/合约违反公共政策,如涉及非法、欺诈等,才可以无视它,不予协助解释或强制执行。但源自美国哈特法的做法,海牙规则却有明文的规定不准订约自由,这是在 Article 3(8)。可以说,哈特法与英美海上运输法(海牙规则)是英美最早保护消费者(班轮业务的货方)与禁止订约自由的立法,岸上同类的立法如英国 1977 年的"不公平合约法"(Unfair Contract Terms Act 1977)与之相比是晚多了。

为方便阅读,不妨先可节录 Article 3(8)如下:"Any clause, covenant, or agreement in a contract of carriage relieving the carrier of the ship from liability for loss or damage to, or in connection with, goods arising from negligence, fault, or failure in the duties and obligations provided in this article[544] or lessening such liability otherwise than as

---

[544] 运输合约(提单)中的任何条款/协议去豁免承运人或船舶对由于他/它的疏忽、过错或未尽本规则条款所加的责任/义务所导致的货损货差的责任……

provided in this convention[545], shall be null and void and of no effect[546]. A benefit of insurance in favour of the carrier or similar clause shall be deemed to be a clause relieving the carrier from liability."

4.2.9.1 有关例子介绍

这方面的例子数不胜数,在此只略作介绍以说明总的精神、原则。首先要提的是上一小段的注[547],这是海牙规则明确禁止的例子,因为当时这种情况很多。若承运人被允许享有货方的保险利益,而保的是"一切险",岂不是等于他/它不必负责了?另外,在本书多处已提及的一个方面,例如本章 4.2.3.1.5 小段详述过的 The "Morviken"(1983)1 Lloyd's Rep. 1 先例,就是涉及提单的适用法条款或/与管辖权条款会因违反海牙/海牙·维斯比规则而被视为无效。而美国法院在 Indussa Corp. v. s. s. Ranborg(1967)2 Lloyd's Rep. 101(2 Cir. 1967)案判提单内的外国管辖条款无效后,一直持这立场,直至最高院判了 The "Sky Reefer"(1995)63 USLW 4617;AMC 1817)一案后才有所改变。

在本章之 4.2.8.6.2 段,还详述了有关船东对堆装货物之责试图推卸的情况,在此不再重复。以下再举一些不同方面的有关先例:

(ⅰ)英国先例曾判规定"承运人不负责货物出汗,有味与弄污"(sweat, smell, taint)的提单条款属无效:Coventry Sheppard & Co. v. Larrinaga Steamship Co. Ltd.(1942)73 Lloyd's Rep. 256 之第 260 页。

(ⅱ)美国曾判提单条款所定的:"承运人不负责因土豆货发热、冻坏、腐烂等损坏"(loss due to heat, frost, rot or decay)属无效:F. W. Pirie v. s. s. Mormactrade, 1970 AMC 1327(SDNY 1970)。

(ⅲ)法国曾判提单条款所讲的"装卸由发货人/收货人监督,并承担费用与风险"属无效,因它意图令承运人逃避"妥善与小心装卸"责任:Cour de Cassation, March 19, 1985, DMF 1986,20。

(ⅳ)提单条款说明冷冻设备的操作属"船舶管理"/"管船"。要知道,管船疏忽与过错可以免责:见本章之 4.2.7.1.1 小段。但承运人在"妥善与小心"照看货物方面有严格的责任,不能对疏忽与过错免责。而冷冻/冷藏设备的使用本质上不属"管船"(请看本章之 4.2.7.1.1.4.1 小段),所以这种"冷冻条款"(refrigeration clause)无效:Heinrich Horn-Marie Horn(1970)1 Lloyd's Rep. 191 之第 202 页(5 Cir. 1968)。

---

[545] 或去减轻本公约(海牙规则)所规定的责任……
[546] 均属无效。
[547] 规定承运人可享有货方的保险利益的条款也属这种条款,因而无效。

(ⅴ）本章第六章之 5.5 小段会详论的美国先例 Tokio M & F Ins. Co. v. Retla. s. s. Co.（1970）2 Lloyd's Rep. 91（9 Cir. 1970），案情涉及一条名为"Retla Rust Clause"的提单条款，它说："表面状况良好"（清洁提单）不表示钢材货物没有生锈或受湿。而发货人若另外要求一份提单去详细列明大副收据所批注的生锈/受湿，可尽管提出，承运人会另签发一套有详细批注的提单。"

这种写法/措辞在部分班轮提单条款中可见到，目的是为了不去批注提单（因为批注不易或/与烦琐），而只去签发一套清洁提单，但提单又加上一条款说"清洁不表示没有批注，想要有批注提单的话可尽管提出要求"。

对这种条款，William Tetley 教授在 Marine Cargo Claims 一书第 3 版第 850 页说道："It would appear, however, that the clause clearly violates art. 3 (3) (c) of the Hague and Hague-Visby Rules whereby a carrier must issue a bill of lading declaring the apparent order and condition of the goods and is bound by that statement in virtue of art. 3(4) in the light of the general rules of estoppel."

（ⅵ）为了便于计算赔偿，会有提单条款说货值以发票价格为准，但发票价格会比货物在卸港的市场价格低，因此有美国案例曾判这种条款无效：Otis, McAllister & Co. v. Skibs,（1959）2 Lloyd's Rep. 210（9 Cir. 1958）。

（ⅶ）美国曾判提单条款所讲的："（汽车）没有保护，货方自己承担损坏风险"（uncrated at owners risk of damage）属无效：Southern Cross, 1940 AMC 59（SDNY 1939）。汽车若没有保护，在传统的运输方法下容易刮花，受碰撞等。今天有专门的运车船舶或/与集装箱运输，这方面问题已大减。若是没有保护的汽车受到一些难以避免的损坏，船东/承运人可以"包装不足"的免责（4.2.7.1.11 小段）或总揽条款的免责（4.2.7.1.16 小段）作为抗辩。但他/它要证明这些损坏是汽车有了足够的外层保护就可以避免的，不能是什么原因造成或加深损坏都可以推在"没有保护"方面。这正是美国法院在 Southern Cross 先例对该提单条款不满的理由，承运人不能单凭汽车"没有保护"，就乘机把所有责任都推到货方身上。法官说："The sentence 'Uncrated at owners（货方）risk of damage' stamped on the bill of lading does not itself mean that the owner assumes the risk of damage to the automobile from whatever cause arising, but only such damage as might be attributable to the fact that the automobile was not crated. The works 'at owners risk of damage' are to be strictly construed. Nor do these words relieve the carrier from any damage sustained by the automobile due to the negligent handling or stowage of the automobile, even though the negligence would not have caused the damage if the automobile had been crated. Any other interpretation of the exception would be contrary to the provisions of the Hatter Act and the Carriage of Goods by Sea Act."

4.2.9.2 有关刑事化之说

从上一小段各先例可见,在许多情况下提单的条款(明示或合并的)会属无效,是海牙规则的 Article 3(8)所禁止的。这种条款有时看来会十分"中性"甚至"公道",也会十分隐蔽,可能船东/承运人自己也在不知不觉中加上了这些无效的条款。而它们所针对的方面更会是多元化的,如条款是去改变或减轻举证责任,扩大绕航权力,缩短一年时效(The "Amazona" (1989) 2 Lloyd's Rep. 130)或增加收货人索赔的困难,等等。

这种无效条款在提单中可能会起误导作用,因为收货人(尤其是班轮业务中的小公司)往往不懂什么海牙规则的 Article 3(8),也怕打官司。所以看了一条实际是无效的提单明示条款,也就自认倒霉,放弃索赔了事。因此在讨论汉堡规则时,笔者曾听过有人提出要把船东/承运人的这种行为刑事化。但这说法很快就因受到强烈反对而不了了之。笔者可以理解这种反应,而且也会加入反对者的行列。若反对不成功,笔者会建议船东/承运人改行,因为触犯刑法可不是开玩笑的。谁会想在做正当生意时无端端犯上刑事官非,况且它还很容易犯,不知不觉就会犯上。

4.2.9.3 提单条款无效后可否重生

这方面可以节录 William Tetley 教授 *Marine Cargo Claims* 一书第 3 版第 844 页所说的如下:"As a general rule, a clause, once null in one set of circumstances, may not revive in other circumstances. In Leather's Best Inc. v. S. S. Mormaclynx (1970) 1 Lloyd's Rep. 527 (EDNY 1970), a clause which was invalid during carriage was not permitted to revive after discharge…

The judgment was upheld in appeal (2 to 1): Leather's Best Inc. v. S. S. Mormaclynx (1971) 2 Lloyd's Rep. 476 (2 Cir. 1971). It is possible nevertheless, in very particular circumstances and depending on the wording of the clause, that an invalid clause may revive."

4.2.9.4 提单条款可否被分割,只判部分无效

这种情况可举 The "Ion" (1971) 1 Lloyd's Rep. 541 为例,该案中提单有一条仲裁条款,只有 3 个月的时效。显然,这违反了海牙规则的一年时效。但到底应判整条条款无效,还是只判 3 个月时效的规定无效而条款其余有关仲裁的部分仍有效呢? 该先例判是后者,即该条款可被分割。但英国法律在这一点也不是十分明确,也曾有不同的先例。

在 Svenska Traktor Akt. v. Maritime Agencies (1953) 2 Lloyd's Rep. 124,判法也是可去分割这无效条款,然后不同对待。但另在 G. H. Renton v. Palmyra (1956) 2 Lloyd's Rep. 379,高院的一审判决是一条"自由条款"前半部分有效(针对卸港罢工可去其他港卸),但后半部分无效。可是因为不能分割,所以整条条款无效。McNair 大法官说

不能分割的理由是:"But there still remains, however, the question whether it is permissible, in order to save the clause, to use the blue pencil and delete only the offending provision. The words of art. Ⅲ r. 8 '*any clause*, covenant or agreement' are quite precise and do not, as I think, permit of any such process of revision in a case where the Act and Rules apply as a matter of law…"

看来在这一方面,目前的法律地位仍是要看个别法官如何判定个别案情的公平合理性而去解释提单条款。例如,条款是否明确可以分割? 有一些条款会把完全不同的两样事项连在一起讲。或是,分割后的判法会否仍有违反海牙规则明示规定的可能性?

4.2.9.5 海牙规则强制适用与纯属合并适用有否分别

众所周知,海牙规则可以对有关航次强制适用,如装港国家有立法(海上运输法之类的立法),也可以纯靠合约去合并引入而适用(因为立法不管)。而合并的做法,往往是靠一条"首要条款";这方面请参阅本章之4.2.3.2.2.2至4.2.3.2.2.6小段。这就带来在解释上的争议:若以合约的形式适用,首要条款只是合约的其中一条条款而已,若它与其他条款发生矛盾,还须整体地去看合约才能作出解释。而印上的首要条款也可能被附加条款或手写/打字的条款超越。依此精神/原则的判法是 W. R. Varnis & Co. Ltd. v. Khoti (1949) 82 Lloyd's Rep. 525。该先例涉及一条"洋葱条款"(onion clause)加在提单前页,说明船东不对洋葱负责。这明显是违反了海牙规则,实属无效。但该航次开始自埃及,而当时埃及尚未立法承认海牙规则。但提单背面条款第11条明示适用英国法与1924年的英国海上运输法。结果法院判是该提单下海牙规则的适用只能以合约法的精神/原则来解释。但在 The "Agios Lazaros" (1976) 2 Lloyd's Rep. 47,Denning 勋爵在第50~51页批评这判法(即以合约的形式适用要比强制适用效力低)不是好的法律(bad law)。

4.2.10 举证的第六步:双方对其他有关方面的争辩

在本章4.2.2小段的有提到这最后一步的举证,即双方对所有关方面的争辩,例如是不合理绕航、时效、责任限制,等等。根据每一案件的不同事实,这种争辩可能有,也可能没有。"有"也可能只是其中一项或多项。以下便对这类常见的争辩分别加以介绍。

4.2.10.1 非法/不合理绕航

海牙规则有两处涉及或针对绕航。一是已在4.2.7.1.15小段论及的免责项目之(1)项("海上救助人命或财产"),二是在 Article 4(4)的如下规定:"Any deviation in saving or attempting to save life or property at sea or any reasonable deviation shall not be deemed to be an infringement or breach of this Convention or of the contract of carriage, and the carrier shall not be liable for any loss or damage resulting therefrom."

显然,海牙规则所明确允许的两种船舶在约定航次中的绕航(这是英美普通法所不允许的)是如下:

(ⅰ)绕航去救助人或财产。正如本章之 4.2.7.1.15 小段讲到的,普通法本是不允许绕航去救财产的:Scaramanga v. Stamp (1880) 5 C. P. D. 295。

(ⅱ)合理绕航。

4.2.10.1.1 非法绕航的历史与严重后果

因为船舶非法绕航会导致货物保险的失效(大道理是若绕航会令保险人原先对风险的估计不足,保费也反映不出这点,因此为了对保险人公平,非法绕航会令保险中断。有关这方面请参阅笔者与汪鹏南教授合著的《英国海上保险条款详论》一书之第 306 页,内有详论)。所以英国在 200 年前已有先例判船一发生非法绕航,船东/承运人即丧失合约的权利,而他/它也从"承运人"的身份变为是"货物保险人"的身份:Ellis v. Turner (1800),8 T. R. 531,101 E. R. 1529;Hain S. S. Co. v. Tate & Lyle (1936) 55 Lloyd's Rep. 159。

而英国法律的"基本违约"(fundamental breach)概念,也在 Hain S. S. Co. 先例由 Wright 勋爵首次提出[在(1936) 55 Lloyd's Rep. 之第 177 页]。判例发展下去,Denning 大法官(当时尚未升任为勋爵)最终确立了这基本违约的理论:Karsales (Harrow) Ltd. v. Wallis, (1956) 1 W. L. R. 936。他讲到"违约若是达到把合约连根拔起的程度"(guilty of a breach which goes to the root of the contract),违约方再也不能享受合约内的免责条款,不论这条款拟定得多么周密/广泛去保护违约方。当时,英国也正开始有了保护消费者的意识,因为拥有优越谈判力量与有关知识的公司(特别是垄断性的公司)往往可以拟定十分周密/广泛的免责条款去保护自己,然后再强加到消费者身上。英国法院若光是依赖解释合约上的有限武器如"针对原则"(contra proferentum)等,实在难以去保护消费者。所以干脆引入一个基本违约的说法,不再在"解释合约"(construction of contract)上去纠缠。直至在 1977 年制定了"不公平合约法"(Unfair Contract Terms Act,1977)去保护消费者,英国贵族院才正式在 Photo Production v. Securicor Transport (1980) 1 Lloyd's Rep. 545 的先例推翻了基本违约的说法。而 Denning 勋爵对此也完全予以跟从:George Mitchell v. Finney Lock Seeds (1983) 1 Lloyd's Rep. 168。

4.2.10.1.2 在海牙规则下的解释

但不合理绕航在海牙规则下的解释,仍被视为是基本违约,这可去看 William Tetley 教授的《Marine Cargo Claims》一书第 3 版之第 107 页。该书虽也有谈及 Photo Production 等先例。但这一基本违约的说法在该书之第 746~747 页被再次重复,不妨节录如下:"The consequence of an unreasonable deviation under the Hague Rules is that the carrier may not rely on the exceptions and limitations in the contract of carriage and the Rules.[548]

Because art. 4 (4) states that a reasonable deviation is not an infringement of the Convention or of the contract of carriage,[549] it follows that an unreasonable deviation does contravene the Convention and the contract.[550] Therefore the carrier will lose the benefit in the Rules of:[551]

a) the package limitation,

b) the one year delay for suit,

c) the defence of due diligence at art. 3 (1),

d) the exculpatory defences at art. 4 (2) (a) to (q),

e) any other contractual limitations and exclusions, which would otherwise be upheld despite art. 3 (8) 's ban on exculpatory provisions.

In other words, if there is a deviation, the carrier cannot invoke the exculpatory exceptions in the Hague Rules, or in the contract of carriage. The principle was stated by Lord Atkin in Stag Line Ltd. v. Foscolo, Mango & Co. (The "Ixia" (1931) 41 Lloyd' Rep. 165) where he said:[552]

I pause here to say that I find no substance in the contention faintly made by the defendants（船东作为被告）that an unauthorized deviation would not displace the statutory exceptions contained in the Carriage of Goods by Sea Act.[553] I am satisfied that the gen-

---

[548] 在海牙规则下不合理绕航的后果是承运人不能再依赖运输合约与海牙规则中的所有免责或限责条款。

[549] 这是因为海牙规则在 Article 4(4)明确讲合理绕航并不破坏本公约（海牙规则）或有关运输合约。

[550] 换言之，就是一有不合理绕航即会破坏公约与运输合约。

[551] 进一步去分析/推理，不合理绕航这一行为本身往往不会造成货损货差，它只是拉长了或/与增加了海上风险的时间。若之后真发生货损货差，也会是其他（与不合理绕航没有直接因果关系）的原因，例如是由于航行疏忽或是海上风险/海难。而且，海牙规则的措辞/用字是针对"不合理绕航"而不是"不合理绕航所导致的损失"。这表示不必有任何货损货差直接是由绕航而导致（也不大可能），该绕航已可被当做是破坏了公约（海牙规则）或有关运输合约。而对这一破坏所作出的惩罚（如果有之），显然包括要剥夺船东/承运人一些权利。其中对后来会造成货损货差的近因如航行疏忽或海上风险/海难等，原可以免责，但不合理绕航后船东就应丧失对这些免责的享受。延伸下去，船东/承运人在海牙规则的其他免责/限责条款下享有的权利，如单位赔偿的限责、时效等，也会丧失。但这还要看规则中的相关措辞/用字，要以一般的解释准则来分析/推理，等等。这方面在接下去的小段会详述。

[552] William Tetley 教授随后节录了有关先例中 Atkin 勋爵的说法。

[553] 他说被告船东的软弱争辩指没有授权的绕航（即没有获货方同意的）在英国海上运输法下并不会导致丧失立法下的免责实在没有说服力。

eral principles of English law are still applicable to the carriage of goods by sea except as modified by the Act,[554] and I can find nothing in the Act which makes its statutory exceptions apply to a voyage which is not the voyage the subject of the 'contract for the carriage of goods by sea' to which the Act applies.[555]"

4.2.10.1.3　不合理绕航后会丧失海牙规则的单位赔偿责任限制

海牙规则的 Article 4(5) 允许船东/承运人在昂贵货物发生货损货差时享有赔偿限责。英文的条款是："Neither the carrier nor the ship shall in any event be or become liable for any loss or damage to or in connection with goods in an amount exceeding 100 pounds sterling per package…"

从以上节录可见，这条条款用了颇广泛的措辞，说是"任何情况下"（in any event）船东都可享有此项单位赔偿限责。那这是否意味着不合理绕航后船东/承运人仍可享有这一条款的限责呢？要知道，这方面的分析也纯粹是解释海牙规则所用的措辞/文字。

William Tetley 教授在其《Marine Cargo Claims》一书第 3 版第 747~748 页提出了三个理由去支持禁止船东/承运人享有这限责条款的权利，具体如下：

（i）对货方不公道："…the shipper assumes that the cargo will not be exposed to risks outside the contract. The shipper《is lulled into a false sense of security》by the carrier's undertakings. If the carrier could rely on the package limitation, he would be immunized against the consequences of his own wilful actions, at the expense of the innocent shipper."

（ii）在英国先例 The "Ixia"（1931）41 Lloyd's Rep. 165，第 170 页是说"任何情况下"（in any event）的措辞/文字并不足够明确/肯定以致可改变法律对绕航的严厉性。

（iii）海牙·维斯比规则虽也保留了"任何情况下"的措辞/文字，但在随后的 Article 4 (5) (e) 却说明了剥夺船东/承运人享有此限责的情况。这表明并非是"任何情况下"船东/承运人都肯定可以限责。

最后请读者看回本章之 4.2.3.5.3.7 小段，它针对的是违约装货于甲板，在美国法律下被称之为"准绕航"（quasi-deviation）。因此，本小段论及的"正宗"地理上的不合理绕航完全适用于那一小段所讲的内容，笔者不再重复。

---

[554]　Atkin 勋爵认为英国普通法对非法绕航的严厉对待完全适用在海牙规则，除非海牙规则对这方面明示作出调整（例如允许合理绕航）。

[555]　Atkin 勋爵认为他没法看出英国海上运输法（海牙规则）有意向让立法下的免责适用在一个并非运输合约所同意的航次（即不合理绕航后的航次）。

有关这一年时效是否仍适用/有效,尤其是在海牙·维斯比规则 Article 3(6)的广泛措辞/文字下,本章 4.2.3.5.3.7 与 4.2.3.5.3.8 小段已有详论,大原则/道理也完全适用于本小段,不必再重复。换言之,海牙·维斯比规则的一年时效应适用在不合理绕航,并不失效。

4.2.10.1.4 美国法律的准绕航说法

在本章之 4.2.3.5.3.7 小段,已略为提到了违约装货于甲板在美国法律下会被视为是"准绕航"(quasi-deviation)。由于这种违约后果严重,所以美国上诉庭(Second Circuit)曾试图去局限这个说法。在 Iligan Int. Steel v. John Weyerhaeuser, 1975 AMC 33 (2 Cir. 1974)的第 38 页是说:"We think the principle of 'quasi-deviation' is not one to be extended.[556] As previously noted, even the holding that a deviation in the geographical sense voids limitations on the carrier's liability seems inconsistent with the language of COSGA.[557] It has been justified in part by what is-or at least was-the especially serious effect of such a deviation on the shipper[558]…

Up to this point the concept of 'quasi-deviation' in the United States has recognized only one instance, deck stowage of cargo which the carrier had agreed to carry below deck,[559] for which the carrier becomes liable in full as an insurer of the shipper's cargo.[560] Whatever may be thought of that principle, it is easy to administer and carriers know the risks[561]."

但美国仍有其他法院判其他情况下的违约,特别是"有意"(intentional)造成的,属"准绕航"。例如是有意/故意不交出货(有关承运人的交货责任在本章之 4.2.3.4.2 小段有详论)。但属无意的交不出货,则不属"准绕航":Hellyer v. N. Y. K. ,1955 AMC 1258 (SDNY 1955)。该先例中,货方(提单持有人)过了一年时效才起诉,美国法院判一年时效适用,说道:"…non-delivery is not to be equated with an unjustifiable deviation which results in abrogating the contract of carriage…The non-delivery of a cargo is an ordinary, even though a material breach of contract and it may be said to be a risk within the contemplation of the parties…"

---

[556] 准绕航的说法不应去扩大。
[557] 因为与海牙规则(美国 1936 年海上运输法)的措词/文字毕竟有不一致之处,例如在本章之 4.2.10.1.3 小段提及的 Article 4 (5)有"任何情况下"(in any event)一词。
[558] 硬去解释只能绕航对发货人(其实最后是收货人)的影响实在是太严重了。
[559] 美国法律至今只承认一种非是地理上绕航的"准绕航",就是违约装甲板货。
[560] 一去违约,承运人身份变为是货物保险人身份。
[561] 不论对此"准绕航"有何看法(同意或异议),好处是遇上这种违约容易审理,与承运人清楚明了他/它的风险而避免去违约。

另一种情况是"运过了站"(overcarriage),即货物原应在第一卸港卸下,因为船东疏忽/过错而忘了卸下,或是货物压在货舱底(这种问题在以前非集装箱运输中经常发生,会是由于原先在装货前的"堆装"(stowage)没有周密地考虑到卸港的次序),导致要把货物带去第二卸港或第三卸港才能卸下再转运回第一卸港。这一来,既延误了这票货物的交货,也延长了运输的风险期。看来,这种违约是否属"准绕航"也应去看船东/承运人是否属有意/故意,虽然这并非是容易确定的事实。若只是疏忽(无心之失),仍去判属"准绕航"就会受到批评了,例如在 William Tetley 教授的《Marine Cargo Claims》一书第 3 版之第 117 页说道:"The "Silvercypress" (Fire), 1943 AMC 224 and 510 (SDNY 1943) is another example of failing to ascertain the carrier's intention. Here the Court held that, because the overcarriage was negligent and therefore a deviation, the carrier could not benefit from the fire exemption under COGSA. It is submitted that, if the overcarriage was merely negligent and not grossly negligent or intentional, the Court should not declared that the contract was fundamentally breached. Instead, the Court should have permitted the carrier to claim the protection of COGSA and the Fire Statute."(该判例显然不允许船东/承运人在"运过了站"后发生火灾造成货损时,去享有火灾的免责。但该案中的"运过了站"只属无心之失)。

最后要略为提一提的是,发生了"准绕航",是否要求将来发生的货损货差仍多少要与"准绕航"的违约"有一点因果关系"(casual relationship 或 connection)呢?这一点在本章4.2.10.1.2也有略及。照理说,在绕航后承运人的身份变了是保险人说法下,应不再要求绕航(地理上的或"准绕航")与后来的货损货差有任何因果关系,否则怎能称得上是保险人呢?但看来,美国判例对这方面的要求仍有不稳定之处,笔者不妨节录《Marine Cargo Claims》一书第 3 版之第 120~121 页所说的如下:

"... More recently the Second Circuit required that the quasi-deviation (deck stowage) be connected to the loss: O'Connell Machinery Co. Inc. v. Americana, 1986 AMC 2822 (2 Cir. 1986).

On the other hand, the Fifth Circuit considers that the carrier who deviates assumes an insurer's liability [Sealane, 1966 AMC 1405 (5 Cir. 1966) cert. den. 1966 AMC 2788 (1966).] The logical conclusion to this is that there need not be any casual connection between the deviation and the loss. Nevertheless a casual connection is usually to be deemed necessary and one is usually discovered in the facts."

4.2.10.1.5 何谓海牙规则下的"合理绕航"

一早已经提到,海牙规则明示允许一种"合理绕航"(reasonable deviation),这是英国普通法所没有。那么这到底是指什么的情况呢?

4.2.10.1.5.1 班轮的约定航线

在不定期船（租约）业务中，什么是约定航线应较容易去确定，因为往往只有为数不多甚至是一个的装/卸港。若只有一个装/卸港，默示的约定航线自然是它们之间在地理上最直接，或是适当与习惯的航线，这样确定后若船舶偏离了此航线，也就构成绕航了。

但在班轮业务中，会有大量的装/卸港，而且在提单上也不会列明具体有多少是什么港口要挂靠，航线是什么。班轮提单往往只是写上该票货装/卸港，但事实上不会是直航。这一来，怎样去确定什么才是双方（承运人与发货人）约定的航线呢？

要知道，班轮提单只是运输合约的证明，它往往也不会包括了运输合约的所有实质内容。故此，要找出双方约定的航线，仍是要看：

（ⅰ）该班轮以往惯常的航线：Mitsubishi Intl. v. Glyfada Spirit, 1978 AMC 480 (SDNY 1978)。

（ⅱ）班轮公司所刊登的广告：Goya Foods, Inc. v. S. S. Italia, 1987 AMC 817 (2 Cir. 1983)。

（ⅲ）双方的订舱合约/订舱单（booking note），或许会有班轮公司对发货人作出直航的承诺：The "Ardennes" (1950) 84 Lloyd's Rep. 340。

4.2.10.1.5.2 "合理"的定义

"合理"与否要看每一事件的事实而定。因为事实总会有不同，而且会千变万化，所以很难预先判定何谓合理绕航，何谓不合理绕航。在海牙规则与相关的立法，虽也有试图去列出一些情况，但那毕竟只是极少数的情况。例如，海牙规则在Article 4 (4) 明显是把绕航去救助人命或财产当做合理绕航。又例如在美国的1936年海上运输法，还多加了一句说明一种情况表面算是不合理绕航，其措辞如下："Provided, however, that if the deviation is for the purpose of loading or unloading cargo or passengers, it shall, prima facie, be regarded as unreasonable."

英国法律对海牙规则的"合理绕航"作出权威性定义的是 The "Ixia" (1931) 41 Lloyd's Rep. 165 先例。上诉庭的 Scrutton 大法官对"合理"的看法是："I think the interests to be considered must be those of the parties to the contract adventure, which may include consideration of the position of their underwriters."

即要考虑所有涉及该航次的当事人的利益，如船东，货方与保险人。一个好的例子是绕航去避开坏天气，而坏天气会在不同程度上影响船货双方的共同利益。

另外 Greer 大法官，讲道："I think the words (reasonable deviation) mean a deviation whether in the interests of the ship or the cargoowner or both, which no reasonably minded cargo-owner would raise any objection to."（即使绕航是为了船东单独的利益或货方单独的利益又或双方共同的利益，如果当时情况下一位合情合理的货方是

第五章　提单作用之二：运输合约下的货损货差责任　495

不会对该绕航提出异议的，那么该绕航应属合理。这其中的一个例子是船舶不适航导致半途需要绕航去加油或紧急修理，绕航本身应算合理）。

在 The "Ixia"案的终审贵族院的 Atkin 勋爵说：

"The true test seems to be what departure from the contract voyage might a prudent person controlling the voyage at the time make and maintain,[562] having in mind all the relevant circumstances existing at the time,[563] including the terms of the contract[564] and the interest of all parties concerned,[565] but without obligation to consider the interests of any one as conclusive[566]."

"Departure from the route so ascertained may also be justified by express stipulations (e. g. 'liberty' or 'deviation' clauses) in the contract; but any such stipulation, however, widely phrased must be construed with reference to the contract route ascertained…"

还有另一方面的"合理"要顾及是即使"合理"决定了去绕航，但绕去哪里呢，因为会有多于一个选择，例如是可进行修理的港口？看来，这方面的"合理"决定更是应去多信任船长，不应多去"事后诸葛亮"形式的批评。比方是说应去较近的 Piraeus 港进行修理，而不是去 Lavrion 港：The "Daffodil B" (1983) 1 Lloyd's Rep. 498。会是去作出决定时，船长会考虑到不同修船地点的优劣与价钱高低，这只是船东自己的利益。但在合情合理范围内，应不多加以批评。但若是选的一个修理港口会令货物风险大增，则该当别论。毕竟，曾有美国先例判"风险因绕航大增应是不合理绕航"（a deviation is unreasonable which substantially increases the exposure of cargo to foreseeable dangers that would have been avoided if no deviation occurred）：General Electric v. Nancy Lykes, 1983 AMC 1947 (2 Cir. 1983)。

4.2.10.1.5.3　总结

有关这方面的课题，本书第四章之 3.2.2 小段也有详论，该段还节录了《程租合约》一书的相关内容；就此不必再多作论述。在此只提以下三点：

（i）在 4.2.10.1.5.2 小段已提到，因船舶不适航导致半途需要绕航（去加油或紧急修理等）不会令绕航变为非法（普通法下）或不合理（海牙规则下）：Kish v. Taylor (1912) 12 Asp. M. C. 217。当然，对不适航的违约自有相针对的惩罚，但这

---

[562]　应该看一个谨慎的人在控制航行方面（一般就是船长）当时会作出什么决定。
[563]　他应考虑当时所有相关的情况，例如船上装载的是否为易腐货物。
[564]　这考虑也包括了运输合约内的条款，其中包括一些所谓的"自由条款"（这方面在本书第四章之 3.2.2 与 3.4.4 小段有详论）。在《Scrutton on Charter-Parties》一书第 19 版之第 260 页也有论及。
[565]　还要考虑所有航次当事人的利益。
[566]　但不必只考虑一方的利益作为最终的定论。毕竟，这"合理"是在海牙规则中的措辞，它是船货双方妥协的产物，合理与自然要全面考虑。

不致于会把承运人变为保险人。是否合法或合理绕航是要看当时的情况与风险（例如燃油不足），而不是去追究这情况与风险为何原因导致（不适航）。这也完全合理：试想想，若船长害怕绕航后有更严重的后果（构成基本违约），宁愿冒不适航的风险勉强支撑往卸港，这绝非好事。这不适航的风险（本来一经绕航可以尽快排除），最终可能导致船货两失。

（ⅱ）若船长错误（不是有意）绕航，例如为了避开坏天气但决定不对，这只属航行疏忽的免责而并非不合理绕航：The "Marilyn L" (1972) 1 Lloyd's Rep. 418 的美国先例。

（ⅲ）若不合理绕航后发生了货损货差，船东互保协将会不予负责/赔偿。一般在船东互保协会的章程内，都会订明像如下的条款："Deviation: Unless and to the extent that the Directors in their discretion otherwise decide, there shall be no recovery from the Association in respect of liabilities costs and expenses which arise out of or which are incurred as a consequence of a deviation, in the sense of a departure from the contractually agreed voyage or adventure which deprives the Owner of the right to rely on defences or rights of limitation which would otherwise have been available to him on the basis of the standard terms of carriage referred…to reduce or eliminate his liability."

如果船舶非要去绕航，尽管估计会构成不合理绕航，船东/承运人应如何应对呢？例如，开航后发觉船上有偷渡客（人蛇），若不回航或绕航而把偷渡客留在船上，带去卸港，会带来无穷的后患或/与罚款。但要知道，去这样做只是为了船东的利益，与货方的利益无关。又或是本章 4.2.8.7.2 小段所讲的情况，即船上除了牛羊的货物，同时还装有其他货物如 1 万吨钢材，甚或是易腐货物。这一来，为去中途港加添饲料而绕航对牛羊的货物是完全合理（与必需），但就其他货物（如 1 万吨钢材或易腐货物）的利益而言就谈不上了，只会增加/延长了海上的风险。

针对以上情况，船东/承运人应到保险市场加保一种 SOL (shipowner's liability) 保险，这可通过船东互保协会安排。在涉及牛羊货物的例子，这加保的保费也应可当做是"特殊费用"(special charges)。

4.2.10.2 索赔时效

海牙规则在 Article 3(6) 针对索赔规定了一个时效，内容如下："In any event the carrier and the ship shall be discharged from all liability…unless suit is brought within one year after delivery of the goods or the date when the goods should have been delivered."

这著名的海牙规则下的 1 年索赔时效，对遭受货损货差的货方而言，是一个十分危险的陷阱。笔者已见过无数的案件因时效已过，慢了一步的货方只好无奈放弃索赔，不论要索赔的金额有多大。

第五章 提单作用之二：运输合约下的货损货差责任 497

4.2.10.2.1 时效过了的各种原因
导致这种局面，主因是不懂。要不是货方自己不懂，甚至是货方所托非人，连他/它的律师也不懂。这不懂在程度上会有不同，严重的会是连海牙规则都不知道。但也会是：

（ⅰ）索赔对象搞错，会是收货人跑去跟发货人（卖方）纠缠不清，但实际却应向承运人/船东索赔，因为针对买卖合约而言，运输风险（导致货损货差）实际已归买方。这方面在本书第三章§2段所节录的《国际货物买卖》一书的相关内容中有详论。要知道，1年时间很短。索赔方向一错，走了弯路，往往就导致时效过去。

（ⅱ）即使知悉索赔对象应是承运人，货方（收货人/提单持有人）仍要有本事根据提单识别谁才是承运人（合约承运人），是应控告的对象。这承运人常会是真正的船东，或提单上抬头的船公司或班轮公司（会只是期租该出事船舶的承租人），还会是更隐蔽的光船承租人。这些巧妙在本书第三章有详论，不去重复。反正是，对象一搞错又会导致一年时效失去，正如第三章4.3.1.4小段所详论的The "Antares" (1981) 1 Lloyd's Rep. 424先例。

（ⅲ）诉讼地点或/与方式搞错，例如在本书第四章之2.6.4.5小段详论的提单合并了一条伦敦仲裁条款，但收货人在中国海事法院对船舶起诉，而罔顾了保护伦敦仲裁的一年时效：Thyssen v. Calypso (2000) 2 Lloyd's Rep. 243。

（ⅳ）货方一知半解，以为与船东/承运人一直在谈判即可保护时效，而不知道海牙规则是要求他/它要起诉才能保护时效。

（ⅴ）货方/货方律师中了圈套，船东/承运人所同意的延长时效其实有附带条件，不是无条件的：The "August Leonhardt" (1985) 2 Lloyd's Rep. 28。

（ⅵ）其他方面。

一年时效过去，货方只会是怪自己疏忽/看漏了眼。笔者认为这常是掩饰的话。若真是懂，自然也包括应懂得时效的严重性，一般看漏了眼的可能性绝低。但人性就是如此：宁可承认一时疏忽也不肯去承认"不懂"。后者会失面子，所以即使是真正原因，也不愿意承认，导致永远学不到教训。顺便再提一提，一年时效实在也是太短。英国一般的民事诉讼（合约与侵权）有长达6年的时效，这在本书第三章之§2段的节录有提及。但海牙规则是国际公约，是各国与各方不同利益的妥协结果。而面对一个国际公约，一个国家要么就承认它，去将其立法，要就不接受，往往不存在分割国际公约，只承认一部分的情况（对公约有保留的除外，但情况毕竟不多）。

4.2.10.2.2 从交货始算一年时效：何谓交货
海牙规则的一年时效是从"交货"（delivery）始算的，所以首先要确定何谓交货。交货不同于卸货，交货是要承运人与收货人互相配合才能实现的。"实际交货"（actual delivery）是由承运人/船东交出货物，放弃占有权，而由收货人接收过去，对货物拥有占有权。还有另一种是"推定交货"(constructive delivery),是承运人/船东给了收货人通知称船已抵达,货已卸下到适当与安全的地方托管,只等待收货人在合理时间内提取。所谓卸下至"适当与安全"(fit and safe)地点,可以是指货已卸下码头或把货物寄存在仓库,让收货人随意来提取:The "Beltana"(1967)1 Lloyd's Rep. 531;The "Hakone Maru"(1973)1 Lloyd's Rep. 46(美国案例)。

要知道,卸货可以是任由承运人(尤其是在班轮业务)一方执行,而收货人并不知悉,无法知悉有否货损货差。所以一年时效从卸货算起不公道,它总得从收货人知悉自己有一个"起诉原因"(cause of action)时算起才合理。海牙规则在这一条款的措辞/文字上以"交货"替代"卸货"不是没有理由的。但"交货"若只局限在"实际交货",又会有收货人迟迟不提取货物的情况难以针对。故另有"推定交货"的说法,强调只要通知了收货人,并给予他/它合理时间来提取即可。

基于上述"交货"的概念,在另一美国先例 The "Aubade"(1971)2 Lloyd's Rep. 423,货物(钢材)已卸下到 Charleston 港交由港口当局托管,但港口当局并非是收货人的代理或与之有任何关系。后因钢材有锈收货人在卸货后1年零1天才起诉,美国法院判时效未过,原告收货人可以向船东/承运人追索。法院也讲到说:"…delivery implies mutual acts of the carrier and the consignees…It is a more inclusive term than 'unloading', implying acceptance or agreement to accept by, or, at least communication to, the consignee, if not actual passing of possession to the consignee, coupled with relinquishment of possession or control by the carrier. The mere discharge of the cargo is not delivery."

4.2.10.2.2.1 大宗或大批货的交货

在这种情况,"交货"应是指把最后一点货物实际或推定的交出,这时才开始算这一年时效。在《Marine Cargo Claims》一书第3版之第673页说:"In the case of a large lot, delivery takes place on the day that the last piece of cargo has been discharged and actually or constructively delivered."

4.2.10.2.2.2 交不出货

会有情况是船货半途全损,或易腐货物半途已因船不适航(冷冻设备发生故障)而全损并遭抛弃。这一来,根本交不出货,船舶(若仍在)也不会再去卸港白跑一趟。这一来,想要索赔的收货人对这一年时效应如何计算呢?

这应该不困难,而海牙规则在条款最后一句说明可自"货物应交付之时"(The date when the goods should have been delivered)起算,这表明它也有针对这"交不出货"的情况。在计算上,可根据正常航线、船速和天气等估算出抵达卸港的日期,然后再进一步估计出应交货的日期。

4.2.10.2.2.3 分不开的货物

看来,若是货物因损坏而分不开或本来就分不开,要分开才能让收货人提取货物,那么交货应是指分开货物的一天。在《Marine Cargo Claims》一书第 3 版,William Tetley 教授在第 673 页介绍了两个法国先例如下:

(i)Tribunal de Commerce de Marseille, February 3, 1948, DMF 1949, 485: The vessel completed discharge of her cargo on October 7, 1945. Survey began on October 8, 1945, and separation of damaged cargo ended on October 20, 1945. Suit brought on October 15, 1946, was held valid. The delay began to run the day cargo was in the effective disposition of the receiver of the goods(货在 1945 年 10 月 7 日从船上卸下,但至 10 月 20 日才把损坏的货物分开。诉讼在 1946 年 10 月 15 日开始,判是时效未过)。

(ii)Tribunal de Commerce de Nantes, April 23, 1951, DMF 1952, 27: Delivery was held to have taken place when all the cargo was ashore, and had been sorted for delivery, and the consignee could see what was short and what was damaged。(判"交货"是指货物卸上了岸,并已分开了以便交货,同时可让收货人看见有何货损货差)。

4.2.10.2.2.4 半途转船的情况之一:全程提单

全程提单的课题在本书第二章之 3.2 小段有详论,不再重复。在此只提提,若一程船签发了全程提单并安排半途转运,交货是指二程船(或最后的承运人)在卸港的交货。在《Marine Cargo Claims》一书第 3 版之第 674 页是说:"In a though bill of lading, delivery would be at the moment when the last carrier has delivered."

4.2.10.2.2.5 半途转船的情况之二:遇上事故

这种情况较为复杂,它会是原船遇上事故(例如是不适航导致的事故),无法继续航次,或是要在货舱内进行修理但把货物寄存在岸上仓库又太昂贵,结果只好安排转船。这里的不同之处是原来运输合约(提单)并没有计划转船,并非是全程提单。而且,转船后还会涉及另要签发一套提单给货方。另外的变数是转船后可能需时良久才能成功抵达原订卸港"交货",但并非是交不出货的情况。这一来,收货方若想向原船的承运人索赔(毕竟损失是由他/它的船舶不适航引起),"交货"是指半途的原船交货,还是指另一船最后在卸港的交货呢?看来,在收货人有被通知半途转船的情况下,交货应是指原船在半途的交出货物。

在《Marine Cargo Claims》一书第 3 版之第 674 页,William Tetley 教授介绍了一个法国先例说:"…where there are two contracts of transport for two successive carriages, suit against the first carrier must be taken within 12 months of the first discharge. Thus a vessel left Los Angeles for Le Havre but was involved in a collision and put into Flushing for repairs. Later it went on to Hamburg where the cargo was discharged and sent by another carrier to Le Havre. The Tribunal de Commerce de Paris, January 2, 1974,

DMF 1974, 492 held that the delay for suit was 12 months from the date of delivery in Hamburg. (船舶从美国洛杉矶去法国勒阿弗尔，半途发生碰撞。结果转折去了德国汉堡，在汉堡把货物卸下并用另船转运去法国勒柯弗尔。法国法院判一年时效是从汉堡交货时算起)"。

在同一页，Tetley 教授还列举了美国先例的 Potter v. North German Lloyd, 1943 AMC 738 (N. D. Cal. 1943)。它涉及一票货物自汉堡运去美国的波特兰，因"二战"爆发而半途在 Costa Rica 放弃了该航次，当时为 1939 年 9 月 7 日。在 Costa Rica 曾安排同一班轮公司的另一条船舶转运，但延误了 20 个月最后仍未成功。收货人在 1941 年 5 月 26 日开始起诉，结果被判时效已过。美国法院认为从 1939 年 9 月 7 日（原船放弃航次）起再多加 6 个月（这算是一段合理时间让收货人去提取货物）应算是"交货"时间。

在另一美国先例 Cerro Sales Corp. v. Atlantic Marine Enterprises, 1976 AMC 375 (SDNY 1975)，涉及航次是从菲律宾去秘鲁。但船舶半途发生火灾而被救助拖往檀香山，并最终在该港宣告航次受阻，时为 1968 年 7 月 26 日。结果货物由另一船舶运去卸港。

若不出此事故（火灾），原船本可在 1968 年 7 月 11 日抵达秘鲁卸港。以此日子计算收货人在 1969 年 7 月 23 日起诉应是一年时效已过。但法院判时效未过，因为实际在檀香山"交货"是在 1968 年 7 月 26 日。

4.2.10.2.3 谁可享有一年时效

海牙规则明确是讲"船舶"(ship)与"承运人"(carrier)可享有一年时效。承运人自然会包括船东、光船承租人或期租承租人等，还有他/它们的雇员（比如船员）。他/它们享有 1 年的时效，可以在面对被诉时以这一方面来作为其中一项"抗辩"(defence)。或者，为了省事，他/它们可以像 The "Aubade" (1971) 2 Lloyd's Rep. 423 先例那样要求法院先对这一项抗辩作出简易判决。显然，若抗辩成功，双方可以不必再花大量的时间/金钱去对货损货差责任作出争辩与举证。当然，若案件不是由国家法院而是由仲裁审理（本书第四章之 2.6.4 小段所讲及），也可向仲裁庭申请先针对时效的抗辩作出一个"中间的裁决"(interim award)。

分包人或"独立承包商"(independent contractor)比如是装卸工不能享受海牙规则的一年时效，因为他/它们不是运输的合约方，而海牙规则只是针对运输合约（以局限提单的订约自由）。而在海牙·维斯比规则即使加上了"侵权"(tort)，也只是指与运输合约有关的"并列诉权"(concurrent actions)，而不是指完全没有合约关系作为大前提的侵权关系：请参阅本书第二章之 5.5.2 小段，第三章之 8.2.1 小段与本章之 4.2.3.3.2 小段，等等。

换言之，若货损发生在装卸作业中，而装卸工又确有疏忽之处，货方可以侵权向装卸工索赔损失,从而避开海牙规则的一年时效或/与单位赔偿限责:Midland Silicones v. Scruttons (1961) 2 Lloyd's Rep. 365; The "Eurymedon" (1974) 1 Lloyd's Rep. 534。

要对付这种针对侵权的起诉,承运人可以把一条"喜马拉雅条款"(Himalaya Clause)加印在提单(一般是班轮提单)上,进而将分包人/独立承包商包括在合约方内。这一方面在本书第三章的8.2.2小段有详论,不再重复。

4.2.10.2.4　双方可否同意延长一年时效

4.2.10.2.4.1　海牙·维斯比规则的明示允许

照理说,在民事诉讼中,若是双方当事人同意(包括同意延长时效),法院/法律不应再去管。要去干预也说不过去。但在1924年的海牙规则,Article 3(6)的措辞/用字是说"任何情况下"(in any event),这会否包括了双方同意也不行? 照说,这有说不通之处,因为去延长时效本身并非减轻了承运人的责任,海牙规则没有理由去反对。但无论如何,1968年的海牙·维斯比规则已明确讲了这一年时效可由双方同意延长,具体如下:"This period may, however, be extended if the parties so agree after the cause of action has arisen."

除了英国外,还会有其他国家禁止双方同意延长时效,好像本书第四章3.4.3小段谈到的希腊。故如果希腊也去承认了海牙·维斯比规则,将其立法,意味着以后也要改为去接受双方同意延长时效为有效了。

4.2.10.2.4.2　双方的同意必须明确、肯定、最终及无先决条件

这一点应该没有什么奥妙,每一个对合约法有基本概念的人对此都应明白,就是任何一个协议要有效,都必须有双方明确、肯定、最终及无先决条件的"发盘"(offer)与"受盘"(acceptance):The "Castle Alpha" (1989) 2 Lloyd's Rep. 383。所以,若是船东/承运人在谈判时效延长时拖泥带水,例如只是说会"慎重考虑"等不确定的话,收货人就应该明白并没有达成协议,应及时开始诉讼以保护时效。

同样的道理,若是船东/承运人同意延长时效,但却附带上先决条件,收货人或他/它的律师也应小心对待。若先决条件不能尽快去除,也应当做没有达成协议,及时采取行动以保护时效。

船东/承运人的货损货差责任通常由国际船东互保协会承保,而在案件处理上包括延长一年时效的谈判,往往也是由互保协会一手包办。它们的雇员多数有良好的法律基础,精明过人,谈判经验丰富。所以收货人或他/它的律师若不是对手,常会上当/犯错。

例如在The "August Leonhardt" (1985) 2 Lloyd's Rep. 28,货方的律师(是伦敦一家著名律师行)与船东互保协会(西英)谈判并同意延长3个月的时效。西英的电传是说:"...our members are prepared to extend time to your clients for a period of three months beyond 26.1.82 on a without prejudice basis and provided charterers agree likewise."

显然，这项时效延长有一个先决条件，就是要求承租人也同意。在该先例也显示这是所有船东互保协会的惯常做法。只要知悉有租约存在，它们在同意延长时效时即会多加一句话"provided charterers agree likewise。"

这样做要起到什么作用笔者也不太清楚。或许是先取得承租人同意延长时效，将来船东赔付了收货人之后（被判败诉或庭外和解），再以租约条款的规定要求承租人作出"补偿"（indemnity）时，承租人难以再指称较早的延长时效有不合理之处。但照理说，只要做法合理，船东不必事事都要先取得承租人的同意。这并不会影响后来的补偿行动。从另一角度看，若承租人什么都不同意，诸如延长时效，庭外和解等，船东也不见得就会不做，只要这明确是合理的做法。

但且不论这起到什么作用，对收货人而言，取得船东这样一个有此先决条件的对延长时效的同意，会是毫无用处，因为根本就没有过有效的协议。

在 The "August Leonhardt"，承租人也在西英投保了货损货差责任险。这给了货方律师一个借口说他收到了西英的电传后，以为西英会向承租人要求授权延长时效，毕竟大家都在同一个互保协会，只是"左右口袋"的分别而已。这之后货方没再听到异议，也就以为先决条件已经解除了。

但法院判是货方律师（收货人）有责任去取得承租人对延长时效的同意。若没有这样做，或者做了但承租人没有同意，即表示没有达成过任何协议。

读者或许会问：双方何必去延长时效呢？毕竟打官司的费用高昂，最后的判决/裁决也不见得会太科学，而且货损货差的赔偿金额也不一定是太大一笔钱。这些因素加起来表示庭外和解仍应是双方最佳，最有利的出路。但要知道，庭外和解的谈判需花时间，而且双方要手段，你退我进，互设地雷，以谋求对自己更有利的和解。还有，和解谈判前必须对事实调查清楚，有一定的掌握，否则这谈判是"赌博"，而且会不知进退。调查需时，会是时效将届仍未完成。这一来，若是一年时效双方不同意延长，收货人就会被迫花钱先去起诉。而一起诉，可能也就带来扣船，承运人要出庭以免被缺席判决，等等。这最终会导致一场原可避免的不必要的"大战"（官司）。

也可能会是，船东/承运人与互保协会在谈判中感觉到收货人心虚没底，多数不会真正去起诉，就会以时效来试探收货人。即是，不同意延长时效。在时效过后，若收货人什么都没有做，船东/承运人也就全胜。但若真的起诉了，出了告票等，船东就赶紧庭外和解，以免进一步推进诉讼。

最后再提一提，若延长了的 3 个月时效将届但和解谈判仍未有定论，收货人务必牢记要另再取得延长时效的协议，比如说再多 3 个月。否则，一样会因时效过去而导致索赔失败。

如果最后有了和解协议,但承运人(或他/它的互保协会)又不肯支付。或者对和解协议又有了其他方面的争议。这会有 6 年时效的保护,因为海牙规则的一年时效只适用在提单与相关的物权凭证(请看本章之 4.2.3.2 小段)。像和解协议、保函等其他的合约,若没有明示不同的条款,在英美法下都应享有长达 6 年的时效:有关保函的 6 年时效可以参阅 Rambler Cycle Co. v. P & O Steam Nav. Co. (1968) 1 Lloyd's Rep. 42。

4.2.10.2.4.3　承运人的弃权/禁止翻供行为

这重要的衡平法概念,在本书多处已有涉及,对其尤为透彻的探讨,可参阅本书第六章之 4.1 小段,在此不提前去讲述。

在双方试图同意延长时效的谈判中,也会出现弃权/禁止翻供的行为。例如,船东/承运人并没有明确、肯定及无条件地同意延长时效,但他/它对收货人带"误导"地说:"我保证双方最终肯定可以友好和解,因此你根本不必担心时效,更不必去出告票保护时效。"而结果收货人也信赖了船东/承运人这个表述。但后者后来却以时效已过为由抗辩。结果会是,虽然延长时效的协议并不存在,但船东/承运人却因上述言行构成弃权/禁止翻供而不得再以时效已过来抗辩。

但弃权/禁止翻供也不是轻易就可成立的。因此,在上一小段详述的 The "August Leonhardt" (1985) 2 Lloyd's Rep. 28,法院并不认为船东互保协会(西英)做了什么不对头的事(如有误导货方律师的表述或行动),以致构成弃权/禁止翻供。

在美国法院,也曾有好几个先例判是弃权/禁止翻供不成立,如:

（ⅰ）在 Schwabach Coffee Co. v. S. S. Suriname, 1967 AMC 604 (E. D. La. 1966),判是承运人知悉有这项索赔和不去理睬对方提出的延长时效的书面要求并不构成弃权/禁止翻供。

（ⅱ）在 Subaru of America v. M/V Ranella, 1972 AMC 722 (M. Md. 1972),也是船东不去理睬收货人有关同意延长时效的书面的要求,收货人说印象上以为船东业已同意,但法院不同意,并且说道:"…plaintiffs were not 'justifiably misled' by anything defendants did or said.（被告船东没有做过或说过任何不当的事去误导原告收货人）。"

（ⅲ）在 Bitchoupan Rug Corp. v. A. S. Atlas,1975 AMC 278 (SDNY 1975),承运人从未同意过延长时效或放弃一年时效,唯一的事实是代理人曾口头表示希望不必经法院就能友好和解。法院判这并不构成"恶意误导"(malicious misrepresentations),所以禁止翻供不成立。

会构成弃权/禁止翻供的,可举以下两个案例:

（ⅰ）在 Armenia Coffee v. Santa Magdalena, 1983 AMC 1249 (SDNY 1982) 的美国先例,判是承运人宣扬公司的政策是会同意延长时效构成禁止翻供。

（ⅱ）在 The "Henry Sif"（1982）1 Lloyd's Rep. 456 的英国先例，涉及班轮公司（它实际是承租人，期租了发生货损的一船）的代理人去延长了时效，但后来在正式被诉时，该公司却抗辩说自己不是提单合约的承运人。因为相关的班轮提单（有它的名字作为抬头）有一条"光船条款"（demise clause）。这肯定会害苦了原告的收货人，因为再回头去找正确的承运人（真正船东）会是时效已过。所以，法院判班轮公司构成禁止翻供，它再不准去否认自己是承运人，也再不准去依赖提单内的光船条款。

4.2.10.2.5　保护时效的唯一方法：开始诉讼

如果一年时效得不到船东/承运人同意延长，而收货人又无意放弃索赔，收货人就要紧记在一年时效届满前开始向船东/承运人提起诉讼。"诉讼"（suit）只包括在国家法院的起诉或仲裁，而不包括像调解/和解等行动。故此，光是双方在谈判，试图和解，这并不能保护一年时效。这也是在其他方面要保护时效的做法，例如 Limitation Act 1980 所针对的合约或/与侵权的 6 年时效。

4.2.10.2.5.1　在国家法院起诉：哪一个国家

这是一个十分复杂的问题，涉及的考虑因素极多，比如"择地行诉"（forum shopping）的考虑，诉人或诉船，谁应是承运人，哪里可获诉前保全（扣到船），等等。这些方面的课题在本书各处均有详述，故在此略过。

仅就保护一年时效而言，英国法律曾相当严格。在 Cia Colombiana de Seguros v. Pacific Steam Navigation Co.（1963）2 Lloyd's Rep. 479，开始诉讼是在一年时效内，但是在纽约法院起诉（"错误"的管辖权地点）。之后，收货人被迫转去"正确"的管辖权地点——英国法院诉讼，但为时已晚，而原先在纽约法院的"及时起诉"并不能保护收货人。此先例在本书第四章之 2.6.4.5 小段已详论过。

但后来，英国法律对此又似有放松，即只要求原告的收货人及时在有适当管辖权的法院（但不必是最后进行诉讼的国家法院）起诉，这样已可保护时效：The "Kapetan Markos"（1986）1 Lloyd's Rep. 211 与 The "Nordglimt"（1987）2 Lloyd's Rep. 470。但再发展下去，到了 Thyssen v. Calypso（2000）2 Lloyd's Rep. 243 一案，英国法律在这点上看来又重趋严格。这方面的复杂问题，已在本书第四章之 2.6.4.5 小段与 3.4.3.3 小段有详论，在此不再重复。

看来，要较彻底地解决收货人/提单持有人在这方面的难题及无所适从的困境，需要有国际社会认同的公约/立法像汉堡规则那样去针对它，明确允许收货人/提单合法持有人有广泛的诉讼地点、国家可作选择，而且不会被剥夺，例如被"中止"（stay）或他国法院作出的 Anti-suit 禁令所干预（这一课题请参阅《禁令》一书之第六章）。在汉堡规则的 Article 21，就明确规定有管辖权的地点/国家包括被告（承运人）所在地，装卸港，提单合约订立地点（签发地不一定在装港），提单合约所明示规定的管辖地,等等。笔者看来,这是汉堡规则真正能保护/维护货方利益的仅有的几处。但在海牙/海牙·维斯比规则,并没有类似的规定。所以即使货物的装或卸港在中国,中国海事法院也不一定保得住对案件的管辖权。

4.2.10.2.5.2 何谓开始仲裁

在英美国家法院,何谓开始诉讼应不难确定。这是出告票的一天,而告票也不必去送达。但若是仲裁,这会不易确定,特别近期有一连串矛盾的案例,又带来一些不肯定的因素。首先可以看看立法对此点的定义。在 Limitation Act 1980, Section 34 对"开始仲裁"的解释是:"an arbitration should be 'treated as being' commenced when one party serves notice on another requiring the appointment, or agreement to appoint, an arbitrator"。

另在英国仲裁法(Arbitration Act, 1996)的 Section 14 (3),也有类似的定义如下:"…arbitral proceedings are commenced… when one party serves on the other party… notice in writing[567] requiring him… to appoint an arbitrator[568] or to agree to the appointment of an arbitrator[569]…"

问题常出在这仲裁的书面通知在措辞上实是太不符合立法的要求,例如只说:"你再不承认责任与作出赔偿,我只好马上去仲裁"。这一来,通知既没有要求对方(被告)去指定仲裁员,也没要求对方去同意任命一位仲裁员,怎会是有效开始了仲裁,保护了时效呢?

有关这个问题,笔者的《国际商务仲裁》一书第七章之§7段有谈到,并举了不少先例,内容如下:

> §7 不够明确的开始仲裁的通知
> 曾有过不少先例是由于当事人给的仲裁通知不够明确,结果带来昂贵的

---

[567] 要求开始仲裁的当事人要先走的第一步是给对方发出书面通知。

[568] 这书面通知是要求对方(被告)去指定他自己的仲裁员。这情况会是相关的仲裁条款明示或默示要有2个或3个仲裁员,而各当事人可以指定/任命自己的仲裁员。这一来,想开始仲裁的一方的正常做法就是先去自己指定,然后书面通知对方要求他也去指定。也就是在这一刻,仲裁算是开始,时效也受到保护。

[569] 这书面通知是要求对方(被告)去同意任命一位仲裁员。这情况会是相关的仲裁条款明示或默示要由独任仲裁员仲裁,导致这仲裁员必须由双方同意才能去指定/任命。在英国仲裁法下双方同意不了,才由法院去指定(而在香港仲裁法则是由香港国际仲裁中心去指定)。至于书面通知应如何向对方提出要求,法律并没有严格规定。故此书面通知可列举出几个名字,或要求对方(被告)选择或另建议适合人士以便双方同意。总之,一发出这书面通知,仲裁就算是开始,时效也受到保护。即使后来双方要谈判1年半载才能同意谁被任命为独任仲裁员,也不影响时效一早已受到保护的事实。

官司以决定仲裁是否在时效届满前已开始。以下我再举几个例子：

（ⅰ）在 The "Agios Lazaros"（1976）2 Lloyd's Rep. 47，涉及一个在租约下的严重货损索赔。该租约是金康（Gencon）格式，有一条简单的伦敦仲裁条款（即会是由独任仲裁员仲裁），还有一条首要条款合并了海牙规则。船在1972年2月左右在汉堡卸完货，照理说海牙规则的一年时效应在1973年2月左右届满。

承租人代理在1972年5月31日写了一封信给船东的代理，提到：

"…Please advise your proposals in order to settle this matter or name your arbitrators. Expecting your reply…"

但之后双方没有进一步行动。直至1974年2月14日，承租人给船东通知要求后者在14天内任命仲裁员。船东当即提出一年时效已过，但上诉庭判是1972年5月31日承租人代理写的书信，已是足够清楚地表明承租人已开始仲裁，所以时效已受到保障。

（ⅱ）在 The "APJ Akash"（1977）1 Lloyd's Rep. 653，也是一个金康租约格式下的程租，航次在1968年6月完成。船东向承租人索赔剩余运费及滞期费，并在1968年（同一年）11月6日寄出一封书信如下：

"…In view of the attitude taken by Charterers in their calculation of laytime, Owners will be putting the matter to arbitration. We will be advising you concerning details of the arbitrator appointed in due course."

在1974年7月19日（注意，6年时效已过），船东任命 Cedric Barclay 先生为仲裁员，但法院判时效已过。法院也不认为船东1968年11月6日的书信通知可算作是开始仲裁，已保障了时效。该信并没有符合1939年 Limitation Act 的要求（这与1980年 Limitation Act 是一样的），即给承租人的通知须要求他指定仲裁员或同意任命一位仲裁员（Served on the other party a notice requiring him…to appoint an arbitrator or to agree to the appointment of an arbitrator）。

（ⅲ）在 The "Sargasso"（1994）1 Lloyd's Rep. 162，又是一个租约下的货损货差争议。货在1991年5月27日卸完，海牙规则的一年时效在1992年的同一天届满。

1991年12月11日船东向承租人发了一份电传如下：

"We confirm that in our conversation with…on the 5th December we did agree that all disputes…should be arbitrated with a tribunal consisting of Messrs. Ferryman and Hamsher."

在第二天的12月12日承租人回电："We awaited resolution of the outstanding matters…in order that the arbitrational tribunals may be complete."

1992年1月31日，承租人给船东一份传真说他已任命 Ferryman 先生为仲裁员并要求船东在7天内任命 Hamsher 先生为仲裁员。

法院判是1991年12月11号与12号的电文来往构成一仲裁协议，另外1992年1月31号的承租人传真已算是开始了仲裁，这发生在卸货后一年内，所以时效未过。

（ⅳ）这方面还有其他很多案例，如近期的 The "Petr Shmidt"（1995）1 Lloyd's Rep. 202，在此不再多作详论了。"

英国法律一向是想宽松地对待仲裁，毕竟这是一般不懂法律的商业人士也可去处理的争议解决方法。所以权威的说法一度是按 The "Agios Lazaros"（1976）2 Lloyd's Rep. 47 先例的判法。除了节录的介绍外，笔者对此先例可再进一步解释如下：

船东说书面通知不能保护海牙规则（被合并在租约内）的一年时效，因为它没有说死（或肯定）要去仲裁。但上诉庭不同意，Denning 勋爵说："Mr. Rokison（船东的大律师）says that request is equivocal. It gives the owners an alternative. It does not amount to an unequivocal request for arbitration. That seems to me too legalistic an approach. In a commercial dispute, a letter requesting arbitration should not be construed too strictly. The writer should not impaled on a time bar because he writes in polite and courteous terms, or because he leaves open the possibility of settlement by agreement. Suppose the charterers had written to the owners: 'Unless you are prepared to settle the matter amicably, we must ask you to agree to the appointment of an arbitrator.' That would, to my mind, be quite sufficient. When such a letter follows upon a genuine claim promptly made, it should be interpreted as a request for arbitration——a request made then and there——coupled with a willingness to come to an amicable settlement. The arbitration is deemed to commence with the sending of the letter, and time no longer runs against him."

这先例也被视为是一个就仲裁的"默示要求"（implied request）已足以构成开始仲裁的通知。但二十年后，在 Vosnoc v. Transglobal（1998）1 Lloyd's Rep. 711 先例，Raymond Jack 大法官却有了不同看法。该案也涉及货损及海牙规则的一年时效，在原告向承运人要求延长时效而没有得到回复后，原告在时效将届时给了承运人以下一份书面通知（一份传真）：

"…During loading, stowage and the voyage and unloading of the pipes serious damage was caused to the pipes in consequence of which（原告）has suffered loss and damage…"

Under the Contract of Affreightment…all disputes between our respective companies shall be referred to the Arbitration of three persons in London.

By this letter the dispute between our respective companies is referred to the Arbitration of three Arbitrators in London pursuant to the provisions of Clause 17.8（仲裁条款）."

而原告真正指定了仲裁员却是在二年后，争议是，该份传真能否去保护时效？要知道，当时原告（货方）自己仍未指定仲裁员，所以谈不上去要求承运人的被告指定他/它的仲裁员，以便成立一个3人的仲裁庭。一般总不会是被告比原告先指定仲裁员。

Raymond Jack 大法官判是该传真不能保护时效，原告并没有要求对方指定仲裁员，而立法对这要求说得明明白白，没有理由可以罔顾。他说："…if all that was needed was a notice referring the matter to arbitration, it made pointless the spelling out in the statutes what was to be done in the situations which they covered;

…provided the notice made plain that the arbitration was to commence at the date of the notice, it was plain that the respondent（承运人）was required to do what the arbitration agreement provided, namely to appoint an arbitrator; English law had taken the policy decision that to stop time running the notice must take a step further than a requirement to arbitrate."（即若是仲裁一句话已是足够，立法又何需去对"开始仲裁"有细致与明确的定义？)

但之后马上又有了对此持异议的判例，它们不认同 Raymond Jack 大法官的看法，认为那样是太严格，"墨守法规"（too legalistic）。第一个案例是 The "Baltic Universal"（1999）1 Lloyd's Rep. 497，它也是货损案件，提单（Congenbill）合并了租约的伦敦仲裁条款。在一年时效将届时，原告（货方）的律师指定了仲裁员，并书面通知了船东（被告）的互保协会说："We hereby notify you that in view of the expiration of the statutory time bar, we have appointed Mr. Michael Baskerville…as arbitrator on behalf of our client…in connection with all disputes arising under the three bills of lading…"

看来，这通知应是够清楚了：它说明是为了保护时效，它也指定了谁是仲裁员。但它漏了一点，就是没有要求船东去指定他/它自己的仲裁员。估计是受了 Vosnoc 先例的鼓舞，船东指该书面通知不能保护一年时效。但 Moore-Bick 大法官不同意（也不认同 Raymond Jack 大法官的观点），他说：

"…in a case such as the present a claimant need not expressly call on the respondent to appoint his arbitrator in order to commence arbitration; what was important was not whether a notice contained a particular form of words but whether it made it clear that the arbitration agreement was being invoked and that they were required to take steps accordingly;[570] provided that that was done both the policy of the Act and the requirements of commercial life were satisfied."

4.2.10.2.6 仲裁上可以申请延长时效的做法

若是在英国法院诉讼,时效一过而没有作出保护,这索赔就彻底完了。但若是去伦敦仲裁(相关合约有仲裁条款),即使时效已过也可能会得以挽救。这是因为英国 1996 年的仲裁法 Section 12 有如下规定：

"12 (1) Where an arbitration agreement to refer future disputes to arbitration provides that a claim shall be barred,[571] or the claimant's right extinguished, unless the claimant takes within a time fixed by the agreement some step—

(a) to begin arbitral proceedings, or

(b) to begin other dispute resolution procedures which must be exhausted before arbitral proceedings can be begun, the court may by order extend the time for taking that step.[572]

(2) Any party to the arbitration agreement may apply for such an order (upon notice to the other parties), but only after a claim has arisen and after exhausting any available arbitral process for obtaining an extension of time.[573]

(3) The court shall make an order only if satisfied[574]

(a) that the circumstances are such as were outside the reasonable contemplation of the parties when they agreed the provision in question,[575] and that it would be just to extend the time, or

(b) that the conduct of one party makes it unjust to hold the other party to the strict terms of the provision in question.[576]"

---

[570] 重要是内容,而不是文字上的形式,内容要清楚说明已开始仲裁并要求进一步的行动,这业已足够。在 2 天内,另有一先例同意 The "Baltic Universal"而不认同 Vosnoc,该先例是 The "Smaro" (1999) 1 Lloyd's Rep. 225。之后,还有 The "Fjellvang" (1999) 2 Lloyd's Rep. 685 先例。

[571] 它是针对一条仲裁条款所明示的时效。

[572] 若时效过了,可向法院申请延长。如果时效只是将届而未届,则原告只需去"开始仲裁"即可(如上一小段所讲的去发出书面通知),这样会更简易、更经济,因此根本无须向法院申请。注意香港仲裁法下是向仲裁庭申请,可以说是更简易、更经济了。

[573] 这一句的后半部分针对的情况是,如有仲裁机构的条例规定延长时效先要由它的委员会决定,则申请方要先走这一步,失败了才能向法院申请。

[574] 法院只有在能满足以下两个条件之一的情况下,才会同意延长时效。

[575] 一是超过时效的情况是双方约定时(订下仲裁协议,另加上明示时效之时)无法合理预见到的。

[576] 二是对方行为不当,主要会是像误导致原告错过了时效,没有采取行动。这情况会是本章 4.2.10.2.4.3 小段所讲的行为。

但这做法对索赔时效已过所能作出的挽救十分有限,原告的货方千万别抱太多幻想。原因是:

(ⅰ)它只是针对仲裁条款内明示的时效,即合约规定的时效。而不是立法的时效:The "Antares" (1987) 1 Lloyd's Rep. 424. 这带来微妙的区别,就是如果海牙/海牙·维斯比规则强制适用,那么一年时效如果过了,即使有仲裁条款也没希望去申请延长。但如果海牙/海牙·维斯比规则是以合约的形式适用(主要是依据一条"首要条款"合并引入合约),则可望能申请延长时效。

考虑到海牙/海牙·维斯比规则在提单通常是强制适用(租约才是以合约形式适用),货方在提单下若让一年时效过去而没有采取保护行动,则其索赔是无可挽救了。

(ⅱ)被允许延长时效必须满足两个条件的其中一个。这比起1980年仲裁法只要求申请人说明有"过度困境"(undue hardship)即可获延长时效在尺度上已是大大收紧。有关这方面的课题,笔者的《国际商务仲裁》一书第七章之§3与§4段有详论,请参阅。

(ⅲ)有关条件能否满足,已有几个先例作出过解释如:The "Catherine Heleh" (1998) 2 Lloyd's Rep. 511; Fox & Widley v. Guram (1998) 3 EG 142; The "Siki Rolette" (1999) 1 WLR 908; Harbour & General v. Environment Agency (2000) 1 Lloyd's Rep. 65 等。看来,条件十分严格,因为绝大部分的时效过去的情况都可在订约时预见到。但法律就是坚持这一点才允许延长时效,正如上诉庭在 Harbour & General 先例所说的:"…the section was concerned not to allow a Court to interfere with a contractual bargain unless the circumstances were such that if they had been drawn to the attention of the parties when they agreed the provision(指有时效的仲裁条款), the parties would at the very least have contemplated that the time bar might not apply; and it would then be for the Court finally to rule as to whether justice required an extension of time to be granted."

而在 The "Catherine Helen" 先例,提到的情况是像原告(货方)的律师突然心脏病发作引致无法及时去保护时效等。可见,申请延长时效已绝非易事。

4.2.10.2.7 修改保护了时效的告票

再回头谈谈国家法院的告票。英国法院的"高院规则"(Rules of Supreme Court)允许法官有裁量权准予原告多加一位或多位被告。所以在 The "Puerto Acevedo" (1978) 1 Lloyd's Rep. 38,货方(原告)在一年时效内出了告票,被告是船东。但之后货方知道了另有光船租船人,后者更可能是提单承运人(这方面请参阅本书第三章之3.1小段),于是马上去法院申请加上光船承租人作为第二被告,但当时一年时效已过,再出新的告票已没有可能。但上诉庭允许原告在有效的一份告票内加上第二被告。Denning 勋爵说:"the cargo-owners had believed honestly and reasonably that the shipowners were the people responsible and were accepting responsibility and it would be most unjust that after the year had expired, the club (which covered both shipowners and demise charterers) should escape; on the material before the Court, the cargo-owners had made out a clear prima facie case for the exercise of the Court's discretion in their favour; and leave would be given to the cargo-owners to join the demise charterers as additional defendants."

至于一年时效过后要在告票上多加一位原告(第二原告),例如收货人怕自己的诉权有问题而欲加上发货人为第二原告,应是更容易了。一般的原则/精神是允许这样做,只要是:

(ⅰ)不会剥夺被告(承运人)原可享有的合法抗辩(the defendant is not deprived of some legal defence otherwise available)。

(ⅱ)增加的第二原告不会带来"新的诉因"(new cause of action)。

另在 The "Kefalonia Wind" (1986) 1 Lloyd's Rep. 273,是一年时效已过但法院允许去修改并增加另外两套提单的索赔。在原来的告票,只针对了一套的提单,是第三装港 Baie Comeau 签发的提单。而另外两套第一装港 Colborne 与第二装港 Windsor 签发的提单则没有包括。

4.2.10.2.8 有关追偿的时效

追偿即是寻求"补偿"(indemnity),这行为常发生在租约提单。总之是有涉及另一份程租/期租租约,不论谁是提单的承运人,或许是船东(多数情况是如此),或许是承租人(情况不多但不是没有,如本书第三章之7.4 小段所介绍的 The "Hector" (1998) 2 Lloyd's Rep. 287),他/它在赔付了收货人/提单持有人之后,都可能要找租约的另一方寻求补偿。这赔付可能是败诉的结果,也可能是合理作出的庭外和解(The "Krapan J" (1999) 1 Lloyd's Rep. 688),但都不影响追偿。船东的另一方自然是承租人,而承租人的另一方则是船东了。

4.2.10.2.8.1 为何要有追偿行为

要去追偿会寻求补偿是因为:

(ⅰ)一方根据海牙/海牙·维斯比规则在提单赔付后,发觉租约的条款对自己较为优待。例如,船东发觉租约有一条款明确规定船东不负责任何原因造成的货损货差。或是,租约是根据金康租约的标准格式,其中第2条对船东比海牙规则优待多了。这一来,意味着对该货损货差,船东不必在租约下负责,但却在提单下负了责。对这种因为营运及签发提单带来的额外责任,承租人要去补偿船东,即使租约没有说明,法律上承租人也有默示的补偿责任:The "C. Joyce" (1986) 2 Lloyd's Rep. 285; The "Nogar Marin" (1988) 1 Lloyd's Rep. 412, The "Island Archon"

(1994) 2 Lloyd's Rep. 227。但不少租约标准格式如 Baltime 或 1993 年的"纽约土产"(NYPE)格式,都已有明示的规定针对这方面的补偿责任。

（ⅱ）即使提单与租约的责任一致,例如租约明示加了一条"首要条款"(Clause Paramount),将海牙或/与海牙·维斯比规则合并引入租约,也存在着双方在承运中有不同责任的分别。例如承租人负责装卸、堆货等,而船东负责适航,照看货物等。故此承租人(也是提单承运人)若在提单下赔付了有关不适航的索赔,就会想到去找船东补偿了。而船东若是提单承运人,赔付了有关装卸/堆货不当的索赔,也会想到去找承租人追偿。

4.2.10.2.8.2　追偿的诉因何时产生

在 The "Caroline P" (1984) 2 Lloyd's Rep. 466,判是追偿的诉因最早产生于原先的索赔诉讼有了结果后(不论是诉讼后还是庭外和解后:Biggin v. Permanite (1951) 2 LB 314)。毕竟,原先的索赔可能完全失败。

这带来的问题是原先的索赔诉讼(指提单的收货人向承运人的索赔)可能会延至几年后才有结果,而要等至其有了结果才开始追偿行动,可能那时一般合约的 6 年时效也已过了。

幸亏,在 The "Himmerland" (1965) 2 Lloyd's Rep. 353 与 The "Catherine Helen" (1998) 2 Lloyd's Rep. 511 等先例,都判是没有可供执行的诉因(enforceable cause of action)并不影响一方先开始仲裁,指定仲裁员,发出书面通知,以保护将来可能追偿的时效。

4.2.10.2.8.3　追偿比原先索赔先走一步的困难

问题是若开始了仲裁,对方(被追偿一方)要推进仲裁程序怎样办？要知道,当时承运人可能对原先的索赔只是一知半解,原索赔只在程序中的很早阶段。或许会是,追偿的原告(比方是船东)可向仲裁庭申请一个"宣示裁决书"(declaratory award),判承租人要就收货人最终能成功索赔的金额向船东作出补偿。但要这样做,也必须是事实方面已能有一定程度的明确,例如租约有一条款说明船东不必负责某些原因造成的货损货差。

如果连主要事实都未能明确,那么船东为保护时效开始了仲裁,也要与承租人同意"暂停",先等待原先向船东索赔的收货人的诉讼行为有了结果。这往往会一拖就是几年。幸亏在这种情况下,承租人(被要求补偿一方)往往也会同意,不会留难,毕竟他/它是被告,也想去拖。

4.2.10.2.8.4　租约合并海牙规则的时效

海牙规则从未有打算要适用在租约:请看本章之 4.2.3.2.2 小段。换言之,海牙规则的一年时效只适用在提单,而之后在租约的追偿行动应可享有 6 年时效。除非,租约另有更短的明示时效,如著名的 Centrocon Arbitration Clause,规定在卸货后

3个月就时效已过：The "Himmerland"（1965）2 Lloyd's Rep. 353。

有6年时效可去寻求补偿，应已十分足够，一般情况下都不会出现时效已过的困境。即使原先在提单下的索赔诉讼6年后尚未了结，追偿方先开始仲裁以保护追偿的时效也不会困难。

但今天的租约大多喜欢以首要条款去合并海牙/海牙·维斯比规则：请参阅本章之4.2.3.2.2.2至4.2.3.2.2.6小段。这一来，船东与承租人之间有关货损货差责任（包括追偿）的诉讼也会有了1年的时效。但这会带来很多方面的困难，接下来的段节将详细加以介绍。

4.2.10.2.8.4.1 一年时效只适用在承租人向船东索赔

由于海牙规则在Article 3（6）的一年时效规定是说明"the carrier and the ship shall be discharged from all liability…"，那么这"carrier"（承运人）在租约下是指谁呢？因为从措辞/文字上看明显是只有他/它才可以享受一年时效。租约毕竟不同于提单，在后者谁是货方，谁是承运人，他/它们之间的区分十分明确，身份错不了。

在The "Khian Zephyr"（1982）1 Lloyd's Rep. 73，判是在租约下"承运人"只能是指船东而不是承租人。这一来，就意味着：

（i）船东向承租人索赔，包括追偿，并不受一年时效影响（即使租约合并了海牙规则），仍可享有一般合约的6年时效，除非另有更短的明示时效。

（ii）承租人向船东索赔，受一年时效影响：The "Stena Pacifica"（1990）2 Lloyd's Rep. 234。这也公道，毕竟承租人可能就是真正的收货人/货方，遭受了货损货差，提单就在他的手中，虽然只是一份收据。

（iii）承租人向船东要求补偿（因为他在提单是承运人），也受一年时效影响，毕竟海牙规则的一年时效在措辞上十分绝对，说明是在"任何情况下"（in any event），也没有再去区分在追偿方面是否有不同的对待。

4.2.10.2.8.4.2 承租人向船东追偿的困境

因为受一年时效的影响，承租人在追偿行动上会遇到困境，这就是原先在提单的索赔，可能1年后才浮现。毕竟收货人有一年时效，出了告票就能保护时效。但出了告票并不需要马上送达，这一来承租人（也是提单承运人）就不会知道有货损货差的索赔。而到了索赔浮现时，承租人再马上采取行动（指定仲裁员）去保护追偿的时效，可能为时已晚，一年时效已过。

以往遇上这情况，承租人会马上向法院申请延长时效，说明有"过度困境"（undue hardship），这往往也会获得法院允许延长：The "Himmerland"（1965）2 Lloyd's Rep. 353。法院也可以这样做，因为海牙规则的适用是源自租约条款（首要条款），而不是立法。这一点在本章之4.2.10.2.6小段有略及。

但今天（1996年英国仲裁法下）法院去延长时效的尺度已大大收紧，承租人可能会面临更严重的困境。这可以节录 Bruce Harris 等人所著的《The Arbitration Act 1996——A Commentary》一书第 2 版之第 96 页所介绍的新形势如下:"In shipping arbitrations, 12 month time limits are not uncommon in charterparty arbitration clauses,[577] whilst cargo claims under bills of lading must almost invariably be brought within 12 months by statute.[578] Accordingly we opined in the first edition, an owner seeking an indemnity from a charterer in respect of a cargo claim the subject of proceedings brought just at the end of the 12 month period might have problems in obtaining and extension since such a situation ought to be quite foreseeable,[579] and so it has been held.[580]"

4.2.10.2.8.5 以 Inter-Club Agreement 延长追偿时效

这国际船东互保协会组织的内部协议,在《期租合约》一书的 24.9 至 24.12 小段有详论,不再在此重复。它经常被合并在以"纽约土产"(NYPE)标准格式为基础的期租合约中,也受到互保协会的支持。它主要是为了简化船东与承租人之间对货损货差责任的分摊。而在时效方面,1996 年版本的第 6 条规定如下:"Recovery under this Agreement by an Owner or Charterer shall be deemed to be waived and absolutely barred unless written notification of the cargo claim has been given to the other party to the charterparty within 24 months of the date of delivery of the cargo or the date the cargo should have been delivered, save that, where the Hamburg Rules or any national legislation giving effect thereto are compulsorily applicable by operation of law to the contract of carriage or to that part of the transit that comprised carriage on the chartered vessel, the period shall be 36 months. Such notification shall if possible include details of the contract of carriage, the nature of the claim and the amount claimed."

简单地说,该条款就是将分摊的时限延长至 24 个月到 36 个月,而且要保护时效也只需"给一个有关货损货差的书面通知"(written notification of the cargo claim)即可,而不是像海牙规则那样必须"开始诉讼"(unless suit is brought)才行。

这一来,若是租约合并了 Inter-Club Agreement,但在追偿行动却让时效过去,这可是严重的疏忽。只要是懂得去保护时效,实属举手之劳。

4.2.10.2.8.6 海牙·维斯比规则有关追偿的时效

本来海牙/海牙·维斯比规则只针对提单,它何必去理会租约(或其他方面)的

---

[577] 该书是指租约有一条明示的 12 个月时效的仲裁条款,适用于租约的所有争议。

[578] 而提单的货损货差索赔诉讼总是要在 12 个月内提起(海牙规则的立法)。

[579] 这会导致租约下的追偿行动过了 12 个月时效。但这情况在订约时并非不可以预见。

[580] 这是指 The "Catherine Helen" (1998) 2 Lloyd's Rep. 511 先例。该先例判追偿行动实效已过,这情况订约时可预见,所以不准延长时效。这再也不是 The "Himmerland" (1965) 2 Lloyd's Rep. 353 宽松的判法。

追偿呢？但可能是考虑到租约经常会合并海牙/海牙·维斯比规则，以及一程船要向二程船追偿等，海牙·维斯比规则是增加（加在海牙规则的 Article 3(6)）了一项针对追偿行动的时效规定，说："An action for indemnity against a third party may be brought even after the expiration of the year provided for in the preceding paragraph if brought within the time allowed by the law of the Court seized of the case, However, the time allowed shall be not less than three months, commencing from the day when the person bringing such action for indemnity has settled the claim or has been served with process in the action against himself."

看来，针对追偿行动，追偿方在海牙·维斯比规则下再也不受一年时效的影响了。而且，该段只是说追偿最少有 3 个月时间（从原先的提单索赔已经了结时开始算），并没有说最多有多久？看来，在英美时效会是一般合约的 6 年（在 Limitation Act 1980），从补偿的诉因浮现时始算：The "Xingcheng" (1987) 2 Lloyd's Rep. 210。

这又会带来另一大问题，就是租约的"首要条款"（Clause Paramount）到底合并的是海牙规则还是海牙·维斯比规则？若是前者，即使是追偿行动也受一年时效影响（只适用于向船东追偿）。若是后者，追偿行为根本不受时效影响（除了 6 年之久外）。

所以租约既然有订约自由，意味着首要条款的措辞或/与内容到底是合并海牙规则还是海牙·维斯比规则会变得事关重大。这在本章的 4.2.3.2.2.2 小段已有详论，其中还介绍了 The "Bukhta Russkaya" (1997) 2 Lloyd's Rep. 744 的有关先例。

4.2.10.2.8.7　一程船/二程船之间的追偿时效

最后，不妨详细介绍一下 The "Xingcheng" 这一有趣的先例。它也涉及追偿行动的时效，但不是在租约下的追偿，而是在一程船与二程船之间的追偿。这会出现在一程船签发了一份"全程提单"（through bill of lading）的情况下：请参阅本章之 4.2.3.1.6 小段与第二章之 3.2 小段。若是二程船犯了过错（如无单放货），这会导致作为全程提单承运人的一程船船东要负上赔偿责任：请参阅本章之 4.2.3.4.2.2 小段。结果会是一程船赔付了收货人之后再向二程船追偿或寻求"补偿"（indemnity）。

该先例中，"Xingcheng"是中远公司的船，它是一程船，而二程船名为"Andros"。货物（成衣）是从上海运去澳洲的墨尔本，经香港装箱转二程船。在香港，二程船签发了清洁提单给中远公司的代理人（招商局）。但货物到了墨尔本，发觉严重损坏。货方（中国进出口公司或简称 CNTIEC）根据全程提单向一程船（中远公司）提出索赔，在香港高院以"诉人"（in personam）告中远公司。另外，货方再以侵权为诉因通过"诉物"（in rem）告二程船，并在香港扣了船（"Andros"）。但不知是什么原因，货方后来放弃了告二程船（表面看来并不明智，个中原因则不明），只继续向中远公司起诉。

该先例主要是针对中远公司向二程船的追偿,它涉及二程船以中远公司"懈怠为由申请撤销后者的诉讼请求"(strike out for want of prosecution)。这一课题在笔者的《国际商务仲裁》一书第八章之§3段有详论,可以节录3.1小段的部分内容如下:

> 首先要说明懈怠(want of prosecution)与时效已过的分别:例如,合约下的索赔依1980年Limitation Act有6年时效,原告在诉因产生后五年又十一个半月开始仲裁。这一来,时效已是无关了。但开始仲裁后,原告却并不推进,连索赔文书请求也不去递交,令人无法明确了解他的请求是什么。对被告而言,因为他没有反索赔,所以也乐意去等待,让原告睡觉好了,因为常有可能是"一睡不醒"。而对仲裁员来说,前面已解释过,他也是不会理会的。
>
> 但仲裁开始后的第10年,即从诉因产生的那一天起达16年之久后,原告突然发难,去递交索赔文书请求(claim submissions),并推进仲裁。这一来,被告惨了。他可能证据全失,文件档案已销毁,落得只有去投降的田地。
>
> 对此,被告能采取什么行动呢?在法院,他可以申请把诉讼请求撤销,依据的理由是原告懈怠,对他的抗辩带来不利。法官也有这个潜在的权力去这样做,而且他也会这样做,因为大原则是要求原告有了诉因就快去推进,以便尽早审理。因为拖得越久,要保证有一个公平的审理就越困难。例如,会失去主要证人与文件,证人记忆衰退,等等。"

该书的3.4.2小段又说:

> "……在申请把诉讼请求撤销(strike out claim)时,该索赔的时效仍未过。例如它在1980年Limitation Act本有6年时效,原告一有了诉因即开始仲裁,但之后却按兵不动。到了5年半后,原告再去推动仲裁,那么被告能否去申请撤销呢?在法院,这是不行的。因为若把这诉讼请求撤销,原告大可再出一张告票,反正时效还差一点点未过。这告票会是与原来相同的诉因,但因它从未审理过,不算是一案两审(res judicata)。所以,这毫无意义的事法院不会做:Birkett v. James (1978) A. C. 297。"

再谈回The "Xingcheng"的先例,该案中,一程船(中远公司)签发的全程提单是中远提单,内有明示的"首要条款"(Clause Paramount)合并了1924年的海牙规则(而并非是海牙·维斯比规则)。而中国也没有承认这些公约以令其可强制适用。故此,海牙规则只是以合约的形式适用,而索赔时效是1年,包括了向船东索赔或追偿,均受这一年时效约束:请看本章之4.2.10.2.8.4.1小段。至于二程船签发给中远公司代理人(招商局)的二程船提单,则合并了海牙·维斯比规则。而且,香港承认海牙·维斯比规则,该规则强制适用在香港签发的提单。而根据海牙·维斯比规则,追偿行动可以有长达 6 年的时效:请看本章之 4.2.10.2.8.6 小段。

而二程船能否成功撤销中远公司的诉讼(追偿)请求,当时很大关键是看到底适用海牙规则还是海牙·维斯比规则?因为当时 1 年早已过了但 6 年时效尚未过。

在香港上诉庭,法官竟判中远公司败诉。笔者当时与中远公司商谈,认为判得没有道理。而且带来的坏影响颇大,因为在香港货物转运甚多。若追偿的时效只有 1 年而不是 6 年,经常会令追偿方赶不上时效而导致像中远公司(作为一程船)那样被夹在中间。故笔者鼓励中远公司再上诉,结果案件打到了英国贵族院(枢密院)。最终判下来中远公司胜诉,Brandon 勋爵说:"r. 6 bis[581] of Art. Ⅲ created a special exception to the generality of r. 6;[582] r. 6 bis, in a case to which it applied,[583] had a separate effect of its own independently of r. 6; the case to which r. 6 bis applied was a case where shipowner A being under actual or potential liability to cargo-owner B claimed an indemnity by way of damages against ship or shipowner C;[584] if that claim was made under a contract of carriage[585] to which the Hague-Visby Rules applied then the time allowed for bringing it was that prescribed by r. 6 bis and not r. 6;[586] there was no requirement in r. 6 bis that the liability to shipowner A should also arise under a contract of carriage to which the Hague-Visby Rules applied and there was no reason why such a requirement should be implied.[587]

最后,再讲讲本章 4.2.3.1.6 小段提及的 Ryoder Machinery v. Anders Maersk (1986) 1 Lloyd's Rep. 483 先例,判是即使货物在香港转船,香港的海牙·维斯比规则也不能适用并帮助收货人获得更高的赔偿。表面看来,这与上述的 The "Xingcheng"先例似有矛盾之处。但其实不然,因 The "Anders Maersk"是针对货方向承运人索赔,而该提单(在美国签发)一早已适用了 1936 年的美国海上运输法(海牙规则),故不应因在香港转船而变为适用海牙·维斯比规则。但 The

---

[581] 这是指海牙规则 Article 3(6)的一年时效在海牙·维斯比规则内的增加/修改,后者说明了追偿行动有较长的时效。

[582] r. 6 是指原来海牙规则的一年时效。

[583] 若遇上适合案件(即属于追偿行为),这海牙·维斯比规则的增加/修改有它独立的效用,而不再是泛泛地都受一年时效的约束。

[584] 这包括船东 A 赔付了或可能要赔付货方 B,因而要向船东 C(二船东)追偿。

[585] 若 A 向 C 索赔所根据的一份运输合约是明示合并或适用海牙·维斯比规则:注意该先例正是如此,A(中远公司)向二程船("Andros"船东)索赔正是根据二程船在香港签发的提单。

[586] 这一来,海牙·维斯比规则针对追偿行为较长时效的增加/修改,完全适用。

[587] 海牙·维斯比规则并没有要求原先的索赔诉讼(CNTIEC 告中远公司)也必须是适用海牙·维斯比规则而不光是海牙规则。公约/立法并没有明示此要求,也没有必要去默示。

"Xingcheng"先例是针对一程船向二程船追偿,他/它们之间的提单(二程船提单,也是合约关系)一早在香港签发,合并并适用海牙·维斯比规则,不存在半途改变的情况。

4.2.10.2.8.8 明示条款规定太短时效的危险

在较早的 4.2.10.2.8.4 小段等,曾提到"租约另有更短的明示时效"的例外,它是指那种往往与仲裁条款写在一起的短时效条款。在本章之 4.2.9.4 小段已略为谈到的 The "Ion" (1971) 1 Lloyd's Rep. 541,就是这类案例。又例如,在 The "Himmerland" (1965) 2 Lloyd's Rep. 353 先例的有关条款是:"Any claim must be made in writing and Claimant's Arbitrator appointed within three months of final discharge and where this provision is not complied with the claim shall be deemed to be waived and absolutely barred."

或是,在 The "Catherine Helen" (1998) 2 Lloyd's Rep. 511 先例的有关条款是:"Any claim must be in writing and claimants' arbitrator appointed within one year of final discharging and where this provision is not complied with the claim shall be deemed waived and absolutely barred."

从这种条款的措辞/内容可见:

(ⅰ)它针对的是所有租约的争议/索赔,它们均受仲裁与时效的约束/影响。

(ⅱ)即使开始不知道有一个争议/索赔存在(典型的例子就是不知道提单持有人有货损货差索赔,需要采取追偿行动去跟进),只是时效过了才知道,也不影响时效的适用。正如 Mocatta 大法官在 The "Himmerland" 先例所说:"that the arbitration clause barred a claim, if the claim was not made in writing and the claimant's arbitrator appointed within three months of final discharge, even though the cause of action giving rise to the claim had not arisen or come to knowledge of claimant until too late to enable him to comply with the clause."

这种条款对追偿行动而言十分危险,它尤其针对船东,因为:

(a)租约提单的承运人一般是船东,赔付后要依租约寻求补偿,一般是船东向承租人追索。这比承租人向船东追偿的可能性大得多。

(b)一直都是,租约不论合并海牙规则还是海牙·维斯比规则,其中的一年时效都不至于影响船东向承租人追偿。

(c)但这种明示的时效条款包括了所有的索赔/争议(包括追偿),不论是来自船东还是承租人,均受其影响,而船东受的影响会更大。

(d)正如本章 4.2.10.2.8.4.2 小段所讲,今天(1996 年英国仲裁法下)向法院申请延长时效尺度上已被大大收紧,成功实属不易。船东若嫌法律不公平,很自然会被反驳道:"谁叫你明知可能有货损货差的追偿行为,会在 1 年后才浮现,你仍这么笨地在租约中答应一条太短时效的条款,令你无法及时去向承租人追偿"。

(e)如果租约有一条很短的明示时效条款,另又有首要条款并入了海牙·维斯比规则,大家对追偿行为的时效产生了争议,也难说首要条款一定可以超越较短时效的明示条款,毕竟明示的时效/仲裁条款更有针对性,更局限在这一方面。

4.2.10.2.8.9 总结

综合以上段节所讲,针对有关追偿行动的时效而言可以总结地说:

(ⅰ)承租人不要接受只合并海牙规则的首要条款。

(ⅱ)船东不要接受太短的明示时效条款。若要接受,则须说明追偿行为的时效除外。租约若另有 Inter-Club Agreement,船东的地位应会较佳,但该协议只用在 NYPE 标准期租格式,不适用在其他众多的租约格式。

4.2.10.2.9 海牙·维斯比规则的修改强化了时效的适用

海牙规则有关一年时效的措辞/用字在前面 4.2.10.2 小段一开始已作了节录,照理说,也讲得十分绝对,说明是"任何情况下"(in any event)这一年时效都适用。但到了海牙·维斯比规则,这方面的绝对性更被进一步强化,规则增加了像"whatsoever"(无论如何)这样极为广泛的用词,变了是:"the carrier and the ship shall in any event be discharged from all liability whatsoever in respect of the goods, unless suit is brought within one year of their delivery or of the date when they should have been delivered."

故此,在本章之 4.2.3.5.3.8 小段与 4.2.10.1.3 小段,都提到这即使是十分严重的违约,如把货物装在甲板上,不合理绕航等,仍适用一年时效。在 The "Captain Gregos" (1990) 1 Lloyd's Rep. 310 一案,涉及承运人偷油(货物是原油),这是再严重不过的违约了,但上诉庭还是推翻了一审判决,认为海牙·维斯比规则的一年时效适用,货方让时效过去也就令其对偷油导致货差的索赔作废了。

该先例中,Bingham 大法官说:"the words in art. Ⅲ, r.6(一年时效)that the carrier was to be discharged from 'all liability whatsoever in respect of the goods' meant exactly what it said; the inference that the one year time bar was intended to apply to all claims arising out of the carriage of goods was strengthened by the consideration that art. Ⅲ, r. 6 was intended to achieve finality and, in this case, enable the shipowner to clear his books."(海牙·维斯比规则的一年时效是为了追求终局性,以便让船东在未被起诉的情况下可把文件档案处理掉)。

Bingham 大法官也提到这样的规定对该案的货方并没有不公道之处,他/它本可以主动采取适当行动去保护时效,法官说:"...A limitation provision can lead to injustice if a party's cause of action may be barred before he knows he has it.[588] But that should not, as it seems to me, happen here.[589] A cargo-owner should know whether he has received short delivery at or about the time of delivery.[590] With a cargo of crude oil such as this he will quickly be able to consider, and if necessary investigate, whether the shortage is reasonably explicable by evaporation, wastage, clingage, unpumpable residue etc.[591] He can investigate what quantity was loaded.[592] If he finds an unjustifiable shortage during carriage he is in a position to sue, and it is not crucial how and why the shortage occurred.[593] He should be ready to sue well within the year, as the rules intend.[594] The only reason why the cargo-owners seek to found on the shipowners' alleged misconduct[595] rather than on the breaches of the rules is, as I infer, that for whatever reason they let the year pass without bringing suit.[596] That is in my view precisely the result the rules were intended to preclude.[597]"

4.2.10.3 单位/单件责任限制

4.2.10.3.1 海牙规则的条款与解释

海牙规则在 Article 4(5)有以下的条款：

"Neither the carrier nor the ship shall in any event be or become liable for any loss or damage to or in connection with goods in an amount exceeding 100 pounds sterling per package or unit,[598] or the equivalent of that sum in other currency unless the nature and

---

[588] 当事人可能在时效过去前完全不知道他自己有一个诉因，这会带来不公平。
[589] 但本案的事实并非如此。
[590] 收货人在交货之时已应马上知道有否货差。
[591] 如果有，可马上去考虑/调查这短少是否属正常的"自然流失/短重"(本章之 4.2.7.1.10.2 小段曾详论过这方面课题)。
[592] 收货人也可查看提单去了解装了多少货物(原油)。
[593] 若发觉有不合理的货差/短少，收货人即可起诉承运人。而在保护时效方面，造成货差的具体原因(严重或较不严重的违约)其实并非关键的因素，不必先去确定区分。
[594] 收货人可在一年时效内起诉承运人，这也是海牙·维斯比规则所希望的。
[595] 在本案收货人只一味针对承运人的"不良行为"(misconduct)，指他/它偷油。
[596] 说穿了，就是因为收货人不知何故自己先忘了去保护 1 年的时效。
[597] 而这正是海牙·维斯比规则想要杜绝的。
[598] 这里订明承运人赔偿的责任是限制在每单件/单位 100 英镑的黄金价格。要知道，海牙规则是国际公约，不能单使用某一国家的货币。而当时英国相当强大，国际上普遍以英镑为结算单位，好像今天的美元一样。故此，责任限制的金额订在 100 英镑的黄金价值，这也在海牙规则的 Article 9 有说明。而之后各国就纷纷去立法，把海牙规则改为本国法律。像英国的 1924 年海上运输法就把 100 英镑的黄金价值改为是 100 英镑的币值，这在 1924 年本来是相同的价值，是同一回事。而美国的 1936 年海上运输法，则把 100 英镑的黄金价值改为 500 美元的币值。

value of such goods have been declared by the shipper before shipment and inserted in the bill of lading.[599]

This declaration if embodied in the bill of lading shall be prima facie evidence, but shall not be binding or conclusive on the carrier.[600]

By agreement between the carrier, master or agent of the carrier and the shipper another maximum amount than that mentioned in this paragraph may be fixed,[601] provided that such maximum shall not be less than the figure above named.[602]"

4.2.10.3.2 问题之一：何谓"单件"(package)

这一方面在 1924 年不是问题。当时的货物都以人手操作（装卸、堆放等），会是一包、一捆、一袋、一桶、一箱、一件等，但不会体积庞大或/与重量过高。当时也没有太大的货物交付运输，如整座的机器、整卡的火车、一个 40 尺的集装箱，等等。甚至没有太多的装卸设备/机械去支持。

随着技术的发展，海上运输方法的改变，海牙规则在这一方面的条款明显过时，无法应付。

4.2.10.3.2.1 可否考虑订约双方的意图以找出何谓单件

这一点并不容易解答，因为订约双方的意图在班轮提单下往往也只是班轮公司的单方面的意图而已。所以若允许加以考虑，岂非班轮公司可以在提单中写上

---

[599] 要想不受单位/单件责任限制的约束（即收货人不想承运人少赔钱），除非发货人提前向承运人申明货物是什么以及它的真正价值，并将此写在提单内。但在本书第四章之 3.4.16 小段提到，发货人若是这样做，意味着出了事船东要多赔，船东/承运人尽可能要收取更高运费（称为 ad valorem 运费）。毕竟，他/它可能会要加保，因为船东互保协会仅以海牙规则的赔偿责任作为基础。所以，现实中发货人申明货价的情况并不多见。而收货人对赔不足（因为有单位/单件责任限制）一般也不太关心，因为最终只是代位的保险人"受害"。但代位的保险人也无所谓，因为他/它本来就把代位所追偿回来的钱当做是天上掉下来的。

[600] 海牙规则有此规定并非是为了帮助承运人少赔钱，海牙规则的工作报告显示在 1924 年海上运输的平均货价是低于每件/每单位 100 英镑的。它的目的在于：(a)让承运人了解自己所负的责任，可在投保时有依据（在互保协会投保责任）；(b)不鼓励发货人隐瞒货物价值令船东少收运费却负额外风险的陋习。故此，一旦申明了货物的真正价值（当然会是高价货），出了事就会以该价值赔偿，这也公道，毕竟船东已就此多收了 ad valorem 运费。但船东/承运人也不想被捆死，毕竟集装箱内实是垃圾，与提单中宣告的货物及价值完全不是同一回事的例子也不是没听过。另一种情况是货物在卸港市场大跌。所以，有此说明的提单宣告只是货物价值的"表面证据"（prima facie evidence），承运人将来可以反证这货物并不值这宣告的金额，没有这损失而部分拒赔。

[601] 发货人可与承运人同意更高的赔偿金额（不论有否宣告货物真正价值）。

[602] 但不能去同意更低（比 100 英镑的黄金）的赔偿金额，因为这是去减轻了承运人的责任，违反海牙规则：这方面请参阅本章之 4.2.9 小段。现实也是，若去允许，保证承运人（班轮公司）可去迫发货人接受只赔 1 毛钱的责任限制。

如"40 尺的集装箱只算一个单件",或是"这 50 吨重的锅炉只算一个单件"的条款呢？看来,这种条款很明显会违反海牙规则的 Article 3(8)而变得无效。

但若罔顾订约双方的意图又会导致更难自圆其说地找出何谓"单件"(package)的局面。例如,双方对运费如何支付？发货人有否申明集装箱内有多少件货物以及是什么货物？如何包装以保护货物,等等。

就这方面不妨节录一些法院的稍为不同的说法,像美国的 Matsushita Elec. Corp. v. S. S. Aegis Spirit, 1976 AMC 779 (W. D. Wash. 1976)先例,是说(指订约双方意图并不重要):"The package limitation provision serves no purpose whatsoever if the courts function in applying it is to merely identify and uphold the parties' private definition of COGSA package. Of course, the parties' characterisation may often be wholly reasonable and consistent with the language and purpose of the statute, but the point to be made is that it is not the parties' characterisation of the shipment, but the court's interpretation of the statute, that controls."

而去强调找出订约双方意图重要性的判法,则可以节录在 The "Aleksandr Serafimovich" (1975) 2 Lloyd's Rep. 346 的加拿大先例中 Smith D. J. 大法官所说的:"…it is clear that the decision whether a large container, a pallet, or a smaller, wrapped parcel in or on a container or pallet, is a 'package' within the meaning of (海牙规则) depends on the facts and circumstances of each case. In particular, it depends upon the intention of the parties as indicated by what is stated in the shipping documents, things said by the parties and the course of dealing between them."

4.2.10.3.2.2 集装箱的问题

自六七十年代发展起来的集装箱运输,在班轮业务中已完全取代了传统的运输方法。无可避免,它也带来了各种新问题,其中的一个方面就是海牙规则的单位/单件责任限制如何适用/套用在集装箱运输？这是在 1924 年想也未想到的情况。

简单地举一个例子,某一票货是装在 4 个集装箱内的 1600 袋的"可可"(cocoa),承运人的赔偿责任是限制在 4×100 英镑的 400 英镑,还是 1600 袋×100 英镑的 16 万英镑呢？

正常情况下,看包装应该漠视"内包装"而只看最后/最外表的包装("外包装")。但针对集装箱而言,它能否算是货物最外的包装呢？

而且,针对集装箱还会有其他的疑问,如:

(ⅰ)发货人自己堆装与铅封的集装箱(现实中常是如此)与承运人去堆装的集装箱有否不同对待的必要？要知道,后者的情况会涉及把几票不同的货物堆放在一个集装箱内,所以若只去算一个"单件"(package),再在几票不同的货物中分摊作为赔偿,会更加不合理。

第五章 提单作用之二：运输合约下的货损货差责任

(ⅱ)船东/承运人根据海牙规则的 Article 3(3)，会可以没有"合理方法"查明集装箱内的货物(包括件数)为由拒签有此内容的提单(这方面课题请参阅本书第六章之 3.2.6.1/3.2.6.2 小段)。也就是，只签 4 个集装箱"可可"的提单，但拒签 4 个集装箱内有 1600 袋"可可"的提单。若是如此，会否影响单件责任限制的计算？

(ⅲ)或者，签发的提单虽注明是 4 个集装箱内有 1600 袋"可可"，但又另加上"否定性批注"(disclaimer)，比如说"重量，数量……不知"(weight, quantity, contents and value unknown)或"据说会有"(said to contain)，这一来影响又如何(这方面课题请参阅本书第六章之§5 段)？

(ⅳ)其他如集装箱内的货物描述得不清楚，或是太细微(如 1.6 万支笔)，这又如何对待？这些问题十分重要，尤其是考虑到 1924 年海牙规则的立法已过去多年，通货膨胀已导致单件/单位责任限制的金额大大偏低，例如美国 1936 年的海上运输法的单位赔偿限额只是 500 美元。但今天一个集装箱内的货物，价值可能是几万至几十万美元不等。如果遭受全损，承运人很可能愿意赔 500 美元了事，懒得再去调查/取证，再诉讼/抗辩。但若要赔 10 万、20 万美元，则是另一回事了。

4.2.10.3.2.2.1 计算方法之一：核实原则(the Verification Principle)

在这原则下，强调的是船东/承运人根本无法去核实集装箱内有什么货物。发货人堆装固然无法核实，就算出事后也不一定能做到，例如集装箱已被冲下大海。这一来，若是以发货人自说自话的内容(包括件数)为准，岂非承运人要完全陷于被动？所以，除非提单毫无保留地接受并注明集装箱内的货物件数，即没有"否定性批注"，只应以 1 个集装箱算 1 单件来计算。有关这种争议，不妨节录 The "River Gurara" (1996) 2 Lloyd's Rep. 53 先例一审时代表船东的大律师所说的如下："(承运人大律师) submitted that even where a container held separate items describable as 'packages' there was no reason, in principle, why the container itself could not be treated as separate package for the purposes of article Ⅲ, rule 5. In order to determine whether a container was to be treated as a separate 'package' it was necessary to look at the wording of the bill of lading. If that wording indicated that the contents of the container described in the bill of lading were not loaded into it under the supervision of the carrier or his agents, the container, as distinct from its contents, was to be treated as the package. Phraseology such as 'one container said to contain...' or 'weight/quantity unknown' or 'shipper's load stow and count' would indicate that the carrier, not having loaded or supervised the loading of the container, did not accept that what was stated on the face of the bill of lading should even be prima facie evidence that such items had been carried in it…

…that if such wording in the bill of lading excluded there being prima facie evidence of the contents of the container it could not be the position that in a case where the shipper had packed the container the carrier could be subjected to a limit of liability calculated by reference to whatever number of packages within the container the shipper had chosen to insert in the bill of lading. The carrier would not be in a position to verify the number of contents and, in a case such as this one where the vessel was a total loss, he never would be. This would place him in a position where the quantification of his liability was at the mmercy of the shipper. That could not be the proper construction of the Rule."

4.2.10.3.2.2.2　计算方法之二:根据提单所注明的集装箱内件数

这个计算船东/承运人责任限制的方法,今天看来是主流。它并不理会集装箱是否由发货人自己堆装/铅封,承运人是否无法核实。总之是以发货人申明的集装箱内件数为准,以此作为"单件"(package)。在此列举一些主要国家的有关先例,它们均有相同的判法,具体如下:

(A)美国

(ⅰ)在 The "Mormaclynx"(1970)1 Lloyd's Rep. 527,提单注明是"1 个集装箱,据说内有99 捆的皮革"(1 container said to contain 99 bales of leather)。法院判是以 99 个"单件"为计算基础,并说:"…we cannot escape the belief that the purposes of sect. 4 (5) of COGSA was to set a reasonable figure below which the carrier should not be permitted to limit his liability and that 'package' is thus more sensibly related to the unit in which the shipper packed the goods and described them than to a large metal object, functionally a part of the ship, in which the carrier caused them to be 'contained'[603]."

(ⅱ)在 The "Aegis Spirit"(1977)1 Lloyd's Rep. 93,涉及集装箱内装有电器/电视。提单注明是(集装箱内)有"601 个纸箱"(601 cartons),并有各种"否定性批注"。Becks 大法官判是以 601 个"单件"为计算基础,并说(节录其中一个理由):"Certainly, if the individual crates or cartons prepared by the shipper and containing his goods can rightly be considered 'packages' standing by themselves, they do not suddenly lose that character upon being stowed in a carrier's container. I would liken these containers to detachable stowage compartments of the ship. They simply serve to divide the ship's overall cargo stowage space into smaller, more serviceable loci. Shippers' packages are quite literally 'stowed' in the containers utilizing stevedoring practices and materials analogous to those employed in traditional on board stowage."

(B)加拿大

---

[603] 这是指集装箱运输的概念来自船东,是船东/承运人要令发货人把已包装好的货物再塞入一个名为"集装箱"的大铁箱内。

在 The "Tindefjell" (1973) 2 Lloyd's Rep. 253, 加拿大联邦法院作出与美国的 The "Mormaclynx" 先例相同的判决。

(C) 澳大利亚

在 P. S. Chellaram & Co. Ltd. v. China Shipping Co. (1989) 1 Lloyd's Ref. 413, 提单注明是"1 个集装箱……发货人堆装, 点算与铅封, 据说内有 900 盒录音带"(1 container…Shipper's load, count and seal, said to contain 900 cartons blank cassette tapes)。Carruthers 大法官认同美国的 The "Mormaclynx" 判例, 判是以 900 个"单件"为计算基础。

(D) 法国

法国相同的判例是 Societe Navale Caennaise v. Gastin (1965) D. M. F. 18。

(E) 荷兰

荷兰相同的判例是 The "Cariba Express" (3.9.80) S. 80 No. 122 与 The "Boknis" (20.12.85) S. & S. 86 No. 49。

(F) 英国

在 The "River Gurara" (1998) 1 Lloyd's Rep. 225, 上诉庭支持第一审的判法, 也与美国的 The "Mormaclynx" 先例相同。Phillips 大法官说: "where the Hague Rules limit fell to be computed in relation to parcels of cargo which were loaded in containers it was the parcels and not the containers which constituted the relevant packages;[604] …the shipowner's limit of liability should be calculated on the basis of the number of packages carried in the containers rather than the number of containers[605] unless the manner in which the cargo had been described in the bills of lading required a contrary approach[606]."

The "River Gurara" 是英国法院针对这方面问题的第一个判决。上诉庭这样判的原因/理由是:

(ⅰ) 海牙规则的立法精神众所周知是为了去对付船东/承运人。所以它解释起来应该去反映这一精神, 而不能让船东/承运人轻易取巧。这一点可以参阅 Diplock 勋爵在 The "Morviken" (1983) 1 Lloyd's Rep. 1 先例的著名发言, 它在本章之 4.2.3.1.5 小段有详论。

(ⅱ) 世界各国的主流是这样判, 作为对一个国际公约的理解, 应尽量协调/统一, 而不是唱反调。

(ⅲ) 以英文自然及通俗的字义理解"单件"(package) 一字, 也不会是指 1 个长

---

[604] 海牙规则下的单件责任限制是以集装箱内货物的件数为基础来计算的。

[605] 而不是以多少个集装箱为准。

[606] 除非提单内对货物描述的方式要求必须另作解释(例如在集装箱内的货物是液体或/与散装货物)。

达 20 尺或 40 尺、庞然巨物般、没有人动得了的集装箱。牛津英文字典对单件的定义只是:"…a bundle of things packed up, whether in a box or receptacle, or merely compactly tied up."

另在 The "River Gurara" 先例,上诉庭也解答了不少疑问,具体如下:

(a)提单根本没有说明(或没有清楚说明)集装箱内的货物有否/可否分开件数——这一来,才会把集装箱当做 1 个单件。一审的 Colman 大法官说:"if the contents of the container were described by words which left it unclear whether they were separately packed for transportation, the container would be the package and not the individual items."

(b)集装箱内的货物如果被分为大包小包——这情况比如是说"2 个集装箱,据说内有 20 个托盘(pallets),各有 30 纸箱(cartons)的皮具"。这一来,单件责任限制应以最小的单件为准,即是:100 英镑 × 20 个托盘 × 30 纸箱 = 6 万英镑(1 个集装箱)。Colman 大法官说:"if the contents of the container were described in the bill of lading as said to contain so many separately packed items the number of packages would be the smallest category of separately packed items so described; the insertion of the lesser separately-packed items was a clear indication that those lesser items were to be treated as the unit of measurement for limitation purposes."

(c)承运人看不见也可以当做单件吗?——Colman 大法官(上诉庭也同意)认为这并没有什么不妥,海牙规则本来也预计到会有情况是承运人无法核实或/与怀疑发货人申明的货物件数/数量的[在 Article 3(3)]。这正是承运人看不见的情况。在这情况下,承运人可拒签说明有此件数/数量的提单。但如果签了,则在 Article 3(4)下构成承运人收取(装上船)了这些件数/数量货物的表面证据。而这一切只是针对提单对货物的"证据价值"(evidential value),与出了事故后承运人的赔偿与限责,没有必然的联系,针对的是两回事。比方说,也不一定是在集装箱运输,发生了承运人对货物件数/数量有怀疑而真的拒签提单的情况,船舶之后随即出事而承运人要去依赖单件责任限制,而货物件数也可事后明确,那么计算照样不受影响。同样,出了事故,货方也可提供证据去证明确有多少件货物装上了船,以供计算。Colman 大法官说:"Thus, the bill of lading regime prescribed by the Hague Rules expressly envisages by the proviso to art. Ⅲ, r. 3 that circumstances may arise where a shipper may furnish in writing to a carrier information as to the number of packages or pieces which the carrier may suspect 'not accurately to represent the goods actually received' or which the carrier ' has had no reasonable means of checking'. In such circumstances the rules give the carrier the opportunity of avoiding making a statement in the bills of lading which could create prima facie evidence of the number of packages or pieces shipped. If, in theory, the carrier was entitled to take such a course and did indeed decline to sign bills of lading indicating how many packages had been received, that would not preclude him from limiting his liability by reference to the number of packages actually received. Nor would it preclude the shipper from asserting how many packages had been shipped so as to quantify the limitation of the carrier's liability. There would, however, be nothing in the bills of lading which provided prima facie evidence of that number. The inability of the carrier to tally the number of packages received for shipment would, therefore, not affect his substantive entitlement to limit his liability."

(d)提单若有"否定性批注"会否有影响？——提单若有"否定性批注"(disclaimer)，如"重量/数量不知"等，这情况会类似于上述的(c)段，即与船东/承运人拒签提单一样。这一来，英国法律承认这种条款的有效性(请参阅本书第六章之5.3.8小段所介绍的 The "Mata K" (1998) 2 Lloyd's Rep. 614)，也只是表示这份提单对货物重量/数量等方面的"证据价值"怀疑，说了等于没说，因为有此"否定性批注"。但正如(c)段所讲，这与单件赔偿责任限制并没有必然的联系。双方照样可以举证货物真正装船的件数是多少，用以计算责任限制。充其量是举证难度增加了，因为提单等于什么都没讲。在上诉庭，Phillips 大法官说："In the present case, the description of the goods in the bills of lading was qualified simply by the letters 'stc'（这是'said to contain'的简写）.（船东大律师）submitted that such a qualification has the same effect as qualifying the description of goods 'weight, quantity, number unknown'. Assuming that this is correct, I do not see how the parties had agreed that containers were to be the relevant packages for limitation purposes. Where the shipper give details of the packages shipped and the carrier clauses the bill of lading to indicate that he does not accept those details, the bill of lading manifestly do not indicate any agreement at all as to the description of what has been shipped…this would not lead to the conclusion that limitation fell to be calculated on the basis of the number of containers rather than the number of packages proved to have been lost."

要注意本段的情况与(a)段并不一样。本段情况下提单虽有"否定性批注"，但仍显示了集装箱内的货物有可分开的件数。

(e)承运人成功推翻提单数字的情况——这情况不多，但不是没有。在著名的 Grant v. Norway (1851) 10 C. B. 665 先例（在本书第六章之4.1.4小段有详论），就有这种情况。毕竟海牙规则的 Article,3(4) 只是把提单的数字（如件数或重量）当做表面证据而已，船东/承运人可以去反证/推翻。若成功了，涉及计算单件责任限制，就必须要发货人/货方去举证到底装了多少件的货物。例如，堆装集装箱当时的记录。对这一点，上诉庭 Phillips 大法官说："It is important to bear in mind that, before any question of limitation of liability can arise, the onus is on the cargo-owner to prove his loss. Where he does so by reliance on the bill of lading as prima facie evidence of what is shipped, the description of the goods in the bill of lading will also form the basis of calculation of the Hague Rules limit of liability. Where, however, the shipowner discharges the heavy burden of displacing the evidential effect of the bill of lading, or the cargo-owner established his claim to damages by reference to evidence extrinsic to the bill of lading, then I am of the opinion that the Hague Rules limit of liability falls to be calculated by reference to the particulars of the cargo and its packaging as it is proved to have been on loading, not by reference to the description in the bill of lading. A consignee who proves that he has lost a container containing three packages will be subject to a limit calculated by reference to those packages, even though they were not enumerated in the bill of lading[607]…"

(f)提单条款说明集装箱只当做1个单件无效——在 The "River Gurara"先例，案中的班轮提单有一条款如下：

"Shipper packed containers

If a Container has not been packed or filled by or on behalf of the Carrier…(B) notwithstanding any provision of law to the contrary the Container shall be considered a package or unit even though it has been used to consolidate the Goods the number of packages or units constituting which have been enumerated on the face hereof as having been packed therein by or on behalf of the Merchant and the liability of the Carrier (if any) shall be calculated accordingly."

据知，有不少从事集装箱业务的班轮公司都在它们的班轮提单印有类似的条款。在 The "River Gurara"先例，这已被判作是无效，违反了海牙规则：这方面请参阅本章之4.2.9小段。

4.2.10.3.2.2.3 计算方法之三：美国的"功能论"(Functional Economic Theory)

首先要说明，这曾经一度在美国法院流行的说法目前已被摒弃。它大致是说发货人自己包装的货物，若再堆放在集装箱内，本身必须是已足够坚固去承受该航次的运输。若是本身的包装不足，要依靠集装箱去提供额外的包装/保护，则要以集装箱作为计算单件/单位的标准了。

估计这说法是出于4.2.10.3.2.2小段所述之(iv)情况的考虑与担心，即货物描述得太细，如"1个集装箱据说内有1.6万支笔"。

---

[607] 单就这一句话而言，似乎与(a)段提到的 Colman 大法官(在一审)的说法有不同之处。

提出这说法的先例是 The "Kulmerland" (1973) 2 Lloyd's Rep. 428, 该案中集装箱内有 350 纸箱的计算器。显然，纸箱本身并不能独自承受该运输。美国第二巡回法院(上诉庭)的 Oakes 大法官说: "The statutory purpose here leads us to suggest what for want of a better term we will call the functional economics test. In this regard, the first question in any container case is whether the contents of the container could have feasibly been shipped overseas in the individual packages or cartons in which they were packed by the shipper. Here it is plain that they could not…

When, as here, the shipper's own individual units are not functional or usable for overseas shipment the burden shifts to the shipper to show why the container should not be treated as the 'package'…"

在该先例提出这一说法后，美国其他法院也随之跟从，如: Nichimen Co. v. M. V. Farland, 462 F. 2d 319 (1972); The "Container Forwarder" (1974) 1 Lloyd's Rep. 119。

但这一说法后来被一连串的案例所否定。首先是 The "Aegis Spirit" (1977) 1 Lloyd's Rep. 93 先例, 该案中两个集装箱内有 601 纸箱电器/电视。显然, 该纸箱无法独自承受运输。但 Becks 大法官判是有 601 个"单件"而并非两个"单件"。该先例后, 另一否定"功能论"说法的案例有 Yeramex International v. S. S. Tendo, (1977) A. M. C. 1807。

相信这说法遭到摒弃的原因是:

(i) 罔顾现实, 因为集装箱运输的优点之一是可以令货物减少包装同时又获得良好的保护。这一来, 岂非要迫货方为取得更高(但合理)的赔偿, 白白去浪费包装呢? 这实在有损集装箱运输的优越性。

(ii) 漠视了海牙规则中"单件"(package)一字应有稳定, 肯定及客观的法律解释的需要, 不应是每次在不同案件要依据不同的事实, 订约方的所作所为, 他/它的意图等, 再给予不同的解释。例如, 对同样的集装箱, 同样的做法(由发货人堆装/铅封等), 同样的货物等, 仅因内包装稍有不同, 就会得出对"单件"有天壤之别的解释。

(iii) 这说法会鼓励诉讼。

4.2.10.3.3　问题之二: 何谓"单位"(unit)

这问题涉及大宗散货和没有任何包装的(或极少包装)货物(例如是一座大机器、一卡火车头、一台庞大的发电机或锅炉等)。这些货物谈不上是"单件"(package), 尤其是后者在英文字义上显示了必须要有"包装"(packaging)。所以, 这类货物在计算责任限制时只能以"单位"(unit)为标准。这一点也在 William Tetley 教授的《Marine Cargo Claims》一书第 3 版之第 880 页有说明如下: "Generally, however, a package is a wrapper, case, bag, envelope or platform etc. in which or on which cargo has been placed for carriage. There must, however, be packaging, otherwise the limitation will be based on the 'unit' or 'customary freight unit'. A package need not completely cover the goods; it can be a box, case, carton, container, skid, pallet or other form of preparation for carriage designed to assist the various handlers of the cargo in loading, stowing and carrying it on its way to delivery."

4.2.10.3.3.1　美国海上运输法对"单位"一词的补充

但"单位"一词也不易解释，它空洞且广泛，甚至"单件"（package）亦是"单位"的一种。为了防止诉讼以及跟美国其他相关立法的措辞靠拢，美国在将海牙规则立为国内法时（即1936年的"海上运输法"）刻意把"unit"改为"customary freight unit"（习惯的运费单位）。现将1936年立法 Section 4（5）的有关部分节录如下："Neither the carrier nor the ship shall in any event be or become liable for any loss or damage to or in connection with the transportation of goods in an amount exceeding $ 500 per package lawful money of the United States, or in case of goods not shipped in packages, per customary freight unit…"

4.2.10.3.3.2　海牙规则的"单位"也应是指"运费单位"的观点

William Tetley教授认为海牙规则虽然不像美国的1936年海上运输法那样对"单位"一词作了补充，但也应解释为是"习惯的运费单位"。在《Marine Cargo Claims》一书第三版之第884、885页说到："The definition of a unit under the Hague Rules is the source of considerable controversy. Is it a freight unit or is it an unpacked object? The question is admittedly a difficult one.

It would appear that the 'unit' referred to in the Hague Rules meansa 'freight unit' and not an unpacked object for the following reasons[608]:

(a) The American COGSA at sect. 4 (5) reads: 'per package lawful money of the United States, or in case of goods not shipped in packages per customary freight unit…' This is very much clearer than the Brussels Convention of 1924. It is noteworthy that the phrase added by the United States Congress was intended to clarify rather than change the meaning of the Brussels Convention.[609]

(b) If the meaning of a unit was to be the unpacked object, then only the word 'unit' would have been used in art. 4 (5) because unit is a generic term and covers a pack-

---

[608] Tetley教授认为有4个原因支持他的看法。
[609] 第一是美国的海上运输法，这一点已在4.2.10.3.3.1小段详论。该处提到的1924年布鲁塞尔公约实际就是海牙规则。而美国的立法并无意去更改海牙规则（国际公约也不应单方面被改变），而只是去澄清与加以明确。

age as well as an unpacked object. There would have been no need to use the terms 'package' as well as 'unit', because 'unit' would have been sufficient. In other words, 'unit' is not merely an unpacked object but a packed one as well.[610]

(c) The unpacked object in the Rules is described as a 'piece' in art. 3 (3) (b) in referring to 'the number of packages or pieces'…If an unpacked object were intended in art. 4 (5), then 'piece' would have been the term used rather than 'unit'. 'Unit' is not equivalent to a 'piece' in consequence.[611]

(d) Unit as a 'freight unit' makes sense for bulk cargo such as tallow, wheat, oil and liquid chemicals. In fact, it is difficult to argue that unit in respect to bulk cargo is anything else than a freight unit.[612] "

4.2.10.3.3.3 有关先例

这样看来，货方在大宗货运输若以"总包运费"（lumpsum freight）一笔过支付船东并不明智，他应尽可能以每吨或每立方尺计算运费，这样效果更好。《Marine Cargo Claims》一书第 3 版之第 886 页曾说道："Cargo shipped on a lumpsum basis is a unit or in the United States a customary freight unit."

对这一点美国有不少先例予以支持，可以选几个介绍如下：

（ⅰ）在 The "Edmund Fanning"，1953 A. M. C. 86（2 Cir. 1953），10 台机车（火车头）及加煤车遭受全损。机车装船时并没有包装，理应按照"运费单位"去计算责任限制。但美国法院根据发货人与承运人议订的运费是以每套机车及加煤车 1 万美元结算，判一台机车加一台加煤车合共为一个"运费单位"，只赔 500 美元。要知道，运费已是 1 万美元，货价可想而知，只赔 500 美元是远远不足的。

（ⅱ）在 G. M. Corp. v. Moore-McCormack Lines, 1971 A. M. C. 2408 （2 Cir. 1971），判一台"发电机组"（power plant）因为是以"总包运费"一笔过支付，所以只算是一个"习惯的运费单位"。

---

[610] "单位"一词含义十分广泛，可包括"单件"。因此它不会单是对应"单件"一词，即有包装的货物称为"单件"，没有包装的货物则称为"单位"。若想法真如此，海牙规则可以干脆只用"单位"一词，因为它可包括有包装和没有包装的货物。因此解释起来，"单位"不应只局限在没有包装的货物。

[611] 没有包装的货物在海牙规则的其他条款是以"一件"（piece）来形容的。但在责任限制方面却改用"单位"一词，这再次表明了"单位"一词不单是指没有包装的货物，只可对应针对有包装货物的"单件"一词。

[612] 把"单位"解释为"运费单位"可以完全适用在大宗的散货，否则散货难以有任何其他计算标准可以确定责任限制。这一来，若有 2 万吨小麦，运费以每吨结算，全损时就很容易得出责任限制为 500 美元（以美国海上运输法为例）×20 000 吨＝10 000 000 美元。或者若只是部分/小量的 50 吨小麦损坏，计算即为 500 美元×50 吨＝25 000 美元。

(ⅲ)在 Barth v. Atl. Container Line, 1985 A. M. C. 1196 (D. Md. 1984),涉及所运"汽车"(automobiles)长度在 3.5 米以下收取运费 259.50 美元,长度在 3.5 米以上则要收取更高运费。法院判"习惯的运费单位"是指每架汽车而非多少米的长度。

4.2.10.3.4 问题之三:通货膨胀

在 4.2.10.3 小段的注脚曾提到海牙规则的 100 英镑是 1924 年的黄金价值。经过之后数十年的通货膨胀,1924 年 100 英镑的价值在今天显然再也不是同一回事。这 40 多年过后,1924 年 100 英镑的购买力会相当于今天的好几百英镑。在 The "Ebn Al Waleed" (2000) 1 Lloyd's Rep. 270 的加拿大先例,曾提到 1924 年的 100 英镑值 732.238 克的黄金,在 1996 年初相当于 12 498.28 加币。

其他有关这方面的著名先例有:The "Rosa S" (1988) 2 Lloyd's Rep. 574; The "Nadezhda Krupskaya" (1989) 1 Lloyd's Rep. 518 等。

但多数国家在把海牙规则立法时已将 100 英镑转换为本国货币/纸币,而且也不再与黄金价值挂钩。当时的国际公约(与立法)也不像今天/近期的国际公约(例如有关海上油污责任的公约),有机制/条款可供日后不断调高金额。这一来,这些国家的立法所定的金额很快就追不上通货膨胀了。

这一问题至少会带来以下不妥或/与危险之处:

(ⅰ)在 4.2.10.3.1 小段之注脚〔3〕曾提到海牙规则当初定下 100 英镑的单件/单位责任限制并非是为了帮助承运人少赔钱。但通货膨胀一来,这可真是帮了船东/承运人了。他/它往往愿意付出这 500 美元,省得去花费更昂贵的律师费以抗辩货方的索赔。但今天这 500 美元简直低得像打发要饭的一样,这对货方公平吗?这对船东/承运人今后克尽职责令船舶适航以及小心谨慎照看货物(以免出了事故又要赔一大笔钱)有健康的促进吗?

(ⅱ)若把海牙规则合并进租约,会有危险,这方面已在本章之 4.2.3.2.2.5 小段有详论,不再重复。

4.2.10.3.5 问题之四:各国货币兑换价的变动

除了罕见的情况如土耳其,各国在将海牙规则立为其国内法时,都把代表黄金价值的 100 英镑转换成本国的货币单位。这是海牙规则第 9 条明示允许的。例如,美国是 500 美元,英国是 100 英镑(纸币),澳洲是 100 澳镑,比利时是 17500 法郎,加拿大是 500 加币,德国是 1800 马克,瑞士是 2000 瑞士法郎,西班牙是 5000Peseta,等等。

由于七十多年来各国经济发展不一样,导致今天各种货币的兑换价几经变迁,已远非当年所代表的价值,例如 100 英镑早已是不足 500 美元,而弱势的货币也只会相当于 100 美元或更少(例如在 The "Texaco Melbourne" (1992) 1 Lloyd's Rep. 303 一案,加纳的 Cedis 因经济恶化变得很不值钱,从原来的 2 886 187 美元(兑换价)下跌为 21 165 美元,简直是百分之一的价值也没有)。而且,兑换价还时常会有重大的波动。

这导致了日益严重的"择地行诉"(forum shopping)行为,收货人/提单持有人在提出索赔诉讼时都会小心选择对自己有利的地方的法院去起诉,这其中的一项考虑便是可获赔偿的责任限制金额更高。当然,能否成功择地行诉并不是一个简单的问题,这在本章之4.2.10.2.5.1小段已有略及。而在4.2.3.15小段详论过的The "Morviken" (1983) 1 Lloyd's Rep. 1 先例,更是这方面的一个典型例子。

英国的1924年海上运输法所定的单位责任限额是100英镑纸币,这金额已明显偏低,根本兑换不了500美元,这带来了严重的择地行诉,而且都是远离英国以免赔偿偏低。为了鼓励大家回到英国法院诉讼,英国的货方,保险人,船东互保协会以及船东的各种组织在英国海事法律协会(British Maritime Law Association)的倡议下,达成了一个"黄金条款协议"(Gold Clause Agreement),自动把单件/单位责任限制从100英镑提高到200英镑,时为1950年8月。这协议在Pyrene v. Scindia Steam Nav. Co. (1954) 1 Lloyd's Rep. 321 之第334页有提及。但要注意的是,单件/单位责任限额在英国海上运输法下仍只是100英镑,毕竟法律不容易改,法院作出判决也只依照这金额计算。只是有了这个"君子协议",船东/承运人会自动多赔(其实是背后的互保协会去赔付),多加一倍钱去赔每件/每单位200英镑。该协议虽是君子协议,但由于英国的船东互保协会与保险人(包括劳合社与保险公司)在国际航运界势力巨大,因此它仍得以顺利执行。至于协议为何要有去英国诉讼的先决条件,估计是除了希望减少择地行诉外,还有其他原因,例如英国的公司/人士为了长远利益也希望诉讼在英国,以便让英国法律去领导国际潮流。也会有看不惯外国法院的判决"较外行"等原因。

这"黄金条款协议"在1977年8月作出了修改,进一步把200英镑提升至400英镑。这修改在The "Omega Leros" (1987) 1 Lloyd's Rep. 530 先例有谈及。这协议一直维持至英国把海牙·维斯比规则立为国内法(1971年海上运输法),另有了一套完全不同的单件/单位责任限制(细节将在4.2.10.3.8小段详谈)的计算方法后,才被完全摒弃。

4.2.10.3.6 问题之五:各国立法的不足/不肯定之处

这个问题可以举The "Ebn Al Wabeed" (2000) 1 Lloyd's Rep. 271 一案为例。它涉及从土耳其运去加拿大的钢材,共2626捆。航次中发生货损,收货人索赔57万加元。双方(收货人与承运人)的争议之一是土耳其立法(根据海牙规则)所定的单件责任限制到底是多少金额。土耳其的立法是在1955年2月22日,而且它罕有地没有把100英镑的黄金价值兑换为本国货币/纸币。这一来,正如4.2.10.3.4小段提到的,这在1996年(交货之日)会相当于12498.28加币。

但造成混乱的是,土耳其在1956年通过了"土耳其商业法典"(Turkish Commercial Code),内将单件/单位的责任限制定在1,500 Lire。这金额在1983年增至10

万Lire,但在1996年,这笔钱也只能去兑换2.3加币而已,与12498.28加币根本有天壤之别。而在立法过程中这商业法典从未把1955年的立法"作废"(repeal)。这导致双方去争议到底什么法律适用:收货人的土耳其法律专家当然是指1955年的立法适用,而承运人的土耳其法律专家则是指1956年/1983年的商业法典适用。最后加拿大法院还是接受了承运人的证据。

4.2.10.3.7 问题之六:船东/承运人恶意/有意违约可否享有责任限制之争

海牙规则的Article 4(5)在单位/单件责任限制方面的措辞用了"在任何情况下"(in any event)这样的措辞/文字,这与Article 3(6)在针对1年索赔时效时的用语一样。但遇上船东/承运人一些恶意,有意或/与极严重的违约这责任限制可否仍适用,大家有不同看法。往往是,若让1年索赔时效过去,原告的货方只能怪自己没有及时行动。或许是因为他/它不懂,但不懂也应被责怪,反正这不能作为一个合理的抗辩理由。可是,单位/单件责任限制就不一样了,原告的货方无法采取及时行动或任何主动以避免或改变这方面。充其量只能说发货人一早应去申明货物的价值,注明在提单上,并支付 ad valorem 运费[请看本章4.2.10.3.1小段之注脚(2)]。但这样去追究货方实在太牵强了,这无论如何也不是近因,收货人/提单持有人本身并无可责怪的地方。

所以,遇上像绕航或美国所称的准绕航(违约把货物装在甲板上等那样的违约),甚至是船员/船东偷窃货物,法院总是要设法否定船东这责任限制的权利。

这一方面的课题已在本章多处有详论,例如4.2.3.5.3.7小段(其中介绍了The "Chanda"(1989)2 Lloyd's Rep. 494的重要先例,是判单位/单件赔偿限责不适用),4.2.10.1.3小段等,在此不再重复。另在本书第二章之5.6.3小段也有谈及。

以上争论的结果是,海牙·维斯比规则为此作出了修改,同时也反映了上述的倾向。对1年的索赔时效,它是加以"强化":请参阅4.2.10.2.9小段。但对单位/单件的责任限制,它则加以"弱化",即多加了一段条款(Article Ⅱ之(e))说明可以剥夺承运人这一项权利不准其享有的情况,其内容如下:"Neither the carrier nor the ship shall be entitled to the benefit of the limitation of liability provided for in this paragraph if it is proved that the damage resulted from an act or omission of the carrier done with intent to cause damage, or recklessly and with knowledge that damage would probably result[613]."

总结说来,像本章之4.2.10.2.9小段详论的The "Captain Gregos"(1990)1

---

[613] 有关这二、三种可以剥夺承运人限责权利的情况,《海事法》一书第二章的4.4小段有详论。因为内容太长,不再节录。该书曾谈到1976年的责任限制公约(伦敦公约),它是根据船舶吨位而不是货物的单位/单件计算责任限额的,而且是适用于各种大事故/意外引起的多种类、多方面的索赔,而并非只适用在货损货差。该公约对于剥夺船东限责权利的情况,在措辞/用字上与海牙·维斯比规则一致。

Lloyd's Rep. 310 先例,承运人涉及偷油(货物是原油),仍可享有 1 年索赔时效。但他/它肯定不能再享有单位/单件的责任限制了:不论是在海牙规则还是海牙·维斯比规则下。

4.2.10.3.8 海牙·维斯比规则对各项问题作出的补救/修改

对较早前各段节谈及的海牙规则相关条款[Article 4(5)]所带来的问题,海牙·维斯比规则都作出了补救/修改(除了 4.2.10.3.6 小段,这是各国自己立法的问题),现简单介绍如下:

(i)它引入了一个全新的责任限制计算方法,就是除了以"单件或单位"(package or unit)为准外,还让货方选择以货物重量作为计算标准,二者以较高的金额为准。这一来,可以解决大型机器,大件货物,甚至是集装箱所带来的问题。因为就算集装箱只当做一个"单件",也可以重量计算而得出更高的责任限制金额。

(ii)针对通货膨胀的问题,海牙·维斯比规则把单位/单件的责任限制金额提高至 1 万金法郎(在 1968 年该规则的议定书谈妥之时,即所谓的 Brussels Protocol,全名"Protocol to Amend the International Convention for the Unification of Certain Rules of Law Relating to Bills of Lading, Brussels, February 23,1968"签订时,1 万金法郎相当于 431 英镑的价值,而按货物重量计算责任限额则是毛重每公斤 30 金法郎)。事实上,若只考虑海牙规则的 100 英镑是指黄金价值,那么它从 1924 年到了 1968 年已相当于约七八百英镑。从这个角度来看,维斯比规则将责任限额定在 431 英镑实际并没有提高。但相比于经多国立为国内法后的海牙规则,因都已兑换为本国货币,维斯比规则所定的金额则有明显提高了。

(iii)出于不想让各国在国内立法时再度把 1 万金法郎转换成本国货币,导致令几年后各国货币因经济强弱不同而再次造成严重偏差,海牙·维斯比规则再也不提这种兑换的做法,而且还说明把金法郎兑换成某国货币/纸币应由审理争议的国家法院决定,这也似乎表明了它并不考虑各国在国内立法时作出兑换。

(iv)海牙·维斯比规则也把金法郎的含金量确定了下来,这又被称为"Poincare 金法郎"。Poincare 是 20 年代法国的一位总理,他在 1928 年主张把法郎的含金量固定下来,金法郎因而得名。它并非是货币单位,而是一个含金量的计算单位。它所代表的含金量是每一金法郎含有 65.5 毫克 90% 纯度的黄金。当时金法郎被国际上及国际公约广为采用作为计算单位。但到了 1971 年 8 月,美国宣布美元与黄金脱钩,导致整个以美元为中心的金汇兑本位制(gold exchange standard)的瓦解,金法郎再也不能稳定、肯定地作为计算单位了。故后来海牙·维斯比规则也改为以国际货币基金组织的"特别提款权"(Special Drawing Rights 或简称 SDR)作为计算单位了:修改公约的议定书名为"Brussels Protocol 1979(SDR Protocol)"。根据该修改,1 万金法郎变为 666.67SDR,30 金法郎变为 2SDR。

（ⅴ）在此不妨节录海牙·维斯比规则的相关条款，以便读者更容易理解，具体如下："Article Ⅱ

Article 4, paragraph 5（海牙规则）shall be deleted and replaced by the following:

(a) Unless the nature and value of such goods have been declared by the shipper before shipment and inserted in the Bill of Lading, neither the carrier nor the ship shall in any event be or become liable for any loss or damage to or in connection with the goods in an amount exceeding the equivalent of Frs. 10.000 per package or unit or Frcs. 30 per kilo of gross weight of the goods lost or damaged, whichever is the higher…

(d) A franc means a unit consisting of 65.5 milligrammes of gold of millesimal fineness 900. The date of conversion of the sum awarded into national currencies shallbe governed by the law of the Court seized of the case…"

（ⅵ）尤其是针对集装箱运输，海牙·维斯比规则也特别加了一条款，就是以4.2.10.3.2.2.2小段的主流计算方法为准。该条的英文措辞如下："(c) Where a container, pallet or similar article of transport is used to consolidate goods, the number of packages or units enumerated in the Bill of Lading as packed in such article of transport shall be deemed the number of package or units for the purpose of this package or units are concerned. Except as aforesaid such article of transport shall be considered the package or unit."

综上所述，有了海牙·维斯比规则，可以说海牙规则在这一方面的漏洞/缺点大部分已得到补救。但由于海牙·维斯比规则的普及(被各国接受并立为国内法的普遍程度)[614]不如海牙规则，所以仍有不少航次只适用海牙规则。或者，海牙规则是基于合约的形式(以"首要条款"合并)而适用。故此，上几个小段谈到的海牙规则的各种问题仍会延续下去。

4.2.10.3.9　单位/单件责任限制与船舶吨位责任限制的关系

有关以船舶吨位计算的责任限制，本章之4.2.10.3.7小段有提及，该段还提到了1976年的伦敦公约。有关这一课题，可以参阅笔者的《海事法》一书第二章。因为内容太多，无法在此节录。这里只提一点，就是即使发生了一次重大的货损货差，船东/承运人一样可以享受这船舶吨位的责任限制：The "Penelope Ⅱ"（1979）2 Lloyd's Rep. 42; The "Waltrand"（1991）1 Lloyd's Rep. 389。若是发生了一次重大意外如碰撞或爆炸，除货损货差外还有其他许多第三者的损失(如被碰的另一船舶，人命伤亡等)，则遭受货损货差的货方要与其受害人一起去摊分这一笔的船舶吨位

---

[614]　虽然，主要的欧洲海运国家均已承认它，如英国、法国、比利时、丹麦、意大利、荷兰、挪威、瑞典，等等。而亚洲主要的海事诉讼/扣船地点如新加坡及香港，也承认了海牙·维斯比规则。

责任限制的金额了,这一来货方可获得的赔偿可能更少。

而船东/承运人要限制责任的做法,一是以它作为抗辩。这会是在只有一项索赔(如货损货差),要面对的也只是一个原告和一桩诉讼的情况下,这时船东/承运人可以抗辩说:"即使我要负责(但我并不承认这项责任),也只需要赔这限制的金额,因为我可以依据 1979 年商船法之 Section 17(这是英国对 1976 年伦敦公约的国内立法)计算责任限制如下……"

而另一做法是船东/承运人去适当国家的法院成立/确立一个责任限制的基金,然后要求所有受害人/索赔人前来分摊。显然,这种做法是针对同一事故中有多项不同种类的索赔,也有多个不同的索赔方。这一来,就不宜在个别不同的诉讼中分别以船舶吨位责任限制去抗辩了。

这一切都在《海事法》一书的第二章有详论。

可以肯定的是:基于船舶吨位责任限制计算出的赔偿限制金额都不会低(例如《海事法》一书的 4.6.1 小段曾计算出一艘 9 万吨船责任限额是 11753500SDR 或 800 多万英镑)。因此,小的货损货差不会涉及这方面,但它仍可能涉及单位/单件的责任限制。例如,只是一个集装箱损失了(装在甲板上被冲下大海),索赔是 20 万英镑。但船东/承运人指出提单并没有注明箱内货物的件数/数量,所以只须赔 666.67SDR(或大约 500 英镑)。这一来,货方(原告)只能改为选择以重量计算,那样便可获赔 17.5 公吨(包括集装箱的)×1000 公斤×2SDR = 35000SDR(或大约是 26,650 英镑)。但这金额与船舶吨位责任限制下的几百万英镑仍是相距甚远,所以后者也不会有关。只有在发生了极严重货损货差时,船舶吨位责任限制才会变得有关,例如高价的 2 万吨散货全损(笔者曾见过最高价一次达 7000 万美元),这一来,船舶吨位责任限制的几百万美元或英镑可就有关了。但一旦有关,则可能导致连海牙规则的单位/单件责任限制金额也赔不足。这看来有减轻船东/承运人赔偿责任的嫌疑,但 1924 年海牙规则的 Article 8 已明确说明这是允许/有效的:"The provisions of this convention shall not affect the rights and obligations of the carrier under any statute for the time being in force relating to the limitation of the liability of owners of seagoing vessels."

4.3 海牙·维斯比规则

有关海牙·维斯比规则对海牙规则所作的各种修正,本书以及本章已在多处有详论。在此段节,不妨先简略介绍一下该公约的历史及立法过程。

到了 20 世纪 50 年代末期,海牙规则在运作上已有了几十年的经验,可以说大部分的海权/海运国家都认为它十分成功,可令大家"有例可循"(certainty),国际间在海运责任方面也有了"统一的看法"(uniformity)。但时代的变迁也的确令 1924 年制定的海牙规则在某些方面显得不合时宜了。而且,随着有关判例的不断涌现,也发觉海牙规则有个别地方/措辞并不够明确,需要改良。因此就有了修改海牙规则的必要,而这一任务最终落在了一个名为"国际海事委员会"(Comite Maritime International 或简称为 CMI)的民间组织的身上。

CMI 是由各国的"海事法组织"(maritime law associations)组成(像中国的海商法协会就是它的重要成员),它受到各国的大力支持。CMI 历史悠久:它于 1897 年在比利时的布鲁塞尔(Brussels)成立。创办人是一个有远见的比利时律师,他认为海运是国际性的行业(当时更是仅有或为数不多的国际性行业),各国间需要在许多方面(例如涉及海上安全,航行规则等)协调和尽量统一。但由于有承认"公海自由"(freedom of the sea)的传统,任何一国都不好去干预其他国家的船舶在公海上的行为。而在 1897 年还没有像国际联盟或联合国那样的国家间组织,若通过正常的外交途径由政府间召开国际会议并派出代表,这种"技术"多于"政治"的课题势必会政治化。而且让并非专家的代表去处理,肯定会缓慢并且不会有好的结果。有鉴于此,CMI 便是由民间组织起来,而参予的人士都是专家,由他们去商讨,草拟有关法律,既可避免政治化,也可保障技术上能过关。一待 CMI 通过,各国的海事法组织的代表会把通过的法律携回本国,向本国政府推荐采纳。由于各国的海事法组织都很有影响力,甚至是半官方机构,所以它若真要去大力推荐该法律被采纳的可能性会颇高。而进一步就是一国通过立法的程序,把该 CMI 通过的法律变为本国立法。

CMI 拟定过不少成功的国际公约,包括像著名的国际避碰规则、船舶吨位责任限制公约等,对国际海事立法推动很大。但随着联合国的出现,特别是通过它的"联合国贸易和发展会议(United Nations Conference on Trade and Development 或简称 UNCTAD)以及国际海事组织(International Maritime Organisation 或简称 IMO)介入到贸易与航运的各个方面,包括在技术方面,CMI 的重要性一度被认为是已大大减低。可这一来,带来的代价便是这方面的议题会变得政治化,而且往往也成不了事,例如 UNCTAD 大力促成的"汉堡规则"(Hamburg Rules)。到了近年,CMI 看来又被再度重视起来。鉴于有关海上运输对货物责任的不同公约、立法或/与规则愈来愈多(像海牙规则、海牙·维斯比规则、汉堡规则、中国海商法等),也互不统一,并带来了混乱,这并非是一件好事,因此联合国就让 CMI 去拟定一套规则或法律,以便让世界上绝大多数国家能去接受并加以立法。这一来,会好像 1924 年的海牙规则,可以带来稳定,肯定与国际上的统一。至于联合国为何"看中"CMI,或许是想做到非政治化吧!

介绍过 CMI,再回头谈谈海牙·维斯比规则的草拟。1959 年在南斯拉夫的"里吉卡"(Rijeka)举行的 24 届大会上,CMI 决定成立专门的附属委员会来策划修改海牙规则一事。事后各国的代表均对修改提出了建议,诸如:克尽职责令船舶适航,提单中注明的证据价值,单位/单件赔偿责任限制,等等。结果在 1963 年,CMl 在瑞典斯德哥尔摩的大会上通过了有关草案。而在1968年,在比利时政府的建议下,CMI在布鲁塞尔召开的外交会议上向各国政府正式提出拟订的草案,名为"1968年布鲁塞尔草案"(Brussels Protocol 1968),这就是后来的海牙·维斯比规则。"维斯比"(Visby)是波罗的海上的一个岛。历史上,中世纪的三大海法之一——维斯比海法就曾以此地来命名。CMI所拟订的草案也是在这里签订,故以此为名。

英国本国在1971年把海牙·维斯比规则立为国内法,成为1971年的海上运输法(Carriage of Goods by Sea Act 1971 或简称 COGSA 1971),从而取代了1924年的海上运输法(这是海牙规则)。

但就国际而言,是到了1977年6月23日才有足够国家承认海牙·维斯比规则而令其得以生效。而至今,在近80个海牙规则的签约国中,也已有一半以上参加/承认了海牙·维斯比规则。

至于海牙·维斯比规则的各项条款(条款准确的措辞/文字请看附录六),对海牙规则有实质性修改的可简略介绍如下:

Article Ⅰ

1. 这有关对提单内容/注明的"法定性禁止翻供(statutory estoppel),可参阅本书第六章之4.2.1与4.2.4小段。

2. 这是针对1年索赔时效的修改,请参阅本章之4.2.10.2.4.1小段与4.2.10.2.9小段。

3. 这是针对货损货差的追偿时效,请参阅本章之4.2.10.2.8.6小段。

Article Ⅱ

这是针对海牙规则的单位/单件赔偿责任限制,作了颇大的修改,对此本章之4.2.10.3.7小段和4.2.10.3.8小段已有详论,请参阅。

Article Ⅲ

这里共有4条条款是去针对合约与侵权的"并列责任"(concurrent liability)问题以及船员/代理人受侵权起诉的问题。这在本章之4.2.3.3.1小段至4.2.3.3.2小段有详论,请参阅。

Article Ⅳ

这是针对海牙规则的第9条(Article 9),该条款说明了100英镑的单位/单件赔偿限额是指黄金价值(这可参阅本章之4.2.10.3与4.2.10.3.4小段)。此外,该条款接着还说明了各国可以将这一金额转换为本国货币,而这也带来了后来因各国币值兑换价大幅变动所引起的困难(这可参阅本章之4.2.10.3.5小段)。

随着海牙·维斯比规则已解决了这方面的问题,这Article 9也显得不必要了。但可能是为了不再多改动随后条款的编号,故在此加上了一条不算重要的条款,作为替代。它是针对原子/核子损失的,内容如下:"This convention shall not affect the provisions of any international convention or national law governing liability for nuclear damage."

Article V

这是针对海牙规则的第 10 条（Article 10），该条款规定海牙规则适用于所有在签约国签发的提单，这一般也会是在装港。这带来了一定局限以及本章 4.2.3.1.2 小段谈到的 Vita Food 案例（The "Hurry on"（1939）63 Lloyd's Rep. 21）的情况。所以海牙·维斯比规则便把其适用的范围（航次）扩大了，这在本章之 4.2.3.1.3 小段有详论，请参阅。

4.4 汉堡规则

因为实用价值较低，现实中较少碰到适用这公约的航次，笔者也不准备在本书详谈该规则。故在此仅将笔者 1982 年在大连海事大学出版社出版的《提单》一书谈及的有关内容节录如下：

汉堡规则简介

汉堡规则——一个代表第三世界发展中国家意愿的国际海上货物运输法虽已制订了多年，但迄今未能成为国际法，（注：汉堡规则已在 1992 年生效，是在 20 个国家承认后，如埃及、尼日利亚等，但都并非主要的航运、货运国）因此对国际海运业现实上仍没有什么大影响。但作为必要的知识，在此不妨作简短介绍如下：

订立的经过

海牙规则制定通过以来，至今已近 60 年历史。在这一时期内，海权国家及先进国家对其能起到有例可循的划一作用是基本满意的。但另一方面，代表第三世界发展中国家的看法却不同，他们对海牙规则甚为不满，主要表现为（1）1924 年制定的海牙规则是殖民主义时代的产物，是海权国家企图通过国际立法进一步垄断国际航运业的证明。（2）太保护船东的利益，把大部分的经济责任放在货方（现阶段主要是第三世界的国家）身上。（3）条款很多地方含糊不清，很多地方不适应时代进步。（4）造成船、货双方重叠保险（over-lapping insurance），是经济上的浪费[615]。他们不认同只改动海牙规则部分章节的维斯

---

[615] 货方认为由于船东对部分情况下的货损货差不负责任（海牙规则的免责条款），货方需对此投保，但货物保单的投保范围却并不以船东是否负责来划分，因此，货损涉及船东责任的一部分其实是重叠保险——既有货方的货物保险，亦有船东的船东互保协会的保险，这实在是浪费，倒不如由船东全部负责货损赔偿，对不涉及船东责任的部分亦由船东互保协会负责安排保险，货方就不用对此投保。其实这样的方式确曾出现过，在半岛及东方（P&O）轮船公司就曾应用过一种"保险提单"（Insured B/L）的形式，但由于种种原因结果并不成功，毕竟向保险人索赔比向船东追索要容易与肯定。

比规则,而主张彻底抛弃海牙规则,另订立更理想(能代表第三世界发展中国家意愿)的国际海上运输法。

1968年联合国贸易和发展会议(UNCTAD)下设了一个"国际航运立法工作组"研究国际海商法,并向联合国际贸易法委员会提出建议,经过1969年11月第一次会议及1971年2月第二次会议,商定了对提单问题的几个需修订的建议。从1971年1月31日第三次会议起,修改海牙规则的工作交由联合国国际贸易法委员会(UNCITRAL, United Nations Commission on International Trade Law)下设的新的航运立法工作组负责进行。该工作组召开了6次会议,制订了"联合国海上货物运输公约"草案(U. N. Draft Convention on the Carriage of Goods by Sea)以代替海牙规则。1978年3月由联合国主持在汉堡召开了海上货物运输会议,通过了以上述草案为基础的"1978年联合国海上货物运输公约",简称为"汉堡规则"。

部分条款简介:

1. 海牙规则规定承运人须于船舶开航前克尽职责,使船舶适航,另一方面给予承运人17项的免责权利。这些在汉堡规则内统统被取消了。取而代之的是一种"推定过失"(presumption of fault)的条款。在汉堡规则第5条(1)中规定:"如果货物的灭失或损坏或延误是发生在承运人管理货物的时候(责任期间)承运人应对所运货物的灭失或损坏或延误负责,除非承运人能证明,他以及他的工作人员或代理人已按要求采取了一切合理必要措施以避免此等事故的发生及其后果。"简言之就是两点:其一,只要货损是发生在承运人管理之下,承运人就要负责。其二,唯一的例外是承运人能证明对此已作了必要有效的预防。这一条很明显是加重了承运人的责任,延长了责任期限。

第三世界国家认为现今的航运业与1924年当时的情况已大不相同。现在科技进步,通信方便,航海已有很大的安全性,而且船东可以很有效地与船上保持通信,现在再给予船东、船长、船员、代理人等诸多的免责权利实在是不应该,更何况海牙规则甚至给予船东"过失免责"的权利,更引起大家的不满。因此,海牙规则中船东可依赖的17项免责权利全被取消了,只有"火灾"(fire)一项被有限度地保留下来,这也是经过激烈的争辩才最后由双方利益的代表妥协下来的。

在该规则下,除非火灾是由于承运方的过失所造成,否则承运方对火灾引起的损失无须负责。这其中对承运方很有利的是,要证明承运方过失造成火灾这一点是由货方负举证责任。有人认为这一点实际上"等于承认原来规定的火灾免责"[616]。

---

[616] 航海手册第四分册:第213页。

2. 海牙规则中承运人的责任期限是一项"吊钩至吊钩"(tackle to tackle)原则,汉堡规则则把范围扩展至自收货到交货在承运人照管下的全部期间。汉堡规则第二条规定:"承运人对货物负责的期间应包括货物在装货港、在运输中以及在卸货港于承运人照管下的全部时间。"这无疑又是企图加重承运人责任的另一个改动。对承运人来说,这不单是令其责任期限延长的问题,更头痛的是世界上很多港口的管理仍未妥善,当地港口当局对此亦未能有效监管,更何况是承运人一家公司呢?就算理论上有他的代理人在照看这些货,但承运人仍要对此负责,这加重了的责任几乎是无可估量的。

3. 单位赔偿限额(package limitation)改为以每件(package)或每一装运单位(shipping unit)835计算单位(特别提款权 SDR)或以每公斤2.5计算单位计算,二者中以高者为准,835计算单位等于12500金法郎;2.5计算单位等于37.5金法郎;换言之比海牙·维斯比规则(10000金法郎,30金法郎)提高了25%。由于第三世界国家的出口货往往都是些低价货,因此在汉堡规则中并没有要求再高的赔偿限额。

4. 索赔时效为两年,比海牙规则的规定多一年。承运人的责任又增加了。

5. 若事故涉及承运人的过失责任,收货人可以拒绝分担共同海损费用或海上救助的费用,现在使用海牙规则尚有很多收货人以船舶不适航为由,拒绝分担共同海损费用,更勿论汉堡规则加在船东身上的责任是这样严格,今后船东在出事后要向货方收取应分担的共同海损费用就更是难上加难了。事实上要船东做到对事故毫无过失,这是很困难的,这简直近乎于要取消共同海损。毕竟今天大的共同海损,往往都是涉及船员疏忽(但海牙规则是免责的)的碰撞搁浅所带来的。

6. 汉堡规则适用的货物范围把舱面货(deck cargo)及活牲畜(live animal)都包括在内。对于舱面货,汉堡规则第9条规定:"承运人只有在符合与托运人所签订的协议,符合特定的货运习惯或法律规则或条例时,才有权在舱面上载运货物",否则,后果由承运人负责,而且不能限制赔偿责任。同时,承运人亦有责任在提单上相应加以注明以提醒提单的受让人。

对活牲畜,规则第5条第5款规定:"活牲畜在运输中灭失,损伤或延迟交货,若是起因于这类货物所固有的任何特殊风险,承运人可免除责任。但承运人必须证明已按托运人的特别指示办理。如活牲畜的灭失、损失或延迟交货的全部或部分是由于承运人、他的雇用人员或代理人的过失或疏忽所引起的,承运人仍应负责。"

这里有一个关键的字眼是含糊不清的,就是"任何特殊风险(special risks)"所指为何,这一未知之数有待将来的判例去补充说明。

7. 汉堡规则增加了一项延误交货(delay)货方可向承运方索赔的规定。同时，第三世界国家认为绕航的后果就包括造成货物延误[617]，因此，规则既然有针对延误交货的处理也就无须再理会绕航的问题，故汉堡规则不再设置针对绕航的规定。事实上英国现在的法律已明确了货方可向承运人索赔延误引起的损失(在"Heron II"(1967) 2 Lloyd's Rep 457)，但由于其他国家有不同看法，很不统一，故需要在汉堡规则中列明。

怎样才算延误交货呢？规则的解释是："如果货物在书面明文约定的时间内(若没有这种约定，则要求在合理的时间内)，没有在运输契约规定的卸货港交付，就构成延误交货。另如果货物在规定的交付日期届满后60天内仍不能交货，对货物灭失拥有请求权的索赔人可以认为货物已经灭失(在第5条第3款)。

这里面仍有很多的问题。例如：延误的损失是怎样计算的？是单指市价下跌的损失还是包括其他间接损失？要注意有些间接的损失是很惊人的。例如：德国一个城镇等候燃油发电，由于油轮延误交货，使整个城镇陷于停顿的损失怎样计算？又如延误非由于承运人过失造成，或是延误超过60天部分是因过失引致而另一部分非因承运人过失所致，承运人对损失是否不须负责呢？或货方过了60天可否仍以货物已视为灭失去处理？当时货方怎可以认为延误60天是承运人的过失呢？若货方明知在延误后的第61天货物确会抵达，是否仍有权认为其已经灭失而提出索赔货价呢？答案仍是一句话："留待以后看有关判例吧！"

8. 汉堡规则第15条规定了提单应记载的内容有13项之多，其中较特别的是第(3)项，它规定必须记载"承运人的姓名和主要营业地点。"这一点是为了让收货人对承运人进行索赔、诉讼时有明确的目标，不会茫无头绪。但这说起来容易，要做却不简单。因为目前在装港由代理等人匆匆出具提单，往往并没有考虑调查谁是承运人及其详细资料，反正发货人也不会要，只要格式符合能结汇便行了(注：这一点在 UCP500 已有了改变，请看第三章之6.2小段)。笔者还要提提的是第10条，这是新的一条。它划分了"承运人"与"实际承运人"。按照海牙规则的条款第1(a)，"承运人"包括船东或租家，只要是他与发货人一方订下了一份运输合约(提单)。这一来，就有了所谓船东提单，船东是"承运人"，而租家提单，租家才是"承运人"之说。在租家提单下，船东只是"实际承运人"，但他与发货人及收货人没有合约关系。要告他也只能以侵权告。而且货方也往往会搞错而错过时效，比方以为某班轮公司出的提单，该公司必定是"承运人"，但其实船只是期

---

[617] 航海手册第四分册，第210页。

租回来的,船东是他人,而提单上也有"光船条款"等说明该人才是"承运人"。这一来,出告票告班轮公司出错了,而要纠正再告船东可能时效已过。

这种情况也出现在其他方面,比如原船/一程船出提单,但二程船才是把货送到目的地的"实际承运人"。如有货损货差,货方也不能以提单去告二程船,要他负责全程。还有一个问题是,一程船在海牙规则下可把货卸下(交二程船)以后的责任全部免掉,因海牙规则是只管"船旁到船旁"的。

但现在汉堡规则对此作出了修改,第10条第1款,要"承运人"对全程负责,虽然运输是由"实际承运人"来执行,比方班轮公司要对租入的船负责,一程船要对二程船负责等。另外,在第10条第4款更说明双方都有责任的,"承运人"和"实际承运人"就要对货方负"共同及连带"(joint and several)的责任。

最后,简略提提汉堡规则重要与创新的第21条。它大大扩大了货方对管辖权的选择,也的确是有利于货方。它在第一款允许货方自由地在多地起诉扣船,即:承运人所在地;出和签提单的地点;装卸两港;提单上注明的地点;甚至在承认汉堡规则的国家的地点(在第2款的a)。因此,货方对去埃及的货肯定可以在该国起诉,不管提单怎样规定须去哪里诉讼。这不是择地行诉或方便诉地(Forum non-convenience)的问题了,而是汉堡规则规定有权如此,为此不得减少承运人的责任。

在今天,船东互保协会及船东组织(包括了欧洲的海权国家如英国)对汉堡规则仍有很大抗拒,互保协会保护船东会员的基础仍只是海牙·维斯比规则。如船东自己在租约、提单上接受汉堡规则,多出来的责任(如本来应时效已过或本来可免责的,又或要赔60天的延误损失等),互保协会是不管的。只有在汉堡规则下的责任是强加在船东身上的,互保协会才会予以赔偿:比方船跑埃及或尼日利亚,以致根本无法避免汉堡规则的强制适用。

前面很简单地介绍了汉堡规则的部分章节,主要是一些改变及影响都比较大的新概念,规则全文共34条,要做到详细分析还需假以时日。但由于汉堡规则要产生重大影响为期尚远,要做这样的分析并无实际意义,目前只须略知一二即可。而且规则中的一些规定是在妥协的情况下达成的,只属含糊地带过,要弄清楚其中的法律解释须留待日后法庭裁定,现在是无法弄通的。

汉堡规则在1978年通过时,有人认为它在短期内(甚至有认为是长期)不会生效,或即使生效也没有影响,而根据的是实力地位理论。汉堡规则并无规定占全球船舶吨位数的比例,而只须有20个国家承认即可生效成国际法。不难想象若马上有20个内陆国家承认汉堡规则,规则马上就可成为国际法,(注:事实也是如此,虽然也开始有影响较大的国家如澳洲快要承认汉堡规则。而目前承认汉堡规则的20余个国家(至1993年9月)有:Barbados、Botswana、

Chile、Tunisia、坦桑尼亚、乌干达、埃及、Guinea、Hungary、肯尼亚、Lebanon、Lesotho、Malaui、Morocco、尼日利亚、Senegal、罗马尼亚、Sierra Leone、Zambia 等）。但占全球外贸或船舶吨位数 90% 的国家均未承认，这样的国际法能起什么作用呢？无疑，汉堡规则是第三世界国家打破霸权垄断，发挥自身政治影响力的一大胜利，但反观规则中加在船东身上的责任如此之重，对羽翼未丰的发展中国家船队来说未尝不是一大障碍，试想一个理智的国家又怎会为迎合一时的精神胜利而置最重要的经济利益于不顾呢？

其实，最使人担心的仍是一个水平的问题。即使像汉堡规则这样保护第三世界国家的海上运输法被通过生效成为国际法，第三世界国家的有关从业人员，包括律师、法官、仲裁员、发货人……又有多少人能深切理解明白汉堡规则对自己的有利之处，以利用和巩固既得的胜利成果呢？相反，现在看来对汉堡规则有充分认识的仍然是过去的那些海权国家，例如英国的劳氏出版社在 1978 年就曾以汉堡规则为主题举行过学术研讨会，从几个角度对汉堡规则作了一个透彻的分析。若将来汉堡规则生效了，但第三世界国家的有关从业人员仍不知此为何物，要说主宰自己的命运仍是奢谈，碰到未明之处，仍要到对此有认识的海权国家的法院裁决，造就他们一大批的律师、仲裁员等专才，这对第三世界国家而言，获益仍有限。

归根到底，还是一句话："业务技术与知识水平最重要，世界变不了，永远是懂的人吃掉不懂的人。要保护自己，最根本的办法就是掌握技术知识。"这是笔者深切的体会，也算是给大家的忠告。毕竟中国仍是发展中国家，而对于一个发展中国家要发展，最关键的就是教育与知识（两者互为结合，相辅相成），对于这一点，笔者从未有过怀疑。"

最后要提提的是笔者曾听说有承运人/船东（其实是背后的互保协会）向英国法院申请"止诉禁令"（anti-suit injunction），阻止货方在汉堡规则允许的管辖地点（承运人所在地，提单合约签订地，装卸港，提单合约明示地点与扣船地点）以汉堡规则起诉索赔，理由是这样做会对承运人/船东造成"欺压或困扰"（oppressive or vexatious）。例如，提单明示适用英国法，但卸港之一是埃及（汉堡规则国家）。索赔的一年时效已过，但汉堡规则的 2 年时效仍未过。至于"止诉禁令"的课题，请参阅笔者与杨大明先生的《禁令》一书之第六章，不再在此重复。

4.5 三个公约的各签约国名单

在此，不妨列出三个公约的各签约国名单，具体如下：
（i）海牙规则

Algeria, Angola, Antigua (Barbuda), Argentina, Bahamas, Belize, Bolivia, Cape Verde Islands, Croatia, Cuba, Cyprus, Dominican Republic, Fiji, Gambia, Ghana, Goa, Grenada, Guinea Bissau, Guyana, Hungary[618], Iran, Ireland, Israel, Ivory Coast, Jamaica, Kenya[619], Kiribati, Kuwait, Malagasy Republic, Malaysia, Mauritius, Monaco, Mozambique, Nauru, Papua New Guinea, Paraguay, Peru, Portugal, Sao Tome & Principe, Seychelles, Solomon Islands, Somalia, St. Christopher & Nevis, St. Lucia, St. Vincent & The Grenadines, Timores, Trinidad & Tobago, Turkey, Tuvalu, United States of America[620], Yugoslavia, Zaire.

(ⅱ)海牙·维斯比规则

Australia, Belgium, Bermuda, British Antarctic Territory, British Virgin Islands, Canada[621], Cayman Islands, Denmark, Ecuador, Egypt[622], Falkland Islands, Finland, France, Germany[623], Gibraltar, Greece, Hong Kong, Isle of Man, Italy, Japan, Lebanon[624], Luxembourg, Montserrat, Netherlands, New Zealand, Norway, Oman, Poland, Singapore, South Africa[625], Spain, Sri Lanka, Sweden, Switzerland, Syria, Tanzania, Tonga, Turks & Caicos Islands, United Kingdom and Northern Ireland[626].

(ⅲ)汉堡规则

Australia,[627] Austria, Barbados, Botswana, Bukina Faso, Cameroon, Chile, Czech Republic, Egypt, Guinea, Hungary, Kenya, Lebanon, Lesotho, Malawi, Morocco, Nigeria, Romania, Senegal, Sierra Leone, Tanzania, Tunisia, Uganda, Zambia.

4.6 各国(包括中国)自己的不同立法

除了以上介绍的三个不同公约外(但海牙/海牙·维斯比规则仍是主流),还有一些国家自己制定不同的法律去针对海运的货物责任。这其中读者最熟悉的应是中国海商法,另外北欧国家也有自己的立法(Scandinavian Law on Carriage of Goods by Sea)。这使国际上在这方面变得很不稳定,也不再统一,大家无所适从。

---

[618] 该国也签署/承认了汉堡规则,但其国内立法情况不明。
[619] 同上。
[620] 美国1936年海上运输法仍是海牙规则的立法。
[621] 该国没有正式参加/签署公约,但本国却私下立了法,以海牙·维斯比规则为准。
[622] 该国也签署/承认了汉堡规则。
[623] 该国也签署/承认了汉堡规则,但其国内立法情况不明。
[624] 该国也签署/承认了汉堡规则。
[625] 该国没有正式参加/签署公约,但本国却私下立了法,以海牙·维斯比规则为准。
[626] 英国国内的立法是1971年海上运输法。
[627] 澳大利亚在1994年10月决定延迟实施汉堡规则。

比如中国的海商法,就是什么公约都不像。它有海牙规则的内容,其中一些是汉堡规则强烈反对的,如海商法第 51 条之(一)的"航行/管理船舶中的过失"免责(这方面请看本章之 4.2.7.11 小段)。但同时,中国海商法又有许多条款来自汉堡规则,其中不少又是反对汉堡规则,支持海牙/海牙·维斯比规则的国家如英国等强烈反对的,如第 50 条规定的迟延交付若满 60 天即可认为货物已经灭失,第 60 条的"实际承运人",等等。

而且,同样的概念下措辞/文字也不尽相同。如汉堡规则的 Article 5(2)在解释何谓"迟延交付"时是说:Delay in delivery occurs when the goods have not been delivered at the port of discharge provided for in the contract of carriage by sea within the time expressly agreed upon[628] or, in the absence[629] of such agreement, within the time which it would be reasonable to require of a diligent carrier, having regard to the circumstances of the case[630].

这概念运用到中国的海商法,其第 50 条只是说:"货物未能在明确约定的时间内,在约定的卸货港交付的,为迟延交付。"它只针对提单上有明示的抵达卸港日期的情况,而这在现实中极少发生。它并没有针对默示的抵达卸港日期,而这才是普遍的情况。这一来,立法这样的措辞下如果提单没有注明/同意抵达卸港的日期,是否仍有迟延交付这回事呢?

总结下来,笔者不禁要问,作出这些不同之处到底有否必要?毫无疑问,能与国际通行的做法协调/统一,总归是好事。若有更好的想法能带来更完善的一些规则,则那与国际主流做法相异也无妨。但这也要一步步地走,例如先向国际推广,试图广泛被认同。而在这现实的世界,大家也不会把虚面子看得太重,意味着中国人若真有好办法,它也会很快被普及、接受并跟从。否则,为了不同而不同,或只是为了很小的理由而不同,笔者认为并不值得。这样做的后果甚至会严重导致令本国被摒弃于国际社会之外以及教育出的下一代青年会变成与国际潮流格格不入的"异物"的程度。

---

[628] 现实中提单(作为运输合约)极少会注明船哪一天抵达卸港。

[629] 这才是现实的情况,即提单对抵达卸港的日期并无任何说明。

[630] 这一来,船舶应抵达卸港的日期就要以合理来推算,即以当时的环境(天气、海况等)以及船舶的状况(船速)作为考虑,这样应不难算出默示的抵达卸港日期。若应抵达而没有抵达,即会是船东/承运人违约,例如是不适航或不合理绕航造成延迟。根据英美法,这时收货人一样可以索赔损失,包括经济损失如市场下跌等:The "Heron Ⅱ" (1967) 2 Lloyd's Rep. 457。英美法的分别只是不像汉堡规则 Article 5(3)那样定死收货人在货物未能在明示或默示的应抵达日期交付且迟延 60 天后可以视为货物已经灭失,而是每次都要看收货人真正的损失,根据"复原"(restitutio in integrum)的通用大原则为准,这方面请参阅《国际商务游戏规则——英国合约法》一书第十四章之 2.1 小段。

4.7 CMI 草拟中的运输公约

这方面在本章 4.3 小段已有略及。在此再多谈一下：在 1996 年考虑将来要做的工作时，联合国国际贸易法委员会（UNCITRAL）已想到要协调与统一国际上的海上运输法。因为其秘书处人员/资金的局限以及手头已有汉堡规则，UNCITRAL 希望多与各民间组织（CMI、国际商会等）及各国政府合作。在 1998 年，CMI 回应说愿意与 UNCITRAL 合作，会收集有关资料并作出分析/报告，以供 UNCITRAL 进一步考虑。为此，CMI 成立了工作小组。据悉，目前工作进度良好，而 CMl 也对承担此任务十分积极。CMl 的秘书长 Ziegler 博士认为这项工作如果能成功将是世纪大事或世纪成就，相比于 1924 年的海牙规则将有过之而无不及。而且，Ziegler 博士估计这次不会像制定汉堡规则那样变得太政治化。毕竟今天国际上再也不是那时的政治环境。再加上 CMl 的声誉与组成应令不少传统的海权/海运国家放心了。

至于最后结果如何，尚待下回分解。看来，本书免不了要在不久的将来再出修定版。

第六章 提单作用之三:货物收据

作为收据的概念很容易理解,把一样东西(或金钱、或货物)从一方交给另一方,双方都会想要一份收据以资证明,记录这一行为。不论这双方之间的关系是买卖,或是托运/承运,或是一个承运人交给另一承运人,或只是岸上的托管,都应有这收据。

像其他方面的证据一样,一份文书而不是口头的收据,经"接收方"(recipient)无条件签字确认,会是优越、稳定和不受时间影响的上佳证据。就一位客观人士(法官或仲裁员或任何第三者)而言,他对想去否定收据部分或全部内容的"接收方"马上会有一个质疑,就是收据如果不是事实你签来干吗?当然,"接收方"可去反证,甚至说他是受误导、受骗等而签发。但他有举证责任,而且责任颇重,因为一份无条件签字的收据(好像一份合约)已构成了事实(曾有东西交接)的"表面"(prima facie)证据。如果1年后"接收方"说我虽签收了但不算数,读者客观去看,恐怕也不会接受这种空泛的"自我否定"。

以上所讲只是一般常识,而提单作为货物收据也就是从很简单道理开始。

§1 收据内容

先去看看提单作为收据一般会有、应有的内容。

1.1 Congenbill 提单

Congenbill 提单(本书附录八)只是上百种不同格式的提单中的一种,估计是因为宣传且名气大,它广泛被使用。像近期报道的案件 The "Atlas" (1996) 1 Lloyd's Rep. 642; The "Mata K" (1998) 2 Lloyd's Rep. 614 等,有关提单都是 Congenbill。而笔者日常工作所见的,更多数是这种提单格式。

Congenbill 是由船东机构的 BIMCO 拟定,故像金康租约(Congenbill 本来就是准备与金康租约一并使用,但现实中并不一定),免不了有偏帮船东之嫌。

有关收据内容,Congenbill 提单只在正面页的当中有一大栏空格以供填上,内容是"发货人对货物的描述"(Shipper's description of goods)与"毛重"(Gross weight)。

显然，Congenbill 的租约提单通常用在大宗散货运输，所以收据只针对重量就已足够，这一般也是惯常做法。但若针对班轮运输的 Conlinebill（附录九），因为货物形状各异，计算运费也会有不同依据，所以也印上其他计量单位如"数量"(quantity)、"度量"(measurement)等。而油轮运输会有像"重力"(gravity)、"容量"(volume)等内容。

要注意的是，Congenbill 与 Conlinebill 都在正页下半页以显著字体印上"重量、度量、数量等等不知"(weight, measure, quality, condition, contents and value unknown)。这看来有点开玩笑，等于去否定这收据有任何内容、任何确认。也等于"接收方"对"给予方"说你交给我的东西我一概不知，也不想知。将来有了争议，仍要你证明到底交了什么东西给我，有多少。这一来，还算是收据吗？如果当时马上可去点算交了什么东西和有多少，"给予方"应对"接收方"说你马上点算，并不去推卸地无条件签收，只要收据符合事实。

是提单都会有船东自说自话，只去保障/偏帮自己的危险。故此也不止是 Congenbill 或 Conlinebill 有此"重量……不知"批注，其他船公司的提单格式也会有。这是订约自由。但随便查看，估计也只有一半多的船公司提单格式印有或打印上广泛至有限的内容（如仅针对重量但不提数量）不知的批注。

这种免责或否定性批注，从英国法律近期的案例（The"Atlas"，The"Mata K"）看来，对货方有颇为不利之处，稍后之 5.3 小段会详论。

1.2 海牙规则

海牙规则强制性要求承运人签发的提单必须有三方面内容，体现在 Article 3 (3)，它们是：

（ⅰ）标号/标记（how the goods are marked for the purposes of identification）；

（ⅱ）件数或数量或重量其中之一（The number of packages or the quantity or the weight）；

（ⅲ）表面状况（the apparent order and condition）。

1.3 汉堡规则

汉堡规则针对提单内容要求细致多了，并且强制程度高多了，是在 Article 15，说：

Article 15. Contents of bill of lading

1. The bill of lading must include, inter alia, the following particulars：

（a）the general nature of the goods, the leading marks necessary for identification of the goods, an express statement, if applicable, as to the dangerous character of the goods, the number of packages or pieces, and the weight of the goods or their quantity otherwise expressed, all such particulars as furnished by the shipper;

(b) the apparent condition of the goods;

(c) the name and principal place of business of the carrier;

(d) the name of the shipper;

(e) the consignee if named by the shipper;

(f) the port of loading under the contract of carriage by sea and the date on which the goods were taken over by the carrier at the port of loading;

(g) the port of discharge under the contract of carriage by sea;

(h) the number of originals of the bill of lading, if more than one;

(i) the place of issuance of the bill of lading;

(j) the signature of the carrier or a person acting on his behalf;

(k) the freight to the extent payable by the consignee or other indication that freight is payable by him;

(l) the statement referred to in para. 3 of art. 23;

(m) the statement, if applicable, that the goods shall or may be carried on deck;

(n) the date or the period of delivery of the goods at the port of discharge if expressly agreed upon between the parties; and

(o) any increased limit or limits of liability where agreed in accordance with para. 4 of art. 6.

以上多项内容,许多与提单作为收据的作用无关或关系不大。例如,发货人名字(d),收货人名字(如果是记名提单)(e),装港(f),卸港(g),签发的一套正本提单的份数(h),提单签发地点(这不必与装港一致,全看发货人与承运人的方便)(i),承运人签字(j),等等。

但与收据作用十分有关的,较之海牙规则,也多了如下好几项:

(ⅰ)货物(包括危险品)一般性质/特性(a);

(ⅱ)承运人接收了货物的日期(f);

(ⅲ)收货人仍要负责支付的运费(k)。

以上多加的内容,部分会给承运人带来沉重的责任/负担,这会在稍后详述。

有关这 Article 15 另有两点看法可以略加说明及如下:

(A)汉堡规则对提单及所有其他付运单证(除了租约)要求包括哪些内容在强制程度上比海牙规则高多了。例如,它采用了"必须"(must)的字眼。而海牙规则下的提单(有3方面内容)是要以有权的发货人提出要求为前提:见本章之5.4.2小段。

（B）依汉堡规则该条款,加上像 Article 16 等条款,应是不再允许一般性印就或印章盖注的免责或否定性批注,如"重量……不知","据说是"（said to contain）,"发货人提供资料"（particulars furnished by shipper）,等等。而在海牙规则,它并没有针对这种批注,而且英国法律也并不认为其无效：The "Mata K"（1998）2 Lloyds Rep. 614（请看本章之 5.6 小段）。

§2 发货人提供准确内容的责任

提单不少内容实际是由发货人提供,例如货物标号/标记。至于货物重量或数量,通常也出自发货人。重量出自岸上仪表或过磅,一般没有船东参与,正如船东在 The "Atlas"（1996）1 Lloyd's Rep. 642 对钢材短缺的索赔抗辩说："the billets must have been weighed, if at all, elsewhere and there was no evidence about when, how or by whom that was done."

在著名的 New Chinese Co. v. Ocean S. S. Co.（1917）2 K. B. 664,有关的货物［937 吨矿（oxide ore）］在汉口过磅,之后在上海转运去伦敦,伦敦再转运去 Newcastle 的目的港。货物有 76 吨短缺,法院认定其中 53 吨是在装卸转运中流失的。

有些货物和航次,重量更会由是独立机构/政府机构提供,例如在加拿大装散粮。外人（发货人与承运人）难以置疑,这情况在英国 1924 年的海上运输法之 Section 5 有针对,目的在于对承运人公平。

货物数量或度量会是通过发货人安排的"理货"（tally）或/与"检验"（survey）得出,一般也不会有船东参与。固然,船东可以自己另行安排理货,这看来也是船东互保协会的建议[631],但船东不一定这样做,这可被视为是船东满足于去依赖发货人提供的货物数量：The "Atlas"。也会有情况是船东根本无法去作出安排,只能去依赖发货人提供的数字。

发货人要就其对提供的提单内容对船东/承运人负责,并要对任何不准确内容造成的损失作出赔偿。这是海牙规则 Article 3（5）的规定："The shipper shall be deemed to have guaranteed to the carrier the accuracy at the time of shipment of the marks, number, quantity and weight, as furnished by him, and the shipper shall indemnify the carrier against all loss, damages and expenses arising or resulting from inaccuracies in such particulars. The right of carrier to such indemnity shall in no way limit his re-

---

[631] 在国际船东互保协会出版的 *Handy Book for Shipowners & Masters* 一书之第 84 页说："Whenever possible the master should arrange for the goods to be tallied as they are delivered to the ship. The immense importance of care and accuracy in keeping the tallies cannot be over-stressed…"

sponsibility and liability under the contract of carriage to any person other than the shipper."

这方面有两个小问题可去探讨。

2.1 发货人的责任是否绝对/严格

一是发货人对承运人的责任是"绝对"(absolute)严格的还是只有犯错、疏忽才负责呢？考虑到承运人将来会对收货人/提单持有人就提单内容负上绝对责任(像海牙·维斯比规则是说明禁止承运人向第三者的提单持有人去反证提单的内容不妥)，则发货人的"补偿"(indemnity)责任也应是绝对的，否则说不通。另外，像危险品方面，发货人的责任也是绝对的：见 The "Giannis NK" (1996) 1 Lloyd's Rep. 577。而危险品方面与其他提单内容须由发货人准确提供本质上是同一回事，在汉堡规则之 Article 15 (1)(a)也将它们归纳在一起。

但这一来，它会与海牙规则的 Article 4 (3)发生正面冲突。该条款是："The shipper shall not be responsible for loss or damage sustained by the carrier or the ship arising or resulting from any cause without the act, fault or neglect of the shipper, his agents or his servants."(发货人对不是他的行为,过失或疏忽造成的损失不负责)。

而既然要对提单内容(与危险品)负上绝对责任，又如何讲得通发货人不必对不是他的过失或疏忽造成的损失负责呢？

看来,英美对这一严重矛盾有不同看法。当然,这对解释一个像海牙规则这样重要的国际公约,非是好事。

美国有 3 个先例判是发货人可以在没有过失或疏忽情况下免责：Serraino v. United States Lines (1965) AMC 1038；Williamson v. C. A. Venezolana (1971) AMC 2083 (上诉庭)；General S. A. General Trades Enterprises and Agencies v. Consorcio Pesquerno Del Peru (1974) AMC 2342。

但英国法院并不同意。在 The "Athanasia Cominos" (1990) 1 Lloyd's Rep. 277，Mustill 大法官面对的其中一个问题是海牙规则 Article 4(3)是否令发货人这方面的责任从"绝对"减为"有条件保证"(qualified warranty)？Mustill 大法官说："The remaining four questions all appear to have been expressly or inferentially answered in the affirmative in 以上的美国先例与加拿大的 The "Erwin Schroder" (1970) Ex C. R. 426. Despite the respect which is due to these Courts, I would for my part be hesitant to answer the four questions in the same way. It is, however, unnecessary to reach a conclusion upon them…"

而在 The "Fiona" (1993) 1 Lloyd's Rep. 257，Diamond 大法官认为唯一能解释这矛盾之处的是把 Article 4 (3)中"行为"(act)这个字不去与"过失或疏忽"同义/等同,而去把危险品装上船已是一个行为:"装船行为"(act of shipment)。Diamond 大法官说:"Third, I conclude from the language of the rule that the carrier's right to an indemnity does not involve any enquiry as to whether the shipper had knowledge of the dangerous nature and character of the goods or was at fault in permitting their shipment of the dangerous nature or character of the goods or was at fault in permitting their shipment or in not warning the carrier before shipment of the dangerous nature or character of the goods. None of these matters are referred to in the rule(指海牙规则)as matters on which the carrier's right to an indemnity depends. It has been discussed in some cases and textbooks whether art. IV, r. 3 operates to reduce the shipper's liability under r. 6 from a absolute obligation to indemnify the carrier to a qualified obligation to indemnify him where the shipper can be shown to have been at fault. In the present case BP disclaimed any reliance on art. IV, r. 3 so as to import into art. IV, r. 6 any requirement of fault or negligence on the part of the shipper. In my judgment they were right to do so. Article IV, r. 3 is expressed in negative terms. That rule provides that the shipper shall not be liable for loss resulting "without the act, fault or neglect of the shipper, his agents or his servants". The shipment of dangerous goods is clearly an act of the shipper whether or not it is due to any fault or neglect on his part. The word "act" occurs elsewhere in the Hague-Visby Rules: see art. IV, r. 2 (a) ("act, neglect or default"); art. IV, r. 2 (i) ("act or omission of the shipper"). The expression "fault or neglect" without the addition of the word "act" occurs in art. IV, r. 2(q). While it would be wrong to expect consistency of language in a private law convention[632], I do not consider that the word "act" in art. IV, r. 3 can properly be disregarded or be treated as synonymous with fault or neglect[633], I was referred to three U. S. cases where "act" in art. IV, r. 3 was interpreted as synonymous with fault or neglect: Serraino v. U. S. Lines, (以上介绍过美国先例)。On the other hand it does not appear to have been argued in the Canadian case of the "Erwin Schroder" that art. IV, r. 3 qualifies art. IV, r. 6 and non of the judgments allude to this possibility. I conclude that art. IV, r. 6 depends on proof of shipment of the goods by the defendant against whom an indemnity is claimed but that otherwise art. IV, r. 3 is not relevant to the right of the carrier to claim an indemnity under r. 6."

Diamond 大法官的判决被 The "Giannis NK" (1996) 1 Lloyd's Rep. 577 案中的上诉庭认同。Hirst 大法官判定:"I would therefore hold that the word "act" in r. 3 bears

---

[632] Diamond 大法官不太瞧得起国际公约的草拟技术,认为它考虑不全面,矛盾/漏洞多难免。

[633] "行为"一字不能漠视,也不能去与"过失或疏忽"当做同义。

its natural and ordinary meaning and is apt to include the act of shipment itself, and that the undertaking under r. 6 is absolute and not qualified."

这样看来,发货人提供的提单内容如果不准确,即使不是他的过失/疏忽导致,也可说是他的"行为"导致。这行为可以是指发货人填上提单内容然后给船东核对与签字的行为。即使提单是船东格式(班轮运输),也是有发货人去取得一份空单然后填妥内容的行为。

2.2 收货人是否承担发货人的责任

这方面在本书第三章已详述,即英国 1855 年提单法(已过时)与 1992 年海上运输法为绕过或/与跨越合约相互关系的障碍,立法去强制把发货人的提单(或其他运输合约)转让给收货人/提单合法持有人。而后者是既有权利(如诉权),也有合约责任。这一来,会有疑问:该转让的责任是否包括对提单内容不正确也要负责? 如果是,这可开玩笑了,因为要求提单内容准确本来就是为了保障收货人/提单的合法持有人,让他/它们对提单有信心。

海牙规则与汉堡规则并没有去针对这方面,这毕竟是各国自己对提单立法带来的问题。但考虑到海牙规则 Article 3 (5)的最后一句,加上海牙·维斯比规则说明承运人禁止向第三者的提单持有人反证提单内容不妥,再加上 1992 年海上运输法也在 Section 4 (注)说明对提单合法持有人而言,提单内容是"结论性证据"(conclusive evidence),从所有这些条款看来,不可能会要收货人/提单持有人负上发货人提供提单内容不准确的责任。

为方便阅读,现节录 1992 年立法的 Section 4 如下:

"Representations in bills of lading

4. A bill of lading which—

(a) represents goods to have been shipped on board a vessel or to have been received for shipment on board a vessel; and

(b) has been signed by the master of the vessel or by a person who was not the master but had the express, implied or apparent authority of the carrier to sign bills of lading, shall, in favour of a person who has become the lawful holder of the bill, be conclusive evidence against the carrier of the shipment of the goods or, as the case may be, of their receipt for shipment."

但这一来,又带来对危险品的责任如何处理的问题? 这是否要收货人/提单持有人共同负起发货人提供资料不正确的责任? 如果是,客观看来很不公道,因为收货人/提单持有人对此发货人的行为(不论有否过失或疏忽)毫无控制可言,而且他/它们往往也是受害方。

再者,已经说过,危险品在这方面本质上与其他提单内容的提供是同一回事或十分接近,怎会相反对待呢?

在 The "Giannis NK"(1996) 1 Lloyd's Rep. 577,有关的立法是已经过时的 1855 年提单法,其中一个争议点是发货人对危险品的责任可否在转让提单(包括所有合约责任)给收货人/提单受让人后自动解除掉。上诉庭说不可以;Hirst 大法官判定:"In my judgment it would require very clear words indeed to divest the owner of his rights against the shipper (with whom he is in contractual relationship) and leave him with his sole remedy against a complete stranger who happens to be the consignee of the goods or the endorsee of the bill of lading, of whose whereabouts and financial stability he knows nothing, and who may be a man (or enterprise) of straw."

虽然,The "Giannis K"先例不是针对收货人要否对危险品造成船东损失负责。但它去针对发货人能否脱身,不负责任,岂非是大家已接受了收货人/提单持有人要对此负责?

1992 年的海上运输法,对提单合法持有人负有的运输合约责任(或海运单的收货人),Section 3 (1) 也写得十分明确和毫无保留,请见下文:"that person shall…become subject to the same liabilities under that contract as if he had been a party to that contract."

由此看来,提单合法持有人要对危险品负责,会被船东/承运人起诉索赔:见 The "Berge Sisar"(1998) 2 Lloyd's Rep. 475。虽然笔者仍未见到案例对此有定论。而且,尚有其他疑点例如像汉堡规则的 Article 15(1)(a),提单内容已包括了对危险品的特征/本质的陈述,这是由发货人所提供的。但若出事后证实并不准确,这一来,究竟是收货人/提单持有人可以要求船东对提单内容负责,不得去反证推翻呢,还是倒过头来要向船东负责呢?

在刚刚出版的 *Bills of Lading: Law and Contracts* 一书(Nicholas Gaskell 教授等著)的 4.53 至 4.55 小段谈及此方面,现节录如下:"The Law Commission(这是指 1992 年立法委员) clearly contemplated that a lawful holder could be liable for pre-shipment liabilities, such as loadport demurrage, and were distinctly unimpressed by arguments that this could be unfair on the holder[634]. They specifically declined to make a special provision exempting the lawful holder from potential liabilities of the shipper arising from the 'warranty' in respect of the shipment of dangerous cargo[635]. The clear in-

---

[634] 立法委员清楚是要提单合法持有人对付运前责任负责,如装港滞期费,并不觉得有任何不公平。

[635] 但他们拒绝订立法律条款说明提单合法持有人不必对发货人托运危险品对承运人所作出的保证一并负责。

ference was that the holder could be liable under the Act for such liabilities[636]. In the Court of Appeal in *The Giannis N. K.*, it was stated that the liabilities under the Bills of Lading Act 1855s. 1 were concurrent, with both the shipper and consignee or indorsee sharing the same obligation in relation to them[637]. The House of Lords agreed that the holder's liability was by way of addition rather than substitution[638]. This suggests that the carrier may have a choice about whether to sue the shipper or the holder[639].

However, it is submitted that the matter has not been decided conclusively against holders[640], as this is another area where the Commissions declined to act, leaving the matter to the courts[641]. In the first place, the reference to 'warranty' may have meant that the Commissions had in mind the typical express clauses on dangerous cargo in bills[642]. In relation to these obligations, it is again submitted that the holder's liability may depend upon the definition clause allocating various rights and liabilities to 'merchants'. Secondly, the Commissions may not have had in mind here Art. IV r. 6 of the Hague and Hague-Visby Rules and Art. 13 of the Hamburg Rules[643]. The better view is that the Rules allocate these responsibilities solely to the original shipper[644]. Article 1 of the Hamburg Rules specifically distinguishes between shipper and consignee and it is unlikely the Hague and Hague-Visby Rules were intended to produce a different result[645]. Under Art. 17. 1 of the Hamburg Rules the shipper is expressly to remain liable to the carrier foe inaccuracies in the bill even if it has been transferred[646]. Article III r. 5 of the Hague and Hague-Visby Rules does not specifically mention the point, but it is submitted that the result is the same.[647]

---

[636] 这显示了提单合法持有人会有负责的可能。
[637] 在 The "Giannis NK", 上诉庭判发货人与收货人共同负责。
[638] 贵族院同意提单持有人的责任是加上而非是替代发货人的责任。
[639] 这表示船东/承运人可选择向发货人还是向提单持有人起诉。
[640] 但这仍是没有定论。
[641] 因为立法委员不肯去针对这一点,让法院将来决定。
[642] 立法委员心目中对危险品保证也会只是指提单内的一些明示条款。
[643] 而并没有想到像海牙/海牙·维斯比规则的 4(6) 条款:有关这条款请参阅第五章之 4.2.7.1.9.2 小段。
[644] 更好的看法(也表示是该书作者是认同的)是这些规则只是把托运危险品的责任加在发货人身上: 请参阅第三章之 11.2.1 小段。
[645] 汉堡规则去区分了发货人与收货人,海牙/海牙·维斯比规则也应是如此。
[646] 汉堡规则说明提单转让后发货人仍对承运人负责提单上不准确的后果。
[647] 海牙/海牙·维斯比规则没有提到此点,但应没有相异之处。

Where a carrier seeks to impose the obligations on a consignee by contract there may also be a question as to whether the suggested liability in some way derogated from the Hague, Hague-Visby Rules or Hamburg Rules[648]. It may be significant that while the Hague and Hague-Visby Rules Art. III r. 8 forbids any clause 'relieving the carrier…from liability for or damage to, or in connection with, the goods', the Hamburg Rules Art. 23 prohibits a clause which 'derogates, directly or indirectly, from the provisions of the Convention'. The wider wording of the latter provision might make it easier to suggest that there is an indirect derogation from the Convention when shipper liabilities are transferred to a consignee or indorsee, rather in the same way that a benefit of insurance clause is void (under Hague, Hague-Visby Rules and Hamburg Rules).[649] "

§3 提单的货物内容

可先去探讨海牙规则的 3 方面内容：

3.1 内容之一：货物标号/标记

这方面官司不多，William Tetley 教授的 *Marine Cargo Claims* 一书第 3 版在第 452～453 页提到二个这方面的案例。

一是法国的 Cour d'Appel d'Alger 12. 12. 1961，DMF 1962,660，涉及木材没有适当标号，导致不同收货人之间分不清是谁的木材。于是装卸工干脆让收货人自己拿。这导致其中有收货人少了木材而提出索赔。

另一是法国的 Cour d'Appel de Rouen，18. 11,1982，DMF 1983,423，涉及俄罗斯棉花在货物上的标记与提单上的不一样。

在本书第五章之 4.2.7.1.7 小段提到 The "Strathewe" (1986) LMLN 180，也是因标记与舱单不符导致货物在转运时遗失，两年后才寻获。

3.2 内容之二：货物重量/数量/度量

有关货物重量，在较早的§2 段已提到发货人填上的提单数字来自岸上仪表或过磅，而且一般没有船东参与，船东也不知详情，也会是发货人无法获得岸上数字而要装毕后靠船舶吃水计算数字，再填入提单内。但对船东而言，倒也不是没有合理办法去确定这岸上数字是否准确。对一般干货船而言，可以依赖船舶吃水计算

---

[648] 承运人若向收货人起诉有关危险品责任还会涉及有否违反像海牙/海牙·维斯比或汉堡规则。
[649] 这些规则都想保护善意的提单持有人，而不让承运人去拥有比规则更大的好处。

出货量。若是油轮,更可以通过船上油柜空档(ullage)计算。

3.2.1 岸上货物重量与船舶吃水重量之争

这方面的做法,在笔者《程租合约》一书之第262~265页有详述,可节录如下:

2.3 对"真正"数量计算的事实认定

2.3.1 岸上仪表或过磅

即使在以上大原则下,对"真正"数量(较少的数量)是否准确仍会有争议。例如,较少的是运抵数量,根据是岸上过磅数,则它会有是否准确之争了。任何计算衡量,都可能有人为的疏忽错误。此外,还要看它过磅的方法:例如是否离开船旁很远,或是岸上仪表是否经常校准,等等。是否准确,可否被接受,在仲裁中是由仲裁员来认定事实。

岸上过磅会有多种做法,例如是一辆辆的卡车去过磅,或是漏斗过磅(hopper weight),或是输送带过磅(conveyer belt weight)。像装散粮,它会是漏斗过磅。它先把散粮经第一个漏斗转去填满第二个漏斗,然后过磅,过了磅再转去第三个漏斗不断装上船舶。只要这第二个漏斗的过磅仪经常校准(calibrate),这方法会相当准确。

输送带过磅也会用在散粮、煤炭等多种货物。它根据输送带上货物的重量及输送带的速度,可以算出装上船(或卸下船)的货物数量。今天加上有计算机等精细设备的协助,这种方法也可以很准确。

2.3.2 船舶吃水

另一个就是否准确、能否代表真正数量常有争议的计算是依船舶吃水的计算。例如,较少的是运抵数量,运费照这数字付没有争议。但岸上是9千吨,船上数字(根据吃水计算)是9千5百吨,它们都比(在提单上的)装载数量1万吨要少,但运费应是照9千还是9千5百吨去支付呢?

原则很简单,看谁能代表真正数量,这纯是对事实的认定。上文已经对岸上过磅、仪表计量的方法讨论过。现在再去看看依船舶吃水的计算方法。除了油轮,这一般是船东对散装货唯一的计算衡量方法。

在做法上很简单,就是看了船舶吃水之后,比较载重标尺(deadweight scale)的船图,找出相关的吨位后去调整海水密度(因海水咸淡各不同,船舶吃水会因此有变化),再作出船舶首尾吃水差更正(trim correction,因首尾吃水有差异,中间水尺不会准,要更正),船舶挠曲更正(hogging and sagging correction,因船体挠曲,如货物重量分布不均,带来首尾或中间水尺有偏差)。

这调整过的吨位再减掉船上的油、水以及常数等重量,余下的便应是货物的重量/数量。

以上计算方法准确与否取决于很多不稳定的因素,如:

(ⅰ)船舶吃水数字看错,对于老船,因造船时烧焊的数字已看不见,吃水标志只靠油漆漆上去,就会有这种问题。

(ⅱ)老爷船,本身已有结构上的挠曲偏差,是船上图表反映不出来的。

(ⅲ)一般而言,愈大愈新的船舶会愈准确。

(ⅳ)人为疏忽错误。

(ⅴ)坏天气,如海浪大,甲板上不断积雪结冰等。

(ⅵ)早上晚上视力不一样,看吃水的角度,近看远看不同等等。

(ⅶ)船在装港停久了会有污底,从而增加船舶载重,但又估计不到。

(ⅷ)其他原因。

可见,依吃水的计算不会太准,它不稳定的因素应比岸上高。这样一来,如果吃水数字与岸上数字有偏差(如在 0~5% 之内),船东不应紧张,因为更大可能是岸上数字(仪表或过磅)会更接近"真正"的货物数量。当然,这仍要细看每一宗事件的不同事实。例如,岸上数字是 1 千吨,但吃水计算明明是 3 千吨,这可能吗?或是在一个混乱落后的港口,或是一艘颇新的 Panamax 散装船去进行了两三次吃水计算(draft survey),结果都一致但却与岸上数量有百分之六、七的差异,等等。

我见过船长在装港坚持要以吃水数量否定岸上数量,结果在卸港的岸上数量或船舶吃水数量都显示船长在装港坚持得不对,从而带来承租人多种损失索赔。

2.3.3 总结

散装货物不易认定"真正"的货物数量,一切都要看事实。油轮则会有一个较准确的船上油舱空档计算(ullage measurement),在船旁管路的仪表一般会很准确,所以问题不大,不像干散货。另外问题不大的还有件装货,因可点数理货(tally)。当然,这也会有人为的疏忽错误。

2.4 租约的写法

为了寻求比普通法地位(见 2.2 小段)更为明确的运费计算的方法,今天租约常会订明以哪一个货物数量为准。只要订得清楚,当然是以写什么为准了。例如,约定运费是以装载数量(或提单数量)为准;或是,以运抵数量(或卸货量的 outturn)为准。它甚至会写明以装港双方参与的船舶吃水计算(joint draft survey)为准,等等。

3.2.2 岸上油柜度量与油轮油柜空档度量之争

以上节录略有提到油轮空档计算较为准确,但仍会被发货人视为不可靠。在 The "Irini M" (1988) 1 Lloyd's Rep. 253 案例,涉及岸上与船上(水尺与油轮空档)数字有严重偏差。在装港的叙利亚 Tartous,岸上数字比船上数字多了 691 立方米。在船长的抗议下,提单填上了岸上数字,而在卸港,岸上数字却比船上数字少了 1006 立方米。换言之,如果岸上两个数字(通过岸上油柜的度量)准确,船东就要对这总共约 1700 立方米 "消失" 的原油负责。

该案中,作为原告的收货人/提单持有人的专家提到的船上空档数字的不可靠之处,似为 Leggatt 大法官所接受。他说:"In his view it is customary to raise bill of lading quantities on shore measurements rather than base custody transfer quantities on vessel's calibration scales. He regarded the experience factor data [650] supplied in the CWA [651] Report as confirming the uncertainty of the vessel's calibration scales and the inadvisability of basing official measurements on vessel's receipts."

而对船舶水尺计算,Leggatt 大法官说是 "不准确":"from their nature, draft figures cannot be very accurate…"

对岸上数字的准确性,针对装港的 Tartous,双方专家都有去当地调查并提取证供。Leggatt 大法官接受其准确性,判是:"In relation to the terminal at Tartous Mr Milligan(船东大律师) argues that errors are possible on account of air in the pipeline [652] or incurrate measurement. He argues that there is doubt whether the Syrians in the terminal did undertake any recheck [653] …now assert that their system was fool-proof. I find that at Tartous the pipeline was full both before and after loading, in accordance with normal practice at what is exclusively a loading terminal. This could readily be done by

---

[650] 这是去为过去的航次做记录,看一直下来船上岸上数字的偏差,希望可从中看出油轮潜在的结构上与 "图表" (ship's calibration table) 上的误差会导致计算不准。这记录当然不会太准,毕竟岸上数字会出自许多不同的港口。

[651] 这是船东的专家。显然,该案例中提供的船舶过往航次的偏差波动颇大,所以被货方专家利用来攻击船上数字不准确。

[652] 船东大律师指油管有空气。法官认定油管一直是满的,因为长期装原油的设施,一般都是这样情况。油管是通过海底接往船上,通过岸上油柜位置较高而引致的重力作用,油管会一直满满的。只有遇上修理油管才会抽干/泵干。

[653] 船东大律师指岸上知悉与船上数字有出入,却没有再去检查自己的数字,法官不同意。

gravity[654]. The three tanks used for the loading had been calibrated by SGS[655] or an associated company in or since 1975 and the calibrations were therefore reliable. The opening and closing measurements which were taken manually to a fixed reference point in each of the tanks are before the Court[656]. There is no reason to doubt their accuracy, either by reference to past experience or to the evidence of the loading in question. Since the ship's figures were given to the shore before the shore figures were released, the need for a check was obvious. On such occasions it was the usual practice of the terminal to re-check measurements[657].

On this evidence I accept as accurate the shore tank figures at Tartons. It follows that 691 cubic metres more crude oil was loaded upon the ship than appears from her own ullage readings."

至于卸港在 Le Havre,是在先进国家的法国,自然在设备上更为先进精确。而且货方专家也曾造访调查,但船东专家却没有。所以,Leggatt 大法官接受货方的作证,判岸上数字比船上数字准确,也就不奇怪了。Leggatt 大法官说:"In my judgment, though not unique, Le Havre is indeed a sophisticated modern terminal with good measuring facilities by means of automatic gauges[658]. At the time of discharge in question, a comparison of the automatic gauge readings was being conducted with manual readings in order to satisfy the Customs[659]. A minimum of two-valve segregation was always maintained[660], and the pipelines were kept fully[661]. The control room was equipped with an automatic gauge level display[662], an automatic temperature display[663], a display which showed how oil was routed and which valves were open or shut[664], and a

---

[654] 船东大律师指油管有空气。法官认定油管一直是满的,因为长期装原油的设施,一般都是这样情况。油管是通过海底接往船上,通过岸上油柜位置较高而引致的重力作用,油管会一直满满的。只有遇上修理油管才会抽干/泵干。

[655] SGS 也是货方专家,它们过往也曾替装港的油柜仪表校准,正好为货方作有利的证供。

[656] Leggatt 大法官也接受货方专家对装港如何度量岸上油柜确定装上船舶货量做法的证供,认为准确。

[657] 船东大律师指岸上知悉与船上数字有出入,却没有再去检查自己的数字,法官不同意。

[658] Le Harve 是一十分先进设施,所有对货物度量都有自动量规仪表。不用人手,表示只要仪表有校准,是精确,会可避免人为误差。

[659] 卸货前亦去把自动量规仪表与人手比较,以满足海关对进口原油数量的统计。

[660] 岸上油柜与管道接口处总有二个开关,表示紧密,不会受一个开关漏而影响。

[661] 油管也一直是满满的。

[662] 有控制室装有自动岸上油柜量规的显示表。

[663] 也有原油货物温度的显示表。

[664] 也有原油货物流向的显示表与开关当时是开是关。

computer read-out by volume and weight for each tank[665]. Preceding stock records were available for checking current figures[666]. The 12 sensors in each tank gave a reliable average temperature of the contents[667]. No free water was ever run off from the tanks[668]. The assessment of the bottom sediment and water content was assessed by the automatic flow sampler, which took 2113 samples of this particular cargo.

The staffing and conduct of the control room was such as in my judgment rendered it impossible in the circumstances for the misrouting of 1000 cubic metres of oil to have passed unnoticed[669]. The unchallenged evidence of the quality of the system at this installation conclusively establishes that no loss of relevant cargo occurred in it."

3.2.2.1 岸上与船上数字差异主因

撇开以上的 The"Irini M"先例,现实中岸上与船上数字常有差异,有时高达1.5%,而谁准确谁不准确也是争议不绝。造成这现象,可归咎于4个或更多原因,略去介绍如下:

（ⅰ）岸上油管半满或是空的——这是重要原因之一,岸上油管会很长,常会有多达6000吨以上的容量。若装货前岸上油管是空的,装货后是满的,就会有好几千吨的货物算为装船数字,但其实根本是另一回事。现实中,也很少有人(特别是船东)去对装货前(或卸货前)的岸上油管作出检查。

（ⅱ）测量上的错误——岸上与船上数字根据对岸上与船上油柜空挡(ullage)计量得出实际是以"容量"(volume)去换算重量。其中像货物(石油)的"密度"(density)与温度等测量都会有误差,造成偏差。其他许多方面与本章3.2.1小段讲到的船舶吃水计算会产生的误差也大同小异,例如船舶结构上的挠曲偏差令船上"图表"(ship's calibration table)不正确。另有像船上油柜在刚装完货物急着开航时测量,货物仍在动态,变得有些测量不会准确。故曾听说有部分英国货物保险人对货物(石油)的数量,如果是根据船上测量得出(例如在黑海港口,阿尔及尼亚的Skikda),保单对短少的免赔额要多加0.5%(本来已有习惯的0.5%)。

（ⅲ）水分——原油从地下钻出来已或多或少含有水分。去判断有多少又是要看一种称为"bottom sediment and water(BSW)"的测量。在装港测量往往没有卸港测量准确,因为水分在航次中会慢慢沉淀到石油下层。所以,可以想象,卸港常会是

---

[665] 与有计算机记录每一岸上油柜的原油货物容量与重量。
[666] 以往的原油存量也一齐有记录,可供核算比较。
[667] 每一岸上油柜上下各处装置有12个感应器,对原油货物的温度有可靠的记录。去准备计算,不论是岸上油柜或船上油柜空挡,货物的温度都是十分重要的因素,因为"容量"(volume)热涨冷缩。
[668] 也没有水分流失。原油含有水分与其他沉淀物,会在油柜底积聚。
[669] 所以不可能在 Le Havre 的岸上会有上千立方米的原油在无法知悉情况下失去。

少了货物(石油),多了水分(free water)而导致货差索赔。

(iv)计算表的不同——一般在使用的计算表是 American Societf for Testing Materials（ASTM）与 Institute of Petroleum（IP）所拟定的"Petroleum Measurement Tables"内容一致。但有新旧版本之分,从而造成数量不一致。旧版是在 1940 年左右,而新版是 1980 年。它们之间主要的实际区别是油温较高时(高出 60°F),旧版会多计算出数量,典型的是对中东原油在 0.1% 左右,而加热后的燃油更会多计算达 0.2% 以上,虽然新版是 1980 年的,但至今仍有大量出口国家(沙特阿拉伯、科威特、印尼、伊朗、叙利亚、阿尔及利亚、印度、阿联酋、卡塔尔、阿根廷和土耳其等)的部分码头仍在使用早已过时的旧版计算。大概是为了保护自己,可是这导致经常性的发生卸港的卸货量(以新版计算)有了短少/货差。另据知像俄罗斯有它一套不同的计算表,也会造成不一致。

3.2.2.2 可依赖船上数字去抗辩货差索赔

虽然提单货量数字通常采用装港岸上数字,船东/承运人也难去抗拒:请看 The "Irini M"(1988)1 Lloyd's Rep. 253。但以卸港的岸上数字去证明有货差,看来会受到不同对待。而以船上油柜空档(ullage)算出来的数字如果在装卸港是一致/相近的,会是货物在运输中、在船东手里没有造成短缺很有力的说明。因为即使有计算上的潜在误差,多数的误差都会同样地反映在装卸港的测量因此而抵消掉。所以,这会可以成功抗辩货差索赔。这方面可去节录一家著名的船东互保协会的通告,它曾提到 5 个美国判例与 1 个纽约仲裁,均对船东/承运人有利,通告最后一段强调在装卸港船上准确测量的重要性。通告(部分)如下:

"The United States District Courts have recently developed a line of cases which have established the principle that a shipper or consignee will not make out a *prima facie* case of short-delivery when he bases his claim on shore tank figures cannot be used against a carrier, since they represent measurements taken when the cargo has passed out of the carrier's possession. The cases are summarized below.

Dow Chemical v. S. S. Giovannella D'Amico (297 F. Supp. 699)

The cargo claimed in this case raised a claim for short-delivery of styrene monomer, based on a comparison of the loading receipt quantities with shore tank and lighter measurements following discharge. The ship's figures actually disclosed an increase in the quantity of cargo discharged over that recorded as loaded. In the face of this clear conflict of evidence, the court held that the claimant had not discharged the burden of proof.

Center Chem Products v. A/S Rederiet (1972 A. M. C. 373)

Here the court relied heavily on the reasoning of the tribunal in Dow Chemical v. S. S. Giovannella D'Amico (above) in holding that a consignee could not rely on shore tank figures to prove a loss, since delivery of the cargo of glyoxal occurred when it entered the consignees' shore installation. The claimant failed to establish a short-delivery, since it failed to show that the cause of the short delivery occurred prior to the discharge of the cargo into the shore installation, for "to require the carrier to inspect a maze of piping and storage tanks over which it had no control or expertise would be burdensome if not impossible" (at page 375).

Esso Nederland v. Trade Fortitude (1977 A. M. C. 2144)

Although the court found against the carrier in this case, it nevertheless rejected the claimants contention that a cargo shortage could be proved by comparing the bill of lading quantities with the shore tank figures following discharge. In citing Center Chem Products v. A/S Rederiet, the court remarked that:

"In the light of the problems, both legal and practical, raised by reliance on either shore-to-shore or ship-to-ship comparisons, the court concludes that the only satisfactory predicate for determining whether there is liability and, if so, its extent is a comparison between the (ship's loading and discharging ullages)."

Note. Because the court found against the carrier in that case—there being no evidence to explain a loss of cargo apparent from the ship's figures—it is often cited against owners as establishing that the customary allowance of 0.5% for loss in transit is bad in law. However, it is submitted that the fact that the court in this case chose to ignore the customary loss is entirely because "the defendants...cited no authority supporting its applicability in litigated cargo shortage eases". This being the case, the court was bound to ignore the owners' contention that it should apply.

North East Petroleum v. Prairie Grove (1977 A. M. C. 2139)

This case concerned a cargo of gasoline and diesel oil loaded in Texas. After loading. The ship's tanks were sealed and the seals were found to be unbroken at the discharging port. There was no evidence of loss of cargo during the voyage. The claimants based their short-delivery claim on a comparison of the bill of lading figures with the shore figures following discharge, notwithstanding the fact that the ship's ullages prior to discharge, when compared with the bill of lading figures, did not reveal any significant shortage. In addition, here was clear evidence that the vessel's tanks had been properly stripped. The court once again dismissed the claim on the grounds that the carrier had fulfilled his obligation to deliver the cargo once it had passed the ship's permanent manifold connections and no evidence had been adduced of any leakage of cargo during transit.

Note. By contrast to Esso Nederland v. Trade Fortitude (above) the court in this case admitted the 0.5% customary allowance.

H. Grunewald & Co. v. S. S. Ginevra, Amoco and Sayboult (U. S. D. C., Eastern District of Virginia—19.12.77).

The court in this case once more relied upon the fact that the ship's ullages showed no significant shortages and that "dry tank" certificates were available. The claimants alleged non-payment of monies due under a sale contract, following a deduction from the full price by the buyer defendant—Amoco—who alleged short-delivery of cargo, following a comparison of shore tank figures on discharge with the bill of lading figures. Giving judgment for the claimants, the court was highly critical of methods used to measure shore tank quantities. The vessel was dismissed from the suit entirely.

The effect of this line of decisions has recently been admirably summed up by an award in arbitration in New York—The "Overseas Discoverer" (S. M. A. 1203—1.3.78):

"Courts and arbitration panels have consistently rejected those methods of calculating bulk oil losses which depend on shore tank measurements, or procedures which measure the oil prior to, or after it has left the custody of the vessel. The intricacies of shore tank piping networks invariably leave open to question what quantity of oil leaving a shore tank actually gets aboard a vessel and conversely. How much of the vessel's oil actually reaches the specific shore tank being measured. It is for these reasons that the most reliable figures of all concerned are those amounts calculated from the ship's calibration tables. Using the jointly taken ullage and temperature readings at the loading and discharge."

It is hoped that courts in other jurisdictions will maintain this approach, which is both just and practical. The principle thus established, however, can only be of advantage to the tanker owner if the most stringent care is taken by the ship's officers to ensure that accurate ullage calculations—and draught surveys, if possible—are taken at the loading and discharging port. Without the evidence that these figures provide, he is at the claimants' mercy."

3.2.3 岸上理货与船舶理货

如果是一包包一件件的货物，一项小心谨慎的"理货"（tally）应可以十分准确地得出货物的数量。而发货人岸上理货得出来的数量也应与船东在船上理货得出来的数量十分接近，甚至一致。在历时多天的装货中，在每天装货结束时双方也会去比较数量，以便有偏差时可以马上去查明原因。

当然理货也并非没有争议。例如，对破包/空包应否点算，特别当这是装卸工所造成的。管理不善的发展中国家港口所作的理货更常会受到质疑：如在 The "Herroe"and"Askoe"(1986)2 Lloyd's Rep.281 的装港,埃及——亚历山大港。故意少点算卸下的货物数量这种事,也不是没有听闻过。

若船东自己为省钱或难安排而不去理货,则会相当被动,到时只能依赖岸上的理货数量(装港与卸港都是一样)。在 The"Atlas"(1996)1 Lloyd's Rep.642 先例正是发生了这种情况。当然,要去质疑岸上理货数量也不是不可以。该先例中,装港俄罗斯的 Nakhodka(海参崴附近)港口负责人作证称一束束的钢材由火车运至港区,卸下时点一次,其记录称为"Type 1"(第一种)文件。之后,在从码头装上船舶时再点一次货,这记录称为"Type 2"(第二种)文件。最后,去把"Type 1"与"Type 2"的总数相比得出一份文件叫"Type 3",而提单的钢材货物(steel billets)数量就是根据"Type 3"的文件。

船东对这些记录提出质疑(但不成功),称"Type 1"与"Type 2"的文件不应被接受为说明重量的证据,因为文件中根本没有资料涉及谁去量重,在哪里进行与怎样进行等。且文件并不可靠,如"Type 1"与"Type 2"实际只有过1次的理货,而理货是针对从火车卸下码头而非是装上船舶等。而船长记得并作供称只是部分钢材自码头装上船,也有从火车直接装船的。

看来,船东并未去 Nakhodka 调查事实,只是在发货人披露的文件中挑毛病。Longmore 大法官相信货方,并指出船东自己没有安排理货实在很难去抗辩岸上理货的数量,他说:

"The master's recollection…says that bundles were mainly loaded directly from the quayside but on a few occasions were taken directly from railway trucks. That is not to my mind, inconsistent with two tallies being done even in cases where cargo was loaded directly from railway trucks into the ship since some clerks may have been standing at the truck to tally bundles off and some near or on the ship to tally bundles on board. Surprisingly, those on board the vessel made no independent tally of the cargo and no mate's receipt were signed. In these circumstances the ship cannot effectively dispute the shore figures and I am satisfied that the number of bundles recorded on the bills of lading were, in fact, loaded[670]…

Since both the tally and the rail tally recorded weights, it is a fair inference that the bundles must have been weighed at some stage perhaps up country at the place of manufacture.

---

[670] 这一段是法官针对船长证供的讲话。船长指部分货物直接从火车装船等,总之很混乱,所以理货不会准确,但这不被法官接受。同时法官也指出船东没有自己理货,故难以质疑岸上数字。难怪本章§2 小段提到国际互保船东协会大力建议船东安排理货。

Mr. Baker（船东大律师）maintained that was not evidence of weight shipped[671]…

It seems to me that the tally records, recording the weight of the billets, are documents compiled by persons(viz. tally clerks) acting under duty to the port authority[672]; the information as to weight(unless an invention[673], which was not suggested) must have been supplied(whether directly or through intermediaries) by someone whose duty was to weigh the billets(or perhaps, supervise the weighing)[674]; such a person may reasonably be supposed to have personal knowledge of the weight and an intermediary through whom the chain of information passed will have been acting under a duty to transmit information[675]. I conclude therefore that the tally documents do afford admissible evidence of weight[676]. I further conclude, on the evidence and on the balance of probabilities that the number of bundles and the weight of billets, recorded in three bills of lading, were in fact shipped."

3.2.4 岸上与船上货物重量/数量之争的其他实例

最后，可去节录曾在《期租合约》一书25.5段详述到的这方面的实例，以加强读者对这方面困难的认识。它是笔者曾涉及的 The "Phassa" (1990) SMA No.2640，节录如下：

25.5 租方在签发提单问题上的苦衷

话又说回来，租方要争取自己直接出提单，也有他的苦衷。要能结汇到货款，提单就必须严格依照信用证要求，一点也差不了，正如一著名先例（Equitable Trust Co. of New York v. Dawson Partners Ltd. (1972) 27 Lloyd's Rep. 第49页

---

[671] 在货物重量方面，二个理货记录（"Type 1"，"Type 2"）都有重量数字。估计曾一度量重/过磅，甚至会是在生产地。而船东争辩这不是装上船舶重量的证明。

[672] 这是针对船东的另一抗辩，称在法院诉讼的证据法下，该理货记录不应被接纳为证据。关于这一点，笔者的《国际商务仲裁》一书第十一章之4段（传闻证据）有提及这一方面说："在1968年民事证据法下，Section 4 允许二手或以上的"传闻证据"在一些特定的情况下可去被"接受"（admissible）。这是在 Section 4(1)：(i) 这文件或记录是由一位"身负职责"（acting under a duty）的人作出的，而这是什么人在 Section 4(3) 也极为广泛，可以是商业、专业或其他职业的人士。一些例子是公安报告（该报告上亦只是其他人士告诉公安的事实），医生或护士报告，工厂检验（factory inspector）报告，等等。(ii) 资料是出自一位估计对这件争议的事实有"个人了解"（personal knowledge）的人士。"
本案例中，Longmore 大法官指理货员"身负职责"（对港口当局）。

[673] 钢材货物重量也记录得很细，不会是凭空想象。

[674] 所以估计应有一位对重量有"个人了解"（personal knowledge）的人士去将数字提供给理货员。

[675] 估计他也是"身负职责"。

[676] 所以有关货物重量的理货文件/记录可被接受为证据。

至 52 页) 所说:"There is no room for documents which are almost the same, or which will do just as well."

对笔者更熟悉的一案是 The"Phassa"(1990) SMA No. 2640.(纽约仲裁),该纽约仲裁被报道出来,表面看很正常合理,判得还可以,但内中可明确看到租方或发货人的困境。在"Time Charter"第 4 版的 345 页这样报道:"The panel held that owners' refusal to issue clean bills of lading based upon suspected shoreside measurement was proper since there was ample reason for owner to conclude that such measurement did not accurately reflect the quantity of crude oil which was loaded on the vessel."该案情为,一艘油轮在日本 Kiire 港装原油,涉及以下的货量数字:

(1) 根据岸上油柜计数器:105904.475 吨;
(2) 根据验船师对船上油柜空档(ullage)的计算,105542.054 吨;
(3) 根据大副单方做的水尺计算:105149.160 吨。

装完货后大约两天,当船航行往美国卸货港途中,估计是大副自己做的水尺计算的数字被船东事后知悉,大为恐慌,马上要求租方把两天前船长授权代理出的提单退回,该提单用的是岸上油柜计数器的数字。在租方拒绝后,船东马上在香港法院出禁止令下令租方(公司在香港)不能去使用该提单,要退还给船东。这一来,租方可惨了,没法去结汇,而时间又很紧迫。

租方可去做两件事:一是去法院争辩,希望尽快说服法院把这禁令撤销;另一方法是去与船东谈判和解。租方选择后者,与船东律师交涉,基本上是指出水尺计算,特别是在晚上装完货赶着开航的情况下,不可能准确。租方也指出提单少写了货量,少收货款是一个问题,但信用证不允许低过某数量会是更大的问题。同时租方也提出给予船东担保,即,如果因提单数字夸大而引致有货物短卸,由租方作出赔偿。但这些建议都被船东拒绝。

到最后,双方总算协调出一份提单,以空档计算的 105,542.054 吨为货物数量,但租方仍要就该数字与水尺计算数字之间的差别给予船东银行担保。问题总算告一段落,租方总算能结汇,法院禁令也自动撤销。

可笑的是,到了美国卸港,虽经过航次的正常消耗(normal loss),竟然是收货人确认卸货数字与提单上的大致一样。这表示考虑到有正常的消耗,该提单的货量很大可能是被低估了。明显是收货人根本没有短缺索赔。

在之后的纽约仲裁,租方收集及提供了大量的证据,如:

(i)Kiire 港以往都是习惯以岸上数字作为提单数字的依据,也只有这样才好控制要装的货量。岸上油柜与码头的油船相近,管道不长,原油不可能在其他地方漏掉。

(ⅱ)Kiire 港的岸上计数器的准确性,包括它不断的校准(calibration)及证明书。

(ⅲ)水尺计算,特别在客观环境不妥下(如晚上,风浪大,老船等),会很不准确。该船东的互保协会出过的告诉船东不可太去依赖水尺数字的通告也被呈堂作为证据。

(ⅳ)在卸港的卸货量明确证明提单数字是被低估了。

租方也力争如果船开了几天后容许船东回头去否定提单数字,这会对租方带来莫大损失与不便。比如,没法再去安排一个共同计算以作确定,不管是油柜空档或是水尺。或是,再加装一些货,以符合买卖合约与信用证。

而船东的争辩,只是依赖大副的水尺计算,并提供了该船以往九个航次的水尺计算误差,所谓 Vessel Experience Factor(VEF),一直与岸上数字相差不大。这 VEF,就是因为油船都会有它潜在的结构与图表误差导致水尺计算的不准确。所以凭经验,可计算出某一油船一贯性的水尺计算都是比岸上数字多或少,以及是多少百分比。有了这 VEF 的经验,可估计以后每一次水尺计算的可靠程度到哪里。

但租方马上指"Phassa"轮以往九个航次的 VEF,"平均"是与岸上数字相差不大,但从每一个别航次去看,却有很大分别,有时水尺计算数字比岸上数字少很多,有时却多很多,等等。所以"平均相差不大"实在是误导,而且 VEF 的先决条件仍是进行水尺计算的环境适当,双方共同参与,等等。

可是,三位仲裁员只是简短地否定了租方的争辩与证据,说船长有权不出清洁提单,如果他对岸上(提单上)的货量数字有怀疑。

其实在大道理上,这判法没有错,谁也会讲。在海牙规则的 Art. Ⅲ(3)已是明确地说明:"Provided that no carrier, master or agent of the carrier shall be bound to state or show in the bill of lading any…quantity, or weight he has 'reasonable' ground(合理理由)for suspecting not accurately to represent the goods actually received, or which he has no reasonable means of checking."

问题是,什么叫"合理理由"? 在"Phassa"仲裁案能否算船长有"合理理由"? 看来,这问题仍是会由个别仲裁员自由发挥,任意去判。但看来,仍是以船长一句话,一份供词(statement)或一份宣誓书(affidavit)作为主要依据。这种纠纷,仍是无日无之,后果可大可小。小则延误一些船期(The "Boukadoura" (1989)1 Lloyd's Rep. 393),租方提供担保给船东要花有关的费用。一般而言,提供担保不失为一种好方法,也常见使用来解决这种纠纷。这种担保往往没有欺诈的味道,所以不像欺诈性的保函(来交换倒签提单,明确不妥的货物去出清洁提单等),法律判是无效(Brown Jenkinson v. Percy Dalton(1957)1 Lloyd's

Rep. 31, SCB v. PNSC(1995)2 Lloyd's Rep. 365)。这种担保的合法性,在汉堡规则的 Art. 17(3)也给予明确。

但这种纠纷严重的后果会是双方损失惨重,船被扣留多月,租方或发货人结不了汇,买方因货物市场下跌乘机赖掉买卖合约;船上已装货物因此完全损失。比如,多年前在黄埔港的"金马"轮事件即是一典型例子。关于船上的农产品有点发霉,到底是否正常、无损货物的质量,可否出清洁提单,连多位聘用的专家也是各说各话,谁能肯定真相?又或是,这种纠纷会否有真相,是否只是意见看法相异而已(a matter of different views)?

因为租方/发货人有此大弱点,我也多次听说有船长为要好处,每每在装完货时乱说这里不妥,那里不妥,不肯签清洁提单,直至租方或发货人给他一封大红包。

总而言之,大家可见在 NYPE 租约下,根据在 25.1 段所介绍的 The "Berkshire"(1974)1 Lloyd's Rep. 185 这一主要案例,租方是可以绕过船长(short-circuit)自己去签发提单的好处。能这样偷偷地去做,租方可免了不少麻烦。

3.2.5 发货人一般以岸上货量为提单货量

从以上详论可见岸上与船舶的数字都会有偏差,而且现实中永远不会这么巧是一致的。在 3.2.1 小段的节录针对运费(以货物重量为准),最后提到租约会订明以哪一个货物数量为准。而针对填在提单上的货量,也常见租约去订明以哪一数字为准,以免争议。例如,在 The "Galatia"(1979)2 Lloyd's Rep. 450,有关租约第 44 条说:"…In exchange of the 'Mate's Receipt', the Bill of Lading shall be issued promptly on demand of the Shipper or his Agents by the Master or owners' agents, after loading of the sugar is completed on board of the vessel, for the quantity as determined by the Shipper's surveyors[677]. If Owners elect to hold a draft survey of the vessel, it will be at their own expense and costs but the loaded quantity as determined by such surveyor shall not be mentioned in the Bill of Lading[678]…"

另在笔者的《期租合约》一书 25.6 段,也提到另一种去强制船东去签发以发货人提供的岸上货量为内容的提单的租约条款,如下:"Unless the Charterers and/or the Shippers have been proven fraudulently and/or intentionally misstating in the Bills of Lad-

---

[677] 提单的重量是由发货人检验师的数字决定。
[678] 船东如果选择去进行船舶水尺计算,他/它自己承担费用而且得出来的数字(肯定或多或少与发货人数字相异)不得在提单中提及,以免提单变得不清洁。

ing with regard to the condition and quantity/weight of the cargo, the Master shall not insist on his own observation and/or determination and/or measurement (such as draft survey). The Master shall sign Bills of Lading as presented and accept the Charterers' or Shippers' letter of undertaking to cover the discrepancies or variations."

对发货人(或收货人)而言,一般总是相信岸上数字。除了会较准确外,发货人也只能以此控制装船货量,而不是等装完了货才凭船上的水尺或空档进行计算。发货人的供货如果涉及其他人士如分卖方/政府当局等,也是以岸上数字为准。

3.2.6 船东/承运人在海牙规则下拒签岸上货量提单的理由

但船东也有它/他的考虑。在极端的例子中,如果发货人提供的岸上重量或数量根本不可能是已装船量,因为船上基本仍未半满,去签发这样内容不准确的提单是自找麻烦。可以预测:收货人(买方)以提单货量支付了货价,但结果发现严重短缺,那几乎肯定会向船东索赔,进而带来一连串的麻烦如扣船、提供诉前保全、延误船期等等。之后,估计败诉的可能性大,律师/官司费用又高,船东会去和解赔偿。再之后,船东会向发货人要求补偿,因为他提供不准确的内容(请看本章之2.1小段)。但补偿不一定会成功,有太多未知的因素例如发货人是皮包公司的中间商、诉讼管辖地不明确等。

3.2.6.1 拒签的两个合法理由

故此,船东对发货人提供的岸上数字有合理怀疑或根本无法查明时,应可以拒绝签发提单。这正是海牙规则的妥协:一方面在发货人要求下,强制船东/承运人签发有件数、数量或重量说明的提单(请看本章之1.2小段)。另一方面,在 Article 3 (3)给予承运人或船长可去拒签的理由如下:"Provided that no carrier, master or agent of the carrier shall be bound to state or show in the bill of lading any marks, number, quantity, or weight which he has reasonable ground for suspecting not accurately to represent the goods actually received, or which he has had no reasonable means of checking."

至于何谓"合理怀疑"(reasonable ground for suspecting),可足够去支持拒签提单,在本章3.2.4小段的 The "Phassa"(1990) SMA No. 2640 有涉及。合理与否要看每一宗不同事件的事实而定,加上看法会因人而异,例如对一位中国船长是否信任,特别是出庭作证,并被反盘问。故判决肯定会有不稳定之处。

而船东另一可以拒签的合法理由是他/它没有"合理方法"(reasonable means)去查明,估计这种情况不多。多数情况下船东都可通过理货,船舶水尺或空档计算等方法去查明/反证发货人提供的货量。船东自己不去安排只能怪自己,毕竟太容易让船东找个理由去拒签发提单会带来严重后果,绝非好事。但注意在 The "Herroe" and "Askoe"(1986)2 Lloyd's Rep. 281 先例中提到,如果船东安排了理货,但认为结果太不可靠,仍不必视为船东已有合理方法去查明货量。

在本章 3.2.2 与 3.2.3 小段详述的 The"Irini M"(1988)1 Lloyd's Rep. 253 与 The"Atlas"(1996)1 Lloyd's Rep. 642 先例,虽不涉及这方面争议而是针对货差纠纷,但也从中可见若是涉及船东拒绝签发岸上货量的提单而造成发货人重大损失或/与延误船期,会在事实认定后(审理后),船东败诉。

3.2.6.2 集装箱会有合法理由拒签或加否定性批注

今天集装箱运输通常是"门到门"(house-to-house 或 door-to-door)的多式联运,由发货人自己把货物堆装好在集装箱内,并去捆绑好与封好(或称铅封、密封),才把整个集装箱交付给多式联运承运人托运。对这种"shipper-stuffed"或"consignor-stuffed"的集装箱,承运人的其中一个困难是无法知悉集装箱内有什么内容的货物。会是,相关内容全要依赖发货人去提供,而船东/承运人在海上运输法/海牙规则下可以他/它没有"合理方法"去查明为由拒签有此内容的提单。

至于船东/承运人是否真正没有"合理方法"去查明也曾有过争议。例如,美国先例 Insurance Company of North America v. Dart Containerline, 629 F. Supp. 781, 1987 AMC (42) 44 (E. D. Va. 1985) 判是承运人/班轮公司有权开封查明集装箱的内容,他/它自己不去做只能怪自己,而不能以没有"合理方法"去查明为理由抗辩。

但有不少人持强烈的相反意见,而且很有说服力,如《Multimodal Transport》一书在 9.25 段说:"The carrier has no general duty of inspecting the goods inside a sealed container, in normal circumstances, he is not even allowed to do so."

也曾有过争议多是船东/承运人有否责任去在装卸港把集装箱过秤计重,间接可去查明集装箱的内容。美国上诉庭在 Bally Inc. v. Zim America (2nd Cir.) 20 April 1994; LMLN #390 判没有这个责任。另在 Daewoo v. Sealand (1999) LMLN #535,也是相同判法。

但另有过美国案例判是若提单有一条款容许承运人有"选择权过秤计重"(option to weigh the cargo),则不去选择就不再是承运人没有合理机会/方法去作出检查了:Continental Distributing Co. Inc. V. Sea-Land Commitment 1994 AMC 95 (2nd Cir) 1993), aff'g 1994 AMC 82 (SDNY 1992), amended 1994 AMC 9 (SDNY 1992)。

估计因有以上这种判例,曾见过某著名班轮公司的提单印有一标准条款如下:"The Carrier shall be entitled, but under no obligation[679], to open any Container at any time and to inspect the contents. If it thereupon appears that the contents or any part thereof cannot safely or properly be carried or carried further, either at all, or without incurring any additional expense or expense to carry or to continue the carriage or to store the same a-

---

[679] 强调船东有权开箱/开封检查,但这只是权利而并非义务。

shore or afload under cover or in the taking any measures in relation to the Container or its contents or any part thereof, the Carrier may abandon the transportation thereof and/or take any measures and/or incur any reasonable additional open, at any place, which storage shall be deemed to constitute due delivery under this Bill of Lading. The Merchant shall indemnity the Carrier against any reasonable additional expense so incurred[680]."

现实中，提单一般仍是会填上发货人提供的集装箱内的货物重量、数量或/与其他内容，因为船东不可能去坚持只签发一份完全没有货物内容的提单。加上海牙·维斯比规则下有关的承运人责任限制，也会需要有货物内容填上在提单表面。但通常，船东/承运人会对这些内容加上免责或否定性批注，如"shipper's count"（发货人理货）；"said to contain"（据说会有）；"contents of package are shipper's declaration"（是由发货人宣告）等等。有关这些批注的有效性及其他方面，本章会在§5段后详述。而只就海牙规则而言，只要认定船东/承运人对密封集装箱确实没有合理方法去查明与/或没有可怀疑之处，这类批注应是合法的。

最后在这小段，可去略微介绍 Daewoo v. Sealand 的美国上诉庭先例，该先例显示了这一点，但它涉及欺诈。作为买方的 Daewoo（美国公司）向香港一公司进口一批录像带架子。集装箱是由香港公司堆装、铅封后，并就交给买方的"无船承运人"（NVOC）运往美国。无船承运人签发了提单给香港公司（作为发货人），提单有如下批注："Shipper's load and count"与"said to weigh"。香港公司也予该提单结了汇。到了美国，Daewoo 打开集装箱发现只有水泥块。再去找香港公司，其有关人士已不知所踪。Daewoo 只好起诉无船承运人，但一审与上诉均败诉。上诉庭说：

（ⅰ）否定性批注有效。

（ⅱ）埋怨无船承运人没有在香港装港过秤计重（确实与提单宣告重量不一样）没有作用，因为尽管觉察到重量有误差也不会自动想到集装箱内是假货。

（ⅲ）无船承运人也没有这个责任。

（ⅳ）错误实属 Daewoo 自己，它：

——不应与骗子打交道。

——可授权无船承运人尽早开封检查集装箱。

——更可派人监督集装箱的堆装与铅封。

——要求银行延迟付款给香港卖方（骗子）或在安排查看集装箱后再付款。

3.2.7 发货人与承运人对货量争议的协调做法

尤其在散货运输，这方面争议经常发生，现实中会如何协调呢？一种常见的做

---

[680] 而如果真去做了，会涉及费用，而只要合理，货方要补偿给船东。

法是船东接受发货人或银行的保函,其中金额方面是岸上(填在提单上)与船上货量差额的货价。

3.2.7.1 欺诈性保函无效

一提到发货人出保函以换取船东/承运人签发他所要求的一份提单,就有人会想到这保函会在法律下无效,所以不要去接受。这方面确有英国著名先例这样判:Brown Jenkinson v. Percy Dalton (1957) 1 Lloyd's Rep. 31。

该著名先例涉及浓缩橙汁装在"破漏桶子"(old and frail containers in a leaking condition),但船东却签发清洁提单,并以发货人保函作为交换,事后法院判这份保函无效。即船东赔给收货人/提单持有人因此不正确提单内容所造成的损失后,不能以保函向发货人索取补偿。

该先例虽不是涉及货量,但大道理一样。等于船东明知只有1万吨货物装上船舶,却以发货人保函去交换签发一份2万吨货物的装船提单。

但一概而论去指是保函就无效并不正确。保函只是千万种合约中的一种。在当今的世界,每天都会有上千上万不同的保函在签发,而法律上完全有效。只有在非法的情况下,它才会无效,因为违反公共政策。而明知与事实不符却签发内容不正确的提单,正是有非法之嫌,这非法是去欺诈银行(信用证下)或买方(买卖合约下)等第三者。

这方面在笔者的《国际商务游戏规则——英国合约法》一书第七章4.3小段有详述,可节录如下:

4.3 欺诈(fraud)

这是对商业活动而言最危险也是最常见的情况,而不少欺诈,其实也是4.1小段所讲的触犯刑法。例如:

(ⅰ)买卖合约同意出假发票去骗海关或是去非法套取外汇:1小段的United City Merchants v. Royal Bank of Canada(1982) 2 Lloyd's Rep. 1;去逃避德国进口税的 Euro-Diam Ltd. v. Bathurst (1988) 1 Lloyd's Rep. 228,以及在一开始谈的先例等等。

(ⅱ)损坏了的货,或是数量不足的货,去出清洁提单来欺骗银行与收货人。常听说这种保函是非法的,因为它针对的是欺诈,所以无法去法院执行,确也是如此:Brown Jenkinson v. Percy Dalton(1957) 1 Lloyd's Rep. 31。这应是非常显浅的道理,但我自己在10多20年来对船东发出过无数警告,仍有不少人在做,而且每次在事后都无法根据保函向发货人取回损失(赔给收货人的钱)。更有一少部分船东连概念也搞不清楚,例如一概而论地说所有保函都没有用,不能要。但保函其实是一份合约,它在法律下完全可以有效,可以执行。只是非法的保函,如同非法的合约,它本身是为去欺诈,才会无效,不能执行。

我常建议船东,要非法保函倒不如要红包,红包内的钱要足够赔付将来会面对的索赔。要是将来没有索赔,船东可能赚一笔。在当时,发货人为了要清洁提单,愿意被船东敲一笔的可能性颇大,船东何苦不要红包,去要一张废纸(非法保函)呢?

要是红包不好意思要,比方是与发货人有交情,那也不必去要非法保函。何不索性不参与,随便发货人或他的代理背后去出假提单呢?这一来,至少可以不沾上非法的恶名,将来可合法去向发货人或他的代理追索赔偿。甚至还会有其他好处,比如在 UK 互保协会这一期的年报提到一个案子,是新港代理在船东毫不知情的情况下出了假提单,令船东面临收货人索赔。因为船东是无辜的,没有参与非法欺诈,UK 互保协会董事会(Board of Directors)根据"酌情条款"(Omnibus Rule)给予该船东保障与代赔付。

(iii)因为过了买卖合约的付运期(shipment date),去出倒签提单来欺诈银行与收货人。同样,这保函也是完全非法无效的:SCB v. PNSC(1995)2 Lloyd's Rep. 365。

我建议的做法与(ii)相同,唯一是红包要大多了,因为倒签提单一出事后果很严重,船东要赔整笔货款。

另外,我曾提到的 UK 互保协会一案的假提单实际是倒签提单。

(iv)我在 3.2.2 小段提到三角贸易的非法性,名义上的装、卸港实际是去欺骗出口、进口当局,虽然这是公开的秘密。这属非法在 1 段的 Regazzoni v. Sethia(1958)A. C. 301 著名先例已是明确。这在做法上常会是去转换第二套提单(switched second set of bills of lading)。

去转换第二套提单,也不一定是欺骗非法。这做法也有其他合法的作用,例如让中间商早日可在第二个信用证结汇,不必去等待发货人的一套单证。这样做对船东而言有它的危险,因为是去允许有两套正本提单在外面流通。将来中间商倒闭,船东会面对发货人(手头有一套正本提单)与收货人(手头也有一套正本提单)要货,两位手上的提单都由船东发出,没得赖账。所以,面对这危险,船东可以接受保函后才出第二套提单。这保函也合法,因本意没有去欺骗任何人,可去法院执行,变得船东要关心的只是谁是保人(一流银行自然佳)与保函文字。

但要是第二套提单是为去欺骗,则这保函又是非法而无效了,不要也罢。

如何知道转换的第二套提单是否为了欺骗呢?太容易了,只要有任何注明不符事实,一般就是有人要去欺骗。比如明明是韩国釜山装的货,第二套提单却去写装港是香港。

3.2.7.2 实例介绍

最后再举一个近期的实例,它将在即将出版的《英美证据法》一书中详论。案情涉及从中国运往波兰的一票散装货,买卖合约中约定允许有少于 10% 的杂质。承运的中国船到了波兰港后,收货人指称杂质大大超出了合约所允许的范围,并意图拒绝收货。据闻,当局也拒绝该票货物入境,称会对环境有影响。总之,买卖双方的争议不知发展如何,反正波兰收货人不久向船东提出整票货价的索赔,并扣船取得诉前保全。索赔理由是船长不应签发清洁提单,因为这过多的杂质是肉眼看得见的。对此,船东的抗辩是船长签发时曾问过发货人指定的商检,他知悉该杂质的百分比是买卖合约所允许才误以为应签发清洁提单。若事实并非如此,则是商检判断错了,也不应再指责船长了。毕竟"清洁"提单只针对表面的、合理的、无须船长对该货物具有较深的专业知识等情况下对货物状况的判断。显然,开庭审理时,船长和商检都会是主要证人,会被货方(波兰收货人)的代表律师严厉的"反盘问"(cross-examination),例如问及商检对该种货物的认识、如何判断杂质、如何知道买卖合约条款、当时检验的情况及与船长的谈话内容等。

尚未开庭而在文件披露后,装港外代给中国船东传真了一份"保函"。该"保函"是针对发货人要求船东签发清洁提单,虽然货物表面状况不妥,而后果将由发货人(也是保函的签发人)负责补偿船东。反正是这类保函的通用措辞/文字。

从该文件来看,船长或/与船东代理实属明知该票货物不妥,仍签发了清洁提单,并接受了发货人的这份"保函"。至于船长虽说是听从了商检专家的意见,以为准确无误,才配合真实情况签发了清洁提单,但完全是不足信的。因为若是如此,还要"保函"干什么?如果说船长/船东根本不知道有此"保函",则外代作为代理人来看是越权了。而发货人若是理所当然有权可获得一份清洁提单(根据中国《海商法》),又何需签发"保函"?再若是当时签发"保函"只是为了万一,则需举证,而且要有非常强的说服力的证据,例如文件证据(传真往来)会是船东通过外代要求发货人签发"保函",发货人回应说为何要签发,货物明明是表面状况符合买卖合约,商检不是已证实了吗?而船东说商检确实证实了,但事实上货物仍看得见有杂质,即使它是 10% 以下的允许范围,所以有"保函"才觉得安心,等等。

在该案件中,当然没有这些证据,也即使没有这事实发生过,仲裁庭也不会相信。这一来,船东可就麻烦了,会难去解释为何有此"保函"。船东对此解释是中国港口一贯是这样做法,不论货物如何"清洁"(表面状况良好),发货人仍一定要签发一份"保函"给船东代理人(外代),以交换清洁提单。换言之,这已成了习惯做法。说真的,多年前笔者也曾听说过,但未想到多年后这"陋习"仍在。

说到这里,笔者不禁有一丝的伤感涌上心头,感觉自己希望走的路实在是太遥远了。可以说,人的思维方式一旦形成,终身都很难改变。社会科学就是如此困难。

笔者已不知多少次大声疾呼这"保函"换取清洁提单的做法是不可取的,它不仅不妥,甚至是欺诈行为,这一点已得到全世界的共识:例如在《国际商务游戏规则——英国合约法》一书第七章之4.3小段。不仅英、美、法,欧洲大陆及第三世界也持此看法(不妨请参考汉堡规则)。故此,中国为何要去与别人不同,做一些与国际上的道德观念完全不一样的事情呢?难道说是中华民族的先贤曾告诉我们这样做吗——即出一份收据/文件(例如提单)内有不准确的事实?或是孙子或是诸葛亮有此教诲?要知道去"普及"这世界不容的做法会害死下一代的中国年轻人,令他/她们是非不分,与外国人永远没有共同语言。要知道这陋习是不会被英、美、法认为是"习惯"做法的,因为其要求之一的"合理"是无法满足的:请看第二章之2.2.2小段。

至于说出了"保函"不一定是需要或有关,货物可以是完全美好的,则无疑应签发清洁提单。笔者可以回应说:"保函"既然是不好的东西,内容是针对坏事的,为什么还要去签发呢?在笔者看来,明智的做法是真去干坏事(签发不准确的文件)也不要这份"保函",以免留下磨灭不掉的"坏"证据,更何况不是干坏事。这等于是给每个中国人,不论好人坏人,签发一份男盗女娼的证明,然后出了事再向外国人(英国仲裁员)说有此证明并不一定就是男盗女娼,这只是中国的"习惯"。

言归正传,中国船东从外代取了这份"保函"副本后,把文件传真给了中国律师,再给了英国律师。但据闻,英国律师把该"保函"披露给了仲裁庭和对方(货方/原告)。这一来,波兰货方可就凶了,马上将"索赔请求"(statement of claim)进行修改,增加了"欺诈"(deceit)的指控。长话短说,自此,中国船东变成了挨打的局面,自己的代表律师也说是难以说服仲裁庭有此"保函",其实船东/船长不知道它的存在。结果,在开庭前以投降方式的"和解",赔了一二百万美元。

据闻后来船东对英国的律师十分不满,认为不该把"保函"披露出去,导致此被动局面。英国律师回应这是他们的专业守则,不能不坦白披露。他们也确有这方面的专业守则。只听一面之辞(笔者只听了中国船东),笔者是对英国律师有以下的疑问(但并非是否定性的质疑):

(i)应在披露前通知中国船东(客户)。或是,估计中国船东难以说服允许这样做,也有"自动辞职"(resign)的选择。再说,可让中国船东在披露前争取与对方庭外和解。

(ii)笔者对外代怎么会把"保函"传真给中国船东的背景不了解。要知道文件披露的责任一直到开庭审结之时,当事人有新文件也要抖露出来的。

(iii)由于"保函"涉及犯罪/欺骗等不法行为,所以有诉讼特权(如果涉及)也会失去。但此案件是伦敦仲裁,并非是法院诉讼。笔者也不是说可以误导/蒙骗仲裁庭,法官面前要规规矩矩。但是有几点是有区别的,例如律师是"**officer of the**

Court"但并不是说他/她也是"officer of the arbitral tribunal"。当然,以此为由也是笔者所不喜欢的,因为它仍是暗示仲裁庭可以被误导/蒙骗。故更重要的区别在于仲裁一般不是自动和全面的披露,而是双方当事人去抖出自己所要依赖的文件证据,然后各自向对方再要求"特定披露"(specific discovery)。这是较为接近大陆法国家的做法,他们没有"披露"这一做法,更谈不上像 Peruvian Guano(1882)11 QBD 550 的英国法院要求的自动与全面披露。故此,除非该伦敦仲裁庭已下令要去披露这方面(包括"保函")文件,代表中国船东的英国律师要否自动抖出严重不利的文件会有商榷之处。

笔者强调不对此案件下任何结论,只想以此例子来企望中国的读者能以此引以为戒。若此案涉及法院诉讼而非伦敦仲裁,中国船东更是难以责怪他的英国律师了。该案例的第一个教训是为何产生/制造这份严重不利的"坏"文件证据:"保函"? 一旦制造了再去千方百计设法隐瞒又何苦呢? 而且,不论如何得千方百计,总会有百密一疏的危险被对方(波兰货方)调查出来的,例如从发货方/卖方的渠道获得。固然,"保函"会来自发货人,是他所制造的。但熟悉这"陋习"的中国船东至少可以通知外代绝不能去习惯性地在它背后接受"保函"吧!

3.2.7.3 非欺诈性保函有效

但常见的岸上货量与船上货量之争,并不涉及欺诈。像本章 3.2.2 小段介绍的 The"Irini M"(1988)1 Lloyd's Rep. 253,总的货量是 5 万吨原油,但岸上与船上相差约 1000 立方米。有这误差并不奇怪,因为两个数字是依据完全不同的测量/计算方法,或不同的人理货。

可以说,提单任填上两个数字的其中一个都不会是欺诈、是所谓的"假"提单。"假"提单能称为"假",表示内容与真相/事实相违。但真相不明,两个数字均有它们依赖的合理依据,又何来真假之争呢?

再者,即使在民事诉讼,去指控欺诈(进而指保函无效)也会有较重的举证责任。

所以,去签发一份以岸上重量/数量为据的提单,并以此交换发货人(或他的银行,特别在对发货人经济背景没有信心的情况下)的保函,不失是一个合理的解决办法。看来,汉堡规则也在鼓励这种做法,在 Article 17(3)说:"Such letter of guarantee or agreement is valid as against the shipper unless the carrier...by omitting the reservation referred to in para. 2 of this Article, intends to defraud a third party, including a consignee, who acts in reliance on the description of the goods in the bill of lading. In the latter case, if the reservation omitted relates to particulars furnished by the shipper for insertion in the bill of lading, the carrier has no right of indemnity from the shipper pursuant to para. 1 of this Article."

以上条款显示,发货人的保函起点是有效的,只除非是为了想去欺诈第三者,如收货人。而且,有看法是汉堡规则"想去欺诈第三者"(intends to defraud a third party)的除外情况比一般法律对"欺诈"(tort of deceit)事实的认定要求更严格,所以不易成立进而可去导致保函无效。R. J. L. Thomas 御用大律师在 1978 年一个有关汉堡规则的会议上曾发言说:"In the usual case where the carrier agrees not to clause the Bill of Lading, he will be aware (1) that the condition of the goods is other than as described in the Bill of Lading and (2) that the false description in the Bill of Lading may be relied on by the indorsee, consignee or some other party such as a bank; thus when consignee, indorsee or other third party suffers some loss as a result of the false description, all the necessary elements of the tort of deceit in English law are present. However, in my submission, something more than this is required before "an intent to defraud" on the part of the carrier is established; to escape liability to the carrier, the shipper will probably have to prove that it was a conscious aim or purpose of the carrier to defraud the consignee, indorsee or other third party or that the carrier acted dishonestly. If this is so then in all but the exceptional case, indemnities given by shippers will be valid and the carrier will be able to enforce them. Thus Brown Jenkinson v. Percy Dalton (1957) 1 Lloyd's Rep. 31 will in effect be overruled."

以上说法是指汉堡规则下去指控承运人"想去欺诈第三者"并不容易,因为这涉及要指控承运人在接受保函当时是有一个主观意图去欺诈收货人等第三者。而这种指控一向不容易,因为一个人的主观意图只有自己知悉。只要他(承运人)一口咬死他当时以为(或说是发货人向他表示)这提单不会去流通/转让(如 Strohmeyer & Arpe Co. v. American Line SS Corp., 97 F. 2d 360, 1938 AMC 875(2nd Cir. 1938)案例),谁有资格去反证他当时不是这样想呢?加上作出这指控的发货人自己也不是好人,不会有法官/仲裁员的同情。他与承运人一起签发假提单,而且发起人总是他,但事后却在保函上扯皮。

换言之,若汉堡规则是世界通用(可惜不是),发货人的保函一般会被尊重,被判有效,除非是极端的案子,欺诈意图明显得不能再明显。至于分水线在哪里,可以说往往是看程度方面或提单最后填上任何货量是否有一些依据(即使是很弱的依据)等事实。

3.3 内容之三:货物表面状况

货物表面状况是不必由发货人提供的提单内容,它是由承运人/船长根据自己看得见的事实准确反映/表述在提单表面上的。一般不去另加批注,已表示对货物表面状况满意,因为一般提单格式都印上"Shipped in apparent good order and condition"字样,这通称为"清洁提单"(clean bill of lading)。而去加上批注针对货物表面状况不妥,这提单通称为"不清洁提单"(dirty 或 foul bill of lading)。

货物表面状况不妥,表示外表有瑕疵,例如:破烂、陈旧、杂质、发霉、锈渍、弯曲及破包等。"表面状况"也不光是针对肉眼看,如果其他方面感觉到不妥,也一样有责任加上批注以保障无辜的提单持有人。例如,货物是食品但发出臭味,或纸箱内似是空的。又或是,估计货物包装或性质(易腐货物)根本无法抵受这个航次完好抵达卸港:Dent v. Glen Line (1940) 45 Com. Cas. 244。

这种情况经常发生,例子多不胜数,只随意举一些来说明问题:

——包装食糖有许多破包,在大副收据注明"Many bags stained, torn and re-sewn",但此批注没有加在提单: Canada & Dominion Sugar v. Canadian National (1946) 80 Lloyd's Rep. 13。

——在本章 3.2.7.1 小段提到的浓缩橙汁装在破漏桶子的 Brown Jenkinson v. Percy Dalton (1957) 1 Lloyd's Rep. 31。

——椰子满布小虫的 M. S. Cowen Co. v. American President Lines 167 F. Supp. 838 at p. 840, 1959 AMC 2525 (N. D. Cal. 1958)。

——袋包不固(bags frail)的 Hellenic Lines v. Louis Dreyfus Corp. 372 F. 2d 753, 1967 AMR 213 (2 Cir. 1967)。

——木薯片(tapioca)在大副收据注明"不干"(not quite dry)的 The "Dona Mari" (1973) 2 Lloyd's Rep. 366。

——钢材表面生锈的 Tokio Marine & Fire Insurance Co. v. Retla SS Co. (1970) 2 Lloyd's Rep. 91;The "Arcadio Forest" (1986) ETL 86 (SDNY 1985)。

——笔者《期租合约》一书 2.5.5 段提到的散装化肥混有废纸:The "Hans Leonhardt" (1991) SMA #2820。

——同一处提到的散粮中有虫:The "Exi" (1990) SMA #2709。

3.3.1 以什么时候的表面状况为准

货物表面状况是针对装上船的一刻。海牙规则的 Article 3(3) 对此也说得清楚:

"After receiving the goods into his charge the carrier or the master or agent of the carrier shall, on demand of the shipper, issue to the shipper a bill of lading showing...

(c) The apparent order and condition of the goods."

这在 The "Galatia" (1980) 1 Lloyd's Rep. 453 有明确陈述。该案例中,在印度的 Kandla 装港作业期间,发生了火灾。这导致已装上船的一部分货物(食糖)受损并要卸回岸上处理掉。这一来,在全部货物装毕后,船长签发了两张提单,该买卖允许

"分开付运"(partial shipment)。一张是火灾后装上船的货物，这些全部没有问题，是清洁提单。CFR 买方也接受了这一份"交单"(tender)，虽然它不是买卖合约的总货量。但另一张针对火灾前装的损坏货物，船长加了批注说："Cargo covered by this Bill of Lading has been discharged Kandla view damaged by fire and/or water used to extinguish fire for which General Average declared."

这一来，买方拒绝这份提单，指是不清洁提单。

上诉庭判这是一份清洁提单，而"清洁"是指货物付运时（装上船的一刻），没有任何事实可去否定货物的表面状况良好：a clean bill of lading is one in which there is nothing to qualify the admission that the goods were in apparent good order and condition at the time of shipment.

至于装上船后发生的货损货差，不管时间上是一个小时后，一天后或一个月后，风险已转移给买方，也只能由买方去向船东或保险公司追偿了。至于像 The "Galatia"那样，船东对火灾可免责，买方又忘了及时投保，那买方可就自己倒霉了。

看来，货物装上船后不久已受到损坏，即使当时仍在装货作业中，仍不影响清洁提单的签发。笔者记得曾处理过一宗案件，涉及要在天安门铺的电缆，装港是日本大阪。装了十几大捆后，突有巨风袭港，船舶被迫紧急离港去避风。因为没有捆绑好，这过程中十几大捆的电缆严重受损。但巨风过后，船舶重靠大阪码头，装下其余的十几大捆电缆（总共 30 捆），并签发了包括所有电缆的已装船清洁提单。可说，中国收货人惨了，因为保险即使赔偿，也只限于合理修理费用，不理会延误。这一来，不说别的，光是延误天安门在赶时间的工程已是大问题了。但试想日本的卖方没有保证安全运送电缆，所以运输风险却是在中国买方。这一来，只要过了风险的分水线，已归中国买方，又何须再去斤斤计较何时何地发生事故。

但仍有疑问是：如果货物在吊上船舶的过程中受到损坏，好像 Pvrene Company Ltd. v. Scindia Steam Navigation Company Ltd (1954) 1 Lloyd's Rep. 321 一案，又应否去签发清洁提单？该案例中，船东安排的装卸工因为疏忽导致船吊所吊起的一架灭火车（货物）掉下码头严重损坏。疑问是，这种情况下应否签发清洁提单？如果答案是"不"，则还要问问灭火车如果掉在船上甲板而损坏会否有分别，因为当时已越过了船舷？再或是，灭火车必须从吊杆脱下，安全着"陆"（船舱或甲板上），才算收了货物，而当时表面状况良好，才能签发清洁提单？

Pvrene 先例并没有针对这一方面，它是针对海牙规则是否适用，船东因此可去限制赔偿责任。该案中根本没有对损坏的灭火车签发提单，所以没有关于清洁提单之争。该案中提单预早备妥，但在一架灭火车损坏后，船东便把其中一架灭火车从提单上删去。发货人（卖方）也收回了损坏的灭火车进行修理，毕竟在买卖合约下，可以同意事故发生时货物风险仍属卖方。

但照说这一切都不应影响发货人与船东的关系,即发货人是否有权要求一份提单(如果不肯收回损坏了的灭火车),而且是一份清洁提单?

在 Pvrene 先例中,Devlin 大法官拒绝将货物是否过船栏/船舷作为风险的分水线,认为船舷的概念已过时。他说了以下的话:"But the division of loading into two parts is suited to more antiquated methods of loading than are now generally adopted and the ship's rail has lost much of its nineteenth century significance. Only the most enthusiastic lawyer could watch with satisfaction the spectacie of liabilities shifting uneasily as the cargo sways at the end of a derrick across a notional perpendicular projecting from the ship's rail."

这样看来,如果可去签发清洁提单,货物掉在码头还是船上受损应没有分别。至于发生损坏时货物是仍在吊杆上还是"刚刚"着"陆",亦看不出有区分的需要或可作为分水线的依据。这样看来,笔者虽不知有否直接先例,但考虑到 Pyrene 先例的情况,估计在发货人要求下,船东/承运人仍要签发清洁提单。

3.3.2 集装箱的表面状况

这方面问题与本章 3.2.6.2 小段所讲的大同小异。如果光是去看一个集装箱的表面状况,实在看不出内中货物有什么不妥之处。集装箱表面已看到破旧漏水的事件不是没听说过,但这毕竟少之又少。也会有特殊情况可去指船东不应签发清洁装船提单,如在 *Multimodal Transport* 一书第 355 页提到的一宗案例是冻肉装在两个由发货人提供的冷藏集装箱内从法国马赛运去加蓬。在装上船前两天,集装箱已交到了承运人手中,并且发货人要求为集装箱提供电力并在所有时间保持 -18℃的低温。法院认定发货人交给承运人之时,这两个集装箱都在 -18℃,因为后来在卸港交货,其中一个完好,温度在 -18℃。只有另一个集装箱出了毛病,导致冻肉解冻而损坏。该出事集装箱估计在待装上船的 2 天,码头没有提供电力以保持 -18℃的低温,因为一般的"电源塞子"(plug)不适用(该集装箱不是一般设计)。它装上船也要另用"接合器"(adaptor)才能提供电源。而在装上船舱时,已有记录是温度高达 9℃。要知道,这已令冻肉毁坏而且不可能再重新急冻,降回 -18℃。法院判船东在这事实下仍去签发清洁提单,不把这不妥之处批注在提单上,是不对的做法。

但这种特殊情况也不多,变得集装箱运输中,由于承运人的确无法看得见一个密封/铅封的集装箱内部,导致承运人签发的清洁提单实际上价值很低。不论船东/承运人是否在提单加上免责或否定性批注如"said to contain","container sealed by shipper"等等,事实是对集装箱表面状况的描述没有代表性,没有价值。

这方面可去节录澳大利亚的案例 The "TNT Express" (1992) 2 Lloyd's Rep. 636,

Carruthers 大法官说:"It is, in my view, apparent from the wording of the receipt clause and the notation inserted in the box beneath that clause that the defendant(承运人) is merely acknowledging the receipt of the 20' container in apparent good order and condition. The acknowledgment could not possibly extend to the apparent good order and condition of the contents of the sealed container which had been consolidated by the shipper. A Canadian case to the same effect is Lufty Ltd. v. Canadian Pacific Railway Co. (The "Alex")(1974) 1 Lloyd's Rep. 106. There are numerous cases in the United States to the same effect. See e. g. Red Arrow Freight Lines, Inc. v. Roy G. Howe 480 S. W. 2d 281."

这显然对收货人/提单持有人不利,因为他无法像散装货那样去依赖一份清洁提单,正如在 Blue Bird Food Products Co. v. Baltimore & Ohio Railway Co., 492 F. 2d (1329)1332 (3 Cir.1974) 的美国案例说:"When merchandise is delivered to a carrier in a sealed trailer, it is not 'open and visible'. In the circumstances the consignee who sues the carrier for damages to the goods cannot establish a *prima facie* case by means of the 'apparent good order' representation in the bill of lading."

这表示拆箱时发觉有货损,想指称这是在船东/承运人负责期间发生,就要去:

(i)检验、调查,以"事后诸葛亮"的方式与福尔摩斯的推理与逻辑本领去证明/说明损坏不太可能发生在装货前。

(ii)取得发货人合作,提供证明集装箱堆装时货物状况良好的证据。

对以上的(ii),一个美国案例曾说发货人的举证责任颇重:"The shipper must prove by a preponderance of the credible evidence that the goods were delivered to the vessel in good order and condition."——Caemint Food, Inc. v. Lloyd Brasileiro, 1981 AMC(1801)1812, 647 F. 2d(347)354 (2 Cir. 1981)。

总结以上所说,笔者至少得出以下观点:

其一,涉及集装箱运输,买方更应与有信誉、可依赖的卖方打交道,因为单凭清洁提单保障不了。

其二,与集装箱运输有关的贸易/海运在今天很少涉及运输中进行买卖并转让/背书提单,难怪常以海运单替代提单。否则问题更大,因为光以单证买卖但清洁提单上对货物表面状况的表述毫无价值,那么买方难以会有信心。这不像清洁提单上说明是20万吨沙特阿拉伯的原油,或2万吨美国玉米,错不了去那里,可以凭一套单证频频在海运中以 CIF 转手/转卖。

本小段结束前,可再简单介绍一下较早提及的 The "TNT Express" 先例,以说明对密封集装箱开封时发觉货损的处理。该案涉及集装箱由印尼发货人堆装并铅封/密封后交付给承运人。集装箱是运去悉尼,但经新加坡中转。到了悉尼开封,发觉货物遭水湿全损。同时检查集装箱,发觉它底部有洞漏水,箱门的密封(seals on the doors)也漏水,箱子陈旧,不再适用。

在双方提供证据后,Carruthers 大法官认定了以下事实:

(a)在印尼雅加达堆装货物进集装箱时,不可能有水湿,也没有证据显示当时会遭受水湿(例如下雨,在露天作业等)。所以,货物是表面状况良好:"On the evidence the goods were in apparent good order and condition when they were loaded into the container"。

(b)在堆装集装箱(承运人提供箱子)时,发货人无法合理察觉该箱漏水有洞等缺陷。因为提单有一条款说明即使承运人提供的集装箱不妥,但若发货人在堆装前可合理察觉却不作声,不另去换一个好的集装箱,则有关损失承运人不负责。

(c)在新加坡中转时,集装箱放置在露天码头多天,而当时发生多次大雨,估计损坏/水湿是在当时造成的。

所以,虽然集装箱的清洁提单不代表什么,但该案中根据发货人提供的其他证据说明货物交付给承运人之时是"清洁"的。而损坏发生在承运人负责的环节中,又没有相关的免责,所以承运人要作出赔偿。

3.3.3 表面状况只需合理判断

对货物表面状况是否良好,应否签发清洁提单,法律只要求一个合理判断。例如,并不需要达到专家程度的判断,这也是现实,毕竟世界上有不少装港,要找专家也不容易。所以不能上纲上线去定下办不到的准则/法律。

这方面在 The "TNT Express" (1992) 2 Lloyd's Rep. 636 先例提到过,Carruthers 大法官在解释何谓合理检查时说:

"I think that the 'reasonable inspection'…contemplates inspection by an unskilled person. An analogous situation is, to my mind, the inspection of breakbulk cargo by the master or agent of the carrier for the purpose of issuing a bill of lading showing the apparent good order and condition of the goods in Compania Naviera Vasconzala v. Churchill & Sim (1906) 1 K. B. 237 at p. 245, Mr. Justice Channell said:

I think that 'condition' refers to external and apparent condition, and 'quality' to something which is usually not apparent, at all events to an unskilled person'."

在 William Tetley 教授的 *Marine Cargo Claims* 一书第 3 版 267 页,也有同样说法:

"…it is clear that the carrier must inspect the goods upon receiving them[681]. The in-

---

[681] 承运人接受货物时必须作出检查。

spection, nevertheless, of the carrier, master or agent is only a reasonable inspection [682]. The master need not be an expert nor need he employ experts [683]. On the other hand, the carrier cannot contradict the clean bill of lading which he gave by relying on the laxity with which the cargo was examined on the ship's behalf [684]."

以上提到的船长不必去聘请专家协助,如果他真的请了专家,若该专家犯了错,而这"错"原本属船长/承运人自己无法合理地检查出来、无须负责的。现在的问题是,请了专家,额外得小心,做对了大家都好,做错了也怪不得承运人,因为他/它本来不必这样做。在The"Hoyanger"(1979) 2 Lloyd's Rep. 79,涉及苹果因无法承受长达45天的航程,在抵达卸货港时过熟。而其在装货时,表面看不出不能承受45天的航程,所以无法让船长/承运人承担责任。但船长/承运人在装港请了专家(名Agrotec),是专家犯了错误,以短航程的"阿根廷标准"为准则。加拿大法院认为船长/承运人没有法定的或合约的责任去请一位专家,故船长/承运人自己无法合理检查出来的原因,属苹果的内在缺陷。Addy大法官说:"…the poor condition of the apples discovered on discharge was caused by their overripeness previous to loading which rendered them unfit to withstand the rigours of a 45 day voyage and that such over-ripeness would not have been evident to the ordinary observer without particular expertise in the physiological condition of the fruit; this constituted an inherent defect, quality or vice within the meaning of article IV 2(m) of the Hague Rules;

it was obvious that neither the defendants(承运人) who issued clean bills of lading, nor Agrotec(专家) who had been engaged to carry out the inspections actually knew or suspected that the cargo was unfit because Agrotec erroneously applied the Argentine standards; the carriers(被告) had not contented themselves with an ordinary inspection and it would be both improper and without legal justification to fix liability on a carrier based on lack of knowledge or expertise of an expert which the carrier was not by law nor by duty to the consignee(原告/收货人) bound to engage."

就以上多提两点如下:

(ⅰ)虽然船长不必雇用专家,但遇上疑问或困难,一般建议仍是找有关货物的专家协助。而特别困难的货物如钢材(除了制成品如steel slab),一般船东互保协会更是要求有专家去协助船长/大副对装船钢材的表面状况作出合理判断后准确地在提单上批注。因为这是船东互保协会要求,所以有关专家费用也不当做是船

---

[682] 这要求只是一个合理检查。
[683] 船长自己不必是专家,也不必去雇用专家协助。
[684] 但如疏懒检查,这不能作为借口去将来否定一份清洁提单。

东营运的一般支出,而是由船东互保协会去承担。

(ⅱ)虽然法律不要求船长是专家(因为他不可能充分了解每一航次都可能不同的货物),但对其有相当高的合理要求,毕竟去保障一份清洁提单的可信性,可靠性仍是至高无上的大原则。像在 The "Athanasia Comminos"(1990)1 Lloyd's Rep. 277 一案曾有船东争辩今天船员水平下降,要求不应订得太高,说:"…the carriage of coal may have become…a "lost art",amongst the general run of seamen."

但 Mustill 大法官拒绝接受这个争辩。

3.3.4 货物表面状况的表述是否足够保护买方

显然,只去针对货物表面状况的清洁提单看来仍有不足保障买方/提单持有人之处。当然,这也是现实,没有办法。若硬是要船东/承运人对看不见、检查不到的货物"内部"也作出"盲目"的保证,他/它们肯定不干,不会妥协,这样恐怕历史上也不会达成海牙规则。

当然,以表面状况去判断货物好坏的准确程度,也各不相同。已经说过,对不少散装货,清洁提单代表好货应是错不了。但针对像集装箱,作为另一极端,清洁提单又代表不了什么。

对清洁提单代表不了什么的买卖,精明的买方可要小心了。正如在本章 3.3.2 小段已提到,他要与有信用的卖方打交道。另外,可考虑在买卖合约/信用证中说明在装货或堆装集装箱前要由独立与著名的检验机构(在香港称之为公证行的公司)检查并出具证书证明有关货物堆装妥善而且当时表面状况良好。这种做法请参阅笔者《国际货物买卖》一书第四章 4.2 小段。

去举出承运人不必对表面状况看不出不妥的货物负责的例子,可以援引 William Tetley 教授在 Marine Cargo Claim 一书第 278 页的两宗案例。第一宗是 The "Carso"(1931)41 Lloyd's Rep. 33,涉及三批损坏的芝士(货物),但只有其中一批的损坏是在签发清洁提单时可从外观看见。美国上诉庭判承运人只对这一批负责。另一宗是 M. S. Cowan Co. v. American President Lines 167 F. Supp. 838 at F. 840,1959 AMC 2525 at P. 2528(N. D. Cal. 1958),因无法证明装货时货物(椰子)已受小虫侵袭而且是肉眼可见,因而判索赔失败。

3.3.5 对货物表面状况作出批注必须准确且有必要

这方面的轻重掌握并不容易,常会有批注是多余/不必要的,或是对船东更不利(但这是他/它自己加的批注,等于自投罗网),又或是不准确。

3.3.5.1 不必要的批注

一个常见的批注是"Quality Unknown"(质量不知道),这实在是不必要/多余的。绝大多数货物的质量(如钢材,化肥等)都不是船长可用肉眼判断出来的,所以本来在清洁提单的法律地位下,船东也不会对货物质量保证什么。

另一例子会是"Goods uncovered on the open quay"(货物装船前摆放在露天码头,没有遮掩)。但这又代表什么呢?批注又不是去讲装货时的表面状况。加了这批注徒然令人不安,因为引起了疑点,但又不说清楚是怎么一回事。

像本章 3.3.1 小段提及的 The "Galatia" (1980) 1 Lloyd's Rep. 453 先例,看来,该提单上的批注也是没有必要,加上了反而引起一场昂贵的诉讼。

另举一例是 The "Garbis" (1982) 2 Lloyd's Rep. 283,它涉及租约内有一条款说:"Charterers agree that some colour drop in the clean Naptha parcel is acceptable and Charterers also agree that the clean Naptha parcel will be loaded into the two tar epoxy painted holds."(大致是讲承租人可接受石脑油的货物受一定程度的变色仍属清洁)。

在签发提单时,船东/船长坚持把租约这一"不正常"条款加在提单上。而承租人坚持一定要签发清洁提单,因加上批注会造成结汇困难。结果双方僵持导致船舶延误。后来在这一点(双方还有其他争议)上,Goff 大法官判承租人胜诉,因为已有一条广泛的合并条款把租约所有有关航次的条款并入提单,故另加批注没有必要。Goff 大法官说:"…the words of incorporation were in very wide terms…therefore if a receiver of goods accepted a bill of lading in this form without ascertaining the term of the charter, he had to accept that his contract with the owner for the carriage of the goods contained or evidenced by the bill of lading was subject to the charter-party terms relevant to loading, carriage and discharge of the goods even though they might be unusual terms and might limit the liability of the owners."

3.3.5.2 对船东自己不利的批注

照说,世界上每个人都不会去做对自己不利的事。但现实中这种情况却多的是,可以说每天都会看到有人自掘坟墓,劝也没法劝。在笔者看来,对这种现象的解释应是十分简单:这往往会是不懂或/与受自己知识所限的必然后果。

船东会在提单上加上对自己不利批注的例子可举"国际船东会"(International Chamber of Shipping)曾针对钢材列出的 37 条常见批注之一的 "Shipment during rain"(下雨时装货)。意思一样但措辞上稍有改动也可以是 "Cargo loaded during rain"。

船东要知道,在海牙规则下,是他/它有责任去"妥善"与"谨慎"装货(properly and carefully load)。若在装货作业中下雨,并且会影响货物,船东应中止装货并关上舱盖。若是为此事与承租人的装卸工有争议,也不必把此事实自动抖出来,在提单批注。只去与承租人交涉,留下文书抗议,不是更好吗?

另一也是对船东自己不利的批注的例子是批注"Damaged by stevedores"(被装卸工弄坏)。即使租约讲明装卸工疏忽是承租人的责任,而且是不必船东承担装卸费用的"free in,stow"条款,又何必把租约的关系扯到提单上去呢?要知道,大多数提单会是约束船东的提单(见本书第三章),将来面对提单下的索赔,装卸工的疏忽仍是作为承运人的船东的责任,再将来另找承租人追偿/补偿并不关收货人/提单持有人的事。所以,船东何必去"自证其罪",自动加上不利的批注呢?毕竟,装卸工在装货堆货时损坏货物,并不影响船东业已应去签发清洁提单:请看本章之 3.3.1 小段。

3.3.5.3 必须准确地批注

这一点理所当然:如果只有两包破包,船东/承运人不应去批注有 200 包破包,毕竟要求是要完全符合事实。而且要考虑到,发货人对付不清洁提单的一个正当解决途径是要求收货人(买方)放弃这不符点,接受这套提单。所以准确的批注,既保障船东/承运人,又没有去夸大,才不会无谓地再增加发货人的困难。

对某些货物准确地批注并不容易,以钢材为例,可节录 1964 年国际船东互保协会曾发表的一份通告如下:

"With reference to our circular dated 22nd October, 1963, relating to Letters of Indemnity, experience has since shown that where signs of rust on steel shipments are apparent at the time of shipment. Mates' receipts and Bills of Lading need not necessarily in all cases be claused with the single word "rusty" as stated in sub-paragraph (c) of that circular. Some qualification to the word "rusty" may be justifiable in certain circumstances.

In appropriate cases, therefore, it is permissible for any of the following clauses to be used when describing steel shipments which show signs of rust or a similar condition on shipment:—

Partly rust stained.	Rust and oil spotted.
Rust stained.	Wet before shipment.
Rust spots apparent.	Wet steel tubes.
Some rust spots apparent.	Wet bars.
Rust spots apparent on top sheets.	Rust on metal envelopes.
Some rust spots apparent on top sheets.	Covered with snow.
Top sheets rusty.	Pitted.
Some top sheets rusty.	Rusty.
Rusty edges.	Rust with pitting.
Some rusty edges.	Goods in rusty condition.

Rusty ends.	Edges bent and rusty.
Some rusty ends.	Partly rusty.
Rust spotted.	

When packed sheet iron is shipped the following two clauses may be used:—

Covers rusty/wet.

Packing rusty/wet.

It must be emphasized that the clause which is used must accurately describe the apparent condition of the steel shipment and must also come within the clauses as set out above.

Apart from sub-paragraph (c) of our circular of 22nd October, 1963, which is accordingly hereby modified by this circular, the remainder of that circular, in particular sub-paragraphs (a) and (b), remains unchanged.

In no case should any reference be made to the degree of rust such as "atmospherically" or "superficially"

Yours faithfully,

The Britannia Steam Ship Insurance Association Limited,

Tindall Riley & Co., Managers.

The London Steam-Ship Owners' Mutual Insurance Association Limited,

A. Bilbrough & Co., Ltd., Managers.

The Steamship Mutual Underwriting Association, Ltd.,

Alfred Stocken & Co., Ltd., Managers.

The Standard Steamship Owners' Protection & Indemnity Association Ltd.,

Charles Taylor & Co., Managers.

Sunderland Steamship Protecting & Indemnity Association,

John Rutherford & Son, Secretaries.

Newcastle Protection & Indemnity Association,

Martin Fryer, Manager.

The North of England Protecting & Indemnity Association Ltd.,

W. Ferguson, General Manager.

United Kingdom Mutual Steam Ship Assurance Association Limited,

Thos. R. Miller & Son, Managers.

The West of England Steam Ship Owners' Protection & Indemnity association, Ltd.,

R. S. Fort, Manager.

3.3.6 发货人与承运人对清洁提单争议的折中做法

3.3.6.1 保函

这方面与本章3.2.7小段所讲的完全一样。即是,欺诈性的保函无效,非欺诈性的保函有效。固然,有许多为交换清洁提单而签发的发货人保函,都有欺诈味道。而且船东在事后要求补偿,也遇过不少赖皮的发货人以保函非法为由而拒绝补偿。所以,船东不要轻信发货人。

但去冒险的船东仍有不少,估计会是在一些货物表面状况虽然有不妥,有瑕疵,但并不严重,损坏也不会在航次加重的情况,船东为了帮助发货人,令后者不必去哀求买方接受不清洁提单而冒上被敲一笔钱的危险,在估计后果不会严重的情况下,答应签发清洁提单。

当然,非欺诈性的保函也有,在3.3.5.1小段提到的 The "Garbis" (1982) 2 Lloyd's Rep. 283,就涉及发货人/承租人以保函交换清洁提单,以打破僵局,好让船舶开航。

毕竟,现实中有不少"边缘案子"(borderline case),真相难分(或根本没有真相),去僵持只会徒然扩大损失,小事变大,故不妨多考虑灵活地以非欺诈性保函来折中[685]。当然,有用的保函,除了非欺诈性还有其他多方面要注意,如措辞、谁是保人等,这些都早已在本书第二章5.2.3小段详述。出了这种争议(或任何争议),别太指望打官司会有满意或正确的结果。这太天真,不大会成事。极为劳民伤财的诉讼加上很可能错判的案子笔者见过不知有多少。在本章3.2.4小段已介绍过 The "Phassa" (1990) SMA #2640,另可介绍《期租合约》一书25.5段也提到的 The "Exi" (1990) SMA #2709——纽约仲裁。案中涉及加拿大装散粮,船长看见货中有虫,于是拒绝签清洁提单。租方并不否认有虫,但提出证明说虫并非是混在货物中装上船的,而是装货时在附近草原被吸引而飞上船来的,这已不应影响清洁提单的签发:请看本章之3.3.1小段。而且,该虫对散粮没有影响,不会污染散粮。而事实上,该散粮在卸港没有被收货人拒收或提出索赔。但仲裁员判船东胜诉,认为船东有权拒签清洁提单,不管这虫是否会对散粮有害。所以,承租人(发货人)要承担所有损失,包括在交涉时的船期损失。

笔者还可多举一例以说明这方面的灵活性。曾有一航次货物是木薯片(tapio-

---

[685] 这只是笔者个人的感受,并非其他权威的说法,如 *Scrutton on Charter-Parties* 一书第19版之第112页,注脚58 是说"The practice, however usual, of employing an indemnity as a means of settling an argument between the shipper and the master is not, it is thought, one which the court would encourage." 估计这说法或看法主要是怕乱来,导致不正确的清洁提单满天飞,而船长都去推卸责任说是"边缘案子",不是欺诈。

ca)，自中国一港口出口去意大利，以 CIF 价格成交。中方通过香港公司出面租了一外轮。在木薯片装毕后，双方对应否签发清洁提单有争议，因为货从表面上看似有一点发霉。中方发货人找了商检局两次上船检查，结果都说货物表面状况良好，应签发清洁提单，并出了报告。外轮船东有互保协会撑腰，也找了一家国际货检/公证行的公司作出检查，但出了与商检局不一致的报告。

这一来，双方僵持不下，船也开航不了，因为中方用行政手段不让船开，而双方损失也就不断扩大。

笔者曾在早期试图大事化小，如建议中方劝外轮接受保函，因为这发霉（如果真有）是双方货检都认为是不严重的。但外轮船东与互保协会坚持这保函是欺诈性的（请看 3.2.7.1 小段），绝不接受。用各种说法（包括汉堡规则对保函有效性的说法），都无法说服船东与互保协会。只好退而建议发货人让船开（当时仍延误不久），别使用行政手段。然后背后把船长签发的有批注提单放置一旁，另去签发一套清洁提单结汇。笔者估计商检局检验正确的可能性极大，所以木薯片最终不会有事。若真是如此，中方将来可以嘲笑外轮船东小题大做，庸人自扰。而即使万一商检局检验不完全正确，果真有货损索赔，但因为不会严重，所以顶多几万元可以解决（补偿船东）。而这套清洁提单由承租人签发，有船东的表面授权（实质授权确是没有），所以在意大利卸港面对收货人/提单持有人，船东也不可以拒绝交出货物。而外轮船东顶多指责承租人/发货人越权在背后签发提单。但即使这是事实，也只涉及民事，又不涉及刑事，又何必担心。

但记得发货人拒绝接受笔者的建议，说这是签发"假"提单，这勾当他/它不干。事隔多年，笔者还记得当时自己很不高兴，申辩绝不会去建议任何人签发假提单、假文件。而何谓真假，应是很容易区分，明知与真相/事实不符的即是假的了。但在该事件中，木薯片是否不妥可说是真相未明，又何来假提单之说。若中方坚持商检局检验正确，笔者也相信如此，更应该前后一贯地坚持一份清洁的提单才是正确的提单。

据知该事件后来越闹越大，笔者并没有再参与，但听闻损失上几百万美元，外轮被扣留几个月，船上木薯片全损后卸下销毁，意大利买方好像借此机会在买卖合约中脱身，等等。

3.3.6.2 租约条款

涉及租约提单，会有另一折中或对付清洁提单的做法，就是一早在租约的条款中有所针对。这方面已在笔者《期租合约》一书的 25.6 段有详述，可节录如下：

25.6 如何加重船东签发提单的责任

考虑到这问题的严重性，笔者在想如果条款格式可以相异（在 25.2 段谈到),可以在一定程度上加重船东在提单上的责任,不得单单因为提单有比租约更苛刻的条款而拒绝签发,反正事后船东可向租方追讨补偿。这在 NYPE'46 默示补偿(The "Nanfri" (1979) 1 Lloyd's Rep. 201)已是在 NYPE'93 明示了,它是在 30(b)的条款,订明如下:

"All bills of lading or waybills shall be without prejudice to his Charter Party and the Charterers shall indemnify the Owners against all consequences or liabilities which may arise from any inconsistency between this Charter Party and any bills of lading or waybills signed by the Charterers or by the Master at their request."

这一来,针对货物清洁与否的争议,只要不是欺诈性(fraudulent),而纯是出于双方诚实与善意的不同意见,为何船东可以去拒绝签发清洁提单,拒绝去接受只是"可能"会(而更大可能是不会)带来的额外责任(如货损或短缺)呢?毕竟真有货损货差发生船东可向租方追讨补偿,正如提单条款或格式与租约不一致一样。

看来,对一些租方,特别是 CIF 或 CFR 卖方来说,考虑到某些货物的品种会带来争议,他们真应该去考虑是否须在租约中(即是使用 NYPE'93 格式)加一些条款来针对,例如要船东接受类似汉堡规则的 Art. 17(3)。这条款的内容可以是:

"Unless the Charterers and/or the Shippers have been proven fraudulently and/or intentionally misstating in the Bill of Lading with regard to the condition and quantity/weight of the cargo, the Master shall not insist on his own observation and/or determination and/or measurement(such as draft survey). The Master shall sign Bills of lading as presented and accept the Charterers' or Shippers' letter of undertaking to cover the discrepancies or variations."

我要再强调的是:我这看法纯是针对非欺诈性的,而且是善意与诚实的争执。这往往是双方均不能确定真相或是没有真相的边缘案子(borderline case)。

这种情况下,船东向租方索偿并不会有问题。而且早有案例(The "Lady Brenda" (1931) 41 Lloyd's Rep. 75)明确,它也是提单数量不准,与船上水尺计算不符,再在卸港量重得以确定,结果租方要对船东作出补偿。

要退而求次,租方只能是在订租约时去取得船东船长一揽子的授权直接出提单,如在 NYPE'46 的本条款。但这并不保证船长将来不会对这方面的问题发难,出面阻止提单的签发或/与流通。

对船东来说,最关键的仍是租方是否是一流租家,将来索偿会否成问题。面对一流租家,船长去干涉"清洁"提单只应是在明确的情况,而不是在边缘案子。不去干涉,还会带来其他好处,即是在索偿时,不会被租方吹毛求疵地指控是因船长自己的疏忽带来不准确提单的损失,所以因果关系被打断(The "Nogar Marin"(1988)1 Lloyd's Rep. 412)。

当然,什么时候应去干涉?什么是明确的情况不容许清洁提单?什么是很可能没有真相的边缘案子?这轻重可不好掌握。

订约自由下,笔者也见过许多其他的租约条款。例如,简短且强硬地要求船东/船长必须签发清洁提单("must issue clean bill of lading")。类似的条款在很早的 Canada & Dominion Sugar v. Canadian National (1946) 80 Lloyd's Rep. 13 先例已出现。这种租约条款的不妥之处是如果货物表面状况在装船时确是不妥(或是船长坚持这是事实并事后获法官/仲裁员同意/认定),再去强制签发清洁提单会有非法的味道。这会导致该租约条款无法被承认而变成空话一句。在订约自由的大原则下,清楚的明示条款被漠视只有在违反公正政策的情况下才会发生,而非法正是如此。

另一种租约条款是针对大量的包装货/件装货。条款要求船长在装货作业中若对任何装上船的货物表面状况不满意,应马上提出并要求更换,以保证装完货物能去顺利签发清洁提单。条款说明如果船长没有这样做而导致后来签发不了清洁提单,所有损失由船东负责。这条款可以增加能顺利签发清洁提单的可能性并不让船东偷懒,免其到装货完毕才吹毛求疵,而届时有问题、有争议的货物已经压在其他货物下,无法再检查或更换。

3.3.6.3 买方/卖方同意某些提单批注

这方面不是发货人与承运人之间的做法,但可一揽子去谈。如果发货人无法取得清洁提单,又与承运人协调不了或不愿意这样做(因为涉及欺诈性),正常的做法自然是找买方协调了。危险会是市场下跌时买方会借机中止合约,或敲一笔货价(迫卖方减价)。故有远见的卖方,明知某种货物签发不了清洁提单的机会颇大,索性一早在订买卖合约时(与开信用证时),说明什么批注的提单可被买方接受(或不能拒绝)。当时去说明,是谈判一部分,买方想有合约,能做成买卖,不能一面倒施加压力在卖方头上,所以容易谈得多。在笔者的《国际货物买卖》一书第501页介绍到一份钢材买卖的合约,内有条款说:"Bills of lading marked 'cargo with atmospheric rust' (or similar wordings) acceptable."(提单注有'货物表面生锈'可以接受)。

同样道理,可引申至适用于过往碰到过的麻烦事,例如船长/船东货检曾多次坚持提单加某些批注,但其实收货人/买方最后不当做一回事的货物/货种。而即使吃不准会是怎样的批注,也可在买卖合约加以下一条条款(为例):"Any remarks concerning the second-hand nature of the goods such as 'old bags', 'appearance old and stained', etc., in the bills of lading are acceptable. Buyer shall without delay waive such discrepancies, if any, in the bills of lading."

而针对货物重量,买卖合约也应避免说死如"minimum/maximum 2 万吨",而应尽量留有余地,有伸缩性,如"2 万吨,卖方选择 10% 上下限"。(20,000 tons, 10% more or less seller's option)。

§4 船东/承运人对提单内容不正确的责任

船东/承运人对提单内容(不论是标号、货量或货物表面状况)不正确,会有多方面的责任。例如涉及提单合约方面会有"禁止翻供"(estoppel)的说法。而禁止翻供又有普通法下的与许多立法下的不同类别。另外,涉及侵权方面,会是"误述侵权"(tortuous misrepresentation)。

4.1 普通法下的禁止翻供

有关这个衡平法下的法律概念,在笔者《国际商务游戏规则——英国合约法》一书的第十一章有详论。内容太多,无法在此节录或重复。但所有相关的大道理,如"诱导"(inducement)在 5.2 小段,"依赖"(reliance)在 5.4 小段,造成"损害"(detriment)在 5.4.2 小段等,都有透彻探讨。

如果提单内容不正确,将来船东/承运人被起诉时想去以损坏不发生在他/它的合约责任范围或/与海牙规则期间内(装船前,发货人交付时,已经存在)为由抗辩,在普通法下会被禁止这样做,这即是所谓的"禁止翻供"。

4.1.1 构成的 4 个要求

这方面可节录 William Tetley 教授的 *Marine Cargo Claims* 一书第三版第 273 页所说:"Under the common law principle of estoppel, a person who issues a clean bill of lading may not claim pre-shipment defects in the cargo as against a person who relied on the bill of lading. For estoppel to arise at common law, there must be:

a) a representation as to a state of facts[686];

b) which is made with the intention of being relied upon[687]; and

c) which is in fact relied upon by the person raising estoppel[688];

---

[686] 对一件事实有过表述(不正确表述),例如事实上是表面状况不良好的货物却去表述为没有不妥,即签发清洁提单。
[687] 明知这表述会被第三者依赖与信赖。
[688] 后来也确实被第三者依赖与信赖了。

d) to his detriment[689].

Estoppel does not arise, however, in favour of a shipper[690] against a carrier, or where reliance on the description by a holder for value is not reasonable[691], or where the holder does not rely on the description at all[692]."

4.1.2 一般情况下很容易证明依赖与损害

基于提单在国际外贸与信用证中的运作及所起的作用,可以说,第三者的提单合法持有人(买方,银行,承押人等)很容易去证明他依赖了提单内容的不正确表述而且遭受到损害。正如 Scrutton 大法官在 Silver v. Ocean SS Co. (1929) 35 Lloyd's Rep. 49 所说:"The mercantile importance of clean bill of lading is so obvious and important that I think the fact that the consignee took the bill of lading, which is in fact unclean, without objection, is quite sufficient evidence that he relied on it."

另要去证明受到损害也不困难,一般买方为取得一套清洁提单都会支付了货款。显然,如果是不清洁的提单,买方不必去支付货款(不论是托收或信用证结汇)。现实中,买方即使接受不清洁提单也会可以向发货人(卖方)敲一笔(要求减货价)。所以,船东签发不正确提单等于是剥夺了买方这种机会。

4.1.3 第三者早知真相,没有真正去依赖不正确提单内容的情况

这一点完全合理公平:如果第三者早知真相(往往通过其他渠道),那他就谈不上有去真正依赖与信赖他明知是不正确的表述。这一来,就不应有禁止翻供了。但这理论/说法引申到针对提单内容要小心而且会有局限,因为动不动去质疑收货人/提单持有人有否或可通过其他渠道知悉货物装船的正确情况,会导致提单至高无上的地位受打击。所以 Wright 大法官在 The "Johnstown" (1928) 32 Lloyd's Rep. 218 警告说:

---

[689] 因此造成第三者的损害/损失。

[690] 禁止翻供的说法不适用在发货人;他不是第三者,他应知道事实真相(货物装船时的真正状况),故也不存在去依赖船东在提单上的表述。

[691] 第三者的依赖与信赖是合理的,毕竟,禁止翻供是衡平法,追求的是公平合理。何谓公平合理会涉及多方面考虑,表述不完全清楚明确会是其中一方面。所以在 Canada & Dominion Sugar v. Canadian National (1946) 80 Lloyd's Rep. 13 一案,清洁提单另有印章加上说:"Signed under guarantee to produce ship's clean receipt." 等于是一份清洁提单上另有条款说我船长是被枪指令下签发,则第三者怎可以只去依赖清洁提单而罔顾加上的条款呢? 该先例中英国贵族院同意船东/承运人的抗辩。不公平合理的另一例子可以举第三者并非以合法手段取得并持有提单为例。

[692] 第三者没有真正去依赖与信赖提单表述的内容,例如,他早已知道真相。这方面在 4.1.3 小段会后详。

"There may be cases where the independent knowledge possessed by the indorsee, to whom the bill of lading is presented, is of such a character as to make it absolutely clear to him that the bill of lading statement is not accurate, but such cases, in my judgment, must be very rare indeed…

Any other view would, I think, tend to diminish the value of bills of lading in commerce and would also tend to promote carelessness, if not fraud, on the part of a ship's master in a foreign port when duly clausing them…"

在该案中，Wright 大法官说到每一案件都要严格分析后才好去下结论说提单持有人没有真正去依赖清洁提单：

"It is said that there could be no estoppel where the truth of the matter was known to both parties, and that a false representation made to a person who knew it to be false was not capable of being relied upon as constituting an estoppel.

As to the soundness of that as a general principle there can, of course, be no question, but it is necessary in my judgment to consider very carefully the precise circumstances of the case in order to see whether there was such information before the bill of lading holder in a case like the present as to debar him from acting upon the statement in the bill of lading."

该 The "Johnstown" 先例涉及木材的货物，装货作业中，船长曾书面抗议装上船舶的木材受污染与有污泥，并且部分掉下水被冲走。但之后，船长签发了清洁提单。而事实上在托收时，买方手中既有一份清洁提单，也有一份船长的书面抗议。所以船东争辩说买方不得指称船东禁止翻供，因为买方要去依赖提单时已知真相，所以不是真正的依赖。

但 Wright 大法官说这两份出自船长、内容相异的文件，提单的地位高多了，所以买方（收货人）完全可去依赖、信赖清洁提单，即使船长另有抗议书写得明明白白。他说："In the present case I do not think the information before (买方/收货人) was of such a character as to justify them in rejecting the bills of lading as not representing the true facts. I assume that the date I to take into account for this purpose is Aug. 17, 1927, that is, the date of the acceptance of the bills of exchange. That, of course, beyond question was an act done to their prejudice in relying on the terms of the bills of lading. They had in their possession the clean bills of lading before them; on the other hand, they had the protests…taking the master's protest their position was that they had on the one side a bill of lading signed by the master, an authoritative document under his signature, and on the other hand they had his protest. Even if the protest is treated as of equal value to the bill of lading, and it cannot be regarded as of superior value, they had in their hands two documents each from the master contradicting each other. With that contradiction it seems to me they would be entitled to treat the statement in the bill of lading as one on which they were justified and bound to act, even if there were no ambiguity in the protest."

照以上 Wright 大法官的判法去考虑,去指称收货人/提单持有人早知真相,故此没有真正依赖提单内容,会是绝不容易。毕竟,有什么文件地位会比一份清洁提单高呢? 岂非收货人通过船长在装港抗议或检验报告有异或代理通知货物的真相(例如有不妥或短装),都可去漠视、继续去依赖一份清洁提单?

当然,也要考虑收货人的难处。除了要维护提单至高无上的地位外,收货人也会面对信用证对一份清洁提单作出支付的要求,而试图去阻止支付会是昂贵且后果很不肯定的法律行为(即"止付禁令"的申请)。也会是在托收,如果拒绝一份清洁提单,但最后被判是毁约就惨了。毕竟,即使有合理怀疑(针对清洁提单内容),也不足以成为毁约的理由。

现实中,仍常见船东或/与船东互保协会一发觉签发清洁提单有错,就马上就事实设法通知所有有关人士:发货人、提单上的通知人(他常会是收货人/买方)、装卸港代理人、银行、承租人等等。目的为去阻止提单转让以及第三者不要再去依赖、信赖提单不正确的内容。但能否成功天知道。或许可能会碰巧单证有不符点,买方(开证人)及时获得错签清洁提单的通知可借机与卖方(发货人、信用证受益人)交涉,并由双方协商解决。这一来,再难说有依赖且曾造成任何损害/损失了。但这种情况不会多,所以,大前提仍是去防止错签内容不实的清洁提单。

4.1.4 不利提单持有人的 Grant v. Norway 先例

英国普通法有一个著名但又令人困扰的先例,是 Grant v. Norway (1851) 10 C. B. 665。它涉及一艘名为"Belle"的船舶,船长签发了 12 捆真丝(货物)的提单,但事实上根本没有过货物装船。提单持有人的原告很有说服力地争辩说如果船东可对船长这种行为不负责,今后怎能再令人对提单有信心?

"It would be hard indeed upon the indorsee of the bill of lading, who has no means of knowing whether the master has received the goods, but takes it upon the faith of his signature, to hold that he has no remedy against the owner. Such a doctrine will go very far to destroy the negotiability of these instruments. If the owner's authority to the master is limited to goods actually received on board, the owner would not be responsible for any wrongful act by the master. Suppose the master receives 6 bales of silk, and signs a bill of lading for 12—is the owner responsible for the 6, and not for the others?"

但 Jervis 大法官判船东胜诉,不必对此提单负责,因为船长没有实质授权去签发无中生有的"空"提单去约束船东。判决说："The authority of the master of a ship is large and extends to all acts that are usual and necessary for the use and enjoyment of the ship; but it is subject to several well-known conditions. He may make contracts for the hire of the ship[693], but cannot vary that which the owner has made…He may make contracts to carry goods or freight.（今天看来，船长连这种订合约的权利都不会有，不论是指实质、默示或表面授权）。but cannot bind his owners by a contract to carry freight free. So, with regard to goods put on board, he may sign a bill of lading, and acknowledge the nature and quality and conditions of the goods…

It is not contended that the captain had any real authority to sign bills of lading, unless the goods had been shipped: nor can we discover any ground upon which a party taking a bill of lading by indorsement, would be justified in assuming that he had authority to sign such bills, whether the goods were on board or not…"

Jervis 大法官的判决很有争议性，也不受欢迎，所以随即在 1855 年"提单法"（Bills of lading Act, 1855）被试图改变。该判决除了严重影响提单作为物权凭证的至高无上的地位外，也会对"代理法"（law of agency）造成无法解释得通之处。照说，船长作为船东的代理人及雇员，他在工作中犯的过错，疏忽与欺诈造成第三者的损失应是由雇主承担。雇主不能说雇员/代理人为我办事，办对了我负责（其实没有责任可负），办错了没有我授权，因为我没有让雇员/代理人去犯错。这正是 Robertson 勋爵在 George Whitechurch Ltd. v. Cavanagh（1902）AC 117 的第 137 页所提的同样看法："It seems to be extremely doubtful whether Grant v. Norway can be held, or has ever been held, to represent the general law, or to do more than determine the law about ship-masters and bills of lading; and whether, assuming it to have the wider bearing, it is reconcilable with the doctrine of Lord Selbourne in Houldsworth v. City of Glasgow Bank. I find it extremely difficult on principle to hold that the scope of an agent's employment can be limited to the right performance of his duties, or to say that an agent within whose province it is truly to record a fact is outside the scope of his duties when he falsely records it, when the question of liability to be decided is whether a loss is to be borne by the principal who placed him there, or by an innocent third party who had no voice in selecting him."

但是，Grant v. Norway 的判例在 100 多年之后一直没有被上诉庭或贵族院推翻，甚至被认同。这从 Sheen 大法官在 The"Nea Tyhi"（1982）1 Lloyd's Rep. 606 之第 616 页的判词中可见："To those who are not familiar with the law relating to the carriage

---

[693] 今天看来，船长连这种订合约的权利都不会有，不论是指实质、默示或表面授权。

of goods by sea, but who are familiar with the general principles of agency and in particular with the decision of the House of Lords in Lloyd v. Grace, Smith(1912) A. C. 716, the decision in Grant v. Norway may come as a surprise. But that decision has survived for 130 years and has been quoted with approval in the Court of Appeal and House of Lords…Accordingly I am bound by it…I confess that I find it impossible to reconcile the (two decisions) …I can only conclude that the decision in Grant v. Norway is to be regarded as an exception and not as laying down a general principle."

另在 *Voyage Charters* 一书的第 372 页也有提到说:"The decision in Grant v. Norway has been convincingly criticized by Lord Robertson in Whitechurch v. Cavanagh (1902) AC 117, 137 as an erroneous application of agency principles, but it has frequently been followed, and was approved by the majority of the House of Lords in that case."

Grant v. Norway 重点是针对船长订约并可去约束船东的权限,如不得签发"空"的提单(提单是可约束船东的运输合约),进而说没有这运输合约的存在。这样一来,如果不是"空"的提单,例如 The "Demdocus"(1966)1 Lloyd's Rep. 1 一案,提单上说有 225 捆橡胶,但实际只有 90 捆装船,这就不好解释了。显然,船长有实质或表面授权去签发提单,这是一份有效的运输合约,只是数字/内容错了,被夸大了。但去这样区分实在是难以接受。

此外,Grant v. Norway 是一个以侵权为基础的诉讼。有说法是以合约为基础的诉讼,因为会更针对"代理人法律",因此结果会不一样。但这也是不理想,正如 *Scrutton on Charter-parties* 一书第 19 版第 112 页的注脚 56 说:"According to Grant v. Norway the master has no authority to bind the shipowner to an estoppel in such a case, and although ostensible authority and course of employment are not the same thing, it would be curious if the master's acts could bind the owner in tort but not in contract."

本段结束前,可请读者回头看本书第三章 5.2 小段,它对此著名先例略有介绍。

4.2 立法下的禁止翻供

因为 Grant v. Norway(1851) 10 C. B. 665 的先例实在令人困扰,所以后来有立法试图以"立法禁止翻供"(statutory estoppel)来替代普通法的禁止翻供。照说,Grant v. Norway 只是英国本土法,而且后来又有立法去改变(1855 年提单法),国际上可不去理会。但为了明确,海牙·维斯比规则这一国际公约也明确规定了这一点。另外,替代 1855 年提单法的 1992 年英国海上运输法(适用在 1992 年 9 月 16 日以后签发的提单)也有条款针对此点,改变了 Grant v. Norway。

4.2.1 各立法的措辞/条款

先去节录有关条款如下：

（ⅰ）1855 年提单法的 Section 3：

"Every bill of lading in the hands of a consignee or endorsee for valuable consideration representing goods to have been shipped on board a vessel shall be conclusive evidence of such shipment as against the master or other persons signing the same[694], notwithstanding that such goods or some part thereof may not have been shipped, unless such holder of the bill of lading shall have had actual notice at the time of receiving the same that the goods had not been in fact laden on board: Provided that the master or other person so signing may exonerate himself in respect of such misrepresentation by showing that it was caused without any default on his part, and wholly by the fraud of the shipper, or of the holder, or some person under whom the holder claims."

（ⅱ）1992 年海上运输法的 Section 4：

"A Bill of lading which—

(a) represents goods to have been shipped on board a vessel or to have been received for shipment on board a vessel; and

(b) has been signed by the master of the vessel or by a person who was not the master but had the express, implied or apparent authority of the carrier to sign bills of lading,

shall, in favour of a person who has become the lawful holder of the bill, be conclusive evidence against the carrier of the shipment of the goods or, as the case may be, of their receipt for shipment."

（ⅲ）1968 年的海牙·维斯比规则，在 Article 1 说明在海牙规则加一句如下：

"In Article 3, paragraph 4 shall be added:

"however, proof to the contrary shall not be admissible when the Bill of Lading has been transferred to a third party acting in good faith."

4.2.2　1855 年提单法的不当措辞

1855 年提单法的 Section 3 其意图明显是去改变 Grant v. Norway (1851) 10 C. B. 665 的说法，例如讲明包括货物未装船（或部分装船）的情况，提单内容对无辜收货人或受让人都构成"结论性证据"（conclusive evidence），即船东/承运人不能再去争议/推翻提单的内容。

---

[694] 请留意措辞只是针对船长或真正签发提单的其他人士，并非针对/包括承运人，十分局限。

但它有一处不妥,这在上一小段的注脚已提及,就是针对的人(不准去推翻结论性证据的内容)太局限。这也不知是立法人故意或无意,反正这一来,这立法的作用就有限了,因为收货人/提单持有人起诉的总是船东/承运人,谁会去起诉"光棍"的船长呢？

有关"other persons signing the same"可否去包括船东/承运人,毕竟是他/它去给予实质或表面授权？Esher 勋爵判是不包括,他在 Thorman v. Burt, Boulton v. Co. (1886)54 L. T. 349 说:"Now I agree that the words "the person signing the same" do not necessarily mean the person who actually signs. If, for instance, a clerk in the shipowner's office signs per pro. , the owner might be the person signing within the section. Or, if the captain had the gout and was thereby prevented from signing himself, and a servant signed for him, the captain would be the person signing. But in the present case, the signature was not that of a mere clerk or servant but of an agent; and he was the agent of the master, not of the shipowner. *Therefore, as the shipowner did not sign the bill of lading in the present case, he incurs no liability under the 3rd Section*…"

这也是在 The"Demodocus"(1966)1 Lloyd's Rep. 1 的判法。

所以,这导致收货人/提单持有人向承运人索赔货损货差时,一去指控后者对提单不正确内容禁止翻供,请求就会是既依据"普通法禁止翻供"(common law estoppel),又"或是"(or alternatively)依据"立法禁止翻供"(statutory estoppel)。这可做到一种依据不能成立时,另一种依据仍有机会被接受,好像 The"Demodocus"先例。

随着 1855 年提单法的不再适用(除了少数国家如加拿大尚未改法),已不必多去理会本小段的内容。因为普通法的困扰或缺陷(Grant v. Norway)与 1855 年提单法的局限(因为措辞)都已被 1992 年海上运输法修正过来了。

4.2.3 1992 年海上运输法的改善

1992 年立法在多方面改善了普通法与 1855 年提单法。比方是:

(ⅰ)它仍是通过立法改变 Grant v. Norway(1851)10 C. B. 665 的普通法地位。

(ⅱ)它适用在各种提单,不光是装船提单:请看本书第三章之 12.2.4.3 小段。

(ⅲ)它是为保障提单合法持有人(看来只排除了发货人而已),也没有措辞文字要求他/它们曾经有去依赖与信赖提单的内容并受到损害/损失。

(ⅳ)"结论性证据"(conclusive evidence)是去针对有实质、默示或表面授权给船长或代理人签发提单的承运人(合约承运人)。

4.2.4 海牙·维斯比规则/1971年海上运输法

海牙·维斯比规则的国际公约在英国已立法成为 1971 年海上运输法,这立法内另有一个对提单内容的"立法禁止翻供"(statutory estoppel)。它的措辞/用字节录在 4.2.1 小段,简短明确,不必去多解释了。

有两处的"立法禁止翻供",难免有重叠之处,特别是在 1971 年海上运输法的 Section X,适用航次十分广泛。这也无所谓,毕竟两个立法的制定是在不同时间,不同背景。但仍会有空隙,例如,非海牙·维斯比国家去中国的航次,提单有伦敦仲裁条款,但未说明适用海牙·维斯比规则(不是海牙规则)。而该规则也非是立法强制适用。

至于海牙规则的适用更是局限了,这方面问题与 The "Hurry On"(Vita Food Products, Inc. v. Unus Shipping Co. Ltd.)(1939)63 Lloyd's Rep. 21 一案已在本书第五章之 4.2.3.1.2 小段详述,不再重复。

4.3 合约下的禁止翻供

大概是以前怕 1855 年提单法与普通法的禁止翻供说法不可靠,所以有一些提单会去加上一条"结论性证据"条款。这在 *Scrutton on Charter Parties* 一书第 19 版之第 115～116 页提及说:"A clause, known as 'the conclusive evidence clause' is commonly inserted in timber bills of lading. This clause reads: 'The bill of lading shall be conclusive evidence against the owner of the quantity of cargo received', or is in similar terms. With such a clause, the shipowner will be liable for short delivery though it is otherwise clear that the timber was not 'received' or 'taken on board'."

类似条款也经常在租约出现,一是为强制船东将来去签发这种注明"结论性证据"的提单;二是货损货差会是只依据租约,提单只是一份收据(持有人是承租人自己,例如是 FOB 买方),则可去依赖这类条款来对抗船东了。这方面在本书第五章之 3.1 与 4.2.3.2.2 小段有详论。

订约自由下,这类条款完全有效。即使是适用海牙·维斯比规则,也不影响,因为这类条款是加重承运人的责任、承担。

在 Lishman v. Christie(1887)19 QBD 333,涉及的租约有这类条款,而案件是索赔木材的货差。Esher 勋爵说:"The provision is that the bill of lading is to be conclusive evidence of the quantity of cargo received as stated therein. How is any quantity stated to have been received by a bill of lading? By the word 'shipped' of course. What can be the meaning of such a provision but to get rid of the liberty of the shipowners to show that the quantity stated to have been shipped was not really put on board and to make the bill of lading an estoppel? The provision is a good business provision for the purpose of avoiding disputes as to quantity shipped where there is no dishonesty on either side. Of course, if there were fraud, such a provision would not take effect, for fraud overrides all such provisions."

在稍后之 5.3.4 小段,会有更完整的同类案例介绍:The "Herroe" and "Askoe" (1986) 2 Lloyd's Rep. 281。

4.4 误述侵权(tortuous misrepresentation)

有关误述这课题,在笔者的《国际商务游戏规则——英国合约法》一书第五章有详论。内容太长,无法全部节录。但有关之处不少,如在 1.1 小段说:

> 一直以来,普通法针对欺诈性误述(fraudulent misrepresentation)导致(induce)的合约有救济,它允许受害方可去取消合约外,对遭受的损失还可以欺骗的侵权行为为由进行诉讼(tortuous action of deceit)取得赔偿……

另在该章的 4 段也提到什么程度可导致欺诈误述,说:

> ……也会一过了火便构成误述,甚至是欺诈性误述。毕竟这不需要万恶不赦,只要是轻率鲁莽(reckless)亦会足够;在 Derry v. Peek (1889) 14 app. Cas. 337,Herschell 勋爵把欺诈误述定义为 "knowingly, without belief in its truth or recklessly" ……

而该章的 10.2 小段亦详述了如何计算损失。

在 The "Saudi Crown" (1986) 1 Lloyd's Rep. 261 先例,Sheen 大法官拒绝采纳或区分造成困扰的 Grant v. Norway (1851) 10 C. B. 665 先例,判是代理人签发的假提单(倒签提单)仍可去约束船东/承运人,令后者要对无辜买方/提单持有人作出赔偿,理由就是有误述侵权。这是承运人的代理人在提单作出欺诈性误述(明知内容不正确仍去签发清洁提单,会十之八九以上是欺诈性误述),而买方依赖该误述从而导致有提单的运输合约。Sheen 大法官说:"If the bills of lading had been correctly dated the plaintiffs(买方) would have rejected them…The complaint made by the plaintiffs (买方) is that they were induced to become endorsees by reason of a misrepresentation as to the date when the cargo was loaded. That misrepresentation was made by the agents of the shipowners in the course of their normal duties. It was a fraud committed by the defendants'(船东) representatives in the course of their employment."

Sheen 大法官判船东要赔偿买方因失去机会拒绝该份提单而遭受的所有损失: damages for loss of opportunity to reject the bills of lading. 可以说, 如果货物在跌价, 这损失赔偿金额可就大了。

还有, 以误述侵权起诉, 所有海牙/海牙·维斯比规则的条款/限责如单位赔偿限责等均不适用: 请看 *Scrutton on Charter-Parties* 一书第 19 版之第 114 页。

在近期的 Alimport v. Soubert Shipping Co. Ltd. (2000) 2 Lloyd's Rep. 447, 涉及在宁波港装大米运往古巴, 宁波代理在没有船长授权的情况下, 将 1998 年 8 月 8 日装船的提单签为 8 月 5 日。英国法院同样判船东要负责。代理人是期租人代理, 代船长签, 所以是"船东提单"。

§5 提单内容的否定性批注

先去说清楚为何这种"否定性批注"(disclaimer)如此重要。这是因为有了它, 对整个提单内容的表述就不是无条件、明确的了。这一来, 禁止翻供(特别是衡平法下的禁止翻供)就难以成立了, 因为它追求的是公平合理。Wright 勋爵在 Canada and Dominion Sugar v. Canadian National (1946) 80 Lloyd's Rep. 13 (案情请看本章 4.1.1 小段) 说得很清楚具体如下: "Their Lordships in so deciding are not in any way weakening the rule that a shipowner who issues a clean bill of lading is bound by the statement in it that the goods are shipped in good or in apparent good order and condition…But the whole case of estoppel fails if the statement is not sufficiently clear and unqualified."

5.1 否定性批注如"重量不知"、"据说是有"等的合理性探讨

"否定性批注"(disclaimer)已在较早段节谈及, 如 1.1 小段(Congenbill 提单)与 3.2.6.2 小段(集装箱)。一份提单从整体看、整体解释, 如果一处是写"据说是重 2 万吨"(said to weigh 20,000 tons), 另一处再说"重量不知"(weight unknown), 实在很难得出结论说承运人是表述了 2 万吨货物装上船。这应是承运人什么都没有表述, 全部都推说不知道。

承运人这样批注可能是合理的, 因为装船时他/它根本无法去查明, 这在海牙规则下也明确被允准, 即是在 Article 3(3), 这已在本章之 3.2.6.1 小段谈及。

但如果承运人装船时实际可去查明, 如去安排"理货"(tally), 但又不去这样做, 这看来就有不合理之处了。等于是自己疏懒或为了节省费用, 但又不肯去依赖发货人提供的货量, 且又说不出不肯去依赖它的任何理由。看来, 这如同船东拒绝签发提单一样。

5.2 海牙规则的对策

海牙规则的对策是允许发货人去要求承运人必须签发有本章 1.2 小段所述 3 项内容的提单：Canada and Dominion Sugar v; Canadi an National (1946) 80 Lloyd's Rep. 13 的 18 页；The "Mata K"(1998) 2 Lloyd's Rep. 614。这是在 Article 3 (3)：

"After receiving the goods into his charge the carrier or the master or agent of the carrier shall, on demand of the shipper, issue to the shipper a bill of lading showing among other things—

(a) The leading marks...

(b) Either the number of packages or pieces, or the quantity, or weight, as the case may be, as furnished in writing by the shipper.

(c) The apparent order and condition of the goods.

Provided that no carrier, master or agent of the carrier shall be bound to state or show in the bill of lading any marks, number, quantity, or weight which he has reasonable ground for suspecting not accurately to represent the goods actually received, or which he has had no reasonable means of checking."

所以如果发货人获得签发的一套提单有注明"重量不知"或"表面状况不明"等字句，而船东/承运人又不是对有关内容有合理怀疑或没有合理办法去查明，正确的做法是发货人去对此提出异议。这在 *Scrutton on Charter-Parties* 一书第 19 版之第 109 页注释 [29] 是说："Sometimes the disclaimer takes an extreme form, such as 'weight, quantity, number, contents, condition and quality unknown'. Although this type of claim reduces the commercial value of the document, it is not objectionable in theory, nor does it offend the Hague-Visby Rules, *unless to shipper has made a demand for a bill of lading in compliance with Article III rule 3.*"

但在现实中，发货人绝少会去为这种常见的，印在像 Congenbill 提单格式的"否定性批注"(disclaimer) 烦恼，原因是：

(i) 一般做法是由发货人自己去填妥一份提单然后让承运人签字，双方这样做，表示同意提单所有的内容，包括否定性批注。

(ii) 发货人不去抗议而接受了这套提单，就要受它约束：Watkins v. Rymill (1883) 10 QBD 178。

(iii) 提单上百种不同格式中，笔者估计一半以上有印上"重量……不知"条款，包括著名且常见的 Congenbill（附录八）。笔者从未见过现实中有把这一批注删除掉的。这一来，发货人自己备妥填妥一份 Congenbill 标准格式的提单，承运人自己未讲发货人已代为说"重量……不知"，这能怪谁呢？

(ⅳ)有说法是发货人对否定性批注不满意再去根据海牙规则 Article 3(3)要求船东另签发提单,船舶会已开航。但今天通讯发达,接触船长/船东不应困难,这不是理由。

(ⅴ)笔者看来更大的理由是发货人漠不关心,因为有这种常见的,印在标准格式内的否定性批注如"重量不知",一般不会被当做是不清洁提单,不会影响信用证结汇:可参阅 1977 年 3 月 14 日国际商会的 ICC Documents 475/304,470/309。

针对另一措辞的"据说是有"(said to contain),国际商会也曾在 Case 123(有关集装箱的询问)回应说:

"There is nothing in the description that you have reproduced"expresslv declaring a defective condition of the goods and/or the packaging". The words" said to contain" are not to be understood as such an express declaration. Therefore they do not render a bill of lading unclean."

(ⅵ)在笔者的《国际货物买卖》一书之第 76 页,也有提及说:

在 The"Galatia"(1980)1 Lloyd's Rep. 450,也针对了提单常有的批注判道:"weight,quantity,condition,contents and value unknown"并不影响它是清洁提单。这也正确,措辞上只说"不知道",这并非是去否定货物的表面状况良好。

故此,CFR 的买方也不能拒绝接受有否定性批注的提单。这一来,卖方(发货人)又有何惧,何必去以海牙规则之 Article 3(3)与承运人交涉呢? 在 The"Galatia"案的一审(1979)2 Lloyd's Rep. 450,Donaldson 大法官判是(并获上诉庭确认):"the bill of lading was not objectionable even though it was claused"weight, measure, quantity, condition, contents and value unknown" since this was a printed form and the words complained of were part of the bill itself; there was no conflict produced by the words in the phrase, and they did not contain any qualification of the acknowledgment contained in the bill rendering it otherwise than" clean"; and the buyers should have accepted and paid for the documents."

5.3　英国法律承认"否定性批注"的有效性

在英国法律下,法官/仲裁员只是去全面解释一份提单合约而不会太理会某一条款出现在合约内的背景或合理与否等等(除非是严重至像非法胁迫等的"公共政策")。以下可去介绍一连串有关的重要先例。

5.3.1　先例之一:New Chinese Antimony 1917

在 New Chinese Co. v. Ocean S. S. Co. (1917) 2 KB 664, Viscount Reading 大法官判"否定性批注"(disclaimer)可保障船东,说:"Where in a bill of lading, which is prepared by the shippers for acceptance by the defendants agent(船东代理人), the agent accepts in the margin a quantity 'said to be 937 tons', and in the body of the bill of lading there is a clause 'weight, etc., unknown,' there is no prima facie evidence that 937 tons have been shipped…I think that the true effect of this bill of lading is that the words 'weight unknown' have the effect of a statement by the shipowners' agent that he has received a quantity of ore which the shippers' representative says weight of 937 tons but which he does not accept as being of that weight, the weight being unknown to him and that he does not accept the weight of 937 tons except for the purpose of calculating freight and for that purpose only."

5.3.2　先例之二:Canada and Dominion Sugar 1946

在这先例中,其中针对没有证据支持发货人曾要求过一份清洁提单这点,清楚说明承运人因此不必去"自动"签发,Wright 勋爵说[Canada and Dominion Sugar v. Canadian National(1946) 80 Lloyd's Rep. 13]:"Rule 3 (海牙规则)expressly applies only if the shipper demands a bill of lading showing the apparent order and condition of the goods. There is no evidence that the shipper here made any such demand: indeed, no demand of this nature is alleged. The condition of the Rule is thus not fulfilled…There is indeed no law which prevents goods being carried at sea without any bill of lading at all…or makes any particular form of bill of lading obligatory…"

5.3.3　先例之三:Scindia Steamship 1961

此先例[Attorney-General of Ceylon v. Scindia SS Co. Ltd. (1961)2 Lloyd's Rep. 173]涉及的货物是10万多袋袋装白米,收货人索赔货差。该提单印有否定性批注说"weight, contents and value when shipped unknown"。

注意该批注没有去针对货物"数量"(quantity),只去针对无关的"重量"(weight),所以贵族院判否定性批注不足保障承运人。但贵族院并没有说"否定性批注"(disclaimer)无效,Morris 勋爵说:"…the bills of lading were not even *prima facie* evidence of the weight or contents or value of such bags…It was for the plaintiff to prove the contents of the bags and the weight of the bags and it was for him to prove his loss by proving what it was that the bags contained and by proving what was the value of what the bags contained."

5.3.4　先例之四:The"Herroe"and"Askoe"1986

这先例[The"Herroe"and"Askoe"(1986)2 Lloyd's Rep. 281]涉及的货物是袋装土豆。承租人(也是 FOB 买方)在租约加了一条保护自己的条款,目的是不让船东将来对提单上的货物数量作出否定,即禁止翻供,它说:

"28. The vessel owners are to be responsible for the number of bags/packages as signed for in the bills of lading.

These bills of lading to be conclusive evidence of the quantity of cargo shipped. At loading and discharging ports owners to appoint through agents official tally and to pay for same at the official local rates."

但该先例的提单格式又是 Congenbill,印有:

(ⅰ)在多少袋的数字上说明是"发货人表述的货物"(Shipper's Description of goods)。

(ⅱ)"重量,……数量……不知"(Weight, Measure, Quality, Quantity, Conditions, Contents and Value Unknown)。

提单也并入了租约,表示包括了上述的第 28 条(提单货物数量是结论性证据)。但要注意解释合约的一般准则是合并的内容如有冲突,无法超越提单表面的明示条款/批注。

承租人(收货人/买方)向船东提出货物短缺索赔,船东抗辩说提单上的货物数量不对,不代表真正装船的数量。

在伦敦仲裁,船东败诉。裁决书主要裁定如下:"The bill of lading record unequivocally the number of bags of potatoes shipped[695], and it is established law[696] that the quantities and types of cargo shown in bills of lading may be taken as evidence of cargo received on board, notwithstanding the inclusion in the bills 'Quantity Unknown'[697] unless there is evidence to show that the bills of lading quantities have been inaccurately stated. We have found no such evidence of inaccuracy[698]…

…Since we are bound to apply strictly the conclusive evidence of Charterparty Clause 28[699] at the loading port, despite having some doubts in our mind concerning the tally at

---

[695]　提单毫无保留地写明装了多少袋土豆。
[696]　英国法律下很明确这就是这种货、这是数量已装船的证明。
[697]　"数量不知"的否定性批注印在提单上也不能改变什么,除非另有证据证明这表述并不准确。
[698]　本案例中,船东没有这种证据。
[699]　我们仲裁员必须给租约第 28 条的"结论性证据"一个解释。

Alexandra[700]……"

但这裁仲书上诉至高院被推翻,而且 Hobhouse 大法官说仲裁庭弄错了英国法律:"The statement of law that I have read out is, in my judgrnent, unquestionably an erroneous statement"。

Hobhouse 大法官也说明有这"否定性批注"(disclaimer)的提单,实在是等于提单上没有签认任何货物数量:"Looking at the bills of lading, it is unquestionable, in my judgment, that…no quantity was signed for. The expression "Quantity Unknown" was allowed to remain in the bill of lading form. The number was merely part of the shipper's description of the goods, and the master simply signed the bill of lading in the usual way at the bottom. So there was no signature for the number of bags."

这一来,既然没有就任何货物数量签发提单,何来租约第28条的"结论性证据"呢?

但其中有一套提单(一票货物有几套提单),因为船长在注明货物数量的数字上多加签了一个名字,Hobhouse 大法官判这套提单不一样,这数量不受"否定性批注"说"数量不知"的影响。他说:"But the first bill of lading… had an additional signature and stamp placed by the master against the numbers that were there stated. It seems to me that the correct view (adopting an objective test) of this bill of lading, is that the master, by attaching that additional signature in that location on this bill was prepared to sign for those numbers and was doing that very thing. Since those numbers are part of the typescript placed on this bill of lading, and also since the signature and the stamp are also specially attached to this bill of lading in that position, then, in my judgment, apply ordinary principles of construction, that must be treated as superseding *protanto* the 'weight…quantity…unknown' provision. In that case, on that bill of lading, the master was prepared to sign for the number of bags in that bill of lading."

读者由此可见,解释合约虽有各种准则或"指引"(guidelines),但实际却可以十分灵活。也往往会是,判断的人(法官或仲裁员)有一定的主观感觉(当然他应客观去解释合约,找出双方的订约意图)。例如,提单上就货物数量发货人打印上的数字被船长删去,而另用红笔写了一个数字,笔者认为很明显这数字不会受"否定性批注"的影响。

5.3.5 先例之五:The"Esmeralda"1988

这先例[The"Esmeralda"(1988)1 Lloyd's Rep. 206]涉及集装箱运输,是澳大利

---

[700] 尽管我们对装港阿历山大港的理货数量准确性有多高也不无疑问。

亚的判例。有关的提单表面上写作"FCL/FCL",表示这是发货人铅封/密封了的满载集装箱("full container load")。另对集装箱内货物的表述(发货人提供)是:

"01-container 20'with 437 cardboard boxes, containing:'cutlery and leaflets and posters'."

而提单表面也在各处印有以下的"否定性批注/条款":

(ⅰ)"据说是有——发货人堆装集装箱"(said to contain-packed by shippers)。

(ⅱ)"货物资料由发货人提供"(particulars furnished by shippers of goods)。

(ⅲ)"……重量……数目……数量……等如果由发货人提供而船长无法查明,签发此提单不表示同意"(shipped on board the above vessel…in apparent good order and condition unless otherwise stated and to be discharged at the aforesaid port of discharge…weight, measure, marks, numbers, quality, quantity, condition, content and value, if mentioned in this bill of lading were furnished by the shippers and were not or could not be ascertained or checked by the Master unless the contrary has been expressly acknowledged and agreed to. The signing of this bill of lading is not to be considered as such an agreement…)

Yeldham 大法官判这提单下承运人对集装箱内有 437 盒厨具的正确性并无任何表述(…plain upon its face that no representation was made by the carrier as to the accuracy of the statement that the container contained 437 cardboard boxes of cutlery. leaflets and posters)。

5.3.6　先例之六:The"Atlas"1996

这个先例(The"Atlas"(1996)1 Lloyd's Rep. 642)已在本章之 3.2.3 小段详述。在该提单,钢材(货物)表述为有 1380 束(bundles)与 12,038.20 吨。但该提单印有一句说:

"All particulars(weight, measure, marks, numbers, quantity, contents, value…) thereof as stated by Merchant but unknown to the Carrier."

Longmore 大法官判定:"Although it could be said that the bills showed the number of packages or weights because they had figures which were in fact supplied by the shippers[701], if the bills provided'weight…number…quantity unknown'it could not be said that the bills'showed'that number or weight[702];they showed nothing at all because the

---

[701] 虽然提单上发货人提供了货物数量/重量。
[702] 但若提单表面同时有否定性批注针对货物数量/重量,则等于没有任何表述。

shipowner was not prepared to say what the number was[703]; he could be required to show it under art. Ⅲ, r. 3[704] but until he did so the provisions of art. Ⅲ, r. 4 as to prima facie evidence could not come into effect."

5.3.7　先例之七:The"River Gurara"1998

这先例[The"River Gurara"(1998)1 Lloyd's Rep. 225]涉及另一个常见的"否定性批注"(disclaimer)——"said to contain"(据说是有)。该先例是针对船东的赔偿责任限制,笔者在此只说双方的大律师都接受/同意这批注与"重量,数目与数量不知"(weight, number, quantity unknown)基本相同(在第234页)。

5.3.8　先例之八:The"Mata K"1998

近期的先例[The"Mata K"(1998) 2 Lloyd's Rep. 614]涉及2.5万吨钾肥(muriate of potash)从俄罗斯的 Ventspils 运往韩国与日本卸下。船舶("Mata K")应是中间商 Agrosin 所程租的,估计是以 FOB 从俄罗斯买入再以 CIF 转卖给韩国与日本的买方(包括著名的 Mitsui)。

租约中,有关签发的提单条款(第50条)说:

"50 BILL OF LADING

…Owners guarantee they authorize their agents…to sign/release Congen bills of lading[705] which will be…in accordance with Charterers' instructions…but not contradictory to Mate's receipts in respect of total loaded weight…"

在装港,共签发了3套提单,加起来货量约为2.5万吨。而其中一套是去日本的较后卸港,货量表述为1.1万吨,Agrosin 是发货人,Mitsui 是通知人(实际是收货人,但这先要通过提单背书、转让、结汇等)。

在日本最后的卸港 Sodeguara,Mitsui 发觉有2700百吨的化肥短缺。Mitsui 于是向卖方 Agrosin 交涉。后者赔偿后作为"受让人"(assignee)就 Mitsui 的货差向船东/承运人索赔。但船东抗辩称船上货物已卸清,这种货物又没有船员会偷会吃,所以如果有短缺,实在是根本没有这个提单重量的货在 Ventspils 装上船。

在英国高院,首先是纯粹针对提单表面的解释,Clarke 大法官不认为提单有1.1万吨货装上船的表述,他说:"If this question is to be answered on the construction of

---

[703] 说了等于没说,因为船东不肯说出货量。
[704] 发货人也没有根据海牙规则向船东提出对提单的有关要求。
[705] 租约讲明使用 Congenbill,本章早在1.1小段已提过,这提单格式内印有一条"极其广泛的否定性批注"(disclaimer takes an extreme form):请看本章之5.2小段 Scrutton on Charter-Parties 一书的节录,说明船东什么(包括货物重量)都不知道。

the bill of lading as it stands, the answer, in my judgment is NO. The reason is that given in a number of decided cases, namely that a bill of lading which states that 11000 tonnes of cargo were shipped 'quantity unknown' is not a representation that 11000 tonnes were shipped. Any other conclusion would give no meaning to the expression 'quantity…unknown'."

原告 Agrosin 的大律师争辩说在海牙规则下（双方接受该提单适用海牙规则），该否定性批注违反了 Article 3(8)，因它减轻了承运人责任。所以 1.1 万吨货物对提单合法持有人 Mitsui 来说，在 1992 年海上运输法（本章之 4.2.3 小段）下，是享有立法的禁止翻供，即不准船东去争议说没有这货量装上船。这方面的争辩是："That provision（指"重量……不知"的批注）is null and void and of no effect under art.Ⅲ, r.8. It follows that the bill of lading should be read as if the 'weight…unknown' provision was not included with two results. The first is that the bill of lading 'shows' the weight within the meaning of art.Ⅲ, r.3 and is thus prima facie evidence of the weight against the defendants（船东）under art.Ⅲ, r.4. The second is that it 'represents' the weight within the meaning of section 4 of the Carriage of Goods by Sea Act, 1992 and is conclusive evidence of the weight in favour of Mitsui as lawful holders of the bill. It further follows that it is conclusive evidence that 11,000 tonnes of cargo were shipped in favour of the plaintiffs (Agrosin) as assignees of Mitsui."

但 Clarke 大法官不接受 Agrosin 的说法，因为根本没有证据证明发货人在装港曾根据海牙规则 Article 3(3) 要求过要有显示货物重量的提单。相反，发货人看来满足于使用 Congenbill 提单格式（正如租约的第 50 条款），尽管明知或应知内中印有这"重量……不知"的否定性批注。这实际是本章 5.3.2 小段曾提到的问题。Clarke 大法官说："The question is whether there was such a demand on the facts here. There is no suggestion or evidence that the plaintiffs (Agrosin) asked the defendants（船东）to issue a bill of lading showing the shipment of 11000 tonnes without the qualification 'weight…unknown'. The only evidence replied upon is the bill of lading itself. I do not however think that it is a fair inference from the form of the bill of lading that the plaintiffs made such a request. On the contrary the natural inference is that the shippers were content with a bill of lading in standard Congenbill form, which includes the prevision 'weight…unknown' as part of its printed form. The plaintiffs signed the bill of lading on behalf of the defendants. They were surely happy with it. If they had wanted a bill of lading in a different form they would surely have drafted one."

根据以上的事实认定，Clarke 大法官判船东胜诉，Agrosin 败诉，说："It is, in my judgment, a reasonable inference from Clause 50 that the plaintiffs and the defendants agreed that the bills of lading issued under the charter-party which would be presented for signature on behalf of the defendants would be in the Congenbill form and thus would include the 'weight...unknown' provision.

In all the circumstances I have reached the conclusion that, on the allegations made by the plaintiffs and on the facts set out in the material before the Court, there was no demand such as would satisfy art. Ⅲ, r. 3 of the Hague Rules. It follows that there is no basis on which the 'weight...unknown' provision could be treated as null and void and of no effect under art. Ⅲ, r. 8. It also follows that art. Ⅲ, r. 4 has no application because the bill of lading is not 'such a bill of lading' (that is a bill of lading of the kind referred to in art. Ⅲ, r. 3) so that the bill is not prima facie evidence of the receipt of 11000 tonnes of cargo under r. 4. Finally (and crucially on the facts of this case) it follows that the bill of lading does not represent that 11000 tonnes were shipped so as to be conclusive evidence against the defendants under Section 4 of the Carriage of Goods by Sea Act, 1992."

笔者看来，是 Agrosin 不太熟悉 Congenbill 格式提单有利于船东的内容与有关法律，结果为此而付出昂贵的学费。

5.4　对英国法律在这一方面的批评

从上述5.3小段的多个案例看来，可以说英国法律在这一方面对船东/承运人是太宽松、太优待了。考虑到今天外贸大环境的现实是 Congenbill 标准提单格式满天飞，流通/转让中的提单十之七八会印有这种极广泛的"否定性批注"（disclaimer），岂非在英国法律看来就类同于提单上根本没有货物重量或数量的记载？或会是，没有填上任何数字更好，至少不会误导不懂的买方/提单受让人，以为可去依赖/信赖提单内容对货量等的表述，而其实却是空话一句。

或许会说，收货人/提单合法持有人只是不能去指称承运人对提单内容禁止翻供而已。他/它仍可去装港收集证据，最后以"可能性"（balance of probability）的民事诉讼举证责任证明有5万、10万或12万袋不等的货物装上船。这毕竟常是集装箱运输的做法：请看本章之3.3.2小段。

但散装货涉及多次的海上转卖，买卖双方又不像集装箱运输的密切关系，收货人这一举证又谈何容易呢？

5.4.1　海牙规则的大精神是不准承运人减轻或逃避责任

海牙/海牙·维斯比规则没有直接针对这方面，但大精神、大原则大家耳熟能详，就是不准船东/承运人去减轻或逃避责任，所以会在各方面去防止其取巧。

这恰恰是 Diplock 勋爵在 The "Morviken" (1983) 1 Lloyd's Rep. 1 案中所提出的警告,他说:"...I have no hesitation in rejecting this narrow construction of art. Ⅲ, r. 8, which looks solely to the form of the clause in the contract of carriage and wholly ignores its substance[706]. The only sensible meaning to be given to the description of provisions in contracts of carriage which are rendered "null and void and of no effect" by this rule is one which would embrace every provision in a contract of carriage which, if it were applied, would have the effect of lessening the carrier's liability otherwise than as provided in the rules[707]. To ascribe to it the narrow meaning...would leave it open to any shipowner to evade the provisions of art. Ⅲ, r. 8 by the simple device of inserting in his bills of lading issued in...providing as the exclusive forum for resolution of disputes that might aptly be described as a Court of convenience[708]..."所以,笔者怀疑 Clarke 大法官在 The "Mata K" (1998) 2 Lloyd's Rep. 614 先例有否必要对 Article 3 (4)这一条款中的"such bill of lading"措辞大做文章,好像是海牙规则适用的提单可再区分为两类。一类是发货人要求的、坚持的,属"such bill of lading"。而另一类则不属,所以虽然海牙规则适用,船东仍可任意去加否定性批注以减轻或/与逃避责任。

5.4.2　以发货人要求签发作为前提并不现实

在本章之 5.3.2 与 5.3.8 小段提到的英国先例是怪发货人自己没有去要求船东/承运人在装港签发有重量或数量等内容的"海牙规则提单"。在本章 5.2 小段也详谈到现实中的做法是发货人不会特别去要求。他/它不一定懂,也没有压力去这样做。

所以英国法律这要求并不现实,正如 William Tetley 教授在 *Marine Cargo Claims* 一书第 3 版第 291 页对此批评说:"Certain clauses on bills of lading are intended to deny or qualify the carrier's statement as to the number or quantity of the goods and their condition. The clauses state that the carrier offers to issue a substitute bill of lading bearing proper notations if the shipper so requests. Such a clause violates the spirit and wording of arts. 3(3) and 3(4). The shipper needs a clean bill of lading immediately in order to meet the demands of the consignee and the cargo underwriter. He is deemed to have re-

---

[706]　去解释海牙规则 Article 3(8)之何谓减轻或免除承运人的责任,不能光看提单运输合约上的写法,还要顾及大原则。不能只给一个狭隘的解释。

[707]　其中要包括可能会涉及货物运输的每一处(显然,应包括像"重量、数量……不知"的否定性批注)。

[708]　否则,船东可以很容易在海牙规则下逃避责任,例如提单上加一条款说有纠纷去南极仲裁,或北极法院审理等。

quested such a bill of lading and it is the centuries old practice, tradition and custom that the shipper has requested such a bill. To now suggest that the shipper upon receiving a clause bill of lading must ask for a proper one under art. 3(3) first para. ('on demand of the shipper') is to stretch reality, the practice and the law."

5.4.3 解决办法

通常认为如果对法律所确定的地位不满意,那就去改变做法好了。毕竟在订约自由的大原则下,发货人(在买方要求下)大可去避免使用 Congenbill(或有类似"否定性批注"的提单格式),或虽使用 Congenbill 但删掉"重量……数量……不知"的一句。说真的,船长或代他签发提单的代理人很可能不会觉察,更谈不上会去抗拒。也可以从 5.3.4 小段的判法(The "Herroe" and "Asroe" (1986) 2 Lloyd's Rep. 281)中获得启示,做法变成是买方在买卖合约与信用证中要求卖方(发货人)提交的提单须有船长/代理人加签名字在注明货物重量或数量的数字上。

总之,会有多种对策/变通可能有效,这要做外贸的人士自己去掌握了。

5.5 美国法律只承认符合事实的否定性批注

在美国 1916 年提单法(U.S. Pomerene Act,1916)(在本书附录三(只适用在美国签发的提单),它的 Sections 20(承运人装货)与 21(发货人装货),针对这一方面,它要求承运人理货与确认货量,并不能随意写上"否定性批注",写上了如果不符合事实,也是无效。这些条款在附录可见,因比较长,不在此重复。

William Tetley 教授的 *Marine Cargo Claims* 一书第 285～286 页也说到 Section 20: "The words 'Shipper's weight, load and count' or similar wording, inserted by the carrier in the bill of lading or any other document, is to be treated as 'null and void' by virtue of sect. 20 of the U.S. Pomerene Act 1916, if the goods have been loaded on board by the carrier."

这等于如果集装箱实际是承运人自己堆装铅封的话,他/它就不能再去依赖像"重量,件数,内容等不知"的否定性批注了。

而 *Marine Cargo Claims* 一书的第 281 页,谈到 Section 21 时说:"The United States Pomerene Act 1916 at sect. 21 permits the carrier to state in a bill of lading, covering either packaged goods or bulk cargo which have been loaded on board by the shipper, that the contents, their kind or quantity or condition are 'said to be' or 'are unknown', *so long as this is in fact true*. The carrier may alternatively insert the words 'shipper's weight, load and count' or similar words, if the goods were in fact loaded and described by the shipper.

Where however the shipper has adequate equipment to weigh bulk cargo and this equipment is available to the carrier, the shipper may request the carrier to do the weighing and to not insert 'Shipper's weight'. If the carrier nevertheless does insert such words, they will be treated as null and void."

另在 William Tetley 教授的 *Marine Cargo Claims* 一书,还介绍了大量美国海上运输法(海牙规则)在这方面的美国案例,而其中之一是 Spanish American Skin v. M/S Ferngulf 242 F. 2d 551, 1957 AMC 611 (2 Cir. 1957),这是在该书第 3 版之第 288 页提到说:"In Spanish American Skin v. M/S Ferngulf, the bill of lading acknowledged receipt of 60 packages and stated 'Shipper's Weight Nett 6.8.2.8'. The bill of lading also bore a rubber stamp imprint reading: 'Steamer not responsible for weight, quality or condition of contents'. The Second Circuit held that the bill of lading was prima facie evidence of receipt by the carrier of both number and weight.

The carrier was responsible for the loss. The Court added that COGSA(美国海上运输法) specifically provides a method for avoiding carrier liability for false information given by the shipper, by not stating it in the bill…The Court said:

'The carrier must utilize that method, rather than the quite general reservation attempted here. The purpose of the Act to promote uniformity and negotiability of the ocean bills of lading includes a purpose to eliminate the practice of rubber stamp exceptions, limiting carrier liability'."

William Tetley 教授接下去说法国、比利时、希腊等国的法律在这方面亦是类同于美国的法律立场。

再接下去,William Tetley 教授提到英国的 Attorney-General of Ceylon v. Scindia SS Co. Ltd. (1961) 2 Lloyd's Rep. 173 判例(请看本章之 5.3.3 小段)与美国不同的法律立场,并说(在第 290 页)美国判例比英国好,更能接受,更符合海牙规则大精神。

本小段最后可去一提的是在美国也不是没有争议性的案例。这可介绍著名的 Tokio Marine & Fire Inc. v. Retla (1970) 2 Lloyd's Rep. 91 先例,案中涉及日本的 Mitsubishi 把一批钢管卖给美国的 Barnett 公司,而承运人是当时出了名专门运输钢材的 Retla 公司。众所周知,钢材经常有锈,不易去准确批注:请参阅本章之 3.3.5.3 小段。而去把每一锈迹都加批注,把提单写得满满另加 10 页、8 页附页,徒然会令这提单无法结汇或被接受。所以该批钢管虽有锈迹,Retla 仍签发了清洁提单(表面上看来),因提单表面印上:"表面状况良好"(in apparent good order and condition)。

但同时在提单表面,又另有批注说有表面生锈不影响签发这清洁提单。这名为"Retla Rust Clause"的准确措辞/用字是:"The term 'apparent good order and condition' when used in this bill of lading with reference to iron, steel or metal products does not mean that the goods, when received, were free of visible rust or moisture[709]. If the shipper so requests, a substitute bill of lading will be issued omitting the above definition and setting forth any notations as to rust or moisture which may appear on the mates' or tally clerks' receipts[710]."

在日本装港，发货人 Mitsubishi 显然没有要求 Retla 另出一套细列锈迹与水迹的提单。只把有这 Retla Rust Clause 的提单背书给了 Barnett。到了美国卸港，Barnett 因货物严重生锈要花钱去除锈。反正最后是保险公司赔偿后代位以自己的名义（依美国保险法律可以这样做）向承运人 Retla 索赔。

Retla 争辩说根本没有签发过清洁提单，这"清洁"已被说明是并不表示没有锈迹与水迹。

Jameson 大法官同意 Retla 的说法（估计是考虑到钢材批注生锈的难处），并说："That where a carrier issued a bill of lading which made no representation as to condition of cargo, the carrier was not estopped from showing that damage to cargo was of pre-shipment origin."

至于与 Spanish American Skin v. M/S Ferngulf 的上诉庭先例看来好像判法不一致，Jameson 大法官说是该先例涉及提单表述了货物件数与重量后，再加一个否定性批注说"重量……数量不知或不负责"，承运人本可不去填上货物件数与重量。这与本案不同，本案中 Retla 从未表述过提单是清洁的。

但看来这区分 Jameson 大法官讲得并没有说服力。加上，这样判既带来危险（对提单持有人而言）又不是美国对"否定性批注"（或类似批注）的一贯立场。所以，美国法院在以后的案例已对此有收紧。这在 Schoenbaum 的 *Admiralty and Maritime Law* 一书第 2 版第 522 页是说："Recognizing the unfairness of this predicament, the courts have refused to extend the Retla Rust Clause holding and except for this one exception, which should be repudiated, the courts reject the validity of qualifying clauses and uphold the prima facie effect of an otherwise clean bill of lading as well as the consignee's right to rely on the bill."

该书并去列出三个先例说明法院不予承认"否定性批注"（disclaimer）：

（ⅰ）Portland Fish Co. v. States Steamship Co. 510 F. 2d 628（9 Cir. 1974）– carrier estopped from relying on qualification of statement of cargo weight.

---

[709] 签发清洁提单不表示货物没有表面生锈或水迹。
[710] 发货人大可以要求承运人另去出一套提单替代，该提单将会细列大副据内注明的每一处锈迹与水迹。这样写是为了显示公平合理，已经提示发货人的权利。

(ii) Plywood Panels, Inc. v. M/V Sun Valley 804 F. Supp. 804, 1993 AMC 516 (E. D. Va. 1992) – Lumber clause is invalid attempt to avoid COGSA requirement to show apparent exterior order and condition of goods.

(iii) Sumitomo Corp. of America v. M/V St. Venture 683 F. Supp. 1361 (M. D. Fla. 1988) – rust clause invalid because of fine print and lack of avoidability of a substitute bill.

5.6 汉堡规则及其他国际公约与美国法律立场一致

在本章之1.3小段最后一段,已略为提及汉堡规则应是不允许这种象加印在Congenbill的一般性"否定性批注"(disclaimer)。主要原因是因为有Article 16的规定,特别是在其(1)项,说明了否定性批注一定要说明承运人为何怀疑发货人提供的提单内容,或为何没有合理机会查明。这等于是符合当时事实的"否定性批注"才会有效,否则歪曲在装港事实的否定性批注根本不能写上提单表面。

汉堡规则虽附在本书附录七,但为方便阅读可去节录 Article 16 如下:

Article 16. Bill of lading: reservations and evidentiary effect

1. If the bill of lading contains particulars concerning the general nature, leading marks, number of packages or pieces, weight or quantity of the goods which the carrier or other person issuing the bill of lading on his behalf knows or has reasonable grounds to suspect do not accurately represent the goods actually taken over or, where a ' shipped ' bill of lading is issued, loaded, or if he had no reasonable means of checking such particulars, the carrier or such other person must insert in the bill of lading a reservation specifying these inaccuracies, grounds of suspicion or the absence of reasonable means of checking.

2. If the carrier or other person issuing the bill of lading on his behalf fails to note on the bill of lading the apparent condition of the goods, he is deemed to have noted on the bill of lading that the goods were in apparent good condition.

3. Except for particulars in respect of which and to the extent to which a reservation permitted under para. I of this article has been entered:

(a) The bill of lading is *prima facie* evidence of the taking over or, where a ' shipped ' bill of lading is issued, loading, by the carrier of the goods as described in the bill of lading; and

(b) Proof to the contrary by the carrier is not admissible if the bill of lading has been transferred to a third party, including a consignee, who in good faith has acted in reliance on the description of the goods therein.

4. A bill of lading which does not, as provided in para. 1, subpara. (k) of art. 15, set forth the freight or otherwise indicate that freight is payable by the consignee or does not set forth demurrage incurred at the port of loading payable by the consignee, is *prima facie* evidence that no freight or such demurrage is payable by him. However, proof to the contrary by the carrier is not admissible when the bill of lading has been transferred to a third party, including a consignee, who in good faith has acted in reliance on the absence in the bill of lading of any such indication.

另在1980年的联合国多式联运公约,也是同样的措辞/用字,它在 Article 9 说:

"Reservations in the multimodal transport document:

1. If the multimodal transport document contains particulars concerning the general nature, leading marks, number of packages or pieces, weight or quantity of the goods which the multimodal transport operator or a person acting on his behalf knows, or has reasonable grounds to suspect, do not accurately represent the goods actually taken in charge, or if he has no reasonable means of checking such particulars, the multimodal transport operator or a person acting on his behalf shall insert in the multimodal transport document a reservation specifying these inaccuracies, grounds of suspicion or the absence of reasonable means of checking."

但英国不会去承认汉堡规则,笔者在此只想带出国际大潮流对"否定性批注"(disclaimer)有效性、合理性的看法。

§6 运费

运费并不是海牙规则或/与英国1992年海上运输法所要针对的。但因为 CIF/CFR 买卖的盛行,所以提单通常去注明"运费已经预付"(freight prepaid),这等于是承运人确认运费已经收到。这一来,对依赖与信赖这一表述的收货方/提单持有人来讲,他一样可去以本章4.1小段所讲的普通法下的禁止翻供对付想去"多收一次运费"的承运人。

船东想去胁迫收货人再收取一次运费,往往也难以成功:The "Alev" (1989) 1 Lloyd's Rep. 138。

当然,4.2小段介绍的各项立法下的禁止翻供,因为立法不针对运费,故并不适用。

不少已详论过的有关禁止翻供的各方面争议的处理在此课题同样适用,如:

6.1 表述运费已经预付必须无条件与明确

这与本章§5段讲述的大原则一样,否则衡平法/普通法下的禁止翻供难以成立。有关运费的"否定性批注"(disclaimer)曾在国际商会的 Publication No. 489, Case 248 报道过一例。它涉及一份"运费已经预付"的提单,但又另加一批注说:"Freight prepaid notation does not mean freight has been paid. It is still due and collectable prior to discharge."

该提单不为银行接受(国际商会同意),认为不是清洁的"运费已经预付"提单,也不符合 UCP 500 的要求。

另在 The "Constanza M" (1980) 1 Lloyd's Rep. 505,中国收货人虽已为一船来自美国的散粮支付了 CFR 的货价,但仍被迫去多支付一次运费给船东,道理也是一样,因为提单并未明确表述"运费已经预付",中国收货人不能去依赖一个不明确的表述。该先例的提单对支付运费的表述是:"freight payable according to terms/conditions and exceptions of C/P dated 18/1/79"。

提单格式通常会印上"运费未付"或"运费到付"(freight collect),若不去删掉就加上"运费已经预付"(freight prepaid)的批注,就会导致提单表面有矛盾之处。但不去吹毛求疵,这冲突其实很容易解释,就是后加的"运费已经预付"批注应有更大份量,可去超越前者。正如 Donaldson 大法官在 The "Galatia" (1979) 2 Lloyd's Rep. 450 之第 456 页说:"This is unarguable…that the bill of lading as tendered was overstamped 'Freight prepaid', whether or not the words 'Freight to pay' were deleted. It was no different from a receipted account."

6.2 禁止翻供只适用在第三者依赖与信赖这表述的情况

换言之,对欠下运费的发货人或/与承租人,船东仍可去向他/它们追索运费,不受签发"运费已经预付"提单所影响。在 Cho Yang Shipping v. Coral (UK) (1997) 2 Lloyd's Rep. 641 的上诉庭先例,曾提到一审的 Hallgarten 大法官说:"the basic commercial function of a 'freight prepaid' clause was to assure the notify party or other consignee that as between himself and the shipowner no liability for freight could be asserted; the expression 'freight prepaid' served in no way to affect the basic liability of the shipper if freight had not in fact been prepaid."

该先例涉及在真正发货人(货方)与合约发货人(货代/无船承运人)相异的情况下谁应支付运费,与目前探讨的题目无关,所以该先例案情就此略过,有兴趣人士可去看笔者的《程租合约》一书第九章之 6.1.2 小段的详论。

船东要先去签发或授权签发表述"运费已经预付"(freight prepaid)的提单,而事实上发货人或/与承租人仍未支付的情况经常有。其中原因是因为时间上的差异：发货人装了货物马上会要求签发提单，但汇出运费需时。而如果还有其他人参与（通常有，例如是"营运人"（operator）的二船东等），更是要转几手运费才能付到真正船东手中。这导致船长在装港不肯签发"这种"提单的争议/纠纷，除非收到运费。要注意的是只要船长愿意马上签发提单，只是少了"运费已经预付"的表述而已，这并不违反海牙规则的 Article 3(3)。所以，今天发货人/承租人都在租船时强迫船东接受一条条款是先签发"运费已经预付"提单，而后 3 天、7 天不等的工作天/银行天内，才需支付租约运费。这是程租，而在期租更已有先例明确船东不能去拒签"运费已经预付"提单，否则承租人在 CIF/CFR 买卖盛行的今天难以经营/营运：见 The "Nanfri" (1979) 1 Lloyd's Rep. 201。这一来，船东针对收货人已是禁止翻供（这是在提单下），但针对承租人（这是在租约下）仍可追索欠下的运费（或租金）。在这种情况下，船东失去了像留置货物那样的有效手段以迫出欠下的运费（或租金），但若是承租人有经济实力，不是光棍公司，船东也不会失去太多。这种大公司一去以仲裁或其他法律行动强硬对付，船东很快会迫其付出这笔欠下的运费。

§7 提单日期

提单既然是货物收据，它的日期理所当然就是货物装上船舶的那一天，这是常识。若是 2 万吨货物只装了 1 万吨上船，船东签发提单也只应是 1 万吨的货量而已。如果船东"好心"帮助发货人去签发了 2 万吨的"预借"提单，但之后发货人反咬一口不再装其余的 1 万吨船东可就惨了。或是，发货人不是"坏蛋"但待装的 1 万吨在岸上遇上意外受损，船东又是惨了。而即使一切顺利，去完全装妥 2 万吨上船，也是将来的日子，所以提早签发也类同于"倒签提单"，这做法会十分危险，稍后会探讨。

在海牙规则，Article 3(3)也针对何时何日签发提单，说得十分清楚，如下："After receiving the goods into his charge the carrier or the master...shall...issue to the shipper a bill of lading..."

7.1 付运日期在买卖合约中的重要性

对这方面问题，首先要了解付运日期（也就是提单日期）在买卖合约中的重要性。不难想象，不少货物都会有季节性、时间性：服装、应节（圣诞节或新年）商品、粮食等等。所以，现实中买卖合约通常会有条款针对最早与最后付运期。这尤其是在 CIF/CFR 买卖，付运是卖方的事，买方完全被动，只能去看提单日期以确定付运是否符合买卖合约的付运期。如果不符，卖方往往无法成功在信用证结汇：见 United City Merchants v. Royal Bank of Canada(1982) 2 Lloyd's Rep. 1。而买方也不必接受这份单证/这批货物。这一点可去节录笔者的《国际货物买卖》一书第二章之 7.3.10.5 小段如下:

7.3.10.5 付运日期

这方面的显示(即提单日期)也算是对货物本身描述的一部分。Benjamin's Sale of Goods 一书第四版的 18~116 段说是:

"It has been settled ever since the decision of the House of Lord in Bowes v. Shand (1877) 2 App. Cas. 455 that stipulations as to the time of shipment form part of the description of the goods, and breach of such stipulations entitles the buyer to reject."

货物描述与付运日期扯上关系,笔者想想也是有道理的,"期货"(futures)买卖的不是"7月份大豆","9月份棉花"吗?

在 Bowes v. Shand 的先例,涉及到了付运。货物(大米)付运期是 1874 年 3 月、4 月份。但大部分在 2 月已装上船,出了 3 套提单。只有另一套的少数大米是 3 月份签发的提单。贵族院判是买方可拒绝全部货物。Blackburn 勋爵说:"If the description of the article tendered is different in any respect it is not the article bargained for and the other party is not bound to take it."

像 Bowes v. Shand 的情况现实中不多,大多数是延迟了付运,这一来,明显是买方可以拒绝这套单证。这带来了"倒签提单"(backdate bill of lading)的恶行。这是欺诈行为而且是会触犯刑法的,这方面已在笔者的《信用证》一书第一章的 3.4.4 小段有详论。

提单日期如果不符合买卖合约,买方可拒绝卖方的"交单(tender)"。但如果倒签,买方在发觉后可拒绝接受货物,并向卖方追偿已支付的货款:见 Panchand Freres S. A. v. Et. General Grain Co. (1970) 1 Lloyd's Rep. 53。

固然,准时付运也不表示货物一定会及时抵达卸港。可能航次会延误,卸港会拥挤压港。但这都是买方的风险,能预见的延误情况也应是买方在买卖合约订下付运期当时已经预计在内的了。不能预见的如船东/承运人违约延误,买方/收货人可向他/它索赔延误损失:见 The "Heron Ⅱ"(1967) 2 Lloyd's Rep. 457。而汉堡规则更有严厉明确的条款(Article 19)针对承运人延误。这一切都不是卖方不能把风险及时按照买卖合约转移给买方的理由。

7.2 发货人无法及时装船的困境与对策

这些年来，船舶好找，谨慎与懂行的发货人一般不应有困难去在付运期内装船。当然，发货人在备货与把货物拉至船旁等方面还有其他安排，但这些都应可去预计。

怕就怕有意外，例如发货人（卖方）租的船舶在装港外发生碰船。事故不算严重，但仍要在装港先修理两个星期才能开始装货。但这一来，就会过了买卖合约的付运期。所以，发货人会面对几个选择与可能出现的矛盾，具体如下：

（ⅰ）马上另去紧急租入替代船舶，而对出事故的船舶将来以错过销约期为由取消租约。但可能会遇上租不到"即时待租船舶"（spot vessel），或要多支付运费而不舍得的情况。

（ⅱ）去与买方协调，要求延长付运期，以便出事故的船舶修理妥后按原计划装货。但这在货价市场下跌时会是自投罗网，买方会狠狠地敲诈或借机解除买卖合约。

（ⅲ）强迫出事故的船舶的承运人答应签发不准确日期（往往是买卖合约内付运期的最后一天）的提单，即所谓的"倒签提单"，否则以错过销约期为由取消租约。这做法会带来严重的不良后果，稍后详述。

以上的选择，在很大部分情况下笔者肯定会视（ⅰ）为最适当，较安全，损失也较有限（运费不会高太多）。但会有短视的发货人，也未去充分认识后果的严重性，就以看来简单的（ⅲ）的"倒签提单"去作为解决困境的选择。

7.3 倒签提单容易被发觉，无可抗辩及后果严重

倒签提单十分危险，相比于本章 3.3 小段的货物表面状况，发货人应更有戒心，原因是：

（ⅰ）这种行为太容易被发觉，而且一发觉就证据确凿。例如，任何人（如收货人）去询问装港当局货物什么时候装船，马上会有准确答案/证据。船舶的航海日志，又会有明确证据。从简单的精明做人道理已可分析：对太容易暴露，留下太多蛛丝马迹的"欺诈行为"千万不要去做。

（ⅱ）倒签提单不像其他提单内容的误述，可以争辩是"边沿案子"（borderline case）。一去倒签，欺诈意图即十分明确，就算有保函也不会有效：请参阅本章之 3.2.7.1 小段。甚至，会带来刑事起诉的对待；而做正当生意会导致犯刑法肯定是不明智。这种刑事案在香港也有听闻，而在美国的 1916 年提单法（在本书附录三）的 Section 41，更是明文规定可以被判入狱高达 5 年与罚款，这可不是开玩笑。

Cresswell 大法官在 SCB v. PNSC（1998）1 Lloyd's Rep. 684 的判词一开始就大

力抨击这种不诚实的做法,说是欺诈,必须严厉对付。他说:"Antedated and false bills of lading are a cancer in international trade. A bill of lading is issued in international trade with the purpose that it should be relied upon by those whose hands it properly comes—consignees, bankers and endorsees. A bank, which receives a bill of lading signed by or on behalf of a shipowner (as one of the documents presented under a letter of credit), relied upon the veracity and authenticity of the bill. Honest commerce requires that those who put bills of lading into circulation do so only where the bill of lading, as far as they know, represents the true facts."

(ⅲ)读者也不要受本章 4.1.4 小段的 Grant v. Norway (1851)10C. B. 665 先例困扰。且不说这先例颇受争议,毕竟它只是针对一种无中生有,货物从不存在的"空"提单。至于货物真装了上船,有实质、默示或表面授权的船长,承租人或代理人去签发的提单内容有错(不论任何内容,包括日期),船东/承运人都要受约束,要对后果负责。而后果就是已在本章 4.4 小段提到的就民事责任而言,这是误述侵权/"欺诈侵权"(tort of deceit),要对受害人作出赔偿:The "Saudi Crown" (1986) 1 Lloyd's Rep. 261;Alimport v. Soubert Shipping Co. Ltd. (2000) 2 Lloyd's Rep. 447。另 Evans 大法官也在近期一个著名的同类先例 SCB v. PNSC (2000) 1 Lloyd's Rep. 218 说:"If a false bill of lading is knowingly issued by the master or agent of the shipowner, and if the claimant(提单持有人) was intended to rely on it as being accurate, did rely upon it and as a result of doing so has suffered loss, then the shipowner is liable in damages for the tort of deceit."

(ⅳ)这种赔偿可以是十分巨大的,正如 4.4 小段所说,买方会失去拒绝提单的机会的所有损失。这不像其他提单内容的不正确,如货量是少量短装或应对货物表面状况加一些小批注,除了像"边沿案子"等多方面可供争辩,它们赔起来涉及的金额也较有限。

第七章　总　结

笔者在讲学中常被问及各种有趣的案件,千奇百怪,什么方面问题都有。往往这也不是三言两语可以说清楚的,但说太复杂倒也不见得,万变不离其宗嘛!那就是,处理问题时要有一个综合全面的知识与精密的逻辑思维。国际上的对手不会跟你有让分竞赛,往往是一子错,全盘皆输。

在此总结全书的一章,笔者想随意挑几个近期讲学中被问及的案件,介绍一下简单粗略的建议做法;但要强调的是,建议只是多种做法之一,而且变化无穷,每一案件的事实稍有不同即可能要调整做法,而其中极为重要的一项事实便是对手是谁?水平如何?强或弱?反应如何?等等。

案例一

问题涉及青岛公司(卖方)以 CIF 货价向日本出口两货柜的胡萝卜,买卖合约要求运输条件是:恒温集装箱,温度 3℃,通风量每小时 20M^3。因为根据以往经验,这样才可确保货物品质良好。但日本买方收到货物后,发现货已出现腐烂。经日本货检机构检验,认为原因是:(i)装箱前品质不良;(ii)运输过程中未按要求保持温度。

由于货在装运前已经过青岛动植物检验机构检验合格,之后才装箱发运,因此日本买方要求船公司提供运输途中集装箱温度的记录。但船公司拒不提供,故疑情无法证实。日本买方要求退货,并提出索赔。出于友好关系,卖方也就接受了买方的要求,退还货款(早已在信用证结汇),货也退回了青岛装港。卖方为此蒙受庞大损失,应如何办?

粗略的建议:

此案件涉及买卖合约以及该买卖合约下的运输合约的双重关系。在买卖合约,日本买方可否因货物腐烂而退货/拒货也难说。他必须证明在该买卖合约下,货物有"货不对板"的不符合描述/样本或不是满意质量等情况,又或卖方有条件条款的违反,才会有权拒货。这方面在《国际货物买卖》一书第四章有详论。

而运输的风险,却是在买方头上。在这过程中,货物照料不当而腐烂,是买方自己的事,与卖方无关。该买卖合约相信是适用英国法,因它在国际合约谈判中常常被坚持适用。所以,笔者的建议也以英国法为依据。由于笔者没有考虑到中国海商法的关系,故笔者提的建议要进一步探究。

有关是否"货不对板",在证据上有相异、冲突。买方检验指货坏有两个原因,一个可能会成为拒货的理由(但不一定,后详),而另一个肯定是日本买方自己应承担的风险(即运输未符合温度要求),这怎可拒货? 但卖方有检验书或证明(在青岛)显示货是检验合格后才装箱的,估计其内容是否定货物有品质不良。这一来,双方的证据就有正面矛盾和冲突了。

若买卖双方将来真打官司,就会涉及底哪一份的文件证据会被接受的问题。而这又会涉及诸多方面:如检验机构的权威性比较;他们如何出具的检验书或证明;内容包括什么;措辞/文字上表述如何与有否漏洞;等等。会是,作出检验的人要出庭(受理的法院或仲裁庭)接受反盘问。例如,日本的检验人会被盘问有关他对胡萝卜这种货物的经验与了解;他有何根据去区分是两个截然不同的原因造成货物腐烂;百分比是多少;等等。

而即使是日本的检验人被相信(压倒青岛的动植物检验合格证书),即货坏的部分原因确是装箱前品质不良,动植物检验合格不足为信,仍不一定足以令买方拒货。这方面不多讲,只请读者看看《国际货物买卖》一书与 The "Hansa Nord" (1975) 2 Lloyd's Rev. 445 先例,便可理解在此案中买方不一定有权拒货。另一变数是要看看买卖合约的确切条文/措辞。

该案中青岛卖方为了友好而向日本买方让步,接受了退货/拒货。一说到友好,就不必多言了。但这样一来,也表示青岛卖方的庞大损失无法去找日本买方追回,否则会与较早的"友好"接受退货有矛盾,毕竟要友好就友好到底呗!

青岛卖方可另找的索赔对象会是:

(ⅰ)保险公司,而且友好地要求日本买方把保单交还或/与同时把保险利益转让。

(ⅱ)船东。

表面看来,若是青岛动植物检验可信,有权威,没有疏忽,显示货物装箱前品质没有问题,则怀疑问题出在运输途中确有道理。而一旦能够去表面证明,即指证更大的可能是在运输中出事,则据此可向保险公司或船公司索赔。

但只是怀疑而没有证据,船东又不合作,这怎么办呢? 没有任何证据,无法了解重要事实,青岛卖方是下不了决心去起诉,也走不出这一步。想去息事宁人地寻求庭外和解又因没有任何证据而致心中没底,故难以成功。

这涉及调查与取证的技巧。青岛卖方可先考虑向船东迫出证据,而这种"诉讼前"(pre-action)的取证方法有好几种,在笔者的《禁令》一书有详述,如著名的 Anton

Piller禁令等等。

但与本案有关的另一方法是在《禁令》一书的第五章9.3/9.4小段有介绍,可节录如下:

9.3 命令交出与允许检查文件东西(Order for delivery up and inspection of goods)

在原告(或将来的原告)作出申请,英国法院可去向被告作出命令。这权力来自Supreme Court Act 1981的Section 33(在香港高院规则之R. S. C. ,Order 29),内容如下:

"(1)On the application of any person in accordance with rules of court, the High Court shall, in such circumstances as may be specified in the rules, have power to make an order providing for any one or more of the following matters, that is to say—

(a)the inspection, photographing, preservation, custody and detention of property which appears to the court to be property which may become the subject-matter of subsequent proceedings in the High Court, or as to which any question may arise in any proceedings; and

(b) the taking of samples of any such property as is mentioned in paragraph (a), and the carrying out of any experiment on or with any such property."

英国法院如果下了命令要被告(或将来可能的被告)交出文件东西,或是允许检查(例如东西太大或固定了位置)与取样本,被告不去依从,又会是蔑视法院。

看来,这个做法与Anton Piller命令也差不多,而且代价便宜多了。例如誓词证据不这么严格(好像不必去达至5.1小段的"极强表面诉因"),可省了监督律师,等等。但它比不上Anton Piller命令的优越(对原告而言)是:

(ⅰ)这命令起交出文件/东西,一定程度仍是要被告知法,畏法,依法行事。否则在打草惊蛇后,他去私下毁灭,推说没有这文件/东西,要去证明他蔑视法院不一定是易事。所以,对付不了像本章§1段及多处提到的万恶盗版等的"海盗"。

(ⅱ)这命令针对的文件东西,从措辞/文字可见,较为局限,只是在"会成为将来诉讼的事物"(may become the subject-matter of subsequent proceedings…)。所以不能去包括有关或可能有关的其他文件证据。例如在涉嫌破坏专利商标,命令被告去交出涉嫌破坏的东西/产品是可以。或是在涉嫌破坏机密,命令前雇员交出原告的机密客户名单也可以。但不能延展去其他方面如第三者之间的通信往来,等。

（iii）这命令不是一个突击行动,被告不会严重受压迫,害怕,无助,等,而导致只能去无条件投降。换言之,这命令并非是"核武",Anton Piller 命令才是。对原告而言如果另有谋图如打击消灭竞争者(也会是对方也有点不干净,反正多数情况会是说不清)。则这命令是远远比不上 Anton Piller 命令(再跟着另一个蔑视法院的指控)。

9.4 诉讼前的检查船舶(Pre-action inspection of ships)

英国海事法院有权下命令去让原告(或将来的原告)去对有关船舶作出检查已有上百年历史。这个做法,已在本书第一章§5段之(vi)详及,不再去重复。在此只是分析这做法与 Anton Piller 命令的不同之处。

与上一小段所讲一样,这命令的申请是比 Anton Piller 命令容易/廉宜得多。只去挑二个方面讲讲:

（i）誓词证据不这么严格,不必去达至5.1小段的"极强表面诉因"。只要是,像 Sheen 大法官在 The "Mare del Nord" (1990) 1 Lloyd's Rep. 40 所说的:

"The evidence on affidavit in support of the claimants' application must show that the claimants have a good arguable case on the merits. The evidence must show *prima facie* that on delivery there was a shortage of cargo which should not be treated as *de minimis*."

（ii）可省了监督律师。

但这命令(检查船舶)比不 Anton Piller 命令对原告优越主要也会在局限性。这局限首先在盗版,侵犯专利/商标/机密等的纠纷不能适用,它们并不涉及船舶。而另一局限来自可去检查的范围,这一点在 The "Mare del Nord"案例显示。

在该案例,涉及较早一个航次的在突尼西亚的 La Skhira 港卸货(汽油)有短缺。这种货物在没有意外而发生有短缺,其中可能是船舶上加装管道去偷油(船舱至燃油框),当然也可能是腐蚀而漏油等等原因(船舶不适航)。

稍后,该船舶另外航次到了英国的 Swansea 港。代表索赔原告的律师向被告(船东)律师提出要求检查并警告说:

"If agreement cannot be reached with regard to the above requests we shall of course have to make the necessary applications to the court …for an order that surveyor be allowed on board."

可见,检查船舶一般是不怕打草惊蛇的,总不成船东会去毁灭证据,只为了一个货损货差案件去把船舶弄沉？当然,太早打草惊蛇是会有一定危险船东去事前改装或出售船舶等行为。

船东律师回答说在考虑,并要求原告如果向法院申请命令,请预先通知与提供一份宣誓书/誓词证据:

"With regard to the question of surveyors, a decision has still not been made, but we shall revert to you just as soon as we are informed." 与,

"If you intend to make an application for an order for inspection we require reasonable notice of such intention and would expect to see copies of any affidavit etc. In advance."

接下去索赔方/原告律师紧急回电传(紧急是船期,船舶一开航就完了),说:

"As mentioned on the telephone we intend to apply to the court this morning for an order that a surveyor on behalf of our clients be permitted to board the vessel for inspection and sampling. We shall forward to you a copy of the affidavit in support of our application shortly."

长话短说,"海事法院常务主任"(Admiralty Registrar)下了命令,上船检查包括是:"…plaintiffs' surveyor access to the vessel for the purpose of inspecting and photographing any part thereof, and to take samples from non-cargo spaces and to consider any relevant ship's documents, and in particular any general and pipe arrangement plans which may assist in the survey, and to take relevant copies of these documents."

以上第一项是检查船舶,这没有问题。第二项也没有问题,是关于取样本,主要是燃油样本,估计是去查会否有可能偷回来的货物混在一起。但问题出在第三项的有关文件。在正常诉讼(更不用说诉讼仍未开始),披露文件是稍后才发生(在该案例)。所以,被告(船东)提出反对了,指这个命令雷同 Anton Piller 命令。若是如此,Admiralty Registrar 无权去作出/给予,高院法官才有权。

但 Sheen 大法官认为原告只是去看这些船舶制图(总布置图的"general arrangement plan"与管道图的"piping plan"),是包括在有关的检查船舶命令的立法内。这立法不光是指"船舶"(ship),也加了"其他财产"(other property)。这立法已在本书第一章§5段有节录,以下只去重复有关与要强调的措辞/文字:

"…The Court may…make an order for the inspection…by any party…of any ship or other property…the inspection of which may be…desirable for the purpose of obtaining full information or evidence in connection with any issue in the action."

所以,判决是原告有权这样做,Admiralty Registrar 也有权作出/给予这个命令,它非是 Anton Piller 命令。Sheen 大法官说:

"…although an order for discovery of documents at this stage was premature a surveyor who was required to consider whether oil could have been leaked from a cargo space to a non-cargo space, could not carry out his task without seeing the general arrangement plan and the piping plan and the inspection of such documents was within(有关高院规则)。

考虑到此案涉及的船公司应是班轮公司,故船舶应重返青岛港。这可让青岛卖方向青岛海事法院申请类似做法的"诉讼前"(pre-action)调查与取证。

调查后若真涉及运输中未按要求保持温度,或可能性很大,青岛卖方可考虑向保险公司与船东索赔,若遭拒绝即去起诉。照说,货物保的若是"一切险"(All Risks),拒赔原因的举证责任是在保险公司。而对船东而言,青岛卖方可以青岛动植物检验证明合格后货物才装箱铅封对比日本货检机构检验证明胡萝卜货物腐烂,说明问题出在运输途中。另外,根据调查结果,可指证船东在保持温度方面没有妥善与小心照看货物:请看第五章之 4.2.8 小段。

就船东的立场而言,若真是没有妥善与小心照看货物,即在此案中没有按要求保持温度,也应承担赔偿之责。但船东在文件披露后,在看到日本货检机构的检验证明后,会试图以货物(胡萝卜)的"固有缺陷"为抗辩(第五章之 4.2.7.1.10 小段)。当然,这方面的举证责任在船东,例如依赖专家意见去分析日本货检机构的检验证明,同时去推翻青岛出的证书,试图把货物腐烂的原因归咎为装箱前品质不良,即"固有缺陷"。

若是估计无法把所有原因推为是货物的"固有缺陷",船东会设法举证有多少腐烂是来自违约(没有妥善与小心照看货物,去保持要求的温度)而又有多少是来自"固有缺陷"。这往往又要依赖专家意见。如果无法明确区分,船东要全部负责。如区分得开,则船东可对证明是"固有缺陷"的部分免责:(第五章之 4.2.8 小段)。

再回去讲青岛卖方,因为在日本卸港提货的收货人/提单持有人是日本买方,他只是后来开箱发觉胡萝卜腐烂才退货的,而退货/拒货权力是来自"友好"而非是合约(法律)。这一来,提单合约的诉权与索赔真正损失的权利会在日本买方手上,青岛卖方会要以日本买方的名义向船东起诉(例如以"对物诉讼"(in rem)在香港告船扣船,或在青岛海事法院等):请看第三章之,12.2.5.2 小段,该段特别谈及英国 1992 年海上运输法之 Section 2(5)。

这些要借助日本买方名义的安排,青岛卖方都要在"友好"让日本买方退货和还钱(货价)前先说好,以防将来日本买方反面不认人。看来,想去"友好"也不是简单一句话。

案例二

问题涉及一批中国进口货物[711],货卸了 2/3 后出入境检验检疫局要求停止卸货,因检验结果是货物含有杂质与有毒,超出安全标准。卸港海关据此决定不准再将未卸货物卸下并要求退运出境。中国买方已以信用证支付进口货物的货款,损失重大,因而在卸港委托律师把船舶扣了。结果双方僵在那里,过了一个多月仍未解决。至于卸到岸上的 2/3 货物,业已部分处理。外国船东先在中国海事法院反索赔扣错船(中国买方同时反索赔货损或/与交货不符),期间,再以提单合并了租约的伦敦仲裁条款为由向中国买方发出仲裁通知。中国买方问笔者如何处理。

粗略建议:

此案件表面看来买方索赔的对象可能不正确,即不应针对船东/承运人,而应针对卖方,因为问题(即货物有杂质与有毒)不是在运输中出的。除非是,货物的杂质涉及不应在装港签发清洁提单,这样才能把船东扯进去。至于这杂质能否合理看得见,船长应否签发清洁提单,这些都是事实问题,恐怕要向船长/大副与在装港的有关人士调查/取证,并会要专家来给予意见证据才能下判断。但笔者被中国的买方询问此案,感觉他对事实了解不够、知道得不多。他没有向船上进行调查/取证;他若运气好,会取得一份出具清洁提单的保函或有杂质批注的大副收据(批注没有在提单出现)。这里也可见到另一危险,是一点不了解事实就贸然起诉(类同宣战),把外国船舶扣下来,会是骑虎难下,泥足深陷。

外国卖方作为索赔对象应是错不了,因为问题明确是出自他所供应的货物。看来,这有毒的杂质会让中国买方有足够理由去拒货/退货,其理由比如是货物没达到满意质量,违反了默示条件条款:见《国际货物买卖》一书的第四章之 2.2.4 小段。但中国买方已处理了部分卸下的货物,令这一步做不了,只能去索赔损失。

可以扯着卖方的另一个原因是因为船舶的承租人是他,变得船舶僵在卸港,仍有 1/3 货物没有卸下,总要有个解决才能还船。但愿卖方不是以皮包公司的名义去租船,否则会令他可以撒手不管,中国买方扯着卖方要去解决的问题有几方面,同时应以谈判加上行动对其施加压力,例如:

(ⅰ)要卖方退回货款或作出赔偿。即使退货已不可能,但总得赔偿损失(1/3 货物卸不下来,岸上 2/3 货物若有杂质/有毒也应有损失,如低价出售,补偿分买方的索赔等)。

(ⅱ)可向卖方同时起诉,如买卖合约有仲裁条款,则要开始仲裁。

(ⅲ)双方考虑如何处理这卸不下的 1/3 货物,如再向中国当局交涉,希望宽待

---

[711] 为了保密,不便说明货物品名。

或寻求转售他港/他国等等。

（ⅳ）最好在适当时机把船东/承运人扯进来，以取得其合作（如开去他港卸货），并可一揽子解决他/它指称扣错船的反索赔。

另一方面，中国买方也非要去继续对付船东/承运人不可，毕竟扣了船舶，已骑上了虎背。若调查/取证后（尽管晚了一点）说明真是船长不应签发清洁提单，这是好事，中国买方也可以理直气壮的跟船东/承运人对着干。至于面对伦敦仲裁的通知如何对付，中国买方可先要求船东/承运人披露合并在提单的一份租约，内有伦敦仲裁条款。这电传抄本送给船东/承运人的仲裁员，迫使对方非要披露不可。据知在该案中，迫出的是一份期租合约。这一来，谈判归谈判，（这会是在"无损害"（without prejudice）基础下进行的），针对伦敦仲裁通知的对策可以是：

（A）不去理睬，冷眼看外国船东走错路，并继续走下去。将来面对缺席裁决书执行时才抗辩称没有有效的伦敦仲裁条款合并进提单。有的也不是期租合约的仲裁条款，因为英国法律也认为租约提单不会合并一份期租合约，双者格格不相入，请看本书第四章之 2.2.3 小段。

同时，大力推进中国卸港的海事法院的审理，务求早日获得判决，促使既成事实，而且船舶仍扣留着，可以马上执行。

（B）或，去与船东/承运人争辩说期租合约合并不了进提单，所以以它的仲裁条款（N.Y.P.E 标准格式的三人仲裁条款）来处理，来通知属无效。这不好的地方是船东/承运人的律师会被提醒，可以很快地找出下一份程租约（很可能会有），再纠正说这才是被合并进提单的租约，而且没有格格不入之处，并重新发出伦敦仲裁通知（程租或许是一条独任仲裁员的条款，谁知道？）：这方面请看本书第四章之 2.2.3 小段。

（C）或，若仲裁无可避免而回复时限将届，为了不失去可自己任命仲裁员的好处，不妨在"抗议下"（under protest）与说明"无损害我方认为提单内无仲裁条款"的基础上，去任命自己的仲裁员。这种做法可见于 The "Heigberg"（1994）2 Lloyd's Rep. 287 先例。

中国买方做了以上（A）或（B）或（C）的一步后，可考虑：

（1）向中国海事法院申请类似"anti-suit 禁令"（请看《禁令》一书的第六章）的裁定，指案件已在中国海事法院审理，不应再起动伦敦仲裁。据知，船东/承运人并没有在中国法院申请中止。而且，它也已在中国海事法院采取了一些行动，可以说是放弃了伦敦仲裁（即使提单有合并）。所以即使依据1958年的纽约公约，中国海事法院不尊重伦敦仲裁条款也是振振有辞。

（2）大力推进中国海事法院的审理。

（3）尽量拖延伦敦的仲裁，若非要推进的话，就要求仲裁庭先做一个中间裁决，以确定其有否管辖权。理由是提单没有有效仲裁条款（提单不能合并期租租约），或/与"争议本身"（substantive dispute）已在中国海事法院审理等[部分伦敦仲裁员是不愿意正面与外国法院抢案件而放手不理的，例如笔者经历过的 The "Nand Nakul"(1999)]。

（4）甚至像 The "Heidberg" 先例，在英国法院起诉，要求一个"宣示判决"（declaration）确定伦敦仲裁不能进行，并出禁令阻止。

以上所做的一切，均是为了寻求《禁令》一书所讲的备战伐谋之管辖地点的知战之地，力图保持在中国海事法院审理，以占天时地利人和之利。这一来也大大增加了外国船东/承运人的疑虑，进而导致其愿意对中国买方作出让步以达成和解。和解会是多方面的，包括如何处置仍在船上的 1/3 货物以及怎样补偿中国买方的所有损失等（外国船东会向承租人/卖方加压）。

话说回来，若是调查/取证后看来责任明确，比如船东的确不应签发清洁提单，则中国买方为了取得诉前保全在中国海事法院扣船也没有做错，照说"争议本身"（substantive dispute）在中国海事法院或在伦敦仲裁审理都应是一样。他/它们都应是公平、合理与懂行的。

最后再去总结的一点是如何处理卸不下来的 1/3 货物，这问题需要马上解决。特别是，调查结果的确不属船东的责任，就真会扣错船。这样拖延下去不是办法，而且事情会越搞越大。笔者想到的几点是：

（Ⅰ）提单若合并期租约或合并什么程租约并不明确，表示没有卸货时间与滞期费条款（请看本书第四章之 2.2.1/2.6.2 小段），这表示一个多月的延误，扣船，货卸不下来，不知如何办等，中国收货人/买方并没有支付滞期费或赔滞期损失的责任。因仍有 1/3 货物未曾卸下，所以船仍在卸货中。虽有严重延误，或可以争辩错不在中国买方：这一方面请看《程租合约》一书的第十一章 1.1.6 - 1.1.9 小段。

（Ⅱ）船东/承运人当然会急于把货物卸下，但一路在支付租金的卖方也不见得不心急，对此中国买方可充分利用，毕竟只有卖方才更有办法去处理仍在船上的货。除非是已提及的卖方以皮包公司租船的情况。

（Ⅲ）船东/承运人可迫使期租承租人卸清货物和还船，但能否去迫收货人就有商榷之处。首先会有类似合约受阻的说法，即针对提单合约而言，有 1/3 货物因当局阻止而无法再卸下。期租合约不同提单合约，在后者收货人没有责任与权利去他港卸货/清除货物，所以收货人解决不了问题。但问题若真出在货物本身，主因/近因不在当局阻止，船东/承运人可以盯着发货人要他负责。而且，依英国 1992 年海上运输法（如果适用）的 Section 2，收货人/提单合法持有人若做了 Section 3 定明的 3 个行动之一，则也要承担上与"原订约方（发货人）"一样的合约责任，好像他/它就是原订约方一样：请看本书第三章之 12.2.5.2/12.2.5.3 小段。这一来，在该案中,中国买方(他/它已做尽了1992年立法的Section 3定明的3个行动)会有卸清货物的责任。顺便再提一提,1992年英国立法可能会适用是因为毕竟要否去伦敦仲裁仍是未知数。

(Ⅳ)所以,中国买方动不动以自己大公司的名义去收货/提货不一定是明智之举:请看本书第三章之11.2.1小段,特别提到了The "Aegean Sea" (1998) 2 Lloyd's Rep. 39先例中的西班牙国家石油公司做法。毕竟,第六章之2.2小段详论了另一可能的责任,就是在危险品方面。当然,本案例中,这已是"既成事实"中国出面的收货人/买方,被外国船东索赔扣错船,确是一家大的国营公司。

(Ⅴ)看来,要马上或尽快解决,中国买方仍须充分利用仅有的有利点去争取卖方同意作出有关安排。有利点会是较早讲的(Ⅰ)与(Ⅱ),以及卖方/船东对中国海事法院的判决会有的疑虑。

案例三

问题涉及一批以CFR货价进口中国的货物,船舶在法国的装港(波尔多)开出,在航道不慎碰上一个油码头,并因此引起火灾,把部分货物烧毁。另在救火时海水再湿损了部分货物。最后船舶获救并回航去波尔多,卖方把剩下的少量完好货物转运回中国。该船在波尔多被油码头所有人扣船并起诉,这看似责任明确,这种侵权是不存在天掉下来的"航行过错或/与疏忽"的免责的。但船东因索赔金额庞大,于是在波尔多成立责任限制基金,试图在1976年的责任限制公约下享有以船舶吨位计算的责任限制:这一方面请看本书第五章之4.2.10.3.9小段与更详尽的《海事法》一书之第二章。但据悉责任限制的申请被波尔多法院拒绝。

在波尔多签发的提单,通知人是中国买方,收货人是"凭指示"(to order):请看本书第二章之3.1.5.2小段。法国卖方以这套单证向银行结汇,中国买方不知道应如何处理。

粗略建议:

中国买方若有投保,应不必担忧。事故虽然严重,但应在保险范围内。故中国买方应快通知保险公司,并相互协调看应采取什么行动,如针对船东的索赔行动。

而针对法国卖方,看来除非买卖合约有较不寻常的规定(请看《国际货物买卖》一书之第六章5.2小段),货物风险应是一装上船舶已转移给了中国买方。故此在发生火灾与碰码头之时,风险已归中国买方。看来法国卖方去安排将剩下的完好货物转运回中国亦是不必要,那应是中国买方自己的事情。

中国买方或/与代位的保险公司若想去针对船东/承运人,首先要想到这货损货差表面看会是由于"航行过错或/疏忽"或/与"火灾"所致,而这些在海牙·维斯比规则下都是免责的:见本书第五章之4.2.7.1.1小段与4.2.7.1.2小段。法国是海牙·维斯比规则签字国,规则应强制适用在本案件的航次:请看第五章之4.5小段。

所以,中方也要小心,不要乱起诉。否则一旦开始了行动,如告船并试图扣船,会变得收不了手,只能一路告下去。当然,海牙·维斯比规则的一年时效也短得很,故要尽快调查/取证以利下决定。

在这案件提供给笔者的有限资料中唯一觉得可疑,应去进一步调查才好决定对不对付船东的是他/它的责任限制申请被波尔多法院拒绝。但照说,船东这个权力应不会轻易被否定,除非能证明船东是"意图去造成损失"或/与"明知可能会造成损失而轻率地作为或不作为":请看《海事法》一书第二章之4.4小段。

这一来,与"案例一"相同,又要涉及"诉讼前"(pre-action)调查与取证的技巧。不同的是,今次对象不是船东,而是第三者的波尔多法院。中国买方或/与保险公司可能要通过波尔多的律师或代理人,去查看并取得船东为何被拒责任限制的有关文件。波尔多法院应会对部分文件公开,这毕竟是司法透明的一部分,令外人看得见或可去复印副本。但实际操作如何,那要去问法国律师了。像英国法院这一方面是在高院规则 Order 63, rule 4 有针对,它区分了诉讼的对方与"外人"(non-parties)。对方当事人可去看与复印所有法院文件,但非当事方的外人受到限制。例如,内庭的"宣誓书"(affidavits)、"书面供词"(deposition)、法官在内庭作出过的判决与命令,都不是外人可去查阅的。正如在 Dobson v. Hastings (1992) Ch. 394 之第401页所说:That is the necessary corollary of the rules granting only a limited right to inspect and take copies. In other words, a court file is not a publicly available register. It is a file maintained by the court for the proper conduct of proceedings. Access to that file is restricted. Non-parties have a right of access to the extent, but only to the extent, provided in the rules. The scheme of the rules is that, by being filed, documents do not become available for inspection or copying save to the extent that access to specified documents or classes of documents is granted either generally under the rules or by leave of the court in a particular case…In all cases, however, the court retains an overriding discretion to permit a person to inspect if he has good reason for doing so[712]。

若调查后最终认为采取行动去对付船东是值得的(例如查出碰上油码头实是因为不适航,舵机严重失修导致失灵引起的),接下来便要涉及一连串的行动,如查明谁是提单下的承运人,以找对要告的对象:见本书第三章之§2段。若承运人是船东(一般租约提单都会是船东提单),就要去查他/它有否姊妹船以及这些船(如有的话)和

---

[712] 看来,单方面向法院作出申请,说明中国买方有正当的利益(legitimate interest),充分的理由,需要查阅法院档案,希望法官会行使裁量权予以允许,是英国的做法。

出事船舶通常航行的港口,以决定如何/何处去告船与扣船。这些资料在 Lloyd's Confidential Index, Lloyd's Maritime Directory 以及 Lloyd's Shipping Index 等刊物内均可找到。或是,发觉一份提单是 Congenbill 1994 格式(本书附录八),合并了租约的巴黎仲裁条款,并从法国卖方处取得有关的一份租约,那买方可考虑向船东提起仲裁,毕竟一年时效将届。至于同时去告船扣船,为的是取得诉前保全,这一般不受仲裁影响。像英国 1996 年仲裁法之 Section 11 与联合国示范法之 Article 9,都明确说可以这样做。

总结:

通过对以上三个案例的简略介绍,读者会发现在实际操作中,取证、收集资料和分析证据的技巧十分重要。这方面与许多其他有关方面,笔者与杨大明先生将在下一本书《英美证据法》中详述,而《英美证据法》亦会是作者最重要的一本书。

案例索引

Aakre 1941 AMC 1263(2 Cir. 1941) ……………………………………… C5/4. 2. 6. 6. 7
Achile Lauro v. Total (1968) 2 Lloyd's Rep. 247 …………………………… C4/3. 4. 4
Adam v. Cape Industries (1990) Ch 433 ……………………………………… C3/14
Adler v. Dickson (1955) 1 QB 158 ………………………… C3/8. 2. 2, C5/4. 2. 3. 3. 2. 4
Aetna Insurance v. Carl Matusek Shipping Co. 1956 AMC 400 (S. D. Fla. 1955) …………
  ……………………………………………………………………………… C5/4. 2. 3. 5. 3. 8
Akt. Ocean v. Harding (1928) 30 Lloyd's Rep. 249 ……………………………… C3/ § 10
Alamo Chemical Transp. Co. v. The Overseas Valdes, 1979 AMC 2033 …………… C4/3. 4. 12
Alimport v. Soubert Shipping Co. Ltd. (2000) 2 Lloyd's Rep. 447 ……… C3/5. 2, C6/4. 4, 7. 3
All American Trading Corp. v. New York Maru, 1988 AMC 2208 (SDNY1987) ……………
  ……………………………………………………………………………… C5/4. 2. 4. 4. 2
Allianz v. Indian Steamship Co. 11 Z. R. , 135/82, 30. 5. 1983 …………………… CA/3. 1
Allied Chemical v. Companhia de Navegacao Lloyd Brasileiro, 775F 2d 476, 483(2d Cir. 1985)
  ……………………………………………………………………………… C2/5. 1. 11
Allseas Maritime v. The Mimosa, 574 F. Supp. 844(S. D. Text. 1993) …………… C4/3. 4. 12
Allstate chs. Co. v. Int'l Shipping Corp. 1985 AMC 760 (11Cir. 1983) ……………… C4/3. 1
Aluminium Industrie Vaassen v. Romalpa (1976) 1 Lloyd's Rep. 443 ……………… C2/3. 1. 2
Amer. Tobacco Co. v. S. S. Katingo Hadjipatera, 81F. Supp. 438, 1949 AMC 49(SDNY 1948)
  ……………………………………………………………………………… C5/4. 2. 7. 1. 2. 1
American Mail Line v. Tokyo M. & F. Ins. Co. , 270 F. 2d 499, 1959 AMC 2220 (9 Cir. 1959)
  ……………………………………………………………………………… C5/4. 2. 7. 1. 2. 6
American Smelting v. Irish Spruce 1977 AMC 780 (2 Cir. 1977) ……………… C5/4. 2. 6. 6. 7
American Union Transport Inc. v. United States, 1976 AMC 1480 ……………… C4/3. 4. 12
Anglo-Saxon Petroleum v. Adamastos Shipping Co. (1958) 1 Lloyd's Rep. 73 ……………
  ……………………………………………………………………… (请看 The "Saxon Star")
Anselme Dewavrim v. Wilsons & North-Eastern (1931) 39 Lloyd's Rep. 289 ……… C5/4. 2. 3. 4
Arbib & Houlberg v. Second Russian Insurance Co. 294 F 811 (2 Cir. 1923) ……… C5/4. 2. 1
Arkwright Mutual Insurance Co. v. Oriental Fortune, 745 F. Supp. 920, 1991 AMC (2237) 2240 –
2241, ref. Cited (SDNY 1990) ……………………………………………… C5/4. 2. 4. 4. 2

Armenia Coffee v. Santa Magdalena,1983 AMC 1249 (SDNY 1982) ········· C5/4. 2. 10. 2. 4. 3
Armour & Co. v. Compania Argentina de Navegacion (1958) 2 Lloyd's Rep. 49 ··· C5/4. 2. 8. 2
Attorney General v. Blake (1998) 1 All ER 833 ·············· C2/5. 5. 1
Attorney-General of Ceylon v. Scindia SS Co. Ltd. (1961) 2 Lloyd's Rep. 173 ············
·· C6/5. 3. 3 ,5. 5
Australasian United Steam Navigation Co. Ltd v. Hiskens (1914) 18 CLR 646 ········· C5/4. 2. 1
Baines v. Holland (1855) 10 Exch. 802 ·············· C5/4. 2. 6. 5
Bally Inc. v. Zim America (2nd Cir.) 20 April 1994; LMLN #390 ················ C6/3. 2. 6. 2
Bank of New Zealand v. Ginivan (1991) 1 NZLR 178 ············· C2/5. 5. 2
Bankers Trust Co. v. State Bank of India (1991) 2 Lloyd's Rep. 443 ················ C2/5. 9. 1. 6
Banque Keyser Ullmann SA v. Skandia (UK) Co. Insurance Ltd. (1990) 1 QB 665, (1991) 2 AC
249 ·· C2/5. 5. 2
Barclays Bank Ltd. v. Commissioners of Custom and Excise (1963) 1 Lloyd's Rep. 81 ············
································ C2/3. 1. 2 ,3. 1. 5. 4 ,5. 1. 12
Barth v. Atl. Container Line, 1985 A. M. C. 1196 (D. Md. 1984) ·········· C5/4. 2. 10. 3. 3. 3
Baumwoll v. Gilchrest (1892) 1 Q. B. 253, (1893) A. C. 8 ············· C3/3. 1
BBMB Finance (Hong Kong) v. Eda Holdings (1991) 2 All ER 129 ·········· C2/5. 5. 1
Bell v. Peter Browne & Co. (1990) 2 QB 495 ·············· C2/5. 5. 2
Beswick v. Beswick (1968) AC 58 ·············· C3/12. 2
Bewise v. Hoi Kong 5th Nov. 1998 (香港) ·············· C5/4. 2. 3. 3. 2. 5, 4. 2. 3. 4. 1
Biggin v. Permanite (1951) 2 LB 314 ·············· C5/4. 2. 10. 2. 8. 2
Birkett v. James (1978) A. C. 297 ·············· C5/4. 2. 10. 2. 8. 7
Bitchoupan Rug Corp. v. A. S. Arias, 1975 AMC 278 (SDNY 1975) ········ C5/4. 2. 10. 2. 4. 3
Blue Bird Food Products Co. v. Baltimore & Ohio Railway Co., 492 F. 2d (1329) 1332 (3
Cir. 1974) ·············· C6/3. 3. 2
Bond, Connolly v. Federal SN Co. (1905) 21 TLR 438 ·············· C5/3. 2
Bowes v. Shand (1877) 2 App. Cas. 455 ·············· C6/7. 1
Brandt v. Liverpool (1924) 1 KB 575 ············· C3/12. 2. 1, 12. 2. 3, 12. 2. 4, 12. 2. 5. 5
Brass v. Maitland (1856) 6E. & B. 470 ·············· C3/11. 2. 1
British and Foreign Marine Insurance Co. v Samuel Sanday & Co. (1916) 1 A. C. 650 ············
·· C5/4. 2. 7. 1. 7
Brown Jenkinson v. Percy Dalton (1957) 1 Lloyd's Rep. 31 (一审) ·············
································ C6/3. 2. 4, 3. 2. 7. 1, 3. 2. 7. 3, 3. 3
Brown Jenkinson v. Percy Dalton (1957) 2 Lloyd's Rep. 1 (上诉庭) ·········· C2/5. 4. 2
Buckeye State, 39F. Supp. 344, 1941 AMC 1238 (WDNY 1941) ········ C5/4. 2. 7. 1. 2. 1
C. N. R. v. E. & S. Barbour Ltd. (1963) S. C. R. 323 ·············· C5/4. 2. 7. 1. 3. 5. 1

Caemint Food, Inc. v. Lloyd Brasileiro, 1981 AMC (1801) 1812, 647 F. 2d (347) 354 (2 Cir. 1981) ·· C6/3. 3. 2
Calif. And Hawaiian S. Corp. V. Columbia SS Co. 173 AMC 676 ················ C5/4. 2. 6. 6. 7
Calmaquip Eng. West Hemisphere v. West Coast Carriers 1984 AMC 839 (5 Cir. 1981) ·········
··· C4/3. 1, C5/4. 2. 3. 1. 6
Canada & Dominion Sugar v. Canadian National (1946) 80 Lloyd's Rep. 13 ·······················
··· C6/3. 3, 3. 3. 6. 2, 4. 1. 1, §5, 5. 2, 5. 3. 2
Caparo Industries v. Dickman (1990) 2 AC 605 ·· C2/5. 5. 2
Cape Asbestos Co. Ltd. v. Lloyds Bank Ltd. (1921) W. N. 274 ·················· C2/3. 1. 5. 2
Captain v. Far Eastern Steamship Co. (1979) 1 Lloyd's Rep. 595 ················ C5/4. 2. 3. 1. 6
Captayannis "S", 1969 AMC 2484 (D. Ore. 1969) ································ C5/4. 2. 6. 2
Carlberg v. Wemyss (1915) S. C. 616 ···························· C2/5. 1. 7, 5. 1. 8, 5. 1. 12, 5. 2. 1
Carle and Montanari Inc. v. American Export Isbrandtsen Lines Inc. and others (1968) 1 Lloyd's Rep. 260 ·· C3/8. 2. 2, C5/4. 2. 3. 3. 2. 4
Cattle v. Stockton Waterworks Co. (1875) L. R. 10 QB 453 ······················ C3/8. 2. 4
Center Chem Products v. A/S Rederiet (1972 A. M. C. 373) ····················· C6/3. 2. 2. 2
Cerro Sales Corp. v. Atlantic Marine Enterprises, 1976 AMC 375 (SDNY 1975) ···············
··· C5/4. 2. 10. 2. 2. 5
Chargeurs Reunis Compagnie Francaise de Navigation a Vapeur v. English & American Shipping Co. (1921) 9 Lloyd's Rep. 464 ··· C3/8. 2. 3, 8. 2. 4
Charles Goodfellow Lumber Sales v. Verreault, Hovingfon and Verreault Navigation Inc. (1971) 1 Lloyd's Rep. 185 ·· C5/4. 2. 7. 1. 3. 2
Chartered Bank v. British Steam Navigation (1909) AC 369 ················ C2/5. 6. 2, C5/3. 1
Cho Yang Shipping v. Coral (UK) (1997) 2 Lloyd's Rep. 641 ······················ C6/6. 2
Cia Colombiana de Seguros v. Pacific Steam Navigation Co. (1963) 2 Lloyd's Rep. 479 ·········
··· C1, C5/4. 2. 10. 2. 4. 3, 4. 2. 10. 2. 5. 1
Ciampa v. British India Steam Navigation Co. (1915) 2 K. B. 774 ················ C5/4. 2. 7. 1. 7
Cie. Tunisienne de Nav. v. Cie. ' Armement Maritime (1970) 2 Lloyd's Rep. 99 ················
··· C4/3. 4. 3. 1,3. 4. 3. 3
Clerk v. Linsell ··· C2/5. 4. 3. 2
Commercial Molasses Corp. v. New York Tank Barge Corp. 314 U. S. 104 (1941), 1941 AMC 1697
··· C5/4. 2. 5. 1
Commercial Trading v. Coordinated Caribbean 178 So 2d 890, 1865 AMC 2539 (Fla Ct of Appl 1965) ··· C5/4. 2. 3. 4. 2. 2
Compagnia Colombiana de Seguros v. Pacific Steam Navigation Co. (1963) 2 Lloyd's Rep. 479
··· C4/2. 6. 4. 5

Compania de Navigacion la Flecha v. Braner, 168 U. S. 104 (1897) ············· C5/4. 2. 1
Compania Importadora de Arroges Collette y. Kamp SA v. P & O Steam Navigation Co. (1927) 28
Lloyd's Rep. 63 ··· C2/5. 6. 2
Compania Naviera Vaseonzala v. Churchill & Sim(1906) 1 K. B. 237 ············· C6/3. 3. 3
Consolidated Mining v. Straits Towing Ltd. (1972) F. C. 804 ················· C5/4. 2. 6. 6. 7
Continental Distributing Co. Inc. v. Sea-Land Commitment 1994 AMC 95 (2nd Cir) 1993), aff'g
1994 AMC 82 (SDNY 1992), amended 1994 AMC 9 (SDNY 1992) ············· C6/3. 2. 6. 2
Coventry Sheppard & Co. v. Larrinage Steamship Co. Ltd. (1942) 73 Lloyd's Rep. 256 ············
··· C5/4. 2. 9. 1
Cour d'Appel d'Aix, October 11, 1960, DMF 1962, 276 ············· C5/4. 2. 7. 1. 11. 3
Cour d'Appel d'Alger 12. 12. 1961 DMF 1962, 660 ································· C6/3. 1
Cour d'appel de Douai, Nov. 22, 1956, DMF 1957, 100 ············· C5/4. 2. 7. 10. 2
Cour d'Appel de Montpellier, January 10, 1974, DMF 1974,341 ············· C5/4. 2. 7. 10. 2
Cour d'Appel de Montpellier, January 7, 1958, DMF 1958, 220 ············· C5/4. 2. 7. 10. 2
Cour d'Appel de Rouen, 18. 11, 1982, DMF 1983, 423 ······················· C6/3. 1
Cour d'Appel de Rouen, December 14, 1956, DMF 1957, 536 ············· C5/4. 2. 7. 10. 2
Cour de Cassation, March 19, 1985, DMF 1986, 20 ··························· C5/4. 2. 9. 1
Court of Appeals, Paris, 11 July 1975; 1976 RFDA 127 ······················· C2/3. 9
Crouch v. Martin (1707)2 Vern. 595 ··· C3/12. 2. 2
Customs and Excise Commissioners v. A. p. S. Samex (1983) 1 All E. R. (1043) 1051 ··········
··· C2/3. 4. 5
Daewoo v. Sealand (1999) LMLN # 535 (美国上诉庭) ······················· C6/3. 2. 6. 2
De Rothschild Freres v. Morrison, Kekewich & Co. (1890) 24 QBD 750 (C. A.) ··· C2/5. 3. 1
Dent v. Glen Line (1940) 45 Com. Cas. 244 ······································· C6/3. 3
Derry v. Peek (1889) 14 app. Cas. 337 ······································· C2/5. 5. 2, C6/4. 4
Diamond Alkali Export Corporation v. Fl. Bourgeois (1921) 3 K. B. 443 ······ C2/3. 4. 3, 3. 4. 4
Dir. Gen. Of India Supp. Miss. V. S. S. Maru, 1972 AMC 1694 (2 Cir. 1972) ······ C5/4. 2. 6. 2
Dobson v. Hastings (1992) Ch. 394 ··· C7
Donald H. Scott & Co. Ltd. v. Barclays Bank Ltd. (1923) 2 K. B. 1 ············· C2/5. 1. 4
Dow Chemical v. S. S. Giovannella D'Amico (297 F. Supp. 699) ············· C6/3. 2. 2. 2
Dracachi v. Anglo-Egyptian Navigation Co. (1868) L. R. 3 C. P. 190 ········ C2/1. 2. 1, 3. 1. 5. 1
Dunlop Pneumatic Tyre Co. Ltd. v. Selfridge & Co. Ltd. (1915) A. C. 847 ············· C3/12. 2
Dunlop v. Lambert (1839) 6 CI & F 600 ··············· C3/12. 2. 1, 12. 2. 4. 4, 12. 2. 5. 2, § 13
E. T. Barwick Mills v. Hellenic Lines, 331 F Supp 161, 1972 AMC 1802 (SD Ga 1971) ··········
··· C5/4. 2. 3. 4. 2. 5
Edmond Weil v. American West African Line 147 F. 2d. 363 (2 Cir. 1945) ··· C5/4. 2. 7. 1. 3. 3

Effort Shipping Co. Ltd. v. Linden Management S. A. (1998) 1 Lloyd's Rep. 337 ················
··· C3/12. 2. 4. 2, C5/4. 2. 3. 3. 2. 4
Eisen and Metall A. G. v. Ceres Stevedoring Co. Ltd. (在 UK Club 1977 年 Legal Decisions 报道)
··· C3/8. 2. 2
Eisenerz GmbH v. Federal Commerce & Navigation Co. Ltd. (1974) SCR 1225 ······ C5/4. 2. 5. 6
Elder, Dempster v. Paterson, Iochonis (1924) 18 Lloyd's Rep. 319 ················ C5/4. 2. 3. 3. 2
Elderslie SS Co. v. Borthwick (1905) AC 93 ·· C5/3. 2
Elliott Steam Tug Co. Ltd. v. Shipping Controller (1922) 1 KB 127 ················· C3/8. 2. 4
Ellis v. Turner (1800), 8 T. R. 531, 101 E. R. 1529 ································ C5/4. 2. 10. 1. 1
Ente Nazionale v. Baliwag Nav. 1986 AMC 1184 (4 Cir. 1985) ··············· C5/4. 2. 7. 1. 9. 2
Epstein v. United States (1949) 86 F. Supp. 740 (SDNY) ························· C3/4. 3. 1. 5
Equitable Trust Co. of New York v. Dawson Partners Ltd. (1972) 27 Lloyd's Rep. 4 ··············
··· C6/3. 2. 4
Erichsen v. Barkworth (1858) 3 H & N 601 ··· C2/5. 1. 9
Esso Nederland v. Trade Fortitude (1977 A. M. C. 2144) ····························· C6/3. 2. 2. 2
Euro-Diam Ltd. v. Bathurst (1988) 1 Lloyd's Rep. 228 ································ C6/3. 2. 7. 1
Evans v. Cunard (1902) 18 T. L. R. 374 ··· C4/3. 4. 4
Evans v. Merzario (1976) 2 Lloyd's Rep. 165 ·· C5/4. 2. 3. 5. 3. 7
F. W. Pirie v. s. s. Mormactrade, 1970 AMC 1327 (SDNY 1970) ······················ C5/4. 2. 9. 1
Federal Commerce & Navigation v. Marathonian (1975) AMC 738 ················· C3/8. 2. 4
Field v. Metropolitan Police Receivers (1907) 2 K. B. 853 ························· C5/4. 2. 7. 1. 14
Finalayson v. Taylor, The Times 14 April 1983 ·· C2/1. 3
Finlay v. Liverpool and Great Western Steamship Co. (1870) 23 L. T. 251 ······ C5/4. 2. 7. 1. 7
Fischel & Co. v. Knowles (1922) 12 Lloyd's Rep. 36 ·· C2/3. 2
Foreman and Ellams v. Federal Steam Navigation Co. (1928) 30 Lloyd's Rep. 52 ··············
·· C5/4. 2. 7. 1. 1. 4. 1
Forestal Land, Timber and Railways Co. Ltd. v. Rickards (1940) 4 All ER 96 ············ C2/5. 8
Forward v. Pittard (1785) 1 TR 27 ·· C5/4. 2. 1; 4. 2. 7. 1. 4
Fox & Widley v. Guram (1998) 3 EG 142 ·· C5/4. 2. 10. 2. 6
Fox v. Nott (1861) 6 Hurl & Nov. 630 ···························· C3/12. 2. 5. 4. 2, 12. 2. 5. 5
Frenkel v. MacAndrews (1929) A. C. 545 ··· C4/3. 4. 4
Fung Ping Shan v. Tong Shun (1918) A. C. 403 ·· C3/1. 3
G. E. Dobell & Co. v. Steamship Rossmore Company Ltd. (1895) 2 Q. B. 408 ··· C5/4. 2. 6. 4. 1
G. E. Crippen and Another v. Vancouver Tug Boat Co. Ltd. (1971) 2 Lloyd's Rep. 207 ············
··· C5/4. 2. 6. 6. 5, 4. 2. 7. 1. 11. 4
G. H. Renton v. Palmyra (1956) 2 Lloyd's Rep. 379 ··· C5/4. 2. 9. 4

G. M. Corp. v. Moore-McCormack Lines, 1971 A. M. C. 2408 (2 Cir. 1971) ·················
··· C5/4. 2. 10. 3. 3. 3
Gagniere & Co. v. Eastern Co. of Warehouses (1921) 7 Lloyd's Rep. 188 ··············· C2/2. 2. 3
Gatliffe v. Bourne (1838) 4 Bing NC 314 ·· C5/4. 2. 3. 4. 2. 1
General Elec. Co. Int' Sales Div. v. The Nancy Lykes, 706 F. 2d 80 (2d Cir. 1983); 1983 AMC
1947 ··· C4/3. 4. 4, C5/4. 2. 10. 1. 5. 2
General S. A. General Trades Enterprises and Agencies v. Consorcio Pesquerno Del Peru (1974)
AMC 2342 ··· C6/2. 1
George Mitchell v. Finney Lock Seeds (1983) 1 Lloyd's Rep. 168 ··············· C5/4. 2. 10. 1. 1
George Whitechurch Ltd. v. Cavanagh, (1902) A. C. 117 ······················· C3/5. 2, C6/4. 1. 4
Gerechtshef te's-Gravenhage, January 12, 1966, (1968) ETL 345 ·····························
·· C5/4. 2. 7. 1. 1. 3, 4. 2. 7. 1. 1. 4. 2
Gill & Duffus v. Rionda (1994) 2 Lloyd's Rep. 670 ·· C4/2. 1
Gillespie Bros. Ltd. v. Bowles Transport Ltd. (1973) 1 Lloyd's Rep. 10 ·······················
·· C5/4. 2. 3. 5. 3. 1, 4. 2. 3. 5. 3. 4
Glyn Mills & Co. v. East and West India Dock Co. (1882) 7 App. Cas. 591 ·················
·· C2/3. 1. 3, 5. 1. 4, 5. 1. 5, 5. 3, 5. 4. 2, 5. 4. 3. 4
Glynn v. Margetson (1893) A. C. 351 ··· C4/3. 4. 4
Goodwin, Ferreira & Co. v. Lamport & Holt (1929) 34 Lloyd's Rep. 192 ······ C5/4. 2. 3. 4. 2. 5
Gosse Millerd v. Canadian Government Merchant Marine (1928) 32 Lloyd's Rep. 91 ···········
·· C5/4. 2. 7. 1. 1. 4. 1, 4. 2. 5. 6, 4. 2. 7. 1. 7, 4. 2. 7. 1. 1. 4. 1
Goya Foods, Inc. v. S. S. Italia, 1987 AMC 817 (2 Cir. 1983) ···················· C5/4. 2. 10. 1. 5. 1
Graanhadel T. Vink B. W. v. European Grain & Shipping Co. (1989) 2 Lloyd's Rep. 531 ········
··· C4/3. 4. 7. 5
Gram &. Royle v. Services Maritimes (1914) 1 K. B. 541 ··· C5/3. 2
Grant v. Norway (1851) 10 C. B. 665 ··
··················· C3/5. 2, C5/4. 2. 10. 3. 2. 2. 2, C6/4. 1. 4, 4. 2, 4. 2. 2, 4. 2. 3, 4. 4, 7. 3
Green v. Fibreglass, Ltd. (1958) 2 Q. B. 245 ·· C5/4. 2. 6. 4. 2
Gullischen v. Stewart (1884) 13 QBD 317 ··· C3/10. 1, 11. 2. 2
H. Grunewald & Co. v. S. S. Ginevra, Amoco and Saybouh (U. S. D. C., Eastern District of Virgini-
a-19. 12. 77) ·· C6/3. 2. 2. 2
Hain S. S. Co. v. Tate & Lyle (1936) 55 Lloyd's Rep. 159 ···························· C5/4. 2. 10. 1. 1
Halcyon Steamship v. Continental Grain (1943) 75 Lloyd's Rep. 80 ······················ C3/9. 1. 3
Hall v. Barclay (1937) 3 All ER 620 ··· C2/5. 5. 1
Hamilton & Co. v. Mackie & Sons (1889) 5 T. L. R. 677 ·································· C4/2. 6. 4. 1
Hamilton Fraser & Co. v. Pandorf & Co. (1881) 12 App. Cas. 518 ·············· C5/4. 2. 7. 1. 3. 6

Hansen v. Harrold Bros. (1984) 1 QB 612 ……………………………………… C3/11.2.2
Hansson v. Hanel and Horley Ltd. (1922) 2 A. C. 36 ………………………………… C2/3.2
Harbour & General v. Environment Agency (2000) 1 Lloyd's Rep. 65 ………… C5/4.2.10.2.6
Harrison v. Huddersfield SS Co. (1903) 19 T. L. R. 386 ……………………………… C3/5.2
Heddernheim 1941 AMC 730 (SDNY 1941) …………………………………… C5/4.2.6.6.7
Heinrich Horn-Marie Horn, 1968 AMC 2548; (1970) 1 Lloyd's Rep. 191 …………………………………
………………………………… C5/4.2.6.2, 4.2.6.6.2, 4.2.8.6.1, 4.2.9.1
Hellenic Lines v. Louis Dreyfus Corp. 372 F. 2d 753, 1967 AMC 213 (2 Cir. 1967) … C6/3.3
Hellyer v. N. Y. K., 155 AMC 1258 (SDNY 1955) ……………………………… C5/4.2.10.1.4
Henderson v. Merrett Syndicates (1994) 2 Lloyd's Rep. 468 ………………………… C2/5.5.2
Heyn v. Ocean S. S. Co. (1927) 27 Lloyd's Rep. 334 ……………………………… C5/4.2.7.1.17.4
Hick v. Raymond & Reid (1893) A. C. 22 ……………………………………… C2/5.1.9
Hindley & Co. v. East Indian Produce (1973) 2 Lloyd's Rep. 515 …………… C5/4.2.3.5.3.6
Hiram Walker & Sons, Ltd. v. Dover Navigation Co. Ltd. (1949) 83 Lloyd's Rep. 84 …………
……………………………………………………………………… C5/4.2.7.1.3, 5.2
Hobbs Padgett & Co. Ltd. v. FC Kirkland Ltd. and Kirdland (1969) 2 Hoyd's Rep. 547 ………
……………………………………………………………………………… C4/2.6.4.3
Hoegh v. Green Truck Sales Inc., 298 F. 2d 240 1962 AMC 431 (9 Cir 1962) ………………
……………………………………………………………………………… C5/4.2.3.4.2.5
Hoffman-Laroche Inc v. TFL Jefferson 1990 AMC 1388; 731 F. Supp. 109 (SDNY 1990) ……
………………………………………………………… C2/5.1.11, 5.2.3.1, 5.4.3.4
Holland Colombo Trading Society, Ltd. v. Alawdeen and Others (1954) 2 Lloyd's Rep. 45 ……
……………………………………………………………………………… C2/3.2
Houldsworth v. City of Glagow Bank (1880) 5 App. Cas. 317 …………… C3/5.2, C6/4.1.4
Hourani v. T. & J. Harrison (1927) 32 Com. Cas. 305 ……………………… C5/4.2.7.1.1.4
Hunt Foods v. Matson Navigation Co. 1966 AMC 50 (E. D. La. 1966) ……… C5/4.2.7.1.11.1
Hurlbut v. Turnure, 81F. 208 (2d Cir. 1897) ……………………………………… C4/3.4.4
Iarembo, 136 F. 2d 320, 1943 AMC 954 (2 Cir. 1943) ………………………… C5/4.2.6.4.3
Iligan Int. Steel v. John Weyerhaeuser, 1975 AMC 33 (2 Cir. 1974) …………… C5/4.2.10.1.4
In re Missouri Steamship Company (1889) 42 Ch. D. 321 ……………………… C5/4.2.1
Indussa Corp. v. s. s. Ranborg (1967) 2 Lloyd's Rep. 101 (2 Cir. 1967) ………………
………………………………………………………… C4/3.4.3.4, C5/4.2.9.1
Ingram &. Royle v. Services Maritimes (1914) 1 K. B. 541 …………………………… C5/3.2
Insurance Company of North America v. Dart Containerline, 629 F. Supp. 781, 1987 AMC (42) 44
(E. D. Va. 1985) ……………………………………………………………… C6/3.2.6.2

Insurance Company of North America v. Italica, 567 F. Supp. 59, 1984 AMC 136 (SDNY1983)
.... C5/4. 2. 4. 4. 2
Iristo 1943 AMC 1043 (2 Cir. 1943) C5/4. 2. 6. 6. 7
James Miller & Partners Ltd. v. Whitworth Street Estates (Mancester) Ltd. (1970) AC 583 ......
.... C4/3. 4. 3. 1
Jones v. Flying Clipper, 116F Supp. 386, 1954 AMC 259 (SDNY 1953) C5/4. 2. 3. 5. 3. 7
Jones v. Hough (1880) 1819 5 Ex. D. 115 .... C4/2. 6. 1
K. Chellaram & Sons Ltd. v. Nissho Shipping Co. Ltd. (1967) 2 Lloyd's Rep. 578 ....
.... C5/4. 2. 3. 4
Kallis (Manufacturers) Ltd. v. Success Insurance Ltd. (1985) 2 Lloyd's Rep. 8 ... C2/3. 4. 1. 2
Karsales (Harrow) Ltd. v. Wallis, (1956) 1 W. L. R. 936 .... C5/4. 2. 10. 1. 1
Kinderman & Sons v. Nippon Yusen Kaisha Lines, 322F Supp 939 1971 AMC 743 (ED Pa 1971)
.... C5/4. 2. 3. 4. 1
Kish v. Cory (1875) LR 10 QB 553 .... C4/2. 6. 2. 1
Kish v. Taylor (1912) A. C. 604; 12 Asp. M. C. 217 .... C4/3. 4. 4, C5/4. 2. 10. 1. 5. 3
Knutsford S. S. Co. Ltd. v. Tillmanns & Co. (1908) A. C. 406 .... C4/3. 2. 2
Kulukundis v. Norwich Union Fire Ins. Society (1936) 55 Lloyd's Rep. 55 .... C4/3. 4. 5
Kum v. Wah Tat Bank (1971) 1 Lloyd's Rep. 439 ....
.... C2/2. 2, 2. 2. 3, 2. 2. 4, 3. 1. 6. 2, 3. 3, 4. 1, 4. 2
Kwei Tek Chao v. British Traders and Shippers Ltd. (1954) 2 Lloyd's Rep. 114 ....
.... C5/4. 2. 3. 5. 3. 6
Lakas & Drivas v. Basil Goulandris, 1962 AMC 2366 .... C5/4. 2. 8. 7. 1
Langdale v. Mason (1780) 2 Park on Insurance 965 .... C5/4. 2. 7. 1. 14
Laveroni v. Drury (1852) 8 Ex. 166 at 170 .... C5/4. 2. 1
Leather's Best Inc. v. SS Mormaclynx (1970) 1 Lloyd's Rep. 527 (EDNY 1970) (一审) ......
.... C5/4. 2. 9. 3
Leather's Best Inc. v. SS Mormaclynx (1971) 2 Lloyd's Rep. 476 (2 Cir. 1971)(美国上诉庭)
.... C5/4. 2. 9. 3
Leduc v. Ward (1888) 20 QBD 475 .... C4/3. 4. 4
Leerdam, (1927) AMC 509, 510 .... C5/4. 2. 8. 6. 2
Leyland Shipping Co. v. Norwich Union Fire Insurance Co. (1918) AC 350 .... C5/4. 2. 5. 5
Liberty Shipping Linm. Procs. , 1973 AMC 2241 (W. D. Wash 1973) C5/4. 2. 6. 6. 2
Lickbarrow v. Mason (1787) 2 T. R. 63 ....
.... 4, 3. 1. 2, 3. 1. 3, 3. 1. 6. 2, 3. 4. 1. 4, 3. 4. 3, 3. 4. 4, C3/12. 1, 12. 2. 1
Limerick v. Coker (1916) 33 T. L. R. 103 .... C3/5. 1
Linden Gardens Trust v. Lenesta Sludge Disposals (1994) 1 AC 85 .... C3/12. 2

Lishman v. Christie (1887) 19 QBD 333 ·· C6/4.3
Liver Alkali Co. v. Johnson (1874) LR 7 Ex. 267; Asp. M. C. 332 (高院一审) ········ C5/§1
Liver Alkali Co. v. Johnson (1875) L. R. 9 Ex. 338 (上诉庭) ············ C5/4.2.1, 4.2.7.1.4
Liverpool and Great Western Steam Co. v. Phoenix Insurance Co. 129 U. S. 397 (1889) ··········
·· C5/4.2.1
Lloyd v. Grace Smith (1912) A. C. 716. ···························· C3/5.2, C6/4.1.4
Lloyd's Bank v. Bank of America (1938) 2 KB 147 ······························ C2/1.2.1.3.2
London and Lancashire Fire Insurance Co. v. Bolands (1924) A. C. 836 ········ C5/4.2.7.1.14
Lossiebank (Massce & Co. Inc. v. Bank Line), 1938 AMC 1033 (Sup Ct of Cal 1938) ··········
·· C5/4.2.3.5.3
Lufty Ltd. v. Canadian Pacific Railway Co. (The "Alex") (1974) 1 Lloyd's Rep. 106 ···········
·· C6/3.3.2
M. Golodetz Export Corp. v. Lake Anja, 1985 AMC 891 (2 Cir. 1985) ······· C5/4.2.7.1.17.3
M. Paquet & Co. v. Dart Cantainerline, 1973 AMC 926 (N. Y. Civ. Ct. 1973) ··· C5/4.2.4.4.2
M. S. Cowan Co. v. American President Lines 167 F. Supp. 838 at F. 840, 1959 AMC 2525 at
P. 2528 (N. D. Cal. 1958) ·· C6/3.3, 3.3.4
Major v. Grant (1902) 7 Com. Cas. 231 ······································· C4/3.4.7.4
Makower, McBeath & Co. Pty. Ltd. v. Dalgety & Co. Pry. Ltd. (1921) VLR 365 ······ C2/1.5.3
Mallozzi v. Carapelli (1976) 1 Lloyd's Rep. 407 ·························· C3/10.1, C4/2.2.1
Marcelino Gonzalez v. Nourse (1935) 53 Lloyd's Rep. 151 ··················· C4/3.4.5
Marfani & Co. Ltd. v. Midland Bank Ltd. (1968) 1 WLR 956 ···················· C2/5.4.3.2
Marifortuna Naviera S. A. v. Government of Ceylon (1970) 1 Lloyd's Rep. 247 ····· C5/4.2.7.1
Marshall, Knott & Baker Ltd. v. Arcos Ltd. (1933) 44 Lloyd's Rep. 384 ················ C2/3.7
Matsushita Elec. Corp. v. S. S. Aegis Spirit, 1976 AMC 779 (W. D. Wash. 1976) ···············
·· C5/4.2.10.3.2.1
Maxine Footwear v. Canada Government Merchant Marine (1959) 2 Lloyd's Rep. 105 ··········
·························· 1.1.4.3, 4.2.7.1.2.2, 4.2.7.1.2.5, 4.2.7.1.2.6, 4.2.7.1.3.6
Mayhew Foods v. OCL (1984) 1 Lloyd's Rep. 317 ······························ C5/4.2.3.1.6
Mc Carren v. Humber International Transport (1982) Lloyd's Rep. 301 ········ C5/4.2.3.1.4
Mc Gregor v. Huddart Parker Ltd. (1919) 26 CLR 336 ··························· C5/4.2.1
Mc Iver & Co. Ltd. v. Tate Steamers Ltd. (1903) 1 K. B. 362 ················· C5/4.2.6.6.6
Metalimport v. S. S. Italia, 1976 AMC 2347 (S. D. N. Y. 1976) ·····························
·· C3/8.2.2, C5/4.2.7.1.17.3
Meyerstein v. Barber (1870) L. R. 4 H. L. 317 ································ C2/3.1.5.4
Micada Compania Naviera S. A. v. Texim (1968) 2 Lloyd's Rep. 57 ············ C5/4.2.7.1.9.2

Midlands & Silicones v. Scruttons (1961) 2 Lloyd's Rep. 365 ··············
················· 3. 3. 2. 1, 4. 2. 3. 3. 2. 3, 4. 2. 3. 3. 2. 4, 4. 2. 3. 3. 2. 7, 4. 2. 10. 2. 3
Mimi Limitation Procs (Matter of Intercontinental Properties Management) 1979 AMC 1680 (4 Cir. 1979) ·· C5/4. 2. 7. 1. 17. 5
Minister of Food v. Reardon Smith Line (1951) 1 Lloyd's Rep. 265 ········· C5/4. 2. 7. 1. 1. 2
Ministry of Food v. Lamport & Holt Line, Ltd. (1952) 2 Lloyd's Rep. 371 ········· C3/11. 2. 1
Miserocchi v. Agricultores (1982) 1 Lloyd's Rep. 202 ······················· C3/9. 1. 2
Mitchell v. Finney Lock Seeds (1983) 2 Lloyd's Rep. 272 ·················· C2/5. 6. 2
Mitsubishi Intl. v. Glyfada Spirit, 1978 AMC 480 (SDNY 1978) ············ C5/4. 2. 10. 1. 5. 1
Morrisey v. S. S. A. & J. Faith, 252 F. Supp. 54, 1966 AMC 71 ··········· C5/4. 2. 6. 6. 8
Morrison v. Shaw Savill (1916) 2 K. B. 783 ······················· C4/3. 4. 4
Motis Exports v. Dampskibsselskabet AF 1912 (1999) 1 Lloyd's Rep. 837 ·················
··············· 3, 5. 4, 5. 4. 2, 5. 4. 3. 3, 5. 4. 3. 4, 5. 6. 2, 5. 6. 4, 5. 6. 5, 5. 8, 5. 10. 2
Moukataff v. B. O. A. C. (1967) 1 Lloyd's Rep. 396 ············ C3/8. 2. 2, C5/4. 2. 3. 3. 2. 5
National Bank of Greece SA v. Pinios Shipping (No. 1) (1990) 1 AC 637 ······ C2/5. 5. 2
Navigas v. Enron (1997) 2 Lloyd's Rep. 759 ············· C3/11. 2. 1, 12. 2. 5. 4. 2
Nebco International v. M/V "National Integrity", 752 F. Supp. 1207 1221 - 1222 (SDNY 1990)
··· C2/5. 1. 11
Nelson Line v. Nelson (No. 2) (1908) AC 16 ························· C5/3. 2
Nugent v. Smith (1876) 45 L. J. (C. L.) 697 ······················· C5/4. 2. 1
Nemeth v. General S. S. Corp. 1983 AMC 885 (9 Cir. 1982) ··············· C4/3. 1
Nesbitt v. Lushington (1792) 4 T. R. 783 ······················· C5/4. 2. 7. 1. 7
New Chinese Co. v. Ocean S. S. Co. (1917) 2 KB 664 ··············· C6/ §2, 5. 3. 1
Nichimen Co. v. M. V. Farland, 462 F. 2d 319; AMC 1573 (2 Cir. 1972) ·············
·············· C5/4. 2. 7. 1. 3. 3, 4. 2. 7. 1. 3. 5. 2, 4. 2. 10. 3. 2. 2. 3
Nippon Fire & Marine Ins. Co. v. M/V Coral Halo, 2000 U. S. Dist. LEXIS 1548 (Ed. La. Feb. 11, 2000) ·· C4/3. 4. 3. 4
Nippon Yusen Kaisha v. Ramjiban Serowjee (1938) 60 Lloyd's Rep. 181 ··············
··· C2/2. 2. 2, 3. 1. 6. 2, 3. 3
North East Petroleum v. Prairie Grove (1977 A. M. C. 2139) ··············· C6/3. 2. 2. 2
Nugent v. Smith (1876) 1 C. P. D. 421 ····················· C5/4. 2. 1, 4. 2. 7. 1. 4
O' Connell Machinery Co. Inc. v. Americana, 1986 AMC 2822 (2 Cir. 1986) ·············
··· C5/4. 2. 10. 1. 4
OK Petroleum v. Vitol (1995) 2 Lloyd's Rep. 160 ·······························
·············· C3/1. 4, 2, 4. 2. 2, 4. 3. 1. 3, 5. 2, C4/2. 4, 2. 6. 4
Orient Ins. Co. v. United S. S. Co. 1961 AMC 1228 (SDNY 1961) ········· C5/4. 2. 6. 5. 3

Otis, McAllister & Co. v. Skibs, (1959) 2 Lloyd' Rep. 210 (9 Cir. 1958) C5/4. 2. 9. 1
P. Samuel v. Dumas (1924) 18 Lloyd's Rep. 211 .... C5/4. 2. 7. 1. 3. 6
P. S. Chellaram & Co. Ltd. v. China Shipping Co. (1989) 1 Lloyd's Rep. 413 ....
.... C5/4. 2. 10. 3. 2. 2. 2
Pan-Alaska Fisheries v. Marine Const & Design Co. 56S F. 2d 1129, 1978 AMC 2315 (9 Cir. 1977) C3/14
Panchand Freres S. A. v. Et. General Grain Co. (1970) 1 Lloyd's Rep. 53 .... C6/7. 1
Paradine v. Jane (1647) Aleyn 26 .... C5/ § 2
Paterson, Zochonis v. Elder Dempster (1922) 12 Lloyd's Rep. 69; 13 Lloyd's Rep. 513 (上诉)
.... C3/1. 4, 4. 3. 1. 3, 5. 2, C4/3. 1
Pendle & Rivett Ltd. v. Ellerman Lines, Ltd. (1927) 29 Lloyd's Rep. 13 ...... C5/4. 2. 7. 1. 17. 2
Pendleton v. Benner Line (1918) 246 U. S. 353 .... C3/4. 3. 1. 5
Peruvian Guano (1882) 11 QBD 550 .... C6/3. 2. 7. 2
Phillips & Co. v. Clan Line Steamers Ltd. (1943) 26 Lloyd's Rep. 58 .... C5/4. 2. 7. 1. 17. 2
Phoenix Insurance Co. v. Erie and Western Transportation Co. 117 U. S. 312 (1886) ....
.... C5/4. 2. 1
Phoenix Timber Co. Ltd. v. Application (1958) 2 QB 1; (1958) 1 All ER 815 .... C2/5. 3
Photo Production Ltd. v. Securicor Transport Ltd. (1980) 1 Lloyd's Rep. 545 ....
.... C2/5. 6. 2, C5/4. 2. 3. 5. 3. 7, 4. 2. 10. 1. 1, 4. 2. 10. 1. 2
Pickering v. Barclay (1648) Styles 132 .... C5/4. 2. 7. 1. 6
Plywood Panels, Inc. v. M/V Sun Valley, 804 F. Supp. 804, 1993 AMC 516 (E. D. Va. 1992)
.... C6/5. 5
Portland Fish Co. v. States Steamship Co. 510 F. 2d 628 (9 Cir. 1974) C6/5. 5
Potter v. Burrell (1897) 1 Q. B. 97 .... C5/4. 2. 7. 1. 15
Potter v. North German Lloyd, 1943 AMC 738 (N. D. Cal. 1943) C5/4. 2. 10. 2. 2. 5
Proctor, Garratt, Marston v. Oakwin SS Co. (1926) 1 K. B. 244 .... C2/5. 1. 9
Propeller Niagara v. Cordes 62 U. S. 7 .... C5/4. 2. 1
Punjab National Park v. de Boinville (1992) 3 All ER 104 .... C2/5. 5. 2
Pyrene Co. Ltd. v. Scindia Steam Navigation Co. Ltd. (1954) 1 Lloyd's Rep. 321 ....
.... 2, § 13, C5/4. 2. 3. 4. 2. 5, 4. 2. 6. 5. 4, 4. 2. 8. 4, 4. 2. 10. 3. 5, C6/3. 3. 1
Railroad Co. v. Lockwood, 84 U. S. 357 (1873) C5/4. 2. 1
Ralston Purina Co. v. U. S. A. 1952 AMC 1496 (E. D. La 1952) C5/4. 2. 5. 3. 3
Rambler Cycle Co. v. P & O Steam Nav. Co. (1968) 1 Lloyd's Rep. 42 ...... C5/4. 2. 10. 2. 4. 2
Rank Enterprises v. Gerard (1999) 2 Lloyd's Rep. 666 .... C2/5. 2. 3. 2
Raymond Burke Motors Ltd. v. The Mersey Docks and Harbour Co. (1986) 1 Lloyd's Rep. 155
.... C3/8. 2. 2, C5/4. 2. 3. 3. 2. 4

Re Richardsons & Samuel (1898) 1 Q. B. 261 ·············· C5/4. 2. 7. 1. 13. 1
Re Stapyton Fletcher (1994) 1 WLR 1181 ················ C4/3. 4. 7. 6
Rechtbank van Koophandel te Antwerpen, September 4, 1979, (1980) ETL 291 ············
················ C5/4. 2. 4. 3. 1
Red Arrow Freight Lines, Inc. v. Roy G. Howe 480 S. W. 2d 281 ············ C6/3. 3. 2
Reed & Barton Corp. v. M/V "Tokio Express", 1999 U. S. Dist. LEXIS 1807, 1999 AMC 1088 (SDNY Feb. 22, 1999) ·················· C4/3. 4. 3. 4
Regazzoni v. Sethia (1958) A. C. 301 ·················· C6/3. 2. 7. 1
Remington Rand v. U. S. A. , 1951 AMC 1364 (S. D. N. Y. 1951) ········ C5/4. 2. 7. 1. 17. 4
Riley v. Horne (1825) 5 Bing 217 ·················· C5/§ 1,4. 2. 2
Robalen Inc v. Generale de Banque SA, 3 September 1999, U. S. District Court (SDNY), LMLN # 525 ·················· C2/3. 4. 5
Rodocanachi v. Milburn (1886) 18 OBD 67 ············ C2/5. 5. 1, C3/4. 2, C4/2. 5
Row v. Dowson (1749) 1 Vern. Sen. 331 ················ C3/12. 2. 2
Rowson v. Atlantic Transport Co. (1903) 2 K. B. 666 ·········· C5/4. 2. 7. 1. 1. 4. 1
Royal Exchange Shipping Co. Ltd. v. Dixon (1886) 12 App. Cas. 11 ············
·················· C5/4. 2. 3. 5. 3. 6, 4. 2. 3. 5. 3. 7
Ryoden Machinery v. Anders Maersk (Sup. Ct. of Hong Kong 1986) (1986) 1 Lloyd's Rep. 483
············ C5/4. 2. 3. 1. 6,4. 2. 3. 3. 1. 2, 4. 2. 3. 5. 3. 3, 4. 2. 10. 2. 8. 7
RT Jones Lumber Co. v. Roen Steamship Co. , 270 F. 2d 456 (2 Cir. 1959) ············
·················· C5/4. 2. 7. 1. 3. 2
Ryall v. Rowles (175) 1 Ves. Sen. 348 ················ C3/12. 2. 2
S. I. A. T. di dal Ferro v. Tradax Overseas S. A. (1978) 2 Lloyd's Rep. 470; (1980) 1 Lloyd's Rep. 53 ·················· C4/2. 6. 4. 2
S. M. Sartori Inc. v. Kastav, 412 F. Supp. 1181, 1977 AMC 126 (SDNY 1976) ············
·················· C5/4. 2. 7. 1. 10. 4
Sabah Flour v. Comfez (1988) 2 Lloyd's Rep. 18 ············ C5/4. 2. 3. 2. 2. 3
Sachs v. Miklos (1948) 2 KB 23 ·················· C2/5. 5. 1
Sale Continuation Ltd. v. Austin Taylor & Co. Ltd. (1967) 2 Lloyd's Rep. 403 ············ C2/4
Salzman Tobacco Co. v. S. S. Mormacwind 1967 AMC 277 (2 Cir. 1967) ······ C5/4. 2. 7. 1. 10. 6
Samuel v. West Hartlepool Co. (1906) 11 Com. Cas. 111 ·················· C3/5. 2
Sanders v. MaClean (1883) 11 QBD 327 ············ C2/2. 2. 1, 3. 1. 2, 5. 1. 4, 5. 4. 3. 1
Scaramanga v. Stamp (1880) 5 C. P. D. 295 ············ C4/3. 4. 4, C5/4. 2. 7. 1. 15, 4. 2. 10. 1
SCB v. PNSC (1995) 2 Lloyd' Rep. 365 ············ C2/5. 4. 2, C6/3. 2. 4, 3. 2. 7. 1, 7. 3
Schooner St. Johns N. F. 263 U. S. 119 1923 AMC 1131 (1923) ············ C5/4. 2. 3. 5. 3. 2
Schwabach Coffee Co. v. S. S. Suriname, 1967 AMC 604 (E. D. La. 1966) ··· C5/4. 2. 10. 2. 4. 3

Sealane (Searoad Shipping Co. v. E. I. Dupont de Nemours), 361 F. 2d 833 1966 AMC 1405 (5 Cir. 1966) ·· C5/4. 2. 3. 5. 3. 7, 4. 2. 10. 1. 4
Searle v. Laverick (1874) L. R. Q. B. 122 ·· C5/4. 2. 6. 4. 2
Seng v. Glencore Grain (1996) 1 Lloyd's Rep. 398 ················ C3/10. 1, 10. 2, C4/2. 5
Serraino v. United States Lines (1965) AMC 1038 ·· C6/2. 1
Sewell v. Burdick (1844) 10 App. Cas. 74 ·· C2/4. 2, C3/12. 2. 4. 1
Sheerwood et al. v. The Lake Eyre et al (1970) Ex C. R. 672 ················ C5/4. 2. 3. 5. 3. 5
Shell Oil Co. v. M. T. Gilda 790 F2d 1209 (5th Cir. 1986) ················ C5/4. 2. 3, 2. 2. 1
Shui Fa Oil Mill Co., Ltd. v. M/S Norma, 1976 AMC 936 (SDNY 1976) ······ C5/4. 2. 7. 10. 2
Silver v. Ocean SS Co. (1929) 35 Lloyd's Rep. 49 ················ C6/4. 1. 2
Simpson & Co. v. Thomson (1877) 3 App. Cas. 279 ················ C3/8. 2. 4
Sims v. Bond (1833) 5 B & Ad. 389, 393 ················ C3/ § 1
Smith & Service v. The Rasario Nitrate Co. (1893) 2 Q. B. 323, affirmed at (1894) 1 Q. B. 174 ·· C5/4. 2. 7. 1. 13. 2
Smurthwaite v. Wilkins (1862) 11 C. B. (N. S.) 842 ············ C3/12. 2. 5. 3, 12. 2. 5. 4. 2
Societe Anonyme de Remorquage a Helice v. Bennetts (1911) 1 KB 243 ············ C3/8. 2. 4
Societe Navale Caennaise v. Gastin (1965) D. M. F. 18 ················ C5/4. 2. 10. 3. 2. 2. 2
Soloway v. McLaughlin (1938) AC 247 ················ C2/5. 5. 1
Soproma SpA v. Marine & Animal By Products Corp. (1966) 1 Lloyd's Rep. 367 ········· C2/3. 2
Southern Cross, 1940 AMC 59 (SDNY 1939) ················ C5/4. 2. 9. 1
Southland Rubber Co. Ltd. v. Bank of China (1997) 3 HKC 569 ················ C3/6. 2
Soya Gmbh v. White (1983) 1 Lloyd's Rep. 122 ················ C5/4. 2. 7. 1. 10. 1
Spanish American Skin v. M/S Ferngulf 242F. 2d551, 1957AMC611 (2Cir. 1957) ······ C6/5. 5
Spence v. Chadwick (1847) 10 QB 517 ················ C5/4. 2. 7. 1. 6
Spinney's (1948) v. Royal Insurance Co. (1980) 1 Lloyd's Rep. 406 ············ C5/4. 2. 7. 1. 14
SS Lord (owners) v. Newsum Son & Co. (1920) 1K. B. 846 ················ C5/4. 2. 7. 1. 1. 3
Stag Line Ltd. v. Foscolo, Mango & Co. ······ [请看 The "Ixia" (1931) 41 Lloyd's Rep. 165]
Standard Brands Inc. v. NY Kaisha, 42F. Supp. 43, 1942 AMC 477 (D Mass 1941) ············ C5/4. 2. 3. 4. 1, 4, 2. 3. 4. 2. 4
Standard Oil Co of California v. United States, 59 F. Supp. 100 (S. D. Calif. 1945) aff'd, 156 F. 2d 312 (9th Cir. 1946) ················ C5/4. 2. 3. 2. 2. 3
State Motors Inc. v. ss Espa, 1967 AMC 1447 (S. D. Ga 1966) ················ C5/4. 2. 3. 5. 3. 7
Steel v. Stateline (1877) 3 App Cas ················ C5/3. 2
Stein Hall & Co. v. Sealand Dock and Terminal Co. 1956 AMC 253 at p. 942 (NY Supr Ct 1956) ················ C5/4. 2. 3. 4. 1
Stephens v. Harris (1887) 17 L. T. 618 ················ C5/4. 2. 7. 1. 13. 1

Strathlorne Steamship v. Andrew Weir (1934) 50 Lloyd's Rep. 185 ················· C2/5.1.12
Strohmeyer & Arpe Co. v. American Line SS Corp., 97F. 2d 360, 1938 AMC 875 (2nd Cir. 1938)
··· C6/3.2.7.2
Stuart v. British & African Nav. Co. (1875) 32 L. T. 257 ················· C5/4.2.7.1.15
Subaru of America v. M/V Ranella, 1972 AMC 722 (M. Md. 1972) ········ C5/4.2.10.2.4.3
Sumitomo Corp. Of America v. M/V St. Venture, 683F. Supp. 1361 (M. D. Fla. 1988) ···········
··· C6/5.5
Sun Company, Inc. S. S. Overseas Arctic, 27 D. 3d 1104 (5th Cir. 1994) ····· C5/4.2.3.2.2.1
Surrey County Council v. Bredero Homes Ltd. (1993) 1 WLR 1361 ················· C2/5.5.1
Suzuki & Co. v. Companhia Mercantile Internacional (1921) 9 Lloyd's Rep. 171 ········ C4/2.1
Svenska Traktor Aktiebolaget v. Maritime Agencies (Southampton) Ltd. (1953) 2 Lloyd's Rep. 124
··· C5/4.2.3.5.3.3,4.2.9.4
Swiss Bank Corp. v. First National City Bank er al., 11 May 1979;15 Avi 17. 631 ······ C2/3.9
Sze Hai Tong Bank Ltd. v. Rambler Cycle Co. Ltd. (1959) 2 Lloyd's Rep. 114 ···············
··· C2/1.4, 5.4.3.4, 5.6.2
T. W. Thomas & Co. Ltd. v. Portsea S. S. Co. Ltd. (1912) A. C. 1 ················· C4/2.6.4.1
Ta Chi Lim Proc. (Eurybates) 5. 3 F. Supp. 148, 1981 AMC 1350 (E. D. La. 1981) ···········
··· C5/4.2.6.6.2
Tai Hing v. Liu Chong Hing Bank (1985) 2 Lloyd's Rep. 313 ················· C2/5.5.2
Tan Hi v. U. S. A., 1951 AMC 127 (N. D. Cal. 1950) ················· C5/4.2.8.4
Temple Bar 1942 AMC 1125 (D. Md. 1942) ················· C5/4.2.6.6.7
The "Adhigunda Meranti" (1981) HKLR 904 ················· C4/2.6.4.5
The "Admiral Zmajevic" (1983) 2 Lloyd's Rep. 86 ········ C5/4.2.6.4.3, 4.2.6.6.9
The "Aegean Sea" (1998) 2 Lloyd's Rep. 39 ···
················· C2/3.1.5.3, 5.2.3.2, C3/11.2.1, 12.2.5.4.1, 12.2.5.5, C7
The "Aegis Britannic" (1987)1 Lloyd's Rep. 119 ················· C3/11.2.2
The "Aegis Spirit" (1977) 1 Lloyd's Rep. 93 ············ C5/4.2.10.3.2.2.2, 4.2.10.3.2.2.3
The "Aeneas" (1929) 35 Lloyd's Rep. 49 ················· C5/4.2.7.1.11.2
The "Agia Skepi"(1992) 2 Lloyd's Rep. 467 ················· C4/3.4.3.1
The "Agios Lazaros" (1976) 2 Lloyd's Rep. 47 ···
················· C5/4.2.3.2.2.2, 4.2.3.2.2.3, 4.2.9.5, 4.2.10.2.5.2
The "Agios Nicolas" (1968) 1 Lloyd's Rep. 57 ················· C3/11.2.1
The "Agios Vlasios" (1965) 2 Llody's Rep. 204 ················· C5/4.2.6.6.7
The "Ahmadu Bello" (1967) 1 Lloyd's Rep. 293 ········ C5/4.2.7.1.10.3, 4.2.7.1.10.5
The "Aiolos" (1983) 2 Lloyd's Rep. 25 ················· C3/12.2.2
The "Al Battani" (1993) 2 Lloyd's Rep. 219 ················· C3/4.1, C4/2.2.4

The "Al Taha" (1990) 2 Lloyd's Rep. 117 ······ C4/3.4.4
The "Al Wahab" (1983) 2 Hoyd's Rep. 365 ······ C4/3.4.3.1
The "Albacora" (1966) 2 Lloyd's Rep. 53 ······ C5/4.2.4
The "Albazero" (1976) 2 Lloyd's Rep. 467 ······ C3/12.2.4.4
The "Aleksandr Serafimovich" (1975) 2 Lloyd's Rep. 346 ······ C5/4.2.10.3.2
The "Alev" (1989) 1 Lloyd's Rep. 138 ······ C6/6
The "Alex" (1974) 1 Lloyd's Rep. 106 ······ C5/4.2.4.4.2, C6/3.3.2
The "Alhambra" (1881) 6 P. D. 68 ······ C4/3.2.2
The "Aliakmon" (1985) 1 Lloyd's Rep. 199 (高院一审) ······ C5/4.2.3.3.1.2
The "Aliakmon" (1986) 2 Lloyd's Rep. 1 (贵族院) ······
······ 2/1.1, 1.2.1.1, 1.2.1.3.2, 3.1.2, C3/8.2.3, 8.2.4, 8.3, 12.2.4.4
The "Amazona" (1989) 2 Lloyd's Rep. 130 ······ C4/2.6.4.5, C5/4.2.9.2
The "Amazonia" (1990) 1 Lloyd's Rep. 236 ······ C5/4.2.3.2.2.3
The "Amphion" (1991) 2 Lloyd's Rep. 101 ······ C3/11.2.1, 12.2.5.5, C5/4.2.7.1.11.4
The "Amstelslot" (1963) 2 Lloyd's Rep. 223 ······ C5/4.2.6.4.3, 4.2.6.6.9
The "Andrea Ursula" (1971) 1 Lloyd's Rep. 145 ······ C3/3.3
The "Angelia" (1972) 2 Lloyd's Rep. 154 ······ C4/3.2.2, C5/4.2.7.1.7
The "Anglo Colombian" (1937) 58 Lloyd's Rep. 188 ······ C5/4.2.6.4.3
The "Anna H" (1994) 1 Lloyd's Rep. 287 ······ C5/4.2.8.4
The "Annefield" (1970) 2 Lloyd's Rep. 252 (高院一审) ······ C4/2.6.4.2
The "Annefield" (1971) 1 Lloyd's Rep. 1 (上诉庭) ······
······ C3/4.2.2, 10.1, C4/2.3, 2.4.6.1, 2.6.4, 2.6.4.1
The "Antaios" (1984) 2 Lloyd's Rep. 235 ······ C2/5.4.1, C3/5.3
The "Antares" (1987) 1 Lloyd's Rep. 424 ······
······ 3.5.3.7, 4.2.3.5.3.8, C5/4.2.5.10.2.6, 4.2.10.2.1, 4.2.10.2.6
The "Anthony II" (1966) 2 Lloyd's Rep. 437 (S. D. N. Y. 1966) ······
······ C3/4.3.1.5, C5/4.2.6.6.5, 4.2.8.6.2
The "Anwar Al Sabar" (1980) 2 Lloyd's Rep. 261 ······ C3/ §4, C4/2.6.2.1
The "Apastolis" (1996) 1 Lloyd's Rep. 475 (高院一审) ······ C5/4.2.6.3, 4.2.6.6.3.1
The "Apastolis" (1997) 2 Lloyd's Rep. 241 (上诉庭) ······ C5/4.2.6.3
The "Apastolis" No. 2 (1999) 2 Lloyd's Rep. 292 ······ C5/4.2.6.3, 4.2.7.1.2.2
The "APJ Akash" (1977) 1 Lloyd's Rep. 653 ······ C5/4.2.10.2.5.2
The "Aramis" (1989) 1 Lloyd's Rep. 213 ······ C3/12.2.3, 12.2.4.4
The "Arawa" (1980) 2 Lloyd's Rep. 135 ······ C5/4.2.3.4, 4.2.7.1.13.1
The "Arcadio Forest" (1986) ETL 86 (SDNY 1985) ······ C6/3.3
The "Ardennes" (1950) 84 Lloyd's Rep. 340 ······ C3/9.1.1, C5/4.2.10.1.5.1

The "Assunzione" (1954) P. 150 .... C4/3. 4. 3. 2
The "Athamas" (1963) 1 Lloyd's Rep. 287 .... C4/3. 2. 2
The "Athanasia Comninos" (1990) 1 Lloyd's Rep. 277 .... C3/11. 2. 1, C6/2. 1, 3. 3. 3
The "Athenian Harmony" (1998) 2 Lloyd's Rep. 410 ...... C5/4. 2. 6. 6. 3. 2. 2 ,4. 2. 6. 6. 3. 2. 2
The "Atlantic Duchess" (1957) 2 Lloyd's Rep. 55 .... C3/11. 2. 1, C5/4. 2. 7. 1. 9. 2
The "Atlas" (1996) 1 Lloyd's Rep. 642 .... C6/1. 1, §2,3. 2. 3,3. 2. 6. 1, 5. 3. 6
The "Atlas" 93 U. S. 302, 315 (1816) C4/3. 4. 12
The "Aubade" (1971) 2 Lloyd's Rep. 423 .... C5/4. 2. 10. 2. 2, 4. 2. 10. 2. 3
The "August Leonhardt" (1985) 2 Lloyd's Rep. 28 ....
.... C5/4. 2. 10. 2. 1, 4. 2. 10. 2. 4, 4. 2. 10. 2. 4. 3
The "Australia Star" (1940) 67 Lloyd's Rep. 110 .... C5/4. 2. 6. 4. 3
The "Bahia" (1864) 2 Asp. M. C. (O. S.) 174 .... C4/3. 4. 5
The "Baltic Universal" (1999) 1 Lloyd's Rep. 497 .... C5/4. 2. 10. 2. 5. 2
The "Bamburi" (1982) 1 Lloyd's Rep. 312 .... C5/4. 2. 7. 1. 7
The "Belle Ville" (1970) AMC 663, 284, F. Supp. 1002 .... C4/3. 4. 7. 5
The "Beltana" (1967) 1 Lloyd's Rep. 531 .... C5/4. 2. 10. 2. 2
The "Berge Sisar" (1998) 2 Lloyd's Rep. 475 ....
.... C3/11. 2. 1, 12. 2, 4. 2, 12. 2. 5. 4. 2, C6/2. 2
The "Berkshire" (1974) 1 Lloyd's Rep. 185 ....
.... C3/3. 5, 4, 4. 2. 3, 4. 3, 4. 3. 1. 2, 9. 1. 3, 12. 2. 4. 2, C4/2. 2. 3, C6/3. 2. 4
The "Biela" (1929) 34 Lloyd's Rep. 192 .... C5/4. 2. 7. 1. 11. 4
The "Blue Wave" (1982) 1 Lloyd's Rep. 151 .... C4/2. 6. 4. 5, 3. 4. 3, 3. 4. 3. 3
The "Boknis" (20. 12. 85) S. & S. 86 No. 49 .... C5/4. 2. 10. 3. 2. 2. 2
The "Boral Gas" (1988) 1 Lloyd's Rep. 342 .... C3/11. 2. 2
The "Boukadoura" (1989) 1 Lloyd's Rep. 393 .... C6/3. 2. 4
The "Brabant" (1965) 2 Lloyd's Rep. 546 .... C5/4. 2. 6. 6. 2, 4. 2. 6. 4
The "Brij" (2001) 1 Lloyd's Rep. 431 (香港案例) C2/5. 10. 3
The "Bukhta Russkaya" (1997) 2 Lloyd's Rep. 744 ....
.... C5/4. 2. 3. 2. 2. 2 ,4. 2. 3. 2. 2. 6 ,4. 2. 10. 2. 8. 6
The "Bundesgerichtshof" May 30, 1983 (1984) ETL217 .... C4/3. 1
The "Bunga Seroja" (1994) 1 Lloyd's Rep. 455 (一审) C5/4. 2. 3. 5. 3. 9. 1, 4. 2. 6. 6. 5
The "Bunga Seroja" (1999) 1 Lloyd's Rep. 512 (上诉) ....
.... C5/4. 2. 1 ,4. 2. 6. 6. 5 ,4. 2. 7. 1. 3. 4 ,4. 2. 7. 1. 3. 5 ,4. 2. 7. 1. 3. 5. 3
The "C. Joyce" (1986) 2 Lloyd's Rep. 285 .... C5/4. 2. 3. 2. 2. 4, 4. 2. 10. 2. 8. 1
The "Caledonia", 157 U. S. 124 (1895) C5/4. 2. 1
The "Cape Comorin" (1991) 24 N. S. W. L. R. 745 .... C2/2. 2. 3

The "Capetan Markos" (1987) 2 Lloyd's Rep. 321 ················· C5/4.2.6.6.9
The "Captain Gregos" (1989) 2 Lloyd's Rep. 63 (高院一审) ········· C2/5.6.1, C3/§2
The "Captain Gregos" (1990) 1 Lloyd's Rep. 310 (上诉庭) ·············
·················· C2/5.6.2, C5/4.2.3.5.3.8, 4.2.10.2.9, 4.2.10.3.7
The "Captain Greges" (No.2) (1990) 2 Lloyd's Rep. 395 ············· C2/1.5.5
The "Carib Prince", 170 U.S. 655 (1898) ························ C5/4.2.1
The "Cariba Express" (3.9.80) S.80 No.122 ················· C5/4.2.10.3.2.2.2
The "Caroline P" (1984) 2 Lloyd's Rep. 466 ················ C5/4.2.10.2.8.2
The "Carron Park" (1890) 15 P.D. 203 ·························· C4/3.4.11
The "Carso" (1931) 41 Lloyd's Rep. 33 ·························· C6/3.3.4
The "Caspiana" (1956) 2 Lloyd's Rep. 379 ················· C4/3.2.2, 3.4.4
The "Castle Alpha" (1989) 2 Lloyd's Rep. 383 ·············· C5/4.2.10.2.4.2
The "Catherine Helen" (1998) 2 Lloyd's Rep. 511 ·····················
················· C5/4.2.10.2.6, 4.2.10.2.8.2, 4.2.10.2.8.4.2, 4.2.10.2.8.8
The "Cathay" (1927) 28 Lloyd's Rep. 202 ····················· C5/4.2.6.4.3
The "Chanda" (1989) 2 Lloyd's Rep. 494 ····························
················· 3.5.3.1, 4.2.3.5.3.6, 4.2.3.5.3.7, 4.2.3.5.3.8, 4.2.10.3.7
The "Chasca" (1875) L.R. 4A. BE. 446 ········· C5/4.2.7.1.3.6, 4.2.10.3.7
The "Chattahoochee" 173 U.S. 540 (1898) ····················· C4/3.4.12
The "Chitral" (2000) (Holmes Hardingham Newsletter No.30) ········ C2/2.2.3
The "Choko Star" (1990) 1 Lloyd's Rep. 516 ···················· C4/3.4.7.5
The "Chrysalis" (1983) 1 Lloyd's Rep. 503 ····················· C5/4.2.7.1.7
The "Chyebassa" (1966) 2 Lloyd's Rep. 193 ········ C5/4.2.6.5.2, 4.2.7.1.17.4
The "Cid" (1909) 2 K.B. 360 ······························ C5/4.2.7.1.10.5
The "City of Baroda" (1962) 25 Lloyd's Rep. 437 ················ C5/4.2.5.4
The "Clan Macdougall" (1943) 76 Lloyd's Rep. 58 ················ C5/4.2.5.4
The "Colima" (1897) 82 Fed. 665 ···························· C5/4.2.6.4.1
The "Constanza M" (1980) 1 Lloyd's Rep. 505 ······················ C6/6.1
The "Container Forwarder" (1974) 1 Lloyd's Rep. 119 ········· C5/4.2.10.3.2.2.3
The "Coral" (1992) 2 Lloyd's Rep. 158 ························ C5/4.2.7.1.3.2
The "Daffodil B" (1983) 1 Lloyd's Rep. 498 ········ C4/3.4.4, C5/4.2.10.1.5.2
The "Delfini" (1988) 2 Lloyd's Rep. 599 (高院一审) ······· C2/3.1.5.4, 5.3.3
The "Delfini" (1990) 1 Lloyd's Rep. 252 (上诉庭) ····················
························ C2/2.2.3, 3.1.5.4, 5.2.2, C3/12.2.4.4
The "Del Sud", 1959 AMC 2143 (5 Cir. 1959) ················· C5/4.2.6.5.3
The "Demodocus" (1966) 1 Lloyd's Rep. 1 ················· C6/4.1.4, 4.2.2

The "Demosthenes" 189 F. 2d 488 (4 Cir. 1951) ················ C5/4. 2. 7. 1. 3. 2
The "Denbighire" (1896) 2 QB 326 ····················· C5/4. 2. 7. 1. 7
The "Destro" (1927) 29 Lloyd's Rep. 133 ··············· C5/4. 2. 5. 3. 1
The "Diamond" (1906) 10 Asp. M. L. C 286 ··············· C5/4. 2. 7. 1. 2. 1
The "Dominator" (1959) 1 Lloyd's Rep. 125 ··············· C5/4. 2. 6. 4
The "Dona Mari" (1973) 2 Lloyd's Rep. 366 ············ C2/3. 3, C3/12. 2. 3, C6/3. 3
The "Dunelmia" (1969) 2 Lloyd's Rep. 476 (上诉庭) ············ C3/4. 2, 9. 1. 2, C4/2. 5
The "Dunelmia" (1969) 1 Lloyd's Rep. 32 (高院一审) ········ C5/4. 2. 3. 2. 2. 7, 4. 2. 3. 2. 3
The "Ebn Al Waleed" (2000) 1 Lloyd's Rep. 270 ········ C5/4. 2. 10. 3. 4, 4. 2. 10. 3. 6
The "Edmund Fanning", 1953 A. M. C. 86 (2 Cir. 1953) ··············· C5/4. 2. 10. 3. 3
The "El Amria" (1982) 2 Lloyd's Rep. 28 ··············· C3/9. 1. 2
The "Elafi" (1981) 2 Hoyd's Rep. 679 ··············· C3/12. 2. 4. 4
The "Elbe Maru" (1978) 1 Lloyd's Rep. 206 ······ C3/8. 2. 2, C5/4. 2. 3. 3. 2. 4, 4. 2. 3. 3. 2. 4
The "Eleftheria" (1969) 1 Lloyd's Rep. 237 ··············· C4/3. 4. 3. 3
The "Elli 2" (1985) 1 Lloyd's Rep. 107 ··············· C3/12. 2. 3, 12. 2. 4. 4
The "Emilian Marie" (1875) 44 LJ Adm 9 ··············· C5/4. 2. 3. 4. 2. 1
The "Emmanuel C" (1983) 1 Lloyd's Rep. 310 ············ C3/8. 2. 4, C5/4. 2. 3. 5. 3. 4
The "Ensley City", 1947 AMC 568 (D. Md. 1947) ··············· C5/4. 2. 8. 2
The "Ermis" SMA No. 2960 (1993) ··············· C4/3. 4. 8
The "Ert Stefanie" (1989) 1 Lloyd's Rep. 349 ··············· C5/4. 2. 6. 6. 2
The "Erwin Schroder" (1970) Ex C. R. 426 ··············· C6/2. 1
The "Esmeralda" (1988) 1 Lloyd's Rep. 206 ··············· C6/5. 3. 5
The "Etalofos" (1995) (伦敦仲裁) ··············· C2/5. 7
The "Europa" (1908) P. 84 ··············· C4/3. 4. 4
The "European Enterprise" (1989) 2 Lloyd's Rep. 185 ··············· C2/3. 5. 5
The "Eurymedon" (1974) 1 Lloyd's Rep. 534 ······ C3/8. 2. 2, C5/4. 2. 3. 3. 2. 4, 4. 2. 10. 2. 3
The "Eurysthenes" (1976) 2 Lloyd's Rep. 171 ··············· C5/4. 2. 6. 6. 2, 4. 2. 6. 6. 7
The "Evgrafov" (1987) 2 Lloyd's Rep. 634 ··············· C5/4. 2. 8. 3
The "Evia" (1982) 2 Lloyd's Rep. 307 ··············· C5/4. 2. 7. 1. 7
The "Evje" (No. 2) (1978) 1 Lloyd's Rep. 351
················ C5/4. 2. 6. 6. 6. 1, 4. 2. 6. 6. 6. 3, 4. 2. 7. 1. 1. 3
The "Exi" (1990) SMA # 2709 ··············· C6/3. 3, 3. 3. 6. 1
The "Fantasy" (1992) 1 Lloyd's Rep. 235 ··············· C5/4. 2. 3. 5. 3. 4
The "Farrandoc" (1961) 2 Lloyd's Rep. 276 ··············· C5/4. 2. 7. 1. 1. 4. 3
The "Fedtrade", 1983 AMC 774 (S. D. Tex. 1981) ··············· C5/4. 2. 4. 4. 2
The "Filiatra Legacy" (1991) 2 Lloyd's Rep. 337 ··············· C3/12. 2. 4. 4

The "Finnrose" (1994) 1 Lloyd's Rep. 559 ·· C4/2.6.4.5
The "Fiona" (1993) 1 Lloyd's Rep. 257（高院一审）················· C3/11.2.1,C6/2.1
The "Fiona" (1994) 2 Lloyd's Rep. 506（上诉庭）····················· C5/4.2.6.6.3.2.2
The "Fjellvang" (1999) 2 Lloyd's Rep. 658 ································ C5/4.2.10.2.5.2
The "Fjord Wind" (1999) 1 Lloyd's Rep. 307 ············· C5/4.2.6.6.6.1, 4.2.7.1.10.3
The "Flecha" (1999) 1 Lloyd's Rep. 612 ·· C3/7.5, 7.6
The "Flowergate" (1967) 1 Lloyd's Rep. 1 ································ C5/4.2.7.1.10.6
The "Frances Hammer" (1975) 1 Lloyd's Rep. 305 ······················· C4/3.4.12
The "Friso" (1980) 1 Lloyd's Rep. 469 ··················· C5/4.2.6.6.5, 4.2.7.1.3.2
The "Future Express" (1992) 2 Lloyd's Rep. 79（高院一审）···············
·· C1, C2/2.4, 4.1, 5.6.1, C3/12.2.4.4
The "Future Express" (1993) 2 Lloyd's Rep. 542（上诉庭）···············
··············· 2.4, 3.1.5.1, 3.1.5.4, 4.1, 5.4.3.1, 5.6.1, 5.6.5, C3/12.2.4.4
The "Galatia" (1979) 2 Lloyd's Rep. 450（上诉庭）········ C6/3.2.5, 5.2, 6.1
The "Galatia" (1980) 1 Lloyd's Rep. 453（高院一审）······················
·· C5/4.2.3.4.2.5, C6/3.3.1, 3.3.5.1
The "Gamlen" (1980) 147 C.L.R. 142 ································ C5/4.2.7.1.3.4
The "Garbis" (1982) 2 Lloyd's Rep. 283 ···
······················ C4/2.5, 2.6.3,2.6.4.2,2.6.5,C6/3.3.5.1,3.3.6.1
The "Gianna M" (1937) 57 Lloyd's Rep. 247 ························ C5/4.2.6.6.3.2.3
The "Giannis NK" (1996) 1 Lloyd's Rep. 577（上诉庭）············ C6/2.1, 2.2
The "Giannis NK" (1998) 1 Lloyd's Rep. 337（贵族院）········ C3/12.2.5.3, 12.2.5.4.2
The "Gippsland" (1994) 1 Lloyd's Rep. 335 ·························· C5/4.2.6.6.3.2.2
The "Good Friend" (1984) 2 Lloyd's Rep. 586 ····················· C5/4.2.6.6.3.2.1
The "Grangefield" (1972) 1 Lloyd's Rep. 53 ··················· C4/3.4.3, 3.4.3.1
The "Granville" (1961) A.M.C. 2229 ···························· C5/4.2.3.2.2.3
The "Grelwen (1924) 18 Lloyd's Rep. 319 ···························· C5/4.2.6.6.5
The "Grumant" (1973) 2 Lloyd's Rep. 531 ········· C5/4.2.7.1.3.3,4.2.7.1.3.5.3
The "Gudermes" (1993) 1 Lloyd's Rep. 311 ····························· C5/4.2.6.6.3.1
The "Hakone Maru" (1973) 1 Lloyd's Rep. 46 ······················· C5/4.2.10.2.2
The "Hans Leonhardt" (1991) SMA # 2820 ································· C6/3.3
The "Hansa Nord" (1975) 2 Lloyd's Rep. 445 ···································· C7
The "Havhelt" (1993) 1 Lloyd's Rep. 523 ································ C4/2.6.4.5
The "Havprins" (1983) 2 Lloyd's Rep. 356 ·································· C3/§1
The "Hector" (1998) 2 Lloyd's Rep. 287 ···
···················· 5.2,6.1, 7.4,7.6,8.2.3,8.3, 8.4, C5/4.2.7.1.1.4.1, 4.2.10.2.8

The "Heidberg" (1994) 2 Lloyd's Rep. 287 ·················· C4/2. 2. 4, 2. 6. 4. 1, C7
The "Hellenic Dolphin" (1978) 2 Lloyd's Rep. 336 ·············· C5/4. 2. 6. 4. 3, 4. 2. 6. 4. 4
The "Henry Sif" (1982) 1 Lloyd's Rep. 456 ················ C5/4. 2. 10. 2. 4. 3
The "Heron Ⅱ" (1967) 2 Lloyd's Rep. 457 ·······················
 ················ 8. 2. 4, C4/3. 4. 10, C5/4. 2. 6. 6. 6. 1, 4. 2. 7. 1, 4. 2. 7. 1. 7, 4. 4, C6/7. 1
The "Herroe" and "Askoe" (1986) 2 Lloyd's Rep. 281 ················
 ················ C6/3. 2. 3, 3. 2. 6. 1, 4. 3, 5. 3. 4, 5. 4. 3
The "Highland Monarch" (1939) 64 Lloyd's Rep. 188 ········ C5/4. 2. 6. 4. 3, C5/4. 2. 7. 1. 16
The "Hill Harmony" (1999) 2 Lloyd's Rep. 209 ············· C5/4. 2. 7. 1. 1. 3, 4. 2. 7. 1. 1. 4. 2
The "Himmerland" (1965) 2 Lloyd's Rep. 353 ·······················
 ············ C5/4. 2. 10. 2. 8. 2, 4. 2. 10. 2. 8. 4, 4. 2. 10. 2. 8. 4. 2, 4. 2. 10. 2. 8. 8
The "Hobsons Bay" (1933) 46 Lloyd's Rep. 189 ················ C5/4. 2. 7. 1. 10. 3
The "Hong Kong Fir" (1961) 2 Lloyd's Rep. 478 ················ C3/ § 2
The "Hong Kong Producer" (1969) 2 Lloyd's Rep. 536 ················
 ············ 5. 3. 1, 4. 2. 3. 5. 3. 2, 4. 2. 3. 5. 3. 3, 4. 2. 3. 5. 3. 7, 4. 2. 3. 5. 3. 9. 2
The "Houda" (1994) 2 Lloyd's Rep. 541 ·······················
 ············ 4, 5. 1. 1, 5. 1. 3, 5. 1. 7, 5. 1. 9, 5. 1. 12, 5. 2, 5. 2. 1, 5. 2. 2, 5. 2. 3. 2
The "Hoyanger" (1979) 2 Lloyd's Rep. 79 ······ C5/4. 2. 7. 1. 10. 3, 4. 2. 7. 1. 10. 5, C6/3. 3. 3
The "Hurry On" (Vita Food Products, Inc. v. Unus Shipping Co. Ltd.) (1939) 63 Lloyd's
Rep. 21 ················ C5/4. 2. 1, 4. 2. 3. 1. 1, 4. 3, 4. 6, C6/4. 2. 4
The "I Congreso del Partido" (1977) 1 Lloyd's Rep. 536 ················ C3/3. 3
The "Ikaraiada" (1999) 2 Lloyd's Rep. 365 ················ C3/4. 2. 2
The "Imvros" (1999) 1 Lloyd's Rep. 848 ················ C5/4. 2. 3. 5. 3. 4
The "Inchmaree" (1881) 12 App. Cas. 484 ················ C5/4. 2. 7. 1. 2. 1, 4. 2. 7. 1. 3. 6
The "Indian City" (1939) 64 Lloyd's Rep. 229 ················ C4/3. 4. 4
The "Ines" (1995) 2 Lloyd's Rep. 144 ·······················
 ············ C1, C2/5. 5. 1, 5. 6. 1, 5. 6. 2, C3/ § 2, 7. 3, 7. 5, 7. 6, 8. 2. 3, C5/3. 1
The "Ion" (1971) 1 Lloyd's Rep. 541 ················ C5/4. 2. 9. 4, 4. 2. 10. 2. 8. 8
The "Iran Bohonar" (1983) 2 Lloyd's Rep. 620 ··········· C2/5. 1. 8, 5. 1. 11, C5/4. 2. 8. 7. 4
The "Iran Vojdan" (1984) 2 Lloyd's Rep. 380 ················ C4/3. 1, 3. 4. 3. 1, 3. 4. 3. 3
The "Irini A" (1999) 1 Lloyd's Rep. 189 ················ C2/5. 3. 3
The "Irini M" (1988) 1 Lloyd's Rep. 253 ·······················
 ············ C6/3. 2. 2, 3. 2. 2. 1, 3. 2. 2. 2, 3. 2. 6. 1, 3. 2. 7. 3
The "Iron Gippland" (1994) 1 Lloyd's Rep. 335 ················ C5/4. 2. 7. 1. 1. 4. 1
The "Irrawaddy" (1898) 171 U. S. 187 ················ C4/3. 4. 11
The "Isis", 290 U. S. 333 (1933) ················ C5/4. 1, 4. 2. 1, 4. 2. 6. 2

The "Island Archon" (1994) 2 Lloyd's Rep. 227 ················· C5/4. 2. 10. 2. 8. 1
The "Isnis" s Gravenhage, 4 Oct. 1988, S & S, 1989, No. 77; aff'd by H. R. , 5 Oct. 1990, S &
S, 1991, No. 98 ··· C5/4. 2. 4. 4. 2
The "Ixia" (1931) 41 Lloyd's Rep. 165 ··································
·························· C4/3. 4. 4, C5/4. 2. 10. 1. 2, 4. 2. 10. 1. 3, 4. 2. 10. 1. 5. 2
The "Jalamohan" (1988) 1 Lloyd's Rep. 443 ················· C3/1. 3, 4. 1
The "Jason" (1910) 225 U. S. ······································· C4/3. 4. 11
The "Johnstown" (1928) 32 Lloyd's Rep. 218 ···················· C6/4. 1. 3
The "Juno" (1986) 1 Lloyd's Rep. 190 ··························· C5/4. 2. 4. 3. 1
The "K. H. Enterprise"(另称 The "Pioneer Container") (1994) 1 Lloyd's Rep. 593 ···········
······················· C3/8. 2, 8. 3, C4/2. 6, 2. 6. 3, 2. 6. 4. 2, 2. 6. 4. 5
The "Kapetan Markos" (1986) 1 Lloyd's Rep. 211 ·····················
························ C4/2. 6. 4. 5, C5/4. 2. 10. 2. 5, 4. 2. 10. 2. 5. 1
The "Kapetan Markos No. 2" (1987) 2 Lloyd's Rep. 321 ······················
······························ C1, C3/12. 2. 4. 4, C5/4. 2. 6. 6. 9
The "Kapitan Sakharov" (2000) 2 Lloyd's Rep. 255 ·····················
·············· 2. 1, 12. 2. 5. 5, C5/4. 2. 6. 6, 4. 2. 6. 6. 5, 4. 2. 7. 1. 9. 2, 4. 2. 7. 1. 16
The "Kavo Peiratis" (1977) 2 Lloyd's Rep. 113 ····················· C3/11. 2. 2
The "Kefalonia Wind" (1986) 1 Lloyd's Rep. 273 ··············· C5/4. 2. 10. 2. 7
The "Kelo" (1985) 2 Lloyd's Rep. 85 ················· C3/12. 2. 2, 12. 2. 4. 4
The "Khian Zephyr" (1982) 1 Lloyd's Rep. 73 ········· C5/4. 2. 3. 2. 2. 2, 4. 2. 10. 2. 8. 4. 1
The "Koeaeli" SMA No. 2417 (1987) ······························· C4/3. 4. 8
The "Komninos S" (1991) 1 Lloyd's Rep. 371 ·········· C4/3. 4. 3, 3. 4. 3. 1, C5/4. 2. 3. 1. 4
The "Krapan J" (1999) 1 Lloyd's Rep. 688 ············ C5/4. 2. 3. 2. 2. 7, 4. 2. 10. 2. 8
The "Kulmerland" (1973) 2 Lloyd's Rep. 428 ················ C5/4. 2. 10. 3. 2. 2. 3
The "Lady Brenda" (1931) 41 Lloyd's Rep. 75 ························ C6/3. 3. 6. 2
The "Lady Gwendolen" (1965) 1 Lloyd's Rep. 335 ··············· C5/4. 2. 6. 6. 2, 4. 2. 7. 1. 2. 3
The "Lady Sophie" (1979) 2 Lloyd's Rep. 173 ···················· C4/3. 4. 16
The "Liepaya" (1999) 1 Lloyd's Rep. 649 ······················· C5/4. 2. 6. 6. 3. 2. 2
The "Lilburn" (1939) 64 Lloyd's Rep. 87 ··············· C5/4. 2. 6. 4. 1, 4. 2. 6. 4. 4
The "Lucille" (1984) 1 Lloyd's Rep. 244 ························ C5/4. 2. 7. 1. 7
The "Lucky Wave" (1985) 1 Lloyd's Rep. 80 ······················ C5/4. 2. 7. 1. 11. 1
The "Lycaon" (1981) 1 Lloyd's Rep. 92; (1983) 2 Lloyd's Rep. 548 ·················
······················ C2/3. 1. 5. 3, 3. 2, 3. 4. 3, 4. 1, 5. 1. 5, 5. 1. 8, 5. 3. 2, 5. 10. 3
The "Macedon" (1955) 1 Lloyd's Rep. 459 ······················· C4/3. 4. 4
The "Maestro Giorgis" (1983) 1 Lloyd's Rep. 66 ···················· C5/4. 2. 6. 6. 8

The "Makedonia" (1962) 1 Lloyd's Rep. 316 ···
················· C5/4. 2. 6. 5, 4. 2. 6. 5. 2, 4. 2. 6. 6. 2, 4. 2. 6. 6. 6, 4. 2. 6. 6. 6. 3
The "Maltasian" (1966) 2 Lloyd's Rep. 53 ···
················· 7. 1. 10. 1, 4. 2. 7. 1. 10. 3, 4. 2. 7. 1. 10. 4, 4. 2. 7. 1. 10. 5, 4. 2. 8. 1
The "Mare del Nord" (1990) 1 Lloyd's Rep. 40 ·················· C5/4. 2. 6. 1. 2, C7
The "Mariasmi" (1970) 1 Lloyd's Rep. 247 ··
················· C5/4. 2. 3. 2. 2. 2, 4. 2. 3. 2. 2. 3, 4. 2. 3. 2. 2. 5, 4. 2. 3. 2. 2. 6
The "Marilyn L" (1972) 1 Lloyd's Rep. 418 ················· C5/4. 2. 10. 1. 5. 3
The "Marinor" (1996) 1 Lloyd's Rep. 301 ······················· C5/4. 2. 3. 2. 2. 6
The "Marion" (1984) 2 Lloyd's Rep. 1 ·············· C5/4. 2. 6. 6. 7, 4. 2. 7. 1. 2. 3
The "Markos N" (2000) 2 Lloyd's Rep. 243 ············· (请看 Thyssen v. Calypso)
The "Marlborough Hill" (1921), A. C. 444 ······················ C2/3. 4. 2, 3. 4. 3
The "Marquette" 480 F. 2d 669 1973 AMC 1683 (2 Cir. 1973) ······ C5/4. 2. 7. 1. 2. 6
The "Mata K" (1998) 2 Lloyd's Rep. 614 ··
··················· C5/4. 2. 10. 3. 2. 2. 2, C6/1. 1, 1. 3, 5. 2, 5. 3. 8, 5. 4. 1
The "Mattasian" (1966) 2 Lloyd's Rep. 53 ······················ C5/4. 2. 7. 1. 10. 4
The "Medina Princess" (1965) 1 Lloyd's Rep. 361 ·························· C4/3. 4. 5
The "Merak" (1964) 2 Lloyd's Rep. 283 (高院一审) ························ C3/4. 2. 2
The "Merak" (1964) 2 Lloyd's Rep. 527 (上诉庭) ················· C4/2. 6. 4. 1, 2. 6. 4. 2
The "Mica" (1973) 2 Lloyd's Rep. 478; (1975) 2 Lloyd's Rep. 371 ········ C3/4. 3. 1. 5
The "Milan" (1861) Lush. 388; 31 L. t. Ad. 105; 5 L. T. 590 ·············· C4/3. 4. 12
The "Mineral Transporter" (1985) 2 Lloyd's Rep. 303 ··············· C3/8. 2. 3, 8. 2. 4
The "Miramar" (1983) 2 Lloyd's Rep. 319 (高院一审) ····················· C4/2. 6. 2. 1
The "Miramar" (1984) 2 Lloyd's Rep. 129 (贵族院) ······ C3/11. 2. 2, C4/2. 6. 2. 2, 2. 6. 5
The "Mormaclynx" (1970) 1 Lloyd's Rep. 527 ···················· C5/4. 2. 10. 3. 2. 2. 2
The "Mormacsaga" (1969) 1 Lloyd's Rep. 515 ········· C5/4. 2. 7. 1. 1. 4. 2, 4. 2. 8. 7. 3
The "Mormacvega" (1974) 1 Lloyd's Rep. 296 ············· C5/4. 2. 3. 5. 3. 7, 4. 2. 3. 5. 3. 9
The "Morviken" (1983) 1 Lloyd's Rep. 1 ··
··············· 5, 4. 2. 3. 1. 6, C5/4. 2. 9. 1, 4. 2. 10. 3. 2. 2. 2, 4. 2. 10. 3. 5, C6/5. 4. 1
The "MSC Samia" (1991) LMLN No. 482 ································ C2/5. 2. 1
The "Muncaster Castle" (1961) 1 Lloyd's Rep. 57 ········· C5/4. 2. 6. 4. 2, 4. 2. 6. 6. 3. 2. 3
The "Nadezhda Krupskaya" (1989) 1 Lloyd's Rep. 518 ·················· C5/4. 2. 10. 3. 4
The "Nai Matteini" (1988) 1 Lloyd's Rep. 452 ········· C2/5. 1. 4, C4/2. 2. 2, 2. 2. 3, 2. 6. 4. 1
The "Nan Fung" 1988 (伦敦仲裁) ························ C5/4. 2. 6. 6. 8, 4. 2. 7. 1. 7
The "Nand Nakul" (1999) (伦敦仲裁) ··· C7
The "Nanfri" (1979) 1 Lloyd's Rep. 201 ········· C3/3. 5, 5. 3, C4/2. 2. 3, C6/3. 3. 6. 2, 6. 2

The "Nea Tyhi" (1982) 1 Lloyd's Rep. 606 ···
··· C2/5.4.2, C3/5.2, C5/4.2.3.5.3.6, C6/4.1.4
The "Nemea" (1980) LMLN # 280 ·· C2/5.2.3.2
The "Neptunes" (1814) 4 Camp. 84 ··· C5/4.2.6.5
The "Nerano" (1994) 2 Lloyd's Rep. 50 ··· C4/2.6.4.1
The "New Horizon" (1975) 2 Lloyd's Rep. 314 ·· C5/4.2.7.1.13.1
The "New York Star" (1980) 2 Lloyd's Rep. 317 ················· C3/8.2.2, C5/4.2.3.3.2.4
The "Newbrough" (1939) 64 Lloyd's Rep. 33 ···
····················· C5/4.2.6.4.1, 4.2.6.6.6, 4.2.6.6.6.1, 4.2.6.6.6.3
The "Nicholas H" (1995) 2 Lloyd's Rep. 299 ·············· C5/4.2.3.3.2.3, 4.2.3.3.2.7
The "Njegos" (1935) 53 Lloyd's Rep. 286 ··· C4/2.6.4.1
The "Noel Bay" (1989) 1 Lloyd's Rep. 361 ··· C4/3.4.4
The "Nogar Marin" (1988) 1 Lloyd's Rep. 412 ··············· C5/4.2.10.2.8.1, C6/3.3.6.2
The "Nordglimt" (1987) 2 Lloyd's Rep. 470 ············ C1, C4/2.6.4.5, C5/4.2.10.2.5.1
The "Norman" (1960) 1 Lloyd's Rep. 1 ·· C5/4.2.6.6.7
The "Ocean Dynamic" (1982) 2 Lloyd's Rep. 88 ···
·· C3/§2, C5/4.2.2, 4.2.4.4.1, 4.2.5.3.1
The "Odessa" (1916) 1 AC 145 ·· C2/4.2
The "Olib" (1991) 2 Lloyd's Rep. 108 ··· C4/3.4.9
The "Omega Leros" (1987) 1 Lloyd's Rep. 530 ····································· C5/4.2.10.3.5
The "Orjula" (1995) 2 Lloyd's Rep. 395 ··· C4/§1
The "Orland" (1933) 44 Lloyd's Rep. 384 ··· C4/3.2.2
The "Oroya" (1926) 25 Lloyd's Rep. 573 ·· C4/3.4.5
The "OT Sonja" (1993) 2 Lloyd's Rep. 435 ··· C5/4.2.3.2.2.6
The "Overseas Discoverer" (S.M.A. # 12031.3.78) ································· C6/3.2.2.2
The "Panaghia Tinnou" (1986) 2 Lloyd's Rep. 586 ································· C5/4.2.7.1.7
The "Paros" (1987) 2 Lloyd's Rep. 269 ·· C3/3.5
The "Penelope II" (1980) 2 Lloyd's Rep. 17 (上诉庭) ······························ C3/4.3.1.3
The "Penelope II" (1979) 2 Lloyd's Rep. 42 (高院一审) ························ C5/4.2.10.3.9
The "Petr Shmidt" (1995) 1 Lloyd's Rep. 202 ·············· C4/2.6.4.3, C5/4.2.10.2.5.2
The "Penrith Castle" (1954) 2 Lloyd's Rep. 544 ·································· C5/4.2.3.2.2.3
The "Phassa" (1990) SMA No. 2640 ············· C3/5.3, C6/3.2.4, 3.2.6.1, 3.3.6.1
The "Phonizien" (1966) 1 Lloyd's Rep. 150 ··· C4/2.6.4.1
The "Pioneer Container" (1994) 1 Lloyd's Rep. 593 (另称 The "K.H. Enterprise") ············
·· C2/1.5.2.1, 3.2, C3/8.2.2, C5/4.2.3.3.2.5
The "Playa Larga" (1983) 2 Lloyd's Rep. 171 ·· C2/5.5.1

The "Popi M" (1958) 2 Lloyd's Rep. 1 ···
·· C5/4. 2. 5. 3. 2, 4. 2. 5. 3. 3, 4. 2. 5. 4, 4. 2. 7. 1. 17. 2
The "Pormovskiy 3068" (1994) 2 Lloyd's Rep. 266 ···················· C5/4. 2. 3. 4. 2. 2
The "Puerto Acevedo" (1978) 1 Lloyd's Rep. 38 ············· C3/3. 1, 5/4. 2. 10. 2. 7
The "Punica" SMA No. 3023 (1993) ·· C4/3. 4. 8
The "Pythia" (1982) 2 Lloyd's Rep. 160 ·· C4/3. 4. 5
The "Raffaella" (1984) 1 Lloyd's Rep. 102; (1985) 2 Lloyd's Rep. 36 ······ C5/4. 2. 3. 5. 3. 6
The "Ragnvald Jarl" (1934) 49 Lloyd's Rep. 183 ·· C4/3. 4. 4
The "Regenstein" (1970) 2 Lloyd's Rep. 1 ···
·· C5/4. 2. 3. 3. 2. 1, 4. 2. 3. 3. 2. 5, 4. 2. 3. 4. 2. 2, 4. 2. 3. 4. 2. 3
The "Rena K" (1978) 1 Lloyd's Rep. 545 ·························· C4/2. 3, 2. 6. 4. 1, 2. 6. 4. 3
The "Rewia" (1991) 2 Lloyd's Rep. 325 ·········· C3/1. 3, 3. 5, 5. 1, 5. 2, 7. 2, C4/3. 4. 3. 3
The "River Gurara" (1996) 2 Lloyd's Rep. 53 (高院一审) ············ C5/4. 2. 10. 3. 2. 2. 1
The "River Gurara" (1998) 1 Lloyd's Rep. 225 (上诉庭) ·······································
·· C2/5. 6. 3, C5/4. 2. 10. 3. 2. 2. 2, C6/5. 3. 7
The "Roberta" (1938) 60 Lloyd's Rep. 84 ·· C5/4. 2. 6. 6. 2
The "Rodney" (1900) p. 112 ·· C5/4. 2. 7. 1. 1. 4
The "Rosa S" (1988) 2 Lloyd's Rep. 574 ················· C5/4. 2. 3. 2. 2. 5, 4. 2. 10. 3. 4
The "Sabine Howaldt" (1971) 2 Lloyd's Rep. 78 ·· C5/4. 2. 6. 6. 4
The "Safe Carrier" (1994) 1 Lloyd's Rep. 589 ·· C5/4. 2. 6. 6. 2
The "Safeer" (1994) 1 Lloyd's Rep. 637 ······················· C5/4. 2. 7. 1. 5, 4. 2. 7. 1. 7
The "Sagona" (1984) 1 Lloyd's Rep. 194 ······················· C2/5. 1. 12, 5. 2. 1, 5. 2. 12
The "San Giuseppe" 122 F. 2d 579, 582 (4th Cir. 1941) ····················· C4/3. 4. 4
The "San Nicholas" (1976) 1 Lloyd's Rep. 8 ··
·· C3/4. 2. 3, 10. 1, 12. 2. 4. 4, C4/2. 2. 2, 2. 2. 3
The "Santa Carina" (1977) 1 Lloyd's Rep. 478 ·· C3/ § 1
The "Sante Malta" (1967) 2 Lloyd's Rep. 391 ·· C5/4. 2. 7. 1. 2. 1
The "Sargasso" (1994) 1 Lloyd's Rep. 162 ·· C5/4. 2. 10. 2. 5. 2
The "Satya Kailash" (1984) 1 Lloyd's Rep. 588 ··
·· C3/8. 2. 4, C5/4. 2. 3. 2. 2. 2, 4. 2. 3. 2. 2. 5
The "Saudi Crown" (1986) 1 Lloyd's Rep. 261 ······················ C3/5. 2, C6/4. 4, 7. 3
The "Saudi Prince" (1986) 1 Lloyd's Rep. 347 ·· C5/4. 2. 8. 4
The "Saxon Star" (1957) 1 Lloyd's Rep. 79 (高院一审) ·························· C5/4. 2. 3. 2. 2
The "Saxon Star" (1958) 1 Lloyd's Rep. 73 (上议院) ·······································
·· C2/3. 5. 3, C4/2. 3, C5/4. 2. 3. 2. 2, 4. 2. 7. 1
The "Scaplake" (1978) 2 Lloyd's Rep. 380 ·· C3/ § 1

The "Segundo" (1941) A. C. 55 ·· C5/4. 2. 7. 1. 3. 6
The "Sevonia Team" (1983) 2 Lloyd's Rep. 640 ············ C3/9. 1. 1, 12. 2. 4. 4, C4/2. 2. 2
The "Siki Rolette" (1999) I WLR 908 ·· C5/4. 2. 10. 2. 6
The "Silvercypress" (Fire), 1943 AMC 224 and 510 (SDNY 1943) ············ C5/4. 2. 10. 1. 4
The "Sinoe" (1972) 1 Lloyd's Rep. 201 ··· C3/11. 2. 2
The "Skulptor Vuchetich" (美国地方法院 Southern District of Texas, 在 UK Club 1981 年 Legal Decisions 报道) ··· C3/8. 2. 2, C5/4. 2. 3. 3. 2. 4
The "Sky Reefer" (1995) 63 USLW 4617; AMC 1817 ·······································
·· C4/2. 6. 4, 2. 6. 4. 4, 2. 6. 4. 5, 3. 4. 3. 4, 3. 4. 12; C5/4. 2. 9. 1
The "Sletter" (1999) (LMLN No. 522) ································· C2/3. 1. 5. 2, 5. 4. 1
The "SLS Everest" (1981) 2 Lloyd's Rep. 389 ········ C3/10. 1, C4/2. 2. 1, 2. 2. 3, 2. 6. 4. 1
The "Smaro" (1999) 1 Lloyd's Rep. 225 ·· C5/4. 2. 10. 2. 5. 2
The "Sormovskiy 3068" (1994) 2 Lloyd's Rep. 266 ·······································
················ C2/2. 2, 2. 2. 1, 5. 1. 2, 5. 1. 11, 5. 1. 12, 5. 2, 5. 4. 3. 4, C5/4. 2. 4. 3. 1
The "Southern Sword", 190 F. 2d 394 AMC 1518 (3 Cir. 1951) ··········· C5/4. 2. 5. 3. 3
The "Spiliada" (1987) 1 Lloyd's Rep. 1 ··············· C3/10. 2, 11. 2. 1, C4/2. 6. 4. 5
The "Standard Ardour" (1988) 2 Lloyd's Rep. 159 ····························· C5/4. 2. 3. 2. 2. 6
The "Star Sea" (1997) 1 Lloyd's Rep. 360 ····································· C5/4. 2. 6. 6. 2
The "Starsin" (2000) 1 Lloyd's Rep. 85 (高院一审) ·······································
················ §5, 5. 2, 6. 1, 7. 6, 8. 1, 8. 2. 3, 8. 3, C5/4. 2. 3. 3. 2. 1, 4. 2. 3. 5. 3. 6
The "Starsin" (2001) 1 Lloyd's Rep. 437 (上诉庭) ······························· C3/7. 6
The "Stena Pacifica" (1990) 2 Lloyd's Rep. 234 ········ C5/4. 2. 3. 2. 2. 6, 4. 2. 10. 2. 8. 4. 1
The "Stettin" (1889) 14 PD 142 ·· C2/3. 1. 2
The "Stone Gemini" (1999) 2 Lloyd's Rep. 255 ···
··································· C1, C2/3. 1. 5. 3, 4. 3, 5. 6. 5, C3/12. 4. 1
The "Storviken" (1927) 27 Lloyd's Rep. 227 ································· C4/3. 4. 10
The "Stranna" (1938) 60 Lloyd's Rep. 51 ·································· C5/4. 2. 7. 1. 3. 6
The "Strathewe" (1986) LMLN 180 ····························· C5/4. 2. 7. 1. 7, C6/3. 1
The "Strathnewton" (1983) 1 Lloyd's Rep. 219 ····························· C5/4. 2. 3. 2. 2. 2
The "Suleyman Stalskiy" (1976) 2 Lloyd's Rep. 609 ············· C3/8. 2. 2, C5/4. 2. 3. 3. 2. 4
The "Sun Happiness" (1984) 1 Lloyd's Rep. 381 ······································ C3/ § 1
The "Sun Pollux" SMA No. 1468 (1980) ··· C4/3. 4. 8
The "Swan" (1968) 1 Lloyd's Rep. 5 ··· C3/ § 1
The "Teutonia" (1872) L. R. 4 P. C. 171 ·· C4/3. 4. 4
The "Texaco Melbourne" (1992) 1 Lloyd's Rep. 303 (高院一审) ············ C5/4. 2. 10. 3. 5
The "Texaco Melbourne" (1994) 1Lloyd's Rep. 473 (贵族院) ···················· C2/5. 5. 1

The "Tilia Gorthon" (1985) 1 Lloyd's Rep. 552 ···
··· C5/4. 2. 6. 4. 3, 4. 2. 6. 6. 5 ,4. 2. 7. 1. 3. 2 ,4. 2. 8. 7. 2
The "Tindefjell" (1973) 2 Lloyd's Rep. 253 ································· C5/4. 2. 10. 3. 2. 2. 2
The "TNT Express" (1992) 2 Lloyd's Rep. 636 ······················ C6/3. 3. 2, 3. 3. 3
The "Torenia" (1983) 2 Lloyd's Rep. 210 ················ C5/4. 2. 5. 3. 3, 4. 2. 5. 4, 4. 2. 5. 5
The "Torni" (1932) p. 78 ··· C5/4. 2. 3. 1. 1
The "Transontario", Antwerp, 15 Jun. 1977, J. P. A. 1977 – 78, 40, aff'g Comm. Antwerp, 19 Mar. 1976, J. P. A. ··· C5/4. 2. 4. 4. 2
The "Uhenbels" (1986) 2 Lloyd's Rep. 294 ··· C3/1. 3
The "Ulvern" (1928) 32 Lloyd's Rep. 7 ································· C5/4. 2. 7. 1. 3. 5. 3
The "Unique Mariner" (1978) 1 Lloyd's Rep. 438 ······················ C4/3. 4. 7. 5
The "Varenna" (1983) 2 Lloyd's Rep. 592 ······························ C4/2. 6. 4. 1
The "Varing" (1931) p. 79 ··· C4/3. 2. 2
The "Vassilios Bacolitsas" SMA No. 2259 (1986) ······················ C4/3. 4. 8
The "Venezuela" (1980) 1 Lloyd's Rep. 393 ········ C3/1. 4, 4. 3. 2, 6. 1, 7. 1, 7. 2, 8. 2. 3
The "Vikfrost" (1980) 1 Lloyd's Rep. 560 ······························ C3/4. 3. 1. 2
The "Virgo" (1976) 2 Lloyd's Rep. 135 ······························ C3/ § 1
The "Visurgis" (1999) 1 Lloyd's Rep. 218 ······························ C5/4. 2. 8. 6
The "Vortigern" (1899) p. 140 ··· C5/4. 2. 6. 5
The "Waltrand" (1991) 1 Lloyd's Rep. 389 ······························ C5/4. 2. 10. 3. 9
The "Washington" (1976) 2 Lloyd's Rep. 453 ············· C5/4. 2. 7. 1. 1. 4. 2 ,4. 2. 7. 1. 3. 5. 3
The "Wear Breeze" (1967) 2 Lloyd's Rep. 315 ······························ C3/8. 2. 3
The "Wenjiang" (1983) 1 Lloyd's Rep. 400 ······························ C5/4. 2. 7. 1. 7
The "Winson" (1982) 1 Lloyd's Rep. 117 ······························ C4/3. 4. 7. 5
The "Wise" (1989) 1 Lloyd's Rep. 96 ······························ C5/4. 2. 7. 1. 5
The "Wondrous" (1991) 1 Lloyd's Rep. 400 ······························ C5/4. 2. 7. 1. 7
The "World Harmony" (1965) 1 Lloyd's Rep. 244 ······················ C3/8. 2. 3, 8. 2. 4
The "Xantho" (1881) 12 App. Cas. 503 ············· C5/4. 2. 7. 1. 3. 2, 4. 2. 7. 1. 3. 6
The "Xingcheng" (1987) 2 Lloyd's Rep. 210 ···
··· C2/3. 2, 9. 1. 4, C3/9. 1. 4, C5/4. 2. 10. 2. 8. 6, 4. 2. 10. 2. 8. 7
The "Yamatogawa" (1990) 2 Lloyd's Rep. 39 ············· C5/4. 2. 6. 1. 1, 4. 2. 6. 2, 4. 2. 6. 4. 3
The "Yoro" 197 F 2d 241, 1952 AMC 1094 (5 Cir 1952) ······················ C5/4. 2. 3. 4. 2. 5
The "Ypatianna" (1987) 2 Lloyd's Rep. 286 ······················ C4/3. 4. 7. 6, C5/4. 2. 7. 10. 2
The "Zhi Jiang Kou" (1991) 1 Lloyd's Rep. 493 ······················ C2/5. 6. 1, 5. 6. 5
The "Zim America" (1994) LMLN # 390 ······························ C5/4. 2. 4. 4. 2
The "Zitella" (1938) 61 Lloyd's Rep. 97 ······························ C3/11. 2. 2

The Eras Eil Actions (1992) 1 Lloyd's Rep. 570 ·················· C2/5. 5. 2
Thompson v. Dominy (1845) 14 M & W 403; 153 E. R. 532 ········ C3/12. 1, 12. 2, 12. 2. 4
Thorman v. Burt, Boulton v. Co. (1886) 54 L. T. 349 ·················· C6/4. 2. 2
Thus Brown Jenkinson v. Percy Dalton (1957) 1 Lloyd's Rep. 31 ········ C6/3. 2. 7. 2
Thyssen Inc. v. S/S Eurounity 21 F. 3d 533 (2d Cir. 1994) ·············· C5/4. 2. 7. 1. 3. 3
Thyssen v. Calypso (The "Markos N") (2000) 2 Lloyd's Rep. 243 ··············
················ C1, C3/4. 2. 2, C4/2. 6. 4. 2, 2. 6. 4. 5, C5/4. 2. 10. 2. 1, 4. 2. 10. 2. 5. 1
Tillmans v. Knutsford (1908) 1 K. B. 185 ······················ C3/3. 5, 5. 2
Tokio Marine & Fire Insurance Co. v. Retla SS Co. (1970) 2 Lloyd's Rep. 91 ··············
·· C5/4. 2. 9. 1, C6/3. 3, 5. 5
Tregelles v. Sewell (1862) 7 H. & N. 574, 158 E. R. 600 ················ C2/3. 1. 1
Tribunal de Commerce de Marseille, Feb. 3, 1948, DMF 1949, 485 (法国案例) ··············
·· C5/4. 2. 10. 2. 2. 3
Tribunal de Commerce de Nantes, Apr. 23, 1951, DMF 1952, 27 (法国案例) ··············
·· C5/4. 2. 10. 2. 2. 3
Tribunal de Commerce de Paris, Jan. 2, 1974, DMF 1974, 492 (法国案例) ··············
·· C5/4. 2. 10. 2. 2. 3
Trucks and Spares Ltd. v. Maritime Agencies (Southampton) Ltd. (1951) 2 Lloyd's Rep. 345 ···
·· C2/5. 1. 6
Turner v. Haji Goolam (1904) A. C. 826 ·························· C3/5. 1
Turner, Nott v. Bristol Corporation (1928) 31 Lloyd's Rep. 359 ················ C2/5. 1. 9
Tweddle v. Atkinson (1861) 1 B & S 393 ·························· C3/12. 2
Union Steel America Co. v. M/V Sanko Spruce, 14F. Supp. 2d 682 (DNJ July 21, 1998) ······
·· C4/3. 4. 3. 4
United City Merchants v. Royal Bank of Canada (1982) 2 Lloyd's Rep. 1 ··· C6/3. 2. 7. 1, 7. 1
United States v. Atlantic Mut. Ins. Co 343 U. S. 236, 1952 AMC 659 (1952) ········ C4/3. 4. 12
United States v. Central Gulf Lines, 699 F. 2d 243 (5 Cir. 1983) ················ C5/4. 2. 7. 10. 2
United States v. Wessel, Duval & Co. 115F. Supp. 678 (SDNY 1953) ········ C5/4. 2. 3. 2. 2. 1
Uxbridge Permanent Benefit Building Society v. Pickard, (1939) 2 K. B. 248 ········ C3/5. 2
Vita Food Products, Inc. v. Unus Shipping Co. Ltd. (1939) 63 Lloyd's Rep. 21 ··············
·· 请看 The "Hurry On"
Vosnoc v. Transglobal (1998) 1 Lloyd's Rep. 711 ·················· C5/4. 2. 10. 2. 5. 2
W. R. Varnis & Co. Ltd. v. Khoti (1949) 82 Lloyd's Rep. 525 ······· C5/4. 2. 3. 2. 2. 3, 4. 2. 9. 5
Walker v. Dover Navigation Co. (1950) 83 Lloyd's Rep. 84 ·················· C5/4. 2. 6. 2
Watkins v. Rymill (1883) 10 QBD 178 ·························· C6/5. 2
Wayne Tank & Pump v. Employers' Liability (1973) 2 Lloyd's Rep. 237 ············ C5/4. 2. 5. 5

Wehner v. Dene (1905) 2 KB 92 ·· C3/5. 1
Weiner & Co. v. Wilsons & Furness-Leyland Line (1910) 15 Com Cas 294 ············ C5/3. 2
Westinghouse v. Leslie Lykev, 734 F. 2d 199, 1985 AMC 247 (5 Cir. 1984) ···············
·· C5/4. 2. 7. 1. 2. 3
Westport Coal Co. v. McPhail (1899) 2 Q. B. 130 ················ C5/4. 2. 7. 1. 1. 2
Westwood Shipping Lines Inc v. Geo International Inc. (1998) 150 FIR 125 ·················
·· C2/ § 5, 5. 7, 5. 10. 3
Whitechurch v. Cavanagh (1902) AC 117, 137 ································ C6/4. 1. 4
William Holyman & Sons Pty. Ltd. v. Foy & Gibson Pry. Ltd. (1945) 73 C. L. R. 622 ············
·· C5/4. 2. 1
Williams Bros. (Hull) v. N. V. W. H. Berghuys Kolenhandel (1915) 21 Com. Cas. 253 ········
·· C5/4. 2. 7. 1. 13. 1
Williamson v. C. A. Venezolana (1971) AMC 2083 ································ C6/2. 1
Wilson v. Cie des Messageries Maritimes (1954) 1 Lloyd's Rep. 229 ················ C4/3. 1
Wilston Steamship Company Ltd. v. Andrew Weir & Co. (1925) 22 Lloyd's Rep. 521 ··· C3/7. 1
Wm. Fergu Harris & Son Ltd. v. China Matual S. N. Co. (1959) 2 Lloyd's Rep. 500 ·············
·· C5/4. 2. 7. 1. 10. 3
Wright v. Wright (1750) Ves. Sen. 409 ································ C3/12. 2. 2
Yeramex International v. S. S. Tendo, (1977) A. M. C. 1807 ················ C5/4. 2. 10. 3. 2. 2. 3
York Products Pry v. Gilchrist Watt & Sanderson Pty (1975) 2 Lloyd's Rep. 1 ······ C5/4. 2. 8. 5

附　录

附录一：英国提单法(1855 年)

Bills of Lading Act 1855

Whereas by the custom of merchants a bill of lading of goods being transferable by endorsement the property in the goods may thereby pass to the endorsee, but nevertheless all rights in respect of the contract contained in the bill of lading continue in the original shipper or owner, and it is expedient that such rights should pass with the property; and whereas it frequently happens that the goods in respect of which bills of lading purport to be signed have not been laden on board, and it is proper that such bills of lading in the hands of a bona fide holder for value should not be questioned by the master or other person signing the same on the ground of the goods not having been laden as aforesaid:

1. Every consignee of goods named in a bill of lading, and every endorsee of a bill of lading to whom the property in the goods therein mentioned shall pass, upon or by reason of such consignment or endorsement, shall have transferred to and vested in him all rights of suit, and be subject to the same liabilities in respect of such goods as if the contract contained in the bill of lading had been made with himself.

2. Nothing herein contained shall prejudice or affect any right of stoppage in transit, or any right to claim freight against the original shipper or owner, or any liability of the consignee or endorsee by reason or in consequence of his being such consignee or endorsee, or of his receipt of the goods by reason or in consequence of such consignment or endorsement.

3. Every bill of lading in the hands of a consignee or endorsee for valuable consideration representing goods to have been shipped on board a vessel shall be conclusive evi-

dence of such shipment as against the master or other persons signing the same, notwithstanding that such goods or some part thereof may not have been so shipped, unless such holder of the bill of lading shall have had actual notice at the time of receiving the same that the goods had not been in fact laden on board: Provided that the master or other person so signing may exonerate himself in respect of such misrepresentation by showing that it was caused without any default on his part, and wholly by the fraud of the shipper, or of the holder, or some person under whom the holder claims.

附录二:英国海上运输法(1992 年)

Carriage of Goods by Sea Act 1992
1992 CHAPTER 50
An act to replace the Bills of Lading Act 1855 with new provision with respect to bills of lading and certain other shipping documents.

[16th July 1992]

Be it enacted by the Queen's most Excellent Majesty, by and with the advice and consent of the Lords Spiritual and Temporal, and Commons, in this present Parliament assembled, and by the authority of the same, as follows: – – – – –

Shipping documents etc. to which Act applies.
1. – (1) This Act applies to the following documents, that is to say – – – – –
 (a) any bill of lading;
 (b) any sea waybill; and
 (c) any ship's delivery order.
(2) References in this Act to a bill of lading – – – – –
 (a) do not include references to a document which is incapable of transfer either by indorsement or, as a bearer bill, by delivery without indorsement; but
 (b) subject to that, do include references to a received for shipment bill of lading.
(3) References in this Act to a sea waybill are references to any document which is not a bill of lading but – – – – –
 (a) is such a receipt for goods as contains or evidences a contract for the carriage of goods by sea; and
 (b) identifies the person to whom delivery of the goods is to be made by the carrier in accordance with that contract.
(4) References in this Act to a ship's delivery order are references to any document which is neither a bill of lading nor a sea waybill but contains an undertaking which – – – – –
 (a) is given under or for the purposes of a contract for the carriage by sea of the goods to which the document relates, or of goods which include those goods; and
 (b) is an undertaking by the carrier to a person identified in the document to deliver

the goods to which the document relates to that person.

(5) The Secretary of State may by regulations make provision for the application of this Act to cases where a telecommunication system or any other information technology is used for effecting transactions corresponding to - - - - -

(a) the issue of a document to which this Act applies;

(b) the indorsement, delivery or other transfer of such a document; or

(c) the doing of anything else in relation to such a document.

(6) Regulations under subsection (5) above may - - - - -

(a) make such modifications of the following provisions of this Act as the Secretary of State considers appropriate in connection with the application of this Act to any case mentioned in that subsection; and

(b) contain supplemental, incidental, consequential and transitional provision;

and the power to make regulations under that subsection shall be exercisable by statutory instrument subject to annulment in pursuance of a resolution of either House of Parliament.

Rights under shipping documents.

2. - (1) Subject to the following provisions of this section, a person who becomes - - - - -

(a) the lawful holder of a bill of lading;

(b) the person who (without being an original party to the contract of carriage) is the person to whom delivery of the goods to which a sea waybill relates is to be made by the carrier in accordance with that contract; or

(c) the person to whom delivery of the goods to which a ship's delivery order relates is to be made in accordance with the undertaking contained in the order,

shall (by virtue of becoming the holder of the bill or, as the case may be, the person to whom delivery is to be made) have transferred to and vested in him all rights of suit under the contract of carriage as if he had been a party to that contract.

(2) Where, when a person becomes the lawful holder of a bill of lading, possession of the bill no longer gives a right (as against the carrier) to possession of the goods to which the bill relates, that person shall not have any rights transferred to him by virtue of subsection (1) above unless he becomes the holder of the bill - - - - -

(a) by virtue of a transaction effected in pursuance of any contractual or other arrangements made before the time when such a right to possession ceased to attach to possession of the bill; or

(b) as a result of the rejection to that person by another person of goods or documents delivered to the other person in pursuance of any such arrangements.

(3) The rights vested in any person by virtue of the operation of subsection (1) above in relation to a ship's delivery order – – – – –

(a) shall be so vested subject to the terms of the order; and

(b) where the goods to which the order relates form a part only of the goods to which the contract of carriage relates, shall be confined to rights in respect of the goods to which the order relates.

(4) Where, in the case of any document to which this Act applies – – – – –

(a) a person with any interest or right in or in relation to goods to which the document relates sustains loss or damage in consequence of a breach of the contract of carriage; but

(b) subsection (1) above operates in relation to that document so that rights of suit in respect of that breach are vested in another person,

the other person shall be entitled to exercise those rights for the benefit of the person who sustained the loss or damage to the same extent as they could have been exercised if they had been vested in the person for whose benefit they are exercised.

(5) Where rights are transferred by virtue of the operation of subsection (1) above in relation to any document, the transfer for which that subsection provides shall extinguish any entitlement to those rights which derives – – – – –

(a) where that document is a bill of lading, from a person's having been an original party to the contract of carriage; or

(b) in the case of any document to which this Act applies, from the previous operation of that subsection in relation to that document;

but the operation of that subsection shall be without prejudice to any rights which derive from a person's having been an original party to the contract contained in, or evidenced by, a sea waybill and, in relation to a ship's delivery order, shall be without prejudice to any rights deriving otherwise than from the previous operation of that subsection in relation to that order.

Liabilities under shipping documents.

3. – (1) Where subsection (1) of section 2 of this Act operates in relation to any document to which this Act applies and the person in whom rights are vested by virtue of that subsection – – – – –

 (a) takes or demands delivery from the carrier of any of the goods to which the document relates;

 (b) makes a claim under the contract of carriage against the carrier in respect of any of those goods; or

 (c) is a person who, at a time before those rights were vested in him, took or demanded delivery from the carrier of any of those goods,

that person shall (by virtue of taking or demanding delivery or making the claim or, in a case falling within paragraph (c) above, of having the rights vested in him) become subject to the same liabilities under that contract as if he had been a party to that contract.

(2) Where the goods to which a ship's delivery order relates form a part only of the goods to which the contract of carriage relates, the liabilities to which any person is subject by virtue of the operation of this section in relation to that order shall exclude liabilities in respect of any goods to which the order does not relate.

(3) This section, so far as it imposes liabilities under any contract on any person, shall be without prejudice to the liabilities under the contract of any person as an original party to the contract.

Representations in bills of lading.

4. A Bill of Lading which – – – – –

 (a) represents goods to have been shipped on board a vessel or to have been received for shipment on board a vessel; and

 (b) has been signed by the master of the vessel or by a person who was not the master but had the express, implied or apparent authority of the carrier to sign bills of lading,

shall, in favour of a person who has become the lawful holder of the bill, be conclusive evidence against the carrier of the shipment of the goods or, as the case may be, of their receipt for shipment.

Interpretation etc.

5. – (1) In this Act – – – – –

 "bill of lading", "sea waybill", and "ship's delivery order" shall be construed in accordance with section 1 above;

"the contract of carriage" – – – – –

(a) in relation to a bill of lading or sea waybill, means the contract contained in or evidenced by that bill or waybill; and

(b) in relation to a ship's delivery order, means the contract under or for the purposes of which the undertaking contained in the order is given;

"holder", in relation to a bill of lading, shall be construed in accordance with subsection (2) below;

"information technology" includes any computer or other technology by means of which information or other matter may be recorded or communicated without being reduced to documentary from; and

"telecommunication system" has the same meaning as in the Telecommunications Act 1984.

(2) References in this Act to the holder of a bill of lading are references to any of the following persons, that is to say – – – – –

(a) a person with possession of the bill who, by virtue of being the person identified in the bill, is the consignee of the goods to which the bill relates;

(b) a person with possession of the bill as a result of the completion, by delivery of the bill, of any indorsement of the bill or, in the case of a bearer bill, of any other transfer of the bill;

(c) a person with possession of the bill as a result of any transaction by virtue of which he would have become a holder falling within paragraph (a) or (b) above had not the transaction been effected at a time when possession of the bill no longer gave a right (as against the carrier) to possession of the goods to which the bill relates; and a person shall be regarded for the purposes of this Act as having become the lawful holder of a bill of lading wherever he has become the holder of the bill in good faith.

(3) References in this Act to a person's being identified in a document include references to his being identified by a description which allows for the identity of the person in question to be varied, in accordance with the terms of the document, after its issue; and the reference in section 1 (3) (b) of this Act to a document's identifying a person shall be construed accordingly.

(4) Without prejudice to sections 2(2) and 4 above, nothing in this Act shall preclude its operation in relation to a case where the goods to which a document relates – – – – –

(a) cease to exist after the issue of the document; or

(b) cannot be identified (whether because they are mixed with other goods or for any other reason); and references in this Act to the goods to which a document relates shall be construed accordingly.

(5) The preceding provisions of this Act shall have effect without prejudice to the application, in relation to any case, of the rules (the Hague-Visby Rules) which for the time being have the force of law by virtue of section 1 of the Carriage of Goods by Sea Act 1971.

Short title, repeal, commencement and extent. 1855 c. 111.

6. - (1) This Act may be cited as the Carriage of Goods by Sea Act 1992.

(2) The Bills of Lading Act 1855 is hereby repealed.

(3) This Act shall come into force at the end of the period of two months beginning with the day on which it is passed; but nothing in this Act shall have effect in relation to any document issued before the coming into force of this Act.

(4) This Act extends to Northern Ireland.

附录三:美国提单法(1916 年)

Pomerene Bills of Lading Act, 1916 Act of August 29, 1916.
chap. 415, 39 Stat. 538 – 45, 49 U. S. Code Appendix 81 – 124

Sect. 1   Transportation included.

Bills of lading issued by any common carrier for the transportation of goods in any Territory of the United States, or the District of Columbia, or from a place in a State to a place in a foreign country, or from a place in one State to a place in another State, or from a place in one State to a place in the same State through another State or foreign country, shall be governed by this chapter. 49 U. S. Code Appendix 81.

Sect. 2   Straight bill of lading.

A bill in which it is stated that the goods are consigned or destined to a specified person is a straight bill. 49 U. S. Code Appendix 82.

Sect. 3   Order bill of lading; negotiability.

A bill in which it is stated that the goods are consigned or destined to the order of any person named in such bill is an order bill. Any provision in such a bill or in any notice, contract, rule, regulation, or tariff that it is nonnegotiable shall be null and void and shall not affect its negotiability within the meaning of this chapter unless upon its face and in writing agreed to by the shipper. 49 U. S. Code Appendix 83.

Sect. 4   Order bills in parts or sets; liability of carrier.

Order bills issued in a State for the transportation of goods to any place in the United States on the Continent of North America, except Alaska and Panama, shall not be issued in parts or sets. If so issued, the carrier issuing them shall be liable for failure to deliver the goods described therein to anyone who purchases a part for value in good faith, even though the purchase be after the delivery of the goods by the carrier to a holder of one of the other parts: Provided, however, That nothing contained in this section shall be interpreted or construed to forbid the issuing of order bills in parts or sets for such transportation of goods to Alaska, Panama, Puerto Rico, Hawaii, or foreign countries, or to impose the liabilities set forth in this section for so doing. 49 U. S. Code Appendix 84.

Sect. 5   Indorsement on duplicate bill; liability.

When more than one order bill is issued in a State for the same goods to be transported to any place in the United States on the Continent of North America, except Alaska and Panama, the word "duplicate", or some other word or words indicating that the document is not an original bill, shall be placed plainly upon the face of every such bill except the one first issued. A carrier shall be liable for the damage caused by his failure so to do to anyone who has purchased the bill for value in good faith as an original, even though the purchase be after the delivery of the goods by the carrier to the holder of the original bill: Provided, however, That nothing contained in this section shall in such case for such transportation of goods to Alaska, Panama, Puerto Rico, Hawaii, or foreign countries be interpreted or construed so as to require the placing of the word "duplicate" thereon, or to impose the liabilities set forth in this section for failure so to do. 49 U. S. Code Appendix 85.

Sect. 6   Indorsement on straight bill.

A straight bill shall have placed plainly upon its face by the carrier issuing it "non-negotiable" or "not negotiable."

This section shall not apply, however, to memoranda or acknowledgments of an informal character. 49 U. S. Code Appendix 86.

Sect. 7   Effect of insertion of name of person to be notified.

The insertion in an order bill of the name of a person to be notified of the arrival of the goods shall not limit the negotiability of the bill or constitute notice to a purchaser thereof of any rights or equities of such person in the goods. 49 U. S. Code Appendix 87.

Sect. 8   Duty to deliver goods on demand; refusal.

A carrier, in the absence of some lawful excuse, is bound to deliver goods upon a demand made either by the consignee named in the bill for the goods or, if the bill is an order bill, by the holder thereof, if such a demand is accompanied by:

(a) An offer in good faith to satisfy the carrier's lawful lien upon the goods;

(b) Possession of the bill of lading and an offer in good faith to surrender, properly indorsed, the bill which was issued for the goods, if the bill is an order bill; and

(c) A readiness and willingness to sign, when the goods are delivered, an acknowledgment that they have been delivered, if such signature is requested by the carrier.

In case the carrier refuses or fails to deliver the goods, in compliance with a demand by the consignee or holder so accompanied, the burden shall be upon the carrier to establish the existence of a lawful excuse for such refusal or failure. 49 U. S. Code Appendix 88.

Sect. 9 Delivery; when justified.

A carrier is justified, subject to the provisions of sections 90 to 92 of this title, in delivering goods to one who is:

(a) A person lawfully entitled to the possession of the goods, or

(b) The consignee named in a straight bill for the goods, or

(c) A person in possession of an order bill for the goods, by the terms of which the goods are deliverable to his order; or which has been indorsed to him, or in blank by the consignee, or by the mediate or immediate indorsee of the consignee. 49 U. S. Code Appendix 89.

Sect. 10 Liability for delivery to person not entitled thereto.

Where a carrier delivers goods to one who is not lawfully entitled to the possession of them, the carrier shall be liable to anyone having a right of property or possession in the goods if he delivered the goods otherwise than as authorized by subdivisions (b) and (c) of section 89 of this title; and, though he delivered the goods as authorized by either of said subdivisions, he shall be so liable if prior to such delivery he:

(a) Had been requested, by or on behalf of a person having a right of property or possession in the goods, not to make such delivery, or

(b) Had information at the time of the delivery that it was to a person not lawfully entitled to the possession of the goods.

Such request or information, to be effective within the meaning of this section, must be given to an officer or agent of the carrier, the actual or apparent scope of whose duties includes action upon such a request or information, and must be given in time to enable the officer or agent to whom it is given, acting with reasonable diligence, to stop delivery of the goods. 49 U. S. Code Appendix 90.

Sect. 11 Liability for delivery without cancellation of bill.

Except as provided in section 106 of this title, and except when compelled by legal process, if a carrier delivers goods for which an order bill had been issued, the negotiation of which would transfer the right to the possession of the goods, and fails to take up and cancel the bill, such carrier shall be liable for failure to deliver the goods to anyone who for value and in good faith purchases such bill, whether such purchaser acquired title to the bill before or after the delivery of the goods by the carrier and notwithstanding delivery was made to the person entitled thereto. 49 U. S. Code Appendix 91.

Sect. 12　Liability in case of delivery of part of goods.

Except as provided in section 106 of this title, and except when compelled by legal process, if a carrier delivers part of the goods for which an order bill had been issued and fails either:

(a) To take up and cancel the bill, or

(b) To place plainly upon it a statement that a portion of the goods has been delivered with a description which may be in general terms either of the goods or packages that have been so delivered or of the goods or packages which still remain in the carrier's possession, he shall be liable for failure to deliver all the goods specified in the bill to anyone who for value and in good faith purchases it, whether such purchaser acquired title to it before or after the delivery of any portion of the goods by the carrier, and notwithstanding such delivery was made to the person entitled thereto. 49 U. S. Code Appendix 92.

Sect. 13　Alteration of bill.

Any alteration, addition, or erasure in a bill after its issue without authority from the carrier issuing the same either in writing or noted on the bill, shall be void whatever be the nature and purpose of the change, and the bill shall be enforceable according to its original tenor. 49 U. S. Code Appendix 93.

Sect. 14　Loss, etc., of bill; delivery of goods on order of court.

Where an order bill has been lost, stolen, or destroyed a court of competent jurisdiction may order the delivery of the goods upon satisfactory proof of such loss, theft, or destruction and upon the giving of a bond, with sufficient surety, to be approved by the court, to protect the carrier or any person injured by such delivery from any liability or loss incurred by reason of the original bill remaining outstanding. The court may also in its discretion order the payment of the carrier's reasonable costs and counsel fees: Provided, A voluntary indemnifying bond without order of court shall be binding on the parties thereto.

The delivery of the goods under an order of the court, as provided in this section, shall not relieve the carrier from liability to a person to whom the order bill has been or shall be negotiated for value without notice of the proceedings or of the delivery of the goods. 49 U. S. Code Appendix 94.

Sect. 15　Liability on bill marked "duplicate".

A bill, upon the face of which the word "duplicate" or some other word or words indicating that the document is not an original bill is placed, plainly shall impose upon the carrier issuing the same the liability of one who represents and warrants that such bill is an accurate copy of an original bill properly issued, but no other liability. 49 U. S. Code Appendix 95.

Sect. 16　Claim of title as excuse for refusal to deliver.

No title to goods or right to their possession asserted by a carrier for his own benefit shall excuse him from liability for refusing to deliver the goods according to the terms of a bill issued for them, unless such title or right is derived directly or indirectly from a transfer made by the consignor or consignee after the shipment, or from the carrier's lien. 49 U. S. Appendix 96.

Sect. 17　Interpleader of conflicting claimants.

If more than one person claim the title or possession of goods, the carrier may require all known claimants to interplead, either as a defense to an action brought against him for nondelivery of the goods or as an original suit, whichever is appropriate. 49 U. S. Code Appendix 97.

Sect. 18　Reasonable time for procedure allowed in case of adverse claim.

If someone other than the consignee or the person in possession of the bill has a claim to the title or possession of the goods, and the carrier has information of such claim, the carrier shall be excused from liability for refusing to deliver the goods, either to the consignee or person in possession of the bill or to the adverse claimant, until the carrier has had a reasonable time to ascertain the validity of the adverse claim or to bring legal proceedings to compel all claimants to interplead. 49 U. S. Code Appendix 98.

Sect. 19　Failure to deliver; claim of third person as defense.

Except as provided in sections 89, 97, and 98 of this title, no right or title of a third person, unless enforced by legal process, shall be a defense to an action brought by the consignee of a straight bill or by the holder of an order bill against the carrier for failure to deliver the goods on demand. 49 U. S. Code Appendix 99.

Sect. 20　Loading by carrier; counting packages, etc., contents of bill.

When goods are loaded by a carrier, such carrier shall count the packages of goods if package freight, and ascertain the kind and quantity if bulk freight, and such carrier shall not, in such cases, insert in the bill of lading or in any notice, receipt, contract, rule, regulation, or tariff, "Shipper's weight, load, and count", or other words of like purport, indicating that the goods were loaded by the shipper and the description of them made by him, or in case of bulk freight and freight not concealed by packages the description made by him. If so inserted contrary to the provisions of this section, said words shall be treated as null and void and as if not inserted therein. 49 U. S. Code Appendix 100.

Sect. 21　Loading by shipper; contents of bill; ascertainment of kind and quantity on request.

When package freight or bulk freight is loaded by a shipper and the goods are described in a bill of lading merely by a statement of marks or labels upon them or upon packages containing them, or by a statement that the goods are said to be goods of a certain kind or quantity, or in a certain condition, or it is stated in the bill of lading that packages are said to contain goods of a certain kind or quantity or in a certain condition, or that the contents or condition of the contents of packages are unknown, or words of like purport are contained in the bill of lading, such statements, if true, shall not make liable the carrier issuing the bill of lading, although the goods are not of the kind or quantity or in the condition which the marks or labels upon them indicate, or of the kind or quantity or in the condition they were said to be by the consignor. The carrier may also by inserting in the bill of lading the words "shipper's weight, load, and count", or other words of like purport, indicate that the goods were loaded by the shipper and the description of them made by him; and if such statement be true, the carrier shall not be liable for damages caused by the improper loading or by the nonreceipt or by the misdescription of the goods described in the bill of lading: Provided, however, Where the shipper of bulk freight installs and maintains adequate facilities for weighing such freight, and the same are available to the carrier, then the carrier, upon written request of such shipper and when given a reasonable opportunity so to do, shall ascertain the kind and quantity of bulk freight within a reasonable time after such written request, and the carriers shall not in such cases insert in the bill of lading the words "Shipper's weight", or other words of like purport, and if so inserted contrary to the provisions of this section, said words shall be treated as null and void and as if not inserted therein. 49 U. S. Code Appendix 101.

Sect. 22 Liability for nonreceipt or misdescription of goods.

If a bill of lading has been issued by a carrier or on his behalf by an agent or employee the scope of whose actual or apparent authority includes the receiving of goods and issuing bills of lading therefor for transportation in commerce among the several States and with foreign nations, the carrier shall be liable to (a) the owner of goods covered by a straight bill subject to existing right of stoppage in transit or (b) the holder of an order bill, who has given value in good faith, relying upon the description therein of the goods, or upon the shipment being made upon the date therein shown, for damages caused by the nonreceipt by the carrier of all or part of the goods upon or prior to the date therein shown, or their failure to correspond with the description thereof in the bill at the time of its issue. 49 U. S. Code Appendix 102.

Sect. 23 Attachment, etc., of goods delivered to carrier.

If goods are delivered to a carrier by the owner or by a person whose act in conveying the title to them to a purchaser for value in good faith would bind the owner, and an order bill is issued for them, they can not thereafter, while in the possession of the carrier, be attached by garnishment or otherwise or be levied upon under an execution unless the bill be first surrendered to the carrier or its negotiation enjoined. The carrier shall in no such case be compelled to deliver the actual possession of the goods until the bill is surrendered to him or impounded by the court. 49 U. S. Code Appendix 103.

Sect. 24 Remedies of creditor of owner of order bill.

A creditor whose debtor is the owner of an order bill shall be entitled to such aid from courts of appropriate jurisdiction by injunction and otherwise in attaching such bill or in satisfying the claim by means thereof as is allowed at law or in equity in regard to property which cannot readily be attached or levied upon by ordinary legal process. 49 U. S. Code Appendix 104.

Sect. 25　Lien of carrier.

If an order bill is issued the carrier shall have a lien on the goods therein mentioned for all charges on those goods for freight, storage, demurrage and terminal charges, and expenses necessary for the preservation of the goods or incident to their transportation subsequent to the date of the bill and all other charges incurred in transportation and delivery, unless the bill expressly enumerates other charges for which a lien is claimed. In such case there shall also be a lien for the charges enumerated so far as they are allowed by law and the contract between the consignor and the carrier. 49 U. S. Code Appendix 105.

Sect. 26　Liability after sale to satisfy lien, etc.

After goods have been lawfully sold to satisfy a carrier's lien, or because they have not been claimed, or because they are perishable or hazardous, the carrier shall not thereafter be liable for failure to deliver the goods themselves to the consignee or owner of the goods, or to a holder of the bill given for the goods when they were shipped, even if such bill be an order bill. 49 U. S. Code Appendix 106.

Sect. 27　Negotiation of order bill by delivery.

An order bill may be negotiated by delivery where, by the terms of the bill, the carrier undertakes to deliver the goods to the order of a specified person, and such person or a subsequent indorsee of the bill has indorsed it in blank. 49 U. S. Code Appendix 107.

Sect. 28　Negotiation of order bill by indorsement.

An order bill may be negotiated by the indorsement of the person to whose order the goods are deliverable by the tenor of the bill. Such indorsement may be in blank or to a specified person. If indorsed to a specified person, it may be negotiated again by the indorsement of such person in blank or to another specified person. Subsequent negotiation may be made in like manner. 49 U. S. Code Appendix 108.

Sect. 29　Transfer of bill by delivery; negotiation of straight bill.

A bill may be transferred by the holder by delivery, accompanied with an agreement, express or implied, to transfer the title to the bill or to the goods represented thereby. A straight bill can not be negotiated free from existing equities, and the indorsement of such a bill gives the transferee no additional right. 49 U. S. Code Appendix 109.

Sect. 30 Negotiation of order bill by person in possession.

An order bill may be negotiated by any person in possession of the same, however such possession may have been acquired, if by the terms of the bill the carrier undertakes to deliver the goods to the order of such person, or if at the time of negotiation the bill is in such form that it may be negotiated by delivery. 49 U. S. Code Appendix 110.

Sect. 31 Title and right acquired by transferee of order bill.

A person to whom an order bill has been duly negotiated acquires thereby:

(a) Such title to the goods as the person negotiation the bill to him had or had ability to convey to a purchaser in good faith for value, and also such title to the goods as the consignee and consignor had or had power to convey to a purchaser in good faith for value; and

(b) The direct obligation of the carrier to hold possession of the goods for him according to the terms of the bill as fully as if the carrier had contracted directly with him. 49 U. S. Code Appendix 111.

Sect. 32 Right of transferee of bill without negotiation; notice to carrier.

A person to whom a bill has been transferred, but not negotiated, acquires thereby as against the transferor the title to the goods, subject to the terms of any agreement with the transferor. If the bill is a straight bill such person also acquires the right to notify the carrier of the transfer to him of such bill and thereby to become the direct obligee of whatever obligations the carrier owed to the transferor of the bill immediately before the notification.

Prior to the notification of the carrier by the transferor or transferee of a straight bill the title of the transferee to the goods and the right to acquire the obligation of the carrier may be defeated by garnishment or by attachment or execution upon the goods by a creditor of the transferor, or by a notification to the carrier by the transferor or a subsequent purchaser from the transferor of a subsequent sale of the goods by the transferor.

A carrier has not received notification within the meaning of this section unless an officer or agent of the carrier, the actual or apparent scope of whose duties includes action upon such a notification, has been notified; and no notification shall be effective until the officer or agent to whom it is given has had time, with the exercise of reasonable diligence, to communicate with the agent or agents having actual possession or control of the goods. 49 U. S. Code Appendix 112.

Sect. 33　Compelling indorsement of order bill transferred by delivery.

Where an order bill is transferred for value by delivery, and the indorsement of the transferor is essential for negotiation, the transferee acquires a right against the transferor to compel him to indorse the bill, unless a contrary intention appears. The negotiation shall take effect as of the time when the indorsement is actually made. This obligation may be specifically enforced. 49 U. S. Code Appendix 113.

Sect. 34　Warranties arising out of transfer of bill.

A person who negotiates or transfers for value a bill by indorsement or delivery, unless a contrary intention appears, warrants:

(a) That the bill is genuine;

(b) That he has a legal right to transfer it;

(c) That he has knowledge of no fact which would impair the validity or worth of the bill;

(d) That he has a right to transfer the title to the goods, and that the goods are merchantable or fit for a particular purpose whenever such warranties would have been implied if the contract of the parties had been to transfer without a bill the goods represented thereby. 49 U. S. Code Appendix 114.

Sect. 35　Liability of indorser of bill.

The indorsement of a bill shall not make the indorser liable for any failure on the part of the carrier or previous indorsers of the bill to fulfill their respective obligations. 49 U. S. Code Appendix 115.

Sect. 36　Warranties by mortgagee, etc., receiving payment of bill.

A mortgagee or pledgee or other holder of a bill for security who in good faith demands or receives payment of the debt for which such bill is security, whether from a party to a draft drawn for such debt or from any other person, shall not be deemed by so doing to represent or warrant the genuineness of such bill or the quantity or quality of the goods therein described. 49 U. S. Code Appendix 116.

Sect. 37　Negotiation of bill; impairment of validity.

The validity of the negotiation of a bill is not impaired by the fact that such negotiation was a breach of duty on the part of the person making the negotiation, or by the fact that the owner of the bill was deprived of the possession of the same by fraud, accident, mistake, duress, loss, theft, or conversion, if the person to whom the bill was negotiated, or a person to whom the bill was subsequently negotiated, gave value therefor in good faith, without notice of the breach of duty, or fraud, accident, mistake, duress, loss, theft, or conversion. 49 U. S. Code Appendix 117.

Sect. 38 Negotiation of bill by seller, mortgagor, etc. , to person without notice.

Where a person, having sold, mortgaged, or pledged goods which are in a carrier's possession and for which an order bill has been issued, or having sold, mortgaged, or pledged the order bill representing such goods, continues in possession of the order bill the subsequent negotiation thereof by that person under any sale, pledge, or other disposition therefor to any person receiving the same in good faith, for value and without notice of the previous sale, sale have the same effect as if the first purchaser of the goods or bill had expressly authorized the subsequent negotiation. 49 U. S. Code Appendix 118.

Sect. 39 Rights of bona fide purchaser as affected by seller's lien or right of stoppage.

Where an order bill has been issued for goods no seller's lien or right of stoppage in transit shall defeat the rights of any purchaser for value in good faith to whom such bill has been negotiated, whether such negotiation be prior or subsequent to the notification to the carrier who issued such bill of the seller's claim to a lien or right of stoppage in transit. Nor shall the carrier be obliged to deliver or justified in delivering the goods to an unpaid seller unless such bill is first surrendered for cancellation. 49 U. S. Code Appendix 119.

Sect. 40 Rights of mortgagee or lien holder; limitation.

Except as provided in section 119 of this title, nothing in this chapter shall limit the rights and remedies of a mortgagee or lien holder whose mortgage or lien on goods would be valid, apart from this chapter, as against one who for value and in good faith purchased from the owner, immediately prior to the time of their delivery to the carrier, the goods which are subject to the mortgage or lien and obtained possession of them. 49 U. S. Code Appendix 120.

Sect. 41 Offenses; penalty.

Any person who, knowingly or with intent to defraud, falsely makes, alters, forges, counterfeits, prints or photographs any bill of lading purporting to represent goods received for shipment among the several States or with foreign nations, or with like intent utters or publishes as true and genuine any such falsely altered, forged, counterfeited, falsely printed or photographed bill of lading, knowing it to be falsely altered, forged, counterfeited, falsely printed or photographed, or aids in making, altering, forging, counterfeiting, printing or photographing, or uttering or publishing the same, or issues or aids in issuing or procuring the issue of, or negotiates or transfers for value a bill which contains a false statement as to the receipt of the goods, or as to any other matter, or who, with intent to defraud, violates, or fails to comply with, or aids in any violation of, or failure to comply with any provision of this chapter, shall be guilty of a misdemeanor, and, upon conviction, shall be punished for each offense by imprisonment not exceeding five years, or by a fine not exceeding 15,000, or both. 49 U. S. Code Appendix 121.

Sect. 42 Terms defined.

In this chapter, unless the context of subject matter otherwise requires:

"Action" includes counterclaim, set-off, and suit in equity.

"Bill" means bill of lading, governed by this chapter.

"Consignee" means the person named in the bill as the person to whom delivery of the goods is to be made.

"Consignor" means the person named in the bill as the person from whom the goods have been received for shipment.

"Goods" means merchandise or chattels in course of transportation or which have been or are about to be transported.

"Holder" of a bill means a person who has both actual possession of such bill and a right of property therein.

"order" means an order by indorsement on the bill.

"Person" includes a corporation or partnership, or two or more persons having a joint or common interest.

To "purchase" includes to take as mortgagee and to take as pledgee.

"State" includes any Territory, District, insular possession, or isthmian possession. 49 U. S. Code Appendix 122.

Sect. 43 Retroactive effect.
CODIFICATION

Section, Act of August 29, 1916, ch. 415, "43, 39 Stat. 545, provided that provisions of this chapter should not apply to bills made and delivered prior to January 1, 1917. 49 U. S. Code Appendix 123.

Sect. 44 Invalidity of part of chapter.

The provisions and each part thereof and the sections and each part thereof of this chapter are independent and severable, and the declaring of any provision or part thereof, or provisions or part thereof, or section or part thereof, or sections or part thereof, unconstitutional shall not impair or render unconstitutional any other provision or part thereof or section or part thereof. 49 U. S. Code Appendix 124.

附录四:美国哈特法(1893 年)

Harter Act, 1893. Act of February 13, 1893, chap. 105,27 Stat. 445 – 56, 46 U. S. Code Appendix 190 – 196.

Sect. 1 Stipulations relieving from liability for negligence.

It shall not be lawful for the manager, agent, master, or owner of any vessel transporting merchandise or property from or between ports of the United States and foreign ports to insert in any bill of lading or shipping document any clause, covenant, or agreement whereby it, he, or they shall be relieved from liability for loss or damage arising from negligence, fault, or failure in proper loading, stowage, custody, care, or proper delivery of any and all lawful merchandise or property committed to its or their charge. Any and all words or clauses of such import inserted in bills of lading or shipping receipts shall be null and void and of no effect. 46 U. S. Code Appendix 190.

Sect. 2 Stipulations relieving from exercise of due diligence in equipping vessels.

It shall not be lawful for any vessel transporting merchandise or property from or between ports of the United States of America and foreign ports, her owner, master, agent, or manager, to insert in any bill of lading or shipping document any covenant or agreement whereby the obligations of the owner or owners of said vessel to exercise due diligence properly equip, man, provision, and outfit said vessel, and to make said vessel seaworthy and capable of performing her intended voyage, or whereby the obligations of the master, officers, agents, or servants to carefully handle and stow her cargo and to care for and properly deliver same, shall in any wise be lessened, weakened, or avoided. 46 U. S. Code Appendix 191.

Sect. 3 Limitation of liability for errors of navigation, dangers of the sea and acts of God.

If the owner of any vessel transporting merchandise or property to or from any port in the United States of America shall exercise due diligence to make the said vessel in all respects seaworthy and properly manned, equipped, and supplied, neither the vessel, her owner or owners, agent, or charterers, shall become or be held responsible for damage or loss resulting from faults or errors in navigation or in the management of said vessel nor shall the vessel, her owner or owners, charterers, agent, or master be held liable for losses arising from dangers of the sea or other navigable waters, acts of God, or public enemies, or the inherent defect, quality, or vice of the thing carried, or from insufficiency of package, or seizure under legal process, or for loss resulting from any act or omission of the shipper or owner of the goods, his agent or representative, or from saving or attempting to save life or property at sea, or from any deviation in rendering such service. 46 U. S. Code Appendix 192.

Sect. 4　Bills of lading to be issued; contents.

It shall be the duty of the owner or owners, masters, or agent of any vessel transporting merchandise or property from or between ports of the United States and foreign ports to issue to shippers of any lawful merchandise a bill of lading, or shipping document, stating, among other things, the marks necessary for identification, number of packages, or quantity, stating whether it be carrier's or shipper's weight, and apparent order or condition of such merchandise or property delivered to and received by the owner, master, or agent of the vessel for transportation, and such document shall be prima facie evidence of the receipt of the merchandise therein described. 46 U. S. Code Appendix 193.

Sect. 5　Penalties; liens; recovery.

For a violation of any of the provisions of sections 190 to 193 of this title the agent, owner, or master of the vessel guilty of such violation, and who refuses to issue on demand the bill of lading provided for, shall be liable to a fine not exceeding $ 2,000. The amount of the fine and costs for such violation shall be a lien upon the vessel, whose agent, owner, or master is guilty of such violation, and such vessel may be libeled therefor in any district court of the United States, within whose jurisdiction the vessel may be found. One-half of such penalty shall go to the party injured by such violation and the remainder to the Government of the United States. 46 U. S. Code Appendix 194.

Sect. 6　Certain provisions inapplicable to transportation of live animals.

Sections 190 and 193 of this title shall not apply to the transportation of live animals. 46 U. S. Code Appendix 195.

Sect. 7　Certain laws unaffected.

Sections 190 to 195 of this title shall not be held to modify or repeal sections 181 to 183 of this title, or any other statute defining the liability of vessels, their owners, or representatives. 46 U. S. Code Appendix 196.

附录五：海牙规则(1924 年)

Brussels Convention – 1924 (Translation) International
Convention for the Unification of Certain Rules of Law Relating
to Bills of Lading, Brussels, August 25, 1924

Article 1

In this convention the following words are employed with the meanings set out below:

(a) "Carrier" includes the owner or the charterer who enters into a contract of carriage with a shipper.

(b) "Contract of carriage" applies only to contracts of carriage covered by a bill of lading or any similar document of title, in so far as such document relates to the carriage of goods by sea, including any bill of lading or any similar document as aforesaid issued under or pursuant to a charter party from the moment at which such bill of lading or similar document of title regulates the relations between a carrier and a holder of the same.

(c) "Goods" includes goods, wares, merchandise, and articles of every kind whatsoever except live animals and cargo which by the contract of carriage is stated as being carried on deck and is so carried.

(d) "Ship" means any vessel used for the carriage of goods by sea.

(e) "Carriage of goods" covers the period from the time when the goods are loaded on to the time they are discharged from the ship.

Article 2

Subject to the provisions of Article 6, under every contract of carriage of goods by sea the carrier, in relation to the loading, handling, stowage, carriage, custody, care and discharge of such goods, shall be subject to the responsibilities and liabilities and entitled to the rights and immunities hereinafter set forth.

Article 3

1. The carrier shall be bound before and at the beginning of the voyage to exercise due diligence to – – – – –

(a) Make the ship seaworthy.

(b) Properly man, equip and supply the ship.

(c) Make the holds, refrigerating and cool chambers, and all other parts of the ship in which goods are carried, fit and safe for their reception, carriage and preservation.

2. Subject to the provisions of Article 4, the carrier shall properly and carefully load, handle, stow, carry, keep, care for, and discharge the goods carried.

3. After receiving the goods into his charge the carrier or the master or agent of the carrier shall, on demand of the shipper, issue to the shipper a bill of lading showing among other things – – – – –

(a) The leading marks necessary for identification of the goods as the same are furnished in writing by the shipper before the loading of such goods starts, provided such marks are stamped or otherwise shown clearly upon the goods if uncovered, or on the cases or coverings in which such goods are contained, in such a manner as should ordinarily remain legible until the end of the voyage.

(b) Either the number of packages or pieces, or the quantity, or weight, as the case may be, as furnished in writing by the shipper.

(c) The apparent order and condition of the goods.

Provided that no carrier, master or agent of the carrier shall be bound to state or show in the bill of lading any marks, number, quantity, or weight which he has reasonable ground for suspecting not accurately to represent the goods actually received, or which he has had no reasonable means of checking.

4. Such a bill of lading shall be prima facie evidence of the receipt by the carrier of the goods as therein described in accordance with paragraph 3(a), (b) and (c).

5. The shipper shall be deemed to have guaranteed to the carrier the accuracy at the time of shipment of the marks, number, quantity and weight, as furnished by him, and the shipper shall indemnify the carrier against all loss, damages and expenses arising or resulting from inaccuracies in such particulars. The right of the carrier to such indemnity shall in no way limit his responsibility and liability under the contract of carriage to any person other than the shipper.

6. Unless notice of loss or damage and the general nature of such loss or damage be given in writing to the carrier or his agent at the port of discharge before or at the time of the removal of the goods into the custody of the person entitled to delivery thereof under the contract of carriage, or, if the loss or damage be not apparent, within three days, such removal shall be prima facie evidence of the delivery by the carrier of the goods as described in the bill of lading.

If the loss or damage is not apparent, the notice must be given within three days of the delivery of the goods.

The notice in writing need not be given if the state of the goods has, at the time of their receipt, been the subject of joint survey or inspection.

In any event the carrier and the ship shall be discharged from all liability in respect of loss or damage unless suit is brought within one year after delivery of the goods or the date when the goods should have been delivered.

In the case of an actual or apprehended loss or damage the carrier and the receiver shall give all reasonable facilities to each other for inspecting and tallying the goods.

7. After the goods are loaded the bill of lading to be issued by the carrier, master, or agent of the carrier, to the shipper shall, if the shipper so demands, be a "shipped" bill of lading, provided that if the shipper shall have previously taken up any document of title to such goods, he shall surrender the same as against the issue of the "shipped" bill of lading, but at the option of the carrier such document of title may be noted at the port of shipment by the carrier, master, or agent with the name or names of the ship or ships upon which the goods have been shipped and the date or dates of shipment, and when so noted, if it shows the particulars mentioned in paragraph 3 of Article 3, shall for the purpose of this article be deemed to constitute a "shipped" bill of lading.

8. Any clause, covenant, or agreement in a contract of carriage relieving the carrier or the ship from liability for loss or damage to, or in connexion with, goods arising from negligence, fault, or failure in the duties and obligations provided in this article or lessening such liability otherwise than as provided in this convention, shall be null and void and of no effect. A benefit of insurance in favour of the carrier or similar clause shall be deemed to be a clause relieving the carrier from liability.

Article 4

1. Neither the carrier nor the ship shall be liable for loss or damage arising or resulting from unseaworthiness unless caused by want of due diligence on the part of the carrier to make the ship seaworthy, and to secure that the ship is properly manned, equipped and supplied, and to made the holds, refrigerating and cool chambers and all other parts of the ship in which goods are carried fit and safe for their reception, carriage and preservation in accordance with the provisions of paragraph 1 of Article 3. Whenever loss or damage has resulted from unseaworthiness the burden of proving the exercise of due diligence shall be on the carrier or other person claiming exemption under this article.

2. Neither the carrier nor the ship shall be responsible for loss or damage arising or

resulting from - - - - -

(a) Act, neglect, or default of the master, mariner, pilot, or the servants of the carrier in the navigation or in the management of the ship.

(b) Fire, unless caused by the actual fault or privity of the carrier.

(c) Perils, dangers and accidents of the sea or other navigable waters.

(d) Act of Cod.

(e) Act of war.

(f) Act of public enemies.

(g) Arrest or restraint of princes, rulers or people, or seizure under legal process.

(h) Quarantine restrictions.

(i) Act of omission of the shipper or owner of the goods, his agent or representative.

(j) Strikes or lockouts or stoppage or restraint of labour from whatever cause, whether partial or general.

(k) Riots and civil commotions.

(l) Saving or attempting to save life or property at sea.

(m) Wastage in bulk or weight or any other loss or damage arising from inherent defect, quality or vice of the goods.

(n) Insufficiency of packing.

(o) Insufficiency or inadequacy of marks.

(p) Latent defects not discoverable by due diligence.

(q) Any other cause arising without the actual fault or privity of the carrier, or without the fault or neglect of the agents or servants of the carrier, but the burden of proof shall be on the person claiming the benefit of this exception to show that neither the actual fault or privity of the carrier nor the fault or neglect of the agents or servants of the carrier contributed to the loss or damage.

3. The shipper shall not be responsible for loss or damage sustained by the carrier or the ship arising or resulting from any cause without the act, fault or neglect of the shipper, his agents or his servants.

4. Any deviation in saving or attempting to save life or property at sea or any reasonable deviation shall not be deemed to be an infringement or breach of this convention or of the contract of carriage, and the carrier shall not be liable for any loss or damage resulting therefrom.

5. Neither the carrier nor the ship shall in any event be or become liable for any loss or damage to or in connexion with goods in an amount exceeding £ 100 per package or u-

nit, or the equivalent of that sum in other currency unless the nature and value of such goods have been declared by the shipper before shipment and inserted in the bill of lading.

This declaration if embodied in the bill of lading shall be prima facie evidence, but shall not be binding or conclusive on the carrier.

By agreement between the carrier, master or agent of the carrier and the shipper another maximum amount than that mentioned in this paragraph may be fixed, provided that such maximum shall not be less than the figure above named.

Neither the carrier nor the ship shall be responsible in any event for loss or damage to, or in connexion with, goods if the nature or value thereof has been knowingly misstated by the shipper in the bill of lading.

6. Goods of an inflammable, explosive or dangerous nature to the shipment whereof the carrier, master or agent of the carrier has not consented with knowledge of their nature and character, may at any time before discharge be landed at any place, or destroyed or rendered innocuous by the carrier without compensation and the shipper of such goods shall be liable for all damages and expenses directly or indirectly arising out of or resulting from such shipment. If any such goods shipped with such knowledge and consent shall become a danger to the ship or cargo, they may in like manner be landed at any place, or destroyed or rendered innocuous by the carrier without liability on the part of the carrier except to general average, if any.

Article 5

A carrier shall be at liberty to surrender in whole or in part all or any of his rights and immunities or to increase any of his responsibilities and obligations under this convention, provided such surrender or increase shall be embodied in the bill of lading issued to the shipper. The provisions of this convention shall not be applicable to charter parties, but if bills of lading are issued in the case of a ship under a charter party they shall comply with the terms of this convention. Nothing in these rules shall be held to prevent the insertion in a bill of lading of any lawful provision regarding general average.

Article 6

Notwithstanding the provisions of the preceding articles, a carrier, master or agent of the carrier and a shipper shall in regard to any particular goods be at liberty to enter into any agreement in any terms as to the responsibility and liability of the carrier for such goods, and as to the rights and immunities of the carrier in respect of such goods, or his obligation as to seaworthiness, so far as this stipulation is not contrary to public policy, or the care or diligence of his servants or agents in regard to the loading, handling, stowage, carriage, custody, care and discharge of the goods carried by sea, provided that in this case no bill of lading has been or shall be issued and that the terms agreed shall be embodied in a receipt which shall be a non-negotiable document and shall be marked as such.

Any agreement so entered into shall have full legal effect.

Provided that this article shall not apply to ordinary commercial shipments made in the ordinary course of trade, but only to other shipments where the character or condition of the property to be carried or the circumstances, terms and conditions under which the carriage is to be performed are such as reasonably to justify a special agreement.

Article 7

Nothing herein contained shall prevent a carrier or a shipper from entering into any agreement, stipulation, condition, reservation or exemption as to the responsibility and liability of the carrier or the ship for the loss or damage to, or in connexion with, the custody and care and handling of goods prior to the loading on, and subsequent to, the discharge from the ship on which the goods are carried by sea.

Article 8

The provisions of this convention shall not affect the rights and obligations of the carrier under any statute for the time being in force relating to the limitation of the liability of owners of seagoing vessels.

Article 9

The monetary units mentioned in this convention are to be taken to be gold value.

Those contracting States in which the pound sterling is not a monetary unit reserve to themselves the right of translating the sums indicated in this convention in terms of pound sterling into terms of their own monetary system in round figures.

The national laws may reserve to the debtor the right of discharging his debt in national currency according to the rate of exchange prevailing on the day of the arrival of the ship at the port of discharge of the goods concerned.

Article 10

The provisions of this convention shall apply to all bills of lading issued in any of the contracting States.

Article 11

After an interval of not more than two years from the day on which the convention is signed the Belgian Government shall place itself in communication with the Governments of the high contracting parties which have declared themselves prepared to ratify the convention, with a view to deciding whether it shall be put into force. The ratifications shall be deposited at Brussels at a date to be fixed by agreement among the said Governments. The first deposit of ratifications shall be recorded in a proces-verbal signed by the representatives of the Powers which take part therein and by the Belgian Minister for Foreign Affairs.

The subsequent deposit of ratifications shall be made by means of a written notification, addressed to the Belgian Government and accompanied by the instrument of ratification.

A duly, certified copy of the proces-verbal relating to the first deposit of ratifications, of the notifications referred to in the previous paragraph, and also of the instruments of ratification accompanying them, shall be immediately sent by the Belgian Government through the diplomatic channel to the Powers who have signed this convention or who have acceded to it. In the cases contemplated in the preceding paragraph, the said Government shall inform them at the same time of the date on which it received the notification.

Article 12

Non-signatory States may accede to the present convention whether or not they have been represented at the International Conference at Brussels.

A State which desires to accede shall notify its intention in writing to the Belgian Government, forwarding to it the document of accession, which shall be deposited in the archives of the said Government.

The Belgian Government shall immediately forward to all the States which have signed or acceded to the convention a duly certified copy of the notification and of the act of accession, mentioning the date on which it received the notification.

Article 13

The high contracting parties may at the time of signature, ratification or accession declare that their acceptance of the present convention does not include any or all of the self-governing dominions, or of the colonies, overseas possessions, protectorates or territories under their sovereignty or authority, and they may subsequently accede separately on behalf of any self-governing dominion, colony, overseas possession, protectorate or territory excluded in their declaration. They may also denounce the convention separately in accordance with its provisions in respect of any self-governing dominion, or any colony, overseas possession, protectorate or territory under their sovereignty or authority.

Article 14

The present convention shall take effect, in the case of the States which have taken part in the first deposit of ratifications, one year after the date of the protocol recording such deposit. As respects the States which ratify subsequently or which accede, and also in cases in which the convention is subsequently put into effect in accordance with Article 13, it shall take effect six months after the notifications specified in paragraph 2 of Article 11 and paragraph 2 of Article 12 have been received by the Belgian Government.

Article 15

In the event of one of the contracting States wishing to denounce the present convention, the denunciation shall be notified in writing to the Belgian Government, which shall immediately communicate a duly certified copy of the notification to all the other States, informing them of the date on which it was received.

The denunciation shall only operate in respect of the State which made the notification, and on the expiry of one year after the notification has reached the Belgian Government.

Article 16

Any one of the contracting States shall have the right to call for a fresh conference with a view to considering possible amendments.

A State which would exercise this right should notify its intention to the other States through the Belgian Government, which would make arrangements for convening the Conference.

Done at Brussels, in a single copy, August 25, 1924.

Signatories: Germany, Belgium, Chile, Spain, Estonia, United States of America, France, Great Britain, Hungary, Italy, Japan, Poland and the Free City of Danzig, Roumania, Kingdom of the Serbs, Croats and Slovenes.

Protocol of signature

At the time of signing the International Convention for the Unification of certain Rules of Law relating to Bills of Lading the Plenipotentiaries whose signatures appear below have adopted this Protocol, which will have the same force and the same value as if its provisions were inserted in the text of the convention to which it relates.

The High Contracting Parties may give effect to this convention either by giving it the force of law or by including in their national legislation in a form appropriate to that legislation the rules adopted under this convention.

They may reserve the right — — — — —

1. To prescribe that in the cases referred to in paragraph 2(c) to (p) of Article 4 the holder of a bill of lading shall be entitled to establish responsibility for loss or damage arising from the personal fault of the carrier or the fault of his servants which are not covered by paragraph (a).

2. To apply Article 6 in so far as the national coasting trade is concerned to all classes of goods without taking account of the restriction set out in the last paragraph of that article.

Done at Brussels, in a single copy, August 25, 1924.

Signatories: Germany, Belgium, Chile, Spain, Estonia, United States of America, France, Great Britain, Hungary, Italy, Poland and the Free City of Danzig, Roumania, Kingdom of the Serbs, Croats and Slovenes.

RATIFICATION:

Belgium	June 2, 1930
France	January 4, 1937
German Democratic Republic Germany,	July 1, 1939
Federal Republic of Great Britain and Northern Ireland	June 2, 1930
Hungary	June 2, 1930
Italy	October 7, 1938
Japan	July 1, 1957

Poland	October 26, 1936
Rumania	August 4, 1937
Spain	June 2, 1930
United States of America	June 29, 1937
Yugoslavia	April 17, 1959

ACCESSION:

Algeria	April 13, 1964
Angola	February 2, 1952
Argentina	April 19, 1961
Australia	July 4, 1955
Papua and Norfolk	July 4, 1955
Nauru and New Guinea	July 4, 1955
Barbados	December 2, 1930
Cameroon	December 2, 1930
Cape Verde Isles	February 2, 1952
Cuba	July 25, 1977
Cyprus	December 2, 1930
Denmark	July 1, 1938
Ecuador	March 23, 1977
Egypt	November 29, 1943
Fiji	October 10, 1970
Finland	July 1, 1939
Gambia	December 2, 1930
Goa	February 2, 1952

Great Britain and Northern Ireland Antigua, Bahamas, Belize, Bermuda, Caicos & Turks Islands, Caymans, Dominica, Falkland Islands, Gibraltar, Grenada, Hong Kong, Montserrat, St. Christopher Nevis, Anguilla, Virgin Islands, Seychelles, Solomon Islands, St. Lucia,

St. Vincent, Ascension	December 2, 1930
St. Helena	November 3, 1931
Guiana	December 2, 1930
Guinee-Bissau	February 2, 1952

Iran	April 26, 1966
Ireland	January 30, 1962
Israel	September 5, 1959
Ivory Coast	December 15, 1961
Jamaica	December 2, 1930
Kenya	December 2, 1930
Kiribati	December 2, 1930
Kuwait	July 25, 1969
Lebanon	July 19, 1975
Macao	February 2, 1952
Federated Malay States	December 2, 1930
Unfederated Malay States	December 2, 1930
Malaysia	December 2, 1930
Malgache Republic	July 13, 1965
Mauritius	August 24, 1970
Monaco	May 15, 1931
Mozambique	February 2, 1952
Netherlands	August 18, 1956
Nigeria	December 2, 1930
Norway	July 1, 1938
Palestine	December 2, 1930
Paraguay	November 22, 1967
Peru	October 29, 1964
Portugal	December 24, 1931
Sabeh (Southern Borneo)	December 2, 1930
Sao Tome e Principe (Iles)	February 2, 1952
Sarawak	November 3, 1931
Senegal	February 14, 1978
Sierra-Leone	December 2, 1930
Singapore	December 2, 1930
Somaliland	December 2, 1930
Sri-Lanka	December 2, 1930
Sweden	July 1, 1938
Switzerland	May 28, 1954

Syrian Arab Republic	August 1, 1974
Tanzania	December 3, 1962
Timor	February 2, 1952
Tonga	December 2, 1930
Trinidad & Tobago	December 2, 1930
Turkey	July 4, 1955
Tuvalu	December 2, 1930
Zaire Republic	July 17, 1967

DENUNCIATION:

Denmark	March 1, 1984
Finland	March 1, 1984
Italy	November 22, 1984
Netherlands	April 26, 1982
Norway	March 1, 1984
Sweden	March 1, 1984
United Kingdom of Great Britain and Northern Ireland	June 13, 1977
Gibraltar	September 22, 1977
Hong Kong	October 20, 1983

附录六:海牙·维斯比规则(1968年)

Brussels Protocol – 1968 (Visby Rules) Protocol to Amend the International Convention for the Unification of Certain Rules of Law Relating to Bills of Lading, Brussels, February 23, 1968

The contracting parties

Considering that it is desirable to amend the International convention for the Unification of certain rules of law relating to bills of lading, signed at Brussels on August 25, 1923,

Have agreed as follows:

Article I.

1. In Article 3, paragraph 4 shall be added:

"However, proof to the contrary shall not be admissible when the Bill of Lading has been transferred to a third party acting in good faith".

2. In Article 3, paragraph 6, sub-paragraph 4 shall be replaced by:

"Subject to paragraph 6 bis the carrier and the ship shall in any event be discharged from all liability whatsoever in respect of the goods, unless suit is brought within one year of their delivery or of the date when they should have been delivered. This period may, however, be extended if the parties so agree after the cause of action has arisen".

3. In Article 3, after paragraph 6 shall be added the following paragraph 6 bis:

"An action for indemnity against a third person may be brought even after the expiration of the year provided for in the preceding paragraph if brought within the time allowed by the law of the Court seized of the case. However, the time allowed shall be not less than three months, commencing from the day when the person bringing such action for indemnity has settled the claim or has been served with process in the action against himself".

Article II

Article 4, paragraph 5 shall be deleted and replaced by the following:

(a) Unless the nature and value of such goods have been declared by the shipper before shipment and inserted in the Bill of Lading, neither the carrier nor the ship shall in any event be or become liable for any loss or damage to or in connection with the goods in an amount exceeding the equivalent of Frcs. 10.000 per package or unit or Frcs. 30 per kilo of gross weight of the goods lost or damaged, whichever is the higher.

(b) The total amount recoverable shall be calculated by reference to the value of such goods at the place and time at which the goods are discharged from the ship in accordance with the contract or should have been so discharged.

The value of the goods shall be fixed according to the commodity exchange price, or, if there be no such price, according to the current market price, or, if there be no commodity exchange price or current market price, by reference to the normal value of goods of the same kind and quality.

(c) Where a container, pallet or similar article of transport is used to consolidate goods, the number of packages or units enumerated in the Bill of Lading as packed in such article of transport shall be deemed the number of packages or units for the purpose of this package or units are concerned. Except as aforesaid such article of transport shall be considered the package or unit.

(d) A franc means a unit consisting of 65.5 milligrammes of gold of millesimal fineness 900. The date of conversion of the sum awarded into national currencies shall be governed by the law of the Court seized of the case.

(e) Neither the carrier nor the ship shall be entitled to the benefit of the limitation of liability provided for in this paragraph if it is proved that the damage resulted from an act or omission of the carrier done with intent to cause damage, or recklessly and with knowledge that damage would probably result.

(f) The declaration mentioned in sub-paragraph (a) of this paragraph, if embodied in the bill of lading, shall be prima facie evidence, but shall not be binding or conclusive on the carrier.

(g) By agreement between the carrier, master or agent of the carrier and the shipper other maximum amounts than those mentioned in sub-paragraph (a) of this paragraph may be fixed, provided that no maximum amounts so fixed shall be less than the appropriate maximum mentioned in that sub-paragraph.

(h) Neither the carrier nor the ship shall be responsible in any event for loss or damage to, or in connection with, goods if the nature or value thereof has been knowingly mis-stated by the shipper in the bill of lading.

Article Ⅲ

Between Articles 4 and 5 of the Convention shall be inserted the following Article 4 bis:

"1. The defences and limits of liability provided for in this Convention shall apply in any action against the carrier in respect of loss or damage to goods covered by a contract of carriage whether the action be founded in contract or in tort.

2. If such an action is brought against a servant or agent of the carrier (such servant or agent not being an independent contractor), such servant or agent shall be entitled to avail himself of the defences and limits of liability which the carrier is entitled to invoke under this Convention.

3. The aggregate of the amounts recoverable from the carrier, and such servants and agents, shall in no case exceed the limit provided for in this Convention.

4. Nevertheless, a servant or agent of the carrier shall not be entitled to avail himself of the provisions of this Article, if it is proved that the damage resulted from an act or omission of the servant

or agent done with intent to cause damage or recklessly and with knowledge that damage would probably result."

Article IV

Article 9 of the Convention shall be replaced by the following:

"This Convention shall not affect the provisions of any international Convention or national law governing liability for nuclear damage."

Article V

Article 10 of the Convention shall be replaced by the following:

"The provisions of the Convention shall apply to every Bill of Lading relating to the carriage of goods between ports in two different States if:

(a) the Bill of Lading is issued in a contracting State, or

(b) the carriage is from port in a contracting State, or

(c) the Contract contained in or evidenced by the Bill of Lading provides that the rules of this Convention or legislation of any State giving effect to them are to govern the contract whatever may be the nationality of the ship, the carrier, the shipper, the consignee, or any other interested person.

Each contracting State shall apply the provisions of this Convention to the Bills of Lading mentioned above.

This Article shall not prevent a Contracting State from applying the Rules of this Convention to Bills of Lading not included in the preceding paragraphs. "

Article VI

As between the Parties to this Protocol the Convention and the Protocol shall be read and interpreted together as one single instrument.

A Party to this Protocol shall have no duty to apply the provisions of this Protocol to Bills of Lading issued in a State which is a Party to the Convention but which is not a party to this Protocol.

Article VII

As between the Parties to this Protocol, denunciation by any of them of the Convention in accordance with article 15 thereof, shall not be construed in any way as a denunciation of the Convention as amended by this Protocol.

Article VIII

Any dispute between two or more contracting parties concerning the interpretation or application of the Convention which cannot be settled through negotiation, shall, at the request on one of them, be submitted to arbitration. If within six months from the date of the request for arbitration the Parties are unable to agree on the organization of the arbitration, any one of those Parties may refer the dispute to the International Court of Justice by request in conformity with the Statute of the Court.

Article IX

1. Each contracting party may at the time of signature of ratification of this Protocol or accession thereto, declare that it does not consider itself bound by Article VIII of this Protocol. The other contracting parties shall not be bound by this Article with respect to any contracting party having made such a reservation.

2. Any contracting party having made a reservation in accordance with paragraph 1 may at any time withdraw this reservation by notification to the Belgian Government.

Article X

This Protocol shall be open for signature by the States which have ratified the Convention or which have adhered thereto before February 23, 1968, and by any State represented at the twelfth session (1967 - 1968) of the Diplomatic Conference on Maritime

Law.

Article XI

1. This Protocol shall be ratified.

2. Ratification of this Protocol by any state which is not a Party to the Convention shall have the effect of accession to the Convention.

3. The instruments of ratification shall be deposited with the Belgian Government.

Article XII

1. States, Members of the United Nations or Members of the specialized agencies of the United Nations, not represented at the twelfth session of the Diplomatic Conference on Maritime Law, may accede to this Protocol.

2. Accession to this Protocol shall have the effect of accession to the Convention.

3. The instruments of accession shall be deposited with the Belgian Government.

Article XIII

1. This Protocol shall come into force three months after the date of the deposit of ten instruments of ratification or accession, of which at least five shall have been deposited by States that have each a tonnage equal or superior to one million gross tons of tonnage.

2. For each State which ratifies this Protocol or accedes thereto after the date of deposit of the instrument of ratification or accession determining the coming into force such as is stipulated in § 1 of this Article, this Protocol shall come into force three months after the deposit of its instrument of ratification or accession.

Article XIV

1. Any contracting state may denounce this Protocol by notification to the Belgian Government.

2. This denunciation shall have the effect of denunciation of the Convention.

3. The denunciation shall take effect one year after the date on which the notification has been received by the Belgian Government.

Article XV

1. Any contracting state may at the time of signature, ratification or accession, or at any time thereafter declare by written notification to the Belgian Government which among

the territories under its sovereignty or for whose international relations it is responsible, are those to which the present Protocol applies.

The Protocol shall three months after the date of the receipt of such notification by the Belgian Government extend to the territories named therein, but not before the date of the coming into force of the Protocol in respect of such State.

2. This extension also shall apply to the Convention if the latter is not yet applicable to those territories.

3. Any contracting state which has made a declaration under § 1 of this Article may at any time thereafter declare by notification given to the Belgian Government that the Protocol shall cease to extend to such territory. This denunciation shall take effect one year after the date on which notification thereof has been received by the Belgian Government; it also shall apply to the Convention.

Article XVI

The Contracting Parties may give effect to this Protocol either by giving it the force of law or by including in their national legislation in a form appropriate to that legislation the rules adopted under this Protocol.

Article XVII

The Belgian Government shall notify the States represented at the twelfth session (1967 - 1968) of the Diplomatic Conference on Maritime Law, the acceding States to this Protocol, and the States Parties to the Convention, of the following:

1. The signatures, ratifications and accessions received in accordance with Articles X, XI and XII.

2. The date on which the present Protocol will come into force in accordance with Article XIII.

3. The notifications with regard to the territorial application in accordance with Article XV.

4. The denunciations received in accordance with Article XIV.

In witness whereof the undersigned Plenipotentiaries, duly authorized, have signed this Protocol.

Done at Brussels, this 23rd day of February 1968, in the French and English languages, both texts being equally authentic, in a single copy, which shall remain deposited in the archives of the Belgian Government, which shall issue certified copies.

RATIFICATION:

Belgium	September 6, 1978
Denmark	November 20, 1975
Egypt Arab Republic	January 31, 1983
Finland	December 1, 1984
France	March 10, 1977
Great Britain	October 1, 1976
Italy	August 22, 1985
Netherlands	April 26, 1982
Norway	March 19, 1974
Poland	February 12, 1980
Sweden	December 9, 1974
Switzerland	December 11, 1975

ACCESSION:

Bermuda	November 1, 1980
Ecuador	March 23, 1977
German Dem. Rep.	February 14, 1979
Gilbraltar	September 22, 1977
Hong Kong	November 1, 1980
Isle of Man	October 1, 1976
Lebanon	July 19, 1975
Singapore	April 25, 1972
Sri Lanka	October 21, 1981
Syrian Arab Republic	August 1, 1974
Tonga	June 13, 1978

附录七:汉堡规则(1978年)

Hamburg Rules – 1978 United Nations Convention on the Carriage of Goods by Sea, 1978

ANNEX I

Preamble

THE STATES PARTIES TO THIS CONVENTION,

HAVING RECOGNIZED the desirability of determining by agreement certain rules relating to the carriage of goods by sea,

HAVE DECIDED to conclude a Convention for this purpose and have thereto agreed as follows:

PART I. GENERAL PROVISIONS

Article 1. Definitions

In this Convention:

1. "Carrier" means any person by whom or in whose name a contract of carriage of goods by sea has been concluded with a shipper.

2. "Actual carrier" means any person to whom the performance of the carriage of the goods, or of part of the carriage, had been entrusted by the carrier, and includes any other person to whom such performance has been entrusted.

3. "Shipper" means any person by whom or in whose name or on whose behalf a contract of carriage of goods by sea has been concluded with a carrier, or any person by whom or in whose name or on whose behalf the goods are actually delivered to the carrier in relation to the contract of carriage by sea.

4. "Consignee" means the person entitled to take delivery of the goods.

5. "Goods" includes live animals; where the goods are consolidated in a container, pallet or similar article of transport or where they are packed, "goods" includes such article of transport or packaging if supplied by the shipper.

6. "Contract of carriage by sea" means any contract whereby the carrier undertakes

against payment of freight to carry goods by sea from one port to another; however, a contract which involves carriage by sea and also carriage by some other means is deemed to be a contract of carriage by sea for the purposes of this Convention only in so far as it relates to the carriage by sea.

7. "Bill of lading" means a document which evidences a contract of carriage by sea and the taking over or loading of the goods by the carrier, and by which the carrier undertakes to deliver the goods against surrender of the document. A provision in the document that the goods are to be delivered to the order of a named person, or to order, or to bearer, constitutes such an undertaking.

8. "Writing" includes, inter alia, telegram and telex.

Article 2. Scope of application

1. The provisions of this Convention are applicable to all contracts of carriage by sea between two different States, if:

(a) the port of loading as provided for in the contract of carriage by sea is located in a Contracting State, or

(b) the port of discharge as provided for in the contract of carriage by sea is located in a Contracting State, or

(c) one of the optional ports of discharge provided for in the contract of carriage by sea is the actual port of discharge and such port is located in a Contracting State, or

(d) the bill of lading or other document evidencing the contract of carriage by sea is issued in a Contracting State, or

(e) the bill of lading or other document evidencing the contract of carriage by sea provides that the provisions of this Convention or the legislation of any State giving effect to them are to govern the contract.

2. The provisions of this Convention are applicable without regard to the nationality of the ship, the carrier, the actual carrier, the shipper, the consignee or any other interested person.

3. The provisions of this Convention are not applicable to charterparties. However, where a bill of lading is issued pursuant to a charterparty, the provisions of the Convention apply to such a bill of lading if it governs the relation between the carrier and the holder of the bill of lading, not being the charterer.

4. If a contract provides for future carriage of goods in a series of shipments during an

agreed period, the provisions of this Convention apply to each shipment. However, where a shipment is made under a charter-party, the provisions of para. 3 of this Article apply.

Article 3. Interpretation of the Convention

In the interpretation and application of the provisions of this Convention regard shall be had to its international character and to the need to promote uniformity.

PART Ⅱ. LIABILITY OF THE CARRIER

Article 4. Period of responsibility

1. The responsibility of the carrier for the goods under this Convention covers the period during which the carrier is in charge of the goods at the port of loading, during the carriage and at the port of discharge.

2. For the purpose of para. 1 of this Article, the carrier is deemed to be in charge of the goods.

(a) from the time he has taken over the goods from:

(ⅰ) the shipper, or a person acting on his behalf; or

(ⅱ) an authority of other third party to whom, pursuant to law or regulations applicable at the port of loading, the goods must be handed over for shipment;

(b) until the time he has delivered the goods:

(ⅰ) by handing over the goods to the consignee; or

(ⅱ) in cases where the consignee does not receive the goods from the carrier, by placing them at the disposal of the consignee in accordance with the contract or with the law or with the usage of the particular trade, applicable at the port of discharge; or

(ⅲ) by handing over the goods to an authority or other third party to whom, pursuant to law or regulations applicable at the port of discharge, the goods must be handed over.

3. In paras. 1 and 2 of this Article, reference to the carrier or to the consignee means, in addition to the carrier or the consignee, the servants or agents, respectively of the carrier or the consignee.

Article 5. Basis of liability

1. The carrier is liable for loss resulting from loss of or damage to the goods, as well as from delay in delivery, if the occurrence which caused the loss, damage or delay took

place while the goods were in his charge as defined in art. 4, unless the carrier proves that he, his servants or agents took all measures that could reasonably be required to avoid the occurrence and its consequences.

2. Delay in delivery occurs when the goods have not been delivered at the port of discharge provided for in the contract of carriage by sea within the time expressly agreed upon or, in the absence of such agreement, within the time which it would be reasonable to require of a diligent carrier, having regard to the circumstances of the case.

3. The person entitled to made a claim for the loss of goods may treat the goods as lost if they have not been delivered as required by art. 4 within 60 consecutive days following the expire of the time for delivery according to para. 2 of this Article.

4. (a) the carrier is liable

(i) for loss of or damage to the goods or delay in delivery caused by fire, if the claimant proves that the fire arose from fault or neglect on the part of the carrier, his servants or agents;

(ii) for such loss, damage or delay in delivery which is proved by the claimant to have resulted from the fault or neglect of the carrier, his servants or agents, in taking all measures that could reasonably be required to put out the fire and avoid or mitigate its consequences.

(b) In case of fire on board the ship affecting the goods, if the claimant or the carrier so desires, a survey in accordance with shipping practices must be held into the cause and circumstances of the fire, and a copy of the surveyor's report shall be made available on demand to the carrier and the claimant.

5. With respect to live animals, the carrier is not liable for loss, damage or delay in delivery resulting from any special risks inherent in that kind of carriage. If the carrier proves that he has complied with any special instructions given to him by the shipper respecting the animals and that, in the circumstances of the case, the loss, damage or delay in delivery could be attributed to such risks, it is presumed that the loss, damage or delay in delivery was so caused, unless there is proof that all or a part of the loss, damage or delay in delivery resulted from fault or neglect on the part of the carrier, his servants or agents.

6. The carrier is not liable, except in general average, where loss, damage or delay in delivery resulted from measures to save life or from reasonable measures to save property at sea.

7. Where fault or neglect on the part of the carrier, his servants or agents combines

with another cause to produce loss, damage or delay in delivery the carrier is liable only to the extent that the loss, damage or delay in delivery is attributable to such fault or neglect, provided that the carrier proves the amount of the loss, damage or delay in delivery not attributable thereto.

Article 6. Limits of liability

1. (a) The liability of the carrier for loss resulting from less of or damage to goods according to the provisions of art. 5 is limited to an amount equivalent to 835 units of account per package or other shipping unit or 2.5 units of account per kilogramme of gross weight of the goods lost or damaged, whichever is the higher.

(b) The liability of the carrier for delay in delivery according to the provisions of art. 5 is limited to an amount equivalent to two and a half times the freight payable for the goods delayed, but not exceeding the total freight payable under the contract of carriage of goods by sea.

(c) In no case shall the aggregate liability of the carrier, under both subparas. (a) and (b) of this paragraph, exceed the limitation which would be established under subpara. (a) of this paragraph for total loss of the goods with respect to which such liability was incurred.

2. For the purpose of calculating which amount is the higher in accordance with para. 1(a) of this Article, the following rules apply:

(a) Where a container, pallet or similar article of transport is used to consolidate goods, the package or other shipping units enumerated in the bill of lading, if issued, or otherwise in any other document evidencing the contract of carriage by sea, as packed in such article of transport are deemed packages or shipping units. Except as aforesaid the goods in such article of transport are deemed one shipping unit.

(b) In cases where the article of transport itself has been lost or damaged, that article of transport, if not owned or otherwise supplied by the carrier, is considered one separate shipping unit.

3. Unit of account means the unit of account mentioned in art. 26.

4. By agreement between the carrier and the shipper, limits of liability exceeding those provided for in para. 1 may be fixed.

Article 7. Application to non-contractual claims

1. The defences and limits of liability provided for in this Convention apply in any ac-

tion against the carrier in respect of loss or damage to the goods covered by the contract of carriage by sea, as well as of delay in delivery whether the action is founded in contract, in tort or otherwise.

2. If such an action is brought against a servant or agent of the carrier, such servant or agent, if he proves that he acted within the scope of his employment, is entitled to avail himself of the defences and limits of liability which the carrier is entitled to invoke under this Convention.

3. Except as provided in art. 8, the aggregate of the amounts recoverable form the carrier and from any persons referred to in para. 2 of this Article shall not exceed the limits of liability provided for in this Convention.

Article 8. Loss of right to limit responsibility

1. The carrier is not entitled to the benefit of the limitation of liability provided for in art. 6 if it is proved that the loss, damage or delay in delivery resulted from an act or omission of the carrier done with the intent to cause such loss, damage or delay, or recklessly and with knowledge that such loss, damage or delay would probably result.

2. Notwithstanding the provisions of para. 2 of art. 7, a servant or agent of the carrier is not entitled to the benefit of the limitation of liability provided for in art. 6 if it is proved that the loss, damage or delay in delivery resulted from an act or omission of such servant or agent, done with the intent to cause such loss, damage or delay, or recklessly and with knowledge that such loss, damage or delay would probably result.

Article 9. Deck cargo

1. The carrier is entitled to carry the goods on deck only if such carriage is in accordance with an agreement with the shipper or with the usage of the particular trade or is required by statutory rules or regulations.

2. If the carrier and the shipper have agreed that the goods shall or may be carried on deck, the carrier must insert in the bill of lading or other document evidencing the contract of carriage by sea a statement to that effect. In the absence of such a statement the carrier has the burden of proving that an agreement for carriage on deck has been entered into; however, the carrier is not entitled to invoke such an agreement against a third party, including a consignee, who has acquired the bill of lading in good faith.

3. Where the goods have been carried on deck contrary to the provisions of para. 1 of this Article or where the carrier may not under para. 2 of this Article invoke an agreement

for carriage on deck, the carrier, notwithstanding the provisions of para. 1 of art. 5, is liable for loss of or damage to the goods, as well as for delay in delivery, resulting solely form the carriage on deck, and the extent of his liability is to be determined in accordance with the provisions of art. 6 or art. 8 of this Convention, as the case may be.

4. Carriage of goods on deck contrary to express agreement for carriage under deck is deemed to be an act or omission of the carrier within the meaning of art. 8.

Article 10. Liability of the carrier and actual carrier

1. Where the performance of the carriage or part thereof has been entrusted to an actual carrier, whether or not in pursuance of a liberty under the contract of carriage by sea to do so, the carrier nevertheless remains responsible for the entire carriage according to the provisions of this Convention. The carrier is responsible, in relation to the carriage performed by the actual carrier, for the acts and omissions of the actual carrier and of his servants and agents acting within the scope of their employment.

2. All the provisions of this Convention governing the responsibility of the carrier also apply to the responsibility of the actual carrier for the carriage performed by him. The provisions of paras. 2 and 3 of art. 7 and of para. 2 of art. 8 apply if an action is brought against a servant or agent of the actual carrier.

3. Any special agreement under which the carrier assumes obligations not imposed by this Convention or waives rights conferred by this Convention affects the actual carrier only if agreed to by him expressly and in writing. Whether or not the actual carrier has agreed, the carrier nevertheless remains bound by the obligations or waivers resulting from such special agreement.

4. Where and to the extent that both the carrier and the actual carrier are liable, their liability is joint and several.

5. The aggregate of the amounts recoverable from the carrier, the actual carrier and their servants and agents shall not exceed the limits of liability provided for in this Convention.

6. Nothing in this Article shall prejudice any right of recourse as between the carrier and the actual carrier.

Article 11. Through carriage

1. Notwithstanding the provisions of para. 1 of art. 10, where a contract of carriage by sea provides explicitly that a specified part of the carriage covered by the said contract

is to be performed by a named person other than the carrier, the contract may also provide that the carrier is not liable for loss, damage or delay in delivery caused by an occurrence which takes place while the goods are in the charge of the actual carrier during such part of the carriage. Nevertheless, any stipulation limiting or excluding such liability is without effect if no judicial proceedings can be instituted against the actual carrier in a court competent under paras. 1 or 2 of art. 21. The burden of proving that any loss, damage or delay in delivery has been caused by such an occurrence rests upon the carrier.

2. The actual carrier is responsible in accordance with the provisions of para. 2 of art. 10 for loss, damage or delay in delivery caused by an occurrence which takes place while the goods are in his charge.

PART III. LIABILITY OF THE SHIPPER

Article 12. **General rule**

The shipper is not liable for loss sustained by the carrier or the actual carrier, or for damage sustained by the ship, unless such loss or damage was caused by the fault or neglect of the shipper, his servants or agents. Nor is any servant or agent of the shipper liable for such loss or damage unless the loss or damage was caused by fault or neglect on his part.

Article 13. **Special rules on dangerous goods**

1. The shipper must mark or label in a suitable manner dangerous goods as dangerous.

2. Where the shipper hands over dangerous goods to the carrier or an actual carrier, as the case may be, the shipper must inform him of the dangerous character of the goods and, if necessary, of the precautions to be taken. If the shipper fails to do so and such carrier or actual carrier does not otherwise have knowledge of their dangerous character:

(a) the shipper is liable to the carrier and any actual carrier for the loss resulting from the shipment of such goods, and

(b) the goods may at any time be unloaded, destroyed or rendered innocuous, as the circumstances may require, without payment of compensation.

3. The provisions of para. 2 of this Article may not be invoked by any person if during the carriage he has taken the goods in his charge with knowledge of their dangerous character.

4. If, in eases where the provisions of para. 2, subpara. (b), of this Article do not apply or may not he invoked, dangerous goods become an actual danger to life or property, they may be unloaded, destroyed or rendered innocuous, as the circumstances may require, without payment of compensation except where there is an obligation to contribute in general average or where the carrier is liable in accordance with the provisions of art. 5.

PART IV. TRANSPORT DOCUMENTS

Article 14. Issue of bill of lading

1. When the carrier or the actual carrier takes the goods in his charge, the carrier must, on demand of the shipper, issue to the shipper a bill of lading.

2. The bill of lading may be signed by a person having authority from the carrier. A bill of lading signed by the master of the ship carrying the goods is deemed to have been signed on behalf of the carrier.

3. The signature on the bill of lading may be in handwriting, printed in facsimile, perforated, stamped, in symbols, or made by any other mechanical or electronic means, if not inconsistent with the law of the country where the bill of lading is issued.

Article 15. Contents of bill of lading

1. The bill of lading must include, inter alia, the following particulars:

(a) the general nature of the goods, the leading marks necessary for identification of the goods, an express statement, if applicable, as to the dangerous character of the goods, the number of packages or pieces, and the weight of the goods or their quantity otherwise expressed, all such particulars as furnished by the shipper;

(b) the apparent condition of the goods;

(c) the name and principal place of business of the carrier;

(d) the name of the shipper;

(e) the consignee if named by the shipper;

(f) the port of loading under the contract of carriage by sea and the date on which the goods were taken over by the carrier at the port of loading;

(g) the port of discharge under the contract of carriage by sea;

(h) the number of originals of the bill of lading, if more than one;

(i) the place of issuance of the bill of lading;

(j) the signature of the carrier or a person acting on his behalf;

(k) the freight to the extent payable by the consignee or other indication that freight is payable by him;

(l) the statement referred to in para. 3 of art. 23;

(m) the statement, if applicable, that the goods shall or may be carried on deck;

(n) the date or the period of delivery of the goods at the port of discharge if expressly agreed upon between the parties; and

(o) any increased limit or limits of liability where agreed in accordance with para. 4 of art. 6.

2. After the goods have been loaded on board, if the shipper so demands, the carrier must issue to the shipper a "shipped" bill of lading which, in addition to the particulars required under para. 1 of this Article, must state that the goods are on board a named ship or ships, and the date or dates of loading. If the carrier has previously issued to the shipper a bill of lading or other document of title with respect to any of such goods, on request of the carrier, the shipper must surrender such document in exchange for a "shipped" bill of lading. The carrier may amend any previously issued document in order to meet the shipper's demand for a "shipped" bill of lading if, as mended, such document includes all the information required to be contained in a "shipped" bill of lading.

3. The absence in the bill of lading of one or more particulars referred to in this Article does not affect the legal character of the document as a bill of lading provided that it nevertheless meets the requirements set out in para. 7 of art. 1.

Article 16. Bills of lading: reservations and evidentiary effect

1. If the bill of lading contains particulars concerning the general nature, leading marks, number of packages or pieces, weight or quantity of the goods which the carrier or other person issuing the bill of lading on his behalf knows or has reasonable grounds to suspect do not accurately represent the goods actually taken over or, where a 'shipped' bill of lading is issued, loaded, or if he had no reasonable means of checking such particulars, the carrier or such other person must insert in the bill of lading a reservation specifying these inaccuracies, grounds of suspicion or the absence of reasonable means of checking.

2. If the carrier or other person issuing the bill of lading on his behalf fails to note on the bill of lading the apparent condition of the goods, he is deemed to have noted on the bill of lading that the goods were in apparent good condition.

3. Except for particulars in respect of which and to the extent to which a reservation permitted under para. 1 of this Article has been entered:

(a) the bill of lading is prima facie evidence of the taking over or, where a ' shipped' bill of lading is issued, loading, by the carrier of the goods as described in the bill of lading; and

(b) proof to the contrary by the carrier is not admissible if the bill of lading has been transferred to a third party, including a consignee, who in good faith has acted in reliance on the description of the goods therein.

4. A bill of lading which does not, as provided in para. 1, subpara. (k) of art. 15, set forth the freight or otherwise indicate that freight is payable by the consignee or does not set forth demurrage incurred at the port of loading payable by the consignee, is prima facie evidence that no freight or such demurrage is payable by him. However, proof to the contrary by the carrier is not admissible when the bill of lading has been transferred to a third party, including a consignee, who in good faith has acted in reliance on the absence in the bill of lading of any such indication.

Article 17. Guarantees by the shipper

1. The shipper is deemed to have guaranteed to the carrier the accuracy of particulars relating to the general nature of the goods, their marks, number, weight and quantity as furnished by him for insertion in the bill of lading. The shipper must indemnify the carrier against the loss resulting from inaccuracies in such particulars. The shipper remains liable even if the bill of lading has been transferred by him. The right of the carrier to such indemnity in no way limits his liability under the contract of carriage by sea to any person other than the shipper.

2. Any letter of guarantee or agreement by which the shipper undertakes to indemnify the carrier against loss resulting from the issuance of the bill of lading by the carrier, or by a person acting on his behalf, without entering a reservation relating to particulars furnished by the shipper for insertion in the bill of lading, or to the apparent condition of the goods, is void and of no effect as against any third party, including a consignee, to whom the bill of lading has been transferred.

3. Such letter of guarantee or agreement is valid as against the shipper unless the carrier or the person acting on his behalf, by omitting the reservation referred to in para. 2 of this Article, intends to defraud a third party, including a consignee, who acts in reliance on the description of the goods in the bill of lading. In the latter case, if the reservation o-

mitted relates to particulars furnished by the shipper for insertion in the bill of lading, the carrier has no right of indemnity from the shipper pursuant to para. 1 of this Article.

4. In the case of intended fraud referred to in para. 3 of this Article the carrier is liable, without the benefit of the limitation of liability provided for in this Convention, for the loss incurred by a third party, including a consignee, because he has acted in reliance on the description of the goods in the bill of lading.

Article 18. Documents other than bills of lading

Where a carrier issues a document other than a bill of lading to evidence the receipt of the goods to be carried, such a document is prima facie evidence of the conclusion of the contract of carriage by sea and the taking over by the carrier of the goods as therein described.

PART V. CLAIMS AND ACTIONS

Article 19. Notice of loss, damage or delay

1. Unless notice of loss or damage, specifying the general nature of such loss or damage, is given in writing by the consignee to the carrier not later than the working day after the day when the goods were handed over to the consignee, such handing over is prima facie evidence of the delivery by the carrier of the goods as described in the document of transport or, if no such document has been issued, in good condition.

2. Where the loss or damage is not apparent, the provisions of para. 1 of this Article apply correspondingly if notice in writing is not given within 15 consecutive days after the day when the goods were handed over to the consignee.

3. If the state of the goods at the time they were handed over to the consignee has been the subject of a joint survey or inspection by the parties, notice in writing need not be given of loss or damage ascertained during such survey or inspection.

4. In the case of any actual or apprehended loss or damage the carrier and the consignee must give all reasonable facilities to each other for inspecting and tallying the goods.

5. No compensation shall be payable for loss resulting from delay in delivery unless a notice has been given in writing to the carrier within 60 consecutive days after the day when the goods were handed over to the consignee.

6. If the goods have been delivered by an actual carrier, any notice given under this

Article to him shall have the same effect as if it had been given to the carrier, and any notice given to the carrier shall have effect as if given to such actual carrier.

7. Unless notice of loss or damage, specifying the general nature of the loss or damage, is given in writing by the carrier or actual carrier to the shipper not later than 90 consecutive day after the occurrence of such loss or damage or after the delivery of the goods in accordance with para. 2 of art. 4, whichever is later, the failure to give such notice is prima facie evidence that the carrier or the actual carrier has sustained no loss or damage due to the fault or neglect of the shipper, his servants or agents.

8. For the purpose of this Article, notice given to a person acting on the carrier's or the actual carrier's behalf, including the master or the officer in charge of the ship, or to a person acting on the shipper's behalf if deemed to have been given to the carrier, to the actual carrier or to the shipper, respectively.

Article 20. Limitation of actions

1. Any action relating to carriage of goods under this Convention is time-barred if judicial or arbitral proceedings have not been instituted within a period of two years.

2. The limitation period commences on the day on which the carrier has delivered the goods or part thereof or, in cases where no goods have been delivered, on the last day on which the goods should have been delivered.

3. The day on which the limitation period commences is not included in the period.

4. The person against whom a claim is made may at any time during the running of the limitation period extend that period by a declaration in writing to the claimant. This period may be further extended by another declaration or declarations.

5. An action for indemnity by a person held liable may be instituted even after the expiration of the limitation period provided for in the preceding paragraphs if instituted within the time allowed by the law of the State where proceedings are instituted. However, the time allowed shall not be less than 90 days commencing from the day when the person instituting such action for indemnity has settled the claim or has been served with process in the action against himself.

Article 21. Jurisdiction

1. In judicial proceedings relating to carriage of goods under this Convention the plaintiff, at his option, may institute an action in a court which, according to the law of the State where the court is situated, is competent and within the jurisdiction of which is

situated one of the following places:

(a) the principal place of business or, in the absence thereof, the habitual residence of the defendant; or

(b) the place where the contract was made provided that the defendant has there a place of business, branch or agency through which the contract was made; or

(c) the port of loading or the port of discharge; or

(d) any additional place designated for that purpose in the contract of carriage by sea.

2. (a) Notwithstanding the preceding provisions of this Article, an action may be instituted in the court of any port or place in a Contracting State at which the carrying vessel of any other vessel of the same ownership may have been arrested in accordance with applicable rules of the law of that State and of international law. However, in such a case, at the petition of the defendant, the claimant must remove the action, at his choice, to one of the jurisdictions referred to in para. 1 of this Article for the determination of the claim, but before such removal the defendant must furnish security sufficient to ensure payment of any judgment that may subsequently be awarded to the claimant in the action.

(b) All questions relating to the sufficiency or otherwise of the security shall be determined by the court of the port or place of the arrest.

3. No judicial proceedings relating to carriage of goods under this Convention may be instituted in a place not specified in paras. 1 or 2 of this Article. The provisions of this paragraph do not constitute an obstacle to the jurisdiction of the Contracting States for provisional or protective measures.

4. (a) Where an action has been instituted in a court competent under paras. 1 or 2 of this Article or where judgment has been delivered by such a court, no new action may be started between the same parties on the same grounds unless the judgment of the court before which the first action was instituted is not enforceable in the country in which the new proceedings are instituted;

(b) for the purpose of this Article the institution of measures with a view to obtaining enforcement of a judgment is not to be considered as the starting of a new action;

(c) for the purpose of this Article, the removal of an action to a different court within the same country, or to a court in another country, in accordance with para. 2 (a) of this Article, is not to be considered as the starting of a new action.

5. Notwithstanding the provisions of the preceding paragraphs, an agreement made by the parties, after a claim under the contract of carriage by sea has arisen, which desig-

nates the place where the claimant may institute an action, is effective.

Article 22. Arbitration

1. Subject to the provisions of this Article, parties may provide by agreement evidenced in writing that any dispute that may arise relating to carriage of goods under this Convention shall be referred to arbitration.

2. Where a charter-party contains a provision that disputes arising thereunder shall be referred to arbitration and a bill of lading issued pursuant to the charter-party does not contain a special annotation providing that such provision shall be binding upon the holder of the bill of lading, the carrier may not invoke such provision as a against a holder having acquired the bill of lading in good faith.

3. The arbitration proceedings shall, at the option of the claimant, be instituted at one of the following places:

(a) a place in a State within whose territory is situated:

(i) the principal place of business of the defendant or, in the absence thereof, the habitual residence of the defendant; or

(ii) the place where the contract was made, provided that the defendant has there a place of business, branch or agency through which the contract was made; or

(iii) the port of loading or the port of discharge; or

(b) any place designated for that purpose in the arbitration clause or agreement.

4. The arbitrator or arbitration tribunal shall apply the rules of this Convention.

5. The provisions of paras. 3 and 4 of this Article are deemed to be part of every arbitration clause or agreement, and any term of such clause of agreement which is inconsistent therewith is null and void.

6. Nothing in this Article affects the validity of an agreement relating to arbitration made by the parties after the claim under the contract of carriage by sea has arisen.

PART VI. SUPPLEMENTARY PROVISIONS

Article 23. Contractual stipulations

1. Any stipulation in a contract of carriage by sea, in a bill of lading, or in any other document evidencing the contract of carriage by sea is null and void the extent that it derogates, directly or indirectly, from the provisions of this Convention. The nullity of such a stipulation does not affect the validity of the other provisions of the contract or document of

which it forms a part. A clause assigning benefit of insurance of the goods in favour of the carrier, or any similar clause, is null and void.

2. Notwithstanding the provisions of para. 1 of this Article, a carrier may increase his responsibilities and obligations under this Convention.

3. Where a bill of lading or any other document evidencing the contract of carriage by sea is issued, it must contain a statement that the carriage is subject to the provisions of this Convention which nullify any stipulation derogating therefrom to the detriment of the shipper or the consignee.

4. Where the claimant in respect of the goods has incurred loss as a result of a stipulation which is null and void by virtue of the present Article, or as a result of the omission of the statement referred to in para. 3 of this Article, the carrier must pay compensation to the extent required in order to give the claimant compensation in accordance with the provisions of this Convention for any loss of or damage to the goods as well as for delay in delivery. The carrier must, in addition, pay compensation for costs incurred by the claimant for the purpose of exercising his right, provided that costs incurred in the action where the foregoing provision is invoked are to be determined in accordance with the law of the State where proceedings are instituted.

Article 24. General average

1. Nothing in this Convention shall prevent the application of provisions in the contract of carriage by sea or national law regarding the adjustment of general average.

2. With the exception of art. 20, the provisions of this Convention relating to the liability of the carrier for loss of or damage to the goods also determine whether the consignee may refuse contribution in general average and the liability of the carrier to indemnify the consignee in respect of any such contribution made or any salvage paid.

Article 25. Other conventions

1. This Convention does not modify the rights or duties of the carrier, the actual carrier and their servants and agents, provided for in international conventions or national law relating to the limitation of liability of owners of seagoing ships.

2. The provisions of arts. 21 and 22 of this Convention do not prevent the application of the mandatory provisions of any other multilateral convention already in force at the date of this Convention relating to matters dealt with in the said Articles, provided that the dispute arises exclusively between parties having their principal place of business in States

member of such other convention. However, this paragraph does not affect the application of para. 4 of art. 22 of this Convention.

3. No liability shall arise under the provisions of this Convention for damage caused by a nuclear incident if the operator of a nuclear installation is liable for such damage:

(a) under either the Paris Convention of July 29, 1960, on Third Party Liability in the Field of Nuclear Energy as amended by the Additional Protocol of Jan. 28, 1964, or the Vienna Convention of May 21, 1963, on Civil Liability for Nuclear Damage, or

(b) by virtue of national law governing the liability for such damage, provided that such law is in all respects as favourable to persons who may suffer damage as either the Paris or Vienna Conventions.

4. No liability shall arise under the provisions of this Convention for any loss of or damage to or delay in delivery of luggage for which the carrier is responsible under any international convention or national law relating to the carriage of passengers and their luggage by sea.

5. Nothing contained in this Convention prevents a Contracting State from applying any other international convention which is already in force at the date of this Convention and which applies mandatorily to contracts of carriage of goods primarily by a mode of transport other than transport by sea. This provision also applies to any subsequent revision or amendment of such international convention.

Article 26. Unit of account

1. The unit of account referred to in art. 6 of this Convention is the Special Drawing Right as defined by the International Monetary Fund. The amounts mentioned in art. 6 are to be converted into the national currency of a State according to the value of such currency at the date of judgment or the date agreed upon by the parties. The value of a national currency, in terms of the Special Drawing Right, of a Contracting State which is a member of the International Monetary Fund is to be calculated in accordance with the method of valuation applied by the International Monetary Fund in effect at the date in question for its operations and transactions. The value of a national currency in terms of the Special Drawing Right of a Contracting State which is not a member of the International Monetary Fund is to be calculated in a manner determined by that State.

2. Nevertheless, those States which are not members of the International Monetary Fund and whose law does not permit the application of the provisions of para. 1 of this Article may, at the time of signature, or at the time of ratification, acceptance, approval or

accession or at any time thereafter, declare that the limit of liability provided for in this Convention to be applied in their territories shall be fixed as: 12,500 monetary units per package or other shipping unit or 37.5 monetary units per kilogramme of gross weight of the goods.

3. The monetary unit referred to in para. 2 of this Article corresponds to sixty-five and a half milligrammes of gold of millesimal fineness nine hundred. The conversion of the amounts referred to in para. 2 into the national currency is to be made according to the law of the State concerned.

4. The calculation mentioned in the last sentence of para. 1 and the conversion mentioned in para. 3 of Article is to be made in such a manner as to express in the national currency of the Contracting State as far as possible the same real value for the amounts in art. 6 as is expressed there in units of account. Contracting States must communicate to the depositary the manner of calculation pursuant to para. 1 of this Article, or the result of the conversion mentioned in para. 3 of this Article, as the case may be, at the time of signature or when depositing their instruments of ratification, acceptance, approval or accession, or when availing themselves of the option provided for in para. 2 of this Article and whenever there is a change in the manner of such calculation or in the result of such conversion.

PART VII. FINAL CLAUSES

Article 27. Depositary

The Secretary-General of the United Nations is hereby designated as the depositary of this Convention.

Article 28. Signature, ratification, acceptance, approval, accession

1. This Convention is open for signature by all States until Apr. 30, 1979, at the Headquarters of the United Nations, New York.

2. This Convention is subject to ratification, acceptance or approval by the signatory States.

3. After Apr. 30, 1979, this Convention will be open for accession by all States which are not signatory States.

4. Instruments of ratification, acceptance, approval and accession are to be deposited with the Secretary-General of the United Nations.

Article 29. Reservations

No reservations may be made to this Convention.

Article 30. Entry into force

1. This Convention enters into force on the first day of the month following the expiration of one year from the date of deposit of the 20th instrument of ratification, acceptance, approval or accession.

2. For each State which becomes a Contracting State to this Convention after the date of the deposit of the 20th instrument of ratification, acceptance, approval or accession, this Convention enters into force on the first day of the month following the expiration of one year after the deposit of the appropriate instrument on behalf of that State.

3. Each Contracting State shall apply the provisions of this Convention to contracts of carriage by sea concluded on or after the date of the entry into force of this Convention in respect of that State.

Article 31. Denunciation of other conventions

1. Upon becoming a Contracting State to this Convention, any State party to the International Convention for the Unification of Certain Rules relating to Bills of lading signed at Brussels on Aug. 25, 1924 (1924 Convention) must notify the Government of Belgium as the depositary of the 1924 Convention of its denunciation of the said Convention with a declaration that the denunciation is to take effect as from the date when this Convention enters into force in respect of that State.

2. Upon the entry into force of this Convention under para. 1 of art. 30, the depositary of this Convention must notify the Government of Belgium as the depositary of the 1924 Convention of the date of such entry into force, and of the names of the Contracting States in respect of which the Convention has entered into force.

3. The provisions of paras. 1 and 2 of this Article apply correspondingly in respect of States parties to the Protocol signed on Feb. 23, 1968, to amend the International Convention for the Unification of Certain Rules relating to Bills of Lading signed at Brussels on Aug. 25, 1924.

4. Notwithstanding art. 2 of this Convention, for the purposes of para. 1 of this Article, a Contracting State may, if it deems it desirable, defer the denunciation of the 1924 Convention as modified by the 1968 Protocol for a maximum period of five years from the entry into force of this Convention. It will then notify the Government of Belgium of its in-

tention. During this transitory period, it must apply to the Contracting States this Convention to the exclusion of any other one.

Article 32. Revision and amendment

1. At the request of not loss than one-third of the Contracting States to this Convention, the depositary shall convene a conference of the Contracting States for revising or amending it.

2. Any instrument of ratification, acceptance, approval or accession deposited after the entry into force of an amendment to this Convention, is deemed to apply to the Convention as amended.

Article 33. Revision of the limitation amounts and unit of account or monetary unit

1. Notwithstanding the provisions of art. 32, a conference only for the purpose of altering the amount specified in art. 6 and para. 2 of art. 26, or of substituting either or both of the units defined in paras. 1 and 3 of art. 26 by other units is to be convened by the depositary in accordance with para. 2 of this Article. An alteration of the amounts shall be made only because of a significant change in their real value.

2. A revision conference is to be convened by the depositary when not less than one-fourth of the Contracting States so request.

3. Any decision by the conference must be taken by a two-thirds majority of the participating States. The amendment is communicated by the depositary to all the Contracting States for acceptance and to all the States signatories of the Convention for information.

4. Any amendment adopted enters into force on the first day of the month following one year after its acceptance by two-thirds of the Contracting States. Acceptance is to be effected by the deposit of a formal instrument to that effect, with the depositary.

5. After entry into force of an amendment a Contracting State which has accepted the amendment is entitled to apply the Convention as amended in its relations with Contracting States which have not within six months after the adoption of the amendment notified the depositary that they are not bound by the amendment.

6. Any instrument of ratification, acceptance, approval or accession deposited after the entry into force of an amendment to this Convention, is deemed to apply to the Convention as amended.

Article 34. Denunciation

1. A Contracting State may denounce this Convention at any time by means of a notification in writing addressed to the depositary.

2. The denunciation takes effect on the first day of the month following the expiration of one year after the notification is received by the depositary. Where a longer period is specified in the notification, the denunciation takes effect upon the expiration of such longer period after the notification is received by the depositary.

DONE at Hamburg, this thirty-first day of March one thousand nine hundred and seventy-eight, in a single original, of which the Arabic, Chinese, English, French, Russian and Spanish texts are equally authentic.

IN WITNESS WHEREOF the undersigned plenipotentiaries, being duly authorized by their respective Governments, have signed the present Convention.

ANNEX II   COMMON UNDERSTANDING ADOPTED BY THE UNITED NATIONS CONFERENCE ON THE CARRIAGE OF GOODS BY SEA

It is the common understanding that the liability of the carrier under this Convention is based on the principle of presumed fault or neglect. This means that, as a rule, the burden of proof rests on the carrier but, with respect to certain cases, the provisions of the Convention modify this rule.

ANNEX III   RESOLUTION ADOPTED BY THE UNITED NATIONS CONFERENCE ON THE CARRIAGE OF GOODS BY SEA

The United Nations Conference on the Carriage of Goods by Sea.

Noting with appreciation the kind invitation of the Federal Republic of Germany to hold the Conference in Hamburg.

Being aware that the facilities placed at the disposal of the Conference and the generous hospitality bestowed on the participants by the Government of the Federal Republic of Germany and by the Free and Hanseatic city of Hamburg, have in no small measure contributed to the success of the Conference.

Expresses its gratitude to the Government and people of the Federal Republic of Germany, and

Having adopted the Convention on the Carriage of goods by Sea on the basis of a draft Convention prepared by the United Nations Commission on International Trade Law at the request of the United Nations Conference on Trade and Development.

Expresses its gratitude to the United Nations Commission on International Trade Law and to the United Nations Conference on Trade and Development for their outstanding contribution to the simplification and harmonization of the law of the carriage of goods by sea, and

Decides to designate the Convention adopted by the Conference as the: 'UNITED NATIONS CONVENTION ON THE CARRIAGE OF GOODS BY SEA, 1978', and

recommends that the rules embodied therein be known as the "HAMBURG ULES".

附录八：CONGENBILL 1994 租约提单

（表格见后）

附录九：CONLINEBILL 2000 班轮提单

（表格正面见后，背面条款如下）

1. Definition.

"Merchant" Includes the Shipper, the receiver, the Consignor, the Consignee, the assignee, the holder of the Bill of Lading and the owner of the cargo.

2. Notification.

Any mention in this Bill of Lading of parties to be notified of the arrival of the cargo is solely for information of the Carrier and failure to give such notification shall not involve the Carrier in any liability nor relieve the Merchant of any obligation hereunder.

3. General Paramount Clause.

The International Convention for the Unification of Certain Rules of Law relating to Bills of Lading signed at Brussels on 25 August 1924 ("the Hague Rules") as amended by the Protocol signed at Brussels on 23 February 1968 ("the Hague-Visby Rules") and as enacted in the country of shipment shall apply to this Contract. When the Hague-Visby Rules are not enacted in the country of shipment, the corresponding legislation of the country of destination shall apply, irrespective of whether such legislation may only regulate outbound shipments.

When there is no enactment of the Hague-Visby Rules in either the country of shipment or in the country of destination, the Hague-Visby Rules shall apply to this Contract save where the Hague Rules as enacted in the country of shipment or, if no such enactment is in place, the Hague Rules as enacted in the country of destination apply compulsorily to this Contract.

The Protocol signed at Brussels on 21 December 1979 ("the SDR Protocol 1979") shall apply where the Hague-Visby Rules apply, whether mandatorily or by this Contract.

The Carrier shall in no case be responsible for loss of or damage to cargo arising prior to loading, after discharging, or while the cargo is in the charge of another carrier, or with respect to deck cargo and live animals.

4. Law and Jurisdiction.

Disputes arising out of or in connection with this Bill of Lading shall be exclusively determined by the courts and in accordance with the law of the place where the Carrier has his principal place of business, except as provided elsewhere herein.

5. The Scope of Carriage.

The intended carriage shall not be limited to the direct route but shall be deemed to include any proceeding or returning to or stopping or slowing down at or off any ports or places for any reasonable purpose connected with the carriage including bunkering, loading, discharging, or other cargo operations and maintenance of Vessel and crew.

6. Substitution of Vessel.

The Carrier shall be at liberty to carry the cargo or part thereof to the Port of discharge by the said or other vessel or vessels either belonging to the Carrier or others, or by other means of transport, proceeding either directly or indirectly to such port.

7. Transhipment.

The Carrier shall be at liberty to tranship, land and store the cargo either on shore or afloat and reship and forward the same to the Port of discharge.

8. Liability for Pre-and On-Carriage.

When the Carrier arranges pre-carriage of the cargo from a place other than the Vessel's Port of loading or on-carriage of the cargo to a place other than the Vessel's Port of discharge, the Carrier shall contract as the Merchant's Agent only and the Carrier shall not be liable for any loss or damage arising during any part of the carriage other than between the Port of loading and the Port of discharge even though the freight for the whole carriage has been collected by him.

9. Lighterage.

Any lightering in or off the Port of loading or the Port of discharge to be for the account of the Carrier.

10. Loading, Discharging and Delivery.

(a) Loading, discharging and delivery of the cargo shall be arranged by the Carrier's Agent unless otherwise agreed.

(b) All costs for storing and handling of the cargo before loading and after discharging shall be for the Merchant's account.

(c) Loading and discharging may commence without previous notice.

(d) The Merchant or his Agent shall tender the cargo when the Vessel is ready to load and as fast as the Vessel can receive and, but only if required by the Carrier, also outside ordinary working hours notwithstanding any custom of the port. Otherwise the Carrier shall be relieved of any obligation to load such cargo and the Vessel shall be entitled to leave the port without further notice and deadfreight is to be paid.

(e) The Merchant or his Agent shall take delivery of the cargo and continue to receive the cargo as fast as the Vessel can deliver and, but only if required by the Carrier, also outside ordinary working hours notwithstanding any custom of the port. The Merchant shall bear all overtime charges in connection with tendering and taking delivery of the cargo as above.

(f) If the Merchant or his Agent fail to take delivery of the cargo the Carrier shall be at liberty to discharge the cargo and any such discharge shall be deemed fulfilment of the contract of carriage. Should the cargo not be applied for within a reasonable time, the Carrier may sell the same privately or by auction.

(g) The Merchant shall accept his reasonable proportion of unidentified loose cargo.

11. Freight and Charges.

(a) Freight, whether paid or not, shall be considered as fully earned upon loading and non-returnable in any event. The Carrier's claim for any charges under this contract shall be payable in like manner as soon as the charges have been incurred. Interest at Libor (or its successor) plus 2 percent., shall run from the date when freight and charges are due.

(b) The Merchant shall be liable for expenses of fumigation, gathering and sorting loose cargo and weighing onboard, expenses incurred in repairing damage to and replacing of packing due to excepted causes and for all expenses caused by extra handling of the cargo for any of the aforementioned reasons.

(c) The Merchant shall be liable for any dues, duties, taxes and charges which under any denomination may be levied on any basis, such as amount of freight, weight of cargo or tonnage of the Vessel.

(d) The Merchant shall be liable for all fines and/or losses which the Carrier, Vessel or cargo may incur through non-observance of Customs House and/or import or export regulations.

(e) The Carrier is entitled in case of incorrect declaration of contents, weights, measurements or value of the cargo to claim double the amount of freight which would have been due if such declaration had been correctly given. For the purpose of ascertaining the actual facts, the Carrier shall have the right to obtain from the Merchant the original invoice and to have the contents inspected and the weight, measurement or value verified.

12. Lien.

The Carrier shall have a lien on all cargo for any amount due under this contract and the costs of recovering the same and shall be entitled to sell the cargo privately or by auction to satisfy any such claims.

13. Delay.

If the Carrier is held liable in respect of delay, consequential loss or damages, other than loss of or damage to the cargo, the liability of the Carrier shall be limited to the freight for the carriage covered by this Bill of Lading, or to the limitation amount as determined in Clause 3 and Clause 4, whichever is the lesser.

14. General Average and Salvage.

General Average shall be adjusted, stated and settled in London according to the York Antwerp Rules 1994, or any modification thereof, in respect of all cargo, whether carried on or under deck. In the event of accident, danger, damage or disaster before or after commencement of the voyage resulting from any cause whatsoever, whether due to negligence or not, for which or for the consequence of which the Carrier is not responsible by statute, contract or otherwise, the Merchant shall contribute with the Carrier in General Average to the payment of any sacrifice, losses or expenses of a General Average nature that may be made or incurred, and shall pay salvage and special charges incurred in respect of the cargo. If a salving vessel is owned or operated by the Carrier, salvage shall be paid for as fully as if the salving vessel or vessels belonged to strangers.

15. Both-to-Blame Collision Clause.

If the Vessel comes into collision with another vessel as a result of the negligence of the other vessel and any act, negligence or default of the Master, Mariner, Pilot or the servants of the Carrier in the navigation or in the management of the Vessel, the Merchant will indemnify the Carrier against all loss or liability to the other or non-carrying vessel or her Owner in so far as such loss or liability represents loss of or damage to or any claim whatsoever of the owner of the cargo paid or payable by the other or non-carrying vessel or her Owner to the owner of the cargo and set-off, recouped or recovered by the other or non-carrying vessel or her Owner as part of his claim against the carrying vessel or Carrier. The foregoing provisions shall also apply where the Owner, operator or those in charge of any vessel or vessels or objects other than, or in addition to, the colliding vessels or objects are at fault in respect of a collision or contact.

16. Government directions, War, Epidemics, Ice, Strikes, etc.

(a) The Master and the Carrier shall have liberty to comply with any order or directions or recommendations in connection with the carriage under this contract given by any Government or Authority, or anybody acting or purporting to act on behalf of such Government or Authority, or having under the terms of the insurance on the Vessel the right to give such orders or directions or recommendations.

(b) Should it appear that the performance of the carriage would expose the Vessel or any cargo onboard to risk of seizure, damage or delay, resulting from war, warlike operations, blockade, riots, civil commotions or piracy, or any person onboard to risk of loss of life or freedom, or that any such risk has increased, the Master may discharge the cargo at the Port of loading or any other safe and convenient port.

(c) Should it appear that epidemics, quarantine, ice, labour troubles, labour obstructions, strikes, lockouts, whether onboard or on shore, difficulties in loading or discharging would prevent the Vessel from leaving the Port of loading or reaching or entering the Port of discharge or there discharging in the usual manner and departing therefrom, all of which safely and without delay, the Master may discharge the cargo at the Port of loading or any other safe and convenient port.

(d) The discharge, under the provisions of this clause, of any cargo for which a Bill of Lading has been issued shall be deemed due fulfilment of the contract of carriage.

(e) If in connection with the exercise of any liberty under this clause any extra expenses are incurred they shall be paid by the Merchant in addition to the freight, together with return freight, if any, and a reasonable compensation for any extra services rendered to the cargo.

17. Himalaya Clause.

It is hereby expressly agreed that no servant or agent d the Carrier (including every independent contractor from time to time employed by the Carrier) shall in any circumstances whatsoever be under any liability whatsoever to the Merchant under this contract of carriage, for any loss, damage or delay of whatsoever kind arising or resulting directly or indirectly from any act. neglect or default on his part while acting in the course of or in connection with his employment.

Without prejudice to the generality of the foregoing provisions in this clause, every exemption from liability, limitation, condition and liberty herein contained and every right, defence and immunity of whatsoever nature applicable to the Carrier or to which the Carrier is entitled hereunder, shall also be available and shall extend to protect every such servant or agent of the Carrier acting as aforesaid.

For the purpose of all the foregoing provisions of this clause the Carrier is or shall be deemed to be acting as agent or trustee on behalf of and for the benefit of all persons who might be his servants or agents from time to time (including independent contractors as aforesaid) and all such persons shall to this extent be or be deemed to be parties to this contract of carriage.

18. Optional Stowage, Unitization.

(a) Cargo may be stowed by the Carrier as received, or, at the Carrier's option, by means of containers, or similar articles of transport used to consolidate cargo.

(b) Containers, trailers and transportable tanks, whether stowed by the Carrier or received by him in a stowed condition from the Merchant, may be carried on or under deck without notice to the Merchant.

ADDITIONAL CLAUSES

(To be added if required in the contemplated trade).

A. Demurrage.

Notwithstanding the entitlement of the Vessel under sub-clause 10(d), the Carrier shall be paid demurrage at the daily rate per gross ton (gt) indicated on Page 1 if the Vessel is not loaded or discharged with the dispatch set out in sub-clause 10(d), any delay in waiting for berth at or off port to count. Provided that if the delay is due to causes beyond the control of the Merchant, 24 hours shall be deducted from the time on demurrage. Each Merchant shall be liable towards the Carrier for a proportionate part of the total demurrage due, based upon the total freight on the cargo to be loaded or discharged at the port in question. No Merchant shall be liable in demurrage for any delay arising only in connection with cargo belonging to other Merchants. The demurrage in respect of each parcel shall not exceed its freight.

The Carrier's Tariff concerning free storage time and demurrage is incorporated herein, subject to applicability.

(This Clause shall only apply if the Demurrage Box on Page 1 is filled in).

B. U. S. Trade. Period of Responsibility.

(ⅰ) In case the Contract evidenced by this Bill of Lading is subject to the Carriage of Goods by Sea Act of the United States of America, 1936 (U. S. COGSA), then the provisions stated in said Act shall govern before loading and after discharge and throughout the entire time the cargo is in the Carrier's custody and in which event freight shall be payable on the cargo coming into the Carrier's custody.

(ⅱ) If the U. S. COGSA applies, and unless the nature and value of the cargo has been declared by the shipper before the cargo has been handed over to the Carrier and inserted in this Bill of Lading, the Carrier shall in no event be or become liable for any loss or damage to the cargo in an amount exceeding USD 500 per package or customary freight unit.

附录十:英国某著名班轮公司装船或多式联运共用提单

(表格正面见后,背面条款如下)

1. DEFINITIONS

"Carrier" means ABC

"Merchant" includes the Shipper, Holder, Consignee, Receiver of the Goods, any person owning or entitled to the possession of the Goods or of this Bill of Lading and anyone acting on behalf of any such person.

"Holder" means any person for the time being in possession of this Bill of Lading to whom the property in the Goods has passed on or by reason of the consignment of the Goods or the endorsement of this Bill of Lading or otherwise.

"Goods" means the whole or any part of the cargo received from the Shipper and includes any Container not supplied by or on behalf of the Carrier.

"Container" includes any container, trailer, transportable tank, flat or pallet, or any similar article used to consolidate goods.

"Carriage" means the whole of the operations and services undertaken by the Carrier in respect of the Goods.

"Combined Transport" arises if the Place of Receipt and/or the Place of Delivery are indicated on the face hereof in the relevant spaces.

"Port to Port Shipment" arises if the Carriage called for by this Bill of Lading is not Combined Transport.

"Freight" includes all charges payable to the Carrier in accordance with the applicable Tariff and this Bill of Lading.

"Hague Rules" means the provisions of the International Convention for the Unification of Certain Rules relating to Bills of Lading signed at Brussels on 25th August. 1924 and include the amendments by the Protocol signed at Brussels on 23rd February. 1968 but only if such amendments are compulsorily applicable to this Bill of Lading.

2. WARRANTY

The Merchant warrants that in agreeing to the terms hereof he is, or has the authority of, the person owning or entitled to the possession of the Goods and this Bill of Lading.

3. CARRIER'S TARIFF

The terms of the Carrier's applicable Tariff are incorporated herein. Particular attention is drawn to the terms therein relating to container and vehicle demurrage. Copies of the relevant provisions of the applicable Tariff are obtainable from the Carrier or his agents upon request. In the case of inconsistency between this Bill of Lading and the applicable Tariff, this Bill of Lading shall prevail.

4. SUB-CONTRACTING AND INDEMNITY, HIMALAYA CLAUSE

(1) The Carrier shall be entitled to sub-contract on any terms the whole or any part of the Carriage.

(2) The Merchant undertakes that no claim or allegation shall be made against any person whomsoever by whom the Carriage or any part of the Carriage is performed or undertaken (other than the Carrier), which imposes or attempts to impose upon any such person, or any vessel owned by any such person, any liability whatsoever in connection with the Goods or the Carriage of the Goods, whether or not arising out of negligence on the part of such person and, if any such claim or allegation should nevertheless be made to indemnify the Carrier against all consequences thereof. Without prejudice to the foregoing every such person shall have the benefit of every exemption, limitation, condition and liberty herein contained and of every right, exemption from liability, defence and immunity of whatsoever nature applicable to the Carrier as if such provisions were expressly for his benefit; and in entering into this contract, the Carrier, to the extent of these provisions, does so not only on his own behalf but also as agent and trustee for such persons.

(3) The provisions of Clause 4 (2), including but not limited to the undertakings of the Merchant contained therein, shall extend to claims or allegations of whatsoever nature against other persons chartering space on the carrying vessel.

(4) The Merchant further undertakes that no claim or allegation in respect of the Goods shall be made against the Carrier by any person other than in accordance with the terms and conditions of this Bill of Lading which imposes or attempts to impose upon the Carrier any liability whatsoever in connection with the Goods or the Carriage of the Goods, whether or not arising out of negligence on the part of the Carrier and, if any such claim or allegation should nevertheless be made, to indemnify the Carrier against all consequences thereof.

5. CARRIER'S RESPONSIBILITY

Port-to-Port Shipment

If the Carriage called for by this Bill of Lading is a Port-to-Port Shipment, the liability (if any) of the Carrier for loss of or damage to the Goods occurring from and during loading onto any seagoing vessel up to and during discharge from that vessel or from another seagoing vessel into which the Goods have been transhipped shall be determined in accordance with any national law making the Hague Rules compulsorily applicable to this Bill of Lading, or in any other case in accordance with the Hague Rules.

Notwithstanding the above, the Carrier shall be under no liability whatsoever for loss of or damage to the Goods, howsoever occurring, if such loss or damage arises prior to loading onto or subsequent to discharge from the vessel.

6. CARRIER'S RESPONSIBILITY

Combined Transport

If the Carriage called for by this Bill of Lading is Combined Transport, the Carrier undertakes to perform and/or in his own name to procure performance of the Carriage from the Place of Receipt or the Port of Loading, whichever is applicable, to the Port of Discharge or the Place of Delivery, whichever is applicable, and, save as is otherwise provided in this Bill of Lading, the Carrier shall be liable for loss or damage occurring during the Carriage to the extent set out below.

(1) **If the stage of the Carriage during which loss or damage occur red is not known**

(a) *exclusions*

If the stage of the Carriage where the loss or damage occurred is not known, the Carrier shall be relieved of liability for any loss or damage if such loss or damage was caused by:

(ⅰ) an act or omission of the Merchant,

(ⅱ) insufficiency of or defective condition of packing or marking,

(ⅲ) handling, loading, stowage or unloading of the Goods by or on behalf of the Merchant,

(ⅳ) inherent vice of the Goods.

(ⅴ) strike, lock-out, stoppage or restraint of labour,

(ⅵ) a nuclear incident,

For the purposes of Clause 6 (2), references in the Hague Rules to carriage by sea shall be deemed to include references to carriage by inland waterways and the Hague Rules shall be construed accordingly.

(3) **If the Place of Receipt or Place of Delivery is not named on the face hereof**

Where the Place of Receipt is not named on the face hereof, the Carrier shall be under no liability whatsoever for loss of or damage to the Goods, howsoever occurring, if such loss or damage arises prior to loading onto the vessel. If the Place of Delivery is not named on the face hereof, the Carrier shall be under no liability whatsoever for loss of or damage to the Goods, howsoever occurring, if such loss or damage arises subsequent to discharge from the vessel.

(4) **Notice of Loss or Damage**

The Carrier shall be deemed prima facie to have delivered the goods as described in this Bill of Lading unless notice of loss of or damage to the Goods, indicating the general nature of such loss or damage, shall have been given in writing to the Carrier or to his representative at the Place of Delivery (or the Port of Discharge if no Place of Delivery is named on the face hereof) before or at the time of removal of the Goods into the custody of the person entitled to delivery thereof under this Bill of Lading, or, if the loss or damage is not apparent, within three working days thereafter.

(5) **Time-bar**

The Carrier shall be discharged of all liability unless suit is brought and notice thereof given to the Carrier within nine months after delivery of the Goods or the date when the Goods should have been delivered.

7. OTHER PROVISIONS ON LIABILITY

(1) **Basis of Compensation**

Compensation shall be calculated by reference to the value of the Goods at the place and time they are delivered to the Merchant, or at the place and time they should have been delivered. For the purpose of determining the extent of the Carrier's liability for loss of or damage to the Goods, the sound value of the Goods is agreed to be the invoice value plus freight and insurance if paid.

(vii) any cause or event which the Carrier could not avoid and the consequences whereof he could not prevent by the exercise of reasonable diligence.

(b) *Burden of Proof*

The burden of proof that the loss or damage was due to one or more of the causes or events specified in this Clause 6 (1) shall rest upon the Carrier. Save that if the Carrier establishes that, in the circumstances of the case, the loss or damage could be attributed to one or more of the causes or events specified in Clause 6 (1) (a) (i), (iii), or (iv), it shall be presumed that it was so caused. The Merchant shall, however, be entitled to prove that the loss or damage was not, in fact, caused either wholly or partly by one or more of these causes or events.

(c) *Limitation of Liability*

Except as provided in Clause 7 (3), total compensation shall in no circumstances whatsoever and howsoever arising exceed US 12.50 per kilo of the gross weight of the Goods lost or damaged.

(2) If the stage of the Carriage during which the loss or damage occurred is known

Notwithstanding anything provided for in Clause 6 (1) and subject to Clauses 15 and 16, if it is known during which stage of the Carriage the loss or damage occurred, the liability of the Carrier in respect of such loss or damage shall be determined:

(a) by the provisions contained in any international convention or national law which provisions—

(i) cannot be departed from by private contract to the detriment of the Merchant; and

(ii) would have applied if the Merchant had made a separate and direct contract with the Carrier in respect of the particular stage of the Carriage during which the loss or damage occurred and received as evidence thereof any particular document which must be issued in order to make such international convention or national law applicable; or

(b) if no international convention or national law would apply by virtue of Clause 6 (2) (a), by the Hague Rules if the loss or damage is known to have occurred at sea or on inland waterways; or

(c) by the provisions of Clause 6 (1) if the provisions of Clause 6 (2) (a) and (b) do not apply.

(2) Hague Rules Limitation

Whenever the Hague Rules are applicable, otherwise than by national law, in determining the liability of the Carrier, the liability shall in no event exceed £ 100 sterling per package or unit.

(3) Ad Valorem

The Merchant agrees and acknowledges that the carrier has no knowledge of the value of the Goods, and that higher compensation than that provided above may not be claimed unless, with the consent of the carrier, the value of the Goods declared by the Shipper prior to the commencement of the Carriage is stated on this Bill of Lading and extra Freight paid, if required. In that case, the amount of the declared value shall be substituted for the limits laid down herein. Any partial loss or damage shall be adjusted pro rata on the basis of such declared value.

(4) Delay

The Carrier does not undertake that the Goods shall arrive at the Port of Discharge or Place of Delivery at any particular time or to meet any particular market or use, and the Carrier shall in no circumstances whatsoever and howsoever arising be liable for direct, indirect or consequential loss or damage caused by delay.

(5) Scope of Application

(a) The terms of this Bill of Lading shall at all times govern all responsibilities of the Carrier in connection with or arising out of the supply of a Container to the Merchant, not only during the Carriage, but also during the periods prior to and/or subsequent to the Carriage.

(b) The exemptions from liability, defences and limits of liability provided for in this Bill of Lading shall apply in any action against the Carrier for loss or damage or delay, howsoever occurring and whether the action be founded in contract or in tort and even if the loss, damage or delay arose as a result of unseaworthiness, negligence or fundamental breach of contract.

(c) Save as is otherwise provided herein, the Carrier shall in no circumstances whatsoever and howsoever arising be liable for direct or indirect or consequential loss or damage.

(6) **Mandatory Inspection by Authorities**

If by order of the authorities at any place, a Container has to be opened for the Goods to be inspected the Carrier will not be liable for any loss or damage incurred as a result of any opening, unpacking, inspection or repacking. The Carrier shall be entitled to recover the cost of such opening, unpacking, inspection and repacking from the Merchant.

8. SHIPPER-PACKED CONTAINERS

If a Container has not been packed by or on behalf of the Carrier:

(1) The Carrier shall not be liable for loss of or damage to the Goods caused by:

(a) the manner in which the Container has been packed, or

(b) the unsuitability of the Goods for carriage in the Container supplied, or

(c) the unsuitability or defective condition of the Container, provided that, if the Container has been supplied by or on behalf of the Carrier, this unsuitability or defective condition could have been apparent upon inspection by the Merchant at or prior to the time when the Container was packed.

(2) The Merchant shall indemnify the Carrier against any loss, damage, liability or expense whatsoever and howsoever arising caused by one or more of the matters referred to in Clause 8 (1), save that where the loss, damage, liability or expense was caused by a matter referred to in Clause 8 (1) (c) the Merchant shall not be liable to indemnify the Carrier in respect thereof unless the proviso referred to in that Clause applies.

9. ENTITLEMENT TO INSPECTION OF GOODS

The Carrier or any person to whom the Carrier has sub-contracted the whole or any part of the Carriage or any person authorised by the Carrier shall be entitled, but under no obligation, to open any Container or package at any time and to inspect the Goods.

10. CARRIAGE AFFECTED BY CONDITION OF GOODS

If it appears at any time that the Goods cannot safely or properly be carried or carried further, either at all or without incurring any additional expense or taking any measure(s) in relation to the Container or the Goods the Carrier may without notice to the Merchant take any measure(s) and/or incur any additional expense to carry or to continue the Carriage thereof, and/or abandon the Carriage and/or store them ashore or afloat, under cover or in the open, at any place, which abandonment or storage shall be deemed to constitute due delivery under this Bill of Lading. The Merchant shall indemnify the Carrier against any additional expense so incurred.

11. DESCRIPTION OF GOODS

(1) This Bill of Lading shall be prima facie evidence of the receipt by the Carrier from the Shipper in apparent good order and condition, except as otherwise noted, of the total number of Containers, package or other units or weight of the Goods specified on the face hereof.

(2) Except as provided in Clause 11 (1), no representation is made by the Carrier as to the weight, contents, measure, quantity, quality, description, condition, marks, numbers or value of Goods, and the Carrier shall be under no responsibility whatsoever in respect of such description or particulars.

(3) If any particulars of any Letter of Credit and/or Import Licence and/or Sale Contract and/or Invoice or Order number and/or details of any contract to which the Carrier is not a party are shown on the face of this Bill of Lading, such particulars are included solely at the request of the Merchant for his convenience. The Merchant agrees that the inclusion of such particulars shall not be regarded as a declaration of value and in no way affects the Carrier's liability under this Bill of Lading. The Merchant further agrees to indemnify the Carrier against all consequences of including such particulars in this Bill of Lading.

The Merchant acknowledges that, except when the provisions of Clause 7 (3) apply, the value of the Goods is unknown to the Carrier.

12. SHIPPER'S/MERCHANT'S RESPONSIBILITY

(1) The Shipper warrants to the Carrier that the particulars relating to the Goods as set out overleaf have been checked by the Shipper on receipt of this Bill of Lading and that such particulars, and any other particulars furnished by or on behalf of the Shipper, are correct.

(2) The Merchant shall indemnify the Carrier against all loss, damage, fines and expenses arising or resulting from inaccuracies in or inadequacy of such particulars or from any other cause in connection with the Goods for which the Carrier is not responsible.

(3) The Merchant shall comply with all regulations or requirements of customs, port and other authorities, and shall bear and pay all duties, taxes, fines, imposts, expenses or losses (including, without prejudice to the generality of the foregoing, the full return Freight for the Goods if returned, or if on-carried, the full Freight from the Port of Dis-

charge or the Place of Delivery nominated herein to the amended Port of Discharge or the amended Place of Delivery) incurred or suffered by reason of any failure to so comply, or by reason of any illegal, incorrect or insufficient marking, numbering or addressing of the Goods, and shall indemnify the Carrier in respect thereof.

(4) If Containers supplied by or on behalf of the Carrier are unpacked at the Merchant's premises, the Merchant is responsible for returning the empty Containers, with interiors brushed and clean, to the point or place designated by the Carrier, his servants or agents, within the time prescribed. Should a Container not be returned within the prescribed time, the Merchant shall be liable for any demurrage, loss or expenses which may arise from such non-return.

13. FREIGHT

(1) Freight shall be deemed fully earned on receipt of the Goods by the Carrier and shall be paid and non-returnable in any event.

(2) The Merchant's attention is drawn to the stipulations concerning currency in which the Freight is to be paid, rate of exchange, devaluation and other contingencies relative to Freight in the applicable Tariff.

(3) Freight has been calculated on the basis of particulars furnished by or on behalf of the Shipper. The Carrier may at any time open any Container or other package or unit in order to identify, weigh, measure or value the contents and, if the particulars furnished by or on behalf of the Shipper are incorrect, it is agreed that a sum equal to double the correct Freight less the Freight charged, shall be payable as liquidated damages to the Carrier.

(4) All Freight shall be paid without any set-off, counter-claim, deduction or stay of execution before delivery of the Goods.

(5) The persons falling within the definition of Merchant in Clause 1 shall be jointly and severally liable for the payment of Freight and liquidated damages as provided in this Clause.

14. Lien

The Carrier shall have a lien on the Goods and any documents relating thereto for all sums payable to the Carrier under this or any other contract by any of the persons defined as Merchant in Clause 1 and for general average contributions, to whomsoever due, and for the cost of recovering the same, and for that purpose shall have the right to sell the

Goods by public auction or private sale without notice to the Merchant.

15. LIVE ANIMALS

The Hague Rules shall not apply to the Carriage of live animals, which are carried at the sole risk of the Merchant. The Carrier shall be under no liability whatsoever for any injury, illness, death, delay or destruction howsoever arising.

Should the Master in his sole discretion consider that any live animal is likely to be injurious to any other live animal or any person or property on board, or to cause the vessel to be delayed or impeded in the prosecution of the Carriage, such live animal may be destroyed and thrown overboard without any liability attaching to the Carrier. The Merchant shall indemnify the Carrier against all or any extra costs incurred for any reason whatsoever in connection with the Carriage of any live animal.

16. OPTIONAL STOWAGE AND DECK CARGO

(1) The Goods may be packed by the Carrier in Containers.

(2) Goods, whether or not packed in Containers, may be carried on deck or under deck without notice to the Merchant. All such Goods (other than live animals). Whether carried on deck or under deck, shall participate in general average and shall be deemed to be within the definition of goods for the purposes of the Hague Rules and shall be carried subject to these Rules.

(3) Notwithstanding Clause 15 (2), in the case of Goods which are stated on the face hereof as being carried on deck and which are so carried, the Hague Rules shall not apply and the Carrier shall be under no liability whatsoever for loss, damage or delay, howsoever arising whether or not arising, out of negligence on the part of the Carrier.

17. METHODS AND ROUTE OF CARRIAGE

(1) The Carrier may at any time and without notice to the Merchant:

(a) use any means of carriage whatsoever,

(b) transfer the Goods from one conveyance to another, including but not limited to transhipping or carrying them on another vessel than that named on the face hereof,

(c) unpack and remove the Goods which have been packed into a Container and forward them in a Container or otherwise.

(d) proceed by any route in his discretion (whether or not the nearest or most direct or customary or advertised route), at any speed, and proceed to or stay at any place or port whatsoever, once or more often and in any order.

(e) load or unload the Goods at any place or port (whether or not such port is named overleaf as the Port of Loading or Port of Discharge) and store the Goods at any such place or port,

(f) comply with any orders or recommendations given by any government or authority, or any person or body acting or purporting to act as or on behalf of such government or authority, or having under the terms of the insurance on the conveyance employed by the Carrier the right to give orders or directions,

(g) permit the vessel to proceed with or without pilots, to tow or be towed, or to be dry-docked.

(2) The liberties set out in Clause 17 (1) may be invoked by the Carrier for any purpose whatsoever, whether or not connected with the Carriage of the Goods, including loading or unloading other goods, bunkering, undergoing repairs, adjusting instruments, picking up or landing any persons, including but not limited to persons involved with the operation or maintenance of the vessel and assisting vessels in all situations. Anything done in accordance with Clause 17 (1) or any delay arising therefrom shall be deemed to be within the Contractual Carriage and shall not be a deviation.

(3) By tendering the Goods for Carriage without any written request for Carriage in a specialised Container, or for Carriage otherwise than in a Container, the Merchant accepts that the Carriage may properly be undertaken in a general purpose container.

18. MATTERS AFFECTING PERFORMANCE

If at any time the Carriage is or is likely to be affected by any hindrance, risk, delay, difficulty or disadvantage of any kind (other than the inability of the Goods safely or properly to be carried or carried further) and howsoever arising (even though the circumstances giving rise to such hindrance, risk, delay, difficulty or disadvantage existed at the time this contract was entered into or the Goods were received for Carriage), the Carrier (whether or not the Carriage is commenced) may either:

(a) Without notice to the Merchant, abandon the Carriage of the Goods and place the Goods at the Merchant's disposal at any place or port which the Carrier may deem safe and convenient, whereupon the responsibility of the Carrier in respect of such Goods shall cease. The Carrier shall nevertheless be entitled to full Freight on the Goods received for Carriage, and the Merchant shall pay any additional costs of the Carriage to, and delivery and storage at, such place or port; or

(b) Upon notice to the Merchant, suspend the Carriage of the Goods and store them ashore or afloat upon the terms of this Bill of Lading and use reasonable endeavours to forward the Goods, the Carriage of which has been suspended, as soon as possible after the cause of hindrance, risk, delay, difficulty or disadvantage has been removed, but the Carrier makes no representations as to the maximum period between such removal and the forwarding of the Goods to the Port of Discharge or Place of Delivery, whichever is applicable, named in this Bill of Lading. The Carrier shall be entitled to payment of such additional Freight as the Carrier may determine, including, but not restricted to, charges for storage, handling and any other services to the Goods, and for Freight from the place of suspension to the Port of Discharge or Place of Delivery, whichever is applicable, without giving credit for Freight already paid in respect of the Carriage.

If the Carrier elects to suspend the Carriage under Clause 18 (b), this shall not prejudice his right subsequently to abandon the Carriage under Clause 18 (a).

19. DANGEROUS GOODS

(1) No Goods which are or may become dangerous, inflammable or damaging (including radio-active materials), or which are or may become liable to damage any property whatsoever, shall be tendered to the Carrier for Carriage without his express consent in writing and without the Container or other covering in which the Goods are to be carried as well as the Goods themselves being distinctly marked on the outside so as to indicate the nature and character of any such Goods and so as to comply with any applicable laws, regulations or requirements. If any such Goods are delivered to the Carrier without such written consent and/or marking, or if in the opinion of the Carrier the Goods are or are liable to become of a dangerous, inflammable or damaging nature, they may at any time be destroyed, disposed of, abandoned, or rendered harmless without compensation to the Merchant and without prejudice to the Carrier's right to Freight.

(2) The Merchant undertakes that such Goods are packed in a manner adequate to withstand the risks of Carriage having regard to their nature and in compliance with all laws or regulations which may be applicable during the Carriage.

(3) Whether or not the Merchant was aware of the nature of the Goods, the Merchant shall indemnify the Carrier against all claims, losses, damages or expenses arising in consequence of the Carriage of such Goods.

(4) Nothing contained in this Clause shall deprive the Carrier of any of his rights provided for elsewhere.

20. NOTIFICATION AND DELIVERY

(1) Any mention herein of parties to be notified of the arrival of the Goods is solely for information of the Carrier, and failure to give such notification shall not involve the Carrier in any liability nor relieve the Merchant of any obligation hereunder.

(2) If no Place of Delivery is named on the face hereof, the Carrier shall be at liberty to discharge the Goods at the Port of Discharge, without notice, directly they come to hand, at or on to any wharf, craft or place, on any day and at any time, whereupon the liability of the Carrier (if any) in respect of the Goods discharged as aforesaid shall wholly cease, notwithstanding any custom of the port to the contrary and notwithstanding any charges, dues or other expenses that may be or become payable. The Merchant shall take delivery of the Goods upon discharge.

(3) If a Place of Delivery is named on the face hereof, the Merchant shall take delivery of the Goods within the time provided for in the Carrier's applicable Tariff (see Clause 2).

(4) If the delivery of the Goods is not taken by the Merchant at the time and place the Carrier is entitled to call upon the Merchant to take delivery thereof, the Carrier shall be entitled, without notice, to unpack the Goods if packed in Containers and/or to store the Goods ashore, afloat, in the open or under cover, at the sole risk of the Merchant. Such storage shall constitute due delivery hereunder, and thereupon the liability of the Carrier in respect of the Goods stored as aforesaid shall wholly cease, and the costs of such storage (if paid or payable by the Carrier or any agent or sub-contractor of the Carrier) shall forthwith upon demand be paid by the Merchant to the Carrier.

(5) If the Merchant fails to take delivery of the Goods within thirty days of delivery becoming due under Clause 20 (2) or (3), or if in the opinion of the Carrier they are likely to deteriorate, decay, become worthless or incur charges whether for storage or otherwise in excess of their value, the Carrier may, without prejudice to any other rights which he may have against the Merchant, without notice and without any responsibility whatsoever attaching to him, sell or dispose of the Goods and apply the proceeds of sale in reduction of the sums due to the Carrier from the Merchant in respect of this Bill of Lading.

(6) If, at the place where the Carrier is entitled to call upon the Merchant to take delivery of the Goods under Clause 20 (2) or (3), the Carrier is obliged to hand-over the Goods into the custody of any customs, port or other authority, such hand-over shall constitute due delivery to the Merchant under this Bill of Lading.

(7) Refusal by the Merchant to take delivery of the Goods in accordance with the terms of this Clause, notwithstanding his having been notified of the availability of the Goods for delivery, shall constitute a waiver by the Merchant to the Carrier of any claim whatsoever relating to the Goods or the Carriage thereof.

(8) In the event of the Carrier agreeing at the request of the Merchant, to any change of destination, the terms of the Bill of Lading shall continue to apply to the extent permitted by the applicable Tariff until the Goods are delivered by the Carrier to the Merchant at the amended Port of Discharge or Place of Delivery, whichever is applicable, unless the Carrier specifically agrees in writing to the contrary. Should the applicable Tariff prohibit the continued application of the terms of the Bill of Lading, the Carrier will act as the agent only of the Merchant to arrange for the delivery of the Goods.

21. FCL MULTIPLE BILLS OF LADING

(1) Goods will only be delivered in a Container to the Merchant if all Bills of Lading in respect of the contents of the Container have been surrendered authorising delivery to a single Merchant at a single Place of Delivery. In the event that this requirement is not fulfilled the Carrier may unpack the Container and, in respect of Goods for which Bills of Lading have been surrendered, deliver these to the Merchant on an LCL basis. Such delivery shall constitute due delivery hereunder, but will only be effected against payment by the Merchant of LCL Service Charges and any charges appropriate to LCL Goods (as laid down in the Tariff) together with the actual costs incurred for any additional services rendered.

(2) Where this is an FCL multiple Bill of Lading (as evidenced by the qualification of the tally acknowledged overleaf to the effect that it is "One of... part cargoes in the Container"), then the Goods detailed overleaf are said to comprise part of the contents of the Container indicated. If the Carrier is required to deliver the Goods to more than one Merchant and if all or part of the total Goods within the Container consists of bulk Goods or unappropriated Goods, or is or becomes mixed or unmarked or unidentifiable, the holders of Bills of Lading relating to Goods within the Container shall take delivery thereof (including any damaged portion) and bear any shortage in such proportions as the Carrier shall in his absolute discretion determine, and such delivery shall constitute due delivery hereunder.

22. BOTH-TO-BLAME COLLISION

If the carrying vessel comes into collision with another vessel as a result of the negligence of the other vessel and any act, neglect or default in the navigation or the management of the carrying vessel, the Merchant undertakes to pay the Carrier, or, if the Carrier is not the owner and in possession of the carrying vessel, to pay to the Carrier as trustee for the owner and/or demise charterer of the carrying vessel a sum sufficient to indemnify the Carrier and/or the owner and/or demise charterer of the carrying vessel against all loss or liability to the other or non-carrying vessel or her owners insofar as such loss or liability represents loss of or damage to, or any claim whatsoever of the Merchant, paid or payable by the other or non-carrying vessel or her owners to the merchant and set-off, recouped or recovered by the other or non-carrying vessel or her owners as part of their claim against the carrying vessel or her owners or demise charterer or the Carrier. The foregoing provisions shall also apply if the owners, operators, or those in charge of any vessel or vessels or objects, other than, or in addition to the colliding vessels or objects, are at fault in respect of a collision, contact, stranding or other accident.

23. GENERAL AVERAGE

(1) In the event of accident, danger, damage or disaster before of after the commencement of the voyage, resulting from any cause whatsoever, due to negligence or not, for which, or for the consequences of which, the Carrier is not responsible, by statute, contract or otherwise, the Merchant shall contribute with the Carrier in general average to the payment of any sacrifices, losses or expenses of a general average nature that may be made or incurred, and shall pay salvage and special charges incurred in respect of the Goods.

(2) General average shall be adjusted according to the York/Antwerp Rules of 1974 at any port or place at the option of the Carrier whether declared by the Carrier or a subcontractor of the Carrier. The Merchant shall give such cash deposit or other security as the Carrier may deem sufficient to cover the estimated general average contribution of the Goods before delivery if the Carrier requires, or, if the Carrier does not so require, within three months of the delivery of the Goods, whether or not at the time of delivery the Merchant had notice of the Carrier's lien. The Carrier shall be under no obligation to exercise any lien for general average contribution due to the Merchant.

In the event of any general average credit balances due to Merchants still being unclaimed 5 years after the date of issue of the adjustment, these shall be paid to the owner or disponent owner of the vessel, who will hold such credit balances pending application by the Merchants entitled thereto.

(3) If a salving vessel is owned or operated by the Carrier, salvage shall be paid for as fully as if the salving vessel or vessels belonged to strangers.

24. VARIATION OF THE CONTRACT

No servant or agent of the Carrier shall have the power to waive or vary any of the terms of this Bill of Lading, unless such waiver or variation is in writing and is specifically authorised or ratified in writing by the Carrier.

25. GOVERNING LAW AND JURISDICTION

Any claim or dispute arising under this Bill of Lading shall be governed by English Law and determined by the High Court of Justice in London to the exclusion of the jurisdiction of the courts of any other country or, if the plaintiff to the claim or dispute shall so elect, by the court of the place where the defendant has his principal place of business and then in accordance with the law of that court.

26. VALIDITY

In the event that anything herein contained is inconsistent with any applicable international convention or national law which cannot be departed from by private contract, the provisions hereof shall to the extent of such inconsistency but no further be null and void.

附录十一:海运单

(表格正面见后,背面条款如下)
Conditions of Carriage.

(1) All the terms, conditions, liberties, clauses and exceptions of the Voyage Charter Party, as dated overleaf, including the Law and Arbitration Clause, shall be deemed to be incorporated in this Waybill and shall govern the transportation of the cargo described on the front page of this Waybill. In addition, the provisions set out below shall apply to this Waybill.

(2) Paramount Clause

(a) This Waybill is a non-negotiable document. It is not a bill of lading and no bill of lading will be issued. However it is agreed that the Hague Rules contained in the International Convention for the Unification of certain rules relating to Bills of Lading, dated Brussels the 25th August 1924 as enacted in the country of shipment shall apply to this Waybill. When no such enactment is in force in the country of shipment, the corresponding legislation of the country of destination shall apply, but in respect of shipments to which no such enactments are compulsorily applicable, the terms of the said convention shall apply in exactly the same way.

(b) Trades Where Hague-Visby Rules apply.

In trades where the International Brussels Convention 1924 as amended by the Protocol signed at Brussels on February 23rd 1968—the Hague-Visby Rules—apply compulsorily, the provisions of the respective legislation shall also apply to this Waybill.

(c) The Carrier shall in no case be responsible for loss of or damage to cargo howsoever arising prior to loading into and after discharge from the Vessel or while the goods are in the charge of another Carrier nor in respect of deck cargo and live animals.

(d) It is agreed that whenever the Brussels Convention and the Brussels Protocol or statutes incorporating same use the words "Bill of Lading" they shall be read and interpreted as meaning "Waybill".

(3) General Average

General Average shall be adjusted, stated and settled according to York-Antwerp Rules 1994 or any modification thereof at the place (if any) agreed in the voyage Charter Party, as dated overleaf, otherwise in London.

Cargo's contribution to General Average shall be paid to the Carrier even when such average is the result of a fault, neglect or error of the Master, Pilot or Crew.

If the adjustment of General Average or the liability for any collision in which the Vessel is involved while performing the carriage under the terms of the Voyage Charter Party, as dated overleaf, which govern the transportation of the cargo described on the front page of this Waybill, falls to be determined in accordance with the law and practice of the United States of America the following clauses shall apply:

New Jason Clause

In the event of accident, danger, damage or disaster before or after the commencement of the voyage, resulting from any cause whatsoever, whether due to negligence or not, for which or for the consequence of which, the Carrier is not responsible, by Statute, contract or otherwise, the cargo, shippers, consignees or owners of the cargo shall contribute with the Carrier in general average to the payment of any sacrifices, losses or expenses of a general average nature that may be made or incurred and shall pay salvage and special charges incurred in respect of the cargo.

If a salving vessel is owned or operated by the Carrier, salvage shall be paid for as fully as if the said salving vessel or vessels belonged to strangers. Such deposit as the Carrier, or his agent, may deem sufficient to cover the estimated contribution of the cargo and any salvage and special charges thereon shall, if required, be made to the cargo, shippers, consignees or owners of the cargo to the carrier before delivery.

Both-to-Blame Collision Clause

If the Vessel comes into collision with another vessel as a result of the negligence of the other vessel and any act, neglect or default of the Master, Mariner, Pilot or the Servants of the Carrier in the navigation or in the management of the Vessel, the owners of the cargo carried hereunder will indemnify the Carrier against all loss or liability to the other or non-carrying vessel or her owners in so far as such loss or liability represents loss of, or damage to, or any claim whatsoever of the owners of the said cargo, paid or payable by the other or non-carrying vessel or her owners to the owners of the said cargo and set-off, recouped or recovered by the other or non-carrying vessel or her owners as part of their claim against the carrying vessel or the Carrier.

The foregoing provisions shall also apply where the owners, operators or those in charge of any vessel or vessels or objects other than, or in addition to, the colliding vessels or objects are at fault in respect of a collision or contact.

附录十二:CMI 电子提单规则

(表格正面见后,背面条款如下)
CMI RULES FOR ELECTRONIC BILLS OF LADING

1. Scope of Application
These rules shall apply whenever the parties so agree.

2. Definitions
a. "Contract of Carriage" means any agreement to carry goods wholly or partly by sea.

b. "EDI" means Electronic Data Interchange, i. e. the interchange of trade data effected by teletransmission.

c. "UN/EDIFACT" means the United Nations Rules for Electronic Date Interchange for Administration, Commerce and Transport.

d. "Transmission" means one or more messages electronically sent together as one unit of dispatch which includes heading and terminating data.

e. "Confirmation" means a Transmission which advises that the content of a Transmission appears to be complete and correct, without prejudice to any subsequent consideration or action that the content may warrant.

f. "Private Key" means any technically appropriate form, such as a combination of numbers and/or letters, which the parties may agree for securing the authenticity and integrity of a Transmission.

g. "Holder" means the party who is entitled to the rights described in Article 7(a) by virtue of its possession of a valid Private Key.

h. "Electronic Monitoring System" means the device by which a computer system can be examined for the transactions that it recorded, such as a Trade Data Log or an Audit Trail.

i. "Electronic Storage" means any temporary, intermediate or permanent storage of electronic data including the primary and the back-up storage of such data.

3. Rules of procedure
a. When not in conflict with these Rules, the Uniform Rules of Conduct for Inter-

change of Trade Data by Teletransmission, 1987 (UNCID) shall govern the conduct between the parties.

b. The EDI under these Rules should conform with the relevant UN/EDIFACT standards. However, the parties may use any other method of trade data interchange acceptable to all of the users.

c. Unless otherwise agreed, the document format for the Contract of Carriage shall conform to the UN Layout Key or compatible national standard for bills of lading.

d. Unless otherwise agreed, a recipient of a Transmission is not authorised to act on a Transmission unless he has sent a Confirmation.

e. In the event of a dispute arising between the parties as to the data actually transmitted, an Electronic Monitoring System may be used to verify the data received. Data concerning other transactions not related to the data in dispute are to be considered as trade secrets and thus not available for examination. If such data are unavoidably revealed as part of the examination of the Electronic Monitoring System, they must be treated as confidential and not released to any outside party or used for any other purpose.

f. Any transfer of rights to the goods shall be considered to be private information, and shall not be released to any outside party not connected to the transport or clearance of the goods.

4. **Form and content of the receipt message**

a. The carrier, upon receiving the goods from the shipper, shall give notice of the receipt of the goods to the shipper by a message at the electronic address specified by the shipper.

b. This receipt message shall include:

(i) the name of the shipper;

(ii) the description of the goods, with any representations and reservations, in the same tenor as would be required if a paper bill of lading were issued;

(iii) the date and place of the receipt of the goods;

(iv) a reference to the carrier's terms and conditions of carriage; and

(v) the Private Key to be used in subsequent Transmissions.

The shipper must confirm this receipt message to the carrier, upon which Confirmation the shipper shall be the Holder.

c. Upon demand of the Holder, the receipt message shall be updated with the date and place of shipment as soon as the goods have been loaded on board.

d. The information contained in (ii), (iii) and (iv) of paragraph (b) above including the date and place of shipment if updated in accordance with paragraph (c) of this Rule, shall have the same force and effect as if the receipt message were contained in a paper bill of lading.

5. Terms and conditions of the Contract of Carriage

a. It is agreed and understood that whenever the carrier makes a reference to its terms and conditions of carriage, these terms and conditions shall form part of the Contract of Carriage.

b. Such terms and conditions must be readily available to the parties to the Contract of Carriage.

c. In the event of any conflict or inconsistency between such terms and conditions and these Rules, these Rules shall prevail.

6. Applicable law

The Contract of Carriage shall be subject to any international convention or national law which would have been compulsorily applicable if a paper bill of lading had been issued.

7. Right of Control and Transfer

a. The Holder is the only party who may, as against the carrier:

(1) claim delivery of the goods;

(2) nominate the consignee or substitute a nominated consignee for any other party including itself;

(3) transfer the Right of Control and Transfer to another party;

(4) instruct the carrier on any other subject concerning the goods, in accordance with the terms and conditions of the Contract of Carriage, as if he were the holder of a paper bill of lading.

b. A transfer of the Right of Control and Transfer shall be effected: (i) by notification of the current Holder to the carrier of its intention to transfer its Right of Control and Transfer to a proposed new Holder, and (ii) confirmation by the carrier of such notification message, whereupon (iii) the carrier shall transmit the information as referred to in article 4 (except for the Private Key) to the proposed new Holder, whereafter (iv) the proposed new Holder shall advise the carrier of its acceptance of the Right of Control and

Transfer, whereupon (V) the carrier shall cancel the current Private Key and issue a new Private Key to the new Holder.

c. If the proposed new Holder advises the carrier that it does not accept the Right of Control and Transfer or fails to advise the carrier of such acceptance within a reasonable time, the proposed transfer of the Right of Control and Transfer shall not take place. The carrier shall notify the current Holder accordingly and the current Private Key shall retain its validity.

d. The transfer of the Right of Control and Transfer in the manner described above shall have the same effects as the transfer of such rights under a paper bill of lading.

8. The Private Key

a. The Private Key is unique to each successive Holder. It is not transferable by the Holder. The carrier and the Holder shall each maintain the security of the Private Key.

b. The carrier shall only be obliged to send a Confirmation of an electronic message to the last Holder to whom it issued a Private Key, when such Holder secures the Transmission containing such electronic message by the use of the Private Key.

c. The Private Key must be separate and distinct from any means used to identify the Contract of Carriage, and any security password or identification used to access the computer network.

9. Delivery

a. The carrier shall notify the Holder of the place and date of intended delivery of the goods. Upon such notification the Holder has a duty to nominate a consignee and to give adequate delivery instructions to the carrier with verification by the Private Key. In the absence of such nomination, the Holder will be deemed to be the consignee.

b. The carrier shall deliver the goods to the consignee upon production of proper identification in accordance with the delivery instructions specified in paragraph (a) above; such delivery shall automatically cancel the Private Key.

c. The carrier shall be under no liability for misdelivery if it can prove that it exercised reasonable care to ascertain that the party who claimed to be the consignee was in fact that party.

10. Option to receive a paper document

a. The Holder has the option at any time prior to delivery of the goods to demand from the carrier a paper bill of lading. Such document shall be made available at a location to be determined by the Holder, provided that no carrier shall be obliged to make such document available at a place where it has no facilities and in such instance the carrier shall only be obliged to make the document available at the facility nearest to the location determined by the Holder. The carrier shall not be responsible for delays in delivering the goods resulting from the Holder exercising the above option.

b. The carrier has the option at any time prior to delivery of the goods to issue to the Holder a paper bill of lading unless the exercise of such option could result in undue delay or disrupts the delivery of the goods.

c. A bill of lading issued under Rules 10(a) or (b) shall include: the information set out in the receipt message referred to in Rule 4 (except for the Private Key); and (ii) a statement to the effect that the bill of lading has been issued upon termination of the procedures for EDI under the CMI Rules for Electronic Bills of Lading. The aforementioned bill of lading shall be issued at the option of the Holder either to the order of the Holder whose name for this purpose shall then be inserted in the bill of lading or "to bearer".

d. The issuance of a paper bill of lading under Rule 10 (a) or (b) shall cancel the Private Key and terminate the Procedures for EDI under these Rules. Termination of these procedures by the Holder or the carrier will not relieve any of the parties to the Contract of Carriage of their rights, obligations or liabilities while performing under the present Rules nor of their rights, obligations or liabilities under the Contract of Carriage.

e. The Holder may demand at any time the issuance of a print-out of the receipt message referred to in Rule 4 (except for the Private Key) marked as "non-negotiable copy". The issuance of such a print-out shall not cancel the Private Key nor terminate the procedures for EDI.

11. **Electronic data is equivalent to writing**

The carrier and the shipper and all subsequent parties utilizing these procedures agree that any national or local law, custom or practice requiring the Contract of Carriage to be evidenced in writing and signed, is satisfied by the transmitted and confirmed electronic data residing on computer data storage media displayable in human language on a video screen or as printed out by a computer. In agreeing to adopt these Rules, the parties shall be taken to have agreed not to raise the defense that this contract is not in writing.

附录十三:海牙规则、海牙·维斯比规则、汉堡规则的比较

Cargo conventions at a glance Comparing Hague, Hague/Visby and Hamburg Rules
1. Which voyages covered?
2. Which contracts covered?
3. Geographical application
4. Who is the carrier?
5. Contract and Tort Claims
6. Carrier's general duty of care
7. Carrier's Defences
8. Burden of proof
9. Fire
10. Live animals
11. Deck cargo
12. Dangerous cargo
13. Limits of liability
14. Loss of right to limit liability
15. Lower limits by agreement?
16. Higher limits by agreement?
17. Deviation
18. What information must the bill contain?
19. What is the effect of statements in the bill?
20. Duties of shipper in supplying carrier with information
21. Letters of indemnity
22. Notification of damage
23. Consequences of failing to notify carrier of loss under 22 above
24. Limitation of actions
25. Where can cargo owner commence proceedings?
26. Arbitration
27. General Average
28. Provisions which conflict with the Rules

	Hague Rules	Hague/Visby Rules	Hamburg Rules
1. Which voyages covered?	Rules are silent.	Art X (a) bill issued in a contracting state (b) carriage from contracting state (c) contract of carriage expressly applies Rules	Art 2 (a) bill issued in a contracting state (b) carriage from contracting state (c) carriage to contracting state (d) bill provides Rules are to apply
2. Which contracts covered?	Art 1(b) Bill of lading or "other similar document of title." Not charterparties.	Art 1(b) Same as Hague Rules.	Art 1.6 Contract of carriage by sea. Need not be a bill or document of title. Not Charterparties.
3. Geographical application	Art 1(e) "covers the period from the time when the goods are loaded on to the time when they are discharged from the ship", Tackle to Tackle.	Art 1(e) Same as Hague Rules.	Art 4 Carrier is responsible while in "charge" of the goods at the port of loading, during the carriage, and at the port of discharge i. e. normally from time taken over from shipper to time delivered to consignee, subject to local port regulations.
4. Who is the Carrier?	Art (a) Owner or Charterer "who enters into contract of carriage with a Shipper".	Art 1 (a) Same as Hague Rules.	Art 1.1, Art 10, Art 11 "any person by whom or in whose name a contract of carriage has been concluded with a shipper". Covers "actual" and "contractual" carrier.

5. Contract and Tort Claims	Ruler are silent. May apply to just contract claims. Applies to both under English law.	Art IV bis Apply to contract and tort claims.	Art 7 Apply to contract and tort claims.
6. Carrier's general duty of care	Art III 1. Carrier must exercise due diligence before and at beginning of voyage to. (a) make ship sea worthy (b) properly man, equip and supply the ship (c) make holds etc. fit and safe for the reception, carriage and preservation of cargo 2. Carrier must properly and carefully load, handle, stow, carry, keep, care for and discharge goods carried.	Art III Same as Hague Rules	Art 5.1 Carrer, his servants and agents, must take all measures that could reasonably be required to avoid the event causing loss and its consequences.
7. Carrier's Defences	Art IV 1. Unseaworthiness only defence is for carrier to show he exercised "due diligence" to ensure vessel seaworthy before and at beginning of voyage. 2. Properly and carefully load etc. The following defences apply (a) Act, neglect, or default of the master, mariner, pilot or the sevants of the carrier in the navigation or in the management of the ship (b) Fire, unless caused by the actual fault or privity of the carrier	Art IV Same as Hague Rules.	Art 5.1 Carrier must prove he, his servants or agents, took all measures that could reasonably be required to avoid the occurrence and its consequences.

	(c) Perils, dangers and accidents of the sea or other navigable waters (d) Act of God (e) Act of War (f) Act of public enemies (g) Arrest or restraint of princes, Rulers or people, or seizure under legal process (h) Quarantine restrictions (j) Striker or lockouts, or stoppage or restraing of labour from whatever cause whether partial or general (k) Riots and civil commotions (l) Saving or attempting to save life or property at sea (m) Wastage in bulk or weight or any other loss or damage arising from inherent defect, quality or vice of the goods. (n) Insufficience of packing (o) Insuffiency or inadequacy of marks (p) Latent defects not discoverable by due diligence (q) Any other cause arising without the actual fault or privity of the carrier, or without the fault or neglect of the agents or servants of the carrier, but the burden of proof shall be on the person claiming the benefit of this exception to show the neither the actual fault or privity of the carrier nor the fault or neglect of the agents or servants of the carrier contributed to the loss or damage.		

8. Burden of proof	Rules are unclear (except under Art IV (2) (q)), Under English las cargo owner must establish inference of unseaworthiness or failure to properly and carefully carry the goods, and then carrier must prove relevant defence in 7 (previous page).	Same as Hague Rules.	Carrier must prove that reasonable steps to avoid loss were taken unless damage is caused by fire, (see 9 below).
9. Fire	Art III & IV if due to e.g. poor stowage, carrier only liable if caused by his actual fault or privity, if caused by unseaworthiness, carrier liable unless he exercised due diligence to ensure vessel seaworthy before and at beginning of voyage.	Art III & IV Same as Hague Rules.	Art 5.4 Carrier liable if claimant proves fire arose from fault or neglect on the part of the carrier, his servants or agents.
10. Live Animals	Art 1(c) Excluded from Rules.	Art 1(c) Same as Hague Rules, c/f UK COGSA 1971, S1 (7) which applies Rules to live animals.	Arts 1.5 & 5.5 Rules apply but carrier not liable for in herent "special risks". If carrier complies with shipper's instructions he wil be presumed not to be liable.

11. Deck cargo	Art 1(c) Excluded from Rules if stated to be carried on deck.	Art 1(c) Same as Hague Rules. c/f UK COGSA 1971, S1 (7) which applies Rules to deck cargo (see e. g. Chanda (1989) 2 Lloyd's Rep. 494).	Art 9 Rules do not exclude deck cargo. Carrier can undertake deck carriage if agreed with shipper or accords with the "usage of a particular trade or is required by statutory rules or regulations". Must be statement in Bill that goods carried on deck. Failure to agree deck carriage makes carrier liable for damage, loss or delay, resulting solely from carriage on deck carriage is in breach of express agreement to carry below deck.
12. Dangerous cargo	Art IV Rule 6 inflammable, explosive or dangerous goods if loaded without knowledge of the Master (or carrier's agent) may be discharged, rendered harmless or destroyed at shipper's expense. If Carrier knows of their nature but they prove dangerous they may still be discharged, rendered harmless or destroyed without liability on the part of the carrier, save in general average.	Art IV Rule 6 Same as Hague Rules.	Art 13 Similar provisions apply, and the shipper is obliged to mark and label dangerous goods in a suitable manner.

13. Limits of liability (a) Goods lost or damaged (b) Goods delayed	Art IV Rule 5 £ 100 per package or unit unless value declared and inserted in bill of lading. No special provisions.	Art IV Rule 5 10,000 Poincare Francs per package or unit or 30 Poincare Francs per kilo of gross weight of damaged or lost goods whichever is higher. By virtue of SDR Protocol 1979 2 SDRs per kg or 666.67 SDRs per package Same as Hague Rules.	Art 6 2.5 SDRs per kg or 835 SDRs per package or shipping unit. Art 6 2.5 x freight payable on goods delayed, subject to upper limit of total freight on all goods or amount of limitation if goods have been lost or destroyed under formula in (a) above.
14. Loss of right to limit liability	No special provisions but carrier's liability may be unlimited if unjustified deviation, or deck carriage.	Art IV Ruly 5(e) Right to limit lost if carrier intends to cause loss or is reckless knowing loss would probably result. May also be lost if unjustified deviation or deck carriage.	Art 8 Carrier will only lose right to limit liability if he intended to cause loss or was reckless knowing such loss would probably result. Deck carriage where expressly prohibited will result in loss of right to limit liability.
15. Lower limits by agreement?	Art IV Only permitted where not an ordinary shipment, and reasonable in special circumstances.	Art VI Same as Hague Rules.	No specific right to agree lower limits.

16. Higher limits by agreement?	Art V Permitted if recorded in bill.	Art V Same as Hague Rules.	Art 6.4 Art 15 Permitted if agreed, Should be recorded in bill.
17. Deviation	Deviating carrier might lose right to rely on defences in Rules and lose right to limit liability. Art Ⅳ Rule 4 Provides "any deviation in saving or attempting to save life or property at sea, or any reasonable deviation shall not be deemed to be an infringement or breach of the Rules or contract of carriage".	Same as Hague Rules.	No special provision. Deviation if it caused loss is subject to general test of carrier's liability. Art 5.6 exempts a carrier from liability where he attempts to save life or "reasonable measures" are taken to save property. This would apply to deviation as much as any other cause of loss.
18. What information must the bill contain?	Art Ⅲ Rule 3 (a) leading marks necessary for identifying goods. (b) number of packages or pieces, or the quantity or weight, as the case may be, as furnished by the shipper.	Art Ⅲ Rule 3 Same as Hague Rules.	Art 15 (a) the general nature of the goods, the leading marks necessary for identification of the goods, an express statement, if applicable, as to the dangerous character of the goods, the number of packages or pieces, and the weight of the goods or their quantity otherwise expressed, all such particulars as furnished by the shipper.

| | | | (b) the apparent condition of the goods
(c) the name and principal place of business of the carrier
(d) the name of the shipper
(e) the consignee if named by shipper
(f) the port of loading under the contract carriage by sea and the date on which the goods were taken over by the carrier at the port of loading
(g) the port of discharge under the contract of carriage by sea
(h) the number of originals of the bill of lading, if more than one
(i) the signature of the carrier or a person acting on his behalf
(k) freight to the extent payable by the consignee
(l) the statement referred to in paragraph 3 of Article 24, i.e. applicability of the Convention.
(m) statement if applicable, that the goods shall or may be carried on deck
(n) the date or the period of delivery of the goods at the port of discharge if expressly agreed upon between the parties.
(o) any increased limit or limits of liability where agreed.
If the carrier is unable to state any of the matters in (a) above he should express his omission in the bill. |
|---|---|---|---|

19. What is the effect of statements in the Bill?	Art Ⅲ Rule 4 *prima facie* evidence of their accuracy.	Art Ⅲ Rule 4 *Prima facie* evidence in hands of shipper, conclusive in hands of third party e. g. consignee to whom bill is transferred in goods faith.	Art 16 prima facie evidence of statement in hands of shipper (whether shipped or received bill). Conclusive in hand of third party who relies on statements. However, if freight is payable by holder of bill failure to state this is evidence that no freight is payable.
20. Duties of shipper in supplying carrier with information	Art Ⅲ Rule 5 Shipper is deemed to guarantee accuracy of statements as to weight and quantity of cargo. Shipper to indemnity carrier for loss resulting from errors.	Art Ⅲ Rule 5 Same as Hague Rules.	Art 17 Same as Hague Rules.
21. Effectiveness of Letter of indemnity is sude by shipper for carrier not clausing bill	No specific provisions Void under English Law (Brown Jenkinson & Co Ltd. v. percy Daltion (ldn) Ltd [1957] 2 Q. B. 621)	Same as Hague Rules.	Art 17 Void for bill in hands of consignee. Valid against shipper unless carrier intended to defraud consignee. If fraud, carrier may not limit liability.

22. Notification of damage	Art Ⅲ Rule 6 Notice of loss or damage must be given in writing to the carrier or his agent. (ⅰ) on day of delivery or (ⅱ) with in 3 days where damage is latent	Art Ⅲ Rule 6 Same as Hague Rules.	Art 19 Notice of loss or damage to be given in writing to carrer. (ⅰ) by working day following delivery to consignee. or (ⅱ) within 15 days of delivery where damage is latentNotice of delay must be given within 60 days of delivery. Carrier must give notice to shipper of complaint within 90 days of delivery.
23. Consequences of failing to notify carrier of loss, damage or delay under 22 above	Art Ⅲ Rule 6 *Prima facie* evidence of delivery of goods in condition described by bill.	Art Ⅲ Rule 6 Same as Hague Rules.	Art 19 *prima facie* evidence of delivery of goods in condition described by bill. If goods delayed and complaint not made within 60 days the carrier is exempted from liability.
24. Limitation of actions	Art Ⅲ Rule 6 " suit " must be brought within one year of deliver or date delivery should have taken place.	Art Ⅲ Rule 6 Same as Hague Rules Art Ⅲ Rule 6 bis indemnity actions may be brought after one year, the period for commencing suit to be not less than 15 months after discharge.	Art 20 Litigation or arbitration to be commenced within 2 years from date of delivery of goods or the last day upon which goods should have been delivered. Indemnity proceedings may be commenced after this period (at least 90 days from date of commencement of action against carrier must be allowed).

25. Where can cargo owner commence proceedings?	Rules are silent.	Same as Hague Rules.	Art 21 May sue in court of: (a) Principal place of business of carrier (b) place contract was made (c) port of loading (d) port of discharge (e) place designated by contract of carriage (f) place of arrest of veddel, may be challenged by the carrier, if he submits to one of the other jurisdictions and provides security for the claim.
26. Arbitration	Rules are silent.	Same as Hague Rules.	Art 22 Arbitration agreement permitted, if incorporating Charterparty arbitration clause, must be comprised in bill of lading as " special annotation ". Claimant may choose where to commence arbitration from: (a) place where defendant has principal place of business (b) place where contract was made (c) port of loading (d) port of discharge (e) place specified in arbitration clause.

27. General Average	Art V "nothing in these rules shall be held to prevent the insertion in a bill of any lawful provision regarding general average.	Art V Same as Hague Rules.	Art 24 "The provisions of this convention relating to the liability of the carrier for loss of or damage to the goods also determine whether the consignee may refuse contribution in general average…"
28. Provisions which conflict with the Rules	Art Ⅲ Rule 8 Void.	Art Ⅲ Rule 8 Void.	Art 23.1 Void and compensation may be payable where claimant has suffered a loss; see Art 23.4

图书在版编目(CIP)数据

提单及其他付运单证/杨良宜著.—北京:中国政法大学出版社,2001.6
ISBN 978-7-5620-2087-5

Ⅰ.提... Ⅱ.杨... Ⅲ.国际贸易-提单-研究 Ⅳ.F740.44

中国版本图书馆 CIP 数据核字(2001)第 031440 号

书　　名	提单及其他付运单证	
出版发行	中国政法大学出版社	
经　　销	全国各地新华书店	
承　　印	固安华明印刷厂	
开　　本	787×960　1/16	
印　　张	49.75	
字　　数	940 千字	
版　　本	2007 年 4 月修订版　　2007 年 4 月第 1 次印刷	
书　　号	ISBN 978-7-5620-2087-5/D·2047	
定　　价	79.00 元	
社　　址	北京市海淀区西土城路 25 号	
电　　话	(010)58908325(发行部)　58908335(储运部)	
	58908285(总编室)　58908334(邮购部)	
通信地址	北京 100088 信箱 8034 分箱　邮政编码 100088	
电子信箱	zf5620@263.net	
网　　址	http://www.cuplpress.com　（网络实名：中国政法大学出版社）

☆　☆　☆　☆　☆

声　　明　1.版权所有，侵权必究。
　　　　　2.如发现缺页、倒装问题，请与出版社联系调换。

本社法律顾问　北京地平线律师事务所